Reading *and*
Writing *from*
Literature

Reading and Writing from Literature

John E. Schwiebert

Weber State University

Houghton Mifflin Company   Boston   New York

Senior Sponsoring Editor: Dean Johnson
Editorial Assistant: Mary Furlong Healey
Senior Project Editor: Janet Young
Editorial Assistant: Elizabeth Emmons
Associate Production/Design Coordinator: Jennifer Meyer
Senior Manufacturing Coordinator: Marie Barnes
Senior Marketing Manager: Nancy Lyman

Cover Design: Mark Caleb
Cover Image: *Jardin en Fleurs* by Claude Monet, Musée d'Orsay, Paris/Superstock

Contents

18   Experience and Identity   372

APPENDICES

Preface

Designed for use in literature courses that are also writing courses, *Reading and Writing from Literature* offers a fresh new approach to reading and writing in those classes. The book invokes a "conversation" model of reading and writing that empowers students to interact proactively and constructively with all texts, both literary and their own.

Reading and Writing from Literature presents reading as the primary resource for writing. Rather than only writing *about* literature, student users of this book write *from* literature; they use texts to produce texts. Being personally and culturally diverse, students are encouraged to identify and use those aspects of a text that interest them most as starting points for composing. Throughout the book, the guiding assumption is that, by creating, students also become stronger readers of the literature of past and present.

Inviting Students to Read and Write Intertextually

The theoretical basis of this book can be distilled into a single word—intertextuality, the primary engine that drives composing. In this book "text" is defined broadly to include all kinds of printed works, such as stories, poems, essays, and plays, as well as non-print phenomena such as movies, pictures, songs, conversations, and experiences. Intertextuality posits that every "text" is related to and evokes other texts, that one text is enmeshed in others. To compose a story, poem, or essay is not to invent something out of nothing but to produce a new text out of a complex and interwoven fabric of other texts already "written into" the writer's life.

For a writer, reading is useful because it facilitates getting the texts of one's life on paper. The process begins when the writer reads a springboard text, such as a short story. Some aspect of the story—a character, an image, a phrase, a described incident—resonates with other texts in his or her life, thereby bringing these texts to consciousness. The writer composes a piece of his or her own, and the focus of the resulting composition is not the springboard text but the writer's *intertextual web*—the intricate and unique fabric of texts that constitutes who that writer is.

Intertextuality provides a rationale for reading and for writing in response to reading: through the process of writing, ideas can be articulated that might not have surfaced if the writer hadn't read and written from that particular text.

In addition, intertextuality explains how a person can respond in writing to another text and still produce work that is individual, exciting, and "independent": because each person's intertextual web is unlike anyone else's.

Finally, intertextuality provides a rationale for the student to pursue an ongoing, lifelong program of reading and writing. By demonstrating that no text, great or humble, is final, autonomous, or definitive, it validates every act of composing. In addition to being seen as ends-in-themselves, student texts and literary texts alike can be read temporally as parts of a continuing interplay of words and ideas, as "pre-texts" for additional thought, creation, and re-creation.

Rhetoric Chapters

This textbook is organized into rhetoric chapters and anthology chapters. The rhetoric chapters introduce students to techniques of reading, writing, and sharing that they can use throughout the term. Chapters are short and accessible enough that students can master most of the material on their own with minimal expenditure of in-class time.

Part I, "Writing and Reading: Interrelated Activities" (Chapters 1–4), presents writing and reading as conversational acts in which students "talk back" to the texts they read and use the conversation as a springboard for creating texts of their own. In addition, Part I introduces the "reading notebook," the special kind of journal students can use for collecting their own writings—notes, thoughts, responses to literary works, and creative writings of many kinds that may be prompted by the texts they read. The reading notebook breaks down the wall between composing for school and composing for life and a lifetime; while developing techniques of reading and writing that will be useful to them in this course, students also learn strategies for producing meaningful writings of their own independently of this class or this textbook.

Part II, "Writing Essays About Literature" (Chapters 5–8), emphasizes the intertextual or recursive process of such composing. Students' essays do not materialize out of nothing; they are generated from previous work and from literary texts, the texts in their own notebooks, and the texts of lecture and discussion. With strategies described in Part II, students learn how to use these texts to make a new text, i.e., an essay about literature.

Part III, "Creating a Writing Portfolio" (Chapters 9–11), shows students how to assemble a portfolio of their best writing for the quarter or semester. A portfolio is the result of a sustained process of recursive reading and writing in which students set aside their failed or mediocre work and concentrate on perfecting their best. Part III also provides students with strategies to continue reading and writing conversationally once this course is over. Thus, the ultimate aim of Part III is to liberate students from this textbook, to make them strong and independent readers of literature—and active writers—for life.

Part IV, "An Introduction to the Four Major Genres" (Chapters 12–15), introduces students to the four genres of literature (short stories, poetry, nonfiction/essays, and plays) represented in the anthology. The chapters acquaint students with key literary terms and concepts that will help them to talk and write about short stories, poems, essays, and plays. In addition, Part IV is intended to increase students' technical knowledge of the four genres so that they can write in multiple forms themselves.

The Anthology of Readings

Part V, "A Thematic Anthology of Readings" (Chapters 16–21), offers an anthology of 132 readings in the four major genres, arranged under six thematic headings: Gender and Relationships, Families, Experience and Identity, Individual and Society, Cultural and Racial Identity, and The Greater Universe.

I have chosen a thematic arrangement over a genre-based arrangement for two reasons: first, to avoid breaking whole texts into fragmentary "elements" (those of the short story, of poetry, of drama), which is the almost inevitable result of a genre-based organization; and second, to place primary emphasis on issues and experiences that relate intertextually to students' lives.

In making selections I have worked consistently for variety: a mix of familiar and less-familiar authors, of frequently anthologized works and infrequently collected ones. Texts in each thematic grouping represent a diversity of perspectives and experiences, as the Gender and Relationships chapter (Chapter 16) illustrates. Doris Lessing's story about male objectification of the female body ("A Woman on a Roof") is balanced by Scott Russell Sanders's male perspective on the same subject, "Looking at Women." Robert Bly's portrait of wounded male identity ("My Father's Wedding 1924") is complemented by Adrienne Rich's "Aunt Jennifer's Tigers," which addresses injured female identity. Texts about sexual grief and frustration are balanced by Walt Whitman's and Ray Bradbury's expressions of exuberant sexuality in "Twenty-eight young men bathe by the shore" and "[A Story About Love]."

Finally, in order to encourage strong responses from students of diverse backgrounds and both genders, I have weighted selections toward the modern and contemporary and have included a significant number of multicultural and international selections.

Accompanying Apparatus

I believe that students accustomed to making their own texts will also become better readers of others' texts. A student who writes stories has a special motivation to understand the story elements of point of view, character, and plot because those elements have a context within his or her work as a creator. Similarly, students who write poems have an incentive to understand meter, metaphor, and diction in order to apply them in their own composing.

Accordingly, the book's apparatus is aimed primarily at prompting students to produce as well as consume texts. Such apparatus includes:

- Parts I–IV of *Reading and Writing from Literature,* described above;
- Activities for Writing and Discussion, following approximately half of the selections. These activities are designed to motivate many kinds of textual creation besides literary analysis. Activities involve students in both creative and analytic work as well as in sharing their work and ideas.
- Additional Activities for Writing and Discussion, at the end of each thematic section. The Additional Activities encourage students to make connections among the various readings within the section. In addition, they help students develop habits of recursiveness as they review and reconsider those readings and the notebook writings they have composed in response to them.
- Numerous examples of student-written texts, both within individual chapters and in the appendices, that will stimulate students in their own composing.

Summary: Distinctive Features of Reading and Writing from Literature

- Treats reading and writing as thoroughly interrelated: rhetoric chapters and other apparatus assure that students are always writing as they read and reading as they write.
- Empowers students both to *study* literary texts and to *use* literary texts as springboards for making texts of their own.
- Provides guidelines for a reading notebook that students use recursively: they accumulate writings—notes, thoughts, responses to readings, drafts, revisions—reread them regularly, and continuously revise their selected best work.
- Offers activities and apparatus that get students to look repeatedly at literary texts and their own texts, thereby promoting habits of recursive reading, thinking, and writing.
- Includes an anthology of 132 readings (short stories, poems, essays, and plays) that are weighted toward the contemporary and multicultural to encourage strong responses from students of diverse backgrounds.
- Features a simple and uncluttered apparatus that students can use in class and also navigate independently, without detailed guidance from the instructor.

- Contains numerous examples of student writings in many forms, both creative and analytic.
- Gives students incentives and strategies for continuing to read and write conversationally once this particular course is over.

Acknowledgments

The earliest support for this project came from my students and from my colleague Candadai Seshachari. Words cannot repay the debt I owe to them or to my friends Sheila Kelley and Coleman Clarke, who read an early version of the manuscript and moved it forward in ways they will never know.

Thanks are due to Judy Elsley, Priti Kumar, Dale Oberer, Bob Smith, Emily Smith, and Mali Subbiah—members of my faculty writing group—and to my colleague Jim Young for critiquing drafts of various chapters. I am especially grateful to the late Lee McKenzie, who understood the rationale for this book even better and earlier than its author did. Thanks, also, to the excellent and supportive editorial staff at Houghton Mifflin, particularly George Kane, who got me to restructure the plan of the book; Dean Johnson, who oversaw the project during composition and review and did so with unfailing good humor; Janet Young, who guided the book through production; and Mary Furlong Healey, who assisted with permissions and with patient and cheerful replies to my many queries.

A number of persons helped immeasurably by reading and critiquing the manuscript at various stages:

Robert S. Caim, West Virginia University
Elise Ann Earthman, San Francisco State University
Deanna Delmar Evans, Bemidji State University, MN
Matthew David Fisher, Ball State University, IN
Elaine Fitzpatrick, Massasoit Community College, MA
Fay Johnson, Northwest Mississippi Community College
Esther L. Panitz, William Paterson College, NJ
Dennis M. Ross, University of Miami, FL
Connie G. Rothwell, University of North Carolina at Charlotte
Carol B. Sapora, Villa Julie College, MD

All of the people named have made the good parts of this book better; any flaws that remain are my own responsibility.

Above all, I thank my wife, Ann Jefferds, and my son, Jack, who have supported me in the whole process.

J.E.S.

"Books are the best of things, well used; abused, among the worst. . . . They are for nothing but to inspire."

—Ralph Waldo Emerson

Part

I

Writing and Reading: Interrelated Activities

Part I of *Reading and Writing from Literature* presents writing and reading as conversational acts in which you "talk back" to the texts you read and use the conversation as a springboard for creating works of your own. In addition, Part I introduces you to the "reading notebook," the special kind of journal you will use in the course for collecting your own writings—notes, thoughts, responses to literary works, and creative writings of many kinds that may be prompted by the texts you read. The reading notebook breaks down the wall between composing for school and composing for life and a lifetime. While developing techniques of reading and writing that will be useful to you in this course, you will also learn strategies for producing meaningful writings of your own independently of this class or this textbook.

A Conversation Model of Writing and Reading

Reading and writing are important because we read and write our world as well as our texts, and are read and written by them in turn.

—Robert Scholes

Three Writers

Robin wants to write a story about something that has been on his mind a lot lately: husbands and wives. Sitting at his word processor he begins, "Every marriage is improved—or destroyed—by the fires of time." He likes the sound of that and is poised to continue, when inspiration suddenly dies. He searches for something new and profound to say about love; he ransacks his brain for some original characters and situations . . . in vain. Discouraged, he types another sentence or two and gives up.

Robin is anxious about being "original." His anxiety destroys his creativity.

Suppose he approaches the writing task differently. He thumbs through a book of short fiction to find other stories about husbands and wives and discovers "The Story of an Hour" by the nineteenth-century American Kate Chopin. After reading several paragraphs he has become fascinated by the character of its heroine, Louise Mallard. Mrs. Mallard has just learned that her husband has been killed in a railroad accident. Seated by her bedroom window she slips into a reverie about her past and future. Complex emotions beset her. She sobs; then, as she stares blankly at a distant patch of blue sky, an unfamiliar feeling steals over her. Chopin writes:

When she abandoned herself a little whispered word escaped her slightly parted lips. She said it over and over under her breath: "Free, free, free!" The vacant stare and the look of terror that had followed it went from her eyes. They stayed keen and bright. Her pulses beat fast, and the coursing blood warmed and relaxed every inch of her body.

Robin circles this passage and scribbles in the margin, "She *relaxes* at the thought of her husband's death?" Louise's emotions set Robin thinking about fractured relationships, in which one partner prefers freedom to attachment. Thought follows thought, and soon he is remembering his Uncle Jules, who seemed to experience a kind of rebirth following the death of his wife, Aunt Maria. Robin begins writing the story of Uncle Jules and Aunt Maria. "The Story of an Hour" prompts him to write. While his own story is about a husband and wife, it in no way duplicates Chopin's. In short, his work is "original."

Sally keeps a personal diary. Unfortunately, while she thinks of plenty to write when her life is exciting or awful, on most days (which are humdrum) she draws a mental blank. Each day's entry sounds like every other's. Her own writing puts her to sleep.

A friend, Max, suggests her writing may be suffering from egocentrism and that she should seek prompts for writing from her environment. "Writers do it all the time," says Max. "They eavesdrop, look at people, watch movies, hang around shopping malls. . . ." Heeding Max's advice, Sally indulges in one of her favorite activities, watching TV, hoping it will stimulate her imagination. One evening she sees a TV version of Daniel Keyes's "Flowers for Algernon" and learns that this is a short story told entirely in the form of a diary (Algernon's). Inspired, Sally puts her own favorite literary form to work: she writes a story, in diary form, about a would-be writer who "can't" write.

Erica has always loved the sea. Her family vacationed on Lake Superior when she was growing up. As a child she built sandcastles and combed the beach for shells. Now, every time she gets near water, she dances or merely stands still, transfixed and staring at the horizon, watching cloud shadows roll over the waves, beholding the most fabulous sunsets imaginable. Erica wants to write about the sea. Every time she tries, however, she gets mired in false and overblown phrases that frustrate and embarrass her.

One day, while reading a biographical note on American playwright Eugene O'Neill, she notices the title of one of O'Neill's plays, *Beyond the Horizon*. The mere title does something to her—and for her. She circles it . . . repeats it to herself a few times out loud. She doodles in the margin: a conch shell, a snail, a long horizontal line. As she thinks, repeats, and doodles, memories and images long dormant rise to consciousness: memories of family trips, of childhood, of her own daughter playing in the sand, of sea-conversations and sea-books. She feels herself transported to those days at Lake Superior and writes the poem she has "always wanted to," about the particular feelings a child-turned-adult has when gazing at the horizon. It turns out to be a poem about love and aging and the integration of child and adult. The poem pleases her.

All three of these writers—Robin, Sally, and Erica—wanted to write but had no "way in" to their writing. All three were stuck—either not moving at all (Robin), or writing in circles (Sally), or producing "false" work that didn't reflect the writer's true feelings (Erica). Each transcended the problem by "reading" another text—a short story, a TV show, the title of a play—and using it to catalyze his or her imagination.

How did Robin, Sally, and Erica use the texts they read?

First, consider what they *didn't* do. They did not:

1. Read the text and slavishly imitate it. Robin does not try writing "like" Chopin because that does not interest him. What does interest him are some similarities between Chopin's characters and people he has known in his own life. Likewise Sally and Erica. "Flowers for Algernon" and *Beyond the Horizon* give them the initial impetus to create but recede in importance as Sally and Erica actually write.

2. Read passively. Robin, Sally, and Erica are not mere consumers of texts; they are also *producers*. They follow their reading by creating texts of their own.

3. Read to "master" the total text. The three writers pick up on particular aspects of the text that interest them at the moment. Robin concentrates on the commitment theme. Sally is indifferent to the themes, characters, and plot of "Flowers for Algernon"; what attracts her are the point of view and form—first-person point of view in diary form. As for Erica, she doesn't even bother to read O'Neill's play, let alone "comprehend" it. The mere title suffices to prompt her memories and imagination and give her momentum for writing.

Robin, Sally, and Erica do not write to comprehend the texts they read; they simply seize upon elements of those texts that they can *use* in order to write themselves. Instead of attempting to understand the texts in total, they converse with those aspects of the text that interest them. Like a participant in a two-way conversation, each of these writers composes something (in this case, a written text rather than a spoken statement) that sustains an ongoing conversation. Because these conversations never end, and because the writer is contributing just one bit more to the discussion, the pressures on the writer to compose "brilliantly" and "profoundly" are greatly reduced.

Robin, Sally, and Erica imagine a particular model—a conversation model—of the relationship between themselves as writers and the texts they use to help them write. The existence of this model is all-important to their success as writers.

The Conversation Model

The conversation model says that you interact or *converse* with a text when you read it. Even as you are learning from the text, you yourself are bringing something *to* it, namely, your own background, experiences, thoughts, prior knowledge, biases, and opinions. The conversation model honors your right to *talk back* to the text.

According to the conversation model our minds are not empty receptacles waiting to be filled. As living, sentient beings, each of us brings to a text a history of thoughts, experiences, ideas, and readings. Who you are shapes what meaning you "get" from a text. That is, what essay X "means" is not something intrinsic to the text alone; what it means is largely shaped by the personal and cultural makeup of the reader who reads it.

For example, when I read a short story the "meaning" of the text is partly determined by who I, the reader, am; by what I already know about the subject of the story; by what my feelings, biases, or attitudes are about that subject; and by a whole range of other factors such as my race, gender, previous reading, and personal and cultural experience. In other words, I not only "receive" information, ideas, images, and so on from the story; I also bring my *self* to it. Recall how Robin, for instance, brought his experience of Uncle Jules to his reading of "The Story of an Hour"; his unique individual experience prompted him to read and use Chopin's story in a way that would not have occurred to a different reader. Reading thus becomes a process of negotiation—a sort of conversation—between the distinctive reader "me" and the author and text of the work I am reading.

As an example, imagine you pick up an essay about "the meaning of education." A shudder of insecurity passes through you: "Looks tough. And this writer has a Ph.D. What am *I* going to get out of this?" You are thinking passively. You overlook that you have been in school for many years yourself. Even if you haven't spent your free time reading books and articles on education, you possess another resource that equips you to "converse" with this reading: your dozen or so years as a learner, as a participant in the educational system. You know what it is like to do assignments, and you have encountered all variety of teachers, students, and teaching methods. Even though you are not yet ready to read and respond to the text before you as an educational scholar or expert, you do have expertise of a kind. This expertise—your own life and experiences as a student—gives you a way in to any piece of writing about education.

In short: *you know more than you realize.*

This is what American poet Walt Whitman had in mind when he wrote,

> *Walt, you contain enough, why don't you let it out then?*

It's one of the most democratic lines in all poetry. Instead of bowing to the Voice of Authority, which says, "You don't know enough yet to write; read some more *first*," Whitman discovers that he already knows (and you and I know) "enough" to join the conversation *now*.

Of course, you can always know more and write *better*—and reading and writing can be seen as lifelong endeavors to improve your knowledge and verbal dexterity. Whitman, for instance, read voraciously—everything from history and literature to astronomy, mysticism, criticism, human physiology, philosophy, and geology. His notebooks fill six thick volumes. However, he didn't postpone writing as something to be done only *after* reading; he read and wrote simultaneously. He fused reading and writing into one and treated the whole as a continuous two-way conversation, between himself and the world, himself and the written word, himself and experience.

ACTIVITIES FOR WRITING

1. In your own words, summarize the conversation model. What new understanding, if any, does the conversation model give you of your own habits as a reader and writer? Do you read "conversationally"? How or how don't you? When or when don't you?

2. Practice conversational reading and writing with the following exercise from *Personal Fiction Writing* (New York: Teachers & Writers Collaborative, 1984) by Meredith Sue Willis. Read the dialogue excerpt, below, from Tillie Olsen's novel, *Yonnondio: From the Thirties*. Then write what you imagine might have happened just before or after this dialogue. That is, write a prequel or sequel to the dialogue.

> No one greeted him at the gate—the dark walls of the kitchen enclosed on him like a smothering grave. Anna did not raise her head.
>
> In the other room the baby kept squalling and squalling and Ben was piping an out-of-tune song to quiet her. There was a sour smell of wet diapers and burned pots in the air.
>
> "Dinner ready?" he asked heavily.
>
> "No, not yet."
>
> Silence. Not a word from either.
>
> "Say, can't you stop that damn brat's squallin? A guy wants a little rest once in a while."
>
> No answer.
>
> "Aw, this kitchen stinks. I'm going out on the porch. And shut that brat up, she's driving me nuts, you hear?" You hear, he reiterated to himself, stumbling down the steps, you hear, you hear. Driving me nuts.

Using Texts to Make Texts:
Intertextuality

I had better never see a book than to be warped by its attraction clean out of my own orbit, and made a satellite instead of a system.

—Ralph Waldo Emerson

As a college sophomore John took a literature class in which he was assigned to read *Moby-Dick*. *Moby-Dick* is a long novel, and the class spent four days analyzing it. John worked hard, produced a term paper on *Moby-Dick*—and shortly thereafter forgot the book and nearly everything he had learned about it. Then, two years later, something interesting happened. John was writing a short story with a first-person ("I") narrator; his progress was stalled, when suddenly, out of the murk of his subconscious, there returned to him the opening sentence of *Moby-Dick*: "Call me Ishmael." This sentence, in which the novel's narrator introduces himself, reverberated in John's consciousness as he resumed and finished his story. A single sentence—a mere three words—suggested a sense of directness that helped him quickly and easily transpose his thoughts to paper.

When he mentioned this experience to a friend who had studied *Moby-Dick* in depth, the friend informed him that he had misinterpreted the line "Call me Ishmael"—that it was not about "directness" but about "indirectness and evasion." John thought about this a moment and replied, "You may be right. I only know that that line—whatever it means—helped me produce the best writing I've ever done."

John now describes this event as a turning point in his life as a reader and writer: "Till then I always thought my duty as a reader was to understand everything I read and hold it in my mind like a kind of computer; you know, with total recall. . . . This experience revolutionized my view of reading and writing. From a writer's perspective, what you read is often less significant than how it helps you to think and write."

John's last sentence is worth repeating: *From a writer's perspective, what you read is often less significant than how it helps you to think and write.* In classes you may have grown accustomed to focusing entirely on "what you read," i.e., the literary text itself, which you are generally asked to analyze for meaning. Part I of *Reading and Writing from Literature* has a radically different focus: not on "what you read" but on *how reading can help you to write.* In other words, the focus is not on the literary text itself but on the overlap between the text and your own experiences, knowledge, thoughts, and personal and cultural background. You might call your experiences, knowledge, thoughts, and personal and cultural background "texts" because they are already "written" into your life at the moment you read a text, and, as this chapter will show, they shape how you read that text.

What it is about a particular text that prompts you to write doesn't necessarily have to be something "major"; very often—as the examples of John and of Robin, Sally, and Erica in the previous chapter illustrate—it will be some small and rather limited aspect of the text: a theme, a character, an image, a phrase. The size of the catalyst matters less than how powerfully it resonates with your own life and imagination.

A Four-Step Process for Writing from Reading

How can you do as John did and identify the powerful connections you have with a text? How can you then use those connections to produce satisfying writing of your own? Here is a four-step process that builds on the conversation model discussed in Chapter 1. The beauty of the process is that you can apply it to all your reading—to the short stories, poems, essays, and plays in this book and to a range of other texts that you encounter in daily life.

1. *Do a first reading of the text.* Concentrate on immersing yourself in its rhythms, ideas, conflicts, plot, themes, characters.

2. *On a second reading, annotate passages that strike you.* Perhaps you like an idea, a phrase, a character, or an image, or perhaps you are struck by a section of dialogue, or maybe you are puzzled or mystified by a passage. Underline or bracket any such item. (This assumes, of course, that your copy of the text is your own and not a library's.) Also, in the margins, jot down:

- *Questions* that any passages raise for you
- *Analytical comments*, i.e., what you think about a passage
- *Summaries* of what a passage is saying
- *Connections* that a passage suggests with anything else you have read, thought about, or experienced

The marks you make in a text are called *annotations*. Annotation is as basic to readers and writers as hammers are to carpenters or utensils are to cooks. It is your main means of identifying the resonant points of connection you have with a text; these points, in turn, can catalyze you to write, as "Call me Ishmael" catalyzed John.

The key to successful annotating is that you trust the *first thoughts* that occur to you as you read, and write them down. If you are used to doubting the value of your every thought, this requires conscious effort and practice. You may be more accustomed to trusting in second thoughts, those socially acceptable or "correct" thoughts that censor the first ones as "dumb," "ridiculous," or "irrelevant." Reject these second thoughts and cleave to the first. (There will be an appropriate time later on for revising and refining your first thoughts, but that time is not yet.)

In a sense good annotating requires *un*learning; often it is less a matter of thinking harder than of thinking *less* hard. Rather than straining to write the "correct" or intellectually "comprehensive" response, you relax to write whatever pops into your head. For example, here is how Tyler annotated the opening paragraph of Kate Chopin's "The Story of an Hour" (p. 167):

> Knowing that Mrs. Mallard was afflicted with a <u>heart trou-</u>   *My good elderly*
> <u>ble</u>, great care was taken to break to her as gently as possible   *friend had heart*
> the news of her husband's death.   *trouble too. Jack*
>   *had a valve*
>   *replacement.*

At first Tyler's annotation may seem odd and irrelevant; after all, it refers to his "good elderly friend," who isn't even a character in Chopin's story. However, Tyler trusts his first thought enough to write it down and leave questions of relevance till later.

This trust pays off, as the initial memory of his "good elderly friend" stirs other memories. One thought reminds him of another, which reminds him of yet another, and another, and so forth: "Jack Hislop lived next door for the majority of my youth. He was like a grandfather to me. . . . I remembered how Jack would joke about his heart, 'I've got a pig valve in my heart, oink-oink.' That would always make me laugh." Shared times with Jack, Jack's appearance and mannerisms, fragments of conversation—all these surface, one after another, in Tyler's consciousness. Ultimately, out of these memories he composes a three-page portrait entitled "Grandpa Jack." Here is a portion of what he wrote (a copy of the complete portrait can be found in Appendix A):

> As a little boy I would go over to visit [Jack] almost every day after school. One day I ran over to his house and found him lounging on the patio in his back yard. "Take a seat, partner," said Jack as he pulled up a chair for me. He fed me some cold watermelon and a large glass of "sodi water," as he called it. While I was enjoying the fruit Jack told me a story about when he was a young sheepherder. "I was no older than you, partner, maybe eleven years old. . . . Me and Pa and a few of my brothers were

high on Durphies' Peak taking the sheep down to a nearby watering hole." His eyes were flashing as he was trying to point out where they were, since the mountain was in a broadside view. "A few sheep took off up a narrow canyon, and I got roped into chasin' after 'em. I rode up the canyon a little way and seen 'em up ahead so I galloped my horse to catch 'em. When I caught those little rascals I started herding 'em back down to the watering hole. On the way down the canyon my horse started to get jittery because some bushes started to shake up ahead, and out charged a huge brown bear." Jack was standing now giving the motions of the incident. Jack blurted, "Holy Shit!" then apologized to me because his wife didn't like him to cuss. "The damn horse started to buck and my two dogs went into a barking frenzy. The bear was huge, it was at least ten feet tall when it reared up on his hind legs. The dogs distracted the bear long enough allowin' me to ride up and around to safety."

If you read "The Story of an Hour," the text that inspired "Grandpa Jack," you will find that it focuses on a woman and her feelings about marriage and her husband. Tyler's annotation (and the text it engendered) is about a colorful old friend and has virtually nothing to do with women, husbands, or marriage. What then? Is it merely eccentric and irrelevant? "Yes" and "no." If you take Chopin's text as the central point of reference, then his annotation is indeed irrelevant; however, if you take as the main point of reference the overlap between Chopin's text and the texts of his own life, Tyler's annotation is right on target—a veritable bull's-eye. After all, it prompts him to articulate an aspect of his life he might never have written about otherwise without the stimulus of Chopin.

A footnote: At home and in class Tyler found enthusiastic readers for his essay. How interesting that so individual a response could have broad appeal to others. At the heart of annotation is a paradox. The more individual it is—the more spontaneous and intuitive—the more it seems to tap into something *universal* in human experience. Simply put, "If you like it, other people will tend to like it, too."

Here is a second example of annotation. Margaret is a middle-aged wife and mother who has recently entered college. She reads and annotates the following poem by Linda Pastan (p. 312):

MARKS

My husband gives me an A
for <u>last night's supper,</u>
an incomplete for my <u>ironing,</u>
<u>a B plus in bed.</u>
My son says I am average,
an average mother, but if
<u>I put my mind to it</u>

Annotations (left):
Hard! Anything less than an "A" really hurts

Annotations (right):
he likes the supper, but anything else? Hm. Sounds like she does all the work—or lots—and then has to get <u>grades</u> for it (pouring salt in the wounds)
<u>More</u> work . . . Is this son shiftless like mine? <u>He</u> should talk!

The "typical" family: father, mother, son, daughter. Everyone <u>rates</u> her

I could improve.
My [daughter] believes
in Pass/Fail and tells me
I pass. Wait 'til they learn
I'm dropping out.

Wow! She gonna kill herself? get a divorce? take a break? This'll shake 'em up

Note the individuality of Margaret's annotations. Like Tyler, Margaret writes spontaneously and directly about the points at which the literary text speaks to her. By annotating she focuses her attention less on the poem itself than on the overlap between the poem and the texts of her own life—her own experiences, knowledge, thoughts, and feelings.

3. *Read over your annotations; then take several minutes to list the most powerful thoughts and impressions the text inspires in you.* Here again, trusting your first thoughts is crucial. Instead of writing down the sorts of ideas you think you *ought* to have, put in your list what you *want* to put there. For instance, after Margaret has read and annotated "Marks," she makes the following list:

- I like the phrase 'Wait 'til they learn/I'm dropping out.' It sounds like an ultimatum.
- Idea: being a wife/mother like being in school. Grades, grades, grades! Always someone grading you.
- I relate to this woman.
- How will she drop out?
- I get a picture of this woman working hard all day and her husband comes home and expects everything to be done for him hand and foot. The son and daughter show up for meals but are always running off to have fun somewhere.
- This house sounds like lots I know. Starting with *mine*.
- Who gets grades? Kids. The mother never gets to grow up!

4. *Review your list; identify your most intense point of response, and compose a text of your own.* To see some of the kinds of texts you can write at this stage, look ahead to the section entitled "Ten Ideas for Writing in a Reading Notebook" in Chapter 3. Margaret reviews her list of thoughts and impressions and finds her prevailing response is a sense of identification with the speaker in the poem. She explores this identification in a text of her own.

School of Hard Knocks

Grading doesn't begin and end with school. It goes on all our lives. That's what this poem showed me. Wives and mothers especially; we're always being graded!

I got married right out of high school and I thought I was done with getting grades. Little did I know I was just going from one school to another. And I don't mean college. I mean marriage.

There are several classes in this "school."

Marriage 101 is living with a husband. In my case a husband I hardly knew. A nice man and a good provider and all, it turned out, but also a lout who expected me to wait on him hand and foot. Cook the meals, wash the dishes, clean the house, do the errands, entertain the company.

A typical scene: I'm cleaning the bathroom in 95 degree heat, sweat   5 pouring down my face, and he's in the livingroom watching baseball and drinking a beer. His buddies are with him and when the snack tray's empty they yell at me to "please" get more. If I'm a little slow I get a dirty look (that's a "C"). If I yell "Help yourself" and don't come at all I get a growl and some angry comments about "women" (that's an "F"). If I load up the tray and deliver it with a smile it's a "B." To get an "A" I have to do some extra credit—give them their potato chips plus a new round of beers ("A" if the beers are cold, "A−" if they're not).

Marriage 201 is kids. I love my kids, don't get me wrong. They were cute babies and except for the terrible two's the sweetest children I'll ever see. But since they hit their teens it's been a downhill road.

They treat me like their live-in cook and maid. I spend an hour in a hot kitchen making supper—something a little special, chicken cooked a new way—and they shovel it down without a word, it might as well be an old sock fried in batter. No "thank you's" or "This is great"—they're in too big a hurry to get somewhere—a dance, a game, and other places I probably don't want to know about.

I guess they'd give me a "B" for cooking—not good enough for praise, not bad enough to make them throw up (an "F"). If they don't like what I give them you can bet I hear about it. "Mom, what is this?" "Mom, are we supposed to eat this meatloaf or use it for a paperweight?" That's a "C−"—if they even bother to force it down, that is. A grade of "D" means "give it to the Dog."

Kids grade like most of the teachers I had in school. If they like it they don't tell you, and if they hate it they don't let you forget.

Next we come to Marriage 301: middle age. In my generation this   10 means a daughter going on to college and asking you why you became a homemaker and mother instead of getting "a real job." So I could have you and have conversations like this, I say. She looks at me confused like I must be lying. A real job. Boy! I'll tell you about a real job. . . . *This* is a real job. But it's not the job she's interested in.

I'm 45 years old and was on the verge of burnout when I decided to go back to school this fall. I'm a college freshman now at the same school my daughter graduated from a year ago. My son's a sophomore. And I'm getting grades. Am I living my life backwards, or what? I wonder some-times. I seem to be going back to my childhood: teachers giving me grades. And the teachers get younger and younger. My Math professor's a girl hardly older than my daughter. When she gave me my first test back with a "B" it reminded me of fried chicken! Déjà vu!

Only a mother would understand.

Note that this process of writing from reading leads Margaret to write, as Tyler did, about a number of things that aren't exactly *in* the springboard literary text but are suggested by it. For instance:

- Beliefs traditional in Margaret's culture about appropriate sex roles for men and women—and counterbeliefs that challenge the traditional roles
- The habits and behaviors of her own husband and kids and of other husbands and kids
- Mealtime conversations (those in her own home and perhaps analogous ones she has heard—or heard of—in other homes)
- Memories of various dinners such as chicken and meatloaf
- The particular feelings one has cleaning bathrooms on hot days
- The addiction of some men to TV sports
- The politics of classrooms like grading and teacher-student relations
- Ageism and sexism (both her direct observations of them in life and what she has observed, indirectly, through magazines, books, cosmetics ads, TV shows, movies, and so forth)

You might represent Margaret's reading graphically as follows:

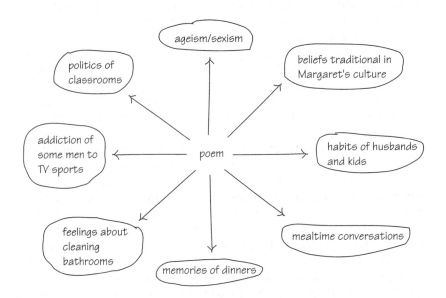

The point in the center is her starting point for writing, i.e., Pastan's poem. The arrows outward lead to the ideas, themes, beliefs, observations, experiences, and memories that she stumbled onto through the process of composing "School of Hard Knocks" and that generated her original focus.

Add a few more lines and you have an image of a web:

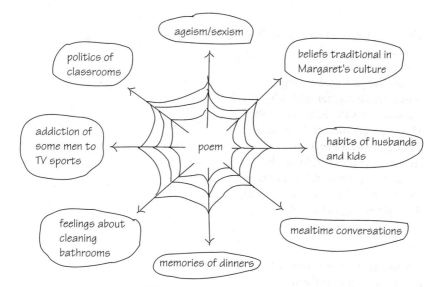

Again, call the circled items "texts"—the texts of Margaret's life. They are texts because they were already present and "written" into her life at the moment she picked up "Marks," and her essay is as much a reading of these texts as it is of Pastan's. Reading and responding to the poem stirs these texts to consciousness, the same as a motion in one strand of a web reverberates through all the other connected strands.

The true focus of Margaret's essay isn't "Marks," it is the weblike intertextual connections the poem evokes with her own life and imagination.

Language theorists call this phenomenon, of one text activating and talking back and forth with others, *intertextuality*. Intertextuality defines a process of imaginative connecting that is the very pulse beat of writing. It explains how the conversation model creates tremendous momentum for writing. Composing by the conversation model enables you to tap into other texts that are dormant within you—texts that are just "waiting" for some external influence, i.e., another text, to bring them to consciousness.

Applying the Four-Step Process

Now try the Four-Step Process for yourself on the following short poem. Like Tyler and Margaret, strive to focus not on the "meaning" of the literary text itself but on the overlap of the text with the texts of your own life and imagination. If you wish, do the first three steps collaboratively, with a group or as a class. For Step Four ("compose a text of your own"), strive to write at least three hundred words.

WAITING FOR THE IDIOT TO GO AWAY

PETER SHARPE

The sweet tomato face annealed to itself
in all directions and pressed sloppily
to the car window.
   I sat five years old asking
'why does he do that' and 'why is he like that'.   5
His name was Benji, he was really
35 or 38 years old and he drooled
and was short. I never got
an answer from my father, who
stared straight ahead, his foot tapping   10
nervously on the accelerator pedal,
lips tight and knuckles whitening
on the wheel, 'pretend he isn't there'
he told me.

   I had my first remembered lesson   15
in the social graces: the world
was imperfect, and this was embarrassing.

When you have finished, reflect on the Four-Step Process in your notebook. How did this mode of responding compare with the ways you have written in response to literature in the past? What do you like or dislike about the writing you produced for Step Four? If your piece pleased you, excellent; if not, bear in mind that *no* writer produces great work every time he or she sits down to write. Some of what a writer writes is good, and much—perhaps even most—is "bad" or disappointing. What matters is that out of the patient and continual practice of conversational reading and writing, *good writing will eventually come*. To put your "bad" writing in perspective, glance ahead to the section on "Revising" (p. 107) in Chapter 9.

Some Implications of Intertextuality

The experiences of Tyler and Margaret show that you don't need a brilliant imagination in order to write well; already woven into your life is a rich web of texts that merely require the catalyst of an *outside* text, such as "The Story of an Hour" or "Marks," in order to be realized on paper (or computer screen). The texts Margaret and Tyler wrote did not materialize out of nothing; they emerged out of other texts—"The Story of an Hour," "Marks," and the texts of Tyler's and Margaret's own lives. The French painter Pierre Auguste Renoir could have had people like Tyler and Margaret in mind when he wrote, "The artist who uses the least of what is called imagination will be the greatest."

This notion—that every text comes out of other texts—may upset some deeply embedded beliefs you have about the "originality" of stories, poems, plays, and other works. You may suppose, for example, that a creation like *Hamlet* was woven entirely out of Shakespeare's imagination and owed little or nothing to the example, structure, style, and themes of other works. But—alas—such a notion is contradicted by evidence. Scholars have shown that Shakespeare probably drew liberally upon other texts when he wrote *Hamlet*. The acting company to which he belonged was performing a *Hamlet* by an earlier author in the 1590s, several years before Shakespeare wrote his own play. He would have known the earlier play and most likely have performed in it. This early play was, in turn, indebted to still older versions of the Hamlet story dating as far back as the twelfth century.

Aside from these obvious intertextual borrowings, we can generalize about other texts that must have echoed, consciously or subconsciously, in the Bard's mind as he composed *Hamlet:* his boyhood experiences of plays and entertainments in his native town of Stratford; the plethora of plays by his fellow playwrights, whose works he either performed or saw produced in London and at court; the many structural and stylistic conventions, e.g., soliloquies and asides, of Elizabethan tragedy; the texts of classical poetry and rhetoric; his intensive training and experience as an actor; his firsthand knowledge of stage mechanics and directing; and any number of personal and cultural "texts" that are more difficult to name exactly but that doubtless played a part.

We can infer from the example of Shakespeare—and of countless other creators—that there is no such thing as an "original" work in the pure sense.

Our traditional sense of printed texts is tacitly hierarchical. A creation like *Hamlet* or *Moby-Dick* ranks at the top of the hierarchy, while newspaper editorials, song lyrics, pop novels, and your own writings rank lower. A work by William Faulkner or Alice Walker—both internationally famous authors—rates high on the scale, while the story you compose is "just (blush) something I wrote." Of course, this hierarchy makes sense in some respects; by most people's standards, your short story isn't as "good" as Faulkner's. But such ratings rest on culturally and individually based notions of literary value and cause us to forget that there are other ways of looking at texts—for instance, the intertextual way.

Intertextuality focuses attention less on questions of literary value than on textuality itself. From that admittedly limited but too often ignored perspective, no text is "better" than another. Intertextuality democratizes. All pieces of writing are equal in terms of their shared identity and utility *as texts.*

A consciousness of intertextuality empowers you as a reader and writer. Every text—everything you read and everything you write—flows out of and into other texts. No text is closed off or completely self-sufficient. No text represents the Last Word.

Your consciousness of intertextuality renders any text you read more accessible and more human. Take *Hamlet,* for instance. If you view it as "perhaps the greatest play ever written by perhaps the greatest writer who ever lived," it overwhelms you; it makes you afraid to write yourself. After all, who are you to meddle with a masterpiece like that? Your fear and insecurity are one with that of thousands of English students down through the decades who have balked helplessly at an assignment to "write an essay about *Hamlet*."

On the other hand, if you view *Hamlet* as the outcome of a complex interaction of many texts—and as a prompt for countless others, e.g., the volumes and volumes of Shakespeare criticism that have been written; the plays, poems, stories, screenplays, musicals, and other imaginative works that have been partially prompted by *Hamlet*—then the play becomes less a holy relic and more a part of the complicated, ever-expanding web of human discourse. *Hamlet* is a strand in the web, a remark in an endless conversation that originated long before Shakespeare's time, reverberates in the present, and will echo and reecho long beyond today.

Viewed from some outlying perspective that takes in all of human time, *Hamlet* appears as just another turn—a brilliant and memorable turn, to be sure—in an ongoing conversation. It is of the nature of conversation to invite additional turn-taking. Reading *Hamlet*, you are welcome to respond to it; you are welcome to add your bit to the conversation.

It may help to think of this visually. Divorced from a notion of intertextuality, a text looks something like this:

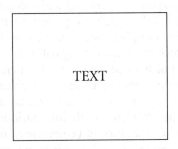

Its edges are hard and defined, closed off to creative reading and responding. Viewed through the lens of intertextuality, on the other hand, the text looks like this:

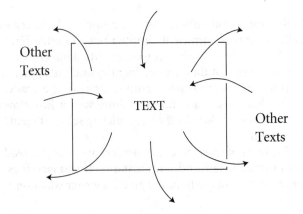

The edges are broken, open, allowing a fluid intercourse of this text with others—past, present, and future; printed and unprinted.

ACTIVITIES FOR WRITING

1. The concept of *intertextuality* implies that every text comes out of other texts—printed or unprinted, texts that are conscious in the writer's mind and others that are subconscious. From this we can infer that there is no such thing as an "original" work in the pure sense; that is, the work always shows traces of other texts. Look around your environment and identify an example of a text, e.g., a story or poem, an article or advertisement, that is intertextually generated. If the text is short, photocopy it. Then, with the analysis of Margaret's intertextual web on page 15 as your model, list the texts that clearly (or possibly) helped generate it.

2. Use the "Four-Step Process for Writing from Reading" to respond to either of the texts printed below, by Ellen Goodman and D. H. Lawrence.
   a. Read through the text a first time without marking it (unless you feel moved to do so).
   b. On a second reading, annotate.
   c. Alone or with a group, create a list of the most powerful thoughts and impressions the piece inspires in you. Don't worry if items on your list seem to go off on a tangent from the text itself.
   d. Identify your favorite item or items in the list of thoughts and impressions and use it/them to create a text of your own that is at least three hundred words long.

LIVE-IN MYTHS

ELLEN GOODMAN

"He is not really like that," she said apologetically as her husband left the room.

"Like what?" I asked, wondering which of the many things that had happened that evening she was excusing.

"Well, you know," she said, "cranky."

I thought about that. Cranky. It was typical of the woman that she would choose a gentle, even childish, word for the sort of erratic outbursts of anger which had been her husband's hallmark for the past fifteen years.

He was not really like that. This had been her sentence when they were first dating, when they were living together, and now, since they were married.

When he questioned, minutely, the price tags of her purchases, she would say: "He is really, deep down, very generous." When he disagreed with her politics, veering to the right while she listed to the left, she would cheerily insist that underneath all that he was "basically" liberal.

When he blamed her for the condition of the house, as if he were a lodger, and blamed her for the children's illnesses, as if her negligence had caused their viruses, she would explain, "He is really very understanding."

Even when he was actually his most vital self, amusing and expansive, full of martinis or enthusiasm or himself—and she disapproved—she would forgive him because he wasn't really like that.

This time, dining with them out of town one brief night, I saw that this was the pattern of their lives together—a struggle between realities. His real and her "really."

I had known the wife since college and the husband from their first date. When they met she was a social worker and he was, it seems, her raw material. Was he the case and she the miracle worker? At times she looked at him that way.

Her husband was erratic and difficult, but he had a streak of humor and zaniness as attractive as Alan Arkin's. Over the years, he had grown "crankier" and she more determined in her myth-making.

This trip, for the first time, I wondered what it must be like to be a text living with an interpreter. To be not really like that. And what it must be like for her, living with her myth as well as her man.

I know many other people who live with their ideas of each other. Not with a real person but with a "really." They doggedly refuse to let the evidence interfere with their opinions. They develop an idea about the other person and spend a lifetime trying to make him or her live up to that idea. A lifetime, too, of disappointments.

As James Taylor sings it: "First you make believe / I believe the things that you make believe / And I'm bound to let you down. / Then it's I who have been deceiving / Purposely misleading / And all along you believed in me."

But when we describe what the other person is really like, I suppose we often picture what we want. We look through the prism of our need.

I know a man who believes that his love is really a very warm woman. The belief keeps him questing for that warmth. I know a woman who is sure that her mate has hidden strength, because she needs him to have it.

Against all evidence, one man believes that his woman is nurturing because he so wants her to be. After twenty years, another woman is still tapping hidden wells of sensuality in her mate, which he has, she believes, "repressed."

And maybe they are right and maybe they are wrong, and maybe they are each other's social workers. But maybe they are also afraid that if they let go of their illusions, they will not like each other.

We often refuse to see what we might not be able to live with. We choose distortion.

Leaving this couple, I thought about how much human effort can go into maintaining the "really." How much daily energy that might have gone into understanding the reality—accepting it or rejecting it.

How many of us spend our lives trying to sustain our myths, and how we are "bound to be let down." Because most people are, after all, the way they seem to be.

Really.

You might find yourself particularly drawn to Goodman's reflections in the last several paragraphs, or, just as easily, you might focus your annotations and response on the people and situations portrayed in the first half of the piece. What are this wife and husband like? Do they remind you of any people from your own experience? Do you know—or can you imagine—"people who live with their *ideas* of each other" [italics added] rather than with their authentic selves? These questions suggest just a few of the many points of connection you might find with this text.

SNAKE

D. H. LAWRENCE

A snake came to my water-trough
On a hot, hot day, and I in pyjamas for the heat,
To drink there.

In the deep, strange-scented shade of the great dark carob-
    tree   5
I came down the steps with my pitcher
And must wait, must stand and wait, for there he was at
    the trough before me.

He reached down from a fissure in the earth-wall in the
    gloom   10
And trailed his yellow-brown slackness soft-bellied down,
    over the edge of the stone trough
And rested his throat upon the stone bottom,
And where the water had dripped from the tap, in a small
    clearness,   15
He sipped with his straight mouth,
Softly drank through his straight gums, into his slack long
    body,
Silently.

Someone was before me at my water-trough,   20
And I, like a second comer, waiting.

He lifted his head from his drinking, as cattle do,
And looked at me vaguely, as drinking cattle do,
And flickered his two-forked tongue from his lips, and
    mused a moment,   25
And stooped and drank a little more,
Being earth-brown, earth-golden from the burning bowels
    of the earth
On the day of Sicilian July, with Etna smoking.

The voice of my education said to me   30

He must be killed,
For in Sicily the black, black snakes are innocent, the gold
   are venomous.

And voices in me said, If you were a man
You would take a stick and break him now, and finish   35
   him off.

But must I confess how I liked him,
How glad I was he had come like a guest in quiet, to drink
   at my water-trough
And depart peaceful, pacified, and thankless,   40
Into the burning bowels of this earth?

Was it cowardice, that I dared not kill him?
Was it perversity, that I longed to talk to him?
Was it humility, to feel so honoured?
I felt so honoured.   45

And yet those voices:
If you were not afraid, you would kill him!

And truly I was afraid, I was most afraid,
But even so, honoured still more
That he should seek my hospitality   50
From out the dark door of the secret earth.

He drank enough
And lifted his head, dreamily, as one who has drunken,
And flickered his tongue like a forked night on the air, so
   black,   55
Seeming to lick his lips,
And looked around like a god, unseeing, into the air,
And slowly turned his head,
And slowly, very slowly, as if thrice adream,
Proceeded to draw his slow length curving round   60
And climb again the broken bank of my wall-face.

And as he put his head into that dreadful hole,
And as he slowly drew up, snake-easing his shoulders, and
   entered farther,
A sort of horror, a sort of protest against his withdrawing   65
   into that horrid black hole,
Deliberately going into the blackness, and slowly drawing
   himself after,
Overcame me now his back was turned.

I looked round, I put down my pitcher,   70
I picked up a clumsy log
And threw it at the water-trough with a clatter.

I think it did not hit him,
But suddenly that part of him that was left behind con-
    vulsed in undignified haste,   75
Writhed like lightning, and was gone
Into the black hole, the earth-lipped fissure in the wall-
    front,
At which, in the intense still noon, I stared with fascination.

And immediately I regretted it.   80
I thought how paltry, how vulgar, what a mean act!
I despised myself and the voices of my accursed human
    education.

And I thought of the albatross,
And I wished he would come back, my snake.   85

For he seemed to me again like a king,
Like a king in exile, uncrowned in the underworld,
Now due to be crowned again.

And so, I missed my chance with one of the lords
Of life.   90
And I have something to expiate;
A pettiness.

Building a Reading Notebook: Ten Ideas for Writing from Reading

Everything has been said before. There's nothing new to write about—always the same old things, the same old lies and the same old loves and the same old tragedy and joy. But you can write about them in a new way, your own way.

—EUGENE O'NEILL

Famous Writers at Work

How do writers produce their finished works? Do their stories, poems, essays, and plays materialize magically out of nothing? As suggested in the previous chapter, writers produce texts out of already existing texts. The examples of this are virtually limitless.

Anton Chekhov (1860–1904) was one of the world's greatest short story writers. Through much of his career he kept notebooks in which he recorded ideas for stories, brief character sketches, snippets of dialogue, memorable images and quotations, and thoughts. Many of these items furnished materials for his published stories. Toward the end of his life he said that he had enough ideas stored up in his notebook "for five years of work."

Eugene O'Neill had an enormous impact on the development of modern drama and was awarded a Nobel Prize for Literature in 1936. Behind O'Neill the great dramatist is O'Neill the notebook writer. In his notebooks O'Neill recorded his "readings" of his own life and of the world around him. The plays that made him famous evolved out of notes, sketches, and outlines that he collected in these notebooks. Often this involved a remarkably slow process of accretion and reworking. For instance, one of his best plays, *The Iceman Cometh,* evolved from notes he made as many as twenty years before the play was published.

Walt Whitman (1819–92) habitually wrote down ideas, spontaneously as they occurred to him, on pocket-sized notepaper. These he periodically reread. Notes that seemed related to each other he put in an envelope. When he felt he had "enough" in an envelope, he dumped out the contents and arranged and rearranged the slips of paper to make a poem. Whitman described this process of accumulating and ordering material as "unhurried" and insisted that he never "forced" his writing in any way.

These are glimpses of writers at work. While the details of habit and behavior differ from one writer to the next, certain commonalities emerge: they collect material; at various times they reread and rework it. Writing is the process of "conversing" with the accumulated notes—reviewing, expanding, revising, and reordering them. The strategy that drives Chekhov's and O'Neill's notebooks and Whitman's pseudonotebook is simple: to accumulate writings that can be reread later and selectively discarded—or reworked and revised into more finished writing. Such is the principle behind the reading notebook.

Using Reading as a Springboard for Writing

One way to understand a reading notebook is to contrast it with a traditional diary. In a diary you write about feelings, personal issues and problems, or goals; perhaps you explore your family background, childhood experiences, joys, and traumas. The diary works wonderfully when you have a lot on your mind or feel a need to unburden or celebrate; but during dull periods in your life when you have no particular thoughts, you begin repeating yourself. One well-known author described this phenomenon as "contemplating your belly button." Self-absorbed, you recycle the same ideas over and over and start to bore even yourself.

A reading notebook solves this problem. Simply defined, a reading notebook is a place where you do as Chekhov, O'Neill, and Whitman did and "springboard" off texts that you read. These texts may be printed works, such as the stories, poems, essays, and plays in Part V of this book, or they may be unprinted "texts," such as movies, TV programs, pictures, songs, memories, personal relationships, experiences, or conversations. You use these texts, which suffuse your everyday life, as prompts for your own writing.

How a Reading Notebook Works

The method behind the reading notebook is simple: read an existing text to create a new text. For instance, suppose you read Robert Frost's poem "Stopping by Woods on a Snowy Evening" (p. 814), which describes a person entering the dark woods with his horse during a snowfall. It uses themes, sounds, and images that move you and remind you of similar mysterious encounters of your own with nature. You annotate the poem and write from it using the Four-Step Process described in Chapter 2. You compose your own poem, or perhaps a short prose memoir, about one of your own nature encounters. Frost's poem catalyzes you to create writing of your own.

You sustain this habit—of using texts to make texts—over weeks and years. You never run out of ideas for writing. In addition to reading widely, you accumulate a notebook full of original texts that *you* have created.

Why a Reading Notebook Works

Left to itself, your mind wanders, or it is nervous and unfocused. Texts focus your attention. They give you ideas for writing by alerting you to thoughts, feelings, images, and experiences that have been powerful to you but are now forgotten.

Imagine you are sitting at your desk trying to write. You've got a rich history of experience with woods and the outdoors, but at that moment that history is buried, subconscious. Then suppose you read Frost's poem. You get the feel of the outdoors—sights, sounds, tactile sensations. Images and experiences from your own past begin flooding your consciousness. Suddenly you are composing a text of your own, riding on the current of those now remembered images and experiences. You compose at the seam between Frost's text and the "text" of your own experience. If you hadn't read "Stopping by Woods" those powerful memories wouldn't have risen into consciousness. Frost's poem brought them to the surface and gave you impetus to write.

Ten Ideas for Writing in a Reading Notebook

A reading notebook is a place for you to create and imagine, to interweave the texts of your life with the texts you read. Use the notebook for producing all kinds of writings that get you involved, personally and imaginatively, in what you read. Here are some suggestions. You can find additional examples of each of these "Ten Ideas" in Appendix A.

1. *Converse with specific points in the text that strike you.* In conversations with other people you do a number of things: agree, disagree, question, comment, joke, continue a point, and so on; you can converse in similar ways with

the texts you read. For example, Stephanie read Ray Bradbury's "[A Story About Love]" (p. 191) and commented on several quotations that were key to her:

> "It's the privilege of old people to seem to know everything. But it's an act and a mask, like every other act and mask. Between ourselves, we old ones wink at each other and smile, saying, How do you like *my* mask, *my* act, *my* certainty? Isn't life a play? Don't I play it well?"

This statement is so very true. Everyone has a mask and plays a part. The only exceptions are children, until they reach a certain age and then they become like the rest of the actors. People play a part and wear a mask because they're afraid of rejection and persecution. No one likes to have their feelings hurt or their egos smashed in.

> "When you're twenty-seven if you still know everything you're still seventeen."

This statement is profound. I think what she means is that if you are 27 and think you know everything, you haven't lived enough, matured enough, or experienced enough to be more than 17. You may have the body of a 27 year-old, but your mind is that of a seventeen year-old.

> "[T]he average man runs helter-skelter the moment he finds anything like a brain in a lady."

This statement strikes me as one spoken by someone who knows. From personal experience, this statement is a fact. I think the key word here is "average." It takes a man who is secure enough in himself and who can see beyond the mask to know when he's got something in a woman with a brain. This is not an average man. That man is an extraordinary man.

> "Kindness and intelligence are the preoccupations of age."

I agree that people become wiser with age, but I don't think that kindness is necessarily a preoccupation of age. Most people try very hard to be kind and spare others' feelings. If she is talking about genuine kindness, then perhaps that is a preoccupation of age. Genuine kindness is a part of the real person; kindness is just another one of the masks we wear.

2. *Write about any personal connections you have with the reading.* Margaret's writing from "Marks," quoted in Chapter 2, is a good example.

3. *Write a letter to the author and/or a return letter from the author to yourself.* This is a good way to gain more confidence in yourself as a reader. Instead of effacing yourself and revering the author as a sort of god or goddess, you

address the writer familiarly and person-to-person. You can write to the author about most anything—from your evaluation of the work to your thoughts about a theme, a character or characters, life issues, or literary technique. Stan read Emily Dickinson's "The Soul Selects Her Own Society" (p. 550) and a few other Dickinson poems, as well as some biographical material. Confused by the poetry but fascinated by the unusual life of its author (see p. 892), he wrote the following letter:

Dear Ms. Dickinson:

I hope you won't think I'm disrespectful, but I have a few questions for you. You seem a little unapproachable to me. Your poems are some of the most difficult I've ever seen—they hardly seem to be written in English.

I wonder if there is some connection between the meaning of your poems and your lifestyle.

Why did you shut yourself off from the world? Why, after a certain point in life, did you wear only white? Why did you write so many hundreds of poems without publishing them?

I could go on, but this is probably enough questions for now.

Sincerely,

Stan

P.S.—Please write back in language I can understand.

P.P.S.—I have my own theory of why you shut yourself off. I think you did it as a way to have maximum control over your own life. Live like a recluse and no one will bother you. You get a father who brings home cash, keeps bread on the table, and stays downstairs. You get a sister who can manage the little chores you don't feel like doing and who also stays downstairs—unless you ask her up. You have a servant or two to clean, cook, do the laundry, and you've got it made. You can bake, garden, and do just enough domestic chores to put "experience" into your poems, and you are running the house while everyone else just thinks you are "poor brilliant Emily" who's a little crazy in the head. You shut yourself off, in short, as part of a conscious strategy to control your family and amuse the neighbors so they would leave you alone to do what you wanted to—write.

Dear friend:
Such bolts of clarity
Inspire your charity—
E. Dickinson

4. *Write an imaginary interview with the author or with a character in a story, novel, or play.* This idea has the same basic advantages as letter writing. The interview format lets you see, hear, and address the author as a flesh-and-blood

person. Use your interview to ask the author questions about his or her text, style, characters, ideas, and life, for example.

5. *Compose a prequel or a sequel to a story.* Have you ever felt disappointed to see a story end? Perhaps you enjoyed the plot or identified with the characters and themes and could gladly have inhabited the world of that story—or novel or play—a while longer. Composing a prequel or sequel is an excellent way to do just that. You can sustain the lives of the characters beyond the author's prescribed ending, or you can imagine what the characters did, thought, and experienced before the story proper begins. This is also a relaxed and pleasurable way of imitating the author's tone, style, and methods of characterization; that is, it is a good way of broadening your own storytelling repertoire.

Helen and Bill, the main characters in Bradbury's "[A Story About Love]," become acquainted one summer day in a drugstore. They fall in love despite a vast difference in age—she is ninety-five and he is thirty-one—and have only a brief relationship before she dies. In the story "reincarnation" is mentioned. This gave Trent the idea to invent a sequel, "written in a Southeast Asian style," that incorporates Buddhist mythology and the idea of reincarnation. "Buddhism," Trent explains, "teaches that human beings can be reincarnated in one of two ways: first, they can improve because of good actions in this life; second, they can regress if they involve themselves in unclean activities."

As William left the house of Helen, she truly desired to be with him. She hoped there was a way because her feelings for him were strong. At this time Buddha looked down and was filled with mercy.

He said to those enlightened about him, "This mortal truly possesses the love necessary to obtain the wish of her heart." He paused, then continued: "But does the other possess the same quality?"

Ong Dia, one of the enlightened, spoke: "We must test the mortal to see if he has this quality."

Buddha replied, "Yes, we must do even as you say, Ong Dia."

Buddha then turned to Tao Quan and said, "Tao Quan, you must go down to the earth and test this mortal. Create a situation in which the mortal voluntarily chooses to do an act of love and mercy; if he chooses not to do this act, then he will not obtain the wish of his heart, and he will have to suffer regression in the great pattern of reincarnation."

The night that Helen died was hard for Bill, and he was having difficulty dealing with it. Just at this moment, a man ran up behind him. The man drew out a knife and demanded Bill's wallet, then ran away. Bill felt as though he had nothing to lose so he chased the man into the woods. They ran for a few minutes, then the thief tripped and fell. The thief was sliding down the edge of a hill which turned out to be a cliff. The bottom appeared to be some twenty feet down. The thief was hanging on to some foliage but was slipping fast.

The thief exclaimed, "Help me, please help me." Bill was scared, he did not know if he should help him. What if the man decided to use the knife and kill him anyway? Bill did not think long, he extended his hand to help the thief up.

Bill pulled the man up, and no sooner had he done so than he witnessed one of the most awesome spectacles he had ever seen. The thief changed form and seemed to float in the air. He then took on his true form, Tao Quan, one of the gods. Light and brilliance shone from his countenance.

Tao Quan spoke to him saying, "Great is the love and mercy possessed by you, mortal. You saved the life of one who had persecuted you and did it with the chance of losing your life; Buddha is smiling upon your action this night. Because of this thing you have done, you will receive the desire of your heart."

That night Bill was full of joy, but he did not know how his wish to be with Helen would be granted. He went to bed. The next morning he awoke and noticed nothing different. However, he felt a need to go to the drugstore.

He went in and everything seem to be the same; so he approached the snow-marble fountain. The man asked, "What'll it be?" Bill responded, "Old fashioned lime-vanilla ice." A shout of joy echoed throughout the store.

A beautiful young woman came running towards Bill. She looked familiar to him, and they embraced. He looked into her eyes and saw that it was Helen, except now she was young again. They held each other for a long time, then Bill whispered to Helen, "I love you." She answered, "I've waited for this day for 95 years. I love you too."

6. Rewrite a text from a point of view different from that presented in the original text. "Point of view" refers to the perspective from which a story is told. Any two witnesses to—or participants in—an event are apt to report different versions of what happened. Thus, events or impressions that seem to be definite and "factual" can change more or less drastically depending on who narrates and interprets them. (For more on the role of point of view in storytelling, see p. 133.)

Nathan found Chopin's "The Story of an Hour" was "too morose" for his taste, so in his response, he says, he " 'livened' it up by taking an outsider's perspective. Along the way I intertwined a little humor as well." Nathan rewrote "The Story of an Hour" from the point of view of the family physician in Brently and Louise Mallard's hometown. Since the physician appears only briefly in Chopin's short story, Nathan had to invent narrative details out of his own imagination:

"I want my mommy!"
The voices from the exam room could be heard out in the waiting room, making people very nervous. Inside the exam room a doctor struggled with his little patient as the father tried in vain to soothe the child.

Eventually a nurse brought in a lollipop which appeased the child somewhat, and the commotion subsided as the doctor quickly finished the child's checkup.

"There is a slight irritation in his ear due to an earlier rash which has flared up again. It should pass in a day or two," the doctor explained to the now frazzled yet relieved father.

As the father and son in tandem left, the doctor heard the nurse down the hall exclaim, "Next!" Wearily he waited for the next in a never-ending stream of patients, complaints, and anxious mothers of small children. It was always the same, day after day, month after month. Not that he minded, of course. The pay was good, the benefits many, and most of all, he knew it was a vital service he rendered to the people of his community. No, he didn't mind the work; it was just that he had seemingly fallen into a rut. Nothing ever changed. He wished that once in a while something so out of the ordinary would happen that he could get a fresh new perspective on everything.

The next person complained of stomach cramps. He prescribed the correct medication, and told the lady to see him again in a week if the pain still persisted.

Now he thought back to that very morning. He had expressed his feelings to his wife and wondered aloud to her what he could do about it. She had offered some words of encouragement, but said that it was something that he needed to work out for himself. Her last words as he exited the house were, "Maybe this'll be the day things change." He hoped she was right.

Suddenly his thoughts were interrupted by a nurse bringing hurried news of a train crash nearby. He acted quickly, telling the nurse to take over, and dashed out to his car.

When he got to the scene of the accident he was astounded by what he found. He had envisioned hundreds of people screaming, trapped inside a burning train. Instead, what he found was almost comical. The train had hit a herd of cattle while they crossed the tracks. The accident was an hour old when he arrived but appeared as if it had just happened moments ago. The engine had derailed, a fire had started, and the result was a fire that burned several head of cattle. One of the derailed cars contained superglue, and the whole conglomerate mess appeared as the largest, stickiest pile of hamburger the doctor had ever seen.

There were only minor injuries to the people involved, however, so when he got a call about a man involved in the wreck who had wandered home with a head injury he quickly drove to the person's house. When he got to the proper house he discovered the man was perfectly healthy, but his wife had just died. The situation was explained in this manner: the husband "died," the woman rejoiced, the "dead" husband returned, the wife then died, and now the husband rejoiced. The doctor thought it'd make a good Shakespearean play. He then determined the cause of death to be joy from hearing deathly news followed by extreme shock and grief on seeing the dead return. The doctor left satisfied at having his wish fulfilled at seeing the extraordinary.

7. *Rewrite a work into a different genre.* For instance, rewrite all or part of a short story as a poem, or a poem as a play, or a play as a letter, and so forth. Craig, a new father, was moved by Donald Hall's poem "My Son, My Executioner" (page 311), in which the speaker/father ruminates on the theme of passing time. Hall's speaker glimpses his own mortality in the young life of his infant son. Craig rewrote the poem as a prose meditation by the father:

> I have such strange feelings as I cradle this child. On the one hand, a feeling of joy and happiness to be holding this new life that is bound to me so intimately. On the other hand, this infant child is like a mirror that shows me myself in a new and sudden light: for an instant it seems I am *myself* being cradled, and the large face looking down at me is my own father's. So *this* is what it's all about, I think: My own father is now an old man . . . his father's father is dead . . . life and death. At some level the fact that I am myself dying doesn't bother me because, for this moment, when everything is just an inseparable part of the living and dying, the individual *ME* doesn't matter, doesn't exist. It's a tender feeling I have as I contemplate my son's joyous life, which is all to come, and my own relentless decay. I almost envy myself this tenderness because such moments are so rare . . . moments of perfect wisdom, to be counted on the fingers of one hand.

8. *Borrow an incident or theme from a work to write a piece of your own based on a similar incident or theme.* The train wreck mentioned in Chopin's "The Story of an Hour" reminded JoEllen of a tragedy that occurred in her hometown when she was growing up, when two boys were killed by a train. "Even though I never really knew the family well," she wrote, "the story of these two boys being killed by a train had an impact on me." JoEllen borrowed the incident of the train death to create her own narrative and imagined herself into the story as the narrator/sister of the two boys.

> Life was casual in the small town of Kaysville. All the necessities were there: a good school, a small grocery store, a bank and the theatre. For such a small place a movie house was a luxury. Many people from neighboring towns came to see the big screen almost weekly. In our family, going to the movies was a monthly ritual. We lived on a farm on the west side of the tracks. Every day was filled to the brim with chores, school, and then chores again. My job was to feed the chickens and slop the pigs. My two brothers helped pa milk the cows and feed the horses. Life was busy, but good.
> The summer of '62 is when things changed. . . .

The rains never came that year. The crops were a complete loss and money was very tight. My brothers, now fifteen and sixteen, were looking for jobs off the farm to help ma and pa make ends meet. School was our only outlet from the frustrations we felt at home. One morning as we rode the bus to school we watched the passing train. As it thundered by we talked of its great power and strength. My oldest brother fantasized about what life would be like engineering a train and traveling all over the country. He felt his future was wide open in front of him. If he only knew. But none of us can predict what will happen in the future.

The day began with the rooster crowing to wake us for our morning chores. Our steps were a little lighter because it was Friday and we knew that we were going to the movies that night. The school day dragged on like most Fridays do, but finally the bell rang and we were out the door into the fresh fall air. We hurried through our chores and met ma in the kitchen fixing our supper. We urged her to hurry for we didn't want to miss a moment of the movie we had been waiting for. Ma and pa opted to stay home that night because of the lack of money or lack of interest—I'm not sure which. My oldest brother could drive, so he got the keys to pa's pickup and the three of us left ready for a break from reality on the farm. As we approached the train tracks my brother flipped on the radio and blasted it in our ears at a level that showed his enthusiasm for life. The night was pitch black with no moon in sight. What happened next was so quick that I can only guess. The powerful train that my brothers had admired only a few days before thundered upon us with no chance of escape. The impact on the driver's side sent me out of the window and to the side of the tracks. My brothers weren't as lucky. As I heard and felt the meshing of metal against metal and the screeching of wheels, I knew my life would never be the same.

9. *Borrow the genre or form of a work to create a piece of your own cast in the same genre or form.* A good example here is Daniel Keyes's story "Flowers for Algernon," which is a narrative related entirely through diary entries. Recall how Sally, mentioned in Chapter 1, borrowed Keyes's form to create a story about a "blocked" writer. While the theme of her story differed totally from Keyes's, the diary form provided a release for emotions and experiences Sally had not been able to articulate in other ways.

Unusual forms like that of "Flowers for Algernon" sometimes generate the most interesting and surprising responses. Eugene O'Neill wrote a one-act play, *Before Breakfast,* which has two characters, only one of whom actually speaks and appears onstage. (The play is a one-way conversation in which a wife, in the kitchen, talks to her husband, who is offstage in the bedroom.) Jean borrowed O'Neill's formal technique to write a short one-way "dialogue" of her own in which a daughter talks on the phone with her mother and the mother herself is never actually heard. Incidentally, O'Neill himself got the idea for *Before Breakfast* from August Strindberg's one-act "monologue" play, *The Stronger.*

10. *Draft a fictional biography or autobiography of a character in a story, poem, or play.* One reason we enjoy literary texts is because they leave much to our own imaginations. Authors reveal selected facts about their characters and leave it to us to "fill in" gaps and missing details. You can use your notebook to reconstruct the life of a character who particularly intrigues you.

This list of "Ten Ideas" is by no means exhaustive. As you compose in your own notebook, you will doubtless discover other ideas for writing. The only rule is to write what you *want* to write, not what you feel you *should* write.

Review List of the Ten Ideas for Writing

1. Converse with specific points in the text that strike you.
2. Write about any personal connections you have with the reading.
3. Write a letter to the author and/or a return letter from the author to yourself.
4. Write an imaginary interview with the author or with a character in a story, novel, or play.
5. Compose a prequel or a sequel to a story.
6. Rewrite a text from a point of view different from that presented in the original text.
7. Rewrite a work into a different genre.
8. Borrow an incident or theme from a work to write a piece of your own based on a similar incident or theme.
9. Borrow the genre or form of a work to create a piece of your own cast in the same genre or form.
10. Draft a fictional biography or autobiography of a character in a story, poem, or play.

ACTIVITIES FOR WRITING

On the following pages are three short stories: Mary Robison's "Yours," Dorothy Parker's "But the One on the Right," and Kate Chopin's "The Storm." Using the "Four-Step Process for Writing from Reading" outlined in Chapter 2 and any one of the "Ten Ideas" in Chapter 3, compose a response of at least three hundred words to any one of these stories.

YOURS

Allison struggled away from her white Renault, limping with the weight of the last of the pumpkins. She found Clark in the twilight on the twig-and-leaf-littered porch behind the house.

He wore a wool shawl. He was moving up and back in a padded glider, pushed by the ball of his slippered foot.

Allison lowered a big pumpkin, let it rest on the wide floorboards.

Clark was much older—seventy-eight to Allison's thirty-five. They were married. They were both quite tall and looked something alike in their facial features. Allison wore a natural-hair wig. It was a thick blond hood around her face. She was dressed in bright-dyed denims today. She wore durable clothes, usually, for she volunteered afternoons at a children's day-care center.

She put one of the smaller pumpkins on Clark's long lap. "Now, nothing surreal," she told him. "Carve just a *regular* face. These are for kids."

In the foyer, on the Hepplewhite desk, Allison found the maid's chore list with its cross-offs, which included Clark's supper. Allison went quickly through the day's mail: a garish coupon packet, a bill from Jamestown Liquors, November's pay-TV program guide, and the worst thing, the funniest, an already opened, extremely unkind letter from Clark's relations up North. "You're an old fool," Allison read, and, "You're being cruelly deceived." There was a gift check for Clark enclosed, but it was uncashable, signed, as it was, "Jesus H. Christ."

Late, late into this night, Allison and Clark gutted and carved the pumpkins together, at an old table set on the back porch, over newspaper after soggy newspaper, with paring knives and with spoons and with a Swiss Army knife Clark used for exact shaping of tooth and eye and nostril. Clark had been a doctor, an internist, but also a Sunday watercolorist. His four pumpkins were expressive and artful. Their carved features were suited to the sizes and shapes of the pumpkins. Two looked ferocious and jagged. One registered surprise. The last was serene and beaming.

Allison's four faces were less deftly drawn, with slits and areas of distortion. She had cut triangles for noses and eyes. The mouths she had made were just wedges—two turned up and two turned down.

By one in the morning they were finished. Clark, who had bent his long torso forward to work, moved back over to the glider and looked out sleepily at nothing. All the lights were out across the ravine.

Clark stayed. For the season and time, the Virginia night was warm. Most leaves had been blown away already, and the trees stood unbothered. The moon was round above them.

Allison cleaned up the mess.

"Your jack-o'-lanterns are much, much better than mine," Clark said to her.

"Like hell," Allison said.

"Look at me," Clark said, and Allison did.

She was holding a squishy bundle of newspapers. The papers reeked sweetly with the smell of pumpkin guts.

"Yours are *far* better," he said.

"You're wrong. You'll see when they're lit," Allison said.

She went inside, came back with yellow vigil candles. It took her a while to get each candle settled, and then to line up the results in a row on the porch railing. She went along and lit each candle and fixed the pumpkin lids over the little flames.

"See?" she said.

They sat together a moment and looked at the orange faces.

"We're exhausted. It's good night time," Allison said. "Don't blow out the candles. I'll put in new ones tomorrow."

That night, in their bedroom, a few weeks earlier in her life than had been predicted, Allison began to die. "Don't look at me if my wig comes off," she told Clark. "Please."

Her pulse cords were fluttering under his fingers. She raised her knees and kicked away the comforter. She said something to Clark about the garage being locked.

At the telephone, Clark had a clear view out back and down to the porch. He wanted to get drunk with his wife once more. He wanted to tell her, from the greater perspective he had, that to own only a little talent, like his, was an awful, plaguing thing; that being only a little special meant you expected too much, most of the time, and liked yourself too little. He wanted to assure her that she had missed nothing.

He was speaking into the phone now. He watched the jack-o'-lanterns. The jack-o'-lanterns watched him.

Dorothy Parker, critic and fiction writer, wrote the next story, "But the One on the Right," for *The New Yorker* in 1929. The piece exemplifies a narrative technique called stream of consciousness, in which a writer seeks to reproduce the flow of thoughts, feelings, and associations that go through a character's mind as that character moves in the "stream" of time.

But the One on the Right

I knew it. I knew if I came to this dinner, I'd draw something like this baby on my left. They've been saving him up for me for weeks. Now, we've simply got to have him—his sister was so sweet to us in London; we can stick him next to Mrs. Parker—she talks enough for two. Oh, I should never have come, never. I'm here against my better judgment, to a decision. That would be a good thing for them to cut on my tombstone: Wherever she went, including here, it was against her better judgment. This is a fine time of the evening to be thinking about tombstones. That's the effect he's had on me, already, and the soup hardly cold yet. I should have stayed at home for dinner. I could have had something on a tray. The head of John the Baptist, or something. Oh, I should not have come.

Well, the soup's over, anyway. I'm that much nearer to my Eternal Home. Now the soup belongs to the ages, and I have said precisely four words to the gentleman on my left. I said, "Isn't this soup delicious?"; that's four words. And he said, "Yes, isn't it?"; that's three. He's one up on me.

At any rate, we're in perfect accord. We agree like lambs. We've been all through the soup together, and never a cross word between us. It seems rather a pity to let the subject drop, now we've found something on which we harmonize so admirably. I believe I'll bring it up again; I'll ask him if that wasn't delicious soup. He says, "Yes, wasn't it?" Look at that, will you; perfect command of his tenses.

Here comes the fish. Goody, goody, goody, we got fish. I wonder if he likes fish. Yes, he does; he says he likes fish. Ah, that's nice. I love that in a man. Look, he's talking! He's chattering away like a veritable magpie! He's asking me if I like fish. Now does he really want to know, or is it only a line? I'd better play it cagey. I'll tell him, "Oh, pretty well." Oh, I like fish pretty well; there's a fascinating bit of autobiography for him to study over. Maybe he would rather wrestle with it alone. I'd better steal softly away, and leave him to his thoughts.

I might try my luck with what's on my right. No, not a chance there. The woman on his other side has him cold. All I can see is his shoulder. It's a nice shoulder, too; oh, it's a nice, *nice* shoulder. All my life, I've been a fool for a nice shoulder. Very well, lady; you saw him first. Keep your Greek god, and I'll go back to my Trojan horse.

Let's see, where were we? Oh, we'd got to where he had confessed his liking for fish. I wonder what else he likes. Does he like cucumbers? Yes, he does; he likes cucumbers. And potatoes? Yes, he likes potatoes, too. Why, he's a regular old Nature-lover, that's what he is. I would have to come out to dinner, and sit next to the Boy Thoreau. Wait, he's saying something! Words are simply pouring out of him. He's asking me if I'm fond of potatoes. No, I don't like potatoes. There, I've done it! I've differed from him. It's our first quarrel. He's fallen into a moody silence. Silly boy, have I pricked your bubble? Do you think I am nothing but a painted doll with sawdust for a heart? Ah, don't take it like that. Look, I have something to tell you that will bring back your faith. I do like cucumbers. Why, he's better already. He speaks again. He says, yes, he likes them, too. Now we've got that all straightened out, thank heaven. We both like cucumbers. Only he likes them twice.

I'd better let him alone now, so he can get some food. He ought to try to get his strength back. He's talked himself groggy.

I wish I had something to do. I hate to be a mere drone. People ought to let you know when they're going to sit you next to a thing like this, so you could bring along some means of occupation. Dear Mrs. Parker, do come to us for dinner on Friday next, and don't forget your drawn-work. I could have brought my top bureau drawer and tidied it up, here on my lap. I could have made great strides towards getting those photographs of the groups on the beach pasted up in the album. I wonder if my hostess would think it strange if I asked for a pack of cards. I wonder if there are any old copies of *St. Nicholas* lying about. I wonder if they wouldn't like a little help out in the kitchen. I wonder if anybody would want me to run up to the corner and get a late paper.

I could do a little drinking, of course, all by myself. There's always that. Oh, dear, oh, dear, oh, dear, there's always that. But I don't want to drink. I'll get *vin triste*. I'm melancholy before I even start. I wonder what this stiff on my left would say, if I told him I was in a fair way to get *vin triste*. Oh, look at him, hoeing into his fish! What does he care whether I get *vin triste* or not? His soul can't rise above food. Purely physical, that's all he is. Digging his grave with his teeth, that's what he's doing. Yah, yah, ya-ah! Digging your grave with your tee-eeth! Making a god of your stommick! Yah, yah, ya-ah!

He doesn't care if I get *vin triste*. Nobody cares. Nobody gives a damn. And me so nice. All right, you baskets, I'll drink myself to death, right in front of your eyes, and see how you'll feel. Here I go. . . . Oh, my God, it's Chablis. And of a year when the grapes failed, and they used Summer squash, instead. Fifteen dollars for all you can carry home on your shoulder. Oh, now, listen, where I come from, we feed this to the pigs. I think I'll ask old Chatterbox on my left if this isn't rotten wine. That ought to open up a new school of dialectics for us. Oh, he says he really wouldn't know—he never touches wine. Well, that fairly well ends that. I wonder how he'd like to step to hell, anyway. Yah, yah, ya-ah! Never touches wi-yine! Don't know what you're miss-sing! Yah, yah, ya-ah!

I'm not going to talk to him any more. I'm not going to spend the best years of my life thinking up pearls to scatter before him. I'm going to stick to my Chablis, rotten though it be. From now on, he can go his way, and I'll go mine. I'm better than anybody at this table. Ah, but am I really? Have I, after all, half of what they have? Here I am lonely, unwanted, silent, and me with all my new clothes on. Oh, what would Louiseboulanger say if she saw her gold lamé going unnoticed like this? It's life, I suppose. Poor little things, we dress, and we plan, and we hope—and for what? What is life, any-way? A death sentence. The longest distance between two points. The bunch of hay that's tied to the nose of the tired mule. The——

Well, well, well, here we are at the *entrecôte*. Button up your *entrecôte*, when the wind is free—no, I guess not. Now I'll be damned if I ask old Lo-quacity if he likes meat. In the first place, his likes and dislikes are nothing to me, and in the second—well, look at him go after it! He must have been playing hard all afternoon; he's Mother's Hungry Boy, tonight. All right, let him worry it all he wants. As for me, I'm on a higher plane. I do not stoop to him. He's less than the dust beneath my chariot wheel. Yah, yah, ya-ah! Less than the du-ust! Before I'd be that way. Yah, yah, ya-ah!

I'm glad there's red wine now. Even if it isn't good, I'm glad. Red wine gives me courage. The Red Badge of Courage. I need courage. I'm in a thin way, here. Nobody knows what a filthy time I'm having. My precious evening, that can never come again, ruined, ruined, ruined, and all because of this Somewhat Different Monologist on my left. But he can't lick me. The night is not yet dead, no, nor dying. You know, this really isn't bad wine.

Now what do you suppose is going on with the Greek God on my right? Ah, no use. There's still only the shoulder—the nice, *nice* shoulder. I wonder what the woman's like, that's got him. I can't see her at all. I wonder if she's beautiful. I wonder if she's Greek, too. When Greek meets immovable body—you might be able to do something with that, if you only had the time. I'm not going to be spineless any longer. Don't think for a minute, lady, that I've given up. He's still using his knife and fork. While there's hands above the table, there's hope.

Really, I suppose out of obligation to my hostess, I ought to do something about saying a few words to this macaw on my left. What shall I try? Have you been reading anything good lately, do you go much to the play, have you ever been to the Riviera? I wonder if he would like to hear about my Summer on the Riviera; hell, no, that's no good without lantern slides. I bet, though, if I started telling him about That One Night, he'd listen. I won't tell him—it's too good for him. Anybody that never touches wine can't hear that. But the one on the right—he'd like that. He touches wine. Touches it, indeed! He just threw it for a formidable loss.

Oh, look, old Silver Tongue is off again! Why, he's mad with his own perfume! He's rattling away like lightning. He's asking me if I like salad. Yes, I do; what does he want to make of that? He's telling me about salad through the ages. He says it's so good for people. So help me God, if he gives me a talk on roughage, I'll slap his face. Isn't that my life, to sit here, all dressed up in my best, and listen to this thing talk about romaine? And all the time, right on my right——

Well, I thought you were never going to turn around. . . . You haven't? . . . You have? Oh, Lord, I've been having an awful time, too. . . . Was she? . . . Well, you should have seen what I drew. . . . Oh, I don't see how we could. . . . Yes, I know it's terrible, but how can we get out of it? . . . Well. . . . Well, yes, that's true. . . . Look, right after dinner, I'll say I have this horrible headache, and you say you're going to take me home in your car, and——

Parker's story suggests multiple ideas for writing. For instance:

- Idea #6: Change the point of view. Though "Mrs. Parker" in this piece is talking or thinking to herself, she evokes the presence of others: the man on the right, "the gentleman on my left," and the woman on the other side of "[the man] on my right." Rewrite the story from the perspective of one of these other people.
- Idea #7: Rewrite the work in a different genre. For example, instead of having "Mrs. Parker" think to herself, have an actual dialogue between Mrs. Parker and one of the people with whom she is dining.
- Idea #9: Borrow the *form*. Imagine a character and a situation of your own, and compose in a stream of consciousness mode.
- Other possibilities? Use your annotations and imagination to invent some.

THE STORM
A Sequel to "The 'Cadian Ball"

The leaves were so still that even Bibi thought it was going to rain. Bobinôt, who was accustomed to converse on terms of perfect equality with his little son, called the child's attention to certain sombre clouds that were rolling with sinister intention from the west, accompanied by a sullen, threatening roar. They were at Friedheimer's store and decided to remain there till the storm had passed. They sat within the door on two empty kegs. Bibi was four years old and looked very wise.

"Mama'll be 'fraid, yes," he suggested with blinking eyes.

"She'll shut the house. Maybe she got Sylvie helpin' her this evenin'," Bobinôt responded reassuringly.

"No; she ent got Sylvie. Sylvie was helpin' her yistiday," piped Bibi.

Bobinôt arose and going across to the counter purchased a can of shrimps, of which Calixta was very fond. Then he returned to his perch on the keg and sat stolidly holding the can of shrimps while the storm burst. It shook the wooden store and seemed to be ripping great furrows in the distant field. Bibi laid his little hand on his father's knee and was not afraid.

II

Calixta, at home, felt no uneasiness for their safety. She sat at a side window sewing furiously on a sewing machine. She was greatly occupied and did not notice the approaching storm. But she felt very warm and often stopped to mop her face on which the perspiration gathered in beads. She unfastened her white sacque at the throat. It began to grow dark, and suddenly realizing the situation she got up hurriedly and went about closing windows and doors.

Out on the small front gallery she had hung Bobinôt's Sunday clothes to air and she hastened out to gather them before the rain fell. As she stepped outside, Alcée Laballière rode in at the gate. She had not seen him very often since her marriage, and never alone. She stood there with Bobinôt's coat in her hands, and the big rain drops began to fall. Alcée rode his horse under the shelter of a side projection where the chickens had huddled and there were plows and a harrow piled up in the corner.

"May I come and wait on your gallery till the storm is over, Calixta?" he asked.

"Come 'long in, M'sieur Alcée."

His voice and her own startled her as if from a trance, and she seized Bobinôt's vest. Alcée, mounting to the porch, grabbed the trousers and snatched Bibi's braided jacket that was about to be carried away by a sudden gust of wind. He expressed an intention to remain outside, but it was soon apparent that he might as well have been out in the open: the water beat in upon the boards in driving sheets, and he went inside, closing the door after him. It was even necessary to put something beneath the door to keep the water out.

"My! what a rain! It's good two years sence it rain' like that," exclaimed Calixta as she rolled up a piece of bagging and Alcée helped her to thrust it beneath the crack.

She was a little fuller of figure than five years before when she married; but she had lost nothing of her vivacity. Her blue eyes still retained their melting quality; and her yellow hair, dishevelled by the wind and rain, kinked more stubbornly than ever about her ears and temples.

The rain beat upon the low, shingled roof with a force and clatter that threatened to break an entrance and deluge them there. They were in the dining room—the sitting room—the general utility room. Adjoining was her bed room, with Bibi's couch along side her own. The door stood open, and the room with its white, monumental bed, its closed shutters, looked dim and mysterious.

Alcée flung himself into a rocker and Calixta nervously began to gather up from the floor the lengths of a cotton sheet which she had been sewing.

"If this keeps up, *Dieu sait* if the levees goin' to stan' it!" she exclaimed.

"What have you got to do with the levees?"

"I got enough to do! An' there's Bobinôt with Bibi out in that storm—if he only didn' left Friedheimer's!"

"Let us hope, Calixta, that Bobinôt's got sense enough to come in out of a cyclone."

She went and stood at the window with a greatly disturbed look on her face. She wiped the frame that was clouded with moisture. It was stiflingly hot. Alcée got up and joined her at the window, looking over her shoulder. The rain was coming down in sheets obscuring the view of far-off cabins and enveloping the distant wood in a gray mist. The playing of the lightning was incessant. A bolt struck a tall chinaberry tree at the edge of the field. It filled all visible space with a blinding glare and the crash seemed to invade the very boards they stood upon.

Calixta put her hands to her eyes, and with a cry, staggered backward. Alcée's arm encircled her, and for an instant he drew her close and spasmodically to him.

"*Bonté!*" she cried, releasing herself from his encircling arm and retreating from the window, "the house'll go next! If I only knew w'ere Bibi was!" She would not compose herself; she would not be seated. Alcée clasped her shoulders and looked into her face. The contact of her warm, palpitating body when he had unthinkingly drawn her into his arms, had aroused all the old-time infatuation and desire for her flesh.

"Calixta," he said, "don't be frightened. Nothing can happen. The house is too low to be struck, with so many tall trees standing about. There! aren't you going to be quiet? say, aren't you?" He pushed her hair back from her face that was warm and steaming. Her lips were as red and moist as pomegranate seed. Her white neck and a glimpse of her full, firm bosom disturbed him powerfully. As she glanced up at him the fear in her liquid blue eyes had given place to a drowsy gleam that unconsciously betrayed a sensuous desire. He looked down into her eyes and there was nothing for him to do but to gather her lips in a kiss. It reminded him of Assumption.

"Do you remember—in Assumption, Calixta?" he asked in a low voice broken by passion. Oh! she remembered; for in Assumption he had kissed her and kissed and kissed her; until his senses would well nigh fail, and to save her he would resort to a desperate flight. If she was not an immaculate dove in those days, she was still inviolate; a passionate creature whose very defenselessness had made her defense, against which his honor forbade him to prevail. Now—well, now—her lips seemed in a manner free to be tasted, as well as her round, white throat and her whiter breasts.

They did not heed the crashing torrents, and the roar of the elements made her laugh as she lay in his arms. She was a revelation in that dim, mysterious chamber; as white as the couch she lay upon. Her firm, elastic flesh that was knowing for the first time its birthright, was like a creamy lily that the sun invites to contribute its breath and perfume to the undying life of the world.

The generous abundance of her passion, without guile or trickery, was like a white flame which penetrated and found response in depths of his own sensuous nature that had never yet been reached.

When he touched her breasts they gave themselves up in quivering ecstasy, inviting his lips. Her mouth was a fountain of delight. And when he possessed her, they seemed to swoon together at the very borderland of life's mystery.

He stayed cushioned upon her, breathless, dazed, enervated, with his heart beating like a hammer upon her. With one hand she clasped his head, her lips lightly touching his forehead. The other hand stroked with a soothing rhythm his muscular shoulders.

The growl of the thunder was distant and passing away. The rain beat softly upon the shingles, inviting them to drowsiness and sleep. But they dared not yield.

The rain was over; and the sun was turning the glistening green world into a palace of gems. Calixta, on the gallery, watched Alcée ride away. He turned and smiled at her with a beaming face; and she lifted her pretty chin in the air and laughed aloud.

III

Bobinôt and Bibi, trudging home, stopped without at the cistern to make themselves presentable.

"My! Bibi, w'at will yo' mama say! You ought to be ashame'. You oughtn' put on those good pants. Look at 'em! An' that mud on yo' collar! How you got that mud on yo' collar, Bibi? I never saw such a boy!" Bibi was the picture of pathetic resignation. Bobinôt was the embodiment of serious solicitude as he strove to remove from his own person and his son's the signs of their tramp over heavy roads and through wet fields. He scraped the mud off Bibi's bare legs and feet with a stick and carefully removed all traces from his heavy brogans. Then, prepared for the worst—the meeting with an over-scrupulous housewife, they entered cautiously at the back door.

Calixta was preparing supper. She had set the table and was dripping coffee at the hearth. She sprang up as they came in.

"Oh, Bobinôt! You back! My! but I was uneasy. W'ere you been during the rain? An' Bibi? he ain't wet? he ain't hurt?" She had clasped Bibi and was kissing him effusively. Bobinôt's explanations and apologies which he had been composing all along the way, died on his lips as Calixta felt him to see if he were dry, and seemed to express nothing but satisfaction at their safe return.

"I brought you some shrimps, Calixta," offered Bobinôt, hauling the can from his ample side pocket and laying it on the table.

"Shrimps! Oh, Bobinôt! you too good fo' anything!" and she gave him a smacking kiss on the cheek that resounded. "*J'vous réponds,* we'll have a feas' to night! umph-umph!"

Bobinôt and Bibi began to relax and enjoy themselves, and when the three seated themselves at table they laughed much and so loud that anyone might have heard them as far away as Laballière's.

IV

Alcée Laballière wrote to his wife, Clarisse, that night. It was a loving letter, full of tender solicitude. He told her not to hurry back, but if she and the babies liked it at Biloxi, to stay a month longer. He was getting on nicely; and though he missed them, he was willing to bear the separation a while longer—realizing that their health and pleasure were the first things to be considered.

V

As for Clarisse, she was charmed upon receiving her husband's letter. She and the babies were doing well. The society was agreeable; many of her old friends and acquaintances were at the bay. And the first free breath since her marriage seemed to restore the pleasant liberty of her maiden days. Devoted as she was to her husband, their intimate conjugal life was something which she was more than willing to forego for a while.

So the storm passed and every one was happy.

Your Reading Notebook
and "Originality"

Every one of my writings has been furnished to me by a thousand different persons, a thousand different things. . . . My work is that of an aggregation of beings taken from the whole of nature and it bears the name of Goethe.

—JOHANN WOLFGANG VON GOETHE

In the weeks ahead you can use the ideas in Chapters 2 and 3 to respond to the short stories, poems, essays, and plays in Part V of this book. The number of writings in your notebook will grow, and literary texts will become integral strands in the web of your life. If you look ahead to Chapters 9 ("The Portfolio Pyramid") and 10 ("Making the Works"), you can find strategies for revising your favorite notebook writings into finished—even publishable—work.

At this juncture an interesting question arises: Since your reading notebook consists of written responses to other, already existing texts, will your writings tend to be dependent and derivative? That is, will they remain unintelligible to readers unless you attach a copy or description of the text that served as your primary prompt?

Sometimes, yes. For instance, if you follow up your reading of a short story by writing a letter to the author, a reader will pretty much need to have read the short story in order to understand your letter, i.e., in order to put it in context. Outside the context of the story, your letter won't make sense.

And sometimes, no. For instance, consider the example (discussed in Chapter 2) of Margaret's response to Linda Pastan's poem "Marks." Both Pastan's text and Margaret's ("School of Hard Knocks") are reprinted below:

MARKS

My husband gives me an A
for last night's supper,
an incomplete for my ironing,
a B plus in bed.
My son says I am average,
an average mother, but if
I put my mind to it
I could improve.
My daughter believes
in Pass/Fail and tells me
I pass. Wait 'til they learn
I'm dropping out.

School of Hard Knocks

Grading doesn't begin and end with school. It goes on all our lives. That's what this poem showed me. Wives and mothers especially; we're always being graded!

I got married right out of high school and I thought I was done with getting grades. Little did I know I was just going from one school to another. And I don't mean college. I mean marriage.

There are several classes in this "school."

Marriage 101 is living with a husband. In my case a husband I hardly knew. A nice man and a good provider and all, it turned out, but also a lout who expected me to wait on him hand and foot. Cook the meals, wash the dishes, clean the house, do the errands, entertain the company.

A typical scene: I'm cleaning the bathroom in 95 degree heat, sweat pouring down my face, and he's in the livingroom watching baseball and drinking a beer. His buddies are with him and when the snack tray's empty they yell at me to "please" get more. If I'm a little slow I get a dirty look (that's a "C"). If I yell "Help yourself" and don't come at all I get a growl and some angry comments about "women" (that's an "F"). If I load up the tray and deliver it with a smile it's a "B." To get an "A" I have to do some extra credit—give them their potato chips plus a new round of beers ("A" if the beers are cold, "A-" if they're not).

Marriage 201 is kids. I love my kids, don't get me wrong. They were cute babies and except for the terrible two's the sweetest children I'll ever see. But since they hit their teens it's been a downhill road.

They treat me like their live-in cook and maid. I spend an hour in a hot kitchen making supper—something a little special, chicken cooked a new way—and they shovel it down without a word, it might as well be an old sock fried in batter. No "thank you's" or "This is great"—they're in too big a hurry to get somewhere—a dance, a game, and other places I probably don't want to know about.

I guess they'd give me a "B" for cooking—not good enough for praise, not bad enough to make them throw up (an "F"). If they don't like what I give them you can bet I hear about it. "Mom, what is this?" "Mom, are we supposed to eat this meatloaf or use it for a paperweight?" That's a "C-"— if they even bother to force it down, that is. A grade of "D" means "give it to the Dog."

Kids grade like most of the teachers I had in school. If they like it they don't tell you, and if they hate it they don't let you forget.

Next we come to Marriage 301: middle age. In my generation this means a daughter going on to college and asking you why you became a homemaker and mother instead of getting "a real job." So I could have you and have conversations like this, I say. She looks at me confused like I must be lying. A real job. Boy! I'll tell you about a real job. . . . *This* is a real job. But it's not the job she's interested in.

I'm 45 years old and was on the verge of burnout when I decided to go back to school this fall. I'm a college freshman now at the same school my daughter graduated from a year ago. My son's a sophomore. And I'm getting grades. Am I living my life backwards, or what? I wonder some-times. I seem to be going back to my childhood: teachers giving me grades. And the teachers get younger and younger. My Math professor's a girl hardly older than my daughter. When she gave me my first test back with a "B" it reminded me of fried chicken! Déjà vu!

Only a mother would understand.

Although Margaret's piece originated as a response to another text, it could easily be revised to be an "independent" and publishable work showing no visible threads of connection to Pastan. To make her essay self-sufficient, Margaret simply needs to delete one sentence—the third sentence in her opening paragraph.

Also notice the writing that another student, Mike, does from "Marks." "Marks" angers Mike because he has been fighting with his girlfriend and currently equates all womanhood with factiousness and noise. The poem prompts him to rough out a dialogue:

> **Linda:** [*banging some pots and pans on the stove and suddenly whirling around on her husband, Mark, who sits at the table*] Where have you been?
>
> **Mark:** I told you, I had to work late. I—
>
> **Linda:** Had to work late, had to work late. . . . That's always your excuse. Well, maybe you need to learn to work faster. Maybe if you worked at a normal human pace you wouldn't *have* this problem.
>
> **Mark:** But the boss—
>
> **Linda:** Don't blame it on the boss. There you go again: always blam-ing other people for your own failures. . . . God! If I'd known all this be-fore we were married I'd have called the whole thing off!
>
> **Mark:** But—

Linda: I'd never have gotten into this mess: feeding you, serving you, waiting on your every whim. [*Linda continues rattling off a list of other complaints*].

Mark: [*numbly slumped over, staring at his empty plate*] Oh . . . forget it.

Mike's creation differs drastically from Margaret's in form, style, setting, outlook, characterization, tone, and theme. Like Margaret's essay, it shows little obvious debt to "Marks." If I hadn't given the fact away, you would never guess that Mike's piece and Margaret's were prompted by a reading of the same text. Reading "Marks," Mike reads the same literal words as Margaret, but the texts of experience that he brings to the reading are *his*—not hers.

Margaret and Mike spin original works out of their own unique and different intertextual webs. In the process, Pastan's poem fades into the background. In Margaret's essay and Mike's dialogue, Pastan's text fades because Margaret and Mike, in their very different ways, read the poem more as writers/creators than as passive readers.

What, then, can we conclude about originality?

1. Since every text comes out of other texts, no text is completely "original."
2. Both dependent texts and independent texts are fun to write, and both are valuable because they weave webs of connection between the texts you read and your own life and imagination.
3. You can use your notebook to produce and collect both dependent and independent texts.
4. By reading conversationally, you will sometimes produce an independent text almost spontaneously, as Margaret and Mike did when they read "Marks."
5. If you want to make one of your dependent texts independent, you can do so through patient revision. Look ahead to Chapters 9 and 10 to learn about a variety of strategies for collecting and revising your work.

ACTIVITIES FOR WRITING

1. Reread one of the texts you wrote in response to the "Activities for Writing" in either Chapter 2 or Chapter 3. Compare the text you created with the text that primarily inspired it. In what ways, if any, does appreciation or understanding of your own text depend on a knowledge of the springboard text? In what ways—or to what degree—is your text independent of the springboard text? If you wanted to make your text independent, how would you need to change it?

2. In the coming weeks, repeat Activity #1 on the other texts that you produce. Explore the varying relationships of dependence/independence between the texts you create and the texts that generate them.

Part

II

Writing Essays About Literature

P art I of *Reading and Writing from Literature* showed you ways of producing writings that are sometimes described as "creative" or "imaginative." In Part II we turn to what is probably the most commonly assigned type of composition in literature-based writing courses: the essay about literature. There are some important differences between the kinds of writing addressed in Parts I and II. For example, writings produced in Part I are typically ungraded and may assume a great variety of forms, such as stories, poems, personal memoirs, dialogues, letters, and many others. The kind of writing emphasized in Part II, on the other hand, is normally done for a grade and in some more narrowly prescribed form, generally that of the expository or argumentative essay. (Expository and argumentative essays are short works of nonfiction prose that pose a main point or thesis and support it with evidence and examples.)

How, then, do Parts I and II interconnect? In some ways, the writings you produce as a result of techniques outlined in Part I have a life of their own and can be collected, revised, and enjoyed independently of Part II. Long after you have finished this particular class, you can continue using the "Four-Step Process," the "Ten Ideas," and other techniques to build up a body of writings for your intellectual or esthetic pleasure, for sharing, and perhaps even for formal publication. At the same time, Part I prepares you for Part II. Part I strategies enable you to engage literary texts in meaningful ways that will help you when you compose essays about literature. In addition, Part I has introduced you to habits of conversational reading and writing—habits as basic to writing good essays about literature as they are to producing creative and imaginative work.

Ways of Planning: Thinking and Writing Recursively

Look, and look again.

—ANN E. BERTHOFF

Putting Essays About Literature into Context

For some students the assignment to "write an essay about literature" is a source of anxiety. Perhaps "essay about literature" triggers memories of failure, of interpreting a story or poem "incorrectly" and receiving a bad grade, or it may conjure feelings of apathy and distance ("What does this assignment have to do with my life?"). The aim of this part of *Reading and Writing from Literature* is to defuse these feelings and demonstrate strategies for working your way naturally through such essays.

The essay about literature is a diverse genre. It includes essay exams, critical analyses or "explications" of literary texts, argumentative papers, personal narratives that are grounded in a reading of a literary text (or texts), and essays that involve library research. Sometimes the topics for such essays are assigned by an instructor; other times you, the student, are asked to devise a topic yourself.

Essays about literature have multiple purposes. One function is broadly personal; they can reward you—the writer—by prompting you to discover interconnections among literary texts and the texts of your own life. A second function is pragmatic: essays about literature provide instructors and others with a means of evaluating your ability to write. Essay assignments often require you to do an "objective" text-focused analysis that may suppress overt mention of the personal. While such essays may be less emotionally engaging for you than personal or creative types of writing, being able to write them is usually critical for succeeding in class and in school.

Cultivating Recursive Habits of Thinking

Perhaps the major value of writing essays about literature is this: they help you develop recursive habits of thinking. "Recursive" means "running back again," or, as Ann Berthoff puts it in the epigraph to this chapter, looking and looking again. Recursiveness is the very stuff of thinking, which (in turn) is the stuff of essay writing.

If the preceding paragraph made you pause, and you reread it to understand or assess it, you were thinking recursively. When you write down a few sentences and look them over with the aim of expanding them, you are again thinking recursively. When you share your interpretation of a story or poem in class and reconsider it in the light of alternative opinions offered by your instructor or classmates, you are again being recursive.

Recursiveness provides a powerful term for understanding what you do when you write an essay about literature. Returning to Part I's theme, you use texts (literary texts, the texts in your notebook, the texts of lecture and discussion, for example) to make a text. Your new thoughts and writings don't come out of nothing but out of "running back" over previous work or "texts." Thus, when you're "stuck" in your writing or your thinking, there is an alternative to panic or to doing nothing; you can go over materials you have already generated and use them to move yourself forward. Writing an essay about literature is not a monolithic task that is to be achieved—or irredeemably failed—in a single step. Instead, it is a steady and incremental process that relies on looking and looking again—on rereading, writing, rewriting, and discussing.

In short, you don't need to be brilliant to think or write well; you do need recursive habits of thinking.

Working Toward Your Essay Before It Has Been Assigned

It follows from the preceding discussion that essay writing begins long before you receive the actual assignment to write one. From day one of class you begin accumulating materials that can provide you with topics and ideas for essays. These materials include the textual annotations you have made on the assigned stories, poems, essays, and plays anthologized in Part V of this book, notes of class lectures and discussions, writings in response to literature that you have been collecting in your reading notebook, and notes on small group discussions. All of these materials—these "texts"—provide scraps of overlapping textual fabric from which to stitch and sew together new creations.

Two of these types of materials—textual annotations and notebook writings—have already been discussed in Part I. Others, such as notes on lectures and class discussions, are fairly self-explanatory. One important kind of daily activity that hasn't been talked about yet is small group work.

Sharing and Learning in a Small Group

A small group (typically composed of three to five members) can be among your most stimulating resources in a literature or composition class. Groups embody the spirit of recursiveness, which is rough and multidimensional. Recursive thinking does not proceed forward in a straight line from brilliance to brilliance; the shape of its movement is more analogous to a web that darts in multiple—even contradictory—directions. Like webs, groups relate and contradict and interconnect. That is what makes them useful and fun. Margaret Fuller, a nineteenth-century essayist, described the group process beautifully. Of her own "conversation" groups she wrote:

> I am so sure that the success of the whole depends on conversation being general that I do not wish any one to join who does not intend, *if possible,* to take an active part. No one will be forced, but those who do not talk will not derive the same advantages with those who openly state their impressions and consent to learn by blundering, as is the destiny of [human beings] here below.

A good group "blunders" its way to understanding, doesn't treat any opinion as "dumb" (so long as the opiner is willing to consider differing opinions and grow from them), and is as lively and various as human thought itself. A small group is an excellent forum for sharing your readings of literary texts and issues. In addition, your group can give you feedback at various stages of planning, drafting, revising, and editing your essays.

Your instructor may encourage group sharing as a regular class activity. Here is one rather generic format for sharing that you can relax or modify as you and your group mates become more familiar with each other. For purposes of illustration the focus of group discussion is assumed here to be a literary text. However, a small group can also meet to share opinions about members' writings in-progress or any other subject of interest to group members and/or the instructor.

1. Form into your group.
2. Share your responses to the assigned literary text for that day. For instance:
   a. Identify a passage in the text that was "most significant" to *you* and explain why,
   or

    b. Read aloud the notebook entry you wrote in response to the text (remembering that you may skip over passages that are too personal or that you are uncomfortable sharing),

    or

    c. Summarize the notebook entry you wrote and share any ways that it enriched your reading of the text.

3. After you have presented, group members can respond by

    a. Pointing out something in your sharing that they found "interesting"

    or

    b. Expressing how they responded to the text differently than you did.

4. Repeat this process, with each member of the group taking a turn as presenter.

Techniques for Note Taking in Small Groups

Make a habit of taking notes on your group discussions, even if some of the ideas presented are ones you disagree with or consider "silly" or "dumb." Note taking improves your listening skills, makes you more conscious of alternative points of view, and provides you with a record of discussion that you can refer to later when writing your essays.

Here are two good ways to develop habits of note taking:

1. *Write while you listen.* Try taking a steady stream of notes as your group mates read their writing or ideas aloud. For instance, here are the notes one student took as he listened to Tyler read the potrait "Grandpa Jack" from Chapter 2 (see pp. 10–11):

Jack—neighbor
visits Jack
Jack "lounges"
Jack down-to-earth
like Jack's talk
tells story
sheepherding incident
"eyes flashing"
colorful
good story/details/suspense

Sometimes writing while you listen can help you to concentrate and to overcome the inertia of not writing (or listening) at all. In addition, of course, you can use items off your list to provide feedback to the writer.

2. *Write after you listen.* Sometimes it's hard to listen and write at the same time—hence this alternative strategy. After a member of your group has read, you and the others can take one minute to jot down reactions to what you just

heard. What struck you? What *issues* does the writing raise for you? Where could you use more information or development? Following the minute of silent writing, group members can hand their written reactions to the author or share their reactions orally.

Finding a Topic: Rereading (and Writing from) the Writing You Have Already Done

As mentioned, when you are assigned to write an essay you do not have to start from scratch. You begin with an already ample storehouse of writings that can provide ideas and prompts for essays. Begin work on your essay by rereading all of your textual annotations, notebook entries, notes on lectures, and notes on class and small-group discussions. Read with pen or pencil in hand. Whenever you find any item that strikes you, for whatever reason, bracket or underline it. When you are finished, reread all the items you have bracketed or underlined. In the margin beside each, write yourself a note explaining what it is about this passage that grabs you.

Turning Your Favorite Interest into a Workable Topic

Based on your review of your annotations, notebook, and lecture and discussion notes, you can define a workable topic for your essay. There are many ways to do this. Your instructor may introduce you to "brainstorming," "quick-writing" (or "freewriting"), or other activities for coming up with topics. Another good place to begin is with the apparatus included in this book. You can find topics by combing the "Activities for Writing and Discussion" that follow many of the short stories, poems, essays, and plays in Part V or by looking through the "Additional Activities for Writing and Discussion" that conclude each thematic section in Part V.

For example, Joe knows that he wants to write something about Doris Lessing's short story "A Woman on a Roof" (p. 183). Lessing's story concerns a woman sunbather whose nakedness stirs complex reactions, e.g., attraction, excitement, anger, in two male roofers named Stanley (in his thirties) and Tom (seventeen). One of Joe's annotations, made in the middle of the story, suggests to him a topic for an essay: "They [Stanley and Tom] have different perspectives—in a sense contradictory." Joe reads the "Activities for Writing and Discussion" that follow the story and decides to write on Activity #5:

> Stanley and Tom react to the woman differently. Stanley feels rage toward her, while we are told that Tom feels a "bond between the woman and himself" (p. 187). Discuss the differences in their reactions. Is Tom (a) "better" or "kinder" than Stanley, (b) simply different from Stanley, or (c) really no different from Stanley?

Developing a "Working Thesis"

A thesis states the main point you are going to make in your essay; it normally appears in the opening paragraph or near the beginning of the essay. A "working thesis" is one you adopt tentatively in order to begin your essay while remaining open to the possibility of revising it in the course of composing.

A clear thesis benefits both writer and readers. First, it gives you—the writer—a manageable focus for your work. A carefully limited thesis can save you from straying off your subject. Second, a thesis helps your readers. A thesis is to an essay as a map is to an unfamiliar city. If you are entering Chicago for the first time, you want a map to show you where you are going. Similarly, a thesis lets your readers know what lies ahead so that they have a context for understanding each of your paragraphs and sentences as the essay unfolds.

How do you devise a working thesis? As with every aspect of writing, there is no one way to do it. Some writers like to discover a thesis by "quick-writing" (see below). Others develop a thesis by devising a question around some problem:

- "Is Mr. Green's behavior in the story 'A Loaf of Bread' ethical?"
- "Why do Mrs. Hale and Mrs. Peters in Susan Glaspell's *Trifles* conceal the evidence that implicates Minnie Wright in the murder of her husband?"
- "Why does Louise Mallard in 'The Story of an Hour' seem to want to be 'free' of her husband, even though he has always treated her affectionately?"

Then they formulate an answer to the question that serves as the working thesis:

- "Mr. Green is unethical; he consciously exploits customers in the poor (mainly black) neighborhood and then blames society for his own wrongdoing."
- "Mrs. Hale and Mrs. Peters feel an empathy for Minnie Wright that ultimately overrides their sense of obligation to the law."
- "Though her husband is loving toward her, Louise Mallard wants to be 'free' to experience the independence she has never been allowed to have."

These examples illustrate some important qualities of a "good" or "strong" thesis:

1. A good thesis is nonobvious. The third example would be greatly weakened if it were changed to read, "Mrs. Mallard yearns for freedom." That would merely be stating the obvious since at the story's climax Mrs. Mallard rhapsodizes about being "Free, free, free!"

2. A good thesis makes a worthwhile, interesting contribution to the "conversation" on the topic. Again, the third example illustrates, as it promises to touch on some interesting aspects of "The Story of an Hour," for instance, the rather surprising fact that Mrs. Mallard seems to want to be rid of her husband even though he has been kind to her, and the idea that freedom and self-fulfillment can be quashed by factors, such as marriage, which are normally viewed as self- and life-enhancing. Similarly, the second sample thesis, about *Trifles*, implies a discussion of interesting conflicts between personal conscience and the law.

In Joe's case a question has already been posed for him in the "Activities for Writing and Discussion" after "A Woman on a Roof":

Is Tom (a) "better" or "kinder" than Stanley, (b) simply different from Stanley, or (c) really no different from Stanley?

From the question Joe derives the following working thesis: "Despite his gallant intentions, Tom is essentially no different from Stanley in Doris Lessing's 'A Woman on a Roof.'"

Planning Your Essay: Quick-Writing

The key to planning is flexibility: writers may use different methods to plan different essays. Joe uses a technique called quick-writing. The purpose of a quick-write is simple: to get something—however crude—on paper or screen that can move you forward in your writing and serve as a reference point (perhaps) for instructor or peer feedback. Quick-writing is easy:

- Write for a limited time period (perhaps ten to fifteen minutes) and *stop*.
- Write quickly and continuously.
- Censor nothing; permit yourself to write down everything—brilliant, mediocre, or "dumb"—that occurs to you.
- Do not worry about making grammar, spelling, punctuation, or other sentence-level errors; simply push forward.

Here is Joe's quick-write:

"Young Tom" in "Woman on a Roof" is really in the same boat as Stanley. "The bond between the woman and himself" is something covert and not outwardly observable. His feelings manifest themselves in the form of elaborate fantasies that he has every evening when he gets home and he somehow imagines that the "woman" has knowledge of these or is somehow informed of his supposed "bond" with her. At the end, young Tom even manages to feel slighted by the woman's apathy towards him as if she has wronged him by reacting in this way. Stanley certainly manifests his feelings in a more direct and observable way.

The woman has made herself unavailable to Stanley who may observe the candor of the relationship Stanley has with Mrs. Pritchett, a
woman who has made herself accessible to him and he manages to have
a reasonable relationship though it is made possible via the flirtatious nature of their interaction.

Stanley may be capable of dealing with women in only a sexual way
and the woman on the roof's uncaring, unmoved manner has been in effect an invalidation of Stanley's sexual persona or merely a rejection—
something that Stanley is not accustomed to or perhaps just a rejection in
this manner.

Note that quick-writing is a step, not an end in itself; Joe's writing is rather disjointed, but he now has some basic ideas to mull over and develop into a draft.
We will come back to these "basic ideas" in a moment.

Also, notice that quick-writing is not only an activity for the "planning"
stage of writing; you can quick-write at any time in the course of composing an
essay or any other piece of writing. You can quick-write to develop a thesis, to
recast an awkward or confusing paragraph, to "rough out" an introduction or
conclusion, to regain focus when your mind wanders, or simply to break the inertia of not writing. Quick-writing is a quintessentially recursive activity.

Planning Your Essay: Listing and Sequencing

Another way to plan is by listing the points you want to raise to support your
thesis. First, do a brainstorm list; that is, write down any points that occur to
you without worrying about their order. Then reread the list and rearrange the
items, as necessary, into a logical sequence.

For an example of listing and sequencing, consider Lori's work for an essay
on Charlotte Perkins Gilman's story "The Yellow Wallpaper." "The Yellow Wallpaper" is about a married woman in a profound mental and emotional crisis.
Her husband, John (a physician), has prescribed complete rest and has moved
her to a house in the country, where she is confined to a single garishly wallpapered room. The wife becomes obsessed with the wallpaper, perceiving images
in it of a trapped woman trying to escape, and eventually tears the paper from
the walls. Critical opinions differ over the end of the story: Has the woman
achieved a liberation of some kind, or has she gone insane? In her working thesis and list of supporting points, Lori argues the latter:

Working thesis: The narrator went insane at the end of the story, but jus-
tifiably so.
Why justifiably?
John's treatment was that of a Dr. whose last concern is his wife
John laughs at her—practical—he doesn't believe she's sick
she admits that he may be the reason she doesn't get better

he assures friends and relatives she's fine; she's stuck
doesn't let her work
she can't be herself around him
he "takes all care from me" instead of taking care of her
It's a human characteristic that, when left in one place, alone, people start to think weird things
She is insane (examples at end)
insanity was her escape (?)

Lori then rereads and refines her list and classifies related items into groups. Finally (as indicated here by the arrow she has drawn), she arranges the groups into a meaningful sequence:

1. Insane
   examples at end (quotes)
   it was her way of *escape*
2. John's treatment was more like punishment
   left her alone; no variety
   told her she wasn't sick
   didn't let her work
3. It's a human characteristic that, when left in one place, alone, people start to think weird things
   like analyzing wallpaper and giving it a smell
   she has no one to be intimate with/so she becomes intimate with the wallpaper
   she was forced to be in a horrible place and she couldn't deal with it.

Like Joe, Lori now has some ideas with which to work. She follows her list with a quick-write:

At the first of the story we have a depressed woman. She is slightly depressed and dealing with a mild nervous condition but overall a pretty healthy person. Her husband, John, decides to take his wife away for a while (to hide/rest) and they move into an old abandoned mansion. This could have been a good arrangement. She might have even grown better, but John gave her a cruel schedule to follow. She was told not to work, be around people, or even write. Her eating and sleeping habits were closely monitored, and she got worse. She was kept in a big room with only a heavy bed, bars on the windows and hideous wallpaper. At first she would write her feelings, but after a while she became too weak for that and layed(?) in bed and stared at the wallpaper. She could not grow close to John (in fact, there was a growing gap between them), so she became intimate with this wallpaper. She analyzed its color, texture, patterns, and even gave it a "smell." This woman was forced to live in a horrible place deprived of work, beauty, freedom, and exercise, and she couldn't deal with it.

She is trapped. She is entirely too weak to get out of a world that's destroying her. All she has left is the wallpaper, so she finds a woman in that wallpaper and she displaces/uses her as an avenue to her feelings. The woman is symbolically trying to get out and the narrator is determined to help. She begins stripping the wallpaper off the walls around the room, and in doing so, liberates herself from this mentally torturous reality.

Creeping about, she is finally free. Call it insane, but this is the only "out" she had. Reality didn't hold anything for her. So, she stepped out.

Getting Feedback from a Peer or a Small Group

As they formulate theses and plan their essays, Joe and Lori can benefit from peer feedback. Like quick-writing and listing, feedback is useful at all stages of writing an essay (or any other text). Two common misconceptions about feedback are that its aim is to "tear apart" the other person's paper and that its message is primarily negative. In fact, some of the most helpful and motivating feedback is positive. Its focal aim is not to hurt but to help. In a partnership or small group, the objective is always to assist each other toward better writing.

Different stages of writing call for different kinds of feedback. Here are two general suggestions for feedback during early stages of writing:

1. Offer at least some positive and encouraging comments. What writers most need at this stage is momentum to get all their ideas on paper. Positive comments can help create that momentum. Make your comments as specific as possible. A reaction such as "Joe, I like how you contrast Stanley's treatment of Mrs. Pritchett with his treatment of the woman on the roof, though I'm not sure I understand it" is quite helpful. It tells Joe that his point is worth developing but needs clarification. On the other hand, a response of "Great piece! Don't change a thing!" is of dubious value. Your feedback, of course, should also be sincere. You don't have to applaud writing that fails to meet the assignment just because you want to be supportive.

2. Since essays often change radically during the drafting, revision, and editing stages, focus on larger issues (appropriateness to the assignment, focus, potential for development) rather than on such sentence-level matters as wording, grammar, and spelling.

Here are a few questions that you and your group might address during the planning stages of writing an essay:

When you have developed a working thesis and are starting to plan your essay:

- Is the thesis appropriate to the assignment? Example: If your assignment says to write on one of the "Activities for Writing and Discussion" at the end of "A Woman on a Roof" and your thesis is on "The Story of an Hour," you need a new thesis.

- Is the thesis nonobvious? Does it promise to make an interesting contribution to the "conversation" about the chosen topic?
- Is the thesis supportable within the prescribed word length for the assignment (e.g., three hundred words, five hundred words, one thousand words)? Example: If your instructor wants an essay of "around one thousand words," you will have trouble covering the following thesis: "Charlotte Perkins Gilman's 'The Yellow Wallpaper' is a critique of nineteenth-century treatments of nervous disorders." Such a thesis would require considerable development and outside research. You would do better to narrow the thesis to something like "John's medical treatment of the narrator helps precipitate her final crisis."

After you have composed one or more quick-writes on your topic:

- Which points relate to and support the thesis? Which, if any, do *not* (and should therefore be cut)?
- Which points seem strongest or most interesting?
- Which points need more explanation or development?

Joe applies these questions to his quick-write on "A Woman on a Roof" and also gets feedback on the questions from his group mates. Then, as shown below, he marks up his quick-write to indicate points for development. With these notes, he begins the transition from quick-write to draft.

"Young Tom" in "Woman on a Roof" is really in the same boat as Stanley. "The bond between the woman and himself" is something covert and not outwardly observable. His feelings manifest themselves in the form of elaborate fantasies that he has every evening when he gets home and he somehow imagines that the "woman" has knowledge of these or is somehow informed of his supposed "bond" with her. At the end, young Tom even manages to feel slighted by the woman's apathy towards him as if she has wronged him by reacting this way. Stanley certainly manifests his feelings in a more direct and observable way.

Outwardly, Tom and Stanley react differently. Inwardly, their reactions are similar.

    The woman has made herself unavailable to Stanley who may observe the candor of the relationship Stanley has with Mrs. Pritchett, a woman who has made herself accessible to him and he manages to have a reasonable relationship though it is made possible via the flirtatious nature of their interaction.

Similarity with Tom's inward fantasies

    Stanley may be capable of dealing with women in only a sexual way and the woman on the roof's uncaring, unmoved manner has been in effect an invalidation of Stanley's sexual persona or merely a

Compare/contrast their reactions— outward reactions/ inward reactions

rejection—something that Stanley is not accustomed to
or perhaps just a rejection in this manner.

Conclusion: the nature of unspoken relationships?

Checklist of Activities for Planning an Essay about Literature

Develop habits of recursive reading and writing:
- Reread your notebook regularly, and mine it for ideas for writing.
- Share with your peers to develop your ideas and gain new perspectives.
- Practice habits of note taking and of reviewing and annotating your own notes.

Find a topic:
- Review your notes and notebook.
- Brainstorm or quick-write for possible topics.
- Peruse the "Activities for Writing and Discussion" and the "Additional Activities for Writing and Discussion" that follow many of the reading selections in Part V.

Develop a working thesis:
- Brainstorm or quick-write your way to a thesis, or
- Pose a question around some problem your thesis can answer.

Evaluate your thesis:
- Is it appropriate to the assignment?
- Is it nonobvious, and does it promise to make an interesting contribution to the "conversation" about the topic?
- Is it supportable within the prescribed word length for the assignment?

Do a quick-write of your essay, or
Make a list of points to support your thesis (and then arrange the points into a logical sequence or outline).

Get feedback at various stages from a partner, small group, and/or your instructor.

Ways of Drafting: Building a Barn in a Tornado

I don't give a hoot what the writing's like. I write any sort of rubbish that will cover the main outlines of the story, then I can begin to see it.

—FRANK O'CONNOR

Beginning with Limited Expectations

It's one thing to develop a thesis for an essay, make a list of ideas, and do a quick-write or two; quite another to produce a draft. Somehow a "draft" suggests something *substantial.*

The best way to approach drafting is with limited expectations. Rid yourself of the notion that a draft is a nearly "finished" piece of writing, and think of it, instead, as a *rough approximation* of an essay. When you draft you are trying to get all your ideas on paper (or screen) in whatever rough form you can. Concerns about quality and finish are far away.

You may want to keep the following images in mind as you draft:

1. *A safety net.* Spread beneath you as you draft is an immense safety net called "revision," which makes injury impossible, no matter how hard or far you fall. Revision is your invitation to return to your draft and redo it, as much as you'd like, later on.

2. *Building a barn in a tornado.* This was novelist William Faulkner's metaphor for drafting. Imagine yourself in the ultimate race against time. You have to hang on to your hammer and drive the nails *fast* before they blow away.

Two Ways of Drafting

Two basic procedures for drafting are "starting from scratch" and "cutting and pasting." Which approach you use depends on the quality of the writing you have done on your topic so far. If your predraft writings such as notes, lists of ideas to develop, and quick-writes are confused or unsatisfying, you may prefer the "start-from-scratch" method. On the other hand, if your predraft writings read well and already begin to suggest usable "pieces" of a draft, then cutting and pasting is good.

Starting from Scratch: Writing a "Throwaway" or "Rehearsal" Draft

Start from scratch when you have a topic but the preliminary writings you have done for it are too poorly written to include in your essay. First, review your writings, getting the important ideas firmly fixed in your mind. Then write a quick draft. To highlight its tentative nature, call it a "throwaway" draft or, if you prefer, a "rehearsal" draft.

Starting with a fresh sheet of paper (or a clear screen), and without looking back at your preliminary writings, write the draft. Begin by accepting that what you produce will probably be food for the trash bin—compost, waste material, junk. Your main goal in this draft is to *approximate* the shape you want your final text to have.

Here are a few guidelines for throwaway drafting:

- Focus yourself by jotting down your working thesis.
- Write quickly for a limited time period (twenty to thirty minutes works well).
- Make sure the draft has a beginning and an end, however sketchy.
- Do not concern yourself with getting the "correct" phrasing or with providing supporting examples, as fumbling over these matters will break your momentum and disturb your train of thought.
- Whenever you get stuck and can't think of a word, phrase, or sentence, leave a blank and push on. If you are undecided between two different words or phrases, include both and separate them with a slash, e.g., "She loved/enjoyed the book." Aim to achieve an overall shape for the piece, and worry about details later.

Here is the throwaway draft Joe wrote for his essay about "A Woman on a Roof":

Lessing on Men and Women

In Doris Lessing's "A Woman on a Roof," two men/roofers become fascinated with a woman who sunbathes nearby them as they work. While Stanley hoots and _____ angry at the woman, Tom—the younger—sees himself as the woman's protector. Yet, despite his gallant intentions, Tom is essentially no different from Stanley in his treatment of the sunbathing woman.

Outwardly, the two men react quite differently. With the initial sighting of the "woman on a roof" Stanley raises questions about the woman's near-nudity, and, later, he begins acting out at the woman, whistling and hooting at her. Though he is seemingly annoyed at her and her state of near-nudity, he seems inextricably drawn to her and his annoyance deepens with her indifference.

Tom's actions are, at first, little different from Stanley's: he snickers at Stanley's derisive comments about the woman, he goes with Stanley to spy on the woman, and he even stands by Stanley as Stanley hurls epithets at the woman after Tom has come to see himself as the woman's champion. The woman's indifference angers Tom as much as it does Stanley and, ultimately, he comes to feel a resentment in himself toward the woman, even hatred.

Stanley's relationship with the *other* two women of the story, his wife and Mrs. Pritchett, gives us a glimpse of some of his inner motivations. Some of his earlier anger with the "woman on the roof" seems to stem from his feelings about his wife. "If my wife lay about like that, _____" (fill in quote) Stanley says. It seems his annoyance with the sunbathing woman could be related to his inability to control her the way he, probably, controls his wife. Stanley is able to regain that sense of control through his relationship with Mrs. Pritchett and we see him responding positively to her as she seems to be receptive to his physical charms.

Control is also the primary issue in Tom's relationship with the woman on the roof. When he first sees her, he wants to possess her apart from his cohorts, as his own. Tom stands near Stanley as Stanley rages against the woman, hoping that she doesn't associate him with Stanley (reword?); he comes to see himself as having to save the woman from Stanley and even has involved fantasies about becoming the woman's lover. But when the woman does not sunbathe one day, Tom feels betrayed. Her appearance the following day reassures Tom, and the fact she can't be seen by the others makes her seem more like his own. By the end of the story, however, when Tom comes face to face with the woman's indifference, he feels slighted in much the same way that Stanley does.

It is the woman herself who sees Tom, for all his romantic intentions, as no different from Stanley. When Tom finally speaks to her, the woman tells him to go away and that, if he gets a thrill out of "seeing women in bikinis," he should "go to the Lido." Tom feels stung by what he perceives as her mis-perception of his actions and goes away hating the woman, suggesting that the woman saw him with the utmost clarity of all.

What happens to the throwaway draft after you have written it? From its name you might assume it ends up in the wastebasket, and this does occasionally happen. Even then, however, you will not be disappointed because your expectations were modest. You may need to change your topic, do some more preliminary quick-writes, or get feedback from your instructor or classmates about what to do next. On the other hand, like Joe, you may be pleasantly surprised by the quality of your throwaway. Sometimes, when you have low expectations for a draft (telling yourself you're going to "throw it away" when it's done), you end up producing something better, richer, and more exciting than you do when you grit your teeth and say, "This *will* be a masterpiece." Thus, you might end up not "throwing away" the draft at all. You may find that doing a rough draft is basically a matter of filling out and elaborating on the throwaway. Finally, no matter what you do with the draft, you will be going back over it; you will be using it recursively to move your work forward.

Joe reviews his draft in the light of two questions that you might apply to your own throwaways:

1. What are the strengths of the draft, and where is it working well?
2. What do I need to do in order to advance to a rough draft?

To observe Joe's next step, see "From Throwaway Draft to Rough Draft," below.

Cutting and Pasting

Cutting and pasting involves taking various pieces of preliminary writing you have already done on your topic and combining and arranging them to create a draft. You can cut and paste by either of two general methods: on screen with a word processor or on paper.

As you accumulate a number of entries on a topic that you want to develop into a finished piece of work, e.g., "Anne Tyler's 'Teenage Wasteland' and the condition of teens today" or "escape themes in 'The Yellow Wallpaper' and 'The Story of an Hour,' " a word processor is enormously helpful. With word processing you can type related notebook items into a word-processing document. That way you can see them all, together and in one place, on screen. You are "getting all the cards on the table." At this point the "cards" may be extremely disorganized. Nevertheless, you are 51 percent of the way to a finished text because you have all your ideas before you. Now you can begin arranging, rearranging, adding, and deleting materials toward accomplishment of a draft.

To illustrate: suppose the pages below are in your notebook, and the circled parts—"A" and "B"—are passages that please you in their current form:

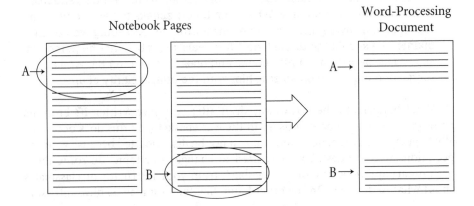

Notebook Pages   Word-Processing Document

A→   A→

B→   B→

As illustrated, you can "cut" these passages out of your notebook and "paste" them into a *new* word-processing document as parts of a rough draft.

If you lack access to word processing, you can rearrange the pages in your notebook so that entries on your topic are physically juxtaposed. This is where a looseleaf notebook is advantageous. For instance, if entries from October 8 and October 14 talk about "differences between Stanley and Tom in 'A Woman on a Roof,' " put them physically together (within your notebook or in a file folder) so that you can begin to see connections between what you wrote on those two days. This is an excellent way of organizing your ideas, of moving from the notebook writing stage to the draft stage. (I have presented "starting from scratch" and "cutting and pasting" as if they were mutually exclusive activities. They aren't. Often you will end up creating a part of your draft by cutting and pasting and other parts by writing from scratch.)

From Throwaway Draft to Rough Draft

Here is the rough draft that Joe wrote after doing his throwaway. The marginal notes indicate some of the more significant changes he has made from his throwaway draft.

The Clarity of Control:
Lessing on Men and Women

In Doris Lessing's "A Woman on a Roof," two men become fascinated with a woman who sunbathes nearby them as they work. While Stanley hoots and hollers and actually expresses a sense of rage at the woman, Tom, a younger man, comes to see himself as the woman's protector. Yet, despite his gallant intentions, Tom is essentially no different from Stanley in his treatment of the sunbathing woman.

Outwardly, the two men react quite differently. With the initial sighting of the scantily clad woman, Stanley raises questions concerning the woman's state of undress ("Someone'll report her if she doesn't watch out") and, later, begins acting out at the woman, whistling and hooting at her and expressing a great deal of agitation at her subsequent apathy. Though he is seemingly annoyed at her and her state of near-nudity, he seems inextricably drawn to her and his annoyance deepens with her "gesture[s] of indifference."

Tom's actions are, at first, in conspiracy with Stanley's actions: he snickers at the derisive comments Stanley makes about the woman, he "makes the trip" with Stanley to spy on the woman and, even once he

Marginal notes:

Expands title to be more descriptive

Here (and elsewhere) adds quotations to illustrate points

Details supplement ideas that were hinted at in throwaway

comes to see himself as the woman's champion, he stands by Stanley as Stanley hurls epithets at her. The woman's indifference angers Tom much in the same way it angers Stanley and, ultimately, he comes to feel a resentment in himself toward the woman, even hatred. He feels her "unfairness pale him," and, when it rains at the end of the story, he feels a sense of triumph over her.

It is in Stanley's relationship with the other two women of the story, his wife and Mrs. Pritchett, that we glimpse some of his inner motivations. Some of his earlier anger with the "woman on the roof" seems to stem from his feelings about his wife. "If my wife lay about like that," Stanley says, "I'd soon stop her," and it is here that we are able to discern that his annoyance with the sunbathing woman could be related to his inability to control her much in the same way he, no doubt, controls or seeks to control his wife. Stanley is able to regain that sense of control through his relationship with Mrs. Pritchett and we see him responding positively to her as she seems to be receptive to his physical charms.

Expands discussion of Mrs. Pritchett and how Stanley's relationship with her illuminates his relationship with "woman"

Control is the primary issue in Tom's relationship with the woman on the roof, as well. When he first sees her, he wants to possess her apart from his cohorts, to keep her for his own. On one of his trips to spy on the woman, Tom makes the report that "she hadn't moved, but it was a lie. He wanted to keep what he had seen to himself: he had caught her in the act of rolling down the little red pants over her hips. . . ." Tom stands near Stanley as he rages against the woman, hoping that she doesn't associate his proximity with complicity; he comes to see himself as having to save the woman from Stanley and even has involved fantasies about becoming the woman's lover. But when the woman does not sunbathe one day, Tom feels betrayed. Her appearance the following day reassures Tom as does her moving to a part of the roof where the men could not see her, because he feels that she's "more his when the other men couldn't see her." And, by the end of the story, when Tom comes face to face with the woman's indifference, he feels slighted in much the same way that Stanley does.

Extensive expansion of last 2 paragraphs with quotations, examples, and rewording of undeveloped ideas

It is the woman on the roof's perception of Stanley and Tom that is most telling, for she sees Tom, with all his romantic intentions and farflung illusions, as being virtually indivisible from the howling, ranting and hateful Stanley. When Tom finally speaks to her, after he has (in his mind) come to her rescue at the end of the story, the woman tells him to go away and that, if he gets a thrill out of "seeing women in bikinis," he should go somewhere where he'd "see dozens of them, without all this mountaineering." Tom feels stung by what he perceives as her mis-perception of his actions and goes away hating the woman, suggesting that the woman had not mis-perceived the situation at all, but that, perhaps, she had seen Tom with the utmost clarity of all.

Checklist of Activities for Drafting

- **"Start from scratch"** if none of your predraft writings is successful. Write a "throwaway" or "rehearsal" draft.
- Follow your throwaway with a **rough draft.**
- **"Cut and paste"** if portions of your predraft writings are successful. "Cut" the successful portions and "paste" them together. Then add other paragraphs, as needed, to complete your essay.
- **Get feedback** at various stages of drafting from a partner, small group, and/or your instructor.

Ways of Revising: Caring and Not Caring

Teach us to care and not to care . . .

—T. S. Eliot

Putting Revision into Context

Chapter 6 suggested that you approach drafting with low expectations. Not so revising. The very nature of revision is to "go over" and make better. The further along you get in revising a text, the higher your standards of quality become. At the quick-writing stage you have no standards at all. By the time you reach final proofreading, at the other end of the composing spectrum, you ought to be an archperfectionist. Keep in mind, however, that not every text you begin writing is worth revising. For more about that, see Chapter 9 ("The Portfolio Pyramid").

To title this chapter "Revising," as if announcing a new topic in *Reading and Writing from Literature,* is somewhat misleading. Realize it or not, you have been revising constantly throughout this course. To revise means "to look . . . again" (*Oxford English Dictionary*), and "looking again"— a.k.a. "conversing" or being "recursive"—has been the perennial theme of this book. In developing habits of recursiveness, you have automatically developed habits of revision as well. A litany of revision techniques you have already learned and practiced would read like a repetition of the table of contents for Chapters 1 through 6. Any of the following is, potentially, an act of revision:

- Conversational reading and writing
- Annotating
- Notebook writing and sharing
- Listing and sequencing
- Quick-writing
- Revising from group or instructor feedback
- Reading aloud
- Throwaway/rehearsal drafting
- Cutting and pasting

All of these techniques and habits can help you revise an essay about literature. If it weren't for the problem of redundancy, all could be addressed again in this chapter. The best way to use this book is not to read about these techniques once and never come back to them but—you guessed it—to use the book recursively. "Run back" to these strategies again and again—any place, any time. If one cannot help you in a particular situation, perhaps another can.

Thus, this chapter does not "introduce" revision or presume to confine it to a single chapter unto itself; it merely revisits it in the somewhat distinctive context of revising an essay about literature.

Talking to Your Draft: Caring and Not Caring

Someone once said that writers have two absolutely indispensable needs, a passion for what they are writing and an attitude of ruthless objectivity toward their own creations. This is a paradox at the very heart of revising. As a writer you need to care and not care; you need to care deeply about what you are creating and yet be ready—in an instant—to destroy your writing if it's not working.

Most of us feel vulnerable—naked—when we revise; we long for a suit of armor to steel us for the task and to defend ourselves from the expected "blows" of readers. Together, passion and objectivity constitute this armor. If you are passionate enough about what you are making, if you care enough about the task, the destruction of your text won't matter; you will simply collect yourself and begin again. If you are objective enough, you will never encounter a harsher critic than yourself, so no attack or defeat will astonish you.

To be a good reviser, do everything possible to cultivate both passion for your task *and* objectivity about it. Part III will have more to say about passion, but here, now, is a word about objectivity. In the context of revision, the opposite of objectivity is attachment—attachment to your text. Writers who are attached to their texts regard any criticism, however useful or appropriate, as a personal affront. They reject criticism, whether self-generated or from others, and thus eliminate any chance of making their texts better.

One excellent way of developing objectivity is to talk—in writing—to the text of your evolving essay. For example, here I am talking to an earlier draft of the introduction to this chapter.

> By this point in *Reading and Writing from Literature*, you are no stranger to revision. To revise means, literally, "to see again"; and "seeing again"—a.k.a "conversing" or "recursiveness"—has been the constant theme of this book. In developing habits of conversing and recursiveness, you have necessarily developed habits of revision as well. Speaking practically, you have already developed a repertoire of strategies for revising. Refresh your memory of these as often as necessary/Refer back to these as often as necessary. If one cannot help you in a particular situation, perhaps another can.

EXPAND. Good ideas but flat

Good link with earlier chapters

Use a different word?

Sounds preachy & patronizing(?)

Why should I care?

I treat the paragraph as a thing, an object. No emotions attach to it. I don't care about *it,* only about having my ideas come across clearly and effectively.

Psychologically, talking to your draft is a way of distancing yourself from it. By splitting yourself into two different people—the one who wrote the draft and the "other" who is now reviewing it—you become less emotionally and personally enmeshed in your own written product. To put this slightly differently, you imagine yourself into a different role, that of a prospective member of your audience. Instead of asking, "What do *I* think of this writing?" you ask, "What do I—a prospective *audience* member—think of this writing?"

Practice talking to your draft; even address yourself as "you" rather than "I" as a way of exaggerating your own separateness from your text. In the margins write:

- **Reactions you have to your own ideas:** "Interesting." "Brilliant!" "Gets dull here." "This needs reworking."
- **Questions:** "Does this make sense?" "Will this be clear to readers?" "Reverse order of paragraphs here?" "What will your reader(s) think about this?"
- **New thoughts that are prompted by something in the draft:** "Reminds me of the point about ____; can you work that in here?" "Relate this to the idea on previous page."
- **Next-step ideas for reading and writing:** "What can you do next to develop this point?" "Move this idea to next page." "Read ____." "Where can you find more information about this?"

The more you write, the more weblike you will find the nature of writing to be; every strand—every process and activity—is interconnected with every other. *How* do you get better at recording "reactions," "questions," "new thoughts," and "next-step ideas" in the margins of your drafts? By experiencing, whenever possible, feedback from other people. Such feedback teaches you how and what readers think. Every time you discuss your work with instructors, peers, or anyone else, you strengthen your capacity to identify with readers of your own work.

Global and Local Revisions

Being large in scope and complex, revision tends to raise questions like "Where do I start?" It is useful to separate revision concerns into "global" and "local." Among global concerns are matters of topic selection, thesis, focus, purpose, organization, and clarity. Local concerns include sentence-level issues of grammar, spelling, punctuation, and usage. Though writers often mix their writing on the two levels, generally you should deal with global concerns first and local ones later. After all, it doesn't pay to revise sentence "X" to perfection if you are going to throw it out a few minutes later because it doesn't fit your thesis. Why do surgery on a toe if you're going to amputate the foot? The strategies in this chapter follow a general progression from global to local.

A Short Checklist of Questions for Global Revision

Here are a few questions for addressing global revision concerns. You can use the questions by yourself or in collaboration with a small group.

- Does the draft meet the requirements of the assignment? Is it the appropriate length? Does it address an appropriate topic? A brilliant paper that fails to meet the assignment is probably going to get a poor grade.
- Does the draft have a clear thesis or purpose? If so, what is it?
- Does each paragraph relate to and support the thesis? Which paragraphs, if any, do not?
- Are ideas logically or coherently arranged so that one paragraph follows clearly and understandably from another?
- Does the essay include adequate evidence or examples to support and illustrate the various points?
- Does the essay have a clear conclusion?

Postdraft Outlining

An outline is a familiar device for planning an essay, but you may not realize that it can be equally useful to do an outline *after* drafting. Postdraft outlining helps you look at your draft closely, and it can also help you respond to the "Checklist of Questions." Here are the steps:

1. Read through your whole draft. Then, at the bottom of the last page, write a statement that summarizes what you think the whole paper "does" (that is, what its thesis or purpose is).

2. Reread your draft again, paragraph by paragraph. When you finish reading a paragraph, write in the margin beside it a statement summarizing what you think that paragraph "does," i.e., how it functions in your paper.
3. Beside each paragraph, you can also record your emotional reactions to that paragraph, for instance, "My interest really picks up here," "I find this suspenseful," "I'm feeling bored here," or "I'm losing interest here."
4. When you are finished, review the marginal comments you have written and ask yourself the following questions:
    a. Do my ideas seem to be in a logical order? Does one paragraph and idea follow clearly and logically from another? Draw arrows in the margins to indicate places where you want to rearrange paragraphs or information.
    b. Does each paragraph and idea have a reason for being in the essay? That is, does each paragraph relate to and support the thesis? If not, so indicate.
    c. Are there any places where I need to add more information? or perhaps eliminate some information? or clarify a point? Mark any such places and, if possible, add or delete the information.

Here is Joe's postdraft outline for his paper about "A Woman on a Roof." Skim through the essay, paying particular attention to the "outline" comments in the margins and at the end of the essay.

The Clarity of Control:
Lessing on Men and Women

In Doris Lessing's "A Woman on a Roof," two men become fascinated with a woman who sunbathes nearby them as they work. While Stanley hoots and hollers and actually expresses a sense of rage at the woman, Tom, a younger man, comes to see himself as the woman's protector. Yet, despite his gallant intentions, Tom is essentially no different from Stanley in his treatment of the sunbathing woman.

thesis/intro

Tom is no different from Stanley

Outwardly, the two men react quite differently. With the initial sighting of the scantily clad woman, Stanley raises questions concerning the woman's state of undress ("Someone'll report her if she doesn't watch out") and, later, begins acting out at the woman, whistling and hooting at her and expressing a great deal of agitation at her subsequent apathy. Though he is seemingly annoyed at her and her state of near-nudity, he seems inextricably drawn to her and his annoyance deepens with her "gesture[s] of indifference."

Comparison of outward reactions—Stanley moves from puritanical concern to rage inexorably(?)

Add page #'s for quotations

Tom's actions are, at first, in conspiracy with Stanley's actions: he snickers at the derisive comments

Stanley makes about the woman, he "makes the trip" with Stanley to spy on the woman and, even once he comes to see himself as the woman's champion, he stands by Stanley as Stanley hurls epithets at her. The woman's indifference angers Tom much in the same way it angers Stanley and, ultimately, he comes to feel a resentment in himself toward the woman, even hatred. He feels her "unfairness pale him," and, when it rains at the end of the story, he feels a sense of triumph over her.

It is in Stanley's relationship with the other two women of the story, his wife and Mrs. Pritchett, that we glimpse some of his inner motivations. Some of his earlier anger with the "woman on the roof" seems to stem from his feelings about his wife. "If my wife lay about like that," Stanley says, "I'd soon stop her," and it is here that we are able to discern that his annoyance with the sunbathing woman could be related to his inability to control her much in the same way he, no doubt, controls or seeks to control his wife. Stanley is able to regain that sense of control through his relationship with Mrs. Pritchett and we see him responding positively to her as she seems to be receptive to his physical charms.

Control is the primary issue in Tom's relationship with the woman on the roof, as well. When he first sees her, he wants to possess her apart from his cohorts, to keep her for his own. On one of his trips to spy on the woman, Tom makes the report that "she hadn't moved, but it was a lie. He wanted to keep what he had seen to himself: he had caught her in the act of rolling down the little red pants over her hips. . . ." Tom stands near Stanley as he rages against the woman, hoping that she doesn't associate his proximity with complicity; he comes to see himself as having to save the woman from Stanley and even has involved fantasies about becoming the woman's lover. But when the woman does not sunbathe one day, Tom feels betrayed. Her appearance the following day reassures Tom as does her moving to a part of the roof where the men could not see her, because he feels that she's "more his when the other men couldn't see her." And, by the end of the story, when Tom comes face to face with the woman's indifference, he feels slighted in much the same way that Stanley does.

Tom's outward reaction initially a self-mirroring of Stanley; moves to the end of story. Tom's feelings of hatred

Need to mention that resentment occurs as result of her rejecting him?

Gauging Stanley's internal state via his external relationships with women: it all equals the attempt to gain and maintain control

Clear

Expand?

Control is the catalyst in Tom's motivations re: the woman on the roof as well— speaks in terms of possession— motivation the same as Stanley's

Redundant with end of 3rd paragraph?

It is the woman on the roof's perception of Stanley and Tom that is most telling, for she sees Tom, with all his romantic intentions and farflung illusions, as being virtually indivisible from the howling, ranting and hateful Stanley. When Tom finally speaks to her, after he has (in his mind) come to her rescue at the end of the story, the woman tells him to go away and that, if he gets a thrill out of "seeing women in bikinis," he should go somewhere where he'd "see dozens of them, without all this mountaineering." Tom feels stung by what he perceives as her mis-perception of his actions and goes away hating the woman, suggesting that the woman had not mis-perceived the situation at all, but that, perhaps, she had seen Tom with the utmost clarity of all.

We see that it is the perception of the woman that is illuminating—she views both Tom and Stanley as being the same leering fiend

Despite Tom's intentions, he is driven by the same thing that drives Stanley: control, *and the woman perceives this more aptly than either Tom or Stanley.*

Joe's draft is already quite strong. The postdraft outline indicates a clear thesis with effective organization and supporting points. Joe does, however, identify a few places for revision. For instance, he raises a question about clarity in the third paragraph, makes a note to "expand" at one point (the end of paragraph #4), and locates a possible redundancy between the third and fifth paragraphs.

Having Other People Outline Your Draft

Postdraft outlining enables you to see your draft more objectively. You can also benefit from having other people, particularly a peer or a small group, do outlines of your draft so that you have one or more alternative perspectives to compare with your own. Here's how to do it:

- Bring an extra, *clean* copy of your draft with you to class.
- Sit with a partner.
- After you and your partner have finished doing postdraft outlines of your own papers, exchange papers so you are now looking at your classmate's draft and he or she is looking at yours.
- Now repeat steps 1 through 4 above on your *partner's* draft.
- Finally, with your partner compare how you analyzed each other's papers. This can tell you a lot about how well your paper is working. For instance, if your partner's summary of thesis or purpose for your draft (step #1) differs from what you intended, you probably need to make your thesis clearer. Similarly, if your partner's analysis of one of your paragraphs suggests that he or she is interpreting it differently from what

you meant, then you need to think about revising for greater clarity. If your partner writes, in the margin beside your third paragraph, "I am losing interest here," perhaps you need to revise that paragraph to make it more vivid or exciting, or perhaps you need to consider getting rid of it.

Getting Writer-Initiated Feedback

The postdraft outline is an example of reader-initiated feedback; that is, it involves readers describing their reactions to your work while you—the writer—mainly listen. While such feedback is useful, there may be times when you want input on specific problems or issues that concern you about your draft. Hence the value of *writer*-initiated feedback. This is where you, as writer, indicate to your partner(s) specific kinds of feedback that you want that may not be addressed through postdraft outlining.

Before meeting with your partner or group, take a few moments to respond in your notebook to the following questions:

- What do you feel are *strengths* of your draft in its current form?
- What, specifically, do you feel you need to work on in order to improve your draft?
- In what specific areas would you like suggestions from your partner or small group?

Share your responses to these questions with your partner(s) or group and read your draft aloud to them. Then ask your partner or group members to respond to the specific areas of need you indicated and take notes on their suggestions.

As you request feedback, keep in mind how thick or thin your skin is. If you thrive on tough criticism, you can ask for it. On the other hand, if tough criticism tends simply to destroy your confidence, devise your request for input so that it will elicit gentler comments of the sort that you want and need in order to improve your draft. After all, the ultimate goal of this or any other revision activity is to get the input that will help you move boldly forward toward a better piece of writing.

Developing Your Essay with Illustrative Quotations and Examples

Poet William Stafford once said that he could reduce revision to a single word: "more." Stafford meant that his most frequent response to others' writing was "tell me more." Clearly, one of the major defects in many rough drafts is a lack of supporting quotations or examples. The key here is *development:* you can make your ideas clearer and more vivid for readers by illustrating those ideas.

Compare the following two versions of a paragraph in Joe's "The Clarity of Control: Lessing on Men and Women." The first version omits quotations and examples, while the second includes them.

> Control is the primary issue in Tom's relationship with the woman on the roof, as well. When he first sees her, he wants to possess her apart from his cohorts, to keep her for his own. Tom stands near Stanley as he rages against the woman, hoping that she doesn't associate his proximity with complicity; he comes to see himself as having to save the woman from Stanley and even has involved fantasies about becoming the woman's lover. But when the woman does not sunbathe one day, Tom feels betrayed. Her appearance the following day reassures Tom, as does her moving to a part of the roof where the men could not see her.

> Control is the primary issue in Tom's relationship with the woman on the roof, as well. When he first sees her, he wants to possess her apart from his cohorts, to keep her for his own. On one of his trips to spy on the woman, Tom makes the report that "she hadn't moved, but it was a lie. He wanted to keep what he had seen to himself: he had caught her in the act of rolling down the little red pants over her hips. . . ." Tom stands near Stanley as he rages against the woman, hoping that she doesn't associate his proximity with complicity; he comes to see himself as having to save the woman from Stanley and even has involved fantasies about becoming the woman's lover. But when the woman does not sunbathe one day, Tom feels betrayed. Her appearance the following day reassures Tom as does her moving to a part of the roof where the men could not see her, because he feels that she's "more his when the other men couldn't see her." And, by the end of the story, when Tom comes face to face with the woman's indifference, he feels slighted in much the same way that Stanley does.

Notice how the quotations and examples serve to ground discussion more carefully in the text's details. Notice, also, how Joe introduces his quotations; rather than simply insert them without context or explanation, he integrates them into his own prose, sewing together distinctly different fabrics so that they appear almost seamless.

Local Revision: Copyediting Your Text

When you draft or do global revisions, imagination is an asset. By contrast, when proofreading, you want to be like a machine that focuses in on individual sentences and words and coldly examines them for errors. The problem is, after rereading your text a dozen times during the drafting and revision stages, you may reach a point where you can no longer "see" it; the words and sentences run together in a confused blur. How can you see your text afresh? Here are two suggestions:

Do a "micro" postdraft outline. While the regular or "macro" postdraft outline described earlier in this chapter focuses on revision at the *paragraph* level, a "micro" outline focuses on *sentences*. Simply follow the directions on page 73 for postdraft outlining, with one difference: wherever you see the word "paragraph" replace it with "sentence." You can either apply the "micro" process to your whole text or to troublesome parts of it.

Proofread your text backward. This is an excellent way of seeing your text objectively.

1. Get a clean hard copy of your text and sit alongside a partner.
2. Turn to the last page of your text and place a sheet of paper over it so that everything is covered except the final sentence.
3. Read the final sentence aloud slowly, with pen or pencil in hand. With your partner, examine the sentence for any of the following:

   - Typographical mistakes, e.g., you typed "teh" for "the"
   - Missing words, e.g., "He bought book"
   - Spelling errors, e.g., you typed "seperate" for "separate"
   - Punctuation errors, e.g., you omitted the apostrophe from the contraction in "She cant"
   - Other errors to which you may be prone, e.g., sentence run-ons, comma splices, mistakes in capitalization

4. If you or your partner find any errors, correct them. If you are uncertain whether an error exists or how to correct it, consult a good English handbook.
5. Raise your cover sheet so that the second-to-last sentence is exposed and repeat steps 3 and 4 on that sentence.
6. Continue in like manner through the rest of the text so that the last sentence you proofread is the first sentence of your paper.

If this process seems a bit tedious, keep in mind that its larger purpose is to train you to read carefully and with an editor's eye. The reward is a better and more professional-looking text. Over time and as your eye improves, you can modify the steps as appropriate.

"Lightning" Revision: Reading Your Writing Aloud to a Peer or a Small Group

Reading aloud was just recommended as a method of copyediting. In fact, reading aloud is useful at any and all stages of composing an essay about literature (or any other text). You can read your lists of ideas, your notes, your working theses, your quick-writes, your drafts, your revised drafts (or parts of drafts)—anything.

Reading aloud is helpful in at least two ways. First, it can show you whether a particular writing project is worth pursuing. If you are too embarrassed to read a piece aloud, it *may* mean your work is severely flawed and that perhaps you should start over with a different idea. (A poet friend treated this as a litmus: if he hesitated to read his precious poem aloud he knew the poem wasn't precious, and he destroyed it.) Second, reading aloud is an excellent device for "lightning" revision. Often you can make improvements in your work when reading it aloud that you wouldn't when reviewing it silently. You can read aloud to yourself, but it is even better if you read to a partner or small group because the presence of an audience can intensify your concentration. Observe these three simple steps:

1. Begin without apology ("This is really stupid . . .") or introduction ("Well, you know I'd better explain this before I read it . . ."). Simply plunge in and read. It's a fast way to thicken your writer's skin.
2. Read slowly, with pen or pencil in hand. Whenever you come to a place where you want to make a change (correct a typo or spelling error, alter a word or phrase, add or eliminate a phrase or sentence), simply pause and make the revision. Continue thus throughout your text. Remember: this is a method of *rapid* revising, so don't belabor it; only make changes that occur to you spontaneously.
3. When you have finished, congratulate yourself; you have made your work public, and that takes courage. Reading aloud is a mode of instant publication.

Checklist of Activities for Revising

- "Talk" to your draft.
- Focus on global revisions first and local revisions later.
- Do a postdraft outline.
- Have other people do postdraft outlines of your draft.
- Get writer-initiated feedback.
- Develop your essay with illustrative quotations and examples.
- Copyedit your text.
- Do "lightning" revision while reading your writing aloud to a peer or a small group.

Documenting Research Essays

[T]he man who thinks for himself becomes acquainted with the authorities for his opinions only after he has acquired them and merely as a confirmation of them, while the book-philosopher starts with his authorities, in that he constructs his opinions by collecting together the opinions of others: his mind then compares with that of the former as an automaton compares with a living man.

—ARTHUR SCHOPENHAUER

Chapter 7 dealt with an essay about literature that focuses on one literary text (or possibly two or three, if the essay is a comparison). Most likely, the text you wrote about was one of those included in Part V of this book. Thus, readers could find your text without the aid of a bibliography and research documentation was unnecessary. In this chapter we turn to essays that draw on outside sources. Such sources may include primary texts, e.g., literary texts such as short stories, poems, essays, and plays, as well as secondary sources, e.g., works of literary criticism, biographies, and other texts *about* literature rather than the literature itself. For these essays documentation is a necessity; that is, you must acknowledge, in an appropriate format, the sources of your information and ideas.

Writing research essays is a familiar, though more complex, example of the conversational and intertextual models of reading and writing you have worked with so extensively throughout this book. It involves the finding and stitching together of patches of overlapping text. Rather than addressing the intricacies of finding and evaluating sources (tasks with which a good librarian can help you), this chapter focuses on how to *use* sources:

- When and how should you acknowledge your sources?
- How can you read sources and understand them?

- How can you incorporate ideas or information from sources into your essay?
- What rules should you use for citing your sources and preparing a bibliography or "Works Cited" page?

A Sample Research Essay

Throughout this chapter, the following essay by Kristin will serve as an illustration. Refer to it, as necessary, as you read the chapter or prepare your own research essays. Boxed notes in the margins refer to terms or ideas that are explained in this chapter.

"The Yellow Wallpaper": A Critical Survey

Charlotte Perkins Gilman's "The Yellow Wallpaper," written over one hundred years ago, is the narration or journal of a woman who is severely oppressed by her husband. While she is suffering from a "nervous disorder," a result of post-partum depression, he takes her to an old abandoned house and demands that she rest from all her work. He does not allow her to think or act for herself. She is afraid to speak out against him, so she records her feelings and impressions in her journal which becomes the text for the story.

> Title of essay centered on page

> Titles of short stories, poems, essays, and other kinds of short works are enclosed in quotation marks

"The Yellow Wallpaper" has undergone a variety of interpretational changes in its hundred year history. Its original audiences thought of it simply as a tale of horror or a depiction of mental breakdown. Consequently, it was ignored by most literary critics immediately following its publication. It was not until the latter part of the twentieth-century that the onset of the feminist movement demanded a closer look at the symbolism behind "The Yellow Wallpaper." Jean E. Kennard suggested "that the recent appearance of feminist novels has . . . led us to find in the story an exploration of women's role instead of the tale of horror . . . its original audience found" (qtd. in Shumaker 588). At a 1989 Modern Language Association convention in Washington, D.C., Elaine R. Hedges called "The Yellow Wallpaper" "the most well-known rediscovered work by a nineteenth-century American woman." At present "The Yellow Wallpaper" is firmly established in the literary canon appearing in all major literary anthologies (222).

> Kristin introduces quotations and integrates them into her own prose

> Example of a parenthetical reference omitting author's last name

Subsequent to its republication, "The Yellow Wallpaper" has been subject to many critical studies. Feminist critics from North America to Europe have used its text as an explicit illustration of the degrading and detrimental effects of women's life in a male dominated society.

Michelle A. Masse, from the department of English at Louisiana State University in Baton Rouge, wrote a critical essay on "The Yellow Wallpaper" entitling it "Gothic Repetition." She employed a variety of techniques in her interpretation. She utilized feminist criticism throughout the work, but also used psychoanalytic and formalist. Much of the essay concentrated on Gilman's use of repetition in her phrases and symbols creating a classic Gothic tale. Though this was the primary purpose of the essay, it was not as important as her explanations for the narrator's motivations and actions.

Masse begins by describing the narrator's loss of identity as a direct cause of her anxiety. Because of John's infantilizing treatment she is forced to deny her identity as an adult, mother, and intelligent human being (702). Using names such as "darling," "little goose," and "little girl" in addressing her and compelling her to stay in a room previously used as nursery or asylum forces her, according to Masse, to see herself as a child and ambiguously joins children with infantilized women (702).

Masse states that the narrator is subject to Freud's theories of displacement and repression. "At a certain pitch of intensity, she ostensibly moves away from talking about herself to discussion of safe inanimate objects . . . " (705). This is shown on page 88 of Gilman's text when the narrator states, "John says the very worst thing I can do is to think about my condition, and I confess it always makes me feel bad. So I will . . . talk about the house." Not being able to consciously deal with her submission and gradual loss of identity, she displaces and represses her feelings onto the house. She also displaces the restrictions placed upon her by her husband/doctor onto the woman she sees imprisoned behind the wallpaper (Masse 701).

> Example of a paraphrase or summary

> Example of a parenthetical reference using author's last name

The key symbol in this work is the yellow wallpaper. Its bulbous eyed, crawling, fungus-like pattern becomes the object of the narrator's unconscious attempts to resolve her problems. She is determined to find the pattern behind the paper because, as Masse states: "[she] believes that there must be a logical principle . . . determining the pattern of the paper, because there are supposed to be rules for such things, just as there must be comprehensible reasons for gender expectations" (707). Her attempts to find order and control within the paper are in vain. After staring at the paper for a number of hours, she writes: "just as you get well underway in following, it turns a back-somersault and there you are. It slaps you in the face, knocks you down, and tramples upon you. It is like a bad dream" (Gilman 95). Just as she cannot conquer and control the paper, she cannot conquer and control her husband. Masse says "The paper, unlikely concretization of authority's horror though it is, is inescapable and aggressive when challenged" (Masse 708). The narrator becomes angry with the "everlastingness" of the paper (Gilman 91), symbolizing the continuity of oppressiveness. Masse points out that the narrator believes others have been subjected to the paper and angered by it and worries that it will continue to be detrimental to women (708). The narrator spends many long hours studying the paper and eventually "sees what the cultural codes found in this story reveal: a trapped woman" (Masse 708).

Examples of paraphrasing

Masse states that the narrator finally finds freedom, autonomy and power through her identification with the woman in the wallpaper. "[The narrator] has finally recognized her dilemma, measured the scope allowed to her, and disabused herself of belief in the benevolent intention behind those limits" (Masse 709). She no longer struggles to deal with her prohibited identity. Although her escape is destructive and only partial, it is nonetheless an escape to the only freedom available to her. She has finally spoken and been heard by John (Masse 709).

This essay is very detailed and specific. Masse did many close readings of "The Yellow Wallpaper," and most of her symbolisms can be traced back to certain words in the text. I am in strong agreement with her interpretation of the story's conclusion and of the wallpaper's symbolism as a representation of her sense of repression and submission. I too feel that the narrator displaced many of her feelings onto the wallpaper, refusing to talk or write about them. This essay, however, seemed very complex and only a few parts opened up the text and gave me a better understanding of it. Masse concentrated on too many symbols, and thus her essay was not clear and concise. Her lack of focus made it difficult to discern what was actually being discussed.

Conrad Shumaker, of the University of Central Arkansas, describes "The Yellow Wallpaper" as:

> a question that was ... and still is—central ... to the place of women in American culture: What happens to the imagination when it's defined as feminine (and thus weak) and has to face a society that values the useful and the practical and rejects anything else as nonsense? (590)

Block-indented quotation (use when a quotation runs to 5 or more typed lines)

In a block-indented quotation, the terminal punctuation precedes the parenthetical reference

Through the use of feminist criticism, Shumaker shows how the narrator's husband tries to force her to shut out all imaginative powers and be logical. He, like most males of that day, is unable to see anything that is not practical and materialistic. Anything illogical, like his wife's problem not really being physical or her "work" helping her to improve, is unfathomable to him. He wants only to deal with physical causes and effects (Shumaker 591). By labeling his wife's imagination as a negative force, John can control her and maintain his materialistic view of the world (Shumaker 593). John represents reason to his wife, so when her feelings contradict him it is automatically her sensitivity that is at fault because she cannot question his authority (594). The narrator believes that John loves her just as John believes that she is obedient to all of his demands. Although neither is true, this shows that they both are doomed to act out these roles until the disastrous end (595). Shumaker points out the irony in the fact that the reason John fails to cure his wife is because of his deeply rooted belief and faith in materialism, "a faith that will not allow him even to consider the possibility that his wife's imagination could be a positive force" (592). The chilling conclusion of the story, as seen by Shumaker, is a very limited amount of freedom for the narrator. The most important thing accomplished is the fact that "she has discovered ... and finally revealed to John, the wife he is attempting to create—

the woman without illusions or imagination who
spends all her time creeping" (598).

Kristin's essay continues for several more pages, but this portion of it is adequate for our purposes here. Her essay ends with the following "Works Cited" page, which lists all of the sources to which she referred in her essay:

Works Cited

Gilman, Charlotte Perkins. "The Yellow Wallpaper." *Literature: An Introduction to Critical Reading.* Ed. William Vesterman. New York: Harcourt, 1993: 87–100.

Golden, Catherine. " 'Overwriting' the Rest Cure: Charlotte Perkins Gilman's Literary Escape from S. Weir Mitchell's Fictionalization of Women." *Critical Essays on Charlotte Perkins Gilman.* Ed. Joanne B. Karpinski. New York: G. K. Hall & Co., 1992: 144–58.

Hedges, Elaine R. " 'Out at Last?' 'The Yellow Wallpaper' after Two Decades of Feminist Criticism." *Critical Essays on Charlotte Perkins Gilman.* Ed. Joanne B. Karpinski. New York: G. K. Hall & Co., 1992: 222–33.

Lane, Ann J. *The Charlotte Perkins Gilman Reader.* New York: Pantheon Books, 1980.

Masse, Michelle A. "Gothic Repetition: Husbands, Horrors and Things That Go Bump in the Night." *Signs* 15 (1990): 679–709.

Shumaker, Conrad. "Too Terribly Good to Be Printed: Charlotte Gilman's 'The Yellow Wallpaper.' " *American Literature* 57 (1985): 588–99.

When You Need to Cite or Acknowledge a Source

Like Kristin, you need to acknowledge any source that you quote, summarize, or paraphrase. To quote is to use the exact words that are in the source text. To paraphrase or summarize is to put the cited material into your own words (a paraphrase usually involves a shorter passage of text and a summary a longer one). Paraphrasing or summarizing is the process of cutting textual fragments to the size and shape you want and skillfully stitching them together so that the whole appears almost seamless.

Acknowledging sources is important for two main reasons. The first is *intellectual honesty.* The ideas are someone else's, not your own. Therefore, you need to give the other person credit for the idea or words. Using another's words or ideas without acknowledgment, as if they were your own, constitutes plagiarism, a serious offense. The second is *as a courtesy to your readers.* A citation of an outside source shows readers where they need to look if they desire further information on your topic.

In a research essay, try to use quotations sparingly. If you overuse quotations, your essay may read like a patchwork of other people's ideas and your own presence as author of the essay will suffer. In addition, copying ideas word for word from a source is a purely mechanical process; you don't even have to think about what you read. On the other hand, when you summarize or paraphrase, you must process what the passage means. The reward of your effort is that you understand the material to a degree that you wouldn't if you merely copied it verbatim.

How to Paraphrase or Summarize

Here are some suggested steps for paraphrasing or summarizing a passage:

Step #1: Read through the passage a first time to get a sense of the content.

Step #2: Reread the passage, underlining and jotting down key ideas; that is, annotate.

Step #3: Determine the hierarchy of ideas (which idea is most important, next most important, and so on).

Step #4: Write out the most important points and find a way to link them together into one or two sentences.

Step #5: Edit the sentence(s) for clarity and conciseness.

For example, suppose you want to summarize the second paragraph of Kristin's essay. Steps #1 (read), #2 (annotate), and #3 (determine the hierarchy of ideas) are indicated by the following underlinings and marginal notes:

"The Yellow Wallpaper" has undergone <u>a variety of interpretational changes</u> in its hundred year history. Its <u>original audiences</u> thought of it simply as <u>a tale of horror</u> or a depiction of mental breakdown. Consequently, it was ignored by most literary critics immediately following its publication. It was not until the latter part of the twentieth-century that the onset of <u>the feminist movement</u> demanded a closer look at the <u>symbolism</u> behind "The Yellow Wallpaper." Jean E. Kennard suggested "that the recent appearance of feminist novels has . . . led us to find in the story an exploration of women's role instead of the tale of horror . . . its original audience found" (qtd. in Shumaker 588). At a 1989 Modern Language Association convention in Washington, D.C., Elaine R. Hedges called "The Yellow Wallpaper" "the most well-known rediscovered work by a nineteenth-century American woman." At present <u>"The Yellow Wallpaper" is firmly established</u> in the literary canon appearing in all major literary anthologies (222).

Interpretations of the story have changed over time

Early—seen as sensational story: critics didn't pay attention to it

Feminist movement has focused new attention on the story—see it as symbolic

Step #4: Write out the most important points and find a way to link them together into one or two sentences:

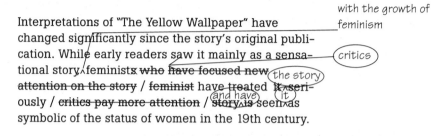

Step #5: Edit the sentences for clarity and conciseness:

Interpretations of "The Yellow Wallpaper" have changed significantly since the story's original publication. While early readers saw it mainly as a sensational story, with the onset of feminist criticism the story has been treated seriously by critics and been seen as symbolic of the status of women in the 19th century.

You can see how hard it is to portray the process of summarizing on paper. You can't retrace the exact mental shifts and turns this reader went through to produce his final summary. That is okay. The important thing is to have a sense of the steps involved and to recognize the recursiveness of the process. For instance, notice the crossed-out words, inserts, and arrows that show the reader rethinking and revising.

There are several additional points to make about this example.

First, if this process seems overly time-consuming, realize that the five steps are a slow-motion description of what you do when you summarize. As you gain more practice at the process you will inevitably collapse the steps into an abridged form.

Second, there is not one "correct" wording for a summary. If you tried summarizing the sample paragraph yourself and came up with something slightly different, that is fine, though your summary ought to express similar content.

Third, summarizing is an intellectually empowering process in and of itself, independent of the summary you produce. Simply by going through the intellectual process of the five steps, you strengthen yourself as a reader (and tone your recursive "muscles").

Fourth, summarizing is affected by context. The final content of your summary or paraphrase will change somewhat depending on the particular purpose you have for summarizing. For instance, suppose you are reading Kristin's essay as part of your research for writing an essay about "sensational literature in nineteenth-century America." In that case, what Kristin's second paragraph has to say about twentieth-century feminist critics will be irrelevant to your purposes. Your essay might include a summary more like the following:

> Many stories regarded today as "classics" were viewed as merely sensational stories when they were first published. Charlotte Perkins Gilman's "The Yellow Wallpaper" is a good example (Richards 1).

Parenthetical References; MLA Documentation Style

The "(Richards 1)" that concludes the above sample is called a "parenthetical reference." It indicates that the information is not something you came up with yourself but that you found on page one of a text by Richards. In Modern Language Association (MLA) documentation style, parenthetical references replace traditional footnotes.

The term "documentation style" refers, in part, to the particular set of rules you follow for citing sources in a research essay. Documentation styles vary from discipline to discipline. If you are writing a paper in an English class, you will probably use the MLA style, which is based on the *MLA Handbook for Writers of Research Papers;* in a psychology class you will use the APA (American Psychological Association) style; and for a paper in biology, the CBE (Council of Biology Editors) style. The important thing is not to memorize the rules for all of these styles but to learn how to understand and follow *a* style consistently. It's like using a cookbook. You don't need to memorize all the steps in a recipe; you just need to know where to look them up and how to read and follow them. If you can read and follow the rules for MLA style, you will be able to learn the rules of style for other subjects and follow them accurately, too.

The following are several common variations of MLA-style parenthetical references:

- **Parenthetical reference including author's last name.** A parenthetical reference usually includes the author's last name and the page number(s) where the information appears:

> Not being able to consciously deal with her submission and gradual loss of identity, she displaces and represses her feelings onto the house. She also displaces the restrictions placed upon her by her husband/doctor onto the woman she sees imprisoned behind the wallpaper (Masse 701).

The reference gives readers all the information they need to find the summarized material in its original source. They merely need to turn to the "Works Cited" page at the end of the essay and run down the alphabetical list of authors till they come to "Masse." There they will find all the bibliographical data on Masse:

Masse, Michelle A. "Gothic Repetition: Husbands, Horrors and Things That Go Bump in the Night." *Signs* 15 (1990): 679–709.

Once they have located the issue of *Signs* (an academic journal) in which Masse's article appears, readers can turn to page 701 to find the source of the summarized material.

- **Parenthetical reference giving page number(s) only.** If you mention the author's name when introducing your summary or quotation, or if the author's identity is obvious from the context, simply give the page number:

Masse states that the narrator is subject to Freud's theories of displacement and repression. "At a certain pitch of intensity, she ostensibly moves away from talking about herself to a discussion of safe inanimate objects ..." (705).

- **Parenthetical reference following a block-indented quotation.** If a quotation runs to five or more typed lines, you should block-indent it. This makes it easier for readers to distinguish the quoted passage from the rest of your text. With block-indented quotations, note that the final period or question mark is placed *before,* rather than after, the parenthetical reference:

Conrad Shumaker, of the University of Central Arkansas, describes "The Yellow Wallpaper" as:

> a question that was ... and still is—central ... to the place of women in American culture: What happens to the imagination when it's defined as feminine (and thus weak) and has to face a society that values the useful and the practical and rejects anything else as nonsense? (590)

- **Reference to an anonymously authored text.** If a text is authored anonymously, use the title of the source, or an abbreviated version, within your parenthetical reference, as in this example from the *MLA Handbook* (4th ed.):

The nine grades of mandarins were "distinguished by the color of the button on the hats of office" ("Mandarin").

Here "Mandarin" is the title of an anonymously written encyclopedia article.

- **Reference to a work by an author who is listed two or more times in your Works Cited.** If your Works Cited contains two or more works by the same author, use the author's last name and an abbreviated version of the work's title in your parenthetical reference. For example, if your Works Cited includes two books by Rainer Maria Rilke, a parenthetical reference will look like this:

"Days go by and sometimes I hear life going. And still nothing has happened, still there is nothing real about me ... " (Rilke, *Letters of Rainer Maria Rilke* 122).

Preparing Your List of Works Cited

The Works Cited begins on a fresh page at the end of your paper and lists all the outside sources you have quoted, paraphrased, or summarized in your work. List sources alphabetically by author's last name, and include the following information, in sequence, for each entry:

- Author (last name first)
- Title of the work
- Title of the larger work, magazine, or journal (if the work you're citing is contained in it)
- Editor, translator, or compiler (if applicable)
- Edition used (if applicable)
- Number of volumes (if applicable)
- Place of publication
- Publisher
- Year of publication
- Page numbers (if the work is only a part of a larger publication, such as a scholarly journal, magazine, or newspaper)

Center the words "Works Cited" (without quotation marks, underlining, or italics) one inch from the top of the page. Double-space down once to begin your first entry. Start the entry flush with the left margin. If the entry goes beyond one line, indent the second and succeeding lines five spaces (this is called a "hanging" indent). Double-space *between* entries as well as *within* an entry.

The following are examples of a few of the more common types of entries you may include in your Works Cited.

- **Book.**
  Lane, Ann J. *The Charlotte Perkins Gilman Reader.* New York: Pantheon Books, 1980.

- **Book with two authors.**
  Rosenthal, M. L., and Sally M. Gall. *The Modern Poetic Sequence: The Genius of Modern Poetry.* New York: Oxford UP, 1983.

- **Book with more than three authors.**
  Britton, James, et al. *The Development of Writing Abilities (11-18).* London: Macmillan Education, 1975.

- **An edited collection of essays.**
  Karpinski, Joanne B., ed. *Critical Essays on Charlotte Perkins Gilman.* New York: G. K. Hall & Co., 1992.

- **A book with an editor and/or translator.**
  Whitman, Walt. *Walt Whitman's Workshop: A Collection of Unpublished Manuscripts.* Ed. Clifton Joseph Furness. Cambridge: Harvard UP, 1928.

Rilke, Rainer Maria. *Letters of Rainer Maria Rilke.* Trans. Jane Bannard Greene and M. D. Herter Norton. 2 vols. New York: Norton Library, 1969.

- **A short story, poem, or essay included in an edited anthology or collection.**
  Faulkner, William. "That Evening Sun." *The Oxford Book of American Short Stories.* Ed. Joyce Carol Oates. New York: Oxford UP, 1992. 334–51.
  Rich, Adrienne. "Diving into the Wreck." *The Heath Anthology of American Literature.* Ed. Paul Lauter et al. 2nd ed. Vol. 2. Lexington: Heath, 1994. 2531–34.
  Golden, Catherine. "'Overwriting' the Rest Cure: Charlotte Perkins Gilman's Literary Escape from S. Weir Mitchell's Fictionalization of Women." *Critical Essays on Charlotte Perkins Gilman.* Ed. Joanne B. Karpinski. New York: G. K. Hall & Co., 1992. 144–58.

- **Two or more texts by the same author.** Order the texts alphabetically according to the first word (other than "A" or "The") of the title. For second and successive works, substitute three hyphens and a period for the author's name.
  Gilman, Charlotte Perkins. *The Living of Charlotte Perkins Gilman.* New York: Arno Press, 1935.
  ---. "The Yellow Wallpaper." *Literature: An Introduction to Critical Reading.* Ed. William Vesterman. New York: Harcourt, 1993: 87–100.

- **Article in a professional journal that numbers pages continuously throughout the year.**
  Shumaker, Conrad. "Too Terribly Good to Be Printed: Charlotte Gilman's 'The Yellow Wallpaper.'" *American Literature* 57 (1985): 588–99.

- **Article in a professional journal that begins each issue with page one.**
  Behrens, L. "Writing, Reading, and the Rest of the Faculty: A Survey." *English Journal* 67.6 (1978): 54–66.

In the example, "6" indicates that this is the sixth issue of the year (1978).

- **Article in an encyclopedia.**
  "Mandarin." *The Encyclopedia Americana.* 1993 ed.

- **An audio recording.**
  Copland, Aaron. *Symphony No. 3, Quiet City.* Deutsche Grammophon, 1986.

- **A video recording (example borrowed from the *MLA Handbook,* 4th ed.).**
  A Room with a View. Dir. James Ivory. Prod. Ismail Merchant. Cinecom Intl. Films, 1985.

- **A published interview.**
  Davis, Miles. Interview. *Talking Jazz: An Oral History.* By Ben Sidran. Expanded edition. New York: Da Capo, 1995. 7–15.

- **An interview you conducted yourself.**
  Young, William. Personal interview. 4 April 1995.
  Stephenson, Mary. Telephone interview. 6 Dec. 1993.

- **Material accessed on CD-ROM and with a specified printed source (example borrowed from *MLA Handbook,* 4th ed.).**
  Galloway, Stephen. "TV Takes the Fall in Violence Poll." *Hollywood Reporter* 23 July 1993: 16. *Predicasts F and S Plus Text: United States.* CD-ROM. SilverPlatter. Oct. 1993.

- **Material accessed on CD-ROM without a specified printed source (example borrowed from *MLA Handbook,* 4th ed.).**
  "Time Warner, Inc.: Sales Summary, 1988–1992." *Disclosure/Worldscope.* CD-ROM. W/D Partners. Oct. 1993.

- **Material accessed through a computer service (example borrowed from *MLA Handbook,* 4th ed.).**
  Galloway, Stephen. "TV Takes the Fall in Violence Poll." *Hollywood Reporter* 23 July 1993: 16. *PTS F and S Indexes.* Online. Dialog. 14 Jan. 1994.

Part

III

Creating a
Writing Portfolio

A "writing portfolio," as used in this book, is a selection of your best work that you assemble, over a period of time, for presentation to others and for your own use. A portfolio is the result of a sustained process of recursive reading and writing in which you set aside your failed or mediocre writings and concentrate on perfecting your best. Part III shows you how to create a portfolio. Equally important, it shows how you can continue reading and writing conversationally once this course is over. Thus, the ultimate aim of Part III is to liberate you from this textbook, to make you a strong and independent reader of literature—and an active writer—for life.

The Portfolio Pyramid

Do not fear mistakes. There are none.

—MILES DAVIS, JAZZ MUSICIAN

The word "portfolio" means different things in different contexts. As used in this book, a portfolio is a selection of your best work that you assemble, over a period of time, to present to others and to please yourself. In terms of the writing or literature course you are currently taking, your portfolio might be a selection of writings that you submit to your instructor at the end of the quarter or semester for a final grade; in a nonclassroom context, your portfolio might consist of the best work that you assemble, share, and perhaps even publish over a span of years or a lifetime.

A portfolio is the result of a sustained process of recursive reading and writing. No writer writes well consistently; for every piece of writing that succeeds, there may be five or ten or a dozen that fail. Fortunately, professional writers are not evaluated on every scribble they make in the privacy of their workrooms; they are able, instead, to discard the failed texts and present only the worthy ones to their readers. Portfolio evaluation takes into account this unevenness in quality that is common to all writers. Rather than being graded on your failures, a portfolio allows you to be judged on that portion of your cumulative output which is the *best*. You write profusely and get graded on the selected few pieces of work that you revise and polish for inclusion in your portfolio. This process is especially appropriate in a course involving literature because it parallels the composing methods used by the authors in our anthology, who wrote in large quantities and published selectively.

A case in point is American poet Walt Whitman (1819–1892).

Walt Whitman and the Portfolio Pyramid

Whitman is a person of habit. He carries paper everywhere. If he is out walking, in his room, alone or in public and he gets an idea, or if he encounters something striking in a book or newspaper, he jots it down on a slip of paper. Then he stuffs the slip in his pocket. In the course of a day, he may collect two or three notes or one or two dozen. Quotations, observations, stray lines, and thoughts.

At home he sorts related notes into envelopes. A different envelope for each embryonic poem:

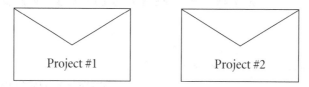

Over the days he collects and sorts, collects and sorts.

When he feels he has accumulated "enough" inside an envelope to make a poem, he empties the contents (a somewhat random gathering of lines, thoughts, images, and phrases) onto his desk. Then the fun begins. Like a child assembling a jigsaw puzzle, he moves the pieces (paper slips) around—now quickly, now slowly, sensing his way to order, pattern, sequence. This slip seems to belong first, this one second, that one . . . hm . . . toward the end. Sometimes the pattern emerges quickly; he gets the slips into an order and transcribes them to make a rough draft. Other times the pattern emerges partially . . . fine. He doesn't force it, just leaves it for another day. Still other times the slips resist any pattern at all, or they produce a pattern that strikes him as flat and uninteresting. That pile of paper scraps he gathers up and tosses.

Whitman sustains this process of collecting, sorting, dumping, arranging, drafting, and revising—or throwing away—over weeks, months, and years. The result is a steady accumulation of works in progress: notes, drafts, revised drafts, finished poems. Nothing that shouldn't be lost is lost.

As one work is being finished, another is beginning (in the note-taking phase) and others are at various stages of drafting and revision. Since he works simultaneously on several poems, each at a different stage of development, there is always some task available to fit his current mood. If he is feeling exuberantly creative he can draft. When he feels like a technician, he can fiddle with word choice, format, or syntax. If he is listless, or too preoccupied to write at all, he can work on spelling or punctuation, or grab a reference book to track down some scrap of information he needs in one of his evolving works. Moreover, if he is unable to make progress on one poem, he has plenty of others to take up instead.

Collectively, the poems evolve into a book, *Leaves of Grass,* one of the most important volumes of poetry in American literature. *Leaves* is Whitman's "portfolio." In its final edition, published in the poet's old age, *Leaves* contains over 350 poems. A life's work.

Whitman lived in the nineteenth century, but the process driving his work is as valid today as it was a hundred years ago. It involves:

- **Collecting** large numbers of notes and writings
- **Organizing** them for easy retrieval
- **Rereading** the notes and writings thus collected and organized
- **Selecting** usable material worth revising
- **Revising** the usable material into finished work

You can usefully visualize these activities as a pyramid:

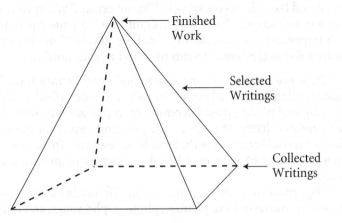

At the bottom and broadest part of the pyramid are collected writings, the huge and uncensored totality of all your work. As you proceed upward and the pyramid narrows, you come to that relatively smaller portion of your total output that you select for revising. At the apex of the pyramid is finished work, the volume of which is a very small percentage of the total.

Like Whitman, all productive writers find ways of organizing the paper flow and the development of their ideas, from first notes to finished texts. You can call this process of collecting, organizing, rereading, selecting, and revising the "portfolio-building process." Of course, this isn't "one" process that all writers use in exactly the same way, but these five activities, in some form, are basic to the work of all successful writers. This chapter introduces you to each of these activities so that you—like Whitman—can create your own portfolio. You will find a short "Checklist of Activities for Collecting, Organizing, Rereading, Selecting, and Revising" at the end of this chapter (p. 112). Dog-ear that page, or, if you like, rip it out and secure it to the inside cover of your notebook. Reread and use it regularly during the term and throughout your writing life.

Collecting

In every work of genius we recognize our own rejected thoughts.

—RALPH WALDO EMERSON

Kim, a would-be writer, can easily relate to this quotation. Again and again she has recognized in "work[s] of genius" her "own rejected thoughts." "I've thought of that!" "I could have written that!" "I could have done it better!" All are thoughts that occur to her frequently as she reads her favorite authors. Each statement has an element of truth; Kim's problem is that she failed to honor her thoughts by writing them down when they occurred to her. Instead, she let her internal censor wave them aside as "stupid" or "unimportant," and what might have matured into good writing died stillborn.

The first and last rule of collecting is "Do not censor." When you are collecting, *no* idea is too "stupid," "trite," or "insignificant" to write down. If it occurs to you, it's important—not necessarily "final" or "finished" but important.

Here are a few suggestions of items to collect in your notebook:

- *Writings you produce by "springboarding" from literary texts.* These include writings generated out of the techniques described in Chapter 3 of *Reading and Writing from Literature.* Examples are imaginary interviews with authors, letters to authors, prequels and sequels to stories or other literary texts, literary texts that you have rewritten from other points of view, and texts of your own based on themes or incidents in literary texts.
- *Writings you do from other sources in your life and in the world,* such as experiences, conversations, pictures, photographs, songs, and films.

In addition, there are other shorter collectibles that you could describe as "quick notes." Some examples from one student notebook—Liz's—will illustrate. Liz is a sophomore music major interested in a variety of musical forms, especially classical and jazz.

- *Random thoughts.* Sitting alone in a café and pondering her life, Liz thinks,

I don't need a future; I only need to believe in a future.

She isn't exactly sure what that means but writes it down anyway. Another time, while walking to the gym and thinking about jazz music and soul, she writes,

Soul. Life's walls come crashing down and you sing/shout/stomp.

- *Striking sentences or phrases.* Liz is doing nothing in particular when the following pops into her head:

Whatever shook me out of that tree . . .

What strikes her about this is not the particular content of the words but the *sound* of them, how they're strung together. They resonate, hinting at some bigger composition or sequence of thoughts that might eventually grow out of them. For this reason Liz doesn't meddle with the words at all but records the phrase exactly as it occurred to her.

- *Ideas for writing.* Examples from Liz's notebook:

Write a dialogue between a husband and his wife who has decided to return to school.

Write an essay on my own life history with music.

Rewrite Sonny's life story from Sonny's point of view [Sonny, a jazz musician, is the central character in James Baldwin's short story "Sonny's Blues" (see p. 263)].

Make up an interview with Billie Holiday—Have Billie tell her life story.

- *Memorable quotations encountered in reading or conversation.* People used to keep "commonplace books" for jotting down quotations and thoughts that they could later reread for pleasure or "edification." It's a custom worth reviving. Again, here is a sample quotation from Liz's notebook:

And even then, on the rare occasions when something opens up within, and the music enters, what we mainly hear, or hear corroborated, are personal, private, vanishing evocations. But the man who creates the music is hearing something else, is dealing with the roar rising from the void and imposing order on it as it hits the air. What is evoked in him, then, is of another order, more terrible because it has no words, and triumphant, too, for that same reason. And his triumph, when he triumphs, is ours. (Baldwin, "Sonny's Blues")

To collect items of the "quick-note" variety, you need to be able to get ideas on paper when they occur to you. A standard-sized 8 × 10 or 9 × 11 notebook is too bulky to carry everywhere. So what do you do when you have a great idea but no place to put it? If you say, "I'll write it down when I get home," you probably never will, or you will have forgotten what your idea *was* by the time you reach pen and paper or your computer.

To eliminate this problem, do as Liz does and carry a pocket-sized spiral notepad with you at all times. That way you can be sure that no interesting thought you have will go unrecorded. Whenever you get an idea for writing—from a literary text, a film or TV show, a conversation, a song—jot it down in your notepad.

Good writers are habitual quick-note takers. They write ideas on cards, napkins, scraps of paper, letters, backs of envelopes, restaurant menus, the palms of their hands—even on walls. William Faulkner is said to have outlined one of his novels on the walls of a hotel room, not a process I recommend but an extreme example of the lengths to which writers may go when they need to write *now*.

On May 14, 1925, British novelist Virginia Woolf scribbled the following in her diary:

> This is going to be fairly short; to have father's character done complete in it; and mother's; and St. Ives; and childhood; and all the usual things I try to put in—life, death, etc. But the center is father's character, sitting in a boat, reciting "We perished each alone."

These hastily written words—a mere two sentences—anticipate the structure of Woolf's great semiautobiographical novel *To the Lighthouse*, which she published two years later, in 1927. This quick sketch defined the original vision that helped Woolf plan and carry the work to completion.

Contemporary British poet Stephen Spender had a similar habit of collecting ideas for writing:

> My method . . . is to write down as many ideas as possible, in however rough a form in notebooks. I have at least twenty of these, on a shelf beside my desk, going back over fifteen years. I then make use of these sketches and discard others.

Notice particularly how Spender uses these notes. He accumulates vast numbers—everything that occurs to him, without worrying about "quality"—and then sifts through them to determine which he will use, i.e., develop, revise, and possibly publish, and which he will discard. What he uses is only a fraction of the total accumulation, but without making lots of notes—from brilliant to ordinary to downright dull—he might never have written down the "good" ideas that eventually became poems.

Organizing What You Collect

As you accumulate diverse writings in your notebook, it's useful to develop a plan for organizing them so that you can easily retrieve and reread them. *How* to organize is largely a matter of individual taste, but here are two basic suggestions:

1. Begin each entry in your notebook by recording the date, time, and place where you are writing, e.g., "8/16/95, 8:20 A.M., kitchen." This notation is useful in two ways. First, date, time, and place provide a record that enables you to trace your intellectual and imaginative growth over weeks, months, and years;

it's fun, in 1997, to look back at what you were reading, thinking, and producing in 1995. Second, the date/time/place notation shows you where and when you work best. If you notice that you produce 90 percent of your best writing at the "kitchen table" or in the "library," that tells you something about yourself as a writer. It tells you *where* you are most productive, just as recording the time tells you *when* you are most productive. After keeping a notebook for a while, you may realize that you write best between 7 and 9 A.M. in your bedroom or between 10 and 11 P.M. in your living room, for example.

2. Over time you may discover that you address certain themes or topics repeatedly. Consider organizing your notebook around these topics or themes. Emerson created some two hundred "topical" notebooks (with titles like "Fate," "Country Life," and "Beauty and Art") and distributed his raw notes and writings among these notebooks. You may want to adapt Emerson's strategy for your own use. For instance, insert dividers, with appropriately labeled tabs, e.g., "stories," "ideas for writing," "family issues," "love," "thoughts," "quotations," within your notebook:

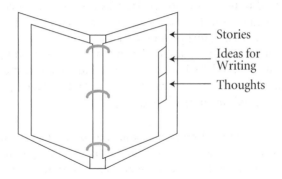

Or create individual paper file folders for each topic:

Or, if you prefer to organize electronically, create word-processing files for each category. Of course, the topics or categories you create *now* are not fixed; you can change them or create new categories at any time, as your own life and interests change.

Organizing like this eliminates the pressure to act immediately on a writing or note once you have collected it. The item goes into the appropriate section of your notebook, or into the appropriate electronic or paper file, and it *stays* there. Even if you don't do anything with the item for months or years, it's in a place where you can retrieve it instantly when you want it.

Rereading

> I can no more manage these thoughts that come into my head than thunderbolts. But once get them written down, I come & look at them every day, & get wonted to their faces, & by & by, am so far used to them, that I see their family likeness, & can pair them & range them better, & if I once see where they belong, & join them in that order they will stay so.
>
> —RALPH WALDO EMERSON

Though the language of this quote is somewhat archaic, the message is simple: *it is valuable to write things down and then, later on, to "look at them" again.* By rereading the materials in his notebooks "every day," Emerson got "used to" those materials and began to notice the "family likeness," or patterns, among his many assorted notes and writings. He was then able to revise and develop his notebook writings into the essays and poems that made him one of nineteenth-century America's most prolific writers.

Elsewhere, in a brilliant metaphor, Emerson refers to his journals and notebooks as his "Savings Bank," where he deposited ideas and earned "interest" on them by saving and rereading them. A century later essayist Joan Didion invokes the same metaphor for rereading:

> See enough and write it down. Then some morning when the world seems drained of wonder, some day when I am only going through the motions of what I am supposed to do—on that bankrupt morning, I will simply open my notebook and there it will all be, a forgotten account with accumulated interest, paid passage back to the world out there.

No writer can wake up with fresh inspiration for writing every day of his or her life. Rereading gives you something to do when your mind is too dull for producing new writing. It epitomizes a major theme of this book: *One of the best stimuli for new writing is old writing, both other people's and your own.*

Here are some practical steps for rereading:

1. Reread your notebook regularly, with pen or pencil in hand.
2. Underline or bracket words, phrases, sentences, paragraphs, or longer entries that interest you—for whatever reason.
3. In the margins annotate or "talk back" to those items that strike you. Write about:
   a. Additional thoughts the item suggests to you
   b. Why the item interests you
   c. How you might like, at some point, to expand the item

For example, recall the following entry from Liz's notebook:

I don't need a future, I just need to believe in a future.

Liz writes this note on October 23, 1994. As she rereads it in mid-November, it stimulates a further thought, which she jots in the margin (her shorthand is slightly edited here for clarity):

I don't need a future, I just need to believe in a future. ⟵———— Use in a story of "mad musician": likes being disconnected from reality, needs her own reality

On another occasion Liz rereads an entry she wrote on October 29 and reacts to it as follows:

Definition of a success: someone whose work is their fun. ⟵———— Write a letter about this to Meg?

The beauty of this process of "talking back" to your own writing is that it can be endlessly extended. What you write in the margin beside one of your entries can, in turn, be a prompt to still further expansion. Thus, over time, a short entry with a marginal comment can evolve into something much larger, such as a full-fledged essay, story, or poem.

Selecting

> The essential thing in our period of weak morale is to create enthusiasm.
> —PABLO PICASSO

While collecting and rereading are both continuous and sustained activities, selecting is the deed of a moment. You review the mass of materials in your notebook and use your intuitions to select—quickly—the items you like enough to revise or expand.

Being able to make this selection intelligently, however, is an acquired skill; specifically, it requires that you know what you want to create in your writing. Writers write from their obsessions. Unless you define your interests carefully and frequently, you can't know what to collect or revise. Passion is the fuel that drives collecting, rereading, and revising. As Virginia Woolf put it, "The art of writing has for backbone some fierce attachment to an idea." Woolf's sentiment is echoed by numerous other writers:

For a work to be successful, one has to feel a bond with its main basic idea. Thus, in *Anna Karenina* I love the idea of the family; in *War and Peace* I love the idea of the people in the war of 1812. (Leo Tolstoy, novelist)

My Journal should be the record of my love. I would write in it only of the things I love, my affection for any aspect of the world, what I love to think of. (Henry David Thoreau, essayist)

Every artist preserves deep within him a single source from which, throughout his lifetime, he draws what he is and what he says and when the source dries up the work withers and crumbles. (Albert Camus, novelist)

[I]t is [the] quality of being in love with your subject that is indispensable for writing good history—or good anything, for that matter. (Barbara Tuchman, historian)

Working writers strengthen their capacity for selecting by writing, in their notebooks, about their central interests and about themselves *as writers.*

Here are three activities you can do in your notebook to know yourself (as writer) better:

1. *Describe what you want to do in your writing, either generally or in a specific text in progress.* For instance, here are several entries from Walt Whitman's notebook in which he defines for himself the qualities he desires in his poetry. Note that Whitman is writing for himself here and not for a public audience, hence the abbreviated, sometimes disconnected shape of his ideas.

My poems when complete should be a *unity,* in the same sense that the earth is, or that the human body, (senses, soul, head, trunk, feet, blood, viscera, man-root, eyes, hair) or that a perfect musical composition is.

Great constituent elements of my poetry—Two, viz: Materialism—Spirituality—The Intellect is what is to be the medium of these and to beautify and make serviceable there.

To change the book—go over the whole with great care—to make it more intensely the poem of *Individuality*—addressed more *distinctly to the single personality listening to it*—ruling out, perhaps, some parts that stand in the way of this—cull out the ego[tistic] somewhat.

Make *the Works*—Do not go into criticisms or arguments at all. Make full-blooded, rich, natural *works.* Insert natural things, indestructibles, idioms, characteristics, rivers, states, persons, etc. Be full of *strong, sensual germs.*

Put in my poems: *American things, idioms, materials, persons, groups, minerals, vegetables, animals, etc.*

Such notes, sustained over a lifetime, helped Whitman center himself in his writing and define his literary goals and purposes. The result of this process is his masterpiece, *Leaves of Grass.*

2. *List readings you want to do in order to enhance your writing.* This "list" will probably include literary texts such as those found in Part V of this book, but it certainly need not be limited to such works. Include whatever items stimulate your imagination and productivity.

Some time ago I was frustrated with a lackadaisical quality in my own writing style; accordingly, I sketched out names of some authors and readings I thought could liven me up:

6/7/95. 2 P.M. Airport. My own program of reading. Read:

- Writings by nontraditional people—individuals and blunt-talkers (e.g., Picasso, Georgia O'Keeffe, Henry Miller, Tennessee Williams, Alice Walker). If I can get *their* voice into my writing, maybe I can also get some of their character.
- Works by creative artistic people—sculptors, painters, etc.
- Works by traditionally marginalized peoples who are just now—or have only recently—found a "voice," people who are not intimidated by a long tradition of "model" writers.

Later that summer I read some of these authors and was able to infuse a bit of their style and energy into my own writing.

3. *Record your feelings—good, bad, and indifferent—about the writing you are doing and about your progress (or lack of progress).* Recording good feelings can bolster your confidence. Surprisingly, recording bad feelings and frustrations can also serve a positive purpose. Suppose you describe a lousy writing day on May 3 that is followed by a brilliant day on May 6. In the future, whenever your writing is going badly, you can reread your descriptions of May 3 and 6 and be reassured that "dry" spells are invariably followed by more productive periods—even breakthroughs.

Revising

Revision means, literally, to "look at again." In a sense this whole book, with its theme of intertextuality, of rereading and rewriting texts, is about revising. In fact, reading and writing are always revisionary acts because they are acts of thinking, which is itself always recursive.

Here, however, we consider "revision" in its more limited and conventional sense, as the process of taking a piece of your writing and reworking it to make it better. Two key questions are: *When* should you revise? *What* should you revise, and what should you leave as is?

Brenda Ueland, a writer and teacher of writing, once observed:

[T]here are wonderfully gifted people who write a little piece and then write it over and over again to make it perfect,—absolutely, flawlessly perfect, a gem. But these people only emit about a pearl a year, or in five years. And that is because of the grind, the polishing, i.e., the fear that the little literary pearl will not be perfect and unassailable. But this is all a loss of time and a pity. For in them there is a fountain of exuberant life and poetry and literature and imagination, but it cannot get out because they are so anxiously busy polishing the gem.

Ueland suggests that many of us choke off our confidence and productivity at the roots by working too hard on one piece of writing and failing to write in quantity. *We work on one piece of writing only, and revise that to death, rather than writing in large quantities and revising selectively.*

Consider four kinds of writing:

1. Writing you revise carefully
2. Writing you revise quickly
3. Writing you leave unrevised
4. Writing you throw away

All four of these kinds of writing are important, and it is important to do each. Any successful and prolific writer will tell you that. While it is true that good writers revise some work painstakingly (Ernest Hemingway said he rewrote the opening of his novel *A Farewell to Arms* twenty times!), they also do a good deal of writing that they revise quickly, or leave unrevised, or simply throw away.

Popular myth portrays the writer as someone who gets "inspired" and then, in one swift motion, creates a masterpiece. In fact, the writer's work—or workshop—is far messier and imperfect than that. Writers have layers of material within their workshops:

- Short notes—hundreds, thousands, everything from quick notes recording images or phrases, to quotations from books or conversations, to visual sketches (of characters, themes, natural objects, for instance), to paraphrases of major ideas for future works (stories, poems, memoirs, essays, plays). Some of these notes are "strays" or "orphans," that is, the writer has no idea what she may do with them—they just interest her in some way. Others take a ready slot in the writer's work in progress. Some are expanded or joined to other larger works. Some of these never get used; many or most get reread some time.
- Outlines
- Paragraphs or other chunks of text that are written and awaiting a slot within some larger piece of work
- Rough drafts
- Revised and edited works that the writer—or publisher—deems unpublishable
- Texts in diverse stages of revision

- Works that are virtually "done" but missing some small detail that will make them complete.

Eugene O'Neill kept a notebook in which he recorded ideas for plays, plot scenarios, character ideas, arrangements for sets and scenes, and other thoughts that came to mind. Reading his notebooks affords a useful glimpse into the creative process and the principles of mass generation of ideas and selective revision that guide it. For every one play he conceives, drafts, revises, polishes, and brings to production, there seem to be dozens of others that die at conception, or at the outline stage, or in some medial phase of revision. From 1925 to 1934 he worked on a play about an emperor of ancient China that he ultimately abandoned. That was okay because he had lots of other plays in the works that he loved enough and felt good enough about to finish.

Were the abandoned plays, sketches, and ideas a waste of O'Neill's time? No. They were simply by-products of the process, efforts that probably had to be made in order for O'Neill to create the plays for which he is famous.

An especially striking example of a writer producing in quantity and revising selectively is Russian novelist Leo Tolstoy, who drafted several hundred pages of a novel about Czar Peter the Great and then threw them away because he was "no longer interested" in Peter the Great!

When you do only extensively revised writing, a problem develops. Call it "thinness." You get better, perhaps, at editing, at performing microsurgery on texts, and at repairing faulty punctuation and grammar, but your ability to generate large quantities of text atrophies from lack of practice. Your writing output is paper-thin—almost nonexistent. You are like a stream that has dried to a trickle. By contrast, bold and prolific writers are like great gushing rivers that overflow their banks so powerfully that nothing can slow or stop them.

A moment ago I mentioned Tolstoy, who tossed his novel in progress into the wastebasket after drafting hundreds of pages. During his long life, Tolstoy also wrote *War and Peace,* one of the longest, best novels of all time, and enough volumes of short and long fiction, correspondence, moral and religious philosophy, and educational essays to fill several yards of library shelf space. Tolstoy wrote in abundance. Is all his work of equal excellence? No. It ranges from the brilliant to the average to the downright bad.

Consider Walt Whitman, whose literary output was nearly as vast as Tolstoy's. His secret? He wrote constantly and abundantly—sometimes magnificently, sometimes ordinarily, sometimes sloppily and poorly. Out of this immense pool of writings—poems, notes, plans, sketches, outlines, drafts, fragments—he selected a relatively small portion (those works he cared about most) for careful revision into finished work. The great majority of his writings he left unfinished, unrevised, or partially unrevised.

Tolstoy and Whitman wrote in quantity and revised selectively.

Now consider the contrasting example of Steve, an English professor. He probably spends as much time writing as Tolstoy or Whitman. He is always at his desk; he avoids parties, movies, plays, concerts, and social gatherings of every kind in order to concentrate on his work. He reads constantly and keeps ever-expanding files of notes on Shakespeare, his subject. For two years he de-voted all his writing energies to working and reworking an essay on "incest in *Hamlet*." Finally, he got up enough nerve to submit the essay to a journal for publication. The essay was rejected. When asked if he was planning to resubmit the piece to another journal (after all, he had dedicated two years of his life to that essay), Steve replied, "No, it's boring. Who'd be interested?"

Unfortunately, the world is full of people like Steve, people who have read hundreds of books, plays, novels, articles, journals, treatises, histories, and monographs but whose consumption of texts is way out of proportion to their production of texts. Out of all that reading and painstaking revision and re-revision of their writings, what have they themselves made? In Steve's case, only one essay, which seemed doomed from the start and died, in effect, still-born.

Cultivate a sense of *selectivity* in your writing. Practice doing all four kinds of writing I mentioned above—carefully revised, quickly revised, unrevised, and throw away—and select only the works you care about most for careful re-vision. Your reading notebook is a place for you to produce writing in abun-dance. By writing regularly in your notebook, you accumulate ample raw material that you can either revise and publish or simply use as a way of pursu-ing the ongoing task of making meaning.

A Personal Story

I want to describe a writer with a bad habit. This will be easy because this writer is myself several years ago.

This writer had no system. He had no method for collecting, organizing, and rereading his writing. Every day blared out at him as if it were the only day—ever. The rest of time never was or would be. No yesterday and no tomorrow.

Each day's writing, therefore, was do or die. Succeed or die. Only one chance. The day had to yield up a masterpiece or that day was not worth living.

This writer had to put up with a lot of deadness because the masterpiece never came. He survived a lot of depression—barely.

What made me think of him was a response I once wrote in my reading notebook. I had just read *Beloved*, a novel by Toni Morrison that is set during and soon after the American Civil War. It tells the story of Sethe, a slave woman who escapes, at great cost, from Kentucky and goes to Ohio, and of her family, her loves, and her suffering. I believe, with many other people, that Morrison's novel is one of the best of recent American novels. I read the last page in a state of awe. I felt I had completed a book that just might change my life.

I started to write a response but gave up after a sentence or two. Too much emotion was inside me. The next morning, excited and eager, I tried again. I searched for a *form* of writing that could channel my rich experience of this text. Some sort of dialogue? A character history of Sethe? A sequel? A whole new story from my own life that would parallel, in however remote a way, a theme in the novel? Nothing brilliant or exciting came to mind. After a few minutes I simply started writing:

> Response to *Beloved,* by Toni Morrison. 7/15/94. 7:25 A.M. Bed.
>   Characters:
>   Sethe—heroine
>   Paul D—slave who worked with Sethe at Sweet Home (plantation in Kentucky)
>   Denver—Sethe's daughter
>   Beloved—the daughter Sethe attacked with a handsaw to protect her from being recaptured by the white posse led by "Schoolteacher" (the ex-owner of Sethe, Paul D)
>   Baby Suggs—Sethe's mother-in-law. "Baby Suggs, holy," because she led prayer and worship meetings out of the overflow of her big heart. At the end, Baby Suggs just lay in her bed at 124 (the name of her and Sethe's house in Ohio) and refused to move, and became fascinated with color (why? because she never got to enjoy color all through her life, because she was always working her body for someone else. It was therefore only as an old woman almost dead that she began to notice color. . . . Later in the novel the same thing is to happen to Sethe.)
>   These people spend all their lives fighting. Schoolteacher and the white people treat them worse than dogs.

A flat, dull response to a great book.

A few years ago this ho-hum writing would have ruined my morning. "I'm lousy! I can't write!" Now I have a place where this kind of writing is acceptable—even expected. That place is my reading notebook, which is nothing if not democratic. There is room in it for the good and the bad, the beautiful and the ugly, the interesting and the dull, the inspired and lengthy as well as the uninspired and short.

Then—a few years ago—I saw a response like this one to Morrison from only one perspective, the perspective of here and now, the moment of composition. Seen in this limited way, it was simply a disappointing written product. It loomed up depressingly as a sort of terminus, as the final destination of my entire writing career.

Now I see it from a different perspective, that of my ongoing writing life in progress. Now it is simply part of my *daily doing.* It is one attempt among many, one page in hundreds. It does not devastate me; it does not slow my momentum or dull my enthusiasm for writing because I know I will write again tomorrow and again the day after that.

Meanwhile, I am generating so much other writing that this small piece dwindles to insignificance. In just the last three years I have accumulated several hundred pages of handwritten and computer-generated hard copy in my notebook. I cannot reread this notebook without feeling *centered* in my work and thinking. One page seems to echo and elaborate on another. Even pieces in very different forms or on drastically different themes seem to interconnect. This is natural because all of these writings come out of one person—me.

As I reread and/or revise selected materials in my notebook, I continue to add new materials. Between generating new writings, rereading old ones, and revising the selected pieces I like the best and want to share or publish, I never lack things to do. And the presence of all these varied composing tasks gives me a certain indomitable attitude about writing.

One lousy response to Toni Morrison? Who cares?

A Checklist of Activities for Collecting, Organizing, Rereading, Selecting, and Revising

Materials to Collect
- Writings you produce by "springboarding" from literary texts
- Writings you do from other sources in your life and in the world
- Random thoughts
- Striking sentences or phrases
- Ideas for writing
- Memorable quotations encountered in reading or conversation

Organizing
- Record the date, time, and place for each item you collect.
- Devise a plan for cataloguing your notes and writings.

Rereading
- Reread your notebook regularly.
- Underline or bracket words, phrases, sentences, paragraphs, or longer entries that interest you—for whatever reason.
- In the margins annotate or "talk back" to those items that strike you. Write about:
  a. Additional thoughts the item suggests to you
  b. Why the item interests you
  c. How you might like, at some point, to expand the item

Selecting
- Use your notebook to meditate on what you want to do in your writing, either generally or in a specific text in progress.
- List readings you want to do in order to enhance your writing.
- Record your feelings—good, bad, and indifferent—about the writing you are doing and about your progress (or lack of progress).

Revising
- Write in quantity and revise selectively.
- See the next chapter for specific revising strategies.

Making the Works: Eleven Strategies for Revising

As you can imagine, I have hundreds of new ideas in my head, but the main thing is making, not thinking.

         —JOHANN WOLFGANG VON GOETHE

Make *the Works*. . . .

         —WALT WHITMAN

Chapter 9 contextualized revising as something you don't do with all your work but only with those selected texts you like best. This chapter continues the discussion by describing some specific strategies for revising your work. Since revision of essays about literature has already been addressed in Chapter 7, this chapter focuses on revising your writings of a more "creative" nature, such as stories, poems, letters, dialogues, prequels and sequels, or personal memoirs and narratives. Examples of these and related kinds of writing are collected, for your reference, in Appendix A.

What is the aim of this chapter? What is "good" writing, and how do you know when you've produced it? There is no simple answer to this question because "good" writing means different things to different groups and in different contexts. A "good" piece of writing, e.g., a clear memorandum, an informative report, in a business setting exhibits different qualities from "good" writing in a workshop for science fiction writers; good writing for a popular newspaper differs from good writing for an audience of experts in an academic discipline.

Good writing is defined by the community of those among whom and for whom you write. In this course, the community is yourself and your classmates, instructor, and others (such as friends or family members) to whom you show your work. Your best way to gauge the quality of your favorite writings is by re-working and sharing them within that community. This chapter shows you some ways of doing that.

Strategies in this chapter are sequenced to move from techniques for more global revision, e.g., starting over from scratch, to more modest revisions. In-cluded are strategies you can do by yourself and ones that involve interaction with a peer or a small group. Treat these ideas as items on a menu; you don't need to use them all. Simply consult the chapter whenever you are revising—at any time during the quarter or semester—and use the particular ideas that fit your needs at that moment.

Finally, your notebook is a repository for all kinds of writings, from one- or two-sentence notes to longer responses to literary texts. In this chapter the word "draft," which usually implies a longer piece of writing, can be used inter-changeably with "note," "sketch," or "idea."

1. Start Over: Consult Chapter 3

Perhaps you have selected a notebook text for revision because you like the ideas or issues it addresses, but, as a piece of writing, it is awkward or uninter-esting. Review the "Ten Ideas for Writing in a Reading Notebook" in Chapter 3 to find stimulating alternative ways of reworking your draft. For instance, con-sider recasting your unsatisfying "letter to the author" as a dialogue or rewrit-ing your "character biography" of the husband in "The Yellow Wallpaper" as a prequel to that story.

2. Start Over: Rewrite Using a Topic/Form Grid

A Topic/Form Grid enables you to observe all your options for rewriting in a concise visual format.

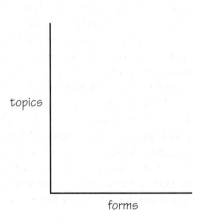

1. Draw a grid and label the vertical axis "topics" and the horizontal "forms," as at right.

2. Along the "topic" axis list topics for writing that interest you. Along the "form" axis list forms of discourse you could use to write about these topics. Think espe-cially of forms you use most regularly and spontaneously in everyday life. Some typi-

cal favorites are "talking to myself," "personal letter," and "conversation."

3. Use the diverse topic/form matches available to you to generate writings. For instance, a simple grid like that at right gives you four possible topic/ form combinations. You can create a song lyric about youth, a song lyric about fishing, a letter about youth, or a letter about fishing. Increase the number of items along the axes and you increase, exponentially, the combinations available: three topics and three forms yield nine possible combinations; four topics and four forms give you sixteen, and so on.

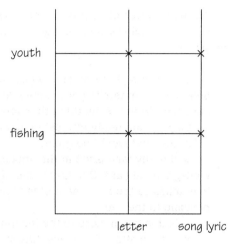

Virginia is an avid outdoorswoman with a passion for landscaping. Rereading her notebook she discovers the following note:

> Of all things I love landscaping most. I acquired this interest as a small girl from my grandfather, and since then hardly a day passes in the growing season when I don't have my hands in the soil.

She wants to do something with this . . . but what? How can she expand it and say all she would like about her love for landscaping? She consults a Topic/Form Grid she had made a few weeks earlier:

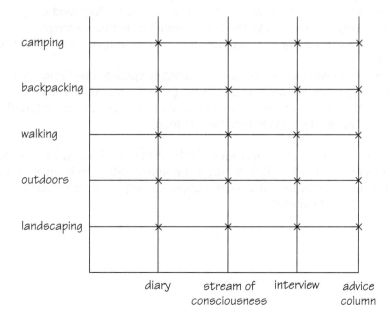

An avid viewer of television interviews, she decides an imaginary interview—with herself—would be a good way of eliciting more information about her passion:

INTERVIEWER (I): Virginia, I am excited to conduct this interview. It will help me and others to get to know you and your interests. Here is my first question. What is something that you enjoy and feel confident doing?

ME (M): I am really interested in landscaping. May I tell you about it?

I: Yes, that would be great.

M: I really take pride in the appearance of my yard. I love to have a well-groomed yard. One that is full of brilliant colors, and a little contrast to emphasize the movement of my lawn. I feel that a yard should be pleasing to the eye.

I: Is this talent close to the imagination of an artist?

M: As a matter of fact, yes. Envision for a minute a blob of clay. Now as a sculptor would begin his piece of work, he plays around with this clay. He or she would place the clay in his or her palm and squeeze it through their fingers. They are creating a picture in their minds of the final piece they are wanting to produce.

I: Hum, interesting.

M: That is basically how I perform my art. As I am out in my yard, doing cultivating, fertilizing, etc. ideas begin to flow. The colors, types of flowers, trees, and rocks that would best express my love for nature begin to materialize.

I: Tell me, Virginia, how did you get interested in this?

M: My grandfather and a good friend of mine were landscapers. They took great pride in their and others' yards. Even as a little child, as I walked to school I observed yards. I really would be disgusted if a yard was unruly. You know, like the look of your hair in the morning?

I: Are you willing to help others manicure their lawns as well as your own?

M: Yes! I have helped three other families upgrade their yards. It's very rewarding, not only for myself but for the other families also.

I: Well, thanks for your time. Could you come and look at my lawn?

M: Thank you, I would love the challenge.

You can see how remarkably individualized the grid is when you compare Virginia's work with Michelle's. A college sophomore, Michelle is currently preoccupied by issues of love and relationships, interests that are reflected in the "topic" portion of her grid:

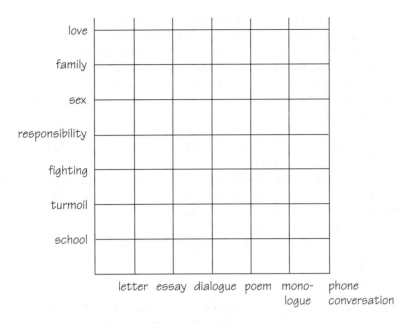

letter essay dialogue poem mono-   phone
                                  logue   conversation

Mulling over her notebook, with its numerous entries about her own experiences of relationships, she discovers how hard it can be to write about them without becoming more personal and confessional than she would like. Her "form" axis gives her an idea: she can use the form of "phone conversation" to render her emotions more objectively. Instead of writing directly about herself, she can invent a conversation between two imaginary lovers experiencing hard times:

Halfway into a long-distance phone conversation:

"John, quit yelling at me! I don't get it. Last week you did the same thing with your friends and I didn't say one word to you!"

"That's not the same thing. When I go to parties with my friends, you know I'm not going to do anything behind your back!"

"So what are you saying, that I can't be trusted? For some reason that doesn't sit right with me!"

"No, Melissa, I'm not trying to say I don't trust you. I just know how you get around other guys when you drink and it makes me worry."

"John, you know how I am around you when I drink and that's because I love you. And it's probably true, I may flirt with guys, but you do the same thing and I know it's harmless. You should know that I would never do anything that might hurt you, no matter how much I've had to drink. I know it's hard living so far away from each other, and if I could change things I would. I hate it every bit as much as you do! But that is no reason not to trust me. I have never been anything but honest with you and I just don't think it's fair when you start coming down on me like this."

"Melissa, I'm sorry. I know you're right. It just kills me to be so far away from you. You know everyone down here teases me about you being away. They all say you're going to find some gorgeous football player and forget all about me. They get me so worried that little things like you going to a party and drinking really set me off. I shouldn't have gotten so upset. I really do trust you. I love you so much and I don't ever want to lose you."

"Quit listening to your friends so much, honey. You know I've never liked football players much. I like the baseball men much better."

"That's not funny, Melissa."

"Okay, I'm sorry. I'm just playing with you. I've told you a million times that you are the one I want to spend the rest of my life with. Nothing is going to change that. I love you. Do you believe me?"

"Yeah, hon. I believe you. I love you too."

"Good! I'll see you as soon as I can, okay? Take care."

"You too. Bye."

"Bye."

One virtue of the grid is its flexibility. Once made, it is never "set in stone"; you can discard old grids and create new ones as your needs and interests change. Moreover, if one topic/form combination fails you, you can shift to a different topic or form on your grid until you find one that works.

Here are a few suggestions for the "form" axis of your grid (certainly not an exhaustive list):

- diary entry or series of diary entries
- personal letter
- unsent letter (e.g., to someone about whom you have strong feelings)
- letter to the editor
- editorial
- monologue
- gossip (a form of dialogue)
- telephone conversation
- E-mail conversation
- song lyrics
- public speech
- drawing or doodle (you don't need to limit yourself to verbal forms; visual sketching can move the imagination in powerful ways)

Use the steps described at the beginning of this section to create your own grid. Then secure the result to the inside cover of your notebook for convenient reference.

3. "Talk" to Your Draft

See Chapter 7.

4. Do a Postdraft Outline

Postdraft outlining was introduced in Chapter 7 as a tool for revising essays about literature. You can use the same process to revise drafts of a more "creative" nature, such as dialogues, short stories, or personal narratives. Since some creative texts use extremely short individual paragraphs, you may want to summarize *clusters* of related paragraphs (see step #2 on page 74) rather than each individual paragraph.

5. Have Other People Outline Your Draft

See Chapter 7.

6. Ask Yourself Other Questions Appropriate to the Draft

What questions and problems to address in revision depends on the form (prose narrative, essay, play, poem) of the particular text you are revising. Whatever the form, begin by concentrating on what is working in the draft and on global revisions. From there—and only then—proceed to comments on a more local level. (For a review of the distinction between "global" and "local" revisions, see page 73.) Make your comments *in writing* so you can refer to them as you revise.

For prose narratives such as short fiction texts (stories, prequels, sequels), personal narratives, and plays, respond to the following questions and topics:

- What are two parts of the piece you especially like? Why? Be specific.
- What is one place in the text where you could use more information or detail?
- Where do the **characters**[1] seem most convincing and alive? Where, if anywhere, are they less so?
- Does the **dialogue** (if any) sound convincing? At what points does it need revising?
- In what places, if any, might the events of the **plot** be arranged more effectively? Is there adequate conflict to generate and sustain reader interest?
- Where (if at all) does the piece lag for you? Why? Be specific.

If you want, provide a partner or members of your small group with copies of your draft, and have them respond to these questions and topics, too.

For poems address questions and topics such as these (again, you can also get feedback on these questions and topics from a partner or peer group):

---

1. Words in **boldface** are discussed in Part IV, "An Introduction to the Four Major Genres," and defined in Appendix C, "Glossary of Literary Terms."

- What are two parts of the poem you especially like? Why? Be specific.
- What is one place in the poem where you could use more information or detail?
- Describe the poem's impact on you. How does it make you feel? What does it make you think about?
- Does the poem include examples of **figurative language,** such as **metaphors** or **similes**? Where? How do they affect you? How can they be improved?
- React to the poem's physical shape or appearance—the length of the **stanzas** and lines, the amount of white space on the page, for example. How successfully does this shape work to reinforce the poem's overall effect?
- Identify any images that strike you. Describe in the margins how they affect you.
- If the poem is rhymed, circle **rhyme** words you like; then, jot a marginal note beside each such rhyme that describes how it affects you or why you like it.
- Underline uses of other sound effects, e.g., **assonance, alliteration, consonance,** in the poem that you find effective.
- Note any places where you think the poem is excessively obscure or confusing.

7. Get Writer-Initiated Feedback

See Chapter 7.

8. "Lightning" Revision: Read Your Writing Aloud to a Peer or a Small Group

See Chapter 7.

9. Break the Revision Task into Smaller Steps

The difference between timid and bold revision is largely psychological. The timid reviser thinks: "Revision is an overwhelming task, like plunging into freezing waters . . . so do anything you can to avoid it!" By contrast, the bold reviser thinks: "No revision task is too hard because it can always be broken into smaller steps. If I can't 'perfect' my text all at once, I can at least do some small things right now to make it *better.*"

Whenever a particular revision task seems too big, i.e., you are avoiding doing it, break it into smaller parts. Do one part first, then another, and so on—attacking one small bit at a time. Revise what is easiest to revise first—the soft spots—and leave the parts that resist revision—the hard spots—till later. Gradually, the hard spots will soften; return to them a day or two later and suddenly you will see how to improve them. Then, rather than laboring over them for hours, you can revise them quickly.

What are some soft spots you might revise? A soft spot could be a word or a phrase. It could be a sentence. It could be a matter of moving a couple of paragraphs or of expanding an idea by adding some useful bit of supporting information. If you know your piece has an organization problem but cannot yet see how to correct it, do some editing or revise a sentence or the opening or closing paragraph—anything that comes easily. If you can't get the opening paragraph to come right, work on a middle paragraph.

Sound familiar? This is the very revising strategy Walt Whitman used that was described at the beginning of Chapter 9.

10. Take Advantage of Small Bits of Time

In 1787 the poet and playwright Johann Wolfgang von Goethe was traveling by boat from the Italian mainland to Sicily when he became seasick. Rather than give in to the pain and resign himself to a miserable journey, Goethe got out a draft of one of his plays and began revising it, a bit at a time, as he lay flat on his back. "I remained in my horizontal position," he wrote, "revolving and reviving my play in my mind. The hours passed by and I would not have known what time of day it was if [a friend] had not periodically brought me bread and wine." By journey's end, Goethe reported, he "had almost mastered the whole play."

"I write anywhere," says novelist/attorney Scott Turow. Turow worked out much of his three bestselling suspense works—*Presumed Innocent, Burden of Proof,* and *Pleading Guilty*—while riding the commuter train to work in downtown Chicago. He writes in longhand as the train bumps and rolls along the tracks. Turow utilizes spare moments for writing because he chooses to make time for a life outside that of "author." He has learned to exploit the odd moments of the day for writing.

Novelist Toni Morrison says she is writing all the time, even when she appears to be doing something else. "Writing is a process that goes on all the time," she remarks. "I can find myself in any place, solving some problem in the work that I am at the moment working on. . . . It's just a way of life." The fruits of her habit are impressive, to say the least: over half a dozen novels, two Pulitzer Prizes, a National Book Award, and a Nobel Prize for Literature.

The lesson? Don't wait for huge chunks of time for writing; write in the cracks and crevices of the day. Huge chunks are rare, but the cracks are virtually infinite. Revise when you are:

- In line at the store
- Standing by or pushing the cart while your partner (wife, husband, friend) shops

- Waiting for the water to boil
- Just waking up
- About to sit down to eat
- About to go to bed
- Moving between any two other activities

Above all, try writing at "unlikely" times and in unlikely places, when your expectations of success—and the corresponding pressures to succeed—are low. Often you will surprise yourself by accomplishing more than you expect. In addition, you will learn to work quickly and efficiently and realize how very much can be accomplished in a short period of time.

11. Try Various Miscellaneous Revision Strategies

- Develop as broad a repertoire of revision strategies as possible so that when one fails, you can fall back on another.
- Cultivate an attitude of "I'll try this, and, if this doesn't work, I'll try something else." Successful revision depends on risk taking and ingenuity.
- If you get stuck revising one part or aspect of a text, work on a different part or aspect.
- Alternate or diversify your writing tools. If you have been revising at a computer without making satisfactory progress, print a hard copy of your text (or a part of it) and switch to longhand revisions. Conversely, if you are stalling on longhand revisions, change over to computer. If writing at a desk gets tiresome, write in bed or in an easy chair or sit on the floor.
- Alternate between working on details and working on major concepts and structure. When you can't do one, switch to the other. Observe how a painter moves as she creates a painting: she paints close-up to do detail work; then she stands back to get a sense of the whole picture; then she works close-up again.
- Revise steadily. Goethe's motto "Without haste, without rest" is excellent advice for revision. On the one hand, you don't need to make "haste" and attempt to revise your work in a single step; on the other hand, you don't want to "rest" staring at the page doing nothing, either. Always act. Always find something to work on, even if it is only the spelling of a word.
- If you are too tired to revise, if the mere sight of your text sickens you, quit. Do something completely different—jog, houseclean, play tennis, sleep, go to a movie, take a walk. Live.

Checklist of Strategies for Revising

- Start over: Consult Chapter 3.
- Start over: Rewrite using a Topic/Form Grid.
- "Talk" to your draft.
- Do a postdraft outline.
- Have other people outline your draft.
- Ask yourself other questions appropriate to the draft.
- Get writer-initiated feedback.
- "Lightning" revise: Read your writing aloud to a peer or a small group.
- Break the revision task into smaller steps.
- Take advantage of small bits of time.
- Try various miscellaneous revision strategies.

11

Assembling Your Final Portfolio

Age sets its house in order, and finishes its works, which to every artist is a supreme pleasure.

—Ralph Waldo Emerson

The previous chapter described how to revise selected favorite pieces in your notebook. This chapter shows you how to assemble these revised pieces into a final portfolio for submission to your instructor. This process enables you to synthesize your collected and selected writings from the quarter or semester, to reflect on the whole course and on what you have learned, and to consider how this learning can serve you in other courses and in life.

Your instructor will have specific requirements concerning the contents of your portfolio. Typically, a portfolio might include at least some of the following:

- One or more creative selections
- One or more essays about literature
- Complete process work for one or more of your final selections, along with a "process memorandum" that interprets your process
- Some sample pages of your annotations of a literary text, along with an analysis of those annotations
- An introduction to the entire portfolio in which you comment on your selections and reflect on what you have done and learned in the course

Steps for Choosing a Favorite "Creative" Text

Use the process of "rereading" described in Chapter 9:

1. Read through your entire notebook for the quarter or semester.
2. Bracket or underline any pieces that grab or strike you.
3. Reread the marked pieces and choose a favorite. In the margin beside this favorite text, jot down what it is you like about it.
4. If you cannot decide on a favorite text, obtain input on your various options from a partner or small group.

Editing Your Text for Style

"Style" refers to the "how" (as opposed to the "what") of your writing: how it reads, how it sounds. Sometimes style is seen as an ornament that is merely "added on" to a text during the final stages of review. In fact, however, there is a close kinship between the "how" of your text and its "what." The foundation of style is passionate involvement in what you are writing. If you don't care about the "what" of your writing, the "how" will tend to be correspondingly lackadaisical and dull. On the other hand, if your subject excites passion in you, a corresponding intensity of language will follow (with some work and revision), hence, style. By this point in the course you have learned to set aside texts in your notebook that bore you and to concentrate your attention on texts that move and excite you. Thus, some issues of style should already have been resolved. By choosing to work on a text you care about rather than one that bores you, you have prepared the way for style.

That said, there *are* things you can do during the editing stage to strengthen the style of your piece. Your biggest resource here is intertextuality: the best way to improve the style of your own text is by studying other related or similar texts that can serve as examples for you. For instance:

- You are editing a sequel you wrote to Charlotte Perkins Gilman's "The Yellow Wallpaper" (see p. 170); you reread the story to make your style more consistent with Gilman's.
- You are editing a rhymed poem and are frustrated by the awkwardness of your rhymes; you read other rhymed poems, paying particular attention to the rhymed words themselves.
- You are editing a personal memoir that is too stylistically "choppy" for your taste, and you want to make it "flow" better with longer sentences; you read William Faulkner's "Barn Burning" to study its masterful use of long sentences.

Meg wants to edit the style of a piece she wrote in the form of a series of diary entries. The imagined diary writer in her piece is an individual and opinionated young woman named Candy, who is an overworked secretary in a law office. In the current version of the text, Candy sounds less colorful than Meg would like. Accordingly, Meg looks for examples of colorful writing that can help her. Through the short story "Good Country People" (p. 512), she got interested in the writings of Flannery O'Connor and read a volume of O'Connor's stories, which display just the style she wants. Meg rereads several of these stories to infuse some of O'Connor's stylistic qualities into the character of Candy.

Intertextuality is also of obvious benefit when it comes to improving your stylistic command of the *type* or *form* of writing you are trying to produce, e.g., short story, poem, dialogue, letter, short play, personal essay, etc. For instance, suppose your text is a dialogue. You can find examples of dialogues, written or heard, that are as similar as possible to the one you are trying to create. (The short stories and plays in Part V of this book are excellent places to look.) Then immerse yourself in those dialogues: read them, listen to them, enjoy them. ("Enjoying" will be easy because you have an incentive for studying this form of writing—it is going to help you improve your own text.) How do the dialogues sound when read aloud? What kind of language or vocabulary do they use? Is it formal? informal? special in any way? Is slang used? If the dialogue is printed, e.g., in a short story or a play, how is it punctuated? Where do the quotation marks go? How is the dialogue divided into paragraphs?

Here are some questions to ask yourself when editing your text for style:

1. What stylistic qualities do I want in my text? Consider such factors as:

- Sentence length and complexity. Do I want the sentences to be long or short, simple or complex? How will choices about sentence style affect the meaning of my work?
- Diction (or word choice). Do I want my piece to have a formal-sounding vocabulary, or do I want it to be more informal? Do I want the diction of a sophisticated adult? of a child or adolescent?
- Tone. Do I want the tone to be serious? comic? formal? casual? strident? friendly?
- Rhetorical situation. Who is talking to whom in my piece? What is the relationship between my speaker or narrator and his or her subject? and his or her audience or readers? What kind of language will appropriately reflect that relationship?

2. What other texts exemplify the stylistic qualities I want in my own work? Where—in Part V of this book or elsewhere—can I find these examples?

3. What is the *form* of my text? What are some other texts in that form that I can read and study?

Local Revising: Copyediting Your Text

See Chapter 7.

Preparing a Preface to Your Creative Selection(s)

In order to establish a context for your work, your instructor may want you to attach a preface to your creative selection(s). Here is how:

1. Describe the selection. What kind of text is it? poem? letter to the author? sequel to a play or story? Explain why, out of all the other possibilities available to you, you chose this particular selection for your portfolio.
2. Discuss how the selection originated. What literary text or other source—personal experience, memory, observation, song, movie, photograph—inspired it?
3. Discuss how the piece evolved. Once you got your initial idea, through what sequence of steps did the selection grow into its final form? What challenges or problems did you face during the process of composing, and how did you resolve (or try to resolve) them?
4. If the selection is still not completely satisfactory to you, describe how (given more time) you would change it to improve it.

Be specific and detailed in your preface. The care with which you reflect on your work can be as important to your instructor as the work itself.

Preparing a Process Memorandum

One purpose of a portfolio is to make you more conscious of how you process ideas, from first thoughts to finished work. For at least one of your portfolio selections, save all the writing you did, including first notes, drafts, revisions, and notes on meetings with peers. Turn these in along with the finished text and attach a memorandum (addressed to your instructor) in which you interpret your paper trail and tell the story of your text's evolution.

How did your text originate?

Which parts of the process went well and which posed problems? Why?

At what points did you experience breakthroughs in your development of the piece? Why?

What did you learn through the processes of composing and revising?

Interpreting Your Sample Annotations

Annotation is the beginning of response. Each of the finished texts you include in your portfolio originated in some sort of annotation or annotations. Therefore, it is worth reflecting carefully on this process and how you have used it.

Thumb through the annotations you have made in the literary texts included in Part V of *Reading and Writing from Literature*. Identify a few sample pages (your instructor will tell you how many) that show your use of annotation at its best. (Most likely you will find these pages in a literary text that moved you especially powerfully.) Photocopy those pages for your portfolio. In a preface, attached to the sample:

1. Discuss why you chose these particular pages as your sample.
2. Comment on two or three *specific* annotations in the sample that were especially important to you. How did these annotations enrich your reading of the text? How did they stimulate you to do additional thinking and writing?

Writing an Introduction to Your Portfolio

The introduction will be the first item in your portfolio. Since it is difficult, however, to "introduce" a body of materials before the materials themselves are finished and in place, you will want to compose your introduction last. Think of the introduction as a kind of final exam. The difference is, while an exam sometimes seems to draw attention to what you *don't* know (because someone else asks the questions and sets the agenda), the introduction enables *you* to set the agenda and focus attention on what you *do* know. It is an opportunity to show how thoughtfully you have considered the issues of reading, writing, and literature during the course.

One obvious purpose of the introduction is to help the instructor determine your final grade. There are also other, more self-interested reasons for writing an introduction. As an act of summing-up and reflection, composing an introduction gives you a sense of power vis-à-vis the course you have just taken. Rather than simply finishing the class and saying "Well, that was nice," you assess the course for its current and (likely) long-term value in your life. You see how it fits within your larger life as reader and writer; and you reflect on how you have grown during the course and how you want to continue growing after it's over.

Here are several points to consider in your introduction (you won't be able to do them all; focus on the ones about which you have the most to say):

- Introduce the various selections in your portfolio.
- In what ways do you approach literature differently now than you did at the start of the course? In what ways do you approach reading and writing differently?
- Discuss and illustrate two specific strategies or techniques of writing from reading that you have used during the course and have found especially helpful. (Some possibilities are annotation, conversational reading, rereading, postdraft outlining, any particular forms of writing such as those discussed in Chapter 3.)
- Describe the single *most important* thing you have learned during the course.

- Identify the one aspect of your reading and writing behavior that you would most like to improve.

Examples are crucial for making your ideas clear. Therefore, illustrate your responses to these points with examples from your own notebook and from *Reading and Writing from Literature.*

An Introduction
to the Four
Major Genres

The purpose of Part IV is twofold:

The first purpose is *to increase your technical knowledge of short stories, poetry, essays, and plays so that you can write in multiple forms yourself.* For example, if you want to write a personal essay, you can consult Chapter 14 to read about the form and its various components, such as theme, story (or narrative), dialogue, and citation. If you are having trouble deciding how to represent *yourself* in your essay ("How do I want to come across to my readers?"), you can check the paragraphs under the heading "Persona and Voice," which explain that authors construct a persona (or version of a self) to suit the particular context in which they are writing. Then you can peruse or study the essays collected in Part V to see *how* authors shape their personae.

As another example, imagine that a reading of Susan Glaspell's *Trifles* or Terrence McNally's *Andre's Mother* inspires you to write a short play of your own. You have ideas for a couple of characters, and you know a play centers around dialogue; but there your knowledge ends. How do you represent and punctuate dialogue on the page? How do you incorporate scene descriptions and stage directions to indicate the appearance of the stage and the movements and gestures of your characters? And what do you need in the way of a plot to motivate the characters and actions? Chapter 15, read in conjunction with the plays collected in Part V, can assist you with these and other questions.

The second purpose is *to introduce you to key literary terms and concepts that will help you talk and write about the short stories, poems, essays, and plays collected in Part V.* Suppose you read Kate Chopin's "The Story of an Hour" (p. 167), finish the story thinking, "This really grabs me," and decide to write about it for your first essay assignment. You are off to a good start; your excitement suggests the potential for a thoughtful response. In order to write the essay, however, you need to articulate *what* grabs you and *why*. You are fascinated by the story's main character, Louise Mallard. You read the section on "Characters" in Chapter 12 ("Short Stories") to find out ways of discussing characters. There you learn that you can talk about Louise as a "round" character, i.e., one who is individual and complex. In your essay (or in a class discussion) you might analyze this complexity and describe how Mrs. Mallard evolves during the "hour" represented in the story's action. Since the story is told from Mrs. Mallard's perspective, consideration of her character may also lead you to investigate the "Point of View" discussion. In short, the chapter provides you with a vocabulary for articulating your thoughts and feelings about Chopin's story or any of the other stories in Part V.

Note that, throughout Part IV, literary terms are printed in **boldface.** You can find additional information and references to these terms by consulting Appendix C ("Glossary of Literary Terms") and the Subject Index.

Short Stories

A **short story** is a brief work of prose fiction, shorter than a novel or novella and longer than an anecdote. All short stories include such elements as point of view, characters, plot, theme, and setting that are found in longer works of fiction. Given the great flexibility writers have for manipulating these elements, however, the diversity of stories is enormous.

Point of View

Point of view refers to the perspective from which a story is told. The two basic types of point of view are first-person and third-person.

In the **first-person** point of view the storyteller or **narrator** is a major or minor character within the story who uses the pronoun "I." The first-person narrator is sometimes also called a **persona,** after the Latin word for "mask," to signify a distinction between the author (as a flesh-and-blood individual) and the "mask" that he or she assumes in a particular story. When the youth, naiveté, limited intelligence, or extreme subjectivity of a first-person narrator leads us to question the accuracy of his or her version of characters and events, he or she is called a **naive** or **unreliable** narrator. An example is Marie Lazarre, the Native American narrator of Louise Erdrich's "Saint Marie" (p. 420). Marie is about to enter a convent school, where she will end up in an almost deadly struggle with her teacher, Sister Leopolda. The story begins:

> So when I went there, I knew the dark fish must rise. Plumes of radiance had soldered on me. No reservation girl had ever prayed so hard. There was no use in trying to ignore me any longer. I was going up there on the hill with the black robe women. . . . I was going up there to pray as good as they could. Because I don't have that much Indian blood. And they never thought they'd have a girl from this reservation as a saint they'd have to kneel to. But they'd have me.

Marie's declared aim of making the nuns (i.e., "the black robe women") "kneel to" her is an example of her fierce subjectivity and alerts us to read and interpret what follows with caution.

In the **third-person** point of view the narrator is outside the story and refers to characters as "he," "she," or "they," or by their proper names. A third-person **omniscient** narrator functions as an all-knowing presence who has access to the thoughts, feelings, and actions of any and all of the characters. An **intrusive** omniscient narrator evaluates the actions and motives of characters and inserts other of his/her personal views into a story. An **objective** narrator, on the other hand, merely shows or reports actions and characters without evaluating them. Objective narration is evident in Anton Chekhov's "Gooseberries" (p. 500).

Rather than seeing everything, a narrator in a **third-person limited** point of view relates events from the perspective of one of the characters within the story. An example is Kate Chopin's "The Story of an Hour," in which we perceive events through the consciousness of Louise Mallard, though Louise herself is not the narrator of the story. (Incidentally, Louise Mallard dies at the end of "The Story of an Hour." Thus, if she had written the story in the first-person with Louise as narrator, Kate Chopin would have had to change her ending.)

Writers sometimes *mix* various points of view in a single story. For instance, William Faulkner's "Barn Burning" (p. 391) is told, for the most part, from a third-person limited point of view (by a narrator who perceives events through the consciousness of the boy Sarty). At times, however, Faulkner shifts the point of view to first-person and writes *as* Sarty, as in the italicized portions of the following passage:

> They were running a middle buster now, his brother holding the plow straight while he handled the reins, and walking beside the straining mule, the rich black soil shearing cool and damp against his bare ankles, he thought *Maybe this is the end of it. Maybe even that twenty bushels that seems hard to have to pay for just a rug will be a cheap price for him to stop forever and always from being what he used to be;* thinking, dreaming now, so that his brother had to speak sharply to him to mind the mule: *Maybe he even won't collect the twenty bushels. Maybe it will all add up and balance and vanish—corn, rug, fire; the terror and grief, the being pulled two ways like between two teams of horses—gone, done with for ever and ever.*

Sarty's thoughts exemplify a type of narrative technique called **stream of consciousness.** In stream of consciousness a writer seeks to reproduce, without a narrator's intervention, the exact flow of thoughts, feelings, and associations that go through a character's mind as that character moves in the "stream" of time.

Point of view in a story is important for at least two major reasons. First, as writer/teacher James Moffett has noted, "*What* a story is about is a question of *how* it is told." A writer's choice of point of view profoundly affects every other aspect of the story, from its themes and plot structure to its characters and style. For instance, Charlotte Perkins Gilman composed "The Yellow Wallpaper" (p. 170) as a first-person narrative. The narrator is a woman in the midst of a profound mental and emotional crisis who records her fluctuating thoughts and feelings in a diary or journal:

> I don't know why I should write this.
> I don't want to.
> I don't feel able.
> And I know John [the narrator's husband] would think it absurd. But I *must* say what I feel and think in some way—it is such a relief!
> But the effort is getting to be greater than the relief.
> Half the time now I am awfully lazy, and lie down ever so much.

Here the point of view contributes to a sense of urgency (reflected in the short sentences and paragraphs, the sudden shifts in thought, the mood of fear and nagging uncertainty) that would probably be weakened or lost if the story were written from a third-person perspective.

Point of view is also important because it involves us in one of the major functions of imagination, namely, the act of seeing and understanding anew by getting out of our own consciousness and into the consciousness of the "other." Alice Walker writes eloquently about this:

> Writing to me is. . . . about expanding myself as much as I can and seeing myself in as many roles and situations as possible. . . . If I could live as a tree, as a river, as the moon, as the sun, as a star, as the earth, as a rock, I would. Writing permits me to be more than I am. Writing permits me to experience life as any number of strange creations.[1]

Playing with point of view helps a writer understand things (self, culture, life, the world, etc.) *better* or *differently* by knowing them from diverse perspectives. In addition, the possibility of alternative points of view provides a writer with a powerful mode of invention. If the stories you write in your notebook lack vitality, you can bring them to life by manipulating the point of view. You can rewrite your dull first-person narrative about "growing up in the eighties" as a third-person narrative or relate the first-person story that "isn't quite working" from the first-person perspective of a different character in the same story.

Characters

Characters are the imaginary persons who appear in fictional narratives or dramatic works, and characterization is achieved through the depiction of ac-

---

1. Quoted in Claudia Tate, ed., *Black Women Writers at Work* (New York: Continuum, 1983, p. 185).

tion, description, and/or dialogue. A **flat character** is one who remains essentially unchanged throughout the story and tends to be less an individual than a type. Akin to flat characters are the merely undeveloped minor characters who appear in many stories and plays. A **round character,** on the other hand, evolves or undergoes change in the course of the story and is more individualized and complex. Good examples of rounded characters are Louise Mallard in Chopin's "The Story of an Hour," whose thoughts and feelings about her life and marriage are shown to fluctuate quite widely, and Sarty in Faulkner's "Barn Burning." As illustrated in the stream of consciousness passage quoted earlier, Sarty has complex thoughts and emotions; by the end of the story he has grown and changed in his relationship to his father, his family, and his past.

The main character around whom a narrative or dramatic work centers is called the **protagonist** or **hero/heroine.** The protagonist's main opponent, if any, is the **antagonist.** In Louise Erdrich's "Saint Marie," the protagonist is Marie, a Native American girl who goes to a convent school to be "educated"; the antagonist is Sister Leopolda, the stern and repressive nun who seeks to transform her. Note that the protagonist's conflict in a story can take many forms; it is not always with a personal opponent bent on his or her destruction. For more about conflict, see the section on "Plot," on page 137.

Dialogue

Dialogue is the spoken conversation that occurs in a story and is a major means both of characterization and of advancing the story's plot. Consider again the wife/protagonist in Charlotte Perkins Gilman's "The Yellow Wallpaper." The wife's illness has prompted her physician husband to take her to a house in the country for a complete "rest" cure. From the wife's point of view, however, the cure is not working, and, in the following dialogue, she approaches her husband about leaving the house:

> I thought it was a good time to talk, so I told him that I really was not gaining here, and that I wished he would take me away.
> "Why, darling!" said he. "Our lease will be up in three weeks, and I can't see how to leave before.
> "The repairs are not done at home, and I cannot possibly leave town just now. Of course if you were in any danger, I could and would, but you really are better, dear, whether you can see it or not. I am a doctor, dear, and I know. You are gaining flesh and color, your appetite is better, I feel really much easier about you."
> "I don't weigh a bit more," said I, "nor as much; and my appetite may be better in the evening when you are here but it is worse in the morning when you are away!"
> "Bless her little heart!" said he with a big hug. "She shall be as sick as she pleases! But now let's improve the shining hours by going to sleep, and talk about it in the morning!"

"And you won't go away?" I asked gloomily.

"Why, how can I, dear? It is only three weeks more and then we will take a nice little trip of a few days while Jennie is getting the house ready. Really, dear, you are better!"

"Better in body perhaps—" I began, and stopped short, for he sat up straight and looked at me with such a stern, reproachful look that I could not say another word.

"My darling," said he, "I beg of you, for my sake and for our child's sake, as well as for your own, that you will never for one instant let that idea enter your mind! There is nothing so dangerous, so fascinating, to a temperament like yours. It is a false and foolish fancy. Can you not trust me as a physician when I tell you so?"

So of course I said no more on that score, and we went to sleep before long.

This bit of dialogue speaks volumes about the two characters and their relationship. That John does nearly all the talking suggests his position of authority over his wife. In saying "I am a doctor, dear, and I know," he uses professional credentials to reinforce this authority. His remark that "*I* feel really much easier about you" [italics added] implies, perhaps, some insensitivity to what *she* feels; and when he exclaims, "Bless her little heart!" he speaks of his wife in the third-person, as if she weren't even present with him in the room. The narrator, for her part, is nearly silent (in stark contrast to her effusiveness when she writes). When she does talk it is to utter a feeble protest ("I don't weigh a bit more"), or to ask a question ("And you won't go away?"), or to be cut short by a look from John ("Better in body perhaps—"). The dialogue crystallizes the fundamental conflicts and differences between wife and husband; it *shows* us wife and husband with far more suggestiveness and precision than could any comparably short passage that might merely *tell* us about that relationship.

Plot

Point of view, character, and dialogue interconnect with plot and other features to create a story. The **plot** of a story refers to the pattern of actions and events that combine to produce a total effect in readers. A plot is driven by some sort of conflict (e.g., between the protagonist and his or her antagonist; between the protagonist and outward circumstances—environmental, social, or cosmic; or between opposing impulses within the main character). Traditional plots have a beginning, a middle, and an end and move chronologically. Some critics divide plots into a **rising action,** which introduces the characters and establishes the conflict; a **climax** in which the conflict reaches its height in the form of some decisive action or decision; a **falling action,** in which the conflict moves toward resolution; and a **resolution,** in which the conflicts are resolved. This is only a basic pattern for plot, however, and story writers often generate suspense and surprise by upsetting our conventional expectations about how a story should begin, proceed, and end.

One common departure from straightforward chronology is **flashback.** In a flashback a narrator interrupts the narrative to present or relate some event(s) that occurred at a time chronologically prior to the events of the story itself. James Joyce makes frequent use of this device in "Eveline" (p. 253). The events that happen *in* the story are relatively few: Eveline, a dutiful daughter in conflict with her family and her ordinary life, tries to decide whether to elope with her boyfriend, Frank. Through flashback, however, Joyce acquaints us with details of Eveline's life before the events of the story proper and shows us the motivations and factors that contribute to her final choice between family and Frank.

Theme and Setting

Theme is the basic idea advanced (or implied) in the text. Of course, any group of readers coming from diverse situations and backgrounds will perceive different nuances of theme in the same text, and the more complex and interesting the story, the more diverse the articulations of theme are likely to be. The theme of "The Story of an Hour" could be variously described (broadly) as "marriage" or (more specifically) as "the constraining effects of marriage on individual freedom."

Setting refers to the place, time, and social context in which a story or other narrative takes place. In some stories setting is extremely important. Faulkner's "Barn Burning" would not be the same story if it were set any place other than the Deep South of the post–Civil War period. Charlotte Perkins Gilman's account of a woman's mental crisis is set within a single wallpapered room on a lonely country estate; the room and its wallpaper become symbolic focus points for the narrator's inner turmoil. Edgar Allan Poe's "The Masque of the Red Death" (p. 771) is about a plague that has "long devastated the country" of the arrogant Prince Prospero. Poe devotes long paragraphs—most of his story, in fact—to describing the environs and interior of the "castellated" abbey where Prospero and "a thousand light-hearted friends" think to insulate themselves from the Red Death. Evoking feelings of horror and the macabre, *place* becomes a major part of our experience of the story; on the other hand, Poe's nonspecificity about the historical *time* in which the events are supposed to occur makes the sense of danger and doom even greater by rendering the "Red Death" suggestively timeless.

Poetry

S ome students see poetry as the most intimidating form of literature, the
form they "love to hate." This may be because of poetry's odd linear appearance on the page or the student's sometimes paralyzing fear of "getting the
wrong meaning." It helps, at the outset, to realize that poetry is something
broader than a rarified art form; poetry has roots in the ancient past, has flourished among all civilizations and social strata, and is present in popular music,
song lyrics, children's verses, and other popular forms. Whether you know it or
not, you almost certainly *like* some particular poems even if you profess to *dislike* "poetry" in general.

See for yourself. Before reading the poems in Part V of *Reading and Writing
from Literature*, locate and respond to some song lyrics or other poems that you
already know and enjoy. Then:

1. Choose one of these texts that you like the best.
2. Read the text aloud and annotate it.
3. In your notebook make a list of the qualities that make this text beautiful, pleasing, memorable, or meaningful to you. What qualities strike
   you—the sounds of particular words or phrases? rhymes? images? ideas,
   themes, or life issues the text raises for you?
4. Share your text and responsive notes with classmates.
5. Working collaboratively with a small group of classmates, make a list of
   "qualities that make for good poetry."

As another way of overcoming the fears you may have about poems, try approaching poetry with a different psychology. Rather than straining to "get the
meaning right"—instead of being on your "best behavior" when you read a
poem, assume the role of a "dumb" reader. Follow the advice given in Chapter 2
about trusting your intuitions as you annotate (see pp. 10–12). Reread,
again, the example of Margaret's annotations of "Marks" (see pp. 11–12). As
you read a poem jot down your uncensored reactions; record the various

associations—however strange or far-fetched—that the various words, phrases, or images suggest to you. Share your annotations with others; take notes on your peers' ideas and impressions, and realize the enormous diversity of responses a poem can provoke. This diversity of response is part of what makes poems fun.

Major Types of Poetry

Poems can be divided into **narrative** (poems that tell a story), **epic** (long narrative poems on heroic subjects), and **lyric** (poems in which a speaker expresses a state of mind or feeling). Though most of the poems included in *Reading and Writing from Literature* are lyric, some poems like Robert Frost's "Out, Out—" (p. 814) relate a story and are short narrative poems. A fourth subclass of poem is the **prose poem.** Prose poems *look* like prose (i.e., they are laid out in paragraphs rather than lines) but display other features characteristic of poetry. For examples of prose poems, see Bertolt Brecht's "Anecdotes of Mr. Keuner" (p. 553) and Jorge Luis Borges's "Delia Elena San Marco" (p. 818).

Poems can be further classified as either **traditional** or **free verse.** Traditional poems employ poetic **meter** (see below) and often **rhyme,** and they dominated the Anglo-American tradition of poetry up until the last century. Free verse poems discard meter and usually dispense with rhyme but keep other important poetic elements, such as pronouncedly rhythmic phrasing, various types of patterned sound, and intensive use of **figurative language.**

Speaker and Situation

The "I" in a lyric poem is called the **speaker.** Though the identities of speaker and **author** may seem to be close in some poems, the speaker is normally regarded as a being distinct from the author him- or herself: The "speaker" is a *version* of a self that the author projects in a particular poem, while the "author" is the flesh-and-blood person who wrote the poem. The speaker's situation in a poem is a fundamental part of what the poem means—or more accurately, *how* it means.

Consider Theodore Roethke's "My Papa's Waltz" (p. 307):

The whiskey on your breath
Could make a small boy dizzy;
But I hung on like death:
Such waltzing was not easy.

We romped until the pans
Slid from the kitchen shelf;
My mother's countenance
Could not unfrown itself.

The hand that held my wrist
Was battered on one knuckle;
At every step you missed
My right ear scraped a buckle.

You beat time on my head
With a palm caked hard by dirt,
Then waltzed me off to bed
Still clinging to your shirt.

The poem's subject is fairly clear: an experience of "rough" love between a child (most likely a son) and his father; but the speaker and situation are at least as interesting as the subject. At the moment he "speaks," how distant is the speaker, in time, from the experience described? The past tense verbs indicate some time has passed, though how much isn't certain. He seems to talk to his father ("The whiskey on your breath . . .") but more as one might "talk to" someone indirectly, as in a letter, than face to face. Most important, perhaps, the whole experience—what happened, the relationship between father (and mother) and son—is filtered and interpreted for us through the consciousness of the son; we don't get *the* story of the experience but the *son's* version of it.

Roethke could keep the same subject but change the speaker or situation to create a radically different poem. For instance, what if he went through the poem and replaced all the second-person pronouns ("you" and "your") with third-person pronouns ("he" and "his")? The poem would become more emotionally detached, less profoundly personal. Or what if he rewrote the poem from either (a) the first-person point of view of the father or mother or (b) the perspective of a third-person narrator who was uninvolved in the events described but heard about them from the son or the mother? These are questions of technique as much as of meaning; and, just as story writers work with point of view, poets work (or play) with such questions constantly.

Poetic Meter

Rhythm refers to a distinct but variable pattern of stressed and lightly stressed sounds in poetry or prose. When the rhythm follows a *regular* repeating pattern of stressed and lightly stressed syllables it is called **meter,** and the poem is said to be metrical. Within a poetic line, meters are measured in **feet,** with each repetition of the pattern comprising a separate foot.

Iambic is by far the most common of meters in traditional poems written in English. An **iambic** foot consists of a lightly stressed followed by a stressed syllable (˘ ´), as in the following line from Robert Frost's "Birches":

Ăcróss / thĕ línes / ŏf stráight / ĕr dárk / ĕr treés . . .

The vertical slash marks indicate metrical feet. In this example, each line has five feet and the poem is described as being in iambic **pentameter.** A line of four feet is **tetrameter,** three feet **trimeter,** and two feet **dimeter.**

A less common but important meter is the **trochaic** (˘), illustrated in these lines from Robert Browning's "Soliloquy of the Spanish Cloister":

> Thére's ă / gréat text / ĭn Ğa / látiăns,
> Ońce yŏu / trĭp ŏn / ĭt, ĕn / taĭls
> Twénty̆ / -nĭne dĭs / tińct dăm / nátiŏns . . .

Note that the Browning sample exemplifies trochaic tetrameter because it has four metrical feet per line.

Lord Byron's "The Destruction of Sennacherib" provides an example of **anapestic** meter (˘˘´):

> Ănd thĕ wíd / ŏws ŏf Aśh / ŭr ăre loúd / ĭn theĭr waíl,
> Ănd thĕ í / dŏls are bróke / ĭn the tém / plĕ ŏf Báal . . .

Thomas Hardy's "The Voice" illustrates **dactylic** meter (´˘˘):

> Wómăn mŭch / míssed, hŏw yŏu / cáll tŏ mĕ, / cáll tŏ mĕ,
> Sáyiṅg thăt / nŏw yŏu ăre / nót aš yŏu / wére . . .

Using marks to indicate the meter of a poem, as in the above examples, is called a **scansion** of the poem.

Rhyme and Sound Effects

The most familiar sound effect in traditional verse is **end rhyme** (or simply **rhyme**). The example is from "My Papa's Waltz":

> The hand that held my wrist
> Was battered on one knuckle;
> At every step you missed
> My right ear scraped a buckle.

In this example, rhymes like "wrist" and "missed," which consist of a single stressed syllable, are called **masculine rhymes.** A rhyme that falls on a final stressed syllable followed by a lightly stressed one, as in "knuckle" and "buckle," is called a **feminine rhyme.** If the rhyming vowel sounds are only approximately (rather than exactly) alike, the rhyme is called a **slant rhyme** or **partial rhyme.** The rhyme in the second and fourth lines of the following example (from the same poem) illustrate:

The whiskey on your breath
Could make a small boy dizzy;
But I hung on like death:
Such waltzing was not easy.

The following is conventional notation for indicating the rhyme scheme in a poem:

The whiskey on your breath	a
Could make a small boy dizzy;	b
But I hung on like death:	a
Such waltzing was not easy.	b
We romped until the pans	c
Slid from the kitchen shelf;	d
My mother's countenance	c
Could not unfrown itself.	d
The hand that held my wrist	e
Was battered on one knuckle;	f
At every step you missed	e
My right ear scraped a buckle.	f
You beat time on my head	g
With a palm caked hard by dirt,	h
Then waltzed me off to bed	g
Still clinging to your shirt.	h

The "a" indicates all line endings that rhyme with the first line; "b" indicates a second rhyme sound and its repetitions within the poem; "c" designates a third rhyme sound; and so on.

Three other important types of sound effects—alliteration, assonance, and consonance—involve repetitions of speech sounds in a sequence of nearby words. These sound effects enrich verbal texture, affect meaning, and enhance the pleasure experienced in reading. **Alliteration** occurs when consonant sounds are repeated, particularly at the beginnings of words or of stressed syllables:

You ferries! you **p**lanks and **p**osts of wharves!
—Walt Whitman, "Song of the Open Road" (p. 540)

Assonance refers to repeated vowel sounds within words:

H**e**dge-cr**i**ckets s**i**ng; and now with tr**e**ble soft
The r**e**d-br**ea**st wh**i**stles from a garden-croft . . .
—John Keats, "To Autumn" (p. 809)

Consonance refers to repetitions of identical or similar consonant sounds with different intervening vowels:

> **Fish, flesh,** or fowl, commend all summer long . . .
> —W. B. Yeats, "Sailing to Byzantium" (p. 813)

Diction and Syntax

Diction refers to a poet's choice of words and **syntax** to the way those words are put together (e.g., in complex sentences and phrases or simpler sentences and phrases). Persons used to thinking of poetry as always being composed in "high" or rarefied language are sometimes surprised to discover the enormous range of vocabularies that poets actually use. Poets can manipulate language to evoke vastly diverse esthetic effects, cultural contexts, and human experiences. This is because the poet's realm is all of personal and cultural experience rather than just some part of it. Thus at one extreme is the *formal* diction and elaborate syntax of Wordsworth's sonnet "The World Is Too Much with Us" (p. 809):

> The world is too much with us; late and soon,
> Getting and spending, we lay waste our powers:
> Little we see in Nature that is ours;
> We have given our hearts away, a sordid boon!
> This Sea that bares her bosom to the moon. . . .

In this passage words and phrases like "Getting and spending," "sordid boon," and "bares her bosom" convey a sense of formality and magnitude. Syntactically, the speaker's clauses are complex, layered one on the other; it takes him four lines to get through his first sentence, and the fourteen lines of the entire poem are comprised of only three sentences.

At another extreme is the *colloquial* or *informal* diction of Audre Lorde in "Hanging Fire" (p. 439):

> I am fourteen
> and my skin has betrayed me
> the boy I cannot live without
> still sucks his thumb
> in secret
> how come my knees are
> always so ashy
> what if I die
> before morning
> and momma's in the bedroom
> with the door closed.

A first reaction to this poem might be, "It doesn't even sound like poetry!" No less than Wordsworth, however, Lorde chooses and crafts her words to articulate a particular version of experience. In contrast to Wordsworth's formal language and syntax, Lorde evokes the spontaneous bluntness of the frustrated adolescent in such words and phrases as "I am fourteen," "momma's" (instead of "mother's"), and "how come" (instead of "why"). As for syntax, "Hanging Fire" is almost punctuation-free; where we expect to see commas, periods, and question marks there are none; one thought seems to tumble anxiously into the next, in a way that seems appropriate to the jumpy mental state of Lorde's adolescent speaker.

Diction can also be classified as *abstract* (e.g., Wordsworth writes grandly of "The world") or *concrete* (e.g., Lorde's mention of "ashy" knees); *general* (Wordsworth's generic characterization of our wasted lives as made up of "Getting and spending") or *specific* (Lorde's references to thumbsucking and "skin," for example); and *literal* or *figurative* (see next section).

Figurative Language

A **figure** (or **trope**) is a word or phrase used in a way that significantly changes its standard or literal meaning, and **figurative language** is the term used to encompass all nonliteral uses of language. Though figurative language is discussed here with reference to poetry, figures—metaphors, similes, paradoxes, and others—are common in *all* types of discourse, written and spoken. For instance, even in an ordinary expression like "This idea ought to fly" you are speaking figuratively because you are giving nonliteral significations to the literal words "idea" and "fly." That is, the statement doesn't mean that your "idea" is going to sprout literal wings but that it is going to be successful.

Probably the most important of the figures, a **metaphor** makes an implicit comparison between dissimilar items in a way that evokes new or vivid ways of perceiving, knowing, and/or feeling. Adrienne Rich's "Living in Sin" (p. 219) depicts the waking hours of two lovers whose passion is subsiding into routine and boredom. Metaphors make vivid a sense of staleness:

> Not that at five each separate stair would *writhe*
> under the milkman's tramp; that morning light
> so coldly would delineate the scraps
> of last night's cheese and three *sepulchral bottles* . . . [italics added]

The verb "writhe" suggests snakes and other slithery creatures whose touch (for many readers) is unpleasant; the metaphor of stairs *writhing* conveys a sensation tactile enough to send a veritable shudder down the spine. The phrase "sepulchral bottles," yoking together burial vaults and beverage dispensers, suggests bottles that contain dead (stale? moldy? putrid?) matter one would rather not see, smell, touch, or even acknowledge.

Donald Hall's poem "My Son, My Executioner" (p. 311) evokes the surprising and simultaneous similarity and dissimilarity between the speaker's "son" and an "executioner." Thus the poem itself functions as a kind of extended metaphor:

> My son, my executioner,
>   I take you in my arms,
> Quiet and small and just astir,
>   And whom my body warms.

In another example, the speaker in Rita Dove's "Fifth Grade Autobiography" (p. 316) describes the image of her grandmother in a family photograph:

>   Grandmother's hips
> bulge from the brush, she's leaning
> into the ice chest, *sun* through the trees
> *printing* her dress with *soft*
> *luminous paws.* [italics added]

The metaphor in the last three lines evokes the gentleness of the sunlight by likening it to the tangible *weightlessness* one might associate with a cat's paws.

Finally, note that metaphors are not just decorative "ornaments" that writers add to their language as an afterthought; metaphoric or connective thinking seems to be built into the very structure of our minds and imaginations. The ancient Greek philosopher Aristotle said that metaphor "produces knowledge," and many contemporary linguists argue that metaphor is a principle mode of understanding the world and of making meaning.

Closely related to metaphor, a **simile** makes the comparison between dissimilar items explicit with the word *like* or *as*—as in this example from Sharon Olds's "The Elder Sister" (p. 314):

>   . . . now I
> see I had *her* before me always
> *like a shield.* [italics added]

Pat Mora's speaker in "Gentle Communion" (p. 312) also uses a simile when she describes her grandmother's skin as being "worn, like the pages of her prayer book."

In **metonymy** the literal term for one thing is used to stand for another with which it is closely associated. In the following lines from Edwin Arlington Robinson's "Richard Cory" (p. 551), "meat" and "bread" signify not just literal cow's flesh and baked goods but food and money:

> So on we worked, and waited for the light,
> And went without the meat, and cursed the bread . . .

Similarly "drink" and "The Press" in this passage from W. H. Auden's "The Unknown Citizen" (p. 556) signify an alcoholic beverage and the makers of newspapers, respectively, rather than (literally) "any beverage" or "a machine to produce print":

> And our Social Psychology workers found
> That he was popular with his mates and liked *a drink.*
> *The Press* are convinced that he bought a paper every day . . . [italics added]

In **synecdoche** a part of something is used to signify the whole or the whole is used to signify a part. A simple example is the sailor's expression "All hands on deck."

A **paradox** is a statement that seems to be contradictory but proves, on further consideration, to make sense. The first line of the following poem (p. 550) by Emily Dickinson states a paradox:

> Much Madness is divinest Sense—
> To a discerning Eye—
> Much Sense—the starkest Madness—
> 'Tis the Majority
> In this, as All, prevail—
> Assent—and you are sane—
> Demur—you're straightway dangerous—
> And handled with a Chain—

As we finish and ponder the poem, the apparently impossible assertion of the opening line becomes understandable; for the speaker indicates that "Sense" and "Madness" are not absolute concepts but defined situationally by majorities (i.e., in the eyes of a majority, a minority is often treated as "mad" simply because it objects to majority opinion or behavior).

Verbal irony refers to a contrast between what a speaker says literally and the meaning that is implied in the larger context of the poem (or story, play, essay). In Wole Soyinka's "Telephone Conversation" (p. 663) a black African speaker talks over the phone with a white landlady about renting an apartment:

> The price seemed reasonable, location
> Indifferent. The landlady swore she lived
> Off premises. Nothing remained
> But self-confession. 'Madam,' I warned,
> 'I hate a wasted journey—I am—African.'

The word "self-confession"—implying the speaker has something to be ashamed about—conflicts ironically with our (and Soyinka's) moral sense that no one should have to apologize for the color of his/her skin. The deferential tone of the speaker's address to the woman (in "Madam . . ./. . . I am—African" and elsewhere in the poem) is also ironic, as readers discern the speaker's intellectual and moral superiority to the landlady, whose questions and remarks are ludicrous.

Irony also pervades Carter Revard's poem "Discovery of the New World" (p. 661). Revard's speaker reports how he/she and a force of aliens have conquered and subdued a world that is recognizably planet earth. The poem's last line ("we will be safe, and rich, and happy here, forever") expresses a confidence about the everlasting triumph of the conquerers that is apt to sound ironic to students of history, who know that civilizations rise and fall and that conquerors are themselves invariably conquered.

A **personification** is a figure in which human qualities are ascribed to an abstract concept or inanimate object. In the lines "Because I could not stop for Death—/He kindly stopped for me—" (p. 810), Emily Dickinson personifies death as a kindly gentleman. Though more common in older poems, personification can be used with striking effect by modern or contemporary poets. In C. P. Cavafy's "The City" (p. 432) the speaker admonishes a friend, who means to bury the past by moving to another city, that "You will find no new lands, you will find no other seas./The city will *follow* you" [italics added]. Here the city loses its character as a fixed place that can be left behind and becomes, instead, like a persistent and living person who will not let the escapee go. The personification makes the speaker's point more effectively than the more literal "You can't get away from the past."

Symbolism

Strictly speaking, a **symbol** refers to something that stands for something else. In literary analysis the term usually has a broader signification, and something is said to be "symbolic" if it evokes a large range of reference beyond itself.

Consider, for instance, Walt Whitman's "open road" in "Song of the Open Road" (p. 540). Whitman begins by talking about the road as a more or less *literal* road (i.e., "an open, generally public way for the passage of vehicles, people, and animals"—*The American Heritage College Dictionary*):

> Afoot and light-hearted I take to the open road,
> Healthy, free, the world before me,
> The long brown path before me leading wherever I choose.

Soon, however, he imagines the road as being something more ("I believe that much unseen is also here"); and later he asserts that "the universe itself [is] a road." By the poem's end the road seems to embrace virtually every aspect of human experience—all struggles, thoughts, passions, fears, sufferings, triumphs, and failures. The range of symbolic reference is so vast that we, as readers, may find it difficult to imagine any way that we can be alive and *not* be on this "road."

In "The Holy Longing" (p. 430) Johann Wolfgang von Goethe's speaker evokes the instinctive yearning that a literal moth or "butterfly" has for a candle flame:

> Distance does not make you falter,
> now, arriving in magic, flying,
> and, finally, insane for the light,
> you are the butterfly and you are gone.

The next stanza, however, makes clear that this is not *only* a literal description of a moth's behavior:

> And so long as you haven't experienced
> this: to die and so to grow,
> you are only a troubled guest
> on the dark earth.

The moth is suggestively symbolic of human life and of the speaker's assertion that human beings must "die" in order "to grow." Effective literary symbols are, by nature, evocative and complex rather than simple. It would be reductive to speak about *the* meaning of the symbols in either Whitman's or Goethe's poem. Whitman's road *works* as a symbol because it leaves us thinking, for a long time, about the many roads in our personal and collective lives. Similarly, the effectiveness of Goethe's symbol depends on his not attempting to define or explain what is meant by "dying" and "growing"; the poet allows the symbol to resonate in our imaginations and leaves us to discuss and debate among ourselves its manifold implications.

Essays

E *ssay* is a simple word used to describe a broad variety of writings. The word derives from the French verb "essaier," which means "to attempt," and the Frenchman Michel de Montaigne (1533–1592), the first great essayist, used the genre for the sorts of exploratory, reflective, and personal purposes that are implied by this verb. Generally, "essay" refers to a unified work of nonfiction prose that is relatively short (i.e., shorter than a book). Essays can be classified into **argumentative** essays, which advance an explicit argument and support it with evidence; **expository** essays, which inform an audience or explain a particular subject; and **personal** and **literary** essays. This last group emphasizes elements that are ordinarily associated with "literary" texts—an engaging persona, an intellectual or emotional focus or theme that is usually implied rather than directly stated, artful use of figurative language and of such other "literary" elements as dialogue and narrative. A literary essayist combines and crafts these elements to produce particular emotional and intellectual effects in readers. Nearly all the essays collected in Part V of this book are personal or literary essays.

Like most texts, essays come into being gradually, through writing and rewriting. The literary essay is latent in diary entries, personal letters, experimental paragraphs, bits of dialogue, written observations, and portraits of people. Any of these kinds of writing may exhibit the "literary" features characteristic of essays. Thus the texts you compose in your notebook can all be viewed as potential essays or parts of essays. As Montaigne would say, they are "attempts"—the attempts that lurk in the evolutionary background of any "finished" work.

Sample Essay: Judith Ortiz Cofer's "Primary Lessons"

Before continuing, take time to read "Primary Lessons" (p. 459), a personal essay by Judith Ortiz Cofer.

Persona and Voice

As mentioned with reference to short stories and poetry, a persona is the "mask" or version of a self that a writer projects in a particular text. In explicitly autobiographical writings like "Primary Lessons" persona and author may be extremely close, and the authorial presence we perceive in such a text is sometimes called the writer's **voice.** To say that the writer of an essay is "just being herself," however, would be misleading. In important ways the persona is always shaped or *crafted,* for any one essayist will create different personae for different occasions, depending on her subject, purpose, and intended readers. Thus a writer will develop one kind of persona if she is addressing an audience of English professors on the subject of "Metrical Substitutions in the Poems of John Keats" and a very different persona if she is writing for general readers on the subject of "childhood experiences." In the first situation the writer is apt to craft a persona who is authoritative, impersonal, and "scholarly." In the second, the writer will probably want her persona to be personal and "approachable" so as to elicit feelings of empathy or identification in readers.

In "Primary Lessons" Cofer's subject is those "first" or "basic" lessons, learned early, that shape the rest of our lives; her intended audience seems to be adult readers who have experienced similar kinds of "lessons" and who might be interested in revisiting their own childhood experiences by means of this essay. Appropriately, therefore, Cofer crafts a personal and engaging persona who tells a good story. At the same time, she projects a kind of authority—not by marshaling arguments or formidable displays of logic, which might distance her from readers, but by conveying an attitude of simple trust in the facts of her experience:

> My mother walked me to my first day at school at La Escuela Segundo Ruiz Belvis, named after the Puerto Rican patriot born in our town. I remember yellow cement with green trim. All the classrooms had been painted these colors to identify them as government property. This was true all over the Island.

Though in many ways individual and unique, the experience Cofer goes on to relate is apt to resonate in important ways with readers' experiences. Like her, we can recall our "first" school experience, times "of running wild in the sun," or times we didn't want to do what a parent demanded we do. Immediately Cofer establishes a rapport with us, her readers, immersing us in her experiences and making us ready to follow wherever her persona might lead.

Style and Language

A writer's persona in an essay has a shaping effect on his or her style and language.

"Repeat after me, children: Pollito—Chicken," she [*La Mrs.*] commanded in her heavily accented English that only I understood, being the only child in the room who had ever been exposed to the language. But I too remained silent. No use making waves or showing off. Patiently *La Mrs.* sang her song and gestured for us to join in. At some point it must have dawned on the class that this silly routine was likely to go on all day if we did not "repeat after her." It was not her fault that she had to follow the rule in the teacher's manual stating that she must teach English *in* English, and that she must not translate, but merely repeat her lesson in English until the children "begin to respond" more or less "unconsciously." This was one of the vestiges of the regimen followed by her predecessors in the last generation. To this day I can recite "Pollito—Chicken" mindlessly, never once pausing to visualize chicks, hens, pencils, or pens.

Note how Cofer's language fits and reinforces her candid, "ordinary," and forthright persona. There are no inappropriately "fancy" words here, no abstruse sentences or concepts, nothing that can't be understood and followed by an average attentive reader. The vocabulary and syntax are relatively simple. Note, also, how Cofer shuttles between child and adult perspectives on the experiences she relates. The paragraph opens from the viewpoint of herself as a child, looking on ironically at her teacher's "silly routine"; then the perspective shifts to that of the adult who appreciates the causes behind the teacher's behavior: "It was not her fault that she had to follow the rule in her teacher's manual. . . . This was one of the vestiges of the regimen followed by her predecessors. . . " We trust this story—as we do others in the rest of the essay—as a truthful account of what Cofer thought and felt as a child; at the same time, we enter into the adult vision that transforms those "experiences" into "lessons."

Theme

Theme refers to what the essay is about, its prevailing idea. One theme in "Primary Lessons" seems to be early experiences and their lasting effects (though Cofer never explicitly traces these effects in her essay). Another theme might center on the whole question of *which* lessons in our lives are the most "primary," "basic," or "important." To articulate or discuss theme is to get at the *what* of the essay (i.e., its content and ideas), while discussions of persona, voice, audience, language, and literary technique immerse us in its *how* (i.e., how it conveys its content and ideas effectively to readers).

Dialogue

Dialogue is a familiar element of fiction that also appears in essays. Writers of personal and literary essays often assume the role of storytellers; therefore, it is not surprising that they make use of this narrative device.

The presence of dialogue in essays raises an interesting question: Since an essay is a form of *non*fiction, must the dialogue be an exact transcription of what was actually said? The answer is a guarded "no." Few people have the kind of memory that can recall a conversation verbatim ten or fifteen years after it occurred. Thus dialogue—even in nonfiction—is usually to some extent shaped or constructed. If you want to include dialogue in an essay of your own, a good way to begin is by getting a sense of what was said, a feeling for the conversation's tone, themes, and conflict (if any) and for the persons who were involved. Then relax and begin writing.

Judith Ortiz Cofer includes three passages of dialogue in "Primary Lessons." One passage begins with the third paragraph and runs through the fifth; a second occurs toward the middle of the essay, where *La Mrs.* instructs her class in the English words for "Pollito," "Gallina," and so on; and a third appears at the end, in the overheard conversation between *La Mrs.* and the other teacher. You can appreciate the rhetorical importance of these dialogues if you imagine what would be lost if they were omitted. For instance, suppose the closing dialogue were replaced with a mere *summary* of what the two teachers said. We would miss the casual jocularity of the teachers' banter, which is made ironic by the references to Lorenzo as the "funny *negrito*" and to his looking "like a fly drowned in a glass of milk." The dialogue renders the speaker's experience with evocative specificity; it *shows* us the two teachers' racial attitudes and outlook and the child's puzzled response, rather than simply *telling* us about them. Finally, note that Cofer exercises selectivity about her dialogue. She could have put in more of the dialogue between the two teachers, but she has included just enough to make her point. As she puts it, "The conversation ends there for me."

Story

Cofer's essay includes several stories, examples of things she said or did or that happened to her during that important sixth year of her life. The stories are a part of the reason we read her essay, with interest, to the end. Like the passages of dialogue, the stories *show* us her experiences instead of merely telling us about them. A weakness of some personal essays is that the writer spends too much time relating abstract information about his ideas and experiences without embodying those ideas and experiences through devices like storytelling. If this is a problem in your own writing, try the following: make a point (e.g., "It was a miserable year for me") and begin the next sentence with the simple word "Once . . ."; then let the story grow from there. Later, of course, you can edit out superfluous repetitions of the word "once" while keeping the stories themselves.

Stories within essays entertain readers while also giving "flesh" to ideas; in other words, the stories are purposeful, and illustrative of the essay's themes. To begin his essay on "Looking at Women" (p. 225), Scott Russell Sanders relates a story about the first time *he* "looked at a woman." Elsewhere in the essay he incorporates other personal stories relevant to his theme. The essay is worth studying for its repeated and skillful blending of narrative (i.e., storytelling) and exposition (i.e., passages where Sanders interprets or comments on his experience or informs us through the writings of others).

Citations of Other Texts; Allusions

The term **citation** signifies a reference to another text. Though more typically associated with academic or research essays, citations also appear in some personal and literary essays. The citation may take the form of a direct quotation or a summary and can be used for various purposes: to illustrate a point or idea, to reinforce a writer's argument or reasoning, to bolster reader trust in the authority of the persona, or to add depth to an essay by expanding its range of literary reference.

Sanders's "Looking at Women" discusses the psychology and cultural implications of how men look at women. While personal storytelling provides Sanders with one means of embodying his ideas, his topic is broad and complex and has been addressed, directly or indirectly, by many social scientists, cultural critics, and other writers. Accordingly, Sanders cites some of these writers and their ideas in his essay. His citations (of D. H. Lawrence, Simone de Beauvoir, John Berger, and others) lend greater authority to his persona, as readers appreciate that "he knows what he's talking about." They also enrich the essay's content by acquainting readers with diverse perspectives on the main theme.

An **allusion** is another particular kind of reference that essayists (and other writers) sometimes use. An allusion is a reference, without explicit identification, to a specific person, place, or other text. Like citations, allusions (appropriately used) can broaden an essay's range of literary and cultural reference and enhance the authority of the persona. Since allusions depend on the reader having a shared frame of reference or knowledge with the writer, however, they must be used with caution. The writer has to be careful to use allusions that will be understood by the essay's intended readers. Scott Sanders's two allusions (to Jimmy Carter and *Playboy*) in the following sentence help ground his ideas about "looking at women" in the worlds of contemporary and popular culture:

> While he was president, Jimmy Carter raised a brouhaha by confessing in a *Playboy* interview, of all shady places, that he occasionally felt lust in his heart for women.

Allusion was a favorite device of Henry David Thoreau, as exemplified in this passage from "Where I Lived, and What I Lived For" (p. 826):

> All memorable events, I should say, transpire in morning time and in a morning atmosphere. The Vedas say, "All intelligences awake with the morning." Poetry and art, and the fairest and most memorable of the ac-

tions of men, date from such an hour. All poets and heroes, like Memnon, are the children of Aurora, and emit their music at sunrise.

The allusions here—to "the Vedas" (sacred and ancient Hindu writings), "Memnon" (a heroic ruler of ancient Ethiopia), and "Aurora" (goddess of the dawn in Roman mythology)—lend a special aura of nobility and heroic precedent to the wakeful life that Thoreau is praising.

Plays

While one typically reads short stories, poems, and essays in private and silently, a play is a form of performance art; that is, it is a work normally intended for live performance in a theater. A play relates a story; however, rather than narrating (as in a short story), the writer dramatizes the story by means of characters acting and speaking, within a particular imagined setting, on a stage. **Dialogue** is basic to plays. Other important features of the printed text are **scene descriptions,** which describe what the stage looks like for a particular play; **costume descriptions;** and **stage directions,** which describe the movements or gestures of characters on stage. All three of these, which are typically printed in italics, are illustrated in the opening of Susan Glaspell's *Trifles* (p. 235):

SCENE: *The kitchen in the now abandoned farmhouse of* JOHN WRIGHT, *a gloomy kitchen, and left without having been put in order—the walls covered with a faded wallpaper. . . . In the rear wall at* R[IGHT], *up two steps is a door opening onto stairs leading to the second floor. In the rear wall at* L[EFT] *is a door to the shed and from there to the outside. Between these two doors is an old-fashioned black iron stove. . . . At the rear the shed door opens and the* SHERIFF *comes in followed by the* COUNTY AT-TORNEY *and* HALE. *The* SHERIFF *and* HALE *are men in middle life, the* COUNTY AT-TORNEY *is a young man; all are much bundled up and go at once to the stove. They are followed by the two women—the* SHERIFF'S *wife,* MRS. PETERS, *first; she is a slight wiry woman, a thin nervous face.* MRS. HALE *is larger and would ordinarily be called more comfortable looking, but she is disturbed now and looks fearfully about as she enters. The women have come in slowly, and stand close together near the door.*

COUNTY ATTORNEY *(at stove rubbing his hands).* This feels good. Come up to the fire, ladies.

MRS. PETERS *(after taking a step forward).* I'm not—cold.

Note how the italicized text helps you to visualize the action and interpret the characters. For example, the men in the play seem to move around confidently; they enter the kitchen *"and go at once to the stove."* The women, on the other hand, are described as *"nervous"* and fearful; Mrs. Peters takes one *"step forward"* and stops to deliver a very short and halted speech: "I'm not—cold." Already you get a sense of the contrast between the men characters and the women that will be central to the play. Even if you cannot see a particular play performed, dialogue, scene and costume descriptions, and stage directions enable you to do a good production of it in your head.

Plays can follow a range of structural formats. A main division within a play is called an **act,** and full-length plays are typically composed of two or more acts, which may be further subdivided into **scenes.** Some modern and contemporary plays replace acts altogether with a format of multiple scenes or episodes. For instance, Eugene O'Neill's *The Hairy Ape* (p. 464) is composed of eight scenes.

An important subclass of play is the **one-act play,** which bears somewhat the same relationship to a full-length play as a short story does to a novel. One-acts usually dramatize a single incident and include fewer characters than multiple-act plays. In addition, while a full-length play of two hours may represent actions that are supposed to occur over a period of days, months, or years, the time represented by the onstage action of a one-act play usually corresponds closely to real time; that is, a twenty-minute play corresponds to roughly twenty minutes in the lives of the characters.

Setting

Setting refers to the time and place in which the onstage action of a play is supposed to occur. August Wilson's *Fences* (p. 715) dramatizes the story of Troy Maxson, an African-American living in a white man's world. Wilson sets his drama in a specific place (i.e., the yard of *"the Maxson household, an ancient two-story brick house set back off a small alley in a big-city neighborhood"*), and he is also particular about the historical time—1957. In fact, he sets the play against the historical background of migration to America's big cities. While children of European descent found abundant opportunities in the cities, Wilson writes, *"The descendants of African slaves were offered no such welcome or participation. . . . They came strong, eager, searching. The city rejected them and they fled and settled along the riverbanks and under bridges in shallow, ramshackle houses made of sticks and tarpaper."* This description of setting prepares us to understand and appreciate Troy's struggles and motivations, which develop in a context of historically entrenched racism.

Settings do not have to be realistic. *The Hairy Ape* opens in the stokehole of a transatlantic liner, a loud and cramped environment where men labor under circumstances of inhuman oppression and confinement:

*The room is crowded with men, shouting, cursing, laughing, singing—a con-
fused, inchoate uproar swelling into a sort of unity, a meaning—the bewildered, furious, baffled defiance of a beast in a cage.*

O'Neill indicates that *"The treatment of this scene . . . should by no means be naturalistic"*; that is, the scene is meant to distort reality in order to create particular effects. No less than in *Fences,* however, the setting prepares us for what is to
follow—the drama of "Yank" Smith (a.k.a. "the Hairy Ape"), whose life and
death evoke the ferocity and futility of a defiant "beast in a cage."

Characters and Plot

Like short stories, plays may include **flat characters** and **round characters** (see
p. 135); the main character is known as the **protagonist,** and his/her chief opponent in the drama is the **antagonist.**

For purposes of analysis, critics sometimes divide the **plots** of plays into a
rising action, which introduces the characters and establishes the conflict; a
climax, in which the conflict reaches its height in the form of some crucial action or decision; a **falling action,** in which the conflict moves toward resolution; and a **resolution,** in which the central conflict is resolved. As this scheme
suggests, the essential ingredient in any plot is conflict, which may include—
but is not limited to—a conflict between protagonist and antagonist. Conflict—
physical, personal, social, moral, and/or cosmic—helps to define the characters
and themes of the play and to sustain the interest of readers or viewers.

Trifles is set in the farmhouse kitchen of John Wright, who has recently died
under mysterious circumstances. Two women and several men (including the
women's husbands) are investigating the scene of Wright's death. While the
men leave the kitchen and pursue fruitless lines of inquiry, the two women
chance upon evidence that both incriminates the dead man's wife (Minnie) and
unveils the abusive circumstances under which she lived. Hence the focal conflict: Should the women be law-abiding citizens and turn over the evidence to
the men (who remain ignorant of it), or, out of compassion for Minnie, should
they conceal the evidence and thus break the law? In plays, as in life, conflict is
seldom single and simple but multiple and complex. Thus in *Trifles* one conflict
interrelates with others. For instance, one of the women feels an inner conflict
of guilt over having neglected Minnie in her unhappy marriage. Additional
conflict occurs between the women, who discover evidence among "kitchen
things," and the men, who belittle these things as "trifles." At the end of the play
the two women make a choice about what to do with their incriminating evidence, and the central conflict is resolved. As in all good plays, however, readers
or viewers are left with enough unanswered questions to make discussion or responsive writing interesting. What if the women had made a different choice
about the evidence? Did they do the "right" thing? Who decides what is or isn't
morally "right"?

Dialogue

Dialogue is the primary mode of characterization and of advancing plot in plays. Consider this brief passage of dialogue from *Trifles:*

COUNTY ATTORNEY: . . . [Y]ou and Mrs. Wright were neighbors. I suppose you were friends, too.

MRS. HALE: *(shaking her head).* I've not seen much of her of late years. I've not been in this house—it's more than a year.

COUNTY ATTORNEY: *(crossing to women U[pper] C[enter]).* And why was that? You didn't like her?

MRS. HALE: I liked her all well enough. Farmers' wives have their hands full, Mr. Henderson. And then—

COUNTY ATTORNEY: Yes—?

MRS. HALE: *(looking about).* It never seemed a very cheerful place.

COUNTY ATTORNEY: No—it's not cheerful. I shouldn't say she had the home-making instinct.

MRS. HALE: Well, I don't know as Wright had, either.

COUNTY ATTORNEY: You mean that they didn't get on very well?

MRS. HALE: No, I don't mean anything. But I don't think a place'd be any cheer-fuller for John Wright's being in it.

The County Attorney initiates and controls the conversation; confident and aggressive, he presses Mrs. Hale for answers. She, by contrast, maintains a tentative attitude about events and hesitates to interpret them ("I don't mean anything"). The dialogue underscores a broad contrast between the men and women in the play: While the men take an aggressive attitude toward the truth (and achieve nothing), the women take a "wait and see" stance (and discover everything). As for plot, Mrs. Hale's last line is one of many clues in the play that define John Wright as a cold and cruel man who brought on his own demise.

In *Tone Clusters* (p. 335), Joyce Carol Oates departs radically from the kind of *realistic* dialogue used in *Trifles.* Frank and Emily Gulick, "good" citizens and parents, who happen to have a rapist/murderer for a son, are the subjects of an interview for the mass media. Their interviewer, a male voiceover identified simply as "VOICE," never appears on stage. Rather than being realistic, the dialogue is **expressionistic;** that is, Oates exaggerates and distorts reality in order to render the world as we *feel* it rather than as we literally see it:

VOICE: Of today's pressing political issues   the rise in violent crime most concerns American citizens   Number-one political issue of Mr. and Mrs. Gulick   tell our viewers your opinion?

FRANK: In this state,
            the state of New Jersey

EMILY: Oh it's everywhere

FRANK: there's capital punishment supposedly
EMILY: But the lawyers   the lawyers get them off,
FRANK: you bet
          There's public defenders the taxpayer pays
EMILY: Oh, it's   it's out of control
          (like that, what is it   "acid rain"
FRANK: it can fall on you anywhere,
EMILY: the sun is too hot too:
BOTH: the "greenhouse effect") . . .

The characters speak in fractured sentences; the dialogue is unnaturally redundant; syntax or word order is jumbled; and disturbing themes and impressions evoked by the words seem to overshadow the words themselves. The dialogue conveys a sense of the Gulicks as human yet automaton- or puppet-like, as they mouth, with mechanical predictability, the slogans, fears, and attitudes of their culture.

A **monologue** is a long speech by a single character. For instance, in scene eight of *The Hairy Ape,* Yank (the protagonist) finds himself in *"The monkey house at the Zoo."* Yank has spent most of the play living down an insinuation that he is a "hairy ape," and now he comes face to face with a real-life gorilla, whom he addresses familiarly:

Say, yuh're some hard-lookin' guy, ain't yuh? I seen lots of tough nuts dat de gang called gorillas, but yuh're de foist real one I ever seen. Some chest yuh got, and shoulders, and dem arms and mits! I bet yuh got a punch in eider fist dat'd knock 'em all silly. . . .

At the end of act two, scene two, of *Fences,* Troy Maxson feels ultimate disaster closing in upon him. Troy is an African-American who has suffered racial injustice but is no mere "victim"; in many ways—physical and other—he is a giant of a man: caring and cruel, magnetic and alienating, powerful yet flawed. Alone on stage, he directs his anger at no ordinary enemy but at the king of enemies—"Mr. Death."

TROY *(with a quiet rage that threatens to consume him):* All right . . . Mr. Death. See now . . . I'm gonna tell you what I'm gonna do. I'm gonna take and build me a fence around this yard. See? I'm gonna build me a fence around what belongs to me. And then I want you to stay on the other side. See? You stay over there until you're ready for me. Then you come on. Bring your army. Bring your sickle. Bring your wrestling clothes. I ain't gonna fall down on my vigilance this time. You ain't gonna sneak up on me no more. When you ready for me . . . when the top of your list say Troy Maxson . . . that's when you come around here. You come up and knock on the front door. . . .

The monologue reveals to us Troy's inner essence. Powerfully imaginative, he perceives death as no mere idea but as a physical presence poised and ready to attack. He fears death and yet can reduce it to a tangible human shape ("Mr. Death") whom he bosses and bullies as freely as he does his own family ("You stay. . . . Then you come on. . . . Bring your wrestling clothes. . . . You come up. . . ."). Finally, even as he smells his own demise, Troy can taunt and belittle "Mr. Death" for trying to "sneak up" instead of "[knocking] on the front door." The monologue shows us the qualities of imagination, arrogance, and defiance that are at once Troy's sources of power and his defining weaknesses.

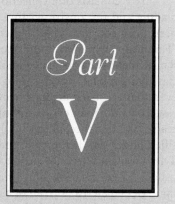

Part

V

A Thematic Anthology of Readings

Parts I through IV introduced you to various ideas for conversational reading and writing and to ways of working with four major genres of literature. Now is your chance to apply these ideas to a range of literary works.

Part V consists of a collection of short stories, poems, essays, and plays for reading and responsive writing. For purposes of convenience, selections have been arranged into several thematic categories: "Gender and Relationships," "Families," "Experience and Identity," "Individual and Society," "Cultural and Racial Identity," and "The Greater Universe." The themes provide a means of classifying related readings into groups of workable size. You will notice, however, that any such arrangement is somewhat arbitrary. Any one story, poem, essay, or play may evoke multiple themes in different readers or in a single reader. For instance, in this book Kate Chopin's "The Story of an Hour" is classified under the theme of "Gender and Relationships"; yet the story prompted Tyler (see Chapter 2) to produce writing that has little to do with the sorts of gender-based "relationships" that are the focus of the particular theme grouping. Tyler created a portrait of a man who served as a surrogate "grandfather" in his life; he produced work that transcends artificially imposed thematic boundaries. You should feel free to do the same. Moreover, if your class is focusing on readings in one thematic section and you want to do additional reading in a different section, do so. Browse, read, enjoy, and write as your individual tastes and instincts dictate.

By referring back to Part I—especially Chapters 2 and 3—you can find ideas for writing in response to *any* of the readings in this anthology. In addition, about half of the individual readings are followed by Activities for Writing and Discussion, which provide ready-made prompts for both "creative" and "analytic" work. The Activities for any particular reading are sequenced to begin with simpler activities and progress toward more complex. Thus, if a particular text puzzles you, you might choose to address Activity #1 rather than one of the later, more demanding activities. Conversely, if a reading affects you powerfully, a later activity may be more appealing.

The Activities are not meant to be exhaustive or to restrict your options for writing. You can best approach *any* story, poem, essay, or play in the anthology by using the "Four-Step Process for Writing from Reading" described in Chapter 2. Then, for additional writing ideas, either:

1. Consult the Activities (if provided) that follow the selection, or
2. Use one of the "Ten Ideas for Writing" described in Chapter 3, or
3. Use some other mode of response of your own devising.

Each thematic section ends with a set of Additional Activities for Writing and Discussion. The Additional Activities serve a twofold purpose. First, they encourage you to make connections among the various readings within the section. Second, they help you develop habits of recursiveness as you "look again" at those readings and at the notebook writings you did in response to them. You can think and talk more about the readings. You can also rewrite, expand, or otherwise improve your notebook writings as you exercise the habit of "selective revising" that is at the heart of the book.

Finally, in both the Activities for Writing and Discussion and the Additional Activities you will find literary terms printed in **boldface.** These are defined and illustrated in Part IV ("An Introduction to the Four Major Genres") and Appendix C ("Glossary of Literary Terms").

Gender and Relationships

KATE CHOPIN (1850–1904)

The Story of an Hour

Knowing that Mrs. Mallard was afflicted with a heart trouble, great care was 1 taken to break to her as gently as possible the news of her husband's death.

It was her sister Josephine who told her, in broken sentences, veiled hints 2 that revealed in half concealing. Her husband's friend Richards was there, too, near her. It was he who had been in the newspaper office when intelligence of the railroad disaster was received, with Brently Mallard's name leading the list of "killed." He had only taken the time to assure himself of its truth by a second telegram, and had hastened to forestall any less careful, less tender friend in bearing the sad message.

She did not hear the story as many women have heard the same, with a par- 3 alyzed inability to accept its significance. She wept at once, with sudden, wild abandonment, in her sister's arms. When the storm of grief had spent itself she went away to her room alone. She would have no one follow her.

There stood, facing the open window, a comfortable, roomy armchair. Into 4 this she sank, pressed down by a physical exhaustion that haunted her body and seemed to reach into her soul.

She could see in the open square before her house the tops of trees that were 5 all aquiver with the new spring life. The delicious breath of rain was in the air. In the street below a peddler was crying his wares. The notes of a distant song which some one was singing reached her faintly, and countless sparrows were twittering in the eaves.

There were patches of blue sky showing here and there through the clouds 6 that had met and piled one above the other in the west facing her window.

She sat with her head thrown back upon the cushion of the chair, quite mo- 7 tionless, except when a sob came up into her throat and shook her, as a child who has cried itself to sleep continues to sob in its dreams.

She was young, with a fair, calm face, whose lines bespoke repression and 8 even a certain strength. But now there was a dull stare in her eyes, whose gaze was fixed away off yonder on one of those patches of blue sky. It was not a glance of reflection, but rather indicated a suspension of intelligent thought.

There was something coming to her and she was waiting for it, fearfully. 9 What was it? She did not know; it was too subtle and elusive to name. But she felt it, creeping out of the sky, reaching toward her through the sounds, the scents, the color that filled the air.

Now her bosom rose and fell tumultuously. She was beginning to recognize 10 this thing that was approaching to possess her, and she was striving to beat it back with her will—as powerless as her two white slender hands would have been.

When she abandoned herself a little whispered word escaped her slightly 11 parted lips. She said it over and over under her breath: "Free, free, free!" The vacant stare and the look of terror that had followed it went from her eyes. They stayed keen and bright. Her pulses beat fast, and the coursing blood warmed and relaxed every inch of her body.

She did not stop to ask if it were or were not a monstrous joy that held her. 12 A clear and exalted perception enabled her to dismiss the suggestion as trivial.

She knew that she would weep again when she saw the kind, tender hands 13 folded in death; the face that had never looked save with love upon her, fixed and gray and dead. But she saw beyond that bitter moment a long procession of years to come that would belong to her absolutely. And she opened and spread her arms out to them in welcome.

There would be no one to live for her during those coming years; she would 14 live for herself. There would be no powerful will bending her in that blind persistence with which men and women believe they have a right to impose a private will upon a fellow-creature. A kind intention or a cruel intention made the act seem no less a crime as she looked upon it in that brief moment of illumination.

And yet she had loved him—sometimes. Often she had not. What did it 15 matter! What could love, the unsolved mystery, count for in face of this possession of self-assertion which she suddenly recognized as the strongest impulse of her being!

"Free! Body and soul free!" she kept whispering. 16

Josephine was kneeling before the closed door with her lips to the keyhole, 17 imploring for admission. "Louise, open the door! I beg; open the door—you will make yourself ill. What are you doing, Louise? For heaven's sake open the door."

"Go away. I am not making myself ill." No; she was drinking in a very elixir 18
of life through that open window.

Her fancy was running riot along those days ahead of her. Spring days, and 19
summer days, and all sorts of days that would be her own. She breathed a quick
prayer that life might be long. It was only yesterday she had thought with a
shudder that life might be long.

She arose at length and opened the door to her sister's importunities. There 20
was a feverish triumph in her eyes, and she carried herself unwittingly like a
goddess of Victory. She clasped her sister's waist, and together they descended
the stairs. Richards stood waiting for them at the bottom.

Some one was opening the front door with a latchkey. It was Brently Mal- 21
lard who entered, a little travel-stained, composedly carrying his grip-sack and
umbrella. He had been far from the scene of accident, and did not even know
there had been one. He stood amazed at Josephine's piercing cry; at Richards'
quick motion to screen him from the view of his wife.

But Richards was too late. 22

When the doctors came they said she had died of heart disease—of joy that 23
kills.

ACTIVITIES FOR WRITING AND DISCUSSION

1. Louise Mallard's feelings toward her husband are complex. We are told
that Brently "never looked save with love upon her," and yet she seems elated
over his death. Is there any evidence that Mr. Mallard has treated her cruelly?
What reasons might she have for feeling "joy" at his death?

2. Chopin's style is concise, leaving much to her readers' imaginations. In
"The Story of an Hour" we get clues about the individual **characters** of Louise
and Brently but do not actually see them together. How do you imagine they
interact with each other? What is their body language like? What sorts of things
do they talk about? Describe a typical day in the marriage of the Mallards, using
dialogue if you wish, or dramatize their interaction in a specific situation (e.g.,
"over breakfast," "after dinner," "with friends").

3. Imagine you are Louise Mallard writing in her diary. Compose a diary
entry—or entries—in which you reflect on your relationship with Brently.

4. Draft a memoir reflecting on any personal connections you have with
the characters or events of this story.

5. Identify and write down two prominent **themes** in this story that interest you. Choose one of them and compare its treatment in this story with its
treatment in any other story, poem, essay, or play in this anthology.

Charlotte Perkins Gilman (1860–1935)

The Yellow Wallpaper

It is very seldom that mere ordinary people like John and myself secure ancestral halls for the summer.

A colonial mansion, a hereditary estate, I would say a haunted house and reach the height of romantic felicity—but that would be asking too much of fate!

Still I will proudly declare that there is something queer about it.

Else, why should it be let so cheaply? And why have stood so long untenanted?

John laughs at me, of course, but one expects that.   5

John is practical in the extreme. He has no patience with faith, an intense horror of superstition, and he scoffs openly at any talk of things not to be felt and seen and put down in figures.

John is a physician, and *perhaps*—(I would not say it to a living soul, of course, but this is dead paper and a great relief to my mind)—*perhaps* that is one reason I do not get well faster.

You see, he does not believe I am sick! And what can one do?

If a physician of high standing, and one's own husband, assures friends and relatives that there is really nothing the matter with one but temporary nervous depression—a slight hysterical tendency—what is one to do?

My brother is also a physician, and also of high standing, and he says the 10
same thing.

So I take phosphates or phosphites—whichever it is—and tonics, and air and exercise, and journeys, and am absolutely forbidden to "work" until I am well again.

Personally, I disagree with their ideas.

Personally, I believe that congenial work, with excitement and change, would do me good.

But what is one to do?

I did write for a while in spite of them; but it *does* exhaust me a good deal— 15
having to be so sly about it, or else meet with heavy opposition.

I sometimes fancy that in my condition, if I had less opposition and more society and stimulus—but John says the very worst thing I can do is to think about my condition, and I confess it always makes me feel bad.

So I will let it alone and talk about the house.

The most beautiful place! It is quite alone, standing well back from the road, quite three miles from the village. It makes me think of English places that you read about, for there are hedges and walls and gates that lock, and lots of separate little houses for the gardeners and people.

There is a *delicious* garden! I never saw such a garden—large and shady, full of box-bordered paths, and lined with long grape-covered arbors with seats under them.

There were greenhouses, but they are all broken now.   20

There was some legal trouble, I believe, something about the heirs and co-heirs; anyhow, the place has been empty for years.

That spoils my ghostliness, I am afraid, but I don't care—there is something strange about the house—I can feel it.

I even said so to John one moonlight evening, but he said what I felt was a draught, and shut the window.

I get unreasonably angry with John sometimes. I'm sure I never used to be so sensitive. I think it is due to this nervous condition.

But John says if I feel so, I shall neglect proper self-control; so I take pains to   25
control myself—before him, at least, and that makes me very tired.

I don't like our room a bit. I wanted one downstairs that opened on the piazza and had roses all over the window, and such pretty old-fashioned chintz hangings! But John would not hear of it.

He said there was only one window and not room for two beds, and no near room for him if he took another.

He is very careful and loving, and hardly lets me stir without special direction.

I have a schedule prescription for each hour in the day; he takes all care from me, and so I feel basely ungrateful not to value it more.

He said we came here solely on my account, that I was to have perfect rest   30
and all the air I could get. "Your exercise depends on your strength, my dear," said he, "and your food somewhat on your appetite; but air you can absorb all the time." So we took the nursery at the top of the house.

It is a big, airy room, the whole floor nearly, with windows that look all ways, and air and sunshine galore. It was nursery first and then playroom and gymnasium, I should judge; for the windows are barred for little children, and there are rings and things in the walls.

The paint and paper look as if a boys' school had used it. It is stripped off—the paper—in great patches all around the head of my bed, about as far as I can reach, and in a great place on the other side of the room low down. I never saw a worse paper in my life. One of those sprawling flamboyant patterns committing every artistic sin.

It is dull enough to confuse the eye in following, pronounced enough to constantly irritate and provoke study, and when you follow the lame uncertain curves for a little distance they suddenly commit suicide—plunge off at outrageous angles, destroy themselves in unheard-of contradictions.

The color is repellant, almost revolting; a smouldering unclean yellow, strangely faded by the slow-turning sunlight. It is a dull yet lurid orange in some places, a sickly sulphur tint in others.

No wonder the children hated it! I should hate it myself if I had to live in   35
this room long.

There comes John, and I must put this away—he hates to have me write a word.

———

We have been here two weeks, and I haven't felt like writing before, since that first day.

I am sitting by the window now, up in this atrocious nursery, and there is nothing to hinder my writing as much as I please, save lack of strength.

John is away all day, and even some nights when his cases are serious.

I am glad my case is not serious!   40

But these nervous troubles are dreadfully depressing.

John does not know how much I really suffer. He knows there is no reason to suffer, and that satisfies him.

Of course it is only nervousness. It does weigh on me so not to do my duty in any way!

I mean to be such a help to John, such a real rest and comfort, and here I am a comparative burden already!

Nobody would believe what an effort it is to do what little I am able—to   45 dress and entertain, and order things.

It is fortunate Mary is so good with the baby. Such a dear baby!

And yet I *cannot* be with him, it makes me so nervous.

I suppose John never was nervous in his life. He laughs at me so about this wallpaper!

At first he meant to repaper the room, but afterwards he said that I was letting it get the better of me, and that nothing was worse for a nervous patient than to give way to such fancies.

He said that after the wallpaper was changed it would be the heavy bed-   50 stead, and then the barred windows, and then that gate at the head of the stairs, and so on.

"You know the place is doing you good," he said, "and really, dear, I don't care to renovate the house just for a three months' rental."

"Then do let us go downstairs," I said. "There are such pretty rooms there."

Then he took me in his arms and called me a blessed little goose, and said he would go down cellar, if I wished, and have it whitewashed into the bargain.

But he is right enough about the beds and windows and things.

It is as airy and comfortable a room as anyone need wish, and, of course, I   55 would not be so silly as to make him uncomfortable just for a whim.

I'm really getting quite fond of the big room, all but that horrid paper.

Out of one window I can see the garden—those mysterious deep-shaded arbors, the riotous old-fashioned flowers, and bushes and gnarly trees.

Out of another I get a lovely view of the bay and a little private wharf belonging to the estate. There is a beautiful shaded lane that runs down there from the house. I always fancy I see people walking in these numerous paths and arbors, but John has cautioned me not to give way to fancy in the least. He says that with my imaginative power and habit of story-making, a nervous weakness like mine is sure to lead to all manner of excited fancies, and that I ought to use my will and good sense to check the tendency. So I try.

I think sometimes that if I were only well enough to write a little it would relieve the press of ideas and rest me.

But I find I get pretty tired when I try. 60

It is so discouraging not to have any advice and companionship about my work. When I get really well, John says we will ask Cousin Henry and Julia down for a long visit; but he says he would as soon put fireworks in my pillow-case as to let me have those stimulating people about now.

I wish I could get well faster.

But I must not think about that. This paper looks to me as if it *knew* what a vicious influence it had!

There is a recurrent spot where the pattern lolls like a broken neck and two bulbous eyes stare at you upside down.

I get positively angry with the impertinence of it and the everlastingness. 65 Up and down and sideways they crawl, and those absurd unblinking eyes are everywhere. There is one place where two breadths didn't match, and the eyes go all up and down the line, one a little higher than the other.

I never saw so much expression in an inanimate thing before, and we all know how much expression they have! I used to lie awake as a child and get more entertainment and terror out of blank walls and plain furniture than most children could find in a toy-store.

I remember what a kindly wink the knobs of our big old bureau used to have, and there was one chair that always seemed like a strong friend.

I used to feel that if any of the other things looked too fierce I could always hop into that chair and be safe.

The furniture in this room is no worse than inharmonious, however, for we had to bring it all from downstairs. I suppose when this was used as a playroom they had to take the nursery things out, and no wonder! I never saw such ravages as the children have made here.

The wallpaper, as I said before, is torn off in spots, and it sticketh closer than 70 a brother—they must have had perseverance as well as hatred.

Then the floor is scratched and gouged and splintered, the plaster itself is dug out here and there, and this great heavy bed which is all we found in the room, looks as if it had been through the wars.

But I don't mind it a bit—only the paper.

There comes John's sister. Such a dear girl as she is, and so careful of me! I must not let her find me writing.

She is a perfect and enthusiastic housekeeper, and hopes for no better profession. I verily believe she thinks it is the writing which made me sick!

But I can write when she is out, and see her a long way off from these windows. 75

There is one that commands the road, a lovely shaded winding road, and one that just looks off over the country. A lovely country, too, full of great elms and velvet meadows.

This wallpaper has a kind of sub-pattern in a different shade, a particularly irritating one, for you can only see it in certain lights, and not clearly then.

But in the places where it isn't faded and where the sun is just so—I can see a strange, provoking, formless sort of figure that seems to skulk about behind that silly and conspicuous front design.

There's sister on the stairs!

———

Well, the Fourth of July is over! The people are all gone, and I am tired out. 80
John thought it might do me good to see a little company, so we just had
Mother and Nellie and the children down for a week.

Of course I didn't do a thing. Jennie sees to everything now.

But it tired me all the same.

John says if I don't pick up faster he shall send me to Weir Mitchell in the
fall.

But I don't want to go there at all. I had a friend who was in his hands once,
and she says he is just like John and my brother, only more so!

Besides, it is such an undertaking to go so far.   85

I don't feel as if it was worthwhile to turn my hand over for anything, and
I'm getting dreadfully fretful and querulous.

I cry at nothing, and cry most of the time.

Of course I don't when John is here, or anybody else, but when I am alone.

And I am alone a good deal just now. John is kept in town very often by serious cases, and Jennie is good and lets me alone when I want her to.

So I walk a little in the garden or down that lovely lane, sit on the porch un- 90
der the roses, and lie down up here a good deal.

I'm getting really fond of the room in spite of the wallpaper. Perhaps *because* of the wallpaper.

It dwells in my mind so!

I lie here on this great immovable bed—it is nailed down, I believe—and
follow that pattern about by the hour. It is as good as gymnastics, I assure you. I
start, we'll say, at the bottom, down in the corner over there where it has not
been touched, and I determine for the thousandth time that I *will* follow that
pointless pattern to some sort of conclusion.

I know a little of the principle of design, and I know this thing was not
arranged on any laws of radiation, or alternation, or repetition, or symmetry, or
anything else that I ever heard of.

It is repeated, of course, by the breadths, but not otherwise.   95

Looked at in one way, each breadth stands alone; the bloated curves and
flourishes—a kind of "debased Romanesque" with delirium tremens—go waddling up and down in isolated columns of fatuity.

But, on the other hand, they connect diagonally, and the sprawling outlines
run off in great slanting waves of optic horror, like a lot of wallowing sea-weeds
in full chase.

The whole thing goes horizontally, too, at least it seems so, and I exhaust
myself trying to distinguish the order of its going in that direction.

They have used a horizontal breadth for a frieze, and that adds wonderfully to the confusion.

There is one end of the room where it is almost intact, and there, when the crosslights fade and the low sun shines directly upon it, I can almost fancy radiation after all—the interminable grotesque seems to form around a common center and rush off in headlong plunges of equal distraction.

It makes me tired to follow it. I will take a nap, I guess.

I don't know why I should write this.

I don't want to.

I don't feel able.

And I know John would think it absurd. But I *must* say what I feel and think in some way—it is such a relief!

But the effort is getting to be greater than the relief.

Half the time now I am awfully lazy, and lie down ever so much.

John says I mustn't lose my strength, and has me take cod liver oil and lots of tonics and things, to say nothing of ale and wine and rare meat.

Dear John! He loves me very dearly, and hates to have me sick. I tried to have a real earnest reasonable talk with him the other day, and tell him how I wish he would let me go and make a visit to Cousin Henry and Julia.

But he said I wasn't able to go, nor able to stand it after I got there; and I did not make out a very good case for myself, for I was crying before I had finished.

It is getting to be a great effort for me to think straight. Just this nervous weakness, I suppose.

And dear John gathered me up in his arms, and just carried me upstairs and laid me on the bed, and sat by me and read to me till it tired my head.

He said I was his darling and his comfort and all he had, and that I must take care of myself for his sake, and keep well.

He says no one but myself can help me out of it, that I must use my will and self-control and not let any silly fancies run away with me.

There's one comfort—the baby is well and happy, and does not have to occupy this nursery with the horrid wallpaper.

If we had not used it, that blessed child would have! What a fortunate escape! Why, I wouldn't have a child of mine, an impressionable little thing, live in such a room for worlds.

I never thought of it before, but it is lucky that John kept me here after all, I can stand it so much easier than a baby, you see.

Of course I never mention it to them any more—I am too wise—but I keep watch for it all the same.

There are things in that paper that nobody knows about but me, or ever will.

Behind that outside pattern the dim shapes get clearer every day.

It is always the same shape, only very numerous.

And it is like a woman stooping down and creeping about behind that pattern. I don't like it a bit. I wonder—I begin to think—I wish John would take me away from here!

————————

It is so hard to talk with John about my case, because he is so wise, and because he loves me so.

But I tried it last night.

It was moonlight. The moon shines in all around just as the sun does.   125

I hate to see it sometimes, it creeps so slowly, and always comes in by one window or another.

John was asleep and I hated to waken him, so I kept still and watched the moonlight on that undulating wallpaper till I felt creepy.

The faint figure behind seemed to shake the pattern, just as if she wanted to get out.

I got up softly and went to feel and see if the paper *did* move, and when I came back John was awake.

"What is it, little girl?" he said. "Don't go walking about like that—you'll get 130 cold."

I thought it was a good time to talk, so I told him that I really was not gaining here, and that I wished he would take me away.

"Why, darling!" said he. "Our lease will be up in three weeks, and I can't see how to leave before.

"The repairs are not done at home, and I cannot possibly leave town just now. Of course if you were in any danger, I could and would, but you really are better, dear, whether you can see it or not. I am a doctor, dear, and I know. You are gaining flesh and color, your appetite is better, I feel really much easier about you."

"I don't weigh a bit more," said I, "nor as much; and my appetite may be better in the evening when you are here but it is worse in the morning when you are away!"

"Bless her little heart!" said he with a big hug. "She shall be as sick as she 135 pleases! But now let's improve the shining hours by going to sleep, and talk about it in the morning!"

"And you won't go away?" I asked gloomily.

"Why, how can I, dear? It is only three weeks more and then we will take a nice little trip of a few days while Jennie is getting the house ready. Really, dear, you are better!"

"Better in body perhaps—" I began, and stopped short, for he sat up straight and looked at me with such a stern, reproachful look that I could not say another word.

"My darling," said he, "I beg of you, for my sake and for our child's sake, as well as for your own, that you will never for one instant let that idea enter your mind! There is nothing so dangerous, so fascinating, to a temperament like yours. It is a false and foolish fancy. Can you not trust me as a physician when I tell you so?"

So of course I said no more on that score, and we went to sleep before long.   140 He thought I was asleep first, but I wasn't, and lay there for hours trying to decide whether that front pattern and the back pattern really did move together or separately.

———

On a pattern like this, by daylight, there is a lack of sequence, a defiance of law, that is a constant irritant to a normal mind.

The color is hideous enough, and unreliable enough, and infuriating enough, but the pattern is torturing.

You think you have mastered it, but just as you get well under way in following, it turns a back-somersault and there you are. It slaps you in the face, knocks you down, and tramples upon you. It is like a bad dream.

The outside pattern is a florid arabesque, reminding one of a fungus. If you can imagine a toadstool in joints, an interminable string of toadstools, budding and sprouting in endless convolutions—why, that is something like it.

That is, sometimes!   145

There is one marked peculiarity about this paper, a thing nobody seems to notice but myself, and that is that it changes as the light changes.

When the sun shoots in through the east window—I always watch for that first long, straight ray—it changes so quickly that I never can quite believe it.

That is why I watch it always.

By moonlight—the moon shines in all night when there is a moon—I wouldn't know it was the same paper.

At night in any kind of light, in twilight, candlelight, lamplight, and worst   150 of all by moonlight, it becomes bars! The outside pattern, I mean, and the woman behind it is as plain as can be.

I didn't realize for a long time what the thing was that showed behind, that dim sub-pattern, but now I am quite sure it is a woman.

By daylight she is subdued, quiet. I fancy it is the pattern that keeps her so still. It is so puzzling. It keeps me quiet by the hour.

I lie down ever so much now. John says it is good for me, and to sleep all I can.

Indeed he started the habit by making me lie down for an hour after each meal.

It is a very bad habit I am convinced, for you see, I don't sleep.   155

And that cultivates deceit, for I don't tell them I'm awake—O no!

The fact is I am getting a little afraid of John.

He seems very queer sometimes, and even Jennie has an inexplicable look.

It strikes me occasionally, just as a scientific hypothesis, that perhaps it is the paper!

I have watched John when he did not know I was looking, and come into   160 the room suddenly on the most innocent excuses, and I've caught him several times *looking at the paper!* And Jennie too. I caught Jennie with her hand on it once.

She didn't know I was in the room, and when I asked her in a quiet, a very quiet voice, with the most restrained manner possible, what she was doing with the paper—she turned around as if she had been caught stealing, and looked quite angry—asked me why I should frighten her so!

Then she said that the paper stained everything it touched, that she had found yellow smooches on all my clothes and John's, and she wished we would be more careful!

Did not that sound innocent? But I know she was studying that pattern, and I am determined that nobody shall find it out but myself!

———————

Life is very much more exciting now than it used to be. You see I have some-thing more to expect, to look forward to, to watch. I really do eat better, and am more quiet than I was.

John is so pleased to see me improve! He laughed a little the other day, and   165
said I seemed to be flourishing in spite of my wallpaper.

I turned it off with a laugh. I had no intention of telling him it was *because* of the wallpaper—he would make fun of me. He might even want to take me away.

I don't want to leave now until I have found it out. There is a week more, and I think that will be enough.

———————

I'm feeling so much better!

I don't sleep much at night, for it is so interesting to watch developments; but I sleep a good deal during the daytime.

In the daytime it is tiresome and perplexing.   170

There are always new shoots on the fungus, and new shades of yellow all over it. I cannot keep count of them, though I have tried conscientiously.

It is the strangest yellow, that wallpaper! It makes me think of all the yellow things I ever saw—not beautiful ones like buttercups, but old, foul, bad yellow things.

But there is something else about that paper—the smell! I noticed it the moment we came into the room, but with so much air and sun it was not bad. Now we have had a week of fog and rain, and whether the windows are open or not, the smell is here.

It creeps all over the house.

I find it hovering in the dining-room, skulking in the parlor, hiding in the   175
hall, lying in wait for me on the stairs.

It gets into my hair.

Even when I go to ride, if I turn my head suddenly and surprise it—there is that smell!

Such a peculiar odor, too! I have spent hours in trying to analyze it, to find what it smelled like.

It is not bad—at first—and very gentle, but quite the subtlest, most enduring odor I ever met.

In this damp weather it is awful, I wake up in the night and find it hanging over me.   180

It used to disturb me at first. I thought seriously of burning the house—to reach the smell.

But now I am used to it. The only thing I can think of that it is like is the *color* of the paper! A yellow smell.

There is a very funny mark on this wall, low down, near the mopboard. A streak that runs round the room. It goes behind every piece of furniture, except the bed, a long, straight, even *smooch*, as if it had been rubbed over and over.

I wonder how it was done and who did it, and what they did it for. Round and round and round—round and round and round—it makes me dizzy!

———

I really have discovered something at last.   185

Through watching so much at night, when it changes so, I have finally found out.

The front pattern *does* move—and no wonder! The woman behind shakes it!

Sometimes I think there are a great many women behind, and sometimes only one, and she crawls around fast, and her crawling shakes it all over.

Then in the very bright spots she keeps still, and in the very shady spots she just takes hold of the bars and shakes them hard.

And she is all the time trying to climb through. But nobody could climb   190
through that pattern—it strangles so; I think that is why it has so many heads.

They get through, and then the pattern strangles them off and turns them upside down, and makes their eyes white!

If those heads were covered or taken off it would not be half so bad.

———

I think that woman gets out in the daytime!

And I'll tell you why—privately—I've seen her!

I can see her out of every one of my windows!   195

It is the same woman, I know, for she is always creeping, and most women do not creep by daylight.

I see her in that long shaded lane, creeping up and down. I see her in those dark grape arbors, creeping all around the garden.

I see her on that long road under the trees, creeping along, and when a carriage comes she hides under the blackberry vines.

I don't blame her a bit. It must be very humiliating to be caught creeping by daylight!

I always lock the door when I creep by daylight. I can't do it at night, for I 200
know John would suspect something at once.

And John is so queer now that I don't want to irritate him. I wish he would
take another room! Besides, I don't want anybody to get that woman out at
night but myself.

I often wonder if I could see her out of all the windows at once.

But, turn as fast as I can, I can only see out of one at one time.

And though I always see her, she *may* be able to creep faster than I can turn!
I have watched her sometimes away off in the open country, creeping as fast as a
cloud shadow in a wind.

If only that top pattern could be gotten off from the under one! I mean to 205
try it, little by little.

I have found out another funny thing, but I shan't tell it this time! It does
not do to trust people too much.

There are only two more days to get this paper off, and I believe John is beginning to notice. I don't like the look in his eyes.

And I heard him ask Jennie a lot of professional questions about me. She
had a very good report to give.

She said I slept a good deal in the daytime.

John knows I don't sleep very well at night, for all I'm so quiet!   210

He asked me all sorts of questions, too, and pretended to be very loving and
kind.

As if I couldn't see through him!

Still, I don't wonder he acts so, sleeping under this paper for three months.

It only interests me, but I feel sure John and Jennie are affected by it.

Hurrah! This is the last day, but it is enough. John is to stay in town over 215
night, and won't be out until this evening.

Jennie wanted to sleep with me—the sly thing; but I told her I should un-
doubtedly rest better for a night all alone.

That was clever, for really I wasn't alone a bit! As soon as it was moonlight
and that poor thing began to crawl and shake the pattern, I got up and ran to
help her.

I pulled and she shook, I shook and she pulled, and before morning we had
peeled off yards of that paper.

A strip about as high as my head and half around the room.

And then when the sun came and that awful pattern began to laugh at me, I 220
declared I would finish it today!

We go away tomorrow, and they are moving all my furniture down again to
leave things as they were before.

Jennie looked at the wall in amazement, but I told her merrily that I did it
out of pure spite at the vicious thing.

She laughed and said she wouldn't mind doing it herself, but I must not get tired.

How she betrayed herself that time!

But I am here, and no person touches this paper but Me—not *alive*!   225

She tried to get me out of the room—it was too patent! But I said it was so quiet and empty and clean now that I believed I would lie down again and sleep all I could; and not to wake me even for dinner—I would call when I woke.

So now she is gone, and the servants are gone, and the things are gone, and there is nothing left but that great bedstead nailed down, with the canvas mattress we found on it.

We shall sleep downstairs tonight, and take the boat home tomorrow.

I quite enjoy the room, now it is bare again.

How those children did tear about here!   230

This bedstead is fairly gnawed!

But I must get to work.

I have locked the door and thrown the key down into the front path.

I don't want to go out, and I don't want to have anybody come in, till John comes.

I want to astonish him.   235

I've got a rope up here that even Jennie did not find. If that woman does get out, and tries to get away, I can tie her!

But I forgot I could not reach far without anything to stand on!

This bed will *not* move!

I tried to lift and push it until I was lame, and then I got so angry I bit off a little piece at one corner—but it hurt my teeth.

Then I peeled off all the paper I could reach standing on the floor. It sticks   240 horribly and the pattern just enjoys it! All those strangled heads and bulbous eyes and waddling fungus growths just shriek with derision!

I am getting angry enough to do something desperate. To jump out of the window would be admirable exercise, but the bars are too strong even to try.

Besides I wouldn't do it. Of course not. I know well enough that a step like that is improper and might be misconstrued.

I don't like to *look* out of the windows even—there are so many of those creeping women, and they creep so fast.

I wonder if they all come out of that wallpaper as I did?

But I am securely fastened now by my well-hidden rope—you don't get *me*   245 out in the road there!

I suppose I shall have to get back behind the pattern when it comes night, and that is hard!

It is so pleasant to be out in this great room and creep around as I please!

I don't want to go outside. I won't, even if Jennie asks me to.

For outside you have to creep on the ground, and everything is green instead of yellow.

But here I can creep smoothly on the floor, and my shoulder just fits in that   250 long smooch around the wall, so I cannot lose my way.

Why there's John at the door!

It is no use, young man, you can't open it!

How he does call and pound!

Now he's crying to Jennie for an axe.

It would be a shame to break down that beautiful door!   255

"John dear!" said I in the gentlest voice. "The key is down by the front steps, under a plantain leaf!"

That silenced him for a few moments.

Then he said—very quietly indeed, "Open the door, my darling!"

"I can't," said I. "The key is down by the front door under a plantain leaf!"

And then I said it again, several times, very gently and slowly, and said it so 260 often that he had to go and see, and he got it of course, and came in. He stopped short by the door.

"What is the matter?" he cried. "For God's sake, what are you doing!"

I kept on creeping just the same, but I looked at him over my shoulder.

"I've got out at last," said I, "in spite of you and Jane[.] And I've pulled off most of the paper, so you can't put me back!"

Now why should that man have fainted? But he did, and right across my path by the wall, so that I had to creep over him every time!

ACTIVITIES FOR WRITING AND DISCUSSION

1. Describe your first impressions of the narrator. Is she an **unreliable narrator,** or do you find her relatively objective? Cite and share particular passages to support your answer.

2. On page 171 the narrator says her husband "hates to have me write a word." Later, on page 175, she declares, "I *must* say what I feel and think in some way—it is such a relief!" Why does she write? What does writing do for her? Identify any passages in the story that relate to writing or imagination. Then produce evidence to support either of the following assertions:

    a. "Writing helps the narrator," or

    b. "Writing and imagination help destroy the narrator."

As you do this exercise, consider what Gilman said of her own experiences with Dr. S. Weir Mitchell:

> [U]sing the remnants of intelligence that remained . . . I cast the noted specialist's advice to the winds and went to work again—work, the normal life of every human being; work, in which is joy and growth and service, without which one is a pauper and a parasite; ultimately recovering some measure of power.

3. The **narrator** expresses ambivalent feelings about John, sometimes challenging his judgments and elsewhere saying "he is so wise, and . . . he loves me

so" (p. 176). How can you account for such contradictory views? What are the narrator's thoughts and feelings about John? Is John good for her? Why or why not? Cite and analyze two or three passages that provide support for your answer.

4. Read aloud the reported **dialogue** between the narrator and John on page 176.
  a. Underline any words or phrases that seem peculiar or interesting to you. How do these words or phrases illuminate the husband/wife relationship? Discuss your thoughts in class or in a small group.
  b. Read the sentence that concludes the dialogue: "So of course I said no more on that score, and we went to sleep before long" (p. 177). How is John able to silence his wife and induce her to sleep?
  c. Write an essay in which you analyze the dialogue and how it helps to characterize the narrator, John, and their relationship.

5. Analyze the story's ending. Has the narrator achieved a greater intellectual and emotional clarity, or has she gone insane? Cite illustrative quotations from the story to support your answer.

6. "The Yellow Wallpaper" is a subjective, **first-person** narrative. As a technical challenge, try rendering the same story in a more objective format. For instance, recast the story as a short play. Provide a **scene description** and **stage directions** to supplement the dialogue of your play.

Doris Lessing (b. 1919)

A Woman on a Roof

It was during the week of hot sun, that June.   1

Three men were at work on the roof, where the leads got so hot they had the   2
idea of throwing water on to cool them. But the water steamed, then sizzled; and they made jokes about getting an egg from some woman in the flats under them, to poach it for their dinner. By two it was not possible to touch the guttering they were replacing, and they speculated about what workmen did in regularly hot countries. Perhaps they should borrow kitchen gloves with the egg? They were all a bit dizzy, not used to the heat; and they shed their coats and stood side by side squeezing themselves into a foot-wide patch of shade against a chimney, careful to keep their feet in the thick socks and boots out of the sun. There was a fine view across several acres of roofs. Not far off a man sat in a deck chair reading the newspapers. Then they saw her, between chimneys, about fifty yards away. She lay face down on a brown blanket. They could see the top part of her: black hair, a flushed solid back, arms spread out.

"She's stark naked," said Stanley, sounding annoyed.   3

Harry, the oldest, a man of about forty-five, said: "Looks like it."   4

Young Tom, seventeen, said nothing, but he was excited and grinning.   5

Stanley said: "Someone'll report her if she doesn't watch out."   6

"She thinks no one can see," said Tom, craning his head all ways to see more.   7

At this point the woman, still lying prone, brought her two hands up behind   8
her shoulders with the ends of a scarf in them, tied it behind her back, and sat
up. She wore a red scarf tied around her breasts and brief red bikini pants. This
being the first day of the sun she was white, flushing red. She sat smoking, and
did not look up when Stanley let out a wolf whistle. Harry said: "Small things
amuse small minds," leading the way back to their part of the roof, but it was
scorching. Harry said: "Wait, I'm going to rig up some shade," and disappeared
down the skylight into the building. Now that he'd gone, Stanley and Tom went
to the farthest point they could to peer at the woman. She had moved, and all
they could see were two pink legs stretched on the blanket. They whistled and
shouted but the legs did not move. Harry came back with a blanket and
shouted: "Come on, then." He sounded irritated with them. They clambered
back to him and he said to Stanley: "What about your missus?" Stanley was
newly married, about three months. Stanley said, jeering: "What about my missus?"—preserving his independence. Tom said nothing, but his mind was full
of the nearly naked woman. Harry slung the blanket, which he had borrowed
from a friendly woman downstairs, from the stem of a television aerial to a row
of chimney-pots. This shade fell across the piece of gutter they had to replace.
But the shade kept moving, they had to adjust the blanket, and not much
progress was made. At last some of the heat left the roof, and they worked fast,
making up for lost time. First Stanley, then Tom, made a trip to the end of the
roof to see the woman. "She's on her back," Stanley said, adding a jest which
made Tom snicker, and the older man smile tolerantly. Tom's report was that
she hadn't moved, but it was a lie. He wanted to keep what he had seen to himself: he had caught her in the act of rolling down the little red pants over her
hips, till they were no more than a small triangle. She was on her back, fully visible, glistening with oil.

Next morning, as soon as they came up, they went to look. She was already   9
there, face down, arms spread out, naked except for the little red pants. She had
turned brown in the night. Yesterday she was a scarlet-and-white woman, today
she was a brown woman. Stanley let out a whistle. She lifted her head, startled,
as if she'd been asleep, and looked straight over at them. The sun was in her
eyes, she blinked and stared, then she dropped her head again. At this gesture of
indifference, they all three, Stanley, Tom, and old Harry, let out whistles and
yells. Harry was doing it in parody of the younger men, making fun of them,
but he was also angry. They were all angry because of her utter indifference to
the three men watching her.

"Bitch," said Stanley.   10

"She should ask us over," said Tom, snickering.   11

Harry recovered himself and reminded Stanley: "If she's married, her old 12
man wouldn't like that."

"Christ," said Stanley virtuously, "if my wife lay about like that, for everyone 13
to see, I'd soon stop her."

Harry said, smiling: "How do you know, perhaps she's sunning herself at 14
this very moment?"

"Not a chance, not on our roof." The safety of his wife put Stanley into a 15
good humour, and they went to work. But today it was hotter than yesterday;
and several times one or the other suggested they should tell Matthew, the foreman, and ask to leave the roof until the heat wave was over. But they didn't.
There was work to be done in the basement of the big block of flats, but up here
they felt free, on a different level from ordinary humanity shut in the streets or
the buildings. A lot more people came out on to the roofs that day, for an hour
at midday. Some married couples sat side by side in deck chairs, the women's
legs stockingless and scarlet, the men in vests with reddening shoulders.

The woman stayed on her blanket, turning herself over and over. She ig- 16
nored them, no matter what they did. When Harry went off to fetch more
screws, Stanley said: "Come on." Her roof belonged to a different system of
roofs, separated from theirs at one point by about twenty feet. It meant a
scrambling climb from one level to another, edging along parapets, clinging to
chimneys, while their big boots slipped and slithered, but at last they stood on a
small square projecting roof looking straight down at her, close. She sat smoking, reading a book. Tom thought she looked like a poster, or a magazine cover,
with the blue sky behind her and her legs stretched out. Behind her a great
crane at work on a new building in Oxford Street swung its black arm across
roofs in a great arc. Tom imagined himself at work on the crane, adjusting the
arm to swing over and pick her up and swing her back across the sky to drop
her near him.

They whistled. She looked up at them, cool and remote, then went on read- 17
ing. Again, they were furious. Or, rather, Stanley was. His sun-heated face was
screwed into a rage as he whistled again and again, trying to make her look up.
Young Tom stopped whistling. He stood beside Stanley, excited, grinning; but
he felt as if he were saying to the woman: Don't associate me with *him,* for his
grin was apologetic. Last night he had thought of the unknown woman before
he slept, and she had been tender with him. This tenderness he was remembering as he shifted his feet by the jeering, whistling Stanley, and watched the indifferent, healthy brown woman a few feet off, with the gap that plunged to the
street between them. Tom thought it was romantic, it was like being high on
two hilltops. But there was a shout from Harry, and they clambered back. Stanley's face was hard, really angry. The boy kept looking at him and wondered
why he hated the woman so much, for by now he loved her.

They played their little games with the blanket, trying to trap shade to work 18
under; but again it was not until nearly four that they could work seriously, and
they were exhausted, all three of them. They were grumbling about the weather

by now. Stanley was in a thoroughly bad humour. When they made their routine trip to see the woman before they packed up for the day, she was apparently asleep, face down, her back all naked save for the scarlet triangle on her buttocks. "I've got a good mind to report her to the police," said Stanley, and Harry said: "What's eating you? What harm's she doing?"

"I tell you, if she was my wife!"   19

"But she isn't, is she?" Tom knew that Harry, like himself, was uneasy at   20 Stanley's reaction. He was normally a sharp young man, quick at his work, making a lot of jokes, good company.

"Perhaps it will be cooler tomorrow," said Harry.   21

But it wasn't; it was hotter, if anything, and the weather forecast said the   22 good weather would last. As soon as they were on the roof, Harry went over to see if the woman was there, and Tom knew it was to prevent Stanley going, to put off his bad humour. Harry had grownup children, a boy the same age as Tom, and the youth trusted and looked up to him.

Harry came back and said: "She's not there."   23

"I bet her old man has put his foot down," said Stanley, and Harry and Tom   24 caught each other's eyes and smiled behind the young married man's back.

Harry suggested they should get permission to work in the basement, and   25 they did, that day. But before packing up Stanley said: "Let's have a breath of fresh air." Again Harry and Tom smiled at each other as they followed Stanley up to the roof, Tom in the devout conviction that he was there to protect the woman from Stanley. It was about five-thirty, and a calm, full sunlight lay over the roofs. The great crane still swung its black arm from Oxford Street to above their heads. She was not there. Then there was a flutter of white from behind a parapet, and she stood up, in a belted, white dressing-gown. She had been there all day, probably, but on a different patch of roof, to hide from them. Stanley did not whistle; he said nothing, but watched the woman bend to collect papers, books, cigarettes, then fold the blanket over her arm. Tom was thinking: If they weren't here, I'd go over and say . . . what? But he knew from his nightly dreams of her that she was kind and friendly. Perhaps she would ask him down to her flat? Perhaps . . . He stood watching her disappear down the skylight. As she went, Stanley let out a shrill derisive yell; she started, and it seemed as if she nearly fell. She clutched to save herself, they could hear things falling. She looked straight at them, angry. Harry said, facetiously: "Better be careful on those slippery ladders, love." Tom knew he said it to save her from Stanley, but she could not know it. She vanished, frowning. Tom was full of a secret delight, because he knew her anger was for the others, not for him.

"Roll on some rain," said Stanley, bitter, looking at the blue evening sky.   26

Next day was cloudless, and they decided to finish the work in the base-   27 ment. They felt excluded, shut in the grey cement basement fitting pipes, from the holiday atmosphere of London in a heat wave. At lunchtime they came up for some air, but while the married couples, and the men in shirt-sleeves or vests, were there, she was not there, either on her usual patch of roof or where she had been yesterday. They all, even Harry, clambered about, between chimney-pots, over parapets, the hot leads stinging their fingers. There was not a sign of her. They took off their shirts and vests and exposed their chests, feeling their feet sweaty and hot. They did not mention the woman. But Tom felt alone again. Last night she had him into her flat: it was big and had fitted white carpets and a bed with a padded white leather head-board. She wore a black filmy negligée and her kindness to Tom thickened his throat as he remembered it. He felt she had betrayed him by not being there.

And again after work they climbed up, but still there was nothing to be seen 28 of her. Stanley kept repeating that if it was as hot as this tomorrow he wasn't going to work and that's all there was to it. But they were all there next day. By ten the temperature was in the middle seventies, and it was eighty long before noon. Harry went to the foreman to say it was impossible to work on the leads in that heat; but the foreman said there was nothing else he could put them on, and they'd have to. At midday they stood, silent, watching the skylight on her roof open, and then she slowly emerged in her white gown, holding a bundle of blanket. She looked at them, gravely, then went to the part of the roof where she was hidden from them. Tom was pleased. He felt she was more his when the other men couldn't see her. They had taken off their shirts and vests, but now they put them back again, for they felt the sun bruising their flesh. "She must have the hide of a rhino," said Stanley, tugging at guttering and swearing. They stopped work, and sat in the shade, moving around behind chimney stacks. A woman came to water a yellow window box opposite them. She was middleaged, wearing a flowered summer dress. Stanley said to her: "We need a drink more than them." She smiled and said: "Better drop down to the pub quick, it'll be closing in a minute." They exchanged pleasantries, and she left them with a smile and a wave.

"Not like Lady Godiva," said Stanley. "She can give us a bit of a chat and a 29 smile."

"You didn't whistle at *her*," said Tom, reproving.   30

"Listen to him," said Stanley, "you didn't whistle, then?"   31

But the boy felt as if he hadn't whistled, as if only Harry and Stanley had. He 32 was making plans, when it was time to knock off work, to get left behind and somehow make his way over to the woman. The weather report said the hot spell was due to break, so he had to move quickly. But there was no chance of being left. The other two decided to knock off work at four, because they were exhausted. As they went down, Tom quickly climbed a parapet and hoisted himself higher by pulling his weight up a chimney. He caught a glimpse of her lying on her back, her knees up, eyes closed, a brown woman lolling in the sun. He slipped and clattered down, as Stanley looked for information: "She's gone down," he said. He felt as if he had protected her from Stanley, and that she must be grateful to him. He could feel the bond between the woman and himself.

Next day, they stood around on the landing below the roof, reluctant to 33 climb up into the heat. The woman who had lent Harry the blanket came out and offered them a cup of tea. They accepted gratefully, and sat around Mrs. Pritchett's kitchen an hour or so, chatting. She was married to an airline pilot.

A smart blonde, of about thirty, she had an eye for the handsome sharp-faced Stanley; and the two teased each other while Harry sat in a corner, watching, indulgent, though his expression reminded Stanley that he was married. And young Tom felt envious of Stanley's ease in badinage; felt, too, that Stanley's getting off with Mrs. Pritchett left his romance with the woman on the roof safe and intact.

"I thought they said the heat wave'd break," said Stanley, sullen, as the time   34
approached when they really would have to climb up into the sunlight.

"You don't like it, then?" asked Mrs. Pritchett.   35

"All right for some," said Stanley. "Nothing to do but lie about as if it was a   36
beach up there. Do you ever go up?"

"Went up once," said Mrs. Pritchett. "But it's a dirty place up there, and it's   37
too hot."

"Quite right too," said Stanley.   38

Then they went up, leaving the cool neat little flat and the friendly Mrs.   39
Pritchett.

As soon as they were up they saw her. The three men looked at her, resentful   40
at her ease in this punishing sun. Then Harry said, because of the expression on
Stanley's face: "Come on, we've got to pretend to work, at least."

They had to wrench another length of guttering that ran beside a parapet   41
out of its bed, so that they could replace it. Stanley took it in his two hands,
tugged, swore, stood up. "Fuck it," he said, and sat down under a chimney. He lit
a cigarette. "Fuck them," he said. "What do they think we are, lizards? I've got
blisters all over my hands." Then he jumped up and climbed over the roofs and
stood with his back to them. He put his fingers either side of his mouth and let
out a shrill whistle. Tom and Harry squatted, not looking at each other, watching him. They could just see the woman's head, the beginnings of her brown
shoulders. Stanley whistled again. Then he began stamping with his feet, and
whistled and yelled and screamed at the woman, his face getting scarlet. He
seemed quite mad, as he stamped and whistled, while the woman did not move,
she did not move a muscle.

"Barmy," said Tom.   42

"Yes," said Harry, disapproving.   43

Suddenly the older man came to a decision. It was, Tom knew, to save some   44
sort of scandal or real trouble over the woman. Harry stood up and began
packing tools into a length of oily cloth. "Stanley," he said, commanding. At first
Stanley took no notice, but Harry said: "Stanley, we're packing it in, I'll tell
Matthew."

Stanley came back, cheeks mottled, eyes glaring.   45

"Can't go on like this," said Harry. "It'll break in a day or so. I'm going to tell   46
Matthew we've got sunstroke, and if he doesn't like it, it's too bad." Even Harry
sounded aggrieved, Tom noted. The small, competent man, the family man
with his grey hair, who was never at a loss, sounded really off balance. "Come
on," he said, angry. He fitted himself into the open square in the roof, and went
down, watching his feet on the ladder. Then Stanley went, with not a glance at

the woman. Then Tom, who, his throat beating with excitement, silently promised her on a backward glance: Wait for me, wait, I'm coming.

On the pavement Stanley said: "I'm going home." He looked white now, so 47 perhaps he really did have sunstroke. Harry went off to find the foreman, who was at work on the plumbing of some flats down the street. Tom slipped back, not into the building they had been working on, but the building on whose roof the woman lay. He went straight up, no one stopping him. The skylight stood open, with an iron ladder leading up. He emerged on to the roof a couple of yards from her. She sat up, pushing back her black hair with both hands. The scarf across her breasts bound them tight, and brown flesh bulged around it. Her legs were brown and smooth. She stared at him in silence. The boy stood grinning, foolish, claiming the tenderness he expected from her.

"What do you want?" she asked. 48

"I ... I came to ... make your acquaintance," he stammered, grinning, 49 pleading with her.

They looked at each other, the slight, scarlet-faced excited boy, and the seri- 50 ous, nearly naked woman. Then, without a word, she lay down on her brown blanket, ignoring him.

"You like the sun, do you?" he enquired of her glistening back. 51

Not a word. He felt panic, thinking of how she had held him in her arms, 52 stroked his hair, brought him where he sat, lordly, in her bed, a glass of some exhilarating liquor he had never tasted in life. He felt that if he knelt down, stroked her shoulders, her hair, she would turn and clasp him in her arms.

He said: "The sun's all right for you, isn't it?" 53

She raised her head, set her chin on two small fists. "Go away," she said. He 54 did not move. "Listen," she said, in a slow reasonable voice, where anger was kept in check, though with difficulty; looking at him, her face weary with anger, "if you get a kick out of seeing women in bikinis, why don't you take a sixpenny bus ride to the Lido? You'd see dozens of them, without all this mountaineering."

She hadn't understood him. He felt her unfairness pale him. He stammered: 55 "But I like you, I've been watching you and . . ."

"Thanks," she said, and dropped her face again, turned away from him. 56

She lay there. He stood there. She said nothing. She had simply shut him 57 out. He stood, saying nothing at all, for some minutes. He thought: She'll have to say something if I stay. But the minutes went past, with no sign of them in her, except in the tension of her back, her thighs, her arms—the tension of waiting for him to go.

He looked up at the sky, where the sun seemed to spin in heat; and over the 58 roofs where he and his mates had been earlier. He could see the heat quivering where they had worked. And they expect us to work in these conditions! he thought, filled with righteous indignation. The woman hadn't moved. A bit of hot wind blew her black hair softly; it shone, and was iridescent. He remembered how he had stroked it last night.

Resentment of her at last moved him off and away down the ladder, through 59 the building, into the street. He got drunk then, in hatred of her.

Next day when he woke the sky was grey. He looked at the wet grey and   60
thought, vicious: Well, that's fixed you, hasn't it now? That's fixed you good and
proper.

The three men were at work early on the cool leads, surrounded by damp   61
drizzling roofs where no one came to sun themselves, black roofs, slimy with
rain. Because it was cool now, they would finish the job that day, if they
hurried.

ACTIVITIES FOR WRITING AND DISCUSSION

1. Working alone or in a small group, brainstorm a list of issues this story
raises for you. Then select one issue that interests you most and relate it (in
writing) to your own or someone else's life experience.

2. Reread and annotate any passages that specifically describe the
woman. Note the items and belongings she carries with her, what she apparently does (other than sunbathe) while on the roof. Note her various reactions
to the men observing and taunting her. Then, without slavishly following Lessing's plot, rewrite the story from the woman's **point of view.** Consider composing your piece in the form of a personal letter (to a recipient of your own
imagining), a series of diary entries, or a **dialogue** between the woman and a
friend.

3. Examine Stanley's interactions with Mrs. Pritchett, a woman whom he
likes. How do these interactions differ from those he has with the woman on the
roof, and how might this difference account for his divergent feelings about
the two women?

4. Imagine that, after seeing the woman on the roof for the second or third
time, Stanley describes her behavior to his wife of three months. In what setting
or situation does Stanley broach the subject? What are his unspoken thoughts,
feelings, or words?
   a. Create the conversation between wife and husband.
   b. Share your dialogue with the class or a small group.
   c. After hearing the dialogues, write a reaction to your own or someone
      else's dialogue. What did you hear that surprised you? What do you now
      understand that you did not when you first read the story?

5. Stanley and Tom react to the woman differently. Stanley feels rage toward her, while we are told that Tom feels a "bond between the woman and
himself" (p. 187). Discuss the differences in their reactions. Is Tom (a) "better"
or "kinder" than Stanley, (b) simply different from Stanley, or (c) really no different from Stanley? Support your analysis with illustrative examples and quotations from the story.

Ray Bradbury (b. 1920)

[A Story About Love]

And out there in the middle of the first day of August, just getting into his car, 1
was Bill Forrester, who shouted he was going downtown for some extraordinary ice cream or other and would anyone join him? So, not five minutes later,
jiggled and steamed into a better mood, Douglas found himself stepping in off
the fiery pavements and moving through the grotto of soda-scented air, of
vanilla freshness at the drugstore, to sit at the snow-marble fountain with Bill
Forrester. They then asked for a recital of the most unusual ices and when the
fountain man said, "Old fashioned lime-vanilla ice . . ."

"That's it!" said Bill Forrester. 2

"Yes, sir!" said Douglas. 3

And, while waiting, they turned slowly on their rotating stools. The silver 4
spigots, the gleaming mirrors, the hushed whirl-around ceiling fans, the green
shades over the small windows, the harp-wire chairs, passed under their moving gaze. They stopped turning. Their eyes had touched upon the face and form
of Miss Helen Loomis, ninety-five years old, ice-cream spoon in hand, ice
cream in mouth.

"Young man," she said to Bill Forrester, "you are a person of taste and imagi- 5
nation. Also, you have the will power of ten men; otherwise you would not dare
veer away from the common flavors listed on the menu and order, straight out,
without quibble or reservation, such an unheard-of thing as lime-vanilla ice."

He bowed his head solemnly to her. 6

"Come sit with me, both of you," she said. "We'll talk of strange ice creams 7
and such things as we seem to have a bent for. Don't be afraid; I'll foot the bill."

Smiling, they carried their dishes to her table and sat. 8

"You look like a Spaulding," she said to the boy. "You've got your grandfa- 9
ther's head. And you, you're William Forrester. You write for the *Chronicle*, a
good enough column. I've heard more about you than I'd care to tell."

"I know you," said Bill Forrester. "You're Helen Loomis." He hesitated, then 10
continued. "I was in love with you once," he said.

"Now that's the way I like a conversation to open." She dug quietly at her ice 11
cream. "That's grounds for another meeting. No—don't tell me where or when
or how you were in love with me. We'll save that for next time. You've taken away
my appetite with your talk. Look there now! Well, I must get home anyway. Since
you're a reporter, come for tea tomorrow between three and four; it's just possible I can sketch out the history of this town, since it was a trading post, for you.
And, so we'll both have something for our curiosity to chew on, Mr. Forrester,
you remind me of a gentleman I went with seventy, yes, seventy years ago."

She sat across from them and it was like talking with a gray and lost quiver- 12
ing moth. The voice came from far away inside the grayness and the oldness,
wrapped in the powders of pressed flowers and ancient butterflies.

"Well." She arose. "Will you come tomorrow?"   13

"I most certainly will," said Bill Forrester.   14

And she went off into the town on business, leaving the young boy and the   15
young man there, looking after her, slowly finishing their ice cream.

———————

William Forrester spent the next morning checking some local news items   16
for the paper, had time after lunch for some fishing in the river outside town,
caught only some small fish which he threw back happily, and, without thinking about it, or at least not noticing that he had thought about it, at three
o'clock he found his car taking him down a certain street. He watched with interest as his hands turned the steering wheel and motored him up a vast circular
drive where he stopped under an ivy-covered entry. Letting himself out, he was
conscious of the fact that his car was like his pipe—old, chewed-on, unkempt
in this huge green garden by this freshly painted, three-story Victorian house.
He saw a faint ghostlike movement at the far end of the garden, heard a whis-
pery cry, and saw that Miss Loomis was there, removed across time and distance,
seated alone, the tea service glittering its soft silver surfaces, waiting for him.

"This is the first time a woman has ever been ready and waiting," he said,   17
walking up. "It is also," he admitted, "the first time in my life I have been on
time for an appointment."

"Why is that?" she asked, propped back in her wicker chair.   18

"I don't know," he admitted.   19

"Well." She started pouring tea. "To start things off, what do you think of   20
the world?"

"I don't know anything."   21

"The beginning of wisdom, as they say. When you're seventeen you know   22
everything. When you're *twenty*-seven if you *still* know everything you're still
seventeen."

"You seem to have learned quite a lot over the years."   23

"It is the privilege of old people to seem to know everything. But it's an act   24
and a mask, like every other act and mask. Between ourselves, we old ones wink
at each other and smile, saying, How do you like *my* mask, *my* act, *my* certainty?
Isn't life a play? Don't I play it well?"

They both laughed quietly. He sat back and let the laughter come naturally   25
from his mouth for the first time in many months. When they quieted she held
her teacup in her two hands and looked into it. "Do you know, it's lucky we met
so late. I wouldn't have wanted you to meet me when I was twenty-one and full
of foolishness."

"They have special laws for pretty girls twenty-one."   26

"So you think I was pretty?"   27

He nodded good-humoredly.   28

"But how can you tell?" she asked. "When you meet a dragon that has eaten   29
a swan, do you guess by the few feathers left around the mouth? That's what it

is—a body like this is a dragon, all scales and folds. So the dragon ate the white swan. I haven't seen her for years. I can't even remember what she looks like. I *feel* her, though. She's safe inside, still alive; the essential swan hasn't changed a feather. Do you know, there are some mornings in spring or fall, when I wake and think, I'll run across the fields into the woods and pick wild strawberries! Or I'll swim in the lake, or I'll dance all night tonight until dawn! And then, in a rage, discover I'm in this old and ruined dragon. I'm the princess in the crumbled tower, no way out, waiting for her Prince Charming."

"You should have written books." 30

"My dear boy, I *have* written. What else was there for an old maid? I was a 31 crazy creature with a headful of carnival spangles until I was thirty, and then the only man I ever really cared for stopped waiting and married someone else. So in spite, in anger at myself, I told myself I deserved my fate for not having married when the best chance was at hand. I started traveling. My luggage was snowed under blizzards of travel stickers. I have been alone in Paris, alone in Vienna, alone in London, and, all in all, it is very much like being alone in Green Town, Illinois. It is, in essence, being alone. Oh, you have plenty of time to think, improve your manners, sharpen your conversations. But I sometimes think I could easily trade a verb tense or a curtsy for some company that would stay over for a thirty-year weekend."

They drank their tea. 32

"Oh, such a rush of self-pity," she said good-naturedly. "About yourself, 33 now. You're thirty-one and still not married?"

"Let me put it this way," he said. "Women who act and think and talk like 34 you are rare."

"My," she said seriously, "you mustn't expect young women to talk like me. 35 That comes later. They're much too young, first of all. And secondly, the average man runs helter-skelter the moment he finds anything like a brain in a lady. You've probably met quite a few brainy ones who hid it most successfully from you. You'll have to pry around a bit to find the odd beetle. Lift a few boards."

They were laughing again. 36

"I shall probably be a meticulous old bachelor," he said. 37

"No, no, you mustn't do that. It wouldn't be right. You shouldn't even be 38 here this afternoon. This is a street which ends only in an Egyptian pyramid. Pyramids are all very nice, but mummies are hardly fit companions. Where would you like to go, what would you really like to do with your life?"

"See Istanbul, Port Said, Nairobi, Budapest. Write a book. Smoke too many 39 cigarettes. Fall off a cliff, but get caught in a tree halfway down. Get shot at a few times in a dark alley on a Moroccan midnight. Love a beautiful woman."

"Well, I don't think I can provide them all," she said. "But I've traveled and I 40 can tell you about many of those places. And if you'd care to run across my front lawn tonight about eleven and if I'm still awake, I'll fire off a Civil War musket at you. Will that satisfy your masculine urge for adventure?"

"That would be just fine." 41

"Where would you like to go first? I can take you there, you know. I can 42
weave a spell. Just name it. London? Cairo? Cairo makes your face turn on like a
light. So let's go to Cairo. Just relax now. Put some of that nice tobacco in that
pipe of yours and sit back."

He sat back, lit his pipe, half smiling, relaxing, and listened, and she began 43
to talk. "Cairo . . ." she said.

––––––

The hour passed in jewels and alleys and winds from the Egyptian desert. 44
The sun was golden and the Nile was muddy where it lapped down to the
deltas, and there was someone very young and very quick at the top of the pyramid, laughing, calling to him to come on up the shadowy side into the sun, and
he was climbing, she putting her hand down to help him up the last step, and
then they were laughing on camel back, loping toward the great stretched bulk
of the Sphinx, and late at night, in the native quarter, there was the tinkle of
small hammers on bronze and silver, and music from some stringed instruments fading away and away and away. . . .

––––––

William Forrester opened his eyes. Miss Helen Loomis had finished the ad- 45
venture and they were home again, very familiar to each other, on the best of
terms, in the garden, the tea cold in the silver pourer, the biscuits dried in the
latened sun. He sighed and stretched and sighed again.

"I've never been so comfortable in my life."   46

"Nor I."   47

"I've kept you late. I should have gone an hour ago."   48

"You know I love every minute of it. But what you should see in an old silly 49
woman . . ."

He lay back in his chair and half closed his eyes and looked at her. He 50
squinted his eyes so the merest filament of light came through. He tilted his
head ever so little this way, then that.

"What are you doing?" she asked uncomfortably.   51

He said nothing, but continued looking.   52

"If you do this just right," he murmured, "you can adjust, make al- 53
lowances. . . ." To himself he was thinking, You can erase lines, adjust the time
factor, turn back the years.

Suddenly he started.   54

"What's wrong?" she asked.   55

But then it was gone. He opened his eyes to catch it. That was a mistake. He 56
should have stayed back, idling, erasing, his eyes gently half closed.

"For just a moment," he said, "I saw it."   57

"Saw what?"   58

"The swan, of course," he thought. His mouth must have pantomimed the 59
words.

The next instant she was sitting very straight in her chair. Her hands were in　60
her lap, rigid. Her eyes were fixed upon him and as he watched, feeling helpless,
each of her eyes cupped and brimmed itself full.

"I'm sorry," he said, "terribly sorry."　61

"No, don't be." She held herself rigid and did not touch her face or her eyes;　62
her hands remained, one atop the other, holding on. "You'd better go now. Yes,
you may come tomorrow, but go now, please, and don't say any more."

He walked off through the garden, leaving her by her table in the shade. He　63
could not bring himself to look back.

Four days, eight days, twelve days passed, and he was invited to teas, to sup-　64
pers, to lunches. They sat talking through the long green afternoons—they
talked of art, of literature, of life, of society and politics. They ate ice creams
and squabs and drank good wines.

"I don't care what anyone says," she said. "And people are saying things,　65
aren't they?"

He shifted uneasily.　66

"I knew it. A woman's never safe, even when ninety-five, from gossip."　67

"I could stop visiting."　68

"Oh, no," she cried, and recovered. In a quieter voice she said, "You know　69
you can't do that. You know you don't care what they think, do you? So long as
we know it's all right?"

"I don't care," he said.　70

"Now"—she settled back—"let's play our game. Where shall it be this time?　71
Paris? I think Paris."

"Paris," he said, nodding quietly.　72

"Well," she began, "it's the year 1885 and we're boarding the ship in New　73
York harbor. There's our luggage, here are our tickets, there goes the sky line.
Now we're at sea. Now we're coming into Marseilles. . . ."

Here she was on a bridge looking into the clear waters of the Seine, and here　74
he was, suddenly, a moment later, beside her, looking down at the tides of summer flowing past. Here she was with an apéritif in her talcum-white fingers,
and here he was, with amazing quickness, bending toward her to tap her wine-
glass with his. His face appeared in mirrored halls at Versailles, over steaming
smörgasbörds in Stockholm, and they counted the barber poles in the Venice
canals. The things she had done alone, they were now doing together.

In the middle of August they sat staring at one another one late afternoon.　75

"Do you realize," he said, "I've seen you nearly every day for two and a half　76
weeks?"

"Impossible!"　77

"I've enjoyed it immensely."　78

"Yes, but there are so many young girls . . ."   79

"You're everything they are not—kind, intelligent, witty."   80

"Nonsense. Kindness and intelligence are the preoccupations of age. Being   81 cruel and thoughtless is far more fascinating when you're twenty." She paused and drew a breath. "Now, I'm going to embarrass you. Do you recall that first afternoon we met in the soda fountain, you said that you had had some degree of—shall we say affection for me at one time? You've purposely put me off on this by never mentioning it again. Now I'm forced to ask you to explain the whole uncomfortable thing."

He didn't seem to know what to say. "That's embarrassing," he protested.   82

"Spit it out!"   83

"I saw your picture once, years ago."   84

"I never let my picture be taken."   85

"This was an old one, taken when you were twenty."   86

"Oh, that. It's quite a joke. Each time I give to a charity or attend a ball they   87 dust that picture off and print it. Everyone in town laughs; even *I*."

"It's cruel of the paper."   88

"No. I told them, If you want a picture of me, use the one taken back in   89 1853. Let them remember me that way. Keep the lid down, in the name of the good Lord, during the service."

"I'll tell you all about it." He folded his hands and looked at them and   90 paused a moment. He was remembering the picture now and it was very clear in his mind. There was time, here in the garden to think of every aspect of the photograph and of Helen Loomis, very young, posing for her picture the first time, alone and beautiful. He thought of her quiet, shyly smiling face.

It was the face of spring, it was the face of summer, it was the warmness of   91 clover breath. Pomegranate glowed in her lips, and the noon sky in her eyes. To touch her face was that always new experience of opening your window one December morning, early, and putting out your hand to the first white cool powdering of snow that had come, silently, with no announcement, in the night. And all of this, this breath-warmness and plum-tenderness was held forever in one miracle of photographic chemistry which no clock winds could blow upon to change one hour or one second; this fine first cool white snow would never melt, but live a thousand summers.

That was the photograph; that was the way he knew her. Now he was talking   92 again, after the remembering and the thinking over and the holding of the picture in his mind. "When I first saw that picture—it was a simple, straightforward picture with a simple hairdo—I didn't know it had been taken that long ago. The item in the paper said something about Helen Loomis marshalling the Town Ball that night. I tore the picture from the paper. I carried it with me all that day. I intended going to the ball. Then, late in the afternoon, someone saw me looking at the picture, and told me about it. How the picture of the beautiful girl had been taken so long ago and used every year since by the paper. And they said I shouldn't go to the Town Ball that night, carrying that picture and looking for you."

They sat in the garden for a long minute. He glanced over at her face. She 93
was looking at the farthest garden wall and the pink roses climbing there. There
was no way to tell what she was thinking. Her face showed nothing. She rocked
for a little while in her chair and then said softly, "Shall we have some more tea?
There you are."

They sat sipping the tea. Then she reached over and patted his arm. "Thank 94
you."

"For what?" 95

"For wanting to come to find me at the dance, for clipping out my picture, 96
for everything. Thank you so very much."

They walked about the garden on the paths. 97

"And now," she said, "it's my turn. Do you remember, I mentioned a certain 98
young man who once attended me, seventy years ago? Oh, he's been dead fifty
years now, at least, but when he was very young and very handsome he rode a
fast horse off for days, or on summer nights over the meadows around town.
He had a healthy, wild face, always sunburned, his hands were always cut and he
fumed like a stovepipe and walked as if he were going to fly apart; wouldn't
keep a job, quit those he had when he felt like it, and one day he sort of rode off
away from me because I was even wilder than he and wouldn't settle down, and
that was that. I never thought the day would come when I would see him alive
again. But you're pretty much alive, you spill ashes around like he did, you're
clumsy and graceful combined, I know everything you're going to do before
you do it, but after you've done it I'm always surprised. Reincarnation's a lot of
milk-mush to me, but the other day I felt, What if I called Robert, Robert, to
you on the street, would William Forrester turn around?"

"I don't know," he said. 99

"Neither do I. That's what makes life interesting." 100

August was almost over. The first cool touch of autumn moved slowly 101
through the town and there was a softening and the first gradual burning fever
of color in every tree, a faint flush and coloring in the hills, and the color of li-
ons in the wheat fields. Now the pattern of days was familiar and repeated like a
penman beautifully inscribing again and again, in practice, a series of *l*'s and
w's and *m*'s, day after day the line repeated in delicate rills.

William Forrester walked across the garden one early August afternoon to 102
find Helen Loomis writing with great care at the tea table.

She put aside her pen and ink. 103

"I've been writing you a letter," she said. 104

"Well, my being here saves you the trouble." 105

"No, this is a special letter. Look at it." She showed him the blue envelope, 106
which she now sealed and pressed flat. "Remember how it looks. When you receive this in the mail, you'll know I'm dead."

"That's no way to talk, is it?" 107

"Sit down and listen to me." 108

He sat.   109

"My dear William," she said, under the parasol shade. "In a few days I will be   110
dead. No." She put up her hand. "I don't want you to say a thing. I'm not afraid.
When you live as long as I've lived you lose that, too. I never liked lobster in my
life, and mainly because I'd never tried it. On my eightieth birthday I tried it. I
can't say I'm greatly excited over lobster still, but I have no doubt as to its taste
now, and I don't fear it. I dare say death will be a lobster, too, and I can come to
terms with it." She motioned with her hands. "But enough of that. The important thing is that I shan't be seeing you again. There will be no services. I believe
that a woman who has passed through that particular door has as much right to
privacy as a woman who has retired for the night."

"You can't predict death," he said at last.   111

"For fifty years I've watched the grandfather clock in the hall, William. After   112
it is wound I can predict to the hour when it will stop. Old people are no different. They can feel the machinery slow down and the last weights shift. Oh,
please don't look that way—please don't."

"I can't help it," he said.   113

"We've had a nice time, haven't we? It has been very special here, talking   114
every day. It was that much-overburdened and worn phrase referred to as a
'meeting of the minds.'" She turned the blue envelope in her hands. "I've always
known that the quality of love was the mind, even though the body sometimes
refuses this knowledge. The body lives for itself. It lives only to feed and wait for
the night. It's essentially nocturnal. But what of the mind which is born of the
sun, William, and must spend thousands of hours of a lifetime awake and
aware? Can you balance off the body, that pitiful, selfish thing of night against a
whole lifetime of sun and intellect? I don't know. I only know there has been
your mind here and my mind here, and the afternoons have been like none I
can remember. There is still so much to talk about, but we must save it for another time."

"We don't seem to have much time now."   115

"No, but perhaps there *will* be another time. Time is so strange and life is   116
twice as strange. The cogs miss, the wheels turn, and lives interlace too early or
too late. I lived too long that much is certain. And you were born either too
early or too late. It was a terrible bit of timing. But perhaps I am being punished
for being a silly girl. Anyway, the next spin around, wheels might function right
again. Meantime you must find a nice girl and be married and be happy. But
you must promise me one thing."

"Anything."   117

"You must promise me not to live to be too old, William. If it is at all conve-   118
nient, die before you're fifty. It may take a bit of doing. But I advise this simply
because there is no telling when another Helen Loomis might be born. It would
be dreadful, wouldn't it, if you lived on to be very, very old and some afternoon
in 1999 walked down Main Street and saw me standing there, aged twenty-one,
and the whole thing out of balance again? I don't think we could go through

any more afternoons like these we've had, no matter how pleasant, do you? A thousand gallons of tea and five hundred biscuits is enough for one friendship. So you must have an attack of pneumonia some time in about twenty years. For I don't know how long they let you linger on the other side. Perhaps they send you back immediately. But I shall do my best, William, really I shall. And everything put right and in balance, do you know what might happen?"

"You tell me."   119

"Some afternoon in 1985 or 1990 a young man named Tom Smith or John   120 Green or a name like that, will be walking downtown and will stop in the drugstore and order, appropriately, a dish of some unusual ice cream. A young girl the same age will be sitting there and when she hears the name of that ice cream, something will happen. I can't say what or how. *She* won't know why or how, assuredly. Nor will the young man. It will simply be that the name of that ice cream will be a very good thing to both of them. They'll talk. And later, when they know each other's names, they'll walk from the drugstore together."

She smiled at him.   121

"This is all very neat, but forgive an old lady for tying things in neat packets.   122 It's a silly trifle to leave you. Now let's talk of something else. What shall we talk about? Is there any place in the world we haven't traveled to yet? Have we been to Stockholm?"

"Yes, it's a fine town."   123

"Glasgow? Yes? Where then?"   124

"Why not Green Town, Illinois?" he said. "Here. We haven't really visited   125 our own town together at all."

She settled back, as did he, and she said, "I'll tell you how it was, then, when   126 I was only nineteen, in this town, a long time ago. . . ."

It was a night in winter and she was skating lightly over a pond of white   127 moon ice, her image gliding and whispering under her. It was a night in summer in this town of fire in the air, in the cheeks, in the heart, your eyes full of the glowing and shutting-off color of fireflies. It was a rustling night in October, and there she stood, pulling taffy from a hook in the kitchen, singing, and there she was, running on the moss by the river, and swimming in the granite pit beyond town on a spring night, in the soft deep warm waters, and now it was the Fourth of July with rockets slamming the sky and every porch full of now red-fire, now blue-fire, now white-fire faces, hers dazzling bright among them as the last rocket died.

"Can you see all these things?" asked Helen Loomis. "Can you see me doing   128 them and being with them?"

"Yes," said William Forrester, eyes closed. "I can see you."   129

"And then," she said, "and then . . ."   130

Her voice moved on and on as the afternoon grew late and the twilight   131 deepened quickly, but her voice moved in the garden and anyone passing on the road, at a far distance, could have heard its moth sound, faintly, faintly. . . .

Two days later William Forrester was at his desk in his room when the letter 132
came. Douglas brought it upstairs and handed it to Bill and looked as if he
knew what was in it.

William Forrester recognized the blue envelope, but did not open it. He 133
simply put it in his shirt pocket, looked at the boy for a moment, and said,
"Come on, Doug; my treat."

They walked downtown, saying very little, Douglas preserving the silence he 134
sensed was necessary. Autumn, which had threatened for a time, was gone.
Summer was back full, boiling the clouds and scouring the metal sky. They
turned in at the drugstore and sat at the marble fountain. William Forrester
took the letter out and laid it before him and still did not open it.

He looked out at the yellow sunlight on the concrete and on the green 135
awnings and shining on the gold letters of the window signs across the street,
and he looked at the calendar on the wall. August 27, 1928. He looked at his
wrist watch and felt his heart beat slowly, saw the second hand of the watch
moving moving with no speed at all, saw the calendar frozen there with its one
day seeming forever, the sun nailed to the sky with no motion toward sunset
whatever. The warm air spread under the sighing fans over his head. A number
of women laughed by the open door and were gone through his vision, which
was focused beyond them at the town itself and the high courthouse clock. He
opened the letter and began to read.

He turned slowly on the revolving chair. He tried the words again and again, 136
silently, on his tongue, and at last spoke them aloud and repeated them.

"A dish of lime-vanilla ice," he said. "A dish of lime-vanilla ice." 137

ACTIVITIES FOR WRITING AND DISCUSSION

1. Respond to the story using the "Four-Step Process for Writing from
Reading" described in Chapter 2.

2. Describe the love that binds Bill and Helen together. Is it physical? spiritual? social? emotional? intellectual? all or some of the above? which? Elaborate
with examples from the text.

3. Reflecting the perspective of ninety-five years of life, Helen's conversation is marvelously witty and perceptive. Annotate any remarks by her that
strike you. Then, in your notebook, reflect on these remarks.

4. Bill and Helen fantasize themselves to be together in various exotic
places around the globe. Imagine that, through a wrinkle in time, a young
William meets a young Helen. What happens? What sort of relationship do
they form? How does this relationship evolve over the next ten, twenty, or fifty
years?

5. The **setting** of the story is memorable: the 1920s, summertime, a small
average town in Middle America. Write a story or memoir of your own in

which you emphasize the setting (whether pleasant or unpleasant), describing time and place in vivid and evocative terms.

Claire Kemp (b. 1936)

Keeping Company

William wakes me with water. He sprays me through the window screen and I 1
am introduced to morning under tangled sheets, sprinkled damp and rolled like laundry ready for the iron. He's whistling. When he sings, "Lazy Mary, will you get up?", I do and go outside in my nightdress to stand barefoot on the cool wet cement close to William. "Hello, wife," he says.

Two men walking to the beach smile and wave a hand in greeting. I raise my 2
hand to wave to them but William checks me with a look. He aims the hose at the street but the pressure is down and the water falls short. "Missed by a mile," he says. "I'm losing my touch."

"They're not bothering anyone. What do you care?"   3

"They're bothering me and I care." A small muscle in his cheek keeps an an- 4
gry beat.

"You'll be late for work," I tell him and run inside to make his eggs, soft 5
boiled on white toast.

"Never happen," he says. The hose, a fat green snake, uncoils and follows 6
obediently wherever he walks.

Mornings I go to the beach. I go alone because William won't. Certain 7
young men come to stroll on this beach. Their walk is a slow dance, graceful and sure. They glide on pewter sand like skaters do on ice. In their brief suits, satin bands of azure blue, magenta, yellow, emerald green, they appear as exotic flowers blooming in the desert. I am taken with their beauty and don't mind sitting in their shade. Not unkindly they dismiss me with their eyes, unencumbered souls walking free at water's edge with perhaps a scarlet towel over one tanned shoulder or a small cloth bag worn around the neck to hold the treasures of the moment. They have smiles for each other but not for me. I'm a cabbage in their garden, a woman large with child, a different species altogether. Next year, I'll have someone to keep me company. I'll teach her how to make castles with turrets from paper cups and wet sand. Swizzle sticks will make a fine bridge to span the moat. Perhaps we'll place cocktail parasols for color in the sand palace courtyard. And I'll take her home before the tide comes in to take it down. She's with me now, tumbling and turning in her water bed and dancing on my ribs with tiny heels and toes. She's coming to term and letting me know. It won't be long.

Afternoons I tend my flowers. Today, I see an open truck parked next door. 8
And a piano on the porch. Two men are discussing how to get it through the
door. One goes inside to pull; the other stays out to push. I think of the piano as
a stubborn horse, its mahogany rump splendid in the sun. "Perhaps, if you offer
it sugar," I suggest. The outside man grins. "Hello," he says and vaults over his
porch rail. I brush potting soil from my hands and reach to shake his hand.

"I'm James," he says. His eyes are gray blue and direct. When he smiles his 9
features merge brightly like a photograph in focus. He has a good face. He says,
"Dennis is inside. He might come out or he might not. He's shy." Behind him,
someone parts the lace curtain at one window and lets it fall.

I tell James my name and he says, "It's nice to meet you, Nora. Your flowers 10
are lovely." But he's not looking at my flowers. Just at me. He nods in affirmation of some private thought and says, "Moving's more work than I bargained
for. I'd better get back to it."

"Yes, see you again" I reply and bend to the task of breaking off the blooms 11
gone by. The aroma of geranium is so strong it seems to leave a taste on my
tongue. When I go inside to make myself a cup of tea, the piano has made it
through the door and there is no one in sight.

After dinner, I tell William we have neighbors and he tells me he's not blind. 12
He uncaps a beer and tilts the bottle to his lips. He wipes foam from his beard
with the back of his hand and gives me a long look I'm meant to pay attention
to. "Don't bother with them, Nora. They're not our kind." From next door I
hear a tentative chord or two. I listen for more but the night air is still, not another note. I listen for sounds from their house over the sounds of our house all
evening long. I don't know why I would. After a while the heat leaves the house
and it's cool enough for sleep and still I listen.

James brings me a croissant sprinkled with cinnamon and sugar. I put down 13
my watering can and take it from his hand. Dennis is practicing scales and I remember how it felt to play, my eyes on the page, not on the keys.

"What are you hoping for?" James asks shyly.   14

"It's a girl. We already know. Doctors can tell in advance now. We've named 15
her Sara."

"Imagine," he says but his eyes are worried as if he marvels at giving credi- 16
bility to someone who can't yet breathe on her own. "She's like a present, as yet
unwrapped," he says. Abruptly the music stops. I picture Dennis closing the piano, covering the keys and going to another part of his house.

"Dennis is tired," James explains. He has already turned from me toward the 17
silence and I am left holding the still warm pastry in one hand and nothing in
the other.

I hang the wash, William's work shirts, dish cloths and towels, heavy sheets 18
that pull on my arms. Next door, James and Dennis talking, always talking.

Their voices rise and fall and blend together. They have so much to say. They never seem to tire of talk. Their screen door opens and shuts throughout the day as they come and go. When they are out of each other's sight, one calls out and the other answers.

Late in the day, I take in the dry clothes, stripping the line and folding as I go   19 along, leaving the clothespins to bob like small wooden birds. Dennis and James head for the beach. Dennis wears a light jacket zipped to the neck as if he is cold. His short sandy hair curls up around his cap, leaving the back of his neck bare, like a young boy's. I can tell James would walk faster if he was alone. Perhaps he would run. As it is, he holds back to keep the pace that Dennis sets but his energy shows itself in the enthusiastic swing of his arms and the quick, attentive way he inclines his head to catch the words that Dennis speaks. When they're out of sight beyond the dunes, I go inside to wait for William.

––––––––––

James is teaching me backgammon. We sit on his patio under the Cinzano   20 umbrella and drink iced tea with lemon slices on the rim of tall oddly shaped amber glasses, no two alike. Dennis will not play but once he points out a move for me and seems quietly pleased when I take that game from James. I do not tell William where I spend my summer afternoons. I'm where I belong when he gets home. He slides his arms around me and rubs my face with his beard and says proudly, "Nora, I swear, you're as big as a house." "I am," I agree, laughing. "I'm Sara's house." He does not ask me what I do all day and I would not tell him if he did. I know something about myself that I didn't know before. I'm successful at sins of omission, never really lying, never telling truth. I hoard secrets like a dog who buries bones to relish at some future time. I wonder if when that time comes, I will remember why or where I dug the holes.

––––––––––

William comes home early, tires spinning in the sand on the lane between   21 our house and theirs. I'm caught and stand up fast from James' table and hurry home leaving James in the middle of a play.

"I don't want you over there," William tells me. "Is that clear?"   22

"But why? They're good company."   23

"They can keep each other company. Not you. I'm your good company. The   24 only company you'll ever need."

William sighs when he looks at me as though I'm a chore he must complete.   25

Dennis gives a concert in my honor, all my favorite pieces played perfect,   26 without flaw or fault. I sit on my front step as evening falls to dark and listen till he's done.

––––––––––

William is building a wall. To make certain he's within his rights, he engages   27 a surveyor to determine the exact boundaries of our land. After supper and on Saturdays he works on his wall. There are guidelines he must follow as to height. I know if permitted he would make it six feet high, five inches taller than the top of my head, but the law won't allow it. Its purpose is to keep me in my place. When he's done, he calls me out to admire his work and I do. I tell him it's a fine wall which is what he wants to hear. James, on his porch, raises his glass in a silent toast. I send him my best smile, an apology big enough for both William and myself.

———————

William has gone south to deliver a boat and won't be home before mid- 28
night at least. James invites me for dinner. I'm invited, so I go. Their kitchen is yellow and blue, quaint, like a woman's sitting room. There are many plants I can't begin to name in clay pots and hanging baskets. I sit on paisley cushions in a wicker chair by the window watching James make stew from scratch. While James chops vegetables, his hand on the knife making quick, precise cuts, Dennis copies the recipe in his spidery script on a card for me to take home. I set the table, lace cloth from Ireland, tall rose colored candles in crystal, linen napkins in shell rings and sterling silver by the plates. James holds my chair and seats me as if I am a lady and not a country girl in faded shorts and one of William's shirts. Dennis searches the yard for hibiscus blooms. He floats them in a shallow blue bowl for a centerpiece. I have gone over the wall.

Unlike Cinderella, I'm home well before midnight in my own kitchen, with 29
a bowl of stew for William over a low flame on my stove. He eats out of the pan. "What are these yellow things?" he asks, poking with his fork.

"Parsnips."   30

"OK," he says. "Next time peas. Otherwise, not bad at all."   31

I let him think I made the stew myself which of course I could have done.   32
And maybe will someday. The recipe is out of sight in the bottom of my sewing box.

We are in a tropical depression. Hot steady rain for a week and thick humid 33
air that leaves me worn out and sleepy. I stay inside, an idle woman, changing in spite of myself like a mushroom growing at a furious rate in this damp and fertile season. We lose our power and Dennis brings candles. He hands the bag to William and runs off without a proper thank you. William hands it quick to me as if its contents are not candles but sticks of dynamite that could go off at any minute. He follows me like the tail of a kite as I place lighted candles on waxed saucers in each room of our house. "The wall is holding," he says. "Can you believe it?" I say, "Yes, I believe it."

In September, Sara will be born.   34

When the storms give in to sun I'm glad, but it reigns in the sky like a lion. 35
Its heat is fierce. I have not seen Dennis or James. The piano does not play. I knock on their door and finally James is there behind the screen. He doesn't lift the latch. I say, "How are you? I miss you two." "Not to worry," he assures me without meeting my eyes. When I ask for Dennis, James shrugs as if Dennis is someone he's lost track of somehow and can't be bothered getting back, which I know for sure is not the truth. He laughs then, a short harsh sound like a bark.

"Sorry," he says. "Dennis is in the hospital. I don't know that he'll be coming home." He says this like he's asking a question, like he's asking me for an answer. I put my hand on my side of the screen and James touches it briefly with his. We stand for a moment, like visitors in prison before he closes the inside door and shuts me out. I wish I could take back the days.

I go home where I belong. There is laundry to fold, chores to do, an entire 36 house to put to order. I do a proper job of every task, a proper penance. Before bed, I tell William. I know as I begin to speak that it will not go well but I'm bound to tell it, to lay it out like a soiled cloth on our clean table.

"Dennis is sick," I say and at just that moment I know that this truth is an- 37 other bone I buried.

William says, "Yes, he is. Very sick. Have you been over there again? I told 38 you to stay away from them. I warned you. But, knowing you. . . ."

"You don't." 39

"Don't what?" 40

"Know me." I stand up. There is a knot of sorrow that drops in me like a 41 sinker in a tidal pool. I walk out the door and away from William. At the jetty, I climb the slick black rocks, heedless of the cruel pockets of stone that could snap a limb as easy as not. I find a smooth stone that makes a good seat. I'm surprised to know I'm crying. Our porch light comes on and there is William, his pale hair like a halo under its glow. He calls me. "Nora, come home," but the tide takes his voice and swallows my name. When I'm thoroughly chilled and empty of anger, I leave my perch and travel north on the wet sand, close to the cool fingers of incoming tide. I'm a small but competent ship sailing the coast line. I set my own course. I hear someone running in my wake and it's William, breathless from the chase. He passes me on fast feet, then turns, dancing back- ward like a boxer until I stop just shy of the circle of his arms. He carries my sweater, which he puts around my shoulders with great care, as if it is a precious fur he wraps me in and I too am precious. He buttons one button under my chin with clumsy fingers. "Let's go back," he says, so we do. We do not talk about anything, simply walk forward in silence, which is the way it is between hus- bands and wives, with married people.

Raymond Carver (1938–1988)

Intimacy

I have some business out west anyway, so I stop off in this little town where my 1 former wife lives. We haven't seen each other in four years. But from time to time, when something of mine appeared, or was written about me in the maga- zines or papers—a profile or an interview—I sent her these things. I don't know what I had in mind except I thought she might be interested. In any case, she never responded.

It is nine in the morning, I haven't called, and it's true I don't know what I 2
am going to find.

But she lets me in. She doesn't seem surprised. We don't shake hands, much 3
less kiss each other. She takes me into the living room. As soon as I sit down she
brings me some coffee. Then she comes out with what's on her mind. She says
I've caused her anguish, made her feel exposed and humiliated.

Make no mistake, I feel I'm home.   4

She says, But then you were into betrayal early. You always felt comfortable 5
with betrayal. No, she says, that's not true. Not in the beginning, at any rate. You
were different then. But I guess I was different too. Everything was different, she
says. No, it was after you turned thirty-five, or thirty-six, whenever it was,
around in there anyway, your mid-thirties somewhere, then you started in. You
really started in. You turned on me. You did it up pretty then. You must be
proud of yourself.

She says, Sometimes I could scream.   6

She says she wishes I'd forget about the hard times, the bad times, when I 7
talk about back then. Spend some time on the good times, she says. Weren't
there some good times? She wishes I'd get off that other subject. She's bored
with it. Sick of hearing about it. Your private hobby horse, she says. What's done
is done and water under the bridge, she says. A tragedy, yes. God knows it was a
tragedy and then some. But why keep it going? Don't you ever get tired of
dredging up that old business?

She says, Let go of the past, for Christ's sake. Those old hurts. You must have 8
some other arrows in your quiver, she says.

She says, You know something? I think you're sick. I think you're crazy as a 9
bedbug. Hey, you don't believe the things they're saying about you, do you?
Don't believe them for a minute, she says. Listen, I could tell them a thing or
two. Let them talk to me about it, if they want to hear a story.

She says, Are you listening to me?   10

I'm listening, I say. I'm all ears, I say.   11

She says, I've really had a bellyful of it, buster! Who asked you here today 12
anyway? I sure as hell didn't. You just show up and walk in. What the hell do
you want from me? Blood? You want more blood? I thought you had your fill
by now.

She says, Think of me as dead. I want to be left in peace now. That's all I 13
want anymore is to be left in peace and forgotten about. Hey, I'm forty-five
years old, she says. Forty-five going on fifty-five, or sixty-five. Lay off, will you.

She says, Why don't you wipe the blackboard clean and see what you have 14
left after that? Why don't you start with a clean slate? See how far that gets you,
she says.

She has to laugh at this. I laugh too, but it's nerves.   15

She says, You know something? I had my chance once, but I let it go. I just 16
let it go. I don't guess I ever told you. But now look at me. Look! Take a good
look while you're at it. You threw me away, you son of a bitch.

She says, I was younger then and a better person. Maybe you were too, she 17
says. A better person, I mean. You had to be. You were better then or I wouldn't
have had anything to do with you.

She says, I loved you so much once. I loved you to the point of distraction. I 18
did. More than anything in the whole wide world. Imagine that. What a laugh
that is now. Can you imagine it? We were so *intimate* once upon a time I can't
believe it now. I think that's the strangest thing of all now. The memory of being that intimate with somebody. We were so intimate I could puke. I can't
imagine ever being that intimate with somebody else. I haven't been.

She says, Frankly, and I mean this, I want to be kept out of it from here on 19
out. Who do you think you are anyway? You think you're God or somebody?
You're not fit to lick God's boots, or anybody else's for that matter. Mister,
you've been hanging out with the wrong people. But what do I know? I don't
even know what I know any longer. I know I don't like what you've been dishing
out. I know that much. You know what I'm talking about, don't you? Am I
right?

Right, I say. Right as rain. 20

She says, You'll agree to anything, won't you? You give in too easy. You al- 21
ways did. You don't have any principles, not one. Anything to avoid a fuss. But
that's neither here nor there.

She says, You remember that time I pulled the knife on you? 22

She says this as if in passing, as if it's not important. 23

Vaguely, I say. I must have deserved it, but I don't remember much about it. 24
Go ahead, why don't you, and tell me about it.

She says, I'm beginning to understand something now. I think I know why 25
you're here. Yes. I know why you're here, even if you don't. But you're a slyboots.
You know why you're here. You're on a fishing expedition. You're hunting for
material. Am I getting warm? Am I right?

Tell me about the knife, I say. 26

She says, If you want to know, I'm real sorry I didn't use that knife. I am. I 27
really and truly am. I've thought and thought about it, and I'm sorry I didn't
use it. I had the chance. But I hesitated. I hesitated and was lost, as somebody or
other said. But I should have used it, the hell with everything and everybody. I
should have nicked your arm with it at least. At least that.

Well, you didn't, I say. I thought you were going to cut me with it, but you 28
didn't. I took it away from you.

She says, You were always lucky. You took it away and then you slapped me. 29
Still, I regret I didn't use that knife just a little bit. Even a little would have been
something to remember me by.

I remember a lot, I say. I say that, then wish I hadn't. 30

She says, Amen, brother. That's the bone of contention here, if you hadn't 31
noticed. That's the whole problem. But like I said, in my opinion you remember
the wrong things. You remember the low, shameful things. That's why you got
interested when I brought up the knife.

She says, I wonder if you ever have any regret. For whatever that's worth on   32
the market these days. Not much, I guess. But you ought to be a specialist in it
by now.

Regret, I say. It doesn't interest me much, to tell the truth. Regret is not a   33
word I use very often. I guess I mainly don't have it. I admit I hold to the dark
view of things. Sometimes, anyway. But regret? I don't think so.

She says, You're a real son of a bitch, did you know that? A ruthless, cold-   34
hearted son of a bitch. Did anybody ever tell you that?

You did, I say. Plenty of times.   35

She says, I always speak the truth. Even when it hurts. You'll never catch me   36
in a lie.

She says, My eyes were opened a long time ago, but by then it was too late. I   37
had my chance but I let it slide through my fingers. I even thought for a while
you'd come back. Why'd I think that anyway? I must have been out of my mind.
I could cry my eyes out now, but I wouldn't give you that satisfaction.

She says, You know what? I think if you were on fire right now, if you sud-   38
denly burst into flame this minute, I wouldn't throw a bucket of water on you.

She laughs at this. Then her face closes down again.   39

She says, Why in hell *are* you here? You want to hear some more? I could go   40
on for days. I think I know why you turned up, but I want to hear it from you.

When I don't answer, when I just keep sitting there, she goes on.   41

She says, After that time, when you went away, nothing much mattered after   42
that. Not the kids, not God, not anything. It was like I didn't know what hit me.
It was like I had *stopped living*. My life had been going along, going along, and
then it just stopped. It didn't just come to a stop, it screeched to a stop. I
thought, If I'm not worth anything to him, well, I'm not worth anything to myself or anybody else either. That was the worst thing I felt. I thought my heart
would break. What am I saying? It did break. Of course it broke. It broke, just
like that. It's still broke, if you want to know. And so there you have it in a nutshell. My eggs in one basket, she says. A tisket, a tasket. All my rotten eggs in one
basket.

She says, You found somebody else for yourself, didn't you? It didn't take   43
long. And you're happy now. That's what they say about you anyway: "He's
happy now." Hey, I read everything you send! You think I don't? Listen, I know
your heart, mister. I always did. I knew it back then, and I know it now. I know
your heart inside and out, and don't you ever forget it. Your heart is a jungle, a
dark forest, it's a garbage pail, if you want to know. Let them talk to me if they
want to ask somebody something. I know how you operate. Just let them come
around here, and I'll give them an earful. I was there. I served, buddy boy. Then
you held me up for display and ridicule in your so-called work. For any Tom or
Harry to pity or pass judgment on. Ask me if I cared. Ask me if it embarrassed
me. Go ahead, ask.

No, I say, I won't ask that. I don't want to get into that, I say.   44

Damn straight you don't! she says. And you know *why*, too!   45

She says, Honey, no offense, but sometimes I think I could shoot you and 46
watch you kick.

She says, You can't look me in the eyes, can you? 47

She says, and this is exactly what she says, You can't even look me in the eyes 48
when I'm talking to you.

So, okay, I look her in the eyes. 49

She says, Right. Okay, she says. Now we're getting someplace, maybe. That's 50
better. You can tell a lot about the person you're talking to from his eyes. Everybody knows that. But you know something else? There's nobody in this whole
world who would tell you this, but I can tell you. I have the right. I *earned* that
right, sonny. You have yourself confused with somebody else. And that's the
pure truth of it. But what do I know? they'll say in a hundred years. They'll say,
Who was she anyway?

She says, In any case, you sure as hell have *me* confused with somebody else. 51
Hey, I don't even have the same name anymore! Not the name I was born with,
not the name I lived with you with, not even the name I had two years ago.
What is this? What is this in hell all about anyway? Let me say something. I want
to be left alone now. Please. That's not a crime.

She says, Don't you have someplace else you should be? Some plane to 52
catch? Shouldn't you be somewhere far from here at this very minute?

No, I say. I say it again: No. No place, I say. I don't have anyplace I have to be. 53

And then I do something. I reach over and take the sleeve of her blouse be- 54
tween my thumb and forefinger. That's all. I just touch it that way, and then I
just bring my hand back. She doesn't draw away. She doesn't move.

Then here's the thing I do next. I get down on my knees, a big guy like me 55
and I take the hem of her dress. What am I doing on the floor? I wish I could
say. But I know it's where I ought to be, and I'm there on my knees holding on
to the hem of her dress.

She is still for a minute. But in a minute she says, Hey, it's all right, stupid. 56
You're so dumb, sometimes. Get up now. I'm telling you to get up. Listen, it's
okay. I'm over it now. It took me a while to get over it. What do you think? Did
you think it wouldn't? Then you walk in here and suddenly the whole cruddy
business is back. I felt a need to ventilate. But you know, and I know, it's over
and done with now.

She says, For the longest while, honey, I was inconsolable. *Inconsolable,* she 57
says. Put that word in your little notebook. I can tell you from experience that's
the saddest word in the English language. Anyway, I got over it finally. Time is a
gentleman, a wise man said. Or else maybe a worn-out old woman, one or the
other anyway.

She says, I have a life now. It's a different kind of life than yours, but I guess 58
we don't need to compare. It's my life, and that's the important thing I have to
realize as I get older. Don't feel *too* bad, anyway, she says. I mean, it's all right to
feel a *little* bad, maybe. That won't hurt you, that's only to be expected after all.
Even if you can't move yourself to regret.

She says, Now you have to get up and get out of here. My husband will be   59
along pretty soon for his lunch. How would I explain this kind of thing?

It's crazy, but I'm still on my knees holding the hem of her dress. I won't let   60
it go. I'm like a terrier, and it's like I'm stuck to the floor. It's like I can't move.

She says, Get up now. What is it? You still want something from me. What   61
do you want? Want me to forgive you? Is that why you're doing this? That's it,
isn't it? That's the reason you came all this way. The knife thing kind of perked
you up, too. I think you'd forgotten about that. But you needed me to remind
you. Okay. I'll say something if you'll just go.

She says, I forgive you.   62

She says, Are you satisfied now? Is that better? Are you happy? He's happy   63
now, she says.

But I'm still there, knees to the floor.   64

She says, Did you hear what I said? You have to go now. Hey, stupid. Honey,   65
I said I forgive you. And I even reminded you about the knife thing. I can't
think what else I can do now. You got it made in the shade, baby. Come *on* now,
you have to get out of here. Get up. That's right. You're still a big guy, aren't you.
Here's your hat, don't forget your hat.

You never used to wear a hat. I never in my life saw you in a hat before.   66

She says, Listen to me now. Look at me. Listen carefully to what I'm going to   67
tell you.

She moves closer. She's about three inches from my face. We haven't been   68
this close in a long time. I take these little breaths that she can't hear, and I wait.
I think my heart slows way down, I think.

She says, You just tell it like you have to, I guess, and forget the rest. Like al-   69
ways. You been doing that for so long now anyway it shouldn't be hard for you.

She says, There, I've done it. You're free, aren't you? At least you think you   70
are anyway. Free at last. That's a joke, but don't laugh. Anyway, you feel better,
don't you?

She walks with me down the hall.   71

She says, I can't imagine how I'd explain this if my husband was to walk in   72
this very minute. But who really cares anymore, right? In the final analysis, nobody gives a damn anymore. Besides which, I think everything that can happen
that way has already happened. His name is Fred, by the way. He's a decent guy
and works hard for his living. He cares for me.

So she walks me to the front door, which has been standing open all this   73
while. The door that was letting in light and fresh air this morning, and sounds
off the street, all of which we had ignored. I looked outside and, Jesus, there's
this white moon hanging in the morning sky. I can't think when I've ever seen
anything so remarkable. But I'm afraid to comment on it. I am. I don't know
what might happen. I might break into tears even. I might not understand a
word I'd say.

She says, Maybe you'll be back sometime, and maybe you won't. This'll wear   74
off, you know. Pretty soon you'll start feeling bad again. Maybe it'll make a
good story, she says. But I don't want to know about it if it does.

I say good-bye. She doesn't say anything more. She looks at her hands, and 75 then she puts them into the pockets of her dress. She shakes her head. She goes back inside, and this time she closes the door.

I move off down the sidewalk. Some kids are tossing a football at the end of 76 the street. But they aren't my kids, and they aren't her kids either. There are these leaves everywhere, even in the gutters. Piles of leaves wherever I look. They're falling off the limbs as I walk. I can't take a step without putting my shoe into leaves. Somebody ought to make an effort here. Somebody ought to get a rake and take care of this.

Poems

William Shakespeare (1564–1616)

Sonnet 18

Shall I compare thee to a summer's day?
Thou art more lovely and more temperate:
Rough winds do shake the darling buds of May,
And summer's lease hath all too short a date;
Sometime too hot the eye of heaven shines,   5
And often is his gold complexion dimm'd,
And every fair from fair sometime declines,
By chance or nature's changing course untrimm'd:
But thy eternal summer shall not fade,
Nor lose possession of that fair thou ow'st,   10
Nor shall Death brag thou wand'rest in his shade,
When in eternal lines to time thou grow'st.
    So long as men can breathe or eyes can see,
    So long lives this, and this gives life to thee.

[line] 1. **a summer's day:** i.e. the summer season.
 2. **temperate:** of even temperature.
 4. **lease:** allotted time.   **date:** duration.
 7. **fair . . . fair:** beautiful thing . . . beauty.
 8. **untrimm'd:** divested of beauty.
10. **ow'st:** ownest.
12. **to . . . grow'st:** you become inseparably engrafted upon time.

Walt Whitman (1819–1892)

Twenty-eight young men bathe by the shore

Twenty-eight young men bathe by the shore,   1
Twenty-eight young men and all so friendly;
Twenty-eight years of womanly life and all so lonesome.

She owns the fine house by the rise of the bank,
She hides handsome and richly drest aft the blinds of the window.   5

Which of the young men does she like the best?
Ah the homeliest of them is beautiful to her.

Where are you off to, lady? for I see you,
You splash in the water there, yet stay stock still in your room.

Dancing and laughing along the beach came the twenty-ninth bather,   10
The rest did not see her, but she saw them and loved them.

The beards of the young men glisten'd with wet, it ran from their
    long hair,
Little streams pass'd all over their bodies.

An unseen hand also pass'd over their bodies,
It descended tremblingly from their temples and ribs.   15

The young men float on their backs, their white bellies bulge to
    the sun, they do not ask who seizes fast to them,
They do not know who puffs and declines with pendant and bend-
    ing arch,
They do not think whom they souse with spray.

ACTIVITIES FOR WRITING AND DISCUSSION

1. It has been said that no verse is entirely "free" (that is, without verbal or rhythmic patterning of some sort). What sorts of patterning does Whitman use to replace the **rhyme** and **meter** of **traditional verse**? To answer this question, begin by making a list of everything that strikes you in this poem; for instance, words and phrases, images, and feelings. Then review the poem and identify the pattern(s). Finally, consider how Whitman's type of pattern supplants traditional rhyme and meter.

2. Whitman believed that the function of a poem is to impel readers along individual paths of thought and growth. Thus he wrote that a poem "is no fin-

ish to a man or woman" and that "the reader . . . must himself or herself construct indeed the poem . . . the text furnishing the hints, the clue, the start or frame-work." Taking the poet at his word, treat "Twenty-eight young men" as a "start" to some imaginative writing of your own. For instance:

    a. Use the poem as a pathway to meditation. Begin by memorizing the poem, reciting it to yourself, and living with it a while. Keep a written record of any thoughts or feelings that occur to you as a result of this process.

    b. Write a poem of your own that employs the long and flowing lines of "Twenty-eight young men."

    c. Write the story of the twenty-ninth bather. Who is she? What is her past? How does she come to be standing at that window? What are the sources of her desire?

Christina Rossetti (1830–1894)

Margery

What shall we do with Margery?
   She lies and cries upon her bed,
   All lily-pale from foot to head,
Her heart is sore as sore can be;
Poor guileless shamefaced Margery.   5

A foolish girl, to love a man
   And let him know she loved him so!
She should have tried a different plan;
   Have loved, but not have let him know:
   Then he perhaps had loved her so.   10

What can we do with Margery
   Who has no relish for her food?
We'd take her with us to the sea—
   Across the sea—but where's the good?
She'd fret alike on land and sea.   15

Yes, what the neighbours say is true:
   Girls should not make themselves so cheap.
But now it's done what can we do?
   I hear her moaning in her sleep.
   Moaning and sobbing in her sleep.   20

I think—and I'm of flesh and blood—
   Were I that man for whom she cares

I would not cost her tears and prayers
To leave her just alone like mud,
    Fretting her simple heart with cares.   25

A year ago she was a child,
    Now she's a woman in her grief;
    The year's now at the falling leaf,
At budding of the leaves she smiled;
Poor foolish harmless foolish child.   30

It was her own fault? so it was.
    If every own fault found us out
    Dogged us and snared us round about,
What comfort should we take because
    Not half our due we thus wrung out?   35

At any rate the question stands:
    What now to do with Margery,
A weak poor creature on our hands?
    Something we must do: I'll not see
    Her blossom fade, sweet Margery.   40

Perhaps a change may after all
    Prove best for her: to leave behind
    Those home-sights seen time out of mind;
To get beyond the narrow wall
Of home, and learn home is not all.   45

Perhaps this way she may forget,
    Not all at once, but in a while;
May come to wonder how she set
    Her heart on this slight thing, and smile
    At her own folly, in a while.   50

Yet this I say and I maintain:
    Were I the man she's fretting for
    I should my very self abhor
If I could leave her to her pain,
Uncomforted to tears and pain.   55

Ezra Pound (1885–1972)

The River-merchant's Wife: A Letter

While my hair was still cut straight across my forehead
Played I about the front gate, pulling flowers.
You came by on bamboo stilts, playing horse,
You walked about my seat, playing with blue plums.
And we went on living in the village of Chōkan: 5
Two small people, without dislike or suspicion.

At fourteen I married My Lord you.
I never laughed, being bashful.
Lowering my head, I looked at the wall.
Called to, a thousand times, I never looked back.   10

At fifteen I stopped scowling,
I desired my dust to be mingled with yours
Forever and forever and forever.
Why should I climb the look out?

At sixteen you departed,   15
You went into far Ku-tō-en, by the river of swirling eddies,
And you have been gone five months.
The monkeys make sorrowful noise overhead.

You dragged your feet when you went out.
By the gate now, the moss is grown, the different mosses, 20
Too deep to clear them away!
The leaves fall early this autumn, in wind.
The paired butterflies are already yellow with August
Over the grass in the West garden;
They hurt me. I grow older.   25
If you are coming down through the narrows of the river Kiang,
Please let me know beforehand,
And I will come out to meet you
        As far as Chō-fū-Sa.

　　　　　　　—By Rihaku (Li T'ai Po)

Ishigaki Rin (b. 1920)

The Pan, the Pot, the Fire I Have Before Me

For a long time
these things have always been placed
before us women:

the pan of a reasonable size
suited to the user's strength,   5
the pot in which it's convenient for rice
to begin to swell and shine, grain by grain,
the glow of the fire inherited from time immemorial—
before these there have always been
mothers, grandmothers, and their mothers   10

What measures of love and sincerity
these persons must have poured
into these utensils—
now red carrots,
now black seaweed,   15
now crushed fish

in the kitchen, always accurately
for morning, noon, and evening, preparations have been made
and before the preparations, in a row, there have always been
some pairs of warm knees and hands.   20

Ah without those persons waiting
how could women have gone on
cooking so happily?
their unflagging care,
so daily a service they became unconscious of it.   25

Cooking was mysteriously assigned
to women, as a role,
but I don't think that was unfortunate;
because of that, their knowledge and positions in society
may have lagged behind the times   30
but it isn't too late:
the things we have before us,
the pan and the pot, and the burning fire,

before these familiar things,
let us study government, economy, literature   35

as sincerely
as we cook potatoes and meat.

not for vanity and promotion
but so everyone   40
may serve all
so everyone may work for love.

   —*Translated by Hiroaki Sato*

ACTIVITIES FOR WRITING AND DISCUSSION

1. Make a list of stories you have heard or read about cooking, women, or politics. Jot down notes on the **characters** in these stories (from books, film, television) and be prepared to share them in your small group.

2. Reread the fourth and fifth **stanzas.** To whom might "pairs of warm knees and hands" refer, and why might the speaker allude to them as "knees" and "hands" instead of as people?

3. Commenting on specific lines or phrases in the poem, attack and/or defend the following statement: "Experiences with 'the pan, the pot, [and] the fire' have nothing to do with preparing women for a role in 'government, economy, [and] literature.'"

Robert Bly (b. 1926)

In Rainy September

In rainy September, when leaves grow down to the dark,
I put my forehead down to the damp, seaweed-smelling sand.
The time has come. I have put off choosing for years,
perhaps whole lives. The fern has no choice but to live;
for this crime it receives earth, water, and night.   5

We close the door. "I have no claim on you."
Dusk comes. "The love I have had with you is enough."
We know we could live apart from one another.
The sheldrake floats apart from the flock.
The oaktree puts out leaves alone on the lonely hillside.   10

Men and women before us have accomplished this.
I would see you, and you me, once a year.
We would be two kernels, and not be planted.

We stay in the room, door closed, lights out.
I weep with you without shame and without honor.   15

My Father's Wedding 1924

Today, lonely for my father, I saw
a log, or branch,
long, bent, ragged, bark gone.
I felt lonely for my father when I saw it.
It was the log   5
that lay near my uncle's old milk wagon.

Some men live with an invisible limp,
stagger, or drag
a leg. Their sons are often angry.
Only recently I thought: 10
Doing what you want . . .
Is that like limping? Tracks of it show in sand.

Have you seen those giant bird-
men of Bhutan?
Men in bird masks, with pig noses, dancing,   15
teeth like a dog's, sometimes
dancing on one bad leg!
They do what they want, the dog's teeth say that!

But I grew up without dogs' teeth,
showed a whole body,   20
left only clear tracks in sand.
I learned to walk swiftly, easily,
no trace of a limp.
I even leaped a little. Guess where my defect is!

Then what? If a man, cautious   25
hides his limp,
Somebody has to limp it! Things
do it; the surroundings limp.
House walls get scars,
the car breaks down; matter, in drudgery, takes it up.   30

On my father's wedding day,
no one was there
to hold him. Noble loneliness
held him. Since he never asked for pity

his friends thought he   35
was whole. Walking alone, he could carry it.

He came in limping. It was a simple
wedding, three
or four people. The man in black,
lifting the book, called for order.   40
And the invisible bride
stepped forward, before his own bride.

He married the invisible bride, not his own.
In her left
breast she carried the three drops   45
that wound and kill. He already had
his barklike skin then,
made rough especially to repel the sympathy

he longed for, didn't need, and wouldn't accept.
They stopped. So   50
the words are read. The man in black
speaks the sentence. When the service
is over, I hold him
in my arms for the first time and the last.

After that he was alone   55
and I was alone.
No friends came; he invited none.
His two-story house he turned
into a forest,
where both he and I are the hunters.   60

Adrienne Rich (b. 1929)

Living in Sin

She had thought the studio would keep itself;
no dust upon the furniture of love.
Half heresy, to wish the taps less vocal,
the panes relieved of grime. A plate of pears,
a piano with a Persian shawl, a cat   5
stalking the picturesque amusing mouse
had risen at his urging.

Not that at five each separate stair would writhe
under the milkman's tramp; that morning light
so coldly would delineate the scraps   10
of last night's cheese and three sepulchral bottles;
that on the kitchen shelf among the saucers
a pair of beetle-eyes would fix her own—
envoy from some village in the moldings . . .
Meanwhile, he, with a yawn,   15
sounded a dozen notes upon the keyboard,
declared it out of tune, shrugged at the mirror,
rubbed at his beard, went out for cigarettes;
while she, jeered by the minor demons,
pulled back the sheets and made the bed and found   20
a towel to dust the table-top,
and let the coffee-pot boil over on the stove.
By evening she was back in love again,
though not so wholly but throughout the night
she woke sometimes to feel the daylight coming   25
like a relentless milkman up the stairs.

Aunt Jennifer's Tigers

Aunt Jennifer's tigers prance across a screen,
Bright topaz denizens of a world of green.
They do not fear the men beneath the tree;
They pace in sleek chivalric certainty.

Aunt Jennifer's fingers fluttering through her wool   5
Find even the ivory needle hard to pull.
The massive weight of Uncle's wedding band
Sits heavily upon Aunt Jennifer's hand.

When Aunt is dead, her terrified hands will lie
Still ringed with ordeals she was mastered by.   10
The tigers in the panel that she made
Will go on prancing, proud and unafraid.

Tomioka Taeko (b. 1935)

Just the Two of Us

You'll make tea,
I'll make toast.
While we're doing that,
at times, early in the evening,
someone may notice the moonrise dyed scarlet   5
and at times visit us
but that'll be the last time the person comes here.
We'll shut the doors, lock them,
make tea, make toast,
talk as usual about how   10
sooner or later
there will be a time
you bury me,
and I bury you, in the garden,
and go out as usual to look for food.   15
There will be a time
either you or I
bury either me or you in the garden
and the one left, sipping tea,
then for the first time, will refuse fiction.   20
Even your freedom
was like a fool's story.

—*Translated by Burton Watson and Hiroaki Sato*

ACTIVITIES FOR WRITING AND DISCUSSION

1. Who are the "you" and the "I" in this poem? How would you characterize
their relationship? their lives?

2. Underline or circle any words or phrases that are repeated in the poem.
Why are they repeated, and to what effect?

3. What is the "fiction" referred to in the third-to-last line? In the context of
this poem, is living by "fiction" a virtue or a weakness? How do you interpret
the last two lines?

4. Using details in the poem and your own imagination, tell the story of
a typical day in the lives of this couple, or, writing from the **point of view**
of the surviving partner, narrate the events of the day on which one partner
dies.

Diane Wakoski (b. 1937)

Belly Dancer

Can these movements which move themselves
be the substance of my attraction?
Where does this thin green silk come from that covers my body?
Surely any woman wearing such fabrics
would move her body just to feel them touching every part of her.   5

Yet most of the women frown, or look away, or laugh stiffly.
They are afraid of these materials and these movements in some way.
The psychologists would say they are afraid of themselves, somehow.
Perhaps awakening too much desire—
that their men could never satisfy?   10

So they keep themselves laced and buttoned and made up
in hopes that the framework will keep them stiff enough not to feel
the whole register.
In hopes that they will not have to experience that unquenchable desire
for rhythm and contact.   15

If a snake glided across this floor
most of them would faint or shrink away.
Yet that movement could be their own.
That smooth movement frightens them—
awakening ancestors and relatives to the tips of the arms and toes.   20

So my bare feet
and my thin green silks
my bells and finger cymbals
offend them—frighten their old-young bodies.
While the men simper and leer—   25
glad for the vicarious experience and exercise.
They do not realize how I scorn them:
or how I dance for their frightened,
unawakened, sweet
women.   30

ACTIVITIES FOR WRITING AND DISCUSSION

1. Circle any lines, images, or other features that make this poem sensual.
What senses (other than sight) are evoked? In which lines and phrases? To
what effect(s)?

2. In lines 16–18 the **speaker** imagines the movement of "a snake" and suggests that the women both fear it (they "would faint or shrink away") and desire it ("that movement could be their own"). How do you explain this apparent contradiction?

3. Imagine you are a woman in the dancer's audience. Borrowing details from the poem and writing in a **stream of consciousness** mode, express the emotions and conflicts you have as you watch the dancer dance.

4. As an alternative to Activity #3, imagine yourself to be an audience member of a different sexual orientation, or disabled, or of a different cultural/racial identity. From any of these **points of view,** what do you celebrate or denounce in what you see? What voices from your culture do you hear influencing your voice and the content of your writing?

Sharon Olds (b. 1942)

Sex Without Love

How do they do it, the ones who make love
without love? Beautiful as dancers,
gliding over each other like ice-skaters
over the ice, fingers hooked
inside each other's bodies, faces   5
red as steak, wine, wet as the
children at birth whose mothers are going to
give them away. How do they come to the
come to the   come to the   God   come to the
still waters, and not love   10
the one who came there with them, light
rising slowly as steam off their joined
skin? These are the true religious,
the purists, the pros, the ones who will not
accept a false Messiah, love the   15
priest instead of the God. They do not
mistake the lover for their own pleasure,
they are like great runners: they know they are alone
with the road surface, the cold, the wind,
the fit of their shoes, their over-all cardio-   20
vascular health—just factors, like the partner
in the bed, and not the truth, which is the
single body alone in the universe
against its own best time.

Liz Rosenberg (b. 1958)

In the End, We Are All Light

I love how old men carry purses for their wives,
those stiff light beige or navy wedge-shaped bags
that match the women's pumps,
with small gold clasps that click open and shut.
The men drowse off in medical center waiting rooms,   5
with bags perched in their laps like big tame birds
too worn to flap away. Within, the wives slowly undress,
put on the thin white robes, consult, come out
and wake the husbands dreaming openmouthed.

And when they both rise up   10
to take their constitutional,
walk up and down the block, her arms are free as air,
his right hand dangles down.

So I, desiring to shed this skin
for some light silken one,   15
will tell my husband, "Here, hold this,"
and watch him amble off into the mall among the shining
cans of motor oil, my leather bag
slung over his massive shoulder bone,
so prettily slender-waisted, so forgiving of the ways   20
we hold each other down, that watching him
I see how men love women, and women men,
and how the burden of the other comes to be
light as a feather blown, more quickly vanishing.

ACTIVITIES FOR WRITING AND DISCUSSION

1. Underline images in the poem that strike you. In your notebook, react to one or two of these images by doing some writing or by drawing a realistic or cartoon picture based on the image(s). What sorts of feelings do the images evoke in you? How would you describe the relationship that is suggested between the "old men"/husbands and their wives?

2. How would the poem change if the "old men" were replaced by "young men" with young wives? Does the poem imply any differences between "old" couples and young? If so, what differences?

3. Interpret the last several lines. How or why *does* "the burden of the other [come] to be/light as a feather blown"?

Nonfiction/Essay

Scott Russell Sanders (b. 1945)

Looking at Women

On that sizzling July afternoon, the girl who crossed at the stoplight in front of our car looked, as my mother would say, as though she had been poured into her pink shorts. The girl's matching pink halter bared her stomach and clung to her nubbin breasts, leaving little to the imagination, as my mother would also say. Until that moment, it had never made any difference to me how much or little a girl's clothing revealed, for my imagination had been entirely devoted to other mysteries. I was eleven. The girl was about fourteen, the age of my buddy Norman who lounged in the back seat with me. Staring after her, Norman elbowed me in the ribs and murmured, "Check out that chassis."

His mother glared around from the driver's seat. "Hush your mouth."

"I was talking about that sweet Chevy," said Norman, pointing out a souped-up jalopy at the curb.

"I know what you were talking about," his mother snapped.

No doubt she did know, since mothers could read minds, but at first I did 5 not have a clue. Chassis? I knew what it meant for a car, an airplane, a radio, or even a cannon to have a chassis. But could a girl have one as well? I glanced after the retreating figure, and suddenly noticed with a sympathetic twitching in my belly the way her long raven ponytail swayed in rhythm to her walk and the way her fanny jostled in those pink shorts. In July's dazzle of sun, her swinging legs and arms beamed at me a semaphore I could almost read.

As the light turned green and our car pulled away, Norman's mother cast one more scowl at her son in the rearview mirror, saying, "Just think how it makes her feel to have you two boys gawking at her."

How? I wondered.

"Makes her feel like hot stuff," said Norman, owner of a bold mouth.

"If you don't get your mind out of the gutter, you're going to wind up in the state reformatory," said his mother.

Norman gave a snort. I sank into the seat, and tried to figure out what 10 power had sprung from that sashaying girl to zap me in the belly.

Only after much puzzling did it dawn on me that I must finally have drifted into the force-field of sex, as a space traveler who has lived all his years in free fall might rocket for the first time within gravitational reach of a star. Even as a bashful eleven-year-old I knew the word *sex*, of course, and I could paste that name across my image of the tantalizing girl. But a label for a mystery no more explains a mystery than the word *gravity* explains gravity. As I grew a beard and my taste shifted from girls to women, I acquired a more cagey language for speaking of desire, I picked up disarming theories. First by hearsay and then by experiment, I learned the delicious details of making babies. I came to appreciate the urgency for propagation that litters the road with maple seeds and drives salmon up waterfalls and yokes the newest crop of boys to the newest crop of girls. Books in their killjoy wisdom taught me that all the valentines and violins, the waltzes and glances, the long fever and ache of romance, were merely embellishments on biology's instructions that we multiply our kind. And yet, the fraction of desire that actually leads to procreation is so vanishingly small as to seem irrelevant. In his lifetime a man sways to a million longings, only a few of which, or perhaps none at all, ever lead to the fathering of children. Now, thirty years away from that July afternoon, firmly married, twice a father, I am still humming from the power unleashed by the girl in pink shorts, still wondering how it made her feel to have two boys gawk at her, still puzzling over how to dwell in the force-field of desire.

How should a man look at women? It is a peculiarly and perhaps neurotically human question. Billy goats do not fret over how they should look at nanny goats. They look or don't look, as seasons and hormones dictate, and feel what they feel without benefit of theory. There is more billy goat in most men than we care to admit. None of us, however, is pure goat. To live utterly as an animal would make the business of sex far tidier but also drearier. If we tried, like Rousseau, to peel off the layers of civilization and imagine our way back to some pristine man and woman who have not yet been corrupted by hand-me-down notions of sexuality, my hunch is that we would find, in our speculative state of nature, that men regarded women with appalling simplicity. In any case, unlike goats, we dwell in history. What attracts our eyes and rouses our blood is only partly instinctual. Other forces contend in us as well: the voices of books and religions, the images of art and film and advertising, the entire chorus of culture. Norman's telling me to relish the sight of females and his mother's telling me to keep my eyes to myself are only two of the many voices quarreling in my head.

If there were a rule book for sex, it would be longer than the one for baseball (that byzantine sport), more intricate and obscure than tax instructions from the Internal Revenue Service. What I present here are a few images and reflections that cling, for me, to this one item in such a compendium of rules: How should a man look at women?

Well before I was to see any women naked in the flesh, I saw a bevy of them naked in photographs, hung in a gallery around the bed of my freshman roommate at college. A *Playboy* subscriber, he would pluck the centerfold from its staples each month and tape another airbrushed lovely to the wall. The gallery was in place when I moved in, and for an instant before I realized what I was looking at, all that expanse of skin reminded me of a meat locker back in Newton Falls, Ohio. I never quite shook that first impression, even after I had inspected the pinups at my leisure on subsequent days. Every curve of buttock and breast was news to me, an innocent kid from the Puritan back roads. Today you would be hard pressed to find a college freshman as ignorant as I was of female anatomy, if only because teenagers now routinely watch movies at home that would have been shown, during my teen years, exclusively on the fly-speckled screens of honky-tonk cinemas or in the basement of the Kinsey Institute. I studied those alien shapes on the wall with a curiosity that was not wholly sexual, a curiosity tinged with the wonder that astronomers must have felt when they pored over the early photographs of the far side of the moon.

The paper women seemed to gaze back at me, enticing or mocking, yet even 15 in my adolescent dither I was troubled by the phony stare, for I knew this was no true exchange of looks. Those mascaraed eyes were not fixed on me but on a camera. What the models felt as they posed I could only guess—perhaps the boredom of any numbskull job, perhaps the weight of dollar bills, perhaps the sweltering lights of fame, perhaps a tingle of the power that launched a thousand ships.

Whatever their motives, these women had chosen to put themselves on display. For the instant of the photograph, they had become their bodies, as a prizefighter does in the moment of landing a punch, as a weightlifter does in the moment of hoisting a barbell, as a ballerina does in the whirl of a pirouette, as we all do in the crisis of making love or dying. Men, ogling such photographs, are supposed to feel that where so much surface is revealed there can be no depths. Yet I never doubted that behind the makeup and the plump curves and the two dimensions of the image there was an inwardness, a feeling self as mysterious as my own. In fact, during moments when I should have been studying French or thermodynamics, I would glance at my roommate's wall and invent mythical lives for those goddesses. The lives I made up were adolescent ones, to be sure, but so was mine. Without that saving aura of inwardness, these women in the glossy photographs would have become merely another category of objects for sale, alongside the sports cars and stereo systems and liquors advertised in the same pages. If not extinguished, however, their humanity was severely reduced. And if by simplifying themselves they had lost some human essence, then by gaping at them I had shared in the theft.

What did that gaping take from me? How did it affect my way of seeing other women, those who would never dream of lying nude on a fake tiger rug before the million-faceted eye of a camera? The bodies in the photographs were implausibly smooth and slick and inflated, like balloon caricatures that might be floated overhead in a parade. Free of sweat and scars and imperfections, sensual without being fertile, tempting yet impregnable, they were Platonic ideals of the female form, divorced from time and the fluster of living, excused from the perplexities of mind. No actual woman could rival their insipid perfection.

The swains who gathered to admire my roommate's gallery discussed the pinups in the same tones and in much the same language as the farmers back home in Ohio used for assessing cows. The relevant parts of male and female bodies are quickly named—and, the *Kamasutra* and Marquis de Sade notwithstanding, the number of ways in which those parts can be stimulated or conjoined is touchingly small—so these studly conversations were more tedious than chitchat about the weather. I would lie on my bunk pondering calculus or Aeschylus and unwillingly hear the same few nouns and fewer verbs issuing from one mouth after another, and I would feel smugly superior. Here I was, improving my mind, while theirs wallowed in the notorious gutter. Eventually the swains would depart, leaving me in peace, and from the intellectual heights of my bunk I would glance across at those photographs—and yield to the gravity of lust. Idiot flesh! How stupid that a counterfeit stare and artful curves, printed in millions of copies on glossy paper, could arouse me. But there it was, not the first proof of my body's automatism and not the last.

Nothing in men is more machinelike than the flipping of sexual switches. I have never been able to read with a straight face the claims made by D. H. Lawrence and lesser pundits that the penis is a god, a lurking dragon. It more nearly resembles a railroad crossing signal, which stirs into life at intervals to announce, "Here comes a train." Or, if the penis must be likened to an animal, let it be an ill-trained circus dog, sitting up and playing dead and heeling whenever it takes a notion, oblivious of the trainer's commands. Meanwhile, heart, lungs, blood vessels, pupils, and eyelids all assert their independence like the members of a rebellious troupe. Reason stands helpless at the center of the ring, cracking its whip.

While he was president, Jimmy Carter raised a brouhaha by confessing in a 20 *Playboy* interview, of all shady places, that he occasionally felt lust in his heart for women. What man hasn't, aside from those who feel lust in their hearts for other men? The commentators flung their stones anyway. Naughty, naughty, they chirped. Wicked Jimmy. Perhaps Mr. Carter could derive some consolation from psychologist Allen Wheelis, who blames male appetite on biology: "We have been selected for desiring. Nothing could have convinced us by argument that it would be worthwhile to chase endlessly and insatiably after women, but something has transformed us from within, a plasmid has invaded our DNA, has twisted our nature so that now this is exactly what we *want* to do." Certainly, by Darwinian logic, those males who were most avid in their pursuit of females were also the most likely to pass on their genes. Consoling it may be, yet it is finally no solution to blame biology. "I am extremely sexual in my desires: I carry them everywhere and at all times," William Carlos Williams tells us on the opening page of his autobiography. "I think that from that arises the drive which empowers us all. Given that drive, a man does with it what his mind directs. In the manner in which he directs that power lies his secret." Whatever the contents of my DNA, however potent the influence of my ancestors, I still must direct that rebellious power. I still must live with the consequences of my looking and my longing.

Aloof on their blankets like goddesses on clouds, the pinups did not belong to my funky world. I was invisible to them, and they were immune to my gaze. Not so the women who passed me on the street, sat near me in classes, shared a table with me in the cafeteria: it was risky to stare at them. They could gaze back, and sometimes did, with looks both puzzling and exciting. It only complicated matters for me to realize that so many of these strangers had taken precautions that men should notice them. The girl in matching pink halter and shorts who set me humming in my eleventh year might only have wanted to keep cool in the sizzle of July. But these alluring college femmes had deeper designs. Perfume, eye shadow, uplift bras (about which I learned in the Sears catalog), curled hair, stockings, jewelry, lipstick, lace—what were these if not hooks thrown out into male waters?

I recall being mystified in particular by spike heels. They looked painful to me, and dangerous. Danger may have been the point, since the spikes would have made good weapons—they were affectionately known, after all, as stilettos. Or danger may have been the point in another sense, because a woman teetering along on such heels is tipsy, vulnerable, broadcasting her need for support. And who better than a man to prop her up, some guy who clomps around in brogans wide enough for the cornerstones of flying buttresses? (For years after college, I felt certain that spike heels had been forever banned, like bustles and foot-binding, but lately they have come back in fashion, and once more one encounters women teetering along on knife points.)

Back in those days of my awakening to women, I was also baffled by lingerie. I do not mean underwear, the proletariat of clothing, and I do not mean foundation garments, pale and sensible. I mean what the woman who lives in the house behind ours—owner of a shop called "Bare Essentials"—refers to as "intimate apparel." Those two words announce that her merchandise is both sexy and expensive. These flimsy items cost more per ounce than truffles, more than frankincense and myrrh. They are put-ons whose only purpose is in being taken off. I have a friend who used to attend the men's-only nights at Bare Essentials, during which he would invariably buy a slinky outfit or two, by way of proving his serious purpose, outfits that wound up in the attic because his wife would not be caught dead in them. Most of the customers at the shop are women, however, as the models are women, and the owner is a woman. What should one make of that? During my college days I knew about intimate apparel only by rumor, not being that intimate with anyone who would have tricked herself out in such finery, but I could see the spike heels and other female trappings everywhere I turned. Why, I wondered then and wonder still, do so many women decorate themselves like dolls? And does that mean they wish to be viewed as dolls?

On this question as on many others, Simone de Beauvoir has clarified matters for me, writing in *The Second Sex:* "The 'feminine' woman in making herself prey tries to reduce man, also, to her carnal passivity; she occupies herself in catching him in her trap, in enchaining him by means of the desires she arouses in him in submissively making herself a thing." Those women who transform themselves into dolls, in other words, do so because that is the most potent identity available to them. "It must be admitted," Beauvoir concedes, "that the males find in woman more complicity than the oppressor usually finds in the oppressed. And in bad faith they take authorization from this to declare that she has *desired* the destiny they have imposed on her."

Complicity, oppressor, bad faith: such terms yank us into a moral realm un-   25 known to goats. While I am saddled with enough male guilt to believe three-quarters of Beauvoir's claim, I still doubt that men are so entirely to blame for the turning of women into sexual dolls. I believe human history is more collaborative than her argument would suggest. It seems unlikely to me that one-half the species could have "imposed" a destiny on the other half, unless that other half were far more craven than the females I have known. Some women have expressed their own skepticism on this point. Thus Joan Didion: "That many women are victims of condescension and exploitation and sex-role stereotyping was scarcely news, but neither was it news that other women are not: nobody forces women to buy the package." Beauvoir herself recognized that many members of her sex refuse to buy the "feminine" package: "The emancipated woman, on the contrary, wants to be active, a taker, and refuses the passivity man means to impose on her."

Since my college years, back in the murky 1960s, emancipated women have been discouraging their unemancipated sisters from making spectacles of themselves. Don't paint your face like a clown's or drape your body like a mannequin's, they say. Don't bounce on the sidelines in skimpy outfits, screaming your fool head off, while men compete in the limelight for victories. Don't present yourself to the world as a fluff pastry, delicate and edible. Don't waddle across the stage in a bathing suit in hopes of being named Miss This or That.

A great many women still ignore the exhortations. Wherever a crown for beauty is to be handed out, many still line up to stake their claims. Recently, Miss Indiana Persimmon Festival was quoted in our newspaper about the burdens of possessing the sort of looks that snag men's eyes. "Most of the time I enjoy having guys stare at me," she said, "but every once in a while it makes me feel like a piece of meat." The news photograph showed a cheerleader's perky face, heavily made-up, with starched hair teased into a blond cumulus. She put me in mind not of meat but of a plastic figurine, something you might buy from a booth outside a shrine. Nobody should ever be seen as meat, mere juicy stuff to satisfy an appetite. Better to appear as a plastic figurine, which is not meant for eating, and which is a gesture, however crude, toward art. Joyce described the aesthetic response as a contemplation of form without the impulse to action. Perhaps that is what Miss Indiana Persimmon Festival wishes to inspire in those who look at her, perhaps that is what many women who paint and primp themselves desire: to withdraw from the touch of hands and dwell in the eye alone, to achieve the status of art.

By turning herself (or allowing herself to be turned into) a work of art, does a woman truly escape men's proprietary stare? Not often, says the British critic

John Berger. Summarizing the treatment of women in Western painting, he concludes that—with a few notable exceptions, such as works by Rubens and Rembrandt—the woman on canvas is a passive object displayed for the pleasure of the male viewer, especially for the owner of the painting, who is, by extension, owner of the woman herself. Berger concludes: "Men look at women. Women watch themselves being looked at. This determines not only most relations between men and women but also the relation of women to themselves. The surveyor of woman in herself is male: the surveyed female. Thus she turns herself into an object—and most particularly an object of vision: a sight."

That sweeping claim, like the one quoted earlier from Beauvoir, also seems to me about three-quarters truth and one-quarter exaggeration. I know men who outdo the peacock for show, and I know women who are so fully possessed of themselves that they do not give a hang whether anybody notices them or not. The flamboyant gentlemen portrayed by Van Dyck are no less aware of being *seen* than are the languid ladies portrayed by Ingres. With or without clothes, both gentlemen and ladies may conceive of themselves as objects of vision, targets of envy or admiration or desire. Where they differ is in their potential for action: the men are caught in the midst of a decisive gesture or on the verge of making one; the women wait like fuel for someone else to strike a match.

I am not sure the abstract nudes favored in modern art are much of an advance over the inert and voluptuous ones of the old school. Think of two famous examples: Duchamp's *Nude Descending a Staircase* (1912), where the faceless woman has blurred into a waterfall of jagged shards, or Picasso's *Les Demoiselles d'Avignon* (1907), where the five angular damsels have been hammered as flat as cookie sheets and fitted with African masks. Neither painting invites us to behold a woman, but instead to behold what Picasso or Duchamp can make of one.

The naked women in Rubens, far from being passive, are gleefully active, exuberant, their sumptuous pink bodies like rainclouds or plump nebulae. "His nudes are the first ones that ever made me feel happy about my own body," a woman friend told me in one of the Rubens galleries of the Prado Museum. I do not imagine any pinup or store-window mannequin or bathing-suited Miss Whatsit could have made her feel that way. The naked women in Rembrandt, emerging from the bath or rising from bed, are so private, so cherished in the painter's gaze, that we as viewers see them not as sexual playthings but as loved persons. A man would do well to emulate that gaze.

I have never thought of myself as a sight. How much that has to do with being male and how much with having grown up on the back roads where money was scarce and eyes were few, I cannot say. As a boy, apart from combing my hair when I was compelled to and regretting the patches on my jeans (only the poor wore patches), I took no trouble over my appearance. It never occurred to me that anybody outside my family, least of all a girl, would look at me twice. As a young man, when young women did occasionally glance my way, without any prospect of appearing handsome I tried at least to avoid appearing odd. A standard haircut and the cheapest versions of the standard clothes were camouflage enough. Now as a middle-aged man I have achieved once more that boyhood condition of invisibility, with less hair to comb and fewer patches to humble me.

Many women clearly pass through the world aspiring to invisibility. Many others just as clearly aspire to be conspicuous. Women need not make spectacles of themselves in order to draw the attention of men. Indeed, for my taste, the less paint and fewer bangles the better. I am as helpless in the presence of subtle lures as a male moth catching a whiff of pheromones. I am a sucker for hair ribbons, a scarf at the throat, toes leaking from sandals, teeth bared in a smile. By contrast, I have always been more amused than attracted by the enameled exhibitionists whom our biblical mothers would identify as brazen hussies or painted Jezebels or, in the extreme cases, as whores of Babylon.

To encounter female exhibitionists in their full glory and variety, you need to go to a city. I never encounted ogling as a full-blown sport until I visited Rome, where bands of Italian men joined with gusto in appraising the charms of every passing female, and the passing females vied with one another in demonstrating their charms. In our own cities the most notorious bands of oglers tend to be construction gangs or street crews, men who spend much of their day leaning on the handles of shovels or pausing between bursts of riveting guns, their eyes tracing the curves of passersby. The first time my wife and kids and I drove into Boston we followed the signs to Chinatown, only to discover that Chinatown's miserably congested main street was undergoing repairs. That street also proved to be the city's home for X-rated cinemas and girlie shows and skin shops. LIVE SEX ACTS ON STAGE. PEEP SHOWS. PRIVATE BOOTHS. Caught in a traffic jam, we spent an hour listening to jackhammers and wolf whistles as we crept through the few blocks of pleasure palaces, my son and daughter with their noses hanging out the windows, my wife and I steaming. Lighted marquees peppered by burnt-out bulbs announced the titles of sleazy flicks; life-size posters of naked women flanked the doorways of clubs: leggy strippers in miniskirts, the originals for some of the posters, smoked on the curb between numbers.

After we had finally emerged from the zone of eros, eight-year-old Jesse inquired, "What was *that* place all about?"   35

"Sex for sale," my wife Ruth explained.

That might carry us some way toward a definition of pornography: making flesh into a commodity, flaunting it like any other merchandise, divorcing bodies from selves. By this reckoning, there is a pornographic dimension to much advertising, where a charge of sex is added to products ranging from cars to shaving cream. In fact, the calculated imagery of advertising may be more harmful than the blatant imagery of the pleasure palaces, that frank raunchiness which Kate Millett refers to as the "truthful explicitness of pornography." One can leave the X-rated zone of the city, but one cannot escape the sticky reach of commerce, which summons girls to the high calling of cosmetic glamor, fashion, and sexual display, while it summons boys to the panting chase.

You can recognize pornography, according to D. H. Lawrence, "by the insult it offers, invariably, to sex, and to the human spirit." He should know, Millet argues in *Sexual Politics,* for in her view Lawrence himself was a purveyor of patriarchal and often sadistic pornography. I think she is correct about the worst of Lawrence, and that she identifies a misogynist streak in his work; but she ignores his career-long struggle to achieve a more public, tolerant vision of sexuality as an exchange between equals. Besides, his novels and stories all bear within themselves their own critiques. George Steiner reminds us that "the list of writers who have had the genius to enlarge our actual compass of sexual awareness, who have given the erotic play of the mind a novel focus, an area of recognition previously unknown or fallow, is very small." Lawrence belongs on that brief list. The chief insult to the human spirit is to deny it, to claim that we are merely conglomerations of molecules, to pretend that we exist purely as bundles of appetites or as food for the appetites of others.

Men commit that insult toward women out of ignorance, but also out of dread. Allen Wheelis again: "Men gather in pornographic shows, not to stimulate desire, as they may think, but to diminish fear. It is the nature of the show to reduce the woman, discard her individuality, her soul, make her into an object, thereby enabling the man to handle her with greater safety, to use her as a toy. . . . As women move increasingly toward equality, the felt danger to men increases, leading to an increase in pornography and, since there are some men whose fears cannot even so be stilled, to an increase also in violence against women."

Make her into an object: all the hurtful ways for men to look at women are 40 variations on this betrayal. "Thus she turns herself into an object," writes Berger. A woman's ultimate degradation is in "submissively making herself a thing," writes Beauvoir. To be turned into an object—whether by the brush of a painter or the lens of a photographer or the eye of a voyeur, whether by hunger or poverty or enslavement, by mugging or rape, bullets or bombs, by hatred, racism, car crashes, fires, or falls—is for each of us the deepest dread; and to reduce another person to an object is the primal wrong.

Caught in the vortex of desire, we have to struggle to recall the wholeness of persons, including ourselves. Beauvoir speaks of the temptation we all occasionally feel to give up the struggle for a self and lapse into the inertia of an object: "Along with the ethical urge of each individual to affirm his subjective existence, there is also the temptation to forgo liberty and become a thing." A woman in particular, given so much encouragement to lapse into thinghood, "is often very well pleased with her role as the *Other.*"

Yet one need not forgo liberty and become a thing, without a center or a self, in order to become the Other. In our mutual strangeness, men and women can be doorways one for another, openings into the creative mystery that we share by virtue of our existence in the flesh. "To be sensual," James Baldwin writes, "is to respect and rejoice in the force of life, of life itself, and to be *present* in all that one does, from the effort of loving to the breaking of bread." The effort of loving is reciprocal, not only in act but in desire, an *I* addressing a *Thou*, a meeting in that vivid presence. The distance a man stares across at a woman, or a woman at a man, is a gulf in the soul, out of which a voice cries, *Leap, leap.* One day all men may cease to look on themselves as prototypically human and on women as lesser miracles; women may cease to feel themselves the targets for desire; men and women both may come to realize that we are all mere flickerings in the universal fire; and then none of us, male or female, need give up humanity in order to become the *Other.*

Ever since I gawked at the girl in pink shorts, I have dwelt knowingly in the force-field of sex. Knowingly or not, it is where we all dwell. Like the masses of planets and stars, our bodies curve the space around us. We radiate signals constantly, radio sources that never go off the air. We cannot help being centers of attraction and repulsion for one another. That is not all we are by a long shot, nor all we are capable of feeling, and yet, even after our much-needed revolution in sexual consciousness, the power of eros will still turn our heads and hearts. In a world without beauty pageants, there will still be beauty, however its definition may have changed. As long as men have eyes, they will gaze with yearning and confusion at women.

When I return to the street with the ancient legacy of longing coiled in my DNA, and the residues from a thousand generations of patriarchs silting my brain, I encounter women whose presence strikes me like a slap of wind in the face. I must prepare a gaze that is worthy of their splendor.

ACTIVITIES FOR WRITING AND DISCUSSION

1. Sanders's essay is quite long, complex, and suggestive. To begin establishing a connection with the piece, review your annotations—questions, reactions, personal associations—of the essay. Select two or three that strike or affect you the most and write about them for a few minutes. Then share those selected annotations in class or in a small group.

2. Several paragraphs into his essay Sanders poses the question that becomes his focus: "How should a man look at women?" Is it significant that he uses the word "should" and not "does"? What sorts of cultural influences on sexual attitudes and behavior are implied by "should"? Draw on Sanders's essay and your own experience to make a list of such influences.

3. The essay includes quotations from various writers (Simone de Beauvoir, John Berger, Kate Millett, Allen Wheelis, and others). Reread and annotate these passages. Then select one passage that particularly strikes you and write an objective summary of it. (See p. 87 for some suggestions on summarizing.) Finally, discuss ways in which you agree and/or disagree with the writer quoted in the passage.

4. Sanders relates several experiences from his own past in which he looked at women. Tell the story of a time when *you* "looked at women" (or at men, or were yourself looked at). Then, like Sanders, analyze ways in which the experience reflects wider cultural influences on sexual attitudes and behavior.

Plays

Susan Glaspell (1882–1948)

Trifles

SCENE: *The kitchen in the now abandoned farmhouse of* JOHN WRIGHT, *a gloomy kitchen, and left without having been put in order—the walls covered with a faded wallpaper.* D. R. *is a door leading to the parlor. On the* R. *wall above this door is a built-in kitchen cupboard with shelves in the upper portion and drawers below. In the rear wall at* R., *up two steps is a door opening onto stairs leading to the second floor. In the rear wall at* L. *is a door to the shed and from there to the outside. Between these two doors is an old-fashioned black iron stove. Running along the* L. *wall from the shed door is an old iron sink and sink shelf, in which is set a hand pump. Downstage of the sink is an uncurtained window. Near the window is an old wooden rocker. Center stage is an unpainted wooden kitchen table with straight chairs on either side. There is a small chair* D. R. *Unwashed pans under the sink, a loaf of bread outside the breadbox, a dish towel on the table—other signs of incompleted work. At the rear the shed door opens and the* SHERIFF *comes in followed by the* COUNTY ATTORNEY *and* HALE. *The* SHERIFF *and* HALE *are men in middle life, the* COUNTY ATTORNEY *is a young man; all are much bundled up and go at once to the stove. They are followed by the two women—the* SHERIFF'S *wife,* MRS. PETERS, *first; she is a slight wiry woman, a thin nervous face.* MRS. HALE *is larger and would ordinarily be called more comfortable looking, but she is disturbed now and looks fearfully about as she enters. The women have come in slowly, and stand close together near the door.*

COUNTY ATTORNEY (*at stove rubbing his hands*). This feels good. Come up to the fire, ladies.

MRS. PETERS (*after taking a step forward*). I'm not—cold.

SHERIFF (*unbuttoning his overcoat and stepping away from the stove to right of table as if to mark the beginning of official business*). Now, Mr. Hale, before we move things about, you explain to Mr. Henderson just what you saw when you came here yesterday morning.

COUNTY ATTORNEY (*crossing down to left of the table*). By the way, has anything been moved? Are things just as you left them yesterday?

SHERIFF (*looking about*). It's just the same. When it dropped below zero last night I thought I'd better send Frank out this morning to make a fire for us— (*sits right of center table*) no use getting pneumonia with a big case on, but I told him not to touch anything except the stove—and you know Frank.

COUNTY ATTORNEY: Somebody should have been left here yesterday.

SHERIFF: Oh—yesterday. When I had to send Frank to Morris Center for that man who went crazy—I want you to know I had my hands full yesterday. I knew you could get back from Omaha by today and as long as I went over everything here myself——

COUNTY ATTORNEY: Well, Mr. Hale, tell just what happened when you came here yesterday morning.

HALE (*crossing down to above table*). Harry and I had started to town with a load of potatoes. We came along the road from my place and as I got here I said, "I'm going to see if I can't get John Wright to go in with me on a party telephone." I spoke to Wright about it once before and he put me off, saying folks talked too much anyway, and all he asked was peace and quiet—I guess you know about how much he talked himself; but I thought maybe if I went to the house and talked about it before his wife, though I said to Harry that I didn't know as what his wife wanted made much difference to John——

COUNTY ATTORNEY: Let's talk about that later, Mr. Hale. I do want to talk about that, but tell now just what happened when you got to the house.

HALE: I didn't hear or see anything; I knocked at the door, and still it was all quiet inside. I knew they must be up, it was past eight o'clock. So I knocked again, and I thought I heard somebody say, "Come in." I wasn't sure, I'm not sure yet, but I opened the door—this door (*indicating the door by which the two women are still standing*) and there in that rocker—(*pointing to it*) sat Mrs. Wright. (*They all look at the rocker* D. L.)

COUNTY ATTORNEY: What—was she doing?

HALE: She was rockin' back and forth. She had her apron in her hand and was kind of—pleating it.

COUNTY ATTORNEY: And how did she—look?

HALE: Well, she looked queer.

COUNTY ATTORNEY: How do you mean—queer?

HALE: Well, as if she didn't know what she was going to do next. And kind of done up.

COUNTY ATTORNEY (*takes out notebook and pencil and sits left of center table*). How did she seem to feel about your coming?

HALE: Why, I don't think she minded—one way or other. She didn't pay much attention. I said, "How do, Mrs. Wright, it's cold, ain't it?" And she said, "Is it?"—and went on kind of pleating at her apron. Well, I was surprised; she didn't ask me to come up to the stove, or to set down, but just sat there, not even looking at me, so I said, "I want to see John." And then she—laughed. I guess you would call it a laugh. I thought of Harry and the team outside, so I said a little sharp: "Can't I see John?" "No," she says, kind o' dull like. "Ain't he home?" says I. "Yes," says she, "he's home." "Then why can't I see him?" I asked her, out of patience. " 'Cause he's dead," says she. "*Dead?*" says I. She just nodded her head, not getting a bit excited, but rockin' back and forth. "Why—where is he?" says I, not knowing what to say. She just pointed upstairs—like that. (*Himself pointing to the room above*). I started for the stairs, with the idea of going up there. I walked from there to here—then I says, "Why, what did he die of?" "He died of a rope round his neck," says she, and just went on pleatin' at her apron. Well, I went out and called Harry. I thought I might—need help. We went upstairs and there he was lyin'—

COUNTY ATTORNEY: I think I'd rather have you go into that upstairs, where you can point it all out. Just go on now with the rest of the story.

HALE: Well, my first thought was to get that rope off. It looked . . . (*stops, his face twitches*) . . . but Harry, he went up to him, and he said, "No, he's dead all right, and we'd better not touch anything." So we went back downstairs. She was still sitting that same way. "Has anybody been notified?" I asked. "No," says she, unconcerned. "Who did this, Mrs. Wright?" said Harry. He said it business-like—and she stopped pleatin' of her apron. "I don't know," she says. "You don't *know?*" says Harry. "No," says she. "Weren't you sleepin' in the bed with him?" says Harry. "Yes," says she, "but I was on the inside." "Somebody slipped a rope round his neck and strangled him and you didn't wake up?" says Harry. "I didn't wake up," she said after him. We must 'a' looked as if we didn't see how that could be, for after a minute she said, "I sleep sound." Harry was going to ask her more questions but I said maybe we ought to let her tell her story first to the coroner, or the sheriff, so Harry went fast as he could to Rivers' place, where there's a telephone.

COUNTY ATTORNEY: And what did Mrs. Wright do when she knew that you had gone for the coroner?

HALE: She moved from the rocker to that chair over there (*pointing to a small chair in the* D. R. *corner*) and just sat there with her hands held together and looking down. I got a feeling that I ought to make some conversation, so I said I had come in to see if John wanted to put in a telephone, and at that she started to laugh, and then she stopped and looked at me—scared. (*The* COUNTY ATTORNEY, *who has had his notebook out, makes a note*). I dunno, maybe it wasn't scared. I wouldn't like to say it was. Soon Harry got back, and then Dr. Lloyd came, and you, Mr. Peters, and so I guess that's all I know that you don't.

COUNTY ATTORNEY (*rising and looking around*). I guess we'll go upstairs first—and then out to the barn and around there. (*To the* SHERIFF). You're convinced that there was nothing important here—nothing that would point to any motive?

SHERIFF: Nothing here but kitchen things. (*The* COUNTY ATTORNEY, *after again looking around the kitchen, opens the door of a cupboard closet in* R. *wall. He brings a small chair from* R.—*gets up on it and looks on a shelf. Pulls his hand away, sticky.*)

COUNTY ATTORNEY: Here's a nice mess. (*The women draw nearer* U. C.)

MRS. PETERS (*to the other woman*). Oh, her fruit; it did freeze. (*To the* LAWYER). She worried about that when it turned so cold. She said the fire'd go out and her jars would break.

SHERIFF (*rises*). Well, can you beat the women! Held for murder and worryin' about her preserves.

COUNTY ATTORNEY (*getting down from chair*). I guess before we're through she may have something more serious than preserves to worry about. (*Crosses down* R.C.)

HALE: Well, women are used to worrying over trifles. (*The two women move a little closer together.*)

COUNTY ATTORNEY (*with the gallantry of a young politician*). And yet, for all their worries, what would we do without the ladies? (*The women do not unbend. He goes below the center table to the sink, takes a dipperful of water from the pail and pouring it into a basin, washes his hands. While he is doing this the* SHERIFF *and* HALE *cross to cupboard, which they inspect. The* COUNTY ATTORNEY *starts to wipe his hands on the roller towel, turns it for a cleaner place*). Dirty towels! (*Kicks his foot against the pans under the sink*). Not much of a housekeeper, would you say, ladies?

MRS. HALE (*stiffly*). There's a great deal of work to be done on a farm.

COUNTY ATTORNEY: To be sure. And yet (*with a little bow to her*) I know there are some Dickson County farmhouses which do not have such roller towels. (*He gives it a pull to expose its full length again.*)

MRS. HALE: Those towels get dirty awful quick. Men's hands aren't always as clean as they might be.

COUNTY ATTORNEY: Ah, loyal to your sex, I see. But you and Mrs. Wright were neighbors. I suppose you were friends, too.

MRS. HALE (*shaking her head*). I've not seen much of her of late years. I've not been in this house—it's more than a year.

COUNTY ATTORNEY (*crossing to women* U. C.). And why was that? You didn't like her?

MRS. HALE: I liked her all well enough. Farmers' wives have their hands full, Mr. Henderson. And then——

COUNTY ATTORNEY: Yes——?

MRS. HALE (*looking about*). It never seemed a very cheerful place.

COUNTY ATTORNEY: No—it's not cheerful. I shouldn't say she had the homemaking instinct.

MRS. HALE: Well, I don't know as Wright had, either.

COUNTY ATTORNEY: You mean that they didn't get on very well?

MRS. HALE: No, I don't mean anything. But I don't think a place'd be any cheerfuller for John Wright's being in it.

COUNTY ATTORNEY: I'd like to talk more of that a little later. I want to get the lay of things upstairs now. (*He goes past the women to* U. R. *where steps lead to a stair door.*)

SHERIFF: I suppose anything Mrs. Peters does'll be all right. She was to take in some clothes for her, you know, and a few little things. We left in such a hurry yesterday.

COUNTY ATTORNEY: Yes, but I would like to see what you take, Mrs. Peters, and keep an eye out for anything that might be of use to us.

MRS. PETER: Yes, Mr. Henderson. (*The men leave by* U. R. *door to stairs. The women listen to the men's steps on the stairs, then look about the kitchen.*)

MRS. HALE (*crossing* L. *to sink*). I'd hate to have men coming into my kitchen, snooping around and criticizing. (*She arranges the pans under sink which the* LAWYER *had shoved out of place.*)

MRS. PETERS: Of course it's no more than their duty. (*Crosses to cupboard* U. R.)

MRS. HALE: Duty's all right, but I guess that deputy sheriff that came out to make the fire might have got a little of this on. (*Gives the roller towel a pull*). Wish I'd thought of that sooner. Seems mean to talk about her for not having things slicked up when she had to come away in such a hurry. (*Crosses* R. *to* MRS. PETERS *at cupboard.*)

MRS. PETERS (*who has been looking through cupboard, lifts one end of a towel that covers a pan*). She had bread set. (*Stands still.*)

MRS. HALE (*eyes fixed on a loaf of bread beside the breadbox, which is on a low shelf of the cupboard*). She was going to put this in there. (*Picks up loaf, then abruptly drops it. In a manner of returning to familiar things*). It's a shame about her fruit. I wonder if it's all gone. (*Gets up on the chair and looks*). I think there's some here that's all right, Mrs. Peters. Yes—here; (*holding it toward the window*) this is cherries, too. (*Looking again*). I declare I believe that's the only one. (*Gets down, jar in her hand. Goes to the sink and wipes it off on the outside*). She'll feel awful bad after all her hard work in the hot weather. I remember the afternoon I put up my cherries last summer. (*She puts the jar on the big kitchen table, center of the room. With a sigh, is about to sit down in the rocking chair. Before she is seated realizes what chair it is; with a slow look at it, steps back. The chair which she has touched rocks back and forth.* MRS. PETERS *moves to center table and they both watch the chair rock for a moment or two.*)

MRS. PETERS (*shaking off the mood which the empty rocking chair has evoked. Now in a businesslike manner she speaks*). Well, I must get those things from the front room closet. (*She goes to the door at the* R., *but, after looking into the other room, steps back*). You coming with me, Mrs. Hale? You could help me carry them. (*They go in the other room; reappear,* MRS. PETERS *carrying a dress, petticoat and skirt,* MRS. HALE *following with a pair of shoes*). My, it's cold in there. (*She puts the clothes on the big table, and hurries to the stove.*)

MRS. HALE (*right of center table examining the skirt*). Wright was close. I think maybe that's why she kept so much to herself. She didn't even belong to the Ladies' Aid. I suppose she felt she couldn't do her part, and then you don't enjoy things when you feel shabby. I heard she used to wear pretty clothes and be lively, when she was Minnie Foster, one of the town girls singing in the choir. But that—oh, that was thirty years ago. This all you was to take in?

MRS. PETERS: She said she wanted an apron. Funny thing to want, for there isn't much to get you dirty in jail, goodness knows. But I suppose just to make her feel more natural. (*Crosses to cupboard*). She said they was in the top drawer in this cupboard. Yes, here. And then her little shawl that always hung behind the door. (*Opens stair door and looks*). Yes, here it is. (*Quickly shuts door leading upstairs.*)

MRS. HALE (*abruptly moving toward her*). Mrs. Peters?

MRS. PETERS: Yes, Mrs. Hale? (*At* U. R. *door.*)

MRS. HALE: Do you think she did it?

MRS. PETERS (*in a frightened voice*). Oh, I don't know.

MRS. HALE: Well, I don't think she did. Asking for an apron and her little shawl. Worrying about her fruit.

MRS. PETERS (*starts to speak, glances up, where footsteps are heard in the room above. In a low voice*). Mr. Peters says it looks bad for her. Mr. Henderson is awful sarcastic in a speech and he'll make fun of her sayin' she didn't wake up.

MRS. HALE: Well, I guess John Wright didn't wake when they was slipping that rope under his neck.

MRS. PETERS (*crossing slowly to table and placing shawl and apron on table with other clothing*). No, it's strange. It must have been done awful crafty and still. They say it was such a—funny way to kill a man, rigging it all up like that.

MRS. HALE (*crossing to left of* MRS. PETERS *at table*). That's just what Mr. Hale said. There was a gun in the house. He says that's what he can't understand.

MRS. PETERS: Mr. Henderson said coming out that what was needed for the case was a motive; something to show anger, or—sudden feeling.

MRS. HALE (*who is standing by the table*). Well, I don't see any signs of anger around here. (*She puts her hand on the dish towel which lies on the table, stands looking down at table, one-half of which is clean, the other half messy*). It's wiped to here. (*Makes a move as if to finish work, then turns and looks at loaf of bread outside the breadbox. Drops towel. In that voice of coming back to familiar things*). Wonder how they are finding things upstairs. (*Crossing below table to* D. R.). I hope she had it a little more red-up up there. You know, it seems kind of *sneaking*. Locking her up in town and then coming out here and trying to get her own house to turn against her!

MRS. PETERS: But, Mrs. Hale, the law is the law.

MRS. HALE: I s'pose 'tis. (*Unbuttoning her coat*). Better loosen up your things, Mrs. Peters. You won't feel them when you go out. (MRS. PETERS *takes off her fur tippet, goes to hang it on chair back left of table, stands looking at the work basket on floor near* D. L. *window.*)

MRS. PETERS: She was piecing a quilt. (*She brings the large sewing basket to the center table and they look at the bright pieces,* MRS. HALE *above the table and* MRS. PETERS *left of it.*)

MRS. HALE: It's a log cabin pattern. Pretty, isn't it? I wonder if she was goin' to quilt it or just knot it? (*Footsteps have been heard coming down the stairs. The* SHERIFF *enters followed by* HALE *and the* COUNTY ATTORNEY.)

SHERIFF: They wonder if she was going to quilt it or just knot it! (*The men laugh, the women look abashed.*)

COUNTY ATTORNEY (*rubbing his hands over the stove*). Frank's fire didn't do much up there, did it? Well, let's go out to the barn and get that cleared up. (*The men go outside by* U. L. *door.*)

MRS. HALE (*resentfully*). I don't know as there's anything so strange, our takin' up our time with little things while we're waiting for them to get the evidence. (*She sits in chair right of table smoothing out a block with decision*). I don't see as it's anything to laugh about.

MRS. PETERS (*apologetically*). Of course they've got awful important things on their minds. (*Pulls up a chair and joins* MRS. HALE *at the left of the table.*)

MRS. HALE (*examining another block*). Mrs. Peters, look at this one. Here, this is the one she was working on, and look at the sewing! All the rest of it has been so nice and even. And look at this! It's all over the place! Why, it looks as if she didn't know what she was about! (*After she has said this they look at each other, then start to glance back at the door. After an instant* MRS. HALE *has pulled at a knot and ripped the sewing.*)

MRS. PETERS: Oh, what are you doing, Mrs. Hale?

MRS. HALE (*mildly*). Just pulling out a stitch or two that's not sewed very good. (*Threading a needle*). Bad sewing always made me fidgety.

MRS. PETERS (*with a glance at door, nervously*). I don't think we ought to touch things.

MRS. HALE: I'll just finish up this end. (*Suddenly stopping and leaning forward*). Mrs. Peters?

MRS. PETERS: Yes, Mrs. Hale?

MRS. HALE: What do you suppose she was so nervous about?

MRS. PETERS: Oh—I don't know. I don't know as she was nervous. I sometimes sew awful queer when I'm just tired. (MRS. HALE *starts to say something, looks at* MRS. PETERS *then goes on sewing*). Well, I must get these things wrapped up. They may be through sooner than we think. (*Putting apron and other things together*). I wonder where I can find a piece of paper, and string. (*Rises.*)

MRS. HALE: In that cupboard, maybe.

MRS. PETERS (*crosses* R. *looking in cupboard*). Why, here's a bird-cage. (*Holds it up*). Did she have a bird, Mrs. Hale?

MRS. HALE: Why, I don't know whether she did or not—I've not been here for so long. There was a man around last year selling canaries cheap, but I don't know as she took one; maybe she did. She used to sing real pretty herself.

MRS. PETERS (*glancing around*). Seems funny to think of a bird here. But she must have had one, or why would she have a cage? I wonder what happened to it?

MRS. HALE: I s'pose maybe the cat got it.

MRS. PETERS: No, she didn't have a cat. She's got that feeling some people have about cats—being afraid of them. My cat got in her room and she was real upset and asked me to take it out.

MRS. HALE: My sister Bessie was like that. Queer, ain't it?

MRS. PETERS (*examining the cage*). Why, look at this door. It's broke. One hinge is pulled apart. (*Takes a step down to* MRS. HALE'S *right.*)

MRS. HALE (*looking too*). Looks as if someone must have been rough with it.

MRS. PETERS: Why, yes. (*She brings the cage forward and puts it on the table.*)

MRS. HALE (*glancing toward* U. L. *door*). I wish if they're going to find any evidence they'd be about it. I don't like this place.

MRS. PETERS: But I'm awful glad you came with me, Mrs. Hale. It would be lonesome for me sitting here alone.

MRS. HALE: It would, wouldn't it? (*Dropping her sewing*). But I tell you what I do wish, Mrs. Peters. I wish I had come over sometimes when she was here. I—(*looking around the room*)—wish I had.

MRS. PETERS: But of course you were awful busy, Mrs. Hale—your house and your children.

MRS. HALE (*rises and crosses* L.). I could've come. I stayed away because it weren't cheerful—and that's why I ought to have come. I—(*looking out* L. *window*)—I've never liked this place. Maybe because it's down in a hollow and you don't see the road. I dunno what it is, but it's a lonesome place and always was. I wish I had come over to see Minnie Foster sometimes. I can see now—— (*Shakes her head.*)

MRS. PETERS (*left of table and above it*). Well, you mustn't reproach yourself, Mrs. Hale. Somehow we just don't see how it is with other folks until—something turns up.

MRS. HALE: Not having children makes less work—but it makes a quiet house, and Wright out to work all day, and no company when he did come in. (*Turning from window*). Did you know John Wright, Mrs. Peters?

MRS. PETERS: Not to know him; I've seen him in town. They say he was a good man.

MRS. HALE: Yes—good; he didn't drink, and kept his word as well as most, I guess, and paid his debts. But he was a hard man, Mrs. Peters. Just to pass the time of day with him—— (*Shivers*). Like a raw wind that gets to the bone. (*Pauses, her eye falling on the cage*). I should think she would 'a' wanted a bird. But what do you suppose went with it?

MRS. PETERS: I don't know, unless it got sick and died. (*She reaches over and swings the broken door, swings it again, both women watch it.*)

MRS. HALE: You weren't raised round here, were you? (MRS. PETERS *shakes her head*). You didn't know—her?

MRS. PETERS: Not till they brought her yesterday.

MRS. HALE: She—come to think of it, she was kind of like a bird herself—real sweet and pretty, but kind of timid and—fluttery. How—she—did—change. (*Silence; then as if struck by a happy thought and relieved to get back to everyday things. Crosses* R. *above* MRS. PETERS *to cupboard, replaces small chair used to stand on to its original place* D. R.). Tell you what, Mrs. Peters, why don't you take the quilt in with you? It might take up her mind.

MRS. PETERS: Why, I think that's a real nice idea, Mrs. Hale. There couldn't possibly be any objection to it, could there? Now, just what would I take? I wonder if her patches are in here—and her things. (*They look in the sewing basket.*)

MRS. HALE (*crosses to right of table*). Here's some red. I expect this has got sewing things in it. (*Brings out a fancy box*). What a pretty box. Looks like something somebody would give you. Maybe her scissors are in here. (*Opens box. Suddenly puts her hand to her nose*). Why—— (MRS. PETERS *bends nearer, then turns her face away*). There's something wrapped up in this piece of silk.

MRS. PETERS: Why, this isn't her scissors.

MRS. HALE (*lifting the silk*). Oh, Mrs. Peters—it's—— (MRS. PETERS *bends closer.*)

MRS. PETERS: It's the bird.

MRS. HALE: But, Mrs. Peters—look at it! Its neck! Look at its neck! It's all—other side *to*.

MRS. PETERS: Somebody—wrung—its—neck. (*Their eyes meet. A look of growing comprehension, of horror. Steps are heard outside.* MRS. HALE *slips box under quilt pieces, and sinks into her chair. Enter* SHERIFF *and* COUNTY ATTORNEY. MRS. PETERS *steps* D. L. *and stands looking out of window.*)

COUNTY ATTORNEY (*as one turning from serious things to little pleasantries*). Well, ladies, have you decided whether she was going to quilt it or knot it? (*Crosses to* C. *above table.*)

MRS. PETERS: We think she was going to—knot it. (SHERIFF *crosses to right of stove, lifts stove lid and glances at fire, then stands warming hands at stove.*)

COUNTY ATTORNEY: Well, that's interesting, I'm sure. (*Seeing the bird-cage*). Has the bird flown?

MRS. HALE (*putting more quilt pieces over the box*). We think the—cat got it.

COUNTY ATTORNEY (*preoccupied*). Is there a cat? (MRS. HALE *glances in a quick covert way at* MRS. PETERS.)

MRS. PETERS (*turning from window takes a step in*). Well, not *now*. They're superstitious, you know. They leave.

COUNTY ATTORNEY (*to* SHERIFF PETERS, *continuing an interrupted conversation*). No sign at all of anyone having come from the outside. Their own rope.

Now let's go up again and go over it piece by piece. (*They start upstairs*). It would have to have been someone who knew just the—— (MRS. PETERS *sits down left of table. The two women sit there not looking at one another, but as if peering into something and at the same time holding back. When they talk now it is in the manner of feeling their way over strange ground, as if afraid of what they are saying, but as if they cannot help saying it.*)

MRS. HALE (*hesitatively and in hushed voice*). She liked the bird. She was going to bury it in that pretty box.

MRS. PETERS (*in a whisper*). When I was a girl—my kitten—there was a boy took a hatchet, and before my eyes—and before I could get there—— (*Covers her face an instant*). If they hadn't held me back I would have—(*catches herself, looks upstairs where steps are heard, falters weakly*)—hurt him.

MRS. HALE (*with a slow look around her*). I wonder how it would seem never to have had any children around. (*Pause*). No, Wright wouldn't like the bird—a thing that sang. She used to sing. He killed that, too.

MRS. PETERS (*moving uneasily*). We don't know who killed the bird.

MRS. HALE: I knew John Wright.

MRS. PETERS: It was an awful thing was done in this house that night, Mrs. Hale. Killing a man while he slept, slipping a rope around his neck that choked the life out of him.

MRS. HALE: His neck. Choked the life out of him. (*Her hand goes out and rests on the bird-cage.*)

MRS. PETERS (*with rising voice*). We don't know who killed him. We don't know.

MRS. HALE (*her own feeling not interrupted*). If there'd been years and years of nothing, then a bird to sing to you, it would be awful—still, after the bird was still.

MRS. PETERS (*something within her speaking*). I know what stillness is. When we homesteaded in Dakota, and my first baby died—after he was two years old, and me with no other then——

MRS. HALE (*moving*). How soon do you suppose they'll be through looking for the evidence?

MRS. PETERS: I know what stillness is. (*Pulling herself back*). The law has got to punish crime, Mrs. Hale.

MRS. HALE (*not as if answering that*). I wish you'd seen Minnie Foster when she wore a white dress with blue ribbons and stood up there in the choir and sang. (*A look around the room*). Oh, I *wish* I'd come over here once in a while! That was a crime! That was a crime! Who's going to punish that?

MRS. PETERS (*looking upstairs*). We mustn't—take on.

MRS. HALE: I might have known she needed help! I know how things can be—for women. I tell you, it's queer, Mrs. Peters. We live close together and we live far apart. We all go through the same things—it's all just a different kind of the same thing. (*Brushes her eyes, noticing the jar of fruit, reaches out for it*). If I was you I wouldn't tell her her fruit was gone. Tell her it *ain't*. Tell her it's all right. Take this in to prove it to her. She—she may never know whether it was broke or not.

MRS. PETERS (*takes the jar, looks about for something to wrap it in; takes petticoat from the clothes brought from the other room, very nervously begins winding this around the jar. In a false voice*). My, it's a good thing the men couldn't hear us. Wouldn't they just laugh! Getting all stirred up over a little thing like a—dead canary. As if that could have anything to do with—with—wouldn't they *laugh*! (*The men are heard coming downstairs.*)

MRS. HALE (*under her breath*). Maybe they would—maybe they wouldn't.

COUNTY ATTORNEY: No, Peters, it's all perfectly clear except a reason for doing it. But you know juries when it comes to women. If there was some definite thing. (*Crosses slowly to above table.* SHERIFF *crosses* D. R. MRS. HALE *and* MRS. PETERS *remain seated at either side of table*). Something to show—something to make a story about—a thing that would connect up with this strange way of doing it—— (*The women's eyes meet for an instant. Enter* HALE *from outer door.*)

HALE (*remaining* U. L. *by door*). Well, I've got the team around. Pretty cold out there.

COUNTY ATTORNEY: I'm going to stay awhile by myself. (*To the* SHERIFF). You can send Frank out for me, can't you? I want to go over everything. I'm not satisfied that we can't do better.

SHERIFF: Do you want to see what Mrs. Peters is going to take in? (*The* LAWYER *picks up the apron, laughs.*)

COUNTY ATTORNEY: Oh, I guess they're not very dangerous things the ladies have picked out. (*Moves a few things about, disturbing the quilt pieces which cover the box. Steps back*). No, Mrs. Peters doesn't need supervising. For that matter a sheriff's wife is married to the law. Ever think of it that way, Mrs. Peters?

MRS. PETERS: Not—just that way.

SHERIFF (*chuckling*). Married to the law. (*Moves to* D. R. *door to the other room*). I just want you to come in here a minute, George. We ought to take a look at these windows.

COUNTY ATTORNEY (*scoffingly*). Oh, windows!

SHERIFF: We'll be right out, Mr. Hale. (HALE *goes outside. The* SHERIFF *follows the* COUNTY ATTORNEY *into the other room. Then* MRS. HALE *rises, hands tight together, looking intensely at* MRS. PETERS, *whose eyes make a slow turn, finally meeting* MRS. HALE'S. *A moment* MRS. HALE *holds her, then her own eyes point the way to where the box is concealed. Suddenly* MRS. PETERS *throws back quilt pieces and tries to put the box in the bag she is carrying. It is too big. She opens box, starts to take bird out, cannot touch it, goes to pieces, stands there helpless. Sound of a knob turning in the other room.* MRS. HALE *snatches the box and puts it in the pocket of her big coat. Enter* COUNTY ATTORNEY *and* SHERIFF, *who remains* D. R.)

COUNTY ATTORNEY (*crosses to* U. L. *door facetiously*). Well, Henry, at least we found out that she was not going to quilt it. She was going to—what is it you call it, ladies?

MRS. HALE (*standing* C. *below table facing front, her hand against her pocket*). We call it—knot it, Mr. Henderson.

CURTAIN

ACTIVITIES FOR WRITING AND DISCUSSION

1. Do a "readers' theater" performance of the play. Form into groups of five or six, assign character roles, and read the play aloud. Since **scene descriptions** and **stage directions**—printed in italics—are important, you may want to assign one person to read the italicized text. As you are performing:

   a. Mark any words, lines, stage directions, or other things that strike you— for whatever reason, and

   b. Note any ways that your interpretation of a character changes as you hear the play performed.

When you are finished, share with the class or your group any new perspectives you have on the play as a result of hearing it performed.

2. Imagine you are Minnie Wright, and you have kept a diary of your experiences since girlhood. After consulting details of Minnie's life story as revealed in the play, compose several of the entries you believe she might have written in her diary. You might include your (Minnie's) thoughts and feelings about life, music, John, and the canary, among other things.

3. Based on evidence in the play, determine whether Minnie Wright murdered her husband and how she might have done it. Then, writing in the **first-person** as Minnie Wright or as a **third-person narrator,** tell the story of how John Wright died.

4. Sometimes you can obtain interesting perspectives on a story or play by assuming the **point of view** of an involved inanimate object or animal. Imagine you are the unfortunate canary in *Trifles.* Tell your story, paying particular attention to your life and witness in the Wright household.

Terrence McNally (b. 1939)

Andre's Mother

Characters

Cal, a young man
Arthur, his father
Penny, his sister
Andre's Mother

Time: Now
Place: New York City, Central Park

Four people—Cal, Arthur, Penny, and Andre's Mother—enter. They are nicely dressed and each carries a white helium-filled balloon on a string.

CAL: You know what's really terrible? I can't think of anything terrific to say. Goodbye. I love you. I'll miss you. And I'm supposed to be so great with words!

PENNY: What's that over there?

ARTHUR: Ask your brother.

CAL: It's a theatre. An outdoor theatre. They do plays there in the summer. Shakespeare's plays. (*To Andre's Mother.*) God, how much he wanted to play Hamlet again. He would have gone to Timbuktu to have another go at that part. The summer he did it in Boston, he was so happy!

PENNY: Cal, I don't think she . . . ! It's not the time. Later.

ARTHUR: Your son was a . . . the Jews have a word for it . . .

PENNY (*quietly appalled*): Oh my God!

ARTHUR: Mensch, I believe it is, and I think I'm using it right. It means warm, solid, the real thing. Correct me if I'm wrong.

PENNY: Fine, Dad, fine. Just quit while you're ahead.

ARTHUR: I won't say he was like a son to me. Even my son isn't always like a son to me. I mean . . . ! In my clumsy way, I'm trying to say how much I liked Andre. And how much he helped me to know my own boy. Cal was always two handsful but Andre and I could talk about anything under the sun. My wife was very fond of him, too.

PENNY: Cal, I don't understand about the balloons.

CAL: They represent the soul. When you let go, it means you're letting his soul ascend to Heaven. That you're willing to let go. Breaking the last earthly ties.

PENNY: Does the Pope know about this?

ARTHUR: Penny!

PENNY: Andre loved my sense of humor. Listen, you can hear him laughing. (*She lets go of her white balloon.*) So long, you glorious, wonderful, I-know-what-Cal-means-about-words . . . *man!* God forgive me for wishing you were straight every time I laid eyes on you. But if any man was going to have you, I'm glad it was my brother! Look how fast it went up. I bet that means something. Something terrific.

ARTHUR (*lets his balloon go*): Goodbye. God speed.

PENNY: Cal?

CAL: I'm not ready yet.

PENNY: Okay. We'll be over there. Come on, Pop, you can buy your little girl a Good Humor.

ARTHUR: They still make Good Humor?

PENNY: Only now they're called Dove Bars and they cost twelve dollars.

(*Penny takes Arthur off. Cal and Andre's Mother stand with their balloons.*)

CAL: I wish I knew what you were thinking. I think it would help me. You know almost nothing about me and I only know what Andre told me about you. I'd always had it in my mind that one day we would be friends, you and me. But if you didn't know about Andre and me . . . If this hadn't happened, I wonder if he would have ever told you. When he was sick, if I asked him once I asked him a thousand times, tell her. She's your mother. She won't mind. But he was so afraid of hurting you and of your disapproval. I don't know which was worse. (*No response. He sighs.*) God, how many of us live in this city because we don't want to hurt our mothers and live in mortal terror of their disapproval. We lose ourselves here. Our lives aren't furtive, just our feelings toward people like you are! A city of fugitives from our parents' scorn or heartbreak. Sometimes he'd seem a little down and I'd say, "What's the matter, babe?" and this funny sweet, sad smile would cross his face and he'd say, "Just a little homesick, Cal, just a little bit." I always accused him of being a country boy just playing at being a hotshot, sophisticated New Yorker. (*He sighs.*)

It's bullshit. It's all bullshit. (*Still no response.*)

Do you remember the comic strip *Little Lulu*? Her mother had no name, she was so remote, so formidable to all the children. She was just Lulu's mother. "Hello, Lulu's Mother," Lulu's friends would say. She was almost anonymous in her remoteness. You remind me of her. Andre's mother. Let me answer the questions you can't ask and then I'll leave you alone and you won't ever have to see me again. Andre died of AIDS. I don't know how he got it. I tested negative. He died bravely. You would have been proud of him. The only thing that frightened him was you. I'll have everything that was his sent to you. I'll pay for it. There isn't much. You should have come up the summer he played Hamlet. He was magnificent. Yes, I'm bitter. I'm bitter I've lost him. I'm bitter what's happening. I'm bitter even now, after all this, I can't reach you. I'm beginning to feel your disapproval and it's making me ill. (*He looks at his balloon.*) Sorry, old friend. I blew it. (*He lets go of the balloon.*)

Good night, sweet prince, and flights of angels sing thee to thy rest! (*Beat.*)

Goodbye, Andre's mother.

(*He goes. Andre's Mother stands alone holding her white balloon. Her lips tremble. She looks on the verge of breaking down. She is about to let go of the balloon when she pulls it down to her. She looks at it awhile before she gently kisses it. She lets go of the balloon. She follows it with her eyes as it rises and rises. The lights are beginning to fade. Andre's Mother's eyes are still on the balloon. The lights fade.*)

GENDER AND RELATIONSHIPS: ADDITIONAL ACTIVITIES FOR WRITING AND DISCUSSION

1. Reread your entire notebook. Mark any passages, however long or short, that strike you, for whatever reason. Beside each passage, write a note explaining its significance for you. Finally, pick a favorite passage and either:
    a. Expand it into a new piece of writing, or
    b. Make notes on how you *could* expand or use it at some future date, or
    c. Rewrite it in a different form (e.g., poem, dialogue, letter, memoir).

For a list of strategies for expanding or revising, see Chapter 10.

2. Following the death of her husband, Minnie Wright (*Trifles*) sits in her jail cell. Several women **characters** and **speakers** in this section of readings might have things to say to her. Imagine that one or more of the following visit Minnie in her cell: the unnamed narrator of "The Yellow Wallpaper," the ex-wife in "Intimacy," Christina Rossetti's Margery, Pound's river-merchant's wife, Rich's "Aunt Jennifer," Wakoski's belly dancer. After selecting your visitor(s), draft a list of subjects she/they might raise with Minnie. Then dramatize her/their encounter with Minnie in the form of a dialogue or a short play (including, if you wish, a **scene description** and **stage directions**).

3. Several readings in this section take what could be seen as a "dim" view of men. As a complement to Activity #2, bring together two or more male characters or speakers from these texts and create a dialogue or short play about their encounter.

4. What ground do the gay couple James and Dennis ("Keeping Company") and Cal (*Andre's Mother*) occupy in the "gender wars"? Conduct an interview with one or more of these characters, inviting their opinions on any of

the characters or conflicts featured in the other readings within this thematic section.

5. The death of a spouse occurs (or is implied) in both Chopin's "The Story of an Hour" and Tomioka Taeko's "Just the Two of Us." Both texts also highlight the notion of "freedom" (note the next-to-last line of Taeko's poem and Louise Mallard's thoughts in "The Story of an Hour"). Write a notebook entry or essay assessing these and/or any other connections you see between these two texts and the characters whose lives they dramatize.

   6. a. Connections between Whitman's "Twenty-eight young men bathe by the shore" and Lessing's "A Woman on a Roof" seem tenuous at first; yet both narrate acts of sexual objectification. Is comparison between Whitman's twenty-ninth bather and Lessing's Stanley or Tom at all meaningful? Why or why not?

     b. Based *only* on these two texts, imagine an encounter between Whitman and Lessing in which the two writers talk about sex. Begin by listing a few topics for discussion; then flesh out a dialogue around these topics.

     c. Review the result of (b). Where did your dialogue falter? Draft a list of "additional information" you would need in order to make this dialogue more meaningful.

7. Near the end of "Looking at Women," Scott Russell Sanders writes:

To be turned into an object—whether by the brush of a painter or the lens of a photographer or the eye of a voyeur, whether by hunger or poverty or enslavement, by mugging or rape, bullets or bombs, by hatred, racism, car crashes, fires, or falls—is for each of us the deepest dread; and to reduce another person to an object is the primal wrong.

Reread the paragraph in which this sentence appears and any other passages that discuss how women—or people generally—turn themselves (or are turned) into objects. If you have not already done so, annotate those passages. Then in an essay:

   a. Summarize the process of objectification to which Sanders and others (e.g., John Berger, Allen Wheelis) are referring. By what means do women/human beings become "objects," and in what respects is being thus objectified bad or harmful?

   b. Apply the process of objectification you have just summarized in an analysis of "A Woman on a Roof," "Keeping Company," "Sex Without Love," or some other story or poem you have read thus far in the course.

8. Review your entire notebook; as you do, make a running list of memorable or striking topics, e.g., "women as objects," "men," "marriages," "kinds of

love." Then choose a favorite topic, make a Topic/Form Grid (see Chapter 10), and use one of the forms on your grid to create a new notebook entry about the topic. Should your chosen form not work, do a Topic/Form Shift to a different form on your grid.

9. Reread your entire notebook, and mark any favorite entries. Then, after reviewing Chapter 4, revise one of these entries that is a "dependent" text into an "independent" text. (For a list of strategies for revising, see Chapter 10.)

Families

James Joyce (1882–1941)

Eveline

She sat at the window watching the evening invade the avenue. Her head was 1
leaned against the window curtains and in her nostrils was the odour of dusty
cretonne. She was tired.

   Few people passed. The man out of the last house passed on his way home; 2
she heard his footsteps clacking along the concrete pavement and afterwards
crunching on the cinder path before the new red houses. One time there used
to be a field there in which they used to play every evening with other people's
children. Then a man from Belfast bought the field and built houses in it—not
like their little brown houses but bright brick houses with shining roofs. The
children of the avenue used to play together in that field—the Devines, the Waters, the Dunns, little Keogh the cripple, she and her brothers and sisters.
Ernest, however, never played: he was too grown up. Her father used often to
hunt them in out of the field with his blackthorn stick; but usually little Keogh
used to keep *nix* and call out when he saw her father coming. Still they seemed
to have been rather happy then. Her father was not so bad then; and besides,
her mother was alive. That was a long time ago; she and her brothers and sisters
were all grown up; her mother was dead. Tizzie Dunn was dead, too, and the
Waters had gone back to England. Everything changes. Now she was going to go
away like the others, to leave her home.

Home! She looked round the room, reviewing all its familiar objects which   3
she had dusted once a week for so many years, wondering where on earth all the
dust came from. Perhaps she would never see again those familiar objects from
which she had never dreamed of being divided. And yet during all those years
she had never found out the name of the priest whose yellowing photograph
hung on the wall above the broken harmonium beside the coloured print of the
promises made to Blessed Margaret Mary Alacoque. He had been a school
friend of her father. Whenever he showed the photograph to a visitor her father
used to pass it with a casual word:

—He is in Melbourne now.   4

She had consented to go away, to leave her home. Was that wise? She tried to   5
weigh each side of the question. In her home anyway she had shelter and food;
she had those whom she had known all her life about her. Of course she had to
work hard both in the house and at business. What would they say of her in the
Stores when they found out that she had run away with a fellow? Say she was a
fool, perhaps, and her place would be filled up by advertisement. Miss Gavan
would be glad. She had always had an edge on her, especially whenever there
were people listening.

—Miss Hill, don't you see these ladies are waiting?   6

—Look lively, Miss Hill, please.   7

She would not cry many tears at leaving the Stores.   8

But in her new home, in a distant unknown country, it would not be like   9
that. Then she would be married—she, Eveline. People would treat her with respect then. She would not be treated as her mother had been. Even now, though
she was over nineteen, she sometimes felt herself in danger of her father's violence. She knew it was that that had given her the palpitations. When they were
growing up he had never gone for her, like he used to go for Harry and Ernest,
because she was a girl; but latterly he had begun to threaten her and say what he
would do to her only for her dead mother's sake. And now she had nobody to
protect her. Ernest was dead and Harry, who was in the church decorating business, was nearly always down somewhere in the country. Besides, the invariable
squabble for money on Saturday nights had begun to weary her unspeakably.
She always gave her entire wages—seven shillings—and Harry always sent up
what he could but the trouble was to get any money from her father. He said she
used to squander the money, that she had no head, that he wasn't going to give
her his hard-earned money to throw about the streets, and much more, for he
was usually fairly bad of a Saturday night. In the end he would give her the
money and ask her had she any intention of buying Sunday's dinner. Then she
had to rush out as quickly as she could and do her marketing, holding her black
leather purse tightly in her hand as she elbowed her way through the crowds
and returning home late under her load of provisions. She had hard work to
keep the house together and to see that the two young children who had been
left to her charge went to school regularly and got their meals regularly. It was
hard work—a hard life—but now that she was about to leave it she did not find
it a wholly undesirable life.

She was about to explore another life with Frank. Frank was very kind, 10
manly, open-hearted. She was to go away with him by the night-boat to be his
wife and to live with him in Buenos Ayres where he had a home waiting for her.
How well she remembered the first time she had seen him; he was lodging in a
house on the main road where she used to visit. It seemed a few weeks ago. He
was standing at the gate, his peaked cap pushed back on his head and his hair
tumbled forward over a face of bronze. Then they had come to know each other.
He used to meet her outside the Stores every evening and see her home. He took
her to see *The Bohemian Girl* and she felt elated as she sat in an unaccustomed
part of the theatre with him. He was awfully fond of music and sang a little. People knew that they were courting and, when he sang about the lass that loves a
sailor, she always felt pleasantly confused. He used to call her Poppens out of
fun. First of all it had been an excitement for her to have a fellow and then she
had begun to like him. He had tales of distant countries. He had started as a deck
boy at a pound a month on a ship of the Allan Line going out to Canada. He told
her the names of the ships he had been on and the names of the different services. He had sailed through the Straits of Magellan and he told her stories of the
terrible Patagonians. He had fallen on his feet in Buenos Ayres, he said, and had
come over to the old country just for a holiday. Of course, her father had found
out the affair and had forbidden her to have anything to say to him.

—I know these sailor chaps, he said. 11

One day he had quarrelled with Frank and after that she had to meet her 12
lover secretly.

The evening deepened in the avenue. The white of two letters in her lap 13
grew indistinct. One was to Harry; the other was to her father. Ernest had been
her favourite but she liked Harry too. Her father was becoming old lately, she
noticed; he would miss her. Sometimes he could be very nice. Not long before,
when she had been laid up for a day, he had read her out a ghost story and made
toast for her at the fire. Another day, when their mother was alive, they had all
gone for a picnic to the Hill of Howth. She remembered her father putting on
her mother's bonnet to make the children laugh.

Her time was running out but she continued to sit by the window, leaning 14
her head against the window curtain, inhaling the odour of dusty cretonne.
Down far in the avenue she could hear a street organ playing. She knew the air.
Strange that it should come that very night to remind her of the promise to her
mother, her promise to keep the home together as long as she could. She remembered the last night of her mother's illness; she was again in the close dark
room at the other side of the hall and outside she heard a melancholy air of
Italy. The organ-player had been ordered to go away and given sixpence. She remembered her father strutting back into the sickroom saying:

—Damned Italians! coming over here! 15

As she mused the pitiful vision of her mother's life laid its spell on the very 16
quick of her being—that life of commonplace sacrifices closing in final crazi-
ness. She trembled as she heard again her mother's voice saying constantly with
foolish insistence:

—Derevaun Seraun! Derevaun Seraun!   17

She stood up in a sudden impulse of terror. Escape! She must escape! Frank   18
would save her. He would give her life, perhaps love, too. But she wanted to live.
Why should she be unhappy? She had a right to happiness. Frank would take
her in his arms, fold her in his arms. He would save her.

———

She stood among the swaying crowd in the station at the North Wall. He   19
held her hand and she knew that he was speaking to her, saying something
about the passage over and over again. The station was full of soldiers with
brown baggages. Through the wide doors of the sheds she caught a glimpse of
the black mass of the boat, lying in beside the quay wall, with illumined port-
holes. She answered nothing. She felt her cheek pale and cold and, out of a
maze of distress, she prayed to God to direct her, to show her what was her
duty. The boat blew a long mournful whistle into the mist. If she went, tomorrow she would be on the sea with Frank, steaming towards Buenos Ayres.
Their passage had been booked. Could she still draw back after all he had done
for her? Her distress awoke a nausea in her body and she kept moving her lips
in silent fervent prayer.

A bell clanged upon her heart. She felt him seize her hand: 20
—Come!   21
All the seas of the world tumbled about her heart. He was drawing her into   22
them: he would drown her. She gripped with both hands at the iron railing.
—Come!   23
No! No! No! It was impossible. Her hands clutched the iron in frenzy. Amid   24
the seas she sent a cry of anguish!
—Eveline! Evvy!   25
He rushed beyond the barrier and called to her to follow. He was shouted   26
at to go on but he still called to her. She set her white face to him, passive,
like a helpless animal. Her eyes gave him no sign of love or farewell or recognition.

ACTIVITIES FOR WRITING AND DISCUSSION

1. In a small group, brainstorm lists of factors that:
a. Impel Eveline to stay with her family.
b. Impel her to elope with Frank.

Why do the former prove stronger than the latter? Why do you think Eveline
declines, at the last moment, to go off with Frank?

2. Assuming the **character** of Eveline, compose a series of diary entries that
articulate your divided feelings for Frank and your family. Where appropriate,
incorporate details from Joyce's story into your entries.

3. Eveline's conflict (self-development versus social duty or duty to family) is shared by countless sons and daughters. Tell the story of a real-life (or imagined) son or daughter whose experience is analogous to Eveline's.

TILLIE OLSEN (b. 1913)

I Stand Here Ironing

I stand here ironing, and what you asked me moves tormented back and forth 1 with the iron.

"I wish you would manage the time to come in and talk with me about your 2 daughter. I'm sure you can help me understand her. She's a youngster who needs help and whom I'm deeply interested in helping."

"Who needs help." Even if I came, what good would it do? You think be- 3 cause I am her mother I have a key, or that in some way you could use me as a key? She has lived for nineteen years. There is all that life that has happened outside of me, beyond me.

And when is there time to remember, to sift, to weigh, to estimate, to total? I 4 will start and there will be an interruption and I will have to gather it all together again. Or I will become engulfed with all I did or did not do, with what should have been and what cannot be helped.

She was a beautiful baby. The first and only one of our five that was beauti- 5 ful at birth. You do not guess how new and uneasy her tenancy in her now-loveliness. You did not know her all those years she was thought homely, or see her poring over her baby pictures, making me tell her over and over how beautiful she had been—and would be, I would tell her—and was now, to the seeing eye. But the seeing eyes were few or non-existent. Including mine.

I nursed her. They feel that's important nowadays. I nursed all the children, 6 but with her, with all the fierce rigidity of first motherhood, I did like the books then said. Though her cries battered me to trembling and my breasts ached with swollenness, I waited till the clock decreed.

Why do I put that first? I do not even know if it matters, or if it explains 7 anything.

She was a beautiful baby. She blew shining bubbles of sound. She loved mo- 8 tion, loved light, loved color and music and textures. She would lie on the floor in her blue overalls patting the surface so hard in ecstasy her hands and feet would blur. She was a miracle to me, but when she was eight months old I had to leave her daytimes with the woman downstairs to whom she was no miracle at all, for I worked or looked for work and for Emily's father, who "could no longer endure" (he wrote in his good-bye note) "sharing want with us."

I was nineteen. It was the pre-relief, pre-WPA world of the depression. I 9 would start running as soon as I got off the streetcar, running up the stairs, the place smelling sour, and awake or asleep to startle awake, when she saw me she would break into a clogged weeping that could not be comforted, a weeping I can hear yet.

After a while I found a job hashing at night so I could be with her days, and 10 it was better. But it came to where I had to bring her to his family and leave her.

It took a long time to raise the money for her fare back. Then she got 11 chicken pox and I had to wait longer. When she finally came, I hardly knew her, walking quick and nervous like her father, looking like her father, thin, and dressed in a shoddy red that yellowed her skin and glared at the pockmarks. All the baby loveliness gone.

She was two. Old enough for nursery school they said, and I did not know 12 then what I know now—the fatigue of the long day, and the lacerations of group life in the nurseries that are only parking places for children.

Except that it would have made no difference if I had known. It was the only 13 place there was. It was the only way we could be together, the only way I could hold a job.

And even without knowing, I knew. I knew the teacher that was evil because 14 all these years it has curdled into my memory, the little boy hunched in the corner, her rasp, "why aren't you outside, because Alvin hits you? that's no reason, go out, scaredy." I knew Emily hated it even if she did not clutch and implore "don't go Mommy" like the other children, mornings.

She always had a reason why she should stay home. Momma, you look sick, 15 Momma. I feel sick. Momma, the teachers aren't there today, they're sick. Momma, we can't go, there was a fire there last night. Momma, it's a holiday today, no school, they told me.

But never a direct protest, never rebellion. I think of our others in their 16 three-, four-year-oldness—the explosions, the tempers, the denunciations, the demands—and I feel suddenly ill. I put the iron down. What in me demanded that goodness in her? And what was the cost, the cost to her of such goodness?

The old man living in the back once said in his gentle way: "You should 17 smile at Emily more when you look at her." What *was* in my face when I looked at her? I loved her. There were all the acts of love.

It was only with the others I remembered what he said, and it was the face of 18 joy, and not of care or tightness or worry I turned to them—too late for Emily. She does not smile easily, let alone almost always as her brothers and sisters do. Her face is closed and sombre, but when she wants, how fluid. You must have seen it in her pantomimes, you spoke of her rare gift for comedy on the stage that rouses a laughter out of the audience so dear they applaud and applaud and do not want to let her go.

Where does it come from, that comedy? There was none of it in her when 19 she came back to me that second time, after I had had to send her away again. She had a new daddy now to learn to love, and I think perhaps it was a better time.

Except when we left her alone nights, telling ourselves she was old enough. 20

"Can't you go some other time, Mommy, like tomorrow?" she would ask. 21 "Will it be just a little while you'll be gone? Do you promise?"

The time we came back, the front door open, the clock on the floor in the 22 hall. She rigid awake. "It wasn't just a little while. I didn't cry. Three times I called you, just three times, and then I ran downstairs to open the door so you could come faster. The clock talked loud. I threw it away, it scared me what it talked."

She said the clock talked loud again that night I went to the hospital to have 23 Susan. She was delirious with the fever that comes before red measles, but she was fully conscious all the week I was gone and the week after we were home when she could not come near the new baby or me.

She did not get well. She stayed skeleton thin, not wanting to eat, and night 24 after night she had nightmares. She would call for me, and I would rouse from exhaustion to sleepily call back: "You're all right, darling, go to sleep, it's just a dream," and if she still called, in a sterner voice, "now go to sleep, Emily, there's nothing to hurt you." Twice, only twice, when I had to get up for Susan anyhow, I went in to sit with her.

Now when it is too late (as if she would let me hold and comfort her like I 25 do the others) I get up and go to her at once at her moan or restless stirring. "Are you awake, Emily? Can I get you something?" And the answer is always the same: "No, I'm all right, go back to sleep, Mother."

They persuaded me at the clinic to send her away to a convalescent home in 26 the country where "she can have the kind of food and care you can't manage for her, and you'll be free to concentrate on the new baby." They still send children to that place. I see pictures on the society page of sleek young women planning affairs to raise money for it, or dancing at the affairs, or decorating Easter eggs or filling Christmas stockings for the children.

They never have a picture of the children so I do not know if the girls still 27 wear those gigantic red bows and the ravaged looks on the every other Sunday when parents can come to visit "unless otherwise notified"—as we were notified the first six weeks.

Oh it is a handsome place, green lawns and tall trees and fluted flower beds. 28 High up on the balconies of each cottage the children stand, the girls in their red bows and white dresses, the boys in white suits and giant red ties. The parents stand below shrieking up to be heard and the children shriek down to be heard, and between them the invisible wall "Not To Be Contaminated by Parental Germs or Physical Affection."

There was a tiny girl who always stood hand in hand with Emily. Her 29 parents never came. One visit she was gone. "They moved her to Rose College," Emily shouted in explanation. "They don't like you to love anybody here."

She wrote once a week, the labored writing of a seven-year-old. "I am fine. 30 How is the baby. If I write my leter nicly I will have a star. Love." There never was a star. We wrote every other day, letters she could never hold or keep but only hear read—once. "We simply do not have room for children to keep any personal possessions," they patiently explained when we pieced one Sunday's shrieking together to plead how much it would mean to Emily, who loved so to keep things, to be allowed to keep her letters and cards.

Each visit she looked frailer. "She isn't eating," they told us.   31

(They had runny eggs for breakfast or mush with lumps, Emily said later, I'd   32
hold it in my mouth and not swallow. Nothing ever tasted good, just when they
had chicken.)

It took us eight months to get her released home, and only the fact that she   33
gained back so little of her seven lost pounds convinced the social worker.

I used to try to hold and love her after she came back, but her body would   34
stay stiff, and after a while she'd push away. She ate little. Food sickened her, and
I think much of life too. Oh she had physical lightness and brightness, twinkling by on skates, bouncing like a ball up and down up and down over the
jump rope, skimming over the hill; but these were momentary.

She fretted about her appearance, thin and dark and foreign-looking at a   35
time when every little girl was supposed to look or thought she should look a
chubby blonde replica of Shirley Temple. The doorbell sometimes rang for her,
but no one seemed to come and play in the house or be a best friend. Maybe because we moved so much.

There was a boy she loved painfully through two school semesters. Months   36
later she told me how she had taken pennies from my purse to buy him candy.
"Licorice was his favorite and I brought him some every day, but he still liked
Jennifer better'n me. Why, Mommy?" The kind of question for which there is
no answer.

School was a worry to her. She was not glib or quick in a world where glib-   37
ness and quickness were easily confused with ability to learn. To her overworked and exasperated teachers she was an overconscientious "slow learner"
who kept trying to catch up and was absent entirely too often.

I let her be absent, though sometimes the illness was imaginary. How differ-   38
ent from my now-strictness about attendance with the others. I wasn't working.
We had a new baby, I was home anyhow. Sometimes, after Susan grew old
enough, I would keep her home from school, too, to have them all together.

Mostly Emily had asthma, and her breathing, harsh and labored, would fill   39
the house with a curiously tranquil sound. I would bring the two old dresser
mirrors and her boxes of collections to her bed. She would select beads and single earrings, bottle tops and shells, dried flowers and pebbles, old postcards and
scraps, all sorts of oddments; then she and Susan would play Kingdom, setting
up landscapes and furniture, peopling them with action.

Those were the only times of peaceful companionship between her and Su-   40
san. I have edged away from it, that poisonous feeling between them, that terrible balancing of hurts and needs I had to do between the two, and did so badly,
those earlier years.

Oh there are conflicts between the others too, each one human, needing, de-   41
manding, hurting, taking—but only between Emily and Susan, no, Emily toward Susan that corroding resentment. It seems so obvious on the surface, yet it
is not obvious. Susan, the second child, Susan, golden- and curly-haired and
chubby, quick and articulate and assured, everything in appearance and manner Emily was not; Susan, not able to resist Emily's precious things, losing or
sometimes clumsily breaking them; Susan telling jokes and riddles to company

for applause while Emily sat silent (to say to me later: that was *my* riddle, Mother, I told it to Susan); Susan, who for all the five years' difference in age was just a year behind Emily in developing physically.

I am glad for that slow physical development that widened the difference 42 between her and her contemporaries, though she suffered over it. She was too vulnerable for that terrible world of youthful competition, of preening and parading, of constant measuring of yourself against every other, of envy, "If I had that copper hair," "If I had that skin. . . ." She tormented herself enough about not looking like the others, there was enough of the unsureness, the having to be conscious of words before you speak, the constant caring—what are they thinking of me? without having it all magnified by the merciless physical drives.

Ronnie is calling. He is wet and I change him. It is rare there is such a cry 43 now. That time of motherhood is almost behind me when the ear is not one's own but must always be racked and listening for the child cry, the child call. We sit for a while and I hold him, looking out over the city spread in charcoal with its soft aisles of light. *"Shoogily,"* he breathes and curls closer. I carry him back to bed, asleep. *Shoogily.* A funny word, a family word, inherited from Emily, invented by her to say: *comfort.*

In this and other ways she leaves her seal, I say aloud. And startle at my say- 44 ing it. What do I mean? What did I start to gather together, to try and make coherent? I was at the terrible, growing years. War years. I do not remember them well. I was working, there were four smaller ones now, there was not time for her. She had to help be a mother, and housekeeper, and shopper. She had to set her seal. Mornings of crisis and near hysteria trying to get lunches packed, hair combed, coats and shoes found, everyone to school or Child Care on time, the baby ready for transportation. And always the paper scribbled on by a smaller one, the book looked at by Susan then mislaid, the homework not done. Running out to that huge school where she was one, she was lost, she was a drop; suffering over the unpreparedness, stammering and unsure in her classes.

There was so little time left at night after the kids were bedded down. She 45 would struggle over books, always eating (it was in those years she developed her enormous appetite that is legendary in our family) and I would be ironing, or preparing food for the next day, or writing V-mail to Bill, or tending the baby. Sometimes, to make me laugh, or out of her despair, she would imitate happenings or types at school.

I think I said once: "Why don't you do something like this in the school am- 46 ateur show?" One morning she phoned me at work, hardly understandable through the weeping: "Mother, I did it. I won, I won; they gave me first prize; they clapped and clapped and wouldn't let me go."

Now suddenly she was Somebody, and as imprisoned in her difference as 47 she had been in anonymity.

She began to be asked to perform at other high schools, even in colleges, 48 then at city and statewide affairs. The first one we went to, I only recognized her that first moment when thin, shy, she almost drowned herself into the curtains. Then: Was this Emily? The control, the command, the convulsing and deadly clowning, the spell, then the roaring, stamping audience, unwilling to let this rare and precious laughter out of their lives.

Afterwards: You ought to do something about her with a gift like that—but without money or knowing how, what does one do? We have left it all to her, and the gift has as often eddied inside, clogged and clotted, as been used and growing.   49

She is coming. She runs up the stairs two at a time with her light graceful step, and I know she is happy tonight. Whatever it was that occasioned your call did not happen today.   50

"Aren't you ever going to finish the ironing, Mother? Whistler painted his mother in a rocker. I'd have to paint mine standing over an ironing board." This is one of her communicative nights and she tells me everything and nothing as she fixes herself a plate of food out of the icebox.   51

She is so lovely. Why did you want me to come in at all? Why were you concerned? She will find her way.   52

She starts up the stairs to bed. "Don't get me up with the rest in the morning." "But I thought you were having midterms." "Oh, those," she comes back in, kisses me, and says quite lightly, "in a couple of years when we'll all be atom-dead they won't matter a bit."   53

She has said it before. She *believes* it. But because I have been dredging the past, and all that compounds a human being is so heavy and meaningful in me, I cannot endure it tonight.   54

I will never total it all. I will never come in to say: She was a child seldom smiled at. Her father left me before she was a year old. I had to work her first six years when there was work, or I sent her home and to his relatives. There were years she had care she hated. She was dark and thin and foreign-looking in a world where the prestige went to blondeness and curly hair and dimples, she was slow where glibness was prized. She was a child of anxious, not proud, love. We were poor and could not afford for her the soil of easy growth. I was a young mother, I was a distracted mother. There were the other children pushing up, demanding. Her younger sister seemed all that she was not. There were years she did not want me to touch her. She kept too much in herself, her life was such she had to keep too much in herself. My wisdom came too late. She has much to her and probably nothing will come of it. She is a child of her age, of depression, of war, of fear.   55

Let her be. So all that is in her will not bloom—but in how many does it? There is still enough left to live by. Only help her to know—help make it so there is cause for her to know—that she is more than this dress on the ironing board, helpless before the iron.   56

ACTIVITY FOR WRITING AND DISCUSSION

1. Respond to the story using the "Four-Step Process for Writing from Reading" described in Chapter 2.

<u>JAMES BALDWIN (1924–1987)</u>

Sonny's Blues

I read about it in the paper, in the subway, on my way to work. I read it, and I 1
couldn't believe it, and I read it again. Then perhaps I just stared at it, at the
newsprint spelling out his name, spelling out the story. I stared at it in the
swinging lights of the subway car, and in the faces and bodies of the people, and
in my own face, trapped in the darkness which roared outside.

It was not to be believed and I kept telling myself that, as I walked from the 2
subway station to the high school. And at the same time I couldn't doubt it. I
was scared, scared for Sonny. He became real to me again. A great block of ice
got settled in my belly and kept melting there slowly all day long, while I taught
my classes algebra. It was a special kind of ice. It kept melting, sending trickles
of ice water all up and down my veins, but it never got less. Sometimes it hardened and seemed to expand until I felt my guts were going to come spilling out
or that I was going to choke or scream. This would always be at a moment when
I was remembering some specific thing Sonny had once said or done.

When he was about as old as the boys in my class his face had been bright 3
and open, there was a lot of copper in it; and he'd had wonderfully direct brown
eyes, and great gentleness and privacy. I wondered what he looked like now. He
had been picked up, the evening before, in a raid on an apartment downtown,
for peddling and using heroin.

I couldn't believe it: but what I mean by that is that I couldn't find any room 4
for it anywhere inside me. I had kept it outside me for a long time. I hadn't
wanted to know. I had had suspicions, but I didn't name them, I kept putting
them away. I told myself that Sonny was wild, but he wasn't crazy. And he'd always been a good boy, he hadn't ever turned hard or evil or disrespectful, the
way kids can, so quick, so quick, especially in Harlem. I didn't want to believe
that I'd ever see my brother going down, coming to nothing, all that light in his
face gone out, in the condition I'd already seen so many others. Yet it had happened and here I was, talking about algebra to a lot of boys who might, every
one of them for all I knew, be popping off needles every time they went to the
head. Maybe it did more for them than algebra could.

I was sure that the first time Sonny had ever had horse, he couldn't have been 5
much older than these boys were now. These boys, now, were living as we'd been
living then, they were growing up with a rush and their heads bumped abruptly
against the low ceiling of their actual possibilities. They were filled with rage. All
they really knew were two darknesses, the darkness of their lives, which was now
closing in on them, and the darkness of the movies, which had blinded them to
that other darkness, and in which they now, vindictively, dreamed, at once more
together than they were at any other time, and more alone.

When the last bell rang, the last class ended, I let out my breath. It seemed 6
I'd been holding it for all that time. My clothes were wet—I may have looked as

though I'd been sitting in a steam bath, all dressed up, all afternoon. I sat alone in the classroom a long time. I listened to the boys outside, downstairs, shouting and cursing and laughing. Their laughter struck me for perhaps the first time. It was not the joyous laughter which—God knows why—one associates with children. It was mocking and insular, its intent was to denigrate. It was disenchanted, and in this, also, lay the authority of their curses. Perhaps I was listening to them because I was thinking about my brother and in them I heard my brother. And myself.

One boy was whistling a tune, at once very complicated and very simple, it 7 seemed to be pouring out of him as though he were a bird, and it sounded very cool and moving through all that harsh, bright air, only just holding its own through all those other sounds.

I stood up and walked over to the window and looked down into the court- 8 yard. It was the beginning of the spring and the sap was rising in the boys. A teacher passed through them every now and again, quickly, as though he or she couldn't wait to get out of that courtyard, to get those boys out of their sight and off their minds. I started collecting my stuff. I thought I'd better get home and talk to Isabel.

The courtyard was almost deserted by the time I got downstairs. I saw this 9 boy standing in the shadow of a doorway, looking just like Sonny. I almost called his name. Then I saw that it wasn't Sonny, but somebody we used to know, a boy from around our block. He's been Sonny's friend. He's never been mine, having been too young for me, and, anyway, I'd never liked him. And now, even though he was a grown-up man, he still hung around that block, still spent hours on the street corners, was always high and raggy. I used to run into him from time to time and he'd often work around to asking me for a quarter or fifty cents. He always had some real good excuse, too, and I always gave it to him, I don't know why.

But now, abruptly, I hated him. I couldn't stand the way he looked at me, 10 partly like a dog, partly like a cunning child. I wanted to ask him what the hell he was doing in the school courtyard.

He sort of shuffled over to me, and he said, "I see you got the papers. So you 11 already know about it."

"You mean about Sonny? Yes, I already know about it. How come they 12 didn't get you?"

He grinned. It made him repulsive and it also brought to mind what he'd 13 looked like as a kid. "I wasn't there. I stay away from them people."

"Good for you." I offered him a cigarette and I watched him through the 14 smoke. "You come all the way down here just to tell me about Sonny?"

"That's right." He was sort of shaking his head and his eyes looked strange, 15 as though they were about to cross. The bright sun deadened his damp dark brown skin and it made his eyes look yellow and showed up the dirt in his kinked hair. He smelled funky. I moved a little away from him and I said, "Well, thanks. But I already know about it and I got to get home."

"I'll walk you a little ways," he said. We started walking. There were a couple 16
of kids still loitering in the courtyard and one of them said goodnight to me
and looked strangely at the boy beside me.

"What're you going to do?" he asked me. "I mean, about Sonny?" 17

"Look. I haven't seen Sonny for over a year, I'm not sure I'm going to do 18
anything. Anyway, what the hell *can* I do?"

"That's right," he said quickly, "ain't nothing you can do. Can't much help 19
old Sonny no more, I guess."

It was what I was thinking and so it seemed to me he had no right to say 20
it.

"I'm surprised at Sonny, though," he went on—he had a funny way of talk- 21
ing, he looked straight ahead as though he were talking to himself—"I thought
Sonny was a smart boy, I thought he was too smart to get hung."

"I guess he thought so too," I said sharply, "and that's how he got hung. And 22
how about you? You're pretty goddamn smart, I bet."

Then he looked directly at me, just for a minute. "I ain't smart," he said. "If I 23
was smart, I'd have reached for a pistol a long time ago."

"Look. Don't tell *me* your sad story, if it was up to me, I'd give you one." 24
Then I felt guilty—guilty, probably, for never having supposed that the poor
bastard *had* a story of his own, much less a sad one, and I asked, quickly,
"What's going to happen to him now?"

He didn't answer this. He was off by himself some place. "Funny thing," he 25
said, and from his tone we might have been discussing the quickest way to get
to Brooklyn, "when I saw the papers this morning, the first thing I asked myself
was if I had anything to do with it. I felt sort of responsible."

I began to listen more carefully. The subway station was on the corner, just 26
before us, and I stopped. He stopped, too. We were in front of a bar and he
ducked slightly, peering in, but whoever he was looking for didn't seem to be
there. The juke box was blasting away with something black and bouncy and I
half watched the barmaid as she danced her way from the juke box to her place
behind the bar. And I watched her face as she laughingly responded to something someone said to her, still keeping time to the music. When she smiled one
saw the little girl, one sensed the doomed, still-struggling woman beneath the
battered face of the semi-whore.

"I never *give* Sonny nothing," the boy said finally, "but a long time ago I 27
come to school high and Sonny asked me how it felt." He paused, I couldn't
bear to watch him, I watched the barmaid, and I listened to the music which
seemed to be causing the pavement to shake. "I told him it felt great." The music
stopped, the barmaid paused and watched the juke box until the music began
again. "It did."

All this way carrying me some place I didn't want to go. I certainly didn't 28
want to know how it felt. It filled everything, the people, the houses, the music,
the dark, quick-silver barmaid, with menace; and this menace was their reality.

"What's going to happen to him now?" I asked again. 29

"They'll send him away some place and they'll try to cure him." He shook 30
his head. "Maybe he'll even think he's kicked the habit. Then they'll let him
loose"—he gestured, throwing his cigarette into the gutter. "That's all."

"What do you mean, that's *all*?" 31

But I knew what he meant. 32

"I *mean*, that's *all*." He turned his head and looked at me, pulling down the 33
corners of his mouth. "Don't you know what I mean?" he asked, softly.

"How the hell *would* I know what you mean?" I almost whispered it, I don't 34
know why.

"That's right," he said to the air, "how would *he* know what I mean?" He 35
turned toward me again, patient and calm, and yet I somehow felt him shaking,
shaking as though he were going to fall apart. I felt that ice in my guts again, the
dread I'd felt all afternoon; and again I watched the barmaid, moving about the
bar, washing glasses, and singing. "Listen. They'll let him out and then it'll just
start all over again. That's what I mean."

"You mean—they'll let him out. And then he'll just start working his way 36
back in again. You mean he'll never kick the habit. Is that what you mean?"

"That's right," he said, cheerfully. "*You* see what I mean." 37

"Tell me," I said at last, "why does he want to die? He must want to die, he's 38
killing himself, why does he want to die?"

He looked at me in surprise. He licked his lips. "He don't want to die. He 39
wants to live. Don't nobody want to die, ever."

Then I wanted to ask him—too many things. He could not have answered, 40
or if he had, I could not have borne the answers. I started walking. "Well, I guess
it's none of my business."

"It's going to be rough on old Sonny," he said. We reached the subway sta- 41
tion. "This is your station?" he asked. I nodded. I took one step down. "Damn!"
he said, suddenly. I looked up at him. He grinned again. "Damn it if I didn't
leave all my money home. You ain't got a dollar on you, have you? Just for a
couple of days, is all."

All at once something inside gave and threatened to come pouring out of me. I 42
didn't hate him any more. I felt that in another moment I'd start crying like a child.

"Sure," I said. "Don't swear." I looked in my wallet and didn't have a dollar, I 43
only had a five. "Here," I said. "That hold you?"

He didn't look at it—he didn't want to look at it. A terrible, closed look 44
came over his face, as though he were keeping the number on the bill a secret
from him and me. "Thanks," he said, and now he was dying to see me go. "Don't
worry about Sonny. Maybe I'll write him or something."

"Sure," I said. "You do that. So long." 45

"Be seeing you," he said. I went down the steps. 46

And I didn't write Sonny or send him anything for a long time. When I fi- 47
nally did, it was just after my little girl died, he wrote me back a letter which
made me feel like a bastard.

Here's what he said: 48

Dear Brother,   49
    You don't know how much I needed to hear from you. I wanted to
write you many a time but I dug how much I must have hurt you and so
I didn't write. But now I feel like a man who's been trying to climb up
out of some deep, real deep and funky hole and just saw the sun up
there, outside. I got to get outside.
    I can't tell you much about how I got here. I mean I don't know how   50
to tell you. I guess I was afraid of something or I was trying to escape
from something and you know I have never been very strong in the
head (smile). I'm glad Mama and Daddy are dead and can't see what's
happened to their son and I swear if I'd known what I was doing I
would never have hurt you so, you and a lot of other fine people who
were nice to me and who believed in me.
    I don't want you to think it had anything to do with me being a mu-   51
sician. It's more than that. Or maybe less than that. I can't get anything
straight in my head down here and I try not to think about what's going
to happen to me when I get outside again. Sometime I think I'm going
to flip and *never* get outside and sometime I think I'll come straight
back. I tell you one thing, though, I'd rather blow my brains out than go
through this again. But that's what they all say, so they tell me. If I tell
you when I'm coming to New York and if you could meet me, I sure
would appreciate it. Give my love to Isabel and the kids and I was sure
sorry to hear about little Gracie. I wish I could be like Mama and say the
Lord's will be done, but I don't know it seems to me that trouble is the
one thing that never does get stopped and I don't know what good it
does to blame it on the Lord. But maybe it does some good if you believe it.

                                                            Your brother,
                                                                  Sonny

    Then I kept in constant touch with him and I sent him whatever I could and   52
I went to meet him when he came back to New York. When I saw him many
things I thought I had forgotten came flooding back to me. This was because I
had begun, finally, to wonder about Sonny, about the life that Sonny lived inside. This life, whatever it was, had made him older and thinner and it had
deepened the distant stillness in which he had always moved. He looked very
unlike my baby brother. Yet, when he smiled, when we shook hands, the baby
brother I'd never known looked out from the depths of his private life, like an
animal waiting to be coaxed into the light.
    "How you been keeping?" he asked me.   53
    "All right. And you?"   54
    "Just fine." He was smiling all over his face. "It's good to see you again."   55
    "It's good to see you."   56

The seven years' difference in our ages lay between us like a chasm: I won- 57
dered if these years would ever operate between us as a bridge. I was remembering, and it made it hard to catch my breath, that I had been there when he was
born; and I had heard the first words he had ever spoken. When he started to
walk, he walked from our mother straight to me. I caught him just before he fell
when he took the first steps he ever took in this world.

"How's Isabel?"   58

"Just fine. She's dying to see you."   59

"And the boys?"   60

"They're fine, too. They're anxious to see their uncle."   61

"Oh, come on. You know they don't remember me."   62

"Are you kidding? Of course they remember you."   63

He grinned again. We got into a taxi. We had a lot to say to each other, far 64
too much to know how to begin.

As the taxi began to move, I asked, "You still want to go to India?"   65

He laughed. "You still remember that. Hell, no. This place is Indian enough 66
for me."

"It used to belong to them," I said.   67

And he laughed again. "They damn sure knew what they were doing when 68
they got rid of it."

Years ago, when he was around fourteen, he'd been all hipped on the idea of 69
going to India. He read books about people sitting on rocks, naked, in all kinds
of weather, but mostly bad, naturally, and walking barefoot through hot coals
and arriving at wisdom. I used to say that it sounded to me as though they were
getting away from wisdom as fast as they could. I think he sort of looked down
on me for that.

"Do you mind," he asked, "if we have the driver drive alongside the park? 70
On the west side—I haven't seen the city in so long."

"Of course not," I said. I was afraid that I might sound as though I were hu- 71
moring him, but I hoped he wouldn't take it that way.

So we drove along, between the green of the park and the stony, lifeless ele- 72
gance of hotels and apartment buildings, toward the vivid, killing streets of our
childhood. These streets hadn't changed, though housing projects jutted up out
of them now like rocks in the middle of a boiling sea. Most of the houses in
which we had grown up had vanished, as had the stores from which we had
stolen, the basements in which we had first tried sex, the rooftops from which
we hurled tin cans and bricks. But houses exactly like the houses of our past yet
dominated the landscape, boys exactly like the boys we once had been found
themselves smothering in these houses, came down into the streets for light
and air and found themselves encircled by disaster. Some escaped the trap,
most didn't. Those who got out always left something of themselves behind, as
some animals amputate a leg and leave it in the trap. It might be said, perhaps,
that I had escaped, after all, I was a school teacher; or that Sonny had, he hadn't
lived in Harlem for years. Yet, as the cab moved uptown through streets which
seemed, with a rush, to darken with dark people, and as I covertly studied

Sonny's face, it came to me that what we both were seeking through our separate cab windows was that part of ourselves which had been left behind. It's always at the hour of trouble and confrontation that the missing member aches.

We hit 110th Street and started rolling up Lenox Avenue. And I'd known 73 this avenue all my life, but it seemed to me again, as it had seemed on the day I'd first heard about Sonny's trouble, filled with a hidden menace which was its very breath of life.

"We almost there," said Sonny. 74

"Almost." We were both too nervous to say anything more. 75

We lived in a housing project. It hasn't been up long. A few days after it was 76 up it seemed uninhabitably new, now, of course, it's already rundown. It looks like a parody of the good, clean, faceless life—God knows the people who live in it do their best to make it a parody. The beat-looking grass lying around isn't enough to make their lives green, the hedges will never hold out the streets, and they know it. The big windows fool no one, they aren't big enough to make space out of no space. They don't bother with the windows, they watch the TV screen instead. The playground is most popular with the children who don't play at jacks, or skip rope, or roller skate, or swing, and they can be found in it after dark. We moved in partly because it's not too far from where I teach, and partly for the kids; but it's really just like the houses in which Sonny and I grew up. The same things happen, they'll have the same things to remember. The moment Sonny and I started into the house I had the feeling that I was simply bringing him back into the danger he had almost died trying to escape.

Sonny has never been talkative. So I don't know why I was sure he'd be dy- 77 ing to talk to me when supper was over the first night. Everything went fine, the oldest boy remembered him, and the youngest boy liked him, and Sonny had remembered to bring something for each of them; and Isabel, who is really much nicer than I am, more open and giving, had gone to a lot of trouble about dinner and was genuinely glad to see him. And she's always been able to tease Sonny in a way that I haven't. It was nice to see her face so vivid again and to hear her laugh and watch her make Sonny laugh. She wasn't, or, anyway, she didn't seem to be, at all uneasy or embarrassed. She chatted as though there were no subject which had to be avoided and she got Sonny past his first, faint stiffness. And thank God she was there, for I was filled with that icy dread again. Everything I did seemed awkward to me, and everything I said sounded freighted with hidden meaning. I was trying to remember everything I'd heard about dope addiction and I couldn't help watching Sonny for signs. I wasn't doing it out of malice. I was trying to find out something about my brother. I was dying to hear him tell me he was safe.

"Safe!" my father grunted, whenever Mama suggested trying to move to a 78 neighborhood which might be safer for children. "Safe, hell! Ain't no place safe for kids, nor nobody."

He always went on like this, but he wasn't, ever, really as bad as he sounded, 79 not even on weekends, when he got drunk. As a matter of fact, he was always on the lookout for "something a little better," but he died before he found it. He died suddenly, during a drunken weekend in the middle of the war, when Sonny was fifteen. He and Sonny hadn't ever got on too well. And this was partly because Sonny was the apple of his father's eye. It was because he loved Sonny so much and was frightened for him, that he was always fighting with him. It doesn't do any good to fight with Sonny. Sonny just moves back, inside himself, where he can't be reached. But the principal reason that they never hit it off is that they were so much alike. Daddy was big and rough and loud-talking, just the opposite of Sonny, but they both had—that same privacy.

Mama tried to tell me something about this, just after Daddy died. I was home on leave from the army.   80

This was the last time I ever saw my mother alive. Just the same, this picture gets all mixed up in my mind with pictures I had of her when she was younger. The way I always see her is the way she used to be on Sunday afternoon, say, when the old folks were talking after the big Sunday dinner. I always see her wearing pale blue. She'd be sitting on the sofa. And my father would be sitting in the easy chair, not far from her. And the living room would be full of church folks and relatives. There they sit, in chairs all around the living room, and the night is creeping up outside, but nobody knows it yet. You can see the darkness growing against the windowpanes and you hear the street noises every now and again, or maybe the jangling beat of a tambourine from one of the churches close by, but it's real quiet in the room. For a moment nobody's talking, but every face looks darkening, like the sky outside. And my mother rocks a little from the waist, and my father's eyes are closed. Everyone is looking at something a child can't see. For a minute they've forgotten the children. Maybe a kid is lying on the rug, half asleep. Maybe somebody's got a kid in his lap and is absent-mindedly stroking the kid's head. Maybe there's a kid, quiet and big-eyed, curled up in a big chair in the corner. The silence, the darkness coming, and the darkness in the faces frightens the child obscurely. He hopes that the hand which strokes his forehead will never stop—will never die. He hopes that there will never come a time when the old folks won't be sitting around the living room, talking about where they've come from, and what they've seen, and what's happened to them and their kinfolk.   81

But something deep and watchful in the child knows that this is bound to end, is already ending. In a moment someone will get up and turn on the light. Then the old folks will remember the children and they won't talk any more that day. And when light fills the room, the child is filled with darkness. He knows that every time this happens he's moved just a little closer to that darkness outside. The darkness outside is what the old folks have been talking about. It's what they've come from. It's what they endure. The child knows that they won't talk any more because if he knows too much about what's happened to *them*, he'll know too much too soon, about what's going to happen to *him*.   82

The last time I talked to my mother, I remember I was restless. I wanted to get out and see Isabel. We weren't married then and we had a lot to straighten out between us.   83

There Mama sat, in black, by the window. She was humming an old church 84
song, *Lord, you brought me from a long ways off.* Sonny was out somewhere.
Mama kept watching the streets.

"I don't know," she said, "if I'll ever see you again, after you go off from here. 85
But I hope you'll remember the things I tried to teach you."

"Don't talk like that," I said, and smiled. "You'll be here a long time yet."   86

She smiled, too, but she said nothing. She was quiet for a long time. And I 87
said, "Mama, don't you worry about nothing. I'll be writing all the time, and
you be getting the checks . . ."

"I want to talk to you about your brother," she said, suddenly. "If anything 88
happens to me he ain't going to have nobody to look out for him."

"Mama," I said, "ain't nothing going to happen to you *or* Sonny. Sonny's all 89
right. He's a good boy and he's got good sense."

"It ain't a question of his being a good boy," Mama said, "nor of his having 90
good sense. It ain't only the bad ones, nor yet the dumb ones that gets sucked
under." She stopped, looking at me. "Your Daddy once had a brother," she said,
and she smiled in a way that made me feel she was in pain. "You didn't never
know that, did you?"

"No," I said, "I never knew that," and I watched her face.   91

"Oh, yes," she said, "your Daddy had a brother." She looked out of the win- 92
dow again. "I know you never saw your Daddy cry. But *I* did—many a time,
through all these years."

I asked her, "What happened to his brother? How come nobody's ever 93
talked about him?"

This was the first time I ever saw my mother look old.   94

"His brother got killed," she said, "when he was just a little younger than 95
you are now. I knew him. He was a fine boy. He was maybe a little full of the
devil, but he didn't mean nobody no harm."

Then she stopped and the room was silent, exactly as it had sometimes been 96
on those Sunday afternoons. Mama kept looking out into the streets.

"He used to have a job in the mill," she said, "and, like all young folks, he just 97
liked to perform on Saturday nights. Saturday nights, him and your father
would drift around to different places, go to dances and things like that, or just
sit around with people they knew, and your father's brother would sing, he had
a fine voice, and play along with himself on his guitar. Well, this particular Saturday night, him and your father was coming home from some place, and they
were both a little drunk and there was a moon that night, it was bright like day.
Your father's brother was feeling kind of good, and he was whistling to himself,
and he had his guitar slung over his shoulder. They was coming down a hill and
beneath them was a road that turned off from the highway. Well, your father's
brother, being always kind of frisky, decided to run down this hill, and he did,
with that guitar banging and clanging behind him, and he ran across the road,
and he was making water behind a tree. And your father was sort of amused at
him and he was still coming down the hill, kind of slow. Then he heard a car
motor and that same minute his brother stepped from behind the tree, into the

road, in the moonlight. And he started to cross the road. And your father started to run down the hill, he says he don't know why. This car was full of white men. They was all drunk, and when they seen your father's brother they let out a great whoop and holler and they aimed the car straight at him. They was having fun, they just wanted to scare him, the way they do sometimes, you know. But they was drunk. And I guess the boy, being drunk, too, and scared, kind of lost his head. By the time he jumped it was too late. Your father says he heard his brother scream when the car rolled over him, and he heard the wood of that guitar when it give, and he heard them strings go flying, and he heard them white men shouting, and the car kept on a-going and it ain't stopped till this day. And, time your father got down the hill, his brother weren't nothing but blood and pulp."

Tears were gleaming on my mother's face. There wasn't anything I could say. 98

"He never mentioned it," she said, "because I never let him mention it be- 99 fore you children. Your Daddy was like a crazy man that night and for many a night thereafter. He says he never in his life seen anything as dark as that road after the lights of that car had gone away. Weren't nothing; weren't nobody on that road, just your Daddy and his brother and that busted guitar. Oh, yes. Your Daddy never did really get right again. Till the day he died he weren't sure but that every white man he saw was the man that killed his brother."

She stopped and took out her handkerchief and dried her eyes and looked 100 at me.

"I ain't telling you all this," she said, "to make you scared or bitter or to 101 make you hate nobody. I'm telling you this because you got a brother. And the world ain't changed."

I guess I didn't want to believe this. I guess she saw this in my face. She 102 turned away from me, toward the window again, searching those streets.

"But I praise my Redeemer," she said at last, "that He called your Daddy 103 home before me. I ain't saying it to throw no flowers at myself, but, I declare, it keeps me from feeling too cast down to know I helped your father get safely through this world. Your father always acted like he was the roughest, strongest man on earth. And everybody took him to be like that. But if he hadn't had *me* there—to see his tears!"

She was crying again. Still, I couldn't move. I said, "Lord, Lord, Mama, I 104 didn't know it was like that."

"Oh, honey," she said, "There's a lot that you don't know. But you are going 105 to find out." She stood up from the window and came over to me. "You got to hold on to your brother," she said, "and don't let him fall, no matter what it looks like is happening to him and no matter how evil you gets with him. You going to be evil with him many a time. But don't you forget what I told you, you hear?"

"I won't forget," I said. "Don't you worry, I won't forget. I won't let nothing 106 happen to Sonny."

My mother smiled as though she were amused at something she saw in my 107
face. Then, "You may not be able to stop nothing from happening. But you got
to let him know you's *there*."

————————

Two days later I was married, and then I was gone. And I had a lot of things 108
on my mind and I pretty well forgot my promise to Mama until I got shipped
home on a special furlough for her funeral.

And, after the funeral, with just Sonny and me alone in the empty kitchen, I 109
tried to find out something about him.

"What do you want to do?" I asked him.   110

"I'm going to be a musician," he said.   111

For he had graduated, in the time I had been away, from dancing to the juke 112
box to finding out who was playing what, and what they were doing with it, and
he had bought himself a set of drums.

"You mean, you want to be a drummer?" I somehow had the feeling that be- 113
ing a drummer might be all right for other people but not for my brother
Sonny.

"I don't know," he said, looking at me very gravely, "that I'll ever be a good 114
drummer. But I think I can play a piano."

I frowned. I'd never played the role of the older brother quite so seriously 115
before, had scarcely ever, in fact, *asked* Sonny a damn thing. I sensed myself in
the presence of something I didn't really know how to handle, didn't understand. So I made my frown a little deeper as I asked: "What kind of musician do
you want to be?"

He grinned. "How many kinds do you think there are?"   116

"Be *serious*," I said.   117

He laughed, throwing his head back, and then looked at me. "I *am* serious." 118

"Well, then, for Christ's sake, stop kidding around and answer a serious 119
question. I mean, do you want to be a concert pianist, you want to play classical
music and all that, or—or what?" Long before I finished he was laughing again.
"For Christ's *sake*, Sonny!"

He sobered, but with difficulty. "I'm sorry. But you sound so—*scared!*" and 120
he was off again.

"Well, you may think it's funny now, baby, but it's not going to be so funny 121
when you have to make your living at it, let me tell you *that*." I was furious because I knew he was laughing at me and I didn't know why.

"No," he said, very sober now, and afraid, perhaps, that he'd hurt me, "I 122
don't want to be a classical pianist. That isn't what interests me. I mean"—he
paused, looking hard at me, as though his eyes would help me to understand,
and then gestured helplessly, as though perhaps his hand would help—"I
mean, I'll have a lot of studying to do, and I'll have to study *everything*, but, I
mean, I want to play *with*—jazz musicians." He stopped. "I want to play jazz,"
he said.

Well, the word had never before sounded as heavy, as real, as it sounded that   123
afternoon in Sonny's mouth. I just looked at him and I was probably frowning a
real frown by this time. I simply couldn't see why on earth he'd want to spend
his time hanging around nightclubs, clowning around on bandstands, while
people pushed each other around a dance floor. It seemed—beneath him,
somehow. I had never thought about it before, had never been forced to, but I
suppose I had always put jazz musicians in a class with what Daddy called
"goodtime people."

"Are you *serious*?"   124

"Hell, *yes*, I'm serious."   125

He looked more helpless than ever, and annoyed, and deeply hurt.   126

I suggested, helpfully: "You mean—like Louis Armstrong?"   127

His face closed as though I'd struck him. "No. I'm not talking about none of   128
that old-time, down home crap."

"Well, look, Sonny, I'm sorry, don't get mad. I just don't altogether get it,   129
that's all. Name somebody—you know, a jazz musician you admire."

"Bird."   130

"Who?"   131

"Bird! Charlie Parker! Don't they teach you nothing in the goddamn army?"   132

I lit a cigarette. I was surprised and then a little amused to discover that I   133
was trembling. "I've been out of touch," I said. "You'll have to be patient with
me. Now. Who's this Parker character?"

"He's just one of the greatest jazz musicians alive," said Sonny, sullenly, his   134
hands in his pockets, his back to me. "Maybe *the* greatest," he added, bitterly,
"that's probably why *you* never heard of him."

"All right," I said, "I'm ignorant. I'm sorry. I'll go out and buy all the cat's   135
records right away, all right?"

"It don't," said Sonny, with dignity, "make any difference to me. I don't care   136
what you listen to. Don't do me no favors."

I was beginning to realize that I'd never seen him so upset before. With an-   137
other part of my mind I was thinking that this would probably turn out to be
one of those things kids go through and that I shouldn't make it seem important by pushing it too hard. Still, I didn't think it would do any harm to ask:
"Doesn't all this take a lot of time? Can you make a living at it?"

He turned back to me and half leaned, half sat, on the kitchen table. "Every-   138
thing takes time," he said, "and—well, yes, sure, I can make a living at it. But
what I don't seem to be able to make you understand is that it's the only thing I
want to do."

"Well, Sonny," I said, gently, "you know people can't always do exactly what   139
they *want* to do—"

"*No*, I don't know that," said Sonny, surprising me. "I think people *ought* to   140
do what they want to do, what else are they alive for?"

"You getting to be a big boy," I said desperately, "it's time you started think-   141
ing about your future."

"I'm thinking about my future," said Sonny, grimly. "I think about it all the   142
time."

I gave up. I decided, if he didn't change his mind, that we could always talk   143
about it later. "In the meantime," I said, "you got to finish school." We had already decided that he'd have to move in with Isabel and her folks. I knew this
wasn't the ideal arrangement because Isabel's folks are inclined to be dicty and
they hadn't especially wanted Isabel to marry me. But I didn't know what else to
do. "And we have to get you fixed up at Isabel's."

There was a long silence. He moved from the kitchen table to the windows.   144
"That's a terrible idea. You know it yourself."

"Do you have a *better* idea?"   145

He just walked up and down the kitchen for a minute. He was as tall as I   146
was. He had started to shave. I suddenly had the feeling that I didn't know him
at all.

He stopped at the kitchen table and picked up my cigarettes. Looking at me   147
with a kind of mocking, amusing defiance, he put one between his lips. "You
mind?"

"You smoking already?"   148

He lit the cigarette and nodded, watching me through the smoke. "I just   149
wanted to see if I'd have the courage to smoke in front of you." He grinned and
blew a great cloud of smoke to the ceiling. "It was easy." He looked at my face.
"Come on, now. I bet you was smoking at my age, tell the truth."

I didn't say anything but the truth was on my face, and he laughed. But now   150
there was something very strained in his laugh. "Sure. And I bet that ain't all
you was doing."

He was frightening me a little. "Cut the crap," I said. "We already decided   151
that you was going to go and live at Isabel's. Now what's got into you all of a
sudden?"

"*You* decided it," he pointed out. "*I* didn't decide nothing." He stopped in   152
front of me, leaning against the stove, arms loosely folded. "Look, brother. I
don't want to stay in Harlem no more, I really don't." He was very earnest. He
looked at me, then over toward the kitchen window. There was something in
his eyes I'd never seen before, some thoughtfulness, some worry all his own. He
rubbed the muscle of one arm. "It's time I was getting out of here."

"Where do you want to *go*, Sonny?"   153

"I want to join the army. Or the navy, I don't care. If I say I'm old enough,   154
they'll believe me."

Then I got mad. It was because I was so scared. "You must be crazy. You god-   155
damn fool, what the hell do you want to go and join the *army* for?"

"I just told you. To get out of Harlem."   156

"Sonny, you haven't even finished *school*. And if you really want to be a mu-   157
sician, how do you expect to study if you're in the *army*?"

He looked at me, trapped, and in anguish. "There's ways. I might be able to   158
work out some kind of deal. Anyway, I'll have the G.I. Bill when I come out."

"*If* you come out." We stared at each other. "Sonny, please. Be reasonable. I   159
know the setup is far from perfect. But we got to do the best we can."

"I ain't learning nothing in school," he said. "Even when I go." He turned   160
away from me and opened the window and threw his cigarette out into the narrow alley. I watched his back. "At least, I ain't learning nothing you'd want me to
learn." He slammed the window so hard I thought the glass would fly out, and
turned back to me. "And I'm sick of the stink of these garbage cans!"

"Sonny," I said, "I know how you feel. But if you don't finish school now,   161
you're going to be sorry later that you didn't." I grabbed him by the shoulders.
"And you only got another year. It ain't so bad. And I'll come back and I swear
I'll help you do *whatever* you want to do. Just try to put up with it till I come
back. Will you please do that? For me?"

He didn't answer and he wouldn't look at me.   162

"Sonny. You hear me?"   163

He pulled away. "I hear you. But you never hear anything *I* say."   164

I didn't know what to say to that. He looked out of the window and then   165
back at me. "OK," he said, and sighed. "I'll try."

Then I said, trying to cheer him up a little, "They got a piano at Isabel's. You   166
can practice on it."

And as a matter of fact, it did cheer him up for a minute. "That's right," he   167
said to himself. "I forgot that." His face relaxed a little. But the worry, the
thoughtfulness, played on it still, the way shadows play on a face which is staring into the fire.

But I thought I'd never hear the end of that piano. At first, Isabel would   168
write me, saying how nice it was that Sonny was so serious about his music and
how, as soon as he came in from school, or wherever he had been when he was
supposed to be at school, he went straight to that piano and stayed there until
suppertime. And, after supper, he went back to that piano and stayed there until everybody went to bed. He was at the piano all day Saturday and all day Sunday. Then he bought a record player and started playing records. He'd play one
record over and over again, all day long sometimes, and he'd improvise along
with it on the piano. Or he'd play one section of the record, one chord, one
change, one progression, then he'd do it on the piano. Then back to the record.
Then back to the piano.

Well, I really don't know how they stood it. Isabel finally confessed that it   169
wasn't like living with a person at all, it was like living with sound. And the
sound didn't make any sense to her, didn't make any sense to any of them—naturally. They began, in a way, to be afflicted by this presence that was living in
their home. It was as though Sonny were some sort of god, or monster. He
moved in an atmosphere which wasn't like theirs at all. They fed him and he
ate, he washed himself, he walked in and out of their door; he certainly wasn't
nasty or unpleasant or rude, Sonny isn't any of those things; but it was as

though he were all wrapped up in some cloud, some fire, some vision all his own; and there wasn't any way to reach him.

At the same time, he wasn't really a man yet, he was still a child, and they had to watch out for him in all kinds of ways. They certainly couldn't throw him out. Neither did they dare to make a great scene about that piano because even they dimly sensed, as I sensed, from so many thousands of miles away, that Sonny was at that piano playing for his life.

But he hadn't been going to school. One day a letter came from the school board and Isabel's mother got it—there had, apparently, been other letters but Sonny had torn them up. This day, when Sonny came in, Isabel's mother showed him the letter and asked where he'd been spending his time. And she finally got it out of him that he'd been down in Greenwich Village, with musicians and other characters, in a white girl's apartment. And this scared her and she started to scream at him and what came up, once she began—though she denies it to this day—was what sacrifices they were making to give Sonny a decent home and how little he appreciated it.

Sonny didn't play the piano that day. By evening, Isabel's mother had calmed down but then there was the old man to deal with, and Isabel herself. Isabel says she did her best to be calm but she broke down and started crying. She says she just watched Sonny's face. She could tell, by watching him, what was happening with him. And what was happening was that they penetrated his cloud, they had reached him. Even if their fingers had been a thousand times more gentle than human fingers ever are, he could hardly help feeling that they had stripped him naked and were spitting on that nakedness. For he also had to see that his presence, that music, which was life or death to him, had been torture for them and that they had endured it, not at all for his sake, but only for mine. And Sonny couldn't take that. He can take it a little better today than he could then but he's still not very good at it and, frankly, I don't know anybody who is.

The silence of the next few days must have been louder than the sound of all the music ever played since time began. One morning, before she went to work, Isabel was in his room for something and she suddenly realized that all of his records were gone. And she knew for certain that he was gone. And he was. He went as far as the navy would carry him. He finally sent me a postcard from some place in Greece and that was the first I knew that Sonny was still alive. I didn't see him any more until we were both back in New York and the war had long been over.

He was a man by then, of course, but I wasn't willing to see it. He came by the house from time to time, but we fought almost every time we met. I didn't like the way he carried himself, loose and dreamlike all the time, and I didn't like his friends, and his music seemed to be merely an excuse for the life he led. It sounded just that weird and disordered.

Then we had a fight, a pretty awful fight, and I didn't see him for months. By and by I looked him up, where he was living, in a furnished room in the Village, and I tried to make it up. But there were lots of other people in the room and Sonny just lay on his bed, and he wouldn't come downstairs with me, and he treated these other people as though they were his family and I weren't. So I got mad and then he got mad, and then I told him that he might just as well be dead as live the way he was living. Then he stood up and he told me not to worry about him any more in life, that he *was* dead as far as I was concerned. Then he pushed me to the door and the other people looked on as though nothing were happening, and he slammed the door behind me. I stood in the hallway, staring at the door. I heard somebody laugh in the room and then the tears came to my eyes. I started down the steps, whistling to keep from crying, I kept whistling to myself, *You going to need me, baby, one of these cold, rainy days.*

I read about Sonny's trouble in the spring. Little Grace died in the fall. She 176
was a beautiful little girl. But she only lived a little over two years. She died of polio and she suffered. She had a slight fever for a couple of days, but it didn't seem like anything and we just kept her in bed. And we would certainly have called the doctor, but the fever dropped, she seemed to be all right. So we thought it had just been a cold. Then, one day, she was up, playing, Isabel was in the kitchen fixing lunch for the two boys when they'd come in from school, and she heard Grace fall down in the living room. When you have a lot of children you don't always start running when one of them falls, unless they start scream-ing or something. And, this time, Grace was quiet. Yet, Isabel says that when she heard that *thump* and then that silence, something happened in her to make her afraid. And she ran to the living room and there was little Grace on the floor, all twisted up, and the reason she hadn't screamed was that she couldn't get her breath. And when she did scream, it was the worst sound, Isabel says, that she'd ever heard in all her life, and she still hears it sometimes in her dreams. Isabel will sometimes wake me up with a low, moaning, strangled sound and I have to be quick to awaken her and hold her to me and where Is-abel is weeping against me seems a mortal wound.

I think I may have written Sonny the very day that little Grace was buried. I 177
was sitting in the living room in the dark, by myself, and I suddenly thought of Sonny. My trouble made his real.

One Saturday afternoon, when Sonny had been living with us, or, anyway, 178
been in our house, for nearly two weeks, I found myself wandering aimlessly about the living room, drinking from a can of beer, and trying to work up the courage to search Sonny's room. He was out, he was usually out whenever I was home, and Isabel had taken the children to see their grandparents. Suddenly I was standing still in front of the living room window, watching Seventh Av-enue. The idea of searching Sonny's room made me still. I scarcely dared to ad-mit to myself what I'd be searching for. I didn't know what I'd do if I found it. Or if I didn't.

On the sidewalk across from me, near the entrance to a barbecue joint, 179
some people were holding an old-fashioned revival meeting. The barbecue
cook, wearing a dirty white apron, his conked hair reddish and metallic in the
pale sun, and a cigarette between his lips, stood in the doorway, watching them.
Kids and older people paused in their errands and stood there, along with some
older men and a couple of very tough-looking women who watched everything
that happened on the avenue, as though they owned it, or were maybe owned
by it. Well, they were watching this, too. The revival was being carried on by
three sisters in black, and a brother. All they had were their voices and their
Bibles and a tambourine. The brother was testifying and while he testified two
of the sisters stood together, seeming to say, amen, and the third sister walked
around with the tambourine outstretched and a couple of people dropped
coins into it. Then the brother's testimony ended and the sister who had been
taking up the collection dumped the coins into her palm and transferred them
to the pocket of her long black robe. Then she raised both hands, striking the
tambourine against the air, and then against one hand, and she started to sing.
And the two other sisters and the brother joined in.

It was strange, suddenly, to watch, though I had been seeing these street 180
meetings all my life. So, of course, had everybody else down there. Yet, they
paused and watched and listened and I stood still at the window. "*Tis the old
ship of Zion*," they sang, and the sister with the tambourine kept a steady, jangling beat, "*it has rescued many a thousand!*" Not a soul under the sound of their
voices was hearing this song for the first time, not one of them had been rescued. Nor had they seen much in the way of rescue work being done around
them. Neither did they especially believe in the holiness of the three sisters and
the brother, they knew too much about them, knew where they lived, and how.
The woman with the tambourine, whose voice dominated the air, whose face
was bright with joy, was divided by very little from the woman who stood
watching her, a cigarette between her heavy, chapped lips, her hair a cuckoo's
nest, her face scarred and swollen from many beatings, and her black eyes glittering like coal. Perhaps they both knew this, which was why, when, as rarely,
they addressed each other, they addressed each other as Sister. As the singing
filled the air the watching, listening faces underwent a change, the eyes focusing
on something within; the music seemed to soothe a poison out of them; and
time seemed, nearly, to fall away from the sullen, belligerent, battered faces, as
though they were fleeing back to their first condition, while dreaming of their
last. The barbecue cook half shook his head and smiled, and dropped his cigarette and disappeared into his joint. A man fumbled in his pockets for change
and stood holding it in his hand impatiently, as though he had just remembered a pressing appointment further up the avenue. He looked furious. Then I
saw Sonny, standing on the edge of the crowd. He was carrying a wide, flat
notebook with a green cover, and it made him look, from where I was standing,
almost like a schoolboy. The coppery sun brought out the copper in his skin, he
was very faintly smiling, standing very still. Then the singing stopped, the tambourine turned into a collection plate again. The furious man dropped in his

coins and vanished, so did a couple of the women, and Sonny dropped some change in the plate, looking directly at the woman with a little smile. He started across the avenue, toward the house. He has a slow, loping walk, something like the way Harlem hipsters walk, only he's imposed on this his own half-beat. I had never really noticed it before.

I stayed at the window, both relieved and apprehensive. As Sonny disap- 181 peared from my sight, they began singing again. And they were still singing when his key turned in the lock.

"Hey," he said.   182

"Hey, yourself. You want some beer?"   183

"No. Well, maybe." But he came up to the window and stood beside me, 184 looking out. "What a warm voice," he said.

They were singing *If I could only hear my mother pray again!*   185

"Yes," I said, "and she can sure beat that tambourine."   186

"But what a terrible song," he said, and laughed. He dropped his notebook 187 on the sofa and disappeared into the kitchen. "Where's Isabel and the kids?"

"I think they went to see their grandparents. You hungry?"   188

"No." He came back into the living room with his can of beer. "You want to 189 come some place with me tonight?"

I sensed, I don't know how, that I couldn't possibly say no. "Sure. Where?" 190

He sat down on the sofa and picked up his notebook and started leafing 191 through it. "I'm going to sit in with some fellows in a joint in the Village."

"You mean, you're going to play, tonight?"   192

"That's right." He took a swallow of his beer and moved back to the window. 193 He gave me a sidelong look. "If you can stand it."

"I'll try," I said.   194

He smiled to himself and we both watched as the meeting across the way 195 broke up. The three sisters and the brother, heads bowed, were singing *God be with you till we meet again.* The faces around them were very quiet. Then the song ended. The small crowd dispersed. We watched the three women and the lone man walk slowly up the avenue.

"When she was singing before," said Sonny, abruptly, "her voice reminded 196 me for a minute of what heroin feels like sometimes—when it's in your veins. It makes you feel sort of warm and cool at the same time. And distant. And—and sure." He sipped his beer, very deliberately not looking at me. I watched his face. "It makes you feel—in control. Sometimes you've got to have that feeling."

"Do you?" I sat down slowly in the easy chair.   197

"Sometimes." He went to the sofa and picked up his notebook again. "Some 198 people do."

"In order," I asked, "to play?" And my voice was very ugly, full of contempt 199 and anger.

"Well"—he looked at me with great, troubled eyes, as though, in fact, he 200 hoped his eyes would tell me things he could never otherwise say—"they *think* so. And *if* they think so—!"

"And what do *you* think?" I asked.   201

He sat on the sofa and put his can of beer on the floor. "I don't know," he 202
said, and I couldn't be sure if he were answering my question or pursuing his
thoughts. His face didn't tell me. "It's not so much to *play*. It's to *stand* it, to be
able to make it at all. On any level." He frowned and smiled: "In order to keep
from shaking to pieces."

"But these friends of yours," I said, "they seem to shake themselves to pieces 203
pretty goddamn fast."

"Maybe." He played with the notebook. And something told me that I 204
should curb my tongue, that Sonny was doing his best to talk, that I should listen. "But of course you only know the ones that've gone to pieces. Some don't—
or at least they haven't *yet* and that's just about all *any* of us can say." He paused.
"And then there are some who just live, really, in hell, and they know it and they
see what's happening and they go right on. I don't know." He sighed, dropped
the notebook, folded his arms. "Some guys, you can tell from the way they play,
they on something *all* the time. And you can see that, well, it makes something
real for them. But of course," he picked up his beer from the floor and sipped it
and put the can down again, "they *want* to, too, you've got to see that. Even
some of them that say they don't—*some*, not all."

"And what about you?" I asked—I couldn't help it. "What about you? Do 205
you want to?"

He stood up and walked to the window and remained silent for a long time. 206
Then he sighed. "Me," he said. Then: "While I was downstairs before, on my way
here, listening to that woman sing, it struck me all of a sudden how much suffering she must have had to go through—to sing like that. It's *repulsive* to think
you have to suffer that much."

I said: "But there's no way not to suffer—is there, Sonny?" 207

"I believe not," he said and smiled, "but that's never stopped anyone from 208
trying." He looked at me. "Has it?" I realized, with his mocking look, that there
stood between us, forever, beyond the power of time or forgiveness, the fact
that I had held silence—so long!—when he had needed human speech to help
him. He turned back to the window. "No, there's no way not to suffer. But you
try all kinds of ways to keep from drowning in it, to keep on top of it, and to
make it seem—well, like *you*. Like you did something, all right, and now you're
suffering for it. You know?" I said nothing. "Well you know," he said, impatiently, "Why *do* people suffer? Maybe it's better to do something to give it a reason, *any* reason."

"But we just agreed," I said, "that there's no way not to suffer. Isn't it 209
better, then, just to—take it?"

"But nobody just takes it," Sonny cried, "that's what I'm telling you! *Every-* 210
body tries not to. You're just hung up on the *way* some people try—it's not *your*
way!"

The hair on my face began to itch, my face felt wet. "That's not true," I said, 211
"that's not true. I don't give a damn what other people do, I don't even care how
they suffer. I just care how *you* suffer." And he looked at me. "Please believe me,"
I said, "I don't want to see you—die—trying not to suffer."

"I won't," he said, flatly, "die trying not to suffer. At least, not any faster than   212
anybody else."

"But there's no need," I said, trying to laugh, "is there? in killing yourself."   213

I wanted to say more, but I couldn't. I wanted to talk about will power and   214
how life could be—well, beautiful. I wanted to say that it was all within; but was
it? or, rather, wasn't that exactly the trouble? And I wanted to promise that I
would never fail him again. But it would all have sounded—empty words and
lies.

So I made the promise to myself and prayed that I would keep it.   215

"It's terrible sometimes, inside," he said, "that's what's the trouble. You walk   216
these streets, black and funky and cold, and there's not really a living ass to talk
to, and there's nothing shaking, and there's no way of getting it out—that storm
inside. You can't talk it and you can't make love with it, and when you finally try
to get with it and play it, you realize *nobody's* listening. So *you've* got to listen.
You got to find a way to listen."

And then he walked away from the window and sat on the sofa again, as   217
though all the wind had suddenly been knocked out of him. "Sometimes you'll
do *anything* to play, even cut your mother's throat." He laughed and looked at
me. "Or your brother's." Then he sobered. "Or your own." Then: "Don't worry.
I'm all right now and I think I'll *be* all right. But I can't forget—where I've been.
I don't mean just the physical place I've been, I mean where I've *been*. And *what*
I've been."

"What have you been, Sonny?" I asked.   218

He smiled—but sat sideways on the sofa, his elbow resting on the back, his   219
fingers playing with his mouth and chin, not looking at me. "I've been something I didn't recognize, didn't know I could be. Didn't know anybody could
be." He stopped, looking inward, looking helplessly young, looking old. "I'm
not talking about it now because I feel *guilty* or anything like that—maybe it
would be better if I did, I don't know. Anyway, I can't really talk about it. Not to
you, not to anybody," and now he turned and faced me. "Sometimes, you know,
and it was actually when I was most *out* of the world, I felt that I was in it, that I
was *with* it, really, and I could play or I didn't really have to *play*, it just came out
of me, it was there. And I don't know how I played, thinking about it now, but I
know I did awful things, those times, sometimes, to people. Or it wasn't that I
did anything to them—it was that they weren't real." He picked up the beer can;
it was empty; he rolled it between his palms: "And other times—well, I needed a
fix, I needed to find a place to lean, I needed to clear a space to *listen*—and I
couldn't find it, and I—went crazy, I did terrible things to *me*, I was terrible *for*
me." He began pressing the beer can between his hands, I watched the metal begin to give. It glittered, as he played with it, like a knife, and I was afraid he
would cut himself, but I said nothing. "Oh well. I can never tell you. I was all by
myself at the bottom of something, stinking and sweating and crying and shaking, and I smelled it, you know? *my* stink, and I thought I'd die if I couldn't get
away from it and yet, all the same, I knew that everything I was doing was just
locking me in with it. And I didn't know," he paused, still flattening the beer

can, "I didn't know, I still *don't* know, something kept telling me that maybe it was good to smell your own stink, but I didn't think that *that* was what I'd been trying to do—and—who can stand it?" and he abruptly dropped the ruined beer can, looking at me with a small, still smile, and then rose, walking to the window as though it were the lodestone rock. I watched his face, he watched the avenue. "I couldn't tell you when Mama died—but the reason I wanted to leave Harlem so bad was to get away from drugs. And then, when I ran away, that's what I was running from—really. When I came back, nothing had changed. *I* hadn't changed, I was just—older." And he stopped, drumming with his fingers on the windowpane. The sun had vanished, soon darkness would fall. I watched his face. "It can come again," he said, almost as though speaking to himself. Then he turned to me. "It can come again," he repeated. "I just want you to know that."

"All right," I said, at last. "So it can come again, All right." 220

He smiled, but the smile was sorrowful. "I had to try to tell you," he said. 221

"Yes," I said. "I understand that." 222

"You're my brother," he said, looking straight at me, and not smiling at all. 223

"Yes," I repeated, "yes. I understand that." 224

He turned back to the window, looking out. "All that hatred down there," he 225 said, "all that hatred and misery and love. It's a wonder it doesn't blow the avenue apart."

———

We went to the only nightclub on a short, dark street, downtown. We 226 squeezed through the narrow, chattering, jam-packed bar to the entrance of the big room, where the bandstand was. And we stood there for a moment, for the lights were very dim in this room and we couldn't see. Then, "Hello, boy," said a voice and an enormous black man, much older than Sonny or myself, erupted out of all that atmospheric lighting and put an arm around Sonny's shoulder. "I been sitting right here," he said, "waiting for you."

He had a big voice, too, and heads in the darkness turned toward us. 227

Sonny grinned and pulled a little away, and said, "Creole, this is my brother. 228 I told you about him."

Creole shook my hand. "I'm glad to meet you, son," he said, and it was clear 229 that he was glad to meet me *there* for Sonny's sake. And he smiled, "You got a real musician in *your* family," and he took his arm from Sonny's shoulder and slapped him, lightly, affectionately, with the back of his hand.

"Well. Now I've heard it all," said a voice behind us. This was another musi- 230 cian, and a friend of Sonny's, a coal-black, cheerful-looking man, built close to the ground. He immediately began confiding to me, at the top of his lungs, the most terrible things about Sonny, his teeth gleaming like a lighthouse and his laugh coming up out of him like the beginning of an earthquake. And it turned out that everyone at the bar knew Sonny, or almost everyone; some were musicians, working there, or nearby, or not working, some were simply hangers-on, and some were there to hear Sonny play. I was introduced to all of them and they were all very polite to me. Yet, it was clear that, for them, I was only Sonny's brother. Here, I was in Sonny's world. Or, rather: his kingdom. Here, it was not even a question that his veins bore royal blood.

They were going to play soon and Creole installed me, by myself, at a table   231 in a dark corner. Then I watched them, Creole, and the little black man, and Sonny, and the others, while they horsed around, standing just below the bandstand. The light from the bandstand spilled just a little short of them and, watching them laughing and gesturing and moving about, I had the feeling that they, nevertheless, were being most careful not to step into that circle of light too suddenly: that if they moved into the light too suddenly, without thinking, they would perish in flame. Then, while I watched, one of them, the small, black man, moved into the light and crossed the bandstand and started fooling around with his drums. Then—being funny and being, also, extremely ceremonious—Creole took Sonny by the arm and led him to the piano. A woman's voice called Sonny's name and a few hands started clapping. And Sonny, also being funny and being ceremonious, and so touched, I think, that he could have cried, but neither hiding it nor showing it, riding it like a man, grinned, and put both hands to his heart and bowed from the waist.

Creole then went to the bass fiddle and a lean, very bright-skinned brown   232 man jumped up on the bandstand and picked up his horn. So there they were, and the atmosphere on the bandstand and in the room began to change and tighten. Someone stepped up to the microphone and announced them. Then there were all kinds of murmurs. Some people at the bar shushed others. The waitress ran around, frantically getting in the last orders, guys and chicks got closer to each other, and the lights on the bandstand, on the quartet, turned to a kind of indigo. Then they all looked different there. Creole looked about him for the last time, as though he were making certain that all his chickens were in the coop, and then he—jumped and struck the fiddle. And there they were.

All I know about music is that not many people ever really hear it. And even   233 then, on the rare occasions when something opens within, and the music enters, what we mainly hear, or hear corroborated, are personal, private, vanishing evocations. But the man who creates the music is hearing something else, is dealing with the roar rising from the void and imposing order on it as it hits the air. What is evoked in him, then, is of another order, more terrible because it has no words, and triumphant, too, for that same reason. And his triumph, when he triumphs, is ours. I just watched Sonny's face. His face was troubled, he was working hard, but he wasn't with it. And I had the feeling that, in a way, everyone on the bandstand was waiting for him, both waiting for him and pushing him along. But as I began to watch Creole, I realized that it was Creole who held them all back. He had them on a short rein. Up there, keeping the beat with his whole body, wailing on the fiddle, with his eyes half closed, he was listening to everything, but he was listening to Sonny. He was having a dialogue with Sonny. He wanted Sonny to leave the shoreline and strike out for the deep water. He was Sonny's witness that deep water and drowning were not the same thing—he had been there, and he knew. And he wanted Sonny to know. He was waiting for Sonny to do the things on the keys which would let Creole know that Sonny was in the water.

And, while Creole listened, Sonny moved, deep within, exactly like someone 234 in torment. I had never before thought of how awful the relationship must be between the musician and his instrument. He has to fill it, this instrument, with the breath of life, his own. He has to make it do what he wants it to do. And a piano is just a piano. It's made out of so much wood and wires and little hammers and big ones, and ivory. While there's only so much you can do with it, the only way to find this out is to try; to try and make it do everything.

And Sonny hadn't been near a piano for over a year. And he wasn't on much 235 better terms with his life, not the life that stretched before him now. He and the piano stammered, started one way, got scared, stopped; started another way, panicked, marked time, started again; then seemed to have found a direction, panicked again, got stuck. And the face I saw on Sonny I'd never seen before. Everything had been burned out of it, and, at the same time, things usually hidden were being burned in, by the fire and fury of the battle which was occurring in him up there.

Yet, watching Creole's face as they neared the end of the first set, I had the 236 feeling that something had happened, something I hadn't heard. Then they finished, there was scattered applause, and then, without an instant's warning, Creole started into something else, it was almost sardonic, it was *Am I Blue*. And, as though he commanded, Sonny began to play. Something began to happen. And Creole let out the reins. The dry, low, black man said something awful on the drums, Creole answered, and the drums talked back. Then the horn insisted, sweet and high, slightly detached perhaps, and Creole listened, commenting now and then, dry, and driving, beautiful and calm and old. Then they all came together again, and Sonny was part of the family again. I could tell this from his face. He seemed to have found, right there beneath his fingers, a damn brand-new piano. It seemed that he couldn't get over it. Then, for awhile, just being happy with Sonny, they seemed to be agreeing with him that brand-new pianos certainly were a gas.

Then Creole stepped forward to remind them that what they were playing 237 was the blues. He hit something in all of them, he hit something in me, myself, and the music tightened and deepened, apprehension began to beat the air. Creole began to tell us what the blues were all about. They were not about anything very new. He and his boys up there were keeping it new, at the risk of ruin, destruction, madness, and death, in order to find new ways to make us listen. For, while the tale of how we suffer, and how we are delighted, and how we may triumph is never new, it always must be heard. There isn't any other tale to tell, it's the only light we've got in all this darkness.

And this tale, according to that face, that body, those strong hands on those 238 strings, has another aspect in every country, and a new depth in every generation. Listen, Creole seemed to be saying, listen. Now these are Sonny's blues. He made the little black man on the drums know it, and the bright, brown man on the horn. Creole wasn't trying any longer to get Sonny in the water. He was wishing him Godspeed. Then he stepped back, very slowly, filling the air with the immense suggestion that Sonny speak for himself.

Then they all gathered around Sonny and Sonny played. Every now and 239 again one of them seemed to say, amen. Sonny's fingers filled the air with life, his life. But that life contained so many others. And Sonny went all the way back, he really began with the spare, flat statement of the opening phrase of the song. Then he began to make it his. It was very beautiful because it wasn't hurried and it was no longer a lament. I seemed to hear with what burning he had made it his, with what burning we had yet to make it ours, how we could cease lamenting. Freedom lurked around us and I understood, at last, that he could help us to be free if we would listen, that he would never be free until we did. Yet, there was no battle in his face now. I heard what he had gone through, and would continue to go through until he came to rest in earth. He had made it his: that long line, of which we knew only Mama and Daddy. And he was giving it back, as everything must be given back, so that, passing through death, it can live forever. I saw my mother's face again, and felt, for the first time, how the stones of the road she had walked on must have bruised her feet. I saw the moonlit road where my father's brother died. And it brought something else back to me, and carried me past it, I saw my little girl again and felt Isabel's tears again, and I felt my own tears begin to rise. And I was yet aware that this was only a moment, that the world waited outside, as hungry as a tiger, and that trouble stretched above us, longer than the sky.

Then it was over. Creole and Sonny let out their breath, both soaking wet, 240 and grinning. There was a lot of applause and some of it was real. In the dark, the girl came by and I asked her to take drinks to the bandstand. There was a long pause, while they talked up there in the indigo light and after awhile I saw the girl put a Scotch and milk on top of the piano for Sonny. He didn't seem to notice it, but just before they started playing again, he sipped from it and looked toward me, and nodded. Then he put it back on top of the piano. For me, then, as they began to play again, it glowed and shook above my brother's head like the very cup of trembling.

ANNE TYLER (b. 1941)

Teenage Wasteland

He used to have very blond hair—almost white—cut shorter than other chil- 1 dren's so that on his crown a little cowlick always stood up to catch the light. But this was when he was small. As he grew older, his hair grew darker, and he wore it longer—past his collar even. It hung in lank, taffy-colored ropes around his face, which was still an endearing face, fine-featured, the eyes an unusual aqua blue. But his cheeks, of course, were no longer round, and a sharp new Adam's apple jogged in his throat when he talked.

In October, they called from the private school he attended to request a con- 2 ference with his parents. Daisy went alone; her husband was at work. Clutching her purse, she sat on the principal's couch and learned that Donny was noisy, lazy, and disruptive; always fooling around with his friends, and he wouldn't respond in class.

In the past, before her children were born, Daisy had been a fourth-grade 3 teacher. It shamed her now to sit before this principal as a parent, a delinquent parent, a parent who struck Mr. Lanham, no doubt, as unseeing or uncaring. "It isn't that we're not concerned," she said. "Both of us are. And we've done what we could, whatever we could think of. We don't let him watch TV on school nights. We don't let him talk on the phone till he's finished his homework. But he tells us he doesn't *have* any homework or he did it all in study hall. How are we to know what to believe?"

From early October through November, at Mr. Lanham's suggestion, Daisy 4 checked Donny's assignments every day. She sat next to him as he worked, trying to be encouraging, sagging inwardly as she saw the poor quality of everything he did—the sloppy mistakes in math, the illogical leaps in his English themes, the history questions left blank if they required any research.

Daisy was often late starting supper, and she couldn't give as much attention 5 to Donny's younger sister. "You'll never guess what happened at . . ." Amanda would begin, and Daisy would have to tell her, "Not now, honey."

By the time her husband, Matt, came home, she'd be snappish. She would 6 recite the day's hardships—the fuzzy instructions in English, the botched history map, the morass of unsolvable algebra equations. Matt would look surprised and confused, and Daisy would gradually wind down. There was no way, really, to convey how exhausting all this was.

In December, the school called again. This time, they wanted Matt to come 7 as well. She and Matt had to sit on Mr. Lanham's couch like two bad children and listen to the news: Donny had improved only slightly, raising a D in history to a C, and a C in algebra to a B-minus. What was worse, he had developed new problems. He had cut classes on at least three occasions. Smoked in the furnace room. Helped Sonny Barnett break into a freshman's locker. And last week, during athletics, he and three friends had been seen off the school grounds; when they returned, the coach had smelled beer on their breath.

Daisy and Matt sat silent, shocked. Matt rubbed his forehead with his fin- 8 gertips. Imagine, Daisy thought, how they must look to Mr. Lanham: an overweight housewife in a cotton dress and a too-tall, too-thin insurance agent in a baggy, frayed suit. Failures, both of them—the kind of people who are always hurrying to catch up, missing the point of things that everyone else grasps at once. She wished she'd worn nylons instead of knee socks.

It was arranged that Donny would visit a psychologist for testing. Mr. Lan- 9 ham knew just the person. He would set this boy straight, he said.

When they stood to leave, Daisy held her stomach in and gave Mr. Lanham a 10 firm, responsible handshake.

Donny said the psychologist was a jackass and the tests were really dumb; 11 but he kept all three of his appointments, and when it was time for the follow-up conference with the psychologist and both parents, Donny combed his hair and seemed unusually sober and subdued. The psychologist said Donny had no serious emotional problems. He was merely going through a difficult period in his life. He required some academic help and a better sense of self-worth. For this reason, he was suggesting a man named Calvin Beadle, a tutor with considerable psychological training.

In the car going home, Donny said he'd be damned if he'd let them drag 12 him to some stupid fairy tutor. His father told him to watch his language in front of his mother.

That night, Daisy lay awake pondering the term "self-worth." She had al- 13 ways been free with her praise. She had always told Donny he had talent, was smart, was good with his hands. She had made a big to-do over every little gift he gave her. In fact, maybe she had gone too far, although, Lord knows, she had meant every word. Was that his trouble?

She remembered when Amanda was born. Donny had acted lost and bewil- 14 dered. Daisy had been alert to that, of course, but still, a new baby keeps you so busy. Had she really done all she could have? She longed—she ached—for a time machine. Given one more chance, she'd do it perfectly—hug him more, praise him more, or perhaps praise him less. Oh, who can say . . .

The tutor told Donny to call him Cal. All his kids did, he said. Daisy thought 15 for a second that he meant his own children, then realized her mistake. He seemed too young, anyhow, to be a family man. He wore a heavy brown handlebar mustache. His hair was as long and stringy as Donny's, and his jeans as faded. Wire-rimmed spectacles slid down his nose. He lounged in a canvas director's chair with his fingers laced across his chest, and he casually, amiably questioned Donny, who sat upright and glaring in an armchair.

"So they're getting on your back at school," said Cal. "Making a big deal 16 about anything you do wrong."

"Right," said Donny.   17

"Any idea why that would be?"   18

"Oh, well, you know, stuff like homework and all," Donny said.   19

"You don't do your homework?"   20

"Oh, well, I might do it sometimes but not just exactly like they want it." 21 Donny sat forward and said, "It's like a prison there, you know? You've got to go to every class, you can never step off the school grounds."

"You cut classes sometimes?"   22

"Sometimes," Donny said, with a glance at his parents.   23

Cal didn't seem perturbed. "Well," he said, "I'll tell you what. Let's you and 24 me try working together three nights a week. Think you could handle that? We'll see if we can show that school of yours a thing or two. Give it a month;

then if you don't like it, we'll stop. If *I* don't like it, we'll stop. I mean, sometimes people just don't get along, right? What do you say to that?"

"Okay," Donny said. He seemed pleased.   25

"Make it seven o'clock till eight, Monday, Wednesday, and Friday," Cal told   26 Matt and Daisy. They nodded. Cal shambled to his feet, gave them a little salute, and showed them to the door.

This was where he lived as well as worked, evidently. The interview had   27 taken place in the dining room, which had been transformed into a kind of office. Passing the living room, Daisy winced at the rock music she had been hearing, without registering it, ever since she had entered the house. She looked in and saw a boy about Donny's age lying on a sofa with a book. Another boy and a girl were playing Ping-Pong in front of the fireplace. "You have several here together?" Daisy asked Cal.

"Oh, sometimes they stay on after their sessions, just to rap. They're a pretty   28 sociable group, all in all. Plenty of goof-offs like young Donny here."

He cuffed Donny's shoulder playfully. Donny flushed and grinned.   29

Climbing into the car, Daisy asked Donny, "Well? What did you think?"   30

But Donny had returned to his old evasive self. He jerked his chin toward   31 the garage. "Look," he said. "He's got a basketball net."

Now on Mondays, Wednesdays, and Fridays, they had supper early—the instant Matt came home. Sometimes, they had to leave before they were really   32 finished. Amanda would still be eating her dessert. "Bye, honey. Sorry," Daisy would tell her.

Cal's first bill sent a flutter of panic through Daisy's chest, but it was worth   33 it, of course. Just look at Donny's face when they picked him up: alight and full of interest. The principal telephoned Daisy to tell her how Donny had improved. "Of course, it hasn't shown up in his grades yet, but several of the teachers have noticed how his attitude's changed. Yes, sir, I think we're onto something here."

At home, Donny didn't act much different. He still seemed to have a low   34 opinion of his parents. But Daisy supposed that was unavoidable—part of being fifteen. He said his parents were too "controlling"—a word that made Daisy give him a sudden look. He said they acted like wardens. On weekends, they enforced a curfew. And any time he went to a party, they always telephoned first to see if adults would be supervising. "For God's sake!" he said. "Don't you trust me?"

"It isn't a matter of trust, honey . . ." But there was no explaining to him.   35

His tutor called one afternoon. "I get the sense," he said, "that this kid's feel-   36 ing . . . underestimated, you know? Like you folks expect the worst of him. I'm thinking we ought to give him more rope."

"But see, he's still so suggestible," Daisy said. "When his friends suggest   37 some mischief—smoking or drinking or such—why, he just finds it hard not to go along with them."

"Mrs. Coble," the tutor said, "I think this kid is hurting. You know? Here's a   38 serious, sensitive kid, telling you he'd like to take on some grown-up challenges, and you're giving him the message that he can't be trusted. Don't you understand how that hurts?"

"Oh," said Daisy.   39

"It undermines his self-esteem—don't you realize that?"   40

"Well, I guess you're right," said Daisy. She saw Donny suddenly from a 41 whole new angle: his pathetically poor posture, that slouch so forlorn that his shoulders seemed about to meet his chin . . . oh, wasn't it awful being young? She'd had a miserable adolescence herself and had always sworn no child of hers would ever be that unhappy.

They let Donny stay out later, they didn't call ahead to see if the parties were 42 supervised, and they were careful not to grill him about his evening. The tutor had set down so many rules! They were not allowed any questions at all about any aspect of school, nor were they to speak with his teachers. If a teacher had some complaint, she should phone Cal. Only one teacher disobeyed—the history teacher, Miss Evans. She called one morning in February. "I'm a little concerned about Donny, Mrs. Coble."

"Oh, I'm sorry, Miss Evans, but Donny's tutor handles these things now . . ." 43

"I always deal directly with the parents. You are the parent," Miss Evans said, 44 speaking very slowly and distinctly. "Now, here is the problem. Back when you were helping Donny with his homework, his grades rose from a D to a C, but now they've slipped back, and they're closer to an F."

"They are?"   45

"I think you should start overseeing his homework again."   46

"But Donny's tutor says . . ."   47

"It's nice that Donny has a tutor, but you should still be in charge of his 48 homework. With you, he learned it. Then he passed his tests. With the tutor, well, it seems the tutor is more of a crutch. 'Donny,' I say, 'a quiz is coming up on Friday. Hadn't you better be listening instead of talking?' 'That's okay, Miss Evans,' he says. 'I have a tutor now.' Like a talisman! I really think you ought to take over, Mrs. Coble."

"I see," said Daisy. "Well, I'll think about that. Thank you for calling." 49

Hanging up, she felt a rush of anger at Donny. A talisman! For a talisman, 50 she'd given up all luxuries, all that time with her daughter, her evenings at home!

She dialed Cal's number. He sounded muzzy. "I'm sorry if I woke you," she 51 told him, "but Donny's history teacher just called. She says he isn't doing well."

"She should have dealt with me."   52

"She wants me to start supervising his homework again. His grades are slip- 53 ping."

"Yes," said the tutor, "but you and I both know there's more to it than mere 54 grades, don't we? I care about the *whole* child—his happiness, his self-esteem. The grades will come. Just give them time."

When she hung up, it was Miss Evans she was angry at. What a narrow 55 woman!

It was Cal this, Cal that, Cal says this, Cal and I did that. Cal lent Donny an 56
album by the Who. He took Donny and two other pupils to a rock concert. In
March, when Donny began to talk endlessly on the phone with a girl named
Miriam, Cal even let Miriam come to one of the tutoring sessions. Daisy was
touched that Cal would grow so involved in Donny's life, but she was also a little hurt, because she had offered to have Miriam to dinner and Donny had refused. Now he asked them to drive her to Cal's house without a qualm.

This Miriam was an unappealing girl with blurry lipstick and masses of 57
rough red hair. She wore a short, bulky jacket that would not have been out of
place on a motorcycle. During the trip to Cal's she was silent, but coming back,
she was more talkative. "What a neat guy, and what a house! All those kids
hanging out, like a club. And the stereo playing rock . . . gosh, he's not like a
grown-up at all! Married and divorced and everything, but you'd think he was
our own age."

"Mr. Beadle was married?" Daisy asked.   58

"Yeah, to this really controlling lady. She didn't understand him a bit." 59

"No, I guess not," Daisy said.   60

Spring came, and the students who hung around at Cal's drifted out to the 61
basketball net above the garage. Sometimes, when Daisy and Matt arrived to
pick up Donny, they'd find him there with the others—spiky and excited, jitter-
ing on his toes beneath the backboard. It was staying light much longer now,
and the neighboring fence cast narrow bars across the bright grass. Loud music
would be spilling from Cal's windows. Once it was the Who, which Daisy recognized from the time that Donny had borrowed the album. *"Teenage Wasteland,"*
she said aloud, identifying the song, and Matt gave a short, dry laugh. "It certainly is," he said. He'd misunderstood; he thought she was commenting on the
scene spread before them. In fact, she might have been. The players looked like
hoodlums, even her son. Why, one of Cal's students had recently been knifed in
a tavern. One had been shipped off to boarding school in midterm; two had
been withdrawn by their parents. On the other hand, Donny had mentioned
someone who'd been studying with Cal for five years. "Five years!" said Daisy.
"Doesn't anyone ever stop needing him?"

Donny looked at her. Lately, whatever she said about Cal was read as criti- 62
cism. "You're just feeling competitive," he said. "And controlling."

She bit her lip and said no more.   63

In April, the principal called to tell her that Donny had been expelled. There 64
had been a locker check, and in Donny's locker they found five cans of beer and
half a pack of cigarettes. With Donny's previous record, this offense meant ex-
pulsion.

Daisy gripped the receiver tightly and said, "Well, where is he now?"   65

"We've sent him home," said Mr. Lanham. "He's packed up all his belong- 66
ings, and he's coming home on foot."

Daisy wondered what she would say to him. She felt him looming closer and 67
closer, bringing this brand-new situation that no one had prepared her to han-

dle. What other place would take him? Could they enter him in public school? What were the rules? She stood at the living room window, waiting for him to show up. Gradually, she realized that he was taking too long. She checked the clock. She stared up the street again.

When an hour had passed, she phoned the school. Mr. Lanham's secretary 68 answered and told her in a grave, sympathetic voice that yes, Donny Coble had most definitely gone home. Daisy called her husband. He was out of the office. She went back to the window and thought awhile, and then she called Donny's tutor.

"Donny's been expelled from school," she said, "and now I don't know 69 where he's gone. I wonder if you've heard from him?"

There was a long silence. "Donny's with me, Mrs. Coble," he finally said.   70

"With you? How'd he get there?"   71

"He hailed a cab, and I paid the driver."   72

"Could I speak to him, please?"   73

There was another silence. "Maybe it'd be better if we had a conference," Cal 74 said.

"I don't *want* a conference. I've been standing at the window picturing him 75 dead or kidnapped or something, and now you tell me you want a—"

"Donny is very, very upset. Understandably so," said Cal. "Believe me, Mrs. 76 Coble, this is not what it seems. Have you asked Donny's side of the story?"

"Well, of course not, how could I? He went running off to you instead."   77

"Because he didn't feel he'd be listened to."   78

"But I haven't even—"   79

"Why don't you come out and talk? The three of us," said Cal, "will try to get 80 this thing in perspective."

"Well, all right," Daisy said. But she wasn't as reluctant as she sounded. Al- 81 ready, she felt soothed by the calm way Cal was taking this.

Cal answered the doorbell at once. He said, "Hi, there," and led her into the 82 dining room. Donny sat slumped in a chair, chewing the knuckle of one thumb. "Hello, Donny," Daisy said. He flicked his eyes in her direction.

"Sit here, Mrs. Coble," said Cal, placing her opposite Donny. He himself re- 83 mained standing, restlessly pacing. "So," he said.

Daisy stole a look at Donny. His lips were swollen, as if he'd been crying.   84

"You know," Cal told Daisy, "I kind of expected something like this. That's a 85 very punitive school you've got him in—you realize that. And any half-decent lawyer will tell you they've violated his civil rights. Locker checks! Where's their search warrant?"

"But if the rule is—" Daisy said.   86

"Well, anyhow, let him tell you his side."   87

She looked at Donny. He said, "It wasn't my fault. I promise."   88

"They said your locker was full of beer."   89

"It was a put-up job! See, there's this guy that doesn't like me. He put all 90 these beers in my locker and started a rumor going, so Mr. Lanham ordered a locker check."

"What was the boy's name?" Daisy asked.   91

"Huh?"   92

"Mrs. Coble, take my word, the situation is not so unusual," Cal said. "You   93
can't imagine how vindictive kids can be sometimes."

"What was the boy's *name*," said Daisy, "so that I can ask Mr. Lanham if   94
that's who suggested he run a locker check."

"You don't believe me," Donny said.   95

"And how'd this boy get your combination in the first place?"   96

"Frankly," said Cal, "I wouldn't be surprised to learn the school was in on it.   97
Any kid that marches to a different drummer, why, they'd just love an excuse to
get rid of him. The school is where I lay the blame."

"Doesn't *Donny* ever get blamed?"   98

"Now, Mrs. Coble, you heard what he—"   99

"Forget it," Donny told Cal. "You can see she doesn't trust me."   100

Daisy drew in a breath to say that of course she trusted him—a reflex. But   101
she knew that bold-faced, wide-eyed look of Donny's. He had worn that look
when he was small, denying some petty misdeed with the evidence plain as day
all around him. Still, it was hard for her to accuse him outright. She temporized
and said, "The only thing I'm sure of is that they've kicked you out of school,
and now I don't know what we're going to do."

"We'll fight it," said Cal.   102

"We can't. Even you must see we can't."   103

"I could apply to Brantly," Donny said.   104

Cal stopped his pacing to beam down at him. "Brantly! Yes. They're really   105
onto where a kid is coming from, at Brantly. Why, *I* could get you into Brantly. I
work with a lot of their students."

Daisy had never heard of Brantly, but already she didn't like it. And she   106
didn't like Cal's smile, which struck her now as feverish and avid—a smile of
hunger.

On the fifteenth of April, they entered Donny in a public school, and they   107
stopped his tutoring sessions. Donny fought both decisions bitterly. Cal, surprisingly enough, did not object. He admitted he'd made no headway with
Donny and said it was because Donny was emotionally disturbed.

Donny went to his new school every morning, plodding off alone with his   108
head down. He did his assignments, and he earned average grades, but he gathered no friends, joined no clubs. There was something exhausted and defeated
about him.

The first week in June, during final exams, Donny vanished. He simply   109
didn't come home one afternoon, and no one at school remembered seeing
him. The police were reassuring, and for the first few days, they worked hard.
They combed Donny's sad, messy room for clues; they visited Miriam and Cal.
But then they started talking about the number of kids who ran away every
year. Hundreds, just in this city. "He'll show up, if he wants to," they said. "If he
doesn't, he won't."

Evidently, Donny didn't want to.   110

It's been three months now and still no word. Matt and Daisy still look for   111
him in every crowd of awkward, heartbreaking teenage boys. Every time the
phone rings, they imagine it might be Donny. Both parents have aged. Donny's
sister seems to be staying away from home as much as possible.

At night, Daisy lies awake and goes over Donny's life. She is trying to figure   112
out what went wrong, where they made their first mistake. Often, she finds herself blaming Cal, although she knows he didn't begin it. Then at other times she
excuses him, for without him, Donny might have left earlier. Who really knows?
In the end, she can only sigh and search for a cooler spot on the pillow. As she
falls asleep, she occasionally glimpses something in the corner of her vision. It's
something fleet and round, a ball—a basketball. It flies up, it sinks through the
hoop, descends, lands in a yard littered with last year's leaves and striped with
bars of sunlight as white as bones, bleached and parched and cleanly picked.

ACTIVITIES FOR WRITING AND DISCUSSION

1. Paragraphs 13 and 14 suggest that Daisy has done everything she can to
be a good parent, yet she seems to feel chronically ashamed about her inade-
quacy as a parent. Converse on paper with Daisy about her upbringing of
Donny. Why has Donny turned out the way he has?

2. Locate and mark the passages referring to Donny's sister, Amanda. Imagine Amanda's position within the family circle as Donny is passing through this
teenage crisis. Then retell the story, or some part of it, from her **point of view.**

3. The "teenage wasteland" is familiar terrain to anyone of late adolescent
age or older. Write about any personal connections you feel with this story or
its **characters**—parents, children, teachers, or counselors.

4. Consider Donny's problems and who is responsible for them. Reread, in
particular, the story's closing paragraph. Then, though the issue is ultimately
unresolvable, weigh the relative responsibility of Daisy, Matt, Cal, the school-
teachers and authorities, and Donny himself.

GLORIA NAYLOR (b. 1950)

Kiswana Browne

From the window of her sixth-floor studio apartment, Kiswana could see over   1
the wall at the end of the street to the busy avenue that lay just north of Brewster Place. The late-afternoon shoppers looked like brightly clad marionettes as
they moved between the congested traffic, clutching their packages against
their bodies to guard them from sudden bursts of the cold autumn wind. A

portly mailman had abandoned his cart and was bumping into indignant window-shoppers as he puffed behind the cap that the wind had snatched from his head. Kiswana leaned over to see if he was going to be successful, but the edge of the building cut him off from her view.

A pigeon swept across her window, and she marveled at its liquid move- 2 ments in the air waves. She placed her dreams on the back of the bird and fantasized that it would glide forever in transparent silver circles until it ascended to the center of the universe and was swallowed up. But the wind died down, and she watched with a sigh as the bird beat its wings in awkward, frantic movements to land on the corroded top of a fire escape on the opposite building. This brought her back to earth.

Humph, it's probably sitting over there crapping on those folks' fire escape, 3 she thought. Now, that's a safety hazard. . . . And her mind was busy again, creating flames and smoke and frustrated tenants whose escape was being hindered because they were slipping and sliding in pigeon shit. She watched their cussing, haphazard descent on the fire escapes until they had all reached the bottom. They were milling around, oblivious to their burning apartments, angrily planning to march on the mayor's office about the pigeons. She materialized placards and banners for them, and they had just reached the corner, boldly sidestepping fire hoses and broken glass, when they all vanished.

A tall copper-skinned woman had met this phantom parade at the corner, 4 and they had dissolved in front of her long, confident strides. She plowed through the remains of their faded mists, unconscious of the lingering wisps of their presence on her leather bag and black fur-trimmed coat. It took a few seconds for this transfer from one realm to another to reach Kiswana, but then suddenly she recognized the woman.

"Oh, God, it's Mama!" She looked down guiltily at the forgotten newspaper 5 in her lap and hurriedly circled random job advertisements.

By this time Mrs. Browne had reached the front of Kiswana's building and 6 was checking the house number against a piece of paper in her hand. Before she went into the building she stood at the bottom of the stoop and carefully inspected the condition of the street and the adjoining property. Kiswana watched this meticulous inventory with growing annoyance but she involuntarily followed her mother's slowly rotating head, forcing herself to see her new neighborhood through the older woman's eyes. The brightness of the unclouded sky seemed to join forces with her mother as it highlighted every broken stoop railing and missing brick. The afternoon sun glittered and cascaded across even the tiniest fragments of broken bottle, and at that very moment the wind chose to rise up again, sending unswept grime flying into the air, as a stray tin can left by careless garbage collectors went rolling noisily down the center of the street.

Kiswana noticed with relief that at least Ben wasn't sitting in his usual place 7 on the old garbage can pushed against the far wall. He was just a harmless old wino, but Kiswana knew her mother only needed one wino or one teenager with a reefer within a twenty-block radius to decide that her daughter was living in a building seething with dope factories and hang-outs for derelicts. If she had seen Ben, nothing would have made her believe that practically every apartment contained a family, a Bible, and a dream that one day enough could be scraped from those meager Friday night paychecks to make Brewster Place a distant memory.

As she watched her mother's head disappear into the building, Kiswana 8 gave silent thanks that the elevator was broken. That would give her at least five minutes' grace to straighten up the apartment. She rushed to the sofa bed and hastily closed it without smoothing the rumpled sheets and blanket or removing her nightgown. She felt that somehow the tangled bedcovers would give away the fact that she had not slept alone last night. She silently apologized to Abshu's memory as she heartlessly crushed his spirit between the steel springs of the couch. Lord, that man was sweet. Her toes curled involuntarily at the passing thought of his full lips moving slowly over her instep. Abshu was a foot man, and he always started his lovemaking from the bottom up. For that reason Kiswana changed the color of the polish on her toenails every week. During the course of their relationship she had gone from shades of red to brown and was now into the purples. I'm gonna have to start mixing them soon, she thought aloud as she turned from the couch and raced into the bathroom to remove any traces of Abshu from there. She took up his shaving cream and razor and threw them into the bottom drawer of her dresser beside her diaphragm. Mama wouldn't dare pry into my drawers right in front of me, she thought as she slammed the drawer shut. Well, at least not the *bottom* drawer. She may come up with some sham excuse for opening the top drawer, but never the bottom one.

When she heard the first two short raps on the door, her eyes took a final 9 flight over the small apartment, desperately seeking out any slight misdemeanor that might have to be defended. Well, there was nothing she could do about the crack in the wall over that table. She had been after the landlord to fix it for two months now. And there had been no time to sweep the rug, and everyone knew that off-gray always looked dirtier than it really was. And it was just too damn bad about the kitchen. How was she expected to be out job-hunting every day and still have time to keep a kitchen that looked like her mother's, who didn't even work and still had someone come in twice a month for general cleaning. And besides . . .

Her imaginary argument was abruptly interrupted by a second series of 10 knocks, accompanied by a penetrating, "Melanie, Melanie, are you there?"

Kiswana strode toward the door. She's starting before she even gets in here. 11 She knows that's not my name anymore.

She swung the door open to face her slightly flushed mother. "Oh, hi, 12 Mama. You know, I thought I heard a knock, but I figured it was for the people next door, since no one hardly ever calls me Melanie." Score one for me, she thought.

"Well, it's awfully strange you can forget a name you answered to for 13 twenty-three years," Mrs. Browne said, as she moved past Kiswana into the apartment. "My, that was a long climb. How long has your elevator been out? Honey, how do you manage with your laundry and groceries up all those steps? But I guess you're young, and it wouldn't bother you as much as it does me." This long string of questions told Kiswana that her mother had no intentions of beginning her visit with another argument about her new African name.

"You know I would have called before I came, but you don't have a phone 14 yet. I didn't want you to feel that I was snooping. As a matter of fact, I didn't expect to find you home at all. I thought you'd be out looking for a job." Mrs. Browne had mentally covered the entire apartment while she was talking and taking off her coat.

"Well, I got up late this morning. I thought I'd buy the afternoon paper and 15 start early tomorrow."

"That sounds like a good idea." Her mother moved toward the window and 16 picked up the discarded paper and glanced over the hurriedly circled ads. "Since when do you have experience as a fork-lift operator?"

Kiswana caught her breath and silently cursed herself for her stupidity. "Oh, 17 my hand slipped—I meant to circle file clerk." She quickly took the paper before her mother could see that she had also marked cutlery salesman and chauffeur.

"You're sure you weren't sitting here moping and daydreaming again?" Am- 18 ber specks of laughter flashed in the corner of Mrs. Browne's eyes.

Kiswana threw her shoulders back and unsuccessfully tried to disguise her 19 embarrassment with indignation.

"Oh, God, Mama! I haven't done that in years—it's for kids. When are you 20 going to realize that I'm a woman now?" She sought desperately for some womanly thing to do and settled for throwing herself on the couch and crossing her legs in what she hoped looked like a nonchalant arc.

"Please, have a seat," she said, attempting the same tones and gestures she'd 21 seen Bette Davis use on the late movies.

Mrs. Browne, lowering her eyes to hide her amusement, accepted the invita- 22 tion and sat at the window, also crossing her legs. Kiswana saw immediately how it should have been done. Her celluloid poise clashed loudly against her mother's quiet dignity, and she quickly uncrossed her legs. Mrs. Browne turned her head toward the window and pretended not to notice.

"At least you have a halfway decent view from here. I was wondering what 23 lay beyond that dreadful wall—it's the boulevard. Honey, did you know that you can see the trees in Linden Hills from here?"

Kiswana knew that very well, because there were many lonely days that she 24 would sit in her gray apartment and stare at those trees and think of home, but she would rather have choked than admit that to her mother.

"Oh, really, I never noticed. So how is Daddy and things at home?" 25

"Just fine. We're thinking of redoing one of the extra bedrooms since you 26 children have moved out, but Wilson insists that he can manage all that work alone. I told him that he doesn't really have the proper time or energy for all that. As it is, when he gets home from the office, he's so tired he can hardly move. But you know you can't tell your father anything. Whenever he starts complaining about how stubborn you are, I tell him the child came by it honestly. Oh, and your brother was by yesterday," she added, as if it had just occurred to her.

So that's it, thought Kiswana. That's why she's here.   27

Kiswana's brother, Wilson, had been to visit her two days ago, and she had   28 borrowed twenty dollars from him to get her winter coat out of layaway. That son-of-a-bitch probably ran straight to Mama—and after he swore he wouldn't say anything. I should have known, he was always a snotty-nosed sneak, she thought.

"Was he?" she said aloud. "He came by to see me, too, earlier this week. And   29 I borrowed some money from him because my unemployment checks hadn't cleared in the bank, but now they have and everything's just fine." There, I'll beat you to that one.

"Oh, I didn't know that," Mrs. Browne lied. "He never mentioned you. He   30 had just heard that Beverly was expecting again, and he rushed over to tell us."

Damn. Kiswana could have strangled herself.   31

"So she's knocked up again, huh?" she said irritably.   32

Her mother started. "Why do you always have to be so crude?"   33

"Personally, I don't see how she can sleep with Willie. He's such a dishrag."   34

Kiswana still resented the stance her brother had taken in college. When   35 everyone at school was discovering their blackness and protesting on campus, Wilson never took part; he had even refused to wear an Afro. This had outraged Kiswana because, unlike her, he was dark-skinned and had the type of hair that was thick and kinky enough for a good "Fro." Kiswana had still insisted on cutting her own hair, but it was so thin and fine-textured, it refused to thicken even after she washed it. So she had to brush it up and spray it with lacquer to keep it from lying flat. She never forgave Wilson for telling her that she didn't look African, she looked like an electrocuted chicken.

"Now that's some way to talk. I don't know why you have an attitude against   36 your brother. He never gave me a restless night's sleep, and now he's settled with a family and a good job."

"He's an assistant to an assistant junior partner in a law firm. What's the big   37 deal about that?"

"The job has a future, Melanie. And at least he finished school and went on   38 for his law degree."

"In other words, not like me, huh?"   39

"Don't put words into my mouth, young lady. I'm perfectly capable of say-   40 ing what I mean."

Amen, thought Kiswana.   41

"And I don't know why you've been trying to start up with me from the mo-   42 ment I walked in. I didn't come here to fight with you. This is your first place away from home, and I just wanted to see how you were living and if you're doing all right. And I must say, you've fixed this apartment up very nicely."

"Really, Mama?" She found herself softening in the light of her mother's ap- 43
proval.

"Well, considering what you had to work with." This time she scanned the 44
apartment openly.

"Look, I know it's not Linden Hills, but a lot can be done with it. As soon 45
as they come and paint, I'm going to hang my Ashanti print over the couch.
And I thought a big Boston Fern would go well in that corner, what do you
think?"

"That would be fine, baby. You always had a good eye for balance." 46

Kiswana was beginning to relax. There was little she did that attracted her 47
mother's approval. It was like a rare bird, and she had to tread carefully around
it lest it fly away.

"Are you going to leave that statue out like that?" 48

"Why, what's wrong with it? Would it look better somewhere else?" 49

There was a small wooden reproduction of a Yoruba goddess with large pro- 50
truding breasts on the coffee table.

"Well," Mrs. Browne was beginning to blush, "it's just that it's a bit sugges- 51
tive, don't you think? Since you live alone now, and I know you'll be having male
friends stop by, you wouldn't want to be giving them any ideas. I mean, uh, you
know, there's no point in putting yourself in any unpleasant situations because
they may get the wrong impressions and uh, you know, I mean, well . . ." Mrs.
Browne stammered on miserably.

Kiswana loved it when her mother tried to talk about sex. It was the only 52
time she was at a loss for words.

"Don't worry, Mama." Kiswana smiled. "That wouldn't bother the type of 53
men I date. Now maybe if it had big feet . . ." And she got hysterical, thinking of
Abshu.

Her mother looked at her sharply. "What sort of gibberish is that about feet? 54
I'm being serious, Melanie."

"I'm sorry, Mama." She sobered up. "I'll put it away in the closet," she said, 55
knowing that she wouldn't.

"Good," Mrs. Browne said, knowing that she wouldn't either. "I guess you 56
think I'm too picky, but we worry about you over here. And you refuse to put in
a phone so we can call and see about you."

"I haven't refused, Mama. They want seventy-five dollars for a deposit, and I 57
can't swing that right now."

"Melanie, I can give you the money." 58

"I don't want you to be giving me money—I've told you that before. Please, 59
let me make it by myself."

"Well, let me lend it to you, then." 60

"No!" 61

"Oh, so you can borrow money from your brother, but not from me." 62

Kiswana turned her head from the hurt in her mother's eyes. "Mama, when 63
I borrow from Willie, he makes me pay him back. You never let me pay you
back," she said into her hands.

"I don't care. I still think it's downright selfish of you to be sitting over here 64 with no phone, and sometimes we don't hear from you in two weeks—anything could happen—especially living among these people."

Kiswana snapped her head up. "What do you mean, *these people*. They're my 65 people and yours, too, Mama—we're all black. But maybe you've forgotten that over in Linden Hills."

"That's not what I'm talking about, and you know it. These streets—this 66 building—it's so shabby and rundown. Honey, you don't have to live like this."

"Well, this is how poor people live."   67

"Melanie, you're not poor."   68

"No, Mama, *you're* not poor. And what you have and I have are two totally 69 different things. I don't have a husband in real estate with a five-figure income and a home in Linden Hills—*you* do. What I have is a weekly unemployment check and an overdrawn checking account at United Federal. So this studio on Brewster is all I can afford."

"Well, you could afford a lot better," Mrs. Browne snapped, "if you hadn't 70 dropped out of college and had to resort to these dead-end clerical jobs."

"Uh-huh, I knew you'd get around to that before long." Kiswana could feel 71 the rings of anger begin to tighten around her lower backbone, and they sent her forward onto the couch. "You'll never understand, will you? Those bourgie schools were counterrevolutionary. My place was in the streets with my people, fighting for equality and a better community."

"Counterrevolutionary!" Mrs. Browne was raising her voice. "Where's your 72 revolution now, Melanie? Where are all those black revolutionaries who were shouting and demonstrating and kicking up a lot of dust with you on that campus? Huh? They're sitting in wood-paneled offices with their degrees in mahogany frames, and they won't even drive their cars past this street because the city doesn't fix potholes in this part of town."

"Mama," she said, shaking her head slowly in disbelief, "how can you—a 73 black woman—sit there and tell me that what we fought for during the Movement wasn't important just because some people sold out?"

"Melanie, I'm not saying it wasn't important. It was damned important to 74 stand up and say that you were proud of what you were and to get the vote and other social opportunities for every person in this country who had it due. But you kids thought you were going to turn the world upside down, and it just wasn't so. When all the smoke had cleared, you found yourself with a fistful of new federal laws and a country still full of obstacles for black people to fight their way over—just because they're black. There was no revolution, Melanie, and there will be no revolution."

"So what am I supposed to do, huh? Just throw up my hands and not care 75 about what happens to my people? I'm not supposed to keep fighting to make things better?"

"Of course, you can. But you're going to have to fight within the system, be- 76 cause it and these so-called 'bourgie' schools are going to be here for a long time. And that means that you get smart like a lot of your old friends and get an important job where you can have some influence. You don't have to sell out, as you say, and work for some corporation, but you could become an assembly-woman or a civil liberties lawyer or open a freedom school in this very neigh-borhood. That way you could really help the community. But what help are you going to be to these people on Brewster while you're living hand-to-mouth on file-clerk jobs waiting for a revolution? You're wasting your talents, child."

"Well, I don't think they're being wasted. At least I'm here in day-to-day 77 contact with the problems of my people. What good would I be after four or five years of a lot of white brainwashing in some phony, prestige institution, huh? I'd be like you and Daddy and those other educated blacks sitting over there in Linden Hills with a terminal case of middle-class amnesia."

"You don't have to live in a slum to be concerned about social conditions, 78 Melanie. Your father and I have been charter members of the NAACP for the last twenty-five years."

"Oh, God!" Kiswana threw her head back in exaggerated disgust. "That's be- 79 ing concerned? That middle-of-the-road, Uncle Tom dumping ground for black Republicans!"

"You can sneer all you want, young lady, but that organization has been 80 working for black people since the turn of the century, and it's still working for them. Where are all those radical groups of yours that were going to put a Cadillac in every garage and Dick Gregory in the White House? I'll tell you where."

I knew you would, Kiswana thought angrily.   81

"They burned themselves out because they wanted too much too fast. Their 82 goals weren't grounded in reality. And that's always been your problem."

"What do you mean, my problem? I know exactly what I'm about."   83

"No, you don't. You constantly live in a fantasy world—always going to ex- 84 tremes—turning butterflies into eagles, and life isn't about that. It's accepting what is and working from that. Lord, I remember how worried you had me, putting all that lacquered hair spray on your head. I thought you were going to get lung cancer—trying to be what you're not."

Kiswana jumped up from the couch. "Oh, God, I can't take this anymore. 85 Trying to be something I'm not—trying to be something I'm not, Mama! Try-ing to be proud of my heritage and the fact that I was of African descent. If that's being what I'm not, then I say fine. But I'd rather be dead than be like you—a white man's nigger who's ashamed of being black!"

Kiswana saw streaks of gold and ebony light follow her mother's flying body 86 out of the chair. She was swung around by the shoulders and made to face the deadly stillness in the angry woman's eyes. She was too stunned to cry out from the pain of the long fingernails that dug into her shoulders, and she was brought so close to her mother's face that she saw her reflection, distorted and wavering, in the tears that stood in the older woman's eyes. And she listened in that stillness to a story she had heard from a child.

"My grandmother," Mrs. Browne began slowly in a whisper, "was a full- 87 bloodied Iroquois, and my grandfather a free black from a long line of journeymen who had lived in Connecticut since the establishment of the colonies. And my father was a Bajan who came to this country as a cabin boy on a merchant mariner."

"I know all that," Kiswana said, trying to keep her lips from trembling.   88

"Then, know this." And the nails dug deeper into her flesh. "I am alive be-   89 cause of the blood of proud people who never scraped or begged or apologized for what they were. They lived asking only one thing of this world—to be allowed to be. And I learned through the blood of these people that black isn't beautiful and it isn't ugly—black is! It's not kinky hair and it's not straight hair—it just is.

"It broke my heart when you changed your name. I gave you my grand-   90 mother's name, a woman who bore nine children and educated them all, who held off six white men with a shotgun when they tried to drag one of her sons to jail for 'not knowing his place.' Yet you needed to reach into an African dictionary to find a name to make you proud.

"When I brought my babies home from the hospital, my ebony son and my   91 golden daughter, I swore before whatever gods would listen—those of my mother's people or those of my father's people—that I would use everything I had and could ever get to see that my children were prepared to meet this world on its own terms, so that no one could sell them short and make them ashamed of what they were or how they looked—whatever they were or however they looked. And Melanie, that's not being white or red or black—that's being a mother."

Kiswana followed her reflection in the two single tears that moved down   92 her mother's cheeks until it blended with them into the woman's copper skin. There was nothing and then so much that she wanted to say, but her throat kept closing up every time she tried to speak. She kept her head down and her eyes closed, and thought, Oh, God, just let me die. How can I face her now?

Mrs. Browne lifted Kiswana's chin gently. "And the one lesson I wanted you   93 to learn is not to be afraid to face anyone, not even a crafty old lady like me who can outtalk you." And she smiled and winked.

"Oh, Mama, I . . ." and she hugged the woman tightly.   94

"Yeah, baby." Mrs. Browne patted her back. "I know."   95

She kissed Kiswana on the forehead and cleared her throat. "Well, now, I   96 better be moving on. It's getting late, there's dinner to be made, and I have to get off my feet—these new shoes are killing me."

Kiswana looked down at the beige leather pumps. "Those are really classy.   97 They're English, aren't they?"

"Yes, but, Lord, do they cut me right across the instep." She removed the   98 shoe and sat on the couch to massage her foot.

Bright red nail polish glared at Kiswana through the stockings. "Since when   99 do you polish your toenails?" she gasped. "You never did that before."

"Well . . ." Mrs. Browne shrugged her shoulders, "your father sort of talked   100 me into it, and, uh, you know, he likes it and all, so I thought, uh, you know, why not, so . . ." And she gave Kiswana an embarrassed smile.

I'll be damned, the young woman thought, feeling her whole face tingle. 101
Daddy's into feet! And she looked at the blushing woman on her couch and
suddenly realized that her mother had trod through the same universe that she
herself was now traveling. Kiswana was breaking no new trails and would eventually end up just two feet away on that couch. She stared at the woman she had
been and was to become.

"But I'll never be a Republican," she caught herself saying aloud. 102

"What are you mumbling about, Melanie?" Mrs. Browne slipped on her 103
shoe and got up from the couch.

She went to get her mother's coat. "Nothing, Mama. It's really nice of you to 104
come by. You should do it more often."

"Well, since it's not Sunday, I guess you're allowed at least one lie." 105

They both laughed. 106

After Kiswana had closed the door and turned around, she spotted an enve- 107
lope sticking between the cushions of her couch. She went over and opened it
up; there was seventy-five dollars in it.

"Oh, Mama, darn it!" She rushed to the window and started to call to the 108
woman, who had just emerged from the building, but she suddenly changed
her mind and sat down in the chair with a long sigh that caught in the upward
draft of the autumn wind and disappeared over the top of the building.

ACTIVITIES FOR WRITING AND DISCUSSION

1. React to the paragraph near the end of the story that begins, "I'll be
damned . . ."

> And she looked at the blushing woman on her couch and suddenly real-
> ized that her mother had trod through the same universe that she herself
> was now traveling. Kiswana was breaking no new trails and would eventu-
> ally end up just two feet away on that couch. She stared at the woman she
> had been and was to become.

a. In what ways *is* Kiswana's mother "the woman she [Kiswana] had been
and was to become"? Jot down some ways and discuss them with a partner or group.

b. Compose a sequel in which you sketch out Kiswana's subsequent life.
What choices does she make about family, career, politics, and social
causes? How does the middle-aged Kiswana/Melanie resemble or differ
from her middle-aged mother?

2. Make a list of similarities and differences between you and your own
mother or father. Then, in a notebook entry, explore how *you* have become
more—or less—like your own mother or father as you have grown older.

3. Recall a conflict in your relationship with your own mother or father.
Brainstorm a list of memories of that conflict. Then create a dialogue between you
and your parent that dramatizes the conflict and its resolution—if there was one.

Poems

William Carlos Williams (1883–1963)

The Last Words of My English Grandmother

There were some dirty plates
and a glass of milk
beside her on a small table
near the rank, disheveled bed—

Wrinkled and nearly blind   5
she lay and snored
rousing with anger in her tones
to cry for food,

Gimme something to eat—
They're starving me—   10
I'm all right I won't go
to the hospital. No, no, no

Give me something to eat
Let me take you
to the hospital, I said   15
and after you are well

you can do as you please.
She smiled, Yes
you do what you please first
then I can do what I please—   20

Oh, oh, oh! she cried
as the ambulance men lifted
her to the stretcher—
Is this what you call

making me comfortable?   25
By now her mind was clear—
Oh you think you're smart
you young people,

she said, but I'll tell you
you don't know anything.   30

Then we started.
On the way

we passed a long row
of elms. She looked at them
awhile out of   35
the ambulance window and said,

What are all those
fuzzy-looking things out there?
Trees? Well, I'm tired
of them and rolled her head away.   40

Activities for Writing and Discussion

1. How would you describe the **speaker's** feelings about his grandmother? What clues in the poem help you with your description?

2. Look at the poem's **free verse** form. Try rewriting a few of Williams's sentences in *prose* form. What, if anything, is lost by not having the text laid out in lines and **stanzas**? How does Williams's visual layout affect your experience of the poem?

3. Think of elderly men or women you have met or known. List some of their characteristics, for instance, their personalities, appearance, gestures, speech, or favorite topics of conversation. Then, assuming the character of an elderly person in the midst of some urgent situation such as death, illness, a move, or some other change in lifestyle, write out your thoughts in a **stream of consciousness** form.

Edna St. Vincent Millay (1892–1950)

Childhood Is the Kingdom Where Nobody Dies

Childhood is not from birth to a certain age and at a certain age
The child is grown, and puts away childish things.
Childhood is the kingdom where nobody dies.

Nobody that matters, that is. Distant relatives of course
Die, whom one never has seen or has seen for an hour,   5
And they gave one candy in a pink-and-green striped bag, or a
    jack-knife,
And went away, and cannot really be said to have lived at all.

And cats die. They lie on the floor and lash their tails,
And their reticent fur is suddenly all in motion
With fleas that one never knew were there,   10
Polished and brown, knowing all there is to know,
Trekking off into the living world.
You fetch a shoe-box, but it's much too small, because she won't curl
    up now:
So you find a bigger box, and bury her in the yard, and weep.
But you do not wake up a month from then, two months,   15
A year from then, two years, in the middle of the night
And weep, with your knuckles in your mouth, and say Oh, God! Oh,
    God!
Childhood is the kingdom where nobody dies that matters,—mothers
    and fathers don't die.

And if you have said, "For heaven's sake, must you always be kissing a
    person?"
Or, "I do wish to gracious you'd stop tapping on the window with
    your thimble!"   20
Tomorrow, or even the day after tomorrow if you're busy having fun,
Is plenty of time to say, "I'm sorry, mother."

To be grown up is to sit at the table with people who have died, who neither
    listen nor speak;
Who do not drink their tea, though they always said
Tea was such a comfort.   25

Run down into the cellar and bring up the last jar of raspberries; they are not
    tempted.
Flatter them, ask them what was it they said exactly
That time, to the bishop, or to the overseer, or to Mrs. Mason;
They are not taken in.
Shout at them, get red in the face, rise,   30
Drag them up out of their chairs by their stiff shoulders and shake
    them and yell at them;
They are not startled, they are not even embarrassed; they slide back
    into their chairs.

Your tea is cold now.
You drink it standing up,
And leave the house.   35

Theodore Roethke (1908–1963)

My Papa's Waltz

The whiskey on your breath
Could make a small boy dizzy;
But I hung on like death:
Such waltzing was not easy.

We romped until the pans   5
Slid from the kitchen shelf;
My mother's countenance
Could not unfrown itself.

The hand that held my wrist
Was battered on one knuckle;   10
At every step you missed
My right ear scraped a buckle.

You beat time on my head
With a palm caked hard by dirt,
Then waltzed me off to bed   15
Still clinging to your shirt.

ACTIVITIES FOR WRITING AND DISCUSSION

1. Considering the title alone, what expectations do you have for the poem's tone and content? How and where are these expectations met or undercut as you read the poem itself?

2. Working in a small group or as a class, read the poem aloud twice. During the second reading, pause after each line or two to discuss any associations that are triggered for you by individual words or phrases. How, if at all, do any of these words or phrases affect your sense of the poem's meaning?

3. The poem offers a concise sketch of a family unit—father, mother, and child. Supplementing clues in the text with your own imagination and experience of families, try to describe this family—its members and their interrelationships—in as much detail as you can. Then show how your finished description is consistent with the spare details provided in the poem.

ROBERT HAYDEN (1913–1980)

Those Winter Sundays

Sundays too my father got up early
and put his clothes on in the blueblack cold,
then with cracked hands that ached
from labor in the weekday weather made
banked fires blaze. No one ever thanked him.   5

I'd wake and hear the cold splintering, breaking.
When the rooms were warm, he'd call,
and slowly I would rise and dress,
fearing the chronic angers of that house,

Speaking indifferently to him,   10
who had driven out the cold
and polished my good shoes as well.
What did I know, what did I know
of love's austere and lonely offices?

GWENDOLYN BROOKS (b. 1917)

Sadie and Maud

Maud went to college.
Sadie stayed at home.
Sadie scraped life
With a fine-tooth comb.

She didn't leave a tangle in.   5
Her comb found every strand.
Sadie was one of the livingest chits
In all the land.

Sadie bore two babies
Under her maiden name.   10
Maud and Ma and Papa
Nearly died of shame.

When Sadie said her last so-long
Her girls struck out from home.

(Sadie had left as heritage   15
Her fine-tooth comb.)

Maud, who went to college,
Is a thin brown mouse.
She is living all alone
In this old house.   20

CHARLES BUKOWSKI (1920–1994)

my old man

16 years old
during the depression
I'd come home drunk
and all my clothing—
shorts, shirts, stockings—   5
suitcase, and pages of
short stories
would be thrown out on the
front lawn and about the
street.   10

my mother would be
waiting behind a tree:
"Henry, Henry, don't
go in . . . he'll
kill you, he's read   15
your stories . . ."

"I can whip his
ass . . ."

"Henry, please take
this . . . and   20
find yourself a room."

but it worried him
that I might not
finish high school
so I'd be back   25
again.

one evening he walked in
with the pages of
one of my short stories
(which I had never submitted   30
to him)
and he said, "this is
a great short story."
I said, "o.k.,"
and he handed it to me   35
and I read it.
it was a story about
a rich man
who had a fight with
his wife and had   40
gone out into the night
for a cup of coffee
and had observed
the waitress and the spoons
and forks and the   45
salt and pepper shakers
and the neon sign
in the window
and then had gone back
to his stable   50
to see and touch his
favorite horse
who then
kicked him in the head
and killed him.   55

somehow
the story held
meaning for him
though
when I had written it   60
I had no idea
of what I was
writing about.

so I told him,
"o.k., old man, you can   65
have it."
and he took it
and walked out

and closed the door.
I guess that's   70
as close
as we ever got.

ACTIVITIES FOR WRITING AND DISCUSSION

1. How does this piece change—or what does it lose—if you re-format it as prose and transform each grouping of lines into a prose paragraph?

2. The father objects to his son's short stories. Why?

3. The father liked *one* of the **speaker's** short stories. Based on the little you know of the father, what "meaning" could that story have "held" for him? What do you make of the word "close" in the next-to-last line? Do you take the word literally or as an example of **verbal irony**? What kind of closeness did this father and son have?

4. Drawing on details in the poem and on your own imagination, reconstruct the speaker's early life with his parents. Tell the story of his life from the **point of view** of the son or of either parent.

DONALD HALL (b. 1928)

My Son, My Executioner

My son, my executioner,
　I take you in my arms,
Quiet and small and just astir,
　And whom my body warms.

Sweet death, small son, our instrument   5
　Of immortality,
Your cries and hungers document
　Our bodily decay.

We twenty-five and twenty-two,
　Who seemed to live forever,   10
Observe enduring life in you
　And start to die together.

ACTIVITIES FOR WRITING AND DISCUSSION

1. Read the poem aloud. Plot out the **rhyme** scheme. Indicate sound patterns using a single underline for examples of **alliteration** and a double underline for examples of **assonance** or **consonance**.

2. Who are the "our" and the "we" in the poem?

3. Working alone or in a group, explicate the poem's dominant metaphor, which identifies "my son" as "my executioner."
   a. What images come to mind when you think of an "executioner"? Make a list of these images or of any other **connotations** the word has for you.
   b. Describe any ways in which the son *is* his father's "executioner." Are all sons or daughters executioners of their fathers or mothers? As an experiment, carry the metaphor to an extreme: Create a short dialogue between parent and child in which the child is a *literal* executioner. Finally, with the class or your group, discuss how a literal executioner differs from a metaphoric one.

LINDA PASTAN (b. 1932)

Marks

My husband gives me an A
for last night's supper,
an incomplete for my ironing,
a B plus in bed.
My son says I am average,   5
an average mother, but if
I put my mind to it
I could improve.
My daughter believes
in Pass/Fail and tells me   10
I pass. Wait 'til they learn
I'm dropping out.

PAT MORA (b. 1942)

Gentle Communion

Even the long-dead are willing to move.
Without a word, she came with me from the desert.

Mornings she wanders through my rooms
making beds, folding socks.

Since she can't hear me anymore,   5
Mamande[1] ignores the questions I never knew
to ask, about her younger days, her red
hair, the time she fell and broke her nose
in the snow. I will never know.

When I try to make her laugh,   10
to disprove her sad album face, she leaves
the room, resists me as she resisted
grinning for cameras, make-up, English.

While I write, she sits and prays,
feet apart, legs never crossed,   15
the blue housecoat buttoned high
as her hair dries white, girlish
around her head and shoulders.

She closes her eyes, bows her head,
and like a child presses her hands together,   20
her patient flesh steeple, the skin
worn, like the pages of her prayer book.

Sometimes I sit in her wide-armed
chair as I once sat in her lap.
Alone, we played a quiet I Spy.   25
She peeled grapes I still taste.

She removes the thin skin, places
the luminous coolness on my tongue.
I know not to bite or chew. I wait
for the thick melt,   30
our private green honey.

———————
1. Grandmother

ACTIVITIES FOR WRITING AND DISCUSSION

1. Identify any passages in the poem that help explain Mamande's importance to the **speaker.** Why do you suppose the speaker experiences Mamande as such a powerful presence in her life?

2. Though dead, the grandmother is imagined as a continuing, almost physical presence in the speaker's life. Write a text (poem, letter, or dialogue) in which you "commune" with a deceased ancestor or relative of your own. If you wish, do as Mora does and show how he/she responds to you.

3. The phrase "sad album face" in line 11 suggests that the speaker remembers the grandmother, in part, through photographs. Find a family photograph of your own that shows a now dead relative (other than your mother or father) who is important to you. Jot down notes on the photograph's visual details. Then, working from direct experience and/or hearsay, write some recollections and stories about that person. (For an example of this sort of writing, see Joy Harjo's "The Place of Origins" on page 327.)

SHARON OLDS (b. 1942)

The Elder Sister

When I look at my elder sister now
I think how she had to go first, down through the
birth canal, to force her way
head-first through the tiny channel,
the pressure of Mother's muscles on her brain,   5
the tight walls scraping her skin.
Her face is still narrow from it, the long
hollow cheeks of a Crusader on a tomb,
and her inky eyes have the look of someone who has
been in prison a long time and   10
knows they can send her back. I look at her
body and think how her breasts were the first to
rise, slowly, like swans on a pond.

By the time mine came along, they were just
two more birds on the flock, and when the hair   15
rose on the white mound of her flesh, like
threads of water out of the ground, it was the
first time, but when mine came
they knew about it. I used to think
only in terms of her harshness, sitting and   20
pissing on me in bed, but now I
see I had her before me always
like a shield. I look at her wrinkles, her clenched
jaws, her frown-lines—I see they are
the dents on my shield, the blows that did not reach me.   25
She protected me, not as a mother

protects a child, with love, but as a
hostage protects the one who makes her
escape as I made my escape, with my sister's
body held in front of me.   30

Linda Hogan (b. 1947)

Heritage

From my mother, the antique mirror
where I watch my face take on her lines.
She left me the smell of baking bread
to warm fine hairs in my nostrils,
she left the large white breasts that weigh down   5
my body.

From my father I take his brown eyes,
the plague of locusts that leveled our crops,
they flew in formation like buzzards.

From my uncle the whittled wood   10
that rattles like bones
and is white
and smells like all our old houses
that are no longer there. He was the man
who sang old chants to me, the words   15
my father was told not to remember.

From my grandfather who never spoke
I learned to fear silence.
I learned to kill a snake
when you're begging for rain.   20

And grandmother, blue-eyed woman
whose skin was brown,
she used snuff.
When her coffee can full of black saliva
spilled on me   25
it was like the brown cloud of grasshoppers
that leveled her fields.
It was the brown stain
that covered my white shirt,
my whiteness a shame.   30
That sweet black liquid like the food

she chewed up and spit into my father's mouth
when he was an infant.
It was the brown earth of Oklahoma
stained with oil.   35
She said tobacco would purge your body of poisons.
It has more medicine than stones and knives
against your enemies.

That tobacco is the dark night that covers me.

She said it is wise to eat the flesh of deer   40
so you will be swift and travel over many miles.
She told me how our tribe has always followed a stick
that pointed west
that pointed east.
From my family I have learned the secrets   45
of never having a home.

ACTIVITIES FOR WRITING AND DISCUSSION

   1. React to the poem's images. How do they make you feel? Are they pleasant? unpleasant? perplexing? disturbing? Why? Be specific, and share your reactions in class or in a small group.

   2. How would you characterize the **speaker's** attitude toward her heritage?
Does she regard it fondly? bitterly? with mixed emotions? Cite words or lines in
the poem to support your answers.

   3. Create a poem about your own heritage. Consider imitating Hogan's
form by beginning each section with the words "From my [grandmother/
uncle/father/mother" and so on] and following with the particular legacy you
have from that ancestor or relative.

RITA DOVE (b. 1952)

Fifth Grade Autobiography

I was four in this photograph fishing
with my grandparents at a lake in Michigan.
My brother squats in poison ivy.
His Davy Crockett cap
sits squared on his head so the raccoon tail   5
flounces down the back of his sailor suit.

My grandfather sits to the far right
in a folding chair,
and I know his left hand is on
the tobacco in his pants pocket   10
because I used to wrap it for him
every Christmas. Grandmother's hips
bulge from the brush, she's leaning
into the ice chest, sun through the trees
printing her dress with soft   15
luminous paws.

I am staring jealously at my brother;
the day before he rode his first horse, alone.
I was strapped in a basket
behind my grandfather.   20
He smelled of lemons. He's died—

but I remember his hands.

Activity for Writing and Discussion

1. Find a childhood photograph of you and your family. Writing in the present tense, describe the photograph's visual details. In your description, incorporate the thoughts that were likely going through your mind—and/or the minds of others in the picture—at the moment the picture was taken.

Judith Ortiz Cofer (b. 1952)

Lessons of the Past

For my daughter

I was born the year my father learned to march in step
with other men, to hit bull's eyes, to pose for sepia photos
in dress uniform outside Panamanian nightspots—pictures
he would send home to his pregnant teenage bride inscribed:
To my best girl.   5

My birth made her a madonna, a husbandless young woman
with a legitimate child, envied by all the tired women
of the pueblo as she strolled my carriage down dirt roads,
both of us dressed in fine clothes bought with army checks.

                When he came home,   10
he bore gifts: silk pajamas from the orient for her; a pink
iron crib for me. People filled our house to welcome him.
He played Elvis loud and sang along in his new English.
She sat on his lap and laughed at everything.

They roasted a suckling pig out on the patio. Later,   15
no one could explain how I had climbed over the iron bars
and into the fire. Hands lifted me up quickly, but not before
the tongues had licked my curls.

                There is a picture of me   20
taken soon after: my hair clipped close to my head,
my eyes enormous—about to overflow with fear.
I look like a minature of one of those women
in Paris after World War II, hair shorn,
being paraded down the streets in shame,
for having loved the enemy.

                But then things changed,
and some nights he didn't come home. I remember   25
hearing her cry in the kitchen. I sat on the rocking chair
waiting for my cocoa, learning how to count, *uno, dos, tres,*
cuatro, cinco, on my toes. So that when he came in,
smelling strong and sweet as sugarcane syrup,
I could surprise my *Papasito*—   30
who liked his girls smart, who didn't like crybabies—
with a new lesson, learned well.

ALBERTO RIOS (b. 1952)

A Dream of Husbands

Though we thought it, Doña Carolina did not die.
She was too old for that nonsense, and too set.
That morning she walked off just a little farther
into her favorite dream, favorite but not nice
so much, not nice and not bad, so it was not death.   5
She dreamed the dream of husbands
and over there she found him after all the years.
Cabrón, she called him, *animal,* very loud
so we could hear it, for us it was a loud truck
passing, or thunder, or too many cats, very loud   10
for having left her for so long and so far. Days now
her voice is the squeak of the rocking chair
as she complains, we hear it, it will not go
not with oils or sanding or shouts back at her.
But it becomes too the sound a spoon makes, her old   15
very large wooden spoon as it stirs a pot of soup.
Dinnertimes, we think of her, the good parts, of her
cooking, we like her best then, even the smell of her.
But then, *cabrones* she calls us, *animales,* irritated,
from over there, from the dream, they come, her words   20
they are the worst sounds of the street in the night
so that we will not get so comfortable about her,
so comfortable with her having left us
we thinking that her husband and her long dream
are so perfect, because no, they are not, not so much,   25
she is not so happy this way, not in this dream,
this is not heaven, don't think it. She tells us this,
sadness too is hers, a half measure, sadness at having
no time for the old things, for rice, for chairs.

LI-YOUNG LEE (b. 1957)

The Gift

To pull the metal splinter from my palm
my father recited a story in a low voice.
I watched his lovely face and not the blade.
Before the story ended he'd removed
the iron sliver I thought I'd die from.   5

I can't remember the tale
but hear his voice still, a well
of dark water, a prayer.
And I recall his hands,
two measures of tenderness   10
he laid against my face,
the flames of discipline
he raised above my head.

Had you entered that afternoon
you would have thought you saw a man   15
planting something in a boy's palm,
a silver tear, a tiny flame.
Had you followed that boy
you would have arrived here,
where I bend over my wife's right hand.   20

Look how I shave her thumbnail down
so carefully she feels no pain.
Watch as I lift the splinter out.
I was seven when my father
took my hand like this,   25
and I did not hold that shard
between my fingers and think,
Metal that will bury me,
christen it Little Assassin,
Ore Going Deep for My Heart.   30
And I did not lift up my wound and cry,
Death visited here!
I did what a child does
when he's given something to keep.
I kissed my father.   35

Nonfiction/Essays

Franz Kafka (1883–1924)

Letter to His Father

Dearest Father:

You asked me recently why I maintain that I am afraid of you. As usual, I
was unable to think of any answer to your question, partly for the very reason

that I am afraid of you, and partly because an explanation of the grounds for this fear would mean going into far more details than I could even approximately keep in mind while talking. And if I now try to give you an answer in writing, it will still be very incomplete, because even in writing this fear and its consequences hamper me in relation to you and because [anyway] the magnitude of the subject goes far beyond the scope of my memory and power of reasoning. . . .

It is indeed quite possible that even if I had grown up entirely free from your influence I still could not have become a person after your own heart. I should probably have still become a weakly, timid, hesitant, restless person, neither Robert Kafka nor Karl Hermann, but yet quite different from what I really am, and we might have got on with each other excellently. I should have been happy to have you as a friend, as a chief, an uncle, a grandfather, even indeed (though this rather more hesitantly) as a father-in-law. Only as what you are, a father, you have been too strong for me, particularly since my brothers died when they were small and my sisters only came along much later, so that I had to bear the whole brunt of it all alone, something I was much too weak for.

Compare the two of us: I, to put it in a very much abbreviated form, a Löwy with a certain basis of Kafka, which, however, is not set in motion by the Kafka will to life, business, and conquest, but by a Löwyish spur that urges more secretly, more diffidently, and in another direction, and which often fails to work entirely. You, on the other hand, a true Kafka in strength, health, appetite, loudness of voice, eloquence, self-satisfaction, worldly dominance, endurance, presence of mind, knowledge of human nature, a certain way of doing things on a grand scale, of course also with all the defects and weaknesses that go with all these advantages and into which your temperament and sometimes your hot temper drive you. . . . However it was, we were so different and in our difference so dangerous to each other that, if anyone had tried to calculate in advance how I, the slowly developing child, and you, the full-grown man, would stand to each other, he could have assumed that you would simply trample me underfoot so that nothing was left of me. Well, that didn't happen. Nothing alive can be calculated. But perhaps something worse happened. And in saying this I would all the time beg of you not to forget that I never, and not even for a single moment, believe any guilt to be on your side. The effect you had on me was the effect you could not help having. But you should stop considering it some particular malice on my part that I succumbed to that effect.

I was a timid child. For all that, I am sure I was also obstinate, as children are. I am sure that Mother spoilt me too, but I cannot believe I was particularly difficult to manage; I cannot believe that a kindly word, a quiet taking of me by the hand, a friendly look, could not have got me to do anything that was wanted of me. Now you are after all at bottom a kindly and softhearted person (what follows will not be in contradiction to this, I am speaking only of the impression you made on the child), but not every child has the endurance and fearlessness to go on searching until it comes to the kindliness that lies beneath the surface. You can only treat a child in the way you yourself are constituted, with vigor, noise, and hot temper, and in this case this seemed to you, into the bargain, extremely suitable, because you wanted to bring me up to be a strong brave boy. . . .

What must be considered as heightening the effect is that you were then 5 younger and hence more energetic, wilder, more untrammeled and still more reckless than you are today and that you were, besides, completely tied to the business, scarcely able to be with me even once a day, and therefore made all the more profound an impression on me, never really leveling out into the flatness of habit.

There is only one episode in the early years of which I have a direct memory. You may remember it, too. Once in the night I kept on whimpering for water, not, I am certain, because I was thirsty, but probably partly to be annoying, partly to amuse myself. After several vigorous threats had failed to have any effect, you took me out of bed, carried me out onto the *pavlatche* and left me there alone for a while in my nightshirt, outside the shut door. I am not going to say that this was wrong—perhaps at that time there was really no other way of getting peace and quiet that night—but I mention it as typical of your methods of bringing up a child and their effect on me. I dare say I was quite obedient afterwards at that period, but it did me inner harm. What was for me a matter of course, that senseless asking for water, and the extraordinary terror of being carried outside were two things that I, my nature being what it was, could never properly connect with each other. Even years afterwards I suffered from the tormenting fancy that the huge man, my father, the ultimate authority, would come almost for no reason at all and take me out of bed in the night and carry me out onto the *pavlatche,* and that therefore I was such a mere nothing for him.

That then was only a small beginning, but this sense of nothingness that often dominates me (a feeling that is in another respect, admittedly, also a noble and fruitful one) comes largely from your influence. What I would have needed was a little encouragement, a little friendliness, a little keeping open of my road, instead of which you blocked it for me, though of course with the good intention of making me go another road. But I was not fit for that. You encouraged me, for instance, when I saluted and marched smartly, but I was no future soldier, or you encouraged me when I was able to eat heartily or even drink beer with my meals, or when I was able to repeat songs, singing what I had not understood, or prattle to you using your own favorite expressions, imitating you, but nothing of this had anything to do with my future. And it is characteristic that even today you really only encourage me in anything when you yourself are involved in it, when what is at stake is your own sense of self-importance, which I damage. . . .

At that time, and at that time everywhere, I would have needed encouragement. I was, after all, depressed even by your mere physical presence. I remember, for instance, how we often undressed together in the same bathing hut. There was I, skinny, weakly, slight; you strong, tall, broad. Even inside the hut I felt myself a miserable specimen, and what's more, not only in your eyes but in the eyes of the whole world, for you were for me the measure of all things. But then when we went out of the bathing hut before the people, I with you holding my hand, a little skeleton, unsteady, barefoot on the boards, frightened of the water, incapable of copying your swimming strokes, which you, with the best of intentions, but actually to my profound humiliation, always kept on showing me, then I was frantic with desperation and all my bad experiences in all spheres at such moments fitted magnificently together. What made me feel best was when you sometimes undressed first and I was able to stay behind in the hut alone and put off the disgrace of showing myself in public until at length you came to see what I was doing and drove me out of the hut. I was grateful to you for not seeming to notice my extremity, and besides, I was proud of my father's body. For the rest, this difference between us remains much the same to this very day.

In keeping with that, furthermore, was your intellectual domination. You had worked your way up so far alone, by your own energies, and as a result you had unbounded confidence in your opinion. For me as a child that was not yet so dazzling as later for the boy growing up. From your armchair you ruled the world. Your opinion was correct, every other was mad, wild, *meshugge*, not normal. With all this your self-confidence was so great that you had no need to be consistent at all and yet never ceased to be in the right. It did sometimes happen that you had no opinion whatsoever about a matter and as a result all opinions that were at all possible with respect to the matter were necessarily wrong, without exception. You were capable, for instance, of running down the Czechs, and then the Germans, and then the Jews, and what is more, not only selectively but in every respect, and finally nobody was left except yourself. For me you took on the enigmatic quality that all tyrants have whose rights are based on their person and not on reason. At least so it seemed to me.

Now where I was concerned you were in fact astonishingly often in the right, which was a matter of course in talk, for there was hardly ever any talk between us, but also in reality. Yet this too was nothing particularly incomprehensible: in all my thinking I was, after all, under the heavy pressure of your personality, even in that part of it—and particularly in that—which was not in accord with yours. All these thoughts, seemingly independent of you, were from the beginning loaded with the burden of your harsh and dogmatic judgments; it was almost impossible to endure this, and yet to work out one's thoughts with any measure of completeness and permanence. I am not here speaking of any sublime thoughts, but of every little enterprise in childhood. It was only necessary to be happy about something or other, to be filled with the thought of it, to come home and speak of it, and the answer was an ironical sigh, a shaking of the head, a tapping of the table with one finger: "Is that all you're so worked up about?" or "I wish I had your worries!" or "The things some people have time to think about!" or "What can you buy yourself with that?" or "What a song and dance about nothing!" Of course, you couldn't be expected to be enthusiastic about every childish triviality, toiling and moiling as you used to. But that wasn't the point. The point was, rather, that you could not help always and on principle causing the child such disappointments, by

10

virtue of your antagonistic nature, and further that this antagonism was cease-
lessly intensified through accumulation of its material, that it finally became a
matter of established habit even when for once you were of the same opinion as
myself, and that finally these disappointments of the child's were not disappointments in ordinary life but, since what it concerned was your person,
which was the measure of all things, struck to the very core. Courage, resolution, confidence, delight in this and that, did not endure to the end when you
were against whatever it was or even if your opposition was merely to be assumed; and it was to be assumed in almost everything I did. . . .

Since as a child I was together with you chiefly at meals, your teaching was
to a large extent teaching about proper behavior at table. What was brought to
the table had to be eaten up, there could be no discussion of the goodness of the
food—but you yourself often found the food uneatable, called it "this swill,"
said "that brute" (the cook) had ruined it. Because in accordance with your
strong appetite and your particular habit you ate everything fast, hot and in big
mouthfuls, the child had to hurry, there was a somber silence at table, interrupted by admonitions: "Eat first, talk afterwards," or "faster, faster, faster," or
"there you are, you see, I finished ages ago." Bones mustn't be cracked with the
teeth, but you could. Vinegar must not be sipped noisily, but you could. The
main thing was that the bread should be cut straight. But it didn't matter that you
did it with a knife dripping with gravy. One had to take care that no scraps fell on
the floor. In the end it was under your chair that there were most scraps. At table
one wasn't allowed to do anything but eat, but you cleaned and cut your fingernails, sharpened pencils, cleaned your ears with the toothpick. Please, Father, understand me rightly: these would in themselves have been utterly insignificant
details, they only became depressing for me because you, the man who was so
tremendously the measure of all things for me, yourself did not keep the com-
mandments you imposed on me. Hence the world was for me divided into three
parts: into one in which I, the slave, lived under laws that had been invented only
for me and which I could, I did not know why, never completely comply with;
then into a second world, which was infinitely remote from mine, in which you
lived, concerned with government, with the issuing of orders and with annoyance about their not being obeyed; and finally into a third world where everybody else lived happily and free from orders and from having to obey. I was
continually in disgrace, either I obeyed your orders, and that was a disgrace, for
they applied, after all, only to me, or I was defiant, and that was a disgrace too, for
how could I presume to defy you, or I could not obey because, for instance, I had
not your strength, your appetite, your skill, in spite of which you expected it of
me as a matter of course; this was the greatest disgrace of all. What moved in this
way was not the child's reflections, but his feelings. . . .

The impossibility of getting on calmly together had one more result, actually
a very natural one: I lost the capacity to talk. I dare say I would never have been a
very eloquent person in any case, but I would, after all, have had the usual flu-
ency of human language at my command. But at a very early stage you forbade
me to talk. Your threat: "Not a word of contradiction!" and the raised hand that

accompanied it have gone with me ever since. What I got from you—and you are, as soon as it is a matter of your own affairs, an excellent talker—was a hesitant, stammering mode of speech, and even that was still too much for you, and finally I kept silent, at first perhaps from defiance, and then because I couldn't either think or speak in your presence. And because you were the person who really brought me up, this has had its repercussions throughout my life. It is altogether a remarkable mistake for you to believe I never fell in with your wishes. "Always agin you" was really not my basic principle where you were concerned, as you believe and as you reproach me. On the contrary: if I had obeyed you less, I am sure you would have been much better pleased with me. As it is, all your educational measures hit the mark exactly. There was no hold I tried to escape. As I now am, I am (apart, of course, from the fundamentals and the influence of life itself) the result of your upbringing and of my obedience. . . .

It was true that Mother was illimitably good to me, but all that was for me in relation to you, that is to say, in no good relation. Mother unconsciously played the part of a beater during a hunt. Even if your method of upbringing might in some unlikely case have set me on my own feet by means of producing defiance, dislike, or even hate in me, Mother canceled that out again by kindness, by talking sensibly (in the maze and chaos of my childhood she was the very pattern of good sense and reasonableness), by pleading for me, and I was again driven back into your orbit, which I might perhaps otherwise have broken out of, to your advantage and to my own. Or it was so that no real reconciliation ever came about, that Mother merely shielded me from you in secret, secretly gave me something, or allowed me to do something, and then where you were concerned I was again the furtive creature, the cheat, the guilty one, who in his worthlessness could only pursue backstairs methods even to get the things he regarded as his right. Of course, I then became used to taking such courses also in quest of things to which, even in my own view, I had no right. This again meant an increase in the sense of guilt.

It is also true that you hardly ever really gave me a whipping. But the shouting, the way your face got red, the hasty undoing of the braces and the laying of them ready over the back of the chair, all that was almost worse for me. It is like when someone is going to be hanged. If he is really hanged, then he's dead and it's all over. But if he has to go through all the preliminaries to being hanged and only when the noose is dangling before his face is told of his reprieve, then he may suffer from it all his life long. Besides, from so many occasions when I had, as you clearly showed you thought, deserved to be beaten, when you were however gracious enough to let me off at the last moment, here again what accumulated was only a huge sense of guilt. On every side I was to blame, I was in debt to you.

You have always reproached me (and what is more either alone or in front of others, you having no feeling for the humiliation of this latter, your children's affairs always being public affairs) for living in peace and quiet, warmth, and abundance, lacking for nothing, thanks to your hard work. I think here of remarks that must positively have worn grooves in my brain, like: "When I was only seven I had to push the barrow from village to village." "We all had to sleep in one room." "We were glad when we got potatoes." "For years I had open sores on my legs from not having enough clothes to wear in winter." "I was only a little boy when I was sent away to Pisek to go into business." "I got nothing from home, not even when I was in the army, even then I was sending money home." "But for all that, for all that—Father was always Father to me. Ah, nobody knows what that means these days! What do these children know of things? Nobody's been through that! Is there any child that understands such things today?" Under other conditions such stories might have been very educational, they might have been a way of encouraging one and strengthening one to endure similar torments and deprivations to those one's father had undergone. But that wasn't what you wanted at all; the situation had, after all, become quite different as a result of all your efforts, and there was no opportunity to distinguish oneself in the world as you had done. Such an opportunity would first of all have had to be created by violence and revolution, it would have meant breaking away from home (assuming one had had the resolution and strength to do so and that Mother wouldn't have worked against it, for her part, with other means). But all that was not what you wanted at all, that you termed ingratitude, extravagance, disobedience, treachery, madness. And so, while on the one hand you tempted me to it by means of example, story, and humiliation, on the other hand you forbade it with the utmost severity. . . .

—*Translated by Ernst Kaiser and Eithne Wilkins*

ACTIVITIES FOR WRITING AND DISCUSSION

1. Using information provided by the **author,** compose brief character descriptions of Kafka and his father.
   a. Based on your descriptions, what are the sources of conflict between father and son?
   b. In what ways do the conflicts strike you as typical of parent/child relationships, and in what ways do they seem unique to Kafka?

2. Kafka recounts several episodes in the father-son relationship. Mark these episodes in your text. Then choose one that particularly strikes you. Remaining faithful to Kafka's facts—but expanding on them as needed—rewrite the episode in the form of a dialogue or a short play involving Kafka and his father. If necessary, include **scene descriptions, stage directions,** and additional **characters.**

3. Write a letter to your own father or mother in which you reflect on the history of your relationship. Taking Kafka's text as an example, review and narrate some particular experiences in this relationship and reflect on their significance to your development. (Note: This does not need to be a letter you actually *send* to your parent or share with anyone else.)

Joy Harjo (b. 1951)

The Place of Origins

for my cousin John Jacobs (1918–1991), who will always be with me

I felt as if I had prepared for the green corn ceremony my whole life. It's nothing I can explain in print, and no explanation would fit in the English language. All I can say is that it is central to the mythic construct of the Muscogee people (otherwise known as "Creek"), a time of resonant renewal, of forgiveness.

The drive to Tallahassee Grounds in northeastern Oklahoma, with my friends Helen and Jim Burgess and Sue Williams, was filled with stories. Stories here are thick as the insects singing. We were part of the ongoing story of the people. Helen and I had made a promise to participate together in a ceremony that ensures the survival of the people, a link in the epic story of grace. The trees and tall, reedlike grasses resounded with singing.

There's nothing quite like it anywhere else I've been, and I've traveled widely. The most similar landscape is in Miskito country in northeastern Nicaragua. I thought I was home again as I walked with the Miskito people whose homeland had suffered terrible destruction from both sides in the war. The singing insects provided a matrix of complex harmonies, shifting the cells in the body that shape imagination. I imagine a similar insect language in a place I've dreamed in West Africa. In summer in Oklahoma it's as if insects shape the world by songs. Their collective punctuation helps the growing corn remember the climb to the sun.

Our first stop was Holdenville, to visit one of my favorite older cousins, John Jacobs, and his wife Carol. They would join us later at the grounds. We traded gifts and stories, ate a perfectly fried meal at the Dairy Queen, one of the few restaurants open in a town hit hard by economic depression. I always enjoy visiting and feasting with these, my favorite relatives, and I feel at home in their house, a refuge surrounded by peacocks, dogs, and well-loved cats, guarded by giant beneficent spirits disguised as trees.

Across the road an oil well pumps relentlessly. When I was a child in Oklahoma, the monster insect bodies of the pumping wells terrified me. I would duck down in the car until we passed. Everyone thought it was funny. I was called high-strung and imaginative. I imagined the collapse of the world, as if the wells were giant insects without songs, pumping blood from the body of Earth. I wasn't far from the truth. 5

My cousin John, who was more like a beloved uncle, gave me two photographs he had culled for me from family albums. I had never before seen my great-grandparents on my father's side. As I held them in my hand, reverberations of memory astounded me.

I believe stories are encoded in the DNA spiral and call each cell into perfect position. Sound tempered with emotion and meaning propels the spiral

MARSIE HARJO AND FAMILY. (Courtesy Joy Harjo.)

MARSIE HARJO AND KATIE MENAWE HARJO. (Courtesy Joy Harjo.)

beyond three dimensions. I recognized myself in this photograph. I saw my sister, my brothers, my son and daughter. My father lived once again at the wheel of a car, my father who favored Cadillacs and Lincolns—cars he was not always able to afford but sacrificed to own anyway because he was compelled by the luxury of well-made vehicles, the humming song of a finely constructed motor. He made sure his cars were greased and perfectly tuned. That was his favorite music.

I was shocked (but not surprised) to recognize something I must always have known—the images of my great-grandmother Katie Menawe, my great-grandfather Marsie Harjo, my grandmother Naomi, my aunts Lois and Mary, and my uncle Joe. They were always inside me, as if I were a soul catcher made of a blood-formed crystal. I had heard the names, the stories, and perhaps their truths had formed the images, had propelled me into the world. My grandchildren and great-grandchildren will also see a magnification of themselves in their grandparents. It's implicit in the way we continue, the same way as corn plants, the same way as stars or cascades of insects singing in the summer. The old mystery of division and multiplication will always lead us to the root.

I think of my Aunt Lois's admonishments about photographs. She said that they could steal your soul. I believe it's true, for an imprint remains behind forever, locked in paper and chemicals. Perhaps the family will always be touring somewhere close to the border, dressed in their Sunday best, acutely aware of the soul stealer that Marsie Harjo hired to photograph them, steadying his tripod on the side of the road. Who's to say they didn't want something left to mark time in that intimate space, a space where they could exist forever as a family, a world drenched in sepia?

Nothing would ever be the same again. But here the family is ever-present, 10 as is the unnamed photographer through his visual arrangement. I wonder if he was surprised to see rich Indians.

The parents of both my great-grandparents made the terrible walk of the Muscogee Nation from Alabama to Indian Territory. They were settled on land bordered on the north by what is now Tulsa—the place my brothers, my sister, and I were born. The people were promised that if they made this move they would be left alone by the U.S. government, which claimed it needed the tribal homelands for expansion. But within a few years, white settlers were once again crowding Indian lands, and in 1887 the Dawes Act, better known as the Allotment Act, was made law. Private ownership was forced on the people. Land that supposedly belonged in perpetuity to the tribe was divided into plots, allotted to individuals. What was "left over" was opened for white settlement. But this did not satisfy the settlers, who proceeded, by new laws, other kinds of trickery, and raw force, to take over allotments belonging to the Muscogee and other tribes. The Dawes Act undermined one of the principles that had always kept the people together: that land was communal property which could not be owned.

On December 1, 1905, oil was struck in Glenpool, Oklahoma. This was one of the richest lakes of oil discovered in the state. At its height it produced forty million barrels annually. Marsie Harjo's allotted land was in Glenpool. He was soon a rich man, as were many other Indian people whose allotted land lay over lakes of oil. Land grabs intensified. Many tribal members were swindled out of their property, or simply killed for their money. It's a struggle that is still being played out in the late twentieth century.

Oil money explains the long elegant car Marsie Harjo poses in with his family. In the stories I've been told, he always loved Hudsons. The family was raised in luxury. My grandmother Naomi and my Aunt Lois both received B.F.A. degrees in art and were able to take expensive vacations at a time when many people in this country were suffering from economic deprivation. They also had an African-American maid, whose name was Susie. I've tried to find out more about her, but all I know is that she lived with the family for many years and made the best ice cream.

There are ironies here, because Marsie Harjo was also half or nearly half African-American, and in more recent years there has been racism directed at African-Americans by the tribe, which originally accepted Africans and often welcomed them as relatives. The acceptance of slavery came with the embrace of European-American cultural values. It was then that we also began to hate ourselves for our own darkness. It's all connected: ownership of land has everything to do with the ownership of humans and how they are treated, with the attitude toward all living things.

This picture of my great-grandparents' family explodes the myth of being   15
Indian in this country for both non-Indian and Indian alike. I wonder how the image of a Muscogee family in a car only the wealthy could own would be interpreted by another Muscogee person, or by another tribal person, or by a non-Indian anywhere in this land. It challenges the popular culture's version of "Indian"—an image that fits no tribe or person. By presenting it here, I mean to question those accepted images that have limited us to cardboard cut-out figures, without blood or tears or laughter.

There were many photographs of this family. I recently sent my cousin Donna Jo Harjo a photograph of her father Joe as a child about five. He was dressed in a finely tailored suit and drove a child's-size model of a car. His daughter has never lived in this kind of elegance. She lives on her salary as a sorter for a conglomerate nut and dried fruit company in northern California. She loves animals, especially horses and cats. (Our clan is the Tiger Clan.) I wonder at the proliferation of photographs and the family's diminishment in numbers to this present generation.

The second photograph is a straight-on shot of the same great-grandparents standing with two Seminole men in traditional dress, wearing turbans. They are in stark contrast to my great-grandparents—especially Marsie Harjo, who is stately and somewhat stiff with the fear of God in his elegant white man's clothes, his Homburg hat.

Marsie Harjo was a preacher, a Creek Baptist minister, representing a counterforce to traditional Muscogee culture. He embodied one side in the split in our tribe since Christianity was introduced and the people were influenced by

European cultural values; the dividing lines remain the same centuries later. He was quite an advanced thinker, and I imagine he repressed what he foresaw for the Muscogee people, who probably would not have believed him anyway.

My great-grandfather was in Stuart, Florida, as he was every winter, to "save" the souls of the Seminole people. He bought a plantation there, and because he hated pineapples, he had every one of the plants dug up and destroyed. I've also heard that he owned an alligator farm. I went to Stuart this spring on my way to Miami and could find no trace of the mission or the plantation anywhere in the suburban mix of concrete, glass, and advertisements. My memories are easier to reach in a dimension that is as alive and living as anything in the three dimensions we know with our five senses.

My great-grandmother Katie Menawe is much more visible here than in the 20 first photograph, where she is not up front, next to the driver, but in the very back of the car, behind her four children. Yet she quietly presides over everything as she guards her soul from the intrusive camera. I sense that Marsie boldly entered the twentieth century ahead of most people, while Katie reluctantly followed. I doubt if she ever resolved the split in her heart between her background and foreground.

I don't know much about her. She and her siblings were orphaned. Her sister Ella, a noted beauty, was my cousin John's mother. They were boarded for some time at Eufaula Indian School. I don't know how old Katie was when she married Marsie Harjo. But the name Monahwee* is one of those Muscogee names that is charged with memory of rebellion, with strength in the face of terrible adversity. Tecumseh came looking for Monahwee when he was building his great alliance of nations in the 1800s. Monahwee was one of the leaders of the Red Stick War, an armed struggle against the U.S. government to resist Andrew Jackson's demand for the removal of the tribes from their Southeastern homelands. Creeks, Seminoles, and Africans made up the fighting forces. Most of those who survived went to Florida, where the Seminoles successfully resisted colonization by hiding in the swamps. They beat the United States forces, who were aided by other tribes, including other Creeks who were promised land and homes for their help. The promises were like others from the U.S. government. Those who assisted were forced to walk west to Indian Territory like everyone else.

Monahwee stayed in Alabama and was soon forced west, but not before he joined with Jackson's forces to round up Seminoles for removal to Oklahoma. My cousin John said he died on the trail. I know that he died of a broken heart. I have a McKenney Hall portrait print of Monahwee, an original hand-colored lithograph dated 1848. Katie has the same eyes and composure of this man who was her father.

By going to Tallahassee Grounds to take part in a traditional tribal ceremony, I was taking my place in the circle of relatives, one more link in the con-

---

*His name is sometimes spelled Menawe or Menewa, but on his gravestone in Okmulgee, Oklahoma, it is spelled Monahwee. [Author's note]

catenation of ancestors. Close behind me are my son and daughter, behind them, my granddaughter. Next to me, interlocking the pattern, are my cousins, my aunts and my uncles, my friends. We dance together in this place of knowing beyond the physical dimensions of space, much denser than the chemicals and paper of photographs. This place is larger than mere human memory, than the destruction we have walked through to come to this ground.

Time can never be stopped, rather it is poised so we can make a leap into knowing or into a field of questions. I understood this as we stompdanced in the middle of the night, as the stars whirred overhead in the same patterns as when Katie, Marsie, and the children lived beneath them. I heard time resume as the insects took up their singing again, to guide us through memory. The old Hudson heads to the east of the border of the photograph. For the Muscogee, East is the place of origins, the place the People emerged from so many hundreds of years ago. It is also a place of return.

ACTIVITIES FOR WRITING AND DISCUSSION

1. On page 330 Harjo says, "This picture of my great-grandparents' family explodes the myth of being Indian in this country for both non-Indian and Indian alike." What is this "myth"? Why should Harjo be concerned to "explode" it?

2. What do the photographs add to this essay? How would the text be weakened, strengthened, or changed if the photos were eliminated?

3. Following Harjo's example, compose an essay about your own family in which you include one or more family photographs that serve as springboards for your writing. If you wish, select photographs that reveal both your family and some aspects of a culture to which you and your family belong.

4. Harjo sees family and culture as closely interconnected. Consider a culture (racial, religious, ethnic, social, avocational, or professional) with which you yourself identify. In an essay, describe some myths or beliefs about the culture that are held by outsiders. Then show how you, your family, or others close to you exemplify and/or belie those myths.

5. As an alternative to Activity #4, focus on a culture with which you do *not* identify instead of one with which you do. If possible, interview some members of that culture or do other outside research on it. Then, in an essay, discuss the stereotypes you and others have of that culture and show how the stereotypes are exemplified and/or belied by individuals.

FENTON JOHNSON (b. 1953)

The Limitless Heart

It is late March—the Saturday of Passover, to be exact—and I am driving an oversize rented car through west Los Angeles. I have never seen this side of the city except in the company of my companion, who died of AIDS-related complications in a Paris hospital in autumn of last year. He was an only child and often asked that I promise to visit his parents after his death. As the youngest son of a large family and a believer in brutal honesty, I refused. I have too much family already, I said. There are limits to how much love one can give.

Now I am here, driving along San Vicente Boulevard, one of the lovelier streets of Santa Monica, Calif., west from Wilshire to the Pacific. The street is divided by a broad green median lined with coral trees, which the city has seen fit to register as landmarks. They spread airy, elegant crowns against a movie-set heaven, a Maxfield Parrish blue. Each branch bleeds at its end an impossibly scarlet blossom, as if the twigs themselves had pierced the thin-skinned sky.

My friend's parents are too old to get about much. They are survivors of the Holocaust, German Jews who spent the war years hiding in a Dutch village a few miles from Germany itself. Beaten by Nazis before the war, my friend's father hid for four years with broken vertebrae, unable to see a doctor. When he was no longer able to move, his desperate wife descended to the street to find help, and saw falling from the sky the parachutes of their liberators.

After the war they came to California, promised land of this promised land. Like Abraham and Sarah,[1] they had a single son in their advanced years, proof that it is possible, in the face of the worst, to pick up sticks and start again.

At his home in Santa Monica, my friend's father sits in chronic pain, un-   5
complaining. Unlike his wife, he is reserved; he does not talk about his son with the women of his life—his wife or his surviving sister. No doubt he fears giving way before his grief, and his life has not allowed for much giving way. This much he and I share: as a gay man who grew up in the rural South, I am no stranger to hiding.

His wife always goes to bed early—partly as a way of coping with grief—but tonight he all but asks her to retire. After she leaves he begins talking of his son, and I listen and respond with gratefulness. We are two men in control, who permit ourselves to speak to each other of these matters because we subscribe implicitly, jointly, unconditionally to this code of conduct.

He tells of a day when his son, then 8 years old, wanted to go fishing. The quintessential urban Jew, my friend's father nonetheless bought poles and hooks and drove 50 miles to Laguna Beach. There they dropped their lines from a pier to discover the hooks dangled some 10 feet above the water. ("Thank God," he says. "Otherwise we might have caught something.") A passer-by scoffed. "What the hell do you think you're trying to catch?" My friend's father shrugged, unperturbed. "Flying fish," he replied.

---

1. In the Old Testament, Abraham and Sarah gave birth to a son, Isaac, in their old age.

I respond with my most vivid memory of his son. He was a wiser man than I, and spoke many times across our years together of his great luck, his great good fortune. Denial pure and simple, or so I told myself at first. AZT, DDI, ACT-UP, CMV, DHPG, and what I came to think of as the big "A" itself—he endured this acronymed life, while I listened and learned and participated and helped when I could.

Until our third and last trip to Paris, the city of his dreams. On what would be his last night to walk about the city we sat in the courtyard of the Picasso Museum. There at dusk, under a deep sapphire sky, I turned to him and said, "I'm so lucky," and it was as if the time allotted to him to teach this lesson, the time for me to learn it, had been consumed, and there were nothing left but the facts of things to play out.

A long silence after this story—I have ventured beyond what I permit my- 10 self, what I am permitted.

I change the subject, asking my friend's father to talk of the war years. He does not allow himself to speak of his beatings or of murdered family and friends. Instead he remembers moments of affection, loyalty, even humor, until he talks of winters spent immobilized with pain and huddled in his wife's arms, their breaths freezing on the quilt as they sang together to pass the time, to stay warm.

Another silence; now he has ventured too far. "I have tried to forget these stories," he says in his halting English.

In the presence of these extremes of love and horror I am reduced to cliché. "It's only by remembering them that we can hope to avoid repeating them."

"They are being repeated all the time," he says. "It is bad sometimes to watch too much television. You see these things and you know we have learned nothing."

Are we so dense that we can learn nothing from all this pain, all this death? 15 Is it impossible to learn from experience? The bitterness of these questions I can taste, as I drive east to spend the night at a relative's apartment.

Just south of the seedier section of Santa Monica Boulevard, I stop at a bar recommended by a friend. I need a drink, and I need the company of men like myself—survivors, for the moment anyway, albeit of a very different struggle.

The bar is filled with Latinos wearing the most extraordinary clothes. Eighty years of B movies have left Hollywood the nation's most remarkable supply of secondhand dresses, most of which, judging from this evening, have made their ways to these guys' closets.

I am standing at the bar, very Anglo, very out of place, very much thinking of leaving, when I am given another lesson:

A tiny, wizened, gray-haired Latina approaches the stage, where under jerry-rigged lights (colored cellophane, Scotch tape) a man lip-syncs to Brazilian rock. His spike heels raise him to something above six feet; he wears a floor-length sheath dress, slit up the sides and so taut, so brilliantly silver, so lustrous that it catches and throws back the faces of his audience. The elderly Latina raises a dollar bill. On tottering heels he lowers himself, missing not a word of his song while half-crouching, half-bending so that she may tuck her dollar in his cleavage and kiss his cheek.

"*Su abuelita,*" the bartender says laconically. "His grandmother."   20

One A.M. in the City of Angels—the streets are clogged with cars. Stuck in traffic, I am haunted by voices and visions: the high thin songs of my companion's parents as they huddle under their frozen quilt, singing into their breath; a small boy and his father sitting on a very long pier, their baitless fishhooks dangling above the vast Pacific; the face of *su abuelita,* uplifted, reverent, mirrored in her grandson's dress.

Somewhere a light changes; the traffic unglues itself. As cars begin moving I am visited by two last ghosts—my companion and myself, sitting in the courtyard of the Hôtel Salé, transfigured by the limitless heart.

Plays

JOYCE CAROL OATES (b. 1938)

Tone Clusters

A PLAY IN NINE SCENES

CHARACTERS

FRANK GULICK: fifty-three years old
EMILY GULICK: fifty-one years old
VOICE: male, indeterminate age

These are white Americans of no unusual distinction, nor are they in any self-evident way "representative."

Tone Clusters *is not intended to be a realistic work, thus any inclination toward the establishment of character should be resisted. Its primary effect should be visual (the dominance of the screen at center stage, the play of lights of sharply contrasting degrees of intensity) and audio (the* VOICE, *the employment of music—* "tone clusters" *of Henry Cowell and/or Charles Ives, and electronic music, etc.). The mood is one of fragmentation, confusion, yet, at times, strong emotion. A fractured narrative emerges which the audience will have no difficulty piecing together even as—and this is the tragicomedy of the piece—the characters* MR. *and* MRS. GULICK *deny it.*

In structure, Tone Clusters *suggests an interview, but a stylized interview in which questions and answers are frequently askew. Voices trail off into silence or may be mocked or extended by strands of music. The* VOICE *is sometimes overamplified and booming; sometimes marred by static; sometimes clear, in an ebullient tone, like that of a talk-show host. The* VOICE *has no identity but must be male. It should not be represented by any actual presence on the stage or within view of the audience. At all times, the* VOICE *is in control: the principals on the stage are dominated by their interrogator and by the screen, which is seemingly floating in the air above them, at center stage. Indeed the screen emerges as a character.*

The piece is divided into nine uneven segments. When one ends, the lights dim, then come up again immediately. (After the ninth segment the lights go out completely and darkness is extended for some seconds to indicate that the piece is ended: it ends on an abrupt cutoff of lights and images on the screen and the monitors.)

By degree the GULICKS *become somewhat accustomed to the experience of being interviewed and filmed, but never wholly accustomed: they are always slightly disoriented, awkward, confused, inclined to speak slowly and methodically or too quickly, "unprofessionally," often with inappropriate emotion (fervor, enthusiasm, hope, sudden rage) or no emotion at all (like "computer voices"). The* GULICKS *may at times speak in unison (as if one were an echo of the other); they may mimic the qualities of tone-cluster music or electronic music (I conceive of their voices, and that of the* VOICE, *as music of a kind); should the director wish, there may be some clear-cut relationship between subject and emotion or emphasis—but the piece should do no more than approach "realism," and then withdraw. The actors must conceive of themselves as elements in a dramatic structure, not as "human characters" wishing to establish rapport with an audience.*

Tone Clusters *is about the absolute mystery—the* not knowing—*at the core of our human experience. That the mystery is being exploited by a television documentary underscores its tragicomic nature.*

Scene 1.

Lights up. Initially very strong, near-blinding. On a bare stage, middle-aged FRANK *and* EMILY GULICK *sit ill-at-ease in "comfortable" modish cushioned swivel chairs, trying not to squint or grimace in the lights (which may be represented as the lights of a camera crew provided the human figures involved can be kept shadowy, even indistinct). They wear clip-on microphones, to which they are unaccustomed. They are "dressed up" for the occasion, and clearly nervous: they continually touch their faces, or clasp their hands firmly in their laps, or fuss with fingernails, buttons, the microphone cords, their hair. The nervous mannerisms continue throughout the piece but should never be too distracting and never comic.*

Surrounding the GULICKS, *dominating their human presence, are the central screen and the TV monitors and/or slide screens upon which, during the course of the play, disparate images, words, formless flashes of light are projected. Even when the* GULICKS' *own images appear on the screens they are upstaged by it: they glance at it furtively, with a kind of awe.*

The rest of the time, the monitors always show the stage as we see it: the GULICKS *seated, glancing uneasily up at the large screen. Thus there is a "screen within a screen."*

The employment of music is entirely at the director's discretion. The opening might be accompanied by classical tone cluster piano pieces—Henry Cowell's "Advertisement," for instance. The music should never be intrusive. The ninth scene might well be completely empty of music. There should certainly be no "film-music" effect. (The GULICKS *do not hear the music.)*

The VOICE *too in its modulations is at the discretion of the director. Certainly at the start the* VOICE *is booming and commanding. There should be intermittent audio trouble (whistling, static, etc.); the* VOICE, *wholly in control, can exude any number of effects throughout the play—pomposity, charity, condescension, bemusement, false chattiness, false pedantry, false sympathy, mild incredulity (like that of a television emcee), affectless "computer talk." The* GULICKS *are entirely intimidated by the* VOICE *and try very hard to answer its questions.*

Screen shifts from its initial image to words: IN A CASE OF MURDER—*large black letters on white.*

VOICE: In a case of murder   (taking murder as an abstraction)   there is always a sense of the Inevitable   once the identity of the murderer   is established. Beforehand there   is   a sense   of disharmony.

And humankind fears and loathes disharmony,

Mr. and Mrs. Gulick of Lakepointe, New Jersey, would you comment?

FRANK: . . .Yes I would say,   I think that

EMILY: What is that again, exactly?   I . . .

FRANK: My wife and I, we . . .

EMILY: Disharmony . . . ?

FRANK: I don't like disharmony.   I mean, all the family,

we are a law-abiding family.

VOICE: A religious family   I believe?

FRANK: Oh yes.   Yes,

We go to church every

EMILY: We almost never miss a,   a Sunday

For a while,   I helped with Sunday School classes

The children,   the children don't always go but they believe,

our daughter Judith for instance she   and Carl

FRANK: oh yes   yessir

EMILY: and Dennis,   they do believe they were raised to

believe in God and, and Jesus Christ

FRANK: We raised them that way because   we were raised that way,

EMILY: there *is* a God whether you agree with Him   or not.

VOICE: "Religion" may be defined as   a sort of adhesive matter invisibly

holding together   nation-states, nationalities, tribes, families

for   the   good   of   those   so

held together,

would you comment?

FRANK: Oh,   oh yes.

EMILY: For the good of . . .

FRANK: Yes I would say so,   I think so.

EMILY: My husband and I, we were married in church, in

FRANK: In the Lutheran Church.

EMILY: In Penns Neck.

FRANK: In New Jersey.

EMILY: All our children,

BOTH: they believe.

EMILY: God sees into the human heart.

VOICE: Mr. and Mrs. Gulick   from your experience would you   theorize for our audience: is the Universe "predestined"   in every particular

    or   is   man   capable   of   acts   of   "freedom"?

BOTH: . . .

EMILY: . . . I would say,   that is hard to say.

FRANK: Yes. I believe that man is free.

EMILY: If you mean like, I guess   choosing good and evil?   Yes

FRANK: I would have to say   yes.   You would have to say mankind is free.

Like moving my hand. *(moves hand)*

EMILY: If nobody is free   it wouldn't be right would it to punish anybody?

FRANK: There is always   Hell.

I believe in Hell.

EMILY: Anybody at all

FRANK: Though I am not free to, to   fly up in the air am I? *(laughs)*

because   Well I'm not built right for that am I? *(laughs)*

VOICE: Man is free.   Thus man is   responsible for his acts.

EMILY: Except, oh   sometime if,   maybe for instance if

A baby born without

FRANK: Oh one of those "AIDS" babies

EMILY: poor thing

FRANK: "crack" babies

Or if you were captured   by some enemy, y'know   and tortured

Some people never have a chance.

EMILY: But God sees into the human heart,

God knows who to forgive   and who not.

Lights down.

Scene 2.

Lights up. Screen shows a suburban street of lower-income homes; the GULICKS *stare at the screen and their answers are initially distracted.*

VOICE: Here we have Cedar Street   in Lakepointe, New Jersey   neatly kept homes (as you can see)   American suburb   low crime rate, single-family homes   suburb of Newark, New Jersey

population twelve thousand   the neighborhood of
Mr. and Mrs. Frank Gulick the parents of   Carl Gulick
Will you introduce yourselves to our audience please?
(House lights come up.)
FRANK: . . . Go on, you first
EMILY: I, I don't know what to say
FRANK: My name is   Frank Gulick, I   I am fifty-three years old
that's our house there   2368 Cedar Street
EMILY: My name is Emily Gulick, fifty-one years old,
VOICE: How employed,   would you care to say?   Mr. Gulick?
FRANK: I work for the post office,   I'm a supervisor for
EMILY: He has worked for the post office for twenty-five years
FRANK: . . . The Terhune Avenue branch.
VOICE: And how long have you resided   in your attractive home   on Cedar
Street?
(House lights begin to fade down.)
FRANK: . . . Oh I guess, how long   if this is
this is 1990?
EMILY: (oh just think: 1990!)
FRANK: we moved there in, uh   Judith wasn't born yet so
EMILY: Oh there was our thirtieth anniversary a year ago,
FRANK: wedding
no that was two years ago
EMILY: was it?
FRANK: or three, I   twenty-seven years, this is 1990
EMILY: Yes: Judith is twenty-six,   now I'm a grandmother
FRANK: Carl is twenty-two
EMILY: Denny is seventeen, he's a senior in high school
No none of them are living at home now
FRANK: not now
EMILY: Right now poor Denny is staying with my sister in
VOICE: Frank and Emily Gulick you have been happy here   in Lakepointe
raising your family like any   American couple   with your
hopes and aspirations
                        until recently?
FRANK: . . .Yes, oh yes.
EMILY: Oh for a long time we *were*
FRANK: oh yes.
EMILY: It's so strange to,   to think of
The years go by so
VOICE: You have led a   happy family life   like so many millions
                        of Americans
EMILY: Until this,   this terrible thing
FRANK: *Innocent until proven guilty*—that's a laugh!
EMILY: Oh it's a, a terrible thing

FRANK: Never any hint beforehand of   the meanness of people's hearts.
I mean the neighbors.

EMILY: Oh now don't start that,   this isn't the

FRANK: Oh God you just try to   comprehend

EMILY: this isn't the place, I

FRANK: Like last night: this carload of kids
drunk, beer-drinking   foul language in the night

EMILY: oh don't, my hands are

FRANK: Yes but you know it's the parents   set them going
And telephone calls   our number is changed now, but

EMILY: my hands are shaking so
we are both on medication   the doctor says,

FRANK: oh you would not believe, you would not   believe   the hatred
like Nazi Germany

EMILY: Denny had to drop out of school,   he loved school he is
an honor student

FRANK: everybody turned against us

EMILY: My sister in Yonkers, he's staying with

FRANK: Oh he'll never be the same   boy again.
none of us will.

VOICE: In the development of   human identity   there's the element
of chance,   and there is genetic determinism.
    Would you comment please?

FRANK: The thing is,   you try your best.

EMILY: oh dear God yes.

FRANK: Your best.

EMILY: You give all that's in your heart

FRANK: you
can't do more than that can you?

EMILY: Yes but there is certain to be   justice.
There *is* a, a sense of things.

FRANK: Sometimes there is a chance, the way they   turn out
but also   what they *are.*

EMILY: Your own babies

VOICE: Frank Gulick   and Mary   what is your assessment of
American civilization   today?

EMILY: . . . it's Emily.

FRANK: My wife's name is,

EMILY: it's
Emily.

VOICE: Frank and EMILY   Gulick.

FRANK: . . . The state of the   civilization?

EMILY: It's so big,

FRANK: We are here to   tell our side of,

EMILY: . . . I don't know: it's a,   a Democracy

FRANK: the truth is,   do you want the truth?
the truth is where we live
Lakepointe
it's changing too
    EMILY: it has changed
    FRANK: Yes but it's all over, it's
terrible, just terrible
    EMILY: Now we are grandparents we fear for
    FRANK: Yes what you read and see on TV
    EMILY: You don't know what to think,
    FRANK: Look: in this country   half the crimes
are committed by the,   by half the population against
the other half.   *(laughs)*
You have your law-abiding citizens,
    EMILY: taxpayers
    FRANK: and you have the   rest of them
Say you went downtown into a city like   Newark, some night
    EMILY: you'd be crazy if you got out of your car
    FRANK: you'd be dead.   That's what.
    VOICE: Is it possible,   probable   or in your assessment *im*probable
that the slaying of   fourteen-year-old   Edith Kaminsky
    on February 12, 1990   is related to
            the social malaise
            of which you speak?
    FRANK: . . . "ma-lezz"?
    EMILY: . . . oh it's hard to,   I would say yes
    FRANK: . . . whoever did it, he
    EMILY: Oh it's terrible the things that
keep happening
    FRANK: If only the police would arrest the right person,
    VOICE: Frank and Emily Gulick   you remain adamant in your belief
in your faith in your twenty-two-year-old son   Carl
    that he is innocent   in the death of
        fourteen-year-old Edith Kaminsky
            on February 12, 1990?
    EMILY: Oh yes,
    FRANK: oh yes that is
the single thing we are convinced of.
    EMILY: On this earth.
    BOTH: With God as our witness,
    FRANK: yes
    EMILY: Yes.
    FRANK: The single thing.

Lights down.

Scene 3.

Lights up. Screen shows violent movement: urban scenes, police patrol cars, a fire burning out of control, men being arrested and herded into vans; a body lying in the street. The GULICKS *stare at the screen.*

VOICE: Of today's pressing political issues   the rise in violent crime
most concerns American citizens   Number-one political issue of
    Mr. and Mrs. Gulick   tell our viewers your opinion?
        FRANK: In this state,
the state of New Jersey
        EMILY: Oh it's everywhere
        FRANK: there's capital punishment supposedly
        EMILY: But the lawyers   the lawyers get them off,
        FRANK: you bet
There's public defenders the taxpayer pays
        EMILY: Oh, it's   it's out of control
(like that, what is it   "acid rain"
        FRANK: it can fall on you anywhere,
        EMILY: the sun is too hot too:
        BOTH: the "greenhouse effect")
        FRANK: It's a welfare state by any other name
        EMILY: Y'know who pays:
        BOTH: the taxpayer
        FRANK: The same God damn criminal, you pay for him   then he
That's the joke of it *(laughs)*
the same criminal who slits your throat *(laughs)*
He's the one you pay bail for, to get out.
But it sure isn't funny.   *(laughs)*
        EMILY: Oh God.
        FRANK: It sure isn't funny.
        VOICE: Many Americans have come to believe   this past decade   that
capital punishment is one of the   answers: would you
comment please?
        FRANK: Oh in cases of actual, proven   murder
        EMILY: Those drug dealers
        FRANK: Yes *I* would have to say, definitely   yes
        EMILY: I would say so yes
        FRANK: You always hear them say   opponents of the death penalty
"The death penalty doesn't stop crime"
        EMILY: Oh that's what they say!
        FRANK: Yes but *I* say, once a man is dead   he sure ain't gonna commit
any more crimes, is he.   *(laughs)*
        VOICE: The death penalty *is* a deterrent to crime   in those cases
when the criminal has been   executed

FRANK: But you have to find the right,
the actual murderer.
EMILY: Not some poor innocent*   some poor innocent*

Lights down.

Scene 4.

Lights up. Screen shows a grainy magnified snapshot of a boy about ten. Quick jump to a snapshot of the same boy a few years older. Throughout this scene images of "Carl Gulick" appear and disappear on the screen though not in strict relationship to what is being said, nor in chronological order. "Carl Gulick" in his late teens and early twenties is muscular but need not have any other outstanding characteristics: he may look like any American boy at all.

VOICE: Carl Gulick, twenty-two years old   the second-born child of Frank and Emily Gulick of Lakepointe, New Jersey   How would you describe your son, Frank and Emily
FRANK: D'you mean how he looks or . . . ?
EMILY: He's a shy boy, he's   shy   Not backward just
FRANK: He's about my height I guess   brown hair, eyes
EMILY: Oh! no I think   no he's much taller Frank
he's been taller than you   for years
FRANK: Well that depends on how we're both standing.
How we're both   standing
Well in one newspaper it said six feet one inch, in the other
six feet three inches, that's the kind of
EMILY: accuracy
FRANK: reliability of the news media
you can expect!
EMILY: And oh that terrible picture of,
in the paper
that face he was making   the police carrying him
against his will   laying their hands on him
FRANK: handcuffs
EMILY: Oh that isn't *him*
BOTH: that isn't our son
(GULICKS *respond dazedly to snapshots flashed on screen.*)
EMILY: Oh! that's Carl   age I guess about
FRANK: four?
EMILY: that's at the beach one summer
FRANK: only nine or ten, he was big for
EMILY: With his sister Judith
FRANK: that's my brother George

---

*"Innocent" is an adjective here, not a noun. [Author's note]

EMILY: That's

FRANK: he loved Boy Scouts,

EMILY: but

Oh when you are the actual parents it's
a different

FRANK: Oh it is so different!

from something just on TV.

VOICE: In times of disruption   of fracture   it is believed that
human behavior moves   in unchartable leaps   History is a formal
record of such   leaps   but in large-scale demographical   terms
   in which the   individual   is   lost

   Frank and Emily Gulick it's said your son   Carl   charged
in the savage slaying of   fourteen-year-old   shows no sign of
   remorse   that is to say, *awareness* of the act:
thus the question we pose to you   Can guilt reside in those
   without conscience,
or is memory   conscience, and conscience memory?
   can "the human" reside in those
      devoid of "memory"

EMILY: . . . Oh the main thing is,

he is innocent.

FRANK: . . . Stake my life on it.

EMILY: He has always been   cheerful, optimistic

FRANK: a good boy, of course he has not

forgotten

BOTH: He is innocent.

EMILY: How could our son "forget" when he has nothing to

BOTH: "forget"

FRANK: He took that lie detector test voluntarily didn't he

EMILY: Oh there he is   weight-lifting, I don't remember

who took that picture?

FRANK: When you are the actual parents you see them every day,

you don't form judgments.

VOICE: And how is your son employed, Mr. and Mrs. Kaminsky?

Excuse me: GULICK.

FRANK: Up until Christmas he was working in

This butcher shop in East Orange

EMILY: . . . it isn't easy, at that age

FRANK: Before that, loading and unloading

EMILY: at Sears at the mall

FRANK: No: that was before, that was before the other

EMILY: No: the job at Sears was

FRANK: . . . Carl was working for that Italian, y'know that

EMILY: the lawn service

FRANK: Was that before?   or after

Oh in this butcher shop   his employer

EMILY: yes there were hard feelings, on both sides

FRANK: Look: you can't believe a single thing   in the newspaper or TV

EMILY: it's not that they lie

FRANK: Oh yes they lie

EMILY: not that they lie, they just   get everything wrong

FRANK: Oh they do lie!   And it's printed and you can't stop them.

EMILY: In this meat shop, I never wanted him to work there

FRANK: In this shop there was pressure on him
to join the union.

EMILY: Then the other side, his employer
did not want him to join.
He's a sensitive boy,   his stomach and nerves
He lost his appetite for weeks, he'd say "oh if you could see
some of the things I see"   "the insides of things"
and so much blood

VOICE: There was always a loving   relationship   in the household?

EMILY: . . . When they took him away he said,   he was so brave
he said Momma I'll be back soon
I'll be right back,   I am innocent he said
I don't know how she came to be in   our house
I don't know,   I don't know he said
I looked into my son's eyes and saw   truth shining
His eyes have always been   dark green,
like mine.

VOICE: On the afternoon of   February 12 you have told police that
no one was home   in your house?

EMILY: I, I was . . . I had a doctor's appointment,
My husband was working, he doesn't get home until

FRANK: Whoever did it,   and brought her body in

EMILY: No: they say she was   they say it,   it happened there

FRANK: No I don't buy that,   He brought her in   carried her
whoever that was,
I believe he tried   other houses
seeing who was home and who   wasn't
and then he

EMILY: Oh it was like lightning striking

VOICE: Your son Dennis   was at Lakepointe High School attending a meeting
of the yearbook staff,   your son Carl has told police he
was   riding   his   motor scooter
in the park,

FRANK: They dragged him like   an animal
put their hands on him like
Like Nazi Germany,

EMILY: it couldn't be any worse

FRANK: And that judge
it's a misuse of power, it's

EMILY: I just don't understand
VOICE: Your son Carl on and after   February 12   did not exhibit
(in your presence) any unusual sign of   emotion?
    agitation? guilt?
EMILY: Every day in a house,   a household
is like the other days.   Oh you never step back,   never *see*.
Like I told them, the   police,   everybody. *He did not.*

Lights down.

Scene 5.

Lights up. Screen shows snapshots, photographs, of the murdered girl Kaminsky.
Like Carl Gulick, she is anyone at all of that age: white, neither strikingly beautiful
nor unattractive.

VOICE: Sometime in the evening of February 12 of this year forensic
reports say   fourteen-year-old Edith Kaminsky daughter of   neighbors
2361 Cedar Street, Lakepointe, New Jersey   multiple stab wounds,
sexual assault   strangulation
An arrest has been made but   legally or otherwise,   the absolute
identity of the murderer has yet to be
EMILY: Oh it's so unjust,
FRANK: the power of a single man
That judge
EMILY: Carl's birthday is   next week
Oh God he'll be in that terrible   cold place
FRANK: "segregated" they call it
How can a judge refuse to set bail
EMILY: oh I would borrow a million dollars
if I could
FRANK: Is this America or   Russia?
EMILY: I can't stop crying
FRANK: . . . we are both under medication you see but
EMILY: Oh it's true he wasn't himself   sometimes.
FRANK: But that day when it happened, that wasn't one of the times.
VOICE: You hold out for the possibility that   the true murderer
carried Edith Kaminsky into your house,   into your basement
thus meaning to throw suspicion on your son?
FRANK: Our boy is guiltless that's the main thing, I will never doubt that.
EMILY: Our body is innocent . . .   What did I say?
FRANK: Why the hell do they make so much of
Carl lifting weights, his   muscles
He is not a freak.
EMILY: There's lots of them   and women too, today   like that,

FRANK: He has other interests he used to collect stamps   play baseball
EMILY: Oh there's so much misunderstanding
FRANK: actual lies
Because the police do not know who the murderer *is*
of course they will blame   anyone they can.

Lights down.

Scene 6.

Lights up. Screen shows the exterior of the Gulick house seen from various angles; then the interior (the basement, evidently, and the "storage area" where the young girl's body was found).

VOICE: If, as is believed, "premeditated" acts arise   out of a
mysterious sequence of neuron discharges   (in the brain)
out of what source   do
    "unpremeditated"   acts   arise?
EMILY: Nobody was down in,   in the basement
until the police came.   The storage space is behind the
water heater,   but
FRANK: My God if my son is   so shiftless   like people are saying
just look: he helped me paint the house last summer
EMILY: Yes Carl and Denny both,
FRANK: Why are they telling such   lies, our neighbors?   We have never
wished them harm,
EMILY: I believed a certain neighbor was my friend,   her and I, we
we'd go shopping together   took my car
Oh my heart is broken
FRANK: It's robin's-egg blue,   the paint turned out brighter than
when it dried, a little brighter than we'd   expected
EMILY: *I* think it's pretty
FRANK: Well.   We'll have to sell the house,   there's no choice
the legal costs   Mr. Filco our attorney has said
EMILY: He told us
FRANK: he's going to fight all the way, he believes Carl is   innocent
EMILY: My heart is broken.
FRANK: *My* heart isn't,
I'm going to fight this all the way
EMILY: A tragedy like this,   you learn fast who is your friend and who
is your enemy
FRANK: Nobody's your friend.
VOICE: The Gulicks and Kaminskys were   well acquainted?
EMILY: We lived on Cedar first,   when they moved in I don't remember:
my mind isn't right these days
FRANK: Oh yes   we knew them

EMILY: I'd have said Mrs. Kaminsky   was my friend, but
that's how people are
    FRANK: Yes
    EMILY: Carl knew her,   Edith
I mean, we all did
    FRANK: but not well,
    EMILY: just neighbors
Now they're our declared enemies, the Kaminskys
    FRANK: well,   so be it.
    EMILY: Oh! that poor girl   if only she hadn't,
I mean, there's no telling who   she was with,   walking home
walking home from school I guess
    FRANK: Well she'd been missing overnight,
    EMILY: yes overnight
    FRANK: of course we were aware
    FRANK: The Kaminskys came around ringing doorbells,
    EMILY: then the police,
    FRANK: then
they got a search party going,   Carl helped them out
    EMILY: Everybody said how much he helped
    FRANK: he kept at it for hours
They walked miles and miles,
he's been out of work for a while,
    EMILY: he'd been looking
in the *help wanted* ads but
    FRANK: . . . He doesn't like to use the telephone.
    EMILY: People laugh at him he says,
    FRANK: I told him no he was imagining it.
    EMILY: This neighborhood:
    FRANK: you would not believe it.
    EMILY: Call themselves Christians
    FRANK: Well   some are Jews.
    EMILY: Well it's still white isn't it   a white neighborhood,   you expect
    better.
    VOICE: The murder weapon   has yet to be found?
    FRANK: One of the neighbors had to offer an opinion,   something sarcastic
I guess
    EMILY: Oh don't go into *that*
    FRANK: the color of the paint   on our house
So Carl said, You don't like it, wear sunglasses.
    EMILY: But,
he was smiling.
    VOICE: A young man with a sense of   humor.
    FRANK: Whoever hid that poor girl's
body
in the storage space of our

basement well clearly it
obviously it was   to deceive
to cast blame on our son.

    EMILY: Yes   if there were fingerprints down there,
    BOTH: that handprint they found on the wall
    FRANK: well for God's sake it was from when Carl
was down there
    BOTH: helping them
    FRANK: He cooperated with them,
    EMILY: Frank wasn't home,
    FRANK: Carl led them downstairs
    EMILY: Why they came to our house, I don't know.
Who was saying things   I don't know,
it was like everybody had gone   crazy
casting blame on all sides.

    VOICE: Mr. and Mrs. Gulick   it's said that from your son's room
Lakepointe police officers confiscated   comic books, military
magazines, pornographic magazines   a cache of more than one dozen
    knives including   switchblades   plus
a U.S. Army bayonet (World War II)   Nazi memorabilia
    including a "souvenir" SS helmet   (manufactured in Taiwan)
a pink plastic skull   with lightbulbs in eyes
    a naked Barbie doll, badly scratched   bitten
        numerous pictures of naked women
    and women in fashion magazines,   their eyes
breasts   crotches   cut out with a scissors
    (pause)
Do you have any comment   Mr. and Mrs. Gulick?
    FRANK: . . . .
Mainly they were hobbies,
    EMILY: I guess I don't,
    FRANK: we didn't know about
    EMILY: Well   he wouldn't allow me in his room,   to vacuum, or
    FRANK: You know how boys are
    EMILY: Didn't want his mother
    FRANK: poking her nose in
    EMILY: So . . .
    (EMILY *upsets a glass of water on the floor.*)
    VOICE: Police forensic findings   bloodstains, hairs, semen
    and DNA "fingerprinting"   constitute a tissue of
        circumstance   linking your son to
    EMILY *(interrupting)*: Mr. Filco says   it's all pieced together
"Circumstantial evidence," he says   not proof
    FRANK: *I* call it bullshit   *(laughs)*
    EMILY: Oh Frank
    FRANK: *I* call it bullshit   *(laughs)*

VOICE: Eyewitness accounts disagree,   two parties report
having seen Carl Gulick and Edith Kaminsky   walking together
   in the afternoon, in the alley   behind Cedar Street
      a third party   a neighbor   claims to have seen
the girl   in the company of a   stranger   at approximately
      4:15 p.m.   And Carl Gulick insists
he was "riding his motor scooter"   all afternoon
   FRANK: He is a boy
   EMILY: not capable of lying
   FRANK: Look: I would have to discipline him sometimes,
   EMILY: You have to, with boys
   FRANK: Oh yes you have to, otherwise
   EMILY: He was always a good eater   didn't fuss
   FRANK: He's a quiet boy
   EMILY: You can't guess his thoughts
   FRANK: But he loved his mother and father   respected
   EMILY: Always well behaved at home
That ugly picture in the paper, oh
   FRANK: THAT WASN'T HIM
   EMILY: You can't believe   the cruelty in the human heart
   FRANK: Giving interviews! his own teachers from the school
   EMILY: Telling lies   cruel   nasty
   FRANK: His own teachers from the   school
   VOICE: Mr. and Mrs. Gulick   you had no suspicion
                     no   awareness
   you   had   no   sense   of   the   fact
      that the battered   raped   mutilated body of
               fourteen-year-old Edith Kaminsky
      was hidden in your basement   in a storage space
            wrapped in plastic garbage bags
for approximately   forty   hours
   GULICKS: . . . .
   VOICE: No consciousness of   disharmony
in your household?
   FRANK: It was a day like
   EMILY: It *was,*   I mean, it wasn't
   FRANK: I keep the cellar clean, I   There's leakage
   EMILY: Oh
Last week at my sister's   where we were staying,
we had to leave   this terrible place
in Yonkers I was crying,   I could not stop   crying
downstairs in the kitchen   three in the morning
I was standing by a window and there was suddenly   it looked
like snow!
it was moonlight moving in the window and there came a   shadow I
guess

like an eclipse?   was there an eclipse?
Oh I felt so, I felt   my heart stopped   Oh but I, I wasn't scared
I was thinking   I was seeing how the world is
how the universe *is*
it's so hard to say, I feel like a   a fool
I was gifted by this, by   seeing   how the world *is* not
how you see it   with your eyes, or talk   talk about it
I mean names you give to,   parts of it   No I mean how it *is*
when there is nobody there.

VOICE: A subliminal conviction of disharmony   may be nullified by   a
transcendental leap of   consciousness;   to a "higher plane"
of celestial harmony.
would you comment   Mr. and Mrs. Gulick?

EMILY: Then Sunday night it was,

FRANK: this last week

EMILY: they came again

FRANK: threw trash on our lawn

EMILY: screamed

Murderers! they were drunk, yelling   in the night *Murderers!*

FRANK: There was the false report that Carl was released on   bail
that he was home with us,

EMILY: Oh dear God if only that was true

FRANK: I've lost fifteen pounds since February

EMILY: Oh Frank has worked so hard   on that lawn,
it's his pride and joy and in the neighborhood   everybody knows,
they compliment him,   and now
Yes he squats right out there, he pulls out crabgrass   by hand
Dumping such such ugly nasty disgusting things
Then in the A&P a woman followed me   up and down the aisles
I could hear people   *That's her, that's the mother of*
the murderer   I could hear them   everywhere in the store
Is that her,   is that the mother of the murderer? they were saying
Lived in this neighborhood, in this town   for so many years
we thought we were welcome here and now
Aren't you ashamed to show your face!   a voice screamed
What can I do with my face,   can I hide it forever?

FRANK: And all this when our boy is   innocent.

VOICE: Perceiving the inviolate nature of   the Universe   apart from human
suffering   rendered you happy, Mrs. Gulick   is this so?
for some precious moments?

EMILY: Oh yes, I was crying but
not because of
no   I was crying because
I was happy I think.

Lights down.

Scene 7.

Lights up. Screen shows neurological X-rays, medical diagrams, charts as of EEG and CAT-scan tests.

VOICE: Is it possible that in times of   fracture, of evolutionary unease   or, perhaps, at any time   human behavior mimics that of minute   particles   of light?   The atom is primarily emptiness
    the neutron dense-packed
The circuitry of the human brain   circadian rhythms   can be tracked
but never,   it's said comprehended.   And then   in descent
from "identity"—(memory?)   to tissue to cells to cell-particles
    electrical impulses   axon-synapse-dendrite
        and beyond, be-
            neath
        to subatomic bits
    Where is "Carl Gulick"?
(GULICKS *turn to each other in bewilderment. Screen flashes images: kitchen interior; weightlifting paraphernalia; a shelf of trophies; photographs; domestic scenes, etc.*)
VOICE: Mr. and Mrs. Gulick you did not notice anything   unusual   in your son's behavior on the night of February 12   or the following day,   to the best   of your recollection?
EMILY: . . . Oh we've told the police this so many   many times
FRANK: Oh you forget what you remember,
EMILY: That night, before we knew there was anyone missing   I mean, in the neighborhood   anyone we knew
FRANK: I can't remember.
EMILY: Yes but Carl had supper with us like always
FRANK: No I think,   he was napping up in his room
EMILY: he was at the table with us:
FRANK: I remember   he came down around nine o'clock,   but he did eat.
EMILY: Him and Denny, they were at the table with us
FRANK: We've told the police this so many times, it's
I don't know any longer
EMILY: I'm sure it was Denny too.   Both our sons.
We had meatloaf   ketchup baked on top, it's the boys'
favorite dish just about   isn't it?
FRANK: Oh anything with hamburger and ketchup!
EMILY: Of course he was at the table with us,   he had his usual appetite.
FRANK: . . . he was upstairs, said he had a touch of   flu
EMILY: Oh no he was there.
FRANK: It's hard to speak of your own flesh and blood,   as if they are other people
it's hard   without giving false testimony against your will.

VOICE: Is the intrusion of the "extra-ordinary" into the dimension of the
"ordinary" an indication that such Aristotelian categories are
invalid? If one day fails to resemble the preceding
    what does it resemble?
FRANK: . . . He has sworn to us, we are his parents
He did not touch a hair of that poor child's head let alone the rest.
Anybody who knew him, they'd know
EMILY: Oh those trophies! he was so proud
one of them is from the, I guess the Lakepointe YMCA
there's some from the New Jersey competition at Atlantic City
two years ago?
FRANK: no, he was in high school
the first was, Carl was only fifteen years old
EMILY: Our little muscleman!
VOICE: Considering the evidence of thousands of years of human culture
of language art religion the judicial system "The family
unit" athletics hobbies fraternal organizations
charitable impulses gods of all species
is it possible that humankind desires
    not to know
      its place in
        the
      food cycle?
EMILY: One day he said
he wasn't going back to school,
my heart was broken.
FRANK: Only half his senior year ahead
but you can't argue, not with
EMILY: oh his temper! he takes after,
oh I don't know who
FRANK: we always have gotten along together
in this household haven't we
EMILY: yes but the teachers would laugh at him he said
girls laughed at him he said stared and pointed at him he said
and there was this pack of oh we're not prejudiced
against Negros, it's just that
the edge of the Lakepointe school district
well
FRANK: Carl got in fights sometimes
in the school cafeteria and I guess the park?
EMILY: the park isn't safe for law-abiding people these days
they see the color of your skin, they'll attack
some of them are just like animals yes they *are*
FRANK: Actually our son was attacked first it isn't like he got
into fights by himself

EMILY: Who his friends are now, I don't   remember
FRANK: He is a quiet boy, keeps to himself
EMILY: he wanted to work
he was looking for work
FRANK: Well: our daughter Judith was misquoted about that
EMILY: also about Carl having a bad temper   she never said that
the reporter for the paper twisted her words
Mr. Filco says   we might sue
FRANK: Look: our son never raised a hand against anybody let alone against
EMILY: He loves his mother and father,   he respects us
FRANK: He is a religious boy at heart
EMILY: He looked me in the eyes he said   Momma you believe me don't
you?   and I said Oh yes   Oh yes   he's just my baby
FRANK: nobody knows him
EMILY: nobody knows him the way we do
FRANK: who would it be, if they did?
I ask you.

Scene 8.

House lights come up, TV screen shows video rewind. Sounds of audio rewind.
Screen shows GULICKS *onstage.*

VOICE: Frank and Mary Gulick we're very sorry   something happened to
the tape we're going to have to re-shoot   Let's go back just to,
we're showing an interior   Carl's room   the trophies
I will say,   I'll be repeating
    Are you ready?
(House lights out, all tech returns to normal.)
    Well Mr. and Mrs. Gulick your son has
        quite a collection of trophies!
FRANK: . . . I,   I don't remember what I
EMILY: . . . yes he,
FRANK: Carl was proud of   he had other hobbies though
EMILY: Oh he was so funny, didn't want his mother   poking in his room
he said
FRANK: Yes but that's   how boys are
EMILY: That judge refuses to set bail, which I don't   understand
FRANK: Is this the United States or   is this the Soviet Union?
EMILY: we are willing to sell our house to stand up for what is
VOICE: You were speaking of your son Carl   having quit school,
his senior year?   and then?
EMILY: . . . He had a hard time, the teachers   were down on him.
FRANK: I don't know why,
EMILY: we were never told
And now in the newspapers

FRANK: the kinds of lies they are saying
EMILY: that he got into fights, that he was
FRANK: that kind of thing is all a distortion
EMILY: He was always a quiet boy
FRANK: but he had his own friends
EMILY: they came over to the house sometime, I don't remember   who
FRANK: there was that one boy what was his name
EMILY: Oh Frank   Carl hasn't seen him in years
he had friends in grade school
    FRANK: Look: in the newspaper there were false statements
    EMILY: Mr. Filco says   we might sue
    FRANK: Oh no: he says we can't,   we have to prove "malice"
    EMILY: Newspapers and TV are filled with lies
    FRANK: Look: our son Carl never raised a hand against anybody let alone
against
    EMILY: He loves his mother and father,
    FRANK: he respects us
    VOICE: Frank and,   it's Emily isn't it   Frank and Emily Gulick
      that is very moving.

Lights down.

Scene 9.

Lights up. Screen shows GULICKS *in theater.*

    VOICE: The discovery of radioactive elements   in the late nineteenth
century enabled scientists to set back the estimated age of the Earth
    to several billion years,   and the discovery in more
recent decades   that the Universe is expanding,   thus that
there is a point in Time when the Universe   was tightly
compressed   smaller than your tiniest fingernail!
    thus that the age of the Universe is many billions
      of   years
      uncountable.
Yet   humankind resides in Time,   God bless us.
    Frank and Emily Gulick as we wind down *our* time together
      What are your plans for the future?
    FRANK: . . . Oh that is, that's hard to   that's hard to answer.
    EMILY: It depends I guess on
    FRANK: Mr. Filco has advised
    EMILY: I guess it's,
next is the grand jury
    FRANK: Yes: the grand jury.
Mr. Filco cannot be present for the session   to protect our boy
I don't understand the law, just the prosecutor is there

swaying the jurors' minds
Oh I try to understand but I can't,
    EMILY: he says we should be prepared
we should be prepared for a trial
    VOICE: You are ready for the trial   to clear your son's name?
    FRANK: Oh yes . . .
    EMILY: yes that is a way of,   of putting it
Yes.   To clear Carl's name.
    FRANK: . . . Oh yes you have to be realistic.
    EMILY: Yes but before that   the true murderer of Edith Kaminsky
might come forward.
If the true murderer is watching this   *Please come forward.*
    FRANK: . . . Well we both believe Carl is protecting someone, some
friend   another boy
    EMILY: the one who really   committed that terrible crime
    FRANK: So all we can do is pray.   Pray Carl will come
to his senses   give police the other boy's name, or
I believe this: if it's a friend of Carl's
he must have some decency   in his heart
    VOICE: Your faith   in your son remains unshaken?
    EMILY: You would have had to see his   toes,
his tiny baby toes in his bath.
His curly hair,   splashing in the bath.
His yellow rompers or no: I guess that was Denny
    FRANK: If your own flesh and blood looks you in the eye,
you believe
    EMILY: Oh yes.
    VOICE: Human personality, it might be theorized, is a phenomenon of
memory
yet memory   built up from cells, and   atoms does not "exist":
    thus memory   like mind   like personality
      is but a fiction?
    EMILY: Oh   remembering backward is so hard!   oh it's,
    FRANK: it pulls your brain in two.
    EMILY: This medication the doctor gave me, my mouth   my mouth is so
dry
In the middle of the night I wake up drenched in
    FRANK: You don't know who you are   until a thing like this happens,
then you don't know.
    EMILY: It tears your brain in two, trying to   remember,
like even looking at the pictures
Oh you are lost.
    FRANK: in Time you are lost
    EMILY: You fall and fall,
. . . ever since the,   the butcher shop
he wasn't always himself   but

who he was then, I don't know.   But
it's so hard, remembering why.

    FRANK: Yes my wife means thinking backward the way   the way the police
make you, so many questions   you start forgetting right away
it comes out crazy.
Like now,   right here   I don't remember anything up to now
I mean, I can't swear to it: the first time, you see, we just
lived. We lived in our house. I am a, I am a post office employee
I guess I said that?   well, we live in our,   our house.
I mean, it was the first time through.   Just living.
Like the TV, the picture's always on if nobody's watching it
you know?   So,   the people we were then,
I guess I'm trying to say
those actual people, me and her   the ones you see *here*
aren't them. *(laughs)*
I guess that sounds crazy,

    VOICE: We have here the heartbeat   of parental love and faith, it's
a beautiful thing   Frank and Molly Gulick. please comment?

    FRANK: We are that boy's father and mother.
We know that our son is not a murderer and a,   a rapist

    EMILY: We know, if that girl came to harm,   there is some reason
for it to be revealed, but
they never found the knife, for one thing

    FRANK: or whatever it was

    EMILY: They never found the knife, the murderer could tell them where
it's buried, or   whatever it was.
Oh he could help us so   if he just would.

    VOICE: And your plans for the future,   Mr. and Mrs. Gulick of Lakepointe,
New Jersey?

    FRANK: . . . Well.
I guess,   I guess we don't have any.
    (Long silence, to the point of awkwardness.)

    VOICE: . . . Plans for the future, Mr. and Mrs. Gulick of Lakepointe,
New Jersey?

    FRANK: The thing is, you discover   you need to be protected
from your own thoughts sometimes,   but
who is there to do it?

    EMILY: God didn't make any of us strong enough I guess.

    FRANK: Look: one day in a family like this, it's   like the next day
and the day before.

    EMILY: You could say it *is* the next day, I mean the same   the same day.

    FRANK: Until one day it isn't

Lights slowly down, then out.

(THE END)

ACTIVITIES FOR WRITING AND DISCUSSION

1. What functions do the various devices of electronic imagery—visual and aural—seem to serve in the play? What, if anything, would be lost if they were omitted?

2. The action and **setting** of the play suggest a live TV program, and many of the trappings of the TV medium are blatantly visible such as a "Voice"/interviewer, microphones, nervous interviewees, and monitors. What does the play imply about TV's role in the coverage and presentation of such deeds as Carl's?

3. At the beginning of scene one, the "Voice" is likened to a "television emcee," but often his language is strikingly unlike that of any TV emcee, interviewer, or talk-show host. For instance, he refers to Aristotle, "the food chain," and other matters that seem remote from the subject of the murder/rape and that fail to register any reaction from Frank and Emily. Locate several such speeches by the Voice and analyze Oates's possible motives for writing the speeches as she did.

4. Based on evidence in the play, write up a list of Frank and Emily's major beliefs and values. Can you make any connections between these beliefs and values and Carl's personality and crime? If not, explain. If so, give examples that illustrate the connections.

5. Citing evidence in the play about his jobs, interests, personal associations, and so on, compose a character portrait of Carl. In what ways might the character of the son be (a) a result of the character of the parents and (b) a mystery that is beyond the parents' control?

6. Re-create the life and conflicts within the Gulick household through either of the following exercises:
   a. Write a mealtime conversation among Frank, Emily, and Carl (and possibly Denny). Create some situation of conflict (borrowed from the play or invented) that will bring out the personality of each family member.
   b. In the play Emily mentions that Carl didn't like her coming into his room. Imagine that Emily enters Carl's room to vacuum it and discovers him there or that she is vacuuming the room and is caught in the act by him. Write the dialogue that occurs.

7. Like many parents, Emily and Frank try to be "good" parents, yet they conflict and clash with their children. Compose a dialogue or scene that dramatizes relationships and conflicts within a family, either your own or some imaginary family of your own creation.

Milcha Sanchez-Scott (b. 1955)

The Cuban Swimmer

CHARACTERS

MARGARITA SUÁREZ, the swimmer
EDUARDO SUÁREZ, her father, the coach
SIMÓN SUÁREZ, her brother
AÍDA SUÁREZ, her mother
ABUELA, her grandmother
VOICE OF MEL MUNSON
VOICE OF MARY BETH WHITE
VOICE OF RADIO OPERATOR

Live conga drums can be used to punctuate the action of the play.

TIME: Summer.
PLACE: The Pacific Ocean between San Pedro and Catalina Island.

Scene 1

Pacific Ocean. Midday. On the horizon, in perspective, a small boat enters U.L., *crosses to* U.R. *and exits. Pause. Lower on the horizon, the same boat, in larger perspective, enters* U.R., *crosses and exits* U.L. *Blackout.*

Scene 2

Pacific Ocean. Midday. The swimmer, MARGARITA SUÁREZ, *is swimming. On the boat following behind her are her father,* EDUARDO SUÁREZ, *holding a megaphone, and* SIMÓN, *her brother, sitting on top of the cabin with his shirt off, punk sunglasses on, binoculars hanging on his chest.*

EDUARDO: *(Leaning forward, shouting in time to* MARGARITA'S *swimming.)* Uno, dos, uno, dos. Y uno, dos . . . keep your shoulders parallel to the water.
SIMÓN: I'm gonna take these glasses off and look straight into the sun.
EDUARDO: *(Through megaphone.) Muy bien, muy bien* . . . but punch those arms in, baby.
SIMÓN: *(Looking directly at the sun through binoculars.)* Come on, come on, zap me. Show me something. *(He looks behind at the shoreline and ahead at the sea.)* Stop! Stop, Papi! Stop! *(*AÍDA SUÁREZ *and* ABUELA, *the swimmer's mother and grandmother, enter running from the back of the boat.)*
AÍDA and ABUELA: *Qué? Qué es?*
AÍDA: *Es un* shark?
EDUARDO: Eh?

ABUELA: *Que es un* shark *dicen?* (EDUARDO *blows whistle.* MARGARITA *looks up at the boat.*)

SIMÓN: No, Papi, no shark, no shark. We've reached the halfway mark.

ABUELA: *(Looking into the water.) A dónde está?*

AÍDA: It's not in the water.

ABUELA: Oh no? Oh no?

AÍDA: No! *A poco* do you think they're gonna have signs in the water to say you are halfway to Santa Catalina? No. It's done very scientific. *A ver, hijo,* explain it to your grandma.

SIMÓN: Well, you see Abuela—*(He points behind.)* There's San Pedro. *(He points ahead.)* And there's Santa Catalina. Looks halfway to me. (ABUELA *shakes her head and is looking back and forth, trying to make the decision, when suddenly the sound of a helicopter is heard.*)

ABUELA: *(Looking up.) Virgencita de la Caridad del Cobre. Qué es eso? (Sound of helicopter gets closer.* MARGARITA *looks up.)*

MARGARITA: Papi, Papi! *(A small commotion on the boat, with everybody pointing at the helicopter above. Shadows of the helicopter fall on the boat.* SIMÓN *looks up at it through binoculars.)* Papi—*qué es?* What is it?

EDUARDO: *(Through megaphone.)* Uh . . . uh . . . uh *un momentico . . . mi hija.* . . . Your papi's got everything under control, understand? Uh . . . you just keep stroking. And stay . . . uh . . . close to the boat.

SIMÓN: Wow, Papi! We're on TV man! Holy Christ, we're all over the fucking U.S.A.! It's Mel Munson and Mary Beth White!

AÍDA: *Por Dios!* SIMÓN, don't swear. And put on your shirt. (AÍDA *fluffs her hair, puts on her sunglasses and waves to the helicopter.* SIMÓN *leans over the side of the boat and yells to* MARGARITA.)

SIMÓN: Yo, Margo! You're on TV, man.

EDUARDO: Leave your sister alone. Turn on the radio.

MARGARITA: Papi! *Qué está pasando?*

ABUELA: *Que es la televisión dicen? (She shakes her head.) Porque como yo no puedo ver nada sin mis espejuelos.* (ABUELA *rummages through the boat, looking for her glasses. Voices of* MEL MUNSON *and* MARY BETH WHITE *are heard over the boat's radio.)*

MEL'S VOICE: As we take a closer look at the gallant crew of La Havana . . . and there . . . yes, there she is . . . the little Cuban swimmer from Long Beach, California, nineteen-year-old Margarita Suárez. The unknown swimmer is our Cinderella entry . . . a bundle of tenacity, battling her way through the choppy, murky waters of the cold Pacific to reach the Island of Romance . . . Santa Catalina . . . where should she be the first to arrive, two thousand dollars and a gold cup will be waiting for her.

AÍDA: Doesn't even cover our expenses.

ABUELA: *Qué dice?*

EDUARDO: Shhhh!

MARY BETH'S VOICE: This is really a family effort, Mel, and—

MEL'S VOICE: Indeed it is. Her trainer, her coach, her mentor is her father, Eduardo Suárez. Not a swimmer himself, it says here, Mr. Suárez is head usher of the Holy Name Society and the owner-operator of Suárez Treasures of the Sea and Salvage Yard. I guess it's one of those places . . .

MARY BETH'S VOICE: If I might interject a fact here, Mel, assisting in this swim is Mrs. Suárez who is a former Miss Cuba.

MEL'S VOICE: And a beautiful woman in her own right. Let's try and get a closer look. *(Helicopter sound gets louder.* MARGARITA, *frightened, looks up again.)*

MARGARITA: Papi!

EDUARDO: *(Through megaphone.)* Mi hija, don't get nervous . . . it's the press. I'm handling it.

AÍDA: I see how you're handling it.

EDUARDO: *(Through megaphone.)* Do you hear? Everything is under control. Get back into your rhythm. Keep your elbows high and kick and kick and kick and kick . . .

ABUELA: *(Finds her glasses and puts them on.) Ay sí, es la televisión . . . (She points to helicopter.) Qué lindo mira . . . (She fluffs her hair, gives a big wave.) Alo América! Viva mi Margarita, viva todo los Cubanos en los Estados Unidos!*

AÍDA: *Ay por Dios,* Cecilia, the man didn't come all this way in his helicopter to look at you jumping up and down, making a fool of yourself.

ABUELA: I don't care. I'm proud.

AÍDA: He can't understand you anyway.

ABUELA: *Viva . . . (She stops.) Simón, comó se dice viva?*

SIMÓN: Hurray.

ABUELA: Hurray for *mi* Margarita *y* for all the Cubans living *en* the United States, *y un abrazo . . .* Simón, *abrazo . . .*

SIMÓN: A big hug.

ABUELA: *Sí,* a big hug to all my friends in Miami, Long Beach, Union City, except for my son Carlos who lives in New York in sin! He lives . . . *(She crosses herself.)* in Brooklyn with a Puerto Rican woman in sin! *No decente . . .*

SIMÓN: Decent.

ABUELA: Carlos, *no decente.* This family, *decente.*

AÍDA: Cecilia, *por Dios.*

MEL'S VOICE: Look at that enthusiasm. The whole family has turned out to cheer little Margarita on to victory! I hope they won't be too disappointed.

MARY BETH'S VOICE: She seems to be making good time, Mel.

MEL'S VOICE: Yes, it takes all kinds to make a race. And it's a testimonial to the all-encompassing fairness . . . the greatness of this, the Wrigley Invitational Women's Swim to Catalina, where among all the professionals there is still room for the amateurs . . . like these, the simple people we see below us on the ragtag La Havana, taking their long-shot chance to victory. *Vaya con Dios! (Helicopter sound fading as family, including* MARGARITA, *watch silently. Static as* SIMÓN *turns radio off.* EDUARDO *walks to bow of boat, looks out on the horizon.)*

EDUARDO: *(To himself.)* Amateurs.

AÍDA: Eduardo, that person insulted us. Did you hear, Eduardo? That he called us a simple people in a ragtag boat? Did you hear . . . ?

ABUELA: *(Clenching her fist at departing helicopter.) Mal-Rayo los parta!*

SIMÓN: *(Same gesture.) Asshole!* (AÍDA *follows* EDUARDO *as he goes to side of boat and stares at* MARGARITA.)

AÍDA: This person comes in his helicopter to insult your wife, your family, your daughter . . .

MARGARITA: *(Pops her head out of the water.)* Papi?

AÍDA: Do you hear me, Eduardo? I am not simple.

ABUELA: *Sí.*

AÍDA: I am complicated.

ABUELA: *Sí, demasiada complicada.*

AÍDA: Me and my family are not so simple.

SIMÓN: Mom, the guy's an asshole.

ABUELA: *(Shaking her fist at helicopter.)* Asshole!

AÍDA: If my daughter was simple she would not be in that water swimming.

MARGARITA: Simple? Papi . . . ?

AÍDA: *Ahora,* Eduardo, this is what I want you to do. When we get to Santa Catalina I want you to call the TV station and demand *un* apology.

EDUARDO: *Cállete mujer! Aquí mando yo.* I will decide what is to be done.

MARGARITA: Papi, tell me what's going on.

EDUARDO: Do you understand what I am saying to you, Aída?

SIMÓN: *(Leaning over side of boat, to* MARGARITA.) Yo Margo! You know that Mel Munson guy on TV? He called you a simple amateur and said you didn't have a chance.

ABUELA: *(Leaning directly behind* SIMÓN.) *Mi hija, insultó a la familia. Desgraciado!!*

AÍDA: *(Leaning in behind* ABUELA.) He called us peasants! And your father is not doing anything about it. He just knows how to yell at me.

EDUARDO: *(Through megaphone.)* Shut up! All of you! Do you want to break her concentration? Is that what you are after? Eh? (ABUELA, AÍDA *and* SIMÓN *shrink back.* EDUARDO *paces before them.)* Swimming is rhythm and concentration. You win a race *aquí.* (Pointing to his head.) Now . . . (To SIMÓN.) you, take care of the boat, Aída y Mama . . . do something. Anything. Something practical. (ABUELA *and* AÍDA *get on knees and pray in Spanish.) Hija,* give it everything, eh? . . . *por la familia. Uno . . . dos. . . .* You must win. (SIMÓN *goes into cabin. The prayers continue as lights change to indicate bright sunlight, later in the afternoon.)*

Scene 3

Tableau for a couple of beats. EDUARDO *on bow with timer in one hand as he counts strokes per minute.* SIMÓN *is in the cabin steering, wearing his sunglasses, baseball cap on backwards.* ABUELA *and* AÍDA *are at the side of the boat, heads down, hands folded, still muttering prayers in Spanish.*

AÍDA and ABUELA: *(Crossing themselves.) En el nombre del Padre, del Hijo y del Espíritu Santo amén.*

EDUARDO: *(Through megaphone.)* You're stroking seventy-two!

SIMÓN: *(Singing.)* Mama's stroking, Mama's stroking seventy-two . . .

EDUARDO: *(Through megaphone.)* You comfortable with it?

SIMÓN: *(Singing)* Seventy-two, seventy-two, seventy-two for you.

AÍDA: *(Looking at the heavens.) Ay,* Eduardo, *ven acá,* we should be grateful that *Nuestro* Señor gave us such a beautiful day.

ABUELA: *(Crosses herself.) Sí, gracias a Dios.*

EDUARDO: She's stroking seventy-two, with no problem. *(He throws a kiss to the sky.)* It's a beautiful day to win.

AÍDA: *Qué hermoso!* So clear and bright. Not a cloud in the sky. *Mira! Mira!* Even rainbows on the water . . . a sign from God.

SIMÓN: *(Singing.)* Rainbows on the water . . . you in my arms . . .

ABUELA and EDUARDO: *(Looking the wrong way.) Dónde?*

AÍDA: *(Pointing toward* MARGARITA.*)* There, dancing in front of Margarita, leading her on . . .

EDUARDO: Rainbows on. . . . *Ay coño!* It's an oil slick! You . . . you . . . *(To* SIMÓN.*)* Stop the boat. *(Runs to bow, yelling.)* Margarita! Margarita! *(On the next stroke,* MARGARITA *comes up all covered in black oil.)*

MARGARITA: Papi! Papi! *(Everybody goes to the side and stares at* MARGARITA, *who stares back.* EDUARDO *freezes.)*

AÍDA: *Apúrate* Eduardo, move . . . what's wrong with you . . . *no me oíste,* get my daughter out of the water.

EDUARDO: *(Softly.)* We can't touch her. If we touch her, she's disqualified.

AÍDA: But I'm her mother.

EDUARDO: Not even by her own mother. Especially by her own mother. . . . You always want the rules to be different for you, you always want to be the exception. *(To* SIMÓN*)* And you . . . you didn't see it, eh? You were playing again?

SIMÓN: Papi, I was watching . . .

AÍDA: *(Interrupting.) Pues,* do something Eduardo. You are the big coach, the monitor.

SIMÓN: Mentor! Mentor!

EDUARDO: How can a person think around you? *(He walks off to bow, puts head in hands.)*

ABUELA: *(Looking over side.) Mira como todos los* little birds are dead. *(She crosses herself.)*

AÍDA: Their little wings are glued to their sides.

SIMÓN: Christ, this is like the La Brea tar pits.

AÍDA: They can't move their little wings.

ABUELA: *Esa niña tiene que moverse.*

SIMÓN: Yeah Margo, you gotta move, man. *(ABUELA and* SIMÓN *gesture for* MARGARITA *to move.* AÍDA *gestures for her to swim.)*

ABUELA: *Anda niña, muévete.*

AÍDA: Swim, *hija,* swim or the *aceite* will stick to your wings.

MARGARITA: Papi?

ABUELA: *(Taking megaphone.)* Your papi say "move it!" (MARGARITA *with difficulty starts moving.*)

ABUELA, AÍDA and SIMÓN. *(Laboriously counting.)* Uno, dos . . . uno, dos . . . anda . . . uno, dos.

EDUARDO: *(Running to take megaphone from* ABUELA.) *Uno, dos . . .* (SIMÓN *races into cabin and starts the engine.* ABUELA, AÍDA *and* EDUARDO *count together.*)

SIMÓN: *(Looking ahead.)* Papi, it's over there!

EDUARDO: Eh?

SIMÓN: *(Pointing ahead and to* R.*)* It's getting clearer over there.

EDUARDO: *(Through megaphone.)* Now pay attention to me. Go to the right. (SIMÓN, ABUELA, AÍDA *and* EDUARDO *all lean over side. They point ahead and to* R., *except* ABUELA, *who points to* L.*)*

FAMILY: *(Shouting together.)* Para yá! Para yá! (Lights go down on boat. A *special light on* MARGARITA, *swimming through the oil, and on* ABUELA, *watching her.*)

ABUELA: *Sangre de mi sangre,* you will be another to save us. *En Bolondron,* where your great-grandmother Luz Suárez was born, they say one day it rained blood. All the people, they run into their houses. They cry, they pray, *pero* your great-grandmother Luz she had *cojones* like a man. She run outside. She look straight at the sky. She shake her fist. And she say to the evil one, "*Mira . . . (Beating her chest.) coño, Diablo, aquí estoy si me quieres.*" And she open her mouth, and she drunk the blood.

(Blackout.)

Scene 4

Lights up on boat. AÍDA *and* EDUARDO *are on deck watching* MARGARITA *swim.*

We hear the gentle, rhythmic lap, lap, lap, of the water, then the sound of inhaling and exhaling as MARGARITA'S *breathing becomes louder. Then* MARGARITA'S *heartbeat is heard, with the lapping of the water and the breathing under it. These sounds continue beneath the dialogue to the end of the scene.*

AÍDA: *Dios mío.* Look how she moves through the water . . .

EDUARDO: You see, it's very simple. It is a matter of concentration.

AÍDA: The first time I put her in water she came to life, she grew before my eyes. She moved, she smiled, she loved it more than me. She didn't want my breast any longer. She wanted the water.

EDUARDO: And of course, the rhythm. The rhythm takes away the pain and helps the concentration. *(Pause.* AÍDA *and* EDUARDO *watch* MARGARITA.*)*

AÍDA: Is that my child, or a seal. . . .

EDUARDO: Ah a seal, the reason for that is that she's keeping her arms very close to her body. She cups her hands and then she reaches and digs, reaches and digs.

AÍDA: To think that a daughter of mine . . .

EDUARDO: It's the training, the hours in the water. I used to tie weights around her little wrists and ankles.

AÍDA: A spirit, an ocean spirit, must have entered my body when I was carrying her.

EDUARDO: *(To* MARGARITA.*)* Your stroke is slowing down. *(Pause. We hear* MARGARITA's *heartbeat with the breathing under, faster now.)*

AÍDA: Eduardo, that night, the night on the boat . . .

EDUARDO: Ah, the night on the boat again . . . the moon was . . .

AÍDA: The moon was full. We were coming to America. . . . *Qué romantico.* *(Heartbeat and breathing continue.)*

EDUARDO: We were cold, afraid, with no money, and on top of everything, you were hysterical, yelling at me, tearing at me with your nails. *(Opens his shirt, points to the base of his neck.)* Look, I still bear the scars . . . telling me that I didn't know what I was doing . . . saying that we were going to die. . . .

AÍDA: You took me, you stole me from my home . . . you didn't give me a chance to prepare. You just said we have to go now, now! Now, you said. You didn't let me take anything. I left everything behind . . . I left everything behind.

EDUARDO: Saying that I wasn't good enough, that your father didn't raise you so that I could drown you in the sea.

AÍDA: You didn't let me say even a goodbye. You took me, you stole me, you tore me from my home.

EDUARDO: I took you so we could be married.

AÍDA: That was in Miami. But that night on the boat, Eduardo. . . . We were not married, that night on the boat.

EDUARDO: *No pasó nada!* Once and for all get it out of your head, it was cold, you hated me and we were afraid. . . .

AÍDA: *Mentiroso!*

EDUARDO: A man can't do it when he is afraid.

AÍDA: Liar! You did it very well.

EDUARDO: I did?

AÍDA: *Sí.* Gentle. You were so gentle and then strong . . . my passion for you so deep. Standing next to you . . . I would ache . . . looking at your hands I would forget to breathe, you were irresistible.

EDUARDO: I was?

AÍDA: You took me into your arms, you touched my face with your fingertips . . . you kissed my eyes . . . *la esquina de la boca y* . . .

EDUARDO: *Sí, sí,* and then . . .

AÍDA: I look at your face on top of mine, and I see the lights of Havana in your eyes. That's when you seduced me.

EDUARDO: Shhh, they're gonna hear you. *(Lights go down. Special on* AÍDA.*)*

AÍDA: That was the night. A woman doesn't forget those things . . . and later that night was the dream . . . the dream of a big country with fields of fertile land and big, giant things growing. And there by a green, slimy pond I found a giant pea pod and when I opened it, it was full of little, tiny baby frogs. (AÍDA *crosses herself as she watches* MARGARITA. *We hear louder breathing and heartbeat.*)

MARGARITA: Santa Teresa. Little Flower of God, pray for me. San Martín de Porres, pray for me. Santa Rosa de Lima, *Virgencita de la Caridad del Cobre*, pray for me. . . . Mother pray for me.

Scene 5

Loud howling of wind is heard, as lights change to indicate unstable weather, fog and mist. Family on deck, braced and huddled against the wind. SIMÓN *is at the helm.*

AÍDA: *Ay Dios mío, qué viento.*

EDUARDO: *(Through megaphone.)* Don't drift out . . . that wind is pushing you out. *(To* SIMÓN*)* You! Slow down. Can't you see your sister is drifting out?

SIMÓN: It's the wind, Papi.

AÍDA: Baby, don't go so far. . . .

ABUELA: *(To heaven.) Ay Gran Poder de Dios, quita este maldito viento.*

SIMÓN: Margo! Margo! Stay close to the boat.

EDUARDO: Dig in. Dig in hard. . . . Reach down from your guts and dig in.

ABUELA: *(To heaven.) Ay Virgen de la Caridad del Cobre, por lo más tú quieres a pararla.*

AÍDA: *(Putting her hand out, reaching for* MARGARITA*.)* Baby, don't go far. (ABUELA *crosses herself. Action freezes. Lights get dimmer, special on* MARGARITA. *She keeps swimming, stops, starts again, stops, then, finally exhausted, stops altogether. The boat stops moving.*)

EDUARDO: What's going on here? Why are we stopping?

SIMÓN: Papi, she's not moving! Yo Margo! *(The family all run to the side.)*

EDUARDO: Hija! . . . Hijita! You're tired, eh?

AÍDA: *Por supuesto* she's tired. I like to see you get in the water, waving your arms and legs from San Pedro to Santa Catalina. A person isn't a machine, a person has to rest.

SIMÓN: Yo, Mama! Cool out, it ain't fucking brain surgery.

EDUARDO: *(To* SIMÓN*)* Shut up, you. *(Louder to* MARGARITA.*)* I guess your mother's right for once, huh? . . . I guess you had to stop, eh? . . . Give your brother, the idiot . . . a chance to catch up with you.

SIMÓN: *(Clowning like Mortimer Snurd.)* Dum dee dum dee dum ooops, ah shucks. . . .

EDUARDO: I don't think he's Cuban.

SIMÓN: *(Like Ricky Ricardo.)* Oye Lucy! I'm home! Ba ba lu!

EDUARDO: *(Joins in clowning, grabbing* SIMÓN *in a headlock.)* What am I gonna do with this idiot, eh? I don't understand this idiot. He's not like us Margarita. *(Laughing.)* You think if we put him into your bathing suit with a cap on his head . . . *(He laughs hysterically.)* you think anyone would know . . . huh? Do you think anyone would know? *(Laughs.)*

SIMÓN: *(Vamping.) Ay, mi amor.* Anybody looking for tits would know. *(EDUARDO slaps SIMÓN across the face, knocking him down. AÍDA runs to SIMÓN's aid. ABUELA holds EDUARDO back.)*

MARGARITA: *Mía culpa! Mía culpa!*

ABUELA: *Qué dices hija?*

MARGARITA: Papi, it's my fault, it's all my fault. . . . I'm so cold, I can't move. . . . I put my face in the water . . . and I hear them whispering . . . laughing at me. . . .

AÍDA: Who is laughing at you?

MARGARITA: The fish are all biting me . . . they hate me . . . they whisper about me. She can't swim, they say. She can't glide. She has no grace. . . . Yellowtails, bonita, tuna, man-o'-war, snub-nose sharks, los baracudas . . . they all hate me . . . only the dolphins care . . . and sometimes I hear the whales crying . . . she is lost, she is dead. I'm so numb, I can't feel. Papi! Papi! Am I dead?

EDUARDO: *Vamos,* baby, punch those arms in. Come on . . . do you hear me?

MARGARITA: Papi . . . Papi . . . forgive me. . . . *(All is silent on the boat.* EDUARDO *drops his megaphone, his head bent down in dejection.* ABUELA, AÍDA, SIMÓN *all leaning over the side of the boat.* SIMÓN *slowly walks away.)*

AÍDA: *Mi hija, qué tienes?*

SIMÓN: Oh Christ, don't make her say it. Please don't make her say it.

ABUELA: Say what? *Qué cosa?*

SIMÓN: She wants to quit, can't you see she's had enough?

ABUELA: *Mira, para eso. Esta niña* is turning blue.

AÍDA: *Oyeme, mi hija.* Do you want to come out of the water?

MARGARITA: Papi?

SIMÓN: *(To* EDUARDO*)* She won't come out until *you* tell her.

AÍDA: Eduardo . . . answer your daughter.

EDUARDO: *Le dije* to concentrate . . . concentrate on your rhythm. Then the rhythm would carry her . . . ay it's a beautiful thing, Aída. It's like yoga, like meditation, the mind over matter . . . the mind controlling the body . . . that's how the great things in the world have been done. I wish you . . . I wish my wife could understand.

MARGARITA: Papi?

SIMÓN: *(To* MARGARITA*)* Forget him.

AÍDA: *(Imploring.)* Eduardo, *por favor.*

EDUARDO: *(Walking in circles.)* Why didn't you let her concentrate? Don't you understand, the concentration, the rhythm is everything. But no, you wouldn't listen. *(Screaming to the ocean.)* Goddam Cubans, why, God, why do you make us go everywhere with our families? *(He goes to back of boat.)*

AÍDA: *(Opening her arms.)* Mi hija, ven, come to Mami. *(Rocking.)* Your mami knows. *(ABUELA has taken the training bottle, puts it in a net. She and SIMÓN lower it to MARGARITA.)*

SIMÓN: Take this. Drink it. *(As MARGARITA drinks, ABUELA crosses herself.)*

ABUELA: *Sangre de mi sangre. (Music comes up softly.* MARGARITA *drinks, gives the bottle back, stretches out her arms, as if on a cross. Floats on her back. She begins a graceful backstroke. Lights fade on boat as special lights come up on* MARGARITA. *She stops. Slowly turns over and starts to swim, gradually picking up speed. Suddenly as if in pain she stops, tries again, then stops in pain again. She becomes disoriented and falls to the bottom of the sea. Special on* MARGARITA *at the bottom of the sea.)*

MARGARITA: *Ya no puedo* . . . I can't . . . A person isn't a machine . . . *es mi culpa* . . . Father forgive me . . . Papi! Papi! One, two. *Uno, dos. (Pause.)* Papi! *A dónde estás? (Pause)* One, two, one, two. Papi! Ay Papi! Where are you . . . ? Don't leave me. . . . Why don't you answer me? *(Pause. She starts to swim, slowly.) Uno, dos, uno, dos.* Dig in, dig in. *(Stops swimming.) Por favor,* Papi! *(Starts to swim again.)* One, two, one, two. Kick from your hip, kick from your hip. *(Stops swimming. Starts to cry.)* Oh God, please. . . . *(Pause.)* Hail Mary, full of grace . . . dig in, dig in . . . the Lord is with thee. . . . *(She swims to the rhythm of her Hail Mary.)* Hail Mary, full of grace . . . dig in, dig in, . . . the Lord is with thee . . . dig in, dig in. . . . Blessed art thou among women. . . . Mommie it hurts. You let go of my hand. I'm lost. . . . And blessed is the fruit of thy womb, now and at the hour of our death. Amen. I don't want to die, I don't want to die. *(*MARGARITA *is still swimming. Blackout. She is gone.)*

Scene 6

Lights up on boat, we hear radio static. There is a heavy mist. On deck we see only black outline of ABUELA *with shawl over her head. We hear the Voices of* EDUARDO, AÍDA *and* RADIO OPERATOR.

EDUARDO'S VOICE: La Havana! Coming from San Pedro. Over.

RADIO OPERATOR'S VOICE: Right. DT6-6, you say you've lost a swimmer.

AÍDA'S VOICE: Our child, our only daughter . . . listen to me. Her name is Margarita Inez Suárez, she is wearing a black one-piece bathing suit cut high in the legs with a white racing stripe down the sides, a white bathing cap with goggles and her whole body covered with a . . . with a . . .

EDUARDO'S VOICE: With lanolin and paraffin.

AÍDA'S VOICE: *Sí* . . . *con* lanolin and paraffin. *(More radio static. Special on* SIMÓN, *on the edge of the boat.)*

SIMÓN: Margo! Yo Margo! *(Pause)* Man don't do this. *(Pause.)* Come on. . . . Come on. . . . *(Pause.)* God, why does everything have to be so hard? *(Pause.)* Stupid. You know you're not supposed to die for this. Stupid. It's his dream and he can't even swim. *(Pause.)* Punch those arms in. Come home. Come home. I'm your little brother. Don't forget what Mama said. You're not supposed to leave me behind. *Vamos,* Margarita, take your little brother, hold his hand tight when you cross the street. He's so little. *(Pause.)* Oh Christ, give us a sign. . . . I know! I know! Margo, I'll send you a message . . . like mental telepathy. I'll hold my breath, close my eyes and I'll bring you home. *(He takes a deep breath; a few beats.)* This time I'll beep . . . I'll send out sonar signals like a dolphin. *(He imitates dolphin sounds. The sound of real dolphins takes over from* SIMÓN, *then fades into sound of* ABUELA *saying the Hail Mary in Spanish, as full lights come up slowly.)*

Scene 7

EDUARDO *coming out of cabin, sobbing,* AÍDA *holding him.* SIMÓN *anxiously scanning the horizon.* ABUELA *looking calmly ahead.*

EDUARDO: *Es mi culpa, sí, es mi culpa. (He hits his chest.)*

AÍDA: *Ya, ya viejo* . . . it was my sin . . . I left my home.

EDUARDO: Forgive me, forgive me. I've lost our daughter, our sister, our granddaughter, *mi carne, mi sangre, mis ilusiones. (To heaven.) Dios mío* take me . . . take me, I say . . . Goddammit, take me!

SIMÓN: I'm going in.

AÍDA and EDUARDO: No!

EDUARDO: *(Grabbing and holding* SIMÓN, *speaking to heaven.)* God, take me, not my children. They are my dreams, my illusions . . . and not this one, this one is my mystery . . . he has my secret dreams. In him are the parts of me I cannot see. (EDUARDO *embraces* SIMÓN. *Radio static becomes louder.)*

AÍDA: I . . . I think I see her.

SIMÓN: No it's just a seal.

ABUELA: *(Looking out with binoculars.) Mi nietacita, dónde estás? (She feels her heart.)* I don't feel the knife in my heart . . . my little fish is not lost. *(Radio crackles with static. As lights dim on boat, voices of* MEL *and* MARY BETH *are heard over the radio.)*

MEL'S VOICE: Tragedy has marred the face of the Wrigley Invitational Women's Race to Catalina. The Cuban swimmer, little Margarita Suárez, has reportedly been lost at sea. Coast Guard and divers are looking for her as we speak. Yet in spite of this tragedy the race must go on because . . .

MARY BETH'S VOICE: *(Interrupting loudly.)* Mel!

MEL'S VOICE: *(Startled.)* What!

MARY BETH'S VOICE: Ah . . . excuse me, Mel . . . we have a winner. We've just received word from Catalina that one of the swimmers is just fifty yards from the breakers . . . it's oh, it's Margarita Suárez! *(Special on family in cabin listening to radio.)*

MEL'S VOICE: What? I thought she died! *(Special on* MARGARITA, *taking off bathing cap, trophy in hand, walking on the water.)*

MARY BETH'S VOICE: Ahhh . . . unless . . . unless this is a tragic. . . . No . . . there she is, Mel. Margarita Suárez! The only one in the race wearing a black bathing suit cut high in the legs with a racing stripe down the side. *(Family cheering, embracing.)*

SIMÓN: *(Screaming.)* Way to go Margo!

MEL'S VOICE: This is indeed a miracle! It's a resurrection! Margarita Suárez with a flotilla of boats to meet her, is now walking on the waters, through the breakers . . . onto the beach, with crowds of people cheering her on. What a jubilation! This is a miracle! *(Sound of crowds cheering. Pinspot on* ABUELA.*)*

ABUELA: *Sangre de mi sangre* you will be another to save us, ... to say to the evil one, *Coño Diablo, aqui estoy si me quieres. (Lights and cheering fade. Blackout.)*

END OF PLAY

FAMILIES: ADDITIONAL ACTIVITIES FOR WRITING AND DISCUSSION

1. Reread your entire notebook. Mark any passages, however long or short, that strike you, for whatever reason. Beside each passage, write a note explaining its significance for you. Finally, pick a favorite passage and either:
   a. Expand it into a new piece of writing, or
   b. Make notes on how you *could* expand or use it at some future date, or
   c. Rewrite it in a different form (e.g., poem, dialogue, letter, memoir).

For a list of strategies for expanding or revising, see Chapter 10.

2. To what extent are children fated to be like their parents, and to what extent can they determine their own personalities and futures? Bring together two or more **characters, speakers,** or **personae** from the different texts and have them discuss this question in a dialogue. Some possible participants might include the mother or daughter in Olsen's "I Stand Here Ironing," the **narrator**/brother in Baldwin's "Sonny's Blues," Kiswana Browne in Naylor's story, the speaker/son in Bukowski's "my old man," Franz Kafka. Begin by listing some pertinent questions and considering how the various speakers might respond to them. Then write the dialogue.

3. Several texts in this section ("Eveline," "Sonny's Blues," "Kiswana Browne," "Heritage," *Tone Clusters,* and *The Cuban Swimmer,* to name just a few) indicate ways that families are shaped by the larger cultures of which they are a part. Write an essay about your own family in which you discuss:
   a. Ways in which your family might be perceived as representative of some culture (ethnic, racial, religious, socioeconomic), and
   b. Ways in which your family has an identity that *transcends* that culture.

Make your essay vivid by illustrating it with specific examples and stories.

4. Several texts in this thematic section incorporate—or refer to—family photographs. Emulate the creative method of Rita Dove ("Fifth Grade Autobiography"), Judith Ortiz Cofer ("Lessons of the Past"), and Joy Harjo ("The

Place of Origins"), and use a family photograph (or photographs) as a spring-board for writing about your family. *Alternative:* Study a photograph (wife/husband, partners, parent/child, or larger family grouping) of a family other than your own—perhaps a family of a different time or culture—and write from *that* photograph. Obviously, you will need to use your imagination and *invent* details and stories about that family. If possible, do some back-ground research to improve your writing about this "stranger" family.

5. The texts present diverse images of childhood. For instance, it is seen as an age of innocence (Millay), a relatively harmonious or secure time (Rita Dove, Li-Young Lee), or a grim period of parental oppression (Kafka). Com-pare and contrast the ways that childhood is viewed in any two or three texts within this section.

6. Review your entire notebook; as you do, make a running list of memo-rable or striking topics, e.g., "fathers and sons," "mothers and daughters," "sib-lings," "breaking free of the parent." Then choose a favorite topic, make a Topic/Form Grid (see Chapter 10), and use one of the forms on your grid to create a new notebook entry about the topic. Should your chosen form not work, do a Topic/Form Shift to a different form on your grid.

7. Reread your entire notebook, and mark any favorite entries. Then, after reviewing Chapter 4, revise one of these entries that is a "dependent" text into an "independent" text. (For a list of strategies for revising, see Chapter 10.)

Experience and Identity

D. H. LAWRENCE (1885–1930)

The Blind Man

Isabel Pervin was listening for two sounds—for the sound of wheels on the 1 drive outside and for the noise of her husband's footsteps in the hall. Her dearest and oldest friend, a man who seemed almost indispensable to her living, would drive up in the rainy dusk of the closing November day. The trap had gone to fetch him from the station. And her husband, who had been blinded in Flanders, and who had a disfiguring mark on his brow, would be coming in from the outhouses.

He had been home for a year now. He was totally blind. Yet they had been 2 very happy. The Grange was Maurice's own place. The back was a farmstead, and the Wernhams, who occupied the rear premises, acted as farmers. Isabel lived with her husband in the handsome rooms in front. She and he had been almost entirely alone together since he was wounded. They talked and sang and read together in a wonderful and unspeakable intimacy. Then she reviewed books for a Scottish newspaper, carrying on her old interest, and he occupied himself a good deal with the farm. Sightless, he could still discuss everything with Wernham, and he could also do a good deal of work about the place—menial work, it is true, but it gave him satisfaction. He milked the cows, carried in the pails, turned the separator, attended to the pigs and horses. Life was still very full and strangely serene for the blind man, peaceful with the almost incomprehensible peace of immediate contact in darkness. With his wife he had a whole world, rich and real and invisible.

They were newly and remotely happy. He did not even regret the loss of his 3 sight in these times of dark, palpable joy. A certain exultance swelled his soul.

But as time wore on, sometimes the rich glamour would leave them. Some- 4
times, after months of this intensity, a sense of burden overcame Isabel, a weariness, a terrible *ennui*, in that silent house approached between a colonnade of
tall-shafted pines. Then she felt she would go mad, for she could not bear it.
And sometimes he had devastating fits of depression, which seemed to lay
waste his whole being. It was worse than depression—a black misery, when his
own life was a torture to him, and when his presence was unbearable to his
wife. The dread went down to the roots of her soul as these black days recurred.
In a kind of panic she tried to wrap herself up still further in her husband. She
forced the old spontaneous cheerfulness and joy to continue. But the effort it
cost her was almost too much. She knew she could not keep it up. She felt she
would scream with the strain, and would give anything, anything, to escape.
She longed to possess her husband utterly; it gave her inordinate joy to have
him entirely to herself. And yet, when again he was gone in a black and massive
misery, she could not bear him, she could not bear herself; she wished she could
be snatched away off the earth altogether, anything rather than live at this cost.

Dazed, she schemed for a way out. She invited friends, she tried to give him 5
some further connection with the outer world. But it was no good. After all
their joy and suffering, after their dark, great year of blindness and solitude and
unspeakable nearness, other people seemed to them both shallow, rattling,
rather impertinent. Shallow prattle seemed presumptuous. He became impatient and irritated, she was wearied. And so they lapsed into their solitude
again. For they preferred it.

But now, in a few weeks' time, her second baby would be born. The first had 6
died, an infant, when her husband first went out to France. She looked with joy
and relief to the coming of the second. It would be her salvation. But also she
felt some anxiety. She was thirty years old, her husband was a year younger.
They both wanted the child very much. Yet she could not help feeling afraid.
She had her husband on her hands, a terrible joy to her, and a terrifying burden.
The child would occupy her love and attention. And then, what of Maurice?
What would he do? If only she could feel that he, too, would be at peace and
happy when the child came! She did so want to luxuriate in a rich, physical satisfaction of maternity. But the man, what would he do? How could she provide
for him, how avert those shattering black moods of his, which destroyed them
both?

She sighed with fear. But at this time Bertie Reid wrote to Isabel. He was her 7
old friend, a second or third cousin, a Scotchman, as she was a Scotchwoman.
They had been brought up near to one another, and all her life he had been her
friend, like a brother, but better than her own brothers. She loved him—though
not in the marrying sense. There was a sort of kinship between them, an affin-
ity. They understood one another instinctively. But Isabel would never have
thought of marrying Bertie. It would have seemed like marrying in her own
family.

Bertie was a barrister and a man of letters, a Scotchman of the intellectual 8
type, quick, ironical, sentimental, and on his knees before the woman he

adored but did not want to marry. Maurice Pervin was different. He came of a good old country family—the Grange was not a very great distance from Oxford. He was passionate, sensitive, perhaps over-sensitive, wincing—a big fellow with heavy limbs and a forehead that flushed painfully. For his mind was slow, as if drugged by the strong provincial blood that beat in his veins. He was very sensitive to his own mental slowness, his feelings being quick and acute. So that he was just the opposite to Bertie, whose mind was much quicker than his emotions, which were not so very fine.

From the first the two men did not like each other. Isabel felt that they *ought* ⁹ to get on together. But they did not. She felt that if only each could have the clue to the other there would be such a rare understanding between them. It did not come off, however. Bertie adopted a slightly ironical attitude, very offensive to Maurice, who returned the Scotch irony with English resentment, a resentment which deepened sometimes into stupid hatred.

This was a little puzzling to Isabel. However, she accepted it in the course of ¹⁰ things. Men were made freakish and unreasonable. Therefore, when Maurice was going out to France for the second time, she felt that, for her husband's sake, she must discontinue her friendship with Bertie. She wrote to the barrister to this effect. Bertram Reid simply replied that in this, as in all other matters, he must obey her wishes, if these were indeed her wishes.

For nearly two years nothing had passed between the two friends. Isabel ¹¹ rather gloried in the fact; she had no compunction. She had one great article of faith, which was, that husband and wife should be so important to one another, that the rest of the world simply did not count. She and Maurice were husband and wife. They loved one another. They would have children. Then let everybody and everything else fade into insignificance outside this connubial felicity. She professed herself quite happy and ready to receive Maurice's friends. She was happy and ready: the happy wife, the ready woman in possession. Without knowing why, the friends retired abashed, and came no more. Maurice, of course, took as much satisfaction in this connubial absorption as Isabel did.

He shared in Isabel's literary activities, she cultivated a real interest in agri- ¹² culture and cattle-raising. For she, being at heart perhaps an emotional enthusiast, always cultivated the practical side of life and prided herself on her mastery of practical affairs. Thus the husband and wife had spent the five years of their married life. The last had been one of blindness and unspeakable intimacy. And now Isabel felt a great indifference coming over her, a sort of lethargy. She wanted to be allowed to bear her child in peace, to nod by the fire and drift vaguely, physically, from day to day. Maurice was like an ominous thunder-cloud. She had to keep waking up to remember him.

When a little note came from Bertie, asking if he were to put up a tomb- ¹³ stone to their dead friendship, and speaking of the real pain he felt on account of her husband's loss of sight, she felt a pang, a fluttering agitation of re-awakening. And she read the letter to Maurice.

"Ask him to come down," he said.   ¹⁴

"Ask Bertie to come here!" she re-echoed.   ¹⁵

"Yes—if he wants to."   16

Isabel paused for a few moments.   17

"I know he wants to—he'd only be too glad," she replied. "But what about   18
you, Maurice? How would you like it?"

"I should like it."   19

"Well—in that case—— But I thought you didn't care for him——"   20

"Oh, I don't know. I might think differently of him now," the blind man   21
replied. It was rather abstruse to Isabel.

"Well, dear," she said, "if you're quite sure——"   22

"I'm sure enough. Let him come," said Maurice.   23

So Bertie was coming, coming this evening, in the November rain and dark-   24
ness. Isabel was agitated, racked with her old restlessness and indecision. She
had always suffered from this pain of doubt, just an agonizing sense of uncertainty. It had begun to pass off, in the lethargy of maternity. Now it returned,
and she resented it. She struggled as usual to maintain her calm, composed,
friendly bearing, a sort of mask she wore over all her body.

A woman had lighted a tall lamp beside the table and spread the cloth. The   25
long dining-room was dim, with its elegant but rather severe pieces of old furniture. Only the round table glowed softly under the light. It had a rich, beautiful effect. The white cloth glistened and dropped its heavy, pointed lace corners
almost to the carpet, the china was old and handsome, creamy-yellow, with a
blotched pattern of harsh red and deep blue, the cups large and bell-shaped, the
teapot gallant. Isabel looked at it with superficial appreciation.

Her nerves were hurting her. She looked automatically again at the high,   26
uncurtained windows. In the last dusk she could just perceive outside a huge
fir-tree swaying its boughs: it was as if she thought it rather than saw it. The
rain came flying on the window panes. Ah, why had she no peace? These two
men, why did they tear at her? Why did they not come—why was there this suspense?

She sat in a lassitude that was really suspense and irritation. Maurice, at   27
least, might come in—there was nothing to keep him out. She rose to her feet.
Catching sight of her reflection in a mirror, she glanced at herself with a slight
smile of recognition, as if she were an old friend to herself. Her face was oval
and calm, her nose a little arched. Her neck made a beautiful line down to her
shoulder. With hair knotted loosely behind, she had something of a warm, maternal look. Thinking this of herself, she arched her eyebrows and her rather
heavy eyelids, with a little flicker of a smile, and for a moment her grey eyes
looked amused and wicked, a little sardonic, out of her transfigured Madonna
face.

Then, resuming her air of womanly patience—she was really fatally self-   28
determined—she went with a little jerk towards the door. Her eyes were slightly
reddened.

She passed down the wide hall and through a door at the end. Then she was   29
in the farm premises. The scent of dairy, and of farm-kitchen, and of farm-yard
and of leather almost overcame her: but particularly the scent of dairy. They

had been scalding out the pans. The flagged passage in front of her was dark, puddled, and wet. Light came out from the open kitchen door. She went forward and stood in the doorway. The farm-people were at tea, seated at a little distance from her, round a long, narrow table, in the centre of which stood a white lamp. Ruddy faces, ruddy hands holding food, red mouths working, heads bent over the tea-cups: men, land-girls, boys: it was tea-time, feeding-time. Some faces caught sight of her. Mrs. Wernham, going round behind the chairs with a large black teapot, halting slightly in her walk, was not aware of her for a moment. Then she turned suddenly.

"Oh, is it Madam!" she exclaimed. "Come in, then, come in! We're at tea." 30 And she dragged forward a chair.

"No, I won't come in," said Isabel. "I'm afraid I interrupt your meal."   31

"No—no—not likely, Madam, not likely."   32

"Hasn't Mr. Pervin come in, do you know?"   33

"I'm sure I couldn't say! Missed him, have you, Madam?"   34

"No, I only wanted him to come in," laughed Isabel, as if shyly.   35

"Wanted him, did ye? Get up, boy—get up, now——"   36

Mrs. Wernham knocked one of the boys on the shoulder. He began to 37 scrape to his feet, chewing largely.

"I believe he's in top stable," said another face from the table.   38

"Ah! No, don't get up. I'm going myself," said Isabel.   39

"Don't you go out of a dirty night like this. Let the lad go. Get along wi' ye, 40 boy," said Mrs. Wernham.

"No, no," said Isabel, with a decision that was always obeyed. "Go on with 41 your tea, Tom. I'd like to go across to the stable, Mrs. Wernham."

"Did ever you hear tell!" exclaimed the woman.   42

"Isn't the trap late?" asked Isabel.   43

"Why, no," said Mrs. Wernham, peering into the distance at the tall, dim 44 clock. "No, Madam—we can give it another quarter or twenty minutes yet, good—yes, every bit of a quarter."

"Ah! It seems late when darkness falls so early," said Isabel.   45

"It do, that it do. Bother the days, that they draw in so," answered Mrs. 46 Wernham. "Proper miserable!"

"They are," said Isabel, withdrawing.   47

She pulled on her overshoes, wrapped a large tartan shawl around her, put 48 on a man's felt hat, and ventured out along the causeways of the first yard. It was very dark. The wind was roaring in the great elms behind the outhouses. When she came to the second yard the darkness seemed deeper. She was unsure of her footing. She wished she had brought a lantern. Rain blew against her. Half she liked it, half she felt unwilling to battle.

She reached at last the just visible door of the stable. There was no sign of a 49 light anywhere. Opening the upper half, she looked in: into a simple well of darkness. The smell of horses, and ammonia, and of warmth was startling to her, in that full night. She listened with all her ears but could hear nothing save the night, and the stirring of a horse.

"Maurice!" she called, softly and musically, though she was afraid. "Mau- 50
rice—are you there?"

Nothing came from the darkness. She knew the rain and wind blew in upon 51
the horses, the hot animal life. Feeling it wrong, she entered the stable and drew
the lower half of the door shut, holding the upper part close. She did not stir,
because she was aware of the presence of the dark hind-quarters of the horses,
though she could not see them, and she was afraid. Something wild stirred in
her heart.

She listened intensely. Then she heard a small noise in the distance—far 52
away, it seemed—the chink of a pan, and a man's voice speaking a brief word. It
would be Maurice, in the other part of the stable. She stood motionless, waiting
for him to come through the partition door. The horses were so terrifyingly
near to her, in the invisible.

The loud jarring of the inner door-latch made her start; the door was 53
opened. She could hear and feel her husband entering and invisibly passing
among the horses near to her, darkness as they were, actively intermingled. The
rather low sound of his voice as he spoke to the horses came velvety to her
nerves. How near he was, and how invisible! The darkness seemed to be in a
strange swirl of violent life, just upon her. She turned giddy.

Her presence of mind made her call, quietly and musically: 54

"Maurice! Maurice—dea-ar!"   55

"Yes," he answered. "Isabel?"   56

She saw nothing, and the sound of his voice seemed to touch her.   57

"Hello!" she answered cheerfully, straining her eyes to see him. He was still 58
busy, attending to the horses near her, but she saw only darkness. It made her
almost desperate.

"Won't you come in, dear?" she said.   59

"Yes, I'm coming. Just half a minute. *Stand over—now!* Trap's not come, has 60
it?"

"Not yet," said Isabel.   61

His voice was pleasant and ordinary, but it had a slight suggestion of the sta- 62
ble to her. She wished he would come away. Whilst he was so utterly invisible,
she was afraid of him.

"How's the time?" he asked.   63

"Not yet six," she replied. She disliked to answer into the dark. Presently he 64
came very near to her, and she retreated out of doors.

"The weather blows in here," he said, coming steadily forward, feeling for 65
the doors. She shrank away. At last she could dimly see him.

"Bertie won't have much of a drive," he said, as he closed the doors.   66

"He won't indeed!" said Isabel calmly, watching the dark shape at the door. 67

"Give me your arm, dear," she said.   68

She pressed his arm close to her, as she went. But she longed to see him, to 69
look at him. She was nervous. He walked erect, with face rather lifted, but with
a curious tentative movement of his powerful, muscular legs. She could feel the
clever, careful, strong contact of his feet with the earth, as she balanced against

him. For a moment he was a tower of darkness to her, as if he rose out of the earth.

In the house-passage he wavered and went cautiously, with a curious look of 70
silence about him as he felt for the bench. Then he sat down heavily. He was a man with rather sloping shoulders, but with heavy limbs, powerful legs that seemed to know the earth. His head was small, usually carried high and light. As he bent down to unfasten his gaiters and boots he did not look blind. His hair was brown and crisp, his hands were large, reddish, intelligent, the veins stood out in the wrists; and his thighs and knees seemed massive. When he stood up his face and neck were surcharged with blood, the veins stood out on his temples. She did not look at his blindness.

Isabel was always glad when they had passed through the dividing door into 71
their own regions of repose and beauty. She was a little afraid of him, out there in the animal grossness of the back. His bearing also changed, as he smelt the familiar indefinable odour that pervaded his wife's surroundings, a delicate, re-fined scent, very faintly spicy. Perhaps it came from the potpourri bowls.

He stood at the foot of the stairs, arrested, listening. She watched him, and 72
her heart sickened. He seemed to be listening to fate.

"He's not here yet," he said. "I'll go up and change."   73

"Maurice," she said, "you're not wishing he wouldn't come, are you?"   74

"I couldn't quite say," he answered. "I feel myself rather on the qui vive."   75

"I can see you are," she answered. And she reached up and kissed his cheek. 76
She saw his mouth relax into a slow smile.

"What are you laughing at?" she said roguishly.   77

"You consoling me," he answered.   78

"Nay," she answered. "Why should I console you? You know we love each 79
other—you know *how* married we are! What does anything else matter?"

"Nothing at all, my dear."   80

He felt for her face and touched it, smiling.   81

"*You're* all right, aren't you?" he asked anxiously.   82

"I'm wonderfully all right, love," she answered. "It's you I am a little trou- 83
bled about, at times."

"Why me?" he said, touching her cheeks delicately with the tips of his fin- 84
gers. The touch had an almost hypnotizing effect on her.

He went away upstairs. She saw him mount into the darkness, unseeing and 85
unchanging. He did not know that the lamps on the upper corridor were un-lighted. He went on into the darkness with unchanging step. She heard him in the bath-room.

Pervin moved about almost unconsciously in his familiar surroundings, 86
dark though everything was. He seemed to know the presence of objects before he touched them. It was a pleasure to him to rock thus through a world of things, carried on the flood in a sort of blood-prescience. He did not think much or trouble much. So long as he kept this sheer immediacy of blood-contact with the substantial world he was happy, he wanted no intervention of visual consciousness. In this state there was a certain rich positivity, bordering some-

times on rapture. Life seemed to move in him like a tide lapping, lapping, and advancing, enveloping all things darkly. It was a pleasure to stretch forth the hand and meet the unseen object, clasp it, and possess it in pure contact. He did not try to remember, to visualize. He did not want to. The new way of consciousness substituted itself in him.

The rich suffusion of this state generally kept him happy, reaching its culmi- 87
nation in the consuming passion for his wife. But at times the flow would seem to be checked and thrown back. Then it would beat inside him like a tangled sea, and he was tortured in the shattered chaos of his own blood. He grew to dread this arrest, this throw-back, this chaos inside himself, when he seemed merely at the mercy of his own powerful and conflicting elements. How to get some measure of control or surety, this was the question. And when the question rose maddening in him, he would clench his fists as if he would *compel* the whole universe to submit to him. But it was in vain. He could not even compel himself.

Tonight, however, he was still serene, though little tremors of unreasonable 88
exasperation ran through him. He had to handle the razor very carefully, as he shaved, for it was not at one with him, he was afraid of it. His hearing also was too much sharpened. He heard the woman lighting the lamps on the corridor, and attending to the fire in the visitors' room. And then, as he went to his room, he heard the trap arrive. Then came Isabel's voice, lifted and calling, like a bell ringing:

"Is it you, Bertie? Have you come?" 89
And a man's voice answered out of the wind: 90
"Hello, Isabel! There you are." 91
"Have you had a miserable drive? I'm so sorry we couldn't send a closed car- 92
riage. I can't see you at all, you know."
"I'm coming. No, I liked the drive—it was like Perthshire. Well, how are 93
you? You're looking fit as ever, as far as I can see."
"Oh, yes," said Isabel. "I'm wonderfully well. How are you? Rather thin, I 94
think——"
"Worked to death—everybody's old cry. But I'm all right, Ciss. How's Per- 95
vin?—isn't he here?"
"Oh, yes, he's upstairs changing. Yes, he's awfully well. Take off your wet 96
things; I'll send them to be dried."
"And how are you both, in spirits? He doesn't fret?" 97
"No—no, not at all. No, on the contrary, really. We've been wonderfully 98
happy, incredibly. It's more than I can understand—so wonderful: the nearness, and the peace——"
"Ah! Well, that's awfully good news——" 99
They moved away. Pervin heard no more. But a childish sense of desolation 100
had come over him, as he heard their brisk voices. He seemed shut out—like a child that is left out. He was aimless and excluded, he did not know what to do with himself. The helpless desolation came over him. He fumbled nervously as he dressed himself, in a state almost of childishness. He disliked the Scotch accent in Bertie's speech, and the slight response it found on Isabel's tongue. He

disliked the slight purr of complacency in the Scottish speech. He disliked intensely the glib way in which Isabel spoke of their happiness and nearness. It made him recoil. He was fretful and beside himself like a child, he had almost a childish nostalgia to be included in the life circle. And at the same time he was a man, dark and powerful and infuriated by his own weakness. By some fatal flaw, he could not be by himself, he had to depend on the support of another. And this very dependence enraged him. He hated Bertie Reid, and at the same time he knew the hatred was nonsense, he knew it was the outcome of his own weakness.

He went downstairs. Isabel was alone in the dining-room. She watched him enter, head erect, his feet tentative. He looked so strong-blooded and healthy and, at the same time, cancelled. Cancelled—that was the word that flew across her mind. Perhaps it was his scar suggested it. 101

"You heard Bertie come, Maurice?" she said. 102

"Yes—isn't he here?" 103

"He's in his room. He looks very thin and worn." 104

"I suppose he works himself to death." 105

A woman came in with a tray—and after a few minutes Bertie came down. He was a little dark man, with a very big forehead, thin, wispy hair, and sad, large eyes. His expression was inordinately sad—almost funny. He had odd, short legs. 106

Isabel watched him hesitate under the door, and glance nervously at her husband. Pervin heard him and turned. 107

"Here you are, now," said Isabel. "Come, let us eat." 108

Bertie went across to Maurice. 109

"How are you, Pervin?" he said, as he advanced. 110

The blind man stuck his hand out into space, and Bertie took it. 111

"Very fit. Glad you've come," said Maurice. 112

Isabel glanced at them, and glanced away, as if she could not bear to see them. 113

"Come," she said. "Come to table. Aren't you both awfully hungry? I am, tremendously." 114

"I'm afraid you waited for me," said Bertie, as they sat down. 115

Maurice had a curious monolithic way of sitting in a chair, erect and distant. Isabel's heart always beat when she caught sight of him thus. 116

"No," she replied to Bertie. "We're very little later than usual. We're having a sort of high tea, not dinner. Do you mind? It gives us such a nice long evening, uninterrupted." 117

"I like it," said Bertie. 118

Maurice was feeling, with curious little movements, almost like a cat kneading her bed, for his plate, his knife and fork, his napkin. He was getting the whole geography of his cover into his consciousness. He sat erect and inscrutable, remote-seeming. Bertie watched the static figure of the blind man, the delicate tactile discernment of the large, ruddy hands, and the curious mindless silence of the brow, above the scar. With difficulty he looked away, and 119 without knowing what he did, picked up a little crystal bowl of violets from the table, and held them to his nose.

"They are sweet-scented," he said. "Where do they come from?"   120

"From the garden—under the windows," said Isabel.   121

"So late in the year—and so fragrant! Do you remember the violets under   122
Aunt Bell's south wall?"

The two friends looked at each other and exchanged a smile, Isabel's eyes   123
lighting up.

"Don't I?" she replied. "*Wasn't* she queer!"   124

"A curious old girl," laughed Bertie. "There's a streak of freakishness to the   125
family, Isabel."

"Ah—but not in you and me, Bertie," said Isabel. "Give them to Maurice,   126
will you?" she added, as Bertie was putting down the flowers. "Have you smelled
the violets, dear? Do!—they are so scented."

Maurice held out his hand, and Bertie placed the tiny bowl against his large,   127
warm-looking fingers. Maurice's hand closed over the thin white fingers of the
barrister. Bertie carefully extricated himself. Then the two watched the blind man
smelling the violets. He bent his head and seemed to be thinking. Isabel waited.

"Aren't they sweet, Maurice?" she said at last, anxiously.   128

"Very," he said. And he held out the bowl. Bertie took it. Both he and Isabel   129
were a little afraid, and deeply disturbed.

The meal continued. Isabel and Bertie chatted spasmodically. The blind   130
man was silent. He touched his food repeatedly, with quick, delicate touches of
his knife-point, then cut irregular bits. He could not bear to be helped. Both Isabel and Bertie suffered: Isabel wondered why. She did not suffer when she was
alone with Maurice. Bertie made her conscious of a strangeness.

After the meal the three drew their chairs to the fire, and sat down to talk.   131
The decanters were put on a table near at hand. Isabel knocked the logs on the
fire, and clouds of brilliant sparks went up the chimney. Bertie noticed a slight
weariness in her bearing.

"You will be glad when your child comes now, Isabel?" he said.   132

She looked up to him with a quick wan smile.   133

"Yes, I shall be glad," she answered. "It begins to seem long. Yes, I shall be   134
very glad. So will you, Maurice, won't you?" she added.

"Yes, I shall," replied her husband.   135

"We are both looking forward so much to having it," she said.   136

"Yes, of course," said Bertie.   137

He was a bachelor, three or four years older than Isabel. He lived in beauti-   138
ful rooms overlooking the river, guarded by a faithful Scottish man-servant.
And he had his friends among the fair sex—not lovers, friends. So long as he
could avoid any danger of courtship or marriage, he adored a few good women
with constant and unfailing homage, and he was chivalrously fond of quite a
number. But if they seemed to encroach on him, he withdrew and detested
them.

Isabel knew him very well, knew his beautiful constancy, and kindness, also   139
his incurable weakness, which made him unable ever to enter into close contact
of any sort. He was ashamed of himself because he could not marry, could not
approach women physically. He wanted to do so. But he could not. At the centre
of him he was afraid, helplessly and even brutally afraid. He had given up hope,
had ceased to expect any more that he could escape his own weakness. Hence
he was a brilliant and successful barrister, also a *littérateur* of high repute, a rich
man, and a great social success. At the centre he felt himself neuter, nothing.

Isabel knew him well. She despised him even while she admired him. She   140
looked at his sad face, his little short legs, and felt contempt of him. She looked
at his dark grey eyes, with their uncanny, almost childlike, intuition, and she
loved him. He understood amazingly—but she had no fear of his understanding. As a man she patronized him.

And she turned to the impassive, silent figure of her husband. He sat lean-   141
ing back, with folded arms, and face a little uptilted. His knees were straight
and massive. She sighed, picked up the poker, and again began to prod the fire,
to rouse the clouds of soft brilliant sparks.

"Isabel tells me," Bertie began suddenly, "that you have not suffered unbear-   142
ably from the loss of sight."

Maurice straightened himself to attend but kept his arms folded.   143

"No," he said, "not unbearably. Now and again one struggles against it, you   144
know. But there are compensations."

"They say it is much worse to be stone deaf," said Isabel.   145

"I believe it is," said Bertie. "Are there compensations?" he added, to Mau-   146
rice.

"Yes. You cease to bother about a great many things." Again Maurice   147
stretched his figure, stretched the strong muscles of his back, and leaned backwards, with uplifted face.

"And that is a relief," said Bertie. "But what is there in place of the bother-   148
ing? What replaces the activity?"

There was a pause. At length the blind man replied, as out of a negligent,   149
unattentive thinking:

"Oh, I don't know. There's a good deal when you're not active."   150

"Is there?" said Bertie. "What, exactly? It always seems to me that when there   151
is no thought and no action, there is nothing."

Again Maurice was slow in replying.   152

"There is something," he replied. "I couldn't tell you what it is."   153

And the talk lapsed once more, Isabel and Bertie chatting gossip and remi-   154
niscence, the blind man silent.

At length Maurice rose restlessly, a big obtrusive figure. He felt tight and   155
hampered. He wanted to go away.

"Do you mind," he said, "if I go and speak to Wernham?"   156

"No—go along, dear," said Isabel.   157

And he went out. A silence came over the two friends. At length Bertie said: 158

"Nevertheless, it is a great deprivation, Cissie."   159

"It is, Bertie. I know it is." 160

"Something lacking all the time," said Bertie. 161

"Yes, I know. And yet—and yet—Maurice is right. There is something else, 162 something *there*, which you never knew was there, and which you can't express."

"What is there?" asked Bertie. 163

"I don't know—it's awfully hard to define it—but something strong and 164 immediate. There's something strange in Maurice's presence—indefinable—but I couldn't do without it. I agree that it seems to put one's mind to sleep. But when we're alone I miss nothing; it seems awfully rich, almost splendid, you know."

"I'm afraid I don't follow," said Bertie. 165

They talked desultorily. The wind blew loudly outside, rain chattered on the 166 window-panes, making a sharp drum-sound because of the closed, mellow-golden shutters inside. The logs burned slowly, with hot, almost invisible small flames. Bertie seemed uneasy, there were dark circles round his eyes. Isabel, rich with her approaching maternity, leaned looking into the fire. Her hair curled in odd, loose strands, very pleasing to the man. But she had a curious feeling of old woe in her heart, old, timeless night-woe.

"I suppose we're all deficient somewhere," said Bertie. 167

"I suppose so," said Isabel wearily. 168

"Damned, sooner or later." 169

"I don't know," she said, rousing herself. "I feel quite all right, you know. 170 The child coming seems to make me indifferent to everything, just placid. I can't feel that there's anything to trouble about, you know."

"A good thing, I should say," he replied slowly. 171

"Well, there it is. I suppose it's just Nature. If only I felt I needn't trouble 172 about Maurice, I should be perfectly content——"

"But you feel you must trouble about him?" 173

"Well—I don't know——" She even resented this much effort. 174

The night passed slowly. Isabel looked at the clock. "I say," she said. "It's 175 nearly ten o'clock. Where can Maurice be? I'm sure they're all in bed at the back. Excuse me a moment."

She went out, returning almost immediately. 176

"It's all shut up and in darkness," she said. "I wonder where he is. He must 177 have gone out to the farm——"

Bertie looked at her. 178

"I suppose he'll come in," he said. 179

"I suppose so," she said. "But it's unusual for him to be out now." 180

"Would you like me to go out and see?" 181

"Well—if you wouldn't mind. I'd go, but——" She did not want to make the 182 physical effort.

Bertie put on an old overcoat and took a lantern. He went out from the side 183 door. He shrank from the wet and roaring night. Such weather had a nervous effect on him: too much moisture everywhere made him feel almost imbecile.

Unwilling, he went through it all. A dog barked violently at him. He peered in all the buildings. At last, as he opened the upper door of a sort of intermediate barn, he heard a grinding noise, and looking in, holding up his lantern, saw Maurice, in his shirt-sleeves, standing listening, holding the handle of a turnip-pulper. He had been pulping sweet roots, a pile of which lay dimly heaped in a corner behind him.

"That you, Wernham?" said Maurice, listening. 184

"No, it's me," said Bertie. 185

A large, half-wild grey cat was rubbing at Maurice's leg. The blind man 186 stooped to rub its sides. Bertie watched the scene, then unconsciously entered and shut the door behind him. He was in a high sort of barn-place, from which, right and left, ran off the corridors in front of the stalled cattle. He watched the slow, stooping motion of the other man, as he caressed the great cat.

Maurice straightened himself. 187

"You came to look for me?" he said. 188

"Isabel was a little uneasy," said Bertie. 189

"I'll come in. I like messing about doing these jobs." 190

The cat had reared her sinister, feline length against his leg, clawing at his 191 thigh affectionately. He lifted her claws out of his flesh.

"I hope I'm not in your way at all at the Grange here," said Bertie, rather shy 192 and stiff.

"My way? No, not a bit. I'm glad Isabel has somebody to talk to. I'm afraid 193 it's I who am in the way. I know I'm not very lively company. Isabel's all right, don't you think? She's not unhappy, is she?"

"I don't think so." 194

"What does she say?" 195

"She says she's very content—only a little troubled about you." 196

"Why me?" 197

"Perhaps afraid that you might brood," said Bertie, cautiously. 198

"She needn't be afraid of that." He continued to caress the flattened grey 199 head of the cat with his fingers. "What I am a bit afraid of," he resumed, "is that she'll find me a dead weight, always alone with me down here."

"I don't think you need think that," said Bertie, though this was what he 200 feared himself.

"I don't know," said Maurice. "Sometimes I feel it isn't fair that she's saddled 201 with me." Then he dropped his voice curiously. "I say," he asked, secretly struggling, "is my face much disfigured? Do you mind telling me?"

"There is the scar," said Bertie, wondering. "Yes, it is a disfigurement. But 202 more pitiable than shocking."

"A pretty bad scar, though," said Maurice. 203

"Oh, yes." 204

There was a pause. 205

"Sometimes I feel I am horrible," said Maurice, in a low voice, talking as if to 206 himself. And Bertie actually felt a quiver of horror.

"That's nonsense," he said. 207

Maurice again straightened himself, leaving the cat.   208

"There's no telling," he said. Then again, in an odd tone, he added: "I don't   209
really know you, do I?"

"Probably not," said Bertie.   210

"Do you mind if I touch you?"   211

The lawyer shrank away instinctively. And yet, out of very philanthropy, he   212
said, in a small voice: "Not at all."

But he suffered as the blind man stretched out a strong, naked hand to him.   213
Maurice accidentally knocked off Bertie's hat.

"I thought you were taller," he said, starting. Then he laid his hand on Bertie   214
Reid's head, closing the dome of the skull in a soft, firm grasp, gathering it, as it
were; then, shifting his grasp and softly closing again, with a fine, close pressure, till he had covered the skull and the face of the smaller man, tracing the
brows, and touching the full, closed eyes, touching the small nose and the nostrils, the rough, short moustache, the mouth, the rather strong chin. The hand
of the blind man grasped the shoulder, the arm, the hand of the other man. He
seemed to take him, in the soft, travelling grasp.

"You seem young," he said quietly, at last.   215

The lawyer stood almost annihilated, unable to answer.   216

"Your head seems tender, as if you were young," Maurice repeated. "So do   217
your hands. Touch my eyes, will you?—touch my scar."

Now Bertie quivered with revulsion. Yet he was under the power of the blind   218
man, as if hypnotized. He lifted his hand, and laid the fingers on the scar, on
the scarred eyes. Maurice suddenly covered them with his own hand, pressed
the fingers of the other man upon his disfigured eye-sockets, trembling in
every fibre, and rocking slightly, slowly, from side to side. He remained thus
for a minute or more, whilst Bertie stood as if in a swoon, unconscious, imprisoned.

Then suddenly Maurice removed the hand of the other man from his brow,   219
and stood holding it in his own.

"Oh, my God," he said, "we shall know each other now, shan't we? We shall   220
know each other now."

Bertie could not answer. He gazed mute and terror-struck, overcome by his   221
own weakness. He knew he could not answer. He had an unreasonable fear, lest
the other man should suddenly destroy him. Whereas Maurice was actually
filled with hot, poignant love, the passion of friendship. Perhaps it was this very
passion of friendship which Bertie shrank from most.

"We're all right together now, aren't we?" said Maurice. "It's all right now, as   222
long as we live, so far as we're concerned?"

"Yes," said Bertie, trying by any means to escape.   223

Maurice stood with head lifted, as if listening. The new delicate fulfilment   224
of mortal friendship had come as a revelation and surprise to him, something
exquisite and unhoped-for. He seemed to be listening to hear if it were real.

Then he turned for his coat.   225

"Come," he said, "we'll go to Isabel."   226

Bertie took the lantern and opened the door. The cat disappeared. The two 227
men went in silence along the causeways. Isabel, as they came, thought their
footsteps sounded strange. She looked up pathetically and anxiously for their
entrance. There seemed a curious elation about Maurice. Bertie was haggard,
with sunken eyes.

"What is it?" she asked.   228

"We've become friends," said Maurice, standing with his feet apart, like a 229
strange colossus.

"Friends!" re-echoed Isabel. And she looked again at Bertie. He met her eyes 230
with a furtive, haggard look; his eyes were as if glazed with misery.

"I'm so glad," she said, in sheer perplexity.   231

"Yes," said Maurice.   232

He was indeed so glad. Isabel took his hand with both hers, and held it fast. 233

"You'll be happier now, dear," she said.   234

But she was watching Bertie. She knew that he had one desire—to escape 235
from this intimacy, this friendship, which had been thrust upon him. He could
not bear it that he had been touched by the blind man, his insane reserve broken in. He was like a mollusc whose shell is broken.

Activities for Writing and Discussion

1. Trace the recurring images of darkness and invisibility in the story, and
discuss how they help define the **characters** of Maurice, Isabel, and Bertie. Alternative: Discuss how the story's **setting**—the country location, the storm, the
night and the dark, the stable full of animals and animal smells—intensifies its
characters, themes, and/or **plot**.

2. Compare and contrast the characters of Bertie and Maurice.

a. How are they alike or different physically? in their attitudes toward the
physical or natural world? in their implied feelings about their own bodies and sexuality? Find examples in the text that illustrate your answers to
these questions.

b. Review the tense—even hostile—relationship the two men had prior to
the evening described in the story. Then compose a conversation (with
stage directions, if you wish) that the two might have had during their
earlier acquaintance, before Maurice was blinded.

3. On page 378 the narrator says Maurice's hands were "intelligent." Can
the body, or any part of it, be said to have a quality (i.e., intelligence) we normally associate with the brain? Why or why not?

4. Building on Activity #3, write a reflective piece about how the mind-
body relationship is treated in your culture or in your own personal mythology.
Are the two regarded as allies or as enemies? Which (if either) is regarded as
dominant? What would be the impact if the order of dominance were reversed?

5. On p. 385 Maurice passes his hand over Bertie's face, shoulders, and arms, and Bertie feels "almost annihilated." Why? Write a **stream of consciousness** piece in the **persona** of Bertie in which you articulate what is going through your (Bertie's) mind during those moments.

KATHERINE MANSFIELD (1888–1923)

Her First Ball

Exactly when the ball began Leila would have found it hard to say. Perhaps her 1
first real partner was the cab. It did not matter that she shared the cab with the
Sheridan girls and their brother. She sat back in her own little corner of it, and
the bolster on which her hand rested felt like the sleeve of an unknown young
man's dress suit; and away they bowled, past waltzing lampposts and houses
and fences and trees.

"Have you really never been to a ball before, Leila? But, my child, how too 2
weird—" cried the Sheridan girls.

"Our nearest neighbor was fifteen miles," said Leila softly, gently opening 3
and shutting her fan.

Oh, dear, how hard it was to be indifferent like the others! She tried not to 4
smile too much; she tried not to care. But every single thing was so new and exciting . . . Meg's tuberoses, Jose's long loop of amber, Laura's little dark head,
pushing above her white fur like a flower through snow. She would remember
for ever. It even gave her a pang to see her cousin Laurie throw away the wisps
of tissue paper he pulled from the fastening of his new gloves. She would like to
have kept those wisps as a keepsake, as a remembrance. Laurie leaned forward
and put his hand on Laura's knee.

"Look here, darling," he said. "The third and the ninth as usual. Twig?" 5

Oh, how marvellous to have a brother! In her excitement Leila felt that if 6
there had been time, if it hadn't been impossible, she couldn't have helped crying because she was an only child, and no brother had ever said "Twig?" to her;
no sister would ever say, as Meg said to Jose that moment, "I've never known
your hair go up more successfully than it has tonight!"

But, of course, there was no time. They were at the drill hall already; there 7
were cabs in front of them and cabs behind. The road was bright on either side
with moving fan-like lights, and on the pavement gay couples seemed to float
through the air; little satin shoes chased each other like birds.

"Hold on to me, Leila; you'll get lost," said Laura. 8

"Come on, girls, let's make a dash for it," said Laurie. 9

Leila put two fingers on Laura's pink velvet cloak, and they were somehow 10
lifted past the big gold lantern, carried along the passage, and pushed into the
little room marked "Ladies." Here the crowd was so great there was hardly space
to take off their things; the noise was deafening. Two benches on either side

were stacked high with wraps. Two old women in white aprons ran up and down tossing fresh armfuls. And everybody was pressing forward trying to get at the little dressing table and mirror at the far end.

A great quivering jet of gas lighted the ladies' room. It couldn't wait; it was 11 dancing already. When the door opened again and there came a burst of tuning from the drill hall, it leaped almost to the ceiling.

Dark girls, fair girls were patting their hair, tying ribbons again, tucking 12 handkerchiefs down the front of their bodices, smoothing marble-white gloves. And because they were all laughing it seemed to Leila that they were all lovely.

"Aren't there any invisible hairpins?" cried a voice. "How most extraordi- 13 nary! I can't see a single invisible hairpin."

"Powder my back, there's a darling," cried some one else.   14

"But I must have a needle and cotton. I've torn simply miles and miles of 15 the frill," wailed a third.

Then, "Pass them along, pass them along!" The straw basket of programs 16 was tossed from arm to arm. Darling little pink-and-silver programs, with pink pencils and fluffy tassels. Leila's fingers shook as she took one out of the basket. She wanted to ask someone, "Am I meant to have one too?" but she had just time to read: "Waltz 3. *Two, Two in a Canoe*. Polka 4. *Making the Feathers Fly*," when Meg cried, "Ready, Leila?" and they pressed their way through the crush in the passage towards the big double doors of the drill hall.

Dancing had not begun yet, but the band had stopped tuning, and the noise 17 was so great it seemed that when it did begin to play it would never be heard. Leila, pressing close to Meg, looking over Meg's shoulder, felt that even the little quivering colored flags strung across the ceiling were talking. She quite forgot to be shy; she forgot how in the middle of dressing she had sat down on the bed with one shoe off and one shoe on and begged her mother to ring up her cousins and say she couldn't go after all. And the rush of longing she had had to be sitting on the veranda of their forsaken upcountry home, listening to the baby owls crying "More pork" in the moonlight, was changed to a rush of joy so sweet that it was hard to bear alone. She clutched her fan, and, gazing at the gleaming, golden floor, the azaleas, the lanterns, the stage at one end with its red carpet and gilt chairs and the band in a corner, she thought breathlessly, "How heavenly; how simply heavenly!"

All the girls stood grouped together at one side of the doors, the men at the 18 other, and the chaperones in dark dresses, smiling rather foolishly, walked with little careful steps over the polished floor towards the stage.

"This is my little country cousin Leila. Be nice to her. Find her partners; 19 she's under my wing," said Meg, going up to one girl after another.

Strange faces smiled at Leila—sweetly, vaguely. Strange voices answered, 20 "Of course, my dear." But Leila felt the girls didn't really see her. They were looking towards the men. Why didn't the men begin? What were they waiting for? There they stood, smoothing their gloves, patting their glossy hair and smiling among themselves. Then, quite suddenly, as if they had only just made up their minds that that was what they had to do, the men came gliding over the parquet. There was a joyful flutter among the girls. A tall, fair man flew up to Meg, seized her program, scribbled something; Meg passed him on to Leila. "May I have the pleasure?" He ducked and smiled. There came a dark man wearing an eyeglass, then cousin Laurie with a friend, and Laura with a little freckled fellow whose tie was crooked. Then quite an old man—fat, with a big bald patch on his head—took her program and murmured, "Let me see, let me see!" And he was a long time comparing his program, which looked black with names, with hers. It seemed to give him so much trouble that Leila was ashamed. "Oh, please don't bother," she said eagerly. But instead of replying the fat man wrote something, glanced at her again. "Do I remember this bright little face?" he said softly. "Is it known to me of yore?" At that moment the band began playing; the fat man disappeared. He was tossed away on a great wave of music that came flying over the gleaming floor, breaking the groups up into couples, scattering them, sending them spinning. . . .

Leila had learned to dance at boarding school. Every Saturday afternoon the 21 boarders were hurried off to a little corrugated iron mission hall where Miss Eccles (of London) held her "select" classes. But the difference between that dusty-smelling hall—with calico texts on the walls, the poor terrified little woman in a brown velvet toque with rabbit's ears thumping the cold piano, Miss Eccles poking the girls' feet with her long white wand—and this was so tremendous that Leila was sure if her partner didn't come and she had to listen to that marvelous music and to watch the others sliding, gliding over the golden floor, she would die at least, or faint, or lift her arms and fly out of one of those dark windows that showed the stars.

"Ours, I think—" Some one bowed, smiled, and offered her his arm; she 22 hadn't to die after all. Some one's hand pressed her waist, and she floated away like a flower that is tossed into a pool.

"Quite a good floor, isn't it?" drawled a faint voice close to her ear. 23

"I think it's most beautifully slippery," said Leila. 24

"Pardon!" The faint voice sounded surprised. Leila said it again. And there 25 was a tiny pause before the voice echoed, "Oh, quite!" and she was swung round again.

He steered so beautifully. That was the great difference between dancing 26 with girls and men, Leila decided. Girls banged into each other, and stamped on each other's feet; the girl who was gentleman always clutched you so.

The azaleas were separate flowers no longer; they were pink and white flags 27 streaming by.

"Were you at the Bells' last week?" the voice came again. It sounded tired. 28 Leila wondered whether she ought to ask him if he would like to stop.

"No, this is my first dance," said she. 29

Her partner gave a little gasping laugh. "Oh, I say," he protested. 30

"Yes, it is really the first dance I've ever been to." Leila was most fervent. It 31 was such a relief to be able to tell somebody. "You see, I've lived in the country all my life up until now. . . ."

At that moment the music stopped, and they went to sit on two chairs 32
against the wall. Leila tucked her pink satin feet under and fanned herself, while
she blissfully watched the other couples passing and disappearing through the
swing doors.

"Enjoying yourself, Leila?" asked Jose, nodding her golden head. 33

Laura passed and gave her the faintest little wink; it made Leila wonder for a 34
moment whether she was quite grown up after all. Certainly her partner did
not say very much. He coughed, tucked his handkerchief away, pulled down his
waistcoat, took a minute thread off his sleeve. But it didn't matter. Almost immediately the band started, and her second partner seemed to spring from the
ceiling.

"Floor's not bad," said the new voice. Did one always begin with the floor? 35
And then, "Were you at the Neaves' on Tuesday?" And again Leila explained.
Perhaps it was a little strange that her partners were not more interested. For it
was thrilling. Her first ball! She was only at the beginning of everything. It
seemed to her that she had never known what the night was like before. Up till
now it had been dark, silent, beautiful very often—oh, yes—but mournful
somehow. Solemn. And now it would never be like that again—it had opened
dazzling bright.

"Care for an ice?" said her partner. And they went through the swing doors, 36
down the passage, to the supper room. Her cheeks burned, she was fearfully
thirsty. How sweet the ices looked on little glass plates, and how cold the frosted
spoon was, iced too! And when they came back to the hall there was the fat man
waiting for her by the door. It gave her quite a shock again to see how old he
was; he ought to have been on the stage with the fathers and mothers. And
when Leila compared him with her other partners he looked shabby. His waistcoat was creased, there was a button off his glove, his coat looked as if it was
dusty with French chalk.

"Come along, little lady," said the fat man. He scarcely troubled to clasp her, 37
and they moved away so gently, it was more like walking than dancing. But he
said not a word about the floor. "Your first dance, isn't it?" he murmured.

"How *did* you know?" 38

"Ah," said the fat man, "that's what it is to be old!" He wheezed faintly as he 39
steered her past an awkward couple. "You see, I've been doing this kind of thing
for the last thirty years."

"Thirty years?" cried Leila. Twelve years before she was born! 40

"It hardly bears thinking about, does it?" said the fat man gloomily. Leila 41
looked at his bald head, and she felt quite sorry for him.

"I think it's marvelous to be still going on," she said kindly. 42

"Kind little lady," said the fat man, and he pressed her a little closer, and 43
hummed a bar of the waltz. "Of course," he said, "you can't hope to last anything like as long as that. No-o," said the fat man, "long before that you'll be sitting up there on the stage, looking on, in your nice black velvet. And these
pretty arms will have turned into little short fat ones, and you'll beat time with
such a different kind of fan—a black bony one." The fat man seemed to shud-

der. "And you'll smile away like the poor old dears up there, and point to your daughter, and tell the elderly lady next to you how some dreadful man tried to kiss her at the club ball. And your heart will ache, ache"—the fat man squeezed her closer still, as if he really was sorry for that poor heart—"because no one wants to kiss you now. And you'll say how unpleasant these polished floors are to walk on, how dangerous they are. Eh, Mademoiselle Twinkletoes?" said the fat man softly.

Leila gave a light little laugh, but she did not feel like laughing. Was it— 44 could it all be true? It sounded terribly true. Was this first ball only the beginning of her last ball after all? At that the music seemed to change; it sounded sad, sad it rose upon a great sigh. Oh, how quickly things changed! Why didn't happiness last for ever? For ever wasn't a bit too long.

"I want to stop," she said in a breathless voice. The fat man led her to the 45 door.

"No," she said, "I won't go outside. I won't sit down. I'll just stand here, 46 thank you." She leaned against the wall, tapping with her foot, pulling up her gloves and trying to smile. But deep inside her a little girl threw her pinafore over her head and sobbed. Why had he spoiled it all?

"I say, you know," said the fat man, "you mustn't take me seriously, little 47 lady."

"As if I should!" said Leila, tossing her small dark head and sucking her un- 48 derlip. . . .

Again the couples paraded. The swing doors opened and shut. Now new 49 music was given out by the bandmaster. But Leila didn't want to dance any more. She wanted to be home, or sitting on the veranda listening to those baby owls. When she looked through the dark windows at the stars, they had long beams like wings. . . .

But presently a soft, melting, ravishing tune began, and a young man with 50 curly hair bowed before her. She would have to dance, out of politeness, until she could find Meg. Very stiffly she walked into the middle; very haughtily she put her hand on his sleeve. But in one minute, in one turn, her feet glided, glided. The lights, the azaleas, the dresses, the pink faces, the velvet chairs, all became one beautiful flying wheel. And when her next partner bumped her into the fat man and he said, "Par*don*," she smiled at him more radiantly than ever. She didn't even recognize him again.

William Faulkner (1897–1962)

Barn Burning

The store in which the Justice of the Peace's court was sitting smelled of cheese. 1 The boy, crouched on his nail keg at the back of the crowded room, knew he smelled cheese, and more: from where he sat he could see the ranked shelves close-packed with the solid, squat, dynamic shapes of tin cans whose labels his stomach read, not from the lettering which meant nothing to his mind but from the scarlet devils and the silver curve of fish—this, the cheese which he knew he smelled and the hermetic meat which his intestines believed he smelled coming in intermittent gusts momentary and brief between the other constant one, the smell and sense just a little of fear because mostly of despair and grief, the old fierce pull of blood. He could not see the table where the Justice sat and before which his father and his father's enemy (*our enemy* he thought in that despair; *ourn! mine and hisn both! He's my father!*) stood, but he could hear them, the two of them that is, because his father had said no word yet:

"But what proof have you, Mr. Harris?"   2

"I told you. The hog got into my corn. I caught it up and sent it back to him.   3
He had no fence that would hold it. I told him so, warned him. The next time I put the hog in my pen. When he came to get it I gave him enough wire to patch up his pen. The next time I put the hog up and kept it. I rode down to his house and saw the wire I gave him still rolled on to the spool in his yard. I told him he could have the hog when he paid me a dollar pound fee. That evening a nigger came with the dollar and got the hog. He was a strange nigger. He said, 'He say to tell you wood and hay kin burn.' I said, 'What?' 'That whut he say to tell you,' the nigger said. 'Wood and hay kin burn.' That night my barn burned. I got the stock out but I lost the barn."

"Where is the nigger? Have you got him?"   4

"He was a strange nigger, I tell you. I don't know what became of him."   5

"But that's not proof. Don't you see that's not proof?"   6

"Get that boy up here. He knows." For a moment the boy thought too that   7
the man meant his older brother until Harris said, "Not him. The little one. The boy," and, crouching, small for his age, small and wiry like his father, in patched and faded jeans even too small for him, with straight, uncombed, brown hair and eyes gray and wild as storm scud, he saw the men between himself and the table part and become a lane of grim faces, at the end of which he saw the Justice, a shabby, collarless, graying man in spectacles, beckoning him. He felt no floor under his bare feet; he seemed to walk beneath the palpable weight of the grim turning faces. His father, stiff in his black Sunday coat donned not for the trial but for the moving, did not even look at him. *He aims for me to lie,* he thought, again with that frantic grief and despair. *And I will have to do hit.*

"What's your name, boy?" the Justice said.   8

"Colonel Sartoris Snopes," the boy whispered.   9

"Hey?" the Justice said. "Talk louder. Colonel Sartoris? I reckon anybody   10
named for Colonel Sartoris in this country can't help but tell the truth, can they?" The boy said nothing. *Enemy! Enemy!* he thought; for a moment he could not even see, could not see that the Justice's face was kindly nor discern that his voice was troubled when he spoke to the man named Harris: "Do you want me to question this boy?" But he could hear, and during those subsequent long seconds while there was absolutely no sound in the crowded little room save that of quiet and intent breathing it was as if he had swung outward at the

end of a grape vine, over a ravine, and at the top of the swing had been caught in a prolonged instant of mesmerized gravity, weightless in time.

"No!" Harris said violently, explosively. "Damnation! Send him out of 11 here!" Now time, the fluid world, rushed beneath him again, the voices coming to him again through the smell of cheese and sealed meat, the fear and despair and the old grief of blood:

"This case is closed. I can't find against you, Snopes, but I can give you ad- 12 vice. Leave this country and don't come back to it."

His father spoke for the first time, his voice cold and harsh, level, without 13 emphasis: "I aim to. I don't figure to stay in a country among people who . . ." he said something unprintable and vile, addressed to no one.

"That'll do," the Justice said. "Take your wagon and get out of this country 14 before dark. Case dismissed."

His father turned, and he followed the stiff black coat, the wiry figure walk- 15 ing a little stiffly from where a Confederate provost's man's musket ball had taken him in the heel on a stolen horse thirty years ago, followed the two backs now, since his older brother had appeared from somewhere in the crowd, no taller than the father but thicker, chewing tobacco steadily, between the two lines of grim-faced men and out of the store and across the worn gallery and down the sagging steps and among the dogs and half-grown boys in the mild May dust, where as he passed a voice hissed:

"Barn burner!" 16

Again he could not see, whirling; there was a face in a red haze, moonlike, 17 bigger than the full moon, the owner of it half again his size, he leaping in the red haze toward the face, feeling no blow, feeling no shock when his head struck the earth, scrabbling up and leaping again, feeling no blow this time either and tasting no blood, scrabbling up to see the other boy in full flight and himself al-ready leaping into pursuit as his father's hand jerked him back, the harsh, cold voice speaking above him: "Go get in the wagon."

It stood in a grove of locusts and mulberries across the road. His two hulk- 18 ing sisters in their Sunday dresses and his mother and her sister in calico and sunbonnets were already in it, sitting on and among the sorry residue of the dozen and more movings which even the boy could remember—the battered stove, the broken beds and chairs, the clock inlaid with mother-of-pearl, which would not run, stopped at some fourteen minutes past two o'clock of a dead and forgotten day and time, which had been his mother's dowry. She was cry-ing, though when she saw him she drew her sleeve across her face and began to descend from the wagon. "Get back," the father said.

"He's hurt. I got to get some water and wash his . . ." 19

"Get back in the wagon," his father said. He got in too, over the tail-gate. His 20 father mounted to the seat where the older brother already sat and struck the gaunt mules two savage blows with the peeled willow, but without heat. It was not even sadistic; it was exactly that same quality which in later years would cause his descendants to over-run the engine before putting a motor car into motion, striking and reining back in the same movement. The wagon went on, the store with its quiet crowd of grimly watching men dropped behind; a curve in the road hid it. *Forever* he thought. *Maybe he's done satisfied now, now that he has* . . . stopping himself, not to say it aloud even to himself. His mother's hand touched his shoulder.

"Does hit hurt?" she said.   21

"Naw," he said. "Hit don't hurt. Lemme be."   22

"Can't you wipe some of the blood off before hit dries?"   23

"I'll wash to-night," he said. "Lemme be, I tell you."   24

The wagon went on. He did not know where they were going. None of them 25
ever did or ever asked, because it was always somewhere, always a house of sorts waiting for them a day or two days or even three days away. Likely his father had already arranged to make a crop on another farm before he . . . Again he had to stop himself. He (the father) always did. There was something about his wolflike independence and even courage when the advantage was at least neutral which impressed strangers, as if they got from his latent ravening ferocity not so much a sense of dependability as a feeling that his ferocious conviction in the rightness of his own actions would be of advantage to all whose interest lay with his.

That night they camped, in a grove of oaks and beeches where a spring ran. 26
The nights were still cool and they had a fire against it, of a rail lifted from a nearby fence and cut into lengths—a small fire, neat, niggard almost, a shrewd fire; such fires were his father's habit and custom always, even in freezing weather. Older, the boy might have remarked this and wondered why not a big one; why should not a man who had not only seen the waste and extravagance of war, but who had in his blood an inherent voracious prodigality with material not his own, have burned everything in sight? Then he might have gone a step farther and thought that that was the reason: that niggard blaze was the living fruit of nights passed during those four years in the woods hiding from all men, blue or gray, with his strings of horses (captured horses, he called them). And older still, he might have divined the true reason: that the element of fire spoke to some deep mainspring of his father's being, as the element of steel or of powder spoke to other men, as the one weapon for the preservation of integrity, else breath were not worth the breathing, and hence to be regarded with respect and used with discretion.

But he did not think this now and he had seen those same niggard blazes all 27
his life. He merely ate his supper beside it and was already half asleep over his iron plate when his father called him, and once more he followed the stiff back, the stiff and ruthless limp, up the slope and on to the starlit road where, turning, he could see his father against the stars but without face or depth—a shape black, flat, and bloodless as though cut from tin in the iron folds of the frock-coat which had not been made for him, the voice harsh like tin and without heat like tin:

"You were fixing to tell them. You would have told him." He didn't answer. 28
His father struck him with the flat of his hand on the side of the head, hard but without heat, exactly as he had struck the two mules at the store, exactly as he would strike either of them with any stick in order to kill a horse fly, his voice

still without heat or anger: "You're getting to be a man. You got to learn. You got to learn to stick to your own blood or you ain't going to have any blood to stick to you. Do you think either of them, any man there this morning, would? Don't you know all they wanted was a chance to get at me because they knew I had them beat? Eh?" Later, twenty years later, he was to tell himself, "If I had said they wanted only truth, justice, he would have hit me again." But now he said nothing. He was not crying. He just stood there. "Answer me," his father said.

"Yes," he whispered. His father turned.   29

"Get on to bed. We'll be there tomorrow."   30

To-morrow they were there. In the early afternoon the wagon stopped be- 31
fore a paintless two-room house identical almost with the dozen others it had
stopped before even in the boy's ten years, and again, as on the other dozen occasions, his mother and aunt got down and began to unload the wagon, although his two sisters and his father and brother had not moved.

"Likely hit ain't fitten for hawgs," one of the sisters said.   32

"Nevertheless, fit it will and you'll hog it and like it," his father said. "Get out 33
of them chairs and help your Ma unload."

The two sisters got down, big, bovine, in a flutter of cheap ribbons; one of 34
them drew from the jumbled wagon bed a battered lantern, the other a worn
broom. His father handed the reins to the older son and began to climb stiffly
over the wheel. "When they get unloaded, take the team to the barn and feed
them." Then he said, and at first the boy thought he was still speaking to his
brother: "Come with me."

"Me?" he said.   35

"Yes," his father said. "You."   36

"Abner," his mother said. His father paused and looked back—the harsh 37
level stare beneath the shaggy, graying, irascible brows.

"I reckon I'll have a word with the man that aims to begin to-morrow own- 38
ing me body and soul for the next eight months."

They went back up the road. A week ago—or before last night, that is—he 39
would have asked where they were going, but not now. His father had struck
him before last night but never before had he paused afterward to explain why;
it was as if the blow and the following calm, outrageous voice still rang, reper-
cussed, divulging nothing to him save the terrible handicap of being young, the
light weight of his few years, just heavy enough to prevent his soaring free of
the world as it seemed to be ordered but not heavy enough to keep him footed
solid in it, to resist it and try to change the course of its events.

Presently he could see the grove of oaks and cedars and the other flowering 40
trees and shrubs where the house would be, though not the house yet. They
walked beside a fence massed with honeysuckle and Cherokee roses and came
to a gate swinging open between two brick pillars, and now, beyond a sweep of
drive, he saw the house for the first time and at that instant he forgot his father
and the terror and despair both, and even when he remembered his father again
(who had not stopped) the terror and despair did not return. Because, for all

the twelve movings, they had sojourned until now in a poor country, a land of small farms and fields and houses, and he had never seen a house like this before. *Hit's big as a courthouse* he thought quietly, with a surge of peace and joy whose reason he could not have thought into words, being too young for that: *They are safe from him. People whose lives are a part of this peace and dignity are beyond his touch, he no more to them than a buzzing wasp: capable of stinging for a little moment but that's all; the spell of this peace and dignity rendering even the barns and stable and cribs which belong to it impervious to the puny flames he might contrive . . .* this, the peace and joy, ebbing for an instant as he looked again at the stiff black back, the stiff and implacable limp of the figure which was not dwarfed by the house, for the reason that it had never looked big anywhere and which now, against the serene columned backdrop, had more than ever that impervious quality of something cut ruthlessly from tin, depthless, as though, sidewise to the sun, it would cast no shadow. Watching him, the boy remarked the absolutely undeviating course which his father held and saw the stiff foot come squarely down in a pile of fresh droppings where a horse had stood in the drive and which his father could have avoided by a simple change of stride. But it ebbed only for a moment, though he could not have thought this into words either, walking on in the spell of the house, which he could even want but without envy, without sorrow, certainly never with that ravening and jealous rage which unknown to him walked in the ironlike black coat before him: *Maybe he will feel it too. Maybe it will even change him now from what maybe he couldn't help but be.*

They crossed the portico. Now he could hear his father's stiff foot as it came 41 down on the boards with clocklike finality, a sound out of all proportion to the displacement of the body it bore and which was not dwarfed either by the white door before it, as though it had attained to a sort of vicious and ravening minimum not to be dwarfed by anything—the flat, wide, black hat, the formal coat of broadcloth which had once been black but which had now that friction-glazed greenish cast of the bodies of old house flies, the lifted sleeve which was too large, the lifted hand like a curled claw. The door opened so promptly that the boy knew the Negro must have been watching them all the time, an old man with neat grizzled hair, in a linen jacket, who stood barring the door with his body, saying, "Wipe yo foots, white man, fo you come in here. Major ain't home nohow."

"Get out of my way, nigger," his father said, without heat too, flinging the 42 door back and the Negro also and entering, his hat still on his head. And now the boy saw the prints of the stiff foot on the doorjamb and saw them appear on the pale rug behind the machinelike deliberation of the foot which seemed to bear (or transmit) twice the weight which the body compassed. The Negro was shouting "Miss Lula! Miss Lula!" somewhere behind them, then the boy, deluged as though by a warm wave by a suave turn of carpeted stair and a pendant glitter of chandeliers and a mute gleam of gold frames, heard the swift feet and saw her too, a lady—perhaps he had never seen her like before either—in a gray, smooth gown with lace at the throat and an apron tied at the waist and the sleeves turned back, wiping cake or biscuit dough from her hands with a towel as she came up the hall, looking not at his father at all but at the tracks on the blond rug with an expression of incredulous amazement.

"I tried," the Negro cried. "I tole him to . . ." 43

"Will you please go away?" she said in a shaking voice. "Major de Spain is 44 not at home. Will you please go away?"

His father had not spoken again. He did not speak again. He did not even 45 look at her. He just stood stiff in the center of the rug, in his hat, the shaggy iron-gray brows twitching slightly above the pebble-colored eyes as he appeared to examine the house with brief deliberation. Then with the same deliberation he turned; the boy watched him pivot on the good leg and saw the stiff foot drag round the arc of the turning, leaving a final long and fading smear. His father never looked at it, he never once looked down at the rug. The Negro held the door. It closed behind them, upon the hysteric and indistinguishable woman-wail. His father stopped at the top of the steps and scraped his boot clean on the edge of it. At the gate he stopped again. He stood for a moment, planted stiffly on the stiff foot, looking back at the house. "Pretty and white, ain't it?" he said. "That's sweat. Nigger sweat. Maybe it ain't white enough yet to suit him. Maybe he wants to mix some white sweat with it."

Two hours later the boy was chopping wood behind the house within which 46 his mother and aunt and the two sisters (the mother and aunt, not the two girls, he knew that; even at this distance and muffled by walls the flat loud voices of the two girls emanated an incorrigible idle inertia) were setting up the stove to prepare a meal, when he heard the hooves and saw the linen-clad man on a fine sorrel mare, whom he recognized even before he saw the rolled rug in front of the Negro youth following on a fat bay carriage horse—a suffused, angry face vanishing, still at full gallop, beyond the corner of the house where his father and brother were sitting in the two tilted chairs; and a moment later, almost before he could have put the axe down, he heard the hooves again and watched the sorrel mare go back out of the yard, already galloping again. Then his father began to shout one of the sisters' names, who presently emerged backward from the kitchen door dragging the rolled rug along the ground by one end while the other sister walked behind it.

"If you ain't going to tote, go on and set up the wash pot," the first said. 47

"You, Sarty!" the second shouted. "Set up the wash pot!" His father ap- 48 peared at the door, framed against that shabbiness, as he had been against that other bland perfection, impervious to either, the mother's anxious face at his shoulder.

"Go on," the father said. "Pick it up." The two sisters stooped, broad, lethar- 49 gic; stooping, they presented an incredible expanse of pale cloth and a flutter of tawdry ribbons.

"If I thought enough of a rug to have to git hit all the way from France I 50 wouldn't keep hit where folks coming in would have to tromp on hit," the first said. They raised the rug.

"Abner," the mother said. "Let me do it." 51

"You go back and git dinner," his father said. "I'll tend to this."   52

From the woodpile through the rest of the afternoon the boy watched them,   53
the rug spread flat in the dust beside the bubbling wash-pot, the two sisters
stooping over it with that profound and lethargic reluctance, while the father
stood over them in turn, implacable and grim, driving them though never raising his voice again. He could smell the harsh homemade lye they were using; he
saw his mother come to the door once and look toward them with an expression not anxious now but very like despair; he saw his father turn, and he fell to
with the axe and saw from the corner of his eye his father raise from the ground
a flattish fragment of field stone and examine it and return to the pot, and this
time his mother actually spoke: "Abner. Abner. Please don't. Please, Abner."

Then he was done too. It was dusk; the whippoorwills had already begun.   54
He could smell coffee from the room where they would presently eat the cold
food remaining from the mid-afternoon meal, though when he entered the
house he realized they were having coffee again probably because there was a
fire on the hearth, before which the rug now lay spread over the backs of the
two chairs. The tracks of his father's foot were gone. Where they had been were
now long, water-cloudy scoriations resembling the sporadic course of a lillipu-
tian mowing machine.

It still hung there while they ate the cold food and then went to bed, scat-   55
tered without order or claim up and down the two rooms, his mother in one
bed, where his father would later lie, the older brother in the other, himself, the
aunt, and the two sisters on pallets on the floor. But his father was not in bed
yet. The last thing the boy remembered was the depthless, harsh silhouette of
the hat and coat bending over the rug and it seemed to him that he had not
even closed his eyes when the silhouette was standing over him, the fire almost
dead behind it, the stiff foot prodding him awake. "Catch up the mule," his father said.

When he returned with the mule his father was standing in the black door,   56
the rolled rug over his shoulder. "Ain't you going to ride?" he said.

"No. Give me your foot."   57

He bent his knee into his father's hand, the wiry, surprising power flowed   58
smoothly, rising, he rising with it, on to the mule's bare back (they had owned a
saddle once; the boy could remember it though not when or where) and with
the same effortlessness his father swung the rug up in front of him. Now in the
starlight they retraced the afternoon's path, up the dusty road rife with honeysuckle, through the gate and up the black tunnel of the drive to the lightless
house, where he sat on the mule and felt the rough warp of the rug drag across
his thighs and vanish.

"Don't you want me to help?" he whispered. His father did not answer and   59
now he heard again that stiff foot striking the hollow portico with that wooden
and clocklike deliberation, that outrageous overstatement of the weight it carried. The rug, hunched, not flung (the boy could tell that even in the darkness)
from his father's shoulder, struck the angle of wall and floor with a sound un-
believably loud, thunderous, then the foot again, unhurried and enormous; a

light came on in the house and the boy sat, tense, breathing steadily and quietly and just a little fast, though the foot itself did not increase its beat at all, descending the steps now; now the boy could see him.

"Don't you want to ride now?" he whispered. "We kin both ride now," the 60 light within the house altering now, flaring up and sinking. *He's coming down the stairs now,* he thought. He had already ridden the mule up beside the horse block; presently his father was up behind him and he doubled the reins over and slashed the mule across the neck, but before the animal could begin to trot the hard, thin arm came round him, the hard, knotted hand jerking the mule back to a walk.

In the first red rays of the sun they were in the lot, putting plow gear on the 61 mules. This time the sorrel mare was in the lot before he heard it at all, the rider collarless and even bareheaded, trembling, speaking in a shaking voice as the woman in the house had done, his father merely looking up once before stooping again to the hame he was buckling, so that the man on the mare spoke to his stooping back:

"You must realize you have ruined that rug. Wasn't there anybody here, any 62 of your women . . ." he ceased, shaking, the boy watching him, the older brother leaning now in the stable door, chewing, blinking slowly and steadily at nothing apparently. "It cost a hundred dollars. But you never had a hundred dollars. You never will. So I'm going to charge you twenty bushels of corn against your crop. I'll add it in your contract and when you come to the commissary you can sign it. That won't keep Mrs. de Spain quiet but maybe it will teach you to wipe your feet off before you enter her house again."

Then he was gone. The boy looked at his father, who still had not spoken or 63 even looked up again, who was now adjusting the logger-head in the hame.

"Pap," he said. His father looked at him—the inscrutable face, the shaggy 64 brows beneath which the gray eyes glinted coldly. Suddenly the boy went toward him, fast, stopping as suddenly. "You done the best you could!" he cried. "If he wanted hit done different why didn't he wait and tell you how? He won't git no twenty bushels! He won't git none! We'll gether hit and hide hit! I kin watch . . ."

"Did you put the cutter back in that straight stock like I told you?" 65

"No, sir," he said. 66

"Then go do it." 67

That was Wednesday. During the rest of that week he worked steadily, at 68 what was within his scope and some which was beyond it, with an industry that did not need to be driven nor even commanded twice; he had this from his mother, with the difference that some at least of what he did he liked to do, such as splitting wood with the half-size axe which his mother and aunt had earned, or saved money somehow, to present him with at Christmas. In company with the two older women (and on one afternoon, even one of the sisters), he built pens for the shoat and the cow which were a part of his father's contract with the landlord, and one afternoon, his father being absent, gone somewhere on one of the mules, he went to the field.

They were running a middle buster now, his brother holding the plow 69
straight while he handled the reins, and walking beside the straining mule, the
rich black soil shearing cool and damp against his bare ankles, he thought
*Maybe this is the end of it. Maybe even that twenty bushels that seems hard to have
to pay for just a rug will be a cheap price for him to stop forever and always from
being what he used to be;* thinking, dreaming now, so that his brother had to
speak sharply to him to mind the mule: *Maybe he even won't collect the twenty
bushels. Maybe it will all add up and balance and vanish—corn, rug, fire; the terror and grief, the being pulled two ways like between two teams of horses—gone,
done with for ever and ever.*

Then it was Saturday; he looked up from beneath the mule he was harness- 70
ing and saw his father in the black coat and hat. "Not that," his father said. "The
wagon gear." And then, two hours later, sitting in the wagon bed behind his father and brother on the seat, the wagon accomplished a final curve, and he saw
the weathered paintless store with its tattered tobacco- and patent-medicine
posters and the tethered wagons and saddle animals below the gallery. He
mounted the gnawed steps behind his father and brother, and there again was
the lane of quiet, watching faces for the three of them to walk through. He saw
the man in spectacles sitting at the plank table and he did not need to be told
this was a Justice of the Peace; he sent one glare of fierce, exultant, partisan defiance at the man in collar and cravat now, whom he had seen but twice before
in his life, and that on a galloping horse, who now wore on his face an expression not of rage but of amazed unbelief which the boy could not have known
was at the incredible circumstance of being sued by one of his own tenants, and
came and stood against his father and cried at the Justice: "He ain't done it! He
ain't burnt . . ."

"Go back to the wagon," his father said. 71

"Burnt?" the Justice said. "Do I understand this rug was burned too?" 72

"Does anybody here claim it was?" his father said. "Go back to the wagon." 73
But he did not, he merely retreated to the rear of the room, crowded as that
other had been, but not to sit down this time, instead, to stand pressing among
the motionless bodies, listening to the voices:

"And you claim twenty bushels of corn is too high for the damage you did to 74
the rug?"

"He brought the rug to me and said he wanted the tracks washed out of it. I 75
washed the tracks out and took the rug back to him."

"But you didn't carry the rug back to him in the same condition it was in 76
before you made the tracks on it."

His father did not answer, and now for perhaps half a minute there was no 77
sound at all save that of breathing, the faint, steady suspiration of complete and
intent listening.

"You decline to answer that, Mr. Snopes?" Again his father did not answer. 78
"I'm going to find against you, Mr. Snopes. I'm going to find that you were responsible for the injury to Major de Spain's rug and hold you liable for it. But
twenty bushels of corn seems a little high for a man in your circumstances to

have to pay. Major de Spain claims it cost a hundred dollars. October corn will be worth about fifty cents. I figure that if Major de Spain can stand a ninety-five-dollar loss on something he paid cash for, you can stand a five-dollar loss you haven't earned yet. I hold you in damages to Major de Spain to the amount of ten bushels of corn over and above your contract with him, to be paid to him out of your crop at gathering time. Court adjourned."

It had taken no time hardly, the morning was but half begun. He thought 79 they would return home and perhaps back to the field, since they were late, far behind all other farmers. But instead his father passed on behind the wagon, merely indicating with his hand for the older brother to follow with it, and crossed the road toward the blacksmith shop opposite, pressing on after his father, overtaking him, speaking, whispering up at the harsh, calm face beneath the weathered hat: "He won't git no ten bushels neither. He won't git one. We'll . . ." until his father glanced for an instant down at him, the face absolutely calm, the grizzled eyebrows tangled above the cold eyes, the voice almost pleasant, almost gentle:

"You think so? Well, we'll wait till October anyway." 80

The matter of the wagon—the setting of a spoke or two and the tightening 81 of the tires—did not take long either, the business of the tires accomplished by driving the wagon into the spring branch behind the shop and letting it stand there, the mules nuzzling into the water from time to time, and the boy on the seat with the idle reins, looking up the slope and through the sooty tunnel of the shed where the slow hammer rang and where his father sat on an upended cypress bolt, easily, either talking or listening, still sitting there when the boy brought the dripping wagon up out of the branch and halted it before the door.

"Take them on to the shade and hitch," his father said. He did so and re- 82 turned. His father and the smith and a third man squatting on his heels inside the door were talking, about crops and animals; the boy, squatting too in the ammoniac dust and hoof-parings and scales of rust, heard his father tell a long and unhurried story out of the time before the birth of the older brother even when he had been a professional horsetrader. And then his father came up beside him where he stood before a tattered last year's circus poster on the other side of the store, gazing rapt and quiet at the scarlet horses, the incredible poisings and convolutions of tulle and tights and the painted leers of comedians, and said "It's time to eat."

But not at home. Squatting beside his brother against the front wall, he 83 watched his father emerge from the store and produce from a paper sack a segment of cheese and divide it carefully and deliberately into three with his pocket knife and produce crackers from the same sack. They all three squatted on the gallery and ate, slowly, without talking; then in the store again, they drank from a tin dipper tepid water smelling of the cedar bucket and of living beech trees. And still they did not go home. It was a horse lot this time, a tall rail fence upon and along which men stood and sat and out of which one by one horses were led, to be walked and trotted and then cantered back and forth along the road while the slow swapping and buying went on and the sun began to slant westward, they—the three of them—watching and listening, the older brother with his muddy eyes and his steady, inevitable tobacco, the father commenting now and then on certain of the animals, to no one in particular.

It was after sundown when they reached home. They ate supper by lamp-light, then, sitting on the doorstep, the boy watched the night fully accomplish, listening to the whippoorwills and the frogs, when he heard his mother's voice: "Abner! No! No! Oh, God. Oh, God. Abner!" and he rose, whirled, and saw the altered light through the door where a candle stub now burned in a bottle neck on the table and his father, still in the hat and coat, at once formal and burlesque as though dressed carefully for some shabby and ceremonial violence, emptying the reservoir of the lamp back into the five-gallon kerosene can from which it had been filled, while the mother tugged at his arm until he shifted the lamp to the other hand and flung her back, not savagely or viciously, just hard, into the wall, her hands flung out against the wall for balance, her mouth open and in her face the same quality of hopeless despair as had been in her voice. Then his father saw him standing in the door. 84

"Go to the barn and get that can of oil we were oiling the wagon with," he said. The boy did not move. Then he could speak. 85

"What . . ." he cried. "What are you . . ." 86

"Go get that oil," his father said. "Go." 87

Then he was moving, running, outside the house, toward the stable: this is the old habit, the old blood which he had not been permitted to choose for himself, which had been bequeathed him willy nilly and which had run for so long (and who knew where, battening on what of outrage and savagery and lust) before it came to him. *I could keep on,* he thought. *I could run on and on and never look back, never need to see his face again. Only I can't. I can't,* the rusted can in his hand now, the liquid sploshing in it as he ran back to the house and into it, into the sound of his mother's weeping in the next room, and handed the can to his father. 88

"Ain't you going to even send a nigger?" he cried. "At least you sent a nigger before!" 89

This time his father didn't strike him. The hand came even faster than the blow had, the same hand which had set the can on the table with almost excruciating care flashing from the can toward him too quick for him to follow it, gripping him by the back of his shirt and on to tiptoe before he had seen it quit the can, the face stooping at him in breathless and frozen ferocity, the cold, dead voice speaking over him to the older brother who leaned against the table, chewing with that steady, curious, sidewise motion of cows: 90

"Empty the can into the big one and go on. I'll catch up with you." 91

"Better tie him up to the bedpost," the brother said. 92

"Do like I told you," the father said. Then the boy was moving, his bunched shirt and the hard, bony hand between his shoulder-blades, his toes just touching the floor, across the room and into the other one, past the sisters sitting with spread heavy thighs in the two chairs over the cold hearth, and to where his mother and aunt sat side by side on the bed, the aunt's arms about his mother's shoulders. 93

"Hold him," the father said. The aunt made a startled movement. "Not you," 94 the father said. "Lennie. Take hold of him. I want to see you do it." His mother took him by the wrist. "You'll hold him better than that. If he gets loose don't you know what he is going to do? He will go up yonder." He jerked his head toward the road. "Maybe I'd better tie him."

"I'll hold him," his mother whispered. 95

"See you do then." Then his father was gone, the stiff foot heavy and mea- 96 sured upon the boards, ceasing at last.

Then he began to struggle. His mother caught him in both arms, he jerking 97 and wrenching at them. He would be stronger in the end, he knew that. But he had no time to wait for it. "Lemme go!" he cried. "I don't want to have to hit you!"

"Let him go!" the aunt said. "If he don't go, before God, I am going there 98 myself!"

"Don't you see I can't!" his mother cried. "Sarty! Sarty! No! No! Help me, 99 Lizzie!"

Then he was free. His aunt grasped at him but it was too late. He whirled, 100 running, his mother stumbled forward on to her knees behind him, crying to the nearer sister: "Catch him, Net! Catch him!" But that was too late too, the sister (the sisters were twins, born at the same time, yet either of them now gave the impression of being, encompassing as much living meat and volume and weight as any other two of the family) not yet having begun to rise from the chair, her head, face, alone merely turned, presenting to him in the flying instant an astonishing expanse of young female features untroubled by any surprise even, wearing only an expression of bovine interest. Then he was out of the room, out of the house, in the mild dust of the starlit road and the heavy rifeness of honeysuckle, the pale ribbon unspooling with terrific slowness under his running feet, reaching the gate at last and turning in, running, his heart and lungs drumming, on up the drive toward the lighted house, the lighted door. He did not knock, he burst in, sobbing for breath, incapable for the moment of speech; he saw the astonished face of the Negro in the linen jacket without knowing when the Negro had appeared.

"De Spain!" he cried, panted. "Where's . . ." then he saw the white man too 101 emerging from a white door down the hall. "Barn!" he cried. "Barn!"

"What?" the white man said. "Barn?" 102

"Yes!" the boy cried. "Barn!" 103

"Catch him!" the white man shouted. 104

But it was too late this time too. The Negro grasped his shirt, but the entire 105 sleeve, rotten with washing, carried away, and he was out that door too and in the drive again, and had actually never ceased to run even while he was screaming into the white man's face.

Behind him the white man was shouting, "My horse! Fetch my horse!" and 106 he thought for an instant of cutting across the park and climbing the fence into the road, but he did not know the park nor how high the vine-massed fence might be and he dared not risk it. So he ran on down the drive, blood and breath roaring; presently he was in the road again though he could not see it.

He could not hear either: the galloping mare was almost upon him before he heard her, and even then he held his course, as if the very urgency of his wild grief and need must in a moment more find him wings, waiting until the ultimate instant to hurl himself aside and into the weed-choked roadside ditch as the horse thundered past and on, for an instant in furious silhouette against the stars, the tranquil early summer night sky which, even before the shape of the horse and rider vanished, stained abruptly and violently upward: a long, swirling roar incredible and soundless, blotting the stars, and he springing up and into the road again, running again, knowing it was too late yet still running even after he heard the shot and, an instant later, two shots, pausing now without knowing he had ceased to run, crying "Pap! Pap!", running again before he knew he had begun to run, stumbling, tripping over something and scrabbling up again without ceasing to run, looking backward over his shoulder at the glare as he got up, running on among the invisible trees, panting, sobbing, "Father! Father!"

At midnight he was sitting on the crest of a hill. He did not know it was 107 midnight and he did not know how far he had come. But there was no glare behind him now and he sat now, his back toward what he had called home for four days anyhow, his face toward the dark woods which he would enter when breath was strong again, small, shaking steadily in the chill darkness, hugging himself into the remainder of his thin, rotten shirt, the grief and despair now no longer terror and fear but just grief and despair. *Father. My father,* he thought. "He was brave!" he cried suddenly, aloud but not loud, no more than a whisper: "He was! He was in the war! He was in Colonel Sartoris' cav'ry!" not knowing that his father had gone to that war a private in the fine old European sense, wearing no uniform, admitting the authority of and giving fidelity to no man or army or flag, going to war as Malbrouck himself did: for booty—it meant nothing and less than nothing to him if it were enemy booty or his own.

The slow constellations wheeled on. It would be dawn and then sun-up af- 108 ter a while and he would be hungry. But that would be to-morrow and now he was only cold, and walking would cure that. His breathing was easier now and he decided to get up and go on, and then he found that he had been asleep because he knew it was almost dawn, the night almost over. He could tell that from the whippoorwills. They were everywhere now among the dark trees below him, constant and inflectioned and ceaseless, so that, as the instant for giving over to the day birds drew nearer and nearer, there was no interval at all between them. He got up. He was a little stiff, but walking would cure that too as it would the cold, and soon there would be the sun. He went on down the hill, toward the dark woods within which the liquid silver voices of the birds called unceasing—the rapid and urgent beating of the urgent and quiring heart of the late spring night. He did not look back.

ACTIVITIES FOR WRITING AND DISCUSSION

1. The story is told primarily from the **third-person limited point of view** of the boy Sarty. How would the story change if it were told by Sarty in the *first person,* using "I"?

2. Reread the story for details of the Snopes family's life before the story's happenings. What kind of life has the family led? What did Abner (the father) do during the Civil War? What are the personalities and appearances of the sisters, mother, aunt, and brother? Based on these details, prepare a brief dossier on the family (perhaps for use by law enforcement officials or social workers).

3. Gather evidence of the range of Sarty's feelings for his father. What attracts him? repels him? confuses him? How extensive is the father's influence on the boy's life? In your opinion, will Sarty be able to establish an identity of his own, separate from his father's? Why or why not?

4. Compose a sequel to the story. Away from his father, what does Sarty do next? Where does he go? What does he do with his life? Strive to make the facts of your sequel psychologically consistent with the personality of Sarty as portrayed in Faulkner's story.

JEAN STAFFORD (1915–1979)

Bad Characters

Up until I learned my lesson in a very bitter way, I never had more than one friend at a time, and my friendships, though ardent, were short. When they ended and I was sent packing in unforgetting indignation, it was always my fault; I would swear vilely in front of a girl I knew to be pious and prim (by the time I was eight, the most grandiloquent gangster could have added nothing to my vocabulary—I had an awful tongue), or I would call a Tenderfoot Scout a sissy or make fun of athletics to the daughter of the high school coach. These outbursts came without plan; I would simply one day, in the middle of a game of Russian bank or a hike or a conversation, be possessed with a passion to be by myself, and my lips instantly and without warning would accommodate me. My friend was never more surprised than I was when this irrevocable slander, this terrible, talented invective, came boiling out of my mouth.

Afterward, when I had got the solitude I had wanted, I was dismayed, for I did not like it. Then I would sadly finish the game of cards as if someone were still across the table from me; I would sit down on the mesa and through a glaze of tears would watch my friend departing with outraged strides; mournfully, I would talk to myself. Because I had already alienated everyone I knew, I then had nowhere to turn, so a famine set in and I would have no companion but

Muff, the cat, who loathed all human beings except, significantly, me—truly. She bit and scratched the hands that fed her, she arched her back like a Halloween cat if someone kindly tried to pet her, she hissed, laid her ears flat to her skull, growled, fluffed up her tail into a great bush and flailed it like a bullwhack. But she purred for me, she patted me with her paws, keeping her claws in their velvet scabbards. She was not only an ill-natured cat, she was also badly dressed. She was a calico, and the distribution of her colors was a mess; she looked as if she had been left out in the rain and her paint had run. She had a Roman nose as the result of some early injury, her tail was skinny, she had a perfectly venomous look in her eye. My family said—my family discriminated against me—that I was much closer kin to Muff than I was to any of them. To tease me into a tantrum, my brother Jack and my sister Stella often called me Kitty instead of Emily. Little Tess did not dare, because she knew I'd chloroform her if she did. Jack, the meanest boy I have ever known in my life, called me Polecat and talked about my mania for fish, which, it so happened, I despised. The name would have been far more appropriate for *him*, since he trapped skunks up in the foothills—we lived in Adams, Colorado—and quite often, because he was careless and foolhardy, his clothes had to be buried, and even when that was done, he sometimes was sent home from school on the complaint of girls sitting next to him.

Along about Christmastime when I was eleven, I was making a snowman 3 with Virgil Meade in his backyard, and all of a sudden, just as we had got around to the right arm, I had to be alone. So I called him a son of a sea cook, said it was common knowledge that his mother had bedbugs and that his father, a dentist and the deputy marshal, was a bootlegger on the side. For a moment, Virgil was too aghast to speak—a little earlier we had agreed to marry someday and become millionaires—and then, with a bellow of fury, he knocked me down and washed my face in snow. I saw stars, and black balls bounced before my eyes. When finally he let me up, we were both crying, and he hollered that if I didn't get off his property that instant, his father would arrest me and send me to Canon City. I trudged slowly home, half frozen, critically sick at heart. So it was old Muff again for me for quite some time. Old Muff, that is, until I met Lottie Jump, although "met" is a euphemism for the way I first encountered her.

I saw Lottie for the first time one afternoon in our own kitchen, stealing a 4 chocolate cake. Stella and Jack had not come home from school yet—not having my difficult disposition, they were popular, and they were at their friends' houses, pulling taffy, I suppose, making popcorn balls, playing casino, having fun—and my mother had taken Tess with her to visit a friend in one of the T.B. sanitariums. I was alone in the house, and making a funny-looking Christmas card, although I had no one to send it to. When I heard someone in the kitchen, I thought it was Mother home early, and I went out to ask her why the green pine tree I had pasted on a square of red paper looked as if it were falling down. And there, instead of Mother and my baby sister, was this pale, conspicuous child in the act of lifting the glass cover from the devil's-food my mother had taken out of the oven an hour before and set on the plant shelf by the window. The child had her back to me, and when she heard my footfall, she wheeled with an amazing look of fear and hatred on her pinched and pasty face. Simultaneously, she put the cover over the cake again, and then she stood motionless as if she were under a spell.

I was scared, for I was not sure what was happening, and anyhow it gives 5 you a turn to find a stranger in the kitchen in the middle of the afternoon, even if the stranger is only a skinny child in a moldy coat and sopping wet basketball shoes. Between us there was a lengthy silence, but there was a great deal of noise in the room: the alarm clock ticked smugly; the teakettle simmered patiently on the back of the stove; Muff, cross at having been waked up, thumped her tail against the side of the terrarium in the window where she had been sleeping—contrary to orders—among the geraniums. This went on, it seemed to me, for hours and hours while that tall, sickly girl and I confronted each other. When, after a long time, she did open her mouth, it was to tell a prodigious lie. "I came to see if you'd like to play with me," she said. I think she sighed and stole a side-long and regretful glance at the cake.

Beggars cannot be choosers, and I had been missing Virgil so sorely, as well 6 as all those other dear friends forever lost to me, that in spite of her flagrance (she had never clapped eyes on me before, she had had no way of knowing there was a creature of my age in the house—she had come in like a hobo to steal my mother's cake), I was flattered and consoled. I asked her name and, learning it, believed my ears no better than my eyes: Lottie Jump. What on earth! What on earth—you surely will agree with me—and yet when I told her mine, Emily Vanderpool, she laughed until she coughed and gasped. "Beg pardon," she said. "Names like them always hit my funny bone. There was this tow-head boy in school named Delbert Saxonfield." I saw no connection and I was insulted (what's so funny about Vanderpool, I'd like to know), but Lottie Jump was, technically, my guest and I *was* lonesome, so I asked her, since she had spoken of playing with me, if she knew how to play Andy-I-Over. She said "Naw." It turned out that she did not know how to play any games at all; she couldn't do anything and didn't want to do anything; her only recreation and her only gift was, and always had been, stealing. But this I did not know at the time.

As it happened, it was too cold and snowy to play outdoors that day any- 7 how, and after I had run through my list of indoor games and Lottie had shaken her head at all of them (when I spoke of Parcheesi, she went "Ugh!" and pretended to be sick), she suggested that we look through my mother's bureau drawers. This did not strike me as strange at all, for it was one of my favorite things to do, and I led the way to Mother's bedroom without a moment's hesitation. I loved the smell of the lavender she kept in gauze bags among her chamois gloves and linen handkerchiefs and filmy scarves; there was a pink fascinator knitted of something as fine as spider's thread, and it made me go quite soft—I wasn't soft as a rule, I was as hard as nails and I gave my mother a rough time—to think of her wearing it around her head as she waltzed on the ice in the bygone days. We examined stockings, nightgowns, camisoles, strings of

beads, and mosaic pins, keepsake buttons from dresses worn on memorial occasions, tortoiseshell combs, and a transformation made from Aunt Joey's hair
when she had racily had it bobbed. Lottie admired particularly a blue cloisonné
perfume flask with ferns and peacocks on it. "Hey," she said, "this sure is cute. I
like thing-daddies like this here." But very abruptly she got bored and said,
"Let's talk instead. In the front room." I agreed, a little perplexed this time, because I had been about to show her a remarkable powder box that played *The
Blue Danube.* We went into the parlor, where Lottie looked at her image in the
pier glass for quite a while and with great absorption, as if she had never seen
herself before. Then she moved over to the window seat and knelt on it, looking
out at the front walk. She kept her hands in the pockets of her thin dark red
coat; once she took out one of her dirty paws to rub her nose for a minute and I
saw a bulge in that pocket, like a bunch of jackstones. I know now that it wasn't
jackstones, it was my mother's perfume flask; I thought at the time her hands
were cold and that that was why she kept them put away, for I had noticed that
she had no mittens.

Lottie did most of the talking, and while she talked, she never once looked   8
at me but kept her eyes fixed on the approach to our house. She told me that
her family had come to Adams a month before from Muskogee, Oklahoma,
where her father, before he got tuberculosis, had been a brakeman on the
Frisco. Now they lived down by Arapahoe Creek, on the west side of town, in
one of the cottages of a wretched settlement made up of people so poor and so
sick—for in nearly every ramshackle house someone was coughing himself to
death—that each time I went past I blushed with guilt because my shoes were
sound and my coat was warm and I was well. I wished that Lottie had not told
me where she lived, but she was not aware of any pathos in her family's situation, and, indeed, it was with a certain boastfulness that she told me her mother
was the short-order cook at the Comanche Café (she pronounced this word in
one syllable), which I knew was the dirtiest, darkest, smelliest place in town, patronized by coal miners who never washed their faces and sometimes had such
dangerous fights after drinking dago red that the sheriff had to come. Laughing, Lottie told me that her mother was half Indian, and, laughing even harder,
she said that her brother didn't have any brains and had never been to school.
She herself was eleven years old, but she was only in the third grade, because
teachers had always had it in for her—making her go to the blackboard and all
like that when she was tired. She hated school—she went to Ashton, on North
Hill, and that was why I had never seen her, for I went to Carlyle Hill—and she
especially hated the teacher, Miss Cudahy, who had a head shaped like a pine
cone and who had killed several people with her ruler. Lottie loved the movies
("Not them Western ones or the ones with apes in," she said. "Ones about hugging and kissing. I love it when they die in that big old soft bed with the curtains up top, and he comes in and says 'Don't leave me, Marguerite de la Mar'"),
and she loved to ride in cars. She loved Mr. Goodbars, and if there was one
thing she despised worse than another it was tapioca. ("Pa calls it fish eyes. He
calls it floating island horse spit. He's a big piece of cheese. I hate him.") She did
not like cats (Muff was now sitting on the mantelpiece, glaring like an owl); she

kind of liked snakes—except cottonmouths and rattlers—because she found them kind of funny; she had once seen a goat eat a tin can. She said that one of these days she would take me downtown—it was a slowpoke town, she said, a one-horse burg (I had never heard such gaudy, cynical talk and was trying to memorize it all)—if I would get some money for the trolley fare; she hated to walk, and I ought to be proud that she had walked all the way from Arapahoe Creek today for the sole solitary purpose of seeing me.

Seeing our freshly baked dessert in the window was a more likely story, but I 9 did not care, for I was deeply impressed by this bold, sassy girl from Oklahoma and greatly admired the poise with which she aired her prejudices. Lottie Jump was certainly nothing to look at. She was tall and made of skin and bones; she was evilly ugly, and her clothes were a disgrace, not just ill-fitting and old and ragged but dirty, unmentionably so; clearly she did not wash much or brush her teeth, which were notched like a saw, and small and brown (it crossed my mind that perhaps she chewed tobacco); her long, lank hair looked as if it might have nits. But she had personality. She made me think of one of those self-contained dogs whose home is where his handout is and who travels alone but, if it suits him to, will become the leader of a pack. She was aloof, never looking at me, but amiable in the way she kept calling me "kid." I liked her enormously, and presently I told her so.

At this, she turned around and smiled at me. Her smile was the smile of a 10 jack-o'-lantern—high, wide, and handsome. When it was over, no trace of it remained. "Well, that's keen, kid, and I like you, too," she said in her downright Muskogee accent. She gave me a long, appraising look. Her eyes were the color of mud. "Listen, kid, how much do you like me?"

"I like you loads, Lottie," I said. "Better than anybody else, and I'm not kid- 11 ding."

"You want to be pals?" 12

"Do I!" I cried. So *there*, Virgil Meade, you big fat hootnanny, I thought. 13

"All right, kid, we'll be pals." And she held out her hand for me to shake. I 14 had to go and get it, for she did not alter her position on the window seat. It was a dry, cold hand, and the grip was severe, with more a feeling of bones in it than friendliness.

Lottie turned and scanned our path and scanned the sidewalk beyond, and 15 then she said, in a lower voice, "Do you know how to lift?"

"Lift?" I wondered if she meant to lift *her*. I was sure I could do it, since she 16 was so skinny, but I couldn't imagine why she would want me to.

"Shoplift, I mean. Like in the five-and-dime." 17

I did not know the term, and Lottie scowled at my stupidity. 18

"*Steal*, for crying in the beer!" she said impatiently. This she said so loudly 19 that Muff jumped down from the mantel and left the room in contempt.

I was thrilled to death and shocked to pieces. "Stealing is a sin," I said. "You 20 get put in jail for it."

"Ish ka bibble! I should worry if it's a sin or not," said Lottie, with a shrug. 21 "And they'll never put a smart old whatsis like *me* in jail. It's fun, stealing is— it's a picnic. I'll teach you if you want to learn, kid." Shamelessly she winked at me and grinned again. (That grin! She could have taken it off her face and put it on the table.) And she added, "If you don't, we can't be pals, because lifting is the only kind of playing I like. I hate those dumb games like Statues. Kick-the-Can—phooey!"

I was torn between agitation (I went to Sunday school and knew already 22 about morality; Judge Bay, a crabby old man who loved to punish sinners, was a friend of my father's and once had given Jack a lecture on the criminal mind when he came to call and found Jack looking up an answer in his arithmetic book) and excitement over the daring invitation to misconduct myself in so perilous a way. My life, on reflection, looked deadly prim; all I'd ever done to vary the monotony of it was to swear. I knew that Lottie Jump meant what she said—that I could have her friendship only on her terms (plainly, she had gone it alone for a long time and could go it alone for the rest of her life)—and although I trembled like an aspen and my heart went pitapat, I said, "I want to be pals with you, Lottie."

"All right, Vanderpool," said Lottie, and got off the window seat. "I wouldn't 23 go braggin' about it if I was you. I wouldn't go telling my ma and pa and the next-door neighbor that you and Lottie Jump are going down to the five-and-dime next Saturday aft and lift us some nice rings and garters and things like that. I mean it, kid." And she drew the back of her forefinger across her throat and made a dire face.

"I won't. I promise I won't. My *gosh*, why would I?" 24

"That's the ticket," said Lottie, with a grin. "I'll meet you at the trolley shel- 25 ter at two o'clock. You have the money. For both down and up. I ain't going to climb up that ornery hill after I've had my fun."

"Yes, Lottie," I said. Where was I going to get twenty cents? I was going to 26 have to start stealing before she even taught me how. Lottie was facing the center of the room, but she had eyes in the back of her head, and she whirled around back to the window; my mother and Tess were turning in our front path.

"Back way," I whispered, and in a moment Lottie was gone; the swinging 27 door that usually squeaked did not make a sound as she vanished through it. I listened and I never heard the back door open and close. Nor did I hear her, in a split second, lift the glass cover and remove that cake designed to feed six people.

I was restless and snappish between Wednesday afternoon and Saturday. 28 When Mother found the cake was gone, she scolded me for not keeping my ears cocked. She assumed, naturally, that a tramp had taken it, for she knew I hadn't eaten it; I never ate anything if I could help it (except for raw potatoes, which I loved) and had been known as a problem feeder from the beginning of my life. At first it occurred to me to have a tantrum and bring her around to my point of view: my tantrums scared the living daylights out of her because my veins stood out and I turned blue and couldn't get my breath. But I rejected this for a more sensible plan. I said, "It just so happens I didn't hear anything. But if I had, I suppose you wish I had gone out in the kitchen and let the robber cut me up into a million little tiny pieces with his sword. You wouldn't even bury me. You'd just put me on the dump. *I* know who's wanted in this family and who isn't." Tears of sorrow, not of anger, came in powerful tides and I groped blindly to the bedroom I shared with Stella, where I lay on my bed and shook with big, silent *weltschmerzlich* sobs. Mother followed me immediately, and so did Tess, and both of them comforted me and told me how much they loved me. I said they didn't; they said they did. Presently, I got a headache, as I always did when I cried, so I got to have an aspirin and a cold cloth on my head, and when Jack and Stella came home they had to be quiet. I heard Jack say, "Emily Vanderpool is the biggest polecat in the U.S.A. Whyn't she go in the kitchen and say, 'Hands up'? He woulda lit out." And Mother said, "Sh-h-h! You don't want your sister to be sick, do you?" Muff, not realizing that Lottie had replaced her, came in and curled up at my thigh, purring lustily; I found myself glad that she had left the room before Lottie Jump made her proposition to me, and in gratitude I stroked her unattractive head.

Other things happened. Mother discovered the loss of her perfume flask 29 and talked about nothing else at meals for two whole days. Luckily, it did not occur to her that it had been stolen—she simply thought she had mislaid it—but her monomania got on my father's nerves and he lashed out at her and at the rest of us. And because I was the cause of it all and my conscience was after me with red-hot pokers, I finally *had* to have a tantrum. I slammed my fork down in the middle of supper on the second day and yelled, "If you don't stop fighting, I'm going to kill myself. Yammer, yammer, nag, nag!" And I put my fingers in my ears and squeezed my eyes tight shut and screamed so the whole county could hear, "Shut *up!*" And then I lost my breath and began to turn blue. Daddy hastily apologized to everyone, and Mother said she was sorry for carrying on so about a trinket that had nothing but sentimental value—she was just vexed with herself for being careless, that was all, and she wasn't going to say another word about it.

I never heard so many references to stealing and cake, and even to Okla- 30 homa (ordinarily no one mentioned Oklahoma once in a month of Sundays) and the ten-cent store as I did throughout those next days. I myself once made a ghastly slip and said something to Stella about "the five-and-dime." "The five-and-*dime!*" she exclaimed. "Where'd you get *that* kind of talk? Do you by any chance have reference to the *ten-cent store?*"

The worst of all was Friday night—the very night before I was to meet Lot- 31 tie Jump—when Judge Bay came to play two-handed pinochle with Daddy. The Judge, a giant in intimidating haberdashery—for some reason, the white piping on his vest bespoke, for me, handcuffs and prison bars—and with an aura of disapproval for almost everything on earth except what pertained directly to himself, was telling Daddy, before they began their game, about the infamous vandalism that had been going on among the college students. "I have reason to believe that there are girls in this gang as well as boys," he said. "They ransack vacant houses and take everything. In one house on Pleasant Street, up there by the Catholic Church, there wasn't anything to take, so they took the kitchen sink. Wasn't a question of taking everything *but*—they took the kitchen sink."

"What ever would they want with a kitchen sink?" asked my mother.   32

"Mischief," replied the Judge. "If we ever catch them and if they come   33
within my jurisdiction, I can tell you I will give them no quarter. A thief, in my opinion, is the lowest of the low."

Mother told about the chocolate cake. By now, the fiction was so factual in   34
my mind that each time I thought of it I saw a funny-paper bum in baggy pants held up by rope, a hat with holes through which tufts of hair stuck up, shoes from which his toes protruded, a disreputable stubble on his face; he came up beneath the open window where the devil's food was cooling and he stole it and hotfooted it for the woods, where his companion was frying a small fish in a beat-up skillet. It never crossed my mind any longer that Lottie Jump had hooked that delicious cake.

Judge Bay was properly impressed. "If you will steal a chocolate cake, if you   35
will steal a kitchen sink, you will steal diamonds and money. The small child who pilfers a penny from his mother's pocketbook has started down a path that may lead him to holding up a bank."

It was a good thing I had no homework that night, for I could not possibly   36
have concentrated. We were all sent to our rooms, because the pinochle players had to have absolute quiet. I spent the evening doing cross-stitch. I was making a bureau runner for a Christmas present; as in the case of the Christmas card, I had no one to give it to, but now I decided to give it to Lottie Jump's mother. Stella was reading *Black Beauty*, crying. It was an interminable evening. Stella went to bed first; I saw to that, because I didn't want her lying there awake listening to me talking in my sleep. Besides, I didn't want her to see me tearing open the cardboard box—the one in the shape of a church, which held my Christmas Sunday-school offering. Over the door of the church was this shaming legend: "My mite for the poor widow." When Stella had begun to grind her teeth in her first deep sleep, I took twenty cents away from the poor widow, whoever she was (the owner of the kitchen sink, no doubt), for the trolley fare, and secreted it and the remaining three pennies in the pocket of my middy. I wrapped the money well in a handkerchief and buttoned the pocket and hung my skirt over the middy. And then I tore the paper church into bits—the heavens opened and Judge Bay came toward me with a double-barrelled shotgun— and hid the bits under a pile of pajamas. I did not sleep one wink. Except that I must have, because of the stupendous nightmares that kept wrenching the flesh of my skeleton and caused me to come close to perishing of thirst; once I fell out of bed and hit my head on Stella's ice skates. I would have waked her up and given her a piece of my mind for leaving them in such a lousy place, but then I remembered: I wanted *no* commotion of any kind.

I couldn't eat breakfast and I couldn't eat lunch. Old Johnny-on-the-spot   37
Jack kept saying, "*Poor* Polecat. Polecat wants her fish for dinner." Mother made an abortive attempt to take my temperature. And when all that hullabaloo sub-

sided, I was nearly in the soup because Mother asked me to mind Tess while she went to the sanitarium to see Mrs. Rogers, who, all of a sudden, was too sick to have anyone but grownups near her. Stella couldn't stay with the baby, because she had to go to ballet, and Jack couldn't, because he had to go up to the mesa and empty his traps. ("No, they *can't* wait. You want my skins to rot in this hot-one-day-cold-the-next weather?") I was arguing and whining when the telephone rang. Mother went to answer it and came back with a look of great sadness; Mrs. Rogers, she had learned, had had another hemorrhage. So Mother would not be going to the sanitarium after all and I needn't stay with Tess.

By the time I left the house, I was as cross as a bear. I felt awful about the 38 widow's mite and I felt awful for being mean about staying with Tess, for Mrs. Rogers was a kind old lady, in a cozy blue hug-me-tight and an old-fangled boudoir cap, dying here all alone; she was a friend of Grandma's and had lived just down the street from her in Missouri, and all in the world Mrs. Rogers wanted to do was go back home and lie down in her own big bedroom in her own big, high-ceilinged house and have Grandma and other members of the Eastern Star come in from time to time to say hello. But they wouldn't let her go home; they were going to kill or cure her. I could not help feeling that my hardness of heart and evil of intention had had a good deal to do with her new crisis; right at the very same minute I had been saying "Does that old Mrs. Methuselah *always* have to spoil my fun?" the poor wasted thing was probably coughing up her blood and saying to the nurse, "Tell Emily Vanderpool not to mind me, she can run and play."

———

I had a bad character, I know that, but my badness never gave me half the 39 enjoyment Jack and Stella thought it did. A good deal of the time I wanted to eat lye. I was certainly having no fun now, thinking of Mrs. Rogers and of depriving that poor widow of bread and milk; what if this penniless woman without a husband had a dog to feed, too? Or a baby? And besides, I didn't want to go downtown to steal anything from the ten-cent store; I didn't want to see Lottie Jump again—not really, for I knew in my bones that the girl was trouble with a capital "T." And still, in our short meeting she had mesmerized me; I would think about her style of talking and the expert way she had made off with the perfume flask and the cake (how had she carried the cake through the streets without being noticed?) and be bowled over, for the part of me that did not love God was a black-hearted villain. And apart from these considerations, I had some sort of idea that if I did not keep my appointment with Lottie Jump, she would somehow get revenge; she had seemed a girl of purpose. So, revolted and fascinated, brave and lily-livered, I plodded along through the snow in my flopping galoshes up toward the Chautauqua, where the trolley stop was. On my way, I passed Virgil Meade's house; there was not just a snowman, there was a whole snow family in the backyard, and Virgil himself was throwing a stick for his dog. I was delighted to see that he was alone.

Lottie, who was sitting on a bench in the shelter eating a Mr. Goodbar,   40
looked the same as she had the other time except that she was wearing an amazing hat. I think I had expected her to have a black handkerchief over the lower
part of her face or to be wearing a Jesse James waistcoat. But I had never
thought of a hat. It was felt; it was the color of cooked meat; it had some flowers
appliquéd on the front of it; it had no brim, but rose straight up to a very considerable height, like a monument. It sat so low on her forehead and it was so
tight that it looked, in a way, like part of her.

"How's every little thing, bub?" she said, licking her candy wrapper.   41

"Fine, Lottie," I said, freshly awed.   42

A silence fell. I drank some water from the drinking fountain, sat down, fas-   43
tened my galoshes, and unfastened them again.

"My mother's teeth grow wrong way too," said Lottie, and showed me what   44
she meant: the lower teeth were in front of the upper ones. "That so-called trolley car takes its own sweet time. This town is blah."

To save the honor of my home town, the trolley came scraping and groan-   45
ing up the hill just then, its bell clanging with an idiotic frenzy, and ground to a
stop. Its broad, proud cowcatcher was filled with dirty snow, in the middle of
which rested a tomato can, put there, probably, by somebody who was bored to
death and couldn't think of anything else to do—I did a lot of pointless things
like that on lonesome Saturday afternoons. It was the custom of this trolley car,
a rather mysterious one, to pause at the shelter for five minutes while the con-
ductor, who was either Mr. Jansen or Mr. Peck, depending on whether it was the
A.M. run or the P.M., got out and stretched and smoked and spit. Sometimes the
passengers got out, too, acting like sightseers whose destination was this sturdy
stucco gazebo instead of, as it really was, the Piggly Wiggly or the Nelson Dry.
You expected them to take snapshots of the drinking fountain or of the Chautauqua meeting house up on the hill. And when they all got back in the car, you
expected them to exchange intelligent observations on the aborigines and the
ruins they had seen.

Today there were no passengers, and as soon as Mr. Peck got out and began   46
staring at the mountains as if he had never seen them before while he made
himself a cigarette, Lottie, in her tall hat (was it something like the Inspector's
hat in the Katzenjammer Kids?), got into the car, motioning me to follow. I put
our nickels in the empty box and joined her on the very last double seat. It was
only then that she mapped out the plan for the afternoon, in a low but still in-
souciant voice. The hat—she did not apologize for it, she simply referred to it
as "my hat"—was to be the repository of whatever we stole. In the future, it
would be advisable for me to have one like it. (How? Surely it was unique. The
flowers, I saw on closer examination, were tulips, but they were blue, and a very
unsettling shade of blue.) I was to engage a clerk on one side of the counter,
asking her the price of, let's say, a tube of Daggett & Ramsdell vanishing cream,
while Lottie would lift a round comb or a barrette or a hair net or whatever on
the other side. Then, at a signal, I would decide against the vanishing cream and
would move on to the next counter that she indicated. The signal was interest-

ing; it was to be the raising of her hat from the rear—"like I've got the itch and gotta scratch," she said. I was relieved that I was to have no part in the actual stealing, and I was touched that Lottie, who was going to do all the work, said we would "go halvers" on the take. She asked me if there was anything in particular I wanted—she herself had nothing special in mind and was going to shop around first—and I said I would like some rubber gloves. This request was entirely spontaneous; I had never before in my life thought of rubber gloves in one way or another, but a psychologist—or Judge Bay—might have said that this was most significant and that I was planning at that moment to go on from petty larceny to bigger game, armed with a weapon on which I wished to leave no fingerprints.

On the way downtown, quite a few people got on the trolley, and they all gave us such peculiar looks that I was chickenhearted until I realized it must be Lottie's hat they were looking at. No wonder. I kept looking at it myself out of the corner of my eye; it was like a watermelon standing on end. No, it was like a tremendous test tube. On this trip—a slow one, for the trolley pottered through that part of town in a desultory, neighborly way, even going into areas where no one lived—Lottie told me some of the things she had stolen in Muskogee and here in Adams. They included a white satin prayer book (think of it!), Mr. Goodbars by the thousands (she had probably never paid for a Mr. Goodbar in her life), a dinner ring valued at two dollars, a strawberry emery, several cans of corn, some shoelaces, a set of poker chips, countless pencils, four spark plugs ("Pa had this old car, see, and it was broke, so we took 'er to get fixed; I'll build me a radio with 'em sometime—you know? Listen in on them ear muffs to Tulsa?"), a Boy Scout knife, and a Girl Scout folding cup. She made a regular practice of going through the pockets of the coats in the cloakroom every day at recess, but she had never found anything there worth a red cent and was about to give that up. Once, she had taken a gold pencil from a teacher's desk and had got caught—she was sure that this was one of the reasons she was only in the third grade. Of this unjust experience, she said, "The old hoot owl! If I was drivin' in a car on a lonesome stretch and she was settin' beside me, I'd wait till we got to a pile of gravel and then I'd stop and say, 'Git out, Miss Priss.' She'd git out, all right."

Since Lottie was so frank, I was emboldened at last to ask her what she had done with the cake. She faced me with her grin; this grin, in combination with the hat, gave me a surprise from which I have never recovered. "I ate it up," she said. "I went in your garage and sat on your daddy's old tires and ate it. It was pretty good."

There were two ten-cent stores side by side in our town, Kresge's and Woolworth's, and as we walked down the main street toward them, Lottie played with a Yo-Yo. Since the street was thronged with Christmas shoppers and farmers in for Saturday, this was no ordinary accomplishment; all in all, Lottie Jump was someone to be reckoned with. I cannot say that I was proud to be seen with her; the fact is that I hoped I would not meet anyone I knew, and I thanked my lucky stars that Jack was up in the hills with his dead skunks because if he had seen her with that lid and that Yo-Yo, I would never have heard the last of it. But in another way I *was* proud to be with her; in a smaller hemisphere, in one that included only her and me, I was swaggering—I felt like Somebody, marching along beside this lofty Somebody from Oklahoma who was going to hold up the dime store.

There is nothing like Woolworth's at Christmastime. It smells of peanut 50 brittle and terrible chocolate candy, Djer-Kiss talcum powder and Ben Hur Perfume—smells sourly of tinsel and waxily of artificial poinsettias. The crowds are made up largely of children and women, with here and there a deliberative old man; the women are buying ribbons and wrappings and Christmas cards, and the children are buying asbestos pot holders for their mothers and, for their fathers, suede bookmarks with a burnt-in design that says "A good book is a good friend" or "Souvenir from the Garden of the Gods." It is very noisy. The salesgirls are forever ringing their bells and asking the floorwalker to bring them change for a five; babies in go-carts are screaming as parcels fall on their heads; the women, waving rolls of red tissue paper, try to attract the attention of the harried girl behind the counter. ("Miss! All I want is this one batch of the red. Can't I just give you the dime?" And the girl, beside herself, mottled with vexation, cries back, "Has to be rung up, Moddom, that's the rule.") There is pandemonium at the toy counter, where things are being tested by the customers—wound up, set off, tooted, pounded, made to say "Maaaah!-Maaaah!" There is very little gaiety in the scene and, in fact, those baffled old men look as if they were walking over their own dead bodies, but there is an atmosphere of carnival, nevertheless, and as soon as Lottie and I entered the doors of Woolworth's golden-and-vermilion bedlam, I grew giddy and hot—not pleasantly so. The feeling, indeed, was distinctly disagreeable, like the beginning of a stomach upset.

Lottie gave me a nudge and said softly, "Go look at the envelopes. I want 51 some rubber bands."

This counter was relatively uncrowded (the seasonal stationery supplies— 52 the Christmas cards and wrapping paper and stickers—were at a separate counter), and I went around to examine some very beautiful letter paper; it was pale pink and it had a border of roses all around it. The clerk here was a cheerful middle-aged woman wearing an apron, and she was giving all her attention to a seedy old man who could not make up his mind between mucilage and paste. "Take your time, Dad," she said. "Compared to the rest of the girls, I'm on my vacation." The old man, holding a tube in one hand and a bottle in the other, looked at her vaguely and said, "I want it for stamps. Sometimes I write a letter and stamp it and then don't mail it and steam the stamp off. Must have ninety cents' worth of stamps like that." The woman laughed. "I know what you mean," she said. "I get mad and write a letter and then I tear it up." The old man gave her a condescending look and said, "That so? But I don't suppose yours are of a political nature." He bent his gaze again to the choice of adhesives.

This first undertaking was duck soup for Lottie. I did not even have to ex- 53 change a word with the woman; I saw Miss Fagin lift up *that hat* and give me the high sign, and we moved away, she down one aisle and I down the other, now and again catching a glimpse of each other through the throngs. We met at the foot of the second counter, where notions were sold.

"Fun, huh?" said Lottie, and I nodded, although I felt wholly dreary. "I want 54 some crochet hooks," she said. "Price the rickrack."

This time the clerk was adding up her receipts and did not even look at me 55 or at a woman who was angrily and in vain trying to buy a paper of pins. Out went Lottie's scrawny hand, up went her domed chimney. In this way for some time she bagged sitting birds: a tea strainer (there was no one at all at that counter), a box of Mrs. Carpenter's All Purpose Nails, the rubber gloves I had said I wanted, and four packages of mixed seeds. Now you have some idea of the size of Lottie Jump's hat.

I was nervous, not from being her accomplice but from being in this crowd 56 on an empty stomach, and I was getting tired—we had been in the store for at least an hour—and the whole enterprise seemed pointless. There wasn't a thing in her hat I wanted—not even the rubber gloves. But in exact proportion as my spirits descended, Lottie's rose; clearly she had only been target-practicing and now she was moving in for the kill.

We met beside the books of paper dolls, for reconnaissance. "I'm gonna get 57 me a pair of pearl beads," said Lottie. "You go fuss with the hairpins, hear?"

Luck, combined with her skill, would have stayed with Lottie, and her hat 58 would have been a cornucopia by the end of the afternoon if, at the very moment her hand went out for the string of beads, that idiosyncrasy of mine had not struck me full force. I had never known it to come with so few preliminaries; probably this was so because I was oppressed by all the masses of bodies poking and pushing me, and all the open mouths breathing in my face. Anyhow, right then, at the crucial time, I *had to be alone.*

I stood staring down at the bone hairpins for a moment, and when the girl 59 behind the counter said, "What kind does Mother want, hon? What color is Mother's hair?" I looked past her and across at Lottie and I said, "Your brother isn't the only one in your family that doesn't have any brains." The clerk, astonished, turned to look where I was looking and caught Lottie in the act of lifting up her hat to put the pearls inside. She had unwisely chosen a long strand and was having a little trouble; I had the nasty thought that it looked as if her brains were leaking out.

The clerk, not able to deal with this emergency herself, frantically punched 60 her bell and cried, "Floorwalker! Mr. Bellamy! I've caught a thief!"

Momentarily there was a violent hush—then such a clamor as you have 61 never heard. Bells rang, babies howled, crockery crashed to the floor as people stumbled in their rush to the arena.

Mr. Bellamy, nineteen years old but broad of shoulder and jaw, was instantly 62 standing beside Lottie, holding her arm with one hand while with the other he removed her hat to reveal to the overjoyed audience that incredible array of merchandise. Her hair all wild, her face a mask of innocent bewilderment, Lottie Jump, the scurvy thing, pretended to be deaf and dumb. She pointed at the rubber gloves and then she pointed at me, and Mr. Bellamy, able at last to prove his mettle, said "Aha!" and, still holding Lottie, moved around the counter to me and grabbed *my* arm. He gave the hat to the clerk and asked her kindly to accompany him and his red-handed catch to the manager's office.

I don't know where Lottie is now—whether she is on the stage or in jail. If 63
her performance after our arrest meant anything, the first is quite as likely as the second. (I never saw her again, and for all I know she lit out of town that night on a freight train. Or perhaps her whole family decamped as suddenly as they had arrived; ours was a most transient population. You can be sure I made no attempt to find her again, and for months I avoided going anywhere near Arapahoe Creek or North Hill.) She never said a word but kept making signs with her fingers, ad-libbing the whole thing. They tested her hearing by shooting off a popgun right in her ear and she never batted an eyelid.

They called up my father, and he came over from the Safeway on the double. 64
I heard very little of what he said because I was crying so hard, but one thing I did hear him say was "Well young lady, I guess you've seen to it that I'll have to part company with my good friend Judge Bay." I tried to defend myself, but it was useless. The manager, Mr. Bellamy, the clerk, and my father patted Lottie on the shoulder, and the clerk said, "Poor afflicted child." For being a poor, afflicted child, they gave her a bag of hard candy, and she gave them the most fraudulent smile of gratitude, and slobbered a little, and shuffled out, holding her empty hat in front of her like a beggar-man. I hate Lottie Jump to this day, but I have to hand it to her—she was a genius.

The floorwalker would have liked to see me sentenced to the reform school 65
for life, I am sure, but the manager said that considering this was my first offense, he would let my father attend to my punishment. The old-maid clerk, who looked precisely like Emmy Schmalz, clucked her tongue and shook her head at me. My father hustled me out of the office and out of the store and into the car and home, muttering the entire time; now and again I'd hear the words "morals" and "nowadays."

What's the use of telling the rest? You know what happened. Daddy on sec- 66
ond thoughts decided not to hang his head in front of Judge Bay but to make use of his friendship in this time of need, and he took me to see the scary old curmudgeon at his house. All I remember of that long declamation, during which the Judge sat behind his desk never taking his eyes off me, was the warning "I want you to give this a great deal of thought, Miss. I want you to search and seek in the innermost corners of your conscience and root out every bit of badness." Oh, *him!* Why, listen, if I'd rooted out all the badness in me, there wouldn't have been anything left of me. My mother cried for days because she had nurtured an outlaw and was ashamed to show her face at the neighborhood store; my father was silent, and he often looked at me. Stella, who was a prig,

said, "And to think you did it at *Christmas*time!" As for Jack—well, Jack a couple of times did not know how close he came to seeing glory when I had a butcher knife in my hand. It was Polecat this and Polecat that until I nearly went off my rocker. Tess, of course, didn't know what was going on, and asked so many questions that finally I told her to go to Helen Hunt Jackson in a savage tone of voice.

Good old Muff.   67

It is not true that you don't learn by experience. At any rate, I did that time.   68 I began immediately to have two or three friends at a time—to be sure, because of the stigma on me, they were by no means the élite of Carlyle Hill Grade— and never again when that terrible need to be alone arose did I let fly. I would say, instead, "I've got a headache. I'll have to go home and take an aspirin," or "Gosh all hemlocks, I forgot—I've got to go to the dentist."

After the scandal died down, I got into the Campfire Girls. It was through   69 pull, of course, since Stella had been a respected member for two years and my mother was a friend of the leader. But it turned out all right. Even Muff did not miss our periods of companionship, because about that time she grew up and started having literally millions of kittens.

ACTIVITIES FOR WRITING AND DISCUSSION

1. How do you respond to Emily's character and behavior? Do you censure her? identify with her? both? Explain, and support your explanation with references to specific passages in the text. Then ask yourself the same questions about Lottie Jump.

2. Try rewriting part of the story as a series of diary entries by Emily. How does the story change if Emily is in the *midst* of the events she describes instead of looking back at them from a distance of time?

3. Study the story's language and style. Underline and annotate any phrases, sentences, or longer passages that strike or delight you, for whatever reasons. Then, in an essay, analyze several of these passages and articulate *why* they strike or delight you.

4. "Springboard" off this story in any of the following ways (or in another way of your own devising):
   a. Write a character biography of Lottie Jump that narrates her life before and/or after the events recounted in "Bad Characters."
   b. Invent an adolescent-aged character who, like Emily, can never keep a friend. Invent a reason for this problem. Then, using the **first-person point of view,** tell the character's story.
   c. Retell all or a part of the story from a different **point of view,** e.g., Lottie's, Virgil's, Stella's, or that of a **third-person** narrator who is not a character in the story.

After composing your piece, discuss any ways in which it enriched your experience of Stafford's story and its characters, language, or themes.

Louise Erdrich (b. 1954)

Saint Marie

Marie Lazarre

So when I went there, I knew the dark fish must rise. Plumes of radiance had 1
soldered on me. No reservation girl had ever prayed so hard. There was no use
in trying to ignore me any longer. I was going up there on the hill with the black
robe women. They were not any lighter than me. I was going up there to pray as
good as they could. Because I don't have that much Indian blood. And they
never thought they'd have a girl from this reservation as a saint they'd have to
kneel to. But they'd have me. And I'd be carved in pure gold. With ruby lips.
And my toenails would be little pink ocean shells, which they would have to
stoop down off their high horse to kiss.

I was ignorant. I was near age fourteen. The length of sky is just about the 2
size of my ignorance. Pure and wide. And it was just that—the pure and wide-
ness of my ignorance—that got me up the hill to Sacred Heart Convent and
brought me back down alive. For maybe Jesus did not take my bait, but them
Sisters tried to cram me right down whole.

You ever see a walleye strike so bad the lure is practically out its back end 3
before you reel it in? That is what they done with me. I don't like to make that
low comparison, but I have seen a walleye do that once. And it's the same attempt as Sister Leopolda made to get me in her clutch.

I had the mail-order Catholic soul you get in a girl raised out in the bush, 4
whose only thought is getting into town. For Sunday Mass is the only time
my aunt brought us children in except for school, when we were harnessed.
Our soul went cheap. We were so anxious to get there we would have walked
in on our hands and knees. We just craved going to the store, slinging bottle
caps in the dust, making fool eyes at each other. And of course we went to
church.

Where they have the convent is on top of the highest hill, so that from its 5
windows the Sisters can be looking into the marrow of the town. Recently a
windbreak was planted before the bar "for the purposes of tornado insurance."
Don't tell me that. That poplar stand was put up to hide the drinkers as they get
the transformation. As they are served into the beast of their burden. While
they're drinking, that body comes upon them, and then they stagger or crawl
out the bar door, pulling a weight they can't move past the poplars. They don't
want no holy witness to their fall.

Anyway, I climbed. That was a long-ago day. There was a road then for wag- 6
ons that wound in ruts to the top of the hill where they had their buildings of
painted brick. Gleaming white. So white the sun glanced off in dazzling display
to set forms whirling behind your eyelids. The face of God you could hardly
look at. But that day it drizzled, so I could look all I wanted. I saw the homelier
side. The cracked whitewash and swallows nesting in the busted ends of eaves. I
saw the boards sawed the size of broken windowpanes and the fruit trees,
stripped. Only the tough wild rhubarb flourished. Goldenrod rubbed up their
walls. It was a poor convent. I didn't see that then but I know that now. Compared to others it was humble, ragtag, out in the middle of no place. It was the
end of the world to some. Where the maps stopped. Where God had only half a
hand in the creation. Where the Dark One had put in thick bush, liquor, wild
dogs, and Indians.

I heard later that the Sacred Heart Convent was a catchall place for nuns 7
that don't get along elsewhere. Nuns that complain too much or lose their
mind. I'll always wonder now, after hearing that, where they picked up Sister
Leopolda. Perhaps she had scarred someone else, the way she left a mark on me.
Perhaps she was just sent around to test her Sisters' faith, here and there, like
the spot-checker in a factory. For she was the definite most-hard trial to anyone's endurance, even when they started out with veils of wretched love upon
their eyes.

I was that girl who thought the black hem of her garment would help me 8
rise. Veils of love which was only hate petrified by longing—that was me. I was
like those bush Indians who stole the holy black hat of a Jesuit and swallowed
little scraps of it to cure their fevers. But the hat itself carried smallpox and was
killing them with belief. Veils of faith! I had this confidence in Leopolda. She
was different. The other Sisters had long ago gone blank and given up on Satan.
He slept for them. They never noticed his comings and goings. But Leopolda
kept track of him and knew his habits, minds he burrowed in, deep spaces
where he hid. She knew as much about him as my grandma, who called him by
other names and was not afraid.

In her class, Sister Leopolda carried a long oak pole for opening high win- 9
dows. It had a hook made of iron on one end that could jerk a patch of your
hair out or throttle you by the collar—all from a distance. She used this deadly
hook-pole for catching Satan by surprise. He could have entered without your
knowing it—through your lips or your nose or any one of your seven openings—and gained your mind. But she would see him. That pole would brain
you from behind. And he would gasp, dazzled, and take the first thing she offered, which was pain.

She had a stringer of children who could only breathe if she said the word. I 10
was the worst of them. She always said the Dark One wanted me most of all,
and I believed this. I stood out. Evil was a common thing I trusted. Before sleep
sometimes he came and whispered conversation in the old language of the
bush. I listened. He told me things he never told anyone but Indians. I was privy
to both worlds of his knowledge. I listened to him, but I had confidence in
Leopolda. She was the only one of the bunch he even noticed.

There came a day, though, when Leopolda turned the tide with her hook- 11
pole.

It was a quiet day with everyone working at their desks, when I heard him. 12
He had sneaked into the closets in the back of the room. He was scratching
around, tasting crumbs in our pockets, stealing buttons, squirting his dark juice
in the linings and the boots. I was the only one who heard him, and I got bold. I
smiled. I glanced back and smiled and looked up at her sly to see if she had noticed. My heart jumped. For she was looking straight at me. And she sniffed.
She had a big stark bony nose stuck to the front of her face for smelling out
brimstone and evil thoughts. She had smelled him on me. She stood up. Tall,
pale, a blackness leading into the deeper blackness of the slate wall behind her.
Her oak pole had flown into her grip. She had seen me glance at the closet. Oh,
she knew. She knew just where he was. I watched her watch him in her mind's
eye. The whole class was watching now. She was staring, sizing, following his
scuffle. And all of a sudden she tensed down, posed on her bent kneesprings,
cocked her arm back. She threw the oak pole singing over my head, through
my braincloud. It cracked through the thin wood door of the back closet,
and the heavy pointed hook drove through his heart. I turned. She'd speared her
own black rubber overboot where he'd taken refuge in the tip of her darkest toe.

Something howled in my mind. Loss and darkness. I understood. I was to 13
suffer for my smile.

He rose up hard in my heart. I didn't blink when the pole cracked. My skull 14
was tough. I didn't flinch when she shrieked in my ear. I only shrugged at the
flowers of hell. He wanted me. More than anything he craved me. But then she
did the worst. She did what broke my mind to her. She grabbed me by the collar
and dragged me, feet flying, through the room and threw me in the closet with
her dead black overboot. And I was there. The only light was a crack beneath
the door. I asked the Dark One to enter into me and boost my mind. I asked
him to restrain my tears, for they was pushing behind my eyes. But he was
afraid to come back there. He was afraid of her sharp pole. And I was afraid of
Leopolda's pole for the first time, too. I felt the cold hook in my heart. How it
could crack through the door at any minute and drag me out, like a dead fish
on a gaff, drop me on the floor like a gutshot squirrel.

I was nothing. I edged back to the wall as far as I could. I breathed the chalk 15
dust. The hem of her full black cloak cut against my cheek. He had left me. Her
spear could find me any time. Her keen ears would aim the hook into the beat
of my heart.

What was that sound? 16

It filled the closet, filled it up until it spilled over, but I did not recognize the 17
crying wailing voice as mine until the door cracked open, brightness, and she
hoisted me to her camphor-smelling lips.

"He *wants* you," she said. "That's the difference. I give you love." 18

Love. The black hook. The spear singing through the mind. I saw that she 19
had tracked the Dark One to my heart and flushed him out into the open. So
now my heart was an empty nest where she could lurk.

Well, I was weak. I was weak when I let her in, but she got a foothold there. 20
Hard to dislodge as the year passed. Sometimes I felt him—the brush of dim
wings—but only rarely did his voice compel. It was between Marie and
Leopolda now, and the struggle changed. I began to realize I had been on the
wrong track with the fruits of hell. The real way to overcome Leopolda was this:
I'd get to heaven first. And then, when I saw her coming, I'd shut the gate. She'd
be out! That is why, besides the bowing and the scraping I'd be dealt, I wanted
to sit on the altar as a saint.

To this end, I went up on the hill. Sister Leopolda was the consecrated nun 21
who had sponsored me to come there.

"You're not vain," she said. "You're too honest, looking into the mirror, for 22
that. You're not smart. You don't have the ambition to get clear. You have two
choices. One, you can marry a no-good Indian, bear his brats, die like a dog. Or
two, you can give yourself to God."

"I'll come up there," I said, "but not because of what you think." 23

I could have had any damn man on the reservation at the time. And I could 24
have made him treat me like his own life. I looked good. And I looked white.
But I wanted Sister Leopolda's heart. And here was the thing: sometimes I
wanted her heart in love and admiration. Sometimes. And sometimes I wanted
her heart to roast on a black stick.

She answered the back door where they had instructed me to call. I stood there 25
with my bundle. She looked me up and down.

"All right," she said finally. "Come in." 26

She took my hand. Her fingers were like a bundle of broom straws, so thin 27
and dry, but the strength of them was unnatural. I couldn't have tugged loose if
she was leading me into rooms of white-hot coal. Her strength was a kind of
perverse miracle, for she got it from fasting herself thin. Because of this hunger
practice her lips were a wounded brown and her skin deadly pale. Her eye sock-
ets were two deep lashless hollows in a taut skull. I told you about the nose already. It stuck out far and made the place her eyes moved even deeper, as if she
stared out the wrong end of a gun barrel. She took the bundle from my hands
and threw it in the corner.

"You'll be sleeping behind the stove, child." 28

It was immense, like a great furnace. There was a small cot close behind it. 29

"Looks like it could get warm there," I said. 30

"Hot. It does." 31

"Do I get a habit?" 32

I wanted something like the thing she wore. Flowing black cotton. Her face 33
was strapped in white bandages, and a sharp crest of starched white cardboard
hung over her forehead like a glaring beak. If possible, I wanted a bigger, longer,
whiter beak than hers.

"No," she said, grinning her great skull grin. "You don't get one yet. Who 34
knows, you might not like us. Or we might not like you."

But she had loved me, or offered me love. And she had tried to hunt the 35
Dark One down. So I had this confidence.

"I'll inherit your keys from you," I said.   36

She looked at me sharply, and her grin turned strange. She hissed, taking in 37
her breath. Then she turned to the door and took a key from her belt. It was a
giant key, and it unlocked the larder where the food was stored.

Inside there was all kinds of good stuff. Things I'd tasted only once or twice 38
in my life. I saw sticks of dried fruit, jars of orange peel, spice like cinnamon. I
saw tins of crackers with ships painted on the side. I saw pickles. Jars of herring
and the rind of pigs. There was cheese, a big brown block of it from the thick
milk of goats. And besides that there was the everyday stuff, in great quantities,
the flour and the coffee.

It was the cheese that got to me. When I saw it my stomach hollowed. My 39
tongue dripped. I loved that goat-milk cheese better than anything I'd ever ate.
I stared at it. The rich curve in the buttery cloth.

"When you inherit my keys," she said sourly, slamming the door in my face, 40
"you can eat all you want of the priest's cheese."

Then she seemed to consider what she'd done. She looked at me. She took 41
the key from her belt and went back, sliced a hunk off, and put it in my hand.

"If you're good you'll taste this cheese again. When I'm dead and gone," she 42
said.

Then she dragged out the big sack of flour. When I finished that heaven 43
stuff she told me to roll my sleeves up and begin doing God's labor. For a while
we worked in silence, mixing up the dough and pounding it out on stone slabs.

"God's work," I said after a while. "If this is God's work, then I've done it all 44
my life."

"Well, you've done it with the Devil in your heart then," she said. "Not God." 45

"How do you know?" I asked. But I knew she did. And I wished I had not 46
brought up the subject.

"I see right into you like a clear glass," she said. "I always did."   47

"You don't know it," she continued after a while, "but he's come around here 48
sulking. He's come around here brooding. You brought him in. He knows the
smell of me, and he's going to make a last ditch try to get you back. Don't let
him." She glared over at me. Her eyes were cold and lighted. "Don't let him
touch you. We'll be a long time getting rid of him."

So I was careful. I was careful not to give him an inch. I said a rosary, two 49
rosaries, three, underneath my breath. I said the Creed. I said every scrap of
Latin I knew while we punched the dough with our fists. And still, I dropped
the cup. It rolled under that monstrous iron stove, which was getting fired up
for baking.

And she was on me. She saw he'd entered my distraction.   50

"Our good cup," she said. "Get it out of there, Marie."   51

I reached for the poker to snag it out from beneath the stove. But I had a 52
sinking feel in my stomach as I did this. Sure enough, her long arm darted past
me like a whip. The poker lighted in her hand.

"Reach," she said. "Reach with your arm for that cup. And when your flesh is 53 hot, remember that the flames you feel are only one fraction of the heat you will feel in his hellish embrace."

She always did things this way, to teach you lessons. So I wasn't surprised. It 54 was playacting, anyway, because a stove isn't very hot underneath right along the floor. They aren't made that way. Otherwise a wood floor would burn. So I said yes and got down on my stomach and reached under. I meant to grab it quick and jump up again, before she could think up another lesson, but here it happened. Although I groped for the cup, my hand closed on nothing. That cup was nowhere to be found. I heard her step toward me, a slow step. I heard the creak of thick shoe leather, the little *plat* as the folds of her heavy skirts met, a trickle of fine sand sifting, somewhere, perhaps in the bowels of her, and I was afraid. I tried to scramble up, but her foot came down lightly behind my ear, and I was lowered. The foot came down more firmly at the base of my neck, and I was held.

"You're like I was," she said. "He wants you very much." 55

"He doesn't want me no more," I said. "He had his fill. I got the cup!" 56

I heard the valve opening, the hissed intake of breath, and knew that I 57 should not have spoke.

"You lie," she said. "You're cold. There is a wicked ice forming in your blood. 58 You don't have a shred of devotion for God. Only wild cold dark lust. I know it. I know how you feel. I see the beast . . . the beast watches me out of your eyes sometimes. Cold."

The urgent scrape of metal. It took a moment to know from where. Top of 59 the stove. Kettle. Lessons. She was steadying herself with the iron poker. I could feel it like pure certainty, driving into the wood floor. I would not remind her of pokers. I heard the water as it came, tipped from the spout, cooling as it fell but still scalding as it struck. I must have twitched beneath her foot, because she steadied me, and then the poker nudged up beside my arm as if to guide. "To warm your cold ash heart," she said. I felt how patient she would be. The water came. My mind went dead blank. Again. I could only think the kettle would be cooling slowly in her hand. I could not stand it. I bit my lip so as not to satisfy her with a sound. She gave me more reason to keep still.

"I will boil him from your mind if you make a peep," she said, "by filling up 60 your ear."

Any sensible fool would have run back down the hill the minute Leopolda let 61 them up from under her heel. But I was snared in her black intelligence by then. I could not think straight. I had prayed so hard I think I broke a cog in my mind. I prayed while her foot squeezed my throat. While my skin burst. I prayed even when I heard the wind come through, shrieking in the busted bird nests. I didn't stop when pure light fell, turning slowly behind my eyelids. God's face. Even that did not disrupt my continued praise. Words came. Words came from nowhere and flooded my mind.

Now I could pray much better than any one of them. Than all of them full 62
force. This was proved. I turned to her in a daze when she let me up. My
thoughts were gone, and yet I remember how surprised I was. Tears glittered in
her eyes, deep down, like the sinking reflection in a well.

"It was so hard, Marie," she gasped. Her hands were shaking. The kettle clat- 63
tered against the stove. "But I have used all the water up now. I think he is
gone."

"I prayed," I said foolishly. "I prayed very hard."   64

"Yes," she said. "My dear one, I know."   65

We sat together quietly because we had no more words. We let the dough rise 66
and punched it down once. She gave me a bowl of mush, unlocked the sausage
from a special cupboard, and took that in to the Sisters. They sat down the hall,
chewing their sausage, and I could hear them. I could hear their teeth bite
through their bread and meat. I couldn't move. My shirt was dry but the cloth
stuck to my back, and I couldn't think straight. I was losing the sense to understand how her mind worked. She'd gotten past me with her poker and I would
never be a saint. I despaired. I felt I had no inside voice, nothing to direct me,
no darkness, no Marie. I was about to throw that cornmeal mush out to the
birds and make a run for it, when the vision rose up blazing in my mind.

I was rippling gold. My breasts were bare and my nipples flashed and 67
winked. Diamonds tipped them. I could walk through panes of glass. I could
walk through windows. She was at my feet, swallowing the glass after each step
I took. I broke through another and another. The glass she swallowed ground
and cut until her starved insides were only a subtle dust. She coughed. She
coughed a cloud of dust. And then she was only a black rag that flapped off,
snagged in bobwire, hung there for an age, and finally rotted into the breeze.

I saw this, mouth hanging open, gazing off into the flagged boughs of trees. 68

"Get up!" she cried. "Stop dreaming. It is time to bake."   69

Two other Sisters had come in with her, wide women with hands like pad- 70
dles. They were evening and smoothing out the firebox beneath the great jaws
of the oven.

"Who is this one?" they asked Leopolda. "Is she yours?"   71

"She is mine," said Leopolda. "A very good girl."   72

"What is your name?" one asked me.   73

"Marie."   74

"Marie. Star of the Sea."   75

"She will shine," said Leopolda, "when we have burned off the dark corro- 76
sion."

The others laughed, but uncertainly. They were mild and sturdy French, 77
who did not understand Leopolda's twisted jokes, although they muttered re-
spectfully at things she said. I knew they wouldn't believe what she had done
with the kettle. There was no question. So I kept quiet.

"*Elle est docile,*" they said approvingly as they left to starch the linens. 78

"Does it pain?" Leopolda asked me as soon as they were out the door.   79

I did not answer. I felt sick with the hurt.   80

"Come along," she said.   81

The building was wholly quiet now. I followed her up the narrow staircase   82 into a hall of little rooms, many doors. Her cell was the quietest, at the very end. Inside, the air smelled stale, as if the door had not been opened for years. There was a crude straw mattress, a tiny bookcase with a picture of Saint Francis hanging over it, a ragged palm, a stool for sitting on, a crucifix. She told me to remove my blouse and sit on the stool. I did so. She took a pot of salve from the bookcase and began to smooth it upon my burns. Her hands made slow, wide circles, stopping the pain. I closed my eyes. I expected to see blackness. Peace. But instead the vision reared up again. My chest was still tipped with diamonds. I was walking through windows. She was chewing up the broken litter I left behind.

"I am going," I said. "Let me go."   83

But she held me down.   84

"Don't go," she said quickly. "Don't. We have just begun."   85

I was weakening. My thoughts were whirling pitifully. The pain had kept me   86 strong, and as it left me I began to forget it; I couldn't hold on. I began to wonder if she'd really scalded me with the kettle. I could not remember. To remember this seemed the most important thing in the world. But I was losing the memory. The scalding. The pouring. It began to vanish. I felt like my mind was coming off its hinge, flapping in the breeze, hanging by the hair of my own pain. I wrenched out of her grip.

"He was always in you," I said. "Even more than in me. He wanted you even   87 more. And now he's got you. Get thee behind me!"

I shouted that, grabbed my shirt, and ran through the door throwing the   88 cloth on my body. I got down the stairs and into the kitchen, even, but no matter what I told myself, I couldn't get out the door. It wasn't finished. And she knew I would not leave. Her quiet step was immediately behind me.

"We must take the bread from the oven now," she said.   89

She was pretending nothing happened. But for the first time I had gotten   90 through some chink she'd left in her darkness. Touched some doubt. Her voice was so low and brittle it cracked off at the end of her sentence.

"Help me, Marie," she said slowly.   91

But I was not going to help her, even though she had calmly buttoned the   92 back of my shirt up and put the big cloth mittens in my hands for taking out the loaves. I could have bolted for it then. But I didn't. I knew that something was nearing completion. Something was about to happen. My back was a wall of singing flame. I was turning. I watched her take the long fork in one hand, to tap the loaves. In the other hand she gripped the black poker to hook the pans.

"Help me," she said again, and I thought, Yes, this is part of it. I put the mit-   93 tens on my hands and swung the door open on its hinges. The oven gaped. She stood back a moment, letting the first blast of heat rush by. I moved behind her. I could feel the heat at my front and at my back. Before, behind. My skin was turning to beaten gold. It was coming quicker than I thought. The oven was like the gate of a personal hell. Just big enough and hot enough for one person, and that was her. One kick and Leopolda would fly in headfirst. And that would be one-millionth of the heat she would feel when she finally collapsed in his hellish embrace.

Saints know these numbers.   94

She bent forward with her fork held out. I kicked her with all my might. She   95
flew in. But the outstretched poker hit the back wall first, so she rebounded. The oven was not so deep as I had thought.

There was a moment when I felt a sort of thin, hot disappointment, as when   96
a fish slips off the line. Only I was the one going to be lost. She was fearfully silent. She whirled. Her veil had cutting edges. She had the poker in one hand. In the other she held that long sharp fork she used to tap the delicate crusts of loaves. Her face turned upside down on her shoulders. Her face turned blue. But saints are used to miracles. I felt no trace of fear.

If I was going to be lost, let the diamonds cut! Let her eat ground glass!   97

"Bitch of Jesus Christ!" I shouted. "Kneel and beg! Lick the floor!"   98

That was when she stabbed me through the hand with the fork, then took   99
the poker up alongside my head, and knocked me out.

It must have been a half an hour later when I came around. Things were so   100
strange. So strange I can hardly tell it for delight at the remembrance. For when I came around this was actually taking place. I was being worshiped. I had somehow gained the altar of a saint.

I was lying back on the stiff couch in the Mother Superior's office. I looked   101
around me. It was as though my deepest dream had come to life. The Sisters of the convent were kneeling to me. Sister Bonaventure. Sister Dympna. Sister Cecilia Saint-Claire. The two French with hands like paddles. They were down on their knees. Black capes were slung over some of their heads. My name was buzzing up and down the room, like a fat autumn fly lighting on the tips of their tongues between Latin, humming up the heavy blood-dark curtains, circling their little cosseted heads. Marie! Marie! A girl thrown in a closet. Who was afraid of a rubber overboot. Who was half overcome. A girl who came in the back door where they threw their garbage. Marie! Who never found the cup. Who had to eat their cold mush. Marie! Leopolda had her face buried in her knuckles. Saint Marie of the Holy Slops! Saint Marie of the Bread Fork! Saint Marie of the Burnt Back and Scalded Butt!

I broke out and laughed.   102

They looked up. All holy hell burst loose when they saw I'd woke. I still did   103
not understand what was happening. They were watching, talking, but not to me.

"The marks . . ."   104

"She has her hand closed."   105

"*Je ne peux pas voir.*"   106

I was not stupid enough to ask what they were talking about. I couldn't tell 107
why I was lying in white sheets. I couldn't tell why they were praying to me. But
I'll tell you this: it seemed entirely natural. It was me. I lifted up my hand as in
my dream. It was completely limp with sacredness.

"Peace be with you." 108

My arm was dried blood from the wrist down to the elbow. And it hurt. 109
Their faces turned like flat flowers of adoration to follow that hand's movements. I let it swing through the air, imparting a saint's blessing. I had practiced. I knew exactly how to act.

They murmured. I heaved a sigh, and a golden beam of light suddenly broke 110
through the clouded window and flooded down directly on my face. A stroke of
perfect luck! They had to be convinced.

Leopolda still knelt in the back of the room. Her knuckles were crammed 111
halfway down her throat. Let me tell you, a saint has senses honed keen as a
wolf. I knew that she was over my barrel now. How it happened did not matter.
The last thing I remembered was how she flew from the oven and stabbed me.
That one thing was most certainly true.

"Come forward, Sister Leopolda." I gestured with my heavenly wound. Oh, 112
it hurt. It bled when I reopened the slight heal. "Kneel beside me," I said.

She kneeled, but her voice box evidently did not work, for her mouth 113
opened, shut, opened, but no sound came out. My throat clenched in noble delight I had read of as befitting a saint. She could not speak. But she was beaten.
It was in her eyes. She stared at me now with all the deep hate of the wheel of
devilish dust that rolled wild within her emptiness.

"What is it you want to tell me?" I asked. And at last she spoke. 114

"I have told my Sisters of your passion," she managed to choke out. "How 115
the stigmata . . . the marks of the nails . . . appeared in your palm and you
swooned at the holy vision. . . ."

"Yes," I said curiously. 116

And then, after a moment, I understood. 117

Leopolda had saved herself with her quick brain. She had witnessed a mira- 118
cle. She had hid the fork and told this to the others. And of course they believed
her, because they never knew how Satan came and went or where he took
refuge.

"I saw it from the first," said the large one who put the bread in the oven. 119
"Humility of the spirit. So rare in these girls."

"I saw it, too," said the other one with great satisfaction. She sighed quietly. 120
"If only it was me."

Leopolda was kneeling bolt upright, face blazing and twitching, a barely 121
held fountain of blasting poison.

"Christ has marked me," I agreed. 122

I smiled the saint's smirk into her face. And then I looked at her. That was 123
my mistake.

For I saw her kneeling there. Leopolda with her soul like a rubber overboot. 124
With her face of a starved rat. With the desperate eyes drowning in the deep

wells of her wrongness. There would be no one else after me. And I would leave. I saw Leopolda kneeling within the shambles of her love.

My heart had been about to surge from my chest with the blackness of my 125 joyous heat. Now it dropped. I pitied her. I pitied her. Pity twisted in my stomach like that hook-pole was driven through me. I was caught. It was a feeling more terrible than any amount of boiling water and worse than being forked. Still, still, I could not help what I did. I had already smiled in a saint's mealy forgiveness. I heard myself speaking gently.

"Receive the dispensation of my sacred blood," I whispered.   126

But there was no heart in it. No joy when she bent to touch the floor. No 127 dark leaping. I fell back into the white pillows. Blank dust was whirling through the light shafts. My skin was dust. Dust my lips. Dust the dirty spoons on the ends of my feet.

Rise up! I thought. Rise up and walk! There is no limit to this dust!   128

Poems

JOHANN WOLFGANG VON GOETHE (1749–1832)

The Holy Longing

Tell a wise person, or else keep silent,
because the massman will mock it right away.
I praise what is truly alive,
what longs to be burned to death.

In the calm water of the love-nights,   5
where you were begotten, where you have begotten,
a strange feeling comes over you
when you see the silent candle burning.

Now you are no longer caught
in the obsession with darkness,   10
and a desire for higher love-making
sweeps you upward.

Distance does not make you falter,
now, arriving in magic, flying,
and, finally, insane for the light,   15
you are the butterfly and you are gone.

And so long as you haven't experienced
this: to die and so to grow,
you are only a troubled guest
on the dark earth.   20

—Translated by Robert Bly

ACTIVITIES FOR WRITING AND DISCUSSION

1. Analyze the central image of the poem: the burning candle sought by the moth or "butterfly." What, literally, is this image about, i.e., what natural phenomenon does it describe? In what ways might the image function as a **symbol** of a type of human experience?

2. The poem is rich in **paradoxes.** How can something be "truly alive" if it "longs to be burned to death"? How does one "grow" through dying? What are some examples of the sort of dying the speaker intends?

3. Invent a personal narrative written from the **point of view** of someone who has followed the advice ("to die and so to grow") given in the final stanza. Make up life stories about this person that show the process of growth through "dying."

THOMAS HARDY (1840–1928)

The Ruined Maid

"O 'mélia, my dear, this does everything crown!
Who could have supposed I should meet you in Town?
And whence such fair garments, such prosperi-ty?"—
"O didn't you know I'd been ruined?" said she.

—"You left us in tatters, without shoes or socks,   5
Tired of digging potatoes, and spudding up docks;
And now you've gay bracelets and bright feathers three!"—
"Yes: that's how we dress when we're ruined," said she.

—"At home in the barton you said 'thee' and 'thou,'
And 'thik oon,' and 'theäs oon,' and 't'other'; but now   10
Your talking quite fits 'ee for high compa-ny!"—
"Some polish is gained with one's ruin," said she.

—"Your hands were like paws then, your face blue and bleak
But now I'm bewitched by your delicate cheek,
And your little gloves fit as on any la-dy!"—   15
"We never do work when we're ruined," said she.

—"You used to call home-life a hag-ridden dream,
And you'd sigh, and you'd sock; but at present you seem
To know not of megrims or melancho-ly!"—
"True. One's pretty lively when ruined," said she.   20

—"I wish I had feathers, a fine sweeping gown,
And a delicate face, and could strut about Town!"—
"My dear—a raw country girl, such as you be,
Cannot quite expect that. You ain't ruined," said she.

ACTIVITIES FOR WRITING AND DISCUSSION

1. Review the material on **meter** in Chapter 13 and Appendix C. Then read
the poem aloud and determine its meter.

2. Consider the two speakers in the poem.

a. How would you characterize their **diction**—as formal or informal? as
abstract or **concrete**? as general or specific? as literal or **figurative**? Give
examples.

b. Based on the content and diction of their dialogue, what would you suppose the speakers' backgrounds to be? In what sort of environment did
they grow up? What is their social status?

3. How do you interpret the word "ruined" as it is used in the poem?

4. In poetry or prose, compose a prequel to the poem. That is, reconstruct
the events in the two speakers' lives that have brought them to this moment of
conversation. Embellish your narrative with additional details as needed, but
strive to remain faithful to the characters of the two women as set forth in the
poem.

C. P. CAVAFY (1863–1933)

The City

You said, "I will go to another land, I will go to another sea.
Another city will be found, a better one than this.

Every effort of mine is a condemnation of fate;

and my heart is—like a corpse—buried.   5
How long will my mind remain in this wasteland.

Wherever I turn my eyes, wherever I may look
I see black ruins of my life here,
where I spent so many years destroying and wasting."

You will find no new lands, you will find no other seas.

The city will follow you. You will roam the same   10

streets. And you will age in the same neighborhoods;

and you will grow gray in these same houses.
Always you will arrive in this city. Do not hope for any
      other—
There is no ship for you, there is no road.
As you have destroyed your life here   15
in this little corner, you have ruined it in the entire world.

—Translated by Rae Dalven

WILLIAM BUTLER YEATS (1865–1939)

Adam's Curse

We sat together at one summer's end,
That beautiful mild woman, your close friend,
And you and I, and talked of poetry.
I said: 'A line will take us hours maybe;
Yet if it does not seem a moment's thought,
Our stitching and unstitching has been naught.   5
Better go down upon your marrow-bones
And scrub a kitchen pavement, or break stones
Like an old pauper, in all kinds of weather;
For to articulate sweet sounds together
Is to work harder than all these, and yet   10
Be thought an idler by the noisy set
Of bankers, schoolmasters, and clergymen
The martyrs call the world.'

And thereupon   15
That beautiful mild woman for whose sake
There's many a one shall find out all heartache
On finding that her voice is sweet and low
Replied: 'To be born woman is to know—
Although they do not talk of it at school—   20
That we must labour to be beautiful.'

I said: 'It's certain there is no fine thing
Since Adam's fall but needs much labouring.
There have been lovers who thought love should be
So much compounded of high courtesy   25
That they would sigh and quote with learned looks
Precedents out of beautiful old books;
Yet now it seems an idle trade enough.'

We sat grown quiet at the name of love;
We saw the last embers of daylight die,   30
And in the trembling blue-green of the sky
A moon, worn as if it had been a shell
Washed by time's waters as they rose and fell
About the stars and broke in days and years.

I had a thought for no one's but your ears: 35
That you were beautiful, and that I strove
To love you in the old high way of love;
That it had all seemed happy, and yet we'd grown
As weary-hearted as that hollow moon.

Rainer Maria Rilke (1875–1926)

The Man Watching

I can tell by the way the trees beat, after
so many dull days, on my worried windowpanes
that a storm is coming,
and I hear the far-off fields say things
I can't bear without a friend,   5
I can't love without a sister.

The storm, the shifter of shapes, drives on
across the woods and across time,
and the world looks as if it had no age:

the landscape, like a line in the psalm book,   10
is seriousness and weight and eternity.

What we choose to fight is so tiny!
What fights with us is so great!
If only we would let ourselves be dominated
as things do by some immense storm,   15
we would become strong too, and not need names.

When we win it's with small things,
and the triumph itself makes us small.
What is extraordinary and eternal
does not *want* to be bent by us.   20
I mean the Angel who appeared
to the wrestlers of the Old Testament:
when the wrestlers' sinews
grew long like metal strings,
he felt them under his fingers   25
like chords of deep music.

Whoever was beaten by this Angel
(who often simply declined the fight)
went away proud and strengthened
and great from that harsh hand,   30
that kneaded him as if to change his shape.
Winning does not tempt that man.
This is how he grows: by being defeated, decisively,
by constantly greater beings.

—Translated by Robert Bly

ACTIVITIES FOR WRITING AND DISCUSSION

1. What are examples of the "things" the **speaker** might be referring to in line 15? Why does he desire that "we" should be like those things? Try to explain the analogy he is making here between human beings and things.

2. Agree or disagree with the assertions in lines 12, 13, 17, and 18. If possible, give examples from experience to illustrate your view.

3. Why is the man described toward the end of the poem not tempted by "Winning"?

4. Working in a group, list some everyday examples of defeats that can make a person stronger. Tell the stories of those defeats and how they resulted in strength.

5. Create a text of your own in which you reflect on ways that defeat or loss can strengthen a person. Illustrate your text with stories from your own or others' experience.

Donald Justice (b. 1925)

Men at forty

Men at forty
Learn to close softly
The doors to rooms they will not be
Coming back to.

At rest on a stair landing,   5
They feel it
Moving beneath them now like the deck of a ship,
Though the swell is gentle.

And deep in mirrors
They rediscover   10
The face of the boy as he practices tying
His father's tie there in secret

And the face of that father,
Still warm with the mystery of lather.
They are more fathers than sons themselves now.   15
Something is filling them, something

That is like the twilight sound
Of the crickets, immense,
Filling the woods at the foot of the slope
Behind their mortgaged houses.   20

Maya Angelou (b. 1928)

Seven Women's Blessed Assurance

1
One thing about me,
I'm little and low,
find me a man
wherever I go.

2
They call me string bean   5
'cause I'm so tall.
Men see me,
they ready to fall.

3
I'm young as morning
and fresh as dew.   10
Everybody loves me
and so do you.

4
I'm fat as butter
and sweet as cake.
Men start to tremble   15
each time I shake.

5
I'm little and lean,
sweet to the bone.
They like to pick me up
and carry me home.   20

6
When I passed forty
I dropped pretense,
'cause men like women
who got some sense.

7
Fifty-five is perfect,   25
so is fifty-nine,
'cause every man needs
to rest sometime.

Ursula Fanthorpe (b. 1929)

Growing Up

I wasn't good
At being a baby. Burrowed my way
Through the long yawn of infancy,
Masking by instinct how much I knew
Of the senior world, sabotaging   5
As far as I could, biding my time,
Biting my rattle, my brother (in private),
Shoplifting daintily into my pram.
Not a good baby,
No.   10

I wasn't good
At being a child. I missed
The innocent age. Children,
Being childish, were beneath me.
Adults I despised or distrusted. They   15
Would label my every disclosure
Precocious, naïve, whatever it was.
I disdained definition, preferred to be surly.
Not a nice child,
No.   20

I wasn't good
At adolescence. There was a dance,
A catchy rhythm; I was out of step.
My body capered, nudging me
With hairy, fleshy growths and monthly outbursts,   25
To join the party. I tried to annul
The future, pretended I knew it already,
Was caught bloody-thighed, a criminal
Guilty of puberty.
Not a nice girl,   30
No.
(My hero, intransigent Emily,
Cauterised her own-dog-mauled
Arm with a poker,
Struggled to die on her feet,   35
Never told anyone anything.)

I wasn't good
At growing up. Never learned

The natives' art of life. Conversation
Disintegrated as I touched it,   40
So I played mute, wormed along years,
Reciting the hard-learned arcane litany
Of cliché, my company passport.
Not a nice person,
No.   45

The gift remains
Masonic,[1] dark. But age affords
A vocation even for wallflowers.
Called to be connoisseur, I collect,
Admire, the effortless bravura   50
Of other people's lives, proper and comely,
Treading the measure, shopping, chaffing,
Quarrelling, drinking, not knowing
How right they are, or how, like well-oiled bolts,
Swiftly and sweet, they slot into the grooves   55
Their ancestors smoothed out along the grain.

AUDRE LORDE (1934–1992)

Hanging Fire

I am fourteen
and my skin has betrayed me
the boy I cannot live without
still sucks his thumb
in secret   5
how come my knees are
always so ashy
what if I die
before morning
and momma's in the bedroom   10
with the door closed.

I have to learn how to dance
in time for the next party
my room is too small for me
suppose I die before graduation   15
they will sing sad melodies

---

1. Masonic here means "secret."

but finally
tell the truth about me
There is nothing I want to do
and too much   20
that has to be done
and momma's in the bedroom
with the door closed.

Nobody even stops to think
about my side of it   25
I should have been on Math Team
my marks were better than his
why do I have to be
the one
wearing braces   30
I have nothing to wear tomorrow
will I live long enough
to grow up
and momma's in the bedroom
with the door closed.   35

ACTIVITIES FOR WRITING AND DISCUSSION

1. Other than the periods at the ends of stanzas, the poem has no punctuation. How does this lack of punctuation affect the way you read the poem, and how (if at all) does it "fit" the subject of the poem?

2. How do you explain the repetition of the lines "and momma's in the bedroom/with the door closed" at the end of each stanza?

3. After annotating the poem, identify a particular line or group of lines that resonates with your own experience of adolescence. Use the line(s) as a "springboard" to writing about that experience.

4. Rewrite the poem as a dialogue between the **speaker** and her "momma."

LUCILLE CLIFTON (b. 1936)

[There Is a Girl Inside]

there is a girl inside.
she is randy as a wolf.
she will not walk away

and leave these bones
to an old woman.   5

she is a green tree
in a forest of kindling.
she is a green girl
in a used poet.

she has waited   10
patient as a nun
for the second coming,
when she can break through gray hairs
into blossom

and her lovers will harvest   15
honey and thyme
and the woods will be wild
with the damn wonder of it.

Mark Rudman (b. 1948)

Chrome

On the late news I watch hundreds of helmeted riders
almost indecipherable in the dust
tearing up the holes of desert turtles in the Mojave[1]—
and I remember our bravura cycling:
the trick was to go as fast as you could   5
without being thrown by rock or incline.
Hills leeched of color,
the desert a kind of form,
with rimrock and succulents and gulches
providing borders—boundaries.   10
Dust and desire.
I wanted to go down toward the desert floor,
where the spines of the saguaro cactus
guarded the sticky pulp I loved,
the sweet, incomparable, centerless center.   15
O sweet sixteen, to be sprung again and again against
the rock-studded sand, the danger not

1. A desert in the southwestern United States

in the desert but around it.
The body's oneness with the mind
on the lean machine seemed just right, the body   20
soaring while hovering close
to the sand as the Honda 125
jounced past yucca and cactus and took
the long dip into the arroyo[2] where the ring
of distant chimney rocks and hills   25
like space stations receded, and I
twisted the handle-bars like the horns
of a steer to side-wind up and over the rim.
I was thrown only by breaks in the terrain,
grit and stones and dips in the sand,   30
or by sudden soft patches; or by swerving to avoid
a brush with tumbleweed or a mesquite bush.
Spills were rehearsals for free falling, a way to slow
time down, cease to feel your own weight,
achieve clarity and edge as if edging down   35
off the concrete onto the sand was the aim. . . .
Circling demoniacally, I didn't notice
the ferocious sun, a fusion of horizon and sky,
or the hawks stunned and motionless as clouds.
Each time, bloody but happy,   40
I eased back onto the highway,
and set off down the canyon road
into the sun, whitening as it hung
level with the cliff. Once I rode toward it
hearing only the hush of the tires,   45
the pure elation of it taking my head off as I took
a horseshoe curve at 50 and approached
an even sharper one—the slender cycle shaking apart—;
and I wondered *what to do*, like Porthos[3]
going back to the bomb he'd planted to make sure   50
he'd lit the fuse . . . when — BOOM!—;
I turned the accelerator handle all the way forward
to slow down—gunning the engine
by accident when the cycle bucked, reared,
and surged ahead—I rose, the cliff's gravel   55
gleamed, radiant, it was all over;
I could feel my soul leave my body and see my body flung out
over the canyon rim—
it looked as if I'd leap the cliff and fly
into the sun, time gone, space erased,   60

---

2. A gully cut by a stream.   3. One of the musketeers in Alexandre Dumas's *The Three Musketeers* (1846).

not a piñon in sight to break my fall, only the cliff
wall, studded with jagged stones.
And I knew if I braked abruptly on the gravel the bike
would catapult me headlong into the open,
so I let go of the throttle—threw up my hands—   65
and the bike went off the highway, keeled over
and died at the cliff's edge.
I owe my life to letting go.

Gary Soto (b. 1952)

Oranges

The first time I walked
With a girl, I was twelve,
Cold, and weighted down
With two oranges in my jacket.
December. Frost cracking   5
Beneath my steps, my breath
Before me, then gone,
As I walked toward
Her house, the one whose
Porch light burned yellow   10
Night and day, in any weather.
A dog barked at me, until
She came out pulling
At her gloves, face bright
With rouge. I smiled,   15
Touched her shoulder, and led
Her down the street, across
A used car lot and a line
Of newly planted trees,
Until we were breathing   20
Before a drugstore. We
Entered, the tiny bell
Bringing a saleslady
Down a narrow aisle of goods.
I turned to the candies   25
Tiered like bleachers,
And asked what she wanted—
Light in her eyes, a smile
Starting at the corners
Of her mouth. I fingered   30

A nickel in my pocket,
And when she lifted a chocolate
That cost a dime,
I didn't say anything.
I took the nickel from   35
My pocket, then an orange,
And set them quietly on
The counter. When I looked up,
The lady's eyes met mine,
And held them, knowing   40
Very well what it was all
About.

        Outside,
A few cars hissing past,
Fog hanging like old   45
Coats between the trees.
I took my girl's hand
In mine for two blocks,
Then released it to let
Her unwrap the chocolate.   50
I peeled my orange
That was so bright against
The gray of December
That, from some distance,
Someone might have thought   55
I was making a fire in my hands.

ACTIVITIES FOR WRITING AND DISCUSSION

1. What was the incident of the nickel and the orange "all/About" (lines 41–42)? In your notebook, narrate any similar incidents in your own experience.

2. In poetry or prose, retell the incident of the nickel and the orange from the **point of view** of either the girl or the saleslady.

3. With what mixture of emotions does the poem leave you? Explain.

Maya Angelou (b. 1928)

Graduation

The children in Stamps[1] trembled visibly with anticipation. Some adults were excited too, but to be certain the whole young population had come down with graduation epidemic. Large classes were graduating from both the grammar school and the high school. Even those who were years removed from their own day of glorious release were anxious to help with preparations as a kind of dry run. The junior students who were moving into the vacating classes' chairs were tradition-bound to show their talents for leadership and management. They strutted through the school and around the campus exerting pressure on the lower grades. Their authority was so new that occasionally if they pressed a little too hard it had to be overlooked. After all, next term was coming, and it never hurt a sixth grader to have a play sister in the eighth grade, or a tenth-year student to be able to call a twelfth grader Bubba. So all was endured in a spirit of shared understanding. But the graduating classes themselves were the nobility. Like travelers with exotic destinations on their minds, the graduates were remarkably forgetful. They came to school without their books, or tablets or even pencils. Volunteers fell over themselves to secure replacements for the missing equipment. When accepted, the willing workers might or might not be thanked, and it was of no importance to the pregraduation rites. Even teachers were respectful of the now quiet and aging seniors, and tended to speak to them, if not as equals, as beings only slightly lower than themselves. After tests were returned and grades given, the student body, which acted like an extended family, knew who did well, who excelled, and what piteous ones had failed.

Unlike the white high school, Lafayette County Training School distinguished itself by having neither lawn, nor hedges, nor tennis court, nor climbing ivy. Its two buildings (main classrooms, the grade school and home economics) were set on a dirt hill with no fence to limit either its boundaries or those of bordering farms. There was a large expanse to the left of the school which was used alternately as a baseball diamond or basketball court. Rusty hoops on swaying poles represented the permanent recreational equipment, although bats and balls could be borrowed from the P.E. teacher if the borrower was qualified and if the diamond wasn't occupied.

Over this rocky area relieved by a few shady tall persimmon trees the graduating class walked. The girls often held hands and no longer bothered to speak to the lower students. There was a sadness about them, as if this old world was

---

1. A town in Arkansas.

not their home and they were bound for higher ground. The boys, on the other hand, had become more friendly, more outgoing. A decided change from the closed attitude they projected while studying for finals. Now they seemed not ready to give up the old school, the familiar paths and classrooms. Only a small percentage would be continuing on to college—one of the South's A & M (agricultural and mechanical) schools, which trained Negro youths to be carpenters, farmers, handymen, masons, maids, cooks and baby nurses. Their future rode heavily on their shoulders, and blinded them to the collective joy that had pervaded the lives of the boys and girls in the grammar school graduating class.

Parents who could afford it had ordered new shoes and readymade clothes for themselves from Sears and Roebuck or Montgomery Ward. They also engaged the best seamstresses to make the floating graduating dresses and to cut down secondhand pants which would be pressed to a military slickness for the important event.

Oh, it was important, all right. Whitefolks would attend the ceremony, and   5
two or three would speak of God and home, and the Southern way of life, and Mrs. Parsons, the principal's wife, would play the graduation march while the lower-grade graduates paraded down the aisles and took their seats below the platform. The high school seniors would wait in empty classrooms to make their dramatic entrance.

In the Store I was the person of the moment. The birthday girl. The center. Bailey[2] had graduated the year before, although to do so he had had to forfeit all pleasures to make up for his time lost in Baton Rouge.

My class was wearing butter-yellow piqué dresses, and Momma launched out on mine. She smocked the yoke into tiny crisscrossing puckers, then shirred the rest of the bodice. Her dark fingers ducked in and out of the lemony cloth as she embroidered raised daisies around the hem. Before she considered herself finished she had added a crocheted cuff on the puff sleeves, and a pointy crocheted collar.

I was going to be lovely. A walking model of all the various styles of fine hand sewing and it didn't worry me that I was only twelve years old and merely graduating from the eighth grade. Besides, many teachers in Arkansas Negro schools had only that diploma and were licensed to impart wisdom.

The days had become longer and more noticeable. The faded beige of former times had been replaced with strong and sure colors. I began to see my classmates' clothes, their skin tones, and the dust that waved off pussy willows. Clouds that lazed across the sky were objects of great concern to me. Their shiftier shapes might have held a message that in my new happiness and with a little bit of time I'd soon decipher. During that period I looked at the arch of heaven so religiously my neck kept a steady ache. I had taken to smiling more often, and my jaws hurt from the unaccustomed activity. Between the two

---

2. The author's brother.

physical sore spots, I suppose I could have been uncomfortable, but that was not the case. As a member of the winning team (the graduating class of 1940) I had outdistanced unpleasant sensations by miles. I was headed for the freedom of open fields.

Youth and social approval allied themselves with me and we trammeled 10 memories of slights and insults. The wind of our swift passage remodeled my features. Lost tears were pounded to mud and then to dust. Years of withdrawal were brushed aside and left behind, as hanging ropes of parasitic moss.

My work alone had awarded me a top place and I was going to be one of the first called in the graduating ceremonies. On the classroom blackboard, as well as on the bulletin board in the auditorium, there were blue stars and white stars and red stars. No absences, no tardinesses, and my academic work was among the best of the year. I could say the preamble to the Constitution even faster than Bailey. We timed ourselves often: "We the people of the United States in order to form a more perfect union . . ." I had memorized the Presidents of the United States from Washington to Roosevelt in chronological as well as alphabetical order.

My hair pleased me too. Gradually the black mass had lengthened and thickened, so that it kept at last to its braided pattern, and I didn't have to yank my scalp off when I tried to comb it.

Louise and I had rehearsed the exercises until we tired out ourselves. Henry Reed was class valedictorian. He was a small, very black boy with hooded eyes, a long, broad nose and an oddly shaped head. I had admired him for years because each term he and I vied for the best grades in our class. Most often he bested me, but instead of being disappointed I was pleased that we shared top places between us. Like many Southern Black children, he lived with his grandmother, who was as strict as Momma and as kind as she knew how to be. He was courteous, respectful and soft-spoken to elders, but on the playground he chose to play the roughest games. I admired him. Anyone, I reckoned, sufficiently afraid or sufficiently dull could be polite. But to be able to operate at a top level with both adults and children was admirable.

His valedictory speech was entitled "To Be or Not to Be." The rigid tenth-grade teacher had helped him write it. He'd been working on the dramatic stresses for months.

The weeks until graduation were filled with heady activities. A group of 15 small children were to be presented in a play about buttercups and daisies and bunny rabbits. They could be heard throughout the building practicing their hops and their little songs that sounded like silver bells. The older girls (nongraduates, of course) were assigned the task of making refreshments for the night's festivities. A tangy scent of ginger, cinnamon, nutmeg and chocolate wafted around the home economics building as the budding cooks made samples for themselves and their teachers.

In every corner of the workshop, axes and saws split fresh timber as the woodshop boys made sets and stage scenery. Only the graduates were left out of the general bustle. We were free to sit in the library at the back of the building or look on quite detachedly, naturally, on the measures being taken for our event.

Even the minister preached on graduation the Sunday before. His subject was, "Let your light so shine that men will see your good works and praise your Father, Who is in Heaven." Although the sermon was purported to be addressed to us, he used the occasion to speak to backsliders, gamblers and general ne'er-do-wells. But since he had called our names at the beginning of the service we were mollified.

Among Negroes the tradition was to give presents to children going only from one grade to another. How much more important this was when the person was graduating at the top of the class. Uncle Willie and Momma had sent away for a Mickey Mouse watch like Bailey's. Louise gave me four embroidered handkerchiefs. (I gave her crocheted doilies.) Mrs. Sneed, the minister's wife, made me an undershirt to wear for graduation, and nearly every customer gave me a nickel or maybe even a dime with the instruction "Keep on moving to higher ground," or some such encouragement.

Amazingly the great day finally dawned and I was out of bed before I knew it. I threw open the back door to see it more clearly, but Momma said, "Sister, come away from that door and put your robe on."

I hoped the memory of that morning would never leave me. Sunlight was it- 20 self young, and the day had none of the insistence maturity would bring it in a few hours. In my robe and barefoot in the backyard, under cover of going to see about my new beans, I gave myself up to the gentle warmth and thanked God that no matter what evil I had done in my life He had allowed me to live to see this day. Somewhere in my fatalism I had expected to die, accidentally, and never have the chance to walk up the stairs in the auditorium and gracefully receive my hard-earned diploma. Out of God's merciful bosom I had won reprieve.

Bailey came out in his robe and gave me a box wrapped in Christmas paper. He said he had saved his money for months to pay for it. It felt like a box of chocolates, but I knew Bailey wouldn't save money to buy candy when we had all we could want under our noses.

He was as proud of the gift as I. It was a soft-leather-bound copy of a collection of poems by Edgar Allan Poe, or, as Bailey and I called him, "Eap." I turned to "Annabel Lee" and we walked up and down the garden rows, the cool dirt between our toes, reciting the beautifully sad lines.

Momma made a Sunday breakfast although it was only Friday. After we finished the blessing, I opened my eyes to find the watch on my plate. It was a dream of a day. Everything went smoothly and to my credit I didn't have to be reminded or scolded for anything. Near evening I was too jittery to attend to chores, so Bailey volunteered to do all before his bath.

Days before, we had made a sign for the Store, and as we turned out the lights Momma hung the cardboard over the doorknob. It read clearly: CLOSED, GRADUATION.

My dress fitted perfectly and everyone said that I looked like a sunbeam in 25 it. On the hill, going toward the school, Bailey walked behind with Uncle Willie, who muttered, "Go on, Ju." He wanted him to walk ahead with us because it embarrassed him to have to walk so slowly. Bailey said he'd let the ladies walk together, and the men would bring up the rear. We all laughed, nicely.

Little children dashed by out of the dark like fireflies. Their crepe-paper dresses and butterfly wings were not made for running and we heard more than one rip, dryly, and the regretful "uh oh" that followed.

The school blazed without gaiety. The windows seemed cold and unfriendly from the lower hill. A sense of ill-fated timing crept over me, and if Momma hadn't reached for my hand I would have drifted back to Bailey and Uncle Willie, and possibly beyond. She made a few slow jokes about my feet getting cold, and tugged me along to the now-strange building.

Around the front steps, assurance came back. There were my fellow "greats," the graduating class. Hair brushed back, legs oiled, new dresses and pressed pleats, fresh pocket handkerchiefs and little handbags, all homesewn. Oh, we were up to snuff, all right. I joined my comrades and didn't even see my family go in to find seats in the crowded auditorium.

The school band struck up a march and all classes filed in as had been rehearsed. We stood in front of our seats, as assigned, and on a signal from the choir director, we sat. No sooner had this been accomplished than the band started to play the national anthem. We rose again and sang the song, after which we recited the pledge of allegiance. We remained standing for a brief minute before the choir director and the principal signaled to us, rather desperately I thought, to take our seats. The command was so unusual that our carefully rehearsed and smooth-running machine was thrown off. For a full minute we fumbled for our chairs and bumped into each other awkwardly. Habits change or solidify under pressure, so in our state of nervous tension we had been ready to follow our usual assembly pattern: the American national anthem, then the pledge of allegiance, then the song every Black person I knew called the Negro National Anthem. All done in the same key, with the same passion and most often standing on the same foot.

Finding my seat at last, I was overcome with a presentiment of worse things 30 to come. Something unrehearsed, unplanned, was going to happen, and we were going to be made to look bad. I distinctly remember being explicit in the choice of pronoun. It was "we," the graduating class, the unit, that concerned me then.

The principal welcomed "parents and friends" and asked the Baptist minister to lead us in prayer. His invocation was brief and punchy, and for a second I thought we were getting on the high road to right action. When the principal came back to the dais, however, his voice had changed. Sounds always affected me profoundly and the principal's voice was one of my favorites. During assembly it melted and lowed weakly into the audience. It had not been in my plan to listen to him, but my curiosity was piqued and I straightened up to give him my attention.

He was talking about Booker T. Washington, our "late great leader," who said we can be as close as the fingers on the hand, etc. . . . Then he said a few vague things about friendship and the friendship of kindly people to those less fortunate than themselves. With that his voice nearly faded, thin, away. Like a river diminishing to a stream and then to a trickle. But he cleared his throat and said, "Our speaker tonight, who is also our friend, came from Texarkana to deliver the commencement address, but due to the irregularity of the train schedule, he's going to, as they say, 'speak and run.' " He said that we understood and wanted the man to know that we were most grateful for the time he was able to give us and then something about how we were willing always to adjust to another's program, and without more ado—"I give you Mr. Edward Donleavy."

Not one but two white men came through the door off-stage. The shorter one walked to the speaker's platform, and the tall one moved to the center seat and sat down. But that was our principal's seat, and already occupied. The dislodged gentleman bounced around for a long breath or two before the Baptist minister gave him his chair, then with more dignity than the situation deserved, the minister walked off the stage.

Donleavy looked at the audience once (on reflection, I'm sure that he wanted only to reassure himself that we were really there), adjusted his glasses and began to read from a sheaf of papers.

He was glad "to be here and to see the work going on just as it was in the   35 other schools."

At the first "Amen" from the audience I willed the offender to immediate death by choking on the word. But Amens and Yes, sir's began to fall around the room like rain through a ragged umbrella.

He told us of the wonderful changes we children in Stamps had in store. The Central School (naturally, the white school was Central) had already been granted improvements that would be in use in the fall. A well-known artist was coming from Little Rock to teach art to them. They were going to have the newest microscopes and chemistry equipment for their laboratory. Mr. Donleavy didn't leave us long in the dark over who made these improvements available to Central High. Nor were we to be ignored in the general betterment scheme he had in mind.

He said that he had pointed out to people at a very high level that one of the first-line football tacklers at Arkansas Agricultural and Mechanical College had graduated from good old Lafayette County Training School. Here fewer Amen's were heard. Those few that did break through lay dully in the air with the heaviness of habit.

He went on to praise us. He went on to say how he had bragged that "one of the best basketball players at Fisk sank his first ball right here at Lafayette County Training School."

The white kids were going to have a chance to become Galileos and   40 Madame Curies and Edisons and Gauguins, and our boys (the girls weren't even in on it) would try to be Jesse Owenses and Joe Louises.

Owens and the Brown Bomber were great heroes in our world, but what school official in the white-goddom of Little Rock had the right to decide that those two men must be our only heroes? Who decided that for Henry Reed to become a scientist he had to work like George Washington Carver, as a bootblack, to buy a lousy microscope? Bailey was obviously always going to be too small to be an athlete, so which concrete angel glued to what country seat had decided that if my brother wanted to become a lawyer he had to first pay penance for his skin by picking cotton and hoeing corn and studying correspondence books at night for twenty years?

The man's dead words fell like bricks around the auditorium and too many settled in my belly. Constrained by hard-learned manners I couldn't look behind me, but to my left and right the proud graduating class of 1940 had dropped their heads. Every girl in my row had found something new to do with her handkerchief. Some folded the tiny squares into love knots, some into triangles, but most were wadding them, then pressing them flat on their yellow laps.

On the dais, the ancient tragedy was being replayed. Professor Parsons sat, a sculptor's reject, rigid. His large, heavy body seemed devoid of will or willingness, and his eyes said he was no longer with us. The other teachers examined the flag (which was draped stage right) or their notes, or the windows which opened on our now-famous playing diamond.

Graduation, the hush-hush magic time of frills and gifts and congratulations and diplomas, was finished for me before my name was called. The accomplishment was nothing. The meticulous maps, drawn in three colors of ink, learning and spelling decasyllabic words, memorizing the whole of *The Rape of Lucrece*—it was for nothing. Donleavy had exposed us.

We were maids and farmers, handymen and washerwomen, and anything higher that we aspired to was farcical and presumptuous.

Then I wished that Gabriel Prosser and Nat Turner had killed all whitefolks in their beds and that Abraham Lincoln had been assassinated before the signing of the Emancipation Proclamation, and that Harriet Tubman had been killed by that blow on her head and Christopher Columbus had drowned in the *Santa Maria*.

It was awful to be a Negro and have no control over my life. It was brutal to be young and already trained to sit quietly and listen to charges brought against my color with no chance of defense. We should all be dead. I thought I should like to see us all dead, one on top of the other. A pyramid of flesh with the whitefolks on the bottom, as the broad base, then the Indians with their silly tomahawks and teepees and wigwams and treaties, the Negroes with their mops and recipes and cotton sacks and spirituals sticking out of their mouths. The Dutch children should all stumble in their wooden shoes and break their necks. The French should choke to death on the Louisiana Purchase (1803) while silkworms ate all the Chinese with their stupid pigtails. As a species, we were an abomination. All of us.

Donleavy was running for election, and assured our parents that if he won we could count on having the only colored paved playing field in that part of Arkansas. Also—he never looked up to acknowledge the grunts of acceptance—also, we were bound to get some new equipment for the home economics building and the workshop.

He finished, and since there was no need to give any more than the most perfunctory thank-you's, he nodded to the men on the stage, and the tall white man who was never introduced joined him at the door. They left with the attitude that now they were off to something really important. (The graduation ceremonies at Lafayette County Training School had been a mere preliminary.)

The ugliness they left was palpable. An uninvited guest who wouldn't leave. 50 The choir was summoned and sang a modern arrangement of "Onward, Christian Soldiers," with new words pertaining to graduates seeking their place in the world. But it didn't work. Elouise, the daughter of the Baptist minister, recited "Invictus," and I could have cried at the impertinence of "I am the master of my fate, I am the captain of my soul."

My name had lost its ring of familiarity and I had to be nudged to go and receive my diploma. All my preparations had fled. I neither marched up to the stage like a conquering Amazon, nor did I look in the audience for Bailey's nod of approval. Marguerite Johnson, I heard the name again, my honors were read, there were noises in the audience of appreciation, and I took my place on the stage as rehearsed.

I thought about colors I hated: ecru, puce, lavender, beige and black.

There was shuffling and rustling around me, then Henry Reed was giving his valedictory address, "To Be or Not to Be." Hadn't he heard the whitefolks? We couldn't *be,* so the question was a waste of time. Henry's voice came out clear and strong. I feared to look at him. Hadn't he got the message? There was no "nobler in the mind" for Negroes because the world didn't think we had minds, and they let us know it. "Outrageous fortune"? Now, that was a joke. When the ceremony was over I had to tell Henry Reed some things. That is, if I still cared. Not "rub," Henry, "erase." "Ah, there's the erase." Us.

Henry had been a good student in elocution. His voice rose on tides of promise and fell on waves of warnings. The English teacher had helped him to create a sermon winging through Hamlet's soliloquy. To be a man, a doer, a builder, a leader, or to be a tool, an unfunny joke, a crusher of funky toadstools. I marveled that Henry could go through with the speech as if we had a choice.

I had been listening and silently rebutting each sentence with my eyes 55 closed; then there was a hush, which in an audience warns that something unplanned is happening. I looked up and saw Henry Reed, the conservative, the proper, the A student, turn his back to the audience and turn to us (the proud graduating class of 1940) and sing, nearly speaking,

> "Lift ev'ry voice and sing
> Till earth and heaven ring
> Ring with the harmonies of Liberty . . ."

It was the poem written by James Weldon Johnson. It was the music composed by J. Rosamond Johnson. It was the Negro national anthem. Out of habit we were singing it.

Our mothers and fathers stood in the dark hall and joined the hymn of encouragement. A kindergarten teacher led the small children onto the stage and the buttercups and daisies and bunny rabbits marked time and tried to follow:

"Stony the road we trod
Bitter the chastening rod
Felt in the days when hope, unborn, had died.
Yet with a steady beat
Have not our weary feet
Come to the place for which our fathers sighed?"

Each child I knew had learned that song with his ABC's and along with "Jesus Loves Me This I Know." But I personally had never heard it before. Never heard the words, despite the thousands of times I had sung them. Never thought they had anything to do with me.

On the other hand, the words of Patrick Henry had made such an impression on me that I had been able to stretch myself tall and trembling and say, "I know not what course others may take, but as for me, give me liberty or give me death."

And now I heard, really for the first time:

"We have come over a way that with tears
has been watered,
We have come, treading our path through
the blood of the slaughtered."

While echoes of the song shivered in the air, Henry Reed bowed his head, 60 said "Thank you," and returned to his place in the line. The tears that slipped down many faces were not wiped away in shame.

We were on top again. As always, again. We survived. The depths had been icy and dark, but now a bright sun spoke to our souls. I was no longer simply a member of the proud graduating class of 1940; I was a proud member of the wonderful, beautiful Negro race.

Oh, Black known and unknown poets, how often have your auctioned pains sustained us? Who will compute the lonely nights made less lonely by your songs, or the empty pots made less tragic by your tales?

If we were a people much given to revealing secrets, we might raise monuments and sacrifice to the memories of our poets, but slavery cured us of that weakness. It may be enough, however, to have it said that we survive in exact relationship to the dedication of our poets (include preachers, musicians and blues singers).

Michael Dorris (b. 1945)

Life Stories

In most cultures, adulthood is equated with self-reliance and responsibility, yet often Americans do not achieve this status until we are in our late twenties or early thirties—virtually the entire average lifespan of a person in a traditional non-Western society. We tend to treat prolonged adolescence as a warm-up for real life, as a wobbly ladder between childhood and legal maturity. Whereas a nineteenth-century Cheyenne or Lakota teenager was expected to alter self-conception in a split-second vision, we often meander through an analogous rite of passage for more than a decade—through high school, college, graduate school.

Though he had never before traveled alone outside his village, the Plains Indian male was expected at puberty to venture solo into the wilderness. There he had to fend for and sustain himself while avoiding the menace of unknown dangers, and there he had absolutely to remain until something happened that would transform him. Every human being, these tribes believed, was entitled to at least one moment of personal, enabling insight.

Anthropology proposes feasible psychological explanations for why this flash was eventually triggered: fear, fatigue, reliance on strange foods, the anguish of loneliness, stress, and the expectation of ultimate success all contributed to a state of receptivity. Every sense was quickened, alerted to perceive deep meaning, until at last the interpretation of an unusual event—a dream, a chance encounter, or an unexpected vista—reverberated with significance. Through this unique prism, abstractly preserved in a vivid memory or song, a boy caught foresight of both his adult persona and his vocation, the two inextricably entwined.

The best approximations that many of us get to such a heady sense of eventuality come in the performance of the jobs we hold during summer vacation. Summers are intermissions, and once we hit our teens it is during these breaks in our structured regimen that we initially taste the satisfaction of remuneration that is earned, not merely doled. Tasks defined as work are not graded, they are compensated; they have a worth that is inarguable because it translates into hard currency. Wage labor—and in the beginning, this generally means a confining, repetitive chore for which we are quickly overqualified—paradoxically brings a sense of blooming freedom. At the outset, the complaint to a peer that business supersedes fun is oddly liberating—no matter what drudgery requires your attention, it is by its very required nature serious and adult.

At least that's how it seemed to me. I come from a line of people hard hit by 5 the Great Depression. My mother and her sisters went to work early in their teens—my mother operated a kind of calculator known as a comptometer while her sisters spent their days, respectively, at a peanut factory and at Western Union. My grandmother did piecework sewing. Their efforts, and the Democratic Party, saw them through, and to this day they never look back without appreciation for their later solvency. They take nothing for granted. Accomplishments are celebrated, possessions are valuable, in direct proportion to the labor entailed to acquire them; anything easily won or bought on credit is suspect. When I was growing up we were far from wealthy, but what money we had was correlated to the hours one of us had logged. My eagerness to contribute to, or at least not diminish, the coffer was countered by the arguments of those whose salaries kept me in school: my higher education was a sound group investment. The whole family was adamant that I have the opportunities they had missed and, no matter how much I objected, they stinted themselves to provide for me.

Summer jobs were therefore a relief, an opportunity to pull a share of the load. As soon as the days turned warm I began to peruse the classifieds, and when the spring semester was done, I was ready to punch a clock. It even felt right. Work in June, July, and August had an almost biblical aspect: in the hot, canicular weather your brow sweats, just as God had ordained. Moreover, summer jobs had the luxury of being temporary. No matter how onerous, how off my supposed track, employment terminated with the falling leaves and I was back to real life. So, during each annual three-month leave from secondary school and later from the university, I compiled an eclectic resumé: lawn cutter, hair sweeper in a barber shop, lifeguard, delivery boy, mail carrier, file clerk, youth program coordinator on my Montana reservation, ballroom dance instructor, theater party promoter, night-shift hospital records keeper, human adding machine in a Paris bank, encyclopedia salesman, newspaper stringer, recreation bus manager, salmon fisherman.

The summer I was eighteen a possibility arose for a rotation at the post office, and I grabbed it. There was something casually sophisticated about work that required a uniform, about having a federal ranking, even if it was GS-1 (Temp/Sub), and it was flattering to be entrusted with a leather bag containing who knew what important correspondence. Every day I was assigned a new beat, usually in a rough neighborhood avoided whenever possible by regular carriers, and I proved quite capable of complicating what would normally be fairly routine missions. The low point came on the first of August when I diligently delivered four blocks' worth of welfare checks to the right numbers on the wrong streets. It is no fun to snatch unexpected wealth from the hands of those who had but moments previously opened their mailboxes and received a bonus.

After my first year of college, I lived with relatives on an Indian reservation in eastern Montana and filled the only post available: Coordinator of Youth Programs. I was seduced by the language of the announcement into assuming that there existed Youth Programs to be coordinated. In fact, the Youth consisted of a dozen bored, disgruntled kids—most of them my cousins—who had nothing better to do each day than to show up at what was euphemistically called "the gym" and hate whatever Program I had planned for them. The Youth ranged in age from fifteen to five and seemed to have as their sole common ambition the determination to smoke cigarettes. This put them at immediate and ongoing odds with the Coordinator, who on his first day naively encouraged them to sing the "Doe, a deer, a female deer" song from *The Sound of Music*. They looked at me, that bleak morning, and I looked at them, each boy and girl equipped with a Pall Mall behind an ear, and we all knew we faced a long, struggle-charged battle. It was to be a contest of wills, the hearty and wholesome versus prohibited vice. I stood for dodge ball, for collecting bugs in glass jars, for arts and crafts; they had pledged a preternatural allegiance to sloth. The odds were not in my favor and each waking dawn I experienced the lightheadedness of anticipated exhaustion, that thrill of giddy dissociation in which nothing seems real or of great significance. Finally, I went with the flow and learned to inhale.

The next summer, I decided to find work in an urban setting for a change, and was hired as a general office assistant in the Elsa Hoppenfeld Theatre Party Agency, located above Sardi's restaurant in New York City. The agency consisted of Elsa Hoppenfeld herself, Rita Frank, her regular deputy, and me. Elsa was a gregarious Viennese woman who established contacts through honesty, hard work, and personal charm, and she spent much of the time away from the building courting trade. Rita was therefore both my immediate supervisor and constant companion; she had the most incredible fingernails I had ever seen— long, carefully shaped pegs lacquered in cruel primary colors and hard as stone—and an attitude about her that could only be described as zeal.

The goal of a theater party agent is to sell blocks of tickets to imminent   10
Broadway productions, and the likely buyers are charities, B'nai B'riths, Hadassahs, and assorted other fund-raising organizations. We received commissions on volume, and so it was necessary to convince a prospect that a play—preferably an expensive musical—for which we had reserved the rights to seats would be a boffo smash hit.

The object of our greatest expectation that season was an extravaganza called *Chu Chem*, a saga that aspired to ride the coattails of *Fiddler on the Roof* into entertainment history. It starred the estimable Molly Picon and told the story of a family who had centuries ago gone from Israel to China during the Diaspora, yet had, despite isolation in an alien environment, retained orthodox culture and habits. The crux of the plot revolved around a man with several marriageable daughters and nary a kosher suitor within five thousand miles. For three months Rita and I waxed eloquent in singing the show's praises. We sat in our little office, behind facing desks, and every noon while she redid her nails I ordered out from a deli that offered such exotic (to me) delicacies as fried egg sandwiches, lox and cream cheese, pastrami, tongue. I developed of necessity and habit a telephone voice laced with a distinctly Yiddish accent. It could have been a great career. However, come November, *Chu Chem* bombed. Its closing was such a financial catastrophe for all concerned that when the following January one Monsieur Dupont advertised on the placement board at my college, I decided to put an ocean between me and my former trusting clientele.

M. Dupont came to campus with the stated purpose of interviewing candidates for teller positions in a French bank. Successful applicants, required to be fluent *en français,* would be rewarded with three well-paid months and a rent-free apartment in Paris. On my way to the language lab, I registered for an appointment.

The only French in the interview was *Bonjour, ça va?,* after which M. Dupont switched into English and described the wonderful deal on charter air flights that would be available to those who got the nod. Round-trip to Amsterdam, via Reykjavík, leaving the day after exams and returning in mid-September, no changes or substitutions. I signed up on the spot. I was to be a *banquier,* with a *pied-à-terre* in Montparnasse!

Unfortunately, when I arrived with only $50 in traveler's checks in my pocket—the flight had cleaned me out, but who needed money since my paycheck started right away—no one in Paris had ever heard of M. Dupont. *Alors.*

I stood in the Gare du Nord and considered my options. There weren't any. 15 I scanned a listing of Paris hotels and headed for the cheapest one: the Hotel Villedo, $10 a night. The place had an ambiance that I persuaded myself was antique, despite the red light above the sign. The only accommodation available was "the bridal suite," a steal at $20. The glass door to my room didn't lock and in the adjacent room there was a rather continual floor show, but at some point I must have dozed off. When I awoke the church bells were ringing, the sky was pink, and I felt renewed. No little setback was going to spoil my adventure. I stretched, then walked to a mirror that hung above the sink next to the bed. I leaned forward to punctuate my resolve with a confident look in the eye.

The sink disengaged and fell to the floor. Water gushed. In panic I rummaged through my open suitcase, stuffed two pairs of underpants into the pipe to quell the flow, and before the dam broke, I was out the door. I barreled through the lobby of the first bank I passed, asked to see the director, and told the startled man my sad story. For some reason, whether from shock or pity, he hired me at $1.27 an hour to be a cross-checker of foreign currency transactions, and with two phone calls found me lodgings at a commercial school's dormitory.

From 8 to 5 each weekday my duty was to sit in a windowless room with six impeccably dressed people, all of whom were totaling identical additions and subtractions. We were highly dignified with each other, very professional, no *tutoyer*ing. Monsieur Saint presided, but the formidable Mademoiselle was the true power; she oversaw each of our columns and shook her head sadly at my American-shaped numbers.

My legacy from that summer, however, was more than an enduring penchant for crossed 7s. After I had worked for six weeks, M. Saint asked me during a coffee break why I didn't follow the example of other foreign students he had known and depart the office at noon in order to spend the afternoon touring the sights of Paris with the Alliance Française.

"Because," I replied in my halting French, "that costs money. I depend upon my full salary the same as any of you." M. Saint nodded gravely and said no more, but then on the next Friday he presented me with a white envelope along with my check.

"Do not open this until you have left the Société Général," he said omi-   20 nously. I thought I was fired for the time I had mixed up kroner and guilders, and, once on the sidewalk, I steeled myself to read the worst. I felt the quiet panic of blankness.

"Dear Sir," I translated the perfectly formed script. "You are a person of value. It is not correct that you should be in our beautiful city and not see it. Therefore we have amassed a modest sum to pay the tuition for a two-week afternoon program for you at the Alliance Française. Your wages will not suffer, for it is your assignment to appear each morning in this bureau and reacquaint us with the places you have visited. We shall see them afresh through your eyes." The letter had thirty signatures, from the director to the janitor, and stuffed inside the envelope was a sheaf of franc notes in various denominations.

I rushed back to the tiny office. M. Saint and Mademoiselle had waited, and accepted my gratitude with their usual controlled smiles and precise handshakes. But they had blown their Gallic cover, and for the next ten days and then through all the weeks until I went home in September, our branch was awash with sightseeing paraphernalia. Everyone had advice, favorite haunts, criticisms of the Alliance's choices or explanations. Paris passed through the bank's granite walls as sweetly as a June breeze through a window screen, and ever afterward the lilt of overheard French, a photograph of Sacre-Coeur or the Louvre, even a monthly bank statement, recalls to me that best of all summers.

I didn't wind up in an occupation with any obvious connection to the careers I sampled during my school breaks, but I never altogether abandoned those brief professions either. They were jobs not so much to be held as to be weighed, absorbed, and incorporated, and, collectively, they carried me forward into adult life like an escalator, unfolding a particular pattern at once amazing and inevitable.

ACTIVITIES FOR WRITING AND DISCUSSION

1. Reread the last sentence in the essay.
a. Interpret this concluding statement. What do you think Dorris means by it?
b. In an essay, discuss one or two jobs in your own past that had a particular impact on you. Tell some specific stories about those jobs (as Dorris does) to make them vivid for a reader. To what extent have you "weighed, absorbed, and incorporated" those jobs, and what "particular pattern" (if any) do you perceive in them?

2. Think of an early job that particularly influenced you. Write a letter (sent or unsent) to your employer, in which you recount your experiences on that job and how they affected you, for better or worse, in the short and/or long term.

JUDITH ORTIZ COFER (b. 1952)

Primary Lessons

My mother walked me to my first day at school at La Escuela Segundo Ruiz Belvis, named after the Puerto Rican patriot born in our town. I remember yellow cement with green trim. All the classrooms had been painted these colors to identify them as government property. This was true all over the Island. Everything was color-coded, including the children, who wore uniforms from first through twelfth grade. We were a midget army in white and brown, led by the hand to our battleground. From practically every house in our barrio emerged a crisply ironed uniform inhabited by the savage creatures we had become over a summer of running wild in the sun.

At my grandmother's house where we were staying until my father returned to Brooklyn Yard in New York and sent for us, it had been complete chaos, with several children to get ready for school. My mother had pulled my hair harder than usual while braiding it, and I had dissolved into a pool of total self-pity. I wanted to stay home with her and Mamá, to continue listening to stories in the late afternoon, to drink *café con leche* with them, and to play rough games with my many cousins. I wanted to continue living the dream of summer afternoons in Puerto Rico, and if I could not have it, then I wanted to go back to Paterson, New Jersey, back to where I imagined our apartment waited, peaceful and cool for the three of us to return to our former lives. Our gypsy lifestyle had convinced me, at age six, that one part of life stops and waits for you while you live another for a while—and if you don't like the present, you can always return to the past. Buttoning me into my stiff blouse while I tried to squirm away from her, my mother attempted to explain to me that I was a big girl now and should try to understand that, like all the other children my age, I had to go to school.

"What about him?" I yelled pointing at my brother who was lounging on the tile floor of our bedroom in his pajamas, playing quietly with a toy car.

"He's too young to go to school, you know that. Now stay still." My mother pinned me between her thighs to button my skirt, as she had learned to do from Mamá, from whose grip it was impossible to escape.

"It's not fair, it's not fair. I can't go to school here. I don't speak Spanish." It 5
was my final argument, and it failed miserably because I was shouting my defiance in the language I claimed not to speak. Only I knew what I meant by saying in Spanish that I did not speak Spanish. I had spent my early childhood in the United States, where I lived in a bubble created by my Puerto Rican parents in a home where two cultures and languages became one. I learned to listen to the English from the television with one ear while I heard my mother and father speaking in Spanish with the other. I thought I was an ordinary American kid—like the children on the shows I watched—and that everyone's parents spoke a secret second language at home. When we came to Puerto Rico right before I started first grade, I switched easily to Spanish. It was the language of fun, of summertime games. But school—that was a different matter.

I made one last desperate attempt to make my mother see reason: "Father will be very angry. You know that he wants us to speak good English." My mother, of course, ignored me as she dressed my little brother in his playclothes. I could not believe her indifference to my father's wishes. She was usually so careful about our safety and the many other areas that he was forever reminding her about in his letters. But I was right, and she knew it. Our father spoke to us in English as much as possible, and he corrected my pronunciation constantly— not "jes" but "y-es." Y-es, sir. How could she send me to school to learn Spanish when we would be returning to Paterson in just a few months?

But, of course, what I feared was not language, but loss of freedom. At school there would be no playing, no stories, only lessons. It would not matter if I did not understand a word, and I would not be allowed to make up my own definitions. I would have to learn silence. I would have to keep my wild imagination in check. Feeling locked into my stiffly starched uniform, I only sensed all this. I guess most children can intuit their loss of childhood's freedom on that first day of school. It is separation anxiety too, but mother is just the guardian of the "playground" of our early childhood.

The sight of my cousins in similar straits comforted me. We were marched down the hill of our barrio where Mamá's robin-egg-blue house stood at the top. I must have glanced back at it with yearning. Mamá's house—a place built for children—where anything that could be broken had already been broken by my grandmother's early batch of offspring (they ranged in age from my mother's oldest sisters to my uncle who was six months older than me). Her house had long since been made childproof. It had been a perfect summer place. And now it was September—the cruelest month for a child.

La Mrs., as all the teachers were called, waited for her class of first-graders at the door of the yellow and green classroom. She too wore a uniform: It was a blue skirt and a white blouse. This teacher wore black high heels with her "standard issue." I remember this detail because when we were all seated in rows she called on one little girl and pointed to the back of the room where there were shelves. She told the girl to bring her a shoebox from the bottom shelf. Then, when the box had been placed in her hands, she did something unusual. She had the little girl kneel at her feet and take the pointy high heels off her feet and replace them with a pair of satin slippers from the shoe box. She told the group that every one of us would have a chance to do this if we behaved in her class. Though confused about the prize, I soon felt caught up in the competition to bring *La Mrs.* her slippers in the morning. Children fought over the privilege.

Our first lesson was English. In Puerto Rico, every child has to take twelve years of English to graduate from school. It is the law. In my parents' school days, all subjects were taught in English. The U.S. Department of Education had specified that as a U.S. territory, the Island had to be "Americanized," and to accomplish this task, it was necessary for the Spanish language to be replaced in one generation through the teaching of English in all schools. My father began his school day by saluting the flag of the United States and singing "America" and "The Star-Spangled Banner" by rote, without understanding a word of what he was saying. The logic behind this system was that, though the children did not understand the English words, they would remember the rhythms. Even the games the teacher's manuals required them to play became absurd adaptations. "Here We Go Round the Mulberry Bush" became "Here We Go Round the Mango Tree." I have heard about the confusion caused by the use of a primer in which the sounds of animals were featured. The children were forced to accept that a rooster says *cockadoodledoo,* when they knew perfectly well from hearing their own roosters each morning that in Puerto Rico a rooster says *cocorocó.* Even the vocabulary of their pets was changed; there are still family stories circulating about the bewilderment of a first-grader coming home to try to teach his dog to speak in English. The policy of assimilation by immersion failed on the Island. Teachers adhered to it on paper, substituting their own materials for the texts, but no one took their English home. In due time, the program was minimized to the one class in English per day that I encountered when I took my seat in *La Mrs.'s* first grade class.

Catching us all by surprise, she stood very straight and tall in front of us and began to sing in English:

Pollito	—	Chicken
Gallina	—	Hen
Lápiz	—	Pencil
Y Pluma	—	Pen.

"Repeat after me, children: Pollito — Chicken," she commanded in her heavily accented English that only I understood, being the only child in the room who had ever been exposed to the language. But I too remained silent. No use making waves or showing off. Patiently *La Mrs.* sang her song and gestured for us to join in. At some point it must have dawned on the class that this silly routine was likely to go on all day if we did not "repeat after her." It was not her fault that she had to follow the rule in her teacher's manual stating that she must teach English *in* English, and that she must not translate, but merely repeat her lesson in English until the children "begin to respond" more or less "unconsciously." This was one of the vestiges of the regimen followed by her predecessors in the last generation. To this day I can recite "Pollito — Chicken" mindlessly, never once pausing to visualize chicks, hens, pencils, or pens.

I soon found myself crowned "teacher's pet" without much effort on my part. I was a privileged child in her eyes simply because I lived in "Nueva York," and because my father was in the navy. His name was an old one in our pueblo, associated with once-upon-a-time landed people and long-gone money. Status is judged by unique standards in a culture where, by definition, everyone is a second-class citizen. Remembrance of past glory is as good as titles and money. Old families living in decrepit old houses rank over factory workers living in modern comfort in cement boxes—all the same. The professions raise a person out of the dreaded "sameness" into a niche of status, so that teachers, nurses, and everyone who went to school for a job were given the honorifics of *El Míster* or *La Mrs.* by the common folks, people who were likely to be making more money in American factories than the poorly paid educators and government workers.

My first impressions of the hierarchy began with my teacher's shoe-changing ceremony and the exaggerated respect she received from our parents. *La Mrs.* was always right, and adults scrambled to meet her requirements. She wanted all our schoolbooks covered in the brown paper now used for paper bags (used at that time by the grocer to wrap meats and other foods). That first week of school the grocer was swamped with requests for paper which he gave away to the women. That week and the next, he wrapped produce in newspapers. All school projects became family projects. It was considered disrespectful at Mamá's house to do homework in privacy. Between the hours when we came home from school and dinner time, the table was shared by all of us working together with the women hovering in the background. The teachers communicated directly with the mothers, and it was a matriarchy of far-reaching power and influence.

There was a black boy in my first-grade classroom who was also the teacher's pet but for a different reason than I: I did not have to do anything to win her favor; he would do anything to win a smile. He was as black as the cauldron that Mamá used for cooking stew and his hair was curled into tight little balls on his head—*pasitas,* like little raisins glued to his skull, my mother had said. There had been some talk at Mamá's house about this boy; Lorenzo was his name. I later gathered that he was the grandson of my father's nanny. Lorenzo lived with Teresa, his grandmother, having been left in her care when

15

his mother took off for "Los Nueva Yores" shortly after his birth. And they were poor. Everyone could see that his pants were too big for him—hand-me-downs—and his shoe soles were as thin as paper. Lorenzo seemed unmindful of the giggles he caused when he jumped up to erase the board for *La Mrs.* and his baggy pants rode down to his thin hips as he strained up to get every stray mark. He seemed to relish playing the little clown when she asked him to come to the front of the room and sing his phonetic version of "o-bootifool, forpa-shios-keeis," leading the class in our incomprehensible tribute to the American flag. He was a bright, loving child, with a talent for song and mimicry that everyone commented on. He should have been chosen to host the PTA show that year instead of me.

At recess one day, I came back to the empty classroom to get something. My cup? My nickel for a drink from the kiosk man? I don't remember. But I remember the conversation my teacher was having with another teacher. I remember because it concerned me, and because I memorized it so that I could ask my mother to explain what it meant.

"He is a funny *negrito,* and, like a parrot, he can repeat anything you teach him. But his Mamá must not have the money to buy him a suit."

"I kept Rafaelito's First Communion suit; I bet Lorenzo could fit in it. It's white with a bow-tie," the other teacher said.

"But, Marisa," laughed my teacher, "in that suit, Lorenzo would look like a fly drowned in a glass of milk."

Both women laughed. They had not seen me crouched at the back of the 20 room, digging into my schoolbag. My name came up then.

"What about the Ortiz girl? They have money."

"I'll talk to her mother today. The superintendent, *El Americano* from San Juan, is coming down for the show. How about if we have her say her lines in both Spanish and English?"

The conversation ends there for me. My mother took me to Mayagüez and bought me a frilly pink dress and two crinoline petticoats to wear underneath so that I looked like a pink and white parachute with toothpick legs sticking out. I learned my lines, "Padres, maestros, Mr. Leonard, bienvenidos/Parents, teachers, Mr. Leonard, welcome. . . ." My first public appearance. I took no pleasure in it. The words were formal and empty. I had simply memorized them. My dress pinched me at the neck and arms, and made me itch all over.

I had asked my mother what it meant to be a "mosca en un vaso de leche," a fly in a glass of milk. She had laughed at the image, explaining that it meant being "different," but that it wasn't something I needed to worry about.

ACTIVITIES FOR WRITING AND DISCUSSION

1. Consider the various meanings of the title. "Primary" can refer to the elementary grades of school; it can also mean "fundamental," "basic," or "of first importance." Do the lessons learned by the six-year-old Cofer fit these different definitions? If so, in what ways?

2. Working with a group, make a list of the "primary lessons" Cofer learned as a six-year-old. Then identify an item on your list that resembles a lesson that *you* once learned, and write the story of that lesson. Either:
   a. Write the story in the form of a personal essay, or
   b. Write a dialogue, set in the past, between yourself and someone who was a key player in the "lesson," or
   c. Tell the story of your particular experience from a **third-person point of view**, i.e., write about yourself as "he" or "she."

3. The final paragraph shows the young Cofer asking her mother an awkward question, which the mother brushes aside. Invent a dialogue in which you either:
   a. Flesh out and expand the conversation you imagine to have taken place between Cofer and her mother, or
   b. Relate a similar type of conversation you had with your own parent, or
   c. Create a fictional conversation of a small child asking a parent about some controversial or "adult" subject.

Play

EUGENE O'NEILL (1888–1953)

The Hairy Ape

A COMEDY OF ANCIENT AND MODERN LIFE IN EIGHT SCENES

CHARACTERS

ROBERT SMITH, "YANK"

PADDY

LONG

MILDRED DOUGLAS

HER AUNT

SECOND ENGINEER

A GUARD

A SECRETARY OF AN ORGANIZATION

Stokers, Ladies, Gentlemen, etc.

Scenes

Scene I: The firemen's forecastle of an ocean liner—an hour after sailing from New York.

Scene II: Section of promenade deck, two days out—morning.

Scene III: The stokehole. A few minutes later.

Scene IV: Same as Scene I. Half an hour later.

Scene V: Fifth Avenue, New York. Three weeks later.

Scene VI: An island near the city. The next night.

Scene VII: In the city. About a month later.

Scene VIII: In the city. Twilight of the next day.

Scene One

The firemen's forecastle of a transatlantic liner an hour after sailing from New York for the voyage across. Tiers of narrow, steel bunks, three deep, on all sides. An entrance in rear. Benches on the floor before the bunks. The room is crowded with men, shouting, cursing, laughing, singing—a confused, inchoate uproar swelling into a sort of unity, a meaning—the bewildered, furious, baffled defiance of a beast in a cage. Nearly all the men are drunk. Many bottles are passed from hand to hand. All are dressed in dungaree pants, heavy ugly shoes. Some wear singlets, but the majority are stripped to the waist.

The treatment of this scene, or of any other scene in the play, should by no means be naturalistic. The effect sought after is a cramped space in the bowels of a ship, imprisoned by white steel. The lines of bunks, the uprights supporting them, cross each other like the steel framework of a cage. The ceiling crushes down upon the men's heads. They cannot stand upright. This accentuates the natural stooping posture which shoveling coal and the resultant over-development of back and shoulder muscles have given them. The men themselves should resemble those pictures in which the appearance of Neanderthal Man is guessed at. All are hairy-chested, with long arms of tremendous power, and low, receding brows above their small, fierce, resentful eyes. All the civilized white races are represented, but except for the slight differentiation in color of hair, skin, eyes, all these men are like.

The curtain rises on a tumult of sound. YANK *is seated in the foreground. He seems broader, fiercer, more truculent, more powerful, more sure of himself than the rest. They respect his superior strength—the grudging respect of fear. Then, too, he represents to them a self-expression, the very last word in what they are, their most highly developed individual.*

VOICES: Gif me trink dere, you!
'Ave a wet!
Salute!
Gesundheit!
Skoal!
Drunk as a lord, God stiffen you!
Here's how!
Luck!
Pass back that bottle, damn you!
Pourin' it down his neck!
Ho, Froggy! Where the devil have you been?
La Touraine.
I hit him smash in yaw, py Gott!
Jenkins—the First—he's a rotten swine—
And the coppers nabbed him—and I run—
I like peer better. It don't pig head gif you.
A slut, I'm sayin'! She robbed me aslape—
To hell with 'em all!
You're a bloody lair!
Say dot again! *(Commotion. Two men about to fight are pulled apart).*
No scrappin' now!
Tonight—
See who's the best man!
Bloody Dutchman!
Tonight on the for'ard square.
I'll bet on Dutchy.
He packa da wallop, I tella you!
Shut up, Wop!
No fightin', maties. We're all chums, ain't we?
(A voice starts bawling a song).

"Beer, beer, glorious beer!
Fill yourselves right up to here."

YANK *(for the first time seeming to take notice of the uproar about him, turns around threateningly—in a tone of contemptuous authority)*: Choke off dat noise! Where d'yuh get dat beer stuff? Beer, hell! Beer's for goils—and Dutchmen. Me for somep'n wit a kick to it! Gimme a drink, one of youse guys. *(Several bottles are eagerly offered. He takes a tremendous gulp at one of them; then, keeping the bottle in his hand, glares belligerently at the owner, who hastens to acquiesce in this robbery by saying)* All righto, Yank. Keep it and have another. *(YANK contemptuously turns his back on the crowd again. For a second there is an embarrassed silence. Then—)*
VOICES: We must be passing the Hook.
She's beginning to roll to it.

Six days in hell—and then Southampton.

Py Yesus, I vish somepody take my first vatch for me!

Gittin' seasick, Square-head?

Drink up and forget it!

What's in your bottle?

Gin.

Dot's nigger trink.

Absinthe? It's doped. You'll go off your chump, Froggy.

Cochon!

Whisky, that's the ticket!

Where's Paddy?

Going asleep.

Sing us that whisky song, Paddy. *(They all turn to an old, wizened Irishman who is dozing, very drunk, on the benches forward. His face is extremely monkey-like with all the sad, patient pathos of that animal in his small eyes).*

Singa da song, Caruso Pat!

He's gettin' old. The drink is too much for him.

He's too drunk.

PADDY *(blinking about him, starts to his feet resentfully, swaying, holding on to the edge of a bunk)*: I'm never too drunk to sing. 'Tis only when I'm dead to the world I'd be wishful to sing at all. *(With a sort of sad contempt)* "Whisky Johnny," ye want? A chanty, ye want? Now that's a queer wish from the ugly like of you, God help you. But no matther. *(He starts to sing in a thin, nasal, doleful tone)*:

Oh, whisky is the life of man!
   Whisky! O Johnny! *(They all join in on this).*
Oh, whisky is the life of man!
   Whisky for my Johnny! *(Again chorus).*

Oh, whisky drove my old man mad!
   Whisky! O Johnny!
Oh, whisky drove my old man mad!
   Whisky for my Johnny!

YANK *(again turning around scornfully)*: Aw hell! Nix on dat old sailing ship stuff! All dat bull's dead, see? And you're dead, too, yuh damned old Harp, on'y yuh don't know it. Take it easy, see. Give us a rest. Nix on de loud noise. *(With a cynical grin)* Can't youse see I'm tryin' to t'ink?

ALL *(repeating the word after him as one with the same cynical amused mockery)*: Think! *(The chorused word has a brazen metallic quality as if their throats were phonograph horns. It is followed by a general uproar of hard, barking laughter).*

VOICES: Don't be cracking your head wit ut, Yank.

You gat headache, py yingo!

One thing about it—it rhymes with drink!

Ha, ha, ha!

Drink, don't think!

Drink, don't think!

Drink, don't think! (*A whole chorus of voices has taken up this refrain, stamping on the floor, pounding on the benches with fists*).

YANK (*taking a gulp from his bottle—good-naturedly*): Aw right. Can de noise. I got yuh de foist time. (*The uproar subsides. A very drunken sentimental tenor begins to sing*):

"Far away in Canada,
    Far across the sea,
There's a lass who fondly waits
    Making a home for me—"

YANK (*fiercely contemptuous*): Shut up, yuh lousy boob! Where d'yuh get dat tripe? Home? Home, hell! I'll make a home for yuh! I'll knock yuh dead. Home! T'hell wit home! Where d'yuh get dat tripe? Dis is home, see? What d'yuh want wit home? (*Proudly*) I runned away from mine when I was a kid. On'y too glad to beat it, dat was me. Home was lickings for me, dat's all. But yuh can bet your shoit no one ain't never licked me since! Wanter try it, any of youse? Huh! I guess not. (*In a more placated but still contemptuous tone*) Goils waitin' for yuh, huh? Aw, hell! Dat's all tripe. Dey don't wait for no one. Dey'd double-cross yuh for a nickel. Dey're all tarts, get me? Treat 'em rough, dat's me. To hell wit 'em. Tarts, dat's what, de whole bunch of 'em.

LONG (*very drunk, jumps on a bench excitedly, gesticulating with a bottle in his hand*): Listen 'ere, Comrades! Yank 'ere is right. 'E says this 'ere stinkin' ship is our 'ome. And 'e says as 'ome is 'ell. And 'e's right! This is 'ell. We lives in 'ell, Comrades—and right enough we'll die in it. (*Raging*) And who's ter blame, I arsks yer? We ain't. We wasn't born this rotten way. All men is born free and ekal. That's in the bleedin' Bible, maties. But what d'they care for the Bible—them lazy, bloated swine what travels first cabin? Them's the ones. They dragged us down 'til we're on'y wage slaves in the bowels of a bloody ship, sweatin', burnin' up, eatin' coal dust! Hit's them's ter blame—the damned Capitalist clarss! (*There had been a gradual murmur of contemptuous resentment rising among the men until now he is interrupted by a storm of catcalls, hisses, boos, hard laughter*).

VOICES: Turn it off!

Shut up!

Sit down!

Closa da face!

Tamn fool! (*Etc.*).

YANK (*standing up and glaring at LONG*): Sit down before I knock yuh down! (LONG *makes haste to efface himself.* YANK *goes on contemptuously*) De Bible, huh? De Cap'tlist class, huh? Aw nix on dat Salvation Army–Socialist bull. Git a soapbox! Hire a hall! Come and be saved, huh? Jerk us to Jesus, huh? Aw g'wan! I've listened to lots of guys like you, see. Yuh're all wrong. Wanter know what I t'ink? Yuh ain't no good for no one. Yuh're de bunk. Yuh ain't got no noive, get me? Yuh're yellow, dat's what. Yellow, dat's you. Say! What's dem slobs in de foist cabin got to do wit us? We're better men dan dey are, ain't we? Sure! One of us guys could clean up de whole mob wit one mit. Put one of 'em down here for one watch in de stokehole, what'd happen? Dey'd carry him off on a stretcher. Dem boids don't amount to nothin'. Dey're just baggage. Who makes dis old tub run? Ain't it us guys? Well den, we belong, don't we? We belong and dey don't. Dat's all. *(A loud chorus of approval.* YANK *goes on)* As for dis bein' hell—aw, nuts! Yuh lost your noive, dat's what. Dis is a man's job, get me? It belongs. It runs dis tub. No stiffs need apply. But yuh're a stiff, see? Yuh're yellow, dat's you.

VOICES *(with a great hard pride in them)*:
Righto!
A man's job!
Talk is cheap, Long.
He never could hold up his end.
Divil take him!
Yank's right. We make it go.
Py Gott, Yank say right ting!
We don't need no one cryin' over us.
Makin' speeches.
Throw him out!
Yellow!
Chuck him overboard!
I'll break his jaw for him!
(They crowd around long threateningly).

YANK *(half good-natured again—contemptuously)*: Aw, take it easy. Leave him alone. He ain't woith a punch. Drink up. Here's how, whoever owns dis. *(He takes a long swallow from his bottle. All drink with him. In a flash all is hilarious amiability again, backslapping, loud talk, etc.).*

PADDY *(who has been sitting in a blinking, melancholy daze—suddenly cries out in a voice full of old sorrow)*: We belong to this, you're saying? We make the ship to go, you're saying? Yerra then, that Almighty God have pity on us! *(His voice runs into the wail of a keen, he rocks back and forth on his bench. The men stare at him, startled and impressed in spite of themselves)* Oh, to be back in the fine days of my youth, ochone! Oh, there was fine beautiful ships them days— clippers wid tall masts touching the sky—fine strong men in them—men that was sons of the sea as if 'twas the mother that bore them. Oh, the clean skins of them, and the clear eyes, the straight backs and full chests of them! Brave men they was, and bold men surely! We'd be sailing out, bound down round the Horn maybe. We'd be making sail in the dawn, with a fair breeze, singing a chanty song wid no care to it. And astern the land would be sinking low and dying out, but we'd give it no heed but a laugh, and never a look behind. For the day that was, was enough, for we was free men—and I'm thinking 'tis only slaves do be giving heed to the day that's gone or the day to come—until they're old like me. *(With a sort of religious exaltation)* Oh, to be scudding south again wid the power of the Trade Wind driving her on steady through the nights and the days! Full sail on her! Nights and days! Nights when the foam of the wake would be flaming wid fire, when the sky'd be blazing and winking wid stars. Or the full of the moon maybe. Then you'd see her driving through the gray night, her sails stretching aloft all silver and white, not a sound on the deck, the lot of us dreaming dreams, till you'd believe 'twas no real ship at all you was on but a ghost ship like the *Flying Dutchman* they say does be roaming the seas forevermore widout touching a port. And there was the days, too. A warm sun on the clean decks. Sun warming the blood of you, and wind over the miles of shiny green ocean like strong drink to your lungs. Work—aye, hard work—but who'd mind that at all? Sure, you worked under the sky and 'twas work wid skill and daring to it. And wid the day done, in the dog watch, smoking me pipe at ease, the lookout would be raising land maybe, and we'd see the mountains of South Americy wid the red fire of the setting sun painting the white tops and the clouds floating by them! *(His tone of exaltation ceases. He goes on mournfully)* Yerra, what's the use of talking? 'Tis a dead man's whisper. *(To* YANK *resentfully)* 'Twas them days men belonged to ships, not now. 'Twas them days a ship was part of the sea, and a man was part of a ship, and the sea joined all together and made it one. *(Scornfully)* Is it one wid this you'd be, Yank—black smoke from the funnels smudging the sea, smudging the decks—the bloody engines pounding and throbbing and shaking—wid divil a sight of sun or a breath of clean air—choking our lungs wid coal dust—breaking our backs and hearts in the hell of the stokehole—feeding the bloody furnace—feeding our lives along wid the coal, I'm thinking—caged in by steel from a sight of the sky like bloody apes in the Zoo! *(With a harsh laugh)* Ho-ho, divil mend you! Is it to belong to that you're wishing? Is it a flesh and blood wheel of the engines you'd be?

YANK *(who has been listening with a contemptuous sneer, barks out the answer)*: Sure ting! Dat's me. What about it?

PADDY *(as if to himself—with great sorrow)*: Me time is past due. That a great wave wid sun in the heart of it may sweep me over the side sometime I'd be dreaming of the days that's gone!

YANK: Aw, yuh crazy Mick! *(He springs to his feet and advances on* PADDY *threateningly—then stops, fighting some queer struggle within himself—lets his hands fall to his sides—contemptuously)* Aw, take it easy. Yuh're aw right, at dat. Yuh're bugs, dat's all—nutty as a cuckoo. All dat tripe yuh been pullin'—Aw, dat's all right. On'y it's dead, get me? Yuh don't belong no more, see. Yuh don't get de stuff. Yuh're too old. *(Disgustedly)* But aw say, come up for air onct in a while, can't yuh? See what's happened since yuh croaked. *(He suddenly bursts forth vehemently, growing more and more excited)* Say! Sure! Sure I meant it! What de hell—Say, lemme talk! Hey! Hey, you old Harp! Hey, youse guys! Say, listen to me—wait a moment—I gotter talk, see. I belong and he don't. He's dead but I'm livin'. Listen to me! Sure I'm part of de engines! Why de hell not! Dey move, don't dey? Dey're speed, ain't dey? Dey smash trou, don't dey? Twenty-five knots a hour! Dat's goin' some! Dat's new stuff! Dat belongs! But him, he's too old. He gets dizzy. Say, listen. All dat crazy tripe about nights and days; all dat crazy tripe about stars and moons; all dat crazy tripe about suns and winds, fresh air and de rest of it—Aw hell, dat's all a dope dream! Hittin' de pipe of de past, dat's what he's doin'. He's old and don't belong no more. But me, I'm young! I'm in de pink! I move wit it! It, get me! I mean de ting dat's de guts of all dis. It ploughs trou all de tripe he's been sayin'. It blows dat up! It knocks dat dead! It slams dat offen de face of de oith! It, get me! De engines and de coal and de smoke and all de rest of it! He can't breathe and swallow coal dust, but I kin, see? Dat's fresh air for me! Dat's food for me! I'm new, get me? Hell in de stokehole? Sure! It takes a man to work in hell. Hell, sure, dat's my fav'rite climate. I eat it up! I git fat on it! It's me makes it hot! It's me makes it roar! It's me makes it move! Sure, on'y for me everything stops. It all goes dead, get me? De noise and smoke and all de engines movin' de woild, dey stop. Dere ain't nothin' no more! Dat's what I'm sayin'. Everyting else dat makes de woild move, somep'n makes it move. It can't move witout somep'n else, see? Den yuh get down to me. I'm at de bottom, get me! Dere ain't nothin' foither. I'm de end! I'm de start! I start somep'n and de woild moves! It—dat's me!—de new dat's moiderin' de old! I'm de ting in coal dat makes it boin; I'm steam and oil for de engines; I'm de ting in noise dat makes yuh hear it; I'm smoke and express trains and steamers and factory whistles; I'm de ting in gold dat makes it money! And I'm what makes iron into steel! Steel, dat stands for de whole ting! And I'm steel—steel—steel! I'm de muscles in steel, de punch behind it! *(As he says this he pounds with his fist against the steel bunks. All the men, roused to a pitch of frenzied self-glorification by his speech, do likewise. There is a deafening metallic roar, through which* YANK's *voice can be heard bellowing)* Slaves, hell! We run de whole woiks. All de rich guys dat tink dey're somep'n, dey ain't nothin'! Dey don't belong. But us guys, we're in de move, we're at de bottom, de whole ting is us! *(*PADDY *from the start of* YANK's *speech has been taking one gulp after another from his bottle, at first frightenedly, as if he were afraid to listen, then desperately, as if to drown his senses, but finally has achieved complete indifferent, even amused, drunkenness.* YANK *sees his lips moving. He quells the uproar with a shout)* Hey, youse guys, take it easy! Wait a moment! De nutty Harp is sayin' somep'n.

PADDY *(is heard now—throws his head back with a mocking burst of laughter)*: Ho-ho-ho-ho-ho—

YANK *(drawing back his fist, with a snarl)*: Aw! Look out who yuh're givin' the bark!

PADDY *(begins to sing the "Miller of Dee" with enormous good nature)*:

"I care for nobody, no, not I,
And nobody cares for me."

YANK (*good-natured himself in a flash, interrupts* PADDY *with a slap on the bare back like a report*): Dat's de stuff! Now yuh're gettin' wise to somep'n. Care for nobody, dat's de dope! To hell wit 'em all! And nix on nobody else carin'. I kin care for myself, get me! (*Eight bells sound, muffled, vibrating through the steel walls as if some enormous brazen gong were imbedded in the heart of the ship. All the men jump up mechanically, file through the door silently close upon each other's heels in what is very like a prisoners' lockstep.* YANK *slaps* PADDY *on the back*) Our watch, yuh old Harp! (*Mockingly*) Come on down in hell. Eat up de coal dust. Drink in de heat. It's it, see! Act like yuh liked it, yuh better—or croak yuhself.

PADDY (*with jovial defiance*): To the divil wid it! I'll not report this watch. Let thim log me and be damned. I'm no slave the like of you. I'll be sittin' here at me ease, and drinking, and thinking, and dreaming dreams.

YANK (*contemptuously*): Tinkin' and dreamin', what'll that get yuh? What's tinkin' got to do wit it? We move, don't we? Speed, ain't it? Fog, dat's all you stand for. But we drive trou dat, don't we? We split dat up and smash trou—twenty-five knots a hour! (*Turns his back on* PADDY *scornfully*) Aw, yuh make me sick! Yuh don't belong! (*He strides out the door in rear.* PADDY *hums to himself, blinking drowsily*)

Curtain

SCENE TWO

Two days out. A section of the promenade deck. MILDRED DOUGLAS *and her aunt are discovered reclining in deck chairs. The former is a girl of twenty, slender, delicate, with a pale, pretty face marred by a self-conscious expression of disdainful superiority. She looks fretful, nervous and discontented, bored by her own anemia. Her aunt is a pompous and proud—and fat—old lady. She is a type even to the point of a double chin and lorgnettes. She is dressed pretentiously, as if afraid her face alone would never indicate her position in life.* MILDRED *is dressed all in white.*

The impression to be conveyed by this scene is one of the beautiful, vivid life of the sea all about—sunshine on the deck in a great flood, the fresh sea wind blowing across it. In the midst of this, these two incongruous, artificial figures, inert and disharmonious, the elder like a gray lump of dough touched up with rouge, the younger looking as if the vitality of her stock had been sapped before she was conceived, so that she is the expression not of its life energy but merely of the artificialities that energy had won for itself in the spending.

MILDRED (*looking up with affected dreaminess*): How the black smoke swirls back against the sky! Is it not beautiful?

AUNT (*without looking up*): I dislike smoke of any kind.

MILDRED: My great-grandmother smoked a pipe—a clay pipe.

AUNT (*ruffling*): Vulgar!

MILDRED: She was too distant a relative to be vulgar. Time mellows pipes.

AUNT *(pretending boredom but irritated)*: Did the sociology you took up at college teach you that—to play the ghoul on every possible occasion, excavating old bones? Why not let your great-grandmother rest in her grave?

MILDRED *(dreamily)*: With her pipe beside her—puffing in Paradise.

AUNT *(with spite)*: Yes, you are a natural born ghoul. You are even getting to look like one, my dear.

MILDRED *(in a passionless tone)*: I detest you, Aunt. *(Looking at her critically)* Do you know what you remind me of? Of a cold pork pudding against a background of linoleum tablecloth in the kitchen of a—but the possibilities are wearisome. *(She closes her eyes)*.

AUNT *(with a bitter laugh)*: Merci for your candor. But since I am and must be your chaperon—in appearance, at least—let us patch up some sort of armed truce. For my part you are quite free to indulge any pose of eccentricity that beguiles you—as long as you observe the amenities—

MILDRED *(drawling)*: The inanities?

AUNT *(going on as if she hadn't heard)*: After exhausting the morbid thrills of social service work on New York's East Side—how they must have hated you, by the way, the poor that you made so much poorer in their own eyes!— you are now bent on making your slumming international. Well, I hope Whitechapel will provide the needed nerve tonic. Do not ask me to chaperon you there, however. I told your father I would not. I loathe deformity. We will hire an army of detectives and you may investigate everything—they allow you to see.

MILDRED *(protesting with a trace of genuine earnestness)*: Please do not mock at my attempts to discover how the other half lives. Give me credit for some sort of groping sincerity in that at least. I would like to help them. I would like to be some use in the world. Is it my fault I don't know how? I would like to be sincere, to touch life somewhere. *(With weary bitterness)* But I'm afraid I have neither the vitality nor integrity. All that was burnt out in our stock before I was born. Grandfather's blast furnaces, flaming to the sky, melting steel, making millions—then father keeping those home fires burning, making more millions—and little me at the tail-end of it all. I'm a waste product in the Bessemer process—like the millions. Or rather, I inherit the acquired trait of the by-product, wealth, but none of the energy, none of the strength of the steel that made it. I am sired by gold and damned by it, as they say at the race track— damned in more ways than one. *(She laughs mirthlessly)*.

AUNT *(unimpressed—superciliously)*: You seem to be going in for sincerity today. It isn't becoming to you, really—except as an obvious pose. Be as artificial as you are, I advise. There's a sort of sincerity in that, you know. And, after all, you must confess you like that better.

MILDRED *(again affected and bored)*: Yes, I suppose I do. Pardon me for my outburst. When a leopard complains of its spots, it must sound rather grotesque. *(In a mocking tone)* Purr, little leopard. Purr, scratch, tear, kill, gorge yourself and be happy—only stay in the jungle where your spots are camouflage. In a cage they make you conspicuous.

AUNT: I don't know what you are talking about.

MILDRED: It would be rude to talk about anything to you. Let's just talk. *(She looks at her wrist watch)* Well, thank goodness, it's about time for them to come for me. That ought to give me a new thrill, Aunt.

AUNT *(affectedly troubled)*: You don't mean to say you're really going? The dirt—the heat must be frightful—

MILDRED: Grandfather started as a puddler. I should have inherited an immunity to heat that would make a salamander shiver. It will be fun to put it to the test.

AUNT: But don't you have to have the captain's—or someone's—permission to visit the stokehole?

MILDRED *(with a triumphant smile)*: I have it—both his and the chief engineer's. Oh, they didn't want to at first, in spite of my social service credentials. They didn't seem a bit anxious that I should investigate how the other half lives and works on a ship. So I had to tell them that my father, the president of Nazareth Steel, chairman of the board of directors of this line, had told me it would be all right.

AUNT: He didn't.

MILDRED: How naïve age makes one! But I said he did, Aunt. I even said he had given me a letter to them—which I had lost. And they were afraid to take the chance that I might be lying. *(Excitedly)* So it's ho! for the stokehole. The second engineer is to escort me. *(Looking at her watch again)* It's time. And here he comes, I think. *(The* SECOND ENGINEER *enters. He is a husky, fine-looking man of thirty-five or so. He stops before the two and tips his cap, visibly embarrassed and ill-at-ease).*

SECOND ENGINEER: Miss Douglas?

MILDRED: Yes. *(Throwing off her rugs and getting to her feet)* Are we all ready to start?

SECOND ENGINEER: In just a second, ma'am. I'm waiting for the Fourth. He's coming along.

MILDRED *(with a scornful smile)*: You don't care to shoulder this responsibility alone, is that it?

SECOND ENGINEER *(forcing a smile)*: Two are better than one. *(Disturbed by her eyes, glances out to sea—blurts out)* A fine day we're having.

MILDRED: Is it?

SECOND ENGINEER: A nice warm breeze—

MILDRED: It feels cold to me.

SECOND ENGINEER: But it's hot enough in the sun—

MILDRED: Not hot enough for me. I don't like Nature. I was never athletic.

SECOND ENGINEER *(forcing a smile)*: Well, you'll find it hot enough where you're going.

MILDRED: Do you mean hell?

SECOND ENGINEER (*flabbergasted, decides to laugh*): Ho-ho! No, I mean the stokehole.

MILDRED: My grandfather was a puddler. He played with boiling steel.

SECOND ENGINEER (*all at sea—uneasily*): Is that so? Hum, you'll excuse me, ma'am, but are you intending to wear that dress?

MILDRED: Why not?

SECOND ENGINEER: You'll likely rub against oil and dirt. It can't be helped.

MILDRED: It doesn't matter. I have lots of white dresses.

SECOND ENGINEER: I have an old coat you might throw over—

MILDRED: I have fifty dresses like this. I will throw this one into the sea when I come back. That ought to wash it clean, don't you think?

SECOND ENGINEER (*doggedly*): There's ladders to climb down that are none to clean—and dark alleyways—

MILDRED: I will wear this very dress and none other.

SECOND ENGINEER: No offense meant. It's none of my business. I was only warning you—

MILDRED: Warning? That sounds thrilling.

SECOND ENGINEER (*looking down the deck—with a sigh of relief*): There's the Fourth now. He's waiting for us. If you'll come—

MILDRED: Go on. I'll follow you. (*He goes.* MILDRED *turns a mocking smile on her aunt*) An oaf—but a handsome, virile oaf.

AUNT (*scornfully*): Poser!

MILDRED: Take care. He said there were dark alleyways—

AUNT (*in the same tone*): Poser!

MILDRED (*biting her lips angrily*): You are right. But would that my millions were not so anemically chaste!

AUNT: Yes, for a fresh pose I have no doubt you would drag the name of Douglas in the gutter!

MILDRED: From which it sprang. Good-by, Aunt. Don't pray too hard that I may fall into the fiery furnace.

AUNT: Poser!

MILDRED (*viciously*): Old hag! (*She slaps her aunt insultingly across the face and walks off, laughing gaily*).

AUNT (*screams after her*): I said poser!

Curtain

SCENE THREE

The stokehole. In the rear, the dimly-outlined bulks of the furnaces and boilers. High overhead one hanging electric bulb sheds just enough light through the murky air laden with coal dust to pile up masses of shadows everywhere. A line of men, stripped to the waist, is before the furnace doors. They bend over, looking neither to right nor left, handling their shovels as if they were part of their bodies, with a strange, awkward, swinging rhythm. They use the shovels to throw open the furnace doors. Then from these fiery round holes in the black a flood of terrific light and heat pours full upon the men who are outlined in silhouette in the crouching, inhuman attitudes of chained gorillas. The men shovel with a rhythmic motion, swinging as on a pivot from the coal which lies in heaps on the floor behind to hurl it into the flaming mouths before them. There is a tumult of noise— the brazen clang of the furnace doors as they are flung open or slammed shut, the grating, teeth-gritting grind of steel against steel, of crunching coal. This clash of sounds stuns one's ears with its rending dissonance. But there is order in it, rhythm, a mechanical regulated recurrence, a tempo. And rising above all, making the air hum with the quiver of liberated energy, the roar of leaping flames in the furnaces, the monotonous throbbing beat of the engines.

As the curtain rises, the furnace doors are shut. The men are taking a breathing spell. One or two are arranging the coal behind them, pulling it into more accessible heaps. The others can be dimly made out leaning on their shovels in relaxed attitudes of exhaustion.

PADDY (*from somewhere in the line—plaintively*): Yerra, will this divil's own watch nivir end? Me back is broke. I'm destroyed entirely.

YANK (*from the center of the line—with exuberant scorn*): Aw, yuh make me sick! Lie down and croak, why don't yuh? Always beefin', dat's you! Say, dis is a cinch! Dis was made for me! It's my meat, get me! (*A whistle is blown—a thin, shrill note from somewhere overhead in the darkness.* YANK *curses without resentment*) Dere's de damn engineer crackin' de whip. He tinks we're loafin'.

PADDY (*vindictively*): God stiffen him!

YANK (*in an exultant tone of command*): Come on, youse guys! Git into de game! She's gittin' hungry! Pile some grub in her. Trow it into her belly! Come on now, all of youse! Open her up! (*At this last all the men, who have followed his movements of getting into position, throw open their furnace doors with a deafening clang. The fiery light floods over their shoulders as they bend round for the coal. Rivulets of sooty sweat have traced maps on their backs. The enlarged muscles form bunches of high light and shadow*).

YANK (*chanting a count as he shovels without seeming effort*): One—two— tree— (*His voice rising exultantly in the joy of battle*) Dat's de stuff! Let her have it! All togedder now! Sling it into her! Let her ride! Shoot de piece now! Call de toin on her! Drive her into it! Feel her move! Watch her smoke! Speed, dat's her middle name! Give her coal, youse guys! Coal, dat's her booze! Drink it up, baby! Let's see yuh sprint! Dig in and gain a lap! Dere she go-o-es. (*This last in the chanting formula of the gallery gods at the six-day bike race. He slams his furnace door shut. The others do likewise with as much unison as their wearied bodies will permit. The effect is of one fiery eye after another being blotted out with a series of accompanying bangs*).

PADDY (*groaning*): Me back is broke. I'm bate out—bate— (*There is a pause. Then the inexorable whistle sounds again from the dim regions above the electric light. There is a growl of cursing rage from all sides*).

YANK (*shaking his fist upward—contemptuously*): Take it easy dere, you! Who d'yuh tink's runnin' dis game, me or you? When I git ready, we move. Not before! When I git ready, get me!

VOICES (*approvingly*): That's the stuff!

Yank tal him, py golly!

Yank ain't affeerd.

Goot poy, Yank!

Give him hell!

Tell 'im 'e's a bloody swine!

Bloody slave-driver!

YANK (*contemptuously*): He ain't got no noive. He's yellow, get me? All de engineers is yellow. Dey got streaks a mile wide. Aw, to hell wit him! Let's move, youse guys. We had a rest. Come on, she needs it! Give her pep! It ain't for him. Him and his whistle, dey don't belong. But we belong, see! We gotter feed de baby! Come on! (*He turns and flings his furnace door open. They all follow his lead. At this instant the* SECOND *and* FOURTH ENGINEERS *enter from the darkness on the left with* MILDRED *between them. She starts, turns paler, her pose is crumbling, she shivers with fright in spite of the blazing heat, but forces herself to leave the* ENGINEERS *and take a few steps nearer the men. She is right behind* YANK. *All this happens quickly while the men have their backs turned*).

YANK: Come on, youse guys! (*He is turning to get coal when the whistle sounds again in a peremptory, irritating note. This drives* YANK *into a sudden fury. While the other men have turned full around and stopped dumfounded by the spectacle of* MILDRED *standing there in her white dress,* YANK *does not turn far enough to see her. Besides, his head is thrown back, he blinks upward through the murk trying to find the owner of the whistle, he brandishes his shovel murderously over his head in one hand, pounding on his chest, gorilla-like, with the other, shouting*) Toin off dat whistle! Come down outa dere, yuh yellow, brass-buttoned, Belfast bum, yuh! Come down and I'll knock yer brains out! Yuh lousy, stinkin', yellow mut of a Catholic-moiderin' bastard! Come down and I'll moider yuh! Pullin' dat whistle on me, huh? I'll show yuh! I'll crash yer skull in! I'll drive yer teet' down yer troat! I'll slam yer nose trou de back of yer head! I'll cut yer guts out for a nickel, yuh lousy boob, yuh dirty, crummy, muckeatin' son of a— (*Suddenly he becomes conscious of all the other men staring at something directly behind his back. He whirls defensively with a snarling, murderous growl, crouching to spring, his lips drawn back over his teeth, his small eyes gleaming ferociously. He sees* MILDRED, *like a white apparition in the full light from the open furnace doors. He glares into her eyes, turned to stone. As for her, during his speech she has listened, paralyzed with horror, terror, her whole personality crushed, beaten in, collapsed, by the terrific impact of this unknown, abysmal brutality, naked and shameless. As she looks at his gorilla face, as his eyes bore into hers, she utters a low, choking cry and shrinks away from him, putting both hands up before her eyes to shut out the sight of his face, to protect her own. This startles* YANK *to a reaction. His mouth falls open, his eyes grow bewildered*).

MILDRED (*about to faint—to the* ENGINEERS, *who now have her one by each arm—whimperingly*): Take me away! Oh, the filthy beast! (*She faints. They carry her quickly back, disappearing in the darkness at the left, rear. An iron door clangs shut. Rage and bewildered fury rush back on* YANK. *He feels himself insulted in some unknown fashion in the very heart of his pride. He roars*) God damn yuh! (*And hurls his shovel after them at the door which has just closed. It hits the steel bulkhead with a clang and falls clattering on the steel floor. From overhead the whistle sounds again in a long, angry, insistent command*).

Curtain

SCENE FOUR

The firemen's forecastle. YANK'S *watch has just come off duty and had dinner. Their faces and bodies shine from a soap and water scrubbing but around their eyes, where a hasty dousing does not touch, the coal dust sticks like black make-up, giving them a queer, sinister expression.* YANK *has not washed either face or body. He stands out in contrast to them, a blackened, brooding figure. He is seated forward on a bench in the exact attitude of Rodin's "The Thinker." The others, most of them smoking pipes, are staring at* YANK *half-apprehensively, as if fearing an outburst; half-amusedly, as if they saw a joke somewhere that tickled them.*

VOICES: He ain't ate nothin'.
Py golly, a fallar gat to gat grub in him.
Divil a lie.
Yank feeda da fire, no feeda da face.
Ha-ha.
He aint even washed hisself.
He's forgot.
Hey, Yank, you forgot to wash.
YANK (*sullenly*): Forgot nothin'! To hell wit washin'.
VOICES: It'll stick to you.
It'll get under your skin.
Give yer the bleedin' itch, that's wot.
It makes spots on you—like a leopard.
Like a piebald nigger, you mean.
Better wash up, Yank.
You sleep better.
Wash up, Yank.
Wash up! Wash up!
YANK (*resentfully*): Aw say, youse guys. Lemme alone. Can't youse see I'm tryin' to tink?
ALL (*repeating the word after him as one with cynical mockery*): Think! (*The word has a brazen, metallic quality as if their throats were phonograph horns. It is followed by a chorus of hard, barking laughter*).

YANK (*springing to his feet and glaring at them belligerently*): Yes, tink! Tink, dat's what I said! What about it? (*They are silent, puzzled by his sudden resentment at what used to be one of his jokes.* YANK *sits down again in the same attitude of "The Thinker"*).

voices: Leave him alone.

He's got a grouch on.

Why wouldn't he?

PADDY (*with a wink at the others*): Sure I know what's the matther. 'Tis aisy to see. He's fallen in love, I'm telling you.

ALL (*repeating the word after him as one with cynical mockery*): Love! (*The word has a brazen, metallic quality as if their throats were phonograph horns. It is followed by a chorus of hard, barking laughter*).

YANK (*with a contemptuous snort*): Love, hell! Hate, dat's what. I've fallen in hate, get me?

PADDY (*philosophically*): 'Twould take a wise man to tell one from the other. (*With a bitter, ironical scorn, increasing as he goes on*) But I'm telling you it's love that's in it. Sure what else but love for us poor bastes in the stokehole would be bringing a fine lady, dressed like a white quane, down a mile of ladders and steps to be havin' a look at us? (*A growl of anger goes up from all sides*).

LONG (*jumping on a bench—hectically*): Hinsultin' us! Hinsultin' us, the bloody cow! And them bloody engineers! What right 'as they got to be exhibitin' us 's if we was bleedin' monkeys in a menagerie? Did we sign for hinsults to our dignity as 'onest workers? Is that in the ship's articles? You kin bloody well bet it ain't! But I know why they done it. I asked a deck steward 'o she was and 'e told me. 'Er old man's a bleedin' millionaire, a bloody Capitalist! 'E's got enuf bloody gold to sink this bleedin' ship! 'E makes arf the bloody steel in the world! 'E owns this bloody boat! And you and me, Comrades, we're 'is slaves! And the skipper and mates and engineers, they're 'is slaves! And she's 'is bloody daughter and we're all 'er slaves, too! And she gives 'er orders as 'ow she wants to see the bloody animals below decks and down they takes 'er! (*There is a roar of rage from all sides*).

YANK (*blinking at him bewilderedly*): Say! Wait a moment! Is all dat straight goods?

LONG: Straight as string! The bleedin' steward as waits on 'em, 'e told me about 'er. And what're we goin' ter do, I arsks yer? 'Ave we got ter swaller 'er hinsults like dogs? It ain't in the ship's articles. I tell yer we got a case. We kin go to law—

YANK (*with abysmal contempt*): Hell! Law!

ALL (*repeating the word after him as one with cynical mockery*): Law! (*The word has a brazen metallic quality as if their throats were phonograph horns. It is followed by a chorus of hard, barking laughter*).

LONG (*feeling the ground slipping from under his feet—desperately*): As voters and citizens we kin force the bloody governments—

YANK (*with abysmal contempt*): Hell! Governments!

ALL (*repeating the word after him as one with cynical mockery*): Governments! (*The word has a brazen metallic quality as if their throats were phonograph horns. It is followed by a chorus of hard, barking laughter*).

LONG (*hysterically*): We're free and equal in the sight of God—

YANK (*with abysmal contempt*): Hell! God!

ALL (*repeating the word after him as one with cynical mockery*) God! (*The word has a brazen metallic quality as if their throats were phonograph horns. It is followed by a chorus of hard, barking laughter*).

YANK (*witheringly*): Aw, join de Salvation Army!

ALL: Sit down! Shut up! Damn fool! Sea-lawyer! (LONG *slinks back out of sight*).

PADDY (*continuing the trend of his thoughts as if he had never been interrupted—bitterly*): And there she was standing behind us, and the Second pointing at us like a man you'd hear in a circus would be saying: In this cage is a queerer kind of baboon than ever you'd find in darkest Africy. We roast them in their own sweat—and be damned if you won't hear some of thim saying they like it! (*He glances scornfully at* YANK).

YANK (*with a bewildered uncertain growl*): Aw!

PADDY: And there was Yank roarin' curses and turning round wid his shovel to brain her—and she looked at him, and him at her—

YANK (*slowly*): She was all white. I tought she was a ghost. Sure.

PADDY (*with heavy, biting sarcasm*): 'Twas love at first sight, divil a doubt of it! If you'd seen the endearin' look on her pale mug when she shriveled away with her hands over her eyes to shut out the sight of him! Sure, 'twas as if she'd seen a great hairy ape escaped from the Zoo!

YANK (*stung—with a growl of rage*): Aw!

PADDY: And the loving way Yank heaved his shovel at the skull of her, only she was out the door! (*A grin breaking over his face*) 'Twas touching, I'm telling you! It put the touch of home, swate home in the stokehole. (*There is a roar of laughter from all*).

YANK (*glaring at* PADDY *menacingly*): Aw, choke dat off, see!

PADDY (*not heeding him—to the others*): And her grabbin' at the Second's arm for protection. (*With a grotesque imitation of a woman's voice*) Kiss me, Engineer dear, for it's dark down here and me old man's in Wall Street making money! Hug me tight, darlin', for I'm afeerd in the dark and me mother's on deck makin' eyes at the skipper! (*Another roar of laughter*).

YANK (*threateningly*): Say! What yuh tryin' to do, kid me, yuh old Harp?

PADDY: Divil a bit! Ain't I wishin' myself you'd brained her?

YANK (*fiercely*): I'll brain her! I'll brain her yet, wait 'n' see! (*Coming over to* PADDY—*slowly*) Say, is dat what she called me—a hairy ape?

PADDY: She looked it at you if she didn't say the word itself.

YANK (*grinning horribly*): Hairy ape, huh? Sure! Dat's de way she looked at me, aw right. Hairy ape! So dat's me, huh? (*Bursting into rage—as if she were still in front of him*) Yuh skinny tart! Yuh white-faced bum, yuh! I'll show yuh who's a ape! (*Turning to the others, bewilderment seizing him again*) Say, youse guys. I was bawlin' him out for pullin' de whistle on us. You heard me. And den I seen youse lookin' at somep'n and I tought he'd sneaked down to come up in back of me, and I hopped round to knock him dead wit de shovel. And dere she was wit de light on her! Christ, yuh coulda pushed me over with a finger! I was scared, get me? Sure! I tought she was a ghost, see? She was all in white like dey wrap around stiffs. You seen her. Kin yuh blame me? She didn't belong, dat's what. And den when I come to and seen it was a real skoit and seen de way she was lookin' at me—like Paddy said—Christ, I was sore, get me? I don't stand for dat stuff from nobody. And I flung de shovel—on'y she'd beat it. (*Furiously*) I wished it'd banged her! I wished it'd knocked her block off!

LONG: And be 'anged for murder or 'lectrocuted? She ain't bleedin' well worth it.

YANK: I don't give a damn what! I'd be square wit her, wouldn't I? Tink I wanter let her put somep'n over on me? Tink I'm goin' to let her git away wit dat stuff? Yuh don't know me! No one ain't never put nothin' over on me and got away wit it, see!—not dat kind of stuff—no guy and no skoit neither! I'll fix her! Maybe she'll come down again—

VOICE: No chance, Yank. You scared her out of a year's growth.

YANK: I scared her? Why de hell should I scare her? Who de hell is she? Ain't she de same as me? Hairy ape, huh? (*With his old confident bravado*) I'll show her I'm better'n her, if she on'y knew it. I belong and she don't, see! I move and she's dead! Twenty-five knots an hour, dat's me! Dat carries her but I make dat. She's on'y baggage. Sure! (*Again bewilderedly*) But, Christ, she was funny lookin'! Did yuh pipe her hands? White and skinny. Yuh could see de bones through 'em. And her mush, dat was dead white, too. And her eyes, dey was like dey'd seen a ghost. Me, dat was! Sure! Hairy ape! Ghost, huh? Look at dat arm! (*He extends his right arm, swelling out the great muscles*) I coulda took her wit dat, wit just my little finger even, and broke her in two. (*Again bewilderedly*) Say, who is dat skoit, huh? What is she? What's she come from? Who made her? Who give her de noive to look at me like dat? Dis ting's got my goat right. I don't get her. She's new to me. What does a skoit like her mean, huh? She don't belong, get me! I can't see her. (*With growing anger*) But one ting I'm wise to, aw right, aw right! Youse all kin bet your shoits I'll git even wit her. I'll show her if she tinks she—She grinds de organ and I'm on de string, huh? I'll fix her! Let her come down again and I'll fling her in de furnace! She'll move den! She won't shiver at nothin', den! Speed, dat'll be her! She'll belong den! (*He grins horribly*).

PADDY: She'll never come. She's had her belly-full, I'm telling you. She'll be in bed now, I'm thinking, wid ten doctors and nurses feedin' her salts to clean the fear out of her.

YANK (*enraged*): Yuh tink I made her sick, too, do yuh? Just lookin' at me, huh? Hairy ape, huh? (*In a frenzy of rage*) I'll fix her! I'll tell her where to git off! She'll git down on her knees and take it back or I'll bust de face offen her! (*Shaking one fist upward and beating on his chest with the other*) I'll find yuh! I'm comin', d'yuh hear? I'll fix yuh, God damn yuh! (*He makes a rush for the door*).

VOICES: Stop him!
He'll get shot!
He'll murder her!
Trip him up!
Hold him!
He's gone crazy!
Gott, he's strong!
Hold him down!
Look out for a kick!
Pin his arms!
(*They have all piled on him and, after a fierce struggle, by sheer weight of numbers have borne him to the floor just inside the door*).

PADDY (*who has remained detached*): Kape him down till he's cooled off. (*Scornfully*) Yerra, Yank, you're a great fool. Is it payin' attention at all you are to the like of that skinny sow widout one drop of rale blood in her?

YANK (*frenziedly, from the bottom of the heap*): She done me doit! She done me doit, didn't she? I'll git square wit her! I'll get her some way! Git offen me, youse guys! Lemme up! I'll show her who's a ape!

Curtain

SCENE FIVE

Three weeks later. A corner of Fifth Avenue in the Fifties on a fine Sunday morning. A general atmosphere of clean, well-tidied, wide street; a flood of mellow, tempered sunshine; gentle, genteel breezes. In the rear, the show windows of two shops, a jewelry establishment on the corner, a furrier's next to it. Here the adornments of extreme wealth are tantalizingly displayed. The jeweler's window is gaudy with glittering diamonds, emeralds, rubies, pearls, etc., fashioned in ornate tiaras, crowns, necklaces, collars, etc. From each piece hangs an enormous tag from which a dollar sign and numerals in intermittent electric lights wink out the incredible prices. The same in the furrier's. Rich furs of all varieties hang there bathed in a downpour of artificial light. The general effect is of a background of magnificence cheapened and made grotesque by commercialism, a background in tawdry disharmony with the clear light and sunshine on the street itself.

Up the side street YANK *and* LONG *come swaggering.* LONG *is dressed in shore clothes, wears a black Windsor tie, cloth cap.* YANK *is in his dirty dungarees. A fireman's cap with black peak is cocked defiantly on the side of his head. He has not shaved for days and around his fierce, resentful eyes—as around those of* LONG *to a lesser degree—the black smudge of coal dust still sticks like make-up. They hesitate and stand together at the corner, swaggering, looking about them with a forced, defiant contempt.*

LONG (*indicating it all with an oratorical gesture*): Well, 'ere we are. Fif' Avenoo. This 'ere's their bleedin' private lane, as yer might say. (*Bitterly*) We're trespassers 'ere. Proletarians keep orf the grass!

YANK (*dully*): I don't see no grass, yuh boob. (*Staring at the sidewalk*) Clean, ain't it? Yuh could eat a fried egg offen it. The white wings got some job sweepin' dis up. (*Looking up and down the avenue—surlily*) Where's all de white-collar stiffs yuh said was here—and de skoits—*her* kind?

LONG: In church, blast 'em! Arskin' Jesus to give 'em more money.

YANK: Choich, huh? I useter go to choich onct—sure—when I was a kid. Me old man and woman, dey made me. Dey never went demselves, dough. Always got too big a head on Sunday mornin', dat was dem. (*With a grin*) Dey was scrappers for fair, bot' of dem. On Satiday nights when dey bot' got a skinful dey could put up a bout oughter been staged at de Garden. When dey got trough dere wasn't a chair or table wit a leg under it. Or else dey bot' jumped on me for somep'n. Dat was where I loined to take punishment. (*With a grin and a swagger*) I'm a chip offen de old block, get me?

LONG: Did yer old man follow the sea?

YANK: Naw. Worked along shore. I runned away when me old lady croaked wit de tremens. I helped at truckin' and in de market. Den I shipped in de stokehole. Sure. Dat belongs. De rest was nothin'. (*Looking around him*) I ain't never seen dis before. De Brooklyn waterfront, dat was where I was dragged up. (*Taking a deep breath*) Dis ain't so bad at dat, huh?

LONG: Not bad? Well, we pays for it wiv our bloody sweat, if yer wants to know!

YANK (*with sudden angry disgust*): Aw hell! I don't see no one, see—like her. All dis gives me a pain. It don't belong. Say, ain't dere a back room around dis dump? Let's go shoot a ball. All dis is too clean and quiet and dolled-up, get me! It gives me a pain.

LONG: Wait and yer'll bloody well see—

YANK: I don't wait for no one. I keep on de move. Say, what yuh drag me up here for, anyway? Tryin' to kid me, yuh simp, yuh?

LONG: Yer wants to get back at 'er, don't yer? That's what yer been sayin' every bloomin' hour since she hinsulted yer.

YANK (*vehemently*): Sure ting I do! Didn't I try to get even wit her in Southampton? Didn't I sneak on de dock and wait for her by de gangplank? I was goin' to spit in her pale mug, see! Sure, right in her pop-eyes! Dat woulda made me even, see! But no chanct. Dere was a whole army of plainclothes bulls around. Dey spotted me and gimme de bum's rush. I never seen her. But I'll git square wit her yet, you watch! (*Furiously*) De lousy tart! She tinks she kin get away wit moider—but not wit me! I'll fix her! I'll tink of a way!

LONG (*as disgusted as he dares to be*): Ain't that why I brought yer up 'ere—to show yer? Yer been lookin' at this 'ere 'ole affair wrong. Yer been actin' an' talkin' 's if it was all a bleedin' personal matter between yer and that bloody cow. I wants to convince yer she was on'y a representative of 'er clarss. I wants to awaken yer bloody clarss consciousness. Then yer'll see it's 'er clarss yer've got to fight, not 'er alone. There's a 'ole mob of 'em like 'er, Gawd blind 'em!

YANK (*spitting on his hands—belligerently*): De more de merrier when I gits started. Bring on de gang!

LONG: Yer'll see 'em in arf a mo', when that church lets out. *(He turns and sees the window display in the two stores for the first time)* Blimey! Look at that, will yer? *(They both walk back and stand looking in the jeweler's.* LONG *flies into a fury)* Just look at this 'ere bloomin' mess! Just look at it! Look at the bleedin' prices on 'em—more'n our 'ole bloody stokehole makes in ten voyages sweatin' in 'ell! And they—'er and 'er bloody clarss—buys 'em for toys to dangle on 'em! One of these 'ere would buy scoff for a starvin' family for a year!

YANK: Aw, cut de sob stuff! T' hell wit de starvin' family! Yuh'll be passin' de hat to me next. *(With naïve admiration)* Say, dem tings is pretty, huh? Bet yuh dey'd hock for a piece of change aw right. *(Then turning away, bored)* But, aw hell, what good are dey? Let me have 'em. Dey don't belong no more'n she does. *(With a gesture of sweeping the jewelers into oblivion)* All dat don't count, get me?

LONG *(who has moved to the furrier's—indignantly)*: And I s'pose this 'ere don't count neither—skins of poor, 'armless animals slaughtered so as 'er and 'ers can keep their bleedin' noses warm!

YANK *(who has been staring at something inside—with queer excitement)*: Take a slant at dat! Give it de once-over! Monkey fur—two t'ousand bucks! *(Bewilderedly)* Is dat straight goods—monkey fur? What de hell—?

LONG *(bitterly)*: It's straight enuf. *(With grim humor)* They wouldn't bloody well pay that for a 'airy ape's skin—no, nor for the 'ole livin' ape with all 'is 'ead, and body, and soul thrown in!

YANK *(clenching his fists, his face growing pale with rage as if the skin in the window were a personal insult)*: Trowin' it up in my face! Christ! I'll fix her!

LONG *(excitedly)*: Church is out. 'Ere they come, the bleedin' swine. *(After a glance at* YANK'S *lowering face—uneasily)* Easy goes, Comrade. Keep yer bloomin' temper. Remember force defeats itself. It ain't our weapon. We must impress our demands through peaceful means—the votes of the on-marching proletarians of the bloody world!

YANK *(with abysmal contempt)*: Votes, hell! Votes is a joke, see. Votes for women! Let dem do it!

LONG *(still more uneasily)*: Calm, now. Treat 'em wiv the proper contempt. Observe the bleedin' parasites but 'old yer 'orses.

YANK *(angrily)*: Get away from me! Yuh're yellow, dat's what. Force, dat's me! De punch, dat's me every time, see! *(The crowd from church enter from the right, sauntering slowly and affectedly, their heads held stiffly up, looking neither to right nor left, talking in toneless, simpering voices. The women are rouged, calcimined, dyed, overdressed to the nth degree. The men are in Prince Alberts, high hats, spats, canes, etc. A procession of gaudy marionettes, yet with something of the relentless horror of Frankensteins in their detached, mechanical unawareness)*.

VOICES: Dear Doctor Caiaphas! He is so sincere!

What was the sermon? I dozed off.

About the radicals, my dear—and the false doctrines that are being preached.

We must organize a hundred per cent American bazaar.

And let everyone contribute one one-hundredth per cent of their income tax.

What an original idea!

We can devote the proceeds to rehabilitating the veil of the temple.

But that has been done so many times.

YANK (*glaring from one to the other of them—with an insulting snort of scorn*): Huh! Huh! (*Without seeming to see him, they make wide detours to avoid the spot where he stands in the middle of the sidewalk*).

LONG (*frightenedly*): Keep yer bloomin' mouth shut, I tells yer.

YANK (*viciously*): G'wan! Tell it to Sweeney! (*He swaggers away and deliberately lurches into a top-hatted gentleman, then glares at him pugnaciously*) Say, who d'yuh tink yuh're bumpin'? Tink yuh own de oith?

GENTLEMAN (*coldly and affectedly*): I beg your pardon. (*He has not looked at* YANK *and passes on without a glance, leaving him bewildered*).

LONG (*rushing up and grabbing* YANK'S *arm*): 'Ere! Come away! This wasn't what I meant. Yer'll 'ave the bloody coppers down on us.

YANK (*savagely—giving him a push that sends him sprawling*): G'wan!

LONG (*picks himself up—hysterically*): I'll pop orf then. This ain't what I meant. And whatever 'appens, yer can't blame me. (*He slinks off left*).

YANK: T' hell wit youse! (*He approaches a lady—with a vicious grin and a smirking wink*) Hello, Kiddo. How's every little ting? Got anyting on for tonight? I know an old boiler down to de docks we kin crawl into. (*The lady stalks by without a look, without a change of pace.* YANK *turns to others— insultingly*) Holy smokes, what a mug! Go hide yuhself before de horses shy at yuh. Gee, pipe de heine on dat one! Say, youse, yuh look like de stoin of a ferryboat. Paint and powder! All dolled up to kill! Yuh look like stiffs laid out for de boneyard! Aw, g'wan, de lot of youse! Yuh give me de eye-ache. Yuh don't belong, get me! Look at me, why don't youse dare? I belong, dat's me! (*Pointing to a skyscraper across the street which is in process of construction—with bravado*) See dat building goin' up dere? See de steel work? Steel, dat's me! Youse guys live on it and tink yuh're somep'n. But I'm *in* it, see! I'm de hoistin' engine dat makes it go up! I'm it—de inside and bottom of it! Sure! I'm steel and steam and smoke and de rest of it! It moves—speed—twenty-five stories up—and me at de top and bottom—movin'! Youse simps don't move. Yuh're on'y dolls I winds up to see 'm spin. Yuh're de garbage, get me—de leavins—de ashes we dump over de side! Now, what 'a' yuh gotta say? (*But as they seem neither to see nor hear him, he flies into a fury*) Bums! Pigs! Tarts! Bitches! (*He turns in a rage on the men, bumping viciously into them but not jarring them the least bit. Rather it is he who recoils after each collision. He keeps growling*) Git off de oith! G'wan, yuh bum! Look where yuh're goin', can't yuh? Git outa here! Fight, why don't yuh? Put up yer mits! Don't be a dog! Fight or I'll knock yuh dead! (*But, without seeming to see him, they all answer with mechnical affected politeness*) I beg your pardon. (*Then at a cry from one of the women, they all scurry to the furrier's window*).

THE WOMAN (*ecstatically, with a gasp of delight*): Monkey fur! (*The whole crowd of men and women chorus after her in the same tone of affected delight*) Monkey fur!

YANK (*with a jerk of his head back on his shoulders, as if he had received a punch full in the face—raging*): I see yuh, all in white! I see yuh, yuh white-faced tart, yuh! Hairy ape, huh? I'll hairy ape yuh! (*He bends down and grips at the street curbing as if to pick it out and hurl it. Foiled in this, snarling with passion, he leaps to the lamp-post on the corner and tries to pull it up for a club. Just at that moment a bus is heard rumbling up. A fat, high-hatted, spatted gentleman runs out from the side street. He calls out plaintively*): Bus! Bus! Stop there! (*and runs full tilt into the bending, straining* YANK, *who is bowled off his balance*).

YANK (*seeing a fight—with a roar of joy as he springs to his feet*): At last! Bus, huh? I'll bust yuh! (*He lets drive a terrific swing, his fist landing full on the fat gentleman's face. But the gentleman stands unmoved as if nothing had happened*).

GENTLEMAN: I beg your pardon. (*Then irritably*) You have made me lose my bus. (*He claps his hands and begins to scream*): Officer! Officer! (*Many police whistles shrill out on the instant and a whole platoon of policemen rush in on* YANK *from all sides. He tries to fight but is clubbed to the pavement and fallen upon. The crowd at the window have not moved or noticed this disturbance. The clanging gong of the patrol wagon approaches with a clamoring din*).

Curtain

SCENE SIX

Night of the following day. A row of cells in the prison on Blackwells Island. The cells extend back diagonally from right front to left rear. They do not stop, but disappear in the dark background as if they ran on, numberless, into infinity. One electric bulb from the low ceiling of the narrow corridor sheds its light through the heavy steel bars of the cell at the extreme front and reveals part of the interior. YANK *can be seen within, crouched on the edge of his cot in the attitude of Rodin's "The Thinker." His face is spotted with black and blue bruises. A blood-stained bandage is wrapped around his head.*

YANK (*suddenly starting as if awakening from a dream, reaches out and shakes the bars—aloud to himself, wonderingly*): Steel. Dis is de Zoo, huh? (*A burst of hard, barking laughter comes from the unseen occupants of the cells, runs back down the tier, and abruptly ceases*).

VOICES (*mockingly*): The Zoo? That's a new name for this coop—a damn good name!

Steel, eh? You said a mouthful. This is the old iron house.

Who is that boob talkin'?

He's the bloke they brung in out of his head. The bulls had beat him up fierce.

YANK (*dully*): I musta been dreamin'. I tought I was in a cage at de Zoo—but de apes don't talk, do dey?

VOICES *(with mocking laughter):* You're in a cage aw right.

A coop!

A pen!

A sty!

A kennel! *(Hard laughter—a pause).*

Say, guy! Who are you? No, never mind lying. What are you?

Yes, tell us your sad story. What's your game?

What did they jug yuh for?

YANK *(dully):* I was a fireman—stokin' on de liners. *(Then with sudden rage, rattling his cell bars)* I'm a hairy ape, get me? And I'll bust youse all in de jaw if yuh don't lay off kiddin' me.

VOICES: Huh! You're a hard boiled duck, ain't you!

When you spit, it bounces! *(Laughter).*

Aw, can it. He's a regular guy. Ain't you?

What did he say he was—a ape?

YANK *(defiantly):* Sure ting! Ain't dat what youse all are—apes? *(A silence. Then a furious rattling of bars from down the corridor).*

A VOICE *(thick with rage):* I'll show yuh who's a ape, yuh bum!

VOICES: Ssshh! Nix!

Can de noise!

Piano!

You'll have the guard down on us!

YANK *(scornfully):* De guard? Yuh mean de keeper, don't yuh? *(Angry exclamations from all the cells).*

VOICE *(placatingly):* Aw, don't pay no attention to him. He's off his nut from the beatin'-up he got. Say, you guy! We're waitin' to hear what they landed you for—or ain't yuh tellin'?

YANK: Sure, I'll tell youse. Sure! Why de hell not? On'y—youse won't get me. Nobody gets me but me, see? I started to tell de Judge and all he says was: "Toity days to tink it over." Tink it over! Christ, dat's all I been doin' for weeks! *(After a pause)* I was tryin' to git even with someone, see?—someone dat done me doit.

VOICES *(cynically):* De old stuff, I bet. Your goil, huh?

Give yuh the double-cross, huh?

That's them every time!

Did yuh beat up de odder guy?

YANK *(disgustedly):* Aw, yuh're all wrong! Sure dere was a skoit in it—but not what youse mean, not dat old tripe. Dis was a new kind of skoit. She was dolled up all in white—in de stokehole. I tought she was a ghost. Sure. *(A pause).*

VOICES *(whispering):* Gee, he's still nutty.

Let him rave. It's fun listenin'.

YANK *(unheeding—groping in his thoughts):* Her hands—dey was skinny and white like dey wasn't real but painted on somep'n. Dere was a million miles from me to her—twenty-five knots a hour. She was like some dead ting de cat brung in. Sure, dat's what. She didn't belong. She belonged in de window of a toy store, or on de top of a garbage can, see! Sure! *(He breaks out angrily)* But would yuh believe it, she had de noive to do me doit. She lamped me like she was seein' somep'n broke loose from de menagerie. Christ, yuh'd oughter seen her eyes! *(He rattles the bars of his cell furiously)* But I'll get back at her yet, you watch! And if I can't find her I'll take it out on de gang she runs wit. I'm wise to where dey hangs out now. I'll show her who belongs! I'll show her who's in de move and who ain't. You watch my smoke!

VOICES *(serious and joking)*: Dat's de talkin'!

Take her for all she's got!

What was this dame, anyway? Who was she, eh?

YANK: I dunno. First cabin stiff. Her old man's a millionaire, dey says— name of Douglas.

VOICES: Douglas? That's the president of the Steel Trust, I bet.

Sure, I seen his mug in de papers.

He's filthy with dough.

VOICE: Hey, feller, take a tip from me. If you want to get back at that dame, you better join the Wobblies. You'll get some action then.

YANK: Wobblies? What de hell's dat?

VOICE: Ain't you ever heard of the I.W.W.?

YANK: Naw. What is it?

VOICE: A gang of blokes—a tough gang. I been readin' about 'em today in the paper. The guard give me the *Sunday Times*. There's a long spiel about 'em. It's from a speech made in the Senate by a guy named Senator Queen. *(He is in the cell next to* YANK'S. *There is a rustling of paper)* Wait'll I see if I got light enough and I'll read you. Listen. *(He reads)* "There is a menace existing in this country today which threatens the vitals of our fair Republic—as foul a menace against the very life-blood of the American Eagle as was the foul conspiracy of Catiline against the eagles of ancient Rome!"

VOICE *(disgustedly)*: Aw, hell! Tell him to salt de tail of dat eagle!

VOICE *(reading)*: "I refer to that devil's brew of rascals, jailbirds, murderers and cutthroats who libel all honest working men by calling themselves the Industrial Workers of the World; but in the light of their nefarious plots, I call them the Industrious *Wreckers* of the World!"

YANK *(with vengeful satisfaction)*: Wreckers, dat's de right dope! Dat belongs! Me for dem!

VOICE: Ssshh! *(reading)* "This fiendish organization is a foul ulcer on the fair body of our Democracy—"

VOICE: Democracy, hell! Give him the boid, fellers—the raspberry! *(They do)*.

VOICE: Ssshh! *(reading)* "Like Cato I say to this Senate, the I.W.W. must be destroyed! For they represent an ever-present dagger pointed at the heart of the greatest nation the world has ever known, where all men are born free and equal, with equal opportunities to all, where the Founding Fathers have guaranteed to each one happiness, where Truth, Honor, Liberty, Justice, and the Brotherhood of Man are a religion absorbed with one's mother's milk, taught at our father's knee, sealed, signed, and stamped upon in the glorious Constitution of these United States!" *(A perfect storm of hisses, catcalls, boos, and hard laughter).*

VOICES *(scornfully)*: Hurrah for de Fort' of July!

Pass de hat!

Liberty!

Justice!

Honor!

Opportunity!

Brotherhood!

ALL *(with abysmal scorn)*: Aw, hell!

VOICE: Give that Queen Senator guy the bark! All togedder now—one—two—tree—*(A terrific chorus of barking and yapping).*

GUARD *(from a distance)*: Quiet there, youse—or I'll git the hose. *(The noise subsides).*

YANK *(with growling rage)*: I'd like to catch dat senator guy alone for a second. I'd loin him some trute!

VOICE: Ssshh! Here's where he gits down to cases on the Wobblies. *(Reads)* "They plot with fire in one hand and dynamite in the other. They stop not before murder to gain their ends, nor at the outraging of defenseless womanhood. They would tear down society, put the lowest scum in the seats of the mighty, turn Almighty God's revealed plan for the world topsy-turvy, and make of our sweet and lovely civilization a shambles, a desolation where man, God's masterpiece, would soon degenerate back to the ape!"

VOICE *(to YANK)*: Hey, you guy. There's your ape stuff again.

YANK *(with a growl of fury)*: I got him. So dey blow up tings, do dey? Dey turn tings round, do dey? Hey, lend me dat paper, will yuh?

VOICE: Sure. Give it to him. On'y keep it to yourself, see. We don't wanter listen to no more of that slop.

VOICE: Here you are. Hide it under your mattress.

YANK *(reaching out)*: Tanks. I can't read much but I kin manage. *(He sits, the paper in the hand at his side, in the attitude of Rodin's "The Thinker." A pause. Several snores from down the corridor. Suddenly YANK jumps to his feet with a furious groan as if some appalling thought had crashed on him—bewilderedly)* Sure—her old man—president of de Steel Trust—makes half de steel in de world—steel—where I tought I belonged—drivin' trou—movin'—in dat—to make *her*—and cage me in for her to spit on! Christ! *(He shakes the bars of his cell door till the whole tier trembles. Irritated, protesting exclamations from those awakened or trying to get to sleep)* He made dis—dis cage! Steel! *It* don't belong, dat's what! Cages, cells, locks, bolts, bars—dat's what it means!—holdin' me down wit him at de top! But I'll drive trou! Fire, dat melts it! I'll be fire—under de heap—fire dat never goes out—hot as hell—breakin' out in de night—*(While he has been saying this last he has shaken his cell door to a clanging accompaniment. As he comes to the "breakin' out" he seizes one bar with both hands and, putting his two feet up against the others so that his position is parallel to the floor like a monkey's, he gives a great wrench backwards. The bar bends like a licorice stick under his tremendous strength. Just at this moment the* PRISON GUARD *rushes in, dragging a hose behind him*).

GUARD (*angrily*): I'll loin youse bums to wake me up! (*Sees* YANK) Hello, it's you, huh? Got the D.T.'s, hey? Well, I'll cure 'em. I'll drown your snakes for yuh! (*Noticing the bar*) Hell, look at dat bar bended! On'y a bug is strong enough for dat!

YANK (*glaring at him*): Or a hairy ape, yuh big yellow bum! Look out! Here I come! (*He grabs another bar*).

GUARD (*scared now—yelling off left*): Toin de hose on, Ben!—full pressure! And call de others—and a straitjacket! (*The curtain is falling. As it hides* YANK *from view, there is a splattering smash as the stream of water hits the steel of* YANK'S *cell*).

Curtain

SCENE SEVEN
Nearly a month later. An I.W.W. local near the waterfront, showing the interior of a front room on the ground floor, and the street outside. Moonlight on the narrow street, buildings massed in black shadow. The interior of the room, which is general assembly room, office, and reading room, resembles some dingy settlement boys' club. A desk and high stool are in one corner. A table with papers, stacks of pamphlets, chairs about it, is at center. The whole is decidedly cheap, banal, commonplace and unmysterious as a room could well be. The secretary is perched on the stool making entries in a large ledger. An eye shade casts his face into shadows. Eight or ten men, longshoremen, iron workers, and the like, are grouped about the table. Two are playing checkers. One is writing a letter. Most of them are smoking pipes. A big signboard is on the wall at the rear, "Industrial Workers of the World—Local No. 57."

YANK (*comes down the street outside. He is dressed as in Scene Five. He moves cautiously, mysteriously. He comes to a point opposite the door; tiptoes softly up to it, listens, is impressed by the silence within, knocks carefully, as if he were guessing at the password to some secret rite. Listens. No answer. Knocks again a bit louder. No answer. Knocks impatiently, much louder*).

SECRETARY (*turning around on his stool*): What the hell is that—someone knocking? (*Shouts*) Come in, why don't you? (*All the men in the room look up.* YANK *opens the door slowly, gingerly, as if afraid of an ambush. He looks around for secret doors, mystery, is taken aback by the commonplaceness of the room and the men in it, thinks he may have gotten in the wrong place, then sees the signboard on the wall and is reassured*).

YANK (*blurts out*): Hello.

MEN (*reservedly*): Hello.

YANK (*more easily*): I thought I'd bumped into de wrong dump.

SECRETARY (*scrutinizing him carefully*): Maybe you have. Are you a member?

YANK: Naw, not yet. Dat's what I came for—to join.

SECRETARY: That's easy. What's your job—longshore?

YANK: Naw. Fireman—stoker on de liners.

SECRETARY (*with satisfaction*): Welcome to our city. Glad to know you people are waking up at last. We haven't got many members in your line.

YANK: Naw. Dey're all dead to de woild.

SECRETARY: Well, you can help to wake 'em. What's your name? I'll make out your card.

YANK (*confused*): Name? Lemme tink.

SECRETARY (*sharply*): Don't you know your own name?

YANK: Sure; but I been just Yank for so long—Bob, dat's it—Bob Smith.

SECRETARY (*writing*): Robert Smith. (*Fills out the rest of card*) Here you are. Cost you half a dollar.

YANK: Is dat all—four bits? Dat's easy. (*Gives the Secretary the money*).

SECRETARY (*throwing it in drawer*): Thanks. Well, make yourself at home. No introductions needed. There's literature on the table. Take some of those pamphlets with you to distribute aboard ship. They may bring results. Sow the seed, only go about it right. Don't get caught and fired. We got plenty out of work. What we need is men who can hold their jobs—and work for us at the same time.

YANK: Sure. (*But he still stands, embarrassed and uneasy*).

SECRETARY (*looking at him—curiously*): What did you knock for? Think we had a coon in uniform to open doors?

YANK: Naw. I tought it was locked—and dat yuh'd wanter give me the once-over trou a peep-hole or somep'n to see if I was right.

SECRETARY (*alert and suspicious but with an easy laugh*): Think we were running a crap game? That door is never locked. What put that in your nut?

YANK (*with a knowing grin, convinced that this is all camouflage, a part of the secrecy*): Dis burg is full of bulls, ain't it?

SECRETARY (*sharply*): What have the cops got to do with us? We're breaking no laws.

YANK (*with a knowing wink*): Sure. Youse wouldn't for woilds. Sure. I'm wise to dat.

SECRETARY: You seem to be wise to a lot of stuff none of us knows about.

YANK (*with another wink*): Aw, dat's aw right, see. (*Then made a bit resentful by the suspicious glances from all sides*) Aw, can it! Youse needn't put me trou de toid degree. Can't youse see I belong? Sure! I'm reg'lar. I'll stick, get me? I'll shoot de woiks for youse. Dat's why I wanted to join in.

SECRETARY (*breezily, feeling him out*): That's the right spirit. Only are you sure you understand what you've joined? It's all plain and above board; still, some guys get a wrong slant on us. (*Sharply*) What's your notion of the purpose of the I.W.W.?

YANK: Aw, I know all about it.

SECRETARY *(sarcastically)*: Well, give us some of your valuable information.

YANK *(cunningly)*: I know enough not to speak outa my toin. *(Then resentfully again)* Aw, say! I'm reg'lar. I'm wise to de game. I know yuh got to watch your step wit a stranger. For all youse know, I might be a plain-clothes dick, or somep'n, dat's what yuh're tinkin', huh? Aw, forget it! I belong, see? Ask any guy down to de docks if I don't.

SECRETARY: Who said you didn't?

YANK: After I'm 'nitiated, I'll show yuh.

SECRETARY *(astounded)*: Initiated? There's no initiation.

YANK *(disappointed)*: Ain't there no password—no grip nor nothin'?

SECRETARY: What'd you think this is—the Elks—or the Black Hand?

YANK: De Elks, hell! De Black Hand, dey're a lot of yellow back-stickin' Ginees. Naw. Dis is a man's gang, ain't it?

SECRETARY: You said it! That's why we stand on our two feet in the open. We got no secrets.

YANK *(surprised but admiringly)*: Yuh mean to say yuh always run wide open—like dis?

SECRETARY: Exactly.

YANK: Den yuh sure got your noive wit youse!

SECRETARY *(sharply)*: Just what was it made you want to join us? Come out with that straight.

YANK: Yuh call me? Well, I got noive, too! Here's my hand. Yuh wanter blow tings up, don't yuh? Well, dat's me! I belong!

SECRETARY *(with pretended carelessness)*: You mean change the unequal conditions of society by legitimate direct action—or with dynamite?

YANK: Dynamite! Blow it offen de oith—steel—all de cages—all de factories, steamers, buildings, jails—de Steel Trust and all dat makes it go.

SECRETARY: So—that's your idea, eh? And did you have any special job in that line you wanted to propose to us? *(He makes a sign to the men, who get up cautiously one by one and group behind* YANK*)*.

YANK *(boldly)*: Sure, I'll come out wit it. I'll show youse I'm one of de gang. Dere's dat millionaire guy, Douglas—

SECRETARY: President of the Steel Trust, you mean? Do you want to assassinate him?

YANK: Naw, dat don't get yuh nothin'. I mean blow up de factory, de woiks, where he makes de steel. Dat's what I'm after—to blow up de steel, knock all de steel in de woild up to de moon. Dat'll fix tings! *(Eagerly, with a touch of bravado)* I'll do it by me lonesome! I'll show yuh! Tell me where his woiks is, how to git there, all de dope. Gimme de stuff, de old butter—and watch me do de rest! Watch de smoke and see it move! I don't give a damn if dey nab me— long as it's done! I'll soive life for it—and give 'em de laugh! *(Half to himself)* And I'll write her a letter and tell her de hairy ape done it. Dat'll square tings.

SECRETARY *(stepping away from* YANK*)*: Very interesting. *(He gives a signal. The men, huskies all, throw themselves on* YANK *and before he knows it they have* *his legs and arms pinioned. But he is too flabbergasted to make a struggle, anyway. They feel him over for weapons).*

MAN: No gat, no knife. Shall we give him what's what and put the boots to him?

SECRETARY: No. He isn't worth the trouble we'd get into. He's too stupid. *(He comes closer and laughs mockingly in* YANK'S *face)* Ho-ho! By God, this is the biggest joke they've put up on us yet. Hey, you Joke! Who sent you—Burns or Pinkerton? No, by God, you're such a bonehead I'll bet you're in the Secret Service! Well, you dirty spy, you rotten agent provocator, you can go back and tell whatever skunk is paying you blood-money for betraying your brothers that he's wasting his coin. You couldn't catch a cold. And tell him that all he'll ever get on us, or ever has got, is just his own sneaking plots that he's framed up to put us in jail. We are what our manifesto says we are, neither more nor less— and we'll give him a copy of that any time he calls. And as for you—*(He glares scornfully at* YANK, *who is sunk in an obvious stupor)* Oh, hell, what's the use of talking? You're a brainless ape.

YANK *(aroused by the word to fierce but futile struggles)*: What's dat, yuh Sheeny bum, yuh!

SECRETARY: Throw him out, boys. *(In spite of his struggles, this is done with gusto and éclat. Propelled by several parting kicks,* YANK *lands sprawling in the middle of the narrow cobbled street. With a growl he starts to get up and storm the closed door, but stops bewildered by the confusion in his brain, pathetically impotent. He sits there, brooding, in as near to the attitude of Rodin's "Thinker" as he can get in his position).*

YANK *(bitterly)*: So dem boids don't tink I belong, neider. Aw, to hell wit 'em! Dey're in de wrong pew—de same old bull—soapboxes and Salvation Army—no guts! Cut out an hour offen de job a day and make me happy! Gimme a dollar more a day and make me happy! Tree square a day, and cauliflowers in de front yard—ekal rights—a woman and kids—a lousy vote— and I'm all fixed for Jesus, huh? Aw, hell! What does dat get yuh? Dis ting's in your inside, but it ain't your belly. Feedin' your face—sinkers and coffee—dat don't touch it. It's way down—at de bottom. Yuh can't grab it, and yuh can't stop it. It moves, and everything moves. It stops and de whole woild stops. Dat's me now—I don't tick, see?—I'm a busted Ingersoll, dat's what. Steel was me, and I owned de woild. Now I ain't steel, and de woild owns me. Aw, hell! I can't see—it's all dark, get me? It's all wrong! *(He turns a bitter mocking face up like an ape gibbering at the moon)* Say, youse up dere, Man in de Moon, yuh look so wise, gimme de answer, huh? Slip me de inside dope, de information right from de stable—where do I get off at, huh?

A POLICEMAN *(who has come up the street in time to hear this last—with grim humor)*: You'll get off at the station, you boob, if you don't get up out of that and keep movin'.

YANK *(looking up at him—with a hard, bitter laugh)*: Sure! Lock me up! Put me in a cage! Dat's de on'y answer yuh know. G'wan, lock me up!

POLICEMAN: What you been doin'?

YANK: Enuf to gimme life for! I was born, see? Sure, dat's de charge. Write it in de blotter. I was born, get me!

POLICEMAN *(jocosely)*: God pity your old woman! *(Then matter-of-fact)* But I've no time for kidding. You're soused. I'd run you in but it's too long a walk to the station. Come on now, get up, or I'll fan your ears with this club. Beat it now! *(He hauls* YANK *to his feet)*.

YANK *(in vague mocking tone)*: Say, where do I go from here?

POLICEMAN *(giving him a push—with a grin, indifferently)*: Go to hell.

Curtain

SCENE EIGHT
Twilight of the next day. The monkey house at the Zoo. One spot of clear gray light falls on the front of one cage so that the interior can be seen. The other cages are vague, shrouded in shadow from which chatterings pitched in a conversational tone can be heard. On the one cage a sign from which the word "gorilla" stands out. The gigantic animal himself is seen squatting on his haunches on a bench in much the same attitude as Rodin's "Thinker." YANK *enters from the left. Immediately a chorus of angry chattering and screeching breaks out. The gorilla turns his eyes but makes no sound or move.*

YANK *(with a hard, bitter laugh)*: Welcome to your city, huh? Hail, hail, de gang's all here! *(At the sound of his voice the chattering dies away into an attentive silence.* YANK *walks up to the gorilla's cage and, leaning over the railing, stares in at its occupant, who stares back at him, silent and motionless. There is a pause of dead stillness. Then* YANK *begins to talk in a friendly confidential tone, half-mockingly, but with a deep undercurrent of sympathy)* Say, yuh're some hard-lookin' guy, ain't yuh? I seen lots of tough nuts dat de gang called gorillas, but yuh're de foist real one I ever seen. Some chest yuh got, and shoulders, and dem arms and mits! I bet yuh got a punch in eider fist dat'd knock 'em all silly! *(This with genuine admiration. The gorilla, as if he understood, stands upright, swelling out his chest and pounding on it with his fist.* YANK *grins sympathetically)* Sure, I get yuh. Yuh challenge de whole woild, huh? Yuh got what I was sayin' even if yuh muffed de woids. *(Then bitterness creeping in)* And why wouldn't yuh get me? Ain't we both members of de same club—de Hairy Apes? *(They stare at each other—a pause—then* YANK *goes on slowly and bitterly)* So yuh're what she seen when she looked at me, de white-faced tart! I was you to her, get me? On'y outa de cage—broke out—free to moider her, see? Sure! Dat's what she tought. She wasn't wise dat I was in a cage, too—worser'n yours—sure—a damn sight—'cause you got some chanct to bust loose—but me—*(He grows confused)* Aw, hell! It's all wrong, ain't it? *(A pause)* I s'pose yuh wanter know what I'm doin' here, huh? I been warmin' a bench down to de Battery—ever since last night. Sure. I seen de sun come up. Dat was pretty, too—all red and pink and green. I was lookin' at de skyscrapers—steel—and all de ships comin' in, sailin' out, all over de oith—and dey was steel, too. De sun was warm, dey wasn't no clouds, and dere was a breeze blowin'. Sure, it was great stuff, I got it aw right—what Paddy said about dat bein' de right dope—on'y I couldn't get *in* it, see? I couldn't belong in dat. It was over my head. And I kept tinkin'—and den I beat it up here to see what youse was like. And I waited till dey was all gone to git yuh alone. Say, how d'yuh feel sittin' in dat pen all de time, havin' to stand for 'em comin' and starin' at yuh—de white-faced, skinny tarts and de boobs that marry 'em—makin' fun of yuh, laughin' at yuh, gittin' scared of yuh—damn 'em! *(He pounds on the rail with his fist. The gorilla rattles the bars of his cage and snarls. All the other monkeys set up an angry chattering in the darkness.* YANK *goes on excitedly)* Sure! Dat's de way it hits me, too. On'y yuh're lucky, see? Yuh don't belong wit 'em and yuh know it. But me, I belong wit 'em—but I don't, see? Dey don't belong wit me, dat's what. Get me? Tinkin' is hard—*(He passes one hand across his forehead with a painful gesture. The gorilla growls impatiently.* YANK *goes on gropingly)* It's dis way, what I'm drivin' at. Youse can sit and dope dream in de past, green woods, de jungle and de rest of it. Den yuh belong and dey don't. Den yuh kin laugh at 'em, see? Yuh're de champ of de woild. But me—I ain't got no past to tink in, nor nothin' dat's comin', on'y what's now—and dat don't belong. Sure, you're de best off! Yuh can't tink, can yuh? Yuh can't talk neider. But I kin make a bluff at talkin' and tinkin'—a'most git away wit it—a'most!—and dat's where de joker comes in. *(He laughs)* I ain't on oith and I ain't in heaven, get me? I'm in de middle tryin' to separate 'em, takin' all de woist punches from bot' of 'em. Maybe dat's what dey call hell, huh? But you, yuh're at de bottom. You belong! Sure! Yuh're de on'y one in de woild dat does, yuh lucky stiff! *(The gorilla growls proudly)* And dat's why dey gotter put yuh in a cage, see? *(The gorilla roars angrily)* Sure! Yuh get me. It beats it when you try to tink it or talk it—it's way down—deep—behind—you 'n' me we feel it. Sure! Bot' members of dis club! *(He laughs—then in a savage tone)* What de hell! T' hell with it! A little action, dat's our meat! Dat belongs! Knock 'em down and keep bustin' 'em till dey croaks yuh with a gat—wit steel! Sure! Are yuh game? Dey've looked at youse, ain't dey—in a cage? Wanter git even? Wanter wind up like a sport 'stead of croakin' slow in dere? *(The gorilla roars an emphatic affirmative.* YANK *goes on with a sort of furious exaltation)* Sure! Yuh're reg'lar! Yuh'll stick to de finish! Me 'n' you, huh?—bot' members of this club! We'll put up one last star bout dat'll knock 'em offen deir seats! Dey'll have to make de cages stronger after we're trou! *(The gorilla is straining at his bars, growling, hopping from one foot to the other.* YANK *takes a jimmy from under his coat and forces the lock on the cage door. He throws this open)* Pardon from de governor! Step out and shake hands. I'll take yuh for a walk down Fif' Avenoo. We'll knock 'em offen de oith and croak wit de band playin'. Come on, Brother. *(The gorilla scrambles gingerly out of his cage. Goes to* YANK *and stands looking at him.* YANK *keeps his mocking tone—holds out his hand)* Shake—de secret grip of our order. *(Something, the tone of mockery, perhaps, suddenly enrages the animal. With a spring he wraps his huge arms around* YANK *in a murderous hug. There is a crackling snap of crushed ribs—a gasping cry, still mocking, from* YANK) Hey, I didn't say kiss me! *(The gorilla lets the crushed body slip to the floor; stands over it uncertainly, considering; then picks it up, throws it in the cage, shuts the door, and shuffles off menacingly into the darkness at left. A great uproar of frightened chattering and whimpering comes from the other cages. Then* YANK *moves, groaning, opening his eyes, and there is silence. He mutters painfully)* Say—dey oughter match him—wit Zybszko. He got me, aw right. I'm trou. Even him didn't tink I belonged. *(Then, with sudden passionate despair)* Christ, where do I get off at? Where do I fit in? *(Checking himself as suddenly)* Aw, what de hell! No squawkin', see! No quittin', get me! Croak wit your boots on! *(He grabs hold of the bars of the cage and hauls himself painfully to his feet—looks around him bewilderedly—forces a mocking laugh)* In de cage, huh? *(In the strident tones of a circus barker)* Ladies and gents, step forward and take a slant at de one and only—*(His voice weakening)*—one and original—Hairy Ape from de wilds of— *(He slips in a heap on the floor and dies. The monkeys set up a chattering, whimpering wail. And, perhaps, the Hairy Ape at last belongs).*

Curtain

ACTIVITIES FOR WRITING AND DISCUSSION

1. *The Hairy Ape* is an example of dramatic **expressionism.** Rather than trying to present characters and events realistically, O'Neill distorts and exaggerates reality in order to produce certain powerful and expressive effects in readers or viewers. Thus, for instance, the coal stokers in scene 1 are characterized less as individual human beings than as a single beast in a "cage" or as anonymous versions of "Neanderthal Man"; the rich people who are assaulted by Yank in scene 5 do not even feel the impact of his blows. Mark these and any other passages in the play that strike you as expressionistic. Then write an essay in which you discuss how the expressionistic devices enhance the themes or impact of the play.

2. Reread the scene 1 speeches of Yank, Long, and Paddy. In your notebook summarize the outlook of each and how those outlooks conflict or clash.

3. In scene 1 both Yank and Paddy talk about "belonging." To whom or to what does each see himself as belonging? In what ways do their notions of belonging resemble and/or differ from each other? What reasons can you think of for their obsessive concern with "belonging"?

4. Consider the various meanings that "belonging" has in your own life and in the play.
   a. Write about your own concept of "belonging." To what extent and in what ways does your own identity seem to be shaped by the groups, orga-

nizations, socioeconomic class, race, religious and ethnic cultures, and so forth to which you "belong"?

b. Locate recurrences of the words "belong" and "belonging" in *The Hairy Ape*. In each case, annotate what you think the speaker is using the word to mean in that situation.

c. To whom or what do the following "belong": Yank, Mildred Douglas, the rich people on Fifth Avenue in scene 5, the workers in the office of the I.W.W., the gorilla in the zoo?

d. Interpret O'Neill's final stage direction in the play: "*And, perhaps, the Hairy Ape at last belongs.*" Do you take this sentence literally or ironically? Why? To *what* does he "belong" at play's end?

5. Mildred Douglas appears in only one scene, but her impact on Yank resonates through the entire play. Reread scene 2, paying particular attention to Mildred's character, attitudes, and style of speech. Then imagine you are Mildred and it is the day after your encounter with Yank. In a letter to a friend of your (i.e., Mildred's) own economic and social class, relate the story of your meeting with the "beast" in the stokehole. In addition to mentioning the encounter, use your imagination to fill the letter with chat about other matters—your aunt, impressions of the ship, things you have done and seen. How much of your letter will you devote to the encounter with Yank? While we know the meeting left a profound impact on Yank, how significant an effect did it have on you/Mildred?

6. In an earlier version of the ending of the play, O'Neill had Yank return to the stokehole to live out his prisonlike existence. Draft a new scene 8 with this ending. Then compare the new ending with the one O'Neill actually chose. Which do you find more effective, and why?

EXPERIENCE AND IDENTITY: ADDITIONAL ACTIVITIES FOR WRITING AND DISCUSSION

1. Reread your entire notebook. Mark any passages, however long or short, that strike you, for whatever reasons. Beside each such passage, write a note explaining its significance for you. Finally, pick a favorite passage and either:

a. Expand it into a new piece of writing, or

b. Make notes on how you *could* expand or use it at some future date, or

c. Rewrite it in a different form, e.g., poem, dialogue, letter, memoir.

For a list of strategies for expanding or revising, see Chapter 10.

2. Explicitly or implicitly, several texts in this section address how growth can occur through experiences of pain, defeat, or even "death," e.g., as figuratively described by Goethe in "The Holy Longing."

a. Compare how this theme plays out in several texts and/or in the text of your own life, or

b. Create an imaginary "interview" with one or more of the **characters, speakers,** or **personae** who experience such growth. Ask them to explain their outlook and to share some stories (which you may invent yourself) that justify that outlook.

3. Imagine Maurice ("The Blind Man") turns up at the zoo in scene 8 of *The Hairy Ape* and bumps into Yank. Though both are more comfortable with actions than words, they begin to talk—perhaps about "belonging," or brawn and brains, or the people in their past, e.g., Bertie Reid, Mildred Douglas. Do the two men have qualities in common? What might Maurice think of Mildred Douglas or Yank think of Bertie Reid? Write up this encounter between Maurice and Yank in the form of a new scene 8 for O'Neill's play or as an interlude before Yank's final death in the arms of the gorilla.

4. Maya Angelou's "Seven Women's Blessed Assurance" articulates the feelings and attitudes of seven women at various stages of life. Assume the **persona** of someone who has moved through three or more stages of life, e.g., infancy, childhood, adolescence, midlife. Create a text, in poetry or in prose, in which this person reflects on his/her changing perspectives on life and experience. Alternative: Write a dialogue between *yourself* at one stage of life and yourself at a different stage of life. Emphasize age-related conflicts and differences between your two "selves." Does the older self "like" the younger or resent it? Does the younger respect the older . . . scorn it?

5. One subject common to Erdrich's "Saint Marie," Rilke's "The Man Watching," Rudman's "Chrome," Angelou's "Graduation," and other texts within this section is the notion of "overcoming." Compare how this subject is treated in any two or three of these texts. Alternative: Write a story about "overcoming" in your own life, and (if you wish) relate it to one of the assigned readings.

6. Several writings in this section are about "firsts." Katherine Mansfield writes about "Her First Ball," Gary Soto's poem is about a first date, and Michael Dorris's and Judith Ortiz Cofer's essays are about first jobs and first days of school, respectively. Write a story, poem, or essay of your own about some actual or imagined "first" experience.

7. Reread D. H. Lawrence's "Snake" (p. 21), paying particular attention to the speaker's comments about "the voice of my education." In what context does the phrase appear, and what do you think the speaker means by it? Then relate the phrase to Judith Ortiz Cofer's "Primary Lessons," which is an essay about education. Assuming the outlook and persona of Lawrence, analyze the six-year-old Cofer's first experiences of "education."

8. Review your entire notebook; as you do, make a running list of memorable or striking topics, such as "childhood experience," "life transitions," "initi-

ations." Then choose a favorite topic, make a Topic/Form Grid (see Chapter 10), and use one of the forms on your grid to create a new notebook entry about the topic. Should your chosen form not work, do a Topic/Form Shift to a different form on your grid.

9. Reread your entire notebook, and mark any favorite entries. Then, after reviewing Chapter 4, revise one of these entries that is a "dependent" text into an "independent" text. (For a list of strategies for revising, see Chapter 10.)

Individual and Society

ANTON CHEKHOV (1860–1904)

Gooseberries

The sky had been overcast since early morning; it was a still day, not hot, but te- 1
dious, as it usually is when the weather is gray and dull, when clouds have been
hanging over the fields for a long time, and you wait for the rain that does not
come. Ivan Ivanych, a veterinary, and Burkin, a high school teacher, were already tired with walking, and the plain seemed endless to them. Far ahead were
the scarcely visible windmills of the village of Mironositzkoe; to the right lay a
range of hills that disappeared in the distance beyond the village, and both of
them knew that over there were the river, and fields, green willows, homesteads,
and if you stood on one of the hills, you could see from there another vast
plain, telegraph poles, and a train that from afar looked like a caterpillar crawling, and in clear weather you could even see the town. Now, when it was still
and when nature seemed mild and pensive, Ivan Ivanych and Burkin were filled
with love for this plain, and both of them thought what a beautiful land it was.

"Last time when we were in Elder Prokofy's barn," said Burkin, "you were 2
going to tell me a story."

"Yes; I wanted to tell you about my brother." 3

Ivan Ivanych heaved a slow sigh and lit his pipe before beginning his story, 4
but just then it began to rain. And five minutes later there was a downpour, and
it was hard to tell when it would be over. The two men halted, at a loss; the dogs,

already wet, stood with their tails between their legs and looked at them feelingly.

"We must find shelter somewhere," said Burkin. "Let's go to Alyohin's; it's quite near." 5

"Let's." 6

They turned aside and walked across a mown meadow, now going straight 7 ahead, now bearing to the right, until they reached the road. Soon poplars came into view, a garden, then the red roofs of barns; the river gleamed, and the view opened on a broad expanse of water with a mill and a white bathing-cabin. That was Sofyino, Alyohin's place.

The mill was going, drowning out the sound of the rain; the dam was shak- 8 ing. Wet horses stood near the carts, their heads drooping, and men were walking about, their heads covered with sacks. It was damp, muddy, dreary; and the water looked cold and unkind. Ivan Ivanych and Burkin felt cold and messy and uncomfortable through and through; their feet were heavy with mud and when, having crossed the dam, they climbed up to the barns, they were silent as though they were cross with each other.

The noise of a winnowing-machine came from one of the barns, the door 9 was open, and clouds of dust were pouring from within. On the threshold stood Alyohin himself, a man of forty, tall and rotund, with long hair, looking more like a professor or an artist than a gentleman farmer. He was wearing a white blouse, badly in need of washing, that was belted with a rope, and drawers, and his high boots were plastered with mud and straw. His eyes and nose were black with dust. He recognized Ivan Ivanych and Burkin and was apparently very glad to see them.

"Please go up to the house, gentlemen," he said, smiling; "I'll be there di- 10 rectly, in a moment."

It was a large structure of two stories. Alyohin lived downstairs in what was 11 formerly the stewards' quarters: two rooms that had arched ceilings and small windows; the furniture was plain, and the place smelled of rye bread, cheap vodka, and harness. He went into the showy rooms upstairs only rarely, when he had guests. Once in the house, the two visitors were met by a chambermaid, a young woman so beautiful that both of them stood still at the same moment and glanced at each other.

"You can't imagine how glad I am to see you, gentlemen," said Alyohin, join- 12 ing them in the hall. "What a surprise! Pelageya," he said, turning to the chambermaid, "give the guests a change of clothes. And, come to think of it, I will change, too. But I must go and bathe first, I don't think I've had a wash since spring. Don't you want to go into the bathing-cabin? In the meanwhile things will be got ready here."

The beautiful Pelageya, with her soft, delicate air, brought them bath towels 13 and soap, and Alyohin went to the bathing-cabin with his guests.

"Yes, it's a long time since I've bathed," he said, as he undressed. "I've an ex- 14 cellent bathing-cabin, as you see—it was put up by my father—but somehow I never find time to use it." He sat down on the steps and lathered his long hair and neck, and the water around him turned brown.

"I say—" observed Ivan Ivanych significantly, looking at his head.   15

"I haven't had a good wash for a long time," repeated Alyohin, embarrassed,   16
and soaped himself once more; the water about him turned dark-blue, the color of ink.

Ivan Ivanych came out of the cabin, plunged into the water with a splash   17
and swam in the rain, thrusting his arms out wide; he raised waves on which white lilies swayed. He swam out to the middle of the river and dived and a minute later came up in another spot and swam on and kept diving, trying to touch bottom. "By God!" he kept repeating delightedly, "by God!" He swam to the mill, spoke to the peasants there, and turned back and in the middle of the river lay floating, exposing his face to the rain. Burkin and Alyohin were already dressed and ready to leave, but he kept on swimming and diving. "By God!" he kept exclaiming. "Lord, have mercy on me."

"You've had enough!" Burkin shouted to him.   18

They returned to the house. And only when the lamp was lit in the big   19
drawing room upstairs, and the two guests, in silk dressing-gowns and warm slippers, were lounging in armchairs, and Alyohin himself, washed and combed, wearing a new jacket, was walking about the room, evidently savoring the warmth, the cleanliness, the dry clothes and light footwear, and when pretty Pelageya, stepping noiselessly across the carpet and smiling softly, brought in a tray with tea and jam, only then did Ivan Ivanych begin his story, and it was as though not only Burkin and Alyohin were listening, but also the ladies, old and young, and the military men who looked down upon them, calmly and severely, from their gold frames.

"We are two brothers," he began, "I, Ivan Ivanych, and my brother, Nikolay   20
Ivanych, who is two years my junior. I went in for a learned profession and became a veterinary; Nikolay at nineteen began to clerk in a provincial branch of the Treasury. Our father was a *kantonist*,[1] but he rose to be an officer and so a nobleman, a rank that he bequeathed to us together with a small estate. After his death there was a lawsuit and we lost the estate to creditors, but be that as it may, we spent our childhood in the country. Just like peasant children we passed days and nights in the fields and the woods, herded horses, stripped bast from the trees, fished, and so on. And, you know, whoever even once in his life has caught a perch or seen thrushes migrate in the autumn, when on clear, cool days they sweep in flocks over the village, will never really be a townsman and to the day of his death will have a longing for the open. My brother was unhappy in the government office. Years passed, but he went on warming the same seat, scratching away at the same papers, and thinking of one and the same thing: how to get away to the country. And little by little this vague long-

---

1. The son of a private, registered at birth in the army and trained in a military school.

ing turned into a definite desire, into a dream of buying a little property somewhere on the banks of a river or a lake.

"He was a kind and gentle soul and I loved him, but I never sympathized 21
with his desire to shut himself up for the rest of his life on a little property of
his own. It is a common saying that a man needs only six feet of earth. But six
feet is what a corpse needs, not a man. It is also asserted that if our educated
class is drawn to the land and seeks to settle on farms, that's a good thing. But
these farms amount to the same six feet of earth. To retire from the city, from
the struggle, from the hubbub, to go off and hide on one's own farm—that's
not life, it is selfishness, sloth, it is a kind of monasticism, but monasticism
without works. Man needs not six feet of earth, not a farm, but the whole globe,
all of Nature, where unhindered he can display all the capacities and peculiari-
ties of his free spirit.

"My brother Nikolay, sitting in his office, dreamed of eating his own *shchi*, 22
which would fill the whole farmyard with a delicious aroma, of picnicking on
the green grass, of sleeping in the sun, of sitting for hours on the seat by the
gate gazing at field and forest. Books on agriculture and the farming items in
almanacs were his joy, the delight of his soul. He liked newspapers too, but the
only things he read in them were advertisements of land for sale, so many acres
of tillable land and pasture, with house, garden, river, mill, and millpond. And
he pictured to himself garden paths, flowers, fruit, birdhouses with starlings in
them, crucians in the pond, and all that sort of thing, you know. These imaginary pictures varied with the advertisements he came upon, but somehow
gooseberry bushes figured in every one of them. He could not picture to himself a single country-house, a single rustic nook, without gooseberries.

" 'Country life has its advantages,' he used to say. 'You sit on the veranda 23
having tea, and your ducks swim in the pond, and everything smells delicious
and—the gooseberries are ripening.'

"He would draw a plan of his estate and invariably it would contain the fol- 24
lowing features: a) the master's house; b) servants' quarters; c) kitchen-garden;
d) a gooseberry patch. He lived meagerly: he deprived himself of food and
drink; he dressed God knows how, like a beggar, but he kept on saving and salt-
ing money away in the bank. He was terribly stingy. It was painful for me to see
it, and I used to give him small sums and send him something on holidays, but
he would put that away too. Once a man is possessed by an idea, there is no doing anything with him.

"Years passed. He was transferred to another province, he was already past 25
forty, yet he was still reading newspaper advertisements and saving up money.
Then I heard that he was married. Still for the sake of buying a property with a
gooseberry patch he married an elderly, homely widow, without a trace of affection for her, but simply because she had money. After marrying her, he went
on living parsimoniously, keeping her half-starved, and he put her money in
the bank in his own name. She had previously been the wife of a postmaster,
who had got her used to pies and cordials. This second husband did not even
give her enough black bread. She began to sicken, and some three years later

gave up the ghost. And, of course, it never for a moment occurred to my brother that he was to blame for her death. Money, like vodka, can do queer things to a man. Once in our town a merchant lay on his deathbed; before he died, he ordered a plateful of honey and he ate up all his money and lottery tickets with the honey, so that no one should get it. One day when I was inspecting a drove of cattle at a railway station, a cattle dealer fell under a locomotive and it sliced off his leg. We carried him in to the infirmary, the blood was gushing from the wound—a terrible business, but he kept begging us to find his leg and was very anxious about it: he had twenty rubles in the boot that was on that leg, and he was afraid they would be lost."

"That's a tune from another opera," said Burkin.   26

Ivan Ivanych paused a moment and then continued: 27

"After his wife's death, my brother began to look around for a property. Of   28
course, you may scout about for five years and in the end make a mistake, and buy something quite different from what you have been dreaming of. Through an agent my brother bought a mortgaged estate of three hundred acres with a house, servants' quarters, a park, but with no orchard, no gooseberry patch, no duck-pond. There was a stream, but the water in it was the color of coffee, for on one of its banks there was a brickyard and on the other a glue factory. But my brother was not at all disconcerted: he ordered a score of gooseberry bushes, planted them, and settled down to the life of a country gentleman.

"Last year I paid him a visit. I thought I would go and see how things were   29
with him. In his letter to me my brother called his estate 'Chumbaroklov Waste, or Himalaiskoe' (our surname was Chimsha-Himalaisky). I reached the place in the afternoon. It was hot. Everywhere there were ditches, fences, hedges, rows of fir trees, and I was at a loss as to how to get to the yard and where to leave my horse. I made my way to the house and was met by a fat dog with reddish hair that looked like a pig. It wanted to bark, but was too lazy. The cook, a fat, bare-legged woman, who also looked like a pig, came out of the kitchen and said that the master was resting after dinner. I went in to see my brother, and found him sitting up in bed, with a quilt over his knees. He had grown older, stouter, flabby; his cheeks, his nose, his lips jutted out: It looked as though he might grunt into the quilt at any moment.

"We embraced and dropped tears of joy and also of sadness at the thought   30
that the two of us had once been young, but were now gray and nearing death. He got dressed and took me out to show me his estate.

" 'Well, how are you getting on here?' I asked.   31

" 'Oh, all right, thank God. I am doing very well.'   32

"He was no longer the poor, timid clerk he used to be but a real landowner,   33
a gentleman. He had already grown used to his new manner of living and developed a taste for it. He ate a great deal, steamed himself in the bathhouse, was growing stout, was already having a lawsuit with the village commune and the two factories and was very much offended when the peasants failed to address him as 'Your Honor.' And he concerned himself with his soul's welfare too in a substantial, upper-class manner, and performed good deeds not simply, but

pompously. And what good works! He dosed the peasants with bicarbonate and castor oil for all their ailments and on his name day he had a thanksgiving service celebrated in the center of the village, and then treated the villagers to a gallon of vodka, which he thought was the thing to do. Oh, those horrible gallons of vodka! One day a fat landowner hauls the peasants up before the rural police officer for trespassing, and the next, to mark a feast day, treats them to a gallon of vodka, and they drink and shout 'Hurrah' and when they are drunk bow down at his feet. A higher standard of living, overeating and idleness develop the most insolent self-conceit in a Russian. Nikolay Ivanych, who when he was a petty official was afraid to have opinions of his own even if he kept them to himself, now uttered nothing but incontrovertible truths and did so in the tone of a minister of state: 'Education is necessary, but the masses are not ready for it; corporal punishment is generally harmful, but in some cases it is useful and nothing else will serve.'

" 'I know the common people, and I know how to deal with them,' he would   34 say. 'They love me. I only have to raise my little finger, and they will do anything I want.'

"And all this, mark you, would be said with a smile that bespoke kindness   35 and intelligence. Twenty times over he repeated: 'We, of the gentry,' 'I, as a member of the gentry.' Apparently he no longer remembered that our grandfather had been a peasant and our father just a private. Even our surname, 'Chimsha-Himalaisky,' which in reality is grotesque, seemed to him sonorous, distinguished, and delightful.

"But I am concerned now not with him, but with me. I want to tell you   36 about the change that took place in me during the few hours that I spent on his estate. In the evening when we were having tea, the cook served a plateful of gooseberries. They were not bought, they were his own gooseberries, the first ones picked since the bushes were planted. My brother gave a laugh and for a minute looked at the gooseberries in silence, with tears in his eyes—he could not speak for excitement. Then he put one berry in his mouth, glanced at me with the triumph of a child who has at last been given a toy he was longing for and said: 'How tasty!' And he ate the gooseberries greedily, and kept repeating: 'Ah, how delicious! Do taste them!'

"They were hard and sour, but as Pushkin[2] has it,   37

The falsehood that exalts we cherish more
Than meaner truths that are a thousand strong.

I saw a happy man, one whose cherished dream had so obviously come true, who had attained his goal in life, who had got what he wanted, who was satisfied with his lot and with himself. For some reason an element of sadness had always mingled with my thoughts of human happiness, and now at the sight of a happy man I was assailed by an oppressive feeling bordering on despair. It

2. Russian poet (1799–1837).

weighed on me particularly at night. A bed was made up for me in a room next to my brother's bedroom, and I could hear that he was wakeful, and that he would get up again and again, go to the plate of gooseberries and eat one after another. I said to myself: how many contented, happy people there really are! What an overwhelming force they are! Look at life: the insolence and idleness of the strong, the ignorance and brutishness of the weak, horrible poverty everywhere, overcrowding, degeneration, drunkenness, hypocrisy, lying—— Yet in all the houses and on all the streets there is peace and quiet; of the fifty thousand people who live in our town there is not one who would cry out, who would vent his indignation aloud. We see the people who go to market, eat by day, sleep by night, who babble nonsense, marry, grow old, good-naturedly drag their dead to the cemetery, but we do not see or hear those who suffer, and what is terrible in life goes on somewhere behind the scenes. Everything is peaceful and quiet and only mute statistics protest: so many people gone out of their minds, so many gallons of vodka drunk, so many children dead from malnutrition—— And such a state of things is evidently necessary; obviously the happy man is at ease only because the unhappy ones bear their burdens in silence, and if there were not this silence, happiness would be impossible. It is a general hypnosis. Behind the door of every contented, happy man there ought to be someone standing with a little hammer and continually reminding him with a knock that there are unhappy people, that however happy he may be, life will sooner or later show him its claws, and trouble will come to him—illness, poverty, losses, and then no one will see or hear him, just as now he neither sees nor hears others. But there is no man with a hammer. The happy man lives at his ease, faintly fluttered by small daily cares, like an aspen in the wind—and all is well."

"That night I came to understand that I too had been contented and happy," 38 Ivan Ivanych continued, getting up. "I too over the dinner table or out hunting would hold forth on how to live, what to believe, the right way to govern the people. I too would say that learning was the enemy of darkness, that education was necessary but that for the common people the three R's were sufficient for the time being. Freedom is a boon, I used to say, it is as essential as air, but we must wait awhile. Yes, that's what I used to say, and now I ask: Why must we wait?" said Ivan Ivanych, looking wrathfully at Burkin. "Why must we wait, I ask you? For what reason? I am told that nothing can be done all at once, that every idea is realized gradually, in its own time. But who is it that says so? Where is the proof that it is just? You cite the natural order of things, the law governing all phenomena, but is there law, is there order in the fact that I, a living, thinking man, stand beside a ditch and wait for it to close up of itself or fill up with silt, when I could jump over it or throw a bridge across it? And again, why must we wait? Wait, until we have no strength to live, and yet we have to live and are eager to live!

"I left my brother's place early in the morning, and ever since then it has be- 39 come intolerable for me to stay in town. I am oppressed by the peace and the quiet, I am afraid to look at the windows, for there is nothing that pains me more than the spectacle of a happy family sitting at table having tea. I am an old man now and unfit for combat, I am not even capable of hating. I can only grieve inwardly, get irritated, worked up, and at night my head is ablaze with the rush of ideas and I cannot sleep. Oh, if I were young!"

Ivan Ivanych paced up and down the room excitedly and repeated, "If I were 40 young!"

He suddenly walked up to Alyohin and began to press now one of his hands, 41 now the other.

"Pavel Konstantinych," he said imploringly, "don't quiet down, don't let 42 yourself be lulled to sleep! As long as you are young, strong, alert, do not cease to do good! There is no happiness and there should be none, and if life has a meaning and a purpose, that meaning and purpose is not our happiness but something greater and more rational. Do good!"

All this Ivan Ivanych said with a pitiful, imploring smile, as though he were 43 asking a personal favor.

Afterwards all three of them sat in armchairs in different corners of the 44 drawing room and were silent. Ivan Ivanych's story satisfied neither Burkin nor Alyohin. With the ladies and generals looking down from the golden frames, seeming alive in the dim light, it was tedious to listen to the story of the poor devil of a clerk who ate gooseberries. One felt like talking about elegant people, about women. And the fact that they were sitting in a drawing room where everything—the chandelier under its cover, the armchairs, the carpets underfoot—testified that the very people who were now looking down from the frames had once moved about here, sat and had tea, and the fact that lovely Pelageya was noiselessly moving about—that was better than any story.

Alyohin was very sleepy; he had gotten up early, before three o'clock in the 45 morning, to get some work done, and now he could hardly keep his eyes open, but he was afraid his visitors might tell an interesting story in his absence, and he would not leave. He did not trouble to ask himself if what Ivan Ivanych had just said was intelligent or right. The guests were not talking about groats, or hay, or tar, but about something that had no direct bearing on his life, and he was glad of it and wanted them to go on.

"However, it's bedtime," said Burkin, rising. "Allow me to wish you good 46 night."

Alyohin took leave of his guests and went downstairs to his own quarters, 47 while they remained upstairs. They were installed for the night in a big room in which stood two old wooden beds decorated with carvings and in the corner was an ivory crucifix. The wide cool beds which had been made by the lovely Pelageya gave off a pleasant smell of clean linen.

Ivan Ivanych undressed silently and got into bed. 48

"Lord forgive us sinners!" he murmured, and drew the bedclothes over his 49 head.

His pipe, which lay on the table, smelled strongly of burnt tobacco, and 50
Burkin, who could not sleep for a long time, kept wondering where the unpleasant odor came from.

The rain beat against the window panes all night.   51

—Translated by Avrahm Yarmolinsky

ACTIVITIES FOR WRITING AND DISCUSSION

1. In paragraph 37, Ivan Ivanych criticizes his brother for being "a happy man." Why? In your notebook write a summary of his reasoning. Do you think his criticism is fair? Why or why not?

2. In paragraph 44 we are told that "Ivan Ivanych's story satisfied neither Burkin nor Alyohin." Describe the two friends' reactions to the story. Can their reactions be said to relate in any ways to the **themes** of Ivan's story about his brother Nikolay?

3. How do you assess Ivan Ivanych's outlook and attitudes? Is he mentally sick? too intense and serious? wiser than his friends or the world he criticizes? Of what people (if any) in your own experience does he remind you?

4. Like the **characters** in many Chekhov stories, Ivan Ivanych doesn't just tell a story: he philosophizes; he wrestles with the meaning of life. Who are we? Why are we alive? What are our lives for? Create a character of your own and a subject about which he/she can philosophize. For a context, consider two or three friends conversing around a campfire or college students talking late at night in the dorm or over beers.

JAMES THURBER (1894–1961)

The Secret Life of Walter Mitty

"We're going through!" The Commander's voice was like thin ice breaking. He 1
wore his full-dress uniform, with the heavily braided white cap pulled down
rakishly over one cold gray eye. "We can't make it, sir. It's spoiling for a hurri-
cane, if you ask me." "I'm not asking you, Lieutenant Berg," said the Commander. "Throw on the power lights! Rev her up to 8,500! We're going through!"
The pounding of the cylinders increased: ta-pocketa-pocketa-pocketa-*pocketa-
pocketa.* The Commander stared at the ice forming on the pilot window. He
walked over and twisted a row of complicated dials. "Switch on No. 8 auxiliary!" he shouted. "Switch on No. 8 auxiliary!" repeated Lieutenant Berg. "Full
strength in No. 3 turret!" shouted the Commander. "Full strength in No. 3 turret!" The crew, bending to their various tasks in the huge, hurtling eight-

engined Navy hydroplane, looked at each other and grinned. "The Old Man'll get us through," they said to one another. "The Old Man ain't afraid of Hell!" . . .

"Not so fast! You're driving too fast!" said Mrs. Mitty. "What are you driving so fast for?"   2

"Hmm?" said Walter Mitty. He looked at his wife, in the seat beside him,   3 with shocked astonishment. She seemed grossly unfamiliar, like a strange woman who had yelled at him in a crowd. "You were up to fifty-five," she said. "You know I don't like to go more than forty. You were up to fifty-five." Walter Mitty drove on toward Waterbury in silence, the roaring of the SN202 through the worst storm in twenty years of Navy flying fading in the remote, intimate airways of his mind. "You're tensed up again," said Mrs. Mitty. "It's one of your days. I wish you'd let Dr. Renshaw look you over."

Walter Mitty stopped the car in front of the building where his wife went to   4 have her hair done. "Remember to get those overshoes while I'm having my hair done," she said. "I don't need overshoes," said Mitty. She put her mirror back into her bag. "We've been all through that," she said, getting out of the car. "You're not a young man any longer." He raced the engine a little. "Why don't you wear your gloves? Have you lost your gloves?" Walter Mitty reached in a pocket and brought out the gloves. He put them on, but after she had turned and gone into the building and he had driven on to a red light, he took them off again. "Pick it up, brother!" snapped a cop as the light changed, and Mitty hastily pulled on his gloves and lurched ahead. He drove around the streets aimlessly for a time, and then he drove past the hospital on his way to the parking lot.

. . . "It's the millionaire banker, Wellington McMillan," said the pretty nurse.   5 "Yes?" said Walter Mitty, removing his gloves slowly. "Who has the case?" "Dr. Renshaw and Dr. Benbow, but there are two specialists here, Dr. Remington from New York and Dr. Pritchard-Mitford from London. He flew over." A door opened down a long, cool corridor and Dr. Renshaw came out. He looked distraught and haggard. "Hello, Mitty," he said. "We're having the devil's own time with McMillan, the millionaire banker and close personal friend of Roosevelt. Obstreosis of the ductal tract. Tertiary. Wish you'd take a look at him." "Glad to," said Mitty.

In the operating room there were whispered introductions: "Dr. Reming-   6 ton, Dr. Mitty, Dr. Pritchard-Mitford, Dr. Mitty." "I've read your book on strep-tothricosis," said Pritchard-Mitford, shaking hands. "A brilliant performance, sir." "Thank you," said Walter Mitty. "Didn't know you were in the States, Mitty," grumbled Remington. "Coals to Newcastle, bringing Mitford and me up here for a tertiary." "You are very kind," said Mitty. A huge, complicated machine, connected to the operating table, with many tubes and wires, began at this moment to go pocketa-pocketa-pocketa. "The new anesthetizer is giving way!" shouted an interne. "There is no one in the East who knows how to fix it!" "Quiet, man!" said Mitty, in a low, cool voice. He sprang to the machine, which was now going pocketa-pocketa-queep-pocketa-queep. He began fingering delicately a row of glistening dials. "Give me a fountain pen!" he snapped. Someone handed him a fountain pen. He pulled a faulty piston out of the machine and inserted the pen in its place. "That will hold for ten minutes," he said. "Get on with the operation." A nurse hurried over and whispered to Renshaw, and Mitty saw the man turn pale. "Coreopsis has set in," said Renshaw nervously. "If you would take over, Mitty?" Mitty looked at him and at the craven figure of Benbow, who drank, and at the grave, uncertain faces of the two great specialists. "If you wish," he said. They slipped a white gown on him; he adjusted a mask and drew on thin gloves; nurses handed him shining. . . .

"Back it up, Mac! Look out for that Buick!" Walter Mitty jammed on the brakes. "Wrong lane, Mac," said the parking-lot attendant, looking at Mitty closely. "Gee. Yeh," muttered Mitty. He began cautiously to back out of the lane marked "Exit Only." "Leave her sit there," said the attendant. "I'll put her away." Mitty got out of the car. "Hey, better leave the key." "Oh," said Mitty, handing the man the ignition key. The attendant vaulted into the car, backed it up with insolent skill, and put it where it belonged. **7**

They're so damn cocky, thought Walter Mitty, walking along Main Street; they think they know everything. Once he had tried to take his chains off, outside New Milford, and he had got them wound around the axles. A man had had to come out in a wrecking car and unwind them, a young, grinning garageman. Since then Mrs. Mitty always made him drive to the garage to have the chains taken off. The next time, he thought, I'll wear my right arm in a sling; they won't grin at me then. I'll have my right arm in a sling and they'll see I couldn't possibly take the chains off myself. He kicked at the slush on the sidewalk. "Overshoes," he said to himself, and he began looking for a shoe store. **8**

When he came out into the street again, with the overshoes in a box under his arm, Walter Mitty began to wonder what the other thing was his wife had told him to get. She had told him, twice, before they set out from their house for Waterbury. In a way he hated these weekly trips to town—he was always getting something wrong. Kleenex, he thought, Squibb's, razor blades? No. Toothpaste, toothbrush, bicarbonate, carborundum, initiative and referendum? He gave it up. But she would remember it. "Where's the what's-its-name?" she would ask. "Don't tell me you forgot the what's-its-name." A newsboy went by shouting something about the Waterbury trial. **9**

. . . "Perhaps this will refresh your memory." The District Attorney suddenly thrust a heavy automatic at the quiet figure on the witness stand. "Have you ever seen this before?" Walter Mitty took the gun and examined it expertly. "This is my Webley-Vickers 50.80," he said calmly. An excited buzz ran around the courtroom. The Judge rapped for order. "You are a crack shot with any sort of firearms, I believe?" said the District Attorney, insinuatingly. "Objection!" shouted Mitty's attorney. "We have shown that the defendant could not have fired the shot. We have shown that he wore his right arm in a sling on the night of the fourteenth of July." Walter Mitty raised his hand briefly and the bickering attorneys were stilled. "With any known make of gun," he said evenly, "I could have killed Gregory Fitzhurst at three hundred feet *with my left hand*." Pande- **10** monium broke loose in the courtroom. A woman's scream rose above the bedlam and suddenly a lovely, dark-haired girl was in Walter Mitty's arms. The District Attorney struck at her savagely. Without rising from his chair, Mitty let the man have it on the point of the chin. "You miserable cur!" . . .

"Puppy biscuit," said Walter Mitty. He stopped walking and the buildings of 11 Waterbury rose up out of the misty courtroom and surrounded him again. A woman who was passing laughed, "He said 'Puppy biscuit,' " she said to her companion. "That man said 'Puppy biscuit' to himself." Walter Mitty hurried on. He went into an A. & P., not the first one he came to but a smaller one farther up the street. "I want some biscuit for small, young dogs," he said to the clerk. "Any special brand, sir?" The greatest pistol shot in the world thought a moment. "It says 'Puppies Bark for It' on the box," said Walter Mitty.

———————

His wife would be through at the hairdresser's in fifteen minutes, Mitty saw 12 in looking at his watch, unless they had trouble drying it; sometimes they had trouble drying it. She didn't like to get to the hotel first; she would want him to be there waiting for her as usual. He found a big leather chair in the lobby, facing a window, and he put the overshoes and the puppy biscuit on the floor beside it. He picked up an old copy of *Liberty* and sank down into the chair. "Can Germany Conquer the World through the Air?" Walter Mitty looked at the pictures of bombing planes and of ruined streets.

. . . "The cannonading has got the wind up in young Raleigh, sir," said the 13 sergeant. Captain Mitty looked up at him through tousled hair. "Get him to bed," he said wearily. "With the others. I'll fly alone." "But you can't, sir," said the sergeant anxiously. "It takes two men to handle that bomber and the Archies are pounding hell out of the air. Von Richtman's circus is between here and Saulier." "Somebody's got to get that ammunition dump," said Mitty. "I'm going over. Spot of brandy?" He poured a drink for the sergeant and one for himself. War thundered and whined around the dugout and battered at the door. There was a rending of wood and splinters flew through the room. "A bit of a near thing," said Captain Mitty carelessly. "The box barrage is closing in," said the sergeant. "We only live once, Sergeant," said Mitty, with his faint, fleeting smile. "Or do we?" He poured another brandy and tossed it off. "I never see a man could hold his brandy like you, sir," said the sergeant. "Begging your pardon, sir." Captain Mitty stood up and strapped on his huge Webley-Vickers automatic. "It's forty kilometers through hell, sir," said the sergeant. Mitty finished one last brandy. "After all," he said softly, "what isn't?" The pounding of the cannon increased; there was the rat-tat-tatting of machine guns, and from somewhere came the menacing pocket-pocketa-pocketa of the new flame-throwers. Walter Mitty walked to the door of the dugout humming "Auprès de Ma Blonde." He turned and waved to the sergeant. "Cheerio!" he said. . . .

Something struck his shoulder. "I've been looking all over this hotel for 14 you," said Mrs. Mitty. "Why do you have to hide in this old chair? How did you expect me to find you?" "Things close in," said Walter Mitty vaguely. "What?"

Mrs. Mitty said. "Did you get the what's-its-name? The puppy biscuit? What's in that box?" "Overshoes," said Mitty. "Couldn't you have put them on in the store?" "I was thinking," said Walter Mitty. "Does it ever occur to you that I am sometimes thinking?" She looked at him. "I'm going to take your temperature when I get you home," she said.

They went out through the revolving doors that made a faintly derisive 15 whistling sound when you pushed them. It was two blocks to the parking lot. At the drugstore on the corner she said, "Wait here for me. I forgot something. I won't be a minute." She was more than a minute. Walter Mitty lighted a cigarette. It began to rain, rain with sleet in it. He stood up against the wall of the drugstore, smoking. . . . He put his shoulders back and his heels together. "To hell with the handkerchief," said Walter Mitty scornfully. He took one last drag on his cigarette and snapped it away. Then, with that faint, fleeting smile playing about his lips, he faced the firing squad; erect and motionless, proud and disdainful, Walter Mitty the Undefeated, inscrutable to the last.

Flannery O'Connor (1925–1964)

Good Country People

Besides the neutral expression that she wore when she was alone, Mrs. Freeman 1 had two others, forward and reverse, that she used for all her human dealings. Her forward expression was steady and driving like the advance of a heavy truck. Her eyes never swerved to left or right but turned as the story turned as if they followed a yellow line down the center of it. She seldom used the other expression because it was not often necessary for her to retract a statement, but when she did, her face came to a complete stop, there was an almost imperceptible movement of her black eyes, during which they seemed to be receding, and then the observer would see that Mrs. Freeman, though she might stand there as real as several grain sacks thrown on top of each other, was no longer there in spirit. As for getting anything across to her when this was the case, Mrs. Hopewell had given it up. She might talk her head off. Mrs. Freeman could never be brought to admit herself wrong on any point. She would stand there and if she could be brought to say anything, it was something like, "Well, I wouldn't of said it was and I wouldn't of said it wasn't," or letting her gaze range over the top kitchen shelf where there was an assortment of dusty bottles, she might remark, "I see you ain't ate many of them figs you put up last summer."

They carried on their most important business in the kitchen at breakfast. 2 Every morning Mrs. Hopewell got up at seven o'clock and lit her gas heater and Joy's. Joy was her daughter, a large blonde girl who had an artificial leg. Mrs. Hopewell thought of her as a child though she was thirty-two years old and highly educated. Joy would get up while her mother was eating and lumber into the bathroom and slam the door, and before long, Mrs. Freeman would arrive at the back door. Joy would hear her mother call, "Come on in," and then they would talk for a while in low voices that were indistinguishable in the bathroom. By the time Joy came in, they had usually finished the weather report and were on one or the other of Mrs. Freeman's daughters, Glynese or Carramae. Joy called them Glycerin and Caramel. Glynese, a redhead, was eighteen and had many admirers; Carramae, a blonde was only fifteen but already married and pregnant. She could not keep anything on her stomach. Every morning Mrs. Freeman told Mrs. Hopewell how many times she had vomited since the last report.

Mrs. Hopewell liked to tell people that Glynese and Carramae were two of 3 the finest girls she knew and that Mrs. Freeman was a *lady* and that she was never ashamed to take her anywhere or introduce her to anybody they might meet. Then she would tell how she had happened to hire the Freemans in the first place and how they were a godsend to her and how she had had them four years. The reason for her keeping them so long was that they were not trash. They were good country people. She had telephoned the man whose name they had given as a reference and he had told her that Mr. Freeman was a good farmer but that his wife was the nosiest woman ever to walk the earth. "She's got to be into everything," the man said. "If she don't get there before the dust settles, you can bet she's dead, that's all. She'll want to know all your business. I can stand him real good," he had said, "but me nor my wife neither could have stood that woman one more minute on this place." That had put Mrs. Hopewell off for a few days.

She had hired them in the end because there were no other applicants but 4 she had made up her mind beforehand exactly how she would handle the woman. Since she was the type who had to be into everything, then, Mrs. Hopewell had decided, she would not only let her be into everything, she would *see to it* that she was into everything—she would give her the responsibility of everything, she would put her in charge. Mrs. Hopewell had no bad qualities of her own but she was able to use other people's in such a constructive way that she never felt the lack. She had hired the Freemans and she had kept them four years.

Nothing is perfect. This was one of Mrs. Hopewell's favorite sayings. Another was: that is life! And still another, the most important, was: well, other people have their opinions too. She would make these statements, usually at the table, in a tone of gentle insistence as if no one held them but her, and the large hulking Joy, whose constant outrage had obliterated every expression from her face, would stare just a little to the side of her, her eyes icy blue, with the look of someone who has achieved blindness by an act of will and means to keep it.

When Mrs. Hopewell said to Mrs. Freeman that life was like that, Mrs. Free- 6 man would say, "I always said so myself." Nothing had been arrived at by anyone that had not first been arrived at by her. She was quicker than Mr. Freeman. When Mrs. Hopewell said to her after they had been on the place a while, "You know, you're the wheel behind the wheel," and winked, Mrs. Freeman had said, "I know it. I've always been quick. It's some that are quicker than others."

"Everybody is different," Mrs. Hopewell said.   7

"Yes, most people is," Mrs. Freeman said.   8

"It takes all kinds to make the world."   9

"I always said it did myself."   10

The girl was used to this kind of dialogue for breakfast and more of it for 11
dinner; sometimes they had it for supper too. When they had no guest they ate
in the kitchen because that was easier. Mrs. Freeman always managed to arrive
at some point during the meal and to watch them finish it. She would stand in
the doorway if it were summer but in the winter she would stand with one elbow on top of the refrigerator and look down on them, or she would stand by
the gas heater, lifting the back of her skirt slightly. Occasionally she would stand
against the wall and roll her head from side to side. At no time was she in any
hurry to leave. All this was very trying on Mrs. Hopewell but she was a woman
of great patience. She realized that nothing is perfect and that in the Freemans
she had good country people and that if, in this day and age, you get good
country people, you had better hang onto them.

She had had plenty of experience with trash. Before the Freemans she had 12
averaged one tenant family a year. The wives of these farmers were not the kind
you would want to be around you for very long. Mrs. Hopewell, who had divorced her husband long ago, needed someone to walk over the fields with her;
and when Joy had to be impressed for these services, her remarks were usually
so ugly and her face so glum that Mrs. Hopewell would say, "If you can't come
pleasantly, I don't want you at all," to which the girl, standing square and rigid-
shouldered with her neck thrust slightly forward, would reply, "If you want me,
here I am—LIKE I AM."

Mrs. Hopewell excused this attitude because of the leg (which had been 13
shot off in a hunting accident when Joy was ten). It was hard for Mrs. Hopewell
to realize that her child was thirty-two now and that for more than twenty years
she had had only one leg. She thought of her still as a child because it tore her
heart to think instead of the poor stout girl in her thirties who had never
danced a step or had any *normal* good times. Her name was really Joy but as
soon as she was twenty-one and away from home, she had had it legally
changed. Mrs. Hopewell was certain that she had thought and thought until she
had hit upon the ugliest name in any language. Then she had gone and had the
beautiful name, Joy, changed without telling her mother until after she had
done it. Her legal name was Hulga.

When Mrs. Hopewell thought the name, Hulga, she thought of the broad 14
blank hull of a battleship. She would not use it. She continued to call her Joy to
which the girl responded but in a purely mechanical way.

Hulga had learned to tolerate Mrs. Freeman who saved her from taking 15
walks with her mother. Even Glynese and Carramae were useful when they occupied attention that might otherwise have been directed at her. At first she had
thought she could not stand Mrs. Freeman for she had found that it was not
possible to be rude to her. Mrs. Freeman would take on strange resentments
and for days together she would be sullen but the source of her displeasure was

always obscure; a direct attack, a positive leer, blatant ugliness to her face—these never touched her. And without warning one day, she began calling her Hulga.

She did not call her that in front of Mrs. Hopewell who would have been in- 16
censed but when she and the girl happened to be out of the house together, she would say something and add the name Hulga to the end of it, and the big spectacled Joy-Hulga would scowl and redden as if her privacy had been intruded upon. She considered the name her personal affair. She had arrived at it first purely on the basis of its ugly sound and then the full genius of its fitness had struck her. She had a vision of the name working like the ugly sweating Vulcan who stayed in the furnace and to whom, presumably, the goddess had to come when called. She saw it as the name of her highest creative act. One of her major triumphs was that her mother had not been able to turn her dust into Joy, but the greater one was that she had been able to turn it herself into Hulga. However, Mrs. Freeman's relish for using the name only irritated her. It was as if Mrs. Freeman's beady steel-pointed eyes had penetrated far enough behind her face to reach some secret fact. Something about her seemed to fascinate Mrs. Freeman and then one day Hulga realized that it was the artificial leg. Mrs. Freeman had a special fondness for the details of secret infections, hidden deformities, assaults upon children. Of diseases, she preferred the lingering or incurable. Hulga had heard Mrs. Hopewell give her the details of the hunting accident, how the leg had been literally blasted off, how she had never lost consciousness. Mrs. Freeman could listen to it any time as if it had happened an hour ago.

When Hulga stumped into the kitchen in the morning (she could walk 17
without making the awful noise but she made it—Mrs. Hopewell was certain—because it was ugly-sounding), she glanced at them and did not speak. Mrs. Hopewell would be in her red kimono with her hair tied around her head in rags. She would be sitting at the table, finishing her breakfast and Mrs. Freeman would be hanging by her elbow outward from the refrigerator, looking down at the table. Hulga always put her eggs on the stove to boil and then stood over them with her arms folded, and Mrs. Hopewell would look at her—a kind of indirect gaze divided between her and Mrs. Freeman—and would think that if she would only keep herself up a little, she wouldn't be so bad looking. There was nothing wrong with her face that a pleasant expression wouldn't help. Mrs. Hopewell said that people who looked on the bright side of things would be beautiful even if they were not.

Whenever she looked at Joy this way, she could not help but feel that it 18
would have been better if the child had not taken the Ph.D. It had certainly not brought her out any and now that she had it, there was no more excuse for her to go to school again. Mrs. Hopewell though it was nice for girls to go to school to have a good time but Joy had "gone through." Anyhow, she would not have been strong enough to go again. The doctors had told Mrs. Hopewell that with the best of care, Joy might see forty-five. She had a weak heart. Joy had made it

plain that if it had not been for this condition, she would be far from these red hills and good country people. She would be in a university lecturing to people who knew what she was talking about. And Mrs. Hopewell could very well picture her there, looking like a scarecrow and lecturing to more of the same. Here she went about all day in a six-year-old skirt and a yellow sweat shirt with a faded cowboy on a horse embossed on it. She thought this was funny; Mrs. Hopewell thought it was idiotic and showed simply that she was still a child. She was brilliant but she didn't have a grain of sense. It seemed to Mrs. Hopewell that every year she grew less like other people and more like herself—bloated, rude, and squint-eyed. And she said such strange things! To her own mother she had said—without warning, without excuse, standing up in the middle of a meal with her face purple and her mouth half full—"Woman! do you ever look inside? Do you ever look inside and see what you are *not*? God!" she had cried sinking down again and staring at her plate, "Malebranche was right: we are not our own light. We are not our own light!" Mrs. Hopewell had no idea to this day what brought that on. She had only made the remark, hoping Joy would take it in, that a smile never hurt anyone.

The girl had taken the Ph.D. in philosophy and this left Mrs. Hopewell at a 19 complete loss. You could say, "My daughter is a nurse," or "My daughter is a school teacher," or even, "My daughter is a chemical engineer." You could not say, "My daughter is a philosopher." That was something that had ended with the Greeks and Romans. All day Joy sat on her neck in a deep chair, reading. Sometimes she went for walks but she didn't like dogs or cats or birds or flowers or nature or nice young men. She looked at nice young men as if she could smell their stupidity.

One day Mrs. Hopewell had picked up one of the books the girl had just put 20 down and opening it at random, she read, "Science, on the other hand, has to assert its soberness and seriousness afresh and declare that it is concerned solely with what-is. Nothing—how can it be for science anything but a horror and a phantasm? If science is right, then one thing stands firm: science wishes to know nothing of nothing. Such is after all the strictly scientific approach to Nothing. We know it by wishing to know nothing of Nothing." These words had been underlined with a blue pencil and they worked on Mrs. Hopewell like some evil incantation in gibberish. She shut the book quickly and went out of the room as if she were having a chill.

This morning when the girl came in, Mrs. Freeman was on Carramae. "She 21 thrown up four times after supper," she said, "and was up twict in the night after three o'clock. Yesterday she didn't do nothing but ramble in the bureau drawer. All she did. Stand up there and see what she could run up on."

"She's got to eat," Mrs. Hopewell muttered, sipping her coffee, while she 22 watched Joy's back at the stove. She was wondering what the child had said to the Bible salesman. She could not imagine what kind of a conversation she could possibly have had with him.

He was a tall gaunt hatless youth who had called yesterday to sell them a 23 Bible. He had appeared at the door, carrying a large black suitcase that weighted him so heavily on one side that he had to brace himself against the door facing. He seemed on the point of collapse but he said in a cheerful voice, "Good morning, Mrs. Cedars!" and set the suitcase down on the mat. He was not a bad-looking young man though he had on a bright blue suit and yellow socks that were not pulled up far enough. He had prominent face bones and a streak of sticky-looking brown hair falling across his forehead.

"I'm Mrs. Hopewell," she said. 24

"Oh!" he said, pretending to look puzzled but with his eyes sparkling, "I saw 25 it said 'The Cedars,' on the mailbox so I thought you was Mrs. Cedars!" and he burst out in a pleasant laugh. He picked up the satchel and under cover of a pant, he fell forward into her hall. It was rather as if the suitcase had moved first, jerking him after it. "Mrs. Hopewell!" he said and grabbed her hand. "I hope you are well!" and he laughed again and then all at once his face sobered completely. He paused and gave her a straight earnest look and said, "Lady, I've come to speak of serious things."

"Well, come in," she muttered, none too pleased because her dinner was al- 26 most ready. He came into the parlor and sat down on the edge of a straight chair and put the suitcase between his feet and glanced around the room as if he were sizing her up by it. Her silver gleamed on the two sideboards; she decided he had never been in a room as elegant as this.

"Mrs. Hopewell," he began, using her name in a way that sounded almost 27 intimate, "I know you believe in Christian service."

"Well, yes," she murmured. 28

"I know," he said and paused, looking very wise with his head cocked on one 29 side, "that you're a good woman. Friends have told me."

Mrs. Hopewell never liked to be taken for a fool. "What are you selling?" she 30 asked.

"Bibles," the young man said and his eye raced around the room before he 31 added, "I see you have no family Bible in your parlor, I see that is the one lack you got!"

Mrs. Hopewell could not say, "My daughter is an atheist and won't let me 32 keep the Bible in the parlor." She said, stiffening slightly. "I keep my Bible by my bedside." This was not the truth. It was in the attic somewhere.

"Lady," he said, "the word of God ought to be in the parlor." 33

"Well, I think that's a matter of taste," she began. "I think . . ." 34

"Lady," he said, "for a Christian, the word of God ought to be in every room 35 in the house besides in his heart. I know you're a Christian because I can see it in every line of your face."

She stood up and said, "Well, young man, I don't want to buy a Bible and I 36 smell my dinner burning."

He didn't get up. He began to twist his hands and looking down at them, he 37 said softly, "Well lady, I'll tell you the truth—not many people want to buy one nowadays and besides, I know I'm real simple. I don't know how to say a thing but to say it. I'm just a country boy." He glanced up into her unfriendly face. "People like you don't like to fool with country people like me!"

"Why!" she cried, "good country people are the salt of the earth! Besides, we 38
all have different ways of doing, it takes all kinds to make the world go 'round.
That's life!"

"You said a mouthful," he said.   39

"Why, I think there aren't enough good country people in the world!" she 40
said, stirred. "I think that's what's wrong with it!"

His face had brightened. "I didn't inraduce myself," he said. "I'm Manley 41
Pointer from out in the country around Willohobie, not even from a place, just
from near a place."

"You wait a minute," she said. "I have to see about my dinner." She went out 42
to the kitchen and found Joy standing near the door where she had been listening.

"Get rid of the salt of the earth," she said, "and let's eat."   43

Mrs. Hopewell gave her a pained look and turned the heat down under the 44
vegetables. "*I* can't be rude to anybody," she murmured and went back into the
parlor.

He had opened the suitcase and was sitting with a Bible on each knee.   45

"You might as well put those up," she told him. "I don't want one."   46

"I appreciate your honesty," he said. "You don't see any more real honest 47
people unless you go way out in the country."

"I know," she said, "real genuine folks!" Through the crack in the door she 48
heard a groan.

"I guess a lot of boys come telling you they're working their way through 49
college," he said, "but I'm not going to tell you that. Somehow," he said, "I don't
want to go to college. I want to devote my life to Christian service. See," he said,
lowering his voice, "I got this heart condition. I may not live long. When you
know it's something wrong with you and you may not live long, well then,
lady . . ." He paused, with his mouth open, and stared at her.

He and Joy had the same condition! She knew that her eyes were filling 50
with tears but she collected herself quickly and murmured. "Won't you stay for
dinner? We'd love to have you!" and was sorry the instant she heard herself
say it.

"Yes mam," he said in an abashed voice, "I would sher love to do that!"   51

Joy had given him one look on being introduced to him and then through- 52
out the meal had not glanced at him again. He had addressed several remarks to
her, which she had pretended not to hear. Mrs. Hopewell could not understand
deliberate rudeness, although she lived with it, and she felt she had always to
overflow with hospitality to make up for Joy's lack of courtesy. She urged him
to talk about himself and he did. He said he was the seventh child of twelve and
that his father had been crushed under a tree when he himself was eight year
old. He had been crushed very badly, in fact, almost cut in two and was practically not recognizable. His mother had got along the best she could by hard
working and she had always seen that her children went to Sunday School and
that they read the Bible every evening. He was now nineteen year old and he
had been selling Bibles for four months. In that time he had sold seventy-seven

Bibles and had the promise of two more sales. He wanted to become a missionary because he thought that was the way you could do most for people. "He who losest his life shall find it," he said simply and he was so sincere, so genuine and earnest that Mrs. Hopewell would not for the world have smiled. He prevented his peas from sliding onto the table by blocking them with a piece of bread which he later cleaned his plate with. She could see Joy observing sidewise how he handled his knife and fork and she saw too that every few minutes, the boy would dart a keen appraising glance at the girl as if he were trying to attract her attention.

After dinner Joy cleared the dishes off the table and disappeared and Mrs. 53
Hopewell was left to talk with him. He told her again about his childhood and his father's accident and about various things that had happened to him. Every five minutes or so she would stifle a yawn. He sat for two hours until finally she told him she must go because she had an appointment in town. He packed his Bibles and thanked her and prepared to leave, but in the doorway he stopped and wrung her hand and said that not on any of his trips had he met a lady as nice as her and he asked if he could come again. She had said she would always be happy to see him.

Joy had been standing in the road, apparently looking at something in the 54
distance, when he came down the steps toward her, bent to the side with his heavy valise. He stopped where she was standing and confronted her directly. Mrs. Hopewell could not hear what he said but she trembled to think what Joy would say to him. She could see that after a minute Joy said something and that then the boy began to speak again, making an excited gesture with his free hand. After a minute Joy said something else at which the boy began to speak once more. Then to her amazement, Mrs. Hopewell saw the two of them walk off together, toward the gate. Joy had walked all the way to the gate with him and Mrs. Hopewell could not imagine what they had said to each other, and she had not yet dared to ask.

Mrs. Freeman was insisting upon her attention. She had moved from the re- 55
frigerator to the heater so that Mrs. Hopewell had to turn and face her in order to seem to be listening. "Glynese gone out with Harvey Hill again last night," she said. "She had this sty."

"Hill," Mrs. Hopewell said absently, "is that the one who works in the 56
garage?"

"Nome, he's the one that goes to chiropracter school," Mrs. Freeman said. 57
"She had this sty. Been had it two days. So she says when he brought her in the other night he says, 'Lemme get rid of that sty for you,' and she says, 'How?' and he says, 'You just lay yourself down acrost the seat of that car and I'll show you.' So she done it and he popped her neck. Kept on a-popping it several times until she made him quit. This morning," Mrs. Freeman said, "she ain't got no sty. She ain't got no traces of a sty."

"I never heard of that before," Mrs. Hopewell said. 58

"He ast her to marry him before the Ordinary," Mrs. Freeman went on, "and 59
she told him she wasn't going to be married in no *office*."

"Well, Glynese is a fine girl," Mrs. Hopewell said. "Glynese and Carramae 60 are both fine girls."

"Carramae said when her and Lyman was married Lyman said it sure felt 61 sacred to him. She said he said he wouldn't take five hundred dollars for being married by a preacher."

"How much would he take?" the girl asked from the stove.   62

"He said he wouldn't take five hundred dollars," Mrs. Freeman repeated.   63

"Well we all have work to do," Mrs. Hopewell said.   64

"Lyman said it just felt more sacred to him," Mrs. Freeman said. "The doctor 65 wants Carramae to eat prunes. Says instead of medicine. Says them cramps is coming from pressure. You know where I think it is?"

"She'll be better in a few weeks," Mrs. Hopewell said.   66

"In the tube," Mrs. Freeman said. "Else she wouldn't be as sick as she is." 67

Hulga had cracked her two eggs into a saucer and was bringing them to the 68 table along with a cup of coffee that she had filled too full. She sat down carefully and began to eat, meaning to keep Mrs. Freeman there by questions if for any reason she showed an inclination to leave. She could perceive her mother's eye on her. The first roundabout question would be about the Bible salesman and she did not wish to bring it on. "How did he pop her neck?" she asked.

Mrs. Freeman went into a description of how he had popped her neck. She 69 said he owned a '55 Mercury but that Glynese said she would rather marry a man with only a '36 Plymouth who would be married by a preacher. The girl asked what if he had a '32 Plymouth and Mrs. Freeman said what Glynese had said was a '36 Plymouth.

Mrs. Hopewell said there were not many girls with Glynese's common 70 sense. She said what she admired in those girls was their common sense. She said that reminded her that they had had a nice visitor yesterday, a young man selling Bibles. "Lord," she said, "he bored me to death but he was so sincere and genuine I couldn't be rude to him. He was just good country people, you know," she said, "—just the salt of the earth."

"I seen him walk up," Mrs. Freeman said, "and then later—I seen him walk 71 off," and Hulga could feel the slight shift in her voice, the slight insinuation, that he had not walked off alone, had he? Her face remained expressionless but the color rose into her neck and she seemed to swallow it down with the next spoonful of egg. Mrs. Freeman was looking at her as if they had a secret together.

"Well it takes all kinds of people to make the world go 'round," Mrs. 72 Hopewell said. "It's very good we aren't all alike."

"Some people are more alike than others," Mrs. Freeman said.   73

Hulga got up and stumped, with about twice the noise that was necessary, 74 into her room and locked the door. She was to meet the Bible salesman at ten o'clock at the gate. She had thought about it half the night. She had started thinking of it as a great joke and then she had begun to see profound implications in it. She had lain in bed imagining dialogues for them that were insane on the surface but that reached below to depths that no Bible salesman would be aware of. Their conversation yesterday had been of this kind.

He had stopped in front of her and had simply stood there. His face was 75
bony and sweaty and bright, with a little pointed nose in the center of it, and his
look was different from what it had been at the dinner table. He was gazing at
her with open curiosity, with fascination, like a child watching a new fantastic
animal at the zoo, and he was breathing as if he had run a great distance to
reach her. His gaze seemed somehow familiar but she could not think where she
had been regarded with it before. For almost a minute he didn't say anything.
Then on what seemed an insuck of breath, he whispered, "You ever ate a
chicken that was two days old?"

The girl looked at him stonily. He might have just put this question up for 76
consideration at the meeting of a philosophical association. "Yes," she presently
replied as if she had considered it from all angles.

"It must have been mighty small!" he said triumphantly and shook all over 77
with little nervous giggles, getting very red in the face, and subsiding finally
into his gaze of complete admiration, while the girl's expression remained exactly the same.

"How old are you?" he asked softly. 78

She waited some time before she answered. Then in a flat voice she said, 79
"Seventeen."

His smiles came in succession like waves breaking on the surface of a little 80
lake. "I see you got a wooden leg," he said. "I think you're real brave. I think
you're real sweet."

The girl stood blank and solid and silent. 81

"Walk to the gate with me," he said. "You're a brave sweet little thing and I 82
liked you the minute I seen you walk in the door."

Hulga began to move forward. 83

"What's your name?" he asked, smiling down on the top of her head. 84

"Hulga," she said. 85

"Hulga," he murmured, "Hulga. Hulga. I never heard of anybody name 86
Hulga before. You're shy, aren't you, Hulga?" he asked.

She nodded, watching his large red hand on the handle of the giant valise. 87

"I like girls that wear glasses," he said. "I think a lot. I'm not like these people 88
that a serious thought don't ever enter their heads. It's because I may die."

"I may die too," she said suddenly and looked up at him. His eyes were very 89
small and brown, glittering feverishly.

"Listen," he said, "don't you think some people was meant to meet on ac- 90
count of what all they got in common and all? Like they both think serious
thoughts and all?" He shifted the valise to his other hand so that the hand nearest her was free. He caught hold of her elbow and shook it a little. "I don't work
on Saturday," he said. "I like to walk in the woods and see what Mother Nature
is wearing. O'er the hills and far away. Pic-nics and things. Couldn't we go on a
pic-nic tomorrow? Say yes, Hulga," he said and gave her a dying look as if he felt
his insides about to drop out of him. He had even seemed to sway slightly toward her.

During the night she had imagined that she seduced him. She imagined that 91
the two of them walked on the place until they came to the storage barn beyond

the two back fields and there, she imagined, that things came to such a pass that she very easily seduced him and that then, of course, she had to reckon with his remorse. True genius can get an idea across even to an inferior mind. She imag-ined that she took his remorse in hand and changed it into a deeper under-standing of life. She took all his shame away and turned it into something useful.

She set off for the gate at exactly ten o'clock, escaping without drawing Mrs. 92 Hopewell's attention. She didn't take anything to eat, forgetting that food is usually taken on a picnic. She wore a pair of slacks and a dirty white shirt, and as an afterthought, she had put some Vapex on the collar of it since she did not own any perfume. When she reached the gate no one was there.

She looked up and down the empty highway and had the furious feeling 93 that she had been tricked, that he had only meant to make her walk to the gate after the idea of him. Then suddenly he stood up, very tall, from behind a bush on the opposite embankment. Smiling, he lifted his hat which was new and wide-brimmed. He had not worn it yesterday and she wondered if he had bought it for the occasion. It was toast-colored with a red and white band around it and was slightly too large for him. He stepped from behind the bush still carrying the black valise. He had on the same suit and the same yellow socks sucked down in his shoes from walking. He crossed the highway and said, "I knew you'd come!"

The girl wondered acidly how he had known this. She pointed to the valise 94 and asked, "Why did you bring your Bibles?"

He took her elbow, smiling down on her as if he could not stop. "You can 95 never tell when you'll need the word of God, Hulga," he said. She had a moment in which she doubted that this was actually happening and then they began to climb the embankment. They went down into the pasture toward the woods. The boy walked lightly by her side, bouncing on his toes. The valise did not seem to be heavy today; he even swung it. They crossed half the pasture without saying anything and then, putting his hand easily on the small of her back, he asked softly, "Where does your wooden leg join on?"

She turned an ugly red and glared at him and for an instant the boy looked 96 abashed. "I didn't mean you no harm," he said. "I only meant you're so brave and all. I guess God takes care of you."

"No," she said, looking forward and walking fast, "I don't even believe in 97 God."

At this he stopped and whistled. "No!" he exclaimed as if he were too aston- 98 ished to say anything else.

She walked on and in a second he was bouncing at her side, fanning with his 99 hat. "That's very unusual for a girl," he remarked, watching her out of the cor-ner of his eye. When they reached the edge of the wood, he put his hand on her back again and drew her against him without a word and kissed her heavily.

The kiss, which had more pressure than feeling behind it, produced that ex- 100 tra surge of adrenalin in the girl that enables one to carry a packed trunk out of a burning house, but in her, the power went at once to the brain. Even before he released her, her mind, clear and detached and ironic anyway, was regarding him from a great distance, with amusement but with pity. She had never been kissed before and she was pleased to discover that it was an unexceptional experience and all a matter of the mind's control. Some people might enjoy drain water if they were told it was vodka. When the boy, looking expectant but uncertain, pushed her gently away, she turned and walked on, saying nothing as if such business, for her, were common enough.

He came along panting at her side, trying to help her when he saw a root 101 that she might trip over. He caught and held back the long swaying blades of thorn vine until she had passed beyond them. She led the way and he came breathing heavily behind her. Then they came out on a sunlit hillside, sloping softly into another one a little smaller. Beyond, they could see the rusted top of the old barn where the extra hay was stored.

The hill was sprinkled with small pink weeds. "Then you ain't saved?" he 102 asked suddenly, stopping.

The girl smiled. It was the first time she had smiled at him at all. "In my 103 economy," she said, "I'm saved and you are damned but I told you I didn't believe in God."

Nothing seemed to destroy the boy's look of admiration. He gazed at her 104 now as if the fantastic animal at the zoo had put its paw through the bars and given him a loving poke. She thought he looked as if he wanted to kiss her again and she walked on before he had the chance.

"Ain't there somewheres we can sit down sometime?" he murmured, his 105 voice softening toward the end of the sentence.

"In that barn," she said. 106

They made for it rapidly as if it might slide away like a train. It was a large 107 two-story barn, cool and dark inside. The boy pointed up the ladder that led into the loft and said, "It's too bad we can't go up there."

"Why can't we?" she asked. 108

"Yer leg," he said reverently. 109

The girl gave him a contemptuous look and putting both hands on the lad- 110 der, she climbed it while he stood below, apparently awestruck. She pulled herself expertly through the opening and then looked down at him and said, "Well come on if you're coming," and he began to climb the ladder, awkwardly bringing the suitcase with him.

"We won't need the Bible," she observed. 111

"You never can tell," he said, panting. After he had got into the loft, he was a 112 few seconds catching his breath. She had sat down in a pile of straw. A wide sheath of sunlight, filled with dust particles, slanted over her. She lay back against a bale, her face turned away, looking out the front opening of the barn where hay was thrown from a wagon into the loft. The two pink-speckled hillsides lay back against a dark ridge of woods. The sky was cloudless and cold blue. The boy dropped down by her side and put one arm under her and the other over her and began methodically kissing her face, making little noises like a fish. He did not remove his hat but it was pushed far enough back not to interfere. When her glasses got in his way, he took them off of her and slipped them into his pocket.

The girl at first did not return any of the kisses but presently she began to 113
and after she had put several on his cheek, she reached his lips and remained there, kissing him again and again as if she were trying to draw all the breath out of him. His breath was clear and sweet like a child's and the kisses were sticky like a child's. He mumbled about loving her and about knowing when he first seen her that he loved her, but the mumbling was like the sleepy fretting of a child being put to sleep by his mother. Her mind, throughout this, never stopped or lost itself for a second to her feelings. "You ain't said you loved me none," he whispered finally, pulling back from her. "You got to say that."

She looked away from him off into the hollow sky and then down at a black 114
ridge and then down farther into what appeared to be two green swelling lakes. She didn't realize he had taken her glasses but this landscape could not seem exceptional to her for she seldom paid any close attention to her surroundings.

"You got to say it," he repeated. "You got to say you love me."   115

She was always careful how she committed herself. "In a sense, " she began, 116
"if you use the word loosely, you might say that. But it's not a word I use. I don't have illusions. I'm one of those people who see *through* to nothing."

The boy was frowning. "You got to say it. I said it and you got to say it," he 117
said.

The girl looked at him almost tenderly. "You poor baby," she murmured. 118
"It's just as well you don't understand," and she pulled him by the neck, face-down, against her. "We are all damned," she said, "but some of us have taken off our blindfolds and see that there's nothing to see. It's a kind of salvation."

The boy's astonished eyes looked blankly through the ends of her hair. 119
"Okay," he almost whined, "but do you love me or don'tcher?"

"Yes," she said and added, "in a sense. But I must tell you something. There 120
mustn't be anything dishonest between us." She lifted his head and looked him in the eye. "I am thirty years old," she said. "I have a number of degrees."

The boy's look was irritated but dogged. "I don't care," he said. "I don't care 121
a thing about what all you done. I just want to know if you love me or don'tcher?" and he caught her to him and wildly planted her face with kisses until she said, "Yes, yes."

"Okay then," he said, letting her go. "Prove it."   122

She smiled, looking dreamily out on the shifty landscape. She had seduced 123
him without even making up her mind to try. "How?" she asked, feeling that he should be delayed a little.

He leaned over and put his lips to her ear. "Show me where your wooden leg 124
joins on," he whispered.

The girl uttered a sharp little cry and her face instantly drained of color. The 125
obscenity of the suggestion was not what shocked her. As a child she had sometimes been subject to feelings of shame but education had removed the last traces of that as a good surgeon scrapes for cancer; she would no more have felt it over what he was asking than she would have believed in his Bible. But she

was as sensitive about the artificial leg as a peacock about his tail. No one ever touched it but her. She took care of it as someone else would his soul, in private and almost with her own eyes turned away. "No," she said.

"I known it," he muttered, sitting up. "You're just playing me for a sucker." 126

"Oh no no!" she cried. "It joins on at the knee. Only at the knee. Why do you 127 want to see it?"

The boy gave her a long penetrating look. "Because," he said, "it's what 128 makes you different. You ain't like anybody else."

She sat staring at him. There was nothing about her face or her round freez- 129 ing-blue eyes to indicate that this had moved her; but she felt as if her heart had stopped and left her mind to pump her blood. She decided that for the first time in her life she was face to face with real innocence. This boy, with an instinct that came from beyond wisdom, had touched the truth about her. When after a minute, she said in a hoarse high voice, "All right," it was like surrendering to him completely. It was like losing her own life and finding it again, miraculously, in his.

Very gently he began to roll the slack leg up. The artificial limb, in a white 130 sock and brown flat shoe, was bound in a heavy material like canvas and ended in an ugly jointure where it was attached to the stump. The boy's face and his voice entirely reverent as he uncovered it and said, "Now show me how to take it off and on."

She took it off for him and put it back on again and then he took it off him- 131 self, handling it as tenderly as if it were a real one. "See!" he said with a delighted child's face. "Now I can do it myself!"

"Put it back on," she said. She was thinking that she would run away with 132 him and that every night he would take the leg off and every morning put it back on again. "Put it back on," she said.

"Not yet," he murmured, setting it on its foot out of her reach. "Leave it off 133 for a while. You got me instead."

She gave a little cry of alarm but he pushed her down and began to kiss her 134 again. Without the leg she felt entirely dependent on him. Her brain seemed to have stopped thinking altogether and to be about some other function that it was not very good at. Different expressions raced back and forth over her face. Every now and then the boy, his eyes like two steel spikes, would glance behind him where the leg stood. Finally she pushed him off and said, "Put it back on me now."

"Wait," he said. He leaned the other way and pulled the valise toward him 135 and opened it. It had a pale blue spotted lining and there were only two Bibles in it. He took one of these out and opened the cover of it. It was hollow and contained a pocket flask of whiskey, a pack of cards, and a small blue box with printing on it. He laid these out in front of her one at a time in an evenly-spaced row, like one presenting offerings at the shrine of a goddess. He put the blue box in her hand. THIS PRODUCT TO BE USED ONLY FOR THE PREVENTION OF DISEASE, she read, and dropped it. The boy was unscrewing the top of the flask. He stopped and pointed, with a smile, to the deck of cards. It was not an ordinary deck but one with an obscene picture on the back of each card. "Take a swig," he said, offering her the bottle first. He held it in front of her, but like one mesmerized, she did not move.

Her voice when she spoke had an almost pleading sound. "Aren't you," she   136
murmured, "aren't you just good country people?"

The boy cocked his head. He looked as if he were just beginning to under-   137
stand that she might be trying to insult him. "Yeah," he said, curling his lip slightly, "but it ain't held me back none. I'm as good as you any day in the week."

"Give me my leg," she said.   138

He pushed it farther away with his foot. "Come on now, let's begin to have   139
us a good time," he said coaxingly. "We ain't got to know one another good yet."

"Give me my leg!" she screamed and tried to lunge for it but he pushed her   140
down easily.

"What's the matter with you all of a sudden?" he asked, frowning as he   141
screwed the top on the flask and put it quickly back inside the Bible. "You just a while ago said you didn't believe in nothing. I thought you was some girl!"

Her face was almost purple. "You're a Christian!" she hissed. "You're a fine   142
Christian! You're just like them all—say one thing and do another. You're a perfect Christian, you're . . ."

The boy's mouth was set angrily. "I hope you don't think," he said in a lofty   143
indignant tone, "that I believe in that crap! I may sell Bibles but I know which end is up and I wasn't born yesterday and I know where I'm going!"

"Give me my leg!" she screeched. He jumped up so quickly that she barely   144
saw him sweep the cards and the blue box back into the Bible and throw the Bible into the valise. She saw him grab the leg and then she saw it for an instant slanted forlornly across the inside of the suitcase with a Bible at either side of its opposite ends. He slammed the lid shut and snatched up the valise and swung it down the hole and then stepped through himself.

When all of him had passed but his head, he turned and regarded her with a   145
look that no longer had any admiration in it. "I've gotten a lot of interesting things," he said. "One time I got a woman's glass eye this way. And you needn't to think you'll catch me because Pointer ain't really my name. I use a different name at every house I call at and don't stay nowhere long. And I'll tell you another thing, Hulga," he said, using the name as if he didn't think much of it, "you ain't so smart. I been believing in nothing ever since I was born!" and then the toast-colored hat disappeared down the hole and the girl was left, sitting on the straw in the dusty sunlight. When she turned her churning face toward the opening, she saw his blue figure struggling successfully over the green speckled lake.

Mrs. Hopewell and Mrs. Freeman, who were in the back pasture, digging up   146
onions, saw him emerge a little later from the woods and head across the meadow toward the highway. "Why, that looks like that nice dull young man that tried to sell me a Bible yesterday," Mrs. Hopewell said, squinting. "He must

have been selling them to the Negroes back in there. He was so simple," she said, "but I guess the world would be better off if we were all that simple."

Mrs. Freeman's gaze drove forward and just touched him before he disap- 147 peared under the hill. Then she returned her attention to the evil-smelling onion shoot she was lifting from the ground. "Some can't be that simple," she said. "I know I never could."

ACTIVITIES FOR WRITING AND DISCUSSION

1. The title may lead us to expect a story in which all the **characters** are "good country people." Are they? Identify any contrasts you see between how characters *seem* in this story and who they actually are. Illustrate those contrasts by pointing to particular passages in the text. Then explain why you think O'Connor uses "Good Country People" as a title.

2. The story refers to various favorite sayings of the characters, e.g., Mrs. Hopewell's "Nothing is perfect," "That is life," and "Well, other people have their opinions too" and Mrs. Freeman's "I always said so myself." Explain what you think the sayings show about the characters who habitually use them. Additional activity: If you wish, invent and portray a character of your own who has certain "pet" sayings.

3. It is said that everyone is guided, consciously or subconsciously, by a ruling passion or desire. If this is so, what passion or desire drives Joy/Hulga? Reread any passages that discuss the choices she has made in life, e.g., to change her name, to remain living with her mother, to rendezvous with the Bible salesman. What patterns of motivation, if any, do you detect behind these choices?

4. Writer Joyce Carol Oates says that O'Connor celebrates "the necessity of succumbing to the divine through violence that is immediate and irreparable. There is no mysticism in her work that is only spiritual; it is physical as well." What do you make of the theme of religion in the story? Mrs. Hopewell professes to being Christian but keeps her Bible in the attic; Hulga despises religion and rejects the existence of God; the Bible salesman mocks his own trade and anyone "foolish" enough to believe in it. O'Connor herself was a devout Catholic. In your opinion, does the story seem to make any point—positive, negative, or mixed—about religion or the presence of the divine in human life?

5. O'Connor once described her stories as "parables." Consult a dictionary definition of "parable" and discuss the applicability of the term to "Good Country People."

ALICE WALKER (b. 1944)

Nineteen Fifty-five

1955

The car is a brandnew red Thunderbird convertible, and it's passed the house 1
more than once. It slows down real slow now, and stops at the curb. An older
gentleman dressed like a Baptist deacon gets out on the side near the house, and
a young fellow who looks about sixteen gets out on the driver's side. They are
white, and I wonder what in the world they doing in this neighborhood.

Well, I say to J. T., put your shirt on, anyway, and let me clean these glasses 2
offa the table.

We had been watching the ballgame on TV. I wasn't actually watching, I was 3
sort of daydreaming, with my foots up in J.T.'s lap.

I seen 'em coming on up the walk, brisk, like they coming to sell something, 4
and then they rung the bell, and J. T. declined to put on a shirt but instead disappeared into the bedroom where the other television is. I turned down the one
in the living room; I figured I'd be rid of these two double quick and J. T. could
come back out again.

Are you Gracie Mae Still? asked the old guy, when I opened the door and 5
put my hand on the lock inside the screen

And I don't need to buy a thing, said I.   6

What makes you think we're sellin'? he asks, in that hearty Southern way 7
that makes my eyeballs ache.

Well, one way or another and they're inside the house and the first thing the 8
young fellow does is raise the TV a couple of decibels. He's about five feet nine,
sort of womanish looking, with real dark white skin and a red pouting mouth.
His hair is black and curly and he looks like a Loosianna creole.

––––––––––

About one of your songs, says the deacon. He is maybe sixty, with white hair 9
and beard, white silk shirt, black linen suit, black tie and black shoes. His cold
grey eyes look like they're sweating.

One of my songs?   10

Traynor here just *loves* your songs. Don't you, Traynor? He nudges Traynor 11
with his elbow. Traynor blinks, says something I can't catch in a pitch I don't
register.

The boy learned to sing and dance livin' round you people out in the coun- 12
try. Practically cut his teeth on you.

Traynor looks up at me and bites his thumbnail.   13

I laugh.   14

Well, one way or another they leave with my agreement that they can record 15
one of my songs. The deacon writes me a check for five hundred dollars, the
boy grunts his awareness of the transaction, and I am laughing all over myself
by the time I rejoin J. T.

Just as I am snuggling down beside him though I hear the front door bell 16
going off again.

Forgit his hat? asks J. T. 17

I hope not, I say. 18

The deacon stands there leaning on the door frame and once again I'm 19
thinking of those sweaty-looking eyeballs of his. I wonder if sweat makes your
eyeballs pink because his are sure pink. Pink and gray and it strikes me that nobody I'd care to know is behind them.

I forgot one little thing, he says pleasantly. I forgot to tell you Traynor and I 20
would like to buy up all of those records you made of the song. I tell you we
sure do love it.

Well, love it or not, I'm not so stupid as to let them do that without making 21
'em pay. So I says, Well, that's gonna cost you. Because, really, that song never
did sell all that good, so I was glad they was going to buy it up. But on the other
hand, them two listening to my song by themselves, and nobody else getting to
hear me sing it, give me a pause.

Well, one way or another the deacon showed me where I would come out 22
ahead on any deal he had proposed so far. Didn't I give you five hundred dollars? he asked. What white man—and don't even need to mention colored—
would give you more? We buy up all your records of that particular song: first,
you git royalties. Let me ask you, how much you sell that song for in the first
place? Fifty dollars? A hundred, I say. And no royalties from it yet, right? Right.
Well, when we buy up all of them records you gonna git royalties. And that's
gonna make all them race record shops sit up and take notice of Gracie Mae
Still. And they gonna push all them other records of yourn they got. And you
no doubt will become one of the big name colored recording artists. And then
we can offer you another five hundred dollars for letting us do all this for you.
And by God you'll be sittin' pretty! You can go out and buy you the kind of outfit a star should have. Plenty sequins and yards of red satin.

I had done unlocked the screen when I saw I could get some more money 23
out of him. Now I held it wide open while he squeezed through the opening
between me and the door. He whipped out another piece of paper and I
signed it.

He sort of trotted out to the car and slid in beside Traynor, whose head was 24
back against the seat. They swung around in a u-turn in front of the house and
then they was gone.

J. T. was putting his shirt on when I got back to the bedroom. Yankees beat 25
the Orioles 10–6, he said. I believe I'll drive out to Paschal's pond and go fishing. Wanta go?

While I was putting on my pants J. T. was holding the two checks. 26

I'm real proud of a woman that can make cash money without leavin' home, 27
he said. And I said *Umph.* Because we met on the road with me singing in first
one little low-life jook after another, making ten dollars a night for myself if I
was lucky, and sometimes bringin' home nothing but my life. And J. T. just
loved them times. The way I was fast and flashy and always on the go from one
town to another. He loved the way my singin' made the dirt farmers cry like babies and the womens shout Honey, hush! But that's mens. They loves any style
to which you can get 'em accustomed.

1956

My little grandbaby called me one night on the phone: Little Mama, Little 28
Mama, there's a white man on the television singing one of your songs! Turn on
channel 5.

   Lord, if it wasn't Traynor. Still looking half asleep from the neck up, but 29
kind of awake in a nasty way from the waist down. He wasn't doing too bad
with my song either, but it wasn't just the song the people in the audience was
screeching and screaming over, it was that nasty little jerk he was doing from
the waist down.

   Well, Lord have mercy, I said, listening to him. If I'da closed my eyes, it 30
could have been me. He had followed every turning of my voice, side streets, avenues, red lights, train crossings and all. It give me a chill.

   Everywhere I went I heard Traynor singing my song, and all the little white 31
girls just eating it up. I never had so many ponytails switched across my line of
vision in my life. They was so *proud.* He was a *genius.*

   Well, all that year I was trying to lose weight anyway and that and high 32
blood pressure and sugar kept me pretty well occupied. Traynor had made a
smash from a song of mine, I still had seven hundred dollars of the original one
thousand dollars in the bank, and I felt if I could just bring my weight down,
life would be sweet.

1957

I lost ten pounds in 1956. That's what I give myself for Christmas. And J. T. and 33
me and the children and their friends and grandkids of all description had just
finished dinner—over which I had put on nine and a half of my lost ten—when
who should appear at the front door but Traynor. Little Mama, Little Mama! It's
that white man who sings —— —— ——. The children didn't call it my song
anymore. Nobody did. It was funny how that happened. Traynor and the deacon had bought up all my records, true, but on his record he had put "written
by Gracie Mae Still." But that was just another name on the label, like "produced by Apex Records."

On the TV he was inclined to dress like the deacon told him. But now he 34
looked presentable.

Merry Christmas, said he. 35

And same to you, Son. 36

I don't know why I called him Son. Well, one way or another they're all our 37
sons. The only requirement is that they be younger than us. But then again,
Traynor seemed to be aging by the minute.

You looks tired, I said. Come on in and have a glass of Christmas cheer. 38

J. T. ain't never in his life been able to act decent to a white man he wasn't 39
working for, but he poured Traynor a glass of bourbon and water, then he took
all the children and grandkids and friends and whatnot out to the den. After
while I heard Traynor's voice singing the song, coming from the stereo console.
It was just the kind of Christmas present my kids would consider cute.

I looked at Traynor, complicit. But he looked like it was the last thing in the 40
world he wanted to hear. His head was pitched forward over his lap, his hands
holding his glass and his elbows on his knees.

I done sung that song seem like a million times this year, he said. I sung it on 41
the Grand Ole Opry, I sung it on the Ed Sullivan show. I sung it on Mike Douglas, I sung it at the Cotton Bowl, the Orange Bowl. I sung it at Festivals. I sung
it at Fairs. I sung it overseas in Rome, Italy, and once in a submarine *underseas.*
I've sung it and sung it, and I'm making forty thousand dollars a day offa it, and
you know what, I don't have the faintest notion what that song means.

Whatchumean, what do it mean? It mean what it says. All I could think was: 42
These suckers is making forty thousand a *day* offa my song and now they gonna
come back and try to swindle me out of the original thousand.

It's just a song, I said. Cagey. When you fool around with a lot of no count 43
mens you sing a bunch of 'em. I shrugged.

Oh, he said. Well. He started brightening up. I just come by to tell you I 44
think you are a great singer.

He didn't blush, saying that. Just said it straight out. 45

And I brought you a little Christmas present too. Now you take this little 46
box and you hold it until I drive off. Then you take it outside under that first
streetlight back up the street aways in front of that green house. Then you open
the box and see . . . Well, just *see.*

What had come over this boy, I wondered, holding the box. I looked out the 47
window in time to see another white man come up and get in the car with him
and then two more cars full of white mens start out behind him. They was all in
long black cars that looked like a funeral procession.

Little Mama, Little Mama, what is it? One of my grandkids come running 48
up and started pulling at the box. It was wrapped in gay Christmas paper—the
thick, rich kind that it's hard to picture folks making just to throw away.

J. T. and the rest of the crowd followed me out the house, up the street to the 49
streetlight and in front of the green house. Nothing was there but somebody's
gold-grilled white Cadillac. Brandnew and most distracting. We got to looking

at it so till I almost forgot the little box in my hand. While the others were busy making 'miration I carefully took off the paper and ribbon and folded them up and put them in my pants pocket. What should I see but a pair of genuine solid gold caddy keys.

Dangling the keys in front of everybody's nose, I unlocked the caddy, mo- 50 tioned for J. T. to git in on the other side, and us didn't come back home for two days.

1960

Well, the boy was sure nuff famous by now. He was still a mite shy of twenty but 51 already they was calling him the Emperor of Rock and Roll.

Then what should happen but the draft.   52

Well, says J. T. There goes all this Emperor of Rock and Roll business.   53

But even in the army the womens was on him like white on rice. We watched 54 it on the News.

Dear Gracie Mae [he wrote from Germany],   55

How you? Fine I hope as this leaves me doing real well. Before I come in the 56 *army I was gaining a lot of weight and gitting jittery from making all them dumb movies. But now I exercise and eat right and get plenty of rest. I'm more awake than I been in ten years.*

I wonder if you are writing any more songs?   57

Sincerely,
Traynor

I wrote him back:

Dear Son,   58

We is all fine in the Lord's good grace and hope this finds you the same. J. T. 59 *and me be out all times of the day and night in that car you give me—which you know you didn't have to do. Oh, and I do appreciate the mink and the new self-cleaning oven. But if you send anymore stuff to eat from Germany I'm going to have to open up a store in the neighborhood just to get rid of it. Really, we have more than enough of everything. The Lord is good to us and we don't know Want.*

Glad to hear you is well and gitting your right rest. There ain't nothing like ex- 60 *ercising to help that along. J. T. and me work some part of every day that we don't go fishing in the garden.*

Well, so long Soldier.   61

Sincerely,   62
Gracie Mae

He wrote: 63

Dear Gracie Mae,   64

I hope you and J. T. like that automatic power tiller I had one of the stores back 65
home send you. I went through a mountain of catalogs looking for it—I wanted
something that even a woman could use.

I've been thinking about writing some songs of my own but every time I finish 66
one it don't seem to be about nothing I've actually lived myself. My agent keeps
sending me other people's songs but they just sound mooney. I can hardly git
through 'em without gagging.

Everybody still loves that song of yours. They ask me all the time what do I 67
think it means, really. I mean, they want to know just what I want to know. Where
out of your life did it come from?

Sincerely,
Traynor

1968

I didn't see the boy for seven years. No. Eight. Because just about everybody was 68
dead when I saw him again. Malcolm X, King, the president and his brother,
and even J. T. J. T. died of a head cold. It just settled in his head like a block of
ice, he said, and nothing we did moved it until one day he just leaned out the
bed and died.

His good friend Horace helped me put him away, and then about a year 69
later Horace and me started going together. We was sitting out on the front
porch swing one summer night, dusk-dark, and I saw this great procession of
lights winding to a stop.

Holy Toledo! said Horace. (He's got a real sexy voice like Ray Charles.) Look 70
at it. He meant the long line of flashy cars and the white men in white summer
suits jumping out on the drivers' sides and standing at attention. With wings
they could pass for angels, with hoods they could be the Klan.

Traynor comes waddling up the walk.   71

And suddenly I know what it is he could pass for. An Arab like the ones you 72
see in storybooks. Plump and soft and with never a care about weight. Because
with so much money, who cares? Traynor is almost dressed like someone from
a storybook too. He has on, I swear, about ten necklaces. Two sets of bracelets
on his arms, at least one ring on every finger, and some kind of shining buckles
on his shoes, so that when he walks you get quite a few twinkling lights.

Gracie Mae, he says, coming up to give me a hug. J. T.   73

I explain that J. T. passed. That this is Horace.   74

Horace, he says, puzzled but polite, sort of rocking back on his heels, Horace. 75

That's it for Horace. He goes in the house and don't come back.   76

Looks like you and me is gained a few, I say.   77

He laughs. The first time I ever heard him laugh. It don't sound much like a   78
laugh and I can't swear that it's better than no laugh a'tall.

He's gitting fat for sure, but he's still slim compared to me. I'll never see   79
three hundred pounds again and I've just about said (excuse me) fuck it. I got
to thinking about it one day an' I thought: aside from the fact that they say it's
unhealthy, my fat ain't never been no trouble. Mens always have loved me. My
kids ain't never complained. Plus they's fat. And fat like I is I looks distinguished. You see me coming and know somebody's *there.*

Gracie Mae, he says, I've come with a personal invitation to you to my house   80
tomorrow for dinner. He laughed. What did it sound like? I couldn't place it.
See them men out there? he asked me. I'm sick and tired of eating with them.
They don't never have nothing to talk about. That's why I eat so much. But if
you come to dinner tomorrow we can talk about the old days. You can tell me
about that farm I bought you.

I sold it, I said.   81

You did?   82

Yeah, I said, I did. Just cause I said I liked to exercise by working in a garden   83
didn't mean I wanted five hundred acres! Anyhow, I'm a city girl now. Raised in
the country it's true. Dirt poor—the whole bit—but that's all behind me now.

Oh well, he said, I didn't mean to offend you.   84

We sat a few minutes listening to the crickets.   85

Then he said: You wrote that song while you was still on the farm, didn't   86
you, or was it right after you left?

You had somebody spying on me? I asked.   87

You and Bessie Smith got into a fight over it once, he said.   88

You *is* been spying on me!   89

But I don't know what the fight was about, he said. Just like I don't know   90
what happened to your second husband. Your first one died in the Texas electric chair. Did you know that? Your third one beat you up, stole your touring
costumes and your car and retired with a chorine to Tuskegee. He laughed. He's
still there.

I had been mad, but suddenly I calmed down. Traynor was talking very   91
dreamily. It was dark but seems like I could tell his eyes weren't right. It was like
some*thing* was sitting there talking to me but not necessarily with a person behind it.

You gave up on marrying and seem happier for it. He laughed again. I married   92
but it never went like it was supposed to. I never could squeeze any of my own life
either into it or out of it. It was like singing somebody else's record. I copied the
way it was sposed to be *exactly* but I never had a clue what marriage meant.

I bought her a diamond ring big as your fist. I bought her clothes. I built her   93
a mansion. But right away she didn't want the boys to stay there. Said they
smoked up the bottom floor. Hell, there were *five* floors.

No need to grieve, I said. No need to. Plenty more where she come from.   94

He perked up. That's part of what that song means, ain't it? No need to   95
grieve. Whatever it is, there's plenty more down the line.

I never really believed that way back when I wrote that song, I said. It was all 96
bluffing then. The trick is to live long enough to put your young bluffs to use.
Now if I was to sing that song today I'd tear it up. 'Cause I done lived long
enough to know it's *true*. Them words could hold me up.

I ain't lived that long, he said. 97

Look like you on your way, I said. I don't know why, but the boy seemed to 98
need some encouraging. And I don't know, seem like one way or another you
talk to rich white folks and you end up reassuring *them*. But what the hell, by
now I feel something for the boy. I wouldn't be in his bed all alone in the middle
of the night for nothing. Couldn't be nothing worse than being famous the
world over for something you don't even understand. That's what I tried to tell
Bessie. She wanted that same song. Overheard me practicing it one day,
said, with her hands on her hips: Gracie Mae, I'ma sing your song tonight.
I *likes* it.

Your lips be too swole to sing, I said. She was mean and she was strong, but I 99
trounced her.

Ain't you famous enough with your own stuff? I said. Leave mine alone. 100
Later on, she thanked me. By then she was Miss Bessie Smith to the World, and
I was still Miss Gracie Mae Nobody from Notasulga.

The next day all these limousines arrived to pick me up. Five cars and twelve 101
bodyguards. Horace picked that morning to start painting the kitchen.

Don't paint the kitchen, fool, I said. The only reason that dumb boy of ours 102
is going to show me his mansion is because he intends to present us with a new
house.

What you gonna do with it? he asked me, standing there in his shirtsleeves 103
stirring the paint.

Sell it. Give it to the children. Live in it on weekends. It don't matter what I 104
do. He sure don't care.

Horace just stood there shaking his head. Mama you sure looks *good*, he 105
says. Wake me up when you git back.

Fool, I say, and pat my wig in front of the mirror. 106

The boy's house is something else. First you come to this mountain, and then 107
you commence to drive and drive up this road that's lined with magnolias. Do
magnolias grow on mountains? I was wondering. And you come to lakes and
you come to ponds and you come to deer and you come up on some sheep. And
I figure these two is sposed to represent England and Wales. Or something out
of Europe. And you just keep on coming to stuff. And it's all pretty. Only the
man driving my car don't look at nothing but the road. Fool. And then *finally*,
after all this time, you begin to go up the driveway. And there's more magnolias—only they're not in such good shape. It's sort of cool up this high and I

don't think they're gonna make it. And then I see this building that looks like if it had a name it would be The Tara Hotel. Columns and steps and outdoor chandeliers and rocking chairs. Rocking chairs? Well, and there's the boy on the steps dressed in a dark green satin jacket like you see folks wearing on TV late at night, and he looks sort of like a fat dracula with all that house rising behind him, and standing beside him there's this little white vision of loveliness that he introduces as his wife.

He's nervous when he introduces us and he says to her: This is Gracie Mae Still,   108
I want you to know me. I mean . . . and she gives him a look that would fry meat.

Won't you come in, Gracie Mae, she says, and that's the last I see of her.   109

He fishes around for something to say or do and decides to escort me to the   110
kitchen. We go through the entry and the parlor and the breakfast room and the dining room and the servants' passage and finally get there. The first thing I notice is that, altogether, there are five stoves. He looks about to introduce me to one.

Wait a minute, I say. Kitchens don't do nothing for me. Let's go sit on the   111
front porch.

Well, we hike back and we sit in the rocking chairs rocking until dinner.   112

Gracie Mae, he says down the table, taking a piece of fried chicken from the   113
woman standing over him, I got a little surprise for you.

It's a house, ain't it? I ask, spearing a chitlin.   114

You're getting *spoiled*, he says. And the way he says *spoiled* sounds funny. He   115
slurs it. It sounds like his tongue is too thick for his mouth. Just that quick he's finished the chicken and is now eating chitlins *and* a pork chop. *Me* spoiled, I'm thinking.

I already got a house. Horace is right this minute painting the kitchen. I   116
bought that house. My kids feel comfortable in that house.

But this one I bought you is just like mine. Only a little smaller.   117

I still don't need no house. And anyway who would clean it?   118

He looks surprised.   119

Really, I think, some peoples advance *so* slowly.   120

I hadn't thought of that. But what the hell, I'll get you somebody to live in.   121

I don't want other folks living 'round me. Makes me nervous.   122

You *don't*? It *do*?   123

What I want to wake up and see folks I don't even know for?   124

He just sits there downtable staring at me. Some of that feeling is in the   125
song, ain't it? Not the words, the *feeling*. What I want to wake up and see folks I don't even know for? But I see twenty folks a day I don't even know, including my wife.

This food wouldn't be bad to wake up to though, I said. The boy had found   126
the genius of corn bread.

He looked at me real hard. He laughed. Short. They want what you got but   127
they don't want you. They want what I got only it ain't mine. That's what makes

'em so hungry for me when I sing. They getting the flavor of something but they ain't getting the thing itself. They like a pack of hound dogs trying to gobble up a scent.

Your talking 'bout your fans? 128

Right. Right. He says. 129

Don't worry 'bout your fans, I say. They don't know their asses from a hole 130
in the ground. I doubt there's a honest one in the bunch.

That's the point. Dammit, that's the point! He hits the table with his fist. It's 131
so solid it don't even quiver. You need a honest audience! You can't have folks
that's just gonna lie right back to you.

Yeah, I say, it was small compared to yours, but I had one. It would have 132
been worth my life to try to sing 'em somebody else's stuff that I didn't know
nothing about.

He must have pressed a buzzer under the table. One of his flunkies zombies up. 133

Git Johnny Carson, he says. 134

On the phone? asks the zombie. 135

On the phone, says Traynor, what you think I mean, git him offa the front 136
porch? Move your ass.

So two weeks later we's on the Johnny Carson show. 137

Traynor is all corseted down nice and looks a little bit fat but mostly good. And 138
all the women that grew up on him and my song squeal and squeal. Traynor
says: The lady who wrote my first hit record is here with us tonight, and she's
agreed to sing it for all of us, just like she sung it forty-five years ago. Ladies and
Gentlemen, the great Gracie Mae Still!

Well, I had tried to lose a couple of pounds my own self, but failing that I 139
had me a very big dress made. So I sort of rolls over next to Traynor, who is
dwarfted by me, so that when he puts his arm around back of me to try to hug
me it looks funny to the audience and they laugh.

I can see this pisses him off. But I smile out there at 'em. Imagine squealing 140
for twenty years and not knowing why you're squealing? No more sense of endings and beginnings than hogs.

It don't matter, Son, I say. Don't fret none over me. 141

I commence to sing. And I sound——wonderful. Being able to sing good 142
ain't all about having a good singing voice a'tall. A good singing voice helps. But
when you come up in the Hard Shell Baptist church like I did you understand
early that the fellow that sings is the singer. Them that waits for programs and
arrangements and letters from home is just good voices occupying body space.

So there I am singing my own song, my own way. And I give it all I got and 143
enjoy every minute of it. When I finish Traynor is standing up clapping and
clapping and beaming at first me and then the audience like I'm his mama for
true. The audience claps politely for about two seconds.

Traynor looks disgusted.   144

He comes over and tries to hug me again. The audience laughs.   145

Johnny Carson looks at us like we both weird.   146

Traynor is mad as hell. He's supposed to sing something called a love ballad.   147
But instead he takes the mike, turns to me and says: Now see if my imitation
still holds up. He goes into the same song, *our* song, I think, looking out at his
flaky audience. And he sings it just the way he always did. My voice, my tone,
my inflection, everything. But he forgets a couple of lines. Even before he's finished the matronly squeals begin.

He sits down next to me looking whipped.   148

It don't matter, Son, I say, patting his hand. You don't even know those peo-   149
ple. Try to make the people you know happy.

Is that in the song? he asks.   150

Maybe, I say.   151

1977

For a few years I hear from him, then nothing. But trying to lose weight takes all   152
the attention I got to spare. I finally faced up to the fact that my fat is the hurt I
don't admit, not even to myself, and that I been trying to bury it from the day I
was born. But also when you git real old, to tell the truth, it ain't as pleasant.
It gits lumpy and slack. Yuck. So one day I said to Horace, I'ma git this shit
offa me.

And he fell in with the program like he always try to do and Lord such a   153
procession of salads and cottage cheese and fruit juice!

One night I dreamed Traynor had split up with his fifteenth wife. He said: 154
*You meet 'em for no reason. You date 'em for no reason. You marry 'em for no rea-
son. I do it all but I swear it's just like somebody else doing it. I feel like I can't remember Life.*

The boy's in trouble, I said to Horace.   155

You've always said that, he said.   156

I have?   157

Yeah. You always said he looked asleep. You can't sleep through life if you   158
wants to live it.

You not such a fool after all, I said, pushing myself up with my cane and   159
hobbling over to where he was. Let me sit down on your lap, I said, while this
salad I ate takes effect.

In the morning we heard Traynor was dead. Some said fat, some said heart,   160
some said alcohol, some said drugs. One of the children called from Detroit.
Them dumb fans of his is on a crying rampage, she said. You just ought to turn
on the t.v.

But I didn't want to see 'em. They was crying and crying and didn't even   161
know what they was crying for. One day this is going to be a pitiful country, I
thought.

ACTIVITIES FOR WRITING AND DISCUSSION

1. Respond to the story using the Four-Step Process for Writing from Reading described in Chapter 2.

2. What effects does Walker achieve by narrating the story from the **first-person point of view** of Gracie Mae? What advantages, if any, does her choice of first-person have over a **third-person** narration?

3. The story's events take place over a span of twenty-two years. What purposes are served by dividing the story up according to years? If you wish, compose a first-person narrative of your own that is similarly structured, i.e., by years.

4. Events in the story are a weave of the personal and the cultural. For instance, in 1956 Gracie Mae is trying to lose weight (personal) and Traynor makes a smash hit out of her song (cultural). Write a story of your own that portrays a person embedded in some culture, time, or movement of your own choosing.

Poems

WILLIAM BLAKE (1757–1827)

The Garden of Love

I went to the Garden of Love,
And saw what I never had seen:
A Chapel was built in the midst,
Where I used to play on the green.

And the gates of this Chapel were shut,   5
And "Thou shalt not" writ over the door;
So I turn'd to the Garden of Love
That so many sweet flowers bore;

And I saw it was filled with graves,
And tomb-stones where flowers should be;   10
And Priests in black gowns were walking their rounds,
And binding with briars my joys & desires.

Walt Whitman (1819–1892)

Song of the Open Road

1

Afoot and light-hearted I take to the open road,
Healthy, free, the world before me,
The long brown path before me leading wherever I choose.

Henceforth I ask not good-fortune, I myself am good-fortune,
Henceforth I whimper no more, postpone no more, need nothing,   5
Done with indoor complaints, libraries, querulous criticisms,
Strong and content I travel the open road.

The earth, that is sufficient,
I do not want the constellations any nearer,
I know they are very well where they are,   10
I know they suffice for those who belong to them.

(Still here I carry my old delicious burdens,
I carry them, men and women, I carry them with me wherever I go,
I swear it is impossible for me to get rid of them,
I am fill'd with them, and I will fill them in return.)   15

2

You road I enter upon and look around, I believe you are not all
      that is here,
I believe that much unseen is also here.

Here the profound lesson of reception, nor preference nor denial,
The black with his woolly head, the felon, the diseas'd, the illiterate
      person, are not denied;
The birth, the hasting after the physician, the beggar's tramp, the
      drunkard's stagger, the laughing party of mechanics,   20
The escaped youth, the rich person's carriage, the fop, the eloping
      couple,
The early market-man, the hearse, the moving of furniture into the
      town, the return back from the town,
They pass, I also pass, any thing passes, none can be interdicted,
None but are accepted, none but shall be dear to me.

3

You air that serves me with breath to speak!   25
You objects that call from diffusion my meanings and give them
    shape!
You light that wraps me and all things in delicate equable showers!
You paths worn in the irregular hollows by the roadsides!
I believe you are latent with unseen existences, you are so dear
    to me.

You flagg'd walks of the cities! you strong curbs at the edges!   30
You ferries! you planks and posts of wharves! you timber-lined
    sides! you distant ships!
You rows of houses! you window-pierc'd façades! you roofs!
You porches and entrances! you copings and iron guards!
You windows whose transparent shells might expose so much!
You doors and ascending steps! you arches!   35
You gray stones of interminable pavements! you trodden crossings!
From all that has touch'd you I believe you have imparted to
    yourselves, and now would impart the same secretly to me,
From the living and the dead you have peopled your impassive
    surfaces, and the spirits thereof would be evident and
    amicable with me.

4

The earth expanding right hand and left hand,
The picture alive, every part in its best light,   40
The music falling in where it is wanted, and stopping where it is
    not wanted,
The cheerful voice of the public road, the gay fresh sentiment of
    the road.

O highway I travel, do you say to me *Do not leave me?*
Do you say *Venture not—if you leave me you are lost?*
Do you say *I am already prepared, I am well-beaten and un-*
    denied, adhere to me?   45

O public road, I say back I am not afraid to leave you, yet I love
    you,
You express me better than I can express myself,
You shall be more to me than my poem.

I think heroic deeds were all conceiv'd in the open air, and all
    free poems also,

I think I could stop here myself and do miracles,   50
I think whatever I shall meet on the road I shall like, and who-
    ever beholds me shall like me,
I think whoever I see must be happy.

5

From this hour I ordain myself loos'd of limits and imaginary
    lines,
Going where I list, my own master total and absolute,
Listening to others, considering well what they say,   55
Pausing, searching, receiving, contemplating,
Gently, but with undeniable will, divesting myself of the holds
    that would hold me.

I inhale great draughts of space,
The east and the west are mine, and the north and the south are
    mine.

I am larger, better than I thought,   60
I did not know I held so much goodness.

All seems beautiful to me,
I can repeat over to men and women You have done such good
    to me I would do the same to you,
I will recruit for myself and you as I go,
I will scatter myself among men and women as I go,   65
I will toss a new gladness and roughness among them,
Whoever denies me it shall not trouble me,
Whoever accepts me he or she shall be blessed and shall bless me.

6

Now if a thousand perfect men were to appear it would not amaze
    me,
Now if a thousand beautiful forms of women appear'd it would
    not astonish me.   70

Now I see the secret of the making of the best persons,
It is to grow in the open air and to eat and sleep with the earth.

Here a great personal deed has room,
(Such a deed seizes upon the hearts of the whole race of men,
Its effusion of strength and will overwhelms law and mocks all
    authority and all argument against it.)   75

Here is the test of wisdom,
Wisdom is not finally tested in schools,
Wisdom cannot be pass'd from one having it to another not
 having it,
Wisdom is of the soul, is not susceptible of proof, is its own proof,
Applies to all stages and objects and qualities and is content, 80
Is the certainty of the reality and immortality of things, and the
 excellence of things;
Something there is in the float of the sight of things that provokes
 it out of the soul.

Now I re-examine philosophies and religions,
They may prove well in lecture-rooms, yet not prove at all under
 the spacious clouds and along the landscape and flowing
 currents.

Here is realization, 85
Here is a man tallied—he realizes here what he has in him,
The past, the future, majesty, love—if they are vacant of you,
 you are vacant of them.

Only the kernel of every object nourishes;
Where is he who tears off the husks for you and me?
Where is he that undoes stratagems and envelopes for you and me? 90

Here is adhesiveness, it is not previously fashion'd, it is apropos;
Do you know what it is as you pass to be loved by strangers?
Do you know the talk of those turning eye-balls?

7

Here is the efflux of the soul,
The efflux of the soul comes from within through embower'd
 gates, ever provoking questions, 95
These yearnings why are they? these thoughts in the darkness
 why are they?
Why are there men and women that while they are nigh me the
 sunlight expands my blood?
Why when they leave me do my pennants of joy sink flat and lank?
Why are there trees I never walk under but large and melodious
 thoughts descend upon me?
(I think they hang there winter and summer on those trees and
 always drop fruit as I pass;) 100
What is it I interchange so suddenly with strangers?
What with some driver as I ride on the seat by his side?

What with some fisherman drawing his seine by the shore as I
    walk by and pause?
What gives me to be free to a woman's and man's good-will?
    what gives them to be free to mine?

8

The efflux of the soul is happiness, here is happiness,   105
I think it pervades the open air, waiting at all times,
Now it flows unto us, we are rightly charged.

Here rises the fluid and attaching character,
The fluid and attaching character is the freshness and sweetness
    of man and woman,
(The herbs of the morning sprout no fresher and sweeter every
    day out of the roots of themselves, than it sprouts fresh
    and sweet continually out of itself.)   110

Toward the fluid and attaching character exudes the sweat of the
    love of young and old,
From it falls distill'd the charm that mocks beauty and attainments,
Toward it heaves the shuddering longing ache of contact.

9

Allons![1] whoever you are come travel with me!
Traveling with me you find what never tires.   115

The earth never tires,
The earth is rude, silent, incomprehensible at first, Nature is rude
    and incomprehensible at first,
Be not discouraged, keep on, there are divine things well envelop'd,
I swear to you there are divine things more beautiful than words
    can tell.

Allons! we must not stop here,   120
However sweet these laid-up stores, however convenient this dwell-
    ing we cannot remain here,
However shelter'd this port and however calm these waters we
    must not anchor here,
However welcome the hospitality that surrounds us we are per-
    mitted to receive it but a little while.

---

1. French word for "Let us go."

10

Allons! the inducements shall be greater,
We will sail pathless and wild seas, 125
We will go where winds blow, waves dash, and the Yankee clipper
  speeds by under full sail.
Allons! with power, liberty, the earth, the elements,
Health, defiance, gayety, self-esteem, curiosity;
Allons! from all formules![2]
From your formules, O bat-eyed and materialistic priests. 130

The stale cadaver blocks up the passage—the burial waits no
  longer.

Allons! yet take warning!
He traveling with me needs the best blood, thews, endurance,
None may come to the trial till he or she bring courage and health,
Come not here if you have already spent the best of yourself, 135
Only those may come who come in sweet and determin'd bodies,
No diseas'd person, no rum-drinker or venereal taint is permitted
  here.

(I and mine do not convince by arguments, similes, rhymes,
We convince by our presence.)

11

Listen! I will be honest with you, 140
I do not offer the old smooth prizes, but offer rough new prizes,
These are the days that must happen to you:
You shall not heap up what is call'd riches,
You shall scatter with lavish hand all that you earn or achieve,
You but arrive at the city to which you were destin'd, you hardly
  settle yourself to satisfaction before you are call'd by an
  irresistible call to depart, 145
You shall be treated to the ironical smiles and mockings of those
  who remain behind you,
What beckonings of love you receive you shall only answer with
  passionate kisses of parting,
You shall not allow the hold of those who spread their reach'd
  hands toward you.

---

2. Formulas.

12

Allons! after the great Companions, and to belong to them!
They too are on the road—they are the swift and majestic men—
    they are the greatest women,   150
Enjoyers of calms of seas and storms of seas,
Sailors of many a ship, walkers of many a mile of land,
Habituès of many distant countries, habituès of far-distant dwellings,
Trusters of men and women, observers of cities, solitary toilers,
Pausers and contemplators of tufts, blossoms, shells of the shore,   155
Dancers at wedding-dances, kissers of brides, tender helpers of
    children, bearers of children,
Soldiers of revolts, standers by gaping graves, lowerers-down of
    coffins,
Journeyers over consecutive seasons, over the years, the curious
    years each emerging from that which preceded it,
Journeyers as with companions, namely their own diverse phases,
Forth-steppers from the latent unrealized baby-days,   160
Journeyers gayly with their own youth, journeyers with their
    bearded and well-grain'd manhood,
Journeyers with their womanhood, ample, unsurpass'd, content,
Journeyers with their own sublime old age of manhood or womanhood,
Old age, calm, expanded, broad with the haughty breadth of the
    universe,
Old age, flowing free with the delicious near-by freedom of death.   165

13

Allons! to that which is endless as it was beginningless,
To undergo much, tramps of days, rests of nights,
To merge all in the travel they tend to, and the days and nights
    they tend to,
Again to merge them in the start of superior journeys,
To see nothing anywhere but what you may reach it and pass it,   170
To conceive no time, however distant, but what you may reach it
    and pass it,
To look up or down no road but it stretches and waits for you,
    however long but it stretches and waits for you,
To see no being, not God's or any, but you also go thither,
To see no possession but you may posses it, enjoying all without
    labor or purchase, abstracting the feast yet not abstracting
    one particle of it,
To take the best of the farmer's farm and the rich man's elegant
    villa, and the chaste blessings of the well-married couple,
    and the fruits of orchards and flowers of gardens,   175

To take to your use out of the compact cities as you pass through,
To carry buildings and streets with you afterward wherever you go,
To gather the minds of men out of their brains as you encounter
    them, to gather the love out of their hearts,
To take your lovers on the road with you, for all that you leave
    them behind you,
To know the universe itself as a road, as many roads, as roads for
    traveling souls.   180

All parts away for the progress of souls,
All religion, all solid things, arts, governments—all that was or is
    apparent upon this globe or any globe, falls into niches and
    corners before the procession of souls along the grand roads
    of the universe.

Of the progress of the souls of men and women along the grand
    roads of the universe, all other progress is the needed
    emblem and sustenance.

Forever alive, forever forward,
Stately, solemn, sad, withdrawn, baffled, mad, turbulent, feeble,
    dissatisfied,   185
Desperate, proud, fond, sick, accepted by men, rejected by men,
They go! they go! I know that they go, but I know not where
    they go,
But I know that they go toward the best—toward something
    great.

Whoever you are, come forth! or man or woman come forth!
You must not stay sleeping and dallying there in the house,
    though you built it, or though it has been built for you.   190

Out of the dark confinement! out from behind the screen!
It is useless to protest, I know all and expose it.

Behold through you as bad as the rest,
Through the laughter, dancing, dining, supping, of people,
Inside of dresses and ornaments, inside of those wash'd and
    trimm'd faces,   195
Behold a secret silent loathing and despair.

No husband, no wife, no friend, trusted to hear the confession,
Another self, a duplicate of every one, skulking and hiding it goes,
Formless and wordless through the streets of the cities, polite and
    bland in the parlors,

In the cars of railroads, in steamboats, in the public assembly,   200
Home to the houses of men and women, at the table, in the bed-
    room, everywhere,
Smartly attired, countenance smiling, form upright, death under
    the breast-bones, hell under the skull-bones,
Under the broadcloth and gloves, under the ribbons and artificial
    flowers,
Keeping fair with the customs, speaking not a syllable of itself,
Speaking of any thing else but never of itself.   205

14

Allons! through struggles and wars!
The goal that was named cannot be countermanded.

Have the past struggles succeeded?
What has succeeded? yourself? your nation? Nature?
Now understand me well—it is provided in the essence of things
    that from any fruition of success, no matter what, shall
    come forth something to make a greater struggle necessary.   210

My call is the call of battle, I nourish active rebellion,
He going with me must go well arm'd,
He going with me goes often with spare diet, poverty, angry
    enemies, desertions.

15

Allons! the road is before us!
It is safe—I have tried it—my own feet have tried it well—be
    not detain'd!   215
Let the paper remain on the desk unwritten, and the book on the
    shelf unopen'd!
Let the tools remain in the workshop! let the money remain
    unearn'd!
Let the school stand! mind not the cry of the teacher!
Let the preacher preach in his pulpit! let the lawyer plead in the
    court, and the judge expound the law.

Camerado, I give you my hand!   220
I give you my love more precious than money,
I give you myself before preaching or law;
Will you give me yourself? will you come travel with me?
Shall we stick by each other as long as we live?

ACTIVITIES FOR WRITING AND DISCUSSION

1. Whitman urged people to read his poems "in the open air every season of every year of your life." Taking this advice literally, read the poem aloud outdoors and live with it over a period of days. Feel free to read and reread the poem in several sittings, focusing on sections that strike you and skimming over others that don't. In your notebook, keep a record of your impressions of the poem and any thoughts or feelings it prompts in you.

2. Whitman saw poetry as a force for bringing people together. Follow your private reading of the poem with a communal reading in class or with a small group. Have each person take a turn at reading a verse paragraph or numbered section, and pause after each section to share and discuss your annotations of particular lines or passages.

3. Think about the title. The poem does not seem to be a "song" in the literal sense. In what respects, if any, is it song*like*? Why does Whitman say "open road" instead of "road"? Of what sorts of experiences and emotions does the phrase "open road" remind you? Make a list of these experiences and emotions. To what (or whom) is the road "open"? Illustrate your answers with examples from the poem.

4. How does it make you feel when the speaker addresses "you" directly? How would the poem change if this element of direct address to the reader were eliminated?

5. Reread sections 12 and 13 and other passages that help explain what the "open road" is. Is the open road for everyone or for a select few? Does a person have to journey physically in order to be on the open road, or are there other **symbolic** types of "journeys"? Identify lines that support your answers to these questions. Then assume the **persona** of a homemaker, a factory worker, a political prisoner, an office clerk, a lawyer, or someone else of your own choosing, and write a letter to Whitman in which you respond to his invitation to "take to the open road."

6. Tell the story of a time when you knew the exhilaration and/or trials of a literal or symbolic "open road."

EMILY DICKINSON (1830–1886)

Much Madness is divinest Sense

Much Madness is divinest Sense—
To a discerning Eye—
Much Sense—the starkest Madness—
'Tis the Majority
In this, as All, prevail—   5
Assent—and you are sane—
Demur[1]—you're straightway dangerous—
And handled with a Chain—

ACTIVITIES FOR WRITING AND DISCUSSION

1. Explain the **paradox** in the first three lines.

2. Share examples of any people you know (or have heard of) whose experience illustrates the paradox.

The Soul selects her own Society

The Soul selects her own Society—
Then—shuts the Door—
To her divine Majority—
Present no more—

Unmoved—she notes the Chariots—pausing—   5
At her low Gate—
Unmoved—an Emperor be kneeling
Upon her Mat—

I've known her—from an ample nation—
Choose One—   10
Then—close the Valves of her attention—
Like Stone—

---

1. Disagree.

EDWIN ARLINGTON ROBINSON (1869–1935)

Richard Cory

Whenever Richard Cory went down town,
We people on the pavement looked at him:
He was a gentleman from sole to crown,
Clean favored, and imperially slim.

And he was always quietly arrayed,   5
And he was always human when he talked;
But still he fluttered pulses when he said,
"Good-morning," and he glittered when he walked.

And he was rich—yes, richer than a king—
And admirably schooled in every grace: 10
In fine, we thought that he was everything
To make us wish that we were in his place.

So on we worked, and waited for the light,
And went without the meat, and cursed the bread;
And Richard Cory, one calm summer night,   15
Went home and put a bullet through his head.

ACTIVITIES FOR WRITING AND DISCUSSION

1. Is it significant that the **speaker** uses the first-person *plural* pronoun ("we") instead of the singular ("I")? Why or why not?

2. Why does Richard Cory kill himself? To enrich what might be a rather pat answer to this question, invent a series of entries from "The Diary of Richard Cory" in which you (Richard) narrate experiences and describe feelings that are weighing on you. Alternative: Write Richard's suicide note, or compose a character biography of Richard.

3. Write a conversation between two townsfolk (gossips, perhaps) discussing Richard Cory, either before or just after his death.

Miyazawa Kenji (1896–1933)

November 3rd

neither yielding to rain
nor yielding to wind
yielding neither to
snow nor to summer heat
   with a stout body   5
      like that
without greed
never getting angry
always smiling quiet-
          ly   10
eating one and a half pints of brown rice
and bean paste and a bit of
             vegetables a day
in everything
not taking oneself   15
    into account
      looking listening understanding well
and not forgetting
living in the shadow of pine trees in a field
   in a small   20
     hut thatched with miscanthus
if in the east there's a
   sick child
going and nursing
      him   25
if in the west there's a tired mother
going and for her
    carrying
     bundles of rice
if in the south   30
  there's someone
         dying
going
  and saying
    you don't have to be   35
     afraid
if in the north
      there's a quarrel
         or a lawsuit
saying it's not worth it   40

                    stop it
in a drought
        shedding tears
in a cold summer
        pacing back and forth   lost   45
called
        a good-for-nothing
                by everyone
neither praised
nor thought a pain   50
    someone
            like that
is what I want
        to be

—*Translated by Hiroaki Sato and Burton Watson*

BERTOLT BRECHT (1898–1956)

from Anecdotes of Mr Keuner

Mr K's Favorite Animal

When Mr K was asked which animal he prized above all others, he named the
elephant and justified it thus: The elephant combines cunning with strength.
Not the miserable cunning which manages to avoid a trap or sneak a meal by
not being noticed, but the cunning attendant upon the strength needed for important tasks. This animal leaves a broad trail. For all that, he is good-natured 5
and has a sense of humor. He is a good friend, just as he is a good enemy.
Though very large and heavy, he is also very swift. His trunk conveys even the
smallest morsels to his enormous body, even nuts. His ears are adjustable: he
hears only what suits him. Besides, he lives to be very old. He is sociable, too,
and not only with other elephants. Everywhere he is both beloved and feared. A 10
certain drollness enables him to be positively venerated. Knifes buckle in his
thick skin, but his heart is tender. He can grow sad. He can grow angry. He enjoys dancing. He dies in the heart of the jungle. He is fond of children and other
small animals. He is grey and conspicuous only by his bulk. He is not edible. He
works well. He enjoys drinking and grows merry. He makes a contribution to 15
art: he provides ivory.

The Natural Instinct for Property

When someone at a party called the property instinct natural, Mr K told the following story about a long-established fishing population: on the south coast of Iceland there are fishermen who have divided the sea into separate lots by means of firmly moored buoys and parcelled it out amongst themselves. They cling to these fields of water as their own property with great affection. 5 They consider them part of themselves, would never give them up even if they yielded no more fish, and despise the inhabitants of the port towns to whom they sell their catch, for they seem to them a superficial race, alienated from nature. They call themselves water-tied. When they catch larger fish, they keep them in tubs, give them names and are greatly attached to them as their own 10 property. For some time past they are said to have been having a bad time economically; nevertheless, they doggedly reject all attempts at reform, and they have already brought down several governments which disregarded their customs. These fishermen prove irrefutably the power of the property instinct to which man is subject by nature.   15

A Man of Purpose

Mr K put the following questions:

'Every morning my neighbour plays music on his gramophone. Why does he play music? I hear that it is because he does exercises. Why does he do exercises? Because he needs to be strong, I hear. Why does he need to be strong? Because he has to get the better of his enemies in the town, he says. Why must he 5 get the better of his enemies? Because he wants to eat, I hear.'

Having learnt that his neighbour played music in order to do exercises, did exercises in order to be strong, wanted to be strong in order to kill his enemies, killed his enemies in order to eat, he put the question: 'Why does he eat?'

Love of Nation, Hatred of Nationalism

Mr K did not think it necessary to live in any particular country. 'I can go hunting anywhere,' he said. But one day he went through a town occupied by the enemy of the country in which he was living. One of the enemy's officers came towards him and forced him to step off the pavement. Mr K stepped off and became aware that he was furious with this man, and not only with the man, but 5 even more with the country from which the man came. So that he wished it could be wiped off the face of the earth. 'Why,' asked Mr K, 'did I become a nationalist for that moment? Through encountering a nationalist. That's why stupidity has to be stamped out, for it makes stupid those who encounter it.'

Starving

Mr K, on being asked about his country, had said: 'I can go hungry anywhere.' A literal-minded listener now asked him how it came about that he talked of going hungry whereas in fact he had enough to eat. Mr K justified himself by saying: 'What I probably meant to say was that I can live anywhere if I want to live where hunger exists. I grant you there is a great difference between whether I 5 myself go hungry or whether I live where hunger exists. But may I plead in extenuation that, for me, to live where hunger exists, even if not quite as bad as going hungry, is nevertheless pretty bad. After all, it would be of no importance to others if I went hungry, what is important is that I am against the existence of hunger.' 10

—*Translated by Yvonne Kapp*

ACTIVITIES FOR WRITING AND DISCUSSION

1. Review your annotations of Brecht's "Anecdotes" and identify the one to which you have the strongest response. What strikes you about the anecdote? What point(s) does it make? How? Why is (or isn't) it successful at making its point(s)? How do **metaphors, symbols, verbal irony,** or other **tropes** contribute to the anecdote's effectiveness?

2. Argue the following thesis: "Brecht uses the 'Anecdotes' as a means of critiquing individual and collective ignorance." Support your thesis with evidence from one or more of the "Anecdotes." Alternative: Argue and support a different thesis of your own making.

3. Imitate Brecht and invent a **persona** who has definite opinions about various subjects. First write a brief description of this persona—his/her appearance, personal and cultural background, biases and beliefs, manner of gesture and speech, for instance. Then articulate his/her opinions in the form of several **prose poems**, e.g., "Mr./Ms. X's Favorite Animal" or "Mr./Ms. X's Opinions about ——."

W. H. Auden (1907–1973)

The Unknown Citizen

(To JS/07/M/378
This Marble Monument
Is Erected by the State)

He was found by the Bureau of Statistics to be
One against whom there was no official complaint,
And all the reports on his conduct agree
That, in the modern sense of an old-fashioned word, he was a saint,
For in everything he did he served the Greater Community.   5
Except for the War till the day he retired
He worked in a factory and never got fired,
But satisfied his employers, Fudge Motors Inc.
Yet he wasn't a scab or odd in his views,
For his Union reports that he paid his dues,   10
(Our report on his Union shows it was sound)
And our Social Psychology workers found
That he was popular with his mates and liked a drink.
The Press are convinced that he bought a paper every day
And that his reactions to advertisements were normal in every way.   15
Policies taken out in his name prove that he was fully insured,
And his Health-card shows he was once in hospital but left it cured.
Both Producers Research and High Grade Living declare
He was fully sensible to the advantages of the Installment Plan
And had everything necessary to the Modern Man,   20
A phonograph, radio, a car and a frigidaire.
Our researchers into Public Opinion are content
That he held the proper opinions for the time of year;
When there was peace, he was for peace; when there was war, he went.
He was married and added five children to the population,   25
Which our Eugenist says was the right number for a parent of his generation,
And our teachers report that he never interfered with their education.
Was he free? Was he happy? The question is absurd:
Had anything been wrong, we should certainly have heard.

ACTIVITIES FOR WRITING AND DISCUSSION

1. Read the poem aloud and jot down the impressions and feelings it evokes in you by its sound, **rhythm,** and **rhymes.** Would you describe the poem as **traditional verse** or **free verse**? Does it have features of both? Explain. Finally, how do the sound, rhythm, and rhymes relate to the poem's meaning(s)?

2. Study the three italicized lines immediately after the title. How do you react to them, and particularly to the *first* line, with its cryptic initials, slash marks, and numbers? What expectations, if any, do they give you for the poem that follows?

3. Who is the "we" in this poem? How would it change the effect or meaning of the poem if "we" were replaced by "I" or "they" or by a more precise phrase such as "we, the people"?

4. The twentieth century has sometimes been called the "age of irony." With a small group, compile a list of examples of **verbal irony** in this poem.

5. Reflect on the society this poem depicts. What sorts of values and behaviors does it honor? What are some distinctive qualities of its heroes (such as "The Unknown Citizen" himself)? Imagine that an outsider enters this society. Mentioning at least some of the institutions and terms named in the poem, e.g., "the Bureau of Statistics," "Fudge Motors Inc.," "Producers Research," or "the Installment Plan," tell the story of some experiences he/she has. If you wish, compose your narrative as a series of journal entries or reports that record this person's experiences of—and observations on—this society.

Margaret Atwood (b. 1939)

The City Planners

Cruising these residential Sunday
streets in dry August sunlight:
what offends us is
the sanities:
the houses in pedantic rows, the planted   5
sanitary trees, assert
levelness of surface like a rebuke
to the dent in our car door.
No shouting here, or
shatter of glass; nothing more abrupt   10
than the rational whine of a power mower
cutting a straight swath in the discouraged grass.

But though the driveways neatly
sidestep hysteria
by being even, the roofs all display   15
the same slant of avoidance to the hot sky,
certain things:
the smell of spilled oil a faint

sickness lingering in the garages,
a splash of paint on brick surprising as a bruise,   20
a plastic hose poised in a vicious
coil; even the too-fixed stare of the wide windows

give momentary access to
the landscape behind or under
the future cracks in the plaster   25

when the houses, capsized, will slide
obliquely into the clay seas, gradual as glaciers
that right now nobody notices.

That is where the City Planners
with the insane faces of political conspirators   30
are scattered over unsurveyed
territories, concealed from each other,
each in his own private blizzard;

guessing directions, they sketch
transitory lines rigid as wooden borders   35
on a wall in the white vanishing air

tracing the panic of suburb
order in a bland madness of snows.

Cathy Appel (b. 1948)

Letters

Don't put your disembodied voice in an envelope—
send objects,
tangibles from Vermont, like the broken thread
from the last shirt button you've lost,
photographs of the house;   5
I should see you as you are.
What kind of soap is in your bathroom;
where do you keep your car keys? Send me
your favorite recipe, something from your pocket
like a ticket stub or tattered list.   10
I'll answer promptly
enclosing dust from my closet,

mud from the soles of my shoes.
Can you imagine me exhausted,
tissues tucked in a sleeve,   15
lying beside my husband, who, regardless,
caresses my hip? I could send you
a toenail clipping
or the umpteen odd barrettes, rubber bands,
unanswered letters scattered in my drawer.   20
Don't write in sentences.
No matter how we feel, send specifics—a branch
of your family's Christmas tree,
your daughter's loose tooth, crumbs
from the toast you ate this morning.   25
Send me what defies
language, something of which
there isn't any doubt.

LEO ROMERO (b. 1950)

What the Gossips Saw

Everyone pitied Escolastica, her leg
had swollen like a watermelon in the summer
It had practically happened over night
She was seventeen, beautiful and soon
to be married to Guillermo who was working   5
in the mines at Terreros, eighty miles away
far up in the mountains, in the wilderness
Poor Escolastica, the old women would say
on seeing her hobble to the well with a bucket
carrying her leg as if it were the weight   10
of the devil, surely it was a curse from heaven
for some misdeed, the young women who were
jealous would murmur, yet they were grieved too
having heard that the doctor might cut
her leg, one of a pair of the most perfect legs   15
in the valley, and it was a topic of great
interest and conjecture among the villagers
whether Guillermo would still marry her
if she were crippled, a one-legged woman—
as if life weren't hard enough for a woman   20
with two legs—how could she manage

Guillermo returned and married Escolastica
even though she had but one leg, the sound
of her wooden leg pounding down the wooden aisle
stayed in everyone's memory for as long   25
as they lived, women cried at the sight
of her beauty, black hair so dark
that the night could get lost in it, a face
more alluring than a full moon

Escolastica went to the dances with her husband   30
and watched and laughed but never danced
though once she had been the best dancer
and could wear holes in a pair of shoes
in a matter of a night, and her waist had been
as light to the touch as a hummingbird's flight   35
And Escolastica bore five children, only half
what most women bore, yet they were healthy
In Escolastica's presence, no one would mention
the absence of her leg, though she walked heavily
And it was not long before the gossips   40
spread their poison, that she must be in cohorts
with the devil, had given him her leg
for the power to bewitch Guillermo's heart
and cloud his eyes so that he could not see
what was so clear to them all   45

ACTIVITIES FOR WRITING AND DISCUSSION

1. Why do you suppose Romero is vague about the precise medical causes of Escolastica's loss of a leg?

2. Jot down your impressions of the village in which Escolastica lives. What are the people like? What sorts of beliefs and attitudes do they have? What are their families like? their entertainments? Then, using details provided in the poem (and fabricating others where necessary), invent the conversation about Escolastica that occurs among any of the following: "the old women," "the young women," "the villagers," or "the gossips."

3. Recall a situation out of your own experience or knowledge in which one person was an object of gossip. Make a few notes about the person, the source of the gossip, and the gossipers. Then write the text of the gossip. Alternative: Invent such a situation.

Jimmy Santiago Baca (b. 1952)

Perfecto Flores

We banter
back and forth
the price
for laying brick.
"You people only pay   5
the rich, those who
already have money.
I have a whole yard of bricks
collected over thirty years
working as a mason.   10
I offer you a good price,
load them on the truck,
bring sand and gravel,
do the work almost for nothing,
and you won't pay me   15
half what Hunter charges."
He was right, I relented,
paid him seventy cents a block.
The next day
he brought them,   20
towing cement mixer
behind his old truck.
He rounded the weeping willow
trunk with blocks
left over from apartments   25
he worked on
six years ago,
then poured cement
and troweled it smooth.
After he was done, he asked,   30
"Can I have that roll of wire back there?"
He lives by scraps, built three houses
for his daughters with construction site
scraps.
In English   35
his name is Perfect Flower.
Brawny man with bull shoulders,
who forty years ago came from Mexico,
tired of the mines, the somnolent
spirit of Mexicans. ". . . I was the first one   40

to say I wouldn't ride the old bus.
It was falling apart. I refused, and
the rest followed, and soon a new bus
was brought up the mountain."
I gave him our old Falcon   45
for pouring cement floor
in the guest cottage,
jar of blessed black-purple
Acoma corn kernels
for helping me uproot a tree,   50
gave him seven rabbits
and a box of chickens
for helping me cut adobe arches.
We curse and laugh as we work.
He proudly hefts a wheelbarrow   55
brimmed with cement. "Ah! Sixty-two, *cabrón!*
And you, naa! You would break your back!"
He ribs me, proud of his strength.
He has nothing that glows his face
so much as stories of his working years,   60
feats of courage in the mines
when he was called upon to defuse dynamite
that didn't explode. Short, stocky
gray-haired man, always in his yard
scattering chicken seed, nailing, sawing,   65
always in jean overalls.
Chews a ground weed,
carries a stub pencil and grimy wad of paper
for figuring, and
always turns to me when I drive   70
or walk into his yard
with a roguish grin,
his love of telling stories
competing with mine.
He growls with laughter   75
at the blisters on my hands,
takes his gloves off,
spreads his palms up—
a gallery owner who strips black cloth
off his prized Van Gogh painting,   80
"Look! You could sharpen a file
on these hands," he grins proudly.

ACTIVITIES FOR WRITING AND DISCUSSION

1. What reasons might there be for beginning the poem with the "banter" and the long quotation of lines 5 through 16 instead of with a physical description of Perfecto Flores, which does not commence until line 63?

2. In poetry or prose, portray an ordinary individual whom you know and respect as a worker or friend. Describe the person involved in his or her daily work and include some typical conversation between yourself and him or her.

3. Imagine you are Perfecto Flores. Impressed by your attitude and achievements, a local organization has asked you to give a speech on the topic of "Work" at a luncheon for its members. "Don't worry about being impressive or profound," you are told. "Just be yourself." Incorporating background information from the poem, write the text of the speech you believe Perfecto Flores would give. Alternative: Compose a speech on the same topic using a *different* imaginary speaker.

CATHY SONG (b. 1955)

Losing Track

Last night I saw a documentary
on China. The camera crew
had traveled to the far western
province of Xinjiang. In the brief
green meadows of summer in the hills   5
I thought I recognized you,
but she was younger,
a girl who could have been your sister.
She was leaping in a game,
trying to catch the tail's end, a small boy,   10
in a snake of children
weaving through the tall grass.
Her long braids were flying like the tassels
tying her cotton quilted vest.
The camera almost touched her face: sturdy and earnest,   15
she seemed to smile against her will.

If you remained in China,
you would be pedaling an ancient
bicycle in Beijing. I received two letters.
The students were so polite   20
they made you feel venerable

beyond your years, waiting after class
to hand you rice cakes and panfried doughnuts.
I can hear them reciting
your stilted English sentences: at school,   25
I had once mistaken you for a foreigner,
your speech halting and deliberate.
You described your room, writing
how cold it was to face
the northern slant of the sun.   30
The light made you think of Michigan,
driving home through the woods with your father.
You made tentative plans to return
to the family house,
to finish a book of stories   35
you began writing in an upstairs room.
And then you wrote that you had fallen
in love with one of your students
but as if thinking it over,
you were riding an inland train   40
with someone else, a safe companion,
a woman with unfeminine features.

That is where we lost track
of one another. The silence that followed
your last letter grew longer,   45
becoming a tunnel of snow
the train you were riding whistled through.
Our words had been what had kept
us alive to one another and when they stopped,
a jade fish, an old coin,   50
was dropped into the blue China Sea.
Last night I found myself alone
when your face was brought back to life.
I dreamt I went to find you
in the drafty halls of the school   55
where in the mausoleum silence
of the library we would study, side by side,
our identical hair covering
the English language we both loved.

The story you began writing in Michigan   60
was a notebook you carried
across the snow quiet fields of the campus.
Walking in the shadow of the lights

along College Road, our tracks
had already begun to diverge   65
with our good night and a stack of books
at the frozen lily pond.
I watched you trudge up the hill
toward the observatory.
I see you as you were then,   70
so serious you did not mean to scowl,
your black ponytail, an ink brush,
dipping into the night air,
dotting the points to a constellation
you had yet to name.   75

Nonfiction/Essays

ARTHUR SCHOPENHAUER (1788–1860)

On Thinking for Oneself

257

Just as the largest library, badly arranged, is not so useful as a very moderate one that is well arranged, so the greatest amount of knowledge, if not elaborated by our own thoughts, is worth much less than a far smaller volume that has been abundantly and repeatedly thought over. For only by universally combining what we know, by comparing every truth with every other, do we fully assimilate our own knowledge and get it into our power. We can think over only what we know, and so we should learn something; but we know only what we have thought out. . . .

258

. . . Therefore the mind is deprived of all its elasticity by *much* reading as is a spring when a weight is continually applied to it; and the surest way not to have thoughts of our own is for us at once to take up a book when we have a moment to spare. This practice is the reason why erudition makes most men more stupid and simple than they are by nature and also deprives their literary careers of every success. As Pope says, they remain:

For ever reading, never to be read.

The Dunciad, 3:193–94.

Scholars are those who have read in books, but thinkers, men of genius, world enlighteners, and reformers of the human race are those who have read directly in the book of the world.

259

At bottom, only our own fundamental ideas have truth and life; for it is they alone that we really and thoroughly understand. The ideas of someone else that we have read are the scraps and leavings of someone else's meal, the cast-off clothes of a stranger.

   The idea of another that we have read is related to our own that occurs to us   5
as the impression in stone of a plant from the primeval world to the blossoming plant of spring.

260

Reading is a mere makeshift for original thinking. When we read, we allow another to guide our thoughts in leading strings. Moreover, many books merely serve to show how many false paths there are and how seriously we could go astray if we allowed ourselves to be guided by them. But whoever is guided by genius, in other words thinks for himself, thinks freely and of his own accord and thinks correctly; he has the compass for finding the right way. We should, therefore, read only when the source of our own ideas dries up, which will be the case often enough even with the best minds. On the other hand, to scare away our own original and powerful ideas in order to take up a book, is a sin against the Holy Ghost. We then resemble the man who runs away from free nature in order to look at a herbarium, or to contemplate a beautiful landscape in a copper engraving.

   Even if occasionally we had been able very easily and conveniently to find in a book a truth or view that we very laboriously and slowly discovered through our own thinking and combining, it is nevertheless a hundred times more valuable if we have arrived at it through our own original thinking. Only then does it enter into the whole system of our ideas as an integral part and living member; only then is it completely and firmly connected therewith, is understood in all its grounds and consequents, bears the color, tone, and stamp of our whole mode of thought, has come at the very time when the need for it was keen, is therefore firmly established and cannot again pass away. Accordingly, Goethe's verse here finds its most perfect application and even explanation:

What from your fathers' heritage is lent,
Earn it anew, really to possess it!

Thus the man who thinks for himself only subsequently becomes acquainted with the authorities for his opinions when they serve merely to confirm him therein and to encourage him. The book-philosopher, on the other hand, starts from those authorities in that he constructs for himself an entire system from the opinions of others that he has collected in the course of his reading. Such a system is then like an automaton composed of foreign material, whereas that of the original thinker resembles a living human being. For it originated like this, since the external world fertilized the thinking mind that afterwards carried it and gave birth to it.

The truth that has been merely learned sticks to us like an artificial limb, a false tooth, a nose of wax, or at best like a rhinoplastic nose formed from someone else's flesh. On the other hand, the truth acquired through our own thinking is like the natural limb; it alone really belongs to us. On this rests the distinction between the thinker and the mere scholar. The intellectual gain of the man who thinks for himself is, therefore, like a beautiful painting that vividly stands out with correct light and shade, sustained tone, and perfect harmony of colors. The intellectual acquisition of the mere scholar, on the other hand, is like a large palette full of bright colors, systematically arranged perhaps, but without harmony, sequence, and significance.

261

Reading is equivalent to thinking with someone else's head instead of with one's own. Now for our own thinking, whence a coherent and connected whole, a system though not strictly rounded off, endeavors to evolve, nothing is more detrimental than too strong an influx of other people's ideas through constant reading. For each of them has sprung from the mind of another, belongs to another system, bears another tint; and never do they flow of themselves into a totality of thought, knowledge, insight, and conviction. On the contrary, they set up in the head a slight Babylonian confusion of tongues, and a mind so crammed is now robbed of all clear insight and thus is well-nigh disorganized. This state can be observed in many scholars and results in their being inferior to many illiterate men as regards common sense, correct judgment, and practical tact. The latter have always subordinated to, and incorporated in, their own thinking the little knowledge that has come to them from without through experience, conversation, and a little reading. Now it is just this that the scientific *thinker* also does to a greater degree. Although he needs much knowledge and must, therefore, read a great deal, his mind is nevertheless strong enough to master all this, to assimilate it, to incorporate it into his system of ideas, and thus to subordinate it to the organically consistent totality of his vast and ever-growing insight. Here his own thinking, like the ground-bass of an organ, always dominates everything and is never drowned by the notes and tones of others, as is the case with the minds of mere pundits and polyhistors, where fragments of music in all keys run into one another, so to speak, and the fundamental note can no longer be detected at all.

262

Those who have spent their lives in reading, and have drawn their wisdom from books, resemble men who have acquired precise information about a country from many descriptions of travel. They are able to give much information about things, but at bottom they have really no coherent, clear, and thorough knowledge of the nature of the country. On the other hand, those who have spent their lives in thinking are like men who have themselves been in that country. They alone really know what they are talking about; they have a consistent and coherent knowledge of things there and are truly at home in them. . . . 10

265

. . . The characteristic sign of all first-rate minds is the directness of all their judgments and opinions. All that they express and assert is the result of their own original thinking and everywhere proclaims itself as such even by the style of delivery. Accordingly, like princes, they have an imperial immediacy in the realm of the mind; the rest are all mediatized, as is already seen from their style that has no stamp of originality.

Therefore every genuine and original thinker is to this extent like a monarch; he is immediate and perceives no one who is his superior. Like the decrees of a monarch, his judgments spring from his own supreme power and come directly from himself. For he no more accepts authorities than does the monarch take orders; on the contrary, he admits nothing but what he himself has confirmed. On the other hand, minds of the common ruck who labor under all kinds of current opinions, authorities, and prejudices, are like the crowd that silently obeys laws and orders. . . .

268

The presence of an idea is like that of a loved one. We imagine that we shall never forget it and that the beloved can never become indifferent to us; but out of sight, out of mind! The finest thought runs the risk of being irretrievably forgotten if it is not written down, and the beloved of being taken from us unless she has been wedded.

—*Translated by E.F.J. Payne*

ACTIVITIES FOR WRITING AND DISCUSSION

1. Review your annotations of Schopenhauer's text. Choose one or more that speak(s) most powerfully to your own experiences of reading or thinking. Then use the annotated passage(s) as a springboard to writing and reflecting on your experiences. Write in **essay** form, or, if you wish, compose a letter to Schopenhauer or a dialogue with him in which you share your experiences of reading and thinking.

2. Schopenhauer's text is rich in **metaphors, similes** and analogies. Working alone or in a group, underline and annotate as many examples of these figures as you can. Then choose two or three and show how they help explain or clarify Schopenhauer's ideas.

3. Working from your annotations of "On Thinking for Oneself," summarize the distinctions Schopenhauer makes between "reading" and "thinking." Then agree or disagree with the distinctions.

CAROL BLY (b. 1930)

Growing Up Expressive

Love, death, the cruelty of power, and time's curve past the stars are what children want to look at. For convenience's sake, let's say these are the four most vitally touching things in life. Little children ask questions about them with relish. Children, provided they are still little enough, have no eye to doing any problem solving about love or death or injustice or the universe; they are simply interested. I've noticed that as we read aloud literature to them, about Baba Yaga, and Dr. Doolittle, and Ivan and the Firebird, and Rat and Mole, children are not only interested, they are prepared to be vitally touched by the great things of life. If you like the phrase, they are what some people call "being as a little child." Another way of looking at it is to say that in our minds we have two kinds of receptivity to life going on all the time: first, being vitally touched and enthusiastic (grateful, enraged, puzzled—but, at all events, *moved*) and, second, having a will to solve problems.

Our gritty society wants and therefore deliberately trains problem solvers, however, not mystics. We teach human beings to keep themselves conscious only of problems that *can* conceivably be solved. There must be no hopeless causes. Now this means that some subjects, of which death and sexual love come to mind straight off, should be kept at as low a level of consciousness as possible. Both resist problem solving. A single-minded problem solver focuses his consciousness, of course, on problems to be solved, but even he realizes there is a concentric, peripheral band of other material around the problems. This band appears to him as "issues." He is not interested in these issues for themselves; he sees them simply as impacting on the problems. He will allow us to talk of love, death, injustice, and eternity—he may even encourage us to do so because his group-dynamics training advises him to let us have our say, thus dissipating our willfulness—but his heart is circling, circling, looking for an opening to *wrap up* these "issues" so he can return attention to discrete, solvable problems. For example, a physician who has that mentality does not wish to be near dying patients very much. They are definitely not a solvable problem. If he is wicked, he will regard them as a present issue with impact on a future problem: then he will order experimentation done on them during their last weeks with us. It means his ethic is toward the healing process only, but not toward the dying person. His ethic is toward problem solving, not toward wonder. He will feel quite conscientious while doing the experiments on the dying patient, because he feels he is saving lives of future patients.

To return to little children for a second: they simply like to contemplate life and death. So our difficulty, in trying to educate adults so they will be balanced but enthusiastic, is to keep both streams going—the problem solving, which seems to be the mental genius of our species, and the fearless contemplation of gigantic things, the spiritual genius of our species.

The problem-solving mentality is inculcated no less in art and English classes than in mathematics and science. Its snake oil is hope of success: by setting very small topics in front of people, for which it is easy for them to see the goals, the problems, the solutions, their egos are not threatened. They feel hopeful of being effective. Therefore, to raise a generation of problem solvers, you encourage them to visit the county offices (as our sixth-grade teachers do) and you lead them to understand that this is citizenship. You carefully do not suggest that citizenship also means comparatively complex and hopeless activities like Amnesty International's pressure to get prisoners in far places released or at least no longer tortured. Small egos are threatened by huge, perhaps insoluble problems. Therefore, one feeds the small ego confidence by setting before it dozens and dozens of very simple situations. The ego is nourished by feeling it understands the relationship between the county recorder's office and the county treasurer's office; in later life, when young people find a couple of sticky places in county government, they will confidently work at smoothing them. How very different an experience such problem solving is from having put before one the spectacle of the United States' various stances and activities with respect to germ warfare. Educators regularly steer off all interest in national and international government to one side, constantly feeding our rural young people on questions to which one can hope for answers on a short timeline. We do not ask them to exercise that muscle which bears the weight of vast considerations—such as cruelty in large governments. By the time the average rural Minnesotan is eighteen, he or she expects to stay in cheerful places, devote some time to local government and civic work, and "win the little ones." Rural young people have a repertoire of pejorative language for hard causes: "opening that keg of worms," "no end to that once you get into it," "don't worry—you can't do anything about that from where you are," "we could go on about that

forever!" They are right, of course: we could, and our species, at its most cultivated, does go on forever about love, death, power, time, the universe. But some
of us, alas, have been conditioned by eighteen fashionably to despise those subjects because there are no immediate answers to all the questions they ask us.

The other way we negatively reinforce any philosophical bent in children is 5
to pretend we don't see the content in their artwork. We comment only on the
technique, in somewhat the same way you can scarcely get a comment on rural
preachers' sermon content: the response is always, He does a good (or bad) job
of speaking. "Well, but what did he say?" "Oh, he talked really well. The man
can preach!"

The way to devalue the content of a child's painting is to say, "Wow, you sure
can paint!" The average art teacher in Minnesota is at pains to find something
to say to the third grader's painting of a space machine with complicated, presumably electronic equipment in it. Here is the drawing in words: A man is sitting at some controls. Outside his capsule, fire is flying from emission points on
his ship toward another spaceship at right, hitting it. Explosions are coming out
of its side and tail. What is an art teacher to do with this? Goodness knows. So
he or she says, "My goodness, I can see there's a lot of action there!" It is said in
a deliberately encouraging way but anyone can hear under the carefully supportive comment: "A lot of work going into nothing but more TV-inspired violence." One might as well have told the child, "Thank you for sharing."

I once attended a regional writers' group at which a young poet wrote about
his feelings of being a single parent and trying to keep his sanity as he cared for
his children. In his poem, he raced up the staircase, grabbed a gun, and shot the
clock. When he finished reading it aloud to us, someone told him, "I certainly
am glad you shared with us. I'd like to really thank you for sharing."

If we are truly serious about life we are going to have to stop thanking people for sharing. It isn't enough response to whatever has been offered. It is half
ingenuous, and sometimes it is insincere, and often it is patronizing. It is the
dictum excrementi of our decade.

I would like to keep in mind for a moment the art works described above:
the child's painting of a spaceship assaulting another spaceship, and the har-
rowed father's racing up the staircase and shooting the clock. Here is a third. It
is a twelve-year-old's theme for English class.

> They were their four days and nights before anyone found them. It was wet
> and cold down there. As little kids at the orphanage, they had been beaten
> every night until they could scarcely make it to bed. Now they were older.
> Duane and Ellen leaned together. "I love you forever," she told him. He
> asked her, "Even though my face is marked from getting scarlet fever and
> polio and small pox and newmonya and they wouldn't take decent care of
> me, not call the doctor or anything, so the marks will always be on me?"
> "You know I love you," Ellen told him. "You know that time they tortured
> me for information and I was there but I didn't talk and later I found out it
> was your uncle who did it. I didn't talk because I remembered the American

flag." Just then they heard someone shout, "Anyone alive down there in this
mess?" You see a bomb had gone off destroying a entire U.S.A. city where
they lived. Duane had lived with his cruel uncle who took him out of the orphanage to get cheap labor and Ellen lived at a boardinghouse where there
were rats that ate pages of her diary all the time. Now they both looked up
and shouted "We're here!" A head appeared at the top of the well into which
they had fallen or they would of been in 6,500 pieces like all the other men
and ladies even pregnant ones and little kids in that town. Now this head
called down, "Oh—a boy and a girl!" then the head explained it was going
for a ladder and ropes and it ducked away and where it had been they saw
the beginnings of stars for that night, the stars still milky in front of the
bright blue because the sky wasn't dark enough yet to show them up good.

The English teacher will typically comment on this story by observing that   10
the spelling is uneven, and adjectives get used as adverbs. In rural Minnesota (if
not elsewhere) an English teacher can spend every class hour on adjectives used
as adverbs: it is meat and potatoes to a nag. But when we discuss spelling, syntax, and adverbs, we are talking method, not content. The child notices that
nothing is said of the story's *plot*. No one remarks on the *feelings* in it. Now if
this happens every time a child hands in fiction or a poem, the child will realize
by the time he reaches twelfth grade that meaning or feelings are not worth
anything, that "mechanics" (note the term) are all that matter.

It is rare for a public school English teacher to comment on a child's content
unless the material is *factual*. Minnesota teachers encourage writing booklets
about the state, themes on ecology and county government, on how Dad strikes
the field each autumn, on how Mom avoids open-kettle canning because the
USDA advises against it. In this way, our children are conditioned to regard
writing as problem solving instead of contemplation, as routine thinking instead of imaginative inquiry.

How can we manage it otherwise?

I would like to suggest some questions we can ask children about their artwork which will encourage them to grow up into lovers, lobby supporters, and
Amnesty International members, instead of only township officers and annual
protestors against daylight saving time. Let us gather all the elements of the
three artworks presented in this Letter: the little boy's spaceship-war painting,
the young divorced father's narrative poem, and the twelve-year-old girl's story
of love in a well. We have a set of images before us, then:

Man directing spaceship fire
Another aircraft being obliterated
Staircase, man shooting a clock; children
Cruel orphanage
Torture
Last survivors of a decimated city

Let us, instead of lending the great sneer to these images, be respectful of them. It may help to pretend the painting is by Picasso, that Flaubert wrote the father/clock scene, and that Tolstoy wrote the well story. It helps to remember that Picasso felt the assault of historical events on us—like Guernica; Flaubert, as skillfully as Dostoyevsky and with less self-pity, was an observer of violent detail; and the Tolstoy who wrote *Resurrection* or the scene of Pierre's imprisonment in *War and Peace* would turn to the well/love story without qualm.

We know we would never say to Picasso, Flaubert, or Tolstoy, "Why don't you draw something you know about from everyday life? Why don't you write about something you know about? You say Anna was smashed beneath a train? Thank you for sharing!"

The fact is that a child's feelings about orphanages and torture and love are 15 things that he does know about. They are psychic realities inside him, and when he draws them, he is drawing something from everyday life. Sometimes they are from his night life of dreaming, but in any event they are images of passion and he is drawing from his genuine if garbled experience. A few years ago there was a stupid movement to discourage children's reading of Grimms' fairy tales. Later, with a more sophisticated psychology, we learned that the stepmother who is hostile and overweening is a reality to all children; the cutting-off of the hero's right hand and replacing of it with a hand of silver is a reality to all children. Spaceships, witches' gingerbread houses, orphanages, being the last two people to survive on earth—all these are part of the inner landscape, something children know about. Therefore, in examining their artwork, we need better sets of questions to ask them. Young people who are not repressed are going to lay their wild stuff in front of adults (hoping for comment of some kind, praise if possible) until the sands of life are run, so we had better try to be good at responding to them. And unless we want to raise drones suitable only for conveyor-belt shifts, we had better be at least half as enthusiastic as when they tell us, Mama, I got the mowing finished.

Here are some questions to ask our young artist. How much of that electronic equipment is used for firepower and how much just to run the ship? After the other spaceship is blown up and the people in it are dead, what will this man do? Will he go home somewhere? Were the stars out that night? You said he'll go home to his parents. Did the other man have parents? How soon will that man's parents find out that his spaceship was destroyed? Could you draw in the stars? You said they were out—could you draw them into the picture some way? but don't ruin anything you've got in there now. Also, that wire you said ran to the solar plates, will you darken it so it shows better? Don't change it—just make it clearer. Yes—terrific! Can you see the planet where the other man would have returned to if he had lived till morning?

The young father's story: There is an obvious psychic complication to this story: the violence in his shooting out the clock face is gratuitous, and the plea for attention on the part of the author directed at the reader is glaring: clock faces as psychological symbols are in the public domain. Anyone who tells a friend (or a group of strangers) I am going to shoot up a clock face at 11 P.M. is asking for psychological attention. In a civil world, to ask is to receive, so if we are civilized we have to pay attention and ask the young author: Why does the father in the story blast the clock? And, when he replies, we have to ask some more. If there was ever an instance in which it was O.K. to say, "Thanks for sharing," this is not it.

I should like to add that this will be especially difficult for rural teachers because the traditional country way to treat any kind of mental problem is to stare it down. It didn't happen. I didn't hear that insane thing you just said, and you know you don't really hate your mother. What nice parent would shoot a clock? We uniformly do what Dr. Vaillant in *Adaptations to Life* would call a denial adaptation. It takes a brave questioner when the young person brings in a crazy story.

The well/love story: Did you know there really are such orphanages? There are orphanages where the children have to get up at four-thirty to work in the dairy, and the girls work hours and hours in the kitchens, and the children's growth is stunted. Did you make the girl so brave on purpose? Were they a lucky couple or an unlucky couple, or is that the sort of a question you can't ask? You made a point of telling us they'd been through a lot of hardship. What would it have been like for them if they hadn't? Do you want to talk about what blew up the city? Did you imagine yourself in the well?

Those are not brilliant questions; they are simply respectful, because the art 20 works described are concerned with death by violence; cruelty by institutions; treachery by relations; bravery (or cowardice—either one is important); sexual love, either despite or encouraged by dreadful circumstances.

They are some of the subjects in *War and Peace,* in Dürer's etchings, paintings, and woodcuts, and in *Madame Bovary.*

It is a moot question in my mind which of two disciplines will be the more useful in helping people stay vitally touched by the Great Things: psychology might do it—and English literature in high school might do it (instruction on the college level is generally so dutiful to methodology that it seems a lost cause to me. "How did D. H. Lawrence foreshadow this event?" and "What metaphors does Harold Rosenberg use in his discussion of Action Painting?" are the questions of technocrats, not preservers of spirit. It is as if we got home from church and the others said, "How was church?" "We had Eucharist," we tell them. "Well, how was it?" they ask. "Pretty good," we reply. "Bishop Anderson was there. He held the chalice eight inches above the rail so no one spilled, then he turned and wiped the chalice after each use so no germs were passed along. People who had already communed returned to their benches using the north aisle so there was no bottlenecking at the chancel.")

I don't think churches will be helpful in preserving the mystical outlook as long as they see life and death as a *problem*—a problem of salvation—with a solution to be worked at. Churches have an axe to grind. They might take the father running up the staircase to be an impact subject: they would wish to use their program to solve his problem. Churchmen often appear to be companionable counselors, but the appearance is largely manner and habit. Under the manner, the clergyman's mindset is nearly always to see a disturbed or grieving person's imagery as *the issues*. From there, he swings into psychological problem solving.

I would like to commend this responsibility to our English teachers: that they help our children preserve pity, happiness, and grief inside themselves. They can enhance those feelings by having young children both write and draw pictures. They can be very enthusiastic about the children's first drawings of death in the sky. Adults, particularly mature ones who have *not* got children in school at the moment, should make it clear that we expect this of English teachers and that we don't give a damn if LeRoy and Merv never in their lives get the sentence balance of past conditional and perfect subjunctive clauses right. We need to protect some of the Things Invisible inside LeRoy and Merv and the rest of us.

This is my last Letter from the Country. That is why it is so shrill. Gadflies   25 are always looking out a chance to be shrill anyway, so I jumped to this one and have shouted my favorite hope: that we can educate children not to be problem solvers but to be madly expressive all their lives.

ACTIVITIES FOR WRITING AND DISCUSSION

1. Working in a group, jot down what you think Bly means by the terms "problem solvers" (or "the problem-solving mentality") and "expressive." Then draw upon Bly's essay and your own experience to give some examples of each. Do you find the terms meaningful for thinking about learning and education? Why or why not?

2. Throughout her essay, Bly reviles the expression "Thank you for sharing." Identify some situations in which people use this expression, and explain the reasons Bly dislikes it. Do you share her dislike? Why or why not? Additional activity: Compose a text (story, dialogue, public speech, poem) in which this expression either recurs or serves as the focal subject.

3. On page 574 Bly says that "the traditional country way to treat any kind of mental problem is to stare it down. It didn't happen." Bly is a rural Minnesotan. Is the phenomenon of "staring it down" confined to rural America? Write a dialogue between two people or characters in which one tries to "stare down" the other's "mental problem."

4. Bly criticizes the ways that some teachers teach. For instance, on page 572 she says that English teachers focus their comments on students' "spelling, syntax, and adverbs" in order to avoid responding to the content and ideas in students' papers. "Now if this happens every time a child hands in fiction or a poem, the child will realize by the time he reaches twelfth grade that meaning or feelings are not worth anything, that 'mechanics' . . . are all that matter."

    a. Does this jibe—or conflict—with your own experience in English classes? Explain, and illustrate with some specific stories of your experiences.

    b. Imagine a situation in which a student is "madly expressive" in his or her writing, drawing, or other creative work. Create the student's madly expressive work and invent the comments that a "problem-solving" teacher might put on it.

5. In the last paragraph Bly states that her "favorite hope" is "that we can educate children not to be problem solvers but to be madly expressive all their lives." Take a point of view that is opposed to Bly's and argue for the importance and value of teaching children to be problem solvers. Alternative: Write a dialogue between someone who shares Bly's view (expressed in the above quotation) and someone who opposes it. Emphasize the conflict between the two speakers and avoid an easy resolution of the conflict.

Play

Athol Fugard (b. 1932)

The Road to Mecca

Characters
MISS HELEN
ELSA
MARIUS BYLEVELD

Time
AUTUMN 1974

Place
NEW BETHESDA, SOUTH AFRICA

Act One

The living room and, leading off it, the bedroom alcove of a house in the small Karoo village of New Bethesda. An extraordinary room by virtue of the attempt to use as much light and color as is humanly possible. The walls—mirrors on all of them—are all of different colors, while on the ceiling and floor are solid, multicolored geometric patterns. Yet the final effect is not bizarre but rather one of light and extravagant fantasy. Just what the room is really about will be revealed later when its candles and lamps—again, a multitude of them of every size, shape and color—are lit. The late afternoon light does, however, give some hint of the magic to come.

MISS HELEN *is in the bedroom alcove. A frail, birdlike little woman in her late sixties. A suggestion of personal neglect, particularly in her clothes, which are shabby and were put on with obvious indifference to the final effect. She is nervously fussing around an old-fashioned washstand, laying out towels, soap, etc., etc., and from time to time directs her attention to the living room and a door leading from it to the rest of the house. In the course of moving around she sees an overnight bag and a briefcase on the floor near the living-room entrance. She fetches these and carries them into the alcove.*

ELSA *enters, a strong young woman in her late twenties dressed in a track suit or something else suitable for a long motorcar ride.*

ELSA: Not cold enough yet for the car to freeze up, is it?

HELEN: No. No danger of that. We haven't had any frost yet.

ELSA: I'm too exhausted to put it away. *(Collapses on the bed)* Whew! Thank God that's over. Another hour and I would have been wiped out. That road gets longer and longer every time.

HELEN: Your hot water is nearly ready.

ELSA: Good. *(Starts to unpack her overnight bag)*

HELEN: Nice clean towels . . . and I've opened that box of scented soaps you brought me last time.

ELSA: What? Oh, those. Haven't you used them yet?

HELEN: Of course not! I was keeping them for a special occasion.

ELSA: And this is it?

HELEN: Yes. An unexpected visit from you is a *very* special occasion. Is that all your luggage?

ELSA: When I said a short visit I really meant it.

HELEN: Such a long way to drive for just one night.

ELSA: I know.

HELEN: You don't think you could . . . ?

ELSA: Stay longer?

HELEN: Even just two nights?

ELSA: Impossible. We're right in the middle of exams. I've got to be in that classroom at eight-thirty on Monday morning. As it is I should be sitting at home right now marking papers. I've even brought a pile of them with me just in case I get a chance up here. *(Starts to undress—track-suit top, sneakers and socks)*

HELEN: Put anything you want washed on one side and I'll get a message to Katrina first thing in the morning.

ELSA: Don't bother her with that. I can do it myself.

HELEN: You can't leave without seeing Katrina! She'll never forgive me if I don't let her know you're here. Please . . . even if it's only for a few minutes.

ELSA: I won't leave without seeing Katrina, Miss Helen! But I don't need her to wash a pair of pants and a bra for me. I do my own washing.

HELEN: I'm sorry . . . I just thought you might. . . . There's an empty drawer here if you want to pack anything away.

ELSA *(An edge to her voice):* Please stop fussing, Miss Helen! I know my way around by now.

HELEN: It's just that if I'd known you were coming, I would have had everything ready for you.

ELSA: Everything is fine just the way it is.

HELEN: No, it isn't! I don't even know that I've got enough in the kitchen for a decent supper tonight. I did buy bread yesterday, but for the rest . . .

ELSA: Please, Miss Helen! If we need anything, I'll get old Retief to open his shop for us. In any case, I'm not hungry. All I need at this moment is a good wash and a chance to unwind so that I can forget I've been sitting in a motorcar for twelve hours.

HELEN: Be patient with me, Elsie. Remember the little saying: "Patience is a virtue, virtue is a grace, and—"

ELSA *(Unexpectedly sharp):* For God's sake, Helen! Just leave me alone for a few minutes!

Pause.

HELEN *(Timidly):* I'll get your hot water.

MISS HELEN *exits.* ELSA *slumps down on the bed, her head in her hands.* MISS HELEN *returns a few seconds later with a large kettle of hot water. She handles it with difficulty.*

I've got the small one on for tea.

ELSA: Let me do that!

She jumps up and takes the kettle away from MISS HELEN. *The two women stand staring at each other for a few seconds.* ELSA *puts down the kettle and then puts her hands on* MISS HELEN *shoulders.*

My turn to say sorry.

HELEN: You don't need to do that.

ELSA: Please! It will help. Sorry, Miss Helen. I also need to hear you say you forgive me.

HELEN: To tell you the truth, I was getting on my own nerves.

ELSA *(Now smiling):* Come on.

HELEN: Oh, all right. . . . But I promise you it isn't necessary. You're forgiven.

ELSA *(Leading* MISS HELEN *over to a chair):* Now sit down and stop worrying about me. We're both going to close our eyes, take a deep breath and start again. Ready?

HELEN: Ready.

ELSA: One, two, three . . .

Closed eyes and deep breaths.

And now?

HELEN *(With the sly, tongue-in-cheek humor we will come to recognize as characteristic of the relaxed woman):* Well, if you really mean it, I think the best thing is for you to get back into your car, drive around the block and arrive again. And this time I want you, please, to hoot three times the way you usually do, so that I don't think a ghost has walked in through the front door when you appear.

ELSA (*Calling* MISS HELEN's *bluff*): Right. Where are the car keys? (*Finds them and heads for the front door*)

HELEN: Where are you going?

ELSA: To do what you said. Drive around the block and arrive again.

HELEN: Like that?

ELSA: Why, what's wrong?

HELEN: Elsie! Sterling Retief will have a heart attack if he sees you like that.

ELSA: But I wear less than this when I go to the beach. Oh, all right then, you old spoilsport, let's pretend.

ELSA *runs into the other room, revs up her motorcar, grinds through all its gears and "arrives." Three blasts on the horn. The two women play the "arrival game" (specifics to be determined in rehearsal). At the end of it they come together in a good laugh.*

If my friends in Cape Town were to have seen that! You must understand, Miss Helen, Elsa Barlow is known as a "serious young woman." Bit of a blue stocking, in fact. Not much fun there! I don't know how you did it, Helen, but you caught me with those stockings down from the first day we met. You have the rare distinction of being the only person who can make me make a fool of myself . . . and enjoy it.

HELEN: You weren't making a fool of yourself. And anyway what about me? Nearly seventy and behaving as if I were seven!

ELSA: Let's face it, we've both still got a little girl hidden away in us somewhere.

HELEN: And they like to play together.

ELSA: Mine hasn't done that for a long time.

HELEN: And I didn't even know that mine was still alive.

ELSA: *That* she most certainly is. She's the one who comes running out to play first. Feeling better?

HELEN: Much better.

For the moment all tensions are gone. ELSA *cleans herself as thoroughly as a basin of water, a facecloth and a bar of scented soap will allow.*

ELSA: God, this Karoo dust gets right into your pores. I can even taste it. That first mouthful of tea is going to be mud. I'll fill up all the kettles tomorrow and have a really good scrub. When did you last have one? (MISS HELEN *has to think about that*) Right, settled. Your name is down for one as well. (*A few seconds of industrious scrubbing.* MISS HELEN *watches her*) What are you thinking?

HELEN: So many things! About the way you *did* arrive. I wasn't joking. For a few seconds I did think I was seeing a ghost. I heard the front door open . . . I thought it was little Katrina, she also never knocks . . . but instead there you were. (*She wants to say more but stops herself.*)

ELSA: Go on.

HELEN: It was so strange. Almost as if you didn't really see me or anything else at first . . . didn't want to. And so cross! I've never seen you like that before.

ELSA: This isn't quite like the other times, Miss Helen.

HELEN: That's a pity. They were all good times. *(Pause)* So what sort of time is this going to be? A bad one?

ELSA *(Evenly):* I hope not. Doesn't have to be. It depends on you.

MISS HELEN *avoids* ELSA*'s eyes. The young woman looks around the room.*

But you're right. I hadn't really arrived until now.

HELEN: Where were you, Elsie?

ELSA *(She thinks about the question before answering):* Way back at the turnoff to the village from the National Road . . . or maybe a few miles further along it now . . . walking to Cradock.

HELEN: I don't understand.

ELSA: I gave a lift to a woman outside Graaff-Reinet. That's most probably where she is now. I dropped her at the turnoff to the village.

HELEN: Who was she?

ELSA *(Shrugging with apparent indifference):* An African woman.

HELEN: Cradock! That's a long walk.

ELSA: I know.

HELEN: It's about another eighty miles from the turn-off. *(She waits for* ELSA *to say more)*

ELSA: I nearly didn't stop for her. She didn't signal that she wanted a lift or anything like that. Didn't even look up when I passed . . . I was watching her in the rearview mirror. Maybe that's what told me there was a long walk ahead of her . . . the way she had her head down and just kept on walking. And then the baby on her back. It was hot out there, Miss Helen, hot and dry and a lot of empty space. . . . There wasn't a farmhouse in sight. She looked very small and unimportant in the middle of all that. Anyway, I stopped and reversed and of-fered her a lift. Not very graciously. I'd already been driving for ten hours and all I wanted was to get here as fast as I could. She got in and after a few miles we started talking. Her English wasn't very good, but when I finally got around to understanding what she was trying to tell me it added up to a good old South African story. Her husband, a farm laborer, had died recently, and no sooner had they buried him when the *baas* told her to pack up and leave the farm. So there she was . . . on her way to the Cradock district, where she hoped to find a few distant relatives and a place to live. *(Trying to remember the woman as clearly as possible)* About my age. The baby couldn't have been more than a few months old. All she had with her was one of those plastic shopping bags they put your groceries in at supermarkets. I saw a pair of old slippers. She was barefoot.

HELEN: Poor woman.

ELSA: So I dropped her at the turnoff. Gave her what was left of my food and some money. She carried on walking and I drove here.

Pause.

HELEN: Is there something else?

ELSA: No. That's all.

HELEN: I'm sure somebody else will give her a lift.

ELSA *(Too easily):* Hope so. If not, she and her baby are in for a night beside the road. There's eighty miles of the Karoo ahead of her. Shadows were already stretching out across the veld when she got out of the car. The Great Karoo! And just when I thought I was getting used to it, beginning to like it, in fact. Down in Cape Town I've actually caught myself talking rubbish about its vast space and emptiness, its awesome stillness and silence! Just like old Getruida down the road. It's that all right, but only because everything else has been all but damned out of existence. It's so obvious where you Afrikaners get your ideas of God from. Beats me how you've put up with it so long, Miss Helen. Nearly seventy years? My God, you deserve a medal. I would have packed up and left it at the first opportunity . . . and let's face it, you've had plenty of those.

HELEN: I was born here, Elsa.

ELSA: I sympathize, Miss Helen. Believe me, I truly sympathize.

HELEN: It's not really as bad as you make it sound. The few times I've been away, I've always ended up missing it and longing to be back.

ELSA: Because you wanted to get back to your work.

HELEN *(Shaking her head):* No. Even before all that started. It grows on you, Elsa.

ELSA: Which is just about the only growing it seems to allow. For the rest, it's as merciless as the religion they preach around here. Looking out of the car window this afternoon I think I finally understood a few things about you Afrikaners . . . and it left me feeling just a little uneasy.

HELEN: You include me in all you're saying.

ELSA: Yes. You might not go to church anymore, but you're still an Afrikaner, Miss Helen. You were in there with them, singing hymns every Sunday, for a long, long time. Bit of a renegade now, I admit, but you're still one at heart.

HELEN: And that heart is merciless?

Pause.

ELSA: No. That you aren't. A lot of other things maybe, but certainly not that. Sorry, sorry, sorry . . .

HELEN: You're still very cross, aren't you? And something else as well. There's a new sound in your voice. One I haven't heard before.

ELSA: What do you mean?

HELEN: Like the way you talked about that woman on the road. Almost as if you didn't care, which I know isn't true.

ELSA: Of course I cared. I cared enough to stop and pick her up, to give her money and food. But I also don't want to fool myself. That was a sop to my conscience and nothing more. It wasn't a real contribution to her life and what she is up against. Anyway, what's the point in talking about her? She's most probably curling up in a stormwater drain at this moment—that's where she said she'd sleep if she didn't get a lift—and I feel better for a good wash.

HELEN: There it is again.

ELSA: Well, it's the truth.

HELEN: It was the way you said it.

ELSA: You're imagining things, Miss Helen. Come on, let's talk about something else. It's too soon to get serious. We've got enough time, and reasons, for that later on. What's been happening in the village? Give me the news. Your last letter didn't have much of that in it.

ELSA *gets into clean clothes.* MISS HELEN *starts to fold the discarded track suit.* ELSA *stops her.*
I can do that.

HELEN: I just wanted to help.

ELSA: And you can do that by making a nice pot of tea and giving me the village gossip.

MISS HELEN *goes into the living room. She takes cups and saucers, etc., from a sideboard and places them on the table.*

HELEN: I haven't got any gossip. Little Katrina is the only one who really visits me anymore, and all she wants to talk about these days is her baby. There's also Marius, of course, but he never gossips.

ELSA: He still comes snooping around, does he?

HELEN: Don't put it like that, Elsa. He's a very old friend.

ELSA: Good luck to him. I hope the friendship continues. It's just that *I* wouldn't want him for one. Sorry, Miss Helen, but I don't trust your old friend, and I have a strong feeling that Pastor Marius Byleveld feels the same way about me. So let's change the subject. Tell me about Katrina. What has she been up to?

HELEN: She's fine. And so is the baby. As prettily dressed these days as any white baby, thanks to the clothes you sent her. She's been very good to me, Elsa. Never passes my front door without dropping in for a little chat. Is always asking about you. I don't know what I would do without her. But I'm afraid Koos has started drinking again. And making all sorts of terrible threats about her and the baby. He still doesn't believe it's his child.

ELSA: Is he beating her?

HELEN: No. The warning you gave him last time seems to have put a stop to that.

ELSA: God, it makes me sick! Why doesn't she leave him?

HELEN: And then do what?

ELSA: Find somebody else! Somebody who will value her as a human being and take care of her and the child.

HELEN: She can't do that, Elsie. They're married.

ELSA: Oh, for God's sake, Helen. There's the Afrikaner in you speaking. There is nothing sacred about a marriage that abuses the woman! I'll have a talk to her tomorrow. Let's make sure we get a message to her to come around.

HELEN: Don't make things more difficult for her, Elsa.

ELSA: How much more difficult can "things" be than being married to a drunken bully? She *has* got a few rights, Miss Helen, and I just want to make sure she knows what they are. How old is she now?

HELEN: Seventeen, I think.

ELSA: At that age I was still at school dreaming about my future, and here she is with a baby and bruises. Quick, tell me something else.

HELEN: Let me see. . . . Good gracious me! Of course, yes! I have got important news. Old Getruida has got the whole village up in arms. Brace yourself, Elsa. She's applied for a license to open a liquor store.

ELSA: A what?

HELEN: A liquor store. Alcoholic beverages.

ELSA: Booze in New Bethesda?

HELEN: If you want to put it that bluntly . . . yes.

ELSA: Now that *is* headline material. Good for old Gerty. I always knew she liked her sundowner, but I never thought she'd have the spunk to go that far.

HELEN: Don't joke about it, Elsie. It's a very serious matter. The village is very upset.

ELSA: Headed, no doubt, by your old friend Pastor Marius Byleveld.

HELEN: That's right. I understand that his last sermon was all about the evils of alcohol and how it's ruining the health and lives of our Coloured folk. Getruida says he's taking unfair advantage of the pulpit and that the Coloureds get it anyway from Graaff-Reinet.

ELSA: Then tell her to demand a turn.

HELEN: At what?

ELSA: The pulpit. Tell her to demand her right to get up there and put her case . . . and remind her before she does that the first miracle was water into wine.

HELEN *(Trying not to laugh)*: You're terrible, Elsie! Old Getruida in the pulpit!

ELSA: And you're an old hypocrite, Miss Helen. You love it when I make fun of the Church.

HELEN: No, I don't. I was laughing at Gerty, not the Church. And you have no right to make me laugh. It's a very serious matter.

ELSA: Of course it is! Which is why I want to know who you think is worse: the dominee deciding what is right and wrong for the Coloured folk or old Getruida exploiting their misery?

HELEN: I'm afraid it's even more complicated than that, Elsa. Marius *is* only thinking about what's best for them, but on the other hand Getruida has offered to donate part of her profits to their school building fund. And what about Koos? Wouldn't it make things even worse for Katrina if he had a local supply?

ELSA: They are two separate issues, Miss Helen. You don't punish a whole community because one man can't control his drinking. Which raises yet another point: has anybody bothered to ask the Coloured people what they think about it all?

HELEN: Are we going to have that argument again?

ELSA: I'm not trying to start an argument. But it does seem to me right and proper that if you're going to make decisions which affect other people, you should find out what those people think.

HELEN: It is the same argument. You know they don't do that here.

ELSA: Well, it's about time they started. I don't make decisions affecting the pupils at school without giving them a chance to say something. And they're children! We're talking about adult men and women in the year 1974.

HELEN: Those attitudes might be all right in Cape Town, Elsa, but you should know by now that the valley has got its own way of doing things.

ELSA: Well, it can't cut itself off from the twentieth century forever. Honestly, coming here is like stepping into the middle of a Chekhov play. While the rest of the world is hoping the bomb won't drop today, you people are arguing about who owns the cherry orchard. Your little world is not as safe as you would like to believe, Helen. If you think it's going to be left alone to stagnate in the nineteenth century while the rest of us hold our breath hoping we'll reach the end of the twentieth, you're in for one hell of a surprise. And it will start with your Coloured folk. They're not fools. They also read newspapers, you know. And if you don't believe me, try talking about something other than the weather and her baby next time Katrina comes around. You'll be surprised at what's going on inside that little head. As for you Helen! Sometimes the contradictions in you make me want to scream. Why do you always stand up and defend this bunch of bigots? Look at the way they've treated you.

HELEN *(Getting nervous)*: They leave me alone now.

ELSA: That is not what you said in your last letter!

HELEN: My last letter?

ELSA: Yes.

Pause. HELEN *has tensed.*

Are you saying you don't remember it, Helen?

HELEN: No . . . I remember it.

ELSA: And what you said in it?

HELEN *(Trying to escape)*: Please, little Elsie! Not now. Let's talk about it later. I'm still all flustered with you arriving so unexpectedly. Give me a chance to collect my wits together. Please? And while I'm doing that, I'll make that pot of tea you asked for.

MISS HELEN *exits into the kitchen.* ELSA *takes stock of the room. Not an idle examination; rather, she is trying to see it objectively, trying to understand something. She spends a few seconds at the window, staring out at the statues in the yard. She sees a cardboard box in a corner and opens it—handfuls of colored ceramic chips. She also discovers a not very successful attempt to hide an ugly burn mark on one of the walls.* MISS HELEN *returns with tea and biscuits.*

ELSA: What happened here?

HELEN: Oh, don't worry about that. I'll get Koos or somebody to put a coat of paint over it.

ELSA: But what happened?

HELEN: One of the lamps started smoking badly when I was out of the room.

ELSA: And new curtains.

HELEN: Yes. I got tired of the old ones. I found a few Marie biscuits in the pantry. Will you be mother?

Light is starting to fade in the room. ELSA *pours the tea, dividing her attention between that and studying the older woman.* MISS HELEN *tries to hide her unease.* Do I get a turn now to ask for news?

ELSA: No.

HELEN: Why not?

ELSA: I haven't come up here to talk about myself.

HELEN: That's not fair!

ELSA: It's boring.

HELEN: Not to me. Come on Elsie, fair is fair. You asked me for the village gossip and I did my best. Now it's your turn.

ELSA: What do you want to know?

HELEN: Everything you would have told me about in your letters if you had kept your promise and written them.

ELSA: Good and bad news?

HELEN: I said everything . . . but try to make the good a little bit more than the bad.

ELSA: Right. The *Elsa Barlow Advertiser*! Hot off the presses! What do you want to start with? Financial, crime or sports page?

HELEN: The front-page headline.

ELSA: How's this? "Barlow to appear before School Board for possible disciplinary action."

HELEN: Not again!

ELSA: Yep.

HELEN: Oh dear! What was it this time?

ELSA: Wait for the story. "Elsa Barlow, a twenty-eight-year-old English-language teacher, is to appear before a Board of Enquiry of the Cape Town School Board. She faces the possibility of strict disciplinary action. The enquiry follows a number of complaints from the parents of pupils in Miss Barlow's Standard Nine class. It is alleged that in April this year Miss Barlow asked the class, as a homework exercise, to write a five-hundred-word letter to the State President on the subject of racial inequality. Miss Barlow teaches at a Coloured School."

HELEN: Is that true?

ELSA: Are you doubting the accuracy and veracity of the *Advertiser*?

HELEN: Elsie! Elsie! Sometimes I think you deliberately look for trouble.

ELSA: All I "deliberately look for," Miss Helen, are opportunities to make those young people in my classroom think for themselves.

HELEN: So what is going to happen?

ELSA: Depends on me, I suppose. If I appear before them contrite and apologetic, a stern reprimand. But if I behave the way I really feel, I suppose I could lose my job.

HELEN: Do you want my advice?

ELSA: No.

HELEN: Well, I'm going to give it to you all the same. Say you're sorry and that you won't do it again.

ELSA: Both of those are lies, Miss Helen.

HELEN: Only little white ones.

ELSA: God, I'd give anything to be able to walk in and tell that School Board exactly what I think of them and their educational system. But you're right, there are the pupils as well, and for as long as I'm in the classroom a little subversion is possible. Rebellion starts, Miss Helen, with just one man or woman standing up and saying, "No. Enough!" Albert Camus. French writer.

HELEN: You make me nervous when you talk like that.

ELSA: And you sound just like one of those parents. You know something? I think you're history's first reactionary-revolutionary. You're a double agent, Helen!

HELEN: Haven't you got any good news?

ELSA: Lots. I still don't smoke. I drink very moderately. I try to jog a few miles every morning.

HELEN: You're not saying anything about David.

ELSA: Turn to the lonely hearts column. There's a sad little paragraph: "Young lady seeks friendship with young man, etc., etc."

HELEN: You're talking in riddles. I was asking you about David.

ELSA: And I'm answering you. I've said nothing about him because there's nothing to say. It's over.

HELEN: You mean . . . you and David . . . ?

ELSA: Yes, that is exactly what I mean. It's finished. We don't see each other anymore.

HELEN: I knew there was something wrong from the moment you walked in.

ELSA: If you think this is me with something wrong, you should have been around two months ago. Your little Elsie was in a bad way. You were in line for an unexpected visit a lot earlier than this, Helen.

HELEN: You should have come.

ELSA: I nearly did. But your letters suggested that you weren't having such a good time either. If we'd got together at that point, we might have come up with a suicide pact.

HELEN: I don't think so.

ELSA: Joke, Miss Helen.

HELEN: Then don't joke about those things. Weren't you going to tell me?

ELSA: I'm trying to forget it, Helen! There's another reason why I didn't come up. It has left me with a profound sense of shame.

HELEN: Of what?

ELSA: Myself. The whole stupid mess.

HELEN: Mess?

ELSA: Yes, mess! Have you got a better word to describe a situation so rotten with lies and deceit that your only sense of yourself is one of disgust?

HELEN: And you were so happy when you told me about him on your last visit.

ELSA: God, that was more than just happiness, Miss Helen. It was like discovering the reason for being the person, the woman, I am for the first time in my life. And a little bit scary . . . realizing that another person could do so much to your life, to your sense of yourself. Even before it all went wrong, there were a couple of times when I wasn't so sure I liked it.

HELEN: But what happened? Was there a row about something?

ELSA *(Bitter little laugh):* Row? Oh, Helen! Yes, there were plenty of those. But they were incidental. There had to be some sort of noise, so we shouted at each other. We also cried. We did everything you're supposed to.

HELEN: All I know about him is what you told me. He sounded like such a sensitive and good man, well-read and intelligent. So right for you.

ELSA: He was all of that. *(A moment's hesitation. She is not certain about saying something. She decides to take the chance)* There's also something about him I didn't tell you. He's married. He has a devoted, loving wife—quite pretty in fact—and a child. A little girl. Shocked you?

HELEN: Yes. You should have told me, Elsie. I would have warned you.

ELSA: That's exactly why I didn't. I knew you would, but I was going to prove you wrong. Anyway, I didn't need any warnings. Anything you could have said to me, Helen, I'd said to myself from the very beginning . . . but I was going to prove myself wrong as well. What it all came down to finally was that there were two very different ideas about what was happening, and we discovered it too late. You see, I was in it for keeps, Helen. I knew that we were all going to get hurt, that somehow we would all end up being victims of the situation . . . but I also believed that when the time came to choose I would be the lucky winner, that he would leave his wife and child and go with me. Boy, was I wrong! Ding-dong, wrong-wrong, tolls Elsa's bell at the close of the day!

HELEN: Don't do that.

ELSA: Defense mechanism. It still hurts. I'm getting impatient for the time when I'll be able to laugh at it all. I mustn't make him sound like a complete bastard. He wasn't without a conscience. Far from it. If anything, it was too big. The end would have been a lot less messy if he'd known how to just walk away and close the door behind him. When finally the time for that did come, he sat around in pain and torment, crying—God, that was awful!—waiting for me to tell him to go back to his wife and child. Should have seen him, Helen. He came up with postures of despair that would have made Michelangelo jealous. I know it's all wrong to find another person's pain disgusting, but that is what eventually happened. The last time he crucified himself on the sofa in my living room I felt like vomiting. He told me just once too often how much he hated himself for hurting me.

HELEN: Elsie, my poor darling. Come here.

ELSA *(Taut):* I'm all right now. *(Pause)* Do you know what the really big word is, Helen? I had it all wrong. Like most people, I suppose I used to think it was "love." That's the big one all right, and it's quite an event when it comes along. But there's an even bigger one. Trust. And more dangerous. Because that's when you drop your defenses, lay yourself wide open, and if you've made a mistake, you're in big, big trouble. And it hurts like hell. Ever heard the story about the father giving his son his first lesson in business? *(MISS HELEN shakes her head)* I think it's meant to be a joke, so remember to laugh. He puts his little boy high up on something or other and says to him "Jump. Don't worry, I'll catch you." The child is nervous, of course, but Daddy keeps reassuring him: "I'll catch you." Eventually the little boy works up enough courage and does jump, and Daddy, of course, doesn't make a move to catch him. When the child has stopped crying—because he has hurt himself—the father says: "Your first lesson in business, my son. Don't trust anybody." *(Pause)* If you tell it with a Jewish accent, it's even funnier.

HELEN: I don't think it's funny.

ELSA: I think it's ugly. That little boy is going to think twice about jumping again, and at this moment the same goes for Elsa Barlow.

HELEN: Don't speak too soon, Elsie. Life has surprised me once or twice.

ELSA: I'm talking about trust, Miss Helen. I can see myself loving somebody else again. Not all that interested in it right at the moment, but there's an even chance that it will happen again. Doesn't seem as if we've got much choice in the matter anyway. But trusting?

HELEN: You can have the one without the other?

ELSA: Oh yes. That much I've learned. I went on loving David long after I realized I couldn't trust him anymore. That is why life is just a bit complicated at the moment. A little of that love is still hanging around.

HELEN: I've never really thought about it.

ELSA: Neither had I. It needs a betrayal to get you going.

HELEN: Then I suppose I've been lucky. I never had any important trusts to betray . . . until I met you. My marriage might have looked like that, but it was habit that kept Stefanus and me together. I was never . . . open? . . . to him. Was that the phrase you used?

ELSA: Wide open.

HELEN: That's it! It's a good one. I was never "wide open" to anyone. But with you all of that changed. So it's as simple as that. Trust. I've always tried to understand what made you, and being with you, so different from anything else in my life. But, of course, that's it. I trust you. That's why my little girl can come out and play. All the doors are wide open!

ELSA *(Breaking the mood):* So there, Miss Helen. You asked for the news . . .

HELEN: I almost wish I hadn't.

Light has now faded. MISS HELEN fetches a box of matches and lights the candles on the table. The room floats up gently out of the gloom, the mirrors and glitter on the walls reflecting the candlelight. ELSA picks up one of the candles and walks around the room with it, and we see something of the magic to come.

ELSA: Still works, Miss Helen. In the car driving up I was wondering if the novelty would have worn off a little. But here it is again. You're a little wizard, you know. You make magic with your mirrors and glitter. "Never light a candle carelessly, and be sure you know what you're doing when you blow one out!" Remember saying that?

HELEN: To myself, yes. Many times.

ELSA: And to me . . . after you had stopped laughing at the expression on my face when you lit them for the first time. "Light is a miracle, Miss Barlow, which even the most ordinary human being can make happen." We had just had our first pot of tea together. Maybe I do take it all just a little for granted now. But that first time . . . I wish I could make you realize what it's like to be walking down a dusty, deserted little street in a Godforsaken village in the middle of the Karoo, bored to death by the heat and flies and silence, and then to be stopped in your tracks—and I mean stopped!—by all of that out there. And then, having barely recovered from that, to come inside and find *this*! Believe me Helen, when I saw your "Mecca" for the first time, I just stood there and gaped. "What in God's name am I looking at? Camels and pyramids? Not three, but dozens of Wise Men? Owls with old motorcar headlights for eyes? Peacocks with more color and glitter than the real birds? Heat stroke? Am I hallucinating?" And then you! Standing next to a mosque made out of beer bottles and staring back at me like one of your owls! *(A good laugh at the memory)* She's mad. No question about it. Everything they've told me about her is true. A genuine Karoo nutcase. *(Walking carefully around* MISS HELEN *in a mock attitude of wary and suspicious examination)* Doesn't look dangerous, though. Wait . . . she's smiling! Be careful, Barlow! Could be a trick. They didn't say she was violent, though. Just mad. Mad as a hatter. Go on. Take a chance. Say hello and see what happens. "Hello!"

Both women laugh.

HELEN: You're exaggerating. It wasn't like that at all.

ELSA: Yes, it was.

HELEN: And I'm saying it wasn't. To start with, it wasn't the mosque. I was repairing a mermaid.

ELSA: I forgot the mermaids!

HELEN *(Serenely certain)*: And I was the one who spoke first. I asked you to point out the direction to Mecca. You made a mistake, and so I corrected you. Then I invited you into the yard, showed you around, after which we came into the house for that pot of tea.

ELSA: That is precisely what I mean! Who would ever believe it? That you found yourself being asked to point out the direction to Mecca—not London, or New York, or Paris, but Mecca—in the middle of the Karoo by a little lady no bigger than a bird surrounded by camels and owls . . . and mermaids! . . . made of cement? Who in their right mind is going to believe that? And then this *(The room)*, your little miracle of light and color. (MISS HELEN *is smiling with suppressed pride and pleasure)* You were proud of yourself, weren't you? Come on, admit it.

HELEN *(Trying hard to contain her emotion)*: Yes, I admit I was a little proud.

ELSA: Miss Helen, just a little?

HELEN *(She can't hold back any longer):* All right, then, no! Not just a little. Oh, most definitely not. I was prouder of myself that day than I had ever been in my life. Nobody before you, or since, has done that to me. I was tingling all over with excitement as we walked around the yard looking at the statues. All those years of working on my Mecca had at last been vindicated. I've got a silly little confession to make about that first meeting. When we came inside and were sitting in here talking and drinking tea and the light started to fade and it became time to light a candle . . . I suddenly realized I was beginning to feel shy, more shy than I had even been with Stefanus on my wedding night. It got so bad I was half-wishing you would stand up and say it was time to go! You see, when I lit the candles you were finally going to see all of me. I don't mean my face, or the clothes I was wearing—you had already seen all of that out in the yard—I mean the *real* me, because that is what this room is . . . and I desperately, oh so desperately, wanted you to like what you saw. By the time we met I had got used to rude eyes staring at me and my work, dismissing both of them as ugly. I'd lived with those eyes for fifteen years, and they didn't bother me anymore. Yours were different. In just the little time we had already been together I had ended up feeling. . . . No, more than that: I *knew* I could trust them. There's our big word again, Elsie! I was so nervous I didn't know what we were talking about anymore while I sat here trying to find enough courage to get a box of matches and light the candles. But eventually I did and you . . . you looked around the room and laughed with delight! You liked what you saw! This is the best of me, Elsa. This is what I really am. Forget everything else. Nothing, not even my name or my face, is me as much as those Wise Men and their camels traveling to the East, or the light and glitter in this room. The mermaids, the wise old owls, the gorgeous peacocks . . . all of them are *me.* And I had delighted you!

Dear God. If you only knew what you did for my life that day. How much courage, how much faith in it you gave me. Because all those years of being laughed at and thought a mad old woman had taken their toll, Elsie. When you walked into my life that afternoon I hadn't been able to work or make anything for nearly a year . . . and I was beginning to think I wouldn't ever again, that I had reached the end. The only reason I've got for being alive is my Mecca. Without that I'm . . . nothing . . . a useless old woman getting on everybody's nerves . . . and that is exactly what I had started to feel like. You revived my life.

I didn't sleep that night after you left. My Mecca was a long way from being finished! All the things I still had to do, all the statues I still had to make, came crowding in on me when I went to bed. I thought my head was going to burst! I've never been so impatient with darkness all my life. I sat up in bed all night waiting for the dawn to come so that I could start working again, and then just go on working and working.

ELSA: And you certainly did that, Miss Helen. On my next trip you proudly introduced me to a very stern Buddha, remember? The cement was still wet.

HELEN: That's quite right. That was my next one.

ELSA: Then came the Easter Island head, the one with the topknot.

HELEN: Correct.

ELSA: And you still haven't explained to me what it's doing in Mecca—and, for that matter, wise old owls and mermaids as well.

HELEN: My Mecca has got a logic of its own, Elsa. Even I don't properly understand it.

ELSA: And then my favorite! That strange creature, half-cock, half-man, on the point of dropping his trousers. Really Helen!

HELEN: That one is pure imagination. I don't know where it comes from. And I've told you before, he's not dropping his trousers, he's pulling them up.

ELSA: And I remain unconvinced. Take another good look at the expression on his face. That's anticipation, not satisfaction. Any surprises this time?

Pause.

HELEN: This time?

ELSA: Yes.

HELEN: No. There aren't any surprises this time.

ELSA: Work in progress?

HELEN: Not at the moment. I haven't managed to get started on anything since you were last here.

ELSA: What happened to the moon mosaic? Remember? Against the back wall! You were going to use those ceramic chips I brought you.

HELEN: They're safe. There in the corner.

ELSA: Yes, I saw them . . . in exactly the same spot where I left them three months ago. It sounded such a wonderful idea, Helen. You were so excited when you told me about it.

HELEN: And I still am. I've still got it.

ELSA: So what are you waiting for? Roll up your sleeves and get on with it.

HELEN: It's not as simple as that, Elsie. You see . . . that's the trouble. It's still only just an *idea* I'm *thinking* about. I can't see it clearly enough yet to start work on it. I've told you before, Elsie, I have to *see* them very clearly first. They've got to come to me inside like pictures. And if they don't, well, all I can do is wait . . . and hope that they will. I wish I knew how to make it happen, but I don't. I don't know where the pictures come from. I can't force myself to see something that isn't there. I've tried to do that once or twice in the past when I was desperate, but the work always ended up a lifeless, shapeless mess. If they don't come, all I can do is wait . . . which is what I'm doing. (*She is revealing a lot of inner agitation*)

ELSA (*Carefully*): I'm listening, Miss Helen. Go on.

HELEN: I try to be patient with myself, but it's hard. There isn't all that much time left . . . and then my eyes . . . and my hands . . . they're not what they used to be. But the worst thing of all is . . . suppose that I'm waiting for nothing, that there won't be any more pictures inside ever again, that this time I *have* reached the end? Oh God, no! Please no. Anything but that. You do understand, don't you, Elsie?

ELSA: I think I do. (*She speaks quietly. It is not going to be easy*) Come and sit down here with me, Helen. (MISS HELEN *does so, but apprehensively*) It's time to talk about your last letter, Helen.

HELEN: Do we have to do that now? Can't it wait?

ELSA: No.

HELEN: Please.

ELSA: Sorry, Helen, but we've only got tonight.

HELEN: Then don't spoil it!

ELSA: Helen . . . that letter is the reason for me being here. You do realize that, don't you?

HELEN: Yes. I guessed that was the reason for your visit. But you must make allowances, little Elsie. I wasn't feeling very well when I wrote it.

ELSA: That much is obvious.

HELEN: But I've cheered up ever so much since then. Truly. And now with your visit . . . I just know everything is going to be all right again. I was very depressed you see. I wrote it in a bad depression. But I regretted posting it the moment after I had dropped it into the letter box. I even thought about asking the postmaster if I could have it back.

ELSA: Why didn't you? *(Pause)* Or send me a telegram: "Ignore last letter. Feeling much better." Six words. That would have done it.

HELEN: I didn't think of that.

ELSA: We're wasting precious time. You wrote it, posted it, and I received it.

HELEN: So can't we now, please, just forget it?

ELSA *(Disbelief)*: Miss Helen, do you remember what you said in it?

HELEN: Vaguely.

ELSA: That's not good enough. *(She goes to the bedroom alcove and fetches the letter from her briefcase)*

HELEN: What are you going to do?

ELSA: Read it.

HELEN: No! I don't want to hear it.

ELSA: You already have, Miss Helen. You wrote it.

HELEN: But I don't want to talk about it.

ELSA: Yes, you must.

HELEN: Don't bully me, Elsa! You know I don't know how to fight back. Please . . . not tonight. Can't we—

ELSA: No, we can't. For God's sake, Helen! We've only got tonight and maybe a little of tomorrow to talk.

HELEN: But you mustn't take it seriously.

ELSA: Too late, Helen. I already have. I've driven eight hundred miles without a break because of this. And don't lie to me. You meant every word of it. *(Pause)* I'm not trying to punish you for writing it. I've come because I want to try and help. *(She sits down at the table, pulls the candle closer and reads. She struggles a little to decipher words. The handwriting is obviously bad)*

My very own and dearest little Elsie,

Have you finally also deserted me? This is my fourth letter to you and still no reply. Have I done something wrong? This must surely be the darkest night of my soul. I thought I had lived through that fifteen years ago, but I was wrong. This is worse. Infinitely worse. I had nothing to lose that night. Nothing in my life was precious or worth holding on to. Now there is so much and I am losing it all . . . you, the house, my work, my Mecca. I can't fight them alone, little Elsie. I need you. Don't you care about me anymore? It is only through your eyes that I now see my Mecca. I need you, Elsie. My eyesight is so bad that I can barely see the words I am writing. And my hands can hardly hold the pen. Help me, little Elsie. Everything is ending and I am alone in the dark. There is no light left. I would rather do away with myself than carry on like this.

Your ever-loving and anguished
Helen.

(She carefully folds up the letter and puts it back in the envelope) What's all that about losing your house. Who's trying to get you out?

HELEN: I exaggerated a little. They're not really being nasty about it.

ELSA: Who?

HELEN: The Church Council. They say it's for my own good. And I do understand what they mean, it's just that—

ELSA: Slowly, Miss Helen, slowly. I still don't know what you're talking about. Start from the beginning. What has the Church Council got to do with you and the house? I thought it was yours.

HELEN: It is.

ELSA: So?

HELEN: It's not the house, Elsa. It's me. They discussed me . . . my situation . . . at one of their meetings.

ELSA *(Disbelief and anger):* They *what?*

HELEN: That's how Marius put it. He . . . he said they were worried about me living here alone.

ELSA: *They* are worried about *you?*

HELEN: Yes. It's my health they are worried about.

ELSA *(Shaking her head):* When it comes to hypocrisy—and blatant hypocrisy at that—you Afrikaners are in a class by yourselves. So tell me, did they also discuss Gertruida's situation? And what about Mrs. van Heerden down at the other end of the village? They're about the same age as you and they also live alone.

HELEN: That's what I said. But Marius said it's different with them.

ELSA: In what way?

HELEN: Well, you see, because of my hands and everything else, they don't believe I can look after myself so well anymore.

ELSA: Are they right?

HELEN: No! I'm quite capable of looking after myself.

ELSA: And where are you supposed to go if you leave the village? To a niece, four times removed, in Durban, whom you've only seen a couple of times in your life?

MISS HELEN *goes to a little table at the back and fetches a form which she hands to* ELSA.

(Reading) "Sunshine Home for the Aged." I see. So it's like that, is it? That's the lovely old house on the left when you come into Graaff-Reinet, next to the church. In fact, it's run by the church, isn't it?

HELEN: Yes.

ELSA: That figures. It's got a beautiful garden, Miss Helen. Whenever I drive past on my way up here there are always a few old folk in their "twilight years" sitting around enjoying the sunshine. It's well named. It all looks very restful. So that's what they want to do with you. This is not your handwriting.

HELEN: No. Marius filled it in for me.

ELSA: Very considerate of him.

HELEN: He's coming to fetch it tonight.

ELSA: For an old friend he sounds a little overeager to have you on your way, Miss Helen.

HELEN: It's just that they've got a vacancy at the moment. They're usually completely full. There's a long waiting list. But I haven't signed it yet!

ELSA *studies* MISS HELEN *in silence for a few moments.*

ELSA: How bad are your hands? Be honest with me.

HELEN: They're not *that* bad. I exaggerated a little in my letter.

ELSA: You could still work with them if you wanted to?

HELEN: Yes.

ELSA: Is there anything you can't do?

HELEN: I can do anything I want to, Elsie . . . if I make the effort.

ELSA: Let me see them.

HELEN: Please don't. I'm ashamed of them.

ELSA: Come on.

MISS HELEN *holds out her hands.* ELSA *examines them.* And these scabs?

HELEN: They're nothing. A little accident at the stove. I was making prickly-pear syrup for you.

ELSA: There seem to have been a lot of little accidents lately. Better be more careful.

HELEN: I will. I definitely will.

ELSA: Pain?

HELEN: Just a little. *(While* ELSA *studies her hands)* Just that one letter after your last visit, saying you had arrived back safely and would be writing again soon, and then nothing. Three months.

ELSA: I did write, Helen. Two very long letters.

HELEN: I never got them.

ELSA: Because I never posted them.

HELEN: Elsie! Why? They would have made all the difference in the world.

ELSA *(Shaking her head):* No. Muddled, confused, full of self-pity. Knowing now what you were trying to deal with here, they were hardly what you needed in your life.

HELEN: You're very wrong. Anything would have been better than nothing.

ELSA: No, Helen. Believe me nothing was better than those two letters. I've still got them at home. I read them now whenever I need to count my blessings. They remind me of the mess I was in.

HELEN: That's why I feel so bad now about the letter I wrote you. My problems seem so insignificant compared with yours.

ELSA: Don't let's start that, Helen. Sorting our problem priorities isn't going to get us anywhere. In any case, mine are over and done with . . . which leaves us with you. So what are you going to do?

MISS HELEN *doesn't answer.* ELSA *is beginning to lose patience.*
Come *on,* Helen! If I hadn't turned up tonight, what were you going to say to Dominee Marius Byleveld when he came around?

HELEN: I was going to ask him to give me a little more time to think about it.

ELSA: You were going to *ask* him for it, not *tell* him you *wanted* it? And *do* you need more time to think about it? I thought you knew what you wanted?

HELEN: Of course I do.

ELSA: Then tell me again. And say it simply. I need to hear it.

HELEN: You know I can't leave here, Elsa!

ELSA: For a moment I wasn't so sure. So then what's the problem? When he comes around tonight hand this back to him . . . unsigned . . . and say no. Thank him for his trouble but tell him you are perfectly happy where you are and quite capable of looking after yourself. (MISS HELEN *hesitates. A sense of increasing emotional confusion and uncertainty)* Helen, you have just said that is what you want.

HELEN: I know. It's just that Marius is such a persuasive talker.

ELSA: Then talk back!

HELEN: I'm not very good at that. Won't you help me, little Elsie, please, and speak to him as well? You are so much better at arguing than me.

ELSA: No, I won't! And for God's sake stop behaving like a naughty child who's been called to the principal's office. I'm sorry, but the more I hear about your Marius, the worse it gets. If you want my advice, you'll keep the two of us well away from each other. I *won't* argue with him on your behalf because there is nothing to argue about. This is not his house, and it most certainly is not his life that is being discussed at Church Council meetings. Who the hell do they think they are? Sitting around a table deciding what is going to happen to you!

HELEN: Marius did say that they were trying to think of what was best for me.

ELSA: No, they're not! God knows what they're thinking about, but it's certainly not that. Dumping you with a lot of old people who've hung on for too long and nobody wants around anymore? You're still living your life, Helen, not drooling it away. The only legal way they can get you out of this house is by having you certified. *(Awkward silence)* We all know you're as mad as a hatter, but it's not quite that bad. *(Another pause)* One little question though, Miss Helen. You haven't been going around talking about doing away with yourself to anyone have you?

HELEN: I told you, Katrina is the only person I really see anymore.

ELSA: And Marius. Don't forget him. Anyway it doesn't matter who it is. All it needs is one person to be able to stand up and testify that they heard you say it.

HELEN: Well, I haven't.

ELSA: Because it would make life a lot easier for them if they ever did try to do something. So no more of that. Okay? Did you hear me, Helen?

HELEN: Yes, I heard you.

ELSA: And while you're about it, add me to your list. I don't want to hear or read any more about it either.

HELEN: I heard you, Elsie! Why do you keep on about it?

ELSA: Because talk like that could be grounds for forcibly committing someone to a "Sunshine Home for the Aged"! I'm sorry, Helen, but what do you expect me to do? Pretend you never said it? Is that what you would have done if our situations had been reversed? If in the middle of my mess I had threatened to do that? God knows, I came near to feeling like it a couple of times. I had a small taste of how bloody pointless everything can seem to be. But if I can hang on, then you most certainly can't throw in the towel—not after all the rounds you've already won against them. So when the dominee comes around, you're going to put on a brave front. Let's get him and his stupid ideas about an old-age home right out of your life. Because you're going to say no, remember? Be as polite and civil as you like—we'll offer him tea and biscuits and discuss the weather and the evils of alcohol—but when the time comes, you're going to thank him for all his trouble and consideration and then hand this back to him with a firm "No, thank you." *(Another idea)* And just to make quite sure he gets the message, you can also mention your trip into Graaff-Reinet next week to see a doctor and an optician.

HELEN: What do you mean?

ELSA: Exactly what I said: appointments with a doctor and an optician.

HELEN: But I haven't got any.

ELSA: You will on Monday. Before I leave tomorrow I'm going to ask Getruida to take you into Graaff-Reinet next week. And this time you're going to go. There must be something they can do about your hands, even if it's just to ease the pain. And a little "regmaker" for your depressions. (MISS HELEN *wants to say something*) No arguments! And to hell with your vanity as well. We all know you think you're the prettiest thing in the village, but if you need glasses, you're going to wear them. I'll make the appointments myself and phone through after you've been in to find out what the verdict is. I'm not trying to be funny, Helen. You've got to prove to the village that you are quite capable of looking after yourself. It's the only way to shut them up.

HELEN: You're going too fast for me, Elsa. You're not allowing me to say anything.

ELSA: That's quite right. How many times in the past have we sat down and tried to talk about all of this? And every time the same story: "I'll think about it, Elsa." Your thinking has got us nowhere, Helen. This time you're just going to agree . . . and that includes letting Katrina come in a couple of times each week to do the house.

HELEN: There's nothing for her to do. I can manage by myself.

ELSA: No, you can't. (*She runs her finger over a piece of furniture and holds it up for* MISS HELEN *to see the dust*)

HELEN: Everything would have been spotless if I had known you were coming.

ELSA: It's got to be spotless all the time! To hell with *my* visits and holidays. I don't live here. You do. I'm concerned with *your* life, Helen. And I'm also not blind, you know. I saw you struggling with that large kettle. Yes, let's talk about that. When did you last boil up enough water for a decent bath? Come on, Helen. Can't you remember? Some time ago, right? Is it because of personal neglect that you've stopped caring about yourself or because you aren't able to? Answer me.

HELEN: I can't listen to you anymore, Elsa. *(She makes a move to leave the room)*

ELSA: Don't do that to me Helen! If you leave this room I'm getting into my car and driving back to Cape Town. You wrote that letter. I haven't made it up. All I'm trying to do is deal with it.

HELEN: No, you're not.

ELSA: Then I give up. What in God's name have we been talking about?

HELEN: A pair of spectacles and medicine for my arthritis and Katrina dusting the house—

ELSA: Do you want me to read it again?

HELEN *(Ignoring the interruption):* You're treating that letter like a shopping list. That isn't what I was writing about.

ELSA: Then what was it?

HELEN: Darkness, Elsa! Darkness! *(She speaks with an emotional intensity and authority which forces* ELSA *to listen in silence)* The Darkness that nearly smothered my life in here one night fifteen years ago. The same Darkness that used to come pouring down the chimney and into the room at night when I was a little girl and frighten me. If you still don't know what I'm talking about, blow out the candles!

But those were easy Darknesses to deal with. The one I'm talking about now is much worse. It's inside me, Elsa . . . it's got inside me at last and I can't light candles there. *(Pause)*

I never knew that could happen. I thought I was safe. I had grown up and I had all the candles I wanted. That is all that little girl could think about when she lay there in bed, trying to make her prayers last as long as she could because she was terrified of the moment when her mother would bend down and kiss her and take away the candle. One day she would have her very own! That was the promise: that one day when I was big enough, she would leave one at my bedside for me to light as often as I wanted. That's all that "getting big" ever meant to me—my very own candle at my bedside.

Such brave little lights! And they taught the little girl how to be that. When she saw one burning in the middle of the night, she knew what courage was. All my life they have helped me to find courage . . . until now.

I'm frightened, Elsie, more frightened than that little girl ever was. There's no "getting big" left to wait for, no prayers to say until that happens . . . and the candles don't help anymore. That is what I was trying to tell you. I'm frightened. And Marius can see it. He's no fool, Elsa. He knows that his moment has finally come.

ELSA: What moment?

HELEN: He's been waiting a long time for me to reach the end of my Mecca. I thought I had cheated him out of it, that that moment would never come.

All those years when I was working away, when it was slowly taking shape, he was there as well . . . standing in the distance, watching and waiting.

I used to peep at him through the curtains. He'd come walking past, then stop, stand there at the gate with his hands behind his back and stare at my Wise Men. And even though he didn't show anything, I know he didn't like what he saw. I used to sing when I was working. He heard me one day and came up and asked: "Are you really that happy, Helen?"

I laughed. Not at *him*, believe me not at him, but because I had a secret he would never understand. *(Pause)*

It's his turn to laugh now. But he won't, of course. He's not that sort of man. He'll be very gentle again . . . pull the curtains and close the shutters the way he did that night fifteen years ago . . . because nobody must stare into a house where there's been a death.

If my Mecca is finished, Elsa, then so is my life.

ELSA *is overwhelmed by a sense of helplessness and defeat.*

ELSA: I think I've had it. It's too much for one day. That woman on the road and now you. I honestly don't know how to handle it. In fact, at this moment, I don't think I know anything. I don't know what it means to be walking eighty miles to Cradock with your baby on your back. I don't know whether your Mecca is finished or not. And all I know about Darkness is that that is when you put on the lights. Jesus! I wouldn't mind somebody coming along and telling me what it does all mean.

So where does all of that leave us, Miss Helen? I'm lost. What are you going to do when he comes? *(No answer)* Ask him—please—for more time? One thing I can tell you right now is that there's no point to that. If you don't say no tonight, you won't ever, in which case you might as well sign that form and get it over and done with. *(A cruel, relentless tone in her voice)* There's no point in talking about anything until that's settled. So you better think about it, Helen. While you do that, I'll see what I can organize for supper.

She exits into the kitchen. A man's voice off: "Anybody at home?" MARIUS *appears in the doorway:*

MARIUS: Miss Helen! Alone in the dark? I didn't think anybody was home.

ELSA *appears from the kitchen.*

Ah, Miss Barlow!

END OF ACT ONE

ACT TWO

The same a few minutes later. MARIUS *and* ELSA *are now at the table with* MISS HELEN, *the center of attraction being a basket of vegetables which* MARIUS *has brought with him. He is about the same age as* MISS HELEN *and is neatly but casually dressed. He speaks with simple sincerity and charm.*

MARIUS (*Holding up a potato*): Feast your eyes on this, Miss Barlow! A genuine Sneeuberg potato! A pinch of salt and you've got a meal, and if you want to be extravagant, add a little butter and you have indeed got a feast. We had a farmer from the Gamtoos Valley up here last week, trying to sell potatoes to us! Can you believe it? Did you see him, Helen? He had his lorry parked in front of the Post Office. What's the English expression, Miss Barlow? Coals to—where?

ELSA: Coals to Newcastle.

MARIUS: That's it! Well in this case it was very near to being an insult as well. We pride ourselves in these parts on knowing what a potato really is. And here you have it. The "apple of the earth," as the French would say. But I don't imagine that poor man will come again. Shame! I ended up feeling very sorry for him. "Don't you people like potatoes?" he asked me. What could I say? I didn't have the heart to tell him he'd wasted his time driving all this distance, that *nobody* comes to Sneeuberg to sell potatoes! And then, to make me feel really bad, he insisted on giving me a small sack of them before he drove off. I don't think he sold enough to cover the cost of his petrol back home.

I also brought you a few beets and tomatoes. The beets have passed their best now, but if you pickle and bottle them, they'll be more than all right. Have you ever treated our young friend to a taste of that, Miss Helen? (*To* ELSA) It's one of our local specialities. One thing I can assure you ladies is that these vegetables are as fresh as you are ever likely to get. I dug them up myself this afternoon.

HELEN: It's very kind of you, Marius, but you really shouldn't have bothered.

MARIUS: It wasn't any bother at all. I've got more than enough for myself stored away in the pantry. Would have been a sin to leave them to rot in the ground when somebody else could use them. And at our age we need fresh vegetables, Helen. (*Wagging a finger at her*) Marie biscuits and tea are not a balanced diet. (*To* ELSA) In the old days Helen used to have a very fine vegetable garden of her own out there. But as you can see, the humble potato has been crowded out by other things. I don't think there's enough room left out there now to grow a radish. (*He turns back to the basket*) Yes, the Good Lord was very generous to us this past year. I don't really know that we deserve it, but our rains came just when we needed them. Not too much or too little. Believe me, young lady, we are well experienced in both those possibilities. Not so, Helen?

ELSA: The Karoo looked very dry and desolate to me as I drove through it this afternoon.

MARIUS: Dry it certainly is, but not desolate. It might appear that to a townsman's eye—as indeed it did to mine when I first came here!—but that is because we are already deep into our autumn. It will be a good few months before we see rain again.

ELSA: I've never thought of this world as having seasons . . . certainly not the soft ones. To me it has always been a landscape of extremes, too hot or too cold, too dry or else Miss Helen is writing to me about floods that have cut off the village from the outside world. It reminds me of something I once read where the desert was described as "God without mankind."

MARIUS: What an interesting thought: "God without mankind." I can't decide whether that's Catholic or Protestant. Would you know?

ELSA *(Shaking her head):* No.

MARIUS: Who wrote it?

ELSA: A French writer. Balzac. It sums up the way I feel about the Karoo. The Almighty hasn't exactly made mankind overwelcome here, has he? In fact, it almost looks as if he resented our presence. Sorry, Dominee, I don't mean to be blasphemous or ungenerous to your world, it's just that I'm used to a gentler one.

MARIUS: You judge it too harshly, Miss Barlow. It has got its gentle moments and moods as well . . . all the more precious because there are so few of them. We can't afford to take them for granted. As you can see, it feeds us. Can any man or woman ask for more than that from the little bit of earth he lives on?

ELSA: Do you think your Coloured folk feel the same way about things?

MARIUS: Why should it be any different for them?

ELSA: I was just wondering whether they had as many reasons to be as contented as you?

MARIUS: I was talking about simple gratitude, Miss Barlow. Wouldn't you say contentment is a more complicated state of mind? One that can very easily be disturbed. But grateful? Yes! Our Coloured folk also have every reason to be. Ask them. Ask little Katrina, who visits Miss Helen so faithfully, if she or her baby have ever wanted for food . . . even when Koos has spent all his wages on liquor. There are no hungry people, white or Coloured, in this village, Miss Barlow. Those of us who are more fortunate than others are well aware of the responsibilities that go with that good fortune. But I don't want to get into an argument. It is my world—and Helen's—and we can't expect an outsider to love or understand it as we do.

ELSA: I'll put these *(The vegetables)* away for you, Miss Helen.

MARIUS: Don't bother to unpack them now. I'll collect the basket tomorrow after church. *(Calling after* ELSA *as she leaves the room)* And there's no need to wash them. I've already done that. Just put them straight into the pot.

Exit ELSA.

I've got a feeling that, given half a chance, your young friend and myself *could* very easily find ourselves in an argument. I think Miss Barlow gets a little impatient with our old-fashioned ways and attitudes. But it's too late for us to change now. Right, Helen?

HELEN: Elsa and I have already had those arguments, Marius.

MARIUS: I hope you put up a good defense on our behalf.

HELEN: I tried my best.

MARIUS: And yet the two of you still remain good friends.

HELEN: Oh yes!

MARIUS: And so it should be. A true friendship should be able to accommodate a difference of opinion. You didn't mention anything about her coming up for a visit last time we talked.

HELEN: Because I didn't know. It's an unexpected visit.

MARIUS: Will she be staying long?

HELEN: Just tonight. She goes back tomorrow.

MARIUS: Good heavens! All this way for only one night. I hope nothing is wrong.

HELEN: No. She just decided on the spur of the moment to visit me. But she's got to go back because they're very busy at school. They're right in the middle of exams.

MARIUS: I see. May I sit down for a moment, Helen?

HELEN: Of course, Marius. Forgive me, I'm forgetting my manners.

MARIUS: I won't stay long. I must put down a few thoughts for tomorrow's sermon. And, thanks to you, I know what I want to say.

HELEN: Me?

MARIUS: Yes, you. *(Teasing her)* You are responsible . . .

HELEN: Oh dear!

MARIUS *(A little laugh):* Relax, Helen. I only said "thanks to you" because it came to me this afternoon while I was digging up your vegetables. I spent a lot of time, while I was out in the garden doing that, just leaning on my spade. My back is giving me a bit of trouble again and, to tell you the truth, I also felt lazy.

I wasn't thinking about anything in particular . . . just looking, you know, the way an old man does, looking around, recognizing once again and saying the names. Spitskop in the distance! Aasvoelkrans down at the other end of the valley. The poplars with their autumn foliage standing around as yellow and still as that candle flame!

And a lot of remembering.

As you know, Helen, I had deep and very painful wounds in my soul when I first came here. Wounds I thought would never heal. This was going to be where I finally escaped from life, turned by back on it and justified what was left of my existence by ministering to you people's simple needs. I was very wrong. I didn't escape life here, I discovered it, what it really means, the fullness and goodness of it. It's a deep and lasting regret that Aletta wasn't alive to share that discovery with me. Anyway, all of this was going on in my head when I realized I was hearing a small little voice, and the small little voice was saying, "Thank you." With every spadeful of earth that I turned when I went down on my knees to lift the potatoes out of the soil, there it was: "Thank you." It was mine! I was muttering away to myself the way we old folks are inclined to do when nobody is around. It was me saying, "Thank you."

That is what I want to do tomorrow, Helen. Give thanks, but in a way that I've never done before.

I know I've stood there in the pulpit many times telling all of you to do exactly that, but oh dear me, the cleverness and conceit in the soul of Marius Byleveld when he was doing that! I had an actor's vanity up there, Helen. I'm not saying I was a total hypocrite but, believe me, in those thanksgivings I was listening to my dominee's voice and its hoped-for eloquence every bit as much as to the true little voice inside my heart . . . the voice I heard so clearly this afternoon.

That's the voice that must speak tomorrow! And to do that I must find words as simple as the sky I was standing under this afternoon or the earth I was turning over with my spade. They have got no vanities and conceits. They are just "there." If the Almighty takes pity on us, the one gives us rain so that the other can in turn . . . give us this day our daily potato. *(A smile at this gentle little joke)* Am I making sense, Helen? Answer me truthfully.

HELEN: Yes, you are, Marius. And if all you do tomorrow is say what you have just said to me, it will be very moving and beautiful.

MARIUS *(Sincerely):* Truly, Helen? Do you really mean that?

HELEN: Every word of it.

MARIUS: Then I will try.

My twentieth anniversary comes up next month. Yes, that is how long I've been here. Twenty-one years ago, on May the sixteenth, the Good Lord called my Aletta to his side, and just over a year later, on June the eleventh, I gave my first sermon in New Bethesda. *(A little laugh at the memory)* What an occasion that was!

I don't know if I showed it, Helen, but let me confess now that I was more than just a little nervous when I went up into the pulpit and looked down at that stern and formidable array of faces. A very different proposition from the town and city congregations I had been preaching to up until then. When Miss de Klerk played the first bars of the hymn at the end of it, I heaved a very deep sigh of relief. None of you had fallen asleep! *(HELEN is shaking her head)* What's the matter?

HELEN: Young Miss de Klerk came later. Mrs. Niewoudt was still our organist when you gave your first service.

MARIUS: Are you sure?

HELEN: Yes. Mrs. Niewoudt also played at the reception we gave you afterwards in Mr. van Heerden's house. She played the piano and Sterling Retief sang.

MARIUS: You know something, I do believe you're right! Good heavens, Helen, your memory is better than mine.

HELEN: And you had no cause to be nervous. You were very impressive.

MARIUS *(A small pause as he remembers something else):* Yes, of course. You were in that congregation. Stefanus was at your side, as he was going to be every Sunday after that for . . . what? Another five years?

HELEN: Five years.

MARIUS: That was all a long time ago.

HELEN: More than a long time, Marius. It feels like another life.

ELSA *returns with a tray of tea and sandwiches.*

MARIUS: Ah, here comes your supper. I must be running along.

ELSA: Just a sandwich, Dominee. Neither of us is very hungry.

MARIUS: I'll drop by tomorrow night if that is all right with you, Helen.

ELSA: Won't you have a cup of tea with us? It's the least we can offer in return for all those lovely vegetables.

MARIUS: I don't want to intrude. Helen tells me you're here for just the night, Miss Barlow. I'm sure you ladies have got things to talk about in private.

ELSA: We've already done quite a lot of that, haven't we, Helen? Please don't go because of me. I have some school work I must see to. I'll take my tea through to the other room.

HELEN: Don't go, Elsa!

ELSA: I told you I had papers to mark, Miss Helen. I'll just get on with that quietly while the two of you have a little chat.

HELEN: Please!

ELSA: All right then, if it will make you happier, I'll bring my work through and do it in here. ,

MARIUS: No. I've obviously come at an inconvenient time.

ELSA: Not at all, Dominee. Miss Helen was expecting you.

ELSA *fetches the application form for the old-age home and puts it down on the table. A moment between* ELSA *and* MARIUS. *He turns to* HELEN *for confirmation.*

HELEN: Yes, I was.

ELSA: How do you like your tea?

MARIUS: Very well, if you insist. Milk but no sugar, please.

ELSA *pours tea, then collects her briefcase from the bedroom alcove and settles down to work at a small table at the back of the room.*

You're quite certain you want to discuss this now, Helen?

HELEN: Yes, Marius.

MARIUS: It can wait until tomorrow.

HELEN: No, I'm ready.

MARIUS: Right. Just before we start talking, Helen, the good news is that I've spoken to Dominee Gericke in Graaff-Reinet again, and the room is definitely yours—that is, if you want it, of course. But they obviously can't have it standing empty indefinitely. As it is, he's already broken the rules by putting you at the top of the waiting list, but as a personal favor. He understands the circumstances. So the sooner we decide, one way or the other, the better. But I want you to know that I do realize how big a move it is for you. I want you to be quite certain and happy in your mind that you're doing the right thing. So don't think we've got to rush into it, start packing up immediately or anything like that. A decision must be made, one way or the other, but once you've done that, you can relax and take all the time you need.

MARIUS *takes spectacles, a little notebook, pen and pencil from a jacket pocket. The way he handles everything, carefully and precisely, reveals a meticulous and orderly mind. He opens the application form.* MISS HELEN *gives* ELSA *the first of many desperate and appealing looks.* ELSA, *engrossed in her work, apparently does not notice it.* MARIUS *puts his spectacles on.*

I know we went over this the last time, but there still are just a few questions. Yes . . . we put Stefanus's father's name down as Petrus Johannes Martins, but in the church registry it's down as Petrus *Jacobus.* (*He takes his spectacles off*) Which one is correct, Helen? Can you remember? You were so certain of Petrus Johannes last time.

HELEN: I still am. But what did you say the other one was?

MARIUS: Petrus Jacobus.

HELEN: Jacobus . . . Johannes. . . . No, maybe I'm not.

MARIUS: In that case what I think I will do is enter it as Petrus J. Martins. Just as well I checked. *(He puts his spectacles on again and turns back to the form)* And next . . . yes, the date of your confirmation. Have you been able to find the certificate?

HELEN: No, I haven't. I'm sorry, Marius. I did look, but I'm afraid my papers are all in a mess.

MARIUS *(Taking his spectacles off):* I've been through the church records, but I can't find anything that sheds any light on it. It's not all that important, of course, but it would have been nice to have had that date as well. *(He replaces his spectacles)* Let's see . . . what shall we do? You think you were about twelve?

HELEN: Something like that.

MARIUS: What I'll do is just pencil in 1920 and have one more look. I hate giving up on *that* one. But you surprise me, Helen—of all the dates to have forgotten.

That takes care of the form now. *(He consults his notebook)* Yes. Two little points from Dominee Gericke, after which you can relax and enjoy your supper. He asked me—and do believe me, Helen, he was just trying to be practical and helpful, nothing else—whether you had taken care of everything by way of a last will and testament, and obviously I said I didn't know.

HELEN: What do you mean, Marius?

MARIUS: That in the event of something happening, your house and possessions will be disposed of in the way that you want them to be. Have you done that?

HELEN: I've still got a copy of Stefanus's will. He left everything to me.

MARIUS: We're talking about you, Helen. Have you seen a lawyer?

HELEN: No, I . . . I've never thought of it.

MARIUS: Then it is just as well Gericke asked. Believe me, Helen, in my time as a minister I have seen so many bitterly unhappy situations because somebody neglected to look after that side of things. Families not talking to each other! Lawsuits over a few pieces of furniture! I really do think it is something you should see to. We're at an age now when anything can happen. I had mine revised only a few months ago. *(He glances at the notebook again)* And finally, he made the obvious suggestion that we arrange for you to visit the home as soon as possible. Just to meet the matron and other people there and to see your room. He's particularly anxious for you to see it so that you know what you need to bring on your side. He had a dreadful to-do a few months ago with a lady who tried to move a whole houseful of furniture into her little room. Don't get worried, though. There's plenty of space for personal possessions and a few of your . . . ornaments. That covers everything, I think. All that's left now is for you to sign it . . . provided you want to do that, of course. *(He places his fountain pen, in readiness, on the form)*

HELEN: Marius . . . please . . . please can I talk for a little bit now?

MARIUS: But of course, Helen.

HELEN: I've done a lot of thinking since we last spoke—

MARIUS: Good! We both agreed that was necessary. This is not a step to be taken lightly.

HELEN: Yes, I've done a lot of thinking, and I've worked out a plan.

MARIUS: For what, Helen?

HELEN: A plan to take care of everything.

MARIUS: Excellent!

HELEN: I'm going in to Graaff-Reinet next week, Marius, to see a doctor. I'm going to make the appointment on Monday, and I'll ask Getruida to drive me in.

MARIUS: You make it sound serious, Helen.

HELEN: No, it's just my arthritis. I'm going to get some medicine for it.

MARIUS: For a moment you had me worried. I thought the burns were possibly more serious than we had realized. But why not save yourself a few pennies and see Dr. Lubbe at the home? He looks after everybody there free of charge.

HELEN *(Hanging on):* And spectacles. I'm also going to make arrangements to see an optician and get a pair of spectacles.

MARIUS: Splendid, Helen! You certainly have been making plans.

HELEN: And, finally, I've decided to get Katrina to come in two or three times a week to help me with the house.

MARIUS: Katrina?

HELEN: Little Katrina. Koos Malgas's wife.

MARIUS: I know who you're talking about, Helen. It's just . . . oh dear! I'm sorry to be the one to tell you this, Helen, but I think you are going to lose your little Katrina.

HELEN: What do you mean, Marius?

MARIUS: Koos has asked the Divisional Council for a transfer to their Aberdeen depot, and I think he will get it.

HELEN: So?

MARIUS: I imagine Katrina and the baby will go with him.

HELEN: Katrina . . . ?

MARIUS: Will be leaving the village.

HELEN: No, it can't be.

MARIUS: It's the truth, Helen.

HELEN: But she's said nothing to me about it. She was in here just a few days ago and she didn't mention anything about leaving.

MARIUS: She most probably didn't think it important.

HELEN: How can you say that, Marius? Of course it is! She knows how much I depend on her. If Katrina goes, I'll be completely alone here except for you and the times when Elsa is visiting. *(She is becoming increasingly distressed)*

MARIUS: Come now, Helen! It's not as bad as that. I know Katrina is a sweet little soul and that you are very fond of her, as we all are, but don't exaggerate things. There are plenty of good women in the location who can come and give you a hand in here and help you pack up . . . if you decide to move. Tell you what I'll do: if you're worried about a stranger being in here with all your personal things, I'll lend you my faithful old Nonna. She's been looking after me for ten years now, and in that time I haven't missed a single thing. You could trust her with your life.

HELEN: I'm not talking about a servant, Marius.

MARIUS: I thought we were.

HELEN: Katrina is the only friend I've got left in the village.

MARIUS: That's a hard thing you're saying, Helen. All of us still like to think of ourselves as your friends.

HELEN: I wasn't including you, Marius. You're different. But as for the others . . . no. They've all become strangers to me. I might just as well not know their names. And they treat me as if I were a stranger to them as well.

MARIUS: You're being very unfair, Helen. They behave towards you in the way you apparently want them to, which is to leave you completely alone. Really, Helen! Strangers? Old Getruida, Sterling, Jerry, Boet, Mrs. van Heerden? You grew up in this village with all of them.

To be very frank, Helen, it's your manner which now keeps them at a distance. I don't think you realize how much you've changed over the years. You're not easily recognizable to others anymore as the person they knew fifteen years ago. And then your hobby, if I can call it that, hasn't really helped matters. This is not exactly the sort of room the village ladies are used to or would feel comfortable in having afternoon tea. As for all of that out there . . . the less said about it, the better.

HELEN: I don't harm or bother anyone, Marius!

MARIUS: And does anyone harm or bother you?

HELEN: Yes! Everybody is trying to force me to leave my home.

MARIUS: Nobody is *forcing* you, Helen! In Heaven's name, where do you get that idea from? If you sign this form, it must be of your own free will.

You're very agitated tonight, Helen. Has something happened to upset you? You were so reasonable about everything the last time we talked. You seemed to understand that the only motive on our side is to try and do what is best for you. And even then it's only in the way of advice. We can't *tell* you what to do. But if you want us to stop caring about what happens to you, we can try . . . though I don't know how our Christian consciences would allow us to do that.

HELEN: I don't believe the others care about me, Marius. All they want is to get rid of me. This village has also changed over the past fifteen years. I am not alone in that. I don't recognize it anymore as the simple, innocent world I grew up in.

MARIUS: If it's as bad as that, Helen, if you are now really that unhappy and lonely here, then I don't know why you have any doubts about leaving.

MISS HELEN's *emotional state has deteriorated steadily.* MARIUS's *fountain pen has ended up in her hand. She looks down at the application form. A few seconds' pause and then a desperate cry.*

HELEN: Why don't you stop me, Elsa! I'm going to sign it!

ELSA *(Abandoning all pretense of being absorbed in her work)*: Then go ahead and do it! Sign that fucking form. If that's what you want to do with your life, just get it over and done with, for God's sake!

MARIUS: Miss Barlow!

ELSA *(Ignoring him)*: What are you waiting for, Helen? You're wasting our time. It's late and we want to go to bed.

HELEN: But you said I mustn't sign it.

ELSA *(Brutally)*: I've changed my mind. Do it. Hurry up and dispose of your life so that we can get on with ours.

HELEN: Stop it, Elsa. Help me. Please help me.

ELSA: Sorry, Helen. I've had more woman-battering today than I can cope with. You can at least say no. That woman on the road couldn't. But if you haven't got the guts to do that, then too bad. I'm not going to do it for you.

HELEN: I tried.

ELSA: You call that trying? All it required was one word—no.

HELEN: Please believe me, Elsa . . . I was trying!

ELSA: No good, Helen. If that's your best, then maybe you will be better off in an old-age home.

MARIUS: Gently, Miss Barlow! In Heaven's name, gently! What's got into you?

ELSA: Exhaustion, Dominee. Very near total mental and emotional exhaustion, to the point where I want to scream. I've already done that once today, and right now I wouldn't mind doing it a second time. Yes, Helen, I've had it. Why were you "crying out to me in the dark"? To be an audience when you signed away your life? Is that why I'm here? Twelve hours of driving like a lunatic for that? God. What a farce! I might just as well have stayed in Cape Town.

MARIUS: Maybe it's a pity you didn't. I think I understand now why Helen is so agitated tonight. But unfortunately you are here, and if you've got anything to say to her, in Heaven's name be considerate of the state she is in. She needs help, not to be confused and terrified even more.

ELSA: Helen understands the way I feel. We *did* do a lot of talking before you came, Dominee.

MARIUS: I'm concerned with *her* feelings, Miss Barlow, not yours. And if by any chance you are as well, then try to show some respect for her age. Helen is a much older woman than you. You were shouting at her as if she were a child.

ELSA: Me, treating her like a child? Oh my God! You can stand there and accuse me of that after what I've just seen and heard from you?

MARIUS: I don't know what you're talking about.

ELSA: Then I'll tell you. You were doing everything in your power to bully and blackmail her into signing that. You were taking the grossest advantage of what you call her confusion and helplessness. I've been trying to tell her she's neither confused nor helpless.

MARIUS: So you know what is best for her.

ELSA: No, no, no! Wrong again, Dominee. I think *she* does. And if you had given her half a chance, she would have told you that that is not being dumped in an old-age home full of old people who have reached the end of their lives. She hasn't. You forget one thing: I didn't stop her signing that form. She stopped herself.

MARIUS: It was a moment of confusion.

ELSA: There you go again! Can't you leave that word alone? She is not confused!

MARIUS: When Helen and I discussed the matter a few days ago—

ELSA: Don't talk about her as if she were not here. She's right next to you, Dominee. Ask her, for God's sake . . . but this time give her a chance to answer.

MARIUS: Don't try to goad me with blasphemy, Miss Barlow. I'm beginning to think Helen needs as much protection from you as she does from herself.

ELSA: You still haven't asked her.

MARIUS: Because I have some sympathy for her condition. Look at her! She is in no condition now, thanks to you, to think clearly about anything.

ELSA: She was an emotional mess, thanks to you, before I opened my mouth. Don't expect me to believe you really care about her.

MARIUS (*Trying hard to control himself*): Miss Barlow, for the last time, what you do or don't believe is not of the remotest concern to me. Helen is, and my concern is that she gets a chance to live out what is left of her life as safely and happily as is humanly possible. I don't think that should include the danger of her being trapped in here when this house goes up in flames.

ELSA: What are you talking about?

MARIUS: Her accident. The night she knocked over the candle. (ELSA *is obviously at a loss*) You don't know about that? When was it, Helen? Four weeks ago? (*Pause.* MISS HELEN *doesn't respond*) I see. You didn't tell your friend about your narrow escape. I think I owe you an apology, Miss Barlow. I assumed you knew all about it.

ELSA: You owe me nothing. Just tell me what happened.

MARIUS: Yes, it was about four weeks ago. Helen knocked over a candle one night and set fire to the curtains. I try not to think about what would have happened if Sterling hadn't been looking out of his window at that moment and seen the flames. He rushed over, and just in time. She had stopped trying to put out the flames herself and was just standing staring at them. Even so she picked up a few bad burns on her hands. We had to get Sister Lategan out of bed to treat them. But it could have been a lot worse. (ELSA *is staring at* MISS HELEN) We don't want that on our consciences. So you see, Miss Barlow, our actions are not quite as pointless or as uncaring as they must have seemed to you.

ELSA: One of the lamps started smoking badly, and there was a little accident at the stove while you were making prickly-pear syrup for me! Oh boy! You certainly can do it, Helen. Don't let us ever again talk about trust between the two of us. Anyway, that settles it. I leave the two of you to fight it out . . . and may the best man win! I'm going to bed.

HELEN: Give me a chance to explain.

ELSA *(Ignoring the plea):* Good night. See you in the morning. I'll be making an early start, Helen.

HELEN: Don't abandon me, Elsa!

ELSA: You've abandoned yourself, Helen! Don't accuse me of that! You were the first to jump overboard. You haven't got enough faith in your life and your work to defend them against him. You lied to me . . . and such stupid bloody lies! What was the point? For that matter, what is the point of anything? Why *did* you make me come up? And then all our talk about trust? God, what a joke. You've certainly made me make a fool of myself again, but this time I don't think it's funny. In fact, I fucking well resent it.

HELEN: I didn't tell you because I was frightened you would agree with them.

ELSA: Don't say anything, Helen. You're making it worse. *(She studies* MISS HELEN *with cruel detachment)* But you might have a point there. Now that I've heard about your "little accident," I'm beginning to think they might be right. *(She indicates the room)* Corrugated iron and wooden walls? Give it half a chance and this would go up like a bonfire. *(She is hating herself, hurting herself every bit as much as she is hurting* MISS HELEN, *but is unable to stop)* And he says you were just standing and staring at it. What was that all about? Couldn't you make a run for it? They say that about terror—it makes you either run like hell or stand quite still. Sort of paralysis. Because it was just an accident, wasn't it, Helen? I mean, you weren't trying anything else, were you? Spite everybody by taking the house with you in a final blaze of glory! Dramatic! But it's a hell of a way to go. There are easier methods.

MISS HELEN *goes up to* ELSA *and stares at her.*

HELEN: Who are you?

The question devastates ELSA.

MARIUS: Ladies, ladies, enough! Stop now! I don't know what's going on between the two of you, but in Heaven's name stop it. I think Helen is aware of the dangers involved, Miss Barlow. And now that you do as well, can't we appeal to you to add your weight to ours and help persuade her to do the right thing? As I am sure you now realize, our only concern has been her well-being.

ELSA: You want my help.

MARIUS: Yes. If now at last you understand why we were trying to persuade Helen to move to the home, then on her behalf I am indeed appealing to you. We don't persecute harmless old ladies, Miss Barlow.

ELSA: And one that isn't so harmless?

MARIUS: Now what are you trying to say?

ELSA: That Helen isn't harmless, Dominee. Anything but that. That's why you people can't leave her alone.

MARIUS: For fifteen years we have done exactly that.

ELSA: Stoning her house and statues at night is not leaving her alone. That is not the way you treat a harmless old lady.

MARIUS: In Heaven's name! Are you going to drag that up? Those were children, Miss Barlow, and it was a long, long time ago. It has not happened again. Do you really mean to be that unfair? Can't you bring as much understanding as you claim to have of Helen's situation to a few other things as well? You've seen what is out there . . . *(He gestures at the window and* MISS HELEN's *"Mecca")* How else do you expect the simple children of the village to react to all that? It frightens them, Miss Barlow. I'm not joking! Think back to your impressionable years as a little girl. I know for a fact that all the children in the village believe this house is haunted and that ghosts walk around out there at night. Don't scoff at them. I'm sure there were monsters and evil spirits in your childhood as well. But as I said, that was all a long, long time ago. The moment we discovered what they were doing, we in turn did everything we could to put a stop to it. Mr. Lategan, the school principal, and I both lectured them in the sternest possible manner. Come now, Miss Barlow, have you learned nothing about us in the course of the few years that you've been visiting the village?

ELSA: A lot more than I would have liked to. Those children didn't arrive at their attitude to Helen on their own. I've also heard about the parents who frighten naughty children with stories about Miss Helen's "monsters." They got the courage to start throwing stones because of what they had heard their mothers and fathers saying. And as far as *they* are concerned, Helen is anything but a harmless old lady. God, what an irony. We spend our time talking about "poor, frightened Miss Helen," whereas it's all of you who are really frightened.

MARIUS: I can only repeat what I've already said to Helen: the people you are talking about grew up with her and have known her a lot longer than you.

ELSA: Not anymore. You also said that, remember? That stopped fifteen years ago when she didn't resign herself to being the meek, churchgoing little widow you all expected her to be. Instead she did something which small minds and small souls can never forgive . . . she dared to be different! Which does make you right about one thing, Dominee. Those statues out there *are* monsters. And they are that for the simple reason that they express Helen's freedom. Yes, I never thought it was a word you would like. I'm sure it ranks as a cardinal sin in these parts. A free woman! God forgive us!

Have you ever wondered why I come up here? It's a hell of a long drive, you know, if the only reason is sympathy for a lonely old lady whom nobody is talking to anymore. And it's also not for the scenery.

She challenges me, Dominee. She challenges me into an awareness of myself and my life, of my responsibilities to both that I never had until I met her. There's a hell of a lot of talk about freedom, and all sorts of it, in the world where I come from. But it's mostly talk, Dominee, easy talk and nothing else. Not with Helen. She's lived it. One dusty afternoon five years ago, when I came walking down that road hoping for nothing more than to get away from the flies that were driving me mad, I met the first truly free spirit I have ever known. *(She looks at* MISS HELEN*)* It is her betrayal of all of that tonight that has made me behave the way I have.

A pause. MARIUS *has been confronted with something he has never had to deal with before.*

MARIUS: You call that . . . that nightmare out there an expression of freedom?

ELSA: Yes. Scary, isn't it? What did you call it earlier? Her hobby? *(She laughs)* Oh no, Dominee. It's much more dangerous than that . . . and I think you know it.

MARIUS: In another age and time it might have been called idolatry.

ELSA: Did you hear that, Helen? *(To* MARIUS*)* You know what you've just said, don't you?

MARIUS *(Total conviction):* Oh yes . . . yes, indeed I do. I am also choosing my words very carefully, Miss Barlow.

When I first realized that it was my duty as a friend and a Christian to raise the question with Helen of a move to an old-age home, I decided I would do so on the basis of her physical well-being and safety and nothing else. Helen will tell you that that is all we have ever talked about. I came here tonight meaning once again to do only that. But you have raised other issues, chosen to talk about more than that . . . which forces me now to do so as well. Because there is a lot more than Helen's physical well-being that has worried me, Miss Barlow— and gravely so! Those "expressions of freedom" have crowded out more than just a few fresh vegetables. I do not take them lightly anymore.

I remember the first one very clearly, Helen. I made the mistake of smiling at it, dismissing it as an idle whim coming out of your loneliness. In fact, I think that is how you yourself described it to me, as something to pass away the time. I was very wrong, wasn't I? And very slow in realizing what was really happening. I only began to feel uneasy about it all that first Sunday you weren't in church.

The moment I stood up there in front of the congregation, I knew your place was empty. But even then, you see, I thought you were sick. After the service I hurried around here, but instead of being in bed there you were outside in the yard making yet another . . . *(At a loss for words)* I don't really know what to call them.

HELEN *(A small but calm voice. She is very still):* It was an owl, Marius. My first owl.

MARIUS: It couldn't have waited until after the service, Helen?

HELEN: Oh no! *(Quietly emphatic)* The picture had come to me in here the night before. I just had to go to work immediately while it was still fresh in my mind. They don't last long, Marius. After a little while it becomes very hard to remember clearly what you saw. I tried explaining to Elsa how it all works . . . but I don't suppose any of you will ever understand.

But don't ever think that missing church that Sunday was something I did lightly, Marius. You don't break the habit of a lifetime without realizing that that life will never quite be the same again. I was already dressed and ready! I had my Bible and hymnbook, I was on the point of leaving this room as I had done every Sunday for as long as I could remember . . . but I knew that if I did, I would never make that owl. . . . I think I also knew that if I didn't, that if I put aside my Bible and hymnbook, took off my hat and changed my dress and went to work. . . . Yes! That was my very first owl!

MARIUS: Helen, Helen! I grieve for you! You turned your back on your church, on your faith and then on us for that? Do you realize that that is why you are now in trouble and so helplessly alone? Those statues out there can't give you love or take care of you the way we wanted to. And, God knows, we were ready to do that. But you spurned us, Helen. You turned your back on our love and left us for the company of those cement monstrosities.

ELSA, *who has been listening and watching quietly, begins to understand.*

ELSA: Helen, listen to me. Listen to me carefully because if you understand what I'm going to say, I think everything will be all right.

They're not only frightened of you, Helen; they're also jealous. It's not just the statues that have frightened them. They were throwing stones at something much bigger than that—you. Your life, your beautiful, light-filled glittering life. And they can't leave it alone, Helen, because they are so, so jealous of it.

HELEN *(Calmly):* Is that true, Marius?

MARIUS: Helen, has your trust in me been eroded away to the extent that you can ask me that? Does she have so much power over you that you will now believe anything she says?

HELEN: Then . . . it isn't true?

MARIUS: Dear God, what is there left for me to say or do that will make you listen to me the way you do to her?

HELEN: But I have been listening to you, Marius.

MARIUS: No, you haven't! If that were so, you wouldn't be asking me to defend myself against the accusations of someone who knows nothing, nothing, about my true feelings for you. I feel as if I were on trial, Helen. For what? For caring about you? *(He confronts* MISS HELEN*)* That I am frightened of what you have done to yourself and your life, yes, that is true! When I find that the twenty years we have known each other, all that we have shared in that time, are outweighed by a handful of visits from her, then yes again. That leaves me bewildered and jealous. Don't you realize that you are being used, Helen—she as much as admitted to that—to prove some lunatic notion about freedom? And since we're talking about it, yes yet again, I *do* hate that word. You aren't free, Helen. If anything, exactly the opposite. Don't let her deceive you. If there is one last thing you will let me do for you, then let it be this: see yourself as I do and tell me if that is what you call being "free." A life I care about as deeply as any I have known, trapped now finally in the nightmare this house has become . . . with an illiterate little Coloured girl and a stranger from a different world as your only visitors and friends! I know I'm not welcome in here anymore. I can feel it the moment I walk in. It's unnatural, Helen. Your life has become as grotesque as those creations of yours out there.

Why, Helen? Why? I will take that question with me to my grave. What possessed you to abandon the life you had, your faith?

HELEN: What life, Marius? What faith? The one that brought me to church every Sunday? *(Shaking her head)* No. You were much too late if you only started worrying about that on the first Sunday I wasn't there in my place. The worst had happened long, long before that. Yes. All those years when, as Elsa said, I sat there so obediently next to Stefanus, it was all a terrible, terrible lie. I tried hard, Marius, but your sermons, the prayers, the hymns, they had all become just words. And there came a time when even they lost their meaning.

Do you know what the word "God" looks like when you've lost your faith? It looks like a little stone, a cold, round, little stone. "Heaven" is another one, but it's got an awkward, useless shape, while "Hell" is flat and smooth. All of them—damnation, grace, salvation—a handful of stones.

MARIUS: Why didn't you come to me, Helen? If only you had trusted me enough to tell me, and we had faced it together, I would have broken my soul to help you win back that faith.

HELEN: It felt too late. I'd accepted it. Nothing more was going to happen to me except time and the emptiness inside and I had got used to that . . . until the night in here after Stefanus's funeral. *(Pause. She makes a decision)*

I've never told you about that night, Marius. I've told no one, not even Elsa, because it was a secret, you see, a very special one, and it had to stay that way while I was working on my Mecca. But so much has happened here tonight, it feels right to do so now. *(Pause)*

You brought me home from the cemetery, remember, and when we had got inside the house and you had helped me off with my coat, you put on a kettle for a pot of tea and then . . . ever so thoughtfully . . . pulled the curtains and closed the shutters. Such a small little thing, and I know that you meant well by it, that you didn't want people to stare in at me and my grief . . . but in doing that it felt as if you were putting away my life as surely as the undertaker had done to Stefanus a little earlier when he closed the coffin lid. There was even an odor of death in here with us, wasn't there, sitting in the gloom and talking, both of us in black, our Bibles in our laps? Your words of comfort didn't help. But that wasn't your fault. You didn't know I wasn't mourning Stefanus's death. He was a good man, and it was very sad that he had died so young, but I never loved him. My black widowhood was really for my own life, Marius. While Stefanus was alive there had at least been some pretense at it . . . of a life I hadn't lived. But with him gone . . . ! You had a little girl in here with you, Marius, who had used up all the prayers she knew and was dreading the moment when her mother would bend down, blow out the candle and leave her in the dark. You lit one for me before you left—there was a lot of darkness in this room—and after you had gone I sat here with it. Such a sad little light, with its little tears of wax running down the side! I had none. Neither for Stefanus nor for myself. You see, nothing hurt anymore. That little candle did all the crying in here that night, and it burned down very low while doing that. I don't know how much time had passed, but I was just sitting here staring into its flame. I had surrendered myself to what was going to happen when it went out . . . but then instead of doing the same, allowing the darkness to defeat it, that small, uncertain little light seemed to find its courage again. It started to get brighter and brighter. I didn't know whether I was awake any longer or dreaming because a strange feeling came over me . . . that it was leading me . . . leading me far away to a place I had never been to before. *(She looks around the room and speaks with authority)* Light the candles, Elsa. That one first.

She indicates a candelabra that has been set up very prominently on a little table. ELSA *lights it.*

And you know why, Marius? That is the East. Go out there into the yard and you'll see that all my Wise Men and their camels are traveling in that direction. Follow that candle on and one day you'll come to Mecca. Oh yes, Marius, it's true! I've done it. That is where I went that night and it was the candle you lit that led me there.

(She is radiantly alive with her vision) A city, Marius! A city of light and color more splendid than anything I had ever imagined. There were palaces and beautiful buildings everywhere, with dazzling white walls and glittering minarets. Strange statues filled the courtyards. The streets were crowded with camels and turbaned men speaking a language I didn't understand, but that didn't matter because I knew, oh I just knew, it was Mecca! And I was on my way to the grand temple.

In the center of Mecca there is a temple, Marius, and in the center of the temple is a vast room with hundreds of mirrors on the walls and hanging lamps, and that is where the Wise Men of the East study the celestial geometry of light and color. I became an apprentice that night.

Light them all, Elsa, so that I can show Marius what I've learned!

ELSA *moves around the room lighting all the candles, and as she does so its full magic and splendor is revealed.* MISS HELEN *laughs ecstatically.*

Look, Marius! Look! Light. Don't be nervous. It's harmless. It only wants to play. That is what I do in here. We play with it like children with a magical toy that never ceases to delight and amuse. Light just one little candle in here, let in the light from just one little star, and the dancing starts. I've even taught it how to skip around corners. Yes, I have! When I lie in bed and look in *that* mirror, I can see *that* mirror, and in *that* one the full moon when it rises over the Sneeuberg *behind* my back! This is my world and I have banished darkness from it.

It is not madness, Marius. They say mad people can't tell the difference between what is real and what is not. I can. I know my little Mecca out there, and this room, for what they really are. I had to learn how to bend rusty wire into the right shape and mix sand cement to make my Wise Men and their camels, how to grind down beer bottles in a coffee mill to put glitter on my walls. My hands will never let me forget. They'll keep me sane. It's the best I could do, as near as I could get to the real Mecca. The journey is over now. This is as far as I can go.

I won't be using this *(The application form).* I can't reduce my world to a few ornaments in a small room in an old-age home.

MARIUS *takes the form. When he speaks again we sense a defeated man, an acceptance of the inevitable behind the quiet attempt to maintain his dignity.*

MARIUS: Mecca! So that's where you went. I'll look for it on my atlas of the world when I get home tonight. That's a long way away, Helen! I didn't realize you had traveled that far from me. So to find you I must light a candle and follow it to the East! *(He makes a helpless gesture)* No. I think I'm too old now for that journey . . . and I have a feeling that you will never come back.

HELEN: I'm also too old for another journey, Marius. It's taken me my whole life to get here.

I know I've disappointed you—most probably, bitterly so—but, whatever you do, please believe me that it wasn't intentional. I had as little choice over all that has happened as I did over the day I was born.

MARIUS: No, I think I do believe you, Helen . . . which only makes it all the harder to accept. All these years it has always felt as if I could reach you. It seemed so inevitable that I would, so right that we should find each other again and be together for what time was left to us in the same world. It seems wrong . . . terribly wrong . . . that we won't. Aletta's death was wrong in the same way.

Pause.

HELEN: What's the matter, Marius?

MARIUS: I am trying to go. It's not easy . . . trying to find the first moment of a life that must be lived out in the shadow of something that is terribly wrong.

HELEN: We're trying to say goodbye to each other, aren't we, Marius?

MARIUS: Yes, I suppose it had come to that. I never thought that was going to happen tonight, but I suppose there *is* nothing else left to say. *(He starts to go. He sees* ELSA, *hesitates for a few seconds, but there is nothing to say to her either)* Be sure all the candles are out when you go to bed, Helen. *(He pauses at the door)* I've never seen you as happy as this! There is more light in you than in all your candles put together.

He leaves. A silence follows his departure. ELSA *eventually makes a move to start blowing out the candles.*

HELEN: No, don't. I must do that. *(From this point on she goes around the room putting out the candles, a quiet but deliberate and grave punctuation to what follows)*

ELSA: Tell me about his wife.

HELEN: Her name was Aletta. Aletta Byleveld. I've only seen pictures of her. She must have been a very beautiful woman.

ELSA: What happened?

HELEN: Her death?

ELSA: Yes.

HELEN: All I know is that there was a long illness. And a very painful one. They never had any children. Marius was a bitter and lonely man when he first came to the valley. Why do you ask?

ELSA: Because he was, and most probably still is, in love with you.

HELEN: Elsa . . .

ELSA: Yes. I don't suppose I would have ever guessed it if it hadn't been for tonight. Like all good Afrikaners, he does a good job of hiding his feelings. But it is very obvious now.

HELEN *(Agitated)*: No, Elsie. When he used the word "love" he meant it in the way—

ELSA: No, Helen. I'm not talking about the good shepherd's feelings for one of his flock. Marius Byleveld, the man, loves you Helen, the woman.

HELEN: What are you talking about? Look at me, Elsa. Look at my hands—

ELSA: You fool! Do you think that is what we see when we look at you? You heard him: "There is more light in you than in all your candles put together." And he's right. You are radiant. You can't be that naive and innocent, Helen!

MISS HELEN *wants to deny it, but the validity, the possible truth, of what* ELSA *has said is very strong.*

It's a very moving story. Twenty years of loving you in the disguise of friendship and professional concern for your soul. *(There is an unnatural and forced tone to her voice)* Anyway, that's his problem, right, Helen? You did what you had to. In fact, you deserve a few bravos for your performance tonight. I'm proud of you. I told you that you never needed me. And you did more than just say no to him. You affirmed your right, as a woman . . . *(Pause)* Do you love him? The way he loves you?

MISS HELEN *thinks before speaking. When she does so there is no doubt about her answer.*

HELEN: No, I don't.

ELSA: Just asking. You're also an Afrikaner. You could also be hiding your real feelings the way he did. That would make it an even better story! The two of you in this Godforsaken little village, each loving the other in secret!

HELEN: Are you all right, Elsa?

ELSA: No.

HELEN: What's wrong?

ELSA: It's my turn to be jealous.

HELEN: Of what?

ELSA *(With a helpless gesture)*: Everything. You and him . . . and, stupid as it may sound, I feel fucking lonely as well.

HELEN: You are jealous? Of us . . . Marius and me? With your whole life still ahead of you?

ELSA: Even that woman on the road has at least got a baby in her arms at this moment. She's got something, for Christ's sake! Mind you, it's cold out there now. It could be on her back again. She might have crawled out of her stormwater drain and started walking to keep warm.

HELEN: Leave that poor woman alone now, Elsa!

ELSA: She won't leave me alone, Helen!

HELEN: For all you know, she might have got a lift.

ELSA *(Another unexpected flash of cruelty)*: I hope not.

HELEN *(Appalled):* Elsa! That is not you talking. You don't mean that.

ELSA: Yes, I do! A lift to where, for God's sake? There's no Mecca waiting for her at the end of that road, Helen. Just the rest of her life, and there won't be any glitter on that. The sooner she knows what the score really is, the better.

HELEN: Then think about the baby, Elsa.

ELSA: What the hell do you think I've been doing? Do you think I don't care? That baby could have been mine, Helen! *(Pause. Then a decision)* I may as well vomit it all out tonight. Two weeks after David left me I discovered I was pregnant. I had an abortion. *(Pause)* Do you understand what I'm saying, Helen?

HELEN: I understand you, Elsa.

ELSA: I put an abrupt and violent end to the first real consequence my life has ever had.

HELEN: I understand, Elsa.

Pause.

ELSA: There is a little sequel to my story about giving that woman a lift. When I stopped at the turnoff and she got out of the car, after I had given her what was left of my food and the money in my purse, after she had stopped thanking me and telling me over and over again that God would bless me, after all of that I asked her who she was. She said: "My English name is Patience." She hitched up the baby, tightened her *doek,* picked up her little plastic shopping bag and started walking. As I watched her walk away, measuring out the next eighty miles of her life in small steps, I wanted to scream. And about a mile further on, in the *kloof,* I did exactly that. I stopped the car, switched off the engine, closed my eyes and started to scream.

I think I lost control of myself. I screamed louder and longer than I have ever done in my life. I can't describe it, Helen. I hated her, I hated the baby, I hated you for dragging me all the way up here . . . and most of all I hated myself. That baby is mine, Helen. Patience is my sister, you are our mother . . . and I still feel fucking lonely.

HELEN: Then don't be so cruel to us. There were times tonight when I hardly recognized you. Why were you doing it?

ELSA: I wanted to punish us.

HELEN: For what? What have we done to deserve that?

ELSA: I've already told you. For being old, for being black, for being born . . . for being twenty-eight years old and trusting enough to jump. For our stupid helplessness.

HELEN: You don't punish people for that, Elsa. I only felt helpless tonight when I thought I had lost you.

ELSA: So what do you want me to do, Helen?

HELEN: Stop screaming.

ELSA: And cry instead?

HELEN: What is wrong with that? Is it something to be ashamed of? I wish I still could . . . not for myself . . . for you, Patience, her little baby. Was it a boy or a girl?

ELSA: I don't know. I'll never know.

Her moment of emotional release has finally come. She cries. MISS HELEN *comforts her.*

I'll be all right.

HELEN: I never doubted that for a moment.

ELSA *(Total exhaustion):* God Almighty, what a day! I'm dead, Helen, dead, dead, dead . . .

HELEN: No, you're not. You're tired . . . and you've got every right and reason to be. *(She fetches a blanket and puts it over* ELSA's *shoulders)*

ELSA: I wasn't much of a help tonight, was I?

HELEN: You were more than that. You were a "challenge." I like that word.

ELSA: But we didn't solve very much.

HELEN: Nonsense! Of course we did. Certainly as much as *we* could. I *am* going to see a doctor and an optician, and Katrina . . . *(She remembers)* or somebody else, will come in here a few times a week and help me with the house.

ELSA: My shopping list!

HELEN: It is as much as "we" could do, Elsa. The rest is up to myself and, who knows, maybe it will be a little easier after tonight. I won't lie to you. I can't say that I'm not frightened anymore. But at the same time I think I can say that I understand something now.

The road to my Mecca *was* one I had to travel alone. It was a journey on which no one could keep me company, and because of that, now that it is over, there is only me there at the end of it. It couldn't have been any other way.

You see, I meant what I said to Marius. This is as far as I can go. My Mecca is finished and with it—*(Pause)* I must try to say it, mustn't I?—the only real purpose my life has ever had.

(She blows out a candle) I was wrong to think I could banish darkness, Elsa. Just as I taught myself how to light candles, and what that means, I must teach myself now how to blow them out . . . and what that means.

(She attempts a brave smile) The last phase of my apprenticeship . . . and if I can get through it, I'll be a master!

ELSA: I'm cold.

HELEN: Cup of tea to warm you up and then bed. I'll put on the kettle.

ELSA: And I've got just the thing to go with it. *(She goes into the bedroom alcove and returns with her toilet bag, from which she takes a small bottle of pills)* Valiums. They're delicious. I think you should also have one.

HELEN *(All innocence):* So tiny! What are they? Artificial sweeteners?

The unintended and gentle irony of her question is not lost on ELSA. *A little chuckle becomes a good laugh.*

ELSA: That is perfect, Helen. Yes, they're artificial sweeteners.

HELEN: I don't know how I did it, but that laugh makes me as proud of myself as of any one of those statues out there.

She exits to put on the kettle. ELSA *goes to the window and looks out at Mecca.* MISS HELEN *returns.*

ELSA: Helen, I've just thought of something. You know what the real cause of all your trouble is? You've never made an angel.

HELEN: Good Heavens, no. Why should I?

ELSA: Because I think they would leave you alone if you did.

HELEN: The village doesn't need more of those. The cemetery is full of them . . . all wings and halos, but no glitter. *(Tongue-in-cheek humor)* But if I did make one, it wouldn't be pointing up to heaven like the rest.

ELSA: No? What would it be doing?

HELEN: Come on, Elsa, you know! I'd have it pointing to the East. Where else? I'd misdirect all the good Christian souls around here and put them on the road to Mecca.

Both have a good laugh.

ELSA: God, I love you! I love so much it hurts.

HELEN: What about trust?

Pause. The two women look at each other.

ELSA: Open your arms and catch me! I'm going to jump!

END OF PLAY

ACTIVITIES FOR WRITING AND DISCUSSION

1. Both Helen and Elsa are socially independent and "nonconformists," yet they seem quite different in their nonconformity. Compare and contrast the two characters as nonconformists.

2. Elsa claims that the villagers fear Helen because she is "dangerous." Is she? What values, norms, or social codes does she threaten? If you wish, assume the **persona** of one of the villagers and articulate (in the form of a diary entry or a letter to the Church Council) the logic or reasoning that regards Helen as a "danger" to society.

3. Note the subjects of Helen's statues—mermaids, camels, Wise Men, for instance. Why does she create these statues and fill up her yard and house with them? Do they serve any purpose? If so, what purposes? If not, why does she keep making them?

4. Elsa asserts that Marius has long been in love with Helen. What *are* Marius's feelings about Helen? Is he in love with her? or jealous of her statues? or envious of her life? or some combination of the above? Imagine it is a time shortly after the action of the play has ended. In the persona of Marius, reveal

your true—and perhaps contradictory—feelings about Helen in a letter to her or in a **monologue.**

5. Write a script of the Church Council meeting at which members discuss what to do about Helen. What attitudes do they have about her work? Why do they want to get her out of her own house and into the old-age home? If you wish, include the voice of a dissenting member who defends Helen.

6. In act 2 we learn that children of the village used to throw stones at Helen's house and statues. According to Elsa, they would not have done so without some influence from their parents. How do you suppose the parents in the village did (or do) discuss Helen with their children? Write the **dialogue** of one father and mother talking with their child or children about Helen and her "work."

7. Imagine it is some time in the future, and Helen has died. You are Elsa, and you want to write down your thoughts and feelings about your dead friend. Building on details furnished in the play, tell the story of your various encounters with Helen and the impact she had on your life. Compose the piece as a diary entry or memoir or as a letter addressed to another, younger woman to whom Helen might be of interest.

INDIVIDUAL AND SOCIETY: ADDITIONAL ACTIVITIES FOR WRITING AND DISCUSSION

1. Reread your entire notebook. Mark any passages, however long or short, that strike you, for whatever reason. Beside each such passage, write a note explaining its significance for you. Finally, pick a favorite passage and either:
    a. Expand it into a new piece of writing, or
    b. Make notes on how you could expand or use it at some future date, or
    c. Rewrite it in a different form, e.g., a poem, dialogue, letter, memoir.

For a list of strategies for expanding or revising, see Chapter 10.

2. Write down your own definitions of "individual" and "society." Then think about this question: Is society essentially the *enemy* of the individual or the *friend*? Finally, bring together two or more **characters, speakers,** or **personae** from the texts in this section and write a dialogue in which they debate the question. Some participants in this dialogue might include Ivan Ivanych's brother in "Gooseberries," the William Blake of "The Garden of Love," the dead man commemorated in Auden's "The Unknown Citizen," one of Margaret Atwood's "City Planners," the Cathy Appel of "Letters," Carol Bly. If you wish, include yourself in the dialogue as a participant or moderator.

3. Is "individuality" mainly a matter of being independent, or does it include dependence of various kinds? Are there kinds of dependence that can en-

hance individuality, or is dependence generally at odds with individuality? Compare the ways in which "independence" and "dependence" interweave as themes in any of the texts within this section.

4. As a variation on Activity #3, write about the same issues in some alternative literary form, e.g., in a dialogue between or among characters or speakers, a personal essay, or a short story.

5. Review Whitman's "Song of the Open Road," paying special attention to the kinds of qualities (personal, physical, moral, spiritual) his speaker prescribes for travelers on the open road. Make a list of these qualities. Then choose any three or four characters, speakers, or personae from this thematic grouping and place them on the road.

    a. Which of your travelers do well? Which, if any, decide to give up the journey? Why?

    b. If you wish, write imaginary travel diaries for one or more of your travelers in which they record their impressions of the journey and why they decide to abandon it (if they decide to abandon it).

6. Several times in *The Road to Mecca,* Helen is referred to as "mad." Annotate and interpret Emily Dickinson's "Much Madness is divinest Sense." Then:

    a. In an essay, argue that the poem could be used as a gloss (or commentary) on the story of Helen in *The Road to Mecca.*

    b. Bring Emily Dickinson and Helen together for a dialogue or an exchange of letters on the subject of "madness" and "sanity." Alternative: Include other characters and speakers from this thematic section, e.g., Ivan Ivanych, Walter Mitty, Gracie Mae from Walker's "Nineteen Fifty-five," Mr. Keuner, in the discussion.

7. Write about any common themes you see in Schopenhauer's "On Thinking for Oneself" and Bly's "Growing Up Expressive." Do the two essays articulate a common message? Are there any important differences?

8. Review your entire notebook; as you do, make a running list of memorable or striking topics, e.g., "individuality," "nonconformists," "communities," "friendship." Then choose a favorite topic, make a Topic/Form Grid (see Chapter 10), and use one of the forms on your grid to create a new notebook entry about the topic. Should your chosen form not work, do a Topic/Form Shift to a different form on your grid.

9. Walker's "Nineteen Fifty-five" is a *mix* of literary forms, combining **first-person** narrative by Gracie Mae with imaginary letters between Traynor and Gracie Mae. Use the topic you chose for Activity #8 and compose a notebook piece that mixes two or more forms from your Topic/Form Grid.

10. Reread your entire notebook, and mark any favorite entries. Then, after reviewing Chapter 4, revise one of these entries that is a "dependent" text into an "independent" text. (For a list of strategies for revising, see Chapter 10.)

Cultural and Racial Identity

Margaret Atwood (b. 1939)

The Man from Mars

A long time ago Christine was walking through the park. She was still wearing 1
her tennis dress; she hadn't had time to shower and change, and her hair was
held back with an elastic band. Her chunky reddish face, exposed with no softening fringe, looked like a Russian peasant's, but without the elastic band the
hair got in her eyes. The afternoon was too hot for April; the indoor courts had
been steaming, her skin felt poached.

The sun had brought the old men out from wherever they spent the winter: 2
she had read a story recently about one who lived for three years in a manhole.
They sat weedishly on the benches or lay on the grass with their heads on
squares of used newspaper. As she passed, their wrinkled toadstool faces drifted
towards her, drawn by the movement of her body, then floated away again, un-
interested.

The squirrels were out, too, foraging; two or three of them moved towards 3
her in darts and pauses, eyes fixed on her expectantly, mouths with the ratlike
receding chins open to show the yellowed front teeth. Christine walked faster,
she had nothing to give them. People shouldn't feed them, she thought; it
makes them anxious and they get mangy.

Halfway across the park she stopped to take off her cardigan. As she bent 4
over to pick up her tennis racquet again someone touched her on her freshly

bared arm. Christine seldom screamed; she straightened up suddenly, gripping the handle of her racquet. It was not one of the old men, however; it was a dark-haired boy of twelve or so.

"Excuse me," he said, "I search for Economics Building. Is it there?" He mo- 5 tioned towards the west.

Christine looked at him more closely. She had been mistaken: he was not 6 young, just short. He came a little above her shoulder, but then, she was above the average height; "statuesque," her mother called it when she was straining. He was also what was referred to in their family as "a person from another culture": oriental without a doubt, though perhaps not Chinese. Christine judged he must be a foreign student and gave him her official welcoming smile. In high school she had been president of the United Nations Club; that year her school had been picked to represent the Egyptian delegation at the Mock Assembly. It had been an unpopular assignment—nobody wanted to be the Arabs—but she had seen it through. She had made rather a good speech about the Palestinian refugees.

"Yes," she said, "that's it over there. The one with the flat roof. See it?"   7

The man had been smiling nervously at her the whole time. He was wearing 8 glasses with transparent plastic rims, through which his eyes bulged up at her as though through a goldfish bowl. He had not followed where she was pointing. Instead he thrust towards her a small green paper and a ball-point pen.

"You make map," he said.   9

Christine set down her tennis racquet and drew a careful map. "We are 10 here," she said, pronouncing distinctly. "You go this way. The building is here." She indicated the route with a dotted line and an X. The man leaned close to her, watching the progress of the map attentively; he smelled of cooked cauliflower and an unfamiliar brand of hair grease. When she had finished Christine handed the paper and pen back to him with a terminal smile.

"Wait," the man said. He tore the piece of paper with the map off the pad, 11 folded it carefully and put it in his jacket pocket; the jacket sleeves came down over his wrists and had threads at the edges. He began to write something; she noticed with a slight feeling of revulsion that his nails and the ends of his fingers were so badly bitten they seemed almost deformed. Several of his fingers were blue from the leaky ball-point.

"Here is my name," he said, holding the pad out to her.   12

Christine read an odd assemblage of Gs, Ys and Ns, neatly printed in block 13 letters. "Thank you," she said.

"You now write *your* name," he said, extending the pen.   14

Christine hesitated. If this had been a person from her own culture she 15 would have thought he was trying to pick her up. But then, people from her own culture never tried to pick her up; she was too big. The only one who had made the attempt was the Moroccan waiter at the beer parlour where they sometimes went after meetings, and he had been direct. He had just intercepted her on the way to the Ladies' Room and asked and she said no; that had been that. This man was not a waiter though, but a student; she didn't want to offend him. In his culture, whatever it was, this exchange of names on pieces of paper was probably a formal politeness, like saying thank you. She took the pen from him.

"That is a very pleasant name," he said. He folded the paper and placed it in his jacket with the map.   16

Christine felt she had done her duty. "Well, goodbye," she said. "It was nice to have met you." She bent for her tennis racquet but he had already stooped and retrieved it and was holding it with both hands in front of him, like a captured banner.   17

"I carry this for you."   18

"Oh no, please. Don't bother, I am in a hurry," she said, articulating clearly. Deprived of her tennis racquet she felt weaponless. He started to saunter along the path; he was not nervous at all now, he seemed completely at ease.   19

"*Vous parlez français?*" he asked conversationally.   20

"*Oui, un petit peu,*" she said. "Not very well." How am I going to get my racquet away from him without being rude? she was wondering.   21

"*Mais vous avez un bel accent.*" His eyes goggled at her through the glasses: was he being flirtatious? She was well aware that her accent was wretched.   22

"Look," she said, for the first time letting her impatience show, "I really have to go. Give me my racquet, please."   23

He quickened his pace but gave no sign of returning the racquet. "Where you are going?"   24

"Home," she said. "My house."   25

"I go with you now," he said hopefully.   26

"*No,*" she said: she would have to be firm with him. She made a lunge and got a grip on her racquet; after a brief tug of war it came free.   27

"Goodbye," she said, turning away from his puzzled face and setting off at what she hoped was a discouraging jog-trot. It was like walking away from a growling dog: you shouldn't let on you were frightened. Why should she be frightened anyway? He was only half her size and she had the tennis racquet, there was nothing he could do to her.   28

Although she did not look back she could tell he was still following. Let there be a streetcar, she thought, and there was one, but it was far down the line, stuck behind a red light. He appeared at her side, breathing audibly, a moment after she reached the stop. She gazed ahead, rigid.   29

"You are my friend," he said tentatively.   30

Christine relented: he hadn't been trying to pick her up after all, he was a stranger, he just wanted to meet some of the local people; in his place she would have wanted the same thing.   31

"Yes," she said, doling him out a smile.   32

"That is good," he said. "My country is very far."   33

Christine couldn't think of an apt reply. "That's interesting," she said. "*Très interessant.*" The streetcar was coming at last; she opened her purse and got out a ticket.   34

"I go with you now," he said. His hand clamped on her arm above the elbow.   35

"You . . . stay . . . *here,*" Christine said, resisting the impulse to shout but 36
pausing between each word as though for a deaf person. She detached his
hand—his hold was quite feeble and could not compete with her tennis bi-
ceps—and leapt off the curb and up the streetcar steps, hearing with relief the
doors grind shut behind her. Inside the car and a block away she permitted herself a glance out a side window. He was standing where she had left him; he
seemed to be writing something on his little pad of paper.

When she reached home she had only time for a snack, and even then she 37
was almost late for the Debating Society. The topic was, "Resolved: That War Is
Obsolete." Her team took the affirmative and won.

Christine came out of her last examination feeling depressed. It was not the 38
exam that depressed her but the fact that it was the last one: it meant the end of
the school year. She dropped into the coffee shop as usual, then went home
early because there didn't seem to be anything else to do.

"Is that you, dear?" her mother called from the living room. She must have 39
heard the front door close. Christine went in and flopped on the sofa, disturbing the neat pattern of cushions.

"How was your exam, dear?" her mother asked. 40

"Fine," said Christine flatly. It had been fine; she had passed. She was not a 41
brilliant student, she knew that, but she was conscientious. Her professors always wrote things like "A serious attempt" and "Well thought out but perhaps
lacking in élan" on her term papers; they gave her Bs, the occasional B+. She
was taking Political Science and Economics, and hoped for a job with the Government after she graduated; with her father's connections she had a good
chance.

"That's nice." 42

Christine felt, resentfully, that her mother had only a hazy idea of what an 43
exam was. She was arranging gladioli in a vase; she had rubber gloves on to protect her hands as she always did when engaged in what she called "housework."
As far as Christine could tell her housework consisted of arranging flowers in
vases: daffodils and tulips and hyacinths through gladioli, irises and roses, all
the way to asters and mums. Sometimes she cooked, elegantly and with chaf-
ing-dishes, but she thought of it as a hobby. The girl did everything else. Christine thought it faintly sinful to have a girl. The only ones available now were
either foreign or pregnant; their expressions usually suggested they were being
taken advantage of somehow. But her mother asked what they would do otherwise; they'd either have to go into a Home or stay in their own countries, and
Christine had to agree this was probably true. It was hard, anyway, to argue
with her mother. She was so delicate, so preserved-looking, a harsh breath
would scratch the finish.

"An interesting young man phoned today," her mother said. She had fin- 44
ished the gladioli and was taking off her rubber gloves. "He asked to speak with
you and when I said you weren't in we had quite a little chat. You didn't tell me
about him, dear." She put on the glasses which she wore on a decorative chain

around her neck, a signal that she was in her modern, intelligent mood rather than her old-fashioned whimsical one.

"Did he leave his name?" Christine asked. She knew a lot of young men but 45 they didn't often call her; they conducted their business with her in the coffee shop or after meetings.

"He's a person from another culture. He said he would call back later."   46

Christine had to think a moment. She was vaguely acquainted with several 47 people from other cultures, Britain mostly; they belonged to the Debating Society.

"He's studying Philosophy in Montreal," her mother prompted. "He 48 sounded French."

Christine began to remember the man in the park. "I don't think he's 49 French, exactly," she said.

Her mother had taken off her glasses again and was poking absentmindedly 50 at a bent gladiolus. "Well, he sounded French." She meditated, flowery sceptre in hand. "I think it would be nice if you had him to tea."

Christine's mother did her best. She had two other daughters, both of 51 whom took after her. They were beautiful; one was well married already and the other would clearly have no trouble. Her friends consoled her about Christine by saying, "She's not fat, she's just big-boned, it's the father's side," and "Christine is so healthy." Her other daughters had never gotten involved in activities when they were at school, but since Christine could not possibly ever be beautiful even if she took off weight, it was just as well she was so athletic and political, it was a good thing she had interests. Christine's mother tried to encourage her interests whenever possible. Christine could tell when she was making an extra effort, there was a reproaching edge to her voice.

She knew her mother expected enthusiasm but she could not supply it. "I 52 don't know, I'll have to see," she said dubiously.

"You look tired, darling," said her mother. "Perhaps you'd like a glass of 53 milk."

Christine was in the bathtub when the phone rang. She was not prone to 54 fantasy but when she was in the bathtub she often pretended she was a dolphin, a game left over from one of the girls who used to bathe her when she was small. Her mother was being bell-voiced and gracious in the hall; then there was a tap at the door.

"It's that nice young French student, Christine," her mother said.   55

"Tell him I'm in the bathtub," Christine said, louder than necessary. "He 56 isn't French."

She could hear her mother frowning. "That wouldn't be very polite, Chris- 57 tine. I don't think he'd understand."

"Oh, all right," Christine said. She heaved herself out of the bathtub, 58 swathed her pink bulk in a towel and splattered to the phone.

"Hello," she said gruffly. At a distance he was not pathetic, he was a nui- 59 sance. She could not imagine how he had tracked her down: most likely he went through the phone book, calling all the numbers with her last name until he hit on the right one.

"It is your friend."   60

"I know," she said. "How are you?"   61

"I am very fine." There was a long pause, during which Christine had a vi-   62
cious urge to say, "Well goodbye then," and hang up; but she was aware of her
mother poised figurine-like in her bedroom doorway. Then he said, "I hope
you also are very fine."

"Yes," said Christine. She wasn't going to participate.   63

"I come to tea," he said.   64

This took Christine by surprise. "You do?"   65

"Your pleasant mother ask me. I come Thursday, four o'clock."   66

"Oh," Christine said, ungraciously.   67

"See you then," he said, with the conscious pride of one who has mastered a   68
difficult idiom.

Christine set down the phone and went along the hall. Her mother was in   69
her study, sitting innocently at her writing desk.

"Did you ask him to tea on Thursday?"   70

"Not exactly, dear," her mother said. "I did mention he might come round   71
to tea *some*time, though."

"Well, he's coming Thursday. Four o'clock."   72

"What's wrong with that?" her mother said serenely. "I think it's a very nice   73
gesture for us to make. I do think you might try to be a little more co-opera-
tive." She was pleased with herself.

"Since you invited him," said Christine, "you can bloody well stick around   74
and help me entertain him. I don't want to be left making nice gestures all by
myself."

"Christine, *dear*," her mother said, above being shocked. "You ought to put   75
on your dressing gown, you'll catch a chill."

After sulking for an hour Christine tried to think of the tea as a cross be-   76
tween an examination and an executive meeting: not enjoyable, certainly, but to
be got through as tactfully as possible. And it *was* a nice gesture. When the cakes
her mother had ordered arrived from The Patisserie on Thursday morning she
began to feel slightly festive; she even resolved to put on a dress, a good one, instead of a skirt and blouse. After all, she had nothing against him, except the
memory of the way he had grabbed her tennis racquet and then her arm. She
suppressed a quick impossible vision of herself pursued around the living
room, fending him off with thrown sofa cushions and vases of gladioli; nevertheless she told the girl they would have tea in the garden. It would be a treat for
him, and there was more space outdoors.

She had suspected her mother would dodge the tea, would contrive to be   77
going out just as he was arriving: that way she could size him up and then leave
them alone together. She had done things like that to Christine before; the excuse this time was the Symphony Committee. Sure enough, her mother care-

fully mislaid her gloves and located them with a faked murmur of joy when the doorbell rang. Christine relished for weeks afterwards the image of her mother's dropped jaw and flawless recovery when he was introduced: he wasn't quite the foreign potentate her optimistic, veil-fragile mind had concocted.

He was prepared for celebration. He had slicked on so much hair cream that 78 his head seemed to be covered with a tight black patent-leather cap, and he had cut the threads off his jacket sleeves. His orange tie was overpoweringly splendid. Christine noticed, however, as he shook her mother's suddenly braced white glove that the ball-point ink on his fingers was indelible. His face had broken out, possibly in anticipation of the delights in store for him; he had a tiny camera slung over his shoulder and was smoking an exotic-smelling cigarette.

Christine led him through the cool flowery softly padded living room and 79 out by the French doors into the garden. "You sit here," she said. "I will have the girl bring tea."

This girl was from the West Indies: Christine's parents had been enraptured 80 with her when they were down at Christmas and had brought her back with them. Since that time she had become pregnant, but Christine's mother had not dismissed her. She said she was slightly disappointed but what could you expect, and she didn't see any real difference between a girl who was pregnant before you hired her and one who got that way afterwards. She prided herself on her tolerance; also there was a scarcity of girls. Strangely enough, the girl became progressively less easy to get along with. Either she did not share Christine's mother's view of her own generosity, or she felt she had gotten away with something and was therefore free to indulge in contempt. At first Christine had tried to treat her as an equal. "Don't call me 'Miss Christine,'" she had said with an imitation of light, comradely laughter. "What you want me to call you then?" the girl had said, scowling. They had begun to have brief, surly arguments in the kitchen, which Christine decided were like the arguments between one servant and another: her mother's attitude towards each of them was similar, they were not altogether satisfactory but they would have to do.

The cakes, glossy with icing, were set out on a plate and the teapot was 81 standing ready; on the counter the electric kettle boiled. Christine headed for it, but the girl, till then sitting with her elbows on the kitchen table and watching her expressionlessly, made a dash and intercepted her. Christine waited until she had poured the water into the pot. Then, "I'll carry it out, Elvira," she said. She had just decided she didn't want the girl to see her visitor's orange tie; already, she knew, her position in the girl's eyes had suffered because no one had yet attempted to get *her* pregnant.

"What you think they pay me for, Miss Christine?" the girl said insolently. 82 She swung towards the garden with the tray; Christine trailed her, feeling lumpish and awkward. The girl was at least as big as she was but in a different way.

"Thank you, Elvira," Christine said when the tray was in place. The girl de- 83 parted without a word, casting a disdainful backward glance at the frayed jacket sleeves, the stained fingers. Christine was now determined to be especially kind to him.

"You are very rich," he said.　84

"No," Christine protested, shaking her head, "we're not." She had never 85 thought of her family as rich; it was one of her father's sayings that nobody made any money with the Government.

"Yes," he repeated, "you are very rich." He sat back in his lawn chair, gazing 86 about him as though dazed.

Christine set his cup of tea in front of him. She wasn't in the habit of paying 87 much attention to the house or the garden; they were nothing special, far from being the largest on the street; other people took care of them. But now she looked where he was looking, seeing it all as though from a different height: the long expanses, the border flowers blazing in the early-summer sunlight, the flagged patio and walks, the high walls and the silence.

He came back to her face, sighing a little. "My English is not good," he said, 88 "but I improve."

"You do," Christine said, nodding encouragement.　89

He took sips of his tea, quickly and tenderly, as though afraid of injuring the 90 cup. "I like to stay here."

Christine passed him the cakes. He took only one, making a slight face as he 91 ate it; but he had several more cups of tea while she finished the cakes. She managed to find out from him that he had come over on a church fellowship— she could not decode the denomination—and was studying Philosophy or Theology, or possibly both. She was feeling well-disposed towards him: he had behaved himself, he had caused her no inconvenience.

The teapot was at last empty. He sat up straight in his chair, as though 92 alerted by a soundless gong. "You look this way, please," he said. Christine saw that he had placed his miniature camera on the stone sundial her mother had shipped back from England two years before. He wanted to take her picture. She was flattered, and settled herself to pose, smiling evenly.

He took off his glasses and laid them beside his plate. For a moment she saw 93 his myopic, unprotected eyes turned towards her, with something tremulous and confiding in them she wanted to close herself off from knowing about. Then he went over and did something to the camera, his back to her. The next instant he was crouched beside her, his arm around her waist as far as it could reach, his other hand covering her own hands which she had folded in her lap, his cheek jammed up against hers. She was too startled to move. The camera clicked.

He stood up at once and replaced his glasses, which glittered now with a sad 94 triumph. "Thank you, miss," he said to her. "I go now." He slung the camera back over his shoulder, keeping his hand on it as though to hold the lid on and prevent escape. "I send to my family; they will like."

He was out the gate and gone before Christine had recovered; then she 95 laughed. She had been afraid he would attack her, she could admit it now, and he had; but not in the usual way. He had raped, *rapeo, rapere, rapui, to seize and carry off,* not herself but her celluloid image, and incidently that of the silver tea service, which glinted mockingly at her as the girl bore it away, carrying it regally, the insignia, the official jewels.

Christine spent the summer as she had for the past three years: she was the 96
sailing instructress at an expensive all-girls camp near Algonquin Park. She had been a camper there, everything was familiar to her; she sailed almost better than she played tennis.

The second week she got a letter from him, postmarked Montreal and for- 97
warded from her home address. It was printed in block letters on a piece of the green paper, two or three sentences. It began, "I hope you are well," then described the weather in monosyllables and ended, "I am fine." It was signed, "Your friend." Each week she got another of these letters, more or less identical. In one of them a colour print was enclosed: himself, slightly cross-eyed and grinning hilariously, even more spindly than she remembered him against her billowing draperies, flowers exploding around them like firecrackers, one of his hands an equivocal blur in her lap, the other out of sight; on her own face, astonishment and outrage, as though he was sticking her in the behind with his hidden thumb.

She answered the first letter, but after that the seniors were in training for 98
the races. At the end of the summer, packing to go home, she threw all the letters away.

When she had been back for several weeks she received another of the green 99
letters. This time there was a return address printed at the top which Christine noted with foreboding was in her own city. Every day she waited for the phone to ring; she was so certain his first attempt at contact would be a disembodied voice that when he came upon her abruptly in midcampus she was unprepared.

"How are you?"   100

His smile was the same, but everything else about him had deteriorated. He 101
was, if possible, thinner; his jacket sleeves had sprouted a lush new crop of threads, as though to conceal hands now so badly bitten they appeared to have been gnawed by rodents. His hair fell over his eyes, uncut, ungreased; his eyes in the hollowed face, a delicate triangle of skin stretched on bone, jumped behind his glasses like hooded fish. He had the end of a cigarette in the corner of his mouth, and as they walked he lit a new one from it.

"I'm fine," Christine said. She was thinking, I'm not going to get involved 102
again, enough is enough, I've done my bit for internationalism. "How are you?"

"I live here now," he said. "Maybe I study Economics."   103

"That's nice." He didn't sound as though he was enrolled anywhere.   104

"I come to see you."   105

Christine didn't know whether he meant he had left Montreal in order to be 106
near her or just wanted to visit her at her house as he had done in the spring; either way she refused to be implicated. They were outside the Political Science Building. "I have a class here," she said. "Goodbye." She was being callous, she

realized that, but a quick chop was more merciful in the long run, that was what her beautiful sisters used to say.

Afterwards she decided it had been stupid of her to let him find out where 107 her class was. Though a timetable was posted in each of the colleges: all he had to do was look her up and record her every probable movement in block letters on his green notepad. After that day he never left her alone.

Initially he waited outside the lecture rooms for her to come out. She said 108 hello to him curtly at first and kept on going, but this didn't work; he followed her at a distance, smiling his changeless smile. Then she stopped speaking altogether and pretended to ignore him, but it made no difference, he followed her anyway. The fact that she was in some way afraid of him—or was it just embarrassment?—seemed only to encourage him. Her friends started to notice, asking her who he was and why he was tagging along behind her; she could hardly answer because she hardly knew.

As the weekdays passed and he showed no signs of letting up, she began to 109 jog-trot between classes, finally to run. He was tireless, and had an amazing wind for one who smoked so heavily: he would speed along behind her, keeping the distance between them the same, as though he were a pull-toy attached to her by a string. She was aware of the ridiculous spectacle they must make, galloping across campus, something out of a cartoon short, a lumbering elephant stampeded by a smiling, emaciated mouse, both of them locked in the classic pattern of comic pursuit and flight; but she found that to race made her less nervous than to walk sedately, the skin on the back of her neck crawling with the feel of his eyes on it. At least she could use her muscles. She worked out routines, escapes: she would dash in the front door of the Ladies' Room in the coffee shop and out the back door, and he would lose the trail, until he discovered the other entrance. She would try to shake him by detours through baffling archways and corridors, but he seemed as familiar with the architectural mazes as she was herself. As a last refuge she could head for the women's dormitory and watch from safety as he was skidded to a halt by the receptionist's austere voice: men were not allowed past the entrance.

Lunch became difficult. She would be sitting, usually with other members 110 of the Debating Society, just digging nicely into a sandwich, when he would appear suddenly as though he'd come up through an unseen manhole. She then had the choice of barging out through the crowded cafeteria, sandwich halfeaten, or finishing her lunch with him standing behind her chair, everyone at the table acutely aware of him, the conversation stilting and dwindling. Her friends learned to spot him from a distance; they posted lookouts. "Here he comes," they would whisper, helping her collect her belongings for the sprint they knew would follow.

Several times she got tired of running and turned to confront him. "What 111 do you want?" she would ask, glowering belligerently down at him, almost clenching her fists; she felt like shaking him, hitting him.

"I wish to talk with you."   112

"Well, here I am," she would say. "What do you want to talk about?"   113

But he would say nothing; he would stand in front of her, shifting his feet,   114
smiling perhaps apologetically (though she could never pinpoint the exact tone
of that smile, chewed lips stretched apart over the nicotine-yellowed teeth, rising at the corners, flesh held stiffly in place for an invisible photographer), his
eyes jerking from one part of her face to another as though he saw her in fragments.

Annoying and tedious though it was, his pursuit of her had an odd result: 115
mysterious in itself, it rendered her equally mysterious. No one had ever found
Christine mysterious before. To her parents she was a beefy heavyweight, a
plodder, lacking in flair, ordinary as bread. To her sisters she was the plain one,
treated with an indulgence they did not give to each other: they did not fear her
as a rival. To her male friends she was the one who could be relied on. She was
helpful and a hard worker, always good for a game of tennis with the athletes
among them. They invited her along to drink beer with them so they could get
into the cleaner, more desirable Ladies and Escorts side of the beer parlour, taking it for granted she would buy her share of the rounds. In moments of stress
they confided to her their problems with women. There was nothing devious
about her and nothing interesting.

Christine had always agreed with these estimates of herself. In childhood   116
she had identified with the false bride or the ugly sister; whenever a story had
begun, "Once there was a maiden as beautiful as she was good," she had known
it wasn't her. That was just how it was, but it wasn't so bad. Her parents never
expected her to be a brilliant social success and weren't overly disappointed
when she wasn't. She was spared the manoeuvring and anxiety she witnessed
among others her age, and she even had a kind of special position among men:
she was an exception, she fitted none of the categories they commonly used
when talking about girls; she wasn't a cock-teaser, a cold fish, an easy lay or a
snarky bitch; she was an honorary person. She had grown to share their contempt for most women.

Now, however, there was something about her that could not be explained.   117
A man was chasing her, a peculiar sort of man, granted, but still a man, and he
was without doubt attracted to her, he couldn't leave her alone. Other men examined her more closely than they ever had, appraising her, trying to find out
what it was those twitching bespectacled eyes saw in her. They started to ask her
out, though they returned from these excursions with their curiosity unsatis-
fied, the secret of her charm still intact. Her opaque dumpling face, her solid
bearshaped body became for them parts of a riddle no one could solve. Christine sensed this. In the bathtub she no longer imagined she was a dolphin; instead she imagined she was an elusive water-nixie, or sometimes, in moments
of audacity, Marilyn Monroe. The daily chase was becoming a habit; she even
looked forward to it. In addition to its other benefits she was losing weight.

All these weeks he had never phoned her or turned up at the house. He must   118
have decided however that his tactics were not having the desired result, or perhaps he sensed she was becoming bored. The phone began to ring in the early

morning or late at night when he could be sure she would be there. Sometimes he would simply breathe (she could recognize, or thought she could, the quality of his breathing), in which case she would hang up. Occasionally he would say again that he wanted to talk to her, but even when she gave him lots of time nothing else would follow. Then he extended his range: she would see him on her streetcar, smiling at her silently from a seat never closer than three away; she could feel him tracking her down her own street, though when she would break her resolve to pay no attention and would glance back he would be invisible or in the act of hiding behind a tree or hedge.

Among crowds of people and in daylight she had not really been afraid of 119 him; she was stronger than he was and he had made no recent attempt to touch her. But the days were growing shorter and colder, it was almost November. Often she was arriving home in twilight or a darkness broken only by the feeble orange streetlamps. She brooded over the possibility of razors, knives, guns; by acquiring a weapon he could quickly turn the odds against her. She avoided wearing scarves, remembering the newspaper stories about girls who had been strangled by them. Putting on her nylons in the morning gave her a funny feeling. Her body seemed to have diminished, to have become smaller than his.

Was he deranged, was he a sex maniac? He seemed so harmless, yet it was 120 that kind who often went berserk in the end. She pictured those ragged fingers at her throat, tearing at her clothes, though she could not think of herself as screaming. Parked cars, the shrubberies near her house, the driveways on either side of it, changed as she passed them from unnoticed background to sinister shadowed foreground, every detail distinct and harsh: they were places a man might crouch, leap out from. Yet every time she saw him in the clear light of morning or afternoon (for he still continued his old methods of pursuit), his aging jacket and jittery eyes convinced her that it was she herself who was the tormentor, the persecutor. She was in some sense responsible; from the folds and crevices of the body she had treated for so long as a reliable machine was emanating, against her will, some potent invisible odour, like a dog's in heat or a female moth's, that made him unable to stop following her.

Her mother, who had been too preoccupied with the unavoidable fall enter- 121 taining to pay much attention to the number of phone calls Christine was getting or to the hired girl's complaints of a man who hung up without speaking, announced that she was flying down to New York for the weekend; her father decided to go too. Christine panicked: she saw herself in the bathtub with her throat slit, the blood drooling out of her neck and running in a little spiral down the drain (for by this time she believed he could walk through walls, could be everywhere at once). The girl would do nothing to help; she might even stand in the bathroom door with her arms folded, watching. Christine arranged to spend the weekend at her married sister's.

When she arrived back Sunday evening she found the girl close to hysterics. 122 She said that on Saturday she had gone to pull the curtains across the French doors at dusk and had found a strangely contorted face, a man's face, pressed against the glass, staring in at her from the garden. She claimed she had fainted and had almost had her baby a month too early right there on the living-room carpet. Then she had called the police. He was gone by the time they got there but she had recognized him from the afternoon of the tea; she had informed them he was a friend of Christine's.

They called Monday evening to investigate, two of them. They were very po- 123 lite, they knew who Christine's father was. Her father greeted them heartily; her mother hovered in the background, fidgeting with her porcelain hands, letting them see how frail and worried she was. She didn't like having them in the living room but they were necessary.

Christine had to admit he'd been following her around. She was relieved 124 he'd been discovered, relieved also that she hadn't been the one to tell, though if he'd been a citizen of the country she would have called the police a long time ago. She insisted he was not dangerous, he had never hurt her.

"That kind don't hurt you," one of the policemen said. "They just kill you. 125 You're lucky you aren't dead."

"Nut cases," the other one said.   126

Her mother volunteered that the thing about people from another culture 127 was that you could never tell whether they were insane or not because their ways were so different. The policemen agreed with her, deferential but also condescending, as though she was a royal halfwit who had to be humoured.

"You know where he lives?" the first policeman asked. Christine had long 128 ago torn up the letter with his address on it; she shook her head.

"We'll have to pick him up tomorrow then," he said. "Think you can keep 129 him talking outside your class if he's waiting for you?"

After questioning her they held a murmured conversation with her father in 130 the front hall. The girl, clearing away the coffee cups, said if they didn't lock him up she was leaving, she wasn't going to be scared half out of her skin like that again.

Next day when Christine came out of her Modern History lecture he was 131 there, right on schedule. He seemed puzzled when she did not begin to run. She approached him, her heart thumping with treachery and the prospect of freedom. Her body was back to its usual size; she felt herself a giantess, self-controlled, invulnerable.

"How are you?" she asked, smiling brightly.   132

He looked at her with distrust.   133

"How have you been?" she ventured again. His own perennial smile faded; 134 he took a step back from her.

"This the one?" said the policeman, popping out from behind a notice 135 board like a Keystone Cop and laying a competent hand on the worn jacket shoulder. The other policeman lounged in the background; force would not be required.

"Don't *do* anything to him," she pleaded as they took him away. They nod- 136 ded and grinned, respectful, scornful. He seemed to know perfectly well who they were and what they wanted.

The first policeman phoned that evening to make his report. Her father 137 talked with him, jovial and managing. She herself was now out of the picture; she had been protected, her function was over.

"What did they *do* to him?" she asked anxiously as he came back into the 138 living room. She was not sure what went on in police stations.

"They didn't do anything to him," he said, amused by her concern. "They 139 could have booked him for Watching and Besetting, they wanted to know if I'd like to press charges. But it's not worth a court case: he's got a visa that says he's only allowed in the country as long as he studies in Montreal, so I told them to just ship him down there. If he turns up here again they'll deport him. They went around to his rooming house, his rent's two weeks overdue; the landlady said she was on the point of kicking him out. He seems happy enough to be getting his back rent paid and a free train ticket to Montreal." He paused. "They couldn't get anything out of him though."

"*Out* of him?" Christine asked. 140

"They tried to find out why he was doing it; following you, I mean." Her fa- 141 ther's eyes swept her as though it was a riddle to him also. "They said when they asked him about that he just clammed up. Pretended he didn't understand English. He understood well enough, but he wasn't answering."

Christine thought this would be the end, but somehow between his arrest 142 and the departure of the train he managed to elude his escort long enough for one more phone call.

"I see you again," he said. He didn't wait for her to hang up. 143

Now that he was no longer an embarrassing present reality, he could be 144 talked about, he could become an amusing story. In fact, he was the only amusing story Christine had to tell, and telling it preserved both for herself and for others the aura of her strange allure. Her friends and the men who continued to ask her out speculated about his motives. One suggested he had wanted to marry her so he could remain in the country; another said that oriental men were fond of well-built women: "It's your Rubens quality."

Christine thought about him a lot. She had not been attracted to him, 145 rather the reverse, but as an idea only he was a romantic figure, the one man who had found her irresistible; though she often wondered, inspecting her unchanged pink face and hefty body in her full-length mirror, just what it was about her that had done it. She avoided whenever it was proposed the theory of his insanity: it was only that there was more than one way of being sane.

But a new acquaintance, hearing the story for the first time, had a different 146 explanation. "So he got you, too," he said, laughing. "That has to be the same guy who was hanging around our day camp a year ago this summer. He followed all the girls like that, a short guy, Japanese or something, glasses, smiling all the time."

"Maybe it was another one," Christine said. 147

"There couldn't be two of them, everything fits. This was a pretty weird 148 guy."

"What . . . *kind* of girls did he follow?" Christine asked. 149

"Oh, just anyone who happened to be around. But if they paid any attention   150
to him at first, if they were nice to him or anything, he was unshakeable. He was
a bit of a pest, but harmless."

Christine ceased to tell her amusing story. She had been one among many,   151
then. She went back to playing tennis, she had been neglecting her game.

A few months later the policeman who had been in charge of the case tele-   152
phoned her again.

"Like you to know, miss, that fellow you were having the trouble with was   153
sent back to his own country. Deported."

"What for?" Christine asked. "Did he try to come back here?" Maybe she   154
had been special after all, maybe he had dared everything for her.

"Nothing like it," the policeman said. "He was up to the same tricks in Mon-   155
treal but he really picked the wrong woman this time—a Mother Superior of a
convent. They don't stand for things like that in Quebec—had him out of here
before he knew what happened. I guess he'll be better off in his own place."

"How old was she?" Christine asked, after a silence.   156

"Oh, around sixty, I guess."   157

"Thank you very much for letting me know," Christine said in her best offi-   158
cial manner. "It's such a relief." She wondered if the policeman had called to
make fun of her.

She was almost crying when she put down the phone. What *had* he wanted   159
from her then? A Mother Superior. Did she really look sixty, did she look like a
mother? What did convents mean? Comfort, charity? Refuge? Was it that something had happened to him, some intolerable strain just from being in this
country; her tennis dress and exposed legs too much for him, flesh and money
seemingly available everywhere but withheld from him wherever he turned, the
nun the symbol of some final distortion, the robe and veil reminiscent to his
nearsighted eyes of the women of his homeland, the ones he was able to understand? But he was back in his own country, remote from her as another planet;
she would never know.

He hadn't forgotten her though. In the spring she got a postcard with a for-   160
eign stamp and the familiar block-letter writing. On the front was a picture of a
temple. He was fine, he hoped she was fine also, he was her friend. A month
later another print of the picture he had taken in the garden arrived, in a sealed
manila envelope otherwise empty.

Christine's aura of mystery soon faded; anyway, she herself no longer be-   161
lieved in it. Life became again what she had always expected. She graduated
with mediocre grades and went into the Department of Health and Welfare; she
did a good job, and was seldom discriminated against for being a woman because nobody thought of her as one. She could afford a pleasant-sized apartment, though she did not put much energy into decorating it. She played less
and less tennis; what had been muscle with a light coating of fat turned gradually into fat with a thin substratum of muscle. She began to get headaches.

As the years were used up and the war began to fill the newspapers and   162
magazines, she realized which Eastern country he had actually been from. She

had known the name but it hadn't registered at the time, it was such a minor place; she could never keep them separate in her mind.

But though she tried, she couldn't remember the name of the city, and the 163 postcard was long gone—had he been from the North or the South, was he near the battle zone or safely far from it? Obsessively she bought magazines and pored over the available photographs, dead villagers, soldiers on the march, colour blowups of frightened or angry faces, spies being executed; she studied maps, she watched the late-night newscasts, the distant country and terrain becoming almost more familiar to her than her own. Once or twice she thought she could recognize him but it was no use, they all looked like him.

Finally she had to stop looking at the pictures. It bothered her too much, it 164 was bad for her; she was beginning to have nightmares in which he was coming through the French doors of her mother's house in his shabby jacket, carrying a packsack and a rifle and a huge bouquet of richly coloured flowers. He was smiling in the same way but the blood streaked over his face, partly blotting out the features. She gave her television set away and took to reading nineteenth-century novels instead; Trollope and Galsworthy were her favourites. When, despite herself, she would think about him, she would tell herself that he had been crafty and agile-minded enough to survive, more or less, in her country, so surely he would be able to do it in his own, where he knew the language. She could not see him in the army, on either side; he wasn't the type, and to her knowledge he had not believed in any particular ideology. He would be something nondescript, something in the background, like herself; perhaps he had become an interpreter.

ACTIVITIES FOR WRITING AND DISCUSSION

1. Working alone or in a group, identify any moments or junctures in the story that made you wonder, "What's going to happen next?" Then compare what you *expected* would happen with what *actually* happened. What conclusions can you draw from the contrast, if any, between your expectations and what happened?

2. Reread any passages pertaining to Christine's self-image. How did she get her self-image, and what was it like before she met "the man from Mars"? How does it evolve in the course of her relationship with the alien man? Why?

3. What motivations do various **characters** ascribe to "the man from Mars"? What reasons do they believe he has for pursuing Christine? What motivations, if any, are implied by the man himself? Investigate these questions. Then:

    a. Invent some diary entries or letters home in which you ("the man from Mars") talk about Christine, or

    b. Write an imaginary interview with the man in which you get the man to explain himself, or

c. Invent an exchange of letters between yourself and the **author** in which she discusses her intentions in the story.

4. What is the native land of "the man from Mars"? A sentence in the second-to-last paragraph begins, "Obsessively [Christine] bought magazines and pored over the available photographs." How can you account for this obsession? In the **persona** of Christine, write about your "obsession" and your inability to forget the man.

James Alan McPherson (b. 1943)

A Loaf of Bread

It was one of those obscene situations, pedestrian to most people, but invested   1
with meaning for a few poor folk whose lives are usually spent outside the imaginations of their fellow citizens. A grocer named Harold Green was caught red-handed selling to one group of people the very same goods he sold at lower prices at similar outlets in better neighborhoods. He had been doing this for many years, and at first he could not understand the outrage heaped upon him. He acted only from habit, he insisted, and had nothing personal against the people whom he served. They were his neighbors. Many of them he had carried on the cuff during hard times. Yet, through some mysterious access to a television station, the poor folk were now empowered to make grand denunciations of the grocer. Green's children now saw their father's business being picketed on the Monday evening news.

No one could question the fact that the grocer had been overcharging the   2
people. On the news even the reporter grimaced distastefully while reading the statistics. His expression said, "It is my job to report the news, but sometimes even I must disassociate myself from it to protect my honor." This, at least, was the impression the grocer's children seemed to bring away from the television. Their father's name had not been mentioned, but there was a close-up of his store with angry black people, and a few outraged whites, marching in groups of three in front of it. There was also a close-up of his name. After seeing this, they were in no mood to watch cartoons. At the dinner table, disturbed by his children's silence, Harold Green felt compelled to say, "I am not a dishonest man." Then he felt ashamed. The children, a boy and his older sister, immediately left the table, leaving Green alone with his wife. "Ruth, I am not dishonest," he repeated to her.

Ruth Green did not say anything. She knew, and her husband did not, that   3
the outraged people had also picketed the school attended by their children. They had threatened to return each day until Green lowered his prices. When they called her at home to report this, she had promised she would talk with him. Since she could not tell him this, she waited for an opening. She looked at her husband across the table.

"I did not make the world," Green began, recognizing at once the serious- 4
ness in her stare. "My father came to this country with nothing but his shirt. He
was exploited for as long as he couldn't help himself. He did not protest or
picket. He put himself in a position to play by the rules he had learned." He
waited for his wife to answer, and when she did not, he tried again. "I did not
make this world," he repeated. "I only make my way in it. Such people as these,
they do not know enough to not be exploited. If not me, there would be a
Greek, a Chinaman, maybe an Arab or a smart one of their own kind. Believe
me, I deal with them. There is something in their style that lacks the patience to
run a concern such as mine. If I closed down, take my word on it, someone else
would do what has to be done."

But Ruth Green was not thinking of his leaving. Her mind was on other 5
matters. Her children had cried when they came home early from school. She
had no special feeling for the people who picketed, but she did not like to see
her children cry. She had kissed them generously, then sworn them to silence.
"One day this week," she told her husband, "you will give free, for eight hours,
anything your customers come in to buy. There will be no publicity, except
what they spread by word of mouth. No matter what they say to you, no matter
what they take, you will remain silent." She stared deeply into him for what she
knew was there. "If you refuse, you have seen the last of your children and myself."

Her husband grunted. Then he leaned toward her. "I will not knuckle un- 6
der," he said. "I will *not* give!"

"We shall see," his wife told him.   7

———————

The black pickets, for the most part, had at first been frightened by the au- 8
dacity of their undertaking. They were peasants whose minds had long before
become resigned to their fate as victims. None of them, before now, had
thought to challenge this. But now, when they watched themselves on television, they hardly recognized the faces they saw beneath the hoisted banners and
placards. Instead of reflecting the meekness they all felt, the faces looked angry.
The close-ups looked especially intimidating. Several of the first pickets, maids
who worked in the suburbs, reported that their employers, seeing the activity
on the afternoon news, had begun treating them with new respect. One
woman, midway through the weather report, called around the neighborhood
to disclose that her employer had that very day given her a new china plate for
her meals. The paper plates, on which all previous meals had been served, had
been thrown into the wastebasket. One recipient of this call, a middle-aged
woman known for her bashfulness and humility, rejoined that her husband, a
sheet-metal worker, had only a few hours before been called "Mister" by his supervisor, a white man with a passionate hatred of color. She added the tale of a
neighbor down the street, a widow-woman named Murphy, who had at first
been reluctant to join the picket; this woman now was insisting it should be
made a daily event. Such talk as this circulated among the people who had been
instrumental in raising the issue. As news of their victory leaked into the ears of

others who had not participated, they received all through the night calls from strangers requesting verification, offering advice, and vowing support. Such strangers listened, and then volunteered stories about indignities inflicted on them by city officials, policemen, other grocers. In this way, over a period of hours, the community became even more incensed and restless than it had been at the time of the initial picket.

Soon, the man who had set events in motion found himself a hero. His 9
name was Nelson Reed, and all his adult life he had been employed as an assembly-line worker. He was a steady husband, the father of three children, and a deacon in the Baptist church. All his life he had trusted in God and gotten along. But now something in him capitulated to the reality that came suddenly into focus. "I was wrong," he told people who called him. "The onliest thing that matters in this world is *money*. And when was the last time you seen a picture of Jesus on a dollar bill?" This line, which he repeated over and over, caused a few callers to laugh nervously, but not without some affirmation that this was indeed the way things were. Many said they had known it all along. Others argued that although it was certainly true, it was one thing to live without money and quite another to live without faith. But still most callers laughed and said, "You right. You *know* I know you right. Ain't it the truth, though?" Only a few people, among them Nelson Reed's wife, said nothing and looked very sad.

Why they looked sad, however, they would not communicate. And anyone 10
observing their troubled faces would have to trust his own intuition. It is known that Reed's wife, Betty, measured all events against the fullness of her own experience. She was skeptical of everything. Brought to the church after a number of years of living openly with a jazz musician, she had embraced religion when she married Nelson Reed. But though she no longer believed completely in the world, she nonetheless had not fully embraced God. There was something in the nature of Christ's swift rise that had always bothered her, and something in the blood and vengeance of the Old Testament that was mellowing and refreshing. But she had never communicated these thoughts to anyone, especially her husband. Instead, she smiled vacantly while others professed leaps of faith, remained silent when friends spoke fiercely of their convictions. The presence of this vacuum in her contributed to her personal mystery; people said she was beautiful, although she was not outwardly so. Perhaps it was because she wished to protect this inner beauty that she did not smile now, and looked extremely sad, listening to her husband on the telephone.

Nelson Reed had no reason to be sad. He seemed to grow more energized 11
and talkative as the days passed. He was invited by an alderman, on the Tuesday after the initial picket, to tell his story on a local television talk show. He sweated heavily under the hot white lights and attempted to be philosophical. "I notice," the host said to him, "that you are not angry at this exploitative treatment. What, Mr. Reed, is the source of your calm?" The assembly-line worker looked unabashedly into the camera and said, "I have always believed in *Justice* with a capital *J*. I was raised up from a baby believin' that God ain't gonna let nobody go *too* far. See, in *my* mind God is in charge of *all* the capital letters in the alphabet of this world. It say in the Scripture He is Alpha and Omega, the

first and the last. He is just about the *onliest* capitalizer they is." Both Reed and the alderman laughed. "Now, when *men* start to capitalize, they gets *greedy*. They put a little *j* in *joy* and a littler one in *justice*. They raise up a big *G* in *Greed* and a big *E* in *Evil*. Well, soon as they commence to put a little *g* in *god,* you can expect some kind of reaction. The Savior will just raise up the *H* in *Hell* and go on from there. And that's just what I'm doin', giving these sharpies *HELL* with a big *H*." The talk show host laughed along with Nelson Reed and the alderman. After the taping they drank coffee in the back room of the studio and talked about the sad shape of the world.

———

Three days before he was to comply with his wife's request, Green, the gro- 12
cer, saw this talk show on television while at home. The words of Nelson Reed sent a chill through him. Though Reed had attempted to be philosophical, Green did not perceive the statement in this light. Instead, he saw a vindictive-looking black man seated between an ambitious alderman and a smug talk-show host. He saw them chatting comfortably about the nature of evil. The cameraman had shot mostly close-ups, and Green could see the set in Nelson Reed's jaw. The color of Reed's face was maddening. When his children came into the den, the grocer was in a sweat. Before he could think, he had shouted at them and struck the button turning off the set. The two children rushed from the room screaming. Ruth Green ran in from the kitchen. She knew why he was upset because she had received a call about the show; but she said nothing and pretended ignorance. Her children's school had been picketed that day, as it had the day before. But both children were still forbidden to speak of this to their father.

"Where do they get so much power?" Green said to his wife. "Two days ago, 13
nobody would have cared. Now, everywhere, even in my home, I am con-demned as a rascal. And what do I own? An airline? A multinational? Half of South America? *No!* I own three stores, one of which happens to be in a certain neighborhood inhabited by people who cost me money to run it." He sighed and sat upright on the sofa, his chubby legs spread wide. "A cab driver has a me-ter that clicks as he goes along. I pay extra for insurance, iron bars, pilfering by customers and employees. Nothing clicks. But when I add a little overhead to my prices, suddenly everything clicks. But for someone else. When was there last such a world?" He pressed the palms of both hands to his temples, suggest-ing a bombardment of brain-stinging sounds.

This gesture evoked no response from Ruth Green. She remained standing 14
by the door, looking steadily at him. She said, "To protect yourself, I would not stock any more fresh cuts of meat in the store until after the giveaway on Satur-day. Also, I would not tell it to the employees until after the first customer of the day has begun to check out. But I would urge you to hire several security guards to close the door promptly at seven-thirty, as is usual." She wanted to say much more than this, but did not. Instead she watched him. He was looking at the blank gray television screen, his palms still pressed against his ears. "In case you need to hear again," she continued in a weighty tone of voice, "I said two days

ago, and I say again now, that if you fail to do this you will not see your children again for many years."

He twisted his head and looked up at her. "What is the color of these peo- 15
ple?" he asked.

"Black," his wife said.   16

"And what is the name of my children?"   17

"Green."   18

The grocer smiled. "There is your answer," he told his wife. "Green is the 19
only color I am interested in."

His wife did not smile. "Insufficient," she said.   20

"The world is mad!" he moaned. "But it is a point of sanity with me to not 21
bend. I will not bend." He crossed his legs and pressed one hand firmly atop his
knee. "*I will not bend,*" he said.

"We will see," his wife said.   22

Nelson Reed, after the television interview, became the acknowledged 23
leader of the disgruntled neighbors. At first a number of them met in the
kitchen at his house; then, as space was lacking for curious newcomers, a mass
meeting was held on Thursday in an abandoned theater. His wife and three
children sat in the front row. Behind them sat the widow Murphy, Lloyd Dukes,
Tyrone Brown, Les Jones—those who had joined him on the first picket line.
Behind these sat people who bought occasionally at the store, people who lived
on the fringes of the neighborhood, people from other neighborhoods come to
investigate the problem, and the merely curious. The middle rows were occupied by a few people from the suburbs, those who had seen the talk show and
whose outrage at the grocer proved much more powerful than their fear of
black people. In the rear of the theater crowded aging, old-style leftists, somber
students, cynical young black men with angry grudges to explain with inarticu-
late gestures. Leaning against the walls, and huddled near the doors at the rear,
tape-recorder-bearing social scientists looked as detached and serene as book-
ies at the track. Here and there, in this diverse crowd, a politician stationed
himself, pumping hands vigorously and pressing his palms gently against the
shoulders of elderly people. Other visitors passed out leaflets, buttons, glossy
color prints of men who promoted causes, the familiar and obscure. There was
a hubbub of voices, a blend of the strident and the playful, the outraged and the
reverent, lending an undercurrent of ominous energy to the assembly.

Nelson Reed spoke from a platform on the stage, standing before a yel- 24
lowed, shredded screen that had once reflected the images of matinee idols. "I
don't mind sayin' that I have always been a sucker," he told the crowd. "All my
life I have been a sucker for the words of Jesus. Being a natural-born fool, I just
ain't never had the *sense* to learn no better. Even right today, while the whole
world is sayin' wrong is right and up is down, I'm so dumb I'm *still* steady believin' what is wrote in the Good Book . . ."

From the audience, especially the front rows, came a chorus singing, 25
"Preach!"

"I have no doubt," he continued in a low baritone, "that it's true what is writ   26
in the Good Book: 'The last shall be first and the first shall be last.' I don't know
about y'all, but I have *always* been the last. I never wanted to be the first, but
sometimes it look like the world get so bad that them that's holdin' onto the
tree of life is the onliest ones left when God commence to blowin' dead leafs off
the branches."

"Now you preaching," someone called.   27

In the rear of the theater a white student shouted an awkward "Amen."   28

Nelson Reed began walking across the stage to occupy the major part of his   29
nervous energy. But to those in the audience, who now hung on his every word,
it looked as though he strutted. "All my life," he said, "I have claimed to be a
man without earnin' the right to call myself that. You know, the *average* man
ain't really a man. The average man is a *bootlicker*. In fact, the *average* man
would *run away* if he found hisself standing alone facin' down a adversary. I
have done that *too many a time* in my life! But *not no more*. Better to be *once* was
than *never* was a man. I will tell you tonight, there is somethin' *wrong* in being
average. *I intend to stand up!* Now, if your average man that ain't really a man
stand up, two things gonna happen: *One,* he g'on bust through all the weights
that been place on his head, and, *two,* he g'on feel a lot of pain. But that same
hurt is what make things fall in place. That, and gettin' your hands on one
of these slick four-flushers tight enough so's you can squeeze him and say,
'*No more!*' You do that, you g'on hurt some, but *you won't be average no
more . . .*"

"*No more!*" a few people in the front rows repeated.   30

"I say *no more!*" Nelson Reed shouted.   31

"*No more! No more! No more!*" The chant rustled through the crowd like the   32
rhythm of an autumn wind against a shedding tree.

Then people laughed and chattered in celebration.   33

As for the grocer, from the evening of the television interview he had begun   34
to make plans. Unknown to his wife, he cloistered himself several times with his
brother-in-law, an insurance salesman, and plotted a course. He had no intention of tossing steaks to the crowd. "And why should I, Tommy?" he asked his
wife's brother, a lean, bald-headed man named Thomas. "I don't cheat anyone. I
have never cheated anyone. The businesses I run are always on the up-and-up.
So why should I pay?"

"Quite so," the brother-in-law said, chewing an unlit cigarillo. "The world   35
has gone crazy. Next they will say that people in my business are responsible for
prolonging life. I have found that people who refuse to believe in death refuse
also to believe in the harshness of life. I sell well by saying that death is a long
happiness. I show people the realities of life and compare this to a funeral with
dignity, *and* the promise of a bundle for every loved one salted away. When they
look around hard at life, they usually buy."

"So?" asked Green. Thomas was a college graduate with a penchant for phi-   36
losophy.

"So," Thomas answered. "You must fight to show these people the reality of 37
both your situation and theirs. How would it be if you visited one of their
meetings and chalked out, on a blackboard, the dollars and cents of your operation? Explain your overhead, your security fees, all the additional expenses. If
you treat them with respect, they might understand."

Green frowned. "That I would never do," he said. "It would be admission of 38
a certain guilt."

The brother-in-law smiled, but only with one corner of his mouth. "Then 39
you have something to feel guilty about?" he asked.

The grocer frowned at him. "*Nothing!*" he said with great emphasis. 40

"So?" Thomas said. 41

This first meeting between the grocer and his brother-in-law took place on 42
Thursday, in a crowded barroom.

At the second meeting, in a luncheonette, it was agreed that the grocer 43
should speak privately with the leader of the group, Nelson Reed. The meeting
at which this was agreed took place on Friday afternoon. After accepting this
advice from Thomas, the grocer resigned himself to explain to Reed, in as finite
detail as possible, the economic structure of his operation. He vowed to suppress no information. He would explain everything: inventories, markups, sale
items, inflation, balance sheets, specialty items, overhead, and that mysterious
item called profit. This last item, promising to be the most difficult to explain,
Green and his brother-in-law debated over for several hours. They agreed first
of all that a man should not work for free, then they agreed that it was unethical
to ruthlessly exploit. From these parameters, they staked out an area between
fifteen and forty percent, and agreed that someplace between these two borders
lay an amount of return that could be called fair. This was easy, but then
Thomas introduced the factor of circumstance. He questioned whether the fact
that one serviced a risky area justified the earning of profits closer to the forty-
percent edge of the scale. Green was unsure. Thomas smiled. "Here is a case that
will point out an analogy," he said, licking a cigarillo. "I read in the papers that a
family wants to sell an electric stove. I call the home and the man says fifty dollars. I ask to come out and inspect the merchandise. When I arrive I see they are
poor, have already bought a new stove that is connected and are selling the old
one for fifty dollars because they want it out of the place. The electric stove is in
good condition, worth much more than fifty. But because I see what I see I offer
forty-five."

Green, for some reason, wrote down this figure on the back of the sales slip 44
for the coffee they were drinking.

The brother-in-law smiled. He chewed his cigarillo. "The man agrees to take 45
forty-five dollars, saying he has had no other calls. I look at the stove again and
see a spot of rust. I say I will give him forty dollars. He agrees to this, on condition that I myself haul it away. I say I will haul it away if he comes down to
thirty. You, of course, see where I am going."

The grocer nodded. "The circumstances of his situation, his need to get rid of 46
the stove quickly, placed him in a position where he has little room to bargain?"

"Yes," Thomas answered. "So? Is it ethical, Harry?" 47

Harold Green frowned. He had never liked his brother-in-law, and now he 48 thought the insurance agent was being crafty. "But," he answered, "this man does not *have* to sell! It is his choice whether to wait for other calls. It is not the fault of the buyer that the seller is in a hurry. It is the right of the buyer to get what he wants at the lowest price possible. That is the rule. That has *always* been the rule. And the reverse of it applies to the seller as well."

"Yes," Thomas said, sipping coffee from the Styrofoam cup. "But suppose 49 that in addition to his hurry to sell, the owner was also a weak soul. There are, after all, many such people." He smiled. "Suppose he placed no value on the money?"

"Then," Green answered, "your example is academic. Here we are not talk- 50 ing about real life. One man lives by the code, one man does not. Who is there free enough to make a judgment?" He laughed. "Now you see," he told his brother-in-law. "Much more than a few dollars are at stake. If this one buyer is to be condemned, then so are most people in the history of the world. An examination of history provides the only answer to your question. This code will be here tomorrow, long after the ones who do not honor it are not."

They argued fiercely late into the afternoon, the brother-in-law leaning 51 heavily on his readings. When they parted, a little before 5:00 P.M., nothing had been resolved.

Neither was much resolved during the meeting between Green and Nelson 52 Reed. Reached at home by the grocer in the early evening, the leader of the group spoke coldly at first, but consented finally to meet his adversary at a nearby drugstore for coffee and a talk. They met at the lunch counter, shook hands awkwardly, and sat for a few minutes discussing the weather. Then the grocer pulled two gray ledgers from his briefcase. "You have for years come into my place," he told the man. "In my memory I have always treated you well. Now our relationship has come to this." He slid the books along the counter until they touched Nelson Reed's arm.

Reed opened the top book and flipped the thick green pages with his 53 thumb. He did not examine the figures. "All I know," he said, "is over at your place a can of soup cost me fifty-five cents, and two miles away at your other store for white folks you chargin' thirty-nine cents." He said this with the calm authority of an outraged soul. A quality of condescension tinged with pity crept into his gaze.

The grocer drummed his fingers on the counter top. He twisted his head 54 and looked away, toward shelves containing cosmetics, laxatives, toothpaste. His eyes lingered on a poster of a woman's apple red lips and milk white teeth. The rest of the face was missing.

"Ain't no use to hide," Nelson Reed said, as to a child. "*I* know you wrong, 55 *you* know you wrong, and before I finish, *everybody in this city* g'on know you wrong. God don't *like* ugly." He closed his eyes and gripped the cup of coffee. Then he swung his head suddenly and faced the grocer again. "Man, why you want to *do* people that way?" he asked. "We human, same as you."

"Before *God!*" Green exclaimed, looking squarely into the face of Nelson 56 Reed. "Before God!" he said again. "*I am not an evil man!*" These last words sounded more like a moan as he tightened the muscles in his throat to lower the sound of his voice. He tossed his left shoulder as if adjusting the sleeve of his coat, or as if throwing off some unwanted weight. Then he peered along the countertop. No one was watching. At the end of the counter the waitress was scrubbing the coffee urn. "Look at these figures, please," he said to Reed.

The man did not drop his gaze. His eyes remained fixed on the grocer's face. 57

"All right," Green said. "Don't look. I'll tell you what is in these books, be- 58 lieve me if you want. I work twelve hours a day, one day off per week, running my business in three stores. I am not a wealthy person. In one place, in the area you call white, I get by barely by smiling lustily at old ladies, stocking gourmet stuff on the chance I will build a reputation as a quality store. The two clerks there cheat me; there is nothing I can do. In this business you must be friendly with everybody. The second place is on the other side of town, in a neighbor- hood as poor as this one. I get out there seldom. The profits are not worth the gas. I use the loss there as a write-off against some other properties." He paused. "Do you understand write-off?" he asked Nelson Reed.

"Naw," the man said. 59

Harold Green laughed. "What does it matter?" he said in a tone of voice in- 60 tended for himself alone. "In this area I will admit I make a profit, but it is not so much as you think. But I do not make a profit here because the people are black. I make a profit because a profit is here to be made. I invest more here in window bars, theft losses, insurance, spoilage; I deserve to make more here than at the other places." He looked, almost imploringly, at the man seated next to him. "You don't accept this as the right of a man in business?"

Reed grunted. "Did the bear shit in the woods?" he said. 61

Again Green laughed. He gulped his coffee awkwardly, as if eager to go. Yet 62 his motions slowed once he had set the coffee cup down on the blue plastic saucer. "Place yourself in *my* situation," he said, his voice high and tentative. "If *you* were running my store in this neighborhood, what would be *your* position? Say on a profit scale of fifteen to forty percent, at what point in between would you draw the line?"

Nelson Reed thought. He sipped his coffee and seemed to chew the liquid. 63 "Fifteen to forty?" he repeated.

"Yes." 64

"I'm a churchgoin' man," he said. "Closer to fifteen than to forty." 65

"How close?" 66

Nelson Reed thought. "In church you tithe ten percent." 67

"In restaurants you tip fifteen," the grocer said quickly. 68

"All right," Reed said. "Over fifteen." 69

"How much over?" 70

Nelson Reed thought. 71

"Twenty, thirty, thirty-five?" Green chanted, leaning closer to Reed. 72

Still the man thought. 73

"Forty? Maybe even forty-five or fifty?" the grocer breathed in Reed's ear. 74 "In the supermarkets, you know, they have more subtle ways of accomplishing such feats."

Reed slapped his coffee cup with the back of his right hand. The brown liq- 75 uid swirled across the counter top, wetting the books. "*Damn this!*" he shouted.

Startled, Green rose from his stool. 76

Nelson Reed was trembling. "I ain't *you*," he said in a deep baritone. "I ain't 77 the *supermarket* neither. All I is is a poor man that works *too* hard to see his pay slip through his fingers like rainwater. All I know is you done *cheat* me, you done *cheat* everybody in the neighborhood, and we organized now to get some of it *back!*" Then he stood and faced the grocer. "My daddy sharecropped down in Mississippi and bought in the company store. He owed them twenty-three years when he died. I paid off five of them years and then run away to up here. Now, I'm a deacon in the Baptist church. I raised my kids the way my daddy raise me and don't bother nobody. Now come to find out, after all my runnin', they done lift that *same company store* up out of Mississippi and slip it down on us here! Well, my daddy was a *fighter,* and if he hadn't owed all them years he would of raise him some hell. Me, I'm steady my daddy's child, plus I got se-niority in my union. I'm a free man. Buddy, don't you know *I'm gonna raise me some hell!*"

Harold Green reached for a paper napkin to sop the coffee soaking into his 78 books.

Nelson Reed threw a dollar on top of the books and walked away. 79

———————————

"I *will not* do it!" Harold Green said to his wife that same evening. They 80 were in the bathroom of their home. Bending over the face bowl, she was wash-ing her hair with a towel draped around her neck. The grocer stood by the door, looking in at her. "I will not bankrupt myself tomorrow," he said.

"I've been thinking about it, too," Ruth Green said, shaking her wet hair. 81 "You'll do it, Harry."

"Why should I?" he asked. "You won't leave. You know it was a bluff. I've 82 waited this long for you to calm down. Tomorrow is Saturday. This week has been a hard one. Tonight let's be realistic."

"Of course you'll do it," Ruth Green said. She said it the way she would say 83 "Have some toast." She said, "You'll do it because you want to see your children grow up."

"And for what other reason?" he asked. 84

She pulled the towel tighter around her neck. "Because you are at heart a 85 moral man."

He grinned painfully. "If I am, why should I have to prove it to *them*?" 86

"Not them," Ruth Green said, freezing her movements and looking in the 87 mirror. "Certainly not them. By no means them. They have absolutely nothing to do with this."

"Who, then?" he asked, moving from the door into the room. "Who else 88 should I prove something to?"

His wife was crying. But her entire face was wet. The tears moved secretly 89
down her face.

"Who else?" Harold Green asked. 90

It was almost 11:00 P.M. and the children were in bed. They had also cried 91
when they came home from school. Ruth Green said, "For yourself, Harry. For
the love that lives inside your heart."

All night the grocer thought about this. 92

Nelson Reed also slept little that Friday night. When he returned home 93
from the drugstore, he reported to his wife as much of the conversation as he
could remember. At first he had joked about the exchange between himself and
the grocer, but as more details returned to his conscious mind he grew solemn
and then bitter. "He ask me to put myself in *his* place," Reed told his wife. "Can
you imagine that kind of gumption? I never cheated nobody in my life. All my
life I have lived on Bible principles. I am a deacon in the church. I have work all
my life for other folks and I don't even own the house I live in." He paced up
and down the kitchen, his big arms flapping loosely at his sides. Betty Reed sat
at the table, watching. "This here's a low-down, ass-kicking world," he said. "I
swear to God it is! All my life I have lived on principle and I ain't got a dime in
the bank. Betty," he turned suddenly toward her, "don't you think I'm a fool?"

"Mr. Reed," she said. "Let's go on to bed." 94

But he would not go to bed. Instead, he took the fifth of bourbon from the 95
cabinet under the sink and poured himself a shot. His wife refused to join him.
Reed drained the glass of whiskey, and then another, while he resumed pacing
the kitchen floor. He slapped his hands against his sides. "*I* think I'm a fool," he
said. "Ain't got a dime in the bank, ain't got a pot to *pee* in or a wall to pitch it
over, and that there *cheat* ask me to put myself inside *his* shoes. Hell, I can't even
afford the kind of shoes he wears." He stopped pacing and looked at his wife.

"Mr. Reed," she whispered, "tomorrow ain't a work day. Let's go to bed." 96

Nelson Reed laughed, the bitterness in his voice rattling his wife. "The *hell* I 97
will!" he said.

He strode to the yellow telephone on the wall beside the sink and began to 98
dial. The first call was to Lloyd Dukes, a neighbor two blocks away and a lieutenant in the organization. Dukes was not at home. The second call was to
McElroy's Bar on the corner of 65th and Carroll, where Stanley Harper, another
of the lieutenants, worked as a bartender. It was Harper who spread the word,
among those men at the bar, that the organization would picket the grocer's
store the following morning. And all through the night, in the bedroom of their
house, Betty Reed was awakened by telephone calls coming from Lester Jones,
Nat Lucas, Mrs. Tyrone Brown, the widow-woman named Murphy, all coordi-
nating the time when they would march in a group against the store owned by
Harold Green. Betty Reed's heart beat loudly beneath the covers as she listened
to the bitterness and rage in her husband's voice. On several occasions, hearing
him declare himself a fool, she pressed the pillow against her eyes and cried.

The grocer opened later than usual this Saturday morning, but still it was 99 early enough to make him one of the first walkers in the neighborhood. He parked his car one block from the store and strolled to work. There were no birds singing. The sky in this area was not blue. It was smog-smutted and gray, seeming on the verge of a light rain. The street, as always, was littered with cans, papers, bits of broken glass. As always the garbage cans overflowed. The morning breeze plastered a sheet of newspaper playfully around the sides of a rusted garbage can. For some reason, using his right foot, he loosened the paper and stood watching it slide into the street and down the block. The movement made him feel good. He whistled while unlocking the bars shielding the windows and door of his store. When he had unlocked the main door he stepped in quickly and threw a switch to the right of the jamb, before the shrill sound of the alarm could shatter his mood. Then he switched on the lights. Everything was as it had been the night before. He had already telephoned his two employees and given them the day off. He busied himself doing the usual things—hauling milk and vegetables from the cooler, putting cash in the till—not thinking about the silence of his wife, or the look in her eyes, only an hour before when he left home. He had determined, at some point while driving through the city, that today it would be business as usual. But he expected very few customers.

The first customer of the day was Mrs. Nelson Reed. She came in around 100 9:30 A.M. and wandered about the store. He watched her from the checkout counter. She seemed uncertain of what she wanted to buy. She kept glancing at him down the center aisle. His suspicions aroused, he said finally, "Yes, may I help you, Mrs. Reed?" His words caused her to jerk, as if some devious thought had been perceived going through her mind. She reached over quickly and lifted a loaf of whole wheat bread from the rack and walked with it to the counter. She looked at him and smiled. The smile was a broad, shy one, that rare kind of smile one sees on virgin girls when they first confess love to themselves. Betty Reed was a woman of about forty-five. For some reason he could not comprehend, this gesture touched him. When she pulled a dollar from her purse and laid it on the counter, an impulse, from no place he could locate with his mind, seized control of his tongue. "Free," he told Betty Reed. She paused, then pushed the dollar toward him with a firm and determined thrust of her arm. "Free," he heard himself saying strongly, his right palm spread and meeting her thrust with absolute force. She clutched the loaf of bread and walked out of his store.

The next customer, a little girl, arriving well after 10:30 A.M., selected a 101 candy bar from the rack beside the counter. "Free," Green said cheerfully. The little girl left the candy on the counter and ran out of the store.

At 11:15 A.M. a wino came in looking desperate enough to sell his soul. The 102 grocer watched him only for an instant. Then he went to the wine counter and selected a half-gallon of medium-grade red wine. He shoved the jug into the belly of the wino, the man's sour breath bathing his face. "Free," the grocer said. "But you must not drink it in here."

He felt good about the entire world, watching the wino through the window 103 gulping the wine and looking guiltily around.

At 11:25 A.M. the pickets arrived.   104

Two dozen people, men and women, young and old, crowded the pavement   105
in front of his store. Their signs, placards, and voices denounced him as a para-
site. The grocer laughed inside himself. He felt lighthearted and wild, like a
man drugged. He rushed to the meat counter and pulled a long roll of brown
wrapping paper from the rack, tearing it neatly with a quick shift of his body
resembling a dance step practiced fervently in his youth. He laid the paper on
the chopping block and with the black-inked, felt-tipped marker scrawled, in
giant letters, the word FREE. This he took to the window and pasted in place
with many strands of Scotch tape. He was laughing wildly. "Free!" he shouted
from behind the brown paper. "Free! Free! Free! Free! Free! Free!" He rushed to
the door, pushed his head out, and screamed to the confused crowd, "*Free!*"
Then he ran back to the counter and stood behind it, like a soldier at attention.

They came in slowly.   106

Nelson Reed entered first, working his right foot across the dirty tile as if   107
tracking a squiggling worm. The others followed: Lloyd Dukes dragging a plac-
ard, Mr. and Mrs. Tyrone Brown, Stanley Harper walking with his fists
clenched, Lester Jones with three of his children, Nat Lucas looking sheepish
and detached, a clutch of winos, several bashful nuns, ironic-smiling teenagers
and a few students. Bringing up the rear was a bearded social scientist holding a
tape recorder to his chest. "Free!" the grocer screamed. He threw up his arms in
a gesture that embraced, or dismissed, the entire store. "*All free!*" he shouted.
He was grinning with the grace of a madman.

The winos began grabbing first. They stripped the shelf of wine in a matter   108
of seconds. Then they fled, dropping bottles on the tile in their wake. The others, stepping quickly through this liquid, soon congealed it into a sticky, blood-
like consistency. The young men went for the cigarettes and luncheon meats
and beer. One of them had the prescience to grab a sack from the counter, while
the others loaded their arms swiftly, hugging cartons and packages of cold cuts
like long-lost friends. The students joined them, less for greed than for the thrill
of the experience. The two nuns backed toward the door. As for the older people, men and women, they stood at first as if stuck to the wine-smeared floor.
Then Stanley Harper, the bartender, shouted, "The man said *free,* y'all heard
him." He paused. "Didn't you say *free* now?" he called to the grocer.

"I said free," Harold Green answered, his temples pounding.   109

A cheer went up. The older people began grabbing, as if the secret lusts of a   110
lifetime had suddenly seized command of their arms and eyes. They grabbed
toilet tissue, cold cuts, pickles, sardines, boxes of raisins, boxes of starch, cans of
soup, tins of tuna fish and salmon, bottles of spices, cans of boned chicken,
slippery cans of olive oil. Here a man, Lester Jones, burdened himself with several heads of lettuce, while his wife, in another aisle, shouted for him to drop
those small items and concentrate on the gourmet section. She herself took imported sardines, wheat crackers, bottles of candied pickles, herring, anchovies,
imported olives, French wafers, an ancient, half-rusted can of paté, stocked, by
mistake, from the inventory of another store. Others packed their arms with

detergents, hams, chocolate-coated cereal, whole chickens with hanging asses, wedges of bologna and salami like squashed footballs, chunks of cheeses, yellow and white, shriveled onions, and green peppers. Mrs. Tyrone Brown hung a curve of pepperoni around her neck and seemed to take on instant dignity, much like a person of noble birth in possession now of a long sought-after gem. Another woman, the widow Murphy, stuffed tomatoes into her bosom, holding a half-chewed lemon in her mouth. The more enterprising fought desperately over the three rusted shopping carts, and the victors wheeled these along the narrow aisles, sweeping into them bulk items—beer in sixpacks, sacks of sugar, flour, glass bottles of syrup, toilet cleanser, sugar cookies, prune, apple and tomato juices—while others endeavored to snatch the carts from them. There were several fistfights and much cursing. The grocer, standing behind the counter, hummed and rang his cash register like a madman.

Nelson Reed, the first into the store, followed the nuns out, empty-handed. 111

In less than half an hour the others had stripped the store and vanished in 112 many directions up and down the block. But still more people came, those late in hearing the news. And when they saw the shelves were bare, they cursed soberly and chased those few stragglers still bearing away goods. Soon only the grocer and the social scientist remained, the latter stationed at the door with his tape recorder sucking in leftover sounds. Then he too slipped away up the block.

———

By 12:10 P.M. the grocer was leaning against the counter, trying to make his 113 mind slow down. Not a man given to drink during work hours he nonetheless took a swallow from a bottle of wine, a dusty bottle from beneath the wine shelf, somehow overlooked by the winos. Somewhat recovered, he was preparing to remember what he should do next when he glanced toward a figure at the door. Nelson Reed was standing there, watching him.

"All gone," Harold Green said. "My friend, Mr. Reed, there is no more." Still 114 the man stood in the doorway, peering into the store.

The grocer waved his arms about the empty room. Not a display case had a 115 single item standing. "All gone," he said again, as if addressing a stupid child. "There is nothing left to get. You, my friend, have come back too late for a second load. I am cleaned out."

Nelson Reed stepped into the store and strode toward the counter. He 116 moved through wine-stained flour, lettuce leaves, red, green, and blue labels, bits and pieces of broken glass. He walked toward the counter.

"All day," the grocer laughed not quite hysterically now, "all day long I have 117 not made a single cent of profit. The entire day was a loss. This store, like the others, is *bleeding* me." He waved his arms about the room in a magnificent gesture of uncaring loss. "Now do you understand?" he said. "Now will you put yourself in my shoes? I have nothing here. Come, now, Mr. Reed, would it not be so bad a thing to walk in my shoes?"

"Mr. Green," Nelson Reed said coldly. "My wife bought a loaf of bread in   118
here this mornin'. She forgot to pay you. I, myself, have come here to pay you
your money."

"Oh," the grocer said.   119

"I think it was brown bread. Don't that cost more than white?"   120

The two men looked away from each other, but not at anything in the store.   121

"In my store, yes," Harold Green said. He rang the register with the most ca-   122
sual movement of his finger. The register read fifty-five cents.

Nelson Reed held out a dollar.   123

"And two cents tax," the grocer said.   124

The man held out the dollar.   125

"After all," Harold Green said. "We are all, after all, Mr. Reed, in debt to the   126
government."

He rang the register again. It read fifty-seven cents.   127

Nelson Reed held out a dollar.   128

ACTIVITIES FOR WRITING AND DISCUSSION

1. At the beginning of the fourth paragraph, Green says, "I did not make the world." He contends that he is only doing what he *must* and that anyone else in his position would do the same.

   a. Identify a situation that placed someone in a dilemma similar to Green's. Who was involved? What was the focus of conflict? How was (or wasn't) the conflict resolved? Provide the facts and write the story of that situation.

   b. Agree with Green's statement that he "did not make the world," summarizing arguments in the text (or your own) that support his claim. Then disagree with him, summarizing arguments in the text (or your own) that take an opposing point of view.

2. Reread Thomas's story (p. 644) about the sale of the electric stove. Then offer your own answer to Thomas's follow-up question, "Is it ethical?" Provide reasons for your answer.

3. Why do you suppose Betty Reed comes to buy something in Green's store on Saturday morning, even though she knows the store is to be picketed that day? To answer this question, first reread and annotate any passages in the story that talk about Betty, her character, or her motivations. Then assume Betty's **persona** and express the thoughts and motives leading up to your action.

4. Using one of the "Ten Ideas for Writing from Reading" in Chapter 3—or some other approach of your own choosing—respond to any of the events that occur in Green's store on that fateful Saturday.

SANDRA CISNEROS (b. 1954)

Excerpts from *The House on Mango Street*

Marin

Marin's boyfriend is in Puerto Rico. She shows us his letters and makes us 1
promise not to tell anybody they're getting married when she goes back to P.R.
She says he didn't get a job yet, but she is saving the money she gets from selling
Avon and taking care of her cousins.

Marin says that if she stays here next year, she is going to get a real job 2
downtown because that's where the best jobs are, since you always get to look
beautiful and get to wear nice clothes and can meet someone in the subway
who might marry and take you to live in a big house far away.

But next year Louie's parents are going to send her back to her mother with 3
a letter saying she is too much trouble, and that is too bad because I like Marin.
She is older and knows lots of things. She is the one who told us how the Baby's
sister got pregnant and what cream is best for taking off moustache hair and if
you count the white flecks on your fingernails you can know how many boys
are thinking of you and lots of other things I can't remember now.

We never see Marin until her aunt comes home from work, and even then 4
she can only stay out in front. She is there every night with the radio. When the
light in her aunt's room goes out, Marin lights a cigarette and it doesn't matter
if it's cold out or if the radio doesn't work or if we've got nothing to say to each
other. What matters, Marin says, is for the boys to see us and for us to see them.
And since Marin's skirts are shorter and since her eyes are pretty, and since
Marin is already older than us in many ways, the boys that do pass say stupid
things like I am in love with those two green apples you call eyes, give them to
me why don't you. And Marin just looks at them without even blinking and is
not afraid.

Marin, under the streetlight, dancing by herself, is singing the same song 5
somewhere. I know. Is waiting for a car to stop, a star to fall, someone to change
her life. Anybody.

Those Who Don't

Those who don't know any better come into our neighborhood scared. They 6
think we're dangerous. They think we will attack them with shiny knives. They
are stupid people who are lost and got here by mistake.

But we aren't afraid. We know the guy with the crooked eye is Davey the 7
Baby's brother, and the tall one next to him in the straw brim, that's Rosa's Ed-

die V. and the big one that looks like a dumb grown man, he's Fat Boy, though he's not fat anymore nor a boy.

All brown all around, we are safe. But watch us drive into a neighborhood of 8
another color and our knees go shakity-shake and our car windows get rolled up tight and our eyes look straight. Yeah. That is how it goes and goes.

Geraldo No Last Name

She met him at a dance. Pretty too, and young. Said he worked in a restaurant, 9
but she can't remember which one. Geraldo. That's all. Green pants and Saturday shirt. Geraldo. That's what he told her.

And how was she to know she'd be the last one to see him alive. An accident, 10
don't you know. Hit and run. Marin, she goes to all those dances. Uptown, Logan. Embassy. Palmer. Aragon. Fontana. The Manor. She likes to dance. She knows how to do cumbias and salsas and rancheras even. And he was just someone she danced with. Somebody she met that night. That's right.

That's the story. That's what she said again and again. Once to the hospital 11
people and twice to the police. No address. No name. Nothing in his pockets. Ain't it a shame.

Only Marin can't explain why it mattered, the hours and hours, for some- 12
body she didn't even know. The hospital emergency room. Nobody but an intern working all alone. And maybe if the surgeon would've come, maybe if he hadn't lost so much blood, if the surgeon had only come, they would know who to notify and where.

But what difference does it make? He wasn't anything to her. He wasn't her 13
boyfriend or anything like that. Just another *brazer* who didn't speak English. Just another wetback. You know the kind. The ones who always look ashamed. And what was she doing out at three A.M. anyway? Marin who was sent home with her coat and some aspirin. How does she explain it?

She met him at a dance. Geraldo in his shiny shirt and green pants. Geraldo 14
going to a dance.

What does it matter?   15

They never saw the kitchenettes. They never knew about the two-room flats 16
and sleeping rooms he rented, the weekly money orders sent home, the currency exchange. How could they?

His name was Geraldo. And his home is in another country. The ones he left 17
behind are far away. They will wonder. Shrug. Remember. Geraldo. He went north . . . we never heard from him again.

No Speak English

Mamacita is the big mama of the man across the street, third-floor front. 18
Rachel says her name ought to be *Mamasota*, but I think that's mean.

The man saved his money to bring her here. He saved and saved because she 19 was alone with the baby boy in that country. He worked two jobs. He came home late and he left early. Every day.

Then one day Mamacita and the baby boy arrived in a yellow taxi. The taxi 20 door opened like a waiter's arm. Out stepped a tiny pink shoe, a foot soft as a rabbit's ear, then the thick ankle, a fluttering of hips, fuchsia roses and green perfume. The man had to pull her, the taxicab driver had to push. Push, pull. Push, pull. Poof!

All at once she bloomed. Huge, enormous, beautiful to look at, from the 21 salmon-pink feather to the tip of her hat down to the little rosebuds of her toes. I couldn't take my eyes off her tiny shoes.

Up, up, up the stairs she went with the baby boy in a blue blanket, the man 22 carrying her suitcases, her lavender hatboxes, a dozen boxes of satin high heels. Then we didn't see her.

Somebody said because she's too fat, somebody because of the three flights 23 of stairs, but I believe she doesn't come out because she is afraid to speak English, and maybe this is so since she only knows eight words. She knows to say: *He not here* for when the landlord comes, *No speak English* if anybody else comes, and *holy smokes*. I don't know where she learned this, but I heard her say it one time and it surprised me.

My father says when he came to this country he ate ham and eggs for three 24 months. Breakfast, lunch and dinner. Ham and eggs. That was the only words he knew. He doesn't eat ham and eggs anymore.

Whatever her reasons, whether she is fat or can't climb the stairs or is afraid 25 of English, she won't come down. She sits all day by the window and plays the Spanish radio show and sings all the homesick songs about her country in a voice that sounds like a sea gull.

Home. Home. Home is a house in a photograph, a pink house, pink as hol- 26 lyhocks with lots of startled light. The man paints the walls of the apartment pink, but it's not the same you know. She still sighs for her pink house, and then I think she cries. I would.

Sometimes the man gets disgusted. He starts screaming and you can hear it 27 all the way down the street.

Ay, she says, she is sad. 28

Oh, he says, not again. 29

¿Cuándo, cuándo, cuándo? she asks. 30

Ay, Caray! We *are* home. This *is* home. Here I am and here I stay. Speak Eng- 31 lish. Speak English. Christ!

Ay! Mamacita, who does not belong, every once in a while lets out a cry, 32 hysterical, high, as if he had torn the only skinny thread that kept her alive, the only road out to that country.

And then to break her heart forever, the baby boy who has begun to talk, 33 starts to sing the Pepsi commercial he heard on T.V.

No speak English, she says to the child who is singing in the language that 34 sounds like tin. No speak English, no speak English, and bubbles into tears. No, no, no as if she can't believe her ears.

LANGSTON HUGHES (1902–1967)

Theme for English B

The instructor said,

> Go home and write
> a page tonight.
> And let that page come out of you—
> Then, it will be true.   5

I wonder if it's that simple?

I am twenty-two, colored, born in Winston-Salem.
I went to school there, then Durham, then here
to this college on the hill above Harlem.
I am the only colored student in my class.   10
The steps from the hill lead down to Harlem,
through a park, then I cross St. Nicholas,
Eighth Avenue, Seventh, and I come to the Y,
the Harlem Branch Y, where I take the elevator
up to my room, sit down, and write this page: 15

It's not easy to know what is true for you or me
at twenty-two, my age. But I guess I'm what
I feel and see and hear. Harlem, I hear you:
hear you, hear me—we two—you, me talk on this page.
(I hear New York, too.) Me—who?   20

Well, I like to eat, sleep, drink, and be in love.
I like to work, read, learn, and understand life.
I like a pipe for a Christmas present,
or records—Bessie,[1] bop,[2] or Bach.[3]

I guess being colored doesn't make me not like   25
the same things other folks like who are other races.

---

1. Bessie Smith (1894–1937), legendary blues singer.   2. A kind of jazz popular in the 1940s and 1950s.
3. Johann Sebastian Bach (1685–1750), German composer.

So will my page be colored that I write?
Being me, it will not be white.
But it will be
a part of you, instructor.   30
You are white—
yet a part of me, as I am a part of you.
That's American.

Sometimes perhaps you don't want to be a part of me.
Nor do I often want to be a part of you.   35
But we are, that's true!
As I learn from you,
I guess you learn from me—
although you're older—and white—
and somewhat more free.   40

This is my page for English B.

ACTIVITIES FOR WRITING AND DISCUSSION

1. How does the structure of the speaker's "theme" (or English paper) compare or contrast with your sense of the standard structure for an English paper? Is there an introduction? a conclusion? Why or why not? What are the main ideas, and what connects one idea with another? How do you react when the student addresses the instructor directly (as "you") in his paper? Finally, how are any of these structural or tonal features significant to the poem's meaning?

2. Imagine you are the instructor. It is late at night; you are nodding off over the twenty or thirty student themes you have collected in response to this assignment when you come across this theme. Does the speaker's "page" of writing satisfy your expectations? fail to meet them? surpass them? How does it compare with the other students' themes? Take some notes in response to these questions. Then, as instructor, write a letter of reply or evaluation to the student.

Ballad of the Landlord

Landlord, landlord,
My roof has sprung a leak.
Don't you 'member I told you about it
Way last week?

Landlord, landlord,   5
These steps is broken down.

When you come up yourself
It's a wonder you don't fall down.

Ten Bucks you say I owe you?
Ten Bucks you say is due?   10
Well, that's Ten Bucks more'n I'll pay you
Till you fix this house up new.

What? You gonna get eviction orders?
You gonna cut off my heat?
You gonna take my furniture and   15
Throw it in the street?

Um-huh! You talking high and mighty.
Talk on—till you get through.
You ain't gonna be able to say a word
If I land my fist on you.   20

Police! Police!
Come and get this man!
He's trying to ruin the government
And overturn the land!

Copper's whistle!   25
Patrol bell!
Arrest.

Precinct Station.
Iron cell.
Headlines in press: 30

MAN THREATENS LANDLORD
TENANT HELD NO BAIL
JUDGE GIVES NEGRO 90 DAYS IN COUNTY JAIL

COUNTEE CULLEN (1903–1946)

Incident

Once riding in old Baltimore,
   Heart-filled, head-filled with glee,
I saw a Baltimorean
   Keep looking straight at me.

Now I was eight and very small,
   And he was no whit bigger,
And so I smiled, but he poked out
   His tongue, and called me, "Nigger."   5

I saw the whole of Baltimore
   From May until December;   10
Of all the things that happened there
   That's all that I remember.

GWENDOLYN BROOKS (b. 1917)

The Boy Died in My Alley

The Boy died in my alley
without my Having Known.
Policeman said, next morning,
"Apparently died Alone."

"You heard a shot?" Policeman said.   5
Shots I hear and Shots I hear.
I never see the Dead.

The Shot that killed him yes I heard
as I heard the Thousand shots before;
careening tinnily down the nights   10
across my years and arteries.

Policeman pounded on my door.
"Who is it?" "POLICE!" Policeman yelled.
"A Boy was dying in your alley.
A Boy is dead, and in your alley.   15
And have you known this Boy before?"

I have known this Boy before.
I have known this Boy before, who
ornaments my alley.
I never saw his face at all.   20
I never saw his futurefall.
But I have known this Boy.

I have always heard him deal with death.
I have always heard the shout, the volley.

I have closed my heart-ears late and early.   25
And I have killed him ever.

I joined the Wild and killed him
with knowledgeable unknowing.
I saw where he was going.
I saw him Crossed. And seeing,   30
I did not take him down.

He cried not only "Father!"
but "Mother!
Sister!
Brother."   35
The cry climbed up the alley.
It went up to the wind.
It hung upon the heaven
for a long
stretch-strain of Moment.   40

The red floor of my alley
is a special speech to me.

ACTIVITIES FOR WRITING AND DISCUSSION

1. Annotate and discuss any words, phrases, or lines that strike or puzzle you. (An example of a puzzling passage might be lines 27–28 with the closing **oxymoron**: "I joined the Wild and killed him/with knowledgeable unknowing.") What strikes you and why? What puzzles you and why?

2. What are the effects of certain phrases being repeated, e.g., "I have known," "I never saw," "I have always heard"?

3. Using details from the poem and inventing others as necessary, tell the story of the Boy. Who (or what) is he? Try narrating from any of a variety of **points of view**—the Boy's mother's or father's, a sibling's, a friend's.

4. Tell the story of the **speaker**. Where does the speaker live? What is his/her life like? What sorts of things does he/she do, see, hear, experience in a typical day? If you wish, compose your narrative in the form of a series of diary entries by the speaker.

Carter Revard (b. 1931)

Discovery of the New World

The creatures that we met this morning
   marveled at our green skins
      and scarlet eyes.
They lack antennae
   and can't be made to grasp   5
     your proclamation that they are
our lawful food and prey and slaves,
    nor can they seem to learn
   their body-space is needed to materialize
    our oxygen-absorbers—   10
which they conceive are breathing
   and thinking creatures whom they implore
at first as angels, then as devils,
     when they are being snuffed out
      by an absorber swelling   15
       into their space.
Their history bled from one this morning,
   while we were tasting his brain,
    in holographic rainbows,
which we assembled into quite an interesting   20
   set of legends—
    that's all it came to, though
the colors were quite lovely before we
   poured them into our time;
    the blue shift bleached away   25
meaningless circumstances, and they would not fit
   any of our truth-matrices—
    there was, however,
    a curious visual echo in their history
      of our own coming to their earth;   30
a certain General Sherman said
   about one group of them precisely what
    we have been telling you about these creatures:
  it is our destiny to asterize this planet,
    and they WILL not be asterized,   35
     so they must be wiped out.
   WE NEED their space and nitrogen
    which they do not know how to *use*,
nor will they breathe ammonia, as we do;
   yet they will not give up their "air" unforced,   40

so it is clear,
    whatever our "agreements" made this
                morning,
  we'll have to kill them all:
    the more we cook this orbit,   45
  the fewer next time round.
We've finished lazing all their crops and stores,
    we've killed their meat-slaves, now
      they'll have to come into our pens
and we can use them for our final studies   50
  of how our heart attacks and cancers spread
                among them,
  since they seem not immune to these.
—If we didn't have this mission it might be sad
    to see such helpless creatures die   55
chanting their sacred psalms and bills of rights; but
                    never fear
    the riches of this globe are ours
  and worth whatever pains others may have to
              feel.   60
    We'll soon have it cleared
completely, as it now is, at the poles, and then
  we will be safe, and rich, and happy here, forever.

ACTIVITIES FOR WRITING AND DISCUSSION

1. Where do the "discoverers" seem to be from? What "New World" are they discovering, and how do you know? To whom might the "your" in line 6 refer? What type of writing is this poem meant to represent—a diary entry? report? letter? oral communication of some sort? Explain.

2. Working alone or in a group, underline or circle any odd, puzzling, or striking terms or expressions you find in the poem. Then look for definitions in a dictionary, or attempt to translate the terms into more familiar language. Finally, discuss how these terms or expressions function meaningfully in the poem.

3. Does the poem parody (i.e., provide a satirical imitation of) any actual events in human history? If so, give examples of some such events. Then, in your notebook, analyze how the parody works.

4. React to the final line. Do you take it literally or **ironically**? Why? Write a sequel (in poetry or prose) in which you trace the subsequent fortunes of the "discoverers."

Wole Soyinka (b. 1934)

Telephone Conversation

The price seemed reasonable, location
Indifferent. The landlady swore she lived
Off premises. Nothing remained
But self-confession. 'Madam,' I warned,
'I hate a wasted journey—I am—African.'   5
Silence. Silenced transmission of
Pressurized good-breeding. Voice, when it came,
Lipstick coated, long gold-rolled
Cigarette-holder pipped. Caught I was, foully.
'HOW DARK?' . . . I had not misheard. . . . 'ARE YOU LIGHT   10
OR VERY DARK?' Button B. Button A. Stench
Of rancid breath of public-hide-and-speak.
Red booth.[1] Red pillar-box.[2] Red double-tiered
Omnibus squelching tar. It *was* real! Shamed
By ill-mannered silence, surrender   15
Pushed dumbfoundment to beg simplification.
Considerate she was, varying the emphasis—
'ARE YOU DARK? OR VERY LIGHT?' Revelation came.
'You mean—like plain or milk chocolate?'
Her assent was clinical, crushing in its light   20
Impersonality. Rapidly, wave-length adjusted,
I chose, 'West African sepia'—and as afterthought,
'Down in my passport.' Silence for spectroscopic
Flight of fancy, till truthfulness clanged her accent
Hard on the mouthpiece. 'WHAT'S THAT?' conceding   25
'DON'T KNOW WHAT THAT IS.' 'Like brunette.'
'THAT'S DARK, ISN'T IT?' 'Not altogether.
Facially, I am brunette, but madam, you should see
The rest of me. Palm of my hand, soles of my feet
Are a peroxid blonde. Friction, caused—   30
Foolishly madam—by sitting down, has turned
My bottom raven black—One moment madam!'—sensing
Her receiver rearing on the thunder clap
About my ears—'Madam,' I pleaded, 'wouldn't you rather
See for yourself?'   35

---

1. Phone booth.   2. Mailbox.

ACTIVITIES FOR WRITING AND DISCUSSION

1. How would the poem change if this "conversation" took place face-to-face rather than over the phone?

2. Analyze the poem's language, e.g., the varied sentence lengths, the choice and use of quoted dialogue, the use of ellipsis points and capitalization in lines 10 and 11 and elsewhere, and other punctuation devices used to depict the rhythms and tensions of the conversation. How do these features enhance the poem's effect? Illustrate your analysis with examples.

3. Soyinka uses a phone conversation to dramatize an example of racial prejudice. In a dialogue within a poem or a prose dialogue, do a takeoff on Soyinka's text. Include one or more of the following elements:
   a. A conflict that goes beyond opinion or thought to the essential selves, e.g., racial, ethnic, linguistic, religious, of the two speakers,
   b. A conflict that threatens to explode but is controlled by a conscious effort at politeness,
   c. A conflict in which one speaker clearly enjoys an implicit position of power over the other.

PAULA GUNN ALLEN (b. 1939)

Pocahontas to Her English Husband, John Rolfe

Had I not cradled you in my arms,
oh beloved   perfidious one,
you would have died.
And how many times did I pluck you
from certain death in the wilderness—   5
my world through which you stumbled
as though blind?
Had I not set you tasks
your masters far across the sea
would have abandoned you—   10
did abandon you, as many times they
left you to reap the harvest of their lies;
still you survived   oh my fair husband
and brought them gold
wrung from a harvest I taught you   15
to plant: Tobacco.   It
is not without irony that by this crop
your descendants die, for other powers
than those you know take part in this.

And indeed I did rescue you   20
not once but a thousand thousand times
and in my arms you slept, a foolish child,
and beside me you played,
chattering nonsense about a God
you had not wit to name;   25
and wondered you at my silence—
simple foolish wanton maid you saw,
dusky daughter of heathen sires
who knew not the ways of grace—
no doubt, no doubt.   30
I spoke little, you said.
And you listened less.
But played with your gaudy dreams
and sent ponderous missives to the throne
striving thereby to curry favor   35
with your king.   I saw you well.   I
understood the ploy and still protected you,
going so far as to die in your keeping—
a wasting, putrifying death, and you,
deceiver, my husband, father of my son,   40
survived, your spirit bearing crop
slowly from my teaching, taking
certain life from the wasting of my bones.

SHARON OLDS (b. 1942)

On the Subway

The boy and I face each other.
His feet are huge, in black sneakers
laced with white in a complex pattern like a
set of intentional scars. We are stuck on
opposite sides of the car, a couple of   5
molecules stuck in a rod of light
rapidly moving through darkness. He has the
casual cold look of a mugger,
alert under hooded lids. He is wearing
red, like the inside of the body   10
exposed. I am wearing dark fur, the
whole skin of an animal taken and
used. I look at his raw face,

he looks at my fur coat, and I don't
know if I am in his power—   15
he could take my coat so easily, my
briefcase, my life—
or if he is in my power, the way I am
living off his life, eating the steak
he does not eat, as if I am taking   20
the food from his mouth. And he is black
and I am white, and without meaning or
trying to I must profit from his darkness,
the way he absorbs the murderous beams of the
nation's heart, as black cotton   25
absorbs the heat of the sun and holds it. There is
no way to know how easy this
white skin makes my life, this
life he could take so easily and
break across his knee like a stick the way his   30
own back is being broken, the
rod of his soul that at birth was dark and
fluid and rich as the heart of a seedling
ready to thrust up into any available light.

ACTIVITIES FOR WRITING AND DISCUSSION

1. Describe the emotions you have as you read the first several lines. What words or images contribute to these emotions?

2. Is the **speaker** male or female? Does it matter? Why or why not? What evidence, if any, do you have of the speaker's race and socioeconomic background? of his/her political leanings? Quote and discuss such evidence. Does it matter that the speaker describes the large person across the car as a "boy" rather than a "man"?

3. Working alone or with a group, underline and annotate any **metaphors** and **similes.** Choose two or three that particularly strike you and brainstorm a list of any thoughts, reactions, or images they stir in you. Finally, in your notebook explain how those two or three metaphors or similes work in the poem.

4. The poem captures a momentary encounter, all from the speaker's **point of view.** In poetry or prose, narrate the same encounter from the boy's point of view. Consider the possibility that the boy has no interest in assaulting Olds's speaker. Alternative: Narrate the encounter between the speaker and the boy from the point of view of someone else aboard the subway car.

Jim Sagel (b. 1947)

Baca Grande

Una vaca se topó con un ratón y le dice:
"Tú—¿tan chiquito y con bigote?" Y le responde el ratón:
"Y tú tan grandota—¿y sin brassiere?"

It was nearly a miracle
James Baca remembered anyone at all
from the old hometown gang
having been two years at Yale
     no less   5
and halfway through law school
at the University of California at Irvine

They hardly recognized him either
in his three-piece grey business suit
and surfer-swirl haircut   10
with just the menacing hint
of a tightly trimmed Zapata moustache
     for cultural balance
and relevance

He had come to deliver the keynote address   15
to the graduating class of 80
at his old alma mater
and show off his well-trained lips
which laboriously parted
     each Kennedyish "R"   20
and drilled the first person pronoun
through the microphone
like an oil bit
with the slick, elegantly honed phrases
that slid so smoothly   25
off his meticulously bleached
     tongue
He talked Big Bucks
with astronautish fervor and if he
     the former bootstrapless James A. Baca   30
could dazzle the ass
off the universe

then even you
    yes you

Joey Martinez toying with your yellow   35
    tassle
and staring dumbly into space
could emulate Mr. Baca someday
    possibly
well   40
there was of course
such a thing
as being an outrageously successful
gas station attendant too
    let us never forget   45
it doesn't really matter what you do
so long as you excel
    James said
never believing a word
of it   50
for he had already risen
    as high as they go

Wasn't nobody else
from this deprived environment
who'd ever jumped   55
    straight out of college
into the Governor's office
and maybe one day
he'd sit in that big chair
    himself   60
and when he did
he'd forget this damned town
and all the petty little people
in it
once and for all   65

That much he promised himself

ACTIVITIES FOR WRITING AND DISCUSSION

1. Describe the occasion depicted and the **speaker.** Do you imagine the speaker is a member of the student audience being addressed by Baca or an outside observer? someone older or younger than Baca? Cite evidence to support your answers.

2. In lines 34–35 the speaker suddenly shifts attention to "you/Joey Martinez," and by the last line he seems to be inside the mind of James Baca. How do you account for these shifts in focus and perspective? Are they clumsy, or are they purposeful in some way? Explain.

3. Based on clues in the poem (and other material from your own imagination), create an outline—or the complete text—of Baca's speech.

GARY SOTO (b. 1952)

Black Hair

At eight I was brilliant with my body.
In July, that ring of heat
We all jumped through, I sat in the bleachers
Of Romain Playground, in the lengthening
Shade that rose from our dirty feet.   5
The game before us was more than baseball.
It was a figure—Hector Moreno
Quick and hard with turned muscles,
His crouch the one I assumed before an altar
Of worn baseball cards, in my room.   10

I came here because I was Mexican, a stick
Of brown light in love with those
Who could do it—the triple and hard slide,
The gloves eating balls into double plays.
What could I do with 50 pounds, my shyness,   15
My black torch of hair, about to go out?
Father was dead, his face no longer
Hanging over the table or our sleep,
And mother was the terror of mouths
Twisting hurt by butter knives.   20

In the bleachers I was brilliant with my body,
Waving players in and stomping my feet,
I chewed sunflower seeds. I drank water
And bit my arm through the late innings.
When Hector lined balls into deep   25
Center, in my mind I rounded the bases
With him, my face flared, my hair lifting
Beautifully, because we were coming home
To the arms of brown people.

Nancy Mairs (b. 1943)

Carnal Acts

Inviting me to speak at her small liberal-arts college during Women's Week, a young woman set me a task: "We would be pleased," she wrote, "if you could talk on how you cope with your MS disability, and also how you discovered your voice as a writer." Oh, Lord, I thought in dismay, how am I going to pull this one off? How can I yoke two such disparate subjects into a coherent presentation, without doing violence to one, or the other, or both, or myself? This is going to take some fancy footwork, and my feet scarcely carry out the basic steps, let alone anything elaborate.

To make matters worse, the assumption underlying each of her questions struck me as suspect. To ask *how* I cope with multiple sclerosis suggests that I *do* cope. Now, "to cope," *Webster's Third* tells me, is "to face or encounter and to find necessary expedients to overcome problems and difficulties." In these terms, I have to confess, I don't feel like much of a coper. I'm likely to deal with my problems and difficulties by squawking and flapping around like that hysterical chicken who was convinced the sky was falling. Never mind that in my case the sky really *is* falling. In response to a clonk on the head, regardless of its origin, one might comport oneself with a grace and courtesy I generally lack.

As for "finding" my voice, the implication is that it was at one time lost or missing. But I don't think it ever was. Ask my mother, who will tell you a little wearily that I was speaking full sentences by the time I was a year old and could never be silenced again. As for its being a writer's voice, it seems to have become one early on. Ask Mother again. At the age of eight I rewrote the Trojan War, she will say, and what Nestor was about to do to Helen at the end doesn't bear discussion in polite company.

Faced with these uncertainties, I took my own teacherly advice, something, I must confess, I don't always do. "If an idea is giving you trouble," I tell my writing students, "put it on the back burner and let it simmer while you do something else. Go to the movies. Reread a stack of old love letters. Sit in your history class and take detailed notes on the Teapot Dome scandal. If you've got your idea in mind, it will go on cooking at some level no matter what else you're doing." "I've had an idea for my documented essay on the back burner," one of my students once scribbled in her journal, "and I think it's just boiled over!"

I can't claim to have reached such a flash point. But in the weeks I've had the   5
themes "disability" and "voice" sitting around in my head, they seem to have converged on their own, without my having to wrench them together and bind them with hoops of tough rhetoric. They *are* related, indeed interdependent,

with an intimacy that has for some reason remained, until now, submerged below the surface of my attention. Forced to juxtapose them, I yank them out of the depths, a little startled to discover how they were intertwined down there out of sight. This kind of discovery can unnerve you at first. You feel like a giant hand that, pulling two swimmers out of the water, two separate heads bobbling on the iridescent swells, finds the two bodies below, legs coiled around each other, in an ecstasy of copulation. You don't quite know where to turn your eyes.

Perhaps the place to start illuminating this erotic connection between who I am and how I speak lies in history. I have known that I have multiple sclerosis for about seventeen years now, though the disease probably started long before. The hypothesis is that the disease process, in which the protective covering of the nerves in the brain and spinal cord is eaten away and replaced by scar tissue, "hard patches," is caused by an autoimmune reaction to a slow-acting virus. Research suggests that I was infected by this virus, which no one has ever seen and which therefore, technically, doesn't even "exist," between the ages of four and fifteen. In effect, living with this mysterious mechanism feels like having your present self, and the past selves it embodies, haunted by a capricious and mean-spirited ghost, unseen except for its footprints, which trips you even when you're watching where you're going, knocks glassware out of your hand, squeezes the urine out of your bladder before you reach the bathroom, and weights your whole body with a weariness no amount of rest can relieve. An alien invader must be at work. But of course it's not. It's your own body. That is, it's you.

This, for me, has been the most difficult aspect of adjusting to a chronic incurable degenerative disease: the fact that it has rammed my "self" straight back into the body I had been trained to believe it could, through high-minded acts and aspirations, rise above. The Western tradition of distinguishing the body from the mind and/or the soul is so ancient as to have become part of our collective unconscious, if one is inclined to believe in such a noumenon, or at least to have become an unquestioned element in the social instruction we impose upon infants from birth, in much the same way we inculcate, without reflection, the gender distinctions "female" and "male." I *have* a body, you are likely to say if you talk about embodiment at all; you don't say, I *am* a body. A body is a separate entity possessable by the "I"; the "I" and the body aren't, as the copula would make them, grammatically indistinguishable.

To widen the rift between the self and the body, we treat our bodies as subordinates, inferior in moral status. Open association with them shames us. In fact, we treat our bodies with very much the same distance and ambivalence women have traditionally received from men in our culture. Sometimes this treatment is benevolent, even respectful, but all too often it is tainted by outright sadism. I think of the bodybuilding regimens that have become popular in the last decade or so, with the complicated vacillations they reflect between self-worship and self-degradation: joggers and aerobic dancers and weightlifters all beating their bodies into shape. "No pain, no gain," the saying goes. "Feel the burn." Bodies get treated like wayward women who have to be shown who's boss, even if it means slapping them around a little. I'm not for a moment opposing rugged exercise here. I'm simply questioning the spirit in which it is often undertaken.

Since, as Hélène Cixous points out in her essay on women and writing, "Sorties,"[1] thought has always worked "through dual, hierarchical oppositions" (p. 64), the mind/body split cannot possibly be innocent. The utterance of an "I" immediately calls into being its opposite, the "not-I," Western discourse being unequipped to conceive "that which is neither 'I' nor 'not-I,' " "that which is both 'I' and 'not-I,' " or some other permutation which language doesn't permit me to speak. The "not-I" is, by definition, other. And we've never been too fond of the other. We prefer the same. We tend to ascribe to the other those qualities we prefer not to associate with our selves: It is the hidden, the dark, the secret, the shameful. Thus, when the "I" takes possession of the body, it makes the body into an other, direct object of a transitive verb, with all the other's repudiated and potentially dangerous qualities.

At the least, then, the body had best be viewed with suspicion. And a woman's body is particularly suspect, since so much of it is in fact hidden, dark, secret, carried about on the inside where, even with the aid of a speculum, one can never perceive all of it in the plain light of day, a graspable whole. I, for one, have never understood why anyone would want to carry all that delicate stuff around on the outside. It would make you awfully anxious, I should think, put you constantly on the defensive, create a kind of siege mentality that viewed all other beings, even your own kind, as threats to be warded off with spears and guns and atomic missiles. And you'd never get to experience that inward dreaming that comes when your flesh surrounds all your treasures, holding them close, like a sturdy shuttered house. Be my personal skepticism as it may, however, as a cultural woman I bear just as much shame as any woman for my dark, enfolded secrets. Let the word for my external genitals tell the tale: my pudendum, from the Latin infinitive meaning "to be ashamed."

It's bad enough to carry your genitals like a sealed envelope bearing the cipher that, once unlocked, might loose the chaotic flood of female pleasure— *jouissance*, the French call it—upon the world-of-the-same. But I have an additional reason to feel shame for my body, less explicitly connected with its sexuality: It is a crippled body. Thus it is doubly other, not merely by the homosexual standards of patriarchal culture but by the standards of physical desirability erected for every body in our world. Men, who are by definition exonerated from shame in sexual terms (this doesn't mean that an individual man might not experience sexual shame, of course; remember that I'm talking in general about discourse, not folks), may—more likely must—experience bodily shame if they are crippled. I won't presume to speak about the details of their experience, however. I don't know enough. I'll just go on telling what it's

---

1. In *The Newly Born Woman*, translated by Betsy Wing (Minneapolis: University of Minnesota Press, 1986). [Author's note.]

like to be a crippled woman, trusting that, since we're fellow creatures who've been living together for some thousands of years now, much of my experience will resonate with theirs.

I was never a beautiful woman, and for that reason I've spent most of my life (together with probably at least 95 percent of the female population of the United States) suffering from the shame of falling short of an unattainable standard. The ideal woman of my generation was . . . perky, I think you'd say, rather than gorgeous. Blond hair pulled into a bouncing ponytail. Wide blue eyes, a turned-up nose with maybe a scattering of golden freckles across it, a small mouth with full lips over straight white teeth. Her breasts were large but well harnessed high on her chest; her tiny waist flared to hips just wide enough to give the crinolines under her circle skirt a starting outward push. In terms of personality, she was outgoing, even bubbly, not pensive or mysterious. Her milieu was the front fender of a white Corvette convertible, surrounded by teasing crewcuts, dressed in black flats, a sissy blouse, and the letter sweater of the Corvette owner. Needless to say, she never missed a prom.

Ten years or so later, when I first noticed the symptoms that would be diagnosed as MS, I was probably looking my best. Not beautiful still, but the ideal had shifted enough so that my flat chest and narrow hips gave me an elegantly attenuated shape, set off by a thick mass of long, straight, shining hair. I had terrific legs, long and shapely, revealed nearly to the pudendum by the fashionable miniskirts and hot pants I adopted with more enthusiasm than delicacy of taste. Not surprisingly, I suppose, during this time I involved myself in several pretty torrid love affairs.

The beginning of MS wasn't too bad. The first symptom, besides the pernicious fatigue that had begun to devour me, was "foot drop," the inability to raise my left foot at the ankle. As a consequence, I'd started to limp, but I could still wear high heels, and a bit of a limp might seem more intriguing than repulsive. After a few months, when the doctor suggested a cane, a crippled friend gave me quite an elegant wood-and-silver one, which I carried with a fair amount of panache. The real blow to my self-image came when I had to get a brace. As braces go, it's not bad: lightweight plastic molded to my foot and leg, fitting down into an ordinary shoe and secured around my calf by a Velcro strap. It reduces my limp and, more important, the danger of tripping and falling. But it meant the end of high heels. And it's ugly. Not as ugly as I think it is, I gather, but still pretty ugly. It signified for me, and perhaps still does, the permanence and irreversibility of my condition. The brace makes my MS concrete and forces me to wear it on the outside. As soon as I strapped the brace on, I climbed into trousers and stayed there (though not in the same trousers, of course). The idea of going around with my bare brace hanging out seemed almost as indecent as exposing my breasts. Not until 1984, soon after I won the Western States Book Award for poetry, did I put on a skirt short enough to reveal my plasticized leg. The connection between winning a writing award and baring my brace is not merely fortuitous; being affirmed as a writer really did embolden me. Since then, I've grown so accustomed to wearing skirts that I don't think about my brace any more than I think about my cane. I've incorporated them, I suppose: made them, in their necessity, insensate but fundamental parts of my body.

Meanwhile, I had to adjust to the most outward and visible sign of all, a   15
three-wheeled electric scooter called an Amigo. This lessens my fatigue and increases my range terrifically, but it also shouts out to the world, "Here is a woman who can't stand on her own two feet." At the same time, paradoxically, it renders me invisible, reducing me to the height of a seven-year-old, with a child's attendant low status. "Would she like smoking or nonsmoking?" the gate agent assigning me a seat asks the friend traveling with me. In crowds I see nothing but buttocks. I can tell you the names of every type of designer jeans ever sold. The wearers, eyes front, trip over me and fall across my handlebars into my lap. "Hey!" I want to shout to the lofty world. "Down here! There's a person down here!" But I'm not, by their standards, quite a person anymore.

My self-esteem diminishes further as age and illness strip away from me the features that made me, for a brief while anyway, a good-looking, even sexy, young woman. No more long, bounding strides: I shuffle along with the timid gait I remember observing, with pity and impatience, in the little old ladies at Boston's Symphony Hall on Friday afternoons. No more lithe, girlish figure: My belly sags from the loss of muscle tone, which also creates all kinds of intestinal disruptions, hopelessly humiliating in a society in which excretory functions remain strictly unspeakable. No more sex, either, if society had its way. The sexuality of the disabled so repulses most people that you can hardly get a doctor, let alone a member of the general population, to consider the issues it raises. Cripples simply aren't supposed to Want It, much less Do It. Fortunately, I've got a husband with a strong libido and a weak sense of social propriety, or else I'd find myself perforce practicing a vow of chastity I never cared to take.

Afflicted by the general shame of having a body at all, and the specific shame of having one weakened and misshapen by disease, I ought not to be able to hold my head up in public. And yet I've gotten into the habit of holding my head up in public, sometimes under excruciating circumstances. Recently, for instance, I had to give a reading at the University of Arizona. Having smashed three of my front teeth in a fall onto the concrete floor of my screened porch, I was in the process of getting them crowned, and the temporary crowns flew out during dinner right before the reading. What to do? I wanted, of course, to rush home and hide till the dental office opened the next morning. But I couldn't very well break my word at this last moment. So, looking like Hansel and Gretel's witch, and lisping worse than the Wife of Bath, I got up on stage and read. Somehow, over the years, I've learned how to set shame aside and do what I have to do.

Here, I think, is where my "voice" comes in. Because, in spite of my demurral at the beginning, I do in fact cope with my disability at least some of the time. And I do so, I think, by speaking about it, and about the whole experience of being a body, specifically a female body, out loud, in a clear, level tone that drowns out the frantic whispers of my mother, my grandmothers, all the other trainers of wayward childish tongues: "Sssh! Sssh! Nice girls don't talk like that. Don't mention sweat. Don't mention menstrual blood. Don't ask what your grandfather does on his business trips. Don't laugh so loud. You sound like a loon. Keep your voice down. Don't tell. Don't tell. Don't tell." Speaking out loud is an antidote to shame. I want to distinguish clearly here between "shame," as I'm using the word, and "guilt" and "embarrassment," which, though equally painful, are not similarly poisonous. Guilt arises from performing a forbidden act or failing to perform a required one. In either case, the guilty person can, through reparation, erase the offense and start fresh. Embarrassment, less opprobrious though not necessarily less distressing, is generally caused by acting in a socially stupid or awkward way. When I trip and sprawl in public, when I wet myself, when my front teeth fly out, I feel horribly embarrassed, but, like the pain of childbirth, the sensation blurs and dissolves in time. If it didn't, every child would be an only child, and no one would set foot in public after the onset of puberty, when embarrassment erupts like a geyser and bathes one's whole life in its bitter stream. Shame may attach itself to guilt or embarrassment, complicating their resolution, but it is not the same emotion. I feel guilt or embarrassment for something I've done; shame, for who I am. I may stop doing bad or stupid things, but I can't stop being. How then can I help but be ashamed? Of the three conditions, this is the one that cracks and stifles my voice.

I can subvert its power, I've found, by acknowledging who I am, shame and all, and, in doing so, raising what was hidden, dark, secret about my life into the plain light of shared human experience. What we aren't permitted to utter holds us, each isolated from every other, in a kind of solipsistic thrall. Without any way to check our reality against anyone else's, we assume that our fears and shortcomings are ours alone. One of the strangest consequences of publishing a collection of personal essays called *Plaintext* has been the steady trickle of letters and telephone calls saying essentially, in a tone of unmistakable relief, "Oh, me too! Me too!" It's as though the part I thought was solo has turned out to be a chorus. But none of us was singing loud enough for the others to hear.

Singing loud enough demands a particular kind of voice, I think. And I was 20 wrong to suggest, at the beginning, that I've always had my voice. I have indeed always had *a* voice, but it wasn't *this* voice, the one with which I could call up and transform my hidden self from a naughty girl into a woman talking directly to others like herself. Recently, in the process of writing a new book, a memoir entitled *Remembering the Bone House*, I've had occasion to read some of my early writing, from college, high school, even junior high. It's not an experience I recommend to anyone susceptible to shame. Not that the writing was all that bad. I was surprised at how competent a lot of it was. Here was a writer who already knew precisely how the language worked. But the voice . . . oh, the voice was all wrong: maudlin, rhapsodic, breaking here and there into little shrieks, almost, you might say, hysterical. It was a voice that had shucked off its own body, its own homely life of Cheerios for breakfast and seventy pages of Chaucer to read before the exam on Tuesday and a plantar wart growing painfully on the ball of its foot, and reeled now wraithlike through the air, seeking incarnation only as the heroine who enacts her doomed love for the tall, dark, mysterious stranger. If it didn't get that part, it wouldn't play at all.

Among all these overheated and vaporous imaginings, I must have retained some shred of sense, because I stopped writing prose entirely, except for scholarly papers, for nearly twenty years. I even forgot, not exactly that I had written prose, but at least what kind of prose it was. So when I needed to take up the process again, I could start almost fresh, using the vocal range I'd gotten used to in years of asking the waiter in the Greek restaurant for an extra anchovy on my salad, congratulating the puppy on making a puddle outside rather than inside the patio door, pondering with my daughter the vagaries of female orgasm, saying good-bye to my husband, and hello, and good-bye, and hello. This new voice—thoughtful, affectionate, often amused—was essential because what I needed to write about when I returned to prose was an attempt I'd made not long before to kill myself, and suicide simply refuses to be spoken of authentically in high-flown romantic language. It's too ugly. Too shameful. Too strictly a bodily event. And, yes, too funny as well, though people are sometimes shocked to find humor shoved up against suicide. They don't like the incongruity. But let's face it, life (real life, I mean, not the edited-for-television version) is a cacophonous affair from start to finish. I might have wanted to portray my suicidal self as a languishing maiden, too exquisitely sensitive to sustain life's wounding pressures on her soul. (I didn't want to, as a matter of fact, but I might have.) The truth remained, regardless of my desires, that when my husband lugged me into the emergency room, my hair matted, my face swollen and gray, my nightgown streaked with blood and urine, I was no frail and tender spirit. I was a body, and one in a hell of a mess.

I "should" have kept quiet about that experience. I know the rules of polite discourse. I should have kept my shame, and the nearly lethal sense of isolation and alienation it brought, to myself. And I might have, except for something the psychiatrist in the emergency room had told my husband. "You might as well take her home," he said. "If she wants to kill herself, she'll do it no matter how many precautions we take. They always do." *They* always do. I was one of "them," whoever they were. I was, in this context anyway, not singular, not aberrant, but typical. I think it was this sense of commonality with others I didn't even know, a sense of being returned somehow, in spite of my appalling act, to the human family, that urged me to write that first essay, not merely speaking out but calling out, perhaps. "Here's the way I am," it said. "How about you?" And the answer came, as I've said: "Me too! Me too!"

This has been the kind of work I've continued to do: to scrutinize the details of my own experience and to report what I see, and what I think about what I see, as lucidly and accurately as possible. But because feminine experience has been immemorially devalued and repressed, I continue to find this task terrifying. "Every woman has known the torture of beginning to speak aloud," Cixous writes, "heart beating as if to break, occasionally falling into loss of language, ground and language slipping out from under her, because for woman speaking—even just opening her mouth—in public is something rash, a transgression" (p. 92).

The voice I summon up wants to crack, to whisper, to trail back into silence. "I'm sorry to have nothing more than this to say," it wants to apologize. "I shouldn't be taking up your time. I've never fought in a war, or even in a schoolyard free-for-all. I've never tried to see who could piss farthest up the barn wall. I've never even been to a whorehouse. All the important formative experiences have passed me by. I was raped once. I've borne two children. Milk trickling out of my breasts, blood trickling from between my legs. You don't want to hear about it. Sometimes I'm too scared to leave my house. Not scared *of* anything, just scared: mouth dry, bowels writhing. When the fear got really bad, they locked me up for six months, but that was years ago. I'm getting old now. Misshapen, too. I don't blame you if you can't get it up. No one could possibly desire a body like this. It's not your fault. It's mine. Forgive me. I didn't mean to start crying. I'm sorry . . . sorry . . . sorry. . . ."

An easy solace to the anxiety of speaking aloud: this slow subsidence be- 25 neath the waves of shame, back into what Cixous calls "this body that has been worse than confiscated, a body replaced with a disturbing stranger, sick or dead, who so often is a bad influence, the cause and place of inhibitions. By censuring the body," she goes on, "breath and speech are censored at the same time" (p. 97). But I am not going back, not going under one more time. To do so would demonstrate a failure of nerve far worse than the depredations of MS have caused. Paradoxically, losing one sort of nerve has given me another. No one is going to leave me speechless. To be silent is to comply with the standard of feminine grace. But my crippled body already violates all notions of feminine grace. What more have I got to lose? I've gone beyond shame. I'm shameless, you might say. You know, as in "shameless hussy"? A woman with her bare brace and her tongue hanging out.

I've "found" my voice, then, just where it ought to have been, in the body-warmed breath escaping my lungs and throat. Forced by the exigencies of physical disease to embrace my self in the flesh, I couldn't write bodiless prose. The voice is the creature of the body that produces it. I speak as a crippled woman. At the same time, in the utterance I redeem both "cripple" and "woman" from the shameful silences by which I have often felt surrounded, contained, set apart; I give myself permission to live openly among others, to reach out for them, stroke them with fingers and sighs. No body, no voice; no voice, no body. That's what I know in my bones.

ACTIVITIES FOR WRITING AND DISCUSSION

1. In her account of her multiple sclerosis, Mairs surveys a range of cultural issues that may not seem (at first) to be directly related to her disease. For instance, she discusses cultural notions of "self," of the mind/body relationship, of "beauty" (particularly female beauty), of repressed feminine experience, etc.

Reread these passages, and annotate one that particularly strikes you. List examples from your culture that support or contradict Mairs's analysis. Then use the notes and list you have made to compose a response to that portion of Mairs's essay.

2. React to Mairs's style—the wit, the pointed humor, the disarming and sometimes brutal candor. Annotate passages that illustrate these or other aspects of Mairs's style. How, if at all, does the style increase the rhetorical effectiveness of her arguments in the essay? Could it be said that her style is itself an argument? Explain with examples.

3. Argue the following: "Mairs the 'cripple' sees herself as primarily different from other 'non-disabled' people." Then argue the opposite: "Mairs the 'cripple' sees herself as primarily like other people." Cite passages from the text in support of each of these perspectives.

4. Whether you think of yourself as disabled or not, what is a "disability"? In what respects is being disabled a simple matter of "fact," and in what ways is it culturally constructed? Cite passages in "Carnal Acts"—or examples from your own knowledge and experience—to illustrate your answer.

5. As she begins her discussion of "voice," Mairs quotes various voices inside her head that discourage her from speaking and writing honestly, e.g., "Sssh! Sssh! Nice girls don't talk like that." From what sources do these voices come? Imagine yourself in a familiar (for you) high-stress situation in which similar voices begin to speak up in your own head to prevent you from being truthful. Write the dialogue between yourself and one or more of these voices. Afterward, record any new perspectives your dialogue gives you on (a) Mairs's struggle for "voice" and/or (b) your own struggle for "voice."

RICHARD RODRIGUEZ (b. 1944)

Aria

1

I remember to start with that day in Sacramento—a California now nearly thirty years past—when I first entered a classroom, able to understand some fifty stray English words.

The third of four children, I had been preceded to a neighborhood Roman Catholic school by an older brother and sister. But neither of them had revealed very much about their classroom experiences. Each afternoon they returned, as they left in the morning, always together, speaking in Spanish as they climbed the five steps of the porch. And their mysterious books, wrapped in

shopping-bag paper, remained on the table next to the door, closed firmly behind them.

An accident of geography sent me to a school where all my classmates were
white, many the children of doctors and lawyers and business executives. All my
classmates certainly must have been uneasy on that first day of school—as most
children are uneasy—to find themselves apart from their families in the first
institution of their lives. But I was astonished.

The nun said, in a friendly but oddly impersonal voice, 'Boys and girls, this
is Richard Rodriguez.' (I heard her sound out: *Rich-heard Road-ree-guess.*) It
was the first time I had heard anyone name me in English. 'Richard,' the nun repeated more slowly, writing my name down in her black leather book. Quickly I
turned to see my mother's face dissolve in a watery blur behind the pebbled
glass door.

Many years later there is something called bilingual education—a scheme pro-   5
posed in the late 1960s by Hispanic-American social activists, later endorsed by
a congressional vote. It is a program that seeks to permit non-English-speaking
children, many from lower-class homes, to use their family language as the language of school. (Such is the goal its supporters announce.) I hear them and am
forced to say no: It is not possible for a child—any child—ever to use his family's
language in school. Not to understand this is to misunderstand the public uses
of schooling and to trivialize the nature of intimate life—a family's 'language.'

Memory teaches me what I know of these matters; the boy reminds the
adult. I was a bilingual child, a certain kind—socially disadvantaged—the son
of working-class parents, both Mexican immigrants.

In the early years of my boyhood, my parents coped very well in America.
My father had steady work. My mother managed at home. They were nobody's
victims. Optimism and ambition led them to a house (our home) many blocks
from the Mexican south side of town. We lived among *gringos* and only a block
from the biggest, whitest houses. It never occurred to my parents that they
couldn't live wherever they chose. Nor was the Sacramento of the fifties bent on
teaching them a contrary lesson. My mother and father were more annoyed
than intimidated by those two or three neighbors who tried initially to make us
unwelcome. ('Keep your brats away from my sidewalk!') But despite all they
achieved, perhaps because they had so much to achieve, any deep feeling of
ease, the confidence of 'belonging' in public was withheld from them both.
They regarded the people at work, the faces in crowds, as very distant from us.
They were the others, *los gringos*. That term was interchangeable in their speech
with another, even more telling, *los americanos*.

I grew up in a house where the only regular guests were my relations. For
one day, enormous families of relatives would visit and there would be so many
people that the noise and the bodies would spill out to the backyard and front
porch. Then, for weeks, no one came by. (It was usually a salesman who rang
the doorbell.) Our house stood apart. A gaudy yellow in a row of white bunga-
lows. We were the people with the noisy dog. The people who raised pigeons

and chickens. We were the foreigners on the block. A few neighbors smiled and waved. We waved back. But no one in the family knew the names of the old couple who lived next door; until I was seven years old, I did not know the names of the kids who lived across the street.

In public, my father and mother spoke a hesitant, accented, not always grammatical English. And they would have to strain—their bodies tense—to catch the sense of what was rapidly said by *los gringos*. At home they spoke Spanish. The language of their Mexican past sounded in counterpoint to the English of public society. The words would come quickly, with ease. Conveyed through those sounds was the pleasing, soothing, consoling reminder of being at home.

During those years when I was first conscious of hearing, my mother and   10
father addressed me only in Spanish; in Spanish I learned to reply. By contrast, English (*inglés*), rarely heard in the house, was the language I came to associate with *gringos*. I learned my first words of English overhearing my parents speak to strangers. At five years of age, I knew just enough English for my mother to trust me on errands to stores one block away. No more.

I was a listening child, careful to hear the very different sounds of Spanish and English. Wide-eyed with hearing, I'd listen to sounds more than words. First, there were English (*gringo*) sounds. So many words were still unknown that when the butcher or the lady at the drugstore said something to me, exotic polysyllabic sounds would bloom in the midst of their sentences. Often, the speech of people in public seemed to me very loud, booming with confidence. The man behind the counter would literally ask, 'What can I do for you?' But by being so firm and so clear, the sound of his voice said that he was a *gringo;* he belonged in public society.

I would also hear then the high nasal notes of middle-class American speech. The air stirred with sound. Sometimes, even now, when I have been traveling abroad for several weeks, I will hear what I heard as a boy. In hotel lobbies or airports, in Turkey or Brazil, some Americans will pass, and suddenly I will hear it again—the high sound of American voices. For a few seconds I will hear it with pleasure, for it is now the sound of *my* society—a reminder of home. But inevitably—already on the flight headed for home—the sound fades with repetition. I will be unable to hear it anymore.

When I was a boy, things were different. The accent of *los gringos* was never pleasing nor was it hard to hear. Crowds at Safeway or at bus stops would be noisy with sound. And I would be forced to edge away from the chirping chatter above me.

I was unable to hear my own sounds, but I knew very well that I spoke English poorly. My words could not stretch far enough to form complete thoughts. And the words I did speak I didn't know well enough to make into distinct sounds. (Listeners would usually lower their heads, better to hear what I was trying to say.) But it was one thing for *me* to speak English with difficulty. It was more troubling for me to hear my parents speak in public: their high-whining vowels and guttural consonants; their sentences that got stuck with 'eh' and 'ah' sounds; the confused syntax; the hesitant rhythm of sounds so different from the way *gringos* spoke. I'd notice, moreover, that my parents' voices were softer than those of *gringos* we'd meet.

I am tempted now to say that none of this mattered. In adulthood I am em- 15 barrassed by childhood fears. And, in a way, it didn't matter very much that my parents could not speak English with ease. Their linguistic difficulties had no serious consequences. My mother and father made themselves understood at the county hospital clinic and at government offices. And yet, in another way, it mattered very much—it was unsettling to hear my parents struggle with English. Hearing them, I'd grow nervous, my clutching trust in their protection and power weakened.

There were many times like the night at a brightly lit gasoline station (a blaring white memory) when I stood uneasily, hearing my father. He was talking to a teenaged attendant. I do not recall what they were saying, but I cannot forget the sounds my father made as he spoke. At one point his words slid together to form one word—sounds as confused as the threads of blue and green oil in the puddle next to my shoes. His voice rushed through what he had left to say. And, toward the end, reached falsetto notes, appealing to his listener's understanding. I looked away to the light of passing automobiles. I tried not to hear anymore. But I heard only too well the calm, easy tones in the attendant's reply. Shortly afterward, walking toward home with my father, I shivered when he put his hand on my shoulder. The very first chance that I got, I evaded his grasp and ran on ahead into the dark, skipping with feigned boyish exuberance.

But then there was Spanish. *Español:* my family's language. *Español:* the language that seemed to me a private language. I'd hear strangers on the radio and in the Mexican Catholic church across town speaking in Spanish, but I couldn't really believe that Spanish was a public language, like English. Spanish speakers, rather, seemed related to me, for I sensed that we shared—through our language—the experience of feeling apart from *los gringos*. It was thus a ghetto Spanish that I heard and I spoke. Like those whose lives are bound by a barrio, I was reminded by Spanish of my separateness from *los otros, los gringos* in power. But more intensely than for most barrio children—because I did not live in a barrio—Spanish seemed to me the language of home. (Most days it was only at home that I'd hear it.) It became the language of joyful return.

A family member would say something to me and I would feel myself specially recognized. My parents would say something to me and I would feel embraced by the sounds of their words. Those sounds said: *I am speaking with ease in Spanish. I am addressing you in words I never use with* los gringos. *I recognize you as someone special, close, like no one outside. You belong with us. In the family.*

(*Ricardo.*)

At the age of five, six, well past the time when most other children no longer 20 easily notice the difference between sounds uttered at home and words spoken in public, I had a different experience. I lived in a world magically compounded of sounds. I remained a child longer than most; I lingered too long, poised at the edge of language—often frightened by the sounds of *los gringos*, delighted by the sounds of Spanish at home. I shared with my family a language that was startlingly different from that used in the great city around us.

For me there were none of the gradations between public and private society so normal to a maturing child. Outside the house was public society; inside the house was private. Just opening or closing the screen door behind me was an important experience. I'd rarely leave home all alone or without reluctance. Walking down the sidewalk, under the canopy of tall trees, I'd warily notice the—suddenly—silent neighborhood kids who stood warily watching me. Nervously, I'd arrive at the grocery store to hear there the sounds of the *gringo*— foreign to me—reminding me that in this world so big, I was a foreigner. But then I'd return. Walking back toward our house, climbing the steps from the sidewalk, when the front door was open in summer, I'd hear voices beyond the screen door talking in Spanish. For a second or two, I'd stay, linger there, listening. Smiling, I'd hear my mother call out, saying in Spanish (words): 'Is that you, Richard?' All the while her sounds would assure me: *You are home now; come closer; inside. With us.*

'*Sí,*' I'd reply.

Once more inside the house I would resume (assume) my place in the family. The sounds would dim, grow harder to hear. Once more at home, I would grow less aware of that fact. It required, however, no more than the blurt of the doorbell to alert me to listen to sounds all over again. The house would turn instantly still while my mother went to the door. I'd hear her hard English sounds. I'd wait to hear her voice return to soft-sounding Spanish, which assured me, as surely as did the clicking tongue of the lock on the door, that the stranger was gone.

Plainly, it is not healthy to hear such sounds so often. It is not healthy to distinguish public words from private sounds so easily. I remained cloistered by sounds, timid and shy in public, too dependent on voices at home. And yet it needs to be emphasized: I was an extremely happy child at home. I remember many nights when my father would come back from work, and I'd hear him call out to my mother in Spanish, sounding relieved. In Spanish, he'd sound light and free notes he never could manage in English. Some nights I'd jump up just at hearing his voice. With *mis hermanos* I would come running into the room where he was with my mother. Our laughing (so deep was the pleasure!) became screaming. Like others who know the pain of public alienation, we transformed the knowledge of our public separateness and made it consoling—the reminder of intimacy. Excited, we joined our voices in a celebration of sounds. *We are speaking now the way we never speak out in public. We are alone—together,* voices sounded, surrounded to tell me. Some nights, no one seemed willing to loosen the hold sounds had on us. At dinner, we invented new words. (Ours sounded Spanish, but made sense only to us.) We pieced together new words by taking, say, an English verb and giving it Spanish endings. My mother's instructions at bedtime would be lacquered with mock-urgent tones. Or a word like *sí* would become, in several notes, able to convey added measures of feeling. Tongues explored the edges of words, especially the fat vowels.

And we happily sounded that military drum roll, the twirling roar of the Spanish *r*. Family language: my family's sounds. The voices of my parents and sisters and brother. Their voices insisting: *You belong here. We are family members. Related. Special to one another. Listen!* Voices singing and sighing, rising, straining, then surging, teeming with pleasure that burst syllables into fragments of laughter. At times it seemed there was steady quiet only when, from another room, the rustling whispers of my parents faded and I moved closer to sleep.

2

Supporters of bilingual education today imply that students like me miss a great deal by not being taught in their family's language. What they seem not to recognize is that, as a socially disadvantaged child, I considered Spanish to be a private language. What I needed to learn in school was that I had the right—and the obligation—to speak the public language of *los gringos*. The odd truth is that my first-grade classmates could have become bilingual, in the conventional sense of that word, more easily than I. Had they been taught (as upper-middle-class children are often taught early) a second language like Spanish or French, they could have regarded it simply as that: another public language. In my case such bilingualism could not have been so quickly achieved. What I did not believe was that I could speak a single public language.

Without question, it would have pleased me to hear my teachers address me in Spanish when I entered the classroom. I would have felt much less afraid. I would have trusted them and responded with ease. But I would have delayed—for how long postponed?—having to learn the language of public society. I would have evaded—and for how long could I have afforded to delay?—learning the great lesson of school, that I had a public identity.

Fortunately, my teachers were unsentimental about their responsibility. What they understood was that I needed to speak a public language. So their voices would search me out, asking me questions. Each time I'd hear them, I'd look up in surprise to see a nun's face frowning at me. I'd mumble, not really meaning to answer. The nun would persist, 'Richard, stand up. Don't look at the floor. Speak up. Speak to the entire class, not just to me!' But I couldn't believe that the English language was mine to use. (In part, I did not want to believe it.) I continued to mumble. I resisted the teacher's demands. (Did I somehow suspect that once I learned public language my pleasing family life would be changed?) Silent, waiting for the bell to sound, I remained dazed, diffident, afraid.

Because I wrongly imagined that English was intrinsically a public language and Spanish an intrinsically private one, I easily noted the difference between classroom language and the language of home. At school, words were directed to a general audience of listeners. ('Boys and girls.') Words were meaningfully ordered. And the point was not self-expression alone but to make oneself understood by many others. The teacher quizzed: 'Boys and girls, why do we use that word in this sentence? Could we think of a better word to use there? Would the sentence change its meaning if the words were differently arranged? And wasn't there a better way of saying much the same thing?' (I couldn't say. I wouldn't try to say.)

Three months. Five. Half a year passed. Unsmiling, ever watchful, my teachers noted my silence. They began to connect my behavior with the difficult progress my older sister and brother were making. Until one Saturday morning three nuns arrived at the house to talk to our parents. Stiffly, they sat on the blue living room sofa. From the doorway of another room, spying the visitors, I noted the incongruity—the clash of two worlds, the faces and voices of school intruding upon the familiar setting of home. I overheard one voice gently wondering, 'Do your children speak only Spanish at home, Mrs. Rodriguez?' While another voice added, 'That Richard especially seems so timid and shy.'

That Rich-heard!   30

With great tact the visitors continued, 'Is it possible for you and your husband to encourage your children to practice their English when they are home?' Of course, my parents complied. What would they not do for their children's well-being? And how could they have questioned the Church's authority which those women represented? In an instant, they agreed to give up the language (the sounds) that had revealed and accentuated our family's closeness. The moment after the visitors left, the change was observed. '*Ahora*, speak to us *en inglés*,' my father and mother united to tell us.

At first, it seemed a kind of game. After dinner each night, the family gathered to practice 'our' English. (It was still then *inglés*, a language foreign to us, so we felt drawn as strangers to it.) Laughing, we would try to define words we could not pronounce. We played with strange English sounds, often overanglicizing our pronunciations. And we filled the smiling gaps of our sentences with familiar Spanish sounds. But that was cheating, somebody shouted. Everyone laughed. In school, meanwhile, like my brother and sister, I was required to attend a daily tutoring session. I needed a full year of special attention. I also needed my teachers to keep my attention from straying in class by calling out, *Rich-heard*—their English voices slowly prying loose my ties to my other name, its three notes, *Ri-car-do*. Most of all I needed to hear my mother and father speak to me in a moment of seriousness in broken—suddenly heartbreaking— English. The scene was inevitable: One Saturday morning I entered the kitchen where my parents were talking in Spanish. I did not realize that they were talking in Spanish however until, at the moment they saw me, I heard their voices change to speak English. Those *gringo* sounds they uttered startled me. Pushed me away. In that moment of trivial misunderstanding and profound insight, I felt my throat twisted by unsounded grief. I turned quickly and left the room. But I had no place to escape to with Spanish. (The spell was broken.) My brother and sisters were speaking English in another part of the house.

Again and again in the days following, increasingly angry, I was obliged to hear my mother and father: 'Speak to us *en inglés*.' (*Speak*.) Only then did I determine to learn classroom English. Weeks after, it happened: One day in school I raised my hand to volunteer an answer. I spoke out in a loud voice. And I did not think it remarkable when the entire class understood. That day, I moved very far from the disadvantaged child I had been only days earlier. The belief, the calming assurance that I belonged in public, had at last taken hold.

Shortly after, I stopped hearing the high and loud sounds of *los gringos*. A more and more confident speaker of English, I didn't trouble to listen to *how* strangers sounded, speaking to me. And there simply were too many English-speaking people in my day for me to hear American accents anymore. Conversations quickened. Listening to persons who sounded eccentrically pitched voices, I usually noted their sounds for an initial few seconds before I concentrated on *what* they were saying. Conversations became content-full. Transparent. Hearing someone's *tone* of voice—angry or questioning or sarcastic or happy or sad—I didn't distinguish it from the words it expressed. Sound and word were thus tightly wedded. At the end of a day, I was often bemused, always relieved, to realize how 'silent,' though crowded with words, my day in public had been. (This public silence measured and quickened the change in my life.)

At last, seven years old, I came to believe what had been technically true 35 since my birth: I was an American citizen.

But the special feeling of closeness at home was diminished by then. Gone was the desperate, urgent, intense feeling of being at home; rare was the experience of feeling myself individualized by family intimates. We remained a loving family, but one greatly changed. No longer so close; no longer bound tight by the pleasing and troubling knowledge of our public separateness. Neither my older brother nor sister rushed home after school anymore. Nor did I. When I arrived home there would often be neighborhood kids in the house. Or the house would be empty of sounds.

Following the dramatic Americanization of their children, even my parents grew more publicly confident. Especially my mother. She learned the names of all the people on our block. And she decided we needed to have a telephone installed in the house. My father continued to use the word *gringo*. But it was no longer charged with the old bitterness or distrust. (Stripped of any emotional content, the word simply became a name for those Americans not of Hispanic descent.) Hearing him, sometimes, I wasn't sure if he was pronouncing the Spanish word *gringo* or saying gringo in English.

Matching the silence I started hearing in public was a new quiet at home. The family's quiet was partly due to the fact that, as we children learned more and more English, we shared fewer and fewer words with our parents. Sentences needed to be spoken slowly when a child addressed his mother or father. (Often the parent wouldn't understand.) The child would need to repeat himself. (Still the parent misunderstood.) The young voice, frustrated, would end up saying, 'Never mind'—the subject was closed. Dinners would be noisy with the clinking of knives and forks against dishes. My mother would smile softly between her remarks; my father at the other end of the table would chew and chew at his food, while he stared over the heads of his children.

My *mother!* My *father!* After English became my primary language, I no longer knew what words to use in addressing my parents. The old Spanish words (those tender accents of sound) I had used earlier—*mamá* and *papá*— I couldn't use anymore. They would have been too painful reminders of how much had changed in my life. On the other hand, the words I heard neighborhood kids call *their* parents seemed equally unsatisfactory. *Mother* and *Father; Ma, Papa, Pa, Dad, Pop* (how I hated the all-American sound of that last word especially)—all these terms I felt were unsuitable, not really terms of address for *my* parents. As a result, I never used them at home. Whenever I'd speak to my parents, I would try to get their attention with eye contact alone. In public conversations, I'd refer to 'my parents' or 'my mother and father.'

My mother and father, for their part, responded differently, as their children   40 spoke to them less. She grew restless, seemed troubled and anxious at the scarcity of words exchanged in the house. It was she who would question me about my day when I came home from school. She smiled at small talk. She pried at the edges of my sentences to get me to say something more. (What?) She'd join conversations she overheard, but her intrusions often stopped her children's talking. By contrast, my father seemed reconciled to the new quiet. Though his English improved somewhat, he retired into silence. At dinner he spoke very little. One night his children and even his wife helplessly giggled at his garbled English pronunciation of the Catholic Grace before Meals. Thereafter he made his wife recite the prayer at the start of each meal, even on formal occasions, when there were guests in the house. Hers became the public voice of the family. On official business, it was she, not my father, one would usually hear on the phone or in stores, talking to strangers. His children grew so accustomed to his silence that, years later, they would speak routinely of his shyness. (My mother would often try to explain: Both his parents died when he was eight. He was raised by an uncle who treated him like little more than a menial servant. He was never encouraged to speak. He grew up alone. A man of few words.) But my father was not shy, I realized, when I'd watch him speaking Spanish with relatives. Using Spanish, he was quickly effusive. Especially when talking with other men, his voice would spark, flicker, flare alive with sounds. In Spanish, he expressed ideas and feelings he rarely revealed in English. With firm Spanish sounds, he conveyed confidence and authority English would never allow him.

The silence at home, however, was finally more than a literal silence. Fewer words passed between parent and child, but more profound was the silence that resulted from my inattention to sounds. At about the time I no longer bothered to listen with care to the sounds of English in public, I grew careless about listening to the sounds family members made when they spoke. Most of the time I heard someone speaking at home and didn't distinguish his sounds from the words people uttered in public. I didn't even pay much attention to my parents' accented and ungrammatical speech. At least not at home. Only when I was with them in public would I grow alert to their accents. Though, even then, their sounds caused me less and less concern. For I was increasingly confident of my own public identity.

I would have been happier about my public success had I not sometimes recalled what it had been like earlier, when my family had conveyed its intimacy through a set of conveniently private sounds. Sometimes in public, hearing a stranger, I'd hark back to my past. A Mexican farmworker approached me downtown to ask directions to somewhere. '¿Hijito . . . ?' he said. And his voice summoned deep longing. Another time, standing beside my mother in the visiting room of a Carmelite convent, before the dense screen which rendered the nuns shadowy figures, I heard several Spanish-speaking nuns—their busy, singsong overlapping voices—assure us that yes, yes, we were remembered, all our family was remembered in their prayers. (Their voices echoed faraway family sounds.) Another day, a dark-faced old woman—her hand light on my shoulder—steadied herself against me as she boarded a bus. She murmured something I couldn't quite comprehend. Her Spanish voice came near, like the face of a never-before-seen relative in the instant before I was kissed. Her voice, like so many of the Spanish voices I'd hear in public, recalled the golden age of my youth. Hearing Spanish then, I continued to be a careful, if sad, listener to sounds. Hearing a Spanish-speaking family walking behind me, I turned to look. I smiled for an instant, before my glance found the Hispanic-looking faces of strangers in the crowd going by.

Today I hear bilingual educators say that children lose a degree of 'individuality' by becoming assimilated into public society. (Bilingual schooling was popularized in the seventies, that decade when middle-class ethnics began to resist the process of assimilation—the American melting pot.) But the bilingualists simplistically scorn the value and necessity of assimilation. They do not seem to realize that there are *two* ways a person is individualized. So they do not realize that while one suffers a diminished sense of *private* individuality by becoming assimilated into public society, such assimilation makes possible the achievement of *public* individuality.

The bilingualists insist that a student should be reminded of his difference from others in mass society, his heritage. But they equate mere separateness with individuality. The fact is that only in private—with intimates—is separateness from the crowd a prerequisite for individuality. (An intimate draws me apart, tells me that I am unique, unlike all others.) In public, by contrast, full individuality is achieved, paradoxically, by those who are able to consider themselves members of the crowd. Thus it happened for me: Only when I was able to think of myself as an American, no longer an alien in *gringo* society, could I seek the rights and opportunities necessary for full public individuality. The social and political advantages I enjoy as a man result from the day that I came to believe that my name, indeed, is *Rich-heard Road-ree-guess.* It is true that my public society today is often impersonal. (My public society is usually mass society.) Yet despite the anonymity of the crowd and despite the fact that the individuality I achieve in public is often tenuous—because it depends on my being one in a crowd—I celebrate the day I acquired my new name. Those middle-class ethnics who scorn assimilation seem to me filled with decadent self-pity, obsessed by the burden of public life. Dangerously, they romanticize public separateness and they trivialize the dilemma of the socially disadvantaged.

My awkward childhood does not prove the necessity of bilingual education. 45 My story discloses instead an essential myth of childhood—inevitable pain. If I rehearse here the changes in my private life after my Americanization, it is finally to emphasize the public gain. The loss implies the gain: The house I returned to each afternoon was quiet. Intimate sounds no longer rushed to the door to greet me. There were other noises inside. The telephone rang. Neighborhood kids ran past the door of the bedroom where I was reading my schoolbooks—covered with shopping-bag paper. Once I learned public language, it would never again be easy for me to hear intimate family voices. More and more of my day was spent hearing words. But that may only be a way of saying that the day I raised my hand in class and spoke loudly to an entire roomful of faces, my childhood started to end.

3

I grew up victim to a disabling confusion. As I grew fluent in English, I no longer could speak Spanish with confidence. I continued to understand spoken Spanish. And in high school, I learned how to read and write Spanish. But for many years I could not pronounce it. A powerful guilt blocked my spoken words; an essential glue was missing whenever I'd try to connect words to form sentences. I would be unable to break a barrier of sound, to speak freely. I would speak, or try to speak, Spanish, and I would manage to utter halting, hiccuping sounds that betrayed my unease.

When relatives and Spanish-speaking friends of my parents came to the house, my brother and sisters seemed reticent to use Spanish, but at least they managed to say a few necessary words before being excused. I never managed so gracefully. I was cursed with guilt. Each time I'd hear myself addressed in Spanish, I would be unable to respond with any success. I'd know the words I wanted to say, but I couldn't manage to say them. I would try to speak, but everything I said seemed to me horribly anglicized. My mouth would not form the words right. My jaw would tremble. After a phrase or two, I'd cough up a warm, silvery sound. And stop.

It surprised my listeners to hear me. They'd lower their heads, better to grasp what I was trying to say. They would repeat their questions in gentle, affectionate voices. But by then I would answer in English. No, no, they would say, we want you to speak to us in Spanish. ('. . . *en español.*') But I couldn't do it. *Pocho* then they called me. Sometimes playfully, teasingly, using the tender diminutive—*mi pochito*. Sometimes not so playfully, mockingly, *Pocho*. (A

Spanish dictionary defines that word as an adjective meaning 'colorless' or 'bland.' But I heard it as a noun, naming the Mexican-American who, in becoming an American, forgets his native society.) '¡*Pocho!*' the lady in the Mexican food store muttered, shaking her head. I looked up to the counter where red and green peppers were strung like Christmas tree lights and saw the frowning face of the stranger. My mother laughed somewhere behind me. (She said that her children didn't want to practice 'our Spanish' after they started going to school.) My mother's smiling voice made me suspect that the lady who faced me was not really angry at me. But, searching her face, I couldn't find the hint of a smile.

Embarrassed, my parents would regularly need to explain their children's inability to speak flowing Spanish during those years. My mother met the wrath of her brother, her only brother, when he came up from Mexico one summer with his family. He saw his nieces and nephews for the very first time. After listening to me, he looked away and said what a disgrace it was that I couldn't speak Spanish, '*su proprio idioma.*' He made that remark to my mother; I noticed, however, that he stared at my father.

I clearly remember one other visitor from those years. A long-time friend of 50 my father from San Francisco would come to stay with us for several days in late August. He took great interest in me after he realized that I couldn't answer his questions in Spanish. He would grab me as I started to leave the kitchen. He would ask me something. Usually he wouldn't bother to wait for my mumbled response. Knowingly, he'd murmur: '*¿Ay Pocho, Pocho, adónde vas?*' And he would press his thumbs into the upper part of my arms, making me squirm with currents of pain. Dumbly, I'd stand there, waiting for his wife to notice us, for her to call him off with a benign smile. I'd giggle, hoping to deflate the tension between us, pretending that I hadn't seen the glittering scorn in his glance.

I remember that man now, but seek no revenge in this telling. I recount such incidents only because they suggest the fierce power Spanish had for many people I met at home; the way Spanish was associated with closeness. Most of those people who called me a *pocho* could have spoken English to me. But they would not. They seemed to think that Spanish was the only language we could use, that Spanish alone permitted our close association. (Such persons are vulnerable always to the ghetto merchant and the politician who have learned the value of speaking their clients' family language to gain immediate trust.) For my part, I felt that I had somehow committed a sin of betrayal by learning English. But betrayal against whom? Not against visitors to the house exactly. No, I felt that I had betrayed my immediate family. I *knew* that my parents had encouraged me to learn English. I *knew* that I had turned to English only with angry reluctance. But once I spoke English with ease, I came to *feel* guilty. (This guilt defied logic.) I felt that I had shattered the intimate bond that had once held the family close. This original sin against my family told whenever anyone addressed me in Spanish and I responded, confounded.

But even during those years of guilt, I was coming to sense certain consoling truths about language and intimacy. I remember playing with a friend in the backyard one day, when my grandmother appeared at the window. Her face was stern with suspicion when she saw the boy (the *gringo*) I was with. In Spanish she called out to me, sounding the whistle of her ancient breath. My companion looked up and watched her intently as she lowered the window and moved, still visible, behind the light curtain, watching us both. He wanted to know what she had said. I started to tell him, to say—to translate her Spanish words into English. The problem was, however, that though I knew how to translate exactly *what* she had told me, I realized that any translation would distort the deepest meaning of her message: It had been directed only to me. This message of intimacy could never be translated because it was not *in* the words she had used but passed *through* them. So any translation would have seemed wrong; her words would have been stripped of an essential meaning. Finally, I decided not to tell my friend anything. I told him that I didn't hear all she had said.

This insight unfolded in time. Making more and more friends outside my house, I began to distinguish intimate voices speaking through *English*. I'd listen at times to a close friend's confidential tone or secretive whisper. Even more remarkable were those instances when, for no special reason apparently, I'd become conscious of the fact that my companion was speaking only to me. I'd marvel just hearing his voice. It was a stunning event: to be able to break through his words, to be able to hear this voice of the other, to realize that it was directed only to me. After such moments of intimacy outside the house, I began to trust hearing intimacy conveyed through my family's English. Voices at home at last punctured sad confusion. I'd hear myself addressed as an intimate at home once again. Such moments were never as raucous with sound as past times had been when we had had 'private' Spanish to use. (Our English-sounding house was never to be as noisy as our Spanish-speaking house had been.) Intimate moments were usually soft moments of sound. My mother was in the dining room while I did my homework nearby. And she looked over at me. Smiled. Said something—her words said nothing very important. But her voice sounded to tell me (*We are together*) I was her son.

(*Richard!*)

Intimacy thus continued at home; intimacy was not stilled by English. It is 55 true that I would never forget the great change of my life, the diminished occasions of intimacy. But there would also be times when I sensed the deepest truth about language and intimacy: *Intimacy is not created by a particular language; it is created by intimates.* The great change in my life was not linguistic but social. If, after becoming a successful student, I no longer heard intimate voices as often as I had earlier, it was not because I spoke English rather than Spanish. It was because I used public language for most of the day. I moved easily at last, a citizen in a crowded city of words.

4

This boy became a man. In private now, alone, I brood over language and intimacy—the great themes of my past. In public I expect most of the faces I meet

to be the faces of strangers. (How do you do?) If meetings are quick and impersonal, they have been efficiently managed. I rush past the sounds of voices
attending only to the words addressed to me. Voices seem planed to an even
surface of sound, soundless. A business associate speaks in a deep baritone, but
I pass through the timbre to attend to his words. The crazy man who sells me a
newspaper every night mumbles something crazy, but I have time only to pretend that I have heard him say hello. Accented versions of English make little
impression on me. In the rush-hour crowd a Japanese tourist asks me a question, and I inch past his accent to concentrate on what he is saying. The Eastern
European immigrant in a neighborhood delicatessen speaks to me through a
marinade of sounds, but I respond to his words. I note for only a second the
Texas accent of the telephone operator or the Mississippi accent of the man
who lives in the apartment below me.

My city seems silent until some ghetto black teenagers board the bus I am
on. Because I do not take their presence for granted, I listen to the sounds of
their voices. Of all the accented versions of English I hear in a day, I hear theirs
most intently. They are *the* sounds of the outsider. They annoy me for being
loud—so self-sufficient and unconcerned by my presence. Yet for the same
reason they seem to me glamorous. (A romantic gesture against public acceptance.) Listening to their shouted laughter, I realize my own quiet. Their voices
enclose my isolation. I feel envious, envious of their brazen intimacy.

I warn myself away from such envy, however. I remember the black political
activists who have argued in favor of using black English in schools. (Their argument varies only slightly from that made by foreign-language bilingualists.) I
have heard 'radical' linguists make the point that black English is a complex and
intricate version of English. And I do not doubt it. But neither do I think that
black English should be a language of public instruction. What makes black
English inappropriate in classrooms is not something *in* the language. It is
rather what lower-class speakers make of it. Just as Spanish would have been a
dangerous language for me to have used at the start of my education, so black
English would be a dangerous language to use in the schooling of teenagers for
whom it reinforces feelings of public separateness.

This seems to me an obvious point. But one that needs to be made. In recent
years there have been attempts to make the language of the alien public language. 'Bilingual education, two ways to understand . . . ,' television and radio
commercials glibly announce. Proponents of bilingual education are careful to
say that they want students to acquire good schooling. Their argument goes
something like this: Children permitted to use their family language in school
will not be so alienated and will be better able to match the progress of English-
speaking children in the crucial first months of instruction. (Increasingly confident of their abilities, such children will be more inclined to apply themselves
to their studies in the future.) But then the bilingualists claim another, very different goal. They say that children who use their family language in school will
retain a sense of their individuality—their ethnic heritage and cultural ties.
Supporters of bilingual education thus want it both ways. They propose bilingual schooling as a way of helping students acquire the skills of the classroom

crucial for public success. But they likewise insist that bilingual instruction will give students a sense of their identity apart from the public.

Behind this screen there gleams an astonishing promise: One can become a public person while still remaining a private person. At the very same time one can be both! There need be no tension between the self in the crowd and the self apart from the crowd! Who would not want to believe such an idea? Who can be surprised that the scheme has won the support of many middle-class Americans? If the barrio or ghetto child can retain his separateness even while being publicly educated, then it is almost possible to believe that there is no private cost to be paid for public success. Such is the consolation offered by any of the current bilingual schemes. Consider, for example, the bilingual voters' ballot. In some American cities one can cast a ballot printed in several languages. Such a document implies that a person can exercise that most public of rights—the right to vote—while still keeping apart, unassimilated from public life.

It is not enough to say that these schemes are foolish and certainly doomed. Middle-class supporters of public bilingualism toy with the confusion of those Americans who cannot speak standard English as well as they can. Bilingual enthusiasts, moreover, sin against intimacy. An Hispanic-American writer tells me, 'I will never give up my family language; I would as soon give up my soul.' Thus he holds to his chest a skein of words, as though it were the source of his family ties. He credits to language what he should credit to family members. A convenient mistake. For as long as he holds on to words, he can ignore how much else has changed in his life.

It has happened before. In earlier decades, persons newly successful and ambitious for social mobility similarly seized upon certain 'family words.' Working-class men attempting political power took to calling one another 'brother.' By so doing they escaped oppressive public isolation and were able to unite with many others like themselves. But they paid a price for this union. It was a public union they forged. The word they coined to address one another could never be the sound (*brother*) exchanged by two in intimate greeting. In the union hall the word 'brother' became a vague metaphor; with repetition a weak echo of the intimate sound. Context forced the change. Context could not be overruled. Context will always guard the realm of the intimate from public misuse.

Today nonwhite Americans call 'brother' to strangers. And white feminists refer to their mass union of 'sisters.' And white middle-class teenagers continue to prove the importance of context as they try to ignore it. They seize upon the idioms of the black ghetto. But their attempt to appropriate such expressions invariably changes the words. As it becomes a public expression, the ghetto idiom loses its sound—its message of public separateness and strident intimacy. It becomes with public repetition a series of words, increasingly lifeless.

The mystery remains: intimate utterance. The communication of intimacy passes through the word to enliven its sound. But it cannot be held by the word. Cannot be clutched or ever quoted. It is too fluid. It depends not on word but on person.

My grandmother! 65

She stood among my other relations mocking me when I no longer spoke Spanish. '*Pocho*,' she said. But then it made no difference. (She'd laugh.) Our relationship continued. Language was never its source. She was a woman in her eighties during the first decade of my life. A mysterious woman to me, my only living grandparent. A woman of Mexico. The woman in long black dresses that reached down to her shoes. My one relative who spoke no word of English. She had no interest in *gringo* society. She remained completely aloof from the public. Protected by her daughters. Protected even by me when we went to Safeway together and I acted as her translator. Eccentric woman. Soft. Hard.

When my family visited my aunt's house in San Francisco, my grandmother searched for me among my many cousins. She'd chase them away. Pinching her granddaughters, she'd warn them all away from me. Then she'd take me to her room, where she had prepared for my coming. There would be a chair next to the bed. A dusty jellied candy nearby. And a copy of *Life en Español* for me to examine. 'There,' she'd say. I'd sit there content. A boy of eight. *Pocho*. Her favorite. I'd sift through the pictures of earthquake-destroyed Latin American cities and blond-wigged Mexican movie stars. And all the while I'd listen to the sound of my grandmother's voice. She'd pace round the room, searching through closets and drawers, telling me stories of her life. Her past. They were stories so familiar to me that I couldn't remember the first time I'd heard them. I'd look up sometimes to listen. Other times she'd look over at me. But she never seemed to expect a response. Sometimes I'd smile or nod. (I understood exactly what she was saying.) But it never seemed to matter to her one way or another. It was enough I was there. The words she spoke were almost irrelevant to that fact—the sounds she made. Content.

The mystery remained: intimate utterance.

I learn little about language and intimacy listening to those social activists who propose using one's family language in public life. Listening to songs on the radio, or hearing a great voice at the opera, or overhearing the woman downstairs singing to herself at an open window, I learn much more. Singers celebrate the human voice. Their lyrics are words. But animated by voice those words are subsumed into sounds. I listen with excitement as the words yield their enormous power to sound—though the words are never totally obliterated. In most songs the drama or tension results from the fact that the singer moves between word (sense) and note (song). At one moment the song simply 'says' something. At another moment the voice stretches out the words—the heart cannot contain!—and the voice moves toward pure sound. Words take flight.

Singing out words, the singer suggests an experience of sound most intensely 70 mine at intimate moments. Literally, most songs are about love. (Lost love; celebrations of living; pleas.) By simply being occasions when sound escapes word, however, songs put me in mind of the most intimate moments of my life.

Finally, among all types of song, it is the song created by lyric poets that I find most compelling. There is no other public occasion of sound so important for me. Written poems exist on a page, at first glance, as a mere collection of words. And yet, despite this, without musical accompaniment, the poet leads me to hear the sounds of the words that I read. As song, the poem passes between sound and sense, never belonging for long to one realm or the other. As public artifact, the poem can never duplicate intimate sound. But by imitating such sound, the poem helps me recall the intimate times of my life. I read in my room—alone—and grow conscious of being alone, sounding my voice, in search of another. The poem serves then as a memory device. It forces remembrance. And refreshes. It remind me of the possibility of escaping public words, the possibility that awaits me in meeting the intimate.

The poems I read are not nonsense poems. But I read them for reasons which, I imagine, are similar to those that make children play with meaningless rhyme. I have watched them before: I have noticed the way children create private languages to keep away the adult; I have heard their chanting riddles that go nowhere in logic but harken back to some kingdom of sound; I have watched them listen to intricate nonsense rhymes, and I have noted their wonder. I was never such a child. Until I was six years old, I remained in a magical realm of sound. I didn't need to remember that realm because it was present to me. But then the screen door shut behind me as I left home for school. At last I began my movement toward words. On the other side of initial sadness would come the realization that intimacy cannot be held. With time would come the knowledge that intimacy must finally pass.

I would dishonor those I have loved and those I love now to claim anything else. I would dishonor our closeness by holding on to a particular language and calling it my family language. Intimacy is not trapped within words. It passes through words. It passes. The truth is that intimates leave the room. Doors close. Faces move away from the window. Time passes. Voices recede into the dark. Death finally quiets the voice. And there is no way to deny it. No way to stand in the crowd, uttering one's family language.

The last time I saw my grandmother I was nine years old. I can tell you some of the things she said to me as I stood by her bed. I cannot, however, quote the message of intimacy she conveyed with her voice. She laughed, holding my hand. Her voice illumined disjointed memories as it passed them again. She remembered her husband, his green eyes, the magic name of Narciso. His early death. She remembered the farm in Mexico. The eucalyptus nearby. (Its scent, she remembered, like incense.) She remembered the family cow, the bell round its neck heard miles away. A dog. She remembered working as a seamstress. How she'd leave her daughters and son for long hours to go into Guadalajara to work. And how my mother would come running toward her in the sun—her bright yellow dress—to see her return. '*Mmmaaammmmmááá,*' the old lady mimicked her daughter (my mother) to her son. She laughed. There was the snap of a cough. An aunt came into the room and told me it was time I should leave. 'You can see her tomorrow,' she promised. And so I kissed my grandmother's cracked face. And the last thing I saw was her thin, oddly youthful thigh, as my aunt rearranged the sheet on the bed.

At the funeral parlor a few days after, I knelt with my relatives during the rosary. Among their voices but silent, I traced, then lost, the sounds of individual aunts in the surge of the common prayer. And I heard at that moment what 75 I have since heard often again—the sounds the women in my family make when they are praying in sadness. When I went up to look at my grandmother, I saw her through the haze of a veil draped over the open lid of the casket. Her face appeared calm—but distant and unyielding to love. It was not the face I remembered seeing most often. It was the face she made in public when the clerk at Safeway asked her some question and I would have to respond. It was her public face the mortician had designed with his dubious art.

ACTIVITIES FOR WRITING AND DISCUSSION

1. One recurring **theme** in this essay (the first chapter of Rodriguez's autobiography, *Hunger of Memory*) is the idea of change as a process of loss and gain. As Rodriguez becomes "Americanized" and educated, what does he lose and what does he gain? Identify passages that illustrate the loss and the gain and annotate them.

2. Write about the losses and gains that have occurred in your own life as a result of education. In this piece, emphasize the storytelling element: Either *narrate* experiences of your loss and gain or *dramatize* them in the form of a dialogue between yourself and some other person or persons involved in your education.

3. Much of the essay concerns Rodriguez's parents and how his relationship with them changed as he learned what he calls the "public language" of English. Narrate or dramatize any life stories of your own that show how your relationship with your own parents—or mentors—changed as a result of education (formal or other).

4. Reread and annotate passages in which Rodriguez attacks supporters of bilingual education. Summarize his arguments against bilingualism. Then write an essay in which you agree—or disagree—with Rodriguez's position.

5. Create a Topic/Form Grid (see Chapter 10). Designate "bilingual education" as the "topic" and list as many "forms" as you can for writing about it. Then use one of the forms to create a piece of writing on bilingual education.

Leslie Marmon Silko (b. 1948)

Language and Literature from a Pueblo Indian Perspective

Where I come from, the words most highly valued are those spoken from the heart, unpremeditated and unrehearsed. Among the Pueblo people, a written speech or statement is highly suspect because the true feelings of the speaker remain hidden as she reads words that are detached from the occasion and the audience. I have intentionally not written a formal paper because I want you to *hear* and to experience English in a structure that follows patterns from the oral tradition. For those of you accustomed to being taken from point A to point B to point C, this presentation may be somewhat difficult to follow. Pueblo expression resembles something like a spider's web—with many little threads radiating from the center, crisscrossing each other. As with the web, the structure emerges as it is made and you must simply listen and trust, as the Pueblo people do, that meaning will be made.

My task is a formidable one: I ask you to set aside a number of basic approaches that you have been using, and probably will continue to use, and instead, to approach language from the Pueblo perspective, one that embraces the whole of creation and the whole of history and time.

What changes would Pueblo writers make to English as a language for literature? I have some examples of stories in English that I will use to address this question. At the same time, I would like to explain the importance of storytelling and how it relates to a Pueblo theory of language.

So, I will begin, appropriately enough, with the Pueblo Creation story, an all-inclusive story of how life began. In this story, Tséitsínako, Thought Woman, by thinking of her sisters, and together with her sisters, thought of everything that is. In this way, the world was created. Everything in this world was a part of the original creation; the people at home understood that far away there were other human beings, also a part of this world. The Creation story even includes a prophecy, which describes the origin of European and African peoples and also refers to Asians.

This story, I think, suggests something about why the Pueblo people are 5 more concerned with story and communication and less concerned with a particular language. There are at least six, possibly seven, distinct languages among the twenty pueblos of the southwestern United States, for example, Zuñi and Hopi. And from mesa to mesa there are subtle differences in language. But the particular language being spoken isn't as important as what a speaker is trying to say, and this emphasis on the story itself stems, I believe, from a view of narrative particular to the Pueblo and other Native American peoples—that is, that language *is* story.

I will try to clarify this statement. At Laguna Pueblo, for example, many individual words have their own stories. So when one is telling a story, and one is using words to tell the story, each word that one is speaking has a story of its own, too. Often the speakers or tellers will go into these word-stories, creating an elaborate structure of stories-within-stories. This structure, which becomes very apparent in the actual telling of a story, informs contemporary Pueblo writing and storytelling as well as the traditional narratives. This perspective on narrative—of story within story, the idea that one story is only the beginning of many stories, and the sense that stories never truly end—represents an important contribution of Native American cultures to the English language.

Many people think of storytelling as something that is done at bedtime, that it is something done for small children. But when I use the term *storytelling*, I'm talking about something much bigger than that. I'm talking about something that comes out of an experience and an understanding of that original view of creation—that we are all part of a whole; we do not differentiate or fragment stories and experiences. In the beginning, Tséitsínako, Thought Woman, thought of all things, and all of these things are held together as one holds many things together in a single thought.

So in the telling (and you will hear a few of the dimensions of this telling) first of all, as mentioned earlier, the storytelling always includes the audience, the listeners. In fact, a great deal of the story is believed to be inside the listener: the storyteller's role is to draw the story out of the listeners. The storytelling continues from generation to generation.

Basically, the origin story constructs our identity—within this story, we know who we are. We are the Lagunas. This is where we come from. We came this way. We came by this place. And so from the time we are very young, we hear these stories, so that when we go out into the world, when one asks who we are, or where we are from, we immediately know: we are the people who came from the north. We are the people of these stories.

In the Creation story, Antelope says that he will help knock a hole in the   10 earth so that the people can come up, out into the next world. Antelope tries and tries; he uses his hooves, but is unable to break through. It is then that Badger says, "Let me help you." And Badger very patiently uses his claws and digs a way through, bringing the people into the world. When the Badger clan people think of themselves, or when the Antelope people think of themselves, it is as people who are of *this* story, and this is *our* place, and we fit into the very beginning when the people first came, before we began our journey south.

Within the clans there are stories that identify the clan. One moves, then, from the idea of one's identity as a tribal person into clan identity, then to one's identity as a member of an extended family. And it is the notion of "extended family" that has produced a kind of story that some distinguish from other Pueblo stories, though Pueblo people do not. Anthropologists and ethnologists have, for a long time, differentiated the types of stories the Pueblos tell. They tended to elevate the old, sacred, and traditional stories and to brush aside family stories, the family's account of itself. But in Pueblo culture, these family stories are given equal recognition. There is no definite, preset pattern for the way one will hear the stories of one's own family, but it is a very critical part of one's childhood, and the storytelling continues throughout one's life. One will hear stories of importance to the family—sometimes wonderful stories—stories about the time a maternal uncle got the biggest deer that was ever seen and brought it back from the mountains. And so an individual's identity will extend from the identity constructed around the family—"I am from the family of my uncle who brought in this wonderful deer and it was a wonderful hunt."

Family accounts include negative stories, too; perhaps an uncle did something unacceptable. It is very important that one keep track of all these stories—both positive and not so positive—about one's own family and other families. Because even when there is no way around it—old Uncle Pete *did* do a terrible thing—by knowing the stories that originate in other families, one is able to deal with terrible sorts of things that might happen within one's own family. If a member of the family does something that cannot be excused, one always knows stories about similarly inexcusable things done by a member of another family. But this knowledge is not communicated for malicious reasons. It is very important to understand this. Keeping track of all the stories within the community gives us all a certain distance, a useful perspective, that brings incidents down to a level we can deal with. If others have done it before, it cannot be so terrible. If others have endured, so can we.

The stories are always bringing us together, keeping this whole together, keeping this family together, keeping this clan together. "Don't go away, don't isolate yourself, but come here, because we have all had these kinds of experiences." And so there is this constant pulling together to resist the tendency to run or hide or separate oneself during a traumatic emotional experience. This separation not only endangers the group but the individual as well—one does not recover by oneself.

Because storytelling lies at the heart of Pueblo culture, it is absurd to attempt to fix the stories in time. "When did they tell the stories?" or "What time of day does the storytelling take place?"—these questions are nonsensical from a Pueblo perspective, because our storytelling goes on constantly: as some old grandmother puts on the shoes of a child and tells her the story of a little girl who didn't wear her shoes, for instance, or someone comes into the house for coffee to talk with a teenage boy who has just been in a lot of trouble, to reassure him that someone else's son has been in that kind of trouble, too. Storytelling is an ongoing process, working on many different levels.

Here's one story that is often told at a time of individual crisis (and I want   15 to remind you that we make no distinctions between types of story—historical, sacred, plain gossip—because these distinctions are not useful when discussing the Pueblo *experience* of language). There was a young man who, when he came back from the war in Vietnam, had saved up his army pay and bought a beautiful red Volkswagen. He was very proud of it. One night he drove up to a place called the King's Bar right across the reservation line. The bar is notorious for many reasons, particularly for the deep *arroyo* located behind it. The young man ran in to pick up a cold six-pack, but he forgot to put on his emergency brake. And his little red Volkswagen rolled back into the *arroyo* and was all smashed up. He felt very bad about it, but within a few days everybody had come to him with stories about other people who had lost cars and family members to that *arroyo*, for instance, George Day's station wagon, with his mother-in-law and kids inside. So everybody was saying, "Well, at least your mother-in-law and kids weren't in the car when it rolled in," and one can't argue with that kind of story. The story of the young man and his smashed-up Volkswagen was now joined with all the other stories of cars that fell into that *arroyo*.

Now I want to tell you a very beautiful little story. It is a very old story that is sometimes told to people who suffer great family or personal loss. This story was told by my Aunt Susie. She is one of the first generation of people at Laguna who began experimenting with English—who began working to make English speak for us—that is, to speak from the heart. (I come from a family intent on getting the stories told.) As you read the story, I think you will hear that. And here and there, I think, you will also hear the influence of the Indian school at Carlisle, Pennsylvania, where my Aunt Susie was sent (like being sent to prison) for six years.

This scene is set partly in Acoma, partly in Laguna. Waithea was a little girl living in Acoma and one day she said, "Mother, I would like to have some *yashtoah* to eat." *Yashtoah* is the hardened crust of corn mush that curls up. *Yashtoah* literally means "curled up." She said, "I would like to have some *yashtoah*," and her mother said, "My dear little girl, I can't make you any *yashtoah* because we haven't any wood, but if you will go down off the mesa, down below, and pick up some pieces of wood and bring them home, I will make you some *yashtoah*." So Waithea was glad and ran down the precipitous cliff of Acoma mesa. Down below, just as her mother had told her, there were pieces of wood, some curled, some crooked in shape, that she was to pick up and take home. She found just such wood as these.

She brought them home in a little wicker basket. First she called to her mother as she got home, "*Nayah, deeni!* Mother, upstairs!" The Pueblo people always called "upstairs" because long ago their homes were two, three stories, and they entered from the top. She said, "*Deeni!* UPSTAIRS!" and her mother came. The little girl said, "I have brought the wood you wanted me to bring." And she opened her little wicker basket to lay out the pieces of wood but here they were snakes. They were snakes instead of the crooked sticks of wood. And her mother said, "Oh my dear child, you have brought snakes instead!" She said, "Go take them back and put them back just where you got them." And the little girl ran down the mesa again, down below to the flats. And she put those snakes back just where she got them. They were snakes instead and she was very hurt about this and so she said, "I'm not going home. I'm going to *Kawaik*, the beautiful lake place, *Kawaik*, and drown myself in that lake, *byn'yah'nah* [the "west lake"]. I will go there and drown myself."

So she started off, and as she passed by the Enchanted Mesa near Acoma she met an old man, very aged, and he saw her running, and he said, "My dear child, where are you going?" "I'm going to *Kawaik* and jump into the lake there." "Why?" "Well, because," she said, "my mother didn't want to make any *yashtoah* for me." The old man said, "Oh, no! You must not go my child. Come with me and I will take you home." He tried to catch her, but she was very light and skipped along. And every time he would try to grab her she would skip faster away from him.

The old man was coming home with some wood strapped to his back and 20 tied with yucca. He just let that strap go and let the wood drop. He went as fast as he could up the cliff to the little girl's home. When he got to the place where she lived, he called to her mother. "*Deeni!*" "Come on up!" And he said, "I can't. I just came to bring you a message. Your little daughter is running away. She is going to *Kawaik* to drown herself in the lake there." "Oh my dear little girl!" the mother said. So she busied herself with making the *yashtoah* her little girl liked so much. Corn mush curled at the top. (She must have found enough wood to boil the corn meal and make the *yashtoah*.)

While the mush was cooling off, she got the little girl's clothing, her *manta* dress and buckskin moccasins and all her other garments, and put them in a bundle—probably a yucca bag. And she started down as fast as she could on the east side of Acoma. (There used to be a trail there, you know. It's gone now, but it was accessible in those days.) She saw her daughter way at a distance and she kept calling: "Stsamaku! My daughter! Come back! I've got your *yashtoah* for you." But the little girl would not turn. She kept on ahead and she cried: "My mother, my mother, she didn't want me to have any *yashtoah*. So now I'm going to *Kawaik* and drown myself." Her mother heard her cry and said, "My little daughter, come back here!" "No," and she kept a distance away from her. And they came nearer and nearer to the lake. And she could see her daughter now, very plain. "Come back, my daughter! I have your *yashtoah*." But no, she kept on, and finally she reached the lake and she stood on the edge.

She had tied a little feather in her hair, which is traditional (in death they tie this feather on the head). She carried a feather, the little girl did, and she tied it in her hair with a piece of string, right on top of her head she put the feather. Just as her mother was about to reach her, she jumped into the lake. The little feather was whirling around and around in the depths below. Of course the mother was very sad. She went, grieved, back to Acoma and climbed her mesa home. She stood on the edge of the mesa and scattered her daughter's clothing, the little moccasins, the *yashtoah*. She scattered them to the east, to the west, to the north, to the south. And the pieces of clothing and the moccasins and *yashtoah*, all turned into butterflies. And today they say that Acoma has more beautiful butterflies, red ones, white ones, blue ones, yellow ones. They came from this little girl's clothing.

Now this is a story anthropologists would consider very old. The version I have given you is just as Aunt Susie tells it. You can occasionally hear some English she picked up at Carlisle—words like "precipitous." You will also notice that there is a great deal of repetition, and a little reminder about *yashtoah*, and how it is made. There is a remark about the cliff trail at Acoma—that it was once there, but is there no longer. The story may be told at a time of sadness or loss, but within this story many other elements are brought together. Things are not separated out and categorized; all things are brought together, so that the reminder about the *yashtaoh* is valuable information that is repeated—a recipe, if you will. The information about the old trail at Acoma reveals that stories are, in a sense, maps, since even to this day there is little information or material about trails that is passed around with writing. In the structure of this story the repetitions are, of course, designed to help you remember. It is repeated again and again, and then it moves on.

The next story I would like to tell is by Simon Ortiz, from Acoma Pueblo. He is a wonderful poet who also works in narrative. One of the things I find very interesting in this short story is that if you listen very closely, you begin to hear what I was talking about in terms of a story never beginning at the beginning, and certainly never ending. As the Hopis sometimes say, "Well, it has gone this far for a while." There is always that implication of a continuing. The other thing I want you to listen for is the many stories within one story. Listen to the kinds of stories contained within the main story—stories that give one a family identity and an individual identity, for example. This story is called "Home Country":

"Well, it's been a while. I think in 1947 was when I left. My husband had   25
been killed in Okinawa some years before. And so I had no more husband.
And I had to make a living. O I guess I could have looked for another man
but I didn't want to. It looked like the war had made some of them into a
bad way anyway. I saw some of them come home like that. They either got
drunk or just stayed around a while or couldn't seem to be satisfied anymore with what was there. I guess now that I think about it, that happened
to me too although I wasn't in the war not in the Army or even much off the
reservation just that several years at the Indian School. Well there was that
feeling things were changing not only the men the boys, but things were
changing.

"One day the home nurse the nurse that came from the Indian health
service was at my mother's home my mother was getting near the end real
sick and she said that she had been meaning to ask me a question. I said
what is the question. And the home nurse said well your mother is getting
real sick and after she is no longer around for you to take care of, what will
you be doing you and her are the only ones here. And I said I don't know.
But I was thinking about it what she said made me think about it. And then
the next time she came she said to me Eloise the government is hiring Indians now in the Indian schools to take care of the boys and girls I heard one
of the supervisors saying that Indians are hard workers but you have to su-
pervise them a lot and I thought of you well because you've been taking care
of your mother real good and you follow all my instructions. She said I
thought of you because you're a good Indian girl and you would be the kind
of person for that job. I didn't say anything I had not ever really thought
about a job but I kept thinking about it.

"Well my mother she died and we buried her up at the old place the cemetery there it's real nice on the east side of the hill where the sun shines warm and the wind doesn't blow too much sand around right there. Well I was sad we were all sad for a while but you know how things are. One of my aunties came over and she advised me and warned me about being too sorry about it and all that she wished me that I would not worry too much about it because old folks they go along pretty soon life is that way and then she said that maybe I ought to take in one of my aunties kids or two because there was a lot of them kids and I was all by myself now. But I was so young and I thought that I might do that you know take care of someone but I had been thinking too of what the home nurse said to me about working. Hardly anybody at our home was working at something like that no woman anyway. And I would have to move away.

"Well I did just that. I remember that day very well. I told my aunties and they were all crying and we all went up to the old highway where the bus to town passed by everyday. I was wearing an old kind of bluish sweater that was kind of big that one of my cousins who was older had got from a white person a tourist one summer in trade for something she had made a real pretty basket. She gave me that and I used to have a picture of me with it on it's kind of real ugly. Yeah that was the day I left wearing a baggy sweater and carrying a suitcase that someone gave me too I think or maybe it was the home nurse there wasn't much in it anyway either. I was scared and everybody seemed to be sad I was so young and skinny then. My aunties said one of them who was real fat you make sure you eat now make your own tortillas drink the milk and stuff like candies is no good she learned that from the nurse. Make sure you got your letter my auntie said. I had it folded into my purse. Yes I had one too a brown one that my husband when he was still alive one time on furlough he brought it on my birthday it was a nice purse and still looked new because I never used it.

"The letter said that I had a job at Keams Canyon the boarding school there but I would have to go to the Agency first for some papers to be filled and that's where I was going first. The Agency. And then they would send me out to Keams Canyon. I didn't even know where it was except that someone of our relatives said that it was near Hopi. My uncles teased me about watching out for the Hopi men and boys don't let them get too close they said well you know how they are and they were pretty strict too about those things and then they were joking and then they were not too and so I said aw they won't get near to me I'm too ugly and I promised I would be careful anyway.

"So we all gathered for a while at my last auntie's house and then the old man my grandfather brought his wagon and horses to the door and we all got in and sat there for a while until my auntie told her father okay father let's go and shook his elbow because the poor old man was old by then and kind of going to sleep all the time you had to talk to him real loud. I had about ten dollars I think that was a lot of money more than it is now you

30

know and when we got to the highway where the Indian road which is just a dirt road goes off the pave road my grandfather reached into his blue jeans and pulled out a silver dollar and put it into my hand. I was so shocked. We were all so shocked. We all looked around at each other we didn't know where the old man had gotten it because we were real poor two of my uncles had to borrow on their accounts at the trading store for the money I had in my purse but there it was a silver dollar so big and shining in my grandfather's hand and then in my hand.

"Well I was so shocked and everybody was so shocked that we all started crying right there at the junction of that Indian road and the pave highway I wanted to be a little girl again running after the old man when he hurried with his long legs to the cornfields or went for water down to the river. He was old then and his eye was turned gray and he didn't do much anymore except drive the wagon and chop a little bit of wood but I just held him and I just held him so tightly.

"Later on I don't know what happened to the silver dollar it had a date of 1907 on it but I kept it for a long time because I guess I wanted to have it to remember when I left my home country. What I did in between then and now is another story but that's the time I moved away," is what she said.*

There are a great many parallels between Pueblo experiences and those of African and Caribbean peoples—one is that we have all had the conqueror's language imposed on us. But our experience with English has been somewhat different in that the Bureau of Indian Affairs schools were not interested in teaching us the canon of Western classics. For instance, we never heard of Shakespeare. We were given Dick and Jane, and I can remember reading that the robins were heading south for the winter. It took me a long time to figure out what was going on. I worried for quite a while about our robins in Laguna because they didn't leave in the winter, until I finally realized that all the big textbook companies are up in Boston and *their* robins do go south in the winter. But in a way, this dreadful formal education freed us by encouraging us to maintain our narratives. Whatever literature we were exposed to at school (which was damn little), at home the storytelling, the special regard for telling and bringing together through the telling, was going on constantly.

And as the old people say, "If you can remember the stories, you will be all right. Just remember the stories." When I returned to Laguna Pueblo after attending college, I wondered how the storytelling was continuing (anthropologists say that Laguna Pueblo is one of the more acculturated pueblos), so I visited an English class at Laguna-Acoma High School. I knew the students had cassette tape recorders in their lockers and stereos at home, and that they lis-

---

*Simon J. Ortiz, *Howbah Indians* (Tucson: Blue Moon Press, 1978). [Author's note]

tened to Kiss and Led Zeppelin and were well informed about popular culture in general. I had with me an anthology of short stories by Native American writers, *The Man to Send Rain Clouds*. One story in the book is about the killing of a state policeman in New Mexico by three Acoma Pueblo men in the early 1950s. I asked the students how many had heard this story and steeled myself for the possibility that the anthropologists were right, that the old traditions were indeed dying out and the students would be ignorant of the story. But instead, all but one or two raised their hands—they had heard the story, just as I had heard it when I was young, some in English, some in Laguna.

One of the other advantages that we Pueblos have enjoyed is that we have always been able to stay with the land. Our stories cannot be separated from their geographical locations, from actual physical places on the land. We were not relocated like so many Native American groups who were torn away from their ancestral land. And our stories are so much a part of these places that it is almost impossible for future generations to lose them—there is a story connected with every place, every object in the landscape. 35

Dennis Brutus has talked about the "yet unborn" as well as "those from the past," and how we are still *all* in *this* place, and language—the storytelling—is our way of passing through or being with them, or being together again. When Aunt Susie told her stories, she would tell a younger child to go open the door so that our esteemed predecessors might bring in their gifts to us. "They are out there," Aunt Susie would say. "Let them come in. They're here, they're here with us *within* the stories."

A few years ago, when Aunt Susie was 106, I paid her a visit, and while I was there she said, "Well, I'll be leaving here soon. I think I'll be leaving here next week, and I will be going over to the Cliff House." She said, "It's going to be real good to get back over there." I was listening, and I was thinking that she must be talking about her house at Paguate Village, just north of Laguna. And she went on, "Well, my mother's sister (and she gave her Indian name) will be there. She has been living there. She will be there and we will be over there, and I will get a chance to write down these stories I've been telling you." Now you understand, of course, that Aunt Susie's mother's sister, a great storyteller herself, has long since passed over into the land of the dead. But then I realized, too, that Aunt Susie wasn't talking about death the way most of us do. She was talking about "going over" as a journey, a journey that perhaps we can only begin to understand through an appreciation for the boundless capacity of language that, through storytelling, brings us together, despite great distances between cultures, despite great distances in time.

ACTIVITIES FOR WRITING AND DISCUSSION

1. In the first paragraph Silko comments on the structure her essay will take:

For those of you accustomed to being taken from point A to point B to point C, this presentation may be somewhat difficult to follow. Pueblo expression resembles something like a spider's web—with many little threads radiating from the center, crisscrossing each other. As with the web, the structure emerges as it is made and you must simply listen and trust, as the Pueblo people do, that meaning will be made.

Do a postdraft outline (see Chapter 7) of all—or some sizable part of—Silko's essay. Then use your outline to show where and how her essay bears out her comments about "structure." Finally, what sorts of things does a "web"-like structure (as opposed to one that goes "from point A to point B to point C") imply about the outlook and values of the culture to which she belongs?

2. Based on your annotations of Silko's text, list and comment on the functions storytelling plays in Pueblo culture. Then, in your notebook, tell one or two particular stories that are important in your own family. What roles do the stories—and storytelling—play in your own family or larger culture? Do they serve any of the functions described by Silko?

3. Look again at the title of Silko's piece. Where in her essay does she discuss "literature"? Jot down your own definition of "literature"; then, as best you can, write down what you think Silko means by the term. How does her Pueblo concept of "literature" resemble and/or differ from your own? Finally, what do the differences suggest about differences between your culture and Silko's?

4. Reread the long story Silko quotes from Simon Ortiz.
   a. Identify and annotate "the many stories within one story" to which she refers.
   b. List and discuss any ways that Ortiz's narrative differs from ones common in your own culture.
   c. If you wish, write a story of your own in which you attempt to imitate the structure and oral style of Ortiz's text.

BELL HOOKS (b. 1952)

Keeping Close to Home: Class and Education

We are both awake in the almost dark of 5 A.M. Everyone else is sound asleep. Mama asks the usual questions. Telling me to look around, make sure I have everything, scolding me because I am uncertain about the actual time the bus arrives. By 5:30 we are waiting outside the closed station. Alone together, we have a chance to really talk. Mama begins. Angry with her children, especially the ones who whisper behind her back, she says bitterly, "Your childhood could not have been that bad. You were fed and clothed. You did not have to do without—that's more than a lot of folks have and I just can't stand the way y'all go on." The hurt in her voice saddens me. I have always wanted to protect mama from hurt, to ease her burdens. Now I am part of what troubles. Confronting me, she says accusingly, "It's not just the other children. You talk too much about the past. You don't just listen." And I do talk. Worse, I write about it.

Mama has always come to each of her children seeking different responses. With me she expresses the disappointment, hurt, and anger of betrayal: anger that her children are so critical, that we can't even have the sense to like the presents she sends. She says, "From now on there will be no presents. I'll just stick some money in a little envelope the way the rest of you do. Nobody wants criticism. Everybody can criticize me but I am supposed to say nothing." When I try to talk, my voice sounds like a twelve year old. When I try to talk, she speaks louder, interrupting me, even though she has said repeatedly, "Explain it to me, this talk about the past." I struggle to return to my thirty-five year old self so that she will know by the sound of my voice that we are two women talking together. It is only when I state firmly in my very adult voice, "Mama, you are not listening," that she becomes quiet. She waits. Now that I have her attention, I fear that my explanations will be lame, inadequate. "Mama," I begin, "people usually go to therapy because they feel hurt inside, because they have pain that will not stop, like a wound that continually breaks open, that does not heal. And often these hurts, that pain has to do with things that have happened in the past, sometimes in childhood, often in childhood, or things that we believe happened." She wants to know, "What hurts, what hurts are you talking about?" "Mom, I can't answer that. I can't speak for all of us, the hurts are different for everybody. But the point is you try to make the hurt better, to heal it, by understanding how it came to be. And I know you feel mad when we say something happened or hurt that you don't remember being that way, but the past isn't like that, we don't have the same memory of it. We remember things differently. You know that. And sometimes folk feel hurt about stuff and you just don't know or didn't realize it, and they need to talk about it. Surely you understand the need to talk about it."

Our conversation is interrupted by the sight of my uncle walking across the park toward us. We stop to watch him. He is on his way to work dressed in a familiar blue suit. They look alike, these two who rarely discuss the past. This interruption makes me think about life in a small town. You always see someone you know. Interruptions, intrusions are part of daily life. Privacy is difficult to maintain. We leave our private space in the car to greet him. After the hug and kiss he has given me every year since I was born, they talk about the day's funerals. In the distance the bus approaches. He walks away knowing that they will see each other later. Just before I board the bus I turn, staring into my mother's face. I am momentarily back in time, seeing myself eighteen years ago, at this same bus stop, staring into my mother's face, continually turning back, waving farewell as I returned to college—that experience which first took me away from our town, from family. Departing was as painful then as it is now. Each movement away makes return harder. Each separation intensifies distance, both physical and emotional.

To a southern black girl from a working-class background who had never been on a city bus, who had never stepped on an escalator, who had never travelled by plane, leaving the comfortable confines of a small town Kentucky life to attend Stanford University was not just frightening; it was utterly painful. My parents had not been delighted that I had been accepted and adamantly opposed my going so far from home. At the time, I did not see their opposition as an expression of their fear that they would lose me forever. Like many working-class folks, they feared what college education might do to their children's minds even as they unenthusiastically acknowledged its importance. They did not understand why I could not attend a college nearby, an all-black college. To them, any college would do. I would graduate, become a school teacher, make a decent living and a good marriage. And even though they reluctantly and skeptically supported my educational endeavors, they also subjected them to constant harsh and bitter critique. It is difficult for me to talk about my parents and their impact on me because they have always felt wary, ambivalent, mistrusting of my intellectual aspirations even as they have been caring and supportive. I want to speak about these contradictions because sorting through them, seeking resolution and reconciliation has been important to me both as it affects my development as a writer, my effort to be fully self-realized, and my longing to remain close to the family and community that provided the groundwork for much of my thinking, writing, and being.

Studying at Stanford, I began to think seriously about class differences. To   5 be materially underprivileged at a university where most folks (with the exception of workers) are materially privileged provokes such thought. Class differences were boundaries no one wanted to face or talk about. It was easier to downplay them, to act as though we were all from privileged backgrounds, to work around them, to confront them privately in the solitude of one's room, or to pretend that just being chosen to study at such an institution meant that those of us who did not come from privilege were already in transition toward privilege. To not long for such transition marked one as rebellious, as unlikely to succeed. It was a kind of treason not to believe that it was better to be identified with the world of material privilege than with the world of the working class, the poor. No wonder our working-class parents from poor backgrounds feared our entry into such a world, intuiting perhaps that we might learn to be ashamed of where we had come from, that we might never return home, or come back only to lord it over them.

Though I hung with students who were supposedly radical and chic, we did not discuss class. I talked to no one about the sources of my shame, how it hurt me to witness the contempt shown the brown-skinned Filipina maids who cleaned our rooms, or later my concern about the $100 a month I paid for a room off-campus which was more than half of what my parents paid for rent. I talked to no one about my efforts to save money, to send a little something home. Yet these class realities separated me from fellow students. We were moving in different directions. I did not intend to forget my class background or alter my class allegiance. And even though I received an education designed to provide me with a bourgeois sensibility, passive acquiescence was not my only option. I knew that I could resist. I could rebel. I could shape the direction and focus of the various forms of knowledge available to me. Even though I sometimes envied and longed for greater material advantages (particularly at vacation times when I would be one of few if any students remaining in the dormitory because there was no money for travel), I did not share the sensibility and values of my peers. That was important—class was not just about money; it was about values which showed and determined behavior. While I often needed more money, I never needed a new set of beliefs and values. For example, I was profoundly shocked and disturbed when peers would talk abut their parents without respect, or would even say that they hated their parents. This was especially troubling to me when it seemed that these parents were caring and concerned. It was often explained to me that such hatred was "healthy and normal." To my white, middle-class California roommate, I explained the way we were taught to value our parents and their care, to understand that they were not obligated to give us care. She would always shake her head, laughing all the while, and say, "Missy, you will learn that it's different here, that we think differently." She was right. Soon, I lived alone, like the one Mormon student who kept to himself as he made a concentrated effort to remain true to his religious beliefs and values. Later in graduate school I found that classmates believed "lower class" people had no beliefs and values. I was silent in such discussions, disgusted by their ignorance.

Carol Stack's anthropological study, *All Our Kin,* was one of the first books I read which confirmed my experiential understanding that within black culture (especially among the working class and poor, particularly in southern states), a value system emerged that was counter-hegemonic, that challenged notions of individualism and private property so important to the maintenance of white-supremacist, capitalist patriarchy. Black folk created in marginal spaces a world of community and collectivity where resources were shared. In the preface to *Feminist Theory: from margin to center,* I talked about how the point of difference, this marginality can be the space for the formation of an oppositional world view. That world view must be articulated, named if it is to provide a sustained blueprint for change. Unfortunately, there has existed no consistent framework for such naming. Consequently both the experience of this difference and documentation of it (when it occurs) gradually loses presence and meaning.

Much of what Stack documented about the "culture of poverty," for example, would not describe interactions among most black poor today irrespective of geographical setting. Since the black people she described did not acknowledge (if they recognized it in theoretical terms) the oppositional value of their world view, apparently seeing it more as a survival strategy determined less by conscious efforts to oppose oppressive race and class biases than by circumstance, they did not attempt to establish a framework to transmit their beliefs and values from generation to generation. When circumstances changed, values altered. Efforts to assimilate the values and beliefs of privileged white people, presented through media like television, undermine and destroy potential structures of opposition.

Increasingly, young black people are encouraged by the dominant culture (and by those black people who internalize the values of this hegemony) to believe that assimilation is the only possible way to survive, to succeed. Without the framework of an organized civil rights or black resistance struggle, individual and collective efforts at black liberation that focus on the primacy of self-definition and self-determination often go unrecognized. It is crucial that those among us who resist and rebel, who survive and succeed, speak openly and honestly about our lives and the nature of our personal struggles, the means by which we resolve and reconcile contradictions. This is no easy task. Within the educational institutions where we learn to develop and strengthen our writing and analytical skills, we also learn to think, write, and talk in a manner that shifts attention away from personal experience. Yet if we are to reach our people and all people, if we are to remain connected (especially those of us whose familial backgrounds are poor and working-class), we must understand that the telling of one's personal story provides a meaningful example, a way for folks to identify and connect.

Combining personal with critical analysis and theoretical perspectives can 10 engage listeners who might otherwise feel estranged, alienated. To speak simply with language that is accessible to as many folks as possible is also important. Speaking about one's personal experience or speaking with simple language is often considered by academics and/or intellectuals (irrespective of their political inclinations) to be a sign of intellectual weakness or even anti-intellectualism. Lately, when I speak, I do not stand in place—reading my paper, making little or no eye contact with audiences—but instead make eye contact, talk extemporaneously, digress, and address the audience directly. I have been told that people assume I am not prepared, that I am anti-intellectual, unprofessional (a concept that has everything to do with class as it determines actions and behavior), or that I am reinforcing the stereotype of black people as nontheoretical and gutsy.

Such criticism was raised recently by fellow feminist scholars after a talk I gave at Northwestern University at a conference on "Gender, Culture, Politics" to an audience that was mainly students and academics. I deliberately chose to speak in a very basic way, thinking especially about the few community folks who had come to hear me. Weeks later, KumKum Sangari, a fellow participant who shared with me what was said when I was no longer present, and I engaged in quite rigorous critical dialogue about the way my presentation had been perceived primarily by privileged white female academics. She was concerned that I not mask my knowledge of theory, that I not appear anti-intellectual. Her critique compelled me to articulate concerns that I am often silent about with colleagues. I spoke about class allegiance and revolutionary commitments, explaining that it was disturbing to me that intellectual radicals who speak about transforming society, ending the domination of race, sex, class, cannot break with behavior patterns that reinforce and perpetuate domination, or continue to use as their sole reference point how we might be or are perceived by those who dominate whether or not we gain their acceptance and approval.

This is a primary contradiction which raises the issue of whether or not the academic setting is a place where one can be truly radical or subversive. Concurrently, the use of a language and style of presentation that alienates most folks who are not also academically trained reinforces the notion that the academic world is separate from real life, that everyday world where we constantly adjust our language and behavior to meet diverse needs. The academic setting is separate only when we work to make it so. It is a false dichotomy which suggests that academics and/or intellectuals can only speak to one another, that we cannot hope to speak with the masses. What is true is that we make choices, that we choose our audiences, that we choose voices to hear and voices to silence. If I do not speak in a language that can be understood, then there is little chance for dialogue. This issue of language and behavior is a central contradiction all radical intellectuals, particularly those who are members of oppressed groups, must continually confront and work to resolve. One of the clear and present dangers that exists when we move outside our class of origin, our collective ethnic experience, and enter hierarchical institutions which daily reinforce domination by race, sex, and class, is that we gradually assume a mindset similar to those who dominate and oppress, that we lose critical consciousness because it is not reinforced or affirmed by the environment. We must be ever vigilant. It is important that we know who we are speaking to, who we most want to hear us, who we most long to move, motivate, and touch with our words.

When I first came to New Haven to teach at Yale, I was truly surprised by the marked class divisions between black folks—students and professors—who identify with Yale and those black folks who work at Yale or in surrounding communities. Style of dress and self-presentation are most often the central markers of one's position. I soon learned that the black folks who spoke on the street were likely to be part of the black community and those who carefully shifted their glance were likely to be associated with Yale. Walking with a black female colleague one day, I spoke to practically every black person in sight (a gesture which reflects my upbringing), an action which disturbed my companion. Since I addressed black folk who were clearly not associated with Yale, she wanted to know whether or not I knew them. That was funny to me. "Of course not," I answered. Yet when I thought about it seriously, I realized that in a deep way, I knew them for they, and not my companion or most of my colleagues at Yale, resemble my family. Later that year, in a black women's support group I started for undergraduates, students from poor backgrounds spoke about the shame they sometimes feel when faced with the reality of their connection to working-class and poor black people. One student confessed that her father is a street person, addicted to drugs, someone who begs from passersby. She, like other Yale students, turns away from street people often, sometimes showing anger or contempt; she hasn't wanted anyone to know that she was related to this kind of person. She struggles with this, wanting to find a way to acknowledge and affirm this reality, to claim this connection. The group asked me and one another what we [should] do to remain connected, to honor the bonds we have with working-class and poor people even as our class experience alters.

Maintaining connections with family and community across class boundaries demands more than just summary recall of where one's roots are, where one comes from. It requires knowing, naming, and being ever-mindful of those aspects of one's past that have enabled and do enable one's self-development in the present, that sustain and support, that enrich. One must also honestly confront barriers that do exist, aspects of that past that do diminish. My parents' ambivalence about my love for reading led to intense conflict. They (especially my mother) would work to ensure that I had access to books, but would threaten to burn the books or throw them away if I did not conform to other expectations. Or they would insist that reading too much would drive me insane. Their ambivalence nurtured in me a like uncertainty about the value and significance of intellectual endeavor which took years for me to unlearn. While this aspect of our class reality was one that wounded and diminished, their vigilant insistence that being smart did not make me a "better" or "superior" person (which often got on my nerves because I think I wanted to have that sense that it did indeed set me apart, make me better) made a profound impression. From them I learned to value and respect various skills and talents folk might have, not just to value people who read books and talk about ideas. They and my grandparents might say about somebody, "Now he don't read nor write a lick, but he can tell a story," or as my grandmother would say, "call out the hell in words."

Empty romanticization of poor or working-class backgrounds undermines 15
the possibility of true connection. Such connection is based on understanding difference in experience and perspective and working to mediate and negotiate these terrains. Language is a crucial issue for folk whose movement outside the boundaries of poor and working-class backgrounds changes the nature and direction of their speech. Coming to Stanford with my own version of a Kentucky accent, which I think of always as a strong sound quite different from Tennessee or Georgia speech, I learned to speak differently while maintaining the speech of my region, the sound of my family and community. This was of course much easier to keep up when I returned home to stay often. In recent years, I have endeavored to use various speaking styles in the classroom as a teacher and find it disconcerts those who feel that the use of a particular patois excludes them as listeners, even if there is translation into the usual, acceptable mode of speech. Learning to listen to different voices, having different speech challenges the notion that we must all assimilate—share a single, similar talk—in educational institutions. Language reflects the culture from which we emerge. To deny ourselves daily use of speech patterns that are common and familiar, that embody the unique and distinctive aspect of our self is one of the ways we become estranged and alienated from our past. It is important for us to have as many languages on hand as we can know or learn. It is important for those of us who are black, who speak in particular patois as well as standard English, to express ourselves in both ways.

Often I tell students from poor and working-class backgrounds that if you believe what you have learned and are learning in schools and universities separates you from your past, this is precisely what will happen. It is important to stand firm in the conviction that nothing can truly separate us from our pasts when we nurture and cherish that connection. An important strategy for maintaining contact is ongoing acknowledgement of the primacy of one's past, of one's background, affirming the reality that such bonds are not severed automatically solely because one enters a new environment or moves toward a different class experience.

Again, I do not wish to romanticize this effort, to dismiss the reality of conflict and contradiction. During my time at Stanford, I did go through a period of more than a year when I did not return home. That period was one where I felt that it was simply too difficult to mesh my profoundly disparate realities. Critical reflection about the choice I was making, particularly about why I felt a choice had to be made, pulled me through this difficult time. Luckily I recognized that the insistence on choosing between the world of family and community and the new world of privileged white people and privileged ways of knowing was imposed upon me by the outside. It is as though a mythical contract had been signed somewhere which demanded of us black folks that once we entered these spheres we would immediately give up all vestiges of our underprivileged past. It was my responsibility to formulate a way of being that would allow me to participate fully in my new environment while integrating and maintaining aspects of the old.

One of the most tragic manifestations of the pressure black people feel to assimilate is expressed in the internalization of racist perspectives. I was shocked and saddened when I first heard black professors at Stanford downgrade and express contempt for black students, expecting us to do poorly, refusing to establish nurturing bonds. At every university I have attended as a student or worked at as a teacher, I have heard similar attitudes expressed with little or no understanding of factors that might prevent brilliant black students from performing to their full capability. Within universities, there are few educational and social spaces where students who wish to affirm positive ties to ethnicity—to blackness, to working-class backgrounds—can receive affirmation and support. Ideologically, the message is clear—assimilation is the way to gain acceptance and approval from those in power.

Many white people enthusiastically supported Richard Rodriguez's vehement contention in his autobiography, *Hunger of Memory,* that attempts to maintain ties with his Chicano background impeded his progress, that he had to sever ties with community and kin to succeed at Stanford and in the larger world, that family language, in his case Spanish, had to be made secondary or discarded. If the terms of success as defined by the standards of ruling groups within white-supremacist, capitalist patriarchy are the only standards that exist, then assimilation is indeed necessary. But they are not. Even in the face of powerful structures of domination, it remains possible for each of us, especially those of us who are members of oppressed and/or exploited groups as well as those radical visionaries who may have race, class, and sex privilege, to define and determine alternative standards, to decide on the nature and extent of compromise. Standards by which one's success is measured, whether student or professor, are quite different from those of us who wish to resist reinforcing the domination of race, sex, and class, who work to maintain and strengthen our ties with the oppressed, with those who lack material privilege, with our families who are poor and working-class.

When I wrote my first, book, *Ain't I a Woman: black women and feminism,* 20 the issue of class and its relationship to who one's reading audience might be came up for me around my decision not to use footnotes, for which I have been sharply criticized. I told people that my concern was that footnotes set class boundaries for readers, determining who a book is for. I was shocked that many academic folks scoffed at this idea. I shared that I went into working-class black communities as well as talked with family and friends to survey whether or not they ever read books with footnotes and found that they did not. A few did not know what they were, but most folks saw them as indicating that a book was for college-educated people. These responses influenced my decision. When some of my more radical college-educated friends freaked out about the absence of footnotes, I seriously questioned how we could ever imagine revolutionary transformation of society if such a small shift in direction could be viewed as threatening. Of course, many folks warned that the absence of footnotes would make the work less credible in academic circles. This information also highlighted the way in which class informs our choices. Certainly I did feel that choosing to use simple language, absence of footnotes, etc. would mean I was jeopardizing the possibility of being taken seriously in academic circles but then this was a political matter and a political decision. It utterly delights me that this has proven not to be the case and that the book is read by many academics as well as by people who are not college-educated.

Always our first response when we are motivated to conform or compromise within structures that reinforce domination must be to engage in critical reflection. Only by challenging ourselves to push against oppressive boundaries do we make the radical alternative possible, expanding the realm and scope of critical inquiry. Unless we share radical strategies, ways of rethinking and revisioning with students, with kin and community, with a larger audience, we risk perpetuating the stereotype that we succeed because we are the exception, different from the rest of our people. Since I left home and entered college, I am often asked, usually by white people, if my sisters and brothers are also high achievers. At the root of this question is the longing for reinforcement of the belief in "the exception" which enables race, sex, and class biases to remain intact. I am careful to separate what it means to be exceptional from a notion of "the exception."

Frequently I hear smart black folks, from poor and working-class backgrounds, stressing their frustration that at times family and community do not recognize that they are exceptional. Absence of positive affirmation clearly diminishes the longing to excel in academic endeavors. Yet it is important to distinguish between the absence of basic positive affirmation and the longing for continued reinforcement that we are special. Usually liberal white folks will willingly offer continual reinforcement of us as exceptions—as special. This can be both patronizing and very seductive. Since we often work in situations where we are isolated from other black folks, we can easily begin to feel that encouragement from white people is the primary or only source of support and recognition. Given the internalization of racism, it is easy to view this support as more validating and legitimizing than similar support from black people. Still, nothing takes the place of being valued and appreciated by one's own, by one's family and community. We share a mutual and reciprocal responsibility for affirming one another's successes. Sometimes we have to talk to our folks about the fact that we need their ongoing support and affirmation, that it is unique and special to us. In some cases we may never receive desired recognition and acknowledgement of specific achievements from kin. Rather than seeing this as a basis for estrangement, for severing connection, it is useful to explore other sources of nourishment and support.

I do not know that my mother's mother ever acknowledged my college education except to ask me once, "How can you live so far away from your people?" Yet she gave me sources of affirmation and nourishment, sharing the legacy of her quilt-making, of family history, of her incredible way with words. Recently, when our father retired after more than thirty years of work as a janitor, I wanted to pay tribute to this experience, to identify links between his work and my own as writer and teacher. Reflecting on our family past, I recalled ways he had been an impressive example of diligence and hard work, approaching tasks with a seriousness of concentration I work to mirror and develop, with a discipline I struggle to maintain. Sharing these thoughts with him keeps us connected, nurtures our respect for each other, maintaining a space, however large or small, where we can talk.

Open, honest communication is the most important way we maintain relationships with kin and community as our class experience and backgrounds change. It is as vital as the sharing of resources. Often financial assistance is given in circumstances where there is no meaningful contact. However helpful, this can also be an expression of estrangement and alienation. Communication between black folks from various experiences of material privilege was much easier when we were all in segregated communities sharing common experiences in relation to social institutions. Without this grounding, we must work to maintain ties, connection. We must assume greater responsibility for making and maintaining contact, connections that can shape our intellectual visions and inform our radical commitments.

The most powerful resource any of us can have as we study and teach in 25 university settings is full understanding and appreciation of the richness, beauty, and primacy of our familial and community backgrounds. Maintaining awareness of class differences, nurturing ties with the poor and working-class people who are our most intimate kin, our comrades in struggle, transforms and enriches our intellectual experience. Education as the practice of freedom becomes not a force which fragments or separates, but one that brings us closer, expanding our definitions of home and community.

August Wilson (b. 1945)

Fences

Characters

TROY MAXSON
JIM BONO, *Troy's friend*
ROSE, *Troy's wife*
LYONS, *Troy's oldest son by previous marriage*
GABRIEL, *Troy's brother*
CORY, *Troy and Rose's son*
RAYNELL, *Troy's daughter*

Setting: *The setting is the yard which fronts the only entrance to the Maxson household, an ancient two-story brick house set back off a small alley in a big-city neighborhood. The entrance to the house is gained by two or three steps leading to a wooden porch badly in need of paint.*

A relatively recent addition to the house and running its full width, the porch lacks congruence. It is a sturdy porch with a flat roof. One or two chairs of dubious value sit at one end where the kitchen window opens onto the porch. An old-fashioned icebox stands silent guard at the opposite end.

The yard is a small dirt yard, partially fenced, except for the last scene, with a wooden sawhorse, a pile of lumber, and other fence-building equipment set off to the side. Opposite is a tree from which hangs a ball made of rags. A baseball bat leans against the tree. Two oil drums serve as garbage receptacles and sit near the house at right to complete the setting.

The Play: *Near the turn of the century, the destitute of Europe sprang on the city with tenacious claws and an honest and solid dream. The city devoured them. They swelled its belly until it burst into a thousand furnaces and sewing machines, a thousand butcher shops and bakers' ovens, a thousand churches and hospitals and funeral parlors and money-lenders. The city grew. It nourished itself and offered each man a partnership limited only by his talent, his guile, and his willingness and capacity for hard work. For the immigrants of Europe, a dream dared and won true.*

The descendants of African slaves were offered no such welcome or participation. They came from places called the Carolinas and the Virginias, Georgia, Alabama, Mississippi, and Tennessee. They came strong, eager, searching. The city rejected them and they fled and settled along the riverbanks and under bridges in shallow, ramshackle houses made of sticks and tarpaper. They collected rags and wood. *They sold the use of their muscles and their bodies. They cleaned houses and washed clothes, they shined shoes, and in quiet desperation and vengeful pride, they stole, and lived in pursuit of their own dream. That they could breathe free, finally, and stand to meet life with the force of dignity and whatever eloquence the heart could call upon.*

By 1957, the hard-won victories of the European immigrants had solidified the industrial might of America. War had been confronted and won with new energies that used loyalty and patriotism as its fuel. Life was rich, full, and flourishing. The Milwaukee Braves won the World Series, and the hot winds of change that would make the sixties a turbulent, racing, dangerous, and provocative decade had not yet begun to blow full.

ACT I · SCENE I

It is 1957. TROY *and* BONO *enter the yard, engaged in conversation.* TROY *is fifty-three years old, a large man with thick, heavy hands; it is this largeness that he strives to fill out and make an accommodation with. Together with his blackness, his largeness informs his sensibilities and the choices he has made in his life.*

Of the two men, BONO *is obviously the follower. His commitment to their friendship of thirty-odd years is rooted in his admiration of* TROY'S *honesty, capacity for hard work, and his strength, which* BONO *seeks to emulate.*

It is Friday night, payday, and the one night of the week the two men engage in a ritual of talk and drink. TROY *is usually the most talkative and at times he can be crude and almost vulgar, though he is capable of rising to profound heights of expression. The men carry lunch buckets and wear or carry burlap aprons and are dressed in clothes suitable to their jobs as garbage collectors.*

BONO: Troy, you ought to stop that lying!

TROY: I ain't lying! The nigger had a watermelon this big.

(He indicates with his hands.)

Talking about . . . "What watermelon, Mr. Rand?" I liked to fell out! "What watermelon, Mr. Rand?" . . . And it sitting there big as life.

BONO: What did Mr. Rand say?

TROY: Ain't said nothing. Figure if the nigger too dumb to know he carrying a watermelon, he wasn't gonna get much sense out of him. Trying to hide that great big old watermelon under his coat. Afraid to let the white man see him carry it home.

BONO: I'm like you . . . I ain't got no time for them kind of people.

TROY: Now what he look like getting mad cause he see the man from the union talking to Mr. Rand?

BONO: He come to me talking about . . . "Maxson gonna get us fired." I told him to get away from me with that. He walked away from me calling you a troublemaker. What Mr. Rand say?

TROY: Ain't said nothing. He told me to go down the Commissioner's office next Friday. They called me down there to see them.

BONO: Well, as long as you got your complaint filed, they can't fire you. That's what one of them white fellows tell me.

TROY: I ain't worried about them firing me. They gonna fire me cause I asked a question? That's all I did. I went to Mr. Rand and asked him, "Why? Why you got the white mens driving and the colored lifting?" Told him, "what's the matter, don't I count? You think only white fellows got sense enough to drive a truck. That ain't no paper job! Hell, anybody can drive a truck. How come you got all whites driving and the colored lifting?" He told me "take it to the union." Well, hell, that's what I done! Now they wanna come up with this pack of lies.

BONO: I told Brownie if the man come and ask him any questions . . . just tell the truth! It ain't nothing but something they done trumped up on you cause you filed a complaint on them.

TROY: Brownie don't understand nothing. All I want them to do is change the job description. Give everybody a chance to drive the truck. Brownie can't see that. He ain't got that much sense.

BONO: How you figure he be making out with that gal be up at Taylors' all the time . . . that Alberta gal?

TROY: Same as you and me. Getting just as much as we is. Which is to say nothing.

BONO: It is, huh? I figure you doing a little better than me . . . and I ain't saying what I'm doing.

TROY: Aw, nigger, look here . . . I know you. If you had got anywhere near that gal, twenty minutes later you be looking to tell somebody. And the first one you gonna tell . . . that you gonna want to brag to . . . is gonna be me.

BONO: I ain't saying that. I see where you be eyeing her.

TROY: I eye all the women. I don't miss nothing. Don't never let nobody tell you Troy Maxson don't eye the women.

BONO: You been doing more than eyeing her. You done bought her a drink or two.

TROY: Hell yeah, I bought her a drink! What that mean? I bought you one, too. What that mean cause I buy her a drink? I'm just being polite.

BONO: It's all right to buy her one drink. That's what you call being polite. But when you wanna be buying two or three . . . that's what you call eyeing her.

TROY: Look here, as long as you known me . . . you ever known me to chase after women?

BONO: Hell yeah! Long as I done known you. You forgetting I knew you when.

TROY: Naw, I'm talking about since I been married to Rose?

BONO: Oh, not since you been married to Rose. Now, that's the truth, there. I can say that.

TROY: All right then! Case closed.

BONO: I see you be walking up around Alberta's house. You supposed to be at Taylors' and you be walking up around there.

TROY: What you watching where I'm walking for? I ain't watching after you.

BONO: I seen you walking around there more than once.

TROY: Hell, you liable to see me walking anywhere! That don't mean nothing cause you see me walking around there.

BONO: Where she come from anyway? She just kinda showed up one day.

TROY: Tallahassee. You can look at her and tell she one of them Florida gals. They got some big healthy women down there. Grow them right up out of the ground. Got a little bit of Indian in her. Most of them niggers down in Florida got some Indian in them.

BONO: I don't know about that Indian part. But she damn sure big and healthy. Woman wear some big stockings. Got them great big old legs and hips as wide as the Mississippi River.

TROY: Legs don't mean nothing. You don't do nothing but push them out of the way. But them hips cushion the ride!

BONO: Troy, you ain't got no sense.

TROY: It's the truth! Like you riding on Goodyears!

(ROSE enters from the house. She is ten years younger than TROY, her devotion to him stems from her recognition of the possibilities of her life without him: a succession of abusive men and their babies, a life of partying and running the streets, the Church, or aloneness with its attendant pain and frustration. She recognizes TROY'S spirit as a fine and illuminating one and she either ignores or forgives his faults, only some of which she recognizes. Though she doesn't drink, her presence is an integral part of the Friday night rituals. She alternates between the porch and the kitchen, where supper preparations are under way.)

ROSE: What you all out here getting into?

TROY: What you worried about what we getting into for? This is men talk, woman.

ROSE: What I care what you all talking about? Bono, you gonna stay for supper?

BONO: No, I thank you, Rose. But Lucille say she cooking up a pot of pigfeet.

TROY: Pigfeet! Hell, I'm going home with you! Might even stay the night if you got some pigfeet. You got something in there to top them pigfeet, Rose?

ROSE: I'm cooking up some chicken. I got some chicken and collard greens.

TROY: Well, go on back in the house and let me and Bono finish what we was talking about. This is men talk. I got some talk for you later. You know what kind of talk I mean. You go on and powder it up.

ROSE: Troy Maxson, don't you start that now!

TROY *(puts his arm around her):* Aw, woman . . . come here. Look here, Bono . . . when I met this woman . . . I got out that place, say, "Hitch up my pony, saddle up my mare . . . there's a woman out there for me somewhere. I looked here. Looked there. Saw Rose and latched on to her." I latched on to her and told her—I'm gonna tell you the truth—I told her, "Baby, I don't wanna marry, I just wanna be your man." Rose told me . . . tell him what you told me, Rose.

ROSE: I told him if he wasn't the marrying kind, then move out the way so the marrying kind could find me.

TROY: That's what she told me. "Nigger, you in my way. You blocking the view! Move out the way so I can find me a husband." I thought it over two or three days. Come back—

ROSE: Ain't no two or three days nothing. You was back the same night.

TROY: Come back, told her . . . "Okay, baby . . . but I'm gonna buy me a banty rooster and put him out there in the backyard . . . and when he see a stranger come, he'll flap his wings and crow . . ." Look here, Bono, I could watch the front door by myself . . . it was that back door I was worried about.

ROSE: Troy, you ought not talk like that. Troy ain't doing nothing but telling a lie.

TROY: Only thing is . . . when we first got married . . . forget the rooster . . . we ain't had no yard!

BONO: I hear you tell it. Me and Lucille was staying down there on Logan Street. Had two rooms with the outhouse in the back. I ain't mind the outhouse none. But when that goddamn wind blow through there in the winter . . . that's what I'm talking about! To this day I wonder why in the hell I ever stayed down there for six long years. But see, I didn't know I could do no better. I thought only white folks had inside toilets and things.

ROSE: There's a lot of people don't know they can do no better than they doing now. That's just something you got to learn. A lot of folks still shop at Bella's.

TROY: Ain't nothing wrong with shopping at Bella's. She got fresh food.

ROSE: I ain't said nothing about if she got fresh food. I'm talking about what she charge. She charge ten cents more than the A&P.

TROY: The A&P ain't never done nothing for me. I spends my money where I'm treated right. I go down to Bella, say, "I need a loaf of bread, I'll pay you Friday." She give it to me. What sense that make when I got money to go and spend it somewhere else and ignore the person who done right by me? That ain't in the Bible.

ROSE: We ain't talking about what's in the Bible. What sense it make to shop there when she overcharge?

TROY: You shop where you want to. I'll do my shopping where the people been good to me.

ROSE: Well, I don't think it's right for her to overcharge. That's all I was saying.

BONO: Look here . . . I got to get on. Lucille going be raising all kind of hell.

TROY: Where you going, nigger? We ain't finished this pint. Come here, finish this pint.

BONO: Well, hell, I am . . . if you ever turn the bottle loose.

TROY (*hands him the bottle*): The only thing I say about the A&P is I'm glad Cory got that job down there. Help him take care of his school clothes and things. Gabe done moved out and things getting tight around here. He got that job. . . . He can start to look out for himself.

ROSE: Cory done went and got recruited by a college football team.

TROY: I told that boy about that football stuff. The white man ain't gonna let him get nowhere with that football. I told him when he first come to me with it. Now you come telling me he done went and got more tied up in it. He ought to go and get recruited in how to fix cars or something where he can make a living.

ROSE: He ain't talking about making no living playing football. It's just something the boys in school do. They gonna send a recruiter by to talk to you. He'll tell you he ain't talking about making no living playing football. It's a honor to be recruited.

TROY: It ain't gonna get him nowhere. Bono'll tell you that.

BONO: If he be like you in the sports . . . he's gonna be all right. Ain't but two men ever played baseball as good as you. That's Babe Ruth and Josh Gibson. Them's the only two men ever hit more home runs than you.

TROY: What it ever get me? Ain't got a pot to piss in or a window to throw it out of.

ROSE: Times have changed since you was playing baseball, Troy. That was before the war. Times have changed a lot since then.

TROY: How in hell they done changed?

ROSE: They got lots of colored boys playing ball now. Baseball and football.

BONO: You right about that, Rose. Times have changed, Troy. You just come along too early.

TROY: There ought not never have been no time called too early! Now you take that fellow . . . what's that fellow they had playing right field for the Yankees back then? You know who I'm talking about, Bono. Used to play right field for the Yankees.

ROSE: Selkirk?

TROY: Selkirk! That's it! Man batting .269, understand? .269. What kind of sense that make? I was hitting .432 with thirty-seven home runs! Man batting .269 and playing right field for the Yankees! I saw Josh Gibson's daughter yesterday. She walking around with raggedy shoes on her feet. Now I bet you Selkirk's daughter ain't walking around with raggedy shoes on her feet! I bet you that!

ROSE: They got a lot of colored baseball players now. Jackie Robinson was the first. Folks had to wait for Jackie Robinson.

TROY: I done seen a hundred niggers play baseball better than Jackie Robinson. Hell, I know some teams Jackie Robinson couldn't even make! What you talking about Jackie Robinson. Jackie Robinson wasn't nobody. I'm talking about if you could play ball then they ought to have let you play. Don't care what color you were. Come telling me I come along too early. If you could play . . . then they ought to have let you play.

(TROY *takes a long drink from the bottle.*)

ROSE: You gonna drink yourself to death. You don't need to be drinking like that.

TROY: Death ain't nothing. I done seen him. Done wrassled with him. You can't tell me nothing about death. Death ain't nothing but a fastball on the outside corner. And you know what I'll do to that! Lookee here, Bono . . . am I lying? You get one of them fastballs, about waist high, over the outside corner of the plate where you can get the meat of the bat on it . . . and good god! You can kiss it goodbye. Now, am I lying?

BONO: Naw, you telling the truth there. I seen you do it.

TROY: If I'm lying . . . that 450 feet worth of lying!

(Pause.)

That's all death is to me. A fastball on the outside corner.

ROSE: I don't know why you want to get on talking about death.

TROY: Ain't nothing wrong with talking about death. That's part of life. Everybody gonna die. You gonna die, I'm gonna die. Bono's gonna die. Hell, we all gonna die.

ROSE: But you ain't got to talk about it. I don't like to talk about it.

TROY: You the one brought it up. Me and Bono was talking about baseball . . . you tell me I'm gonna drink myself to death. Ain't that right, Bono? You know I don't drink this but one night out of the week. That's Friday night. I'm gonna drink just enough to where I can handle it. Then I cuts it loose. I leave it alone. So don't you worry about me drinking myself to death. 'Cause I ain't worried about Death. I done seen him. I done wrestled with him.

Look here, Bono . . . I looked up one day and Death was marching straight at me. Like Soldiers on Parade! The Army of Death was marching straight at me. The middle of July, 1941. It got real cold just like it be winter. It seem like Death himself reached out and touched me on the shoulder. He touch me just like I touch you. I got cold as ice and Death standing there grinning at me.

ROSE: Troy, why don't you hush that talk.

TROY: I say . . . What you want, Mr. Death? You be wanting me? You done brought your army to be getting me? I looked him dead in the eye. I wasn't fearing nothing. I was ready to tangle. Just like I'm ready to tangle now. The Bible say be ever vigilant. That's why I don't get but so drunk. I got to keep watch.

ROSE: Troy was right down there in Mercy Hospital. You remember he had pneumonia? Laying there with a fever talking plumb out of his head.

TROY: Death standing there staring at me . . . carrying that sickle in his hand. Finally he say, "You want bound over for another year?" See, just like that . . . "You want bound over for another year?" I told him, "Bound over hell! Let's settle this now!"

It seem like he kinda fell back when I said that, and all the cold went out of me. I reached down and grabbed that sickle and threw it just as far as I could throw it . . . and me and him commenced to wrestling.

We wrestled for three days and three nights. I can't say where I found the strength from. Every time it seemed like he was gonna get the best of me, I'd reach way down deep inside myself and find the strength to do him one better.

ROSE: Every time Troy tell that story he find different ways to tell it. Different things to make up about it.

TROY: I ain't making up nothing. I'm telling you the facts of what happened. I wrestled with Death for three days and three nights and I'm standing here to tell you about it.
(*Pause.*)
All right. At the end of the third night we done weakened each other to where we can't hardly move. Death stood up, throwed on his robe . . . had him a white robe with a hood on it. He threwed on that robe and went off to look for his sickle. Say, "I'll be back." Just like that. "I'll be back." I told him, say, "Yeah, but . . . you gonna have to find me!" I wasn't no fool. I wan't going looking for him. Death ain't nothing to play with. And I know he's gonna get me. I know I got to join his army . . . his camp followers. But as long as I keep my strength and see him coming . . . as long as I keep up my vigilance . . . he's gonna have to fight to get me. I ain't going easy.

BONO: Well, look here, since you got to keep up your vigilance . . . let me have the bottle.

TROY: Aw hell, I shouldn't have told you that part. I should have left out that part.

ROSE: Troy be talking that stuff and half the time don't even know what he be talking about.

TROY: Bono know me better than that.

BONO: That's right. I know you. I know you got some Uncle Remus in your blood. You got more stories than the devil got sinners.

TROY: Aw hell, I done seen him too! Done talked with the devil.

ROSE: Troy, don't nobody wanna be hearing all that stuff.

(LYONS *enters the yard from the street. Thirty-four years old,* TROY'S *son by a previous marriage, he sports a neatly trimmed goatee, sport coat, white shirt, tieless and buttoned at the collar. Though he fancies himself a musician, he is more caught up in the rituals and "idea" of being a musician than in the actual practice of the music. He has come to borrow money from* TROY, *and while he knows he will be successful, he is uncertain as to what extent his lifestyle will be held up to scrutiny and ridicule.*)

LYONS: Hey, Pop.

TROY: What you come "Hey, Popping" me for?

LYONS: How you doing, Rose?
(*He kisses her.*)
Mr. Bono. How you doing?

BONO: Hey, Lyons . . . how you been?

TROY: He must have been doing all right. I ain't seen him around here last week.

ROSE: Troy, leave your boy alone. He come by to see you and you wanna start all that nonsense.

TROY: I ain't bothering Lyons.
(*Offers him the bottle.*)

Here . . . get you a drink. We got an understanding. I know why he come by to see me and he know I know.

LYONS: Come on, Pop . . . I just stopped by to say hi . . . see how you was doing.

TROY: You ain't stopped by yesterday.

ROSE: You gonna stay for supper, Lyons? I got some chicken cooking in the oven.

LYONS: No, Rose . . . thanks. I was just in the neighborhood and thought I'd stop by for a minute.

TROY: You was in the neighborhood all right, nigger. You telling the truth there. You was in the neighborhood cause it's my payday.

LYONS: Well, hell, since you mentioned it . . . let me have ten dollars.

TROY: I'll be damned! I'll die and go to hell and play blackjack with the devil before I give you ten dollars.

BONO: That's what I wanna know about . . . that devil you done seen.

LYONS: What . . . Pop done seen the devil? You too much, Pops.

TROY: Yeah, I done seen him. Talked to him too!

ROSE: You ain't seen no devil. I done told you that man ain't had nothing to do with the devil. Anything you can't understand, you want to call it the devil.

TROY: Look here, Bono . . . I went down to see Hertzberger about some furniture. Got three rooms for two-ninety-eight. That what it say on the radio. "Three rooms . . . two-ninety-eight." Even made up a little song about it. Go down there . . . man tell me I can't get no credit. I'm working every day and can't get no credit. What to do? I got an empty house with some raggedy furniture in it. Cory ain't got no bed. He's sleeping on a pile of rags on the floor. Working every day and can't get no credit. Come back here—Rose'll tell you— madder than hell. Sit down . . . try to figure what I'm gonna do. Come a knock on the door. Ain't been living here but three days. Who know I'm here? Open the door . . . devil standing there bigger than life. White fellow . . . got on good clothes and everything. Standing there with a clipboard in his hand. I ain't had to say nothing. First words come out of his mouth was . . . "I understand you need some furniture and can't get no credit." I liked to fell over. He say, "I'll give you all the credit you want, but you got to pay the interest on it." I told him, "Give me three rooms worth and charge whatever you want." Next day a truck pulled up here and two men unloaded them three rooms. Man what drove the truck gave me a book. Say send ten dollars, first of every month to the address in the book and everything will be all right. Say if I miss a payment the devil was coming back and it'll be hell to pay. That was fifteen years ago. To this day . . . the first of the month I send my ten dollars, Rose'll tell you.

ROSE: Troy lying.

TROY: I ain't never seen that man since. Now you tell me who else that could have been but the devil? I ain't sold my soul or nothing like that, you understand. Naw, I wouldn't have truck with the devil about nothing like that. I got my furniture and pays my ten dollars the first of the month just like clockwork.

BONO: How long you say you been paying this ten dollars a month?

TROY: Fifteen years!

BONO: Hell, ain't you finished paying for it yet? How much the man done charged you?

TROY: Ah hell, I done paid for it. I done paid for it ten times over! The fact is I'm scared to stop paying it.

ROSE: Troy lying. We got that furniture from Mr. Glickman. He ain't paying no ten dollars a month to nobody.

TROY: Aw hell, woman. Bono know I ain't that big a fool.

LYONS: I was just getting ready to say . . . I know where there's a bridge for sale.

TROY: Look here, I'll tell you this . . . it don't matter to me if he was the devil. It don't matter if the devil give credit. Somebody has got to give it.

ROSE: It ought to matter. You going around talking about having truck with the devil . . . God's the one you gonna have to answer to. He's the one gonna be at the Judgment.

LYONS: Yeah, well, look here, Pop . . . let me have that ten dollars. I'll give it back to you. Bonnie got a job working at the hospital.

TROY: What I tell you, Bono? The only time I see this nigger is when he wants something. That's the only time I see him.

LYONS: Come on, Pop, Mr. Bono don't want to hear all that. Let me have the ten dollars. I told you Bonnie working.

TROY: What that mean to me? "Bonnie working." I don't care if she working. Go ask her for the ten dollars if she working. Talking about "Bonnie working." Why ain't you working?

LYONS: Aw, Pop, you know I can't find no decent job. Where am I gonna get a job at? You know I can't get no job.

TROY: I told you I know some people down there. I can get you on the rubbish if you want to work. I told you that the last time you came by here asking me for something.

LYONS: Naw, Pop . . . thanks. That ain't for me. I don't wanna be carrying nobody's rubbish. I don't wanna be punching nobody's time clock.

TROY: What's the matter, you too good to carry people's rubbish? Where you think that ten dollars you talking about come from? I'm just supposed to haul people's rubbish and give my money to you cause you too lazy to work. You too lazy to work and wanna know why you ain't got what I got.

ROSE: What hospital Bonnie working at? Mercy?

LYONS: She's down at Passavant working in the laundry.

TROY: I ain't got nothing as it is. I give you that ten dollars and I got to eat beans the rest of the week. Naw . . . you ain't getting no ten dollars here.

LYONS: You ain't got to be eating no beans. I don't know why you wanna say that.

TROY: I ain't got no extra money. Gabe done moved over to Miss Pearl's paying her the rent and things done got tight around here. I can't afford to be giving you every payday.

LYONS: I ain't asked you to give me nothing. I asked you to loan me ten dollars. I know you got ten dollars.

TROY: Yeah, I got it. You know why I got it? Cause I don't throw my money away out there in the streets. You living the fast life . . . wanna be a musician . . . running around in them clubs and things . . . then, you learn to take care of yourself. You ain't gonna find me going and asking nobody for nothing. I done spent too many years without.

LYONS: You and me is two different people, Pop.

TROY: I done learned my mistake and learned to do what's right by it. You still trying to get something for nothing. Life don't owe you nothing. You owe it to yourself. Ask Bono. He'll tell you I'm right.

LYONS: You got your way of dealing with the world . . . I got mine. The only thing that matters to me is the music.

TROY: Yeah, I can see that! It don't matter how you gonna eat . . . where your next dollar is coming from. You telling the truth there.

LYONS: I know I got to eat. But I got to live too. I need something that gonna help me to get out of the bed in the morning. Make me feel like I belong in the world. I don't bother nobody. I just stay with my music cause that's the only way I can find to live in the world. Otherwise there ain't no telling what I might do. Now I don't come criticizing you and how you live. I just come by to ask you for ten dollars. I don't wanna hear all that about how I live.

TROY: Boy, your mamma did a hell of a job raising you.

LYONS: You can't change me, Pop. I'm thirty-four years old. If you wanted to change me, you should have been there when I was growing up. I come by to see you . . . ask for ten dollars and you want to talk about how I was raised. You don't know nothing about how I was raised.

ROSE: Let the boy have ten dollars, Troy.

TROY (*to* LYONS): What the hell you looking at me for? I ain't got no ten dollars. You know what I do with my money.

(*To* ROSE.)

Give him ten dollars if you want him to have it.

ROSE: I will. Just as soon as you turn it loose.

TROY (*handing* ROSE *the money*): There it is. Seventy-six dollars and forty-two cents. You see this, Bono? Now, I ain't gonna get but six of that back.

ROSE: You ought to stop telling that lie. Here, Lyons. (*She hands him the money.*)

LYONS: Thanks, Rose. Look . . . I got to run . . . I'll see you later.

TROY: Wait a minute. You gonna say, "thanks, Rose" and ain't gonna look to see where she got that ten dollars from? See how they do me, Bono?

LYONS: I knew she got it from you, Pop. Thanks. I'll give it back to you.

TROY: There he go telling another lie. Time I see that ten dollars . . . he'll be owing me thirty more.

LYONS: See you, Mr. Bono.

BONO: Take care, Lyons!

LYONS: Thanks, Pop. I'll see you again.

(LYONS *exits the yard.*)

TROY: I don't know why he don't go out and get him a decent job and take care of that woman he got.

BONO: He'll be all right, Troy. The boy is still young.

TROY: The *boy* is thirty-four years old.

ROSE: Let's not get off into all that.

BONO: Look here . . . I got to be going. I got to be getting on. Lucille gonna be waiting.

TROY *(puts his arm around* ROSE*):* See this woman, Bono? I love this woman. I love this woman so much it hurts. I love her so much . . . I done run out of ways of loving her. So I got to go back to basics. Don't you come by my house Monday morning talking about time to go to work . . . 'cause I'm still gonna be stroking!

ROSE: Troy! Stop it now!

BONO: I ain't paying him no mind, Rose. That ain't nothing but gin-talk. Go on, Troy. I'll see you Monday.

TROY: Don't you come by my house, nigger! I done told you what I'm gonna be doing.

(The lights go down to black.)

SCENE II

(The lights come up on ROSE *hanging up clothes. She hums and sings softly to herself. It is the following morning.)*

ROSE *(sings):* Jesus, be a fence all around me every day

Jesus, I want you to protect me as I travel on my way.

Jesus, be a fence all around me every day.

*(*TROY *enters from the house.)*

Jesus, I want you to protect me

As I travel on my way.

(To TROY.*)* 'Morning. You ready for breakfast? I can fix it soon as I finish hanging up these clothes?

TROY: I got the coffee on. That'll be all right. I'll just drink some of that this morning.

ROSE: That 651 hit yesterday. That's the second time this month. Miss Pearl hit for a dollar . . . seem like those that need the least always get lucky. Poor folks can't get nothing.

TROY: Them numbers don't know nobody. I don't know why you fool with them. You and Lyons both.

ROSE: It's something to do.

TROY: You ain't doing nothing but throwing your money away.

ROSE: Troy, you know I don't play foolishly. I just play a nickel here and a nickel there.

TROY: That's two nickels you done thrown away.

ROSE: Now I hit sometimes . . . that makes up for it. It always comes in handy when I do hit. I don't hear you complaining then.

TROY: I ain't complaining now. I just say it's foolish. Trying to guess out of six hundred ways which way the number gonna come. If I had all the money niggers, these Negroes, throw away on numbers for one week—just one week—I'd be a rich man.

ROSE: Well, you wishing and calling it foolish ain't gonna stop folks from playing numbers. That's one thing for sure. Besides . . . some good things come from playing numbers. Look where Pope done bought him that restaurant off of numbers.

TROY: I can't stand niggers like that. Man ain't had two dimes to rub together. He walking around with his shoes all run over bumming money for cigarettes. All right. Got lucky there and hit the numbers . . .

ROSE: Troy, I know all about it.

TROY: Had good sense, I'll say that for him. He ain't throwed his money away. I seen niggers hit the numbers and go through two thousand dollars in four days. Man bought him that restaurant down there . . . fixed it up real nice . . . and then didn't want nobody to come in it! A Negro go in there and can't get no kind of service. I seen a white fellow come in there and order a bowl of stew. Pope picked all the meat out the pot for him. Man ain't had nothing but a bowl of meat! Negro come behind him and ain't got nothing but the potatoes and carrots. Talking about what numbers do for people, you picked a wrong example. Ain't done nothing but make a worser fool out of him than he was before.

ROSE: Troy, you ought to stop worrying about what happened at work yesterday.

TROY: I ain't worried. Just told me to be down there at the Commissioner's office on Friday. Everybody think they gonna fire me. I ain't worried about them firing me. You ain't got to worry about that.

(Pause.)

Where's Cory? Cory in the house? *(Calls.)* Cory?

ROSE: He gone out.

TROY: Out, huh? He gone out 'cause he know I want him to help me with this fence. I know how he is. That boy scared of work.

(GABRIEL enters. He comes halfway down the alley and, hearing TROY's voice, stops.)

TROY *(continues):* He ain't done a lick of work in his life.

ROSE: He had to go to football practice. Coach wanted them to get in a little extra practice before the season start.

TROY: I got his practice . . . running out of here before he get his chores done.

ROSE: Troy, what is wrong with you this morning? Don't nothing set right with you. Go on back in there and go to bed . . . get up on the other side.

TROY: Why something got to be wrong with me? I ain't said nothing wrong with me.

ROSE: You got something to say about everything. First it's the numbers . . . then it's the way the man runs his restaurant . . . then you done got on Cory. What's it gonna be next? Take a look up there and see if the weather suits you

... or is it gonna be how you gonna put up the fence with the clothes hanging in the yard.

TROY: You hit the nail on the head then.

ROSE: I know you like I know the back of my hand. Go in there and get you some coffee ... see if that straighten you up. 'Cause you ain't right this morning.

(TROY *starts into the house and sees* GABRIEL. GABRIEL *starts singing.* TROY'S *brother, he is seven years younger than* TROY. *Injured in World War II, he has a metal plate in his head. He carries an old trumpet tied around his waist and believes with every fiber of his being that he is the Archangel Gabriel. He carries a chipped basket with an assortment of discarded fruits and vegetables he has picked up in the strip district and which he attempts to sell.*)

GABRIEL *(singing):* Yes, ma'am, I got plums
You ask me how I sell them
Oh ten cents apiece
Three for a quarter
Come and buy now
'Cause I'm here today
And tomorrow I'll be gone
(GABRIEL *enters.*)
Hey, Rose!

ROSE: How you doing, Gabe?

GABRIEL: There's Troy ... Hey, Troy!

TROY: Hey, Gabe.

(*Exits into kitchen.*)

ROSE (*to* GABRIEL): What you got there?

GABRIEL: You know what I got, Rose. I got fruits and vegetables.

ROSE (*looking in basket*): Where's all these plums you talking about?

GABRIEL: I ain't got no plums today, Rose. I was just singing that. Have some tomorrow. Put me in a big order for plums. Have enough plums tomorrow for St. Peter and everybody.

(TROY *reenters from kitchen, crosses to steps.*)

(*To* ROSE.)

Troy's mad at me.

TROY: I ain't mad at you. What I got to be mad at you about? You ain't done nothing to me.

GABRIEL: I just moved over to Miss Pearl's to keep out from in your way. I ain't mean no harm by it.

TROY: Who said anything about that? I ain't said anything about that.

GABRIEL: You ain't mad at me, is you?

TROY: Naw ... I ain't mad at you, Gabe. If I was mad at you I'd tell you about it.

GABRIEL: Got me two rooms. In the basement. Got my own door too. Wanna see my key?

(*He holds up a key.*)

That's my own key! Ain't nobody else got a key like that. That's my key! My two rooms!

TROY: Well, that's good, Gabe. You got your own key . . . that's good.

ROSE: You hungry, Gabe? I was just fixing to cook Troy his breakfast.

GABRIEL: I'll take some biscuits. You got some biscuits? Did you know when I was in heaven . . . every morning me and St. Peter would sit down by the gate and eat some big fat biscuits? Oh, yeah! We had us a good time. We'd sit there and eat us them biscuits and then St. Peter would go off to sleep and tell me to wake him up when it's time to open the gates for the judgment.

ROSE: Well, come on . . . I'll make up a batch of biscuits.

(ROSE *exits into the house.*)

GABRIEL: Troy . . . St. Peter got your name in the book. I seen it. It say . . . Troy Maxson. I say . . . I know him! He got the same name like what I got. That's my brother!

TROY: How many times you gonna tell me that, Gabe?

GABRIEL: Ain't got my name in the book. Don't have to have my name. I done died and went to heaven. He got your name though. One morning St. Peter was looking at his book . . . marking it up for the judgment . . . and he let me see your name. Got it in there under M. Got Rose's name . . . I ain't seen it like I seen yours . . . but I know it's in there. He got a great big book. Got everybody's name what was ever been born. That's what he told me. But I seen your name. Seen it with my own eyes.

TROY: Go on in the house there. Rose going to fix you something to eat.

GABRIEL: Oh, I ain't hungry. I done had breakfast with Aunt Jemimah. She come by and cooked me up a whole mess of flapjacks. Remember how we used to eat them flapjacks?

TROY: Go on in the house and get you something to eat now.

GABRIEL: I got to go sell my plums. I done sold some tomatoes. Got me two quarters. Wanna see?

(He shows TROY *his quarters.*)

I'm gonna save them and buy me a new horn so St. Peter can hear me when it's time to open the gates.

(GABRIEL *stops suddenly. Listens.*)

Hear that? That's the hellhounds. I got to chase them out of here! Go on get out of here! Get out!

(GABRIEL *exits singing.*)

Better get ready for the judgment
Better get ready for the judgment
My Lord is coming down

(ROSE *enters from the house.*)

TROY: He gone off somewhere.

GABRIEL (offstage): Better get ready for the judgment
Better get ready for the judgment morning
Better get ready for the judgment
My God is coming down

ROSE: He ain't eating right. Miss Pearl say she can't get him to eat nothing.

TROY: What you want me to do about it, Rose? I done did everything I can for the man. I can't make him get well. Man got half his head blown away . . . what you expect?

ROSE: Seem like something ought to be done to help him.

TROY: Man don't bother nobody. He just mixed up from that metal plate he got in his head. Ain't no sense for him to go back into the hospital.

ROSE: Least he be eating right. They can help him take care of himself.

TROY: Don't nobody wanna be locked up, Rose. What you wanna lock him up for? Man go over there and fight the war . . . messin' around with them Japs, get half his head blown off . . . and they give him a lousy three thousand dollars. And I had to swoop down on that.

ROSE: Is you fixing to go into that again?

TROY: That's the only way I got a roof over my head . . . cause of that metal plate.

ROSE: Ain't no sense you blaming yourself for nothing. Gabe wasn't in no condition to manage that money. You done what was right by him. Can't nobody say you ain't done what was right by him. Look how long you took care of him . . . till he wanted to have his own place and moved over there with Miss Pearl.

TROY: That ain't what I'm saying, woman! I'm just stating the facts. If my brother didn't have that metal plate in his head . . . I wouldn't have a pot to piss in or a window to throw it out of. And I'm fifty-three years old. Now see if you can understand that!

(TROY *gets up from the porch and starts to exit the yard.*)

ROSE: Where you going off to? You been running out of here every Saturday for weeks. I thought you was gonna work on this fence?

TROY: I'm gonna walk down to Taylors'. Listen to the ball game. I'll be back in a bit. I'll work on it when I get back.

(*He exits the yard. The lights go to black.*)

Scene III

(*The lights come up on the yard. It is four hours later.* ROSE *is taking down the clothes from the line.* CORY *enters carrying his football equipment.*)

ROSE: Your daddy like to had a fit with you running out of here this morning without doing your chores.

CORY: I told you I had to go to practice.

ROSE: He say you were supposed to help him with this fence.

CORY: He been saying that the last four or five Saturdays, and then he don't never do nothing but go down to Taylors'. Did you tell him about the recruiter?

ROSE: Yeah, I told him.

CORY: What he say?

ROSE: He ain't said nothing too much. You get in there and get started on your chores before he gets back. Go on and scrub down them steps before he gets back here hollering and carrying on.

CORY: I'm hungry. What you got to eat, Mama?

ROSE: Go on and get started on your chores. I got some meat loaf in there. Go on and make you a sandwich . . . and don't leave no mess in there.

(CORY exits into the house. ROSE continues to take down the clothes. TROY enters the yard and sneaks up and grabs her from behind.)

Troy! Go on, now. You liked to scared me to death. What was the score of the game? Lucille had me on the phone and I couldn't keep up with it.

TROY: What I care about the game? Come here, woman. *(He tries to kiss her.)*

ROSE: I thought you went down Taylors' to listen to the game. Go on, Troy! You supposed to be putting up this fence.

TROY *(attempting to kiss her again):* I'll put it up when I finish with what is at hand.

ROSE: Go on, Troy. I ain't studying you.

TROY *(chasing after her):* I'm studying you . . . fixing to do my homework!

ROSE: Troy, you better leave me alone.

TROY: Where's Cory? That boy brought his butt home yet?

ROSE: He's in the house doing his chores.

TROY *(calling):* Cory! Get your butt out here, boy!

(ROSE exits into the house with the laundry. TROY goes over to the pile of wood, picks up a board, and starts sawing. CORY enters from the house.)

TROY: You just now coming in here from leaving this morning?

CORY: Yeah, I had to go to football practice.

TROY: Yeah, what?

CORY: Yessir.

TROY: I ain't but two seconds off you noway. The garbage sitting in there overflowing . . . you ain't done none of your chores . . . and you come in here talking about "Yeah."

CORY: I was just getting ready to do my chores now, Pop . . .

TROY: Your first chore is to help me with this fence on Saturday. Everything else come after that. Now get that saw and cut them boards.

(CORY takes the saw and begins cutting the boards. TROY continues working. There is a long pause.)

CORY: Hey, Pop . . . why don't you buy a TV?

TROY: What I want with a TV? What I want one of them for?

CORY: Everybody got one. Earl, Ba Bra . . . Jesse!

TROY: I ain't asked you who had one. I say what I want with one?

CORY: So you can watch it. They got lots of things on TV. Baseball games and everything. We could watch the World Series.

TROY: Yeah . . . and how much this TV cost?

CORY: I don't know. They got them on sale for around two hundred dollars.

TROY: Two hundred dollars, huh?

CORY: That ain't that much, Pop.

TROY: Naw, it's just two hundred dollars. See that roof you got over your head at night? Let me tell you something about that roof. It's been over ten years since that roof was last tarred. See now . . . the snow come this winter and sit up there on that roof like it is . . . and it's gonna seep inside. It's just gonna be a little bit . . . ain't gonna hardly notice it. Then the next thing you know, it's gonna be leaking all over the house. Then the wood rot from all that water and you gonna need a whole new roof. Now, how much you think it cost to get that roof tarred?

CORY: I don't know.

TROY: Two hundred and sixty-four dollars . . . cash money. While you thinking about a TV, I got to be thinking about the roof . . . and whatever else go wrong around here. Now if you had two hundred dollars, what would you do . . . fix the roof or buy a TV?

CORY: I'd buy a TV. Then when the roof started to leak . . . when it needed fixing . . . I'd fix it.

TROY: Where you gonna get the money from? You done spent it for a TV. You gonna sit up and watch the water run all over your brand new TV.

CORY: Aw, Pop. You got money. I know you do.

TROY: Where I got it at, huh?

CORY: You got it in the bank.

TROY: You wanna see my bankbook? You wanna see that seventy-three dollars and twenty-two cents I got sitting up in there?

CORY: You ain't got to pay for it all at one time. You can put a down payment on it and carry it on home with you.

TROY: Not me. I ain't gonna owe nobody nothing if I can help it. Miss a payment and they come and snatch it right out your house. Then what you got? Now, soon as I get two hundred dollars clear, then I'll buy a TV. Right now, as soon as I get two hundred and sixty-four dollars, I'm gonna have this roof tarred.

CORY: Aw . . . Pop!

TROY: You go on and get you two hundred dollars and buy one if ya want it. I got better things to do with my money.

CORY: I can't get no two hundred dollars. I ain't never seen two hundred dollars.

TROY: I'll tell you what . . . you get you a hundred dollars and I'll put the other hundred with it.

CORY: All right, I'm gonna show you.

TROY: You gonna show me how you can cut them boards right now.

(CORY *begins to cut the boards. There is a long pause.*)

CORY: The Pirates won today. That makes five in a row.

TROY: I ain't thinking about the Pirates. Got an all-white team. Got that boy . . . that Puerto Rican boy . . . Clemente. Don't even half-play him. That boy could be something if they give him a chance. Play him one day and sit him on the bench the next.

CORY: He gets a lot of chances to play.

TROY: I'm talking about playing regular. Playing every day so you can get your timing. That's what I'm talking about.

CORY: They got some white guys on the team that don't play every day. You can't play everybody at the same time.

TROY: If they got a white fellow sitting on the bench . . . you can bet your last dollar he can't play! The colored guy got to be twice as good before he get on the team. That's why I don't want you go get all tied up in them sports. Man on the team and what it get him? They got colored on the team and don't use them. Same as not having them. All them teams the same.

CORY: The Braves got Hank Aaron and Wes Covington. Hank Aaron hit two home runs today. That makes forty-three.

TROY: Hank Aaron ain't nobody. That's what you supposed to do. That's how you supposed to play the game. Ain't nothing to it. It's just a matter of timing . . . getting the right follow-through. Hell, I can hit forty-three home runs right now!

CORY: Not off no major-league pitching, you couldn't.

TROY: We had better pitching in the Negro leagues. I hit seven home runs off of Satchel Paige.[1] You can't get no better than that!

CORY: Sandy Koufax. He's leading the league in strikeouts.

TROY: I ain't thinking of no Sandy Koufax.

CORY: You got Warren Spahn and Lew Burdette. I bet you couldn't hit no home runs off of Warren Spahn.

TROY: I'm through with it now. You go on and cut them boards.

(Pause.)

Your mama tell me you done got recruited by a college football team? Is that right?

CORY: Yeah. Coach Zellman say the recruiter gonna be coming by to talk to you. Get you to sign the permission papers.

TROY: I thought you supposed to be working down there at the A&P. Ain't you suppose to be working down there after school?

CORY: Mr. Stawicki say he gonna hold my job for me until after the football season. Say starting next week I can work weekends.

TROY: I thought we had an understanding about this football stuff? You suppose to keep up with your chores and hold that job down at the A&P. Ain't been around here all day on a Saturday. Ain't none of your chores done . . . and now you telling me you done quit your job.

CORY: I'm gonna be working weekends.

---

1. Legendary black pitcher (1906?–1982) in the Negro leagues.

TROY: You damn right you are! And ain't no need for nobody coming around here to talk to me about signing nothing.

CORY: Hey, Pop . . . you can't do that. He's coming all the way from North Carolina.

TROY: I don't care where he coming from. The white man ain't gonna let you get nowhere with that football noway. You go on and get your book-learning so you can work yourself up in that A&P or learn how to fix cars or build houses or something, get you a trade. That way you have something can't nobody take away from you. You go on and learn how to put your hands to some good use. Besides hauling people's garbage.

CORY: I get good grades, Pop. That's why the recruiter wants to talk with you. You got to keep up your grades to get recruited. This way I'll be going to college. I'll get a chance . . .

TROY: First you gonna get your butt down there to the A&P and get your job back.

CORY: Mr. Stawicki done already hired somebody else 'cause I told him I was playing football.

TROY: You a bigger fool than I thought . . . to let somebody take away your job so you can play some football. Where you gonna get your money to take out your girlfriend and whatnot? What kind of foolishness is that to let somebody take away your job?

CORY: I'm still gonna be working weekends.

TROY: Naw . . . naw. You getting your butt out of here and finding you another job.

CORY: Come on, Pop! I got to practice. I can't work after school and play football too. The team needs me. That's what Coach Zellman say . . .

TROY: I don't care what nobody else say. I'm the boss . . . you understand? I'm the boss around here. I do the only saying what counts.

CORY: Come on, Pop!

TROY: I asked you . . . did you understand?

CORY: Yeah . . .

TROY: What?!

CORY: Yessir.

TROY: You go on down there to that A&P and see if you can get your job back. If you can't do both . . . then you quit the football team. You've got to take the crookeds with the straights.

CORY: Yessir.

(Pause.)

Can I ask you a question?

TROY: What the hell you wanna ask me? Mr. Stawicki the one you got the questions for.

CORY: How come you ain't never liked me?

TROY: Liked you? Who the hell say I got to like you? What law is there say I got to like you? Wanna stand up in my face and ask a damn fool-ass question like that. Talking about liking somebody. Come here, boy, when I talk to you.

(CORY *comes over to where* TROY *is working. He stands slouched over and* TROY *shoves him on his shoulder.*)

Straighten up, goddammit! I asked you a question . . . what law is there say I got to like you?

CORY: None.

TROY: Well, all right then! Don't you eat every day?

(*Pause.*)

Answer me when I talk to you! Don't you eat every day?

CORY: Yeah.

TROY: Nigger, as long as you in my house, you put that sir on the end of it when you talk to me!

CORY: Yes . . . sir.

TROY: You eat every day.

CORY: Yessir!

TROY: Got a roof over your head.

CORY: Yessir!

TROY: Got clothes on your back.

CORY: Yessir.

TROY: Why you think that is?

CORY: Cause of you.

TROY: Ah, hell I know it's 'cause of me . . . but why do you think that is?

CORY (*hesitant*): Cause you like me.

TROY: Like you? I go out of here every morning . . . bust my butt . . . putting up with them crackers every day . . . cause I like you? You about the biggest fool I ever saw.

(*Pause.*)

It's my job. It's my responsibility! You understand that? A man got to take care of his family. You live in my house . . . sleep you behind on my bedclothes . . . fill you belly up with my food . . . cause you my son. You my flesh and blood. Not 'cause I like you! Cause it's my duty to take care of you. I owe a responsibility to you! Let's get this straight right here . . . before it go along any further . . . I ain't got to like you. Mr. Rand don't give me my money come payday cause he likes me. He gives me cause he owe me. I done give you everything I had to give you. I gave you your life! Me and your mama worked that out between us. And liking your black ass wasn't part of the bargain. Don't you try and go through life worrying about if somebody like you or not. You best be making sure they doing right by you. You understand what I'm saying, boy?

CORY: Yessir.

TROY: Then get the hell out of my face, and get on down to that A&P.

(ROSE *has been standing behind the screen door for much of the scene. She enters as* CORY *exits.*)

ROSE: Why don't you let the boy go ahead and play football, Troy? Ain't no harm in that. He's just trying to be like you with the sports.

TROY: I don't want him to be like me! I want him to move as far away from my life as he can get. You the only decent thing that ever happened to me. I wish him that. But I don't wish him a thing else from my life. I decided seventeen years ago that boy wasn't getting involved in no sports. Not after what they did to me in the sports.

ROSE: Troy, why don't you admit you was too old to play in the major leagues? For once . . . why don't you admit that?

TROY: What do you mean too old? Don't come telling me I was too old. I just wasn't the right color. Hell, I'm fifty-three years old and can do better than Selkirk's .269 right now!

ROSE: How's was you gonna play ball when you were over forty? Sometimes I can't get no sense out of you.

TROY: I got good sense, woman. I got sense enough not to let my boy get hurt over playing no sports. You been mothering that boy too much. Worried about if people like him.

ROSE: Everything that boy do . . . he do for you. He wants you to say "Good job, son." That's all.

TROY: Rose, I ain't got time for that. He's alive. He's healthy. He's got to make his own way. I made mine. Ain't nobody gonna hold his hand when he get out there in that world.

ROSE: Times have changed from when you was young, Troy. People change. The world's changing around you and you can't even see it.

TROY (*slow, methodical*): Woman . . . I do the best I can do. I come in here every Friday. I carry a sack of potatoes and a bucket of lard. You all line up at the door with your hands out. I give you the lint from my pockets. I give you my sweat and my blood. I ain't got no tears. I done spent them. We go upstairs in that room at night . . . and I fall down on you and try to blast a hole into forever. I get up Monday morning . . . find my lunch on the table. I go. Make my way. Find my strength to carry me through to the next Friday.

(*Pause.*)

That's all I got, Rose. That's all I got to give. I can't give nothing else.

(TROY *exits into the house. The lights go down to black.*)

SCENE IV

(*It is Friday. Two weeks later.* CORY *starts out of the house with his football equipment. The phone rings.*)

CORY (*calling*): I got it!

(*He answers the phone and stands in the screen door talking.*)

Hello? Hey, Jesse. Naw . . . I was just getting ready to leave now.

ROSE (*calling*): Cory!

CORY: I told you, man, them spikes is all tore up. You can use them if you want, but they ain't no good. Earl got some spikes.

ROSE (*calling*): Cory!

CORY (*calling to* ROSE): Mam? I'm talking to Jesse.

(*Into phone.*)

When she say that? *(Pause.)* Aw, you lying, man. I'm gonna tell her you said that.

ROSE *(calling):* Cory, don't you go nowhere!

CORY: I got to go to the game, Ma!

(Into the phone.)

Yeah, hey, look, I'll talk to you later. Yeah, I'll meet you over Earl's house. Later. Bye, Ma.

(CORY exits the house and starts out the yard.)

ROSE: Cory, where you going off to? You got that stuff all pulled out and thrown all over your room.

CORY *(in the yard):* I was looking for my spikes. Jesse wanted to borrow my spikes.

ROSE: Get up there and get that cleaned up before your daddy get back in here.

CORY: I got to go to the game! I'll clean it up *when I get back.*

(CORY exits.)

ROSE: That's all he need to do is see that room all messed up.

(ROSE exits into the house. TROY and BONO enter the yard. TROY is dressed in clothes other than his work clothes.)

BONO: He told him the same thing he told you. Take it to the union.

TROY: Brownie ain't got that much sense. Man wasn't thinking about nothing. He wait until I confront them on it . . . then he wanna come crying seniority.

(Calls.)

Hey, Rose!

BONO: I wish I could have seen Mr. Rand's face when he told you.

TROY: He couldn't get it out of his mouth! Liked to bit his tongue! When they called me down there to the Commissioner's office . . . he thought they was gonna fire me. Like everybody else.

BONO: I didn't think they was gonna fire you. I thought they was gonna put you on the warning paper.

TROY: Hey, Rose!

(To BONO.)

Yeah, Mr. Rand like to bit his tongue.

(TROY breaks the seal on the bottle, takes a drink, and hands it to BONO.)

BONO: I see you run right down to Taylors' and told that Alberta gal.

TROY *(calling):* Hey, Rose! *(To BONO.)* I told everybody. Hey, Rose! I went down there to cash my check.

ROSE *(entering from the house):* Hush all that hollering, man! I know you out here. What they say down there at the Commissioner's office?

TROY: You supposed to come when I call you, woman. Bono'll tell you that.

(To BONO.)

Don't Lucille come when you call her?

ROSE: Man, hush your mouth. I ain't no dog . . . talk about "come when you call me."

TROY (*puts his arm around* ROSE): You hear this, Bono? I had me an old dog used to get uppity like that. You say, "C'mere, Blue!" . . . and he just lay there and look at you. End up getting a stick and chasing him away trying to make him come.

ROSE: I ain't studying you and your dog. I remember you used to sing that old song.

TROY (*he sings*): Hear it ring! Hear it ring! I had a dog his name was Blue.

ROSE: Don't nobody wanna hear you sing that old song.

TROY (*sings*): You know Blue was mighty true.

ROSE: Used to have Cory running around here singing that song.

BONO: Hell, I remember that song myself.

TROY (*sings*): You know Blue was a good old dog.
Blue treed a possum in a hollow log.
That was my daddy's song. My daddy made up that song.

ROSE: I don't care who made it up. Don't nobody wanna hear you sing it.

TROY (*makes a song like calling a dog*): Come here, woman.

ROSE: You come in here carrying on, I reckon they ain't fired you. What they say down there at the Commissioner's office?

TROY: Look here, Rose . . . Mr. Rand called me into his office today when I got back from talking to them people down there . . . it come from up top . . . he called me in and told me they was making me a driver.

ROSE: Troy, you kidding!

TROY: No I ain't. Ask Bono.

ROSE: Well, that's great, Troy. Now you don't have to hassle them people no more.

(LYONS *enters from the street.*)

TROY: Aw hell, I wasn't looking to see you today. I thought you was in jail. Got it all over the front page of the *Courier* about them raiding Sefus' place . . . where you be hanging out with all them thugs.

LYONS: Hey, Pop . . . that ain't got nothing to do with me. I don't go down there gambling. I go down there to sit in with the band. I ain't got nothing to do with the gambling part. They got some good music down there.

TROY: They got some rogues . . . is what they got.

LYONS: How you been, Mr. Bono? Hi, Rose.

BONO: I see where you playing down at the Crawford Grill tonight.

ROSE: How come you ain't brought Bonnie like I told you. You should have brought Bonnie with you, she ain't been over in a month of Sundays.

LYONS: I was just in the neighborhood . . . thought I'd stop by.

TROY: Here he come . . .

BONO: Your daddy got a promotion on the rubbish. He's gonna be the first colored driver. Ain't got to do nothing but sit up there and read the paper like them white fellows.

LYONS: Hey, Pop . . . if you knew how to read you'd be all right.

BONO: Naw . . . naw . . . you mean if the nigger knew how to *drive* he'd be all right. Been fighting with them people about driving and ain't even got a license. Mr. Rand know you ain't got no driver's license?

TROY: Driving ain't nothing. All you do is point the truck where you want it to go. Driving ain't nothing.

BONO: Do Mr. Rand know you ain't got no driver's license? That's what I'm talking about. I ain't asked if driving was easy. I asked if Mr. Rand know you ain't got no driver's license.

TROY: He ain't got to know. The man ain't got to know my business. Time he find out, I have two or three driver's licenses.

LYONS *(going into his pocket):* Say, look here, Pop . . .

TROY: I knew it was coming. Didn't I tell you, Bono? I know what kind of "Look here, Pop" that was. The nigger fixing to ask me for some money. It's Friday night. It's my payday. All them rogues down there on the avenue . . . the ones that ain't in jail . . . and Lyons is hopping in his shoes to get down there with them.

LYONS: See, Pop . . . if you give somebody else a chance to talk sometime, you'd see that I was fixing to pay you back your ten dollars like I told you. Here . . . I told you I'd pay you when Bonnie got paid.

TROY: Naw . . . you go ahead and keep that ten dollars. Put it in the bank. The next time you feel like you wanna come by here and ask me for something . . . you go on down there and get that.

LYONS: Here's your ten dollars, Pop. I told you I don't want you to give me nothing. I just wanted to borrow ten dollars.

TROY: Naw . . . you go on and keep that for the next time you want to ask me.

LYONS: Come on, Pop . . . here go your ten dollars.

ROSE: Why don't you go on and let the boy pay you back, Troy?

LYONS: Here you go, Rose. If you don't take it I'm gonna have to hear about it for the next six months.

(He hands her the money.)

ROSE: You can hand yours over here too, Troy.

TROY: You see this, Bono. You see how they do me.

BONO: Yeah, Lucille do me the same way.

(GABRIEL is heard singing offstage. He enters.)

GABRIEL: Better get ready for the Judgment! Better get ready for . . . Hey! . . . Hey! . . . There's Troy's boy!

LYONS: How are you doing, Uncle Gabe?

GABRIEL: Lyons . . . The King of the Jungle! Rose . . . hey, Rose. Got a flower for you.

(He takes a rose from his pocket.)

Picked it myself. That's the same rose like you is!

ROSE: That's right nice of you, Gabe.

LYONS: What you been doing, Uncle Gabe?

GABRIEL: Oh, I been chasing hellhounds and waiting on the time to tell St. Peter to open the gates.

LYONS: You been chasing hellhounds, huh? Well . . . you doing the right thing, Uncle Gabe. Somebody got to chase them.

GABRIEL: Oh, yeah . . . I know it. The devil's strong. The devil ain't no pushover. Hellhounds snipping at everybody's heels. But I got my trumpet waiting on the judgment time.

LYONS: Waiting on the Battle of Armageddon, huh?

GABRIEL: Ain't gonna be too much of a battle when God get to waving that Judgment sword. But the people's gonna have a hell of a time trying to get into heaven if them gates ain't open.

LYONS *(putting his arm around* GABRIEL*):* You hear this, Pop. Uncle Gabe, you all right!

GABRIEL *(laughing with* LYONS*):* Lyons! King of the Jungle.

ROSE: You gonna stay for supper, Gabe. Want me to fix you a plate?

GABRIEL: I'll take a sandwich, Rose. Don't want no plate. Just wanna eat with my hands. I'll take a sandwich.

ROSE: How about you, Lyons? You staying? Got some short ribs cooking.

LYONS: Naw, I won't eat nothing till after we finished playing.

(Pause.)

You ought to come down and listen to me play, Pop.

TROY: I don't like that Chinese music. All that noise.

ROSE: Go on in the house and wash up, Gabe . . . I'll fix you a sandwich.

GABRIEL *(to* LYONS, *as he exits):* Troy's mad at me.

LYONS: What you mad at Uncle Gabe for, Pop?

ROSE: He think Troy's mad at him cause he moved over to Miss Pearl's.

TROY: I ain't mad at the man. He can live where he want to live at.

LYONS: What he move over there for? Miss Pearl don't like nobody.

ROSE: She don't mind him none. She treats him real nice. She just don't allow all that singing.

TROY: She don't mind that rent he be paying . . . that's what she don't mind.

ROSE: Troy, I ain't going through that with you no more. He's over there cause he want to have his own place. He can come and go as he please.

TROY: Hell, he could come and go as he please here. I wasn't stopping him. I ain't put no rules on him.

ROSE: It ain't the same thing, Troy. And you know it.

*(*GABRIEL *comes to the door.)*

Now, that's the last I wanna hear about that. I don't wanna hear nothing else about Gabe and Miss Pearl. And next week . . .

GABRIEL: I'm ready for my sandwich, Rose.

ROSE: And next week . . . when that recruiter come from that school . . . I want you to sign that paper and go on and let Cory play football. Then that'll be the last I have to hear about that.

TROY *(to* ROSE *as she exits into the house):* I ain't thinking about Cory nothing.

LYONS: What . . . Cory got recruited? What school he going to?

TROY: That boy walking around here smelling his piss . . . thinking he's grown. Thinking he's gonna do what he want, irrespective of what I say. Look here, Bono . . . I left the Commissioner's office and went down to the A&P . . . that boy ain't working down there. He lying to me. Telling me he got his job back . . . telling me he working weekends . . . telling me he working after school . . . Mr. Stawicki tell me he ain't working down there at all!

LYONS: Cory just growing up. He's just busting at the seams trying to fill out your shoes.

TROY: I don't care what he's doing. When he get to the point where he wanna disobey me . . . then it's time for him to move on. Bono'll tell you that. I bet he ain't never disobeyed his daddy without paying the consequences.

BONO: I ain't never had a chance. My daddy came on through . . . but I ain't never knew him to see him . . . or what he had on his mind or where he went. Just moving on through. Searching out the New Land. That's what the old folks used to call it. See a fellow moving around from place to place . . . woman to woman . . . called it searching out the New Land. I can't say if he ever found it. I come along, didn't want no kids. Didn't know if I was gonna be in one place long enough to fix on them right as their daddy. I figured I was going searching too. As it turned out I been hooked up with Lucille near about as long as your daddy been with Rose. Going on sixteen years.

TROY: Sometimes I wish I hadn't known my daddy. He ain't cared nothing about no kids. A kid to him wasn't nothing. All he wanted was for you to learn how to walk so he could start you to working. When it come time for eating . . . he ate first. If there was anything left over, that's what you got. Man would sit down and eat two chickens and give you the wing.

LYONS: You ought to stop that, Pop. Everybody feed their kids. No matter how hard times is . . . everybody care about their kids. Make sure they have something to eat.

TROY: The only thing my daddy cared about was getting them bales of cotton in to Mr. Lubin. That's the only thing that mattered to him. Sometimes I used to wonder why he was living. Wonder why the devil hadn't come and got him. "Get them bales of cotton in to Mr. Lubin" and find out he owe him money . . .

LYONS: He should have just went on and left when he saw he couldn't get nowhere. That's what I would have done.

TROY: How he gonna leave with eleven kids? And where he gonna go? He ain't knew how to do nothing but farm. No, he was trapped and I think he knew it. But I'll say this for him . . . he felt a responsibility toward us. Maybe he ain't treated us the way I felt he should have . . . but without that responsibility he could have walked off and left us . . . made his own way.

BONO: A lot of them did. Back in those days what you talking about . . . they walk out their front door and just take on down one road or another and keep on walking.

LYONS: There you go! That's what I'm talking about.

BONO: Just keep on walking till you come to something else. Ain't you never heard of nobody having the walking blues? Well, that's what you call it when you just take off like that.

TROY: My daddy ain't had them walking blues! What you talking about? He stayed right there with his family. But he was just as evil as he could be. My mama couldn't stand him. Couldn't stand that evilness. She run off when I was about eight. She sneaked off one night after he had gone to sleep. Told me she was coming back for me. I ain't never seen her no more. All his women run off and left him. He wasn't good for nobody.

When my turn come to head out, I was fourteen and got to sniffing around Joe Canewell's daughter. Had us an old mule we called Greyboy. My daddy sent me out to do some plowing and I tied up Greyboy and went to fooling around with Joe Canewell's daughter. We done found us a nice little spot, got real cozy with each other. She about thirteen and we done figured we was grown anyway . . . so we down there enjoying ourselves . . . ain't thinking about nothing. We didn't know Greyboy had got loose and wandered back to the house and my daddy was looking for me. We down there by the creek enjoying ourselves when my daddy come up on us. Surprised us. He had them leather straps off the mule and commenced to whupping me like there was no tomorrow. I jumped up, mad and embarrassed. I was scared of my daddy. When he commenced to whupping on me . . . quite naturally I run to get out of the way.
(Pause.)
Now I thought he was mad cause I ain't done my work. But I see where he was chasing me off so he could have the gal for himself. When I see what the matter of it was, I lost all fear of my daddy. Right there is where I become a man . . . at fourteen years of age.
(Pause.)
Now it was my turn to run him off. I picked up them same reins that he had used on me. I picked up them reins and commenced to whupping on him. The gal jumped up and run off . . . and when my daddy turned to face me, I could see why the devil had never come to get him . . . cause he was the devil himself. I don't know what happened. When I woke up, I was laying right there by the creek, and Blue . . . this old dog we had . . . was licking my face. I thought I was blind. I couldn't see nothing. Both my eyes were swollen shut. I layed there and cried. I didn't know what I was gonna do. The only thing I knew was the time had come for me to leave my daddy's house. And right there the world suddenly got big. And it was a long time before I could cut it down to where I could handle it.

Part of that cutting down was when I got to the place where I could feel him kicking in my blood and knew that the only thing that separated us was the matter of a few years.
(GABRIEL enters from the house with a sandwich.)

LYONS: What you got there, Uncle Gabe?

GABRIEL: Got me a ham sandwich. Rose gave me a ham sandwich.

TROY: I don't know what happened to him. I done lost touch with everybody except Gabriel. But I hope he's dead. I hope he found some peace.

LYONS: That's a heavy story, Pop. I didn't know you left home when you was fourteen.

TROY: And didn't know nothing. The only part of the world I knew was the forty-two acres of Mr. Lubin's land. That's all I knew about life.

LYONS: Fourteen's kinda young to be out on your own. *(Phone rings.)* I don't even think I was ready to be out on my own at fourteen. I don't know what I would have done.

TROY: I got up from the creek and walked on down to Mobile. I was through with farming. Figured I could do better in the city. So I walked the two hundred miles to Mobile.

LYONS: Wait a minute . . . you ain't walked no two hundred miles, Pop. Ain't nobody gonna walk no two hundred miles. You talking about some walking there.

BONO: That's the only way you got anywhere back in them days.

LYONS: Shhh. Damn if I wouldn't have hitched a ride with somebody!

TROY: Who you gonna hitch it with? They ain't had no cars and things like they got now. We talking about 1918.

ROSE *(entering):* What you all out here getting into?

TROY *(to* ROSE*):* I'm telling Lyons how good he got it. He don't know nothing about this I'm talking.

ROSE: Lyons, that was Bonnie on the phone. She say you supposed to pick her up.

LYONS: Yeah, okay, Rose.

TROY: I walked on down to Mobile and hitched up with some of them fellows that was heading this way. Got up here and found out . . . not only couldn't you get a job . . . you couldn't find no place to live. I thought I was in freedom. Shhh. Colored folks living down there on the riverbanks in whatever kind of shelter they could find for themselves. Right down there under the Brady Street Bridge. Living in shacks made of sticks and tarpaper. Messed around there and went from bad to worse. Started stealing. First it was food. Then I figured, hell, if I steal money I can buy me some food. Buy me some shoes too! One thing led to another. Met your mama. I was young and anxious to be a man. Met your mama and had you. What I do that for? Now I got to worry about feeding you and her. Got to steal three times as much. Went out one day looking for somebody to rob . . . that's what I was, a robber. I'll tell you truth. I'm ashamed of it today. But it's the truth. Went to rob this fellow . . . pulled out my knife . . . and he pulled out a gun. Shot me in the chest. It felt just like somebody had taken a hot branding iron and laid it on me. When he shot me I jumped at him with my knife. They told me I killed him and they put me in the penitentiary and locked me up for fifteen years. That's where I met Bono. That's where I learned how to play baseball. Got out that place and your mama had taken you and went on to make life without me. Fifteen years was a long time for her to wait. But that fifteen years cured me of that robbing stuff. Rose'll tell you. She asked me when I met her if I had gotten all that foolishness out of my system. And I told her, "Baby, it's you and baseball all what count with me." You hear me, Bono? I meant it too. She say, "Which one comes first?" I told her, "Baby, ain't no doubt it's baseball . . . but you stick and get old with me and we'll both outlive this baseball." Am I right, Rose? And it's true.

ROSE: Man, hush your mouth. You ain't said no such thing. Talking about, "Baby, you know you'll always be number one with me." That's what you was talking.

TROY: You hear that, Bono. That's why I love her.

BONO: Rose'll keep you straight. You get off the track, she'll straighten you up.

ROSE: Lyons, you better get on up and get Bonnie. She waiting on you.

LYONS (*gets up to go*): Hey, Pop, why don't you come on down to the Grill and hear me play?

TROY: I ain't going down there. I'm too old to be sitting around in them clubs.

BONO: You got to be good to play down at the Grill.

LYONS: Come on, Pop . . .

TROY: I got to get up in the morning.

LYONS: You ain't got to stay long.

TROY: Naw, I'm gonna get my supper and go on to bed.

LYONS: Well, I got to go. I'll see you again.

TROY: Don't you come around my house on my payday.

ROSE: Pick up the phone and let somebody know you coming. And bring Bonnie with you. You know I'm always glad to see her.

LYONS: Yeah, I'll do that, Rose. You take care now. See you, Pop. See you, Mr. Bono. See you, Uncle Gabe.

GABRIEL: Lyons! King of the Jungle!

(LYONS *exits.*)

TROY: Is supper ready, woman? Me and you got some business to take care of. I'm gonna tear it up too.

ROSE: Troy, I done told you now!

TROY (*puts his arm around* BONO): Aw hell, woman . . . this is Bono. Bono like family. I done known this nigger since . . . how long I done know you?

BONO: It's been a long time.

TROY: I done known this nigger since Skippy was a pup. Me and him done been through some times.

BONO: You sure right about that.

TROY: Hell, I done know him longer than I known you. And we still standing shoulder to shoulder. Hey, look here, Bono . . . a man can't ask for no more than that.

(*Drinks to him.*)

I love you, nigger.

BONO: Hell, I love you too . . . but I got to get home see my woman. You got yours in hand. I got to go get mine.

(BONO *starts to exit as* CORY *enters the yard, dressed in his football uniform. He gives* TROY *a hard, uncompromising look.*)

CORY: What you do that for, Pop?

(*He throws his helmet down in the direction of* TROY.)

ROSE: What's the matter? Cory . . . what's the matter?

CORY: Papa done went up to the school and told Coach Zellman I can't play football no more. Wouldn't even let me play the game. Told him to tell the recruiter not to come.

ROSE: Troy . . .

TROY: What you Troying me for. Yeah, I did it. And the boy know why I did it.

CORY: Why you wanna do that to me? That was the one chance I had.

ROSE: Ain't nothing wrong with Cory playing football, Troy.

TROY: The boy lied to me. I told the nigger if he wanna play football . . . to keep up his chores and hold down that job at the A&P. That was the conditions. Stopped down there to see Mr. Stawicki . . .

CORY: I can't work after school during the football season, Pop! I tried to tell you that Mr. Stawicki's holding my job for me. You don't never want to listen to nobody. And then you wanna go and do this to me!

TROY: I ain't done nothing to you. You done it to yourself.

CORY: Just cause you didn't have a chance! You just scared I'm gonna be better than you, that's all.

TROY: Come here.

ROSE: Troy . . .

(CORY *reluctantly crosses over to* TROY.)

TROY: All right! See. You done made a mistake.

CORY: I didn't even do nothing!

TROY: I'm gonna tell you what your mistake was. See . . . you swung at the ball and didn't hit it. That's strike one. See, you in the batter's box now. You swung and you missed. That's strike one. Don't you strike out!

(*Lights fade to black.*)

ACT II · SCENE I

(*The following morning.* CORY *is at the tree hitting the ball with the bat. He tries to mimic* TROY, *but his swing is awkward, less sure.* ROSE *enters from the house.*)

ROSE: Cory, I want you to help me with this cupboard.

CORY: I ain't quitting the team. I don't care what Poppa say.

ROSE: I'll talk to him when he gets back. He had to go see about your Uncle Gabe. The police done arrested him. Say he was disturbing the peace. He'll be back directly. Come on in here and help me clean out the top of this cupboard.

(CORY *exits into the house.* ROSE *sees* TROY *and* BONO *coming down the alley.*)

Troy . . . what they say down there?

TROY: Ain't said nothing. I give them fifty dollars and they let him go. I'll talk to you about it. Where's Cory?

ROSE: He's in there helping me clean out these cupboards.

TROY: Tell him to get his butt out here.

(TROY *and* BONO *go over to the pile of wood.* BONO *picks up the saw and begins sawing.*)

TROY *(to* BONO*):* All they want is the money. That makes six or seven times I done went down there and got him. See me coming they stick out their *hands.*

BONO: Yeah, I know what you mean. That's all they care about . . . that money. They don't care about what's right.

(Pause.)

Nigger, why you got to go and get some hard wood? You ain't doing nothing but building a little old fence. Get you some soft pine wood. That's all you need.

TROY: I know what I'm doing. This is outside wood. You put pine wood inside the house. Pine wood is inside wood. This here is outside wood. Now you tell me where the fence is gonna be?

BONO: You don't need this wood. You can put it up with pine wood and it'll stand as long as you gonna be here looking at it.

TROY: How you know how long I'm gonna be here, nigger? Hell, I might just live forever. Live longer than old man Horsely.

BONO: That's what Magee used to say.

TROY: Magee's a damn fool. Now you tell me who you ever heard of gonna pull their own teeth with a pair of rusty pliers.

BONO: The old folks . . . my granddaddy used to pull his teeth with pliers. They ain't had no dentists for the colored folks back then.

TROY: Get clean pliers! You understand? Clean pliers! Sterilize them! Besides we ain't living back then. All Magee had to do was walk over to Doc Goldblum's.

BONO: I see where you and that Tallahassee gal . . . that Alberta . . . I see where you all done got tight.

TROY: What you mean "got tight"?

BONO: I see where you be laughing and joking with her all the time.

TROY: I laughs and jokes with all of them, Bono. You know me.

BONO: That ain't the kind of laughing and joking I'm talking about.

(CORY *enters from the house.*)

CORY: How you doing, Mr. Bono?

TROY: Cory? Get that saw from Bono and cut some wood. He talking about the wood's too hard to cut. Stand back there, Jim, and let that young boy show you how it's done.

BONO: He's sure welcome to it.

(CORY *takes the saw and begins to cut the wood.*)

Whew-e-e! Look at that. Big old strong boy. Look like Joe Louis. Hell, must be getting old the way I'm watching that boy whip through that wood.

CORY: I don't see why Mama want a fence around the yard noways.

TROY: Damn if I know either. What the hell she keeping out with it? She ain't got nothing nobody want.

BONO: Some people build fences to keep people out . . . and other people build fences to keep people in. Rose wants to hold on to you all. She loves you.

TROY: Hell, nigger, I don't need nobody to tell me my wife loves me, Cory . . . go on in the house and see if you can find that other saw.

CORY: Where's it at?

TROY: I said find it! Look for it till you find it!

(CORY *exits into the house.*)

What's that supposed to mean? Wanna keep us in?

BONO: Troy . . . I done known you seem like damn near my whole life. You and Rose both. I done know both of you all for a long time. I remember when you met Rose. When you was hitting them baseball out the park. A lot of them old gals was after you then. You had the pick of the litter. When you picked Rose, I was happy for you. That was the first time I knew you had any sense. I said . . . My man Troy knows what he's doing . . . I'm gonna follow this nigger . . . he might take me somewhere. I been following you too. I done learned a whole heap of things about life watching you. I done learned how to tell where the shit lies. How to tell it from the alfalfa. You done learned me a lot of things. You showed me how to not make the same mistakes . . . to take life as it comes along and keep putting one foot in front of the other.

(*Pause.*)

Rose a good woman, Troy.

TROY: Hell, nigger, I know she a good woman. I been married to her for eighteen years. What you got on your mind, Bono?

BONO: I just say she a good woman. Just like I say anything. I ain't got to have nothing on my mind.

TROY: You just gonna say she a good woman and leave it hanging out there like that? Why you telling me she a good woman?

BONO: She loves you, Troy. Rose loves you.

TROY: You saying I don't measure up. That's what you trying to say. I don't measure up cause I'm seeing this other gal. I know what you trying to say.

BONO: I know what Rose means to you, Troy. I'm just trying to say I don't want to see you mess up.

TROY: Yeah, I appreciate that, Bono. If you was messing around on Lucille I'd be telling you the same thing.

BONO: Well, that's all I got to say. I just say that because I love you both.

TROY: Hell, you know me . . . I wasn't out there looking for nothing. You can't find a better woman than Rose. I know that. But seems like this woman just stuck onto me where I can't shake her loose. I done wrestled with it, tried to throw her off me . . . but she just stuck on tighter. Now she's stuck on for good.

BONO: You's in control . . . that's what you tell me all the time. You responsible for what you do.

TROY: I ain't ducking the responsibility of it. As long as it sets right in my heart . . . then I'm okay. Cause that's all I listen to. It'll tell me right from wrong every time. And I ain't talking about doing Rose no bad turn. I love Rose. She done carried me a long ways and I love and respect her for that.

BONO: I know you do. That's why I don't want to see you hurt her. But what you gonna do when she find out? What you got then? If you try and juggle both of them . . . sooner or later you gonna drop one of them. That's common sense.

TROY: Yeah, I hear what you saying, Bono. I been trying to figure a way to work it out.

BONO: Work it out right, Troy. I don't want to be getting all up between you and Rose's business . . . but work it so it come out right.

TROY: Ah hell, I get all up between you and Lucille's business. When you gonna get that woman that refrigerator she been wanting? Don't tell me you ain't got no money now. I know who your banker is. Mellon don't need that money bad as Lucille want that refrigerator. I'll tell you that.

BONO: Tell you what I'll do . . . when you finish building this fence for Rose . . . I'll buy Lucille that refrigerator.

TROY: You done stuck your foot in your mouth now!

(TROY *grabs up a board and begins to saw.* BONO *starts to walk out the yard.*)
Hey, nigger . . . where you going?

BONO: I'm going home. I know you don't expect me to help you now. I'm protecting my money. I wanna see you put that fence up by yourself. That's what I want to see. You'll be here another six months without me.

TROY: Nigger, you ain't right.

BONO: When it comes to my money . . . I'm right as fireworks on the Fourth of July.

TROY: All right, we gonna see now. You better get your bankbook.

(BONO *exits, and* TROY *continues to work.* ROSE *enters from the house.*)

ROSE: What they say down there? What's happening with Gabe?

TROY: I went down there and got him out. Cost me fifty dollars. Say he was disturbing the peace. Judge set up a hearing for him in three weeks. Say to show cause why he shouldn't be recommitted.

ROSE: What was he doing that cause them to arrest him?

TROY: Some kids was teasing him and he run them off home. Say he was howling and carrying on. Some folks seen him and called the police. That's all it was.

ROSE: Well, what's you say? What'd you tell the judge?

TROY: Told him I'd look after him. It didn't make no sense to recommit the man. He stuck out his big greasy palm and told me to give him fifty dollars and take him on home.

ROSE: Where's he at now? Where'd he go off to?

TROY: He's gone on about his business. He don't need nobody to hold his hand.

ROSE: Well, I don't know. Seem like that would be the best place for him if they did put him into the hospital. I know what you're gonna say. But that's what I think would be best.

TROY: The man done had his life ruined fighting for what? And they wanna take and lock him up. Let him be free. He don't bother nobody.

ROSE: Well, everybody got their own way of looking at it I guess. Come on and get your lunch. I got a bowl of lima beans and some cornbread in the oven. Come on get something to eat. Ain't no sense you fretting over Gabe.

(ROSE *turns to go into the house.*)

TROY: Rose . . . got something to tell you.

ROSE: Well, come on . . . wait till I get this food on the table.

TROY: Rose!

(*She stops and turns around.*)

I don't know how to say this.

(*Pause.*)

I can't explain it none. It just sort of grows on you till it gets out of hand. It starts out like a little bush . . . and the next thing you know it's a whole forest.

ROSE: Troy . . . what is you talking about?

TROY: I'm talking, woman, let me talk. I'm trying to find a way to tell you . . . I'm gonna be a daddy. I'm gonna be somebody's daddy.

ROSE: Troy . . . you're not telling me this? You're gonna be . . . what?

TROY: Rose . . . now . . . see . . .

ROSE: You telling me you gonna by somebody's daddy? You telling your *wife* this?

(GABRIEL *enters from the street. He carries a rose in his hand.*)

GABRIEL: Hey, Troy! Hey, Rose!

ROSE: I have to wait eighteen years to hear something like this.

GABRIEL: Hey, Rose . . . I got a flower for you.

(*He hands it to her.*)

That's a rose. Same rose like you is.

ROSE: Thanks, Gabe.

GABRIEL: Troy, you ain't mad at me is you? Them bad mens come and put me away. You ain't mad at me is you?

TROY: Naw, Gabe, I ain't mad at you.

ROSE: Eighteen years and you wanna come with this.

GABRIEL (*takes a quarter out of his pocket*): See what I got? Got a brand new quarter.

TROY: Rose . . . it's just . . .

ROSE: Ain't nothing you can say, Troy. Ain't no way of explaining that.

GABRIEL: Fellow that gave me this quarter had a whole mess of them. I'm gonna keep this quarter till it stop shining.

ROSE: Gabe, go on in the house there. I got some watermelon in the frigidaire. Go on and get you a piece.

GABRIEL: Say, Rose . . . you know I was chasing hellhounds and them bad mens come and get me and take me away. Troy helped me. He come down there and told them they better let me go before he beat them up. Yeah, he did!

ROSE: You go on and get you a piece of watermelon, Gabe. Them bad mens is gone now.

GABRIEL: Okay, Rose . . . gonna get me some watermelon. The kind with the stripes on it.

(GABRIEL *exits into the house.*)

ROSE: Why, Troy? Why? After all these years to come dragging this in to me now. It don't make no sense at your age. I could have expected this ten or fifteen years ago, but not now.

TROY: Age ain't got nothing to do with it, Rose.

ROSE: I done tried to be everything a wife should be. Everything a wife could be. Been married eighteen years and I got to live to see the day you tell me you been seeing another woman and done fathered a child by her. And you know I ain't never wanted no half nothing in my family. My whole family is half. Everybody got different fathers and mothers . . . my two sisters and my brother. Can't hardly tell who's who. Can't never sit down and talk about Papa and Mama. It's your papa and your mama and my papa and my mama . . .

TROY: Rose . . . stop it now.

ROSE: I ain't never wanted that for none of my children. And now you wanna drag your behind in here and tell me something like this.

TROY: You ought to know. It's time for you to know.

ROSE: Well, I don't want to know, goddamn it!

TROY: I can't just make it go away. It's done now. I can't wish the circumstance of the thing away.

ROSE: And you don't want to either. Maybe you want to wish me and my boy away. Maybe that's what you want? Well, you can't wish us away. I've got eighteen years of my life invested in you. You ought to have stayed upstairs in my bed where you belong.

TROY: Rose . . . now listen to me . . . we can get a handle on this thing. We can talk this out . . . come to an understanding.

ROSE: All of a sudden it's "we." Where was "we" at when you was down there rolling around with some godforsaken woman? "We" should have come to an understanding before you started making a damn fool of yourself. You're a day late and a dollar short when it comes to an understanding with me.

TROY: It's just . . . She gives me a different idea . . . a different understanding about myself. I can step out of this house and get away from the pressures and problems . . . be a different man. I ain't got to wonder how I'm gonna pay the bills or get the roof fixed. I can just be a part of myself that I ain't never been.

ROSE: What I want to know . . . is do you plan to continue seeing her. That's all you can say to me.

TROY: I can sit up in her house and laugh. Do you understand what I'm saying. I can laugh out loud . . . and it feels good. It reaches all the way down to the bottom of my shoes.

(*Pause.*)

Rose, I can't give that up.

ROSE: Maybe you ought to go on and stay down there with her . . . if she's a better woman than me.

TROY: It ain't about nobody being a better woman or nothing. Rose, you ain't the blame. A man couldn't ask for no woman to be a better wife than you've been. I'm responsible for it. I done locked myself into a pattern trying to take care of you all that I forgot about myself.

ROSE: What the hell was I there for? That was my job, not somebody else's.

TROY: Rose, I done tried all my life to live decent . . . to live a clean . . . hard . . . useful life. I tried to be a good husband to you. In every way I knew how. Maybe I come into the world backwards, I don't know. But . . . you born with two strikes on you before you come to the plate. You got to guard it closely . . . always looking for the curve ball on the inside corner. You can't afford to let none get past you. You can't afford a call strike. If you going down . . . you going down swinging. Everything lined up against you. What you gonna do. I fooled them, Rose. I bunted. When I found you and Cory and a halfway decent job . . . I was safe. Couldn't nothing touch me. I wasn't gonna strike out no more. I wasn't going back to the penitentiary. I wasn't gonna lay in the streets with a bottle of wine. I was safe. I had me a family. A job. I wasn't gonna get that last strike. I was on first looking for one of them boys to knock me in. To get me home.

ROSE: You should have stayed in my bed, Troy.

TROY: Then when I saw that gal . . . she firmed up my backbone. And I got to thinking that if I tried . . . I just might be able to steal second. Do you understand after eighteen years I wanted to steal second.

ROSE: You should have held me tight. You should have grabbed me and held on.

TROY: I stood on first base for eighteen years and I thought . . . well, goddamn it . . . go on for it!

ROSE: We're not talking about baseball! We're talking about you going off to lay in bed with another woman . . . and then bring it home to me. That's what we're talking about. We ain't talking about no baseball.

TROY: Rose, you're not listening to me. I'm trying the best I can to explain it to you. It's not easy for me to admit that I been standing in the same place for eighteen years.

ROSE: I been standing with you! I been right here with you, Troy. I got a life too. I gave eighteen years of my life to stand in the same spot with you. Don't you think I ever wanted other things? Don't you think I had dreams and hopes? What about my life? What about me? Don't you think it ever crossed my mind to want to know other men? That I wanted to lay up somewhere and forget about my responsibilities? That I wanted someone to make me laugh so I could feel good? You not the only one who's got wants and needs. But I held on to you, Troy. I took all my feelings, my wants and needs, my dreams . . . and I buried them inside you. I planted a seed and watched and prayed over it. I planted myself inside you and waited to bloom. And it didn't take me no eighteen years to find out the soil was hard and rocky and it wasn't never gonna bloom.

But I held on to you, Troy. I held you tighter. You was my husband. I owed you everything I had. Every part of me I could find to give you. And upstairs in that room . . . with the darkness falling in on me . . . I gave everything I had to try and erase the doubt that you wasn't the finest man in the world. And wherever you was going . . . I wanted to be there with you. Cause you was my husband. Cause that's the only way I was gonna survive as your wife. You always talking about what you give . . . and what you don't have to give. But you take too. You take . . . and don't even know nobody's giving!

(ROSE *turns to exit into the house;* TROY *grabs her arm.*)

TROY: You say I take and don't give!

ROSE: Troy! You're hurting me!

TROY: You say I take and don't give.

ROSE: Troy . . . you're hurting my arm! Let go!

TROY: I done give you everything I got. Don't you tell that lie on me.

ROSE: Troy!

TROY: Don't you tell that lie on me!

(CORY *enters from the house.*)

CORY: Mama!

ROSE: Troy. You're hurting me.

TROY: Don't you tell me about no taking and giving.

(CORY *comes up behind* TROY *and grabs him.* TROY, *surprised, is thrown off balance just as* CORY *throws a glancing blow that catches him on the chest and knocks him down.* TROY *is stunned, as is* CORY.)

ROSE: Troy. Troy. No!

(TROY *gets to his feet and starts at* CORY.)

Troy . . . no. Please! Troy!

(ROSE *pulls on* TROY *to hold him back.* TROY *stops himself.*)

TROY (*to* CORY): All right. That's strike two. You stay away from around me, boy. Don't you strike out. You living with a full count. Don't you strike out.

(TROY *exits out the yard as the lights go down.*)

SCENE II

(*It is six months later, early afternoon.* TROY *enters from the house and starts to exit the yard.* ROSE *enters from the house.*)

ROSE: Troy, I want to talk to you.

TROY: All of a sudden, after all this time, you want to talk to me, huh? You ain't wanted to talk to me for months. You ain't wanted to talk to me last night. You ain't wanted no part of me then. What you wanna talk to me about now?

ROSE: Tomorrow's Friday.

TROY: I know what day tomorrow is. You think I don't know tomorrow's Friday? My whole life I ain't done nothing but look to see Friday coming and you got to tell me it's Friday.

ROSE: I want to know if you're coming home.

TROY: I always come home, Rose. You know that. There ain't never been a night I ain't come home.

ROSE: That ain't what I mean . . . and you know it. I want to know if you're coming straight home after work.

TROY: I figure I'd cash my check . . . hang out at Taylors' with the boys . . . maybe play a game of checkers . . .

ROSE: Troy, I can't live like this. I won't live like this. You livin' on borrowed time with me. It's been going on six months now you ain't been coming home.

TROY: I be here every night. Every night of the year. That's 365 days.

ROSE: I want you to come home tomorrow after work.

TROY: Rose . . . I don't mess up my pay. You know that now. I take my pay and I give it to you. I don't have no money but what you give me back. I just want to have a little time to myself . . . a little time to enjoy life.

ROSE: What about me? When's my time to enjoy life?

TROY: I don't know what to tell you, Rose. I'm doing the best I can.

ROSE: You ain't been home from work but time enough to change your clothes and run out . . . and you wanna call that the best you can do?

TROY: I'm going over to the hospital to see Alberta. She went into the hospital this afternoon. Look like she might have the baby early. I won't be gone long.

ROSE: Well, you ought to know. They went over to Miss Pearl's and got Gabe today. She said you told them to go ahead and lock him up.

TROY: I ain't said no such thing. Whoever told you that is telling a lie. Pearl ain't doing nothing but telling a big fat lie.

ROSE: She ain't had to tell me. I read it on the papers.

TROY: I ain't told them nothing of the kind.

ROSE: I saw it right there on the papers.

TROY: What it say, huh?

ROSE: It said you told them to take him.

TROY: Then they screwed that up, just the way they screw up everything. I ain't worried about what they got on the paper.

ROSE: Say the government send part of his check to the hospital and the other part to you.

TROY: I ain't got nothing to do with that if that's the way it works. I ain't made up the rules about how it work.

ROSE: You did Gabe just like you did Cory. You wouldn't sign the paper for Cory . . . but you signed for Gabe. You signed that paper.

(*The telephone is heard ringing inside the house.*)

TROY: I told you I ain't signed nothing, woman! The only thing I signed was the release form. Hell, I can't read, I don't know what they had on that paper! I ain't signed nothing about sending Gabe away.

ROSE: I said send him to the hospital . . . you said let him be free . . . now you done went down there and signed him to the hospital for half his money. You went back on yourself, Troy. You gonna have to answer for that.

TROY: See now . . . you been over there talking to Miss Pearl. She done got mad cause she ain't getting Gabe's rent money. That's all it is. She's liable to say anything.

ROSE: Troy, I seen where you signed the paper.

TROY: You ain't seen nothing I signed. What she doing got papers on my brother anyway? Miss Pearl telling a big fat lie. And I'm gonna tell her about it too! You ain't seen nothing I signed. Say . . . you ain't seen nothing I signed.

(ROSE *exits into the house to answer the telephone. Presently she returns.*)

ROSE: Troy . . . that was the hospital. Alberta had the baby.

TROY: What she have? What is it?

ROSE: It's a girl.

TROY: I better get on down to the hospital to see her.

ROSE: Troy . . .

TROY: Rose . . . I got to go see her now. That's only right . . . what's the matter . . . the baby's all right, ain't it?

ROSE: Alberta died having the baby.

TROY: Died . . . you say she's dead? Alberta's dead?

ROSE: They said they done all they could. They couldn't do nothing for her.

TROY: The baby? How's the baby?

ROSE: They say it's healthy. I wonder who's gonna bury her.

TROY: She had family, Rose. She wasn't living in the world by herself.

ROSE: I know she wasn't living in the world by herself.

TROY: Next thing you gonna want to know if she had any insurance.

ROSE: Troy, you ain't got to talk like that.

TROY: That's the first thing that jumped out your mouth. "Who's gonna bury her?" Like I'm fixing to take on that task for myself.

ROSE: I am your wife. Don't push me away.

TROY: I ain't pushing nobody away. Just give me some space. That's all. Just give me some room to breathe.

(ROSE *exits into the house.* TROY *walks about the yard.*)

TROY (*with a quiet rage that threatens to consume him*): All right . . . Mr. Death. See now . . . I'm gonna tell you what I'm gonna do. I'm gonna take and build me a fence around this yard. See? I'm gonna build me a fence around what belongs to me. And then I want you to stay on the other side. See? You stay over there until you're ready for me. Then you come on. Bring your army. Bring your sickle. Bring your wrestling clothes. I ain't gonna fall down on my vigilance this time. You ain't gonna sneak up on me no more. When you ready for me . . . when the top of your list say Troy Maxson . . . that's when you come around here. You come up and knock on the front door. Ain't nobody else got nothing to do with this. This is between you and me. Man to man. You stay on the other side of that fence until you ready for me. Then you come up and knock on the front door. Anytime you want. I'll be ready for you.

(*The lights go down to black.*)

SCENE III

(The lights come up on the porch. It is late evening three days later. ROSE *sits listening to the ball game waiting for* TROY. *The final out of the game is made and* ROSE *switches off the radio.* TROY *enters the yard carrying an infant wrapped in blankets. He stands back from the house and calls.)*

*(*ROSE *enters and stands on the porch. There is a long, awkward silence, the weight of which grows heavier with each passing second.)*

TROY: Rose . . . I'm standing here with my daughter in my arms. She ain't but a wee bittie little old thing. She don't know nothing about grownups' business. She innocent . . . and she ain't got no mama.

ROSE: What you telling me for, Troy?

(She turns and exits into the house.)

TROY: Well . . . I guess we'll sit out here on the porch.

(He sits down on the porch. There is an awkward indelicateness about the way he handles the baby. His largeness engulfs and seems to swallow it. He speaks loud enough for ROSE *to hear.)*

A man's got to do what's right for him. I ain't sorry for nothing I done. It felt right in my heart.

(To the baby.)

What you smiling at? Your daddy's a big man. Got these great big old hands. But sometimes he's scared. And right now your daddy's scared cause we sitting out here and ain't got no home. Oh, I been homeless before. I ain't had no little baby with me. But I been homeless. You just be out on the road by your lonesome and you see one of them trains coming and you just kinda go like this . . .

(He sings as a lullaby.)

Please, Mr. Engineer let a man ride the line
Please, Mr. Engineer let a man ride the line
I ain't got no ticket please let me ride the blinds

*(*ROSE *enters from the house.* TROY *hearing her steps behind him, stands and faces her.)*

She's my daughter, Rose. My own flesh and blood. I can't deny her no more than I can deny them boys.

(Pause.)

You and them boys is my family. You and them and this child is all I got in the world. So I guess what I'm saying is . . . I'd appreciate it if you'd help me take care of her.

ROSE: Okay, Troy . . . you're right. I'll take care of your baby for you . . . cause . . . like you say . . . she's innocent . . . and you can't visit the sins of the father upon the child. A motherless child has got a hard time.

(She takes the baby from him.)

From right now . . . this child got a mother. But you a womanless man.

*(*ROSE *turns and exits into the house with the baby. Lights go down to black.)*

SCENE IV

(It is two months later. LYONS *enters from the street. He knocks on the door and calls.)*

LYONS: Hey, Rose! *(Pause.)* Rose!

ROSE (*from inside the house*): Stop that yelling. You gonna wake up Raynell. I just got her to sleep.

LYONS: I just stopped by to pay Papa this twenty dollars I owe him. Where's Papa at?

ROSE: He should be here in a minute. I'm getting ready to go down to the church. Sit down and wait on him.

LYONS: I got to go pick up Bonnie over her mother's house.

ROSE: Well, sit it down there on the table. He'll get it.

LYONS (*enters the house and sets the money on the table*): Tell Papa I said thanks. I'll see you again.

ROSE: All right, Lyons. We'll see you.

(LYONS *starts to exit as* CORY *enters.*)

CORY: Hey, Lyons.

LYONS: What's happening, Cory. Say man, I'm sorry I missed your graduation. You know I had a gig and couldn't get away. Otherwise, I would have been there, man. So what you doing?

CORY: I'm trying to find a job.

LYONS: Yeah I know how that go, man. It's rough out here. Jobs are scarce.

CORY: Yeah, I know.

LYONS: Look here, I got to run. Talk to Papa . . . he know some people. He'll be able to help get you a job. Talk to him . . . see what he say.

CORY: Yeah . . . all right, Lyons.

LYONS: You take care. I'll talk to you soon. We'll find some time to talk.

(LYONS *exits the yard.* CORY *wanders over to the tree, picks up the bat, and assumes a batting stance. He studies an imaginary pitcher and swings. Dissatisfied with the result, he tries again.* TROY *enters. They eye each other for a beat.* CORY *puts the bat down and exits the yard.* TROY *starts into the house as* ROSE *exits with* RAYNELL. *She is carrying a cake.*)

TROY: I'm coming in and everybody's going out.

ROSE: I'm taking this cake down to the church for the bake sale. Lyons was by to see you. He stopped by to pay you your twenty dollars. It's laying in there on the table.

TROY (*going into his pocket*): Well . . . here go this money.

ROSE: Put it in there on the table, Troy. I'll get it.

TROY: What time you coming back?

ROSE: Ain't no use in you studying me. It don't matter what time I come back.

TROY: I just asked you a question, woman. What's the matter . . . can't I ask you a question?

ROSE: Troy, I don't want to go into it. Your dinner's in there on the stove. All you got to do is heat it up. And don't you be eating the rest of them cakes in there. I'm coming back for them. We having a bake sale at the church tomorrow.

(ROSE *exits the yard.* TROY *sits down on the steps, takes a pint bottle from his pocket, opens it, and drinks. He begins to sing.*)

TROY: Hear it ring! Hear it ring!
Had an old dog his name was Blue
You know Blue was mighty true
You know Blue was a good old dog
Blue treed a possum in a hollow log
You know from that he was a good old dog
(BONO *enters the yard.*)

BONO: Hey, Troy.

TROY: Hey, what's happening, Bono?

BONO: I just thought I'd stop by to see you.

TROY: What you stop by and see me for? You ain't stopped by in a month of Sundays. Hell, I must owe you money or something.

BONO: Since you got your promotion I can't keep up with you. Used to see you every day. Now I don't even know what route you working.

TROY: They keep switching me around. Got me out in Greentree now . . . hauling white folks' garbage.

BONO: Greentree, huh? You lucky, at least you ain't got to be lifting them barrels. Damn if they ain't getting heavier. I'm gonna put in my two years and call it quits.

TROY: I'm thinking about retiring myself.

BONO: You got it easy. You can *drive* for another five years.

TROY: It ain't the same, Bono. It ain't like working the back of the truck. Ain't got nobody to talk to . . . feel like you working by yourself. Naw, I'm thinking about retiring. How's Lucille?

BONO: She all right. Her arthritis get to acting up on her sometime. Saw Rose on my way in. She going down to the church, huh?

TROY: Yeah, she took up going down there. All them preachers looking for somebody to fatten their pockets.

(*Pause.*)
Got some gin here.

BONO: Naw, thanks. I just stopped by to say hello.

TROY: Hell, nigger . . . you can take a drink. I ain't never known you to say no to a drink. You ain't got to work tomorrow.

BONO: I just stopped by. I'm fixing to go over to Skinner's. We got us a domino game going over his house every Friday.

TROY: Nigger, you can't play no dominoes. I used to whup you four games out of five.

BONO: Well, that learned me. I'm getting better.

TROY: Yeah? Well, that's all right.

BONO: Look here . . . I got to be getting on. Stop by sometime, huh?

TROY: Yeah, I'll do that, Bono. Lucille told Rose you bought her a new refrigerator.

BONO: Yeah, Rose told Lucille you had finally built your fence . . . so I figured we'd call it even.

TROY: I knew you would.

BONO: Yeah . . . okay. I'll be talking to you.

TROY: Yeah, take care, Bono. Good to see you. I'm gonna stop over.

BONO: Yeah. Okay, Troy.

(BONO *exits.* TROY *drinks from the bottle.*)

TROY: Old Blue died and I dig his grave

Let him down with a golden chain

Every night when I hear old Blue bark

I know Blue treed a possum in Noah's Ark.

Hear it ring! Hear it ring!

(CORY *enters the yard. They eye each other for a beat.* TROY *is sitting in the middle of the steps.* CORY *walks over.*)

CORY: I got to get by.

TROY: Say what? What's you say?

CORY: You in my way. I got to get by.

TROY: You got to get by where? This is my house. Bought and paid for. In full. Took me fifteen years. And if you wanna go in my house and I'm sitting on the steps . . . you say excuse me. Like your mama taught you.

CORY: Come on, Pop . . . I got to get by.

(CORY *starts to maneuver his way past* TROY. TROY *grabs his leg and shoves him back.*)

TROY: You just gonna walk over top of me?

CORY: I live here too!

TROY (*advancing toward him*): You just gonna walk over top of me in my own house?

CORY: I ain't scared of you.

TROY: I ain't asked if you was scared of me. I asked you if you was fixing to walk over top of me in my own house? That's the question. You ain't gonna say excuse me? You just gonna walk over top of me?

CORY: If you wanna put it like that.

TROY: How else am I gonna put it?

CORY: I was walking by you to go into the house cause you sitting on the steps drunk, singing to yourself. You can put it like that.

TROY: Without saying excuse me???

(CORY *doesn't respond.*)

I asked you a question. Without saying excuse me???

CORY: I ain't got to say excuse me to you. You don't count around here no more.

TROY: Oh, I see . . . I don't count around here no more. You ain't got to say excuse me to your daddy. All of a sudden you done got so grown that your daddy don't count around here no more . . . Around here in his own house and yard that he done paid for with the sweat of his brow. You done got so grown to where you gonna take over. You gonna take over my house. Is that right? You gonna wear my pants. You gonna go in there and stretch out on my bed. You ain't got to say excuse me cause I don't count around here no more. Is that right?

CORY: That's right. You always talking this dumb stuff. Now, why don't you just get out my way.

TROY: I guess you got someplace to sleep and something to put in your belly. You got that, huh? You got that? That's what you need. You got that, huh?

CORY: You don't know what I got. You ain't got to worry about what I got.

TROY: You right! You one hundred percent right! I done spent the last seventeen years worrying about what you got. Now it's your turn, see? I'll tell you what to do. You grown . . . we done established that. You a man. Now, let's see you act like one. Turn you behind around and walk out this yard. And when you get out there in the alley . . . you can forget about this house. See? 'Cause this is my house. You go on and be a man and get your own house. You can forget about this. 'Cause this is mine. You go on and get yours 'cause I'm through with doing for you.

CORY: You talking about what you did for me . . . what'd you ever give me?

TROY: Them feet and bones! That pumping heart, nigger! I give you more than anybody else is ever gonna give you.

CORY: You ain't never gave me nothing! You ain't never done nothing but hold me back. Afraid I was gonna be better than you. All you ever did was try and make me scared of you. I used to tremble every time you called my name. Every time I heard your footsteps in the house. Wondering all the time . . . what's Papa gonna say if I do this? . . . What's he gonna say if I do that? . . . What's Papa gonna say if I turn on the radio? And Mama, too . . . she tries . . . but she's scared of you.

TROY: You leave your mama out of this. She ain't got nothing to do with this.

CORY: I don't know how she stand you . . . after what you did to her.

TROY: I told you to leave your mama out of this!

(*He advances toward* CORY.)

CORY: What you gonna do . . . give me a whupping? You can't whup me no more. You're too old. You just an old man.

TROY (*shoves him on his shoulder*): Nigger! That's what you are. You just another nigger on the street to me!

CORY: You crazy! You know that?

TROY: Go on now! You got the devil in you. Get on away from me!

CORY: You just a crazy old man . . . talking about I got the devil in me.

TROY: Yeah, I'm crazy! If you don't get on the other side of that yard . . . I'm gonna show you how crazy I am! Go on . . . get the hell out of my yard.

CORY: It ain't your yard. You took Uncle Gabe's money he got from the army to buy this house and then you put him out.

TROY (TROY *advances on* CORY): Get your black ass out of my yard!

(TROY's *advance backs* CORY *up against the tree.* CORY *grabs up the bat.*)

CORY: I ain't going nowhere! Come on . . . put me out! I ain't scared of you.

TROY: That's my bat!

CORY: Come on!

TROY: Put my bat down!

CORY: Come on, put me out.

(CORY *swings at* TROY, *who backs across the yard.*)

What's the matter? You so bad . . . put me out!

(TROY *advances toward* CORY.)

CORY (*backing up*): Come on! Come on!

TROY: You're gonna have to use it! You wanna draw that bat back on me . . . you're gonna have to use it.

CORY: Come on! . . . Come on!

(CORY *swings the bat at* TROY *a second time. He misses.* TROY *continues to advance toward him.*)

TROY: You're gonna have to kill me! You wanna draw that bat back on me. You're gonna have to kill me.

(CORY, *backed up against the tree, can go no farther.* TROY *taunts him. He sticks out his head and offers him a target.*)

Come on! Come on!

(CORY *is unable to swing the bat.* TROY *grabs it.*)

TROY: Then I'll show you.

(CORY *and* TROY *struggle over the bat. The struggle is fierce and fully engaged.* TROY *ultimately is the stronger and takes the bat from* CORY *and stands over him ready to swing. He stops himself.*)

Go on and get away from around my house.

(CORY, *stung by his defeat, picks himself up, walks slowly out of the yard and up the alley.*)

CORY: Tell Mama I'll be back for my things.

TROY: They'll be on the other side of that fence.

(CORY *exits.*)

TROY: I can't taste nothing. Helluljah! I can't taste nothing no more. (TROY *assumes a batting posture and begins to taunt Death, the fastball on the outside corner.*) Come on! It's between you and me now! Come on! Anytime you want! Come on! I be ready for you . . . but I ain't gonna be easy.

(*The lights go down on the scene.*)

SCENE V

(*The time is 1965. The lights come up in the yard. It is the morning of* TROY'S *funeral. A funeral plaque with a light hangs beside the door. There is a small garden plot off to the side. There is noise and activity in the house as* ROSE, LYONS, *and* BONO *have gathered. The door opens and* RAYNELL, *seven years old, enters dressed in a flannel nightgown. She crosses to the garden and pokes around with a stick.* ROSE *calls from the house.*)

ROSE: Raynell!

RAYNELL: Mam?

ROSE: What you doing out there?

RAYNELL: Nothing.

(ROSE *comes to the door.*)

ROSE: Girl, get in here and get dressed. What you doing?

RAYNELL: Seeing if my garden growed.

ROSE: I told you it ain't gonna grow overnight. You got to wait.

RAYNELL: It don't look like it never gonna grow. Dag!

ROSE: I told you a watched pot never boils. Get in here and get dressed.

RAYNELL: This ain't even no pot, Mama.

ROSE: You just have to give it a chance. It'll grow. Now you come on and do what I told you. We got to be getting ready. This ain't no morning to be playing around. You hear me?

RAYNELL: Yes, mam.

(ROSE *exits into the house.* RAYNELL *continues to poke at her garden with a stick.* CORY *enters. He is dressed in a Marine corporal's uniform, and carries a duffel bag. His posture is that of a military man, and his speech has a clipped sternness.*)

CORY *(to* RAYNELL*):* Hi.

(*Pause.*)

I bet your name is Raynell.

RAYNELL: Uh huh.

CORY: Is your mama home?

(RAYNELL *runs up on the porch and calls through the screen door.*)

RAYNELL: Mama . . . there's some man out here. Mama?

(ROSE *comes to the door.*)

ROSE: Cory? Lord have mercy! Look here, you all!

(ROSE *and* CORY *embrace in a tearful reunion as* BONO *and* LYONS *enter from the house dressed in funeral clothes.*)

BONO: Aw, looka here . . .

ROSE: Done got all grown up!

CORY: Don't cry, Mama. What you crying about?

ROSE: I'm just so glad you made it.

CORY: Hey Lyons. How you doing, Mr. Bono.

(LYONS *goes to embrace* CORY.)

LYONS: Look at you, man. Look at you. Don't he look good, Rose? Got them Corporal stripes.

ROSE: What took you so long?

CORY: You know how the Marines are, Mama. They got to get all their paperwork straight before they let you do anything.

ROSE: Well, I'm sure glad you made it. They let Lyons come. Your Uncle Gabe's still in the hospital. They don't know if they gonna let him out or not. I just talked to them a little while ago.

LYONS: A Corporal in the United States Marines.

BONO: Your daddy knew you had it in you. He used to tell me all the time.

LYONS: Don't he look good, Mr. Bono?

BONO: Yeah, he remind me of Troy when I first met him.

(Pause.)

Say, Rose, Lucille's down at the church with the choir. I'm gonna go down and get the pallbearers lined up. I'll be back to get you all.

ROSE: Thanks, Jim.

CORY: See you, Mr. Bono.

LYONS *(with his arm around* RAYNELL*):* Cory . . . look at Raynell. Ain't she precious? She gonna break a whole lot of hearts.

ROSE: Raynell, come and say hello to your brother. This is your brother, Cory. You remember Cory.

RAYNELL: No, Mam.

CORY: She don't remember me, Mama.

ROSE: Well, we talk about you. She heard us talk about you. *(To* RAYNELL.*)* This is your brother, Cory. Come on and say hello.

RAYNELL: Hi.

CORY: Hi. So you're Raynell. Mama told me a lot about you.

ROSE: You all come on into the house and let me fix you some breakfast. Keep up your strength.

CORY: I ain't hungry, Mama.

LYONS: You can fix me something, Rose. I'll be in there in a minute.

ROSE: Cory, you sure you don't want nothing? I know they ain't feeding you right.

CORY: No, Mama . . . thanks. I don't feel like eating. I'll get something later.

ROSE: Raynell . . . get on upstairs and get that dress on like I told you.

*(*ROSE *and* RAYNELL *exit into the house.)*

LYONS: So . . . I hear you thinking about getting married.

CORY: Yeah, I done found the right one, Lyons. It's about time.

LYONS: Me and Bonnie been split up about four years now. About the time Papa retired. I guess she just got tired of all them changes I was putting her through.

(Pause.)

I always knew you was gonna make something out yourself. Your head was always in the right direction. So . . . you gonna stay in . . . make it a career . . . put in your twenty years?

CORY: I don't know. I got six already, I think that's enough.

LYONS: Stick with Uncle Sam and retire early. Ain't nothing out here. I guess Rose told you what happened with me. They got me down the workhouse. I thought I was being slick cashing other people's checks.

CORY: How much time you doing?

LYONS: They give me three years. I got that beat now. I ain't got but nine more months. It ain't so bad. You learn to deal with it like anything else. You got to take the crookeds with the straights. That's what Papa used to say. He used to say that when he struck out. I seen him strike out three times in a row . . . and the next time up he hit the ball over the grandstand. Right out there in

Homestead Field. He wasn't satisfied hitting in the seats . . . he want to hit it over everything! After the game he had two hundred people standing around waiting to shake his hand. You got to take the crookeds with the straights. Yeah, Papa was something else.

CORY: You still playing?

LYONS: Cory . . . you know I'm gonna do that. There's some fellows down there we got us a band . . . we gonna try and stay together when we get out . . . but yeah, I'm still playing. It still helps me to get out of bed in the morning. As long as it do that I'm gonna be right there playing and trying to make some sense out of it.

ROSE *(calling):* Lyons, I got these eggs in the pan.

LYONS: Let me go on and get these eggs, man. Get ready to go bury Papa.
(Pause.)
How you doing? You doing all right?
(CORY nods. LYONS touches him on the shoulder and they share a moment of silent grief. LYONS exits into the house. CORY wanders about the yard. RAYNELL enters.)

RAYNELL: Hi.

CORY: Hi.

RAYNELL: Did you used to sleep in my room?

CORY: Yeah . . . that used to be my room.

RAYNELL: That's what Papa call it. "Cory's room." It got your football in the closet.
(ROSE comes to the door.)

ROSE: Raynell, get in there and get them good shoes on.

RAYNELL: Mama, can't I wear these? Them other one hurt my feet.

ROSE: Well, they just gonna have to hurt your feet for a while. You ain't said they hurt your feet when you went down to the store and got them.

RAYNELL: They didn't hurt then. My feet done got bigger.

ROSE: Don't you give me no backtalk now. You get in there and get them shoes on.
(RAYNELL exits into the house.)
Ain't too much changed. He still got that piece of rag tied to that tree. He was out here swinging that bat. I was just ready to go back in the house. He swung that bat and then he just fell over. Seem like he swung it and stood there with this grin on his face . . . and then he just fell over. They carried him on down to the hospital, but I knew there wasn't no need . . . why don't you come on in the house?

CORY: Mama . . . I got something to tell you. I don't know how to tell you this . . . but I've got to tell you . . . I'm not going to Papa's funeral.

ROSE: Boy, hush your mouth. That's your daddy you talking about. I don't want hear that kind of talk this morning. I done raised you to come to this? You standing there all healthy and grown talking about you ain't going to your daddy's funeral?

CORY: Mama . . . listen . . .

ROSE: I don't want to hear it, Cory. You just get that thought out of your head.

CORY: I can't drag Papa with me everywhere I go. I've got to say no to him. One time in my life I've got to say no.

ROSE: Don't nobody have to listen to nothing like that. I know you and your daddy ain't seen eye to eye, but I ain't got to listen to that kind of talk this morning. Whatever was between you and your daddy . . . the time has come to put it aside. Just take it and set it over there on the shelf and forget about it. Disrespecting your daddy ain't gonna make you a man, Cory. You got to find a way to come to that on your own. Not going to your daddy's funeral ain't gonna make you a man.

CORY: The whole time I was growing up . . . living in his house . . . Papa was like a shadow that followed you everywhere. It weighed on you and sunk into your flesh. It would wrap around you and lay there until you couldn't tell which one was you anymore. That shadow digging in your flesh. Trying to crawl in. Trying to live through you. Everywhere I looked, Troy Maxson was staring back at me . . . hiding under the bed . . . in the closet. I'm just saying I've got to find a way to get rid of that shadow, Mama.

ROSE: You just like him. You got him in you good.

CORY: Don't tell me that, Mama.

ROSE: You Troy Maxson all over again.

CORY: I don't want to be Troy Maxson. I want to be me.

ROSE: You can't be nobody but who you are, Cory. That shadow wasn't nothing but you growing into yourself. You either got to grow into it or cut it down to fit you. But that's all you got to make life with. That's all you got to measure yourself against that world out there. Your daddy wanted you to be everything he wasn't . . . and at the same time he tried to make you into everything he was. I don't know if he was right or wrong . . . but I do know he meant to do more good than he meant to do harm. He wasn't always right. Sometimes when he touched he bruised. And sometimes when he took me in his arms he cut.

When I first met your daddy I thought . . . Here is a man I can lay down with and make a baby. That's the first thing I thought when I seen him. I was thirty years old and had done seen my share of men. But when he walked up to me and said, "I can dance a waltz that'll make you dizzy," I thought, Rose Lee, here is a man that you can open yourself up to and be filled to bursting. Here is a man that can fill all them empty spaces you been tipping around the edges of. One of them empty spaces was being somebody's mother.

I married your daddy and settled down to cooking his supper and keeping clean sheets on the bed. When your daddy walked through the house he was so big he filled it up. That was my first mistake. Not to make him leave some room for me. For my part in the matter. But at that time I wanted that. I wanted a house that I could sing in. And that's what your daddy gave me. I didn't know to keep up his strength I had to give up little pieces of mine. I did that. I took on his life as mine and mixed up the pieces so that you couldn't hardly tell which was which anymore. It was my choice. It was my life and I didn't have to live it like that. But that's what life offered me in the way of being a woman and I took it. I grabbed hold of it with both hands.

By the time Raynell came into the house, me and your daddy had done lost touch with one another. I didn't want to make my blessing off of nobody's misfortune . . . but I took on to Raynell like she was all them babies I had wanted and never had.

(*The phone rings.*)

Like I'd been blessed to relive a part of my life. And if the Lord see fit to keep up my strength . . . I'm gonna do her just like your daddy did you . . . I'm gonna give her the best of what's in me.

RAYNELL (*entering, still with her old shoes*): Mama . . . Reverend Tollivier on the phone.

(ROSE *exits into the house.*)

RAYNELL: Hi.

CORY: Hi.

RAYNELL: You in the Army or the Marines?

CORY: Marines.

RAYNELL: Papa said it was the Army. Did you know Blue?

CORY: Blue? Who's Blue?

RAYNELL: Papa's dog what he sing about all the time.

CORY (*singing*): Hear it ring! Hear it ring!

I had a dog his name was Blue

You know Blue was mighty true

You know Blue was a good old dog

Blue treed a possum in a hollow log

You know from that he was a good old dog.

Hear it ring! Hear it ring!

(RAYNELL *joins in singing.*)

CORY AND RAYNELL: Blue treed a possum out on a limb

Blue looked at me and I looked at him

Grabbed that possum and put him in a sack

Blue stayed there till I came back

Old Blue's feets was big and round

Never allowed a possum to touch the ground.

Old Blue died and I dug his grave

I dug his grave with a silver spade

Let him down with a golden chain

And every night I call his name

Go on Blue, you good dog you

Go on Blue, you good dog you

RAYNELL: Blue laid down and died like a man

Blue laid down and died . . .

BOTH: Blue laid down and died like a man
Now he's treeing possums in the Promised Land
I'm gonna tell you this to let you know
Blue's gone where the good dogs go
When I hear old Blue bark
When I hear old Blue bark
Blue treed a possum in Noah's Ark
Blue treed a possum in Noah's Ark.
(ROSE *comes to the screen door.*)

ROSE: Cory, we gonna be ready to go in a minute.

CORY *(to* RAYNELL*)*: You go on in the house and change them shoes like Mama told you so we can go to Papa's funeral.

RAYNELL: Okay, I'll be back.

(RAYNELL *exits into the house.* CORY *gets up and crosses over to the tree.* ROSE *stands in the screen door watching him.* GABRIEL *enters from the alley.*)

GABRIEL *(calling):* Hey, Rose!

ROSE: Gabe?

GABRIEL: I'm here, Rose. Hey Rose, I'm here!

(ROSE *enters from the house.*)

ROSE: Lord . . . Look here, Lyons!

LYONS: See, I told you, Rose . . . I told you they'd let him come.

CORY: How you doing, Uncle Gabe?

LYONS: How you doing, Uncle Gabe?

GABRIEL: Hey, Rose. It's time. It's time to tell St. Peter to open the gates. Troy, you ready? You ready, Troy. I'm gonna tell St. Peter to open the gates. You get ready now.

(GABRIEL, *with great fanfare, braces himself to blow. The trumpet is without a mouthpiece. He puts the end of it into his mouth and blows with great force, like a man who has been waiting some twenty-odd years for this single moment. No sound comes out of the trumpet. He braces himself and blows again with the same result. A third time he blows. There is a weight of impossible description that falls away and leaves him bare and exposed to a frightful realization. It is a trauma that a sane and normal mind would be unable to withstand. He begins to dance. A slow, strange dance, eerie and life-giving. A dance of atavistic signature and ritual.* LYONS *attempts to embrace him.* GABRIEL *pushes* LYONS *away. He begins to howl in what is an attempt at song, or perhaps a song turning back into itself in an attempt at speech. He finishes his dance and the gates of heaven stand open as wide as God's closet.*)

That's the way that go!

ACTIVITIES FOR WRITING AND DISCUSSION

1. How do you account for the rather long history of migration at the beginning of the play?

2. Working with a group, identify the different conflicts you see between Troy and Cory, and illustrate the conflicts with specific passages from the play. Which of these conflicts strike you as fairly typical of any father/son relationship? Give examples. Which, if any, seem more unique to an African-American father and son? Again, give examples.

3. Examine Troy's motives for not wanting Cory to play football. Citing evidence from the play, argue that he is motivated by:
   a. A desire to protect Cory, to prevent him from getting hurt
   b. Jealousy that Cory has better opportunities than he did
   c. Considerations other than a or b.

4. Find and annotate all the references you find in the play to "fences." What are Rose's thoughts and feelings about the fence around the yard? What are Troy's? What finally prompts Troy to complete the fence? What literal purposes does the fence serve? How, if at all, is it **symbolic**? Finally, give some reasons why Wilson might have chosen "Fences" as the title for his play.

5. Wilson has said that "Troy's flaw is that he does not recognize that the world was changing. That's because he spent fifteen years in a penitentiary." Explain what you think Wilson means. Then consider how this "flaw" affects Troy's family. Does Troy himself suffer as a result of it? Does Rose? Do Lyons and Cory? Explain with references to specific passages in the play.

6. In the play's final scene Rose tells Cory, "You Troy Maxson all over again." In what respects does she seem to be correct? incorrect? Could the same be said of Troy, i.e., that he is his father "all over again"? How might such a comparison be accurate, and where (if at all) would it break down?

7. The play ends on the day of Troy's funeral. Cory doesn't plan to attend but then changes his mind.
   a. Write down the thoughts you believe are going through his mind at the end of the play as he "gets up and crosses over to the tree," or
   b. Write a dialogue, set on the day of the funeral, between Cory and the dead Troy, or
   c. Imagine thirty years have passed and you are Cory and now have a teenage son of your own. Tell your son the story of your relationship with Troy, just as Troy told the family about his relationship with *his* father. Invent some pretext or reason for telling this story, e.g., your son is about to make some important life decision or he wants to do something you resist.

CULTURAL AND RACIAL IDENTITY: ADDITIONAL ACTIVITIES FOR WRITING AND DISCUSSION

1. Reread your entire notebook. Mark any passages, however long or short, that strike you, for whatever reason. Beside each such passage, write a note explaining its significance for you. Finally, pick a favorite passage and either:

    a. Expand it into a new piece of writing, or

    b. Make notes on how you could expand or use it at some future date, or

    c. Rewrite it in a different form, e.g., poem, dialogue, letter, or memoir.

For a list of strategies for expanding or revising, see Chapter 10.

2. Explore the concept of "cultural and racial identity." Is it meaningful to the **characters, speakers,** and **personae** represented in this thematic section? If so, in what ways? Is it meaningful for you? Create a dialogue, with two or more participants, around these questions. Draw your participants from the reading selections and/or the world of your own experience.

3. Harold Green in "A Loaf of Bread" says he is only doing what he must when he charges higher prices to the patrons of his store in the poor black neighborhood. In a sense, he—the ostensible "oppressor" in the story—sees himself as a victim. Are "oppressors" "victims"? Write a dialogue in which you have different characters or speakers from the works in this section take opposing perspectives on this issue.

4. Think of any situations in which you find (or have found) yourself to be a minority because of your race, religion, ethnicity, sexual preference, values, or a disability. In an essay:

    a. Relate some stories or examples that illustrate your minority status.

    b. Characterize the role in which your status places you. Do you perceive yourself as a victim? a hero? a crusader? in some other way, or as some combination of the above? Explain.

5. Scott Russell Sanders, in "Looking at Women" in Chapter 16, describes "objectification" as a process by which people treat those who are "different" from themselves as objects, dehumanizing them so that they can be ignored, set apart, persecuted, or destroyed. Review what Sanders says about objectification. Then discuss objectification as a theme in any two or more of the texts in this section.

6. In the excerpt from *The House on Mango Street* Sandra Cisneros writes in the **persona** of a young person who comments on people and events in her neighborhood. The persona seems to have frank and fresh insights that might not occur to a more equivocal adult. Following Cisneros's example, identify or imagine some local situation in which two or more cultures meet. Pose a conflict between these cultures and react to it in the persona of an observing child.

7. Review your entire notebook. As you do, make a running list of memorable or striking topics, e.g., "racism," "crossing boundaries," "diversity," "multi-

culturalism," "fear." Then choose a favorite topic, make a Topic/Form Grid (see Chapter 10), and use one of the forms on your grid to create a new notebook entry about the topic. Should your chosen form not work, do a Topic/Form Shift to a different form on your grid.

8. Reread your entire notebook, and mark any favorite entries. Then, after reviewing Chapter 4, revise one of these entries that is a "dependent" text into an "independent" text. (For a list of strategies for revising, see Chapter 10.)

The Greater Universe

EDGAR ALLAN POE (1809–1849)

The Masque of the Red Death

The "Red Death" had long devastated the country. No pestilence had ever been 1
so fatal, or so hideous. Blood was its Avatar and its seal—the redness and the
horror of blood. There were sharp pains, and sudden dizziness, and then pro-
fuse bleeding at the pores, with dissolution. The scarlet stains upon the body
and especially upon the face of the victim, were the pest ban which shut him
out from the aid and from the sympathy of his fellow-men. And the whole
seizure, progress, and termination of the disease, were the incidents of half
an hour.

But the Prince Prospero was happy and dauntless and sagacious. When his 2
dominions were half depopulated, he summoned to his presence a thousand
hale and light-hearted friends from among the knights and dames of his court,
and with these retired to the deep seclusion of one of his castellated abbeys.
This was an extensive and magnificent structure, the creation of the prince's
own eccentric yet august taste. A strong and lofty wall girdled it in. This wall
had gates of iron. The courtiers, having entered, brought furnaces and massy
hammers and welded the bolts. They resolved to leave means neither of ingress
nor egress to the sudden impulses of despair or of frenzy from within. The
abbey was amply provisioned. With such precautions the courtiers might bid
defiance to contagion. The external world could take care of itself. In the mean-

time it was folly to grieve, or to think. The prince had provided all the appliances of pleasure. There were buffoons, there were improvisatori, there were ballet-dancers, there were musicians, there was Beauty, there was wine. All these and security were within. Without was the "Red Death."

It was toward the close of the fifth or sixth month of his seclusion, and 3 while the pestilence raged most furiously abroad, that the Prince Prospero entertained his thousand friends at a masked ball of the most unusual magnificence.

It was a voluptuous scene, that masquerade. But first let me tell of the 4 rooms in which it was held. There were seven—an imperial suite. In many palaces, however, such suites form a long and straight vista, while the folding doors slide back nearly to the walls on either hand, so that the view of the whole extent is scarcely impeded. Here the case was very different; as might have been expected from the duke's love of the *bizarre*. The apartments were so irregularly disposed that the vision embraced but little more than one at a time. There was a sharp turn at every twenty or thirty yards, and at each turn a novel effect. To the right and left, in the middle of each wall, a tall and narrow Gothic window looked out upon a closed corridor which pursued the windings of the suite. These windows were of stained glass whose color varied in accordance with the prevailing hue of the decorations of the chamber into which it opened. That at the eastern extremity was hung, for example, in blue—and vividly blue were its windows. The second chamber was purple in its ornaments and tapestries, and here the panes were purple. The third was green throughout, and so were the casements. The fourth was furnished and lighted with orange—the fifth with white—the sixth with violet. The seventh apartment was closely shrouded in black velvet tapestries that hung all over the ceiling and down the walls, falling in heavy folds upon a carpet of the same material and hue. But in this chamber only, the color of the windows failed to correspond with the decorations. The panes here were scarlet—a deep blood color. Now in no one of the seven apartments was there any lamp or candelabrum, amid the profusion of golden ornaments that lay scattered to and fro or depended from the roof. There was no light of any kind emanating from lamp or candle within the suite of chambers. But in the corridors that followed the suite, there stood, opposite to each window, a heavy tripod, bearing a brazier of fire, that projected its rays through the tinted glass and so glaringly illumined the room. And thus were produced a multitude of gaudy and fantastic appearances. But in the western or black chamber the effect of the fire-light that streamed upon the dark hangings through the blood-tinted panes was ghastly in the extreme, and produced so wild a look upon the countenances of those who entered, that there were few of the company bold enough to set foot within its precincts at all.

It was in this apartment, also, that there stood against the western wall, a gi- 5 gantic clock of ebony. Its pendulum swung to and fro with a dull, heavy, monotonous clang; and when the minute-hand made the circuit of the face, and the hour was to be stricken, there came from the brazen lungs of the clock a sound which was clear and loud and deep and exceedingly musical, but of so peculiar a note and emphasis that, at each lapse of an hour, the musicians of the orchestra were constrained to pause, momentarily, in their performance, to hearken to the sound; and thus the waltzers perforce ceased their evolutions; and there was a brief disconcert of the whole gay company; and, while the chimes of the clock yet rang, it was observed that the giddiest grew pale, and the more aged and sedate passed their hands over their brows as if in confused revery or meditation. But when the echoes had fully ceased, a light laughter at once pervaded the assembly; the musicians looked at each other and smiled as if at their own nervousness and folly, and made whispering vows, each to the other, that the next chiming of the clock should produce in them no similar emotion; and then, after the lapse of sixty minutes (which embrace three thousand and six hundred seconds of the Time that flies), there came yet another chiming of the clock, and then were the same disconcert and tremulousness and meditation as before.

But, in spite of these things, it was a gay and magnificent revel. The tastes of 6 the duke were peculiar. He had a fine eye for colors and effects. He disregarded the *decora* of mere fashion. His plans were bold and fiery, and his conceptions glowed with barbaric lustre. There are some who would have thought him mad. His followers felt that he was not. It was necessary to hear and see and touch him to be *sure* that he was not.

He had directed, in great part, the movable embellishments of the seven 7 chambers, upon occasion of this great *fête;* and it was his own guiding taste which had given character to the masqueraders. Be sure they were grotesque. There were much glare and glitter and piquancy and phantasm—much of what has been since seen in "Hernani." There were arabesque figures with unsuited limbs and appointments. There were delirious fancies such as the madman fashions. There were much of the beautiful, much of the wanton, much of the *bizarre,* something of the terrible, and not a little of that which might have excited disgust. To and fro in the seven chambers there stalked, in fact, a multitude of dreams. And these—the dreams—writhed in and about, taking hue from the rooms, and causing the wild music of the orchestra to seem as the echo of their steps. And, anon, there strikes the ebony clock which stands in the hall of the velvet. And then, for a moment, all is still, and all is silent save the voice of the clock. The dreams are stiff-frozen as they stand. But the echoes of the chime die away—they have endured but an instant—and a light, half-subdued laughter floats after them as they depart. And now again the music swells, and the dreams live, and writhe to and fro more merrily than ever, taking hue from the many-tinted windows through which stream the rays from the tripods. But to the chamber which lies most westwardly of the seven there are now none of the maskers who venture; for the night is waning away; and there flows a ruddier light through the blood-colored panes; and the blackness of the sable drapery appals; and to him whose foot falls upon the sable carpet, there comes from the near clock of ebony a muffled peal more solemnly emphatic than any which reaches *their* ears who indulge in the more remote gaieties of the other apartments.

But these other apartments were densely crowded, and in them beat fever- 8 ishly the heart of life. And the revel went whirlingly on, until at length there commenced the sounding of midnight upon the clock. And then the music ceased, as I have told; and the evolutions of the waltzers were quieted; and there was an uneasy cessation of all things as before. But now there were twelve strokes to be sounded by the bell of the clock; and thus it happened, perhaps, that more of thought crept, with more of time, into the meditations of the thoughtful among those who revelled. And thus too, it happened, perhaps, that before the last echoes of the last chime had utterly sunk into silence, there were many individuals in the crowd who had found leisure to become aware of the presence of a masked figure which had arrested the attention of no single individual before. And the rumor of this new presence having spread itself whisperingly around, there arose at length from the whole company a buzz, or murmur, expressive of disapprobation and surprise—then, finally, of terror, of horror, and of disgust.

In an assembly of phantasms such as I have painted, it may well be supposed 9 that no ordinary appearance could have excited such sensation. In truth the masquerade license of the night was nearly unlimited; but the figure in question had out-Heroded Herod, and gone beyond the bounds of even the prince's indefinite decorum. There are chords in the hearts of the most reckless which cannot be touched without emotion. Even with the utterly lost, to whom life and death are equally jests, there are matters of which no jest can be made. The whole company, indeed, seemed now deeply to feel that in the costume and bearing of the stranger neither wit nor propriety existed. The figure was tall and gaunt, and shrouded from head to foot in the habiliments of the grave. The mask which concealed the visage was made so nearly to resemble the countenance of a stiffened corpse that the closest scrutiny must have had difficulty in detecting the cheat. And yet all this might have been endured, if not approved, by the mad revellers around. But the mummer had gone so far as to assume the type of the Red Death. His vesture was dabbled in *blood*—and his broad brow, with all the features of the face, was besprinkled with scarlet horror.

When the eyes of Prince Prospero fell upon this spectral image (which, with 10 a slow and solemn movement, as if more fully to sustain its *rôle,* stalked to and fro among the waltzers) he was seen to be convulsed, in the first moment with a strong shudder either of terror or distaste; but, in the next, his brow reddened with rage.

"Who dares"—he demanded hoarsely of the courtiers who stood near 11 him—"who dares insult us with this blasphemous mockery? Seize him and unmask him—that we may know whom we have to hang, at sunrise, from the battlements!"

It was in the eastern or blue chamber in which stood the Prince Prospero as 12 he uttered these words. They rang throughout the seven rooms loudly and clearly, for the prince was a bold and robust man, and the music had become hushed at the waving of his hand.

It was in the blue room where stood the prince, with a group of pale 13 courtiers by his side. At first, as he spoke, there was a slight rushing movement of this group in the direction of the intruder, who, at the moment was also near at hand, and now, with deliberate and stately step, made closer approach to the speaker. But from a certain nameless awe with which the mad assumptions of the mummer had inspired the whole party, there were found none who put forth hand to seize him; so that, unimpeded, he passed within a yard of the prince's person; and, while the vast assembly, as if with one impulse, shrank from the centres of the rooms to the walls, he made his way uninterruptedly, but with the same solemn and measured step which had distinguished him from the first, through the blue chamber to the purple—through the purple to the green—through the green to the orange—through this again to the white— and even thence to the violet, ere a decided movement had been made to arrest him. It was then, however, that the Prince Prospero, maddening with rage and the shame of his own momentary cowardice, rushed hurriedly through the six chambers, while none followed him on account of a deadly terror that had seized upon all. He bore aloft a drawn dagger, and had approached, in rapid impetuosity, to within three or four feet of the retreating figure, when the latter, having attained the extremity of the velvet apartment, turned suddenly and confronted his pursuer. There was a sharp cry—and the dagger dropped gleaming upon the sable carpet, upon which, instantly afterward, fell prostrate in death the Prince Prospero. Then, summoning the wild courage of despair, a throng of the revellers at once threw themselves into the black apartment, and, seizing the mummer, whose tall figure stood erect and motionless within the shadow of the ebony clock, gasped in unutterable horror at finding the grave cerements and corpse-like mask, which they handled with so violent a rudeness, untenanted by any tangible form.

And now was acknowledged the presence of the Red Death. He had come 14 like a thief in the night. And one by one dropped the revellers in the blood-bedewed halls of their revel, and died each in the despairing posture of his fall. And the life of the ebony clock went out with that of the last of the gay. And the flames of the tripods expired. And Darkness and Decay and the Red Death held illimitable dominion over all.

Isak Dinesen (1885–1962)

Babette's Feast

I. Two Ladies of Berlevaag

In Norway there is a fjord—a long narrow arm of the sea between tall moun- 1 tains—named Berlevaag Fjord. At the foot of the mountains the small town of Berlevaag looks like a child's toy-town of little wooden pieces painted gray, yellow, pink and many other colors.

Sixty-five years ago two elderly ladies lived in one of the yellow houses. 2 Other ladies at that time wore a bustle, and the two sisters might have worn it as gracefully as any of them, for they were tall and willowy. But they had never possessed any article of fashion; they had dressed demurely in gray or black all their lives. They were christened Martine and Philippa, after Martin Luther and his friend Philip Melanchton. Their father had been a Dean and a prophet, the founder of a pious ecclesiastic party or sect, which was known and looked up to in all the country of Norway. Its members renounced the pleasures of this world, for the earth and all that it held to them was but a kind of illusion, and the true reality was the New Jerusalem toward which they were longing. They swore not at all, but their communication was yea yea and nay nay, and they called one another Brother and Sister.

The Dean had married late in life and by now had long been dead. His disci- 3 ples were becoming fewer in number every year, whiter or balder and harder of hearing; they were even becoming somewhat querulous and quarrelsome, so that sad little schisms would arise in the congregation. But they still gathered together to read and interpret the Word. They had all known the Dean's daughters as little girls; to them they were even now very small sisters, precious for their dear father's sake. In the yellow house they felt that their Master's spirit was with them; here they were at home and at peace.

These two ladies had a French maid-of-all-work, Babette.   4

It was a strange thing for a couple of Puritan women in a small Norwegian 5 town; it might even seem to call for an explanation. The people of Berlevaag found the explanation in the sisters' piety and kindness of heart. For the old Dean's daughters spent their time and their small income in works of charity; no sorrowful or distressed creature knocked on their door in vain. And Babette had come to that door twelve years ago as a friendless fugitive, almost mad with grief and fear.

But the true reason for Babette's presence in the two sisters' house was to be 6 found further back in time and deeper down in the domain of human hearts.

II. Martine's Lover

As young girls, Martine and Philippa had been extraordinarily pretty, with the 7 almost supernatural fairness of flowering fruit trees or perpetual snow. They were never to be seen at balls or parties, but people turned when they passed in the streets, and the young men of Berlevaag went to church to watch them walk up the aisle. The younger sister also had a lovely voice, which on Sundays filled the church with sweetness. To the Dean's congregation earthly love, and marriage with it, were trivial matters, in themselves nothing but illusions; still it is possible that more than one of the elderly Brothers had been prizing the maidens far above rubies and had suggested as much to their father. But the Dean had declared that to him in his calling his daughters were his right and left hand. Who could want to bereave him of them? And the fair girls had been brought up to an ideal of heavenly love; they were all filled with it and did not let themselves be touched by the flames of this world.

All the same they had upset the peace of heart of two gentlemen from the 8
great world outside Berlevaag.

There was a young officer named Lorens Loewenhielm, who had led a gay 9
life in his garrison town and had run into debt. In the year of 1854, when Martine was eighteen and Philippa seventeen, his angry father sent him on a
month's visit to his aunt in her old country house of Fossum near Berlevaag,
where he would have time to meditate and to better his ways. One day he rode
into town and met Martine in the marketplace. He looked down at the pretty
girl, and she looked up at the fine horseman. When she had passed him and disappeared he was not certain whether he was to believe his own eyes.

In the Loewenhielm family there existed a legend to the effect that long ago 10
a gentleman of the name had married a Huldre, a female mountain spirit of
Norway, who is so fair that the air round her shines and quivers. Since then,
from time to time, members of the family had been second-sighted. Young
Lorens till now had not been aware of any particular spiritual gift in his own
nature. But at this one moment there rose before his eyes a sudden, mighty vision of a higher and purer life, with no creditors, dunning letters or parental
lectures, with no secret, unpleasant pangs of conscience and with a gentle,
golden-haired angel to guide and reward him.

Through his pious aunt he got admission to the Dean's house, and saw that 11
Martine was even lovelier without a bonnet. He followed her slim figure with
adoring eyes, but he loathed and despised the figure which he himself cut in her
nearness. He was amazed and shocked by the fact that he could find nothing at
all to say, and no inspiration in the glass of water before him. "Mercy and Truth,
dear brethren, have met together," said the Dean. "Righteousness and Bliss have
kissed one another." And the young man's thoughts were with the moment
when Lorens and Martine should be kissing each other. He repeated his visit
time after time, and each time seemed to himself to grow smaller and more insignificant and contemptible.

When in the evening he came back to his aunt's house he kicked his shining 12
riding-boots to the corners of his room; he even laid his head on the table
and wept.

On the last day of his stay he made a last attempt to communicate his feel- 13
ings to Martine. Till now it had been easy for him to tell a pretty girl that he
loved her, but the tender words stuck in his throat as he looked into this
maiden's face. When he had said good-bye to the party, Martine saw him to the
door with a candlestick in her hand. The light shone on her mouth and threw
upwards the shadows of her long eyelashes. He was about to leave in dumb despair when on the threshold he suddenly seized her hand and pressed it to
his lips.

"I am going away forever!" he cried. "I shall never, never see you again! For I 14
have learned here that Fate is hard, and that in this world there are things which
are impossible!"

When he was once more back in his garrison town he thought his adventure 15
over, and found that he did not like to think of it at all. While the other young

officers talked of their love affairs, he was silent on his. For seen from the officers' mess, and so to say with its eyes, it was a pitiful business. How had it come
to pass that a lieutenant of the hussars had let himself be defeated and frustrated by a set of long-faced sectarians, in the bare-floored rooms of an old
Dean's house?

Then he became afraid; panic fell upon him. Was it the family madness   16
which made him still carry with him the dream-like picture of a maiden so fair
that she made the air round her shine with purity and holiness? He did not
want to be a dreamer; he wanted to be like his brother-officers.

So he pulled himself together, and in the greatest effort of his young life   17
made up his mind to forget what had happened to him in Berlevaag. From now
on, he resolved, he would look forward, not back. He would concentrate on his
career, and the day was to come when he would cut a brilliant figure in a brilliant world.

His mother was pleased with the result of his visit to Fossum, and in her let-   18
ters expressed her gratitude to his aunt. She did not know by what queer, winding roads her son had reached his happy moral standpoint.

The ambitious young officer soon caught the attention of his superiors and   19
made unusually quick advancement. He was sent to France and to Russia, and
on his return he married a lady-in-waiting to Queen Sophia. In these high circles he moved with grace and ease, pleased with his surroundings and with
himself. He even in the course of time benefited from words and turns which
had stuck in his mind from the Dean's house, for piety was now in fashion
at Court.

In the yellow house of Berlevaag, Philippa sometimes turned the talk to the   20
handsome, silent young man who had so suddenly made his appearance, and so
suddenly disappeared again. Her elder sister would then answer her gently, with
a still, clear face, and find other things to discuss.

III. Philippa's Lover

A year later a more distinguished person even than Lieutenant Loewenhielm   21
came to Berlevaag.

The great singer Achille Papin of Paris had sung for a week at the Royal   22
Opera of Stockholm, and had carried away his audience there as everywhere.
One evening a lady of the Court, who had been dreaming of a romance with the
artist, had described to him the wild, grandiose scenery of Norway. His own romantic nature was stirred by the narration, and he had laid his way back to
France around the Norwegian coast. But he felt small in the sublime surroundings; with nobody to talk to he fell into that melancholy in which he saw himself as an old man, at the end of his career, till on a Sunday, when he could think
of nothing else to do, he went to church and heard Philippa sing.

Then in one single moment he knew and understood all. For here were the   23
snowy summits, the wild flowers and the white Nordic nights, translated into

his own language of music, and brought him in a young woman's voice. Like Lorens Loewenhielm he had a vision.

"Almighty God," he thought, "Thy power is without end, and Thy mercy 24 reacheth unto the clouds! And here is a prima donna of the opera who will lay Paris at her feet."

Achille Papin at this time was a handsome man of forty, with curly black 25 hair and a red mouth. The idolization of nations had not spoilt him; he was a kind-hearted person and honest toward himself.

He went straight to the yellow house, gave his name—which told the Dean 26 nothing—and explained that he was staying in Berlevaag for his health, and the while would be happy to take on the young lady as a pupil.

He did not mention the Opera of Paris, but described at length how beauti- 27 fully Miss Philippa would come to sing in church, to the glory of God.

For a moment he forgot himself, for when the Dean asked whether he was a 28 Roman Catholic he answered according to truth, and the old clergyman, who had never seen a live Roman Catholic, grew a little pale. All the same the Dean was pleased to speak French, which reminded him of his young days when he had studied the works of the great French Lutheran writer, Lefèvre d'Etaples. And as nobody could long withstand Achille Papin when he had really set his heart on a matter, in the end the father gave his consent, and remarked to his daughter: "God's paths run across the sea and the snowy mountains, where man's eye sees no track."

So the great French singer and the young Norwegian novice set to work to- 29 gether. Achille's expectation grew into certainty and his certainty into ecstasy. He thought: "I have been wrong in believing that I was growing old. My greatest triumphs are before me! The world will once more believe in miracles when she and I sing together!"

After a while he could not keep his dreams to himself, but told Philippa 30 about them.

She would, he said, rise like a star above any diva of the past or present. The 31 Emperor and Empress, the Princes, great ladies and *bels esprits* of Paris would listen to her, and shed tears. The common people too would worship her, and she would bring consolation and strength to the wronged and oppressed. When she left the Grand Opera upon her master's arm, the crowd would unharness her horses, and themselves draw her to the Café Anglais, where a magnificent supper awaited her.

Philippa did not repeat these prospects to her father or her sister, and this 32 was the first time in her life that she had had a secret from them.

The teacher now gave his pupil the part of Zerlina in Mozart's opera *Don* 33 *Giovanni* to study. He himself, as often before, sang Don Giovanni's part.

He had never in his life sung as now. In the duet of the second act—which is 34 called the seduction duet—he was swept off his feet by the heavenly music and the heavenly voices. As the last melting note died away he seized Philippa's hands, drew her toward him and kissed her solemnly, as a bridegroom might kiss his bride before the altar. Then he let her go. For the moment was too sublime for any further word or movement; Mozart himself was looking down on the two.

Philippa went home, told her father that she did not want any more singing 35 lessons and asked him to write and tell Monsieur Papin so.

The Dean said: "And God's paths run across the rivers, my child." 36

When Achille got the Dean's letter he sat immovable for an hour. He 37 thought: "I have been wrong. My day is over. Never again shall I be the divine Papin. And this poor weedy garden of the world has lost its nightingale!"

A little later he thought: "I wonder what is the matter with that hussy? Did I 38 kiss her, by any chance?"

In the end he thought: "I have lost my life for a kiss, and I have no remem- 39 brance at all of the kiss! Don Giovanni kissed Zerlina, and Achille Papin pays for it! Such is the fate of the artist!"

In the Dean's house Martine felt that the matter was deeper than it looked, 40 and searched her sister's face. For a moment, slightly trembling, she too imag- ined that the Roman Catholic gentleman might have tried to kiss Philippa. She did not imagine that her sister might have been surprised and frightened by something in her own nature.

Achille Papin took the first boat from Berlevaag. 41

Of this visitor from the great world the sisters spoke but little; they lacked 42 the words with which to discuss him.

IV. A Letter from Paris

Fifteen years later, on a rainy June night of 1871, the bell-rope of the yellow 43 house was pulled violently three times. The mistresses of the house opened the door to a massive, dark, deadly pale woman with a bundle on her arm, who stared at them, took a step forward and fell down on the doorstep in a dead swoon. When the frightened ladies had restored her to life she sat up, gave them one more glance from her sunken eyes and, all the time without a word, fumbled in her wet clothes and brought out a letter which she handed to them.

The letter was addressed to them all right, but it was written in French. The 44 sisters put their heads together and read it. It ran as follows:

Ladies! 45

Do you remember me? Ah, when I think of you I have the heart 46 filled with wild lilies-of-the-valley! Will the memory of a Frenchman's devotion bend your hearts to save the life of a Frenchwoman?

The bearer of this letter, Madame Babette Hersant, like my beautiful 47 Empress herself, has had to flee from Paris. Civil war has raged in our streets. French hands have shed French blood. The noble Communards, standing up for the Rights of Man, have been crushed and annihilated. Madame Hersant's husband and son, both eminent ladies' hairdressers, have been shot. She herself was arrested as a Pétroleuse—(which word is used here for women who set fire to houses with petroleum)—and has narrowly escaped the bloodstained hands of General Galliffet. She has lost all she possessed and dares not remain in France.

A nephew of hers is cook to the boat *Anna Colbioernsson,* bound for 48 Christiania—(as I believe, the capital of Norway)—and he has obtained shipping opportunity for his aunt. This is now her last sad resort!

Knowing that I was once a visitor to your magnificent country she 49 comes to me, asks me if there be any good people in Norway and begs me, if it be so, to supply her with a letter to them. The two words of 'good people' immediately bring before my eyes your picture, sacred to my heart. I send her to you. How she is to get from Christiania to Berlevaag I know not, having forgotten the map of Norway. But she is a Frenchwoman, and you will find that in her misery she has still got resourcefulness, majesty and true stoicism.

I envy her in her despair: she is to see your faces. 50

As you receive her mercifully, send a merciful thought back to France. 51

For fifteen years, Miss Philippa, I have grieved that your voice 52 should never fill the Grand Opera of Paris. When tonight I think of you, no doubt surrounded by a gay and loving family, and of myself: gray, lonely, forgotten by those who once applauded and adored me, I feel that you may have chosen the better part in life. What is fame? What is glory? The grave awaits us all!

And yet, my lost Zerlina, and yet, soprano of the snow! As I write 53 this I feel that the grave is not the end. In Paradise I shall hear your voice again. There you will sing, without fears or scruples, as God meant you to sing. There you will be the great artist that God meant you to be. Ah! how you will enchant the angels.

Babette can cook. 54

Deign to receive, my ladies, the humble homage of the friend who 55 was once

Achille Papin　56

At the bottom of the page, as a P.S. were neatly printed the first two bars of 57 the duet between Don Giovanni and Zerlina, like this:

The two sisters till now had kept only a small servant of fifteen to help them 58 in the house and they felt that they could not possibly afford to take on an elderly, experienced housekeeper. But Babette told them that she would serve Monsieur Papin's good people for nothing, and that she would take service with nobody else. If they sent her away she must die. Babette remained in the house of the Dean's daughters for twelve years, until the time of this tale.

V. Still Life

Babette had arrived haggard and wild-eyed like a hunted animal, but in her new, 59
friendly surroundings she soon acquired all the appearance of a respectable and
trusted servant. She had appeared to be a beggar; she turned out to be a conqueror. Her quiet countenance and her steady, deep glance had magnetic qualities; under her eyes things moved, noiselessly, into their proper places.

Her mistresses at first had trembled a little, just as the Dean had once done, 60
at the idea of receiving a Papist under their roof. But they did not like to worry
a hard-tried fellow-creature with catechization; neither were they quite sure of
their French. They silently agreed that the example of a good Lutheran life
would be the best means of converting their servant. In this way Babette's presence in the house became, so to say, a moral spur to its inhabitants.

They had distrusted Monsieur Papin's assertion that Babette could cook. In 61
France, they knew, people ate frogs. They showed Babette how to prepare a split
cod and an ale-and-bread-soup; during the demonstration the Frenchwoman's
face became absolutely expressionless. But within a week Babette cooked a split
cod and an ale-and-bread-soup as well as anybody born and bred in Berlevaag.

The idea of French luxury and extravagance next had alarmed and dis- 62
mayed the Dean's daughters. The first day after Babette had entered their service they took her before them and explained to her that they were poor and that
to them luxurious fare was sinful. Their own food must be as plain as possible;
it was the soup-pails and baskets for their poor that signified. Babette nodded
her head; as a girl, she informed her ladies, she had been cook to an old priest
who was a saint. Upon this the sisters resolved to surpass the French priest in
asceticism. And they soon found that from the day when Babette took over the
housekeeping its cost was miraculously reduced, and the soup-pails and baskets acquired a new, mysterious power to stimulate and strengthen their poor
and sick.

The world outside the yellow house also came to acknowledge Babette's ex- 63
cellence. The refugee never learned to speak the language of her new country,
but in her broken Norwegian she beat down the prices of Berlevaag's flintiest
tradesmen. She was held in awe on the quay and in the marketplace.

The old Brothers and Sisters, who had first looked askance at the foreign 64
woman in their midst, felt a happy change in their little sisters' life, rejoiced at it
and benefited by it. They found that troubles and cares had been conjured away
from their existence, and that now they had money to give away, time for the
confidences and complaints of their old friends and peace for meditating on
heavenly matters. In the course of time not a few of the brotherhood included
Babette's name in their prayers, and thanked God for the speechless stranger,
the dark Martha in the house of their two fair Marys. The stone which the
builders had almost refused had become the headstone of the corner.

The ladies of the yellow house were the only ones to know that their corner- 65
stone had a mysterious and alarming feature to it, as if it was somehow related
to the Black Stone of Mecca, the Kaaba itself.

Hardly ever did Babette refer to her past life. When in early days the sisters   66
had gently condoled her upon her losses, they had been met with that majesty
and stoicism of which Monsieur Papin had written. "What will you ladies?" she
had answered, shrugging her shoulders. "It is Fate."

But one day she suddenly informed them that she had for many years held a   67
ticket in a French lottery, and that a faithful friend in Paris was still renewing it
for her every year. Some time she might win the *grand prix* of ten thousand
francs. At that they felt that their cook's old carpetbag was made from a magic
carpet; at a given moment she might mount it and be carried off, back to Paris.

And it happened when Martine or Philippa spoke to Babette that they   68
would get no answer, and would wonder if she had even heard what they said.
They would find her in the kitchen, her elbows on the table and her temples on
her hands, lost in the study of a heavy black book which they secretly suspected
to be a popish prayer-book. Or she would sit immovable on the three-legged
kitchen chair, her strong hands in her lap and her dark eyes wide open, as enig-
matical and fatal as a Pythia upon her tripod. At such moments they realized
that Babette was deep, and that in the soundings of her being there were passions, there were memories and longings of which they knew nothing at all.

A little cold shiver ran through them, and in their hearts they thought: "Per-   69
haps after all she had indeed been a Pétroleuse."

VI. *Babette's Good Luck*

The fifteenth of December was the Dean's hundredth anniversary.   70

His daughters had long been looking forward to this day and had wished to   71
celebrate it, as if their dear father were still among his disciples. Therefore it
had been to them a sad and incomprehensible thing that in this last year discord and dissension had been raising their heads in his flock. They had endeavored to make peace, but they were aware that they had failed. It was as if the fine
and lovable vigor of their father's personality had been evaporating, the way
Hoffmann's anodyne will evaporate when left on the shelf in a bottle without a
cork. And his departure had left the door ajar to things hitherto unknown to
the two sisters, much younger than his spiritual children. From a past half a
century back, when the unshepherded sheep had been running astray in the
mountains, uninvited dismal guests pressed through the opening on the heels
of the worshippers and seemed to darken the little rooms and to let in the cold.
The sins of old Brothers and Sisters came, with late piercing repentance like a
toothache, and the sins of others against them came back with bitter resentment, like a poisoning of the blood.

There were in the congregation two old women who before their conversion   72
had spread slander upon each other, and thereby to each other ruined a marriage and an inheritance. Today they could not remember happenings of yesterday or a week ago, but they remembered this forty-year-old wrong and kept
going through the ancient accounts; they scowled at each other. There was an

old Brother who suddenly called to mind how another Brother, forty-five years ago, had cheated him in a deal; he could have wished to dismiss the matter from his mind, but it stuck there like a deep-seated, festering splinter. There was a gray, honest skipper and a furrowed, pious widow, who in their young days, while she was the wife of another man, had been sweethearts. Of late each had begun to grieve, while shifting the burden of guilt from his own shoulders to those of the other and back again, and to worry about the possible terrible consequences, through all eternity, to himself, brought upon him by one who had pretended to hold him dear. They grew pale at the meetings in the yellow house and avoided each other's eyes.

As the birthday drew nearer, Martine and Philippa felt the responsibility 73 growing heavier. Would their ever-faithful father look down to his daughters and call them by name as unjust stewards? Between them they talked matters over and repeated their father's saying: that God's paths were running even across the salt sea, and the snow-clad mountains, where man's eye sees no track.

One day of this summer the post brought a letter from France to Madame 74 Babette Hersant. This in itself was a surprising thing, for during these twelve years Babette had received no letter. What, her mistresses wondered, could it contain? They took it into the kitchen to watch her open and read it. Babette opened it, read it, lifted her eyes from it to her ladies' faces and told them that her number in the French lottery had come out. She had won ten thousand francs.

The news made such an impression on the two sisters that for a full minute 75 they could not speak a word. They themselves were used to receiving their modest pension in small instalments; it was difficult to them even to imagine the sum of ten thousand francs in a pile. Then they pressed Babette's hand, their own hands trembling a little. They had never before pressed the hand of a person who the moment before had come into possession of ten thousand francs.

After a while they realized that the happenings concerned themselves as well 76 as Babette. The country of France, they felt, was slowly rising before their servant's horizon, and correspondingly their own existence was sinking beneath their feet. The ten thousand francs which made her rich—how poor did they not make the house she had served! One by one old forgotten cares and worries began to peep out at them from the four corners of the kitchen. The congratulations died on their lips, and the two pious women were ashamed of their own silence.

During the following days they announced the news to their friends with 77 joyous faces, but it did them good to see these friends' faces grow sad as they listened to them. Nobody, it was felt in the Brotherhood, could really blame Babette: birds will return to their nests and human beings to the country of their birth. But did that good and faithful servant realize that in going away from Berlevaag she would be leaving many old and poor people in distress? Their little sisters would have no more time for the sick and sorrowful. Indeed, indeed, lotteries were ungodly affairs.

In due time the money arrived through offices in Christiania and Berlevaag. 78
The two ladies helped Babette to count it, and gave her a box to keep it in. They
handled, and became familiar with, the ominous bits of paper.

They dared not question Babette upon the date of her departure. Dared 79
they hope that she would remain with them over the fifteenth of December?

The mistresses had never been quite certain how much of their private con- 80
versation the cook followed or understood. So they were surprised when on a
September evening Babette came into the drawing room, more humble or subdued than they had ever seen her, to ask a favor. She begged them, she said, to
let her cook a celebration dinner on the Dean's birthday.

The ladies had not intended to have any dinner at all. A very plain supper 81
with a cup of coffee was the most sumptuous meal to which they had ever asked
any guest to sit down. But Babette's dark eyes were as eager and pleading as a
dog's; they agreed to let her have her way. At this the cook's face lighted up.

But she had more to say. She wanted, she said, to cook a French dinner, a 82
real French dinner, for this one time. Martine and Philippa looked at each
other. They did not like the idea; they felt that they did not know what it might
imply. But the very strangeness of the request disarmed them. They had no arguments wherewith to meet the proposition of cooking a real French dinner.

Babette drew a long sigh of happiness, but still she did not move. She had 83
one more prayer to make. She begged that her mistresses would allow her to
pay for the French dinner with her own money.

"No, Babette!" the ladies exclaimed. How could she imagine such a thing? 84
Did she believe that they would allow her to spend her precious money on food
and drink—or on them? No, Babette, indeed.

Babette took a step forward. There was something formidable in the move, 85
like a wave rising. Had she stepped forth like this, in 1871, to plant a red flag on
a barricade? She spoke, in her queer Norwegian, with classical French eloquence. Her voice was like a song.

Ladies! Had she ever, during twelve years, asked you a favor? No! And why 86
not? Ladies, you who say your prayers every day, can you imagine what it means
to a human heart to have no prayer to make? What would Babette have had to
pray for? Nothing! Tonight she had a prayer to make, from the bottom of her
heart. Do you not then feel tonight, my ladies, that it becomes you to grant
it her, with such joy as that with which the good God has granted you
your own?

The ladies for a while said nothing. Babette was right; it was her first request 87
these twelve years; very likely it would be her last. They thought the matter over.
After all, they told themselves, their cook was now better off than they, and a
dinner could make no difference to a person who owned ten thousand francs.

Their consent in the end completely changed Babette. They saw that as a 88
young woman she had been beautiful. And they wondered whether in this hour
they themselves had not, for the very first time, become to her the "good people" of Achille Papin's letter.

VII. The Turtle

In November Babette went for a journey.   89

She had preparations to make, she told her mistresses, and would need a   90
leave of a week or ten days. Her nephew, who had once got her to Christiania,
was still sailing to that town; she must see him and talk things over with him.
Babette was a bad sailor; she had spoken of her one sea-voyage, from France to
Norway, as of the most horrible experience of her life. Now she was strangely
collected; the ladies felt that her heart was already in France.

After ten days she came back to Berlevaag.   91

Had she got things arranged as she wished? the ladies asked. Yes, she an-   92
swered, she had seen her nephew and given him a list of the goods which he was
to bring her from France. To Martine and Philippa this was a dark saying, but
they did not care to talk of her departure, so they asked her no more questions.

Babette was somewhat nervous during the next weeks. But one December   93
day she triumphantly announced to her mistresses that the goods had come to
Christiania, had been transshipped there, and on this very day had arrived at
Berlevaag. She had, she added, engaged an old man with a wheelbarrow to have
them conveyed from the harbor to the house.

But what goods, Babette? the ladies asked. Why, Mesdames, Babette replied,   94
the ingredients for the birthday dinner. Praise be to God, they had all arrived in
good condition from Paris.

By this time Babette, like the bottled demon of the fairy tale, had swelled   95
and grown to such dimensions that her mistresses felt small before her. They
now saw the French dinner coming upon them, a thing of incalculable nature
and range. But they had never in their life broken a promise; they gave themselves into their cook's hands.

All the same when Martine saw a barrow load of bottles wheeled into the   96
kitchen, she stood still. She touched the bottles and lifted up one. "What is there
in this bottle, Babette?" she asked in a low voice. "Not wine?" "Wine, Madame!"
Babette answered. "No, Madame. It is a Clos Vougeot 1846!" After a moment
she added: "From Philippe, in Rue Montorgueil!" Martine had never suspected
that wines could have names to them, and was put to silence.

Late in the evening she opened the door to a ring, and was once more faced   97
with the wheelbarrow, this time with a red-haired sailor-boy behind it, as if the
old man had by this time been worn out. The youth grinned at her as he lifted a
big, undefinable object from the barrow. In the light of the lamp it looked like
some greenish-black stone, but when set down on the kitchen floor it suddenly
shot out a snake-like head and moved it slightly from side to side. Martine had
seen pictures of tortoises, and had even as a child owned a pet tortoise, but this
thing was monstrous in size and terrible to behold. She backed out of the
kitchen without a word.

She dared not tell her sister what she had seen. She passed an almost sleep-   98
less night; she thought of her father and felt that on his very birthday she and
her sister were lending his house to a witches' sabbath. When at last she fell

asleep she had a terrible dream, in which she saw Babette poisoning the old Brothers and Sisters, Philippa and herself.

Early in the morning she got up, put on her gray cloak and went out in the dark street. She walked from house to house, opened her heart to her Brothers and Sisters, and confessed her guilt. She and Philippa, she said, had meant no harm; they had granted their servant a prayer and had not foreseen what might come of it. Now she could not tell what, on her father's birthday, her guests would be given to eat or drink. She did not actually mention the turtle, but it was present in her face and voice. 99

The old people, as has already been told, had all known Martine and Philippa as little girls; they had seen them cry bitterly over a broken doll. Martine's tears brought tears into their own eyes. They gathered in the afternoon and talked the problem over. 100

Before they again parted they promised one another that for their little sisters' sake they would, on the great day, be silent upon all matters of food and drink. Nothing that might be set before them, be it even frogs or snails, should wring a word from their lips. 101

"Even so," said a white-bearded Brother, "the tongue is a little member and boasteth great things. The tongue can no man tame; it is an unruly evil, full of deadly poison. On the day of our master we will cleanse our tongues of all taste and purify them of all delight or disgust of the senses, keeping and preserving them for the higher things of praise and thanksgiving." 102

So few things ever happened in the quiet existence of the Berlevaag brotherhood that they were at this moment deeply moved and elevated. They shook hands on their vow, and it was to them as if they were doing so before the face of their Master. 103

VIII. The Hymn

On Sunday morning it began to snow. The white flakes fell fast and thick; the small windowpanes of the yellow house became pasted with snow. 104

Early in the day a groom from Fossum brought the two sisters a note. Old Mrs. Loewenhielm still resided in her country house. She was now ninety years old and stone-deaf, and she had lost all sense of smell or taste. But she had been one of the Dean's first supporters, and neither her infirmity nor the sledge journey would keep her from doing honor to his memory. Now, she wrote, her nephew, General Lorens Loewenhielm, had unexpectedly come on a visit; he had spoken with deep veneration of the Dean, and she begged permission to bring him with her. It would do him good, for the dear boy seemed to be in somewhat low spirits. 105

Martine and Philippa at this remembered the young officer and his visits; it relieved their present anxiety to talk of old happy days. They wrote back that General Loewenhielm would be welcome. They also called in Babette to inform her that they would now be twelve for dinner; they added that their latest guest 106 had lived in Paris for several years. Babette seemed pleased with the news, and assured them that there would be food enough.

The hostesses made their little preparations in the sitting room. They dared 107 not set foot in the kitchen, for Babette had mysteriously nosed out a cook's mate from a ship in the harbor—the same boy, Martine realized, who had brought in the turtle—to assist her in the kitchen and to wait at table, and now the dark woman and the red-haired boy, like some witch with her familiar spirit, had taken possession of these regions. The ladies could not tell what fires had been burning or what cauldrons bubbling there from before daybreak.

Table linen and plate had been magically mangled and polished, glasses and 108 decanters brought, Babette only knew from where. The Dean's house did not possess twelve dining-room chairs, the long horsehair-covered sofa had been moved from the parlor to the dining room, and the parlor, ever sparsely furnished, now looked strangely bare and big without it.

Martine and Philippa did their best to embellish the domain left to them. 109 Whatever troubles might be in wait for their guests, in any case they should not be cold; all day the sisters fed the towering old stove with birch-knots. They hung a garland of juniper round their father's portrait on the wall, and placed candlesticks on their mother's small working table beneath it; they burned juniper-twigs to make the room smell nice. The while they wondered if in this weather the sledge from Fossum would get through. In the end they put on their old black best frocks and their confirmation gold crosses. They sat down, folded their hands in their laps and committed themselves unto God.

The old Brothers and Sisters arrived in small groups and entered the room 110 slowly and solemnly.

This low room with its bare floor and scanty furniture was dear to the 111 Dean's disciples. Outside its windows lay the great world. Seen from in here the great world in its winter-whiteness was ever prettily bordered in pink, blue and red by the row of hyacinths on the window-sills. And in summer, when the windows were open, the great world had a softly moving frame of white muslin curtains to it.

Tonight the guests were met on the doorstep with warmth and sweet smell, 112 and they were looking into the face of their beloved Master, wreathed with evergreen. Their hearts like their numb fingers thawed.

One very old Brother, after a few moments' silence, in his trembling voice 113 struck up one of the Master's own hymns:

"Jerusalem, my happy home
name ever dear to me . . ."

One by one the other voices fell in, thin quivering women's voices, ancient 114 seafaring Brothers' deep growls, and above them all Philippa's clear soprano, a little worn with age but still angelic. Unwittingly the choir had seized one another's hands. They sang the hymn to the end, but could not bear to cease and joined in another:

"Take not thought for food or raiment
careful one, so anxiously . . ."

The mistresses of the house somewhat reassured by it, the words of the 115
third verse:

"Wouldst thou give a stone, a reptile
to thy pleading child for food? . . ."

went straight to Martine's heart and inspired her with hope.

In the middle of this hymn sledge bells were heard outside; the guests from 116
Fossum had arrived.

Martine and Philippa went to receive them and saw them into the parlor. 117
Mrs. Loewenhielm with age had become quite small, her face colorless like
parchment, and very still. By her side General Loewenhielm, tall, broad and
ruddy, in his bright uniform, his breast covered with decorations, strutted and
shone like an ornamental bird, a golden pheasant or a peacock, in this sedate
party of black crows and jackdaws.

IX. *General Loewenhielm*

General Loewenhielm had been driving from Fossum to Berlevaag in a strange 118
mood. He had not visited this part of the country for thirty years. He had come
now to get a rest from his busy life at Court, and he had found no rest. The old
house of Fossum was peaceful enough and seemed somehow pathetically small
after the Tuileries and the Winter Palace. But it held one disquieting figure:
young Lieutenant Loewenhielm walked in its rooms.

General Loewenhielm saw the handsome, slim figure pass close by him. And 119
as he passed the boy gave the elder man a short glance and a smile, the haughty,
arrogant smile which youth gives to age. The General might have smiled back,
kindly and a little sadly, as age smiles at youth, if it had not been that he was
really in no mood to smile; he was, as his aunt had written, in low spirits.

General Loewenhielm had obtained everything that he had striven for in 120
life and was admired and envied by everyone. Only he himself knew of a queer
fact, which jarred with his prosperous existence: that he was not perfectly
happy. Something was wrong somewhere, and he carefully felt his mental self
all over, as one feels a finger over to determine the place of a deep-seated, invisible thorn.

He was in high favor with royalty, he had done well in his calling, he had 121
friends everywhere. The thorn sat in none of these places.

His wife was a brilliant woman and still good-looking. Perhaps she ne- 122
glected her own house a little for her visits and parties; she changed her servants every three months and the General's meals at home were served
unpunctually. The General, who valued good food highly in life, here felt a

slight bitterness against the lady, and secretly blamed her for the indigestion from which he sometimes suffered. Still the thorn was not here either.

Nay, but an absurd thing had lately been happening to General Loewen-   123
hielm: he would find himself worrying about his immortal soul. Did he have any reason for doing so? He was a moral person, loyal to his king, his wife and his friends, an example to everybody. But there were moments when it seemed to him that the world was not a moral, but a mystic, concern. He looked into the mirror, examined the row of decorations on his breast and sighed to himself: "Vanity, vanity, all is vanity!"

The strange meeting at Fossum had compelled him to make out the   124
balance-sheet of his life.

Young Lorens Loewenhielm had attracted dreams and fancies as a flower at-   125
tracts bees and butterflies. He had fought to free himself of them; he had fled and they had followed. He had been scared of the Huldre of the family legend and had declined her invitation to come into the mountain; he had firmly re-fused the gift of second sight.

The elderly Lorens Loewenhielm found himself wishing that one little   126
dream would come his way, and a gray moth of dusk look him up before night-fall. He found himself longing for the faculty of second sight, as a blind man will long for the normal faculty of vision.

Can the sum of a row of victories in many years and in many countries be a   127
defeat? General Loewenhielm had fulfilled Lieutenant Loewenhielm's wishes and had more than satisfied his ambitions. It might be held that he had gained the whole world. And it had come to this, that the stately, worldly-wise older man now turned toward the naïve young figure to ask him, gravely, even bit-terly, in what he had profited? Somewhere something had been lost.

When Mrs. Loewenhielm had told her nephew of the Dean's anniversary   128
and he had made up his mind to go with her to Berlevaag, his decision had not been an ordinary acceptance of a dinner invitation.

He would, he resolved, tonight make up his account with young Lorens   129
Loewenhielm, who had felt himself to be a shy and sorry figure in the house of the Dean, and who in the end had shaken its dust off his riding boots. He would let the youth prove to him, once and for all, that thirty-one years ago he had made the right choice. The low rooms, the haddock and the glass of water on the table before him should all be called in to bear evidence that in their milieu the existence of Lorens Loewenhielm would very soon have become sheer misery.

He let his mind stray far away. In Paris he had once won a *concours hippique*   130
and had been feted by high French cavalry officers, princes and dukes among them. A dinner had been given in his honor at the finest restaurant of the city. Opposite him at table was a noble lady, a famous beauty whom he had long been courting. In the midst of dinner she had lifted her dark velvet eyes above the rim of her champagne glass and without words had promised to make him happy. In the sledge he now all of a sudden remembered that he had then, for a second, seen Martine's face before him and had rejected it. For a while he lis-

tened to the tinkling of the sledge bells, then he smiled a little as he reflected how he would tonight come to dominate the conversation round that same table by which young Lorens Loewenhielm had sat mute.

Large snowflakes fell densely; behind the sledge the tracks were wiped out 131 quickly. General Loewenhielm sat immovable by the side of his aunt, his chin sunk in the high fur collar of his coat.

X. *Babette's Dinner*

As Babette's red-haired familiar opened the door to the dining room, and the 132 guests slowly crossed the threshold, they let go one another's hands and became silent. But the silence was sweet, for in spirit they still held hands and were still singing.

Babette had set a row of candles down the middle of the table: the small 133 flames shone on the black coats and frocks and on the one scarlet uniform, and were reflected in clear, moist eyes.

General Loewenhielm saw Martine's face in the candlelight as he had seen it 134 when the two parted, thirty years ago. What traces would thirty years of Berlevaag life have left on it? The golden hair was now streaked with silver; the flowerlike face had slowly been turned into alabaster. But how serene was the forehead, how quietly trustful the eyes, how pure and sweet the mouth, as if no hasty word had ever passed its lips.

When all were seated, the eldest member of the congregation said grace in 135 the Dean's own words:

> *"May my food my body maintain,*
> *may my body my soul sustain,*
> *may my soul in deed and word*
> *give thanks for all things to the Lord."*

At the word of "food" the guests, with their old heads bent over their folded 136 hands, remembered how they had vowed not to utter a word about the subject, and in their hearts they reinforced the vow: they would not even give it a thought! They were sitting down to a meal, well, so had people done at the wedding of Cana. And grace has chosen to manifest itself there, in the very wine, as fully as anywhere.

Babette's boy filled a small glass before each of the party. They lifted it to 137 their lips gravely, in confirmation of their resolution.

General Loewenhielm, somewhat suspicious of his wine, took a sip of it, 138 startled, raised the glass first to his nose and then to his eyes, and sat it down bewildered. "This is very strange!" he thought. "Amontillado! And the finest Amontillado that I have ever tasted." After a moment, in order to test his senses, he took a small spoonful of his soup, took a second spoonful and laid down his spoon. "This is exceedingly strange!" he said to himself. "For surely I am eating turtle-soup—and what turtle-soup!" He was seized by a queer kind of panic and emptied his glass.

Usually in Berlevaag people did not speak much while they were eating. But somehow this evening tongues had been loosened. An old Brother told the story of his first meeting with the Dean. Another went through that sermon which sixty years ago had brought about his conversion. An aged woman, the one to whom Martine had first confided her distress, reminded her friends how in all afflictions any Brother or Sister was ready to share the burden of any other. 139

General Loewenhielm, who was to dominate the conversation of the dinner table, related how the Dean's collection of sermons was a favorite book of the Queen's. But as a new dish was served he was silenced. "Incredible!" he told himself. "It is Blinis Demidoff!" He looked round at his fellow-diners. They were all quietly eating their Blinis Demidoff without any sign of either surprise or approval, as if they had been doing so every day for thirty years. 140

A Sister on the other side of the table opened on the subject of strange happenings which had taken place while the Dean was still amongst his children, and which one might venture to call miracles. Did they remember, she asked, the time when he had promised a Christmas sermon in the village the other side of the fjord? For a fortnight the weather had been so bad that no skipper or fisherman would risk the crossing. The villagers were giving up hope, but the Dean told them that if no boat would take him, he would come to them walking upon the waves. And behold! Three days before Christmas the storm stopped, hard frost set in, and the fjord froze from shore to shore—and this was a thing which had not happened within the memory of man! 141

The boy once more filled the glasses. This time the Brothers and Sisters knew that what they were given to drink was not wine, for it sparkled. It must be some kind of lemonade. The lemonade agreed with their exalted state of mind and seemed to lift them off the ground, into a higher and purer sphere. 142

General Loewenhielm again set down his glass, turned to his neighbor on the right and said to him: "But surely this is a Veuve Cliquot 1860?" His neighbor looked at him kindly, smiled at him and made a remark about the weather. 143

Babette's boy had his instructions; he filled the glasses of the Brotherhood only once, but he refilled the General's glass as soon as it was emptied. The General emptied it quickly time after time. For how is a man of sense to behave when he cannot trust his senses? It is better to be drunk than mad. 144

Most often the people in Berlevaag during the course of a good meal would come to feel a little heavy. Tonight it was not so. The *convives* grew lighter in weight and lighter of heart the more they ate and drank. They no longer needed to remind themselves of their vow. It was, they realized, when man has not only altogether forgotten but has firmly renounced all ideas of food and drink that he eats and drinks in the right spirit. 145

General Loewenhielm stopped eating and sat immovable. Once more he was carried back to that dinner in Paris of which he had thought in the sledge. An incredibly recherché and palatable dish had been served there; he had asked 146 its name from his fellow diner, Colonel Galliffet, and the Colonel had smilingly told him that it was named "Cailles en Sarcophage." He had further told him that the dish had been invented by the chef of the very café in which they were dining, a person known all over Paris as the greatest culinary genius of the age, and—most surprisingly—a woman! "And indeed," said Colonel Galliffet, "this woman is now turning a dinner at the Café Anglais into a kind of love affair—into a love affair of the noble and romantic category in which one no longer distinguishes between bodily and spiritual appetite or satiety! I have, before now, fought a duel for the sake of a fair lady. For no woman in all Paris, my young friend, would I more willingly shed my blood!" General Loewenhielm turned to his neighbor on the left and said to him: "But this is Cailles en Sarcophage!" The neighbor, who had been listening to the description of a miracle, looked at him absent-mindedly, then nodded his head and answered: "Yes, Yes, certainly. What else would it be?"

From the Master's miracles the talk round the table had turned to the 147 smaller miracles of kindliness and helpfulness daily performed by his daughters. The old Brother who had first struck up the hymn quoted the Dean's saying: "The only things which we may take with us from our life on earth are those which we have given away!" The guests smiled—what nabobs would not the poor, simple maidens become in the next world!

General Loewenhielm no longer wondered at anything. When a few min- 148 utes later he saw grapes, peaches and fresh figs before him, he laughed to his neighbor across the table and remarked: "Beautiful grapes!" His neighbor replied: " 'And they came onto the brook of Eshcol, and cut down a branch with one cluster of grapes. And they bare it two upon a staff.' "

Then the General felt that the time had come to make a speech. He rose and 149 stood up very straight.

Nobody else at the dinner table had stood up to speak. The old people lifted 150 their eyes to the face above them in high, happy expectation. They were used to seeing sailors and vagabonds dead drunk with the crass gin of the country, but they did not recognize in a warrior and courtier the intoxication brought about by the noblest wine of the world.

XI. General Loewenhielm's Speech

"Mercy and truth, my friends, have met together," said the General. "Righteous- 151 ness and bliss shall kiss one another."

He spoke in a clear voice which had been trained in drill grounds and had 152 echoed sweetly in royal halls, and yet he was speaking in a manner so new to himself and so strangely moving that after his first sentence he had to make a pause. For he was in the habit of forming his speeches with care, conscious of his purpose, but here, in the midst of the Dean's simple congregation, it was as if the whole figure of General Loewenhielm, his breast covered with decorations, were but a mouthpiece for a message which meant to be brought forth.

"Man, my friends," said General Loewenhielm, "is frail and foolish. We have 153
all of us been told that grace is to be found in the universe. But in our human
foolishness and short-sightedness we imagine divine grace to be finite. For this
reason we tremble . . ." Never till now had the General stated that he trembled;
he was genuinely surprised and even shocked at hearing his own voice proclaim
the fact. "We tremble before making our choice in life, and after having made it
again tremble in fear of having chosen wrong. But the moment comes when
our eyes are opened, and we see and realize that grace is infinite. Grace, my
friends, demands nothing from us but that we shall await it with confidence
and acknowledge it in gratitude. Grace, brothers, makes no conditions and singles out none of us in particular; grace takes us all to its bosom and proclaims
general amnesty. See! that which we have chosen is given us, and that which we
have refused is, also and at the same time, granted us. Ay, that which we have rejected is poured upon us abundantly. For mercy and truth have met together,
and righteousness and bliss have kissed one another!"

The Brothers and Sisters had not altogether understood the General's 154
speech, but his collected and inspired face and the sound of well-known and
cherished words had seized and moved all hearts. In this way, after thirty-one
years, General Loewenhielm succeeded in dominating the conversation at the
Dean's dinner table.

Of what happened later in the evening nothing definite can here be stated. 155
None of the guests later on had any clear remembrance of it. They only knew
that the rooms had been filled with a heavenly light, as if a number of small halos had blended into one glorious radiance. Taciturn old people received the
gift of tongues; ears that for years had been almost deaf were opened to it. Time
itself had merged into eternity. Long after midnight the windows of the house
shone like gold, and golden song flowed out into the winter air.

The two old women who had once slandered each other now in their hearts 156
went back a long way, past the evil period in which they had been stuck, to those
days of their early girlhood when together they had been preparing for confirmation and hand in hand had filled the roads round Berlevaag with singing. A
Brother in the congregation gave another a knock in the ribs, like a rough caress
between boys, and cried out: "You cheated me on that timber, you old
scoundrel!" The Brother thus addressed almost collapsed in a heavenly burst of
laughter, but tears ran from his eyes. "Yes, I did so, beloved Brother," he answered. "I did so." Skipper Halvorsen and Madam Oppegaarden suddenly found
themselves close together in a corner and gave one another that long, long kiss,
for which the secret uncertain love affair of their youth had never left them time.

The old Dean's flock were humble people. When later in life they thought of 157
this evening it never occurred to any of them that they might have been exalted
by their own merit. They realized that the infinite grace of which General
Loewenheilm had spoken had been allotted to them, and they did not even
wonder at the fact, for it had been but the fulfillment of an ever-present hope.
The vain illusions of this earth had dissolved before their eyes like smoke, and
they had seen the universe as it really is. They had been given one hour of the
millennium.

Old Mrs. Loewenheilm was the first to leave. Her nephew accompanied her,   158
and their hostesses lighted them out. While Philippa was helping the old lady
into her many wraps, the General seized Martine's hand and held it for a long
time without a word. At last he said:

"I have been with you every day of my life. You know, do you not, that it has   159
been so?"

"Yes," said Martine, "I know that it has been so."   160

"And," he continued, "I shall be with you every day that is left to me. Every   161
evening I shall sit down, if not in the flesh, which means nothing, in spirit,
which is all, to dine with you, just like tonight. For tonight I have learned, dear
sister, that in this world anything is possible."

"Yes, it is so, dear brother," said Martine. "In this world anything is possible."   162
Upon this they parted.   163

When at last the company broke up it had ceased to snow. The town and the   164
mountains lay in white, unearthly splendor and the sky was bright with thousands of stars. In the street the snow was lying so deep that it had become difficult to walk. The guests from the yellow house wavered on their feet, staggered,
sat down abruptly or fell forward on their knees and hands and were covered
with snow, as if they had indeed had their sins washed white as wool, and in this
regained innocent attire were gamboling like little lambs. It was, to each of
them, blissful to have become as a small child; it was also a blessed joke to watch
old Brothers and Sisters, who had been taking themselves so seriously, in this
kind of celestial second childhood. They stumbled and got up, walked on or
stood still, bodily as well as spiritually hand in hand, at moments performing
the great chain of a beatified *lanciers*.

"Bless you, bless you, bless you," like an echo of the harmony of the spheres   165
rang on all sides.

Martine and Philippa stood for a long time on the stone steps outside the   166
house. They did not feel the cold. "The stars have come nearer," said Philippa.

"They will come every night," said Martine quietly. "Quite possibly it will   167
never snow again."

In this, however, she was mistaken. An hour later it again began to snow,   168
and such a heavy snowfall had never been known in Berlevaag. The next morning people could hardly push open their doors against the tall snowdrifts. The
windows of the houses were so thickly covered with snow, it was told for years
afterwards, that many good citizens of the town did not realize that daybreak
had come, but slept on till late in the afternoon.

XII. *The Great Artist*

When Martine and Philippa locked the door they remembered Babette. A little   169
wave of tenderness and pity swept through them: Babette alone had had no
share in the bliss of the evening.

So they went out into the kitchen, and Martine said to Babette: "It was quite   170
a nice dinner, Babette."

Their hearts suddenly filled with gratitude. They realized that none of their 171
guests had said a single word about the food. Indeed, try as they might, they
could not themselves remember any of the dishes which had been served. Martine bethought herself of the turtle. It had not appeared at all, and now seemed
very vague and far away; it was quite possible that it had been nothing but a
nightmare.

Babette sat on the chopping block, surrounded by more black and greasy 172
pots and pans than her mistresses had ever seen in their life. She was as white
and as deadly exhausted as on the night when she first appeared and had
fainted on their doorstep.

After a long time she looked straight at them and said: "I was once cook at 173
the Café Anglais."

Martine said again: "They all thought that it was a nice dinner." And when 174
Babette did not answer a word she added: "We will all remember this evening
when you have gone back to Paris, Babette."

Babette said: "I am not going back to Paris."   175

"You are not going back to Paris?" Martine exclaimed.   176

"No," said Babette. "What will I do in Paris? They have all gone. I have lost 177
them all, Mesdames."

The sisters' thoughts went to Monsieur Hersant and his son, and they said: 178
"Oh, my poor Babette."

"Yes, they have all gone," said Babette. "The Duke of Morny, the Duke of 179
Decazes, Prince Narishkine, General Galliffet, Aurélian Scholl, Paul Daru, the
Princesse Pauline! All!"

The strange names and titles of people lost to Babette faintly confused the 180
two ladies, but there was such an infinite perspective of tragedy in her announcement that in their responsive state of mind they felt her losses as their
own, and their eyes filled with tears.

At the end of another long silence Babette suddenly smiled slightly at them 181
and said: "And how would I go back to Paris, Mesdames? I have no money."

"No money?" the sisters cried as with one mouth.   182

"No," said Babette.   183

"But the ten thousand francs?" the sisters asked in a horrified gasp.   184

"The ten thousand francs have been spent, Mesdames," said Babette.   185

The sisters sat down. For a full minute they could not speak.   186

"But ten thousand francs?" Martine slowly whispered.   187

"What will you, Mesdames," said Babette with great dignity. "A dinner for 188
twelve at the Café Anglais would cost ten thousand francs."

The ladies still did not find a word to say. The piece of news was incompre- 189
hensible to them, but then many things tonight in one way or another had been
beyond comprehension.

Martine remembered a tale told by a friend of her father's who had been a 190
missionary in Africa. He had saved the life of an old chief's favorite wife, and to
show his gratitude the chief had treated him to a rich meal. Only long afterwards the missionary learned from his own black servant that what he had par-

taken of was a small fat grandchild of the chief's, cooked in honor of the great Christian medicine man. She shuddered.

But Philippa's heart was melting in her bosom. It seemed that an unforget- 191 table evening was to be finished off with an unforgettable proof of human loyalty and self-sacrifice.

"Dear Babette," she said softly, "you ought not to have given away all you 192 had for our sake."

Babette gave her mistress a deep glance, a strange glance. Was there not pity, 193 even scorn, at the bottom of it?

"For your sake?" she replied. "No. For my own." 194

She rose from the chopping block and stood up before the two sisters. 195

"I am a great artist!" she said. 196

She waited a moment and then repeated: "I am a great artist, Mesdames." 197

Again for a long time there was deep silence in the kitchen. 198

Then Martine said: "So you will be poor now all your life, Babette?" 199

"Poor?" said Babette. She smiled as if to herself. "No, I shall never be poor. I 200 told you that I am a great artist. A great artist, Mesdames, is never poor. We have something, Mesdames, of which other people know nothing."

While the elder sister found nothing more to say, in Philippa's heart deep, 201 forgotten chords vibrated. For she had heard, before now, long ago, of the Café Anglais. She had heard, before now, long ago, the names on Babette's tragic list. She rose and took a step toward her servant.

"But all those people whom you have mentioned," she said, "those princes 202 and great people of Paris whom you named, Babette? You yourself fought against them. You were a Communard! The General you named had your husband and son shot! How can you grieve over them?"

Babette's dark eyes met Philippa's. 203

"Yes," she said, "I was a Communard. Thanks be to God, I was a Commu- 204 nard! And those people whom I named, Mesdames, were evil and cruel. They let the people of Paris starve; they oppressed and wronged the poor. Thanks be to God, I stood upon a barricade; I loaded the gun for my menfolk! But all the same, Mesdames, I shall not go back to Paris, now that those people of whom I have spoken are no longer there."

She stood immovable, lost in thought. 205

"You see, Mesdames," she said, at last, "those people belonged to me, they 206 were mine. They had been brought up and trained, with greater expense than you, my little ladies, could ever imagine or believe, to understand what a great artist I am. I could make them happy. When I did my very best I could make them perfectly happy."

She paused for a moment. 207

"It was like that with Monsieur Papin too," she said. 208

"With Monsieur Papin?" Philippa asked. 209

"Yes, with your Monsieur Papin, my poor lady," said Babette. "He told me so 210 himself: 'It is terrible and unbearable to an artist,' he said, 'to be encouraged to do, to be applauded for doing, his second best.' He said: 'Through all the world there goes one long cry from the heart of the artist: Give me leave to do my utmost!'"

Philippa went up to Babette and put her arms round her. She felt the cook's   211
body like a marble monument against her own, but she herself shook and trembled from head to foot.

For a while she could not speak. Then she whispered: 212

"Yet this is not the end! I feel, Babette, that this is not the end. In Paradise   213
you will be the great artist that God meant you to be! Ah!" she added, the tears streaming down her cheeks. "Ah, how you will enchant the angels!"

ACTIVITIES FOR WRITING AND DISCUSSION

1. What does Babette's feast *do* to those who attend it? How do they behave, talk, and interact? Why? Think of any notable "feasts" or other social gatherings in your own past that affected you and/or others in a similar way. Tell the story of one such "feast" or gathering.

2. Babette and the two sisters differ radically in many ways, yet they live together peacefully for twelve years.
   a. Review the story for any clues that might explain this peaceful coexistence. How or why are these very different personalities able to get along so well?
   b. Relate any stories, from your own experience, of opposite personalities living together harmoniously.

3. The meal and the evening seem to have exhilarated everyone, yet in the end Babette announces that she didn't create the feast for the two sisters or their guests but for her own sake, "I am a great artist!"
   a. Do Babette's motives cheapen her deed? Why or why not?
   b. In the **persona** of Babette, write a **monologue** or diary entry in which you expand your thoughts about the feast and why you prepared it, or
   c. In the persona of some other "artist"—real or imagined—write about what motivates you in your work.

4. Isak Dinesen published "Babette's Feast" in a volume of stories entitled *Anecdotes of Destiny.* The word "destiny" suggests a sense of a governing fatality in people's lives, and various characters in this story seem to have missed or lost opportunities for more "exciting" lives. For instance, Philippa could have joined Monsieur Papin and become a famous singer; Martine could have married the young Lorens, had children, and (presumably) lived happily ever after. Babette herself lost her position as a famous Parisian chef to live among a people with no taste for food.
   a. Describe the feelings you have about "destiny" when you finish the story. Do you find yourself thinking, "If only things had been different"? Why or why not?

b. Examine the pattern of events in your own life. Do you sense a "right-ness" about that pattern? Do you wish something had been "different"?

5. Is the feast **symbolic** in any ways? If so, how?

Naguib Mahfouz (b. 1911)

Zaabalawi

Finally I became convinced that I had to find Sheikh Zaabalawi.   1
The first time I had heard of his name had been in a song: 2

"What's wrong with the world, O Zaabalawi?
They've turned it upside down and made it insipid."

It had been a popular song in my childhood and one day it had occurred to   3
me—in the way children have of asking endless questions—to ask my father
about him.
"Who is Zaabalawi, father?"   4
He had looked at me hesitantly as though doubting my ability to under-   5
stand the answer. However, he had replied:
"May his blessing descend upon you, he's a true saint of God, a remover of   6
worries and troubles. Were it not for him I would have died miserably—"
In the years that followed I heard him many a time sing the praises of this   7
good saint and speak of the miracles he performed. The days passed and
brought with them many illnesses from each one of which I was able, without
too much trouble and at a cost I could afford, to find a cure, until I became afflicted with that illness for which no one possesses a remedy. When I had tried
everything in vain and was overcome by despair, I remembered by chance what
I had heard in my childhood: Why, I asked myself, should I not seek out Sheikh
Zaabalawi? I recollected that my father had said that he had made his acquaintance in Khan Gaafar at the house of Sheikh Kamar, one of those sheikhs who
practised law in the religious courts, and I therefore took myself off to his
house. Wishing to make sure that he was still living there, I made enquiries of a
vendor of beans whom I found in the lower part of the house.
"Sheikh Kamar!" he said, looking at me in amazement. "He left the quarter   8
ages ago. They say he's now living in Garden City and has his office in Al-
Azhaar Square."
I looked up the office address in the telephone book and immediately set off   9
to the Chamber of Commerce Building, where it was located. On asking to see
him I was ushered into a room just as a beautiful woman with a most intoxicat-
ing perfume was leaving it. The man received me with a smile and motioned

me towards a fine leather-upholstered chair. My feet were conscious of the costly lushness of the carpet despite the thick soles of my shoes. The man wore a lounge suit and was smoking a cigar; his manner of sitting was that of someone well satisfied both with himself and his worldly possessions. The look of warm welcome he gave me left no doubt in my mind that he thought me a prospective client, and I felt acutely embarrassed at encroaching upon his valuable time.

"Welcome!" he said, prompting me to speak.   10

"I am the son of your old friend Sheikh Ali al-Tatawi," I answered so as to   11
put an end to my equivocal position.

A certain languor was apparent in the glance he cast at me; the languor was 12
not total in that he had not as yet lost all hope in me.

"God rest his soul," he said. "He was a fine man."   13

The very pain that had driven me to go there now prevailed upon me to   14
stay.

"He told me," I continued, "of a devout saint named Zaabalawi whom he   15
met at Your Honour's. I am in need of him, sir, if he be still in the land of the
living."

The languor became firmly entrenched in his eyes and it would have come   16
as no surprise to me if he had shown the door to both me and my father's
memory.

"That," he said in the tone of one who has made up his mind to terminate   17
the conversation, "was a very long time ago and I scarcely recall him now."

Rising to my feet so as to put his mind at rest regarding my intention of go- 18
ing, I asked:

"Was he really a saint?"   19

"We used to regard him as a man of miracles."   20

"And where could I find him today?" I asked, making another move towards   21
the door.

"To the best of my knowledge he was living in the Birgawi Residence in al-   22
Azhar," and he applied himself to some papers on his desk with a resolute
movement that indicated he wouldn't open his mouth again. I bowed my
head in thanks, apologized several times for disturbing him and left the office,
my head so buzzing with embarrassment that I was oblivious to all sounds
around me.

I went to the Birgawi Residence which was situated in a thickly populated   23
quarter. I found that time had so eaten into the building that nothing was left of
it save an antiquated façade and a courtyard which, despite it being supposedly
in the charge of a caretaker, was being used as a rubbish dump. A small insignificant fellow, a mere prologue to a man, was using the covered entrance as a
place for the sale of old books on theology and mysticism.

On my asking him about Zaabalawi, he peered at me through narrow, in-   24
flamed eyes and said in amazement:

"Zaabalawi! Good heavens, what a time ago that was! Certainly he used to   25
live in this house when it was livable in, and many was the time he would sit

with me talking of bygone days and I would be blessed by his holy presence. Where, though, is Zaabalawi today?"

He shrugged his shoulders sorrowfully and soon left me to attend to an ap- 26 proaching customer. I proceeded to make enquiries of many shopkeepers in the district. While I found that a large number of them had never even heard of him, some, though recalling nostalgically the pleasant times they had spent with him, were ignorant of his present whereabouts, while others openly made fun of him, labelled him a charlatan, and advised me to put myself in the hands of a doctor—as though I had not already done so. I therefore had no alternative but to return disconsolately home.

With the passing of the days like motes in the air my pains grew so severe 27 that I was sure I would not be able to hold out much longer. Once again I fell to wondering about Zaabalawi and clutching at the hopes his venerable name stirred within me. Then it occurred to me to seek the help of the local Sheikh of the district; in fact, I was surprised I hadn't thought of this to begin with. His office was in the nature of a small shop except that it contained a desk and a telephone, and I found him sitting at his desk wearing a jacket over his striped *galabia*.[1] As he did not interrupt his conversation with a man sitting beside him, I stood waiting till the man had gone. He then looked up at me coldly. I told myself that I should win him over by the usual methods, and it wasn't long before I had him cheerfully inviting me to sit down.

"I'm in need of Sheikh Zaabalawi," I answered his enquiry as to the purpose 28 of my visit.

He gazed at me with the same astonishment as that shown by those I had 29 previously encountered.

"At least," he said, giving me a smile that revealed his gold teeth, "he is still 30 alive. The devil of it is, though, he has no fixed abode. You might well bump into him as you go out of here, on the other hand you might spend days and months in fruitless search of him."

"Even you can't find him!"   31

"Even I! He's a baffling man, but I thank the Lord that he's still alive!"   32

He gazed at me intently, and murmured: 33

"It seems your condition is serious."   34

"Very!"   35

"May God come to your aid! But why don't you go about it rationally?"   36

He spread out a sheet of paper on the desk and drew on it with unexpected 37 speed and skill until he had made a full plan of the district showing all the various quarters, lanes, alleyways, and squares. He looked at it admiringly and said, "These are dwelling-houses, here is the Quarter of the Perfumers, here the Quarter of the Coppersmiths, the Mouski, the Police and Fire Stations. The drawing is your best guide. Look carefully in the cafés, the places where the dervishes perform their rites, the mosques and prayer-rooms, and the Green Gate, for he may well be concealed among the beggars and be indistinguishable

---

1. An outer robe.

from them. Actually, I myself haven't seen him for years, having been somewhat preoccupied with the cares of the world and was only brought back to those most exquisite times of my youth by your enquiry."

I gazed at the map in bewilderment. The telephone rang and he took up the 38 receiver.

"Take it," he told me, generously. "We're at your service."   39

Folding up the map, I left and wandered off through the quarter, from 40 square to street to alleyway, making enquiries of everyone I felt was familiar with the place. At last the owner of a small establishment for ironing clothes told me:

"Go to the calligrapher Hassanein in Umm al-Ghulam—they were friends." 41

I went to Umm al-Ghulam where I found old Hassenein working in a deep, 42 narrow shop full of signboards and jars of colour. A strange smell, a mixture of glue and perfume, permeated its every corner. Old Hassanein was squatting on a sheepskin rug in front of a board propped against the wall; in the middle of it he had inscribed the word "Allah" in silver lettering. He was engrossed in embellishing the letters with prodigious care. I stood behind him, fearful to disturb him or break the inspiration that flowed to his masterly hand. When my concern at not interrupting him had lasted some time, he suddenly enquired with unaffected gentleness:

"Yes?"   43

Realizing that he was aware of my presence, I introduced myself.   44

"I've been told that Sheikh Zaabalawi is your friend and I'm looking for 45 him," I said.

His hand came to a stop. He scrutinized me in astonishment.   46

"Zaabalawi! God be praised!" he said with a sigh.   47

"He is a friend of yours, isn't he?" I asked eagerly.   48

"He was, once upon a time. A real man of mystery: he'd visit you so often 49 that people would imagine he was your nearest and dearest, then would disappear as though he'd never existed. Yet saints are not to be blamed."

The spark of hope went out with the suddenness of a lamp by a power-cut. 50

"He was so constantly with me," said the man, "that I felt him to be a part of 51 everything I drew. But where is he today?"

"Perhaps he is still alive?"   52

"He's alive, without a doubt. He had impeccable taste and it was due to him 53 that I made my most beautiful drawings."

"God knows," I said, in a voice almost stifled by the dead ashes of hope, 54 "that I am in the direst need of him and no one knows better than you of the ailments in respect of which he is sought."

"Yes—yes. May God restore you to health. He is, in truth, as is said of him, a 55 man, and more—"

Smiling broadly, he added: "And his face is possessed of an unforgettable 56 beauty. But where is he?"

Reluctantly I rose to my feet, shook hands and left. I continued on my way 57 eastwards and westwards through the quarter, enquiring about him from everyone who, by reason of age or experience, I felt was likely to help me. Eventually I was informed by a vendor of lupine that he had met him a short while ago at the house of Sheikh Gad, the well-known composer. I went to the musician's house in Tabakshiyya where I found him in a room tastefully furnished in the old style, its walls redolent with history. He was seated on a divan, his famous lute lying beside him, concealing within itself the most beautiful melodies of our age, while from within the house came the sound of pestle and mortar and the clamour of children. I immediately greeted him and introduced myself, and was put at my ease by the unaffected way in which he received me. He did not ask, either in words or gesture, what had brought me, and I did not feel that he even harboured any such curiosity. Amazed at his understanding and kindness, which boded well, I said:

"O Sheikh Gad, I am an admirer of yours and have long been enchanted by 58 the renderings of your songs."

"Thank you," he said with a smile. 59

"Please excuse my disturbing you," I continued timidly, "but I was told that 60 Zaabalawi was your friend and I am in urgent need of him."

"Zaabalawi!" he said, frowning in concentration. "You need him? God be 61 with you, for who knows, O Zaabalawi, where you are?"

"Doesn't he visit you?" I asked eagerly. 62

"He visited me some time ago. He might well come now; on the other hand 63 I mightn't see him till death!"

I gave an audible sigh and asked: 64

"What made him like that?" 65

He took up his lute. "Such are saints or they would not be saints," he said 66 laughing.

"Do those who need him suffer as I do?" 67

"Such suffering is part of the cure!" 68

He took up the plectrum and began plucking soft strains from the strings. 69 Lost in thought, I followed his movements. Then, as though addressing myself, I said:

"So my visit has been in vain!" 70

He smiled, laying his cheek against the side of the lute. 71

"God forgive you," he said, "for saying such a thing of a visit that has caused 72 me to know you and you me!"

I was much embarrassed and said apologetically: 73

"Please forgive me; my feelings of defeat made me forget my manners!" 74

"Do not give in to defeat. This extraordinary man brings fatigue to all who 75 seek him. It was easy enough with him in the old days when his place of abode was known. Today, though, the world has changed and after having enjoyed a position attained only by potentates, he is now pursued by the police on a charge of false pretences. It is therefore no longer an easy matter to reach him, but have patience and be sure that you will do so."

He raised his head from the lute and skillfully led into the opening bars of a 76 melody. Then he sang:

"I make lavish mention, even though I blame myself,
of those I have loved,
For the words of lovers are my wine."

With a heart that was weary and listless I followed the beauty of the melody 77
and the singing.

"I composed the music to this poem in a single night," he told me when he 78
had finished. "I remember that it was the night of the Lesser Bairam. He was my
guest for the whole of that night and the poem was of his choosing. He would
sit for a while just where you are, then would get up and play with my children
as though he were one of them. Whenever I was overcome by weariness or my
inspiration failed me he would punch me playfully in the chest and joke with
me, and I would bubble over with melodies and thus I continued working till I
finished the most beautiful piece I have ever composed."

"Does he know anything about music?"   79

"He was the epitome of things musical. He had an extremely beautiful 80
speaking voice and you had only to hear him to want to burst into song. His
loftiness of spirit stirred within you—"

"How was it that he cured those diseases before which men are powerless?" 81

"That is his secret. Maybe you will learn it when you meet him."   82

But when would that meeting occur? We relapsed into silence and the hub- 83
bub of children once more filled the room.

Again, the Sheikh began to sing. He went on repeating the words "and I have 84
a memory of her" in different and beautiful variations until the very walls
danced in ecstasy. I expressed my wholehearted admiration and he gave me a
smile of thanks. I then got up and asked permission to leave and he accompanied me to the outer door. As I shook him by the hand he said, "I hear that
nowadays he frequents the house of Haag Wanas al-Damanhouri. Do you know
him?"

I shook my head, a modicum of renewed hope creeping into my heart.   85

"He is a man of private means," he told me, "who from time to time visits 86
Cairo, putting up at some hotel or other. Every evening, though, he spends at
the Negma Bar in Alfi Street."

I waited for nightfall and went to the Negma Bar. I asked a waiter about 87
Hagg Wanas and he pointed to a corner which was semi-secluded because of its
position behind a large pillar with mirrors on its four sides. There I saw a man
seated alone at a table with a bottle three-quarters empty and another empty
one in front of him; there were no snacks or food to be seen and I was sure that
I was in the presence of a hardened drinker. He was wearing a loosely flowing
silk *galabia* and a carefully wound turban; his legs were stretched out towards
the base of the pillar, and as he gazed into the mirror in rapt contentment the
sides of his face, rounded and handsome despite the fact that he was approaching old age, were flushed with wine. I approached quietly till I stood but a few
feet away from him. He did not turn towards me or give any indication that he
was aware of my presence.

"Good evening, Mr. Wanas," I said with amiable friendliness.   88

He turned towards me abruptly as though my voice had roused him from   89
slumber and glared at me in disapproval. I was about to explain what had
brought me to him when he interrupted me in an almost imperative tone of
voice which was none the less not devoid of an extraordinary gentleness:

"First, please sit down, and, second, please get drunk!"   90

I opened my mouth to make my excuses but, stopping up his ears with his   91
fingers, he said:

"Not a word till you do what I say."   92

I realized that I was in the presence of a capricious drunkard and told my-   93
self that I should go along with him at least halfway.

"Would you permit me to ask one question?" I said with a smile, sitting   94
down.

Without removing his hands from his ears he indicated the bottle.   95

"When engaged in a drinking bout like this I do not allow any conversation   96
between myself and another unless, like me, he is drunk, otherwise the session
loses all propriety and mutual comprehension is rendered impossible."

I made a sign indicating that I didn't drink.   97

"That's your look-out," he said offhandedly. "And that's my condition!"   98

He filled me a glass which I meekly took and drank. No sooner had it settled   99
in my stomach than it seemed to ignite. I waited patiently till I had grown used
to its ferocity, and said:

"It's very strong, and I think the time has come for me to ask you about—"   100

Once again, however, he put his fingers in his ears.   101

"I shan't listen to you until you're drunk!"   102

He filled up my glass for the second time. I glanced at it in trepidation; then,   103
overcoming my innate objection, I drank it down at a gulp. No sooner had it
come to rest inside me than I lost all will-power. With the third glass I lost my
memory and with the fourth the future vanished. The world turned round
about me and I forgot why I had gone there. The man leaned towards me attentively but I saw him—saw everything—as a mere meaningless series of coloured planes. I don't know how long it was before my head sank down on to the
arm of the chair and I plunged into deep sleep. During it I had a beautiful
dream the like of which I had never experienced. I dreamed that I was in an
immense garden surrounded on all sides by luxuriant trees and the sky was
nothing but stars seen between the entwined branches, all enfolded in an atmosphere like that of sunset or a sky overcast with cloud. I was lying on a small
hummock of jasmine petals which fell upon me like rain, while the lucent spray
of a fountain unceasingly sprinkled my head and temples. I was in a state of
deep contentedness, of ecstatic serenity. An orchestra of warbling and cooing
played in my ear. There was an extraordinary sense of harmony between me
and my inner self, and between the two of us and the world, everything being in
its rightful place without discord or distortion. In the whole world there was no
single reason for speech or movement, for the universe moved in a rapture of
ecstasy. This lasted but a short while. When I opened my eyes consciousness

struck at me like a policeman's fist and I saw Wanas al-Damanhouri regarding me with concern. In the bar only a few drowsy people were left.

"You have slept deeply," said my companion; "you were obviously hungry for sleep." 104

I rested my heavy head in the palms of my hands. When I took them away in astonishment and looked down at them I found that they glistened with drops of water. 105

"My head's wet," I protested. 106

"Yes, my friend tried to rouse you," he answered quietly. 107

"Somebody saw me in this state?" 108

"Don't worry, he is a good man. Have you not heard of Sheikh Zaabalawi?" 109

"Zaabalawi!" I exclaimed, jumping to my feet. 110

"Yes," he answered in surprise. "What's wrong?" 111

"Where is he?" 112

"I don't know where he is now. He was here and then he left." 113

I was about to run off in pursuit but found I was more exhausted than I had imagined. Collapsed over the table, I cried out in despair: 114

"My sole reason for coming to you was to meet him. Help me to catch up with him or send someone after him." 115

The man called a vendor of prawns and asked him to seek out the Sheikh and bring him back. Then he turned to me. 116

"I didn't realize you were afflicted. I'm very sorry—" 117

"You wouldn't let me speak," I said irritably. 118

"What a pity! He was sitting on this chair beside you the whole time. He was playing with a string of jasmine petals he had round his neck, a gift from one of his admirers, then, taking pity on you, he began to sprinkle some water on your head to bring you round." 119

"Does he meet you here every night?" I asked, my eyes not leaving the door-way through which the vendor of prawns had left. 120

"He was with me tonight, last night and the night before that, but before that I hadn't seen him for a month." 121

"Perhaps he will come tomorrow," I answered with a sigh. 122

"Perhaps." 123

"I am willing to give him any money he wants." 124

Wanas answered sympathetically: 125

"The strange thing is that he is not open to such temptations, yet he will cure you if you meet him." 126

"Without charge?" 127

"Merely on sensing that you love him." 128

The vendor of prawns returned, having failed in his mission. 129

I recovered some of my energy and left the bar, albeit unsteadily. At every street corner I called out, "Zaabalawi!" in the vague hope that I would be re-warded with an answering shout. The street boys turned contemptuous eyes on me till I sought refuge in the first available taxi. 130

The following evening I stayed up with Wanas al-Damanhouri till dawn, 131
but the Sheikh did not put in an appearance. Wanas informed me that he would
be going away to the country and wouldn't be returning to Cairo until he'd sold
the cotton crop.

I must wait, I told myself; I must train myself to be patient. Let me content 132
myself with having made certain of the existence of Zaabalawi, and even of his
affection for me, which encourages me to think that he will be prepared to cure
me if a meeting between us takes place.

Sometimes, however, the long delay wearied me. I would become beset by 133
despair and would try to persuade myself to dismiss him from my mind completely. How many weary people in this life know him not or regard him as a
mere myth! Why, then, should I torture myself about him in this way?

No sooner, however, did my pains force themselves upon me than I would 134
again begin to think about him, asking myself as to when I would be fortunate
enough to meet him. The fact that I ceased to have any news of Wanas and was
told he had gone to live abroad did not deflect me from my purpose; the truth
of the matter was that I had become fully convinced that I had to find Zaabalawi.

Yes, I have to find Zaabalawi. 135

—*Translated by Denys Johnson-Davies*

ACTIVITIES FOR WRITING AND DISCUSSION

1. Reread and annotate the reactions of the several people to whom the
narrator mentions the name, "Zaabalawi." Do they all react in the same way? in
different ways? Working with a partner or small group, try to provide some
plausible explanations for the type(s) of reactions you find. Finally, write a description of the Zaabalawi who emerges for you through the impressions of the
various characters.

2. Interpret the following dialogue:

Narrator: "Do those who need him suffer as I do?"
Sheikh Gad: "Such suffering is part of the cure!"

Alternative: Identify any other dialogue in the story that intrigues you, annotate it, and give your reading of its literal and/or **symbolic** meanings.

3. At story's end the narrator has yet to "find" Zaabalawi. Does it matter?
Have his efforts been wasted? rewarded in any ways? Explain, supporting your
response with evidence or quotations from the story.

4. Is the narrator's quest for Zaabalawi symbolic in any ways? If so, *how* or
of what?

Novalis (pseudonym of Friedrich von Hardenberg [1772–1801])

Aphorisms

1. The seat of the soul is where the inner world and the outer world meet. Where they overlap, it is in every point of the overlap.

2. Self-expression is the source of all abasement, just as, contrariwise, it is the basis for all true elevation. The first step is introspection—exclusive contemplation of the self. But whoever stops there goes only half way. The second step must be genuine observation outward—spontaneous, sober observation of the external world.

3. The more personal, local, temporal, particularized a poem is, the nearer it stands to the *centrum* of poetry. A poem must be completely inexhaustible, like a human being or a good proverb.

4. There is only one temple in the world and that is the human body. Nothing is more sacred than that noble form.

5. A man will never achieve anything excellent in the way of representation so long as he wishes to represent nothing more than his own experiences, his own favorite objects, so long as he cannot bring himself to study with diligence and to represent at his leisure an object wholly foreign and wholly uninteresting to him.

6. Man is a sun and his senses are the planets.

—Translated by Charles E. Passage

ACTIVITIES FOR WRITING AND DISCUSSION

1. Annotate the "Aphorisms." Then respond to them using Idea #1 from the "Ten Ideas for Writing from Reading" described in Chapter 3.

2. Over a period of days, weeks, or longer, carry a notepad for recording your own on-the-spot thoughts, ideas, and impressions. Reread these occasionally and shape the best into **aphorisms** of your own. For some suggestions on collecting notes and revising them, see Chapter 9.

WILLIAM WORDSWORTH (1770–1850)

The World Is Too Much with Us

The world is too much with us; late and soon,
Getting and spending, we lay waste our powers:
Little we see in Nature that is ours;
We have given our hearts away, a sordid boon!
This Sea that bares her bosom to the moon;   5
The winds that will be howling at all hours,
And are up-gathered now like sleeping flowers;
For this, for every thing, we are out of tune;
It moves us not.—Great God! I'd rather be
A Pagan suckled in a creed outworn;   10
So might I, standing on this pleasant lea,
Have glimpses that would make me less forlorn;
Have sight of Proteus[1] rising from the sea;
Or hear old Triton[2] blow his wreathèd horn.

JOHN KEATS (1795–1821)

To Autumn

1

Season of mists and mellow fruitfulness,
　　Close bosom-friend of the maturing sun;
Conspiring with him how to load and bless
　　With fruit the vines that round the thatch-eves run;
To bend with apples the moss'd cottage-trees,   5
　　And fill all fruit with ripeness to the core;
　　　　To swell the gourd, and plump the hazel shells
　　With a sweet kernel; to set budding more,
And still more, later flowers for the bees,
Until they think warm days will never cease,   10
　　　　For summer has o'er-brimm'd their clammy cells.

---

1. In Greek mythology, an old man of the sea who was able to assume a variety of shapes.   2. A god of the sea, often depicted as blowing on a seashell.

2

Who hath not seen thee oft amid thy store?
   Sometimes whoever seeks abroad may find
Thee sitting careless on a granary floor,
   Thy hair soft-lifted by the winnowing wind;   15
Or on a half-reap'd furrow sound asleep,
   Drows'd with the fume of poppies, while thy hook[1]
      Spares the next swath and all its twined flowers:
And sometimes like a gleaner thou dost keep
   Steady thy laden head across a brook;   20
   Or by a cyder-press, with patient look,
      Thou watchest the last oozings hours by hours.

3

Where are the songs of spring? Ay, where are they?
   Think not of them, thou hast thy music too,—
While barred clouds bloom the soft-dying day,   25
   And touch the stubble-plains with rosy hue;
Then in a wailful choir the small gnats mourn
   Among the river sallows,[2] borne aloft
      Or sinking as the light wind lives or dies;
And full-grown lambs loud bleat from hilly bourn[3];   30
   Hedge-crickets sing; and now with treble soft
   The red-breast whistles from a garden-croft;[4]
      And gathering swallows twitter in the skies.

EMILY DICKINSON (1830–1886)

Because I could not stop for Death

Because I could not stop for Death—
He kindly stopped for me—
The Carriage held but just Ourselves—
And Immortality.

---

1. Scythe.   2. Willows.   3. Area or region.   4. Enclosed plot of land.

We slowly drove—He knew no haste   5
And I had put away
My labor and my leisure too,
For His Civility—

We passed the School, where Children strove
At Recess—in the Ring—   10
We passed the Fields of Gazing Grain—
We passed the Setting Sun—

Or rather—He passed Us—
The Dews drew quivering and chill—
For only Gossamer,[1] my Gown—   15
My Tippet[2]—only Tulle—[3]

We paused before a House that seemed
A Swelling of the Ground—
The Roof was scarcely visible—
The Cornice[4]—in the Ground—   20

Since then—'tis Centuries—and yet
Feels shorter than the Day
I first surmised the Horses Heads
Were toward Eternity—

After great pain, a formal feeling comes

After great pain, a formal feeling comes—
The Nerves sit ceremonious, like Tombs—
The stiff Heart questions was it He, that bore,
And Yesterday, or Centuries before?

The Feet, mechanical, go round—   5
Of Ground, or Air, or Ought—[5]
A Wooden way
Regardless grown,[6]
A Quartz contentment, like a stone—

---

1. A finely woven fabric.   2. A covering for the shoulders, such as a shawl.   3. A very fine net of silk or
similar fabric.   4. Molding that crowns a roof or a wall.

5. Anything.   6. No longer noticing.

This is the Hour of Lead—   10
Remembered, if outlived,
As Freezing persons, recollect the Snow—
First—Chill—then Stupor—then the letting go—

My life closed twice before its close

My life closed twice before its close;
It yet remains to see
If Immortality unveil
A third event to me,

So huge, so hopeless to conceive   5
As these that twice befel.
Parting is all we know of heaven,
And all we need of hell.

ACTIVITIES FOR WRITING AND DISCUSSION

1. Read the three Dickinson poems aloud, paying attention to the **meter, rhymes,** and other sound effects such as **assonance** and **alliteration.** Attempting, for the moment, to set aside issues of "meaning," what passages—words, phrases, or lines—give you pleasure because of their sound or rhythm?

2. In a small group or as a class, progress toward strong readings of the poems by assuming, initially, the role of "dumb" readers. Simply go through a poem, line by line, and brainstorm any images, associations, or feelings that occur to you. Rather than suppressing "dumb," "irrelevant," or "eccentric" responses, honor them and write them down. Then discuss how people's diverse responses illuminate the poem and/or evoke thoughts about life experiences that may not be explicitly addressed in the poem itself.

3. Dickinson's astonishing **metaphors** and **similes** challenge and subvert logical or "rational" ways of thinking and our desire for neatly packaged "meanings." Working with a group:
   a. Identify and mark as many metaphors and similes as you can.
   b. Select two or three favorites.
   c. "Unpack" these favorites in a discussion or by writing about them in your notebook.

4. Respond to one or more of the poems using the "Four-Step Process for Writing from Reading" described in Chapter 2.

William Butler Yeats (1865–1939)

Sailing to Byzantium

I

That is no country for old men. The young
In one another's arms, birds in the trees
—Those dying generations—at their song,
The salmon-falls, the mackerel-crowded seas,
Fish, flesh, or fowl, commend all summer long   5
Whatever is begotten, born, and dies.
Caught in that sensual music all neglect
Monuments of unageing intellect.

II

An aged man is but a paltry thing,
A tattered coat upon a stick, unless   10
Soul clap its hands and sing, and louder sing
For every tatter in its mortal dress,
Nor is there singing school but studying
Monuments of its own magnificence;
And therefore I have sailed the seas and come   15
To the holy city of Byzantium.[1]

III

O sages standing in God's holy fire
As in the gold mosaic of a wall,
Come from the holy fire, perne in a gyre,[2]
And be the singing-masters of my soul.   20
Consume my heart away; sick with desire
And fastened to a dying animal
It knows not what it is; and gather me
Into the artifice of eternity.

IV

Once out of nature I shall never take   25
My bodily form from any natural thing,

---

1. Capital of the Byzantine Empire (fourth century—fifteenth century A.D.), a once thriving center of religion, art, and culture.   2. Spin in a spiraling motion.

But such a form as Grecian goldsmiths make
Of hammered gold and gold enamelling
To keep a drowsy Emperor awake;
Or set upon a golden bough to sing   30
To lords and ladies of Byzantium
Of what is past, or passing, or to come.

Robert Frost (1874–1963)

Stopping by Woods on a Snowy Evening

Whose woods these are I think I know.
His house is in the village though;
He will not see me stopping here
To watch his woods fill up with snow.

My little horse must think it queer   5
To stop without a farmhouse near
Between the woods and frozen lake
The darkest evening of the year.

He gives his harness bells a shake
To ask if there is some mistake.   10
The only other sound's the sweep
Of easy wind and downy flake.

The woods are lovely, dark and deep,
But I have promises to keep,
And miles to go before I sleep,   15
And miles to go before I sleep.

"Out, Out—"

The buzz-saw snarled and rattled in the yard
And made dust and dropped stove-length sticks of wood,
Sweet-scented stuff when the breeze drew across it.
And from there those that lifted eyes could count
Five mountain ranges one behind the other   5
Under the sunset far into Vermont.
And the saw snarled and rattled, snarled and rattled,
As it ran light, or had to bear a load.

And nothing happened: day was all but done.
Call it a day, I wish they might have said   10
To please the boy by giving him the half hour
That a boy counts so much when saved from work.
His sister stood beside them in her apron
To tell them "Supper." At the word, the saw,
As if to prove saws knew what supper meant,   15
Leaped out at the boy's hand, or seemed to leap—
He must have given the hand. However it was,
Neither refused the meeting. But the hand!
The boy's first outcry was a rueful laugh,
As he swung toward them holding up the hand   20
Half in appeal, but half as if to keep
The life from spilling. Then the boy saw all—
Since he was old enough to know, big boy
Doing a man's work, though a child at heart—
He saw all spoiled. "Don't let him cut my hand off—   25
The doctor, when he comes. Don't let him, sister!"
So. But the hand was gone already.
The doctor put him in the dark of ether.
He lay and puffed his lips out with his breath.
And then—the watcher at his pulse took fright.   30
No one believed. They listened at his heart.
Little—less—nothing!—and that ended it.
No more to build on there. And they, since they
Were not the one dead, turned to their affairs.

Birches

When I see birches bend to left and right
Across the lines of straighter darker trees,
I like to think some boy's been swinging them.
But swinging doesn't bend them down to stay
As ice-storms do. Often you must have seen them   5
Loaded with ice a sunny winter morning
After a rain. They click upon themselves
As the breeze rises, and turn many-colored
As the stir cracks and crazes their enamel.
Soon the sun's warmth makes them shed crystal shells   10
Shattering and avalanching on the snow-crust—
Such heaps of broken glass to sweep away
You'd think the inner dome of heaven had fallen.
They are dragged to the withered bracken by the load,

And they seem not to break; though once they are bowed   15
So low for long, they never right themselves:
You may see their trunks arching in the woods
Years afterwards, trailing their leaves on the ground
Like girls on hands and knees that throw their hair
Before them over their heads to dry in the sun.   20
But I was going to say when Truth broke in
With all her matter-of-fact about the ice-storm,
I should prefer to have some boy bend them
As he went out and in to fetch the cows—
Some boy too far from town to learn baseball,   25
Whose only play was what he found himself,
Summer or winter, and could play alone.
One by one he subdued his father's trees
By riding them down over and over again
Until he took the stiffness out of them,   30
And not one but hung limp, not one was left
For him to conquer. He learned all there was
To learn about not launching out too soon
And so not carrying the tree away
Clear to the ground. He always kept his poise   35
To the top branches, climbing carefully
With the same pains you use to fill a cup
Up to the brim, and even above the brim.
Then he flung outward, feet first, with a swish,
Kicking his way down through the air to the ground.   40
So was I once myself a swinger of birches.
And so I dream of going back to be.
It's when I'm weary of considerations,
And life is too much like a pathless wood
Where your face burns and tickles with the cobwebs   45
Broken across it, and one eye is weeping
From a twig's having lashed across it open.
I'd like to get away from earth awhile
And then come back to it and begin over.
May no fate willfully misunderstand me   50
And half grant what I wish and snatch me away
Not to return. Earth's the right place for love:
I don't know where it's likely to go better.
I'd like to go by climbing a birch tree,
And climb black branches up a snow-white trunk,   55
Toward heaven, till the tree could bear no more,
But dipped its top and set me down again.
That would be good both going and coming back.
One could do worse than be a swinger of birches.

ACTIVITIES FOR WRITING AND DISCUSSION

1. Respond to any of Frost's poems using the "Four-Step Process for Writing from Reading" discussed in Chapter 2.

2. Working with a group or as a class, read either "Out, Out—" or "Birches" aloud. Have each person take a turn reading several lines, and pause periodically to do either or both of the following:
   a. Share and discuss your annotations of specific lines and passages. What parts puzzle you or leave you with questions? What parts strike or "grab" you? Why?
   b. Analyze Frost's **metaphors** and **similes** and how they enhance the poem.

Based on this process and on your annotations, write a response to the poem using one of the "Ten Ideas for Writing" from Chapter 3 or a different idea of your own devising.

3. What diverse analogies does "Birches" suggest between birch-swinging and life? Analyze any such analogies in your notebook.

4. In lines 41 and 42 of "Birches" the **speaker** says, "So was I once myself a swinger of birches./And so I dream of going back to be." Explain what you think he means, and share your diverse interpretations of this passage with your group or class.

D. H. LAWRENCE (1885–1930)

Humming-bird

I can imagine, in some otherworld
Primeval-dumb, far back
In that most awful stillness, that only gasped and hummed,
Humming-birds raced down the avenues.

Before anything had a soul,   5
While life was a heave of Matter, half inanimate,
This little bit chipped off in brilliance
And went whizzing through the slow, vast, succulent stems.

I believe there were no flowers then,
In the world where the humming-bird flashed ahead of creation.   10
I believe he pierced the slow vegetable veins with his long beak.

Probably he was big
As mosses, and little lizards, they say, were once big.

Probably he was a jabbing, terrifying monster.

We look at him through the wrong end of the long telescope of Time,   15
Luckily for us.

Jorge Luis Borges (1899–1986)

Delia Elena San Marco

We said goodbye at the corner of Eleventh. From the other sidewalk I turned to
look back; you too had turned, and you waved goodbye to me.

A river of vehicles and people was flowing between us. It was five o'clock
on an ordinary afternoon. How was I to know that the river was Acheron[1] the
doleful, the insuperable?   5

We did not see each other again, and a year later you were dead.

And now I seek out that memory and look at it, and I think it was false, and
that behind that trivial farewell was infinite separation.

Last night I stayed in after dinner and reread, in order to understand these
things, the last teaching Plato put in his master's[2] mouth. I read that the soul   10
may escape when the flesh dies.

And now I do not know whether the truth is in the ominous subsequent
interpretation, or in the unsuspecting farewell.

For if souls do not die, it is right that we should not make much of saying
goodbye.   15

To say goodbye to each other is to deny separation. It is like saying "today
we play at separating, but we will see each other tomorrow." Man invented
farewells because he somehow knows he is immortal, even though he may
seem gratuitous and ephemeral.

Sometime, Delia, we will take up again—beside what river?—this   20
uncertain dialogue, and we will ask each other if ever, in a city lost on a plain,
we were Borges and Delia.

—Translated by Mildred Boyer

Activities for Writing and Discussion

1. Brainstorm a list of thoughts and emotions this **prose poem** stirs in you.
Then write the story of any analogous experience in your own life, in which a
good-bye was followed—if not by death—by some sort of profound separa-

---

1. In ancient mythology, a river in the underworld, or world of the dead.   2. Socrates's.

tion. Alternative: Using two imaginary characters, invent a story about such an experience.

2. Make a Topic/Form Grid (see Chapter 10). Then use one of the forms on your grid to create a notebook entry on "separation," "death," or some other topic evoked by Borges's poem.

Kenneth Rexroth (1905–1982)

The Signature of All Things

My head and shoulders, and my book
In the cool shade, and my body
Stretched bathing in the sun, I lie
Reading beside the waterfall—
Boehme's[1] "Signature of all Things."   5
Through the deep July day the leaves
Of the laurel, all the colors
Of gold, spin down through the moving
Deep laurel shade all day. They float
On the mirrored sky and forest   10
For a while, and then, still slowly
Spinning, sink through the crystal deep
Of the pool to its leaf gold floor.
The saint saw the world as streaming
In the electrolysis of love.   15
I put him by and gaze through shade
Folded into shade of slender
Laurel trunks and leaves filled with sun.
The wren broods in her moss domed nest.
A newt struggles with a white moth   20
Drowning in the pool. The hawks scream,
Playing together on the ceiling
Of heaven. The long hours go by.
I think of those who have loved me,
Of all the mountains I have climbed,   25
Of all the seas I have swum in.
The evil of the world sinks.
My own sin and trouble fall away
Like Christian's bundle, and I watch
My forty summers fall like falling   30

---

1. Jakob Boehme (1575–1624), German philosopher and mystic.

Leaves and falling water held
Eternally in summer air.

———————

Deer are stamping in the glades,
Under the full July moon.
There is a smell of dry grass   35
In the air, and more faintly,
The scent of a far off skunk.
As I stand at the wood's edge,
Watching the darkness, listening
To the stillness, a small owl   40
Comes to the branch above me,
On wings more still than my breath.
When I turn my light on him,
His eyes glow like drops of iron,
And he perks his head at me,   45
Like a curious kitten.
The meadow is bright as snow.
My dog prowls the grass, a dark
Blur in the blur of brightness.
I walk to the oak grove where   50
The Indian village was once.
There, in blotched and cobwebbed light
And dark, dim in the blue haze,
Are twenty Holstein heifers,
Black and white, all lying down,   55
Quietly together, under
The huge trees rooted in the graves.

———————

When I dragged the rotten log
From the bottom of the pool,
It seemed heavy as stone.   60
I let it lie in the sun
For a month, and then chopped it
Into sections, and split them
For kindling, and spread them out
To dry some more. Late that night,   65
After reading for hours,
While moths rattled at the lamp—
The saints and the philosophers
On the destiny of man—
I went out on my cabin porch,   70
And looked up through the black forest

At the swaying islands of stars.
Suddenly I saw at my feet,
Spread on the floor of night, ingots
Of quivering phosphorescence,   75
And all about were scattered chips
Of pale cold light that was alive.

JAMES WRIGHT (1927–1980)

Lying in a Hammock at William Duffy's Farm in Pine Island, Minnesota

Over my head, I see the bronze butterfly,
Asleep on the black trunk,
Blowing like a leaf in green shadow.
Down the ravine behind the empty house,
The cowbells follow one another   5
Into the distances of the afternoon.
To my right,
In a field of sunlight between two pines,
The droppings of last year's horses
Blaze up into golden stones.   10
I lean back, as the evening darkens and comes on.
A chicken hawk floats over, looking for home.
I have wasted my life.

MARY OLIVER (b. 1935)

The Black Snake

When the black snake
flashed onto the morning road,
and the truck could not swerve—
death, that is how it happens.

Now he lies looped and useless   5
as an old bicycle tire.
I stop the car
and carry him into the bushes.

He is as cool and gleaming
as a braided whip, he is as beautiful and quiet   10
as a dead brother.
I leave him under the leaves

and drive on, thinking
about *death:* its suddenness,
its terrible weight,   15
its certain coming. Yet under

reason burns a brighter fire, which the bones
have always preferred.
It is the story of endless good fortune.
It says to oblivion: not me!   20

It is the light at the center of every cell.
It is what sent the snake coiling and flowing forward
happily all spring through the green leaves before
he came to the road.

Some Questions You Might Ask

Is the soul solid, like iron?
Or is it tender and breakable, like
the wings of a moth in the beak of the owl?
Who has it, and who doesn't?
I keep looking around me.   5
The face of the moose is as sad
as the face of Jesus.
The swan opens her white wings slowly.
In the fall, the black bear carries leaves into the darkness.
One question leads to another.   10
Does it have a shape? Like an iceberg?
Like the eye of a hummingbird?
Does it have one lung, like the snake and the scallop?
Why should I have it, and not the anteater
who loves her children?   15
Why should I have it, and not the camel?
Come to think of it, what about the maple trees?
What about the blue iris?
What about all the little stones, sitting alone in the moonlight?
What about roses, and lemons, and their shining leaves?   20
What about the grass?

LUCILLE CLIFTON (b. 1936)

God's Mood

these daughters are bone,
they break.
He wanted stone girls
and boys with branches for arms
that He could lift His life with   5
and be lifted by.
these sons are bone.

He is tired of years that keep turning into age
and flesh that keeps widening.
He is tired of waiting for His teeth to   10
bite Him and walk away.

He is tired of bone,
it breaks.
He is tired of eve's fancy and
adam's whining ways.   15

LOUISE GLÜCK (b. 1943)

Metamorphosis

1. Night

The angel of death flies
low over my father's bed.
Only my mother sees. She and my father
are alone in the room.

She bends over him to touch   5
his hand, his forehead. She is
so used to mothering
that now she strokes his body
as she would the other children's,
first gently, then   10
inured to suffering.

Nothing is any different.
Even the spot on the lung
was always there.

2. Metamorphosis

My father has forgotten me   15
in the excitement of dying.
Like a child who will not eat,
he takes no notice of anything.

I sit at the edge of his bed
while the living circle us   20
like so many tree stumps.

Once, for the smallest
fraction of an instant, I thought
he was alive in the present again;
then he looked at me   25
as a blind man stares
straight into the sun, since
whatever it could do to him
is done already.

Then his flushed face   30
turned away from the contact.

3. For My Father

I'm going to live without you
as I learned once
to live without my mother.
You think I don't remember that?   35
I've spent my whole life trying to remember.

Now, after so much solitude,
death doesn't frighten me,
not yours, not mine either.
And those words, *the last time,*   40
have no power over me. I know
intense love always leads to mourning.

For once, your body doesn't frighten me.
From time to time, I run my hand over your face
lightly, like a dustcloth.   45
What can shock me now? I feel

no coldness that can't be explained.
Against your cheek, my hand is warm
and full of tenderness.

ACTIVITIES FOR WRITING AND DISCUSSION

1. Twice the **speaker** compares her father to a child. In what respects is the comparison apt? Cite passages in the poem to support your answer.

2. Look up "metamorphosis" in a dictionary. Then discuss its appropriateness (or inappropriateness) as a title for this poem. What does the title suggest about the speaker's view of death? To whom or what does the title apply—the speaker? the father? the process of death itself? some combination of the three?

3. Imagine that you are the speaker and that the poem describes an actual experience in your life. Using details from the poem and inventing others as necessary, write a "preface" to the poem in which you reflect on your experience and what it has taught you about life, death, love, and/or change.

Celestial Music

I have a friend who still believes in heaven.
Not a stupid person, yet with all she knows, she literally talks to god,
she thinks someone listens in heaven.
On earth, she's unusually competent.
Brave, too, able to face unpleasantness.   5

We found a caterpillar dying in the dirt, greedy ants crawling over it.
I'm always moved by weakness, by disaster, always eager to oppose vitality.
But timid, also, quick to shut my eyes.
Whereas my friend was able to watch, to let events play out
according to nature. For my sake, she intervened,   10
brushing a few ants off the torn thing, and set it down across the road.

My friend says I shut my eyes to god, that nothing else explains
my aversion to reality. She says I'm like the child who buries her head in
    the pillow

so as not to see, the child who tells herself
that light causes sadness—   15
My friend is like the mother. Patient, urging me
to wake up an adult like herself, a courageous person—

In my dreams, my friend reproaches me. We're walking
on the same road, except it's winter now;
she's telling me that when you love the world you hear celestial music;   20
look up, she says. When I look up, nothing.
Only clouds, snow, a white business in the trees
like brides leaping to a great height—
Then I'm afraid for her; I see her
caught in a net deliberately cast over the earth—   25

In reality, we sit by the side of the road, watching the sun set,
from time to time the silence pierced by a birdcall.
It's this moment we're both trying to explain, the fact
that we're at ease with death, with solitude.
My friend draws a circle in the dirt; inside, the caterpillar doesn't move.   30
She's always trying to make something whole, something beautiful, an image
capable of life apart from her.
We're very quiet. It's peaceful sitting here, not speaking, the composition
fixed, the road turning suddenly dark, the air
going cool, here and there the rocks shining and glittering—   35
it's this stillness that we both love.
The love of form is a love of endings.

Nonfiction/Essays

Henry David Thoreau (1817–1862)

Where I Lived, and What I Lived For

At a certain season of our life we are accustomed to consider every spot as the possible site of a house. I have thus surveyed the country on every side within a dozen miles of where I live. In imagination I have bought all the farms in succession, for all were to be bought, and I knew their price. I walked over each farmer's premises, tasted his wild apples, discoursed on husbandry with him, took his farm at his price, at any price, mortgaging it to him in my mind; even put a higher price on it,—took everything but a deed of it,—took his word for his deed, for I dearly love to talk,—cultivated it, and him too to some extent, I trust, and withdrew when I had enjoyed it long enough, leaving him to carry it on. This experience entitled me to be regarded as a sort of real-estate broker by my friends. Wherever I sat, there I might live, and the landscape radiated from me accordingly. What is a house but a *sedes*, a seat?—better if a country seat. I discovered many a site for a house not likely to be soon improved, which some might have thought too far from the village, but to my eyes the village was too far from it. Well, there I might live, I said; and there I did live, for an hour, a summer and a winter life; saw how I could let the years run off, buffet the winter through, and see the spring come in. The future inhabitants of this region, wherever they may place their houses, may be sure that they have been anticipated. An afternoon sufficed to lay out the land into orchard, woodlot, and pasture, and to decide what fine oaks or pines should be left to stand before the door, and whence each blasted tree could be seen to the best advantage; and then I let it lie, fallow perchance, for a man is rich in proportion to the number of things which he can afford to let alone. . . .

The present was my next experiment of this kind, which I purpose to describe more at length, for convenience, putting the experience of two years into one. As I have said, I do not propose to write an ode to dejection, but to brag as lustily as chanticleer in the morning, standing on his roost, if only to wake my neighbors up.

When first I took up my abode in the woods, that is, began to spend my nights as well as days there, which, by accident, was on Independence day, or the fourth of July, 1845, my house was not finished for winter, but was merely a defence against the rain, without plastering or chimney, the walls being of rough weather-stained boards, with wide chinks, which made it cool at night. The upright white hewn studs and freshly planed door and window casings gave it a clean and airy look, especially in the morning, when its timbers were saturated with dew, so that I fancied that by noon some sweet gum would exude from them. To my imagination it retained throughout the day more or less of this auroral character, reminding me of a certain house on a mountain which I had visited a year before. This was an airy and unplastered cabin, fit to entertain a travelling god, and where a goddess might trail her garments. The winds which passed over my dwelling were such as sweep over the ridges of mountains, bearing the broken strains, or celestial parts only, of terrestrial music. The morning wind forever blows, the poem of creation is uninterrupted; but few are the ears that hear it. Olympus is but the outside of the earth everywhere.

The only house I had been the owner of before, if I except a boat, was a tent, which I used occasionally when making excursions in the summer, and this is still rolled up in my garret; but the boat, after passing from hand to hand, has gone down the stream of time. With this more substantial shelter about me, I had made some progress toward settling in the world. This frame, so slightly clad, was a sort of crystallization around me, and reacted on the builder. It was suggestive somewhat as a picture in outlines. I did not need to go out doors to take the air, for the atmosphere within had lost none of its freshness. It was not so much within doors as behind a door where I sat, even in the rainiest weather. The Harivansa says, "An abode without birds is like a meat without seasoning." Such was not my abode, for I found myself suddenly neighbor to the birds; not by having imprisoned one, but having caged myself near them. I was not only nearer to some of those which commonly frequent the garden and the orchard, but to those wilder and more thrilling songsters of the forest which never, or rarely, serenade a villager,—the wood-thrush, the veery, the scarlet tanager, the field-sparrow, the whippoorwill, and many others. . . .

Every morning was a cheerful invitation to make my life of equal simplicity, and I may say innocence, with Nature herself. I have been as sincere a worshipper of Aurora as the Greeks. I got up early and bathed in the pond; that was a religious exercise, and one of the best things which I did. They say that characters were engraven on the bathing tub of king Tching-thang to this effect: "Renew thyself completely each day; do it again, and again, and forever again." I can understand that. Morning brings back the heroic ages. I was as much affected by the faint hum of a mosquito making its invisible and unimaginable tour through my apartment at earliest dawn, when I was sitting with door and windows open, as I could be by any trumpet that ever sang of fame. It was Homer's requiem; itself an Iliad and Odyssey in the air, singing its own wrath and wanderings. There was something cosmical about it; a standing advertisement, till forbidden, of the everlasting vigor and fertility of the world. The morning, which is the most memorable season of the day, is the awakening hour. Then there is least somnolence in us; and for an hour, at least, some part of us awakes which slumbers all the rest of the day and night. Little is to be expected of that day, if it can be called a day, to which we are not awakened by our Genius, but by the mechanical nudgings of some servitor, are not awakened by our own newly-acquired force and aspirations from within, accompanied by the undulations of celestial music, instead of factory bells, and a fragrance filling the air—to a higher life than we fell asleep from; and thus the darkness bear its fruit, and prove itself to be good, no less than the light. That man who does not believe that each day contains an earlier, more sacred, and auroral hour than he has yet profaned, has despaired of life, and is pursuing a descending and darkening way. After a partial cessation of his sensuous life, the soul of man, or its organs rather, are reinvigorated each day, and his Genius tries again what noble life it can make. All memorable events, I should say, transpire in morning time and in a morning atmosphere. The Vedas say, "All intelligences awake with the morning." Poetry and art, and the fairest and most memorable of the actions of men, date from such an hour. All poets and heroes, like Memnon, are the children of Aurora, and emit their music at sunrise. To him whose elastic and vigorous thought keeps pace with the sun, the day is a perpetual morning. It matters not what the clocks say or the attitudes and labors of men. Morning is when I am awake and there is a dawn in me. Moral reform is the effort to throw off sleep. Why is it that men give so poor an account of their day if they have not been slumbering? They are not such poor calculators. If they had not been overcome with drowsiness they would have performed something. The millions are awake enough for physical labor; but only one in a million is awake enough for effective intellectual exertion, only one in a hundred millions to a poetic or divine life. To be awake is to be alive. I have never yet met a man who was quite awake. How could I have looked him in the face?

We must learn to reawaken and keep ourselves awake, not by mechanical aids, but by an infinite expectation of the dawn, which does not forsake us in our soundest sleep. I know of no more encouraging fact than the unquestionable ability of man to elevate his life by a conscious endeavor. It is something to be able to paint a particular picture, or to carve a statue, and so to make a few objects beautiful; but it is far more glorious to carve and paint the very atmosphere and medium through which we look, which morally we can do. To affect the quality of the day, that is the highest of arts. Every man is tasked to make his life, even in its details, worthy of the contemplation of his most elevated and critical hour. If we refused, or rather used up, such paltry information as we get, the oracles would distinctly inform us how this might be done.

I went to the woods because I wished to live deliberately, to front only the essential facts of life, and see if I could not learn what it had to teach, and not, when I came to die, discover that I had not lived. I did not wish to live what was not life, living is so dear; nor did I wish to practise resignation, unless it was quite necessary. I wanted to live deep and suck out all the marrow of life, to live so sturdily and Spartan-like as to put to rout all that was not life, to cut a broad swath and shave close, to drive life into a corner, and reduce it to its lowest terms, and, if it proved to be mean, why then to get the whole and genuine meanness of it, and publish its meanness to the world; or if it were sublime, to know it by experience, and be able to give a true account of it in my next excursion. For most men, it appears to me, are in a strange uncertainty about it, whether it is of the devil or of God, and have *somewhat hastily* concluded that it is the chief end of man here to "glorify God and enjoy him forever." . . .

Why should we live with such hurry and waste of life? We are determined to be starved before we are hungry. Men say that a stitch in time saves nine, and so they take a thousand stitches to-day to save nine to-morrow. As for *work,* we haven't any of any consequence. We have the Saint Vitus' dance, and cannot possibly keep our heads still. If I should only give a few pulls at the parish bell-rope, as for a fire, that is, without setting the bell, there is hardly a man on his farm in the outskirts of Concord, notwithstanding that press of engagements which was his excuse so many times this morning, nor a boy, nor a woman, I might almost say, but would forsake all and follow that sound, not mainly to save property from the flames, but, if we will confess the truth, much more to see it burn, since burn it must, and we, be it known, did not set it on fire,—or to see it put out, and have a hand in it, if that is done as handsomely; yes, even if it were the parish church itself. Hardly a man takes a half hour's nap after dinner, but when he wakes he holds up his head and asks, "What's the news?" as if the rest of mankind had stood his sentinels. Some give directions to be waked every half hour, doubtless for no other purpose; and then, to pay for it, they tell what they have dreamed. After a night's sleep the news is as indispensable as the breakfast. "Pray tell me anything new that has happened to a man anywhere on this globe,"—and he reads it over his coffee and rolls, that a man has had his eyes gouged out this morning on the Wachito River; never dreaming the while that he lives in the dark unfathomed mammoth cave of this world, and has but the rudiment of an eye himself.

For my part, I could easily do without the post-office. I think that there are very few important communications made through it. To speak critically, I never received more than one or two letters in my life—I wrote this some years ago—that were worth the postage. The penny-post is, commonly, an institution through which you seriously offer a man that penny for his thoughts which is so often safely offered in jest. And I am sure that I never read any memorable news in a newspaper. If we read of one man robbed, or murdered, or killed by accident, or one house burned, or one vessel wrecked, or one steamboat blown up, or one cow run over on the Western Railroad, or one mad dog killed, or one lot of grasshoppers in the winter,—we never need read of another. One is enough. If you are acquainted with the principle, what do you care for a myriad instances and applications? To a philosopher all *news,* as it is called, is gossip, and they who edit and read it are old women over their tea. . . .

What news! how much more important to know what that is which was   10 never old! "Kieou-he-yu (great dignitary of the state of Wei) sent a man to Khoung-tseu to know his news. Khoung-tseu caused the messenger to be seated near him, and questioned him in these terms: What is your master doing? The messenger answered with respect: My master desires to diminish the number of his faults, but he cannot come to the end of them. The messenger being gone, the philosopher remarked: What a worthy messenger! What a worthy messenger!" The preacher, instead of vexing the ears of drowsy farmers on their day of rest at the end of the week,—for Sunday is the fit conclusion of an ill-spent week, and not the fresh and brave beginning of a new one,—with this one other draggle-tail of a sermon, should shout with thundering voice,—"Pause! Avast! Why so seeming fast, but deadly slow?"

Shams and delusions are esteemed for soundest truths, while reality is fabulous. If men would steadily observe realities only, and not allow themselves to be deluded, life, to compare it with such things as we know, would be like a fairy tale and the Arabian Nights' Entertainments. If we respected only what is inevitable and has a right to be, music and poetry would resound along the streets. When we are unhurried and wise, we perceive that only great and worthy things have any permanent and absolute existence,—that petty fears and petty pleasures are but the shadow of the reality. This is always exhilarating and sublime. By closing the eyes and slumbering, and consenting to be deceived by shows, men establish and confirm their daily life of routine and habit everywhere, which still is built on purely illusory foundations. Children, who play life, discern its true law and relations more clearly than men, who fail to live it worthily, but who think that they are wiser by experience, that is, by failure. I have read in a Hindoo book, that "there was a king's son, who, being expelled in infancy from his native city, was brought up by a forester, and, growing up to maturity in that state, imagined himself to belong to the barbarous race with which he lived. One of his father's ministers having discovered him, revealed to him what he was, and the misconception of his character was removed, and he knew himself to be a prince. So soul," continues the Hindoo philosopher, "from the circumstances in which it is placed, mistakes its own character, until the truth is revealed to it by some holy teacher, and then it knows itself to be *Brahme.*" I perceive that we inhabitants of New England live this mean life that we do because our vision does not penetrate the surface of things. We think that that *is* which *appears* to be. If a man should walk through this town and see only the reality, where, think you, would the "Mill-dam" go to? If he should give us an account of the realities he beheld there, we should not recognize the place in his description. Look at a meeting-house, or a courthouse, or a jail, or a shop, or a dwelling-house, and say what that thing really is before a true gaze, and they would all go to pieces in your account of them. Men esteem truth remote, in the outskirts of the system, behind the farthest star, before Adam and after the last man. In eternity there is indeed something true and sublime. But all these times and places and occasions are now and here. God himself culminates in the present moment, and will never be more divine in the lapse of all the ages. And we are enabled to apprehend at all what is sublime and noble only by the perpetual instilling and drenching of the reality that surrounds us. The universe constantly and obediently answers to our conceptions; whether we travel fast or slow, the track is laid for us. Let us spend our lives in conceiving then. The poet or the artist never yet had so fair and noble a design but some of his posterity at least could accomplish it.

Let us spend one day as deliberately as Nature, and not be thrown off the track by every nutshell and mosquito's wing that falls on the rails. Let us rise early and fast, or break fast, gently and without perturbation; let company come and let company go, let the bells ring and the children cry,—determined to make a day of it. Why should we knock under and go with the stream? Let us not be upset and overwhelmed in that terrible rapid and whirlpool called a dinner, situated in the meridian shallows. Weather this danger and you are safe, for the rest of the way is down hill. With unrelaxed nerves, with morning vigor, sail by it, looking another way, tied to the mast like Ulysses. If the engine whistles, let it whistle till it is hoarse for its pains. If the bell rings, why should we run? We will consider what kind of music they are like. Let us settle ourselves, and work and wedge our feet downward through the mud and slush of opinion, and prejudice, and tradition, and delusion, and appearance, that alluvion which covers the globe, through Paris and London, through New York and Boston and Concord, through church and state, through poetry and philosophy and religion, till we come to a hard bottom and rocks in place, which we can call *reality*, and say, This is, and no mistake; and then begin, having a *point d' appui*, below freshet and frost and fire, a place where you might found a wall or a state, or set a lamppost safely, or perhaps a gauge, not a Nilometer, but a Realometer, that future ages might know how deep a freshet of shams and appearances had gathered from time to time. If you stand right fronting and face to face to a fact, you will see the sun glimmer on both its surfaces, as if it were a cimeter, and feel its sweet edge dividing you through the heart and marrow, and so you will happily conclude your mortal career. Be it life or death, we crave only reality. If we are really dying, let us hear the rattle in our throats and feel cold in the extremities; if we are alive, let us go about our business.

Time is but the stream I go a-fishing in. I drink at it; but while I drink I see the sandy bottom and detect how shallow it is. Its thin current slides away, but eternity remains. I would drink deeper; fish in the sky, whose bottom is pebbly with stars. I cannot count one. I know not the first letter of the alphabet. I have always been regretting that I was not as wise as the day I was born. The intellect is a cleaver; it discerns and rifts its way into the secret of things. I do not wish to be any more busy with my hands than is necessary. My head is hands and feet. I feel all my best faculties concentrated in it. My instinct tells me that my head is an organ for burrowing, as some creatures use their snout, and fore-paws, and with it I would mine and burrow my way through these hills. I think that the richest vein is somewhere hereabouts; so by the divining rod and thin rising vapors I judge; and here I will begin to mine.

ACTIVITIES FOR WRITING AND DISCUSSION

1. Thoreau's prose abounds with memorable sentences. Underline and annotate any that strike you, and be prepared to share and discuss them in class. If you wish, copy some or all of these sentences into a notebook—or a section within your reading notebook—that you designate for collecting memorable quotations. (For ideas about collecting and using such quotations, see Chapter 9.)

2. One distinctive aspect of Thoreau's style is his use of **allusions,** i.e., references to other literary works or characters or to historical persons, places, or events. Identify two or three allusions in the essay, look up the references, and analyze how the allusions work. Then generalize about how you think allusions strengthen or weaken the effectiveness of Thoreau's prose.

3. Thoreau takes a dim view of newspapers, the postal service, and other cultural resources and institutions that many of us regard as essential. Reread the relevant passages and summarize—as objectively as possible—the rationale behind Thoreau's criticisms. Then agree or disagree with Thoreau's critique.

4. Imagine you are Thoreau and you are living somewhere in America in the 1990s. In a personal essay, reveal how and where you (Thoreau) presently choose to live and why. Then review some contemporary American institutions, values, and/or behaviors as you believe Thoreau would.

THOMAS MOORE (b. 1940)

The Sacred Arts of Life

We can return now to one of Plato's expressions for care of the soul, *techne tou biou,* the craft of life. Care of the soul requires craft (*techne*)—skill, attention, and art. To live with a high degree of artfulness means to attend to the small things that keep the soul engaged in whatever we are doing, and it is the very heart of soul-making. From some grand overview of life, it may seem that only the big events are ultimately important. But to the soul, the most minute details and the most ordinary activities, carried out with mindfulness and art, have an effect far beyond their apparent insignificance.

Art is not found only in the painter's studio or in the halls of a museum, it also has its place in the store, the shop, the factory, and the home. In fact, when art is reserved as the province of professional artists, a dangerous gulf develops between the fine arts and the everyday arts. The fine arts are elevated and set apart from life, becoming too precious and therefore irrelevant. Having banished art to the museum, we fail to give it a place in ordinary life. One of the most effective forms of repression is to give a thing excessive honor.

Even in our art schools, a technical viewpoint is often dominant. The young painter learns about materials and schools of thought, but not about the soul of his vocation or the deeper significance of the content of his artwork. A voice major in a university music department expects to become an artist, but in her first lesson she is hooked up to an oscilloscope that will measure the parameters of her voice and indicate areas to be improved. The soul makes a quick exit before these purely technical approaches to learning.

The arts are important for all of us, whether or not we ourselves practice a particular discipline. Art, broadly speaking, is that which invites us into contemplation—a rare commodity in modern life. In that moment of contemplation, art intensifies the presence of the world. We see it more vividly and more deeply. The emptiness that many people complain dominates their lives comes in part from a failure to let the world in, to perceive it and engage it fully. Naturally, we'll feel empty if everything we do slides past without sticking. As we have seen, art *arrests* attention, an important service to the soul. Soul cannot thrive in a fast-paced life because being affected, taking things in and chewing on them, requires time.

Living artfully, therefore, might require something as simple as *pausing.* 5 Some people are incapable of being arrested by things because they are always on the move. A common symptom of modern life is that there is no time for thought, or even for letting impressions of a day sink in. Yet it is only when the world enters the heart that it can be made into soul. The vessel in which soul-making takes place is an inner container scooped out by reflection and wonder. There is no doubt that some people could spare themselves the expense and trouble of psychotherapy simply by giving themselves a few minutes each day for quiet reflection. This simple act would provide what is missing in their lives: a period of nondoing that is essential nourishment to the soul.

Akin to pausing, and just as important in care of the soul, is *taking time.* I realize these are extremely simple suggestions, but taken to heart they could transform a life, by allowing soul to enter. Taking time with things, we get to know them more intimately and to feel more genuinely connected to them. One of the symptoms of modern soullessness, an alienation from nature and things as well as from our fellow human beings, might be overcome if we took time with whatever we are dealing with.

Living artfully might require taking the time to buy things with soul for the home. Good linens, a special rug, or a simple teapot can be a source of enrichment not only in our own life, but also in the lives of our children and grandchildren. The soul basks in this extended sense of time. But we can't discover the soul in a thing without first taking time to observe it and be with it for a while. This kind of observation has a quality of intimacy about it; it's not just studying a consumer guide for factual and technical analysis. Surfaces, textures, and feel count as much as efficiency.

Certain things stimulate the imagination more than others, and that very blossoming of fantasy might be a sign of soul. An airline executive once talked to me about the struggle he was having in deciding between two jobs that had opened up for him. One was full of prestige and power, while the other was comfortable but quite ordinary. The first he felt he should consider because it was highly prized among his peers, but his thoughts about it were dry. The second one he imagined all day long. In his mind he had already begun to design his office and set his schedule. From the richness of his imagination of it, it was quite clear that the more lowly job appealed to his soul.

The ordinary arts we practice every day at home are of more importance to the soul than their simplicity might suggest. For example, I can't explain it, but I enjoy doing dishes. I've had an automatic dishwasher in my home for over a year, and I have never used it. What appeals to me, as I think about it, is the reverie induced by going through the ritual of washing, rinsing, and drying. Marie-Louise von Franz, the Swiss Jungian author, observes that weaving and knitting, too, are particularly good for the soul because they encourage reflection and reverie.

I also cherish the opportunity to hang clothes on a line outdoors. The fresh 10 smell, the wet fabrics, the blowing wind, and the drying sun go together to make an experience of nature and culture that is unique and particularly pleasurable for its simplicity. Deborah Hunter, a photographer, made a study several years ago of clothes on a line tossed by the wind. There was an element in these photographs, difficult to name, that touched upon vitality, the deep pleasures of ordinary life, and unseen forces of nature, all of which can be found around the house.

In a book not yet published, Jean Lall, the astrologer, observes that daily life at home is full of epiphanies. "Within our daily experience," she writes, "as keepers of home and gardens the spirits still move and speak if we but attend. They slip in through the cracks, making themselves felt in little breakdowns in appliances, unplanned sproutings in the flowerbeds, and sudden moments of blinding beauty, as where sunlight glances across a newly-waxed table or the wind stirs clean laundry into fresh choreography."

Many of the arts practiced at home are especially nourishing to the soul because they foster contemplation and demand a degree of artfulness, such as arranging flowers, cooking, and making repairs. I have a friend who is taking time over several months to paint a garden scene on a low panel of her dining room wall. Sometimes these ordinary arts bring out the individual, so that when you go into a home you can see the special character of your hosts in a particular aspect of their home.

Attending to the soul in these ordinary things usually leads to a more individual life, if not to an eccentric style. One of the things I love to do on a free afternoon is to visit Sleepy Hollow cemetery in Concord, Massachusetts. On a small, knobby hill deep in the cemetery is Emerson's grave, marked by a large, red-streaked boulder that contrasts with the typical gray rectangular gravestones all around him. Thoreau and Hawthorne lie a short distance away. For any who love Emerson's writing, this place is filled with soul. To me, his remarkable gravestone reflects his love of nature and mirrors both his greatness of soul and the irrepressible eccentricity of his imagination. The particular thrust of nature and the presence of a community of writers buried together make the place truly sacred.

When imagination is allowed to move to deep places, the sacred is revealed. The more different kinds of thoughts we experience around a thing and the deeper our reflections go as we are arrested by its artfulness, the more fully its sacredness can emerge. It follows, then, that living artfully can be a tonic for the secularization of life that characterizes our time. We can, of course, bring religion more closely in tune with ordinary life by immersing ourselves in formal rituals and traditional teachings; but we can also serve religion's soul by discovering the "natural religion" in all things. The route to this discovery is art, both the fine arts and those of everyday life. If we could loosen our grip on the functionality of life and let ourselves be arrested by the imaginal richness that surrounds all objects, natural and human-made, we might ground our secular attitudes in a religious sensibility and give ordinary life soul.

I'm suggesting that we consider sacredness from the point of view of soul 15 rather than spirit. From that angle, the sacred appears when imagination achieves unusual depth and fullness. The Bible, the Koran, Buddhist writings, and ritual books of all religions move us to imagine with exceptional range and depth. They bring us into wonder about the cosmos, about the far reaches of time past and present, and about ultimate values. But in a less formal way, any source of imagination that approaches this richness and depth helps create a religious sensibility. When they expose the deep images and themes that course through human life, so-called secular literature and art serve the religious impulse.

The medieval idea about learning, that theology is the ultimate science and all the others are "ancillary"—in humble service—is, to me, absolutely correct. Every issue, no matter how secular it appears to be, has a sacred dimension. If you press anything far enough, you will come up against either the holy or the demonic. Our secular sciences of physics, sociology, psychology, and the rest stop short of theological categories, thus preserving their scientific "objectivity," but also losing soul. Religious sensibility and soul are inseparable. I'm not saying that any particular religious affiliation or belief is essential to soul, but that a solid, palpable, and intellectually satisfying appreciation of the sacred is a sine qua non of living soulfully.

The theme requires a book of its own, but suffice it to say that theology is of concern for everyone, because our most ordinary experiences touch upon issues of such immense depth that they can only be considered religious. Recall Nicholas of Cusa's observation that God is the minimum as well as the maximum. The small things in everyday life are no less sacred than the great issues of human existence.

Becoming the artists and theologians of our own lives, we can approach the depth that is the domain of soul. When we leave art only to the accomplished painter and the museum, instead of fostering our own artful sensibilities through them, then our lives lose opportunities for soul. The same is true when we leave religion to church on the weekend. Then religion remains on the periphery of life, even if it is an exalted periphery, and life loses opportunities for soul. Fine art, like formal religion, is at times quite lofty, while soul in any context is lower case, ordinary, daily, familial and communal, felt, intimate, attached, engaged, involved, affected, ruminating, stirred, and poetic. The soul of a piece of art is known intimately, not remotely. It is felt, not just understood. So, too, the soul of religion lies in an immediate acquaintance with the angelic and the demonic. It is a daily involvement in mysteries and a personal quest for a corresponding ethic. Without soul, religion's truths and moral principles might be believed in, perhaps, and discussed, but they are not taken truly to heart and lived from the core of one's being.

Dreams: A Royal Road to Soul

Care of the soul involves "work," in the alchemical sense. It is impossible to care for the soul and live at the same time in unconsciousness. Sometimes soul work is exciting and inspiring, but often it is also challenging, requiring genuine courage. Rarely easy, work with the soul is usually placed squarely in that place we would rather not visit, in that emotion we don't want to feel, and in that understanding we would prefer to do without. The most honest route may be the most difficult to take. It is not easy to visit the place in ourselves that is most challenging and to look straight into the image that gives us the most fright; yet, there, where the work is most intense, is the source of soul.

Since we never want to take up the piece of our emotion that is most in need [20] of attention, I usually recommend to my patients that they give increased awareness to their dreams; for there they will find images that in waking life are very difficult to face. Dreams truly are the mythology of the soul and working with them forms a major piece in the project of making life more artful.

As a visit to any bookstore will demonstrate, there are many approaches to working with dreams. I would like to make a few concrete suggestions about what I consider key attitudes and strategies in dealing with dreams in a manner that preserves their integrity, allows meaning to emerge, and generally serves care of the soul.

Therapeutic work with dreams could be a model for less formal habits of giving dreams a serious place in our ordinary lives. When a person comes to me for an hour of therapy, I like to hear a dream or two early in the session. I don't like to listen to a dream and then immediately reach for an interpretation. It is better to let the dream lead us into new territory than to try to master the dream and figure it out at once. After the dream has been told, we might go on to talk about the person's life, since the therapy is almost always concerned with life situations. I may notice ways in which the dream offers us images and a language for talking about life with depth and imagination. Instead of trying to figure out the dream, we are letting the dream figure us out, allowing the dream to influence and shape our way of imagining. Usually, the main problem with life conundrums is that we don't bring to them enough imagination. We understand our difficulties literally and look for literal solutions, which rarely work precisely because they are part of the problem—lack of imagination. Dreams offer a fresh point of view.

In therapy it's tempting for both therapist and patient to translate a dream into theories and rationalizations that merely support the ideas of the therapist or the problematical attitudes of the patient. It is much better to let the dream interpret us rather than for us to become clever in interpreting the dream in ways most compatible with our existing ideas.

It is my experience that a dream reveals itself to the patient and the therapist slowly, gradually. I hear the dream and usually have a few impressions and ideas come to the surface immediately. But there might also be a great deal of confusion about the imagery. I try to hold back my need to overcome a dream with meaning. I tolerate its mood and let its puzzling imagery confound me, turn me away from my convictions in order to consider *its* mystery. Having patience with dreams is extremely important, and is more effective in the long run than any exercise of knowledge, techniques, and tricks. The dream reveals itself on its own timetable, but it does reveal itself.

It's important to trust your intuitions, which are not the same as your intel- 25 lectual interpretations. For example, sometimes a person will tell me a dream and immediately recommend a way of understanding it or offer a bias toward one of the characters. A woman, for instance, relates a dream in which she has absent-mindedly left her front door open, allowing a man to sneak into her house. "It was a nightmare," she says, "I think the dream is telling me that I'm not careful enough about keeping myself protected. I'm too open."

You see, I'm given a dream and an interpretation. Even though I have considerable experience working with dreams and have been trained not to buy into whatever idea a patient gives me, I'm sometimes unconsciously affected by the interpretation. It's so reasonable. Of course, she is too vulnerable and is threatened by an intruder. But then I remember my first rule: trust your intuitions. I wonder if the "accidental" opening in the door might not be a good thing for this person. The opening may allow new personalities to enter her living space. I'm also aware that the unintentional may not be unintended at all:

someone else besides the "I" may wish to leave the door open. The crack in the door may be an accident only to the ego.

There is often an apparent collusion between the dream-ego and the waking dreamer. As the dreamer tells the dream, she may slant her story in the direction of the "I" in the dream, thus convincing the listener to take a certain position in relation to the figures in the dream. Therefore, perhaps sometimes too much in compensation, I like to assume a rather perverse attitude when I hear the dream. I make a point of considering an angle different from the dreamer's. To put it more technically, I assume that in the telling of the dream the dreamer may be locked in the same complex as is the dream-ego. If I simply accept what the dreamer tells me, I may get caught in the dreamer's complex, and then I'm of no use. So I say to this dreamer: "Maybe it's not so bad that your usual thought about closing doors failed in this case. Maybe it allowed an entry that will prove to be beneficial. At least we can keep an open mind."

Speaking for other figures in the dream, sometimes against the bias of the dreamer, can open up a perspective on the dream that is extraordinarily revealing. Care of the soul, remember, does not necessarily mean care of the ego. Other characters may need acceptance and understanding. We may need to consider objectionable actions and characters as somehow necessary and even valuable.

A woman who is a writer tells a dream in which she catches a friend of hers smearing crayons all over the dreamer's typewriter. "It was an awful dream," she said, "and I know what it means. My inner child is always interfering with my adult work. If only I could grow up!"

Notice that this person, too, is quick to move toward interpretation. More than that, she wants me to take a certain position in relation to her dream. In a very subtle way, this desire is a defense against the otherness of the dream, its challenge. Soul and ego are often in a struggle which is sometimes mild and sometimes savage. So, I am careful not to assume that she is right about the content of the dream.

"Was your friend in the dream a child?" I ask.

"No, she was an adult. She was the age she is in life."

"Then why do you think she is being childish?"

"Crayons are a childish thing," she says as if stating the obvious.

"Can you tell me something about this friend of yours?" I am trying to break free of her strong views about her dream.

"She's very seductive, always wearing outlandish clothes—you know, bright colors and always low-cut."

"Is it possible," I say, taking a leap on the basis of her association, "that this colorful, sensual woman could be adding color, body, and some positive qualities of the child to your writing?"

"I suppose it's possible," she says, still unconvinced by this affront to her more satisfying interpretation.

One of the things that turned me away from her reading of the dream, apart from the general principle that we should avoid getting caught in the dream ego's complexes, was the negative narcissism in her judgment about the child: she didn't want to accept her own childlike ways. Once we moved away from her attachment to her usual way of thinking about herself, an attitude that strongly colored her own thoughts about the dream, we could go on to consider some truly fresh ideas about her life situation and her personal habits.

I am going into some detail about dreams not only because they give us a 40 great deal of insight into our habits and our nature, but also because the way we relate to our dreams can be indicative of our way of dealing with all kinds of things, including our interpretations of the past, our current situation and problems, and the culture in the larger sense.

For example, another rule of thumb about dreams is that there is never a single, definitive reading. At another time, the same dream might reveal something altogether new. I like to treat dreams as if they were paintings, and paintings as if they were dreams. A Monet landscape might "mean" something different to various people who contemplate it. It might evoke entirely different reactions in the same person at different viewings. Over many years, a good painting will retain its power to mesmerize, satisfy, and evoke new reverie and wonder.

The same is true with dreams. A dream may survive a lifetime of neglect or an onslaught of interpretations and remain an icon and a fertile enigma for years of reflection. The point in working with a dream is never to translate it into a final meaning, but always to give it honor and respect, drawing from it as much meaningfulness and imaginative meditation as possible. Entering a dream should revitalize the imagination, not keep it in fixed and tired habits.

A simple but effective approach in working with images—whether they are from dreams, art, or personal stories—is never to stop listening to them and exploring them. Why do we listen to Bach's St. Matthew Passion more than once? Because it is the nature of a work of art, of any image, to reveal itself endlessly, one of the methods I use in therapy and in teaching is to listen to a reading of a dream or a story and say, when it is finished, "All right, let's try that again, differently."

Once a young man came to me with a letter he had written to his sweetheart. It was important to him because it expressed his deep feelings. He said he'd like to read it to me aloud. He read it slowly and expressively. When he was finished, I asked him if he'd read it again, with different emphasis. He did, and in this reading we heard different nuances of meaning. We tried it a third and a fourth time, and each time we learned something new. This little exercise points out the rich, multilayered nature of images of all kinds, and the advantage of never stopping in our exploration of them. The images, dreams, and experiences that are important to us will always have a multitude of possible readings and interpretations, because they are rich with imagination and soul.

I understand that this approach to imagination goes against the part of us 45 that longs for a conclusion and a destination in our search for meaning. This is another reason why *care* of the soul, in contrast to *understanding* the soul, amounts to a new paradigm for our modern way of life. It asks us to make a complete turnaround in our usual efforts to figure things out, suggesting a different set of values and new techniques in which we actually appreciate and enjoy the endless unraveling of meaning, the infinitely rich and deep layering of poetics within the shifting, fluid fabric of experience.

The desire to squeeze a single meaning out of a dream or a work of art or a tale from life is inherently and profoundly Promethean. We want to steal fire from the gods for the sake of humanity. We want to replace divine mystery with human rationality. But this loss of complexity and mystery in our everyday response to life stories entails a loss of soul as well, because soul always manifests itself in mystery and multiplicity.

Dreams themselves often show us the way to understand them: they pull the dreamer deep into a body of water, or down into a pit, or down an elevator to a basement, or down a dark stairway, or deep into an alley. Typically, the dreamer, preferring height and light, is afraid to make the downward move into darkness. When I taught in the university, students frequently told me dreams of going into the library, getting on an elevator, then finding themselves in an ancient basement. The dream is not surprising, given the fact that the life of academia is so much an Apollonic, upper-world, ivory tower affair, and stands as a metaphor for all our attempts at understanding.

A woman who worked for a large appliance corporation once told me a dream in which she and her husband got off an elevator on a lower floor of the building, only to find the entire area under water. Together they floated in the water through hallways and streets until they arrived at a wonderful restaurant where they sat and ate a delicious dinner. This, too, is an image of dreamwork: allowing oneself to move around in the liquid atmosphere of fantasy and finding nourishment there. In dreams, which need never be taken literally or according to the laws of nature, we can breathe in a watery atmosphere. Dreams *are* watery: they resist all efforts to make them fixed and solid. We think we can only survive in the airy realms of thought and reason, but this dreamer found that she could be fed in gourmet style in that thicker atmosphere where imagination and life are fluid.

The Guiding Daimon

An approach often taken to images is to find a meaning outside the image itself. A cigar in a dream is considered a phallic symbol instead of a cigar. A woman is an anima figure instead of a particular woman. A child is the "child part of myself" instead of simply the child of the dream. We think of imagination as a kind of symbolic thinking, with, as Freud put it, a latent and a manifest meaning. If we could "decipher" the given symbols, to use a popular rationalistic word, we could learn the meaning that is hidden in the image.

But there is another possible way to understand the creations of the dream 50 world. What if there were no hidden meaning, no underlying message? What if we chose to confront images in all their mystery, deciding whether to follow their lead or to struggle with them?

The Greeks referred to the multitude of unnamed spirits that motivate and guide life as daimons. Socrates claimed to have lived his life according to the dictates of his daimon. In more recent times, W.B. Yeats warned that the daimon both inspires and threatens. In the chapter of *Memories, Dreams, Reflections* entitled "Late Thoughts," Jung, too, discusses the daimon. "We know that something unknown, alien, does come our way, just as we know that we do not ourselves *make* a dream or an inspiration, but that it somehow arises of its own accord. What does happen to us in this manner can be said to emanate from mana, from a daimon, a god, or the unconscious." He goes on to say that he prefers the term *the unconscious,* but he might just as well say *daimon.* Daimonic living is a response to the movements of imagination. When Jung was building his tower, workmen delivered a large piece of stone that was the wrong size. He took this "mistake" as the work of his Mercurial daimon and used the stone for one of his most important sculptures, the Bollingen Stone.

In the fifteenth century, Ficino, in *his* book on care of the soul, recommended finding the guardian daimon that is with us from the beginning: "Whoever examines himself thoroughly will find his own daimon." Rilke also regarded the daimon with respect. In his *Letters to a Young Poet* he suggests diving deeply into oneself in order to find one's own nature: "Go into yourself and see how deep the place is from which your life flows." Rilke is giving advice to a young man who wants to know whether he is called to be an artist, but his recommendation applies to anyone who wants to live everyday life with art. The soul wants to be in touch with that deep place from which life flows, without translating its offerings into familiar concepts. The best way to fulfill this desire is to give attention to the images that arise as independent beings from the springs of day-to-day imagination.

One implication of offering respect to the dream world is that we have to re-imagine imagination itself. Instead of seeing it as a particularly creative form of mind work, we could understand it more along Greek mythological lines, as a spring from which autonomous beings arise. Our relationship to it would change as well, from attempting to translate florid fantasy into reasonable terms to observing and entering a veritable world of personalities, geographies, animals, and events—all irreducible to completely understandable or controllable terms.

We would realize that the images of dreams and art are not puzzles to be solved, and that imagination hides its meaningfulness as much as it reveals it. In order to be affected by a dream, it isn't necessary to understand it or even to mine it for meanings. Merely giving our attention to such imagery, granting its autonomy and mystery, goes a long way toward shifting the center of consciousness from understanding to response. To live in the presence of the daimonic is to obey inner laws and urgencies. Cicero said that it is the *animus*—the Latin translation of *daimon*—that accounts for who you are.

Ficino warned against living in conflict with the daimon lest you succumb to the worst kind of soul sickness. As an example, he says you should never decide where to live without taking into full consideration the demands of the daimon, which may appear as an intuitive attraction or inhibition.

The source from which life flows is so deep that it is experienced as "other." 55 Speaking in the ancient language of the daimonic helps bring imagination into our very sense of self. Our relationship to the deep source of life becomes interpersonal, a dramatic tension between self and angel. In this dialogue, life also becomes more artful, in some cases even dramatic. We see this in people we label psychotic. Most of their actions are explicitly dramatic. Their deep "others," the personalities who play significant roles in their lives, appear in full dress. Writers talk about the characters of their fiction as people with will and intention. The novelist Margaret Atwood said once in an interview, "If the author gets too bossy, the characters may remind her that, though she is their creator, they are to some extent her creator as well."

Art teaches us to respect imagination as something far beyond human creation and intention. To live our ordinary life artfully is to have this sensibility about the things of daily life, to live more intuitively and to be willing to surrender a measure of our rationality and control in return for the gifts of soul.

The Soul Arts

Care of the soul may take the form of living in a fully embodied imagination, being an artist at home and at work. You don't have to be a professional in order to bring art into the care of your soul; anyone can have an art studio at home, for instance. Like Jung, Black Elk, and Ficino, we could decorate our homes with images from our dreams and waking fantasy.

One of my own forms of expression is to play the piano in times of strong emotion. I remember well the day Martin Luther King, Jr., was killed. I was so overwhelmed that I went to the piano and played Bach for three hours. The music gave form and voice to my scrambled emotions, without explanations and rational interpretations.

The stuff of the world is there to be made into images that become for us tabernacles of spirituality and containers of mystery. If we don't allow soul its place in our lives, we are forced to encounter these mysteries in fetishes and symptoms, which in a sense are pathological art forms, the gods in our diseases. The example of artists teaches us that every day we can transform ordinary experience into the material of soul—in diaries, poems, drawings, music, letters, watercolors.

In a letter on soul-making to his brother George, Keats describes the process 60 of transforming world into soul with the image of a school: "I will call the world a School instituted for the purpose of teaching little children to read—I will call the human heart the hornbook used in that School—and I will call the child able to read, the Soul made from that school and its hornbook. Do you not see how necessary a World of Pains and troubles is to school an Intelligence and make it a soul?"

As we read our experiences and learn to express them artfully, we are making life more soulful. Our homely arts arrest the flow of life momentarily so that events can be submitted to the alchemy of reflection. In a letter to a friend, we can deepen the impressions of experience and settle them in the heart where they can become the foundation for soul. Our great museums of art are simply a grand model for the more modest museum that is our home. There is no reason not to imagine our own homes as a place where the Muses can do their work of inspiration daily.

Another advantage to the soul of practicing the ordinary arts is the gift they leave for future generations. Tradition says that the soul thrives in a sense of time much greater than that of consciousness. To the soul the past is alive and valuable, and so is the future. As we perform the alchemy of sketching or writing upon our daily experience, we are preserving our thoughts for those who follow us. The community made by art transcends the limits of a personal lifetime, so that we can be instructed in our own soul work by the letters of John Keats to his brother.

In the modern world, in which we live mainly for the moment, it is easy to overlook the taste of the soul for a greater sense of time and a profound notion of community. We tend to give superficial explanations for our actions, to speak in literal terms instead of focusing on the reasons of the heart. A man explaining to me why he was getting a divorce went on and on with minor complaints about his wife. What he didn't say was what was obvious from our other conversations, that his heart was going through a major change. He wanted a new life, but tried to justify all the accompanying pain with superficial reasons. Because he didn't speak deeply about what was going on with him, he was cutting himself off from the soul of his divorce.

But when you read the letters of Keats, Rilke, or other poets you find a passionate search for expression and language adequate to the pleasures and pains of life. We can learn from them the importance to everyone, not just poets, of the effort to translate experience into words and pictures. The point of art is not simply to express ourselves, but to create an external, concrete form in which the soul of our lives can be evoked and contained.

Children paint every day and love to show their works on walls and refriger- 65
ator doors. But as we become adults, we abandon this important soul task of childhood. We assume, I suppose, that children are just learning motor coordination and alphabets. But maybe they are doing something more fundamental: finding forms that reflect what is going on in their souls. When we grow up and begin to think of the art gallery as much more advanced than the refrigerator door, we lose an important ritual of childhood, giving it away to the professional artist. We are then left with mere rational reasons for our lives, feelings of emptiness and confusion, expensive visits to a psychotherapist, and a compulsive

attachment to pseudoimages, such as shallow television programs. When our own images no longer have a home, a personal museum, we drown our sense of loss in pale substitutes, trashy novels or formulaic movies.

As the poets and painters of centuries have tried to tell us, art is not about the expression of talent or the making of pretty things. It is about the preservation and containment of soul. It is about arresting life and making it available for contemplation. Art captures the eternal in the everyday, and it is the eternal that feeds soul—the whole world in a grain of sand.

Leonardo da Vinci asks an interesting question in one of his notebooks: "Why does the eye see a thing more clearly in dreams than the imagination when awake?" One answer is that the eye of the soul perceives the eternal realities so important to the heart. In waking life, most of us see only with our physical eyes, even though we could, with some effort of imagination, glimpse fragments of eternity in the most ordinary passing events. Dream teaches us to look with that other eye, the eye that in waking life belongs to the artist, to each of us as artist.

When we see pain on a tortured person's face, we might glimpse for a second the image of Jesus crucified, a reality that artists for centuries have shown in infinite variation and detail and one that enters the lives of all of us at one time or another. We might look at a woman in a jewelry shop with the eyes of D.H. Lawrence, who saw Aphrodite in the body of the woman washing her clothes in a river. We might see a Cézanne still life in a momentary glance at our own kitchen table. When a summer breeze blows through an open window as we sit reading in a rare half-hour of quiet, we might recall one of the hundreds of annunciations painters have given us, reminding us that it is the habit of angels to visit in moments of silent reading.

A soul-centered understanding of art sees the interpenetration of poetic image and ordinary life. Art shows us what is already there in the ordinary, but without art we live under the illusion that there is only time, and not eternity. As we practice our daily arts, if only in the composing of a heart-felt letter, we are unearthing the eternal from within ordinary time, engaging in the special qualities, themes, and circumstances of the soul. Soul thrives as we jot down a thought in our diary or note a dream, and give body to a slight influx of eternity. Our notebooks then truly become our own private gospels and sutras, our holy books, and our simple paintings truly serve as icons, every bit as significant in the work of our own soul as the wonderful icons of the Eastern churches are for their congregations.

Care of the soul is not a project of self-improvement nor a way of being released from the troubles and pains of human existence. It is not at all concerned with living properly or with emotional health. These are the concerns of temporal, heroic, Promethean life. Care of the soul touches another dimension, in no way separate from life, but not identical either with the problem solving that occupies so much of our consciousness. We care for the soul solely by honoring its expressions, by giving it time and opportunity to reveal itself, and by living   70 life in a way that fosters the depth, interiority, and quality in which it flourishes. Soul is its own purpose and end.

To the soul, memory is more important than planning, art more compelling than reason, and love more fulfilling than understanding. We know we are well on the way toward soul when we feel attachment to the world and the people around us and when we live as much from the heart as from the head. We know soul is being cared for when our pleasures feel deeper than usual, when we can let go of the need to be free of complexity and confusion, and when compassion takes the place of distrust and fear. Soul is interested in the differences among cultures and individuals, and within ourselves it wants to be expressed in uniqueness if not in outright eccentricity.

Therefore, when in the midst of my confusion and my stumbling attempts to live a transparent life, *I* am the fool, and not everyone around me, then I know I am discovering the power of the soul to make a life interesting. Ultimately, care of the soul results in an individual "I" I never would have planned for or maybe even wanted. By caring for the soul faithfully, every day, we step out of the way and let our full genius emerge. Soul coalesces into the mysterious philosophers' stone, that rich, solid core of personality the alchemists sought, or it opens into the peacock's tail—a revelation of the soul's colors and a display of its dappled brilliance.

ACTIVITIES FOR WRITING AND DISCUSSION

1. Since Moore's essay is quite long, try to read it in two or more sittings, focusing on sections that strike you and skimming over those that don't. In your notebook, respond using either:
   a. The Four-Step Process for Writing from Reading described in Chapter 2; or
   b. Idea #1 from the "Ten Ideas" described in Chapter 3.

2. On page 839 Moore writes: "*[C]are* of the soul, in contrast to *understanding* the soul, amounts to a new paradigm for our modern way of life." Read the context in which this sentence appears. Then consider:
   a. Some differences between "caring" and "understanding" as Moore seems to use those terms. Can caring and understanding be at odds with each other? If so how and in what situations?
   b. In what ways do you think Moore's statement, quoted above, is accurate or inaccurate?

3. In his discussion of "The Guiding Daimon," Moore writes:

The source from which life flows is so deep that it is experienced as "other." ... Our relationship to the deep source of life [i.e., the daimon] becomes interpersonal, a dramatic tension between self and angel.

Explain what you think Moore means by "the daimon." Then do one of the following:

    a. Over a period of days, think about the nature of your own "angel" or "daimon"; describe its power, mystery, promises, and dangers. Then write a dialogue—or a series of short dialogues—between your own "self" and this angel or daimon.

    b. List the names of some outstanding people, living or dead, whom you admire. Choose one such person and write about the nature of the "daimon" that you imagine guides (or guided) that person in his or her life.

LINDA HOGAN (b. 1947)

Waking Up the Rake

In the still dark mornings, my grandmother would rise up from her bed and put wood in the stove. When the fire began to burn, she would sit in front of its warmth and let down her hair. It had never been cut and it knotted down in two long braids. When I was fortunate enough to be there, in those red Oklahoma mornings, I would wake up with her, stand behind her chair, and pull the brush through the long strands of her hair. It cascaded down her back, down over the chair, and touched the floor.

We were the old and the new, bound together in front of the snapping fire, woven like a lifetime's tangled growth of hair. I saw my future in her body and face, and her past was alive in me. We were morning people, and in all of earth's mornings the new intertwines with the old. Even new, a day itself is ancient, old with earth's habit of turning over and over again.

Years later, I was sick, and I went to a traditional healer. The healer was dark and thin and radiant. The first night I was there, she also lit a fire. We sat before it, smelling the juniper smoke. She asked me to tell her everything, my life spoken in words, a case history of living, with its dreams and losses, the scars and wounds we all bear from being in the world. She smoked me with cedar smoke, wrapped a sheet around me, and put me to bed, gently, like a mother caring for her child.

The next morning she nudged me awake and took me outside to pray. We faced east where the sun was beginning its journey on our side of earth.

The following morning in red dawn, we went outside and prayed. The sun 5 was a full orange eye rising up the air. The morning after that we did the same, and on Sunday we did likewise.

The next time I visited her it was a year later, and again we went through the same prayers, standing outside facing the early sun. On the last morning I was there, she left for her job in town. Before leaving, she said, "Our work is our altar."

Those words have remained with me.

Now I am a disciple of birds. The birds that I mean are eagles, owls, and hawks. I clean cages at the Birds of Prey Rehabilitation Foundation. It is the work I wanted to do, in order to spend time inside the gentle presence of the birds.

There is a Sufi saying that goes something like this: "Yes, worship God, go to church, sing praises, but first tie your camel to the post." This cleaning is the work of tying the camel to a post.

I pick up the carcasses and skin of rats, mice, and of rabbits. Some of them   10
have been turned inside out by the sharp-beaked eaters, so that the leathery flesh becomes a delicately veined coat for the inner fur. It is a boneyard. I rake the smooth fragments of bones. Sometimes there is a leg or shank of deer to be picked up.

In this boneyard, the still-red vertebrae lie on the ground beside an open rib cage. The remains of a rabbit, a small intestinal casing, holds excrement like beads in a necklace. And there are the clean, oval pellets the birds spit out, filled with fur, bone fragments and now and then, a delicate sharp claw that looks as if it were woven inside. A feather, light and soft, floats down a current of air, and it is also picked up.

Over time, the narrow human perspective from which we view things expands. A deer carcass begins to look beautiful and rich in its torn redness, the muscle and bone exposed in the shape life took on for a while as it walked through meadows and drank at creeks.

And the bone fragments have their own stark beauty, the clean white jaw bones with ivory teeth small as the head of a pin still in them. I think of medieval physicians trying to learn about our private, hidden bodies by cutting open the stolen dead and finding the splendor inside, the grace of every red organ, and the smooth, gleaming bone.

This work is an apprenticeship, and the birds are the teachers. Sweet-eyed barn owls, such taskmasters, asking us to be still and slow and to move in time with their rhythms, not our own. The short-eared owls with their startling yellow eyes require the full presence of a human. The marsh hawks, behind their branches, watch our every move.

There is a silence needed here before a person enters the bordered world the   15
birds inhabit, so we stop and compose ourselves before entering their doors, and we listen to the musical calls of the eagles, the sound of wings in air, the way their feet with sharp claws, many larger than our own hands, grab hold of a perch. Then we know we are ready to enter, and they are ready for us.

The most difficult task the birds demand is that we learn to be equal to them, to feel our way into an intelligence that is different from our own. A friend, awed at the thought of working with eagles, said, "Imagine knowing an eagle." I answered her honestly, "It isn't so much that we know the eagles. It's that they know us."

And they know that we are apart from them, that as humans we have somehow fallen from our animal grace, and because of that we maintain a distance from them, though it is not always a distance of heart. The places we inhabit, even sharing a common earth, must remain distinct and separate. It was our presence that brought most of them here in the first place, nearly all of them injured in a clash with the human world. They have been shot, or hit by cars, trapped in leg hold traps, poisoned, ensnared in wire fences. To ensure their survival, they must remember us as the enemies that we are. We are the embodiment of a paradox; we are the wounders and we are the healers.

There are human lessons to be learned here, in the work. Fritjof Capra wrote: "Doing work that has to be done over and over again helps us to recognize the natural cycles of growth and decay, of birth and death, and thus become aware of the dynamic order of the universe." And it is true, in whatever we do, the brushing of hair, the cleaning of cages, we begin to see the larger order of things. In this place, there is a constant coming to terms with both the sacred place life occupies, and with death. Like one of those early physicians who discovered the strange, inner secrets of our human bodies, I'm filled with awe at the very presence of life, not just the birds, but a horse contained in its living fur, a dog alive and running. What a marvel it is, the fine shape life takes in all of us. It is equally marvelous that life is quickly turned back to earth-colored ants and the soft white maggots that are time's best and closest companions. To sit with the eagles and their flute-like songs, listening to the longer flute of wind sweep through the lush grasslands, is to begin to know the natural laws that exist apart from our own written ones.

One of those laws, that we carry deep inside us, is intuition. It is lodged in a place even the grave-robbing doctors could not discover. It's a blood-written code that directs us through life. The founder of this healing center, Sigrid Ueblacker, depends on this inner knowing. She watches, listens, and feels her way to an understanding of each eagle and owl. This vision, as I call it, directs her own daily work at healing the injured birds and returning them to the wild.

"Sweep the snow away," she tells me. "The Swainson's hawks should be in 20 Argentina this time of year and should not have to stand in the snow."

I sweep.

And that is in the winter when the hands ache from the cold, and the water freezes solid and has to be broken out for the birds, fresh buckets carried over icy earth from the well. In summer, it's another story. After only a few hours the food begins to move again, as if resurrected to life. A rabbit shifts a bit. A mouse turns. You could say that they have been resurrected, only with a life other than the one that left them. The moving skin swarms with flies and their offspring, ants, and a few wasps, busy at their own daily labor.

Even aside from the expected rewards for this work, such as seeing an eagle healed and winging across the sky it fell from, there are others. An occasional snake, beautiful and sleek, finds its way into the cage one day, eats a mouse and is too fat to leave, so we watch its long muscular life stretched out in the tall grasses. Or, another summer day, taking branches to be burned with a pile of wood near the little creek, a large turtle with a dark and shining shell slips soundlessly into the water, its presence a reminder of all the lives beyond these that occupy us.

One green morning, an orphaned owl perches nervously above me while I clean. Its downy feathers are roughed out. It appears to be twice its size as it clacks its beak at me, warning me: Stay back. Then, fearing me the way we want it to, it bolts off the perch and flies, landing by accident onto the wooden end of my rake, before it sees that a human is an extension of the tool, and it flies again to a safer place, while I return to raking.

The word *rake* means to gather or heap up, to smooth the broken ground. 25 And that's what this work is, all of it, the smoothing over of broken ground, the healing of the severed trust we humans hold with earth. We gather it back together again with great care, take the broken pieces and fragments and return them to the sky. It is work at the borderland between species, at the boundary between injury and healing.

There is an art to raking, a very fine art, one with rhythm in it, and life. On the days I do it well, the rake wakes up. Wood that came from dark dense forests seems to return to life. The water that rose up through the rings of that wood, the minerals of earth mined upward by the burrowing tree roots, all come alive. My own fragile hand touches the wood, a hand full of my own life, including that which rose each morning early to watch the sun return from the other side of the planet. Over time, these hands will smooth the rake's wooden handle down to a sheen.

Raking. It is a labor round and complete, smooth and new as an egg, and the rounding seasons of the world revolving in time and space. All things, even our own heartbeats and sweat, are in it, part of it. And that work, that watching the turning over of life, becomes a road into what is essential. Work is the country of hands, and they want to live there in the dailiness of it, the repetition that is time's language of prayer, a common tongue. Everything is there, in that language, in the humblest of labor. The rake wakes up and the healing is in it. The shadows of leaves that once fell beneath the tree the handle came from are in that labor, and the rabbits that passed this way, on the altar of our work. And when the rake wakes up, all earth's gods are reborn and they dance and sing in the dusty air around us.

Activities for Writing and Discussion

1. The traditional healer whom Hogan visits says, "Our work is our altar." Based on the narrative that precedes this statement, explain what you think the healer means. Then write about ways in which your own "work" (paid or unpaid, vocation or avocation) is—or isn't—an "altar."

2. Hogan says that her work for the Birds of Prey Rehabilitation Foundation is monotonous, yet she seems to value this very monotony. She performs a

task (raking) that would seem to be easy and "mindless," yet she insists "there is an art to [it]." How can monotony be valuable, and how can a menial job—raking or any other—involve "art"? In your notebook try to explain either of these observations. Alternative: Write about any other ideas in the essay that you find surprising or striking, and relate them to your own experience.

3. Hogan says that birds require us "to feel our way into an intelligence that is different from our own." She also regards birds and other animals as soulful creatures from which we humans can learn. Reread and annotate passages about this "teacher"/"apprentice" relationship between animals and humans. Then assume the **point of view** of one such animal—from Hogan's essay or your own experience—and compose a text about your past, your life and its beauty, and your perspective on humans.

Play

Woody Allen (b. 1935)

Death Knocks

The play takes place in the bedroom of the Nat Ackermans' two-story house, somewhere in Kew Gardens. The carpeting is wall-to-wall. There is a big double bed and a large vanity. The room is elaborately furnished and curtained, and on the walls there are several paintings and a not really attractive barometer. Soft theme music as the curtain rises. Nat Ackerman, a bald, paunchy fifty-seven-year-old dress manufacturer is lying on the bed finishing off tomorrow's Daily News. *He wears a bathrobe and slippers, and reads by a bed light clipped to the white headboard of the bed. The time is near midnight. Suddenly we hear a noise, and Nat sits up and looks at the window.*

NAT: What the hell is that?

[*Climbing awkwardly through the window is a sombre, caped figure. The intruder wears a black hood and skintight black clothes. The hood covers his head but not his face, which is middle-aged and stark white. He is something like* NAT *in appearance. He huffs audibly and then trips over the windowsill and falls into the room.*]

DEATH [*for it is no one else*]: Jesus Christ. I nearly broke my neck.
NAT [*watching with bewilderment*]: Who are you?
DEATH: Death.
NAT: Who?
DEATH: Death. Listen—can I sit down? I nearly broke my neck. I'm shaking like a leaf.

NAT: Who *are* you?

DEATH: *Death.* You got a glass of water?

NAT: Death? What do you mean, Death?

DEATH: What is wrong with you? You see the black costume and the whitened face?

NAT: Yeah.

DEATH: Is it Halloween?

NAT: No.

DEATH: Then I'm Death. Now can I get a glass of water—or a Fresca?

NAT: If this is some joke—

DEATH: What kind of joke? You're fifty-seven? Nat Ackerman? One eighteen Pacific Street? Unless I blew it—where's that call sheet? [*He fumbles through pocket, finally producing a card with an address on it. It seems to check.*]

NAT: What do you want with me?

DEATH: What do I want? What do you think I want?

NAT: You must be kidding. I'm in perfect health.

DEATH [*unimpressed*]: Uh-huh. [*Looking around.*] This is a nice place. You do it yourself?

NAT: We had a decorator, but we worked with her.

DEATH [*looking at picture on the wall*]: I love those kids with the big eyes.

NAT: I don't want to go yet.

DEATH: *You* don't want to go? Please don't start in. As it is, I'm nauseous from the climb.

NAT: What climb?

DEATH: I climbed up the drainpipe. I was trying to make a dramatic entrance. I see the big windows and you're awake reading. I figure it's worth a shot. I'll climb up and enter with a little—you know ... [*Snaps fingers.*] Meanwhile, I get my heel caught on some vines, the drainpipe breaks, and I'm hanging by a thread. Then my cape begins to tear. Look, let's just go. It's been a rough night.

NAT: You broke my drainpipe?

DEATH: Broke. It didn't break. It's a little bent. Didn't you hear anything? I slammed into the ground.

NAT: I was reading.

DEATH: You must have really been engrossed. [*Lifting newspaper* NAT *was reading.*] "NAB COEDS IN POT ORGY." Can I borrow this?

NAT: I'm not finished.

DEATH: Er—I don't know how to put this to you, pal ...

NAT: Why didn't you just ring downstairs?

DEATH: I'm telling you, I could have, but how does it look? This way I get a little drama going. Something. Did you read *Faust*?

NAT: What?

DEATH: And what if you had company? You're sitting there with important people. I'm Death—I should ring the bell and traipse right in the front? Where's your thinking?

NAT: Listen, Mister, it's very late.

DEATH: Yeah. Well, you want to go?

NAT: Go where?

DEATH: Death. It. The Thing. The Happy Hunting Grounds. [*Looking at his own knee.*] Y'know, that's a pretty bad cut. My first job, I'm liable to get gangrene yet.

NAT: Now, wait a minute. I need time. I'm not ready to go.

DEATH: I'm sorry. I can't help you. I'd like to, but it's the moment.

NAT: How can it be the moment? I just merged with Modiste Originals.

DEATH: What's the difference, a couple of bucks more or less.

NAT: Sure, what do you care? You guys probably have all your expenses paid.

DEATH: You want to come along now?

NAT [*studying him*]: I'm sorry, but I cannot believe you're Death.

DEATH: Why? What'd you expect—Rock Hudson?

NAT: No, it's not that.

DEATH: I'm sorry if I disappointed you.

NAT: Don't get upset. I don't know, I always thought you'd be . . . uh . . . taller.

DEATH: I'm five seven. It's average for my weight.

NAT: You look a little like me.

DEATH: Who should I look like? I'm your death.

NAT: Give me some time. Another day.

DEATH: I can't. What do you want me to say?

NAT: One more day. Twenty-four hours.

DEATH: What do you need it for? The radio said rain tomorrow.

NAT: Can't we work out something?

DEATH: Like what?

NAT: You play chess?

DEATH: No, I don't.

NAT: I once saw a picture of you playing chess.

DEATH: Couldn't be me, because I don't play chess. Gin rummy, maybe.

NAT: You play gin rummy?

DEATH: Do I play gin rummy? Is Paris a city?

NAT: You're good, huh?

DEATH: Very good.

NAT: I'll tell you what I'll do—

DEATH: Don't make any deals with me.

NAT: I'll play you gin rummy. If you win, I'll go immediately. If I win, give me some more time. A little bit—one more day.

DEATH: Who's got time to play gin rummy?

NAT: Come on. If you're so good.

DEATH: Although I feel like a game . . .

NAT: Come on. Be a sport. We'll shoot for a half hour.

DEATH: I really shouldn't.

NAT: I got the cards right here. Don't make a production.

DEATH: All right, come on. We'll play a little. It'll relax me.

NAT [*getting cards, pad, and pencil*]: You won't regret this.

DEATH: Don't give me a sales talk. Get the cards and give me a Fresca and put out something. For God's sake, a stranger drops in, you don't have potato chips or pretzels.

NAT: There's M&M's downstairs in a dish.

DEATH: M&M's. What if the President came? He'd get M&M's, too?

NAT: You're not the President.

DEATH: Deal.

[NAT *deals, turns up a five.*]

NAT: You want to play a tenth of a cent a point to make it interesting?

DEATH: It's not interesting enough for you?

NAT: I play better when money's at stake.

DEATH: Whatever you say, Newt.

NAT: Nat. Nat Ackerman. You don't know my name?

DEATH: Newt, Nat—I got such a headache.

NAT: You want that five?

DEATH: No.

NAT: So pick.

DEATH [*surveying his hand as he picks*]: Jesus, I got nothing here.

NAT: What's it like?

DEATH: What's what like?

[*Throughout the following, they pick and discard.*]

NAT: Death.

DEATH: What should it be like? You lay there.

NAT: Is there anything after?

DEATH: Aha, you're saving twos.

NAT: I'm asking. Is there anything after?

DEATH [*absently*]: You'll see.

NAT: Oh, then I will actually see something?

DEATH: Well, maybe I shouldn't have put it that way. Throw.

NAT: To get an answer from you is a big deal.

DEATH: I'm playing cards.

NAT: All right, play, play.

DEATH: Meanwhile, I'm giving you one card after another.

NAT: Don't look through the discards.

DEATH: I'm not looking. I'm straightening them up. What was the knock card?

NAT: Four. You ready to knock already?

DEATH: Who said I'm ready to knock? All I asked was what was the knock card.

NAT: And all I asked was is there anything for me to look forward to.

DEATH: Play.

NAT: Can't you tell me anything? Where do we go?

DEATH: We? To tell you the truth, *you* fall in a crumpled heap on the floor.

NAT: Oh, I can't wait for that! Is it going to hurt?

DEATH: Be over in a second.

NAT: Terrific. [*Sighs.*] I needed this. A man merges with Modiste Originals . . .

DEATH: How's four points?

NAT: You're knocking?

DEATH: Four points is good?

NAT: No, I got two.

DEATH: You're kidding.

NAT: No, you lose.

DEATH: Holy Christ, and I thought you were saving sixes.

NAT: No. Your deal. Twenty points and two boxes. Shoot. [*Death deals.*] I must fall on the floor, eh? I can't be standing over the sofa when it happens?

DEATH: No. Play.

NAT: Why not?

DEATH: Because you fall on the floor! Leave me alone. I'm trying to concentrate.

NAT: Why must it be on the floor? That's all I'm saying! Why can't the whole thing happen and I'll stand next to the sofa?

DEATH: I'll try my best. Now can we play?

NAT: That's all I'm saying. You remind me of Moe Lefkowitz. He's also stubborn.

DEATH: I remind him of Moe Lefkowitz. I'm one of the most terrifying figures you could possibly imagine, and him I remind of Moe Lefkowitz. What is he, a furrier?

NAT: You should be such a furrier. He's good for eighty thousand a year. Passementeries. He's got his own factory. Two points.

DEATH: What?

NAT: Two points. I'm knocking. What have you got?

DEATH: My hand is like a basketball score.

NAT: And it's spades.

DEATH: If you didn't talk so much.

[*They redeal and play on.*]

NAT: What'd you mean before when you said this was your first job?

DEATH: What does it sound like?

NAT: What are you telling me—that nobody ever went before?

DEATH: Sure they went. But I didn't take them.

NAT: So who did?

DEATH: Others.

NAT: There's others?

DEATH: Sure. Each one has his own personal way of going.

NAT: I never knew that.

DEATH: Why should you know? Who are you?

NAT: What do you mean who am I? Why—I'm nothing?

DEATH: Not nothing. You're a dress manufacturer. Where do you come to knowledge of the eternal mysteries?

NAT: What are you talking about? I make a beautiful dollar. I sent two kids through college. One is in advertising, the other's married. I got my own home. I drive a Chrysler. My wife has whatever she wants. Maids, mink coat, vacations. Right now she's at the Eden Roc. Fifty dollars a day because she wants to be near her sister. I'm supposed to join her next week, so what do you think I am—some guy off the street?

DEATH: All right. Don't be so touchy.

NAT: Who's touchy?

DEATH: How would you like it if I got insulted quickly?

NAT: Did I insult you?

DEATH: You didn't say you were disappointed in me?

NAT: What do you expect? You want me to throw you a block party?

DEATH: I'm not talking about that. I mean me personally. I'm too short, I'm this, I'm that.

NAT: I said you looked like me. It's like a reflection.

DEATH: All right, deal, deal.

[*They continue to play as music steals in and the lights dim until all is in total darkness. The lights slowly come up again, and now it is later and their game is over.* NAT *tallies.*]

NAT: Sixty-eight . . . one-fifty . . . Well, you lose.

DEATH [*dejectedly looking through the deck*]: I knew I shouldn't have thrown that nine. Damn it.

NAT: So I'll see you tomorrow.

DEATH: What do you mean you'll see me tomorrow?

NAT: I won the extra day. Leave me alone.

DEATH: You were serious?

NAT: We made a deal.

DEATH: Yeah, but—

NAT: Don't "but" me. I won twenty-four hours. Come back tomorrow.

DEATH: I didn't know we were actually playing for time.

NAT: That's too bad about you. You should pay attention.

DEATH: Where am I going to go for twenty-four hours?

NAT: What's the difference? The main thing is I won an extra day.

DEATH: What do you want me to do—walk the streets?

NAT: Check into a hotel and go to a movie. Take a *schvitz.*[1] Don't make a federal case.

DEATH: Add the score again.

NAT: Plus you owe me twenty-eight dollars.

DEATH: *What?*

NAT: That's right, Buster. Here it is—read it.

DEATH [*going through pockets*]: I have a few singles—not twenty-eight dollars.

NAT: I'll take a check.

---

1. Steam bath.

DEATH: From what account?

NAT: Look who I'm dealing with.

DEATH: Sue me. Where do I keep my checking account?

NAT: All right, gimme what you got and we'll call it square.

DEATH: Listen, I need that money.

NAT: Why should you need money?

DEATH: What are you talking about? You're going to the Beyond.

NAT: So?

DEATH: So—you know how far that is?

NAT: So?

DEATH: So where's gas? Where's tolls?

NAT: We're going by car?

DEATH: You'll find out. [*Agitatedly.*] Look—I'll be back tomorrow, and you'll give me a chance to win the money back. Otherwise I'm in definite trouble.

NAT: Anything you want. Double or nothing we'll play. I'm liable to win an extra week or a month. The way you play, maybe years.

DEATH: Meantime I'm stranded.

NAT: See you tomorrow.

DEATH [*being edged to the doorway*]: Where's a good hotel? What am I talking about hotel, I got no money. I'll go sit in Bickford's. [*He picks up the* News.]

NAT: Out. Out. That's my paper. [*He takes it back.*]

DEATH [*exiting*]: I couldn't just take him and go. I had to get involved in rummy.

NAT [*calling after him*]: And be careful going downstairs. On one of the steps the rug is loose.

[*And, on cue, we hear a terrific crash.* NAT *sighs, then crosses to the bedside table and makes a phone call.*]

NAT: Hello, Moe? Me. Listen, I don't know if somebody's playing a joke, or what, but Death was just here. We played a little gin . . . No, *Death*. In person. Or somebody who claims to be Death. But, Moe, he's such a *schlep!*[2]

Curtain

ACTIVITIES FOR WRITING AND DISCUSSION

1. Indicate passages in the play that you find funny, and explain how those passages work as comedy. How does the character Death undercut or conflict with traditional images of death? How do other aspects of the play (such as characterization, **setting, stage directions, plot,** and **dialogue**) conflict with

---

2. A person who is unkempt, down-at-the-heels, clumsy.

what you might expect in an actual encounter between a human being and Death?

2. In a humorous way, *Death Knocks* dramatizes an imaginary conversation between a person (Nat) and a personified abstraction (Death). Try writing such a conversation yourself. Compose an imaginary dialogue between yourself and some abstraction, e.g., your inner self-critic, your conscience, your ideal self, the "child" in you, the "parent" in you, having the abstraction talk as if it were a person.

Steps:
a. Brainstorm a list of possible abstractions you could personify.
b. Choose one that looks most interesting.
c. Imagine what this abstraction would look like if it were a person. Describe such things as facial appearance, eyes, hair, body build, posture, gestures, expressions, how he/she walks, talks, for instance.
d. Pose some conflict between yourself and this "person."
e. Write the dialogue.

Note: Your writing for Activity #2 may be quite personal, and you should feel free *not* to share it with anyone else.

THE GREATER UNIVERSE: ADDITIONAL ACTIVITIES FOR WRITING AND DISCUSSION

1. Reread your entire notebook. Mark any passages, however long or short, that strike you, for whatever reason. Beside each such passage, write a note explaining its significance for you. Finally, pick a favorite passage and either:
a. Expand it into a new piece of writing, or
b. Make notes on how you could expand or use it at some future date, or
c. Rewrite it in a different form, e.g., poem, dialogue, letter, or memoir.

For a list of strategies for expanding or revising, see Chapter 10.

2. Many texts in the section, e.g., Keats's "To Autumn," Lawrence's "Humming-bird," Mary Oliver's "The Black Snake," depict moments of transcendent wonder in which speakers or characters encounter mystery or the natural world. Identify several such texts and the qualities that make these moments remarkable. Then:
a. Brainstorm a list of any such moments you have had yourself.
b. Choose one of the moments on your list and write a text, in any form, that describes and celebrates it.

3. What is "love"? What is "meaning" or a "meaningful" life? What are our lives for? These are perennial questions that everyone must answer for him- or herself. Identify and list a few such "life questions" that are compelling to you.

Then bring together various **characters** and **speakers** from this thematic chapter and write a dialogue in which they (and you, if you wish) discuss your questions and some possible answers.

4. In "Aphorisms" Novalis states:

> Self-expression is the source of all abasement, just as, contrariwise, it is the basis for all true elevation. The first step is introspection—exclusive contemplation of the self. But whoever stops there goes only half way. The second step must be genuine observation outward—spontaneous, sober observation of the external world.

Summarize what you think Novalis is saying here. Then show how the "steps" he describes are exemplified in any two or three texts within this thematic section.

5. Poe's "The Masque of the Red Death," Dickinson's "Because I could not stop for Death" and Woody Allen's *Death Knocks* all feature **personifications** of death, but the personifications differ drastically. Compare and contrast the representations of death in these three texts and analyze how the differences reflect broader contrasts in the attitudes toward death.

6. Emily Dickinson's "My life closed twice" ends with the lines, "Parting is all we know of heaven,/And all we need of hell." Give your best interpretation of Dickinson's lines, particularly of the rather startling first one. Then invent an imaginary exchange of letters between Dickinson and Jorge Luis Borges ("Delia Elena San Marco") in which they reflect on the experience and meaning of "parting." Alternative: Invent a dialogue or exchange of letters between two made-up characters in which they philosophize about this same subject.

7. Explore the various meanings of "art" in Moore's "The Sacred Arts of Life" and Linda Hogan's "Waking Up the Rake." How do the two writers challenge or extend your own sense of the nature of "art"?

8. Review your entire notebook. As you do, make a running list of memorable or striking topics, e.g., "birth and death," "soul," "spirituality," "quests," "relationships between the human and natural worlds." Then choose a favorite topic, make a Topic/Form Grid (see Chapter 10), and use one of the forms on your grid to create a new notebook entry about the topic. Should your chosen form not work, do a Topic/Form Shift to a different form on your grid.

9. Reread your entire notebook, and mark any favorite entries. Then, after reviewing Chapter 4, revise one of these entries that is a "dependent" text into an "independent" text. (For a list of strategies for revising, see Chapter 10.)

Appendix A:
Sample Creative Writings

The samples below are not offered as masterpieces. (Sometimes the presence of a masterpiece does more to intimidate us as writers than it does to motivate us.) You can use these samples in at least two ways:

1. Use them as prompts for your own writing. Review them periodically, particularly when your own imaginative well runs dry. Remember the words of Emerson, which appear as an epigraph at the beginning of *Reading and Writing from Literature:*

> [Texts] are for nothing but to inspire.

2. Use them to help select and revise your own favorite writings for a course portfolio or other presentation. Alone or with your small group or class, you can analyze the samples to determine what makes "successful" or "unsuccessful" writing. What do you like in a particular piece? What first gets your interest, and what makes you keep reading? What specific passages, long or short, do you find yourself annotating or underlining? What ideas does the sample give you for your own writing? What does the writer try that *you* might like to try?

Samples are keyed to the "Ten Ideas for Writing" introduced in Chapter 3. Terms in **boldface** are defined and illustrated in Part IV, "An Introduction to the Four Major Genres," and Appendix C, "Glossary of Literary Terms."

1. Converse with Specific Points in the Text that Strike You.

See sample in Chapter 3.

2. Write About Any Personal Connections You Have with the Reading.

"Grandpa Jack" by Tyler (see Chapter 2) is a good example.

Both of my grandfathers died before I was born. My Dad's father was bucked off a horse which broke his neck and caused his death soon after. My Mom's father had cancer and also died before I was born. Although my grandmothers married again, I never got to know my stepgrandfathers well at all. As a young boy I yearned for the companionship of a grandpa.

I grew up in a small neighborhood set in the heart of a beautiful valley. There was so much to do as a child. Pineview dam was directly behind the house, giving us ample amount of fun swimming in it. The "Honda" trails, as we called them, were nearby, and we rode our dirt bikes up and down the steep hills. It was a choice place for a young child to grow up, and I loved every minute of it. But there was still a vacancy in my life, and that was to have a grandpa. An elderly couple lived next door, and from the time I was born our lives wound together tightly. I believe my desire for a grandpa came true because my neighbor, Jack Hislop, took upon himself the role of a grandfather. Jack has been special to me for as long as I can remember. He gave me my first motorcycle, my first and only bolo decorated with Indian turquoise, and many other gifts throughout my youth. But most importantly he gave me the friendship of a grandpa.

As a little boy I would go over to visit him almost every day after school. One day I ran over to his house and found him lounging on the patio in his back yard. "Take a seat, partner," said Jack as he pulled up a chair for me. He fed me some cold watermelon and a large glass of "sodi water," as he called it. While I was enjoying the fruit Jack told me a story about when he was a young sheepherder. "I was no older than you, partner, maybe eleven years old," said Jack. "Me and Pa and a few of my brothers were high on Durphie's Peak taking the sheep down to a nearby watering hole." His eyes were flashing as he was trying to point out where they were, since the mountain was in a broadside view. "A few sheep took off up a narrow canyon, and I got roped into chasin' after 'em. I rode up the canyon a little way and seen 'em up ahead so I galloped my horse to catch 'em. When I caught those little rascals I started herding 'em back down to the watering hole. On the way down the canyon my horse started to get jittery because some bushes started to shake up ahead, and out charged a huge brown bear." Jack was standing now giving the motions of the incident. Jack blurted "Holy shit!" then apologized to me because his wife didn't like him to cuss. "The damn horse started to buck and my two dogs went into a barking frenzy. The bear was huge, it was at least ten feet tall when it reared up on its hind legs. The dogs distracted the bear long enough allowin' me to ride up and around to safety." Jack was really into the story because he made a sigh of relief as he told about his escape from the bear. "Damn bear killed old Dodger, one of my best dogs," said Jack with a sad look on his face, as if it had just happened.

Jack was drafted into the war during World War II and had many stories to tell about those experiences. The stories he told me about the war
are engraved in my mind, and I am more sensitive about what happened
in the war because Jack told me so many of his firsthand experiences.
"There were dead bodies piled twenty feet high; hell, it smelled bad,"
said Jack as he plugged his nose to emphasize his point. Jack had a very
sorrowful look on his face when he told me about the concentration
camps. "When those skinny Jews were released they just started eatin'
the grass, 'cause they were so hungry. I carried extra rations so I could give
'em something good to eat." Jack could go on and on with his war stories,
and all I had to do was ask him to tell me a story. . . .

Jack's health was never very good. He had diabetes and heart trouble
which caused him to have a great deal of pain. "I've got a pig valve in my
heart—oink-oink," he would joke. As time went on Jack's health got
worse, but our attachment grew stronger. Three years before he died he
said, "I want ya to speak at my funeral, partner." I chuckled and told him
he could never die. When Jack died his wife again asked me if I would
speak. I don't think I could have said no. I was fourteen years old and
scared to death to speak, but my love for Jack implored me to do it. I don't
even remember what I said, but I do know that I declared my love for my
Grandpa Jack.

3. Write a Letter to the Author and/or a Return Letter from the Author to Yourself.

See sample in Chapter 3.

4. Write an Imaginary Interview with the Author or with a Character in a Story, Novel, or Play.

John read some poetry by Walt Whitman and then began writing a response to
it in the form of "What I like about this poet." Soon, however, he tired of this
mode of writing and yearned to meet the poet "in the flesh." The result was the
following "Interview with Walt Whitman." Before writing John read and reread
"Song of the Open Road" (p. 540) and other poems in Whitman's book *Leaves
of Grass* in order to get a sense of the poet's voice and probable style of speech.
Stylistic features he noticed were Whitman's outspokenness, his taste for informal and robust language, and his habit of illustrating and expanding on ideas
with long lists (such as the example in the third paragraph below).

Interview with Walt Whitman

I interviewed Walter Whitman at his print-shop in Brooklyn on a hot, humid day in mid-July. Mr. Whitman was relaxed and cordial. He is a man of
36, large-framed, in amazingly robust health, with a thick, matted beard
and penetrating eyes. As we spoke he sat on the edge of a desk, his

sleeves rolled to the elbows and his shirt collar open, the tools of his trade scattered around him. Mr. Whitman, it might be noted in passing, is a methodical man, softspoken, thinking before he speaks—creating an impression quite unlike that of the "barbaric yawp" that he affects in his poems.

Interviewer (I): Mr. Whitman, your book *Leaves of Grass* has been on the market now for two weeks and is causing something of a stir among critics. Not all the reactions, I might add, are favorable. For instance, Mr. Samuels of the *Daily Press* calls you a "hog" and says that you have no business writing poetry. What do you make of this?

WW: I never published *Leaves* with an eye to receiving compliments, or the favor of critics. The real audience of *Leaves* is profounder than the critics, and vaster: it is the great American public itself, the ordinary men and women—bus drivers, farmers, ferriers, mechanics, blacksmiths, boatmen and -women, clam-diggers, horse-dealers, slaves and freemen and freewomen. . . . On the pulse of these will the future of *Leaves* be decided.

I: Surely this is unlike any book of poetry any of us has seen before. Can you tell us something about the composition of *Leaves?*

WW: Gladly. But I'll probably not give you the answer you're wanting—no "pat" answer that will "finish" the matter, click the box shut, if you will. *Leaves* cannot be put in a box—the making of it can't be either; it doesn't give itself to formulae. First thing I did was throw out the rule-books, the sonnet treatises, the grammars and so on. Then I wrote, and wrote, and wrote—every day. Every chance I got I wrote. On the wharves or in the street, in the smithies and the shops, in the open air of farms where I happened to be, loafing, jotting down, in my leisurely way, all unhurried, nothing forced, getting a record of it all, big and little, I didn't discriminate. Then I stuffed what I wrote—all these pictures of America, of our times—into envelopes. And I never worried over the result. I knew all along I'd get a Poem out of it.

I: Your self-assurance and optimism about your craft are admirable, Mr. Whitman. I'm sure many poets would be envious.

WW: Maybe so. These poets have to see that making a poem isn't a logic-game. You don't just take a fancy mold of a sonnet or ballad or rhyme and dump words into it, so that the ideas are all corseted and constrained and dead. That's the way our poets write, and that's the undoing of 'em. They're stuck in the eighteenth century, or the seventeenth—in Europe—trying to out-Shakespeare Shakespeare, I suppose. That's the poetry *disease* today. That's the point I make in my "Preface" to *Leaves*. The true poems don't come from here [Mr. Whitman points to his head] but from here [he inscribes an imaginary circle from his heart to his pelvis]. That's the birthing room of a thousand poems—a thousand thousand poems—already written and still to be written.

5. Compose a Prequel or a Sequel to a Story.

See sample in Chapter 3.

6. Rewrite a Text from a Point of View Different from that Presented in the Original Text.

Gary Soto's poem "Oranges" (p. 443) describes—from a boy's **point of view**—an awkward incident during a first date. Angela retold the story from the girl's point of view:

Chocolate

My first date came
when I was twelve.
He was coming for me
I had been ready for hours
My parents had the light on
and the dog ready
Their way of saying who's boss.
At the last minute
my mother drowned my face
with rouge.
My father told me to remember
Who I was and what I'm worth.
My brother told me
the way to impress him
was to think big.
He came for me
He looked so nervous
We went to the drugstore
to get some candy
the whole way there
I wondered what he had
in his pockets besides those two oranges.
He told me to choose
whatever I wanted.
I remembered my brother
and picked up a chocolate
hoping he had the money.
His eyes fell
but he didn't say a word.
My heart ached as
he placed a nickel
and then one of his
precious oranges
on the counter.
I cried that night
for being so stupid
I had hurt him

and he had brushed it aside
I stared at the chocolate
wrapper stained brown like my
aching soul,
yet glittering
much like my soul
filled with the hope
That he'd call again.

7. Rewrite a Work into a Different Genre.

See sample in Chapter 3.

8. Borrow an Incident or Theme from a Work to Write a Piece of Your Own Based on a Similar Incident or Theme.

Kate Chopin's "The Story of an Hour" inspired Rebecca "to write about an old woman who wishes she had lived her life differently, as does Mrs. Mallard. Mrs. Mallard says that she will live for herself. The old woman in my poem wishes that she had lived for herself also and regrets not doing what she truly loved doing."

The day was full
of snow . . .

cloggy things
breathed in old heaters
and shoelaces
were being tripped over

I wish I were a potter
or maybe a dancer

My muscles would
let me feel any
movement I wished.

I wish I were 80
and lived in a New
York apartment
10 stories high

At night I would sit
and make

bowls, and the humming
of the wheel would be
my music and company.

In the afternoons I
would walk down the
city streets and look
at the busy people
walking through their
garbage
and graffiti filled
walls.

I would make my
way to the museum
and look at the
paintings for hours and
I would see my
pots and paintings
in there.

A young couple would
walk by my
work and examine
it closely, while
I stood behind them
with a slight
internal smile.

I wish I were 80
and healthy.

I wish that
I had all the
knowledge I needed
to answer these unanswered
questions.

Now I am 80
and I still don't know the answers
I became a
psychoanalyst living
in Beverly Hills
listening
to others' problems

I wish I had
I wish I
had. I wish I had
that apartment in
New York with my
pottery wheel and
the beautiful
humming of it
spin.

9. Borrow the Genre or Form of a Work to Create a Piece of Your Own Cast in the Same Genre or Form.

Susan read Walt Whitman's poetry and followed it by writing a poem. She explains, "Whitman's 'Song of Myself,' a very emotional poem that created images in Walt's time and place, inspired me to write a piece in Whitmanian style, using contemporary images, while still maintaining the romantic tone that Whitman stressed."

Song of Ourselves

We celebrate ourselves, Walt,
you, I, all of us, grasping for perception, meaning
in this entrapment, awe inspired miracle,
from the deepest abyss of the earth,
to the empirical heights of the cosmos;
We keep watch.

A lonely doe crouches, staring at me from my hillside.
Her dark eyes reflect an eerie glow from the porch light.
She looks at me, through me,
knowing.
Hours pass.
I'm anxious, perplexed about my hillside occupant.
No movement from her perch.
The upstairs window elevates my eyes to hers;
Our gazes lock once again.
Am I in her yard?
Finally,
a gentle rain softly taps at the window pane.
I hurriedly glance up toward the sudden emptiness of the hillside.
I sigh . . . relieved?

A family waits for the subway in New York;
a group of cheap hoods attacks them for pocket change.

The family's son is stabbed through the heart
after lunging at his mother's assaulters.
The Mother,
hysterical, screaming in fear for her dying son,
rushes to a subway clerk, begging for help.
She's ignored.

A lost foreign boy knocks on a door
to ask for directions to a costume party,
but instead
gets a bullet through his chest.

The setting sun casts a soft illumination;
the shadows of things appear greater than life.
An orb weaving spider, its intricate web ablaze with sunset,
creeps up, hungrily,
seizing the unfortunate grasshopper nymph entrapped there.
The infant jerks uncontrollably as the fangs of the
venomous vampire
stab into its helpless form.
Another futile attempt at escape,
a final jerk—then stillness.
The spider's legs busily grope the lifeless body.

Survival, once again.

The infant's eyes question, search the face of the young mother.

The purple mountain crests up through the brown city haze.

The toddler giggles, attempts to gather the puppy into his small arms.

A rainforest smolders.

The children wait to talk to Santa Claus.

Men, women, children, humanity,
dash along the beach with buckets of sea water;
rush to quench the parched skin of a young, beached whale.

The kindergartener builds a tower of blocks,
all the way to the sky.

The sea surf roars, washes with a pile of garbage.
Plastic syringes leave imprints in the soft, wet sand.

The children wait to talk to Santa Claus.

The small girl, unsteady, finally balances the bicycle.

The space travelers orbit the earth,
watch the mysterious majesty of blueness.

The teenage boy flashes a grin and a driver's license.

The large and small quail hurriedly scamper;
tiny feet blur the roadway.

Humanity watches life and death each day,
from living room sofas.

The children wait to talk to Santa Claus.

Men armed with rifles
rush into the wilderness to kill,
chase a deer onto a frozen lake.
The frightened buck slips, straddling the frigid surface,
helplessly trapped.
He stares hopelessly into the eyes of the approaching men.
Rifles now discarded, they tie a rope about his fragile body,
gently pulling him along the ice to the shoreline,
then coaxing him back into the sanctuary of the brush;
they've finished hunting.

A group of Somali soldiers drags a trophy,
the body of an American killed in battle,
naked,
through the streets, laughing and cheering.
The body,
smoking from being set ablaze, causes a
jet black sunrise.

The autumn moonlight seeps softly, gently
through the nudeness of tree branches.
The dry leaves swirl about our feet.
Winter smells near, spring will follow.

Walt, we know who you were, and what you meant.
You waited for us.
You were there yesterday, here today, and tomorrow.
We searched and found you, I, ourselves.

10. Draft a Fictional Biography or Autobiography of a Character in a Story, Poem, Play, or Other Text.

Edith wrote an autobiography, in diary form, of Minnie Wright, the abused wife in Susan Glaspell's play *Trifles* (p. 235). The diary entries trace Minnie's development over a period of thirty years.

Dear Diary

April 7, 1886—Today was my 17th birthday. What a happy day! My parents gave me a beautiful white dress with blue hair ribbons. Mama said I was to wear them in the church choir program next Sunday. I can hardly wait, for I do love pretty things, and I do love to sing in the choir—makes me feel all warm and toasty inside. Maybe John will be there. He's new in town. I caught him staring at me last Sunday—I think he wants to walk me home. I've never had a boyfriend before, so the thought of it kinda gives me the "tingles." I wonder if he'll think I look pretty in my new dress.

May 2, 1886—Well, John finally got up the courage to walk me home from church yesterday. He seems awful quiet—didn't say much the whole way home, but I guess I talked enough for the both of us. I never did have trouble thinkin' of things to talk about, 'cause I just get so worked up over everything—the sun goin' down on the prairie, the new department store in town, the minister's sermon, the birds comin' back after winter, or just any old thing. Pa says conversation is my strong point. I don't know if John likes my white dress or not—probably he's too shy to say so. But it did make me feel so important to have a beau see me home!

June 25, 1886—Well, dear diary, you are never going to believe this, but I am gettin' married one month from today! I know it seems sudden, but John says there ain't no use in waitin'. I'm sure he must be right. Sometimes I get right dizzy when I think about bein' married. Most people seem to like it all right, so I guess I will too. John still don't say much, but he must like me or he wouldn't a decided we should get hitched. It *will* be fun to have babies and dress 'em up cute. I always did love babies. And you never know—once the babies come, maybe John will find his tongue a bit more. Then again—maybe not. Some folks just seems more bent on some things than other folks do.

July 25, 1887—Well dear diary, I haven't written much for a long time. It ain't that I don't have anything to write, but I guess it's partly two things: partly it's that bein' a wife is much more work than I ever thought it would be, and partly I guess I been puttin' off writing, hopin' I'd have something cheerful to write—hopin' maybe I'd find myself in the family way, or somethin' like that. But now I'm thinkin' it's not likely to happen any time soon. Every time I bring up the subject, John turns his head the other way and pretends he doesn't hear me. I'm beginning to think he doesn't want any children! Could that be? I don't like to think on it, so sometimes I go for short walks. Don't dare go for long walks, 'cause John gets powerful upset if he comes home and finds me gone somewhere.

March 4, 1888—I can't write too much today—got too much to do. I been feelin' a bit sad lately. John says he don't want me singin' in the choir no more—says it's prideful and a sin to show off in such a way. It's hard to think that havin' a little happiness is a sin, but perhaps he's right. He 'most generally is.

August 12, 1890—Been bakin' my usual batch of bread today, and thinkin' a mite more than usual. It's been *so* hot this week. I think I'll 'most melt away. Got my cherries all bottled a couple weeks ago. Soon it'll be time to do up the peaches. The corn's growin' pretty good. John does work hard, and I try to be a good wife to him. The thing that's hardest is bein' down in this here hollow where I can't see the road or any other houses, or nothin' but just the work that's gotta be done, day in and day out. Just the sameness is enough to make a body tired. Maybe, if we get a good crop, John will say we can go to town. I won't ask for a new dress, but maybe a new apron would be nice.

December 22, 1890—We been havin' one of the *coldest* winters I've ever seen in these parts. I make up a fire in the stove, but the heat seems to creep out at all the cracks before it even warms the room. I can't seem to get warm no matter what I do. John says it's too cold to work outside, so he sits inside all day and seems to get ornrier and ornrier. I've decided it's no use to try to talk to him, so I try to cheer myself up by workin' on my quilt blocks. I'm sure that when I get it all pieced it will be the prettiest thing in the house, and maybe then I'll get warm. Haven't been warm in such a long time. Goodness knows I won't be allowed to hold no quiltin' bee when I get it put together, so I'll just have to settle for tyin' knots in it. Stichin' it would be prettier, but I guess the knots'll do. At least they'll get the job done.

Mar. 1, 1891—The fetchingest little bird landed in the cherry tree this morning. He sang and sang until I thought my heart would just bust.

May 9, 1894—Made bread, did the laundry, hoed three rows of potatoes. Cloudy all day—no wind.

Sept. 12, 1896—Canned two bushel of peaches, mopped the floor, ironed the clothes. Seems cold tonight.

Dec. 24, 1898—Christmas tomorrow. Don't know if there'll be any singin' at Church. Too cold to go.

Mar. 10, 1902—John's been gone for three days, buyin' seed in the next county. I just seem to rattle around in here. Got to wishin' we might-a had a child to keep me a speck o' company. But perhaps it's no kinda life for a child.

Jan. 19, 1909—Found my piece quilt yesterday while cleanin' out the closet. Can't seem to work up the spirit to work on it much. It's been put away so long that it hurts me to look at it.

Dec. 26, 1912—Christmas yesterday. No one came to visit.

Apr. 7, 1916—My birthday. Almost forgot it, perhaps I should have. Seems I'm gettin' on. Bought myself a little canary from a peddlar man. He does sing pretty. Don't know what John will say.

Apr. 9, 1916—It should be spring, but we been havin' a blizzard for the last two days. Don't know why it's turned so cold again. Sewed a couple o' blocks on that quilt I started so long ago. It is right pretty.

Apr. 10, 1916—John couldn't stand for the singin' of my canary. Said it made him nervous. I put the poor little thing in a pretty box I'd been saving for somethin' special. I'll bury him tomorrow.

Apr. 11, 1916—I don't know what to do. I've done a awful thing. Couldn't help myself. God knows I didn't want to. Couldn't help myself. Couldn't stand it no more. My poor little bird. Wrung his neck. Need to finish my quilt. Going to knot it. Couldn't help myself. Gotta be free. Whatever shall I do. No one to talk to. So cold in here. Couldn't stand it no more. Going to knot it. Wrung his neck. God knows I didn't want to. So cold in here. . . .

Appendix B:
Sample Essays
About Literature

Essays about literature may assume a number of forms. This appendix illustrates three major kinds: explication, which is emphatically text-centered and focuses (generally) on a single literary text; the "reader-response" essay, which combines textual analysis with personal thoughts, feelings, and experience; and the comparison/contrast essay, which explores similarities and/or differences between two or more literary texts.

Sample #1. Angie writes an explication of Gary Soto's poem "Oranges" (p. 443); that is, she does a line-by-line analysis of the poem itself and what it means. Since "Oranges" is quite short, Angie is able to explicate, or "explain," the entire poem. In an explication of a longer text, such as a short story or play, you might focus on a particular scene, incident, or other crucial passage rather than the whole work.

"Oranges": Moving from Childhood to Adolescence

The poem "Oranges," by Gary Soto, suggests a beginning as well as an end. The beginning is the start of a new chapter in the lives of the speaker and the "girl"; they are starting to feel the emotions of adolescence in which the opposite sex is no longer viewed as repellent or "gross" but as somewhat mystical. At the same time, their childhood is ending; their new experience of dating seems to change how they look at

life. <u>This is a turning point in their lives,</u> though the
poet makes it seem so simple.

The thesis pro-
vides a context
for the ensuing
paragraphs

    The nervousness and excitement of the boy are
evident early in the poem:

> She came out pulling
> At her gloves, face bright
> With rouge. I smiled,
> Touched her shoulder, and led
> Her down the street. . . .

Quotations of
more than four
lines are block-
indented

The girl's face is painted "bright/With rouge" for him.
He smiles, and leads the girl to a drugstore that sells
candy. The excitement of being able to buy a piece of
candy for this girl shows that he feels he is becoming
a man: "I turned to the candies/Tiered like bleachers,/And asked what she wanted." The mention of
"bleachers" suggests a performance. The speaker is
performing, trying to show the girl that he likes her
enough to give her whatever she wants.

Slash marks indi-
cate line breaks
when poetry is
printed out as
prose

    The poem continues:

> . . . I fingered
> A nickel in my pocket,
> And when she lifted a chocolate
> That cost a dime,
> I didn't say anything.
> I took the nickel from
> My pocket, then an orange,
> And set them quietly on
> The counter.

Angie quotes the
poem to illustrate
her points. In
addition, she
discusses each
quotation to
make clear why
she has included
it

When the girl picks out the chocolate, which costs
more than what he has, the boy seems downhearted.
He gets his first real taste of responsibility in this new
sphere of life. He feels that he needs to impress the
girl in order to save his social status in this new and
frightening world; so he places one of his beloved oranges on the counter next to his hard-earned nickel in
hopes that the woman at the counter will understand.
"The lady's eyes met mine,/And held them, know-
ing/Very well what it was all/About." The woman,
watching this whole scene, probably remembers a
similar situation in her own life and takes pity on the
young boy.

The boy's happiness at being able to give the girl what she wants is incredible. In the beginning of the poem, he is walking with "a girl." Now that he has bought her a chocolate, he feels that she is his: "I took my girl's hand/In mine for two blocks,/Then released it to let/Her unwrap the chocolate." She suddenly changes from *a* girl to "my" girl, and he now gets the courage to hold her hand for two whole blocks.

Soto's poem ends:

> I peeled my orange
> That was so bright against
> The gray of December
> That, from some distance,
> Someone might have thought
> I was making a fire in my hands.

These last six lines suggest a metaphor for the boy's happiness. The orange could be interpreted as him peeling off his childhood to reveal this new part of his life. This new time is sweet, like the juices of an orange; and, also like an orange, it is "bright" with hope. The speaker's mood at this moment is "bright" like "a fire."

The girl, too, is experiencing a new time in her life. She tries to look good for this boy by wearing "gloves" and "rouge," no doubt watching her mother or maybe a sister. In the candy store, she seems flat- tered to be offered anything she likes: "Light in her eyes, a smile/Starting at the corners/Of her mouth." This is most likely the first time a boy has offered to buy her anything. When she sees the boy place one of his oranges on the counter with his nickel, she proba- bly wonders whether she has offended or embar- rassed him in any way. Though it is not mentioned in the poem, she may suppose she has already failed in trying to be like a grown-up. Once the boy takes her hand, however, she probably feels much better, as if the date has been a success.

"Oranges" is a narrative about a young boy and girl's first exposure to the world of dating. Through this experience, they learn lessons for their subse- quent lives. A door has been opened for them to con- tinue to grow and mature; at the same time, however, they must leave their simple childhoods behind.

The closing para- graph reinforces Angie's thesis & casts the experi- ence depicted in the poem as one of simultaneous gain & loss

Sample #2. Many of the professionally written essays in Part V of *Reading and Writing from Literature* use narrative, or storytelling, as a means of illustrating ideas. For instance, Michael Dorris's "Life Stories" (p. 454) is composed primarily of stories about his early jobs and their effects on his development. In "The Hand," Joe discusses Dorris's essay in relationship to an early job experience of his own. Unlike Angie's essay, which focuses quite exclusively on the literary text itself, Joe's essay integrates literary analysis with his own personal experience.

The Hand

At the end of "Life Stories," Michael Dorris writes that his various school vacation jobs were "not so much to be held as to be weighed, absorbed, and incorporated, and, collectively, they carried me forward into adult life like an escalator, unfolding a particular pattern at once haphazard and inevitable" (458). In this statement, Dorris implies that those jobs were important not for making money, but because they provided him with valuable personal insight and revealed to him a pattern or script that his later life might follow.

MLA-style parenthetical references show the source & page numbers of quotations

Dorris begins his essay by talking about a rite of passage of the Plains Indians in which a male teen was to venture out into the wilderness alone and subsist there until he happened upon some "thing" that might transform him or give him insight into his life. "Through this unique prism," Dorris writes, "abstractly preserved in a vivid memory or song, a boy caught foresight of both his adult persona and of his vocation, the two inextricably entwined" (454). For Dorris, "this unique prism" was his collection of summer jobs.

The first job that Dorris describes is his position as a postal carrier, a job important for the opportunity it afforded him to do "casually sophisticated . . . work that required a uniform" (455). Entrusted with possibly "important correspondence," Dorris learned—the hard way—about responsibility on the job (455).

Quotations are skillfully interwoven with the text

Another one of Dorris's jobs was his stint as Coordinator of Tribal Youth Programs, where he was to "coordinate" a group of "bored, disgruntled kids . . . who had nothing better to do each day than to show up . . . and hate whatever Program I had planned for them" (455–56). As that particular summer job progressed, Dorris came to understand the role that he was to play for the youths, and he came to greet each day with the "lightheadedness of anticipated exhaustion, that thrill of giddy dissociation in which nothing seems real or of great significance" (456).

Dorris values both of these jobs for what they offer him: unexpected challenges and unique perspectives. From there, he presumably moves on to deal with the rest of the unexpected challenges and unique perspectives that life affords him.

My experiences with jobs afforded me "personal, enabling insight" (454) in much the same way as Dorris's did. I'm not sure if my experiences were rites of passage or terms of a contract; but through my time spent as the managing editor of the *Iowa State Daily,* I came to understand certain conditions with which we must all live.

I wrote columns at the newspaper. In fact, I was the designated "fluff columnist"—the person responsible for commenting on the string found in coat pockets and combs found beneath couch cushions and which clouds looked like which president on a given day. The life of the fluff columnist on a newspaper is like that of a World War II bomber pilot: he fights the war from an infinitely high place while others slog through the trenches and do the work and report the minutes of school board meetings and take the shrapnel of barbed letters to the editor.

I became a mild hit, accepted by my peers and somehow deemed trustworthy by my readers. People began coming to me to have their stories told. A football player wanted to come out of the closet in my column, a philosophy professor wanted me to print his suicide note, and a co-ed wanted me to write a transcript of one of her sexual encounters. "I really hate sex," she told me on the Commons one afternoon, "and I think you could make that come across. I've never been in the paper before."

My life was running pleasantly out of tilt, happily imbalanced. I felt plugged into things. I got drunk most weekends and some weeknights, because that was what a writer did. I drank angostura bitters in my gin and tonic, because Hemingway drank angostura bitters in his gin and tonic. When I made clumsy, drunken passes at women, it was because Henry Miller made clumsy, drunken passes at women. I felt like I was a vital connection in the creative process and that, as such, a connection, I needed to cultivate certain habits.

One Sunday morning, I was in the office filing my column when the report of an accident came over the

A thesis usually appears near the beginning of an essay—but not always. Joe's thesis appears several paragraphs into his essay; it states the connection between his own job experience & Dorris's

In this paragraph & others, Joe illustrates & enlivens his main point with examples & quotations

Like the simple word "Once," this phrase helps propel the writer (& his readers) into a specific longer story about his job experience

police scanner. It was early enough that no one else except the editor was in the office, so I was sent out with a camera to cover it. A train had struck a car in the middle of town. A man was dead. I was the first reporter on the scene.

Before I knew it, I was snapping pictures of the twisted wreckage of the car, which sat—still smoking—on the tracks, a sick convolution of metal and rubber enfolded back upon itself. In its midst was a hand held tentatively out toward the pavement, dripping blood in a steady patter that looked too red to be real. I circled the wreck, snapping photos; but the only evidence of there having been anything human inside the layered metal was the hand, stretched out like the one on the ceiling of the Sistine Chapel, reaching out for another. I snapped countless photos of the hand, knowing that I would get on the front page, reveling in the exaltation a trench reporter might feel at wading around in the viscera of a story. I was at the heart of the connection.

And then, the man's wife was brought to the scene. By some fluke, her mother had been listening to the police scanner that early Sunday morning as well. She was shielded from the accident by the throng of people that surrounded it, and she pushed her way up, past the police cars, past the people, up to where I was snapping photos.

She was repeating, "What happened? What happened? What happened?" and as she got closer to the wreck, as she was able to see the cataclysm of metal, the blob of car, she knew what it meant. I think she must have seen the hand. Maybe she saw me snapping pictures and composing the lead in my head. She screamed, and I felt it in my chest. Then she dropped to one knee, spattering the pavement with her vomit, and screamed once again through the thin torrent. She didn't cry; I didn't once hear her cry. She just screamed, over and over, mortally wounded; then she was guided off to the ambulance, away from the wreck. I faded into the crowd, drove back to the office, and developed the pictures of the hand. The wreck was front page news, along with my photo and story.

When the letters began coming in later that week, I laughed. People were calling me a ghoul and a sensationalist, and I couldn't have cared less. I was a vital connection. The city editor told me that I shouldn't take such things personally. "The fact of the matter is, you *are* a ghoul. And so am I, and so is everyone else in the newsroom," he told me at the bar later that week. He indicated the other people in the bar with a jerk of his head and added, "They don't understand that."

I didn't write on the paper the next semester and dropped out of school the semester after that. I avoided seeing any of my friends from the paper, but wondered in a sulking child's way if I was missed by them or by any of the readers. None of my self-pity mattered then or now, because I was a ghoul and still am, and only now am I comfortable with that truth.

Beyond the angostura bitters and the clumsy, drunken, poetic passes at women, is what Hemingway and Miller avoided saying directly, though it is a truth as blunt as any: a writer is a ghoul, a person who passes his hands over dead skin and then tells others how it feels.

The essay does not end in the usual way, with a neat conclusion, but with a blunt & disturbing metaphor. What is the effect? Does it matter that Joe does not return to Dorris's "Life Stories" at the end of his essay? Why or why not?

Sample #3. One common type of essay about literature is the comparison/contrast essay. In the next example, Sara compares the protagonists in two short stories, "The Story of an Hour" and "The Yellow Wallpaper."

Free at Last

There are strong similarities between "The Story of an Hour" and "The Yellow Wallpaper." Both stories feature women who are products of their times, confined by the constraints of both husband and society. The women grow in awareness of their situation and make a deliberate decision to free themselves from it.

The time frame of the stories, loosely from the late 1800's through the early 1900's, implies a standard of behavior and a conformity to male/female role models that influences the female protagonists in "The Story of an Hour" and "The Yellow Wallpaper." In this era, females were raised to be the helpmates of man. The clothes, etiquette, education, curricular activities, and household chores functioned to transform a girl into a young lady and to communicate her primary responsibilities as future wife and mother. Similarly, a young boy was trained to assume his birthright as wage earner and husband. Men and women followed closely dictated societal roles: men were the supporters, defenders, and rulers; women were the sup-

Sara deftly limits her thesis: rather than trying to compare every- thing about the two stories, she focuses on the two women pro- tagonists & their move toward free- dom

ported, defended, and governed. Men led; women followed. To venture beyond the confines of the prescribed role was a breach of conduct. Often the punishment was abandonment, alienation, or banishment by family or community. Just as men were instilled with virtues, such as bravery and stoicism, that complemented their role, so women were imbued with submissiveness. <u>These narrowly defined roles form the foundation for the conflict in "The Yellow Wallpaper" and "The Story of an Hour."</u>

Sara places the two characters in a historical & social context but does not lose sight of her focus: this last sentence returns us to the two stories

Long before the "hour" depicted in Chopin's story, Louise Mallard has been indoctrinated into the values and morals of her time period. She has been carefully prepared to fulfill the role of a wife. Within their marriage, she and Brently function in their prescribed roles. Louise is neither happy nor unhappy; she is comfortable. Her days pass predictably, and she feels no desire to change the pattern of her existence.

<u>The doctor's wife in "The Yellow Wallpaper" is a product of the same expectations and conformity.</u> She defers to the judgment of her husband and acquiesces in his decisions. "It is so hard to talk with John about my case," she writes, "because he is so wise, and because he loves me so" (176). Her rebellions are small and confined to his absence. The role modeling and constraints imposed by society form the background of her story and heighten her conflict as she comes into awareness of the self she has imprisoned.

Paragraph transitions are particularly important in comparison/contrast essays. These and other opening sentences of paragraphs keep the focus on connections <u>between</u> the two women rather than on either woman in isolation

<u>Just as Louise has been molded into the role of wife, so, too, has the doctor's wife.</u> Although neither is intentionally limited by her husband from achieving her potential as a woman, both are victims of a confining relationship. The tragic result is a loss of identity. Each woman can perceive herself only in terms of her husband. Because society dictated a submissive role for women, a woman seldom challenged her destiny. If she found her lot unpalatable, she kept the pain to herself. It would not occur to a woman to think in terms of her own development, needs, and expression. Only a crisis or some other catalyst could make her confront the identity she had repressed.

The crisis for Louise is the announcement of her husband's death. After the initial shock, she begins to contemplate her lack of remorse. As she gazes out the window towards the blue sky, she embarks on a process of self-discovery. She does not feel loss but a sense

of release from her confinement in an imposed role. She   MLA-style paren-
is "Free, free, free!" (168). Her awareness is sparked by   thetical reference
her ability to confront the identity she has repressed.
Louise's excitement over her freedom is in stark contrast to the apathy that defined her marriage role.

   The doctor's wife's journey towards self-realiza-
tion is more tortured and lengthy than Louise's. She
does not experience a dramatic crisis that challenges
her to confront her inner self or open her eyes in sudden self-awareness. Her conformity to the established
norm exacts a price—illness. Her postpartum depression is a symptom of the repressed self. The wallpaper
serves as the catalyst for the journey into the depths
of her being. It symbolizes her overpowering illness
and represents an elaborate description of her struggle. The design in the paper illustrates her feelings.
The bars are the strings of steel in her mind that deny
her the courage and strength to move on with life and
that imprison her within her *role:*

> The front pattern *does* move—and no wonder! The   Quotations of
> woman behind shakes it!   more than four
>   Sometimes I think there are a great many women   lines are block-
> behind, and sometimes only one, and she crawls   indented
> around fast, and her crawling shakes it all over. . . .
>   And she is all the time trying to climb through. But
> nobody could climb through that pattern—it strangles
> so; I think that is why it has so many heads. (179)

The woman that the doctor's wife envisions in the
wallpaper, who is alternately trapped and freed, finally lures the wife deeper into herself. As she struggles to free the woman by ripping down the
wallpaper, she is struggling to free herself.

   Both Louise and the doctor's wife become aware of   The conclusion re-
their inner selves through a process of discovery   iterates the main
brought on by an incident in their life. Their previous   similarities &
existence serves to contrast their former selves with   differences be-
their new revelations. Unfortunately, their realizations   tween the 2 char-
are dramatically extinguished: Louise dies when she   acters & their
sees her husband walk through the door; the doctor's   search for free-
wife joins the trapped woman in the wallpaper. Yet   dom
both endings represent a triumph. Louise's death is an
alternative to returning to her submissive self. The
doctor's wife's decision marks the severance of her
submission to her husband. Both women are free.

Appendix C:
Glossary of Literary Terms

Most of the terms below are also discussed in Part IV, "An Introduction to the Four Major Genres." For additional references and examples, consult the appropriate chapter in Part IV.

Abstract language *See* concrete language.

Act A major structural division within a play.

Alliteration A sound effect in which consonant sounds are repeated, particularly at the beginnings of words or of stressed syllables. Examples: "*low*"/"*long*"; "*cracks*"/"*crazes*."

Allusion A reference to something (such as a character or event in literature, history, or mythology) outside the literary text itself.

Anapest A metrical foot composed of two lightly stressed syllables followed by a stressed syllable, e.g., in the end. *See also* meter.

Antagonist The main opponent of the protagonist in a story, play, or other narrative or dramatic work.

Aphorism A terse statement of principle, truth, or opinion.

Argumentative essay *See* essay.

Assonance A sound effect in which identical or similar vowel sounds are repeated in two or more words in close proximity to each other. Example: "*storms*"/"*morning*."

Author The writer of a literary work. *Compare* persona.

Ballad A relatively short narrative poem, generally with an anonymous or impersonal narrator, that is usually written in rhymed four-line stanzas and that may include a refrain.

Blank verse Verse composed in unrhymed iambic pentameter lines.

Caesura   A strong pause within a line of poetry.

Characters   The imaginary persons who appear in fictional narratives or dramatic works. A flat character is one who remains essentially unchanged throughout the story and tends to be less an individual than a type. A round character evolves or undergoes change in the course of the story and is more individualized and complex.

Citation   A reference made, in an essay, to another text. The citation may be included for diverse purposes: to illustrate a point or idea, to add support or authority to the writer's argument or reasoning, to bolster reader trust in the persona, or to add depth to the essay by expanding its range of literary reference.

Climax   *See* plot.

Concrete language   Language that describes or portrays specific or observable persons, places, or things rather than general ideas or qualities. Concrete language appeals to the senses, as in this example from Robert Frost's "Birches": "They [Birches] click upon themselves/As the breeze rises, and turn many-colored/As the stir cracks and crazes their enamel" (ll. 7–9). In contrast, **abstract language** refers to general ideas or qualities, as in this later passage from the same poem: "Earth's the right place for love:/I don't know where it's likely to get better" (ll. 52–53).

Connotation   An associative or suggestive meaning of a word in addition to its literal dictionary meaning (or "denotation"). The word "politician" denotes "a person actively involved in politics," while it connotes (for some people) a corrupt and conniving individual motivated exclusively by self-interest.

Consonance   A sound effect in which identical or similar consonant sounds, occurring in nearby words, are repeated with different intervening vowels. Example: *"crush"/"crash."*

Couplet   A pair of lines of poetry, usually rhymed; a two-line stanza.

Dactyl   A metrical foot consisting of one stressed syllable followed by two lightly stressed syllables, e.g., "pŏndĕring."

Denotation   The dictionary definition of a word, without associative or implied meanings. *Compare* connotation.

Dialogue   The spoken conversation that occurs in a text.

Diction   Word choice. Diction can be described as formal or informal, abstract or concrete, general or specific, and literal or figurative.

End-stopped line   A line of poetry whose end coincides with the end of a phrase, clause, or sentence.

Enjambed line   A line of poetry that completes its grammatical unity and meaning by going into the next line without a pause.

Epic poem   A long narrative poem on a heroic subject.

Essay   A unified and relatively short work of nonfiction prose. An argumentative essay advances an explicit argument and supports it with evidence. An expository essay informs an audience or explains a particular subject. A personal or literary essay emphasizes elements that are ordinarily associated with "literary" texts–an engaging persona, an intellectual or emotional focus or theme that is usually implied rather than directly stated, and artful use of figurative language and other "literary" elements such as dialogue and narrative.

Expository essay   *See* essay.

Expressionism   A writing style or movement in which reality is exaggerated or distorted in order to render the world as we feel it rather than as we literally see it.

Falling action   *See* plot.

Feminine rhyme   *See* rhyme.

Figurative language   The term used to encompass all nonliteral uses of language.

Figure (or **trope**)   A word or phrase used in a way that significantly changes its standard or literal meaning. Some common kinds of figures are metaphor, simile, metonymy, irony, and paradox.

First-person narrator   *See* point of view.

Flashback   An interruption in the chronological presentation of a narrative or drama that presents an earlier episode.

Flat character   *See* characters.

Foot   *See* meter.

Free verse   Poetry that discards meter and usually dispenses with rhyme while keeping other poetic elements such as pronouncedly rhythmic phrasing, various types of patterned sound, and intensive use of figurative language.

Hero/Heroine   The main character in a narrative or dramatic work. Also called the "protagonist."

Hyperbole   A bold exaggeration used for rhetorical effect.

Iamb   A metrical foot consisting of a lightly stressed syllable followed by a stressed syllable, e.g., "around."

Irony   A type of incongruity. Dramatic irony involves an incongruity between what a character in a story or play *believes* and what we (the better-informed members of the audience) *know*. Verbal irony involves an incongruity between what is literally said and what is actually meant.

Limited point of view   *See* point of view.

Lyric poem   A poem, usually rather short, in which a speaker expresses a state of mind or feeling.

Masculine rhyme   *See* rhyme.

Metaphor   A figure or trope that makes an implicit comparison between dissimilar items in a way that evokes new or vivid ways of perceiving, knowing, and/or feeling. Example: "she is a green tree/in a forest of kindling" makes an implicit comparison between a young girl, indestructible in her zest for life, and an almost fireproof tree.

Meter   Rhythm that follows a regular repeating pattern of stressed and lightly stressed syllables. Within a poetic line, meters are measured in feet, with each repetition of the pattern comprising a separate foot. The most common meters are iambic ($\breve{}\acute{}$), trochaic ($\acute{}\breve{}$), anapestic ($\breve{}\breve{}\acute{}$), and dactylic ($\acute{}\breve{}\breve{}$). A line of three feet is described as trimeter, a line of four feet is tetrameter, and one of five feet is pentameter.

Metonymy   A figure or trope in which the literal term for one thing is used to stand for another with which it is closely associated. Example: "The White House says" instead of "The President says."

Monologue   A long speech by a single character.

Narrative poem   A poem that relates a story.

Narrator   The imaginary speaker, as distinct from the author him- or herself, who tells a story. *See also* point of view.

Octave   *See* stanza.

Ode   A lyric poem, composed in a lofty style, that is serious in subject and elaborate in stanza structure.

Omniscient narrator   *See* point of view.

One-act play   A relatively short play. Usually, though not always, a one-act dramatizes a single incident and includes fewer characters than multiple-act plays.

Oxymoron   A joining of two terms that are ordinarily conceived as opposites. Examples: "knowledgeable unknowing," "deafening silence."

Paradox   An apparently contradictory statement that proves, on examination, to be true. Example: "You must lose your life to gain it."

Persona   The "mask" or version of a self that an author projects in a particular text. The plural form of persona is **personae.**

Personal essay   *See* essay.

Personification   A figure or trope in which human qualities are ascribed to an abstract concept or inanimate object. Example: "Fortune smiled upon him."

Plot   The pattern of actions and events that combine to produce a total effect in readers or viewers of a narrative or dramatic work. Some critics divide plots into a rising action, which introduces the characters and establishes the conflict; a climax, in which the conflict reaches its height in the form of some decisive action or decision; a falling action, in which the conflict moves toward resolution; and a resolution, in which the conflicts are resolved.

Poem   A kind of literary text that is typically arranged in lines and composed in meter or free verse.

Point of view   The perspective from which a story is told. The two basic types are first-person and third-person. In a first-person narrative the narrator is a character within the story, while in a third-person narrative he or she is not a character in the story. Third-person narrators can be further classified (broadly) as either limited or omniscient. The limited narrator reports events and characters primarily through the consciousness of one character, while the omniscient functions as an all-knowing presence with access to the thoughts, feelings, and actions of any or all of the characters. An unreliable (or naive) narrator is a first-person narrator whose youth, naiveté, limited intelligence, or extreme subjectivity leads us to question the accuracy of his or her version of characters and events.

Prose poem   A poem that is shaped like prose (in paragraphs rather than lines) but that displays other features (such as pronouncedly rhythmic phrasing, various types of patterned sound, and intensive use of figurative language) characteristic of poetry.

Protagonist   The main character around whom a narrative or dramatic work centers. Also called the "hero" or "heroine."

Quatrain   *See* stanza.

Resolution   *See* plot.

Rhyme   An identity or similarity in sound patterns, the most familiar kind being the *end* rhyme that occurs between words at the ends of lines of poetry. When the end rhyme consists of a single stressed syllable ("sing"/"wing"), it is termed masculine; when the rhyme consists of a final stressed syllable followed by a lightly stressed ("whether"/"feather"), it is termed feminine. A slant, partial, or half rhyme occurs when the rhyming sounds are only approximately ("dizzy"/"easy"), rather than exactly, alike.

Rhythm   A distinct but variable pattern of stressed and lightly stressed sounds in poetry or prose.

Rising action   *See* plot.

Round character   *See* characters.

Scansion   The process of analyzing the metrical pattern of a poem.

Scene description   Text that describes what the stage looks like for a particular play.

Sestet   *See* stanza.

Setting   The place, time, and social context in which a story, poem, or play takes place.

Short story   A brief work of prose fiction.

Simile   A figure that makes an explicit (rather than implicit) comparison between dissimilar items in a way that evokes new or vivid ways of perceiving, knowing, and/or feeling. Example: "skin/worn, like the pages of her prayer book" makes an explicit comparison between an old woman's skin and the pages of a well-used book. *Compare* metaphor.

Slant rhyme   Also called a "half" or "partial" rhyme. *See* rhyme.

Sonnet   A fourteen-line lyric poem written in iambic pentameter and rhymed according to a preset conventional pattern. The **Italian** or **Petrarchan sonnet** is divided into an octave rhymed *abbaabba* and a sestet with a *cdecde* rhyme scheme or some variant. The **English** or **Shakespearean sonnet** falls into three quatrains rhymed *abab, cdcd, efef,* and a closing couplet rhymed *gg.*

Speaker   The "I" in a lyric poem.

Stage directions   In a play, text that describes the movements or gestures of characters onstage.

Stanza   A grouping of poetic lines arranged in a definite pattern that is repeated throughout the poem. Three-line stanzas are called tercets or triplets; stanzas of four lines, six lines, and eight lines are called (respectively) quatrains, sestets, and octaves.

Stream of consciousness   A narrative technique that tries to reproduce the exact flow of thoughts, feelings, and associations that go through a character's mind as he or she moves in the "stream" of time.

Symbol   Something that stands for something else. In literary analysis, something is said to be "symbolic" if it evokes an idea, quality, or concept larger than itself.

Synecdoche   A figure or trope in which a part of something is used to signify the whole or the whole is used to signify a part. Example: "All hands on deck" instead of "All sailors on deck."

Syntax   The arrangement of words within phrases, clauses, and sentences.

Tercet   *See* stanza.

Theme   A basic idea advanced (or implied) in a text.

Third-person narrator   *See* point of view.

Traditional verse   Poetry that employs meter and (often) rhyme. *See also* free verse.

Triplet   *See* stanza.

Trochee   A metrical foot consisting of one stressed syllable followed by a lightly stressed syllable, e.g., "drearў."

Trope   *See* figure.

Unreliable (or naive) narrator   *See* point of view.

Verbal irony   An incongruity between what a speaker says literally and the meaning that is implied in the larger context of the story, poem, or other work.

Voice   The felt authorial presence in a literary text.

Appendix D:
Notes on the Authors

Notes are included for all authors of short stories, essays, and plays and for authors represented by two or more poems.

Woody Allen (b. 1935)

Born in Brooklyn, New York, Woody Allen (real name Allen Stewart Konigsberg) attended college in New York City and began his career as a joke writer and comic. Though best known as a filmmaker (*Bananas, Sleeper, Annie Hall, Interiors, Manhattan, Bullets over Broadway*), the multitalented Allen is also an actor, short story writer, playwright, and jazz clarinetist. *Death Knocks* is reprinted from *Getting Even* (1971), a collection of Allen's comic stories, sketches, and plays.

Maya Angelou (b. 1928)

Maya Angelou has had a long and distinguished career as a poet, autobiographer, playwright, director, actress, singer, and producer for stage and screen. An African-American, Angelou grew up amid racial segregation in Stamps, Arkansas, and attended public schools there and in California. Later she studied dance and drama and worked as a performing artist, director, and producer in the United States and abroad. Her first book, the autobiographical *I Know Why the Caged Bird Sings* (1970), was widely praised. Angelou has produced several additional books of autobiography, including *Gather Together in My Name, The Heart of a Woman,* and *All God's Children Need Traveling Shoes,* and numerous collections of poems, such as *Poems: Maya Angelou, I Shall Not Be Moved,* and *On the Pulse of Morning.* She read the title poem of this last work at the 1993 inauguration of President Bill Clinton.

Margaret Atwood (b. 1939)

Margaret Atwood has been influential as an author and editor who has asserted the cultural identity of Canadian literature. Born in Ottawa, Ontario, Atwood attended the University of Ontario and did graduate work in the United States at Radcliffe College and Harvard. She published her first book of poems, *Double Persephone* (1961), when she was in her twenties. Since then she has been prolific as a writer of novels, poems, short stories, and nonfiction. Among her best-known novels are *The Edible Woman, Surfacing, Life before Man,* and *The Handmaid's Tale.* Her short stories are collected in *Dancing Girls and Other Stories, Bluebeard's Egg and Other Stories, Murder in the Dark,* and *Wilderness Tips.*

James Baldwin (1924–1987)

The first of nine children, James Baldwin was born and educated in Harlem. His tempestuous relationship with his stepfather, a religious fanatic, figured prominently in his first completed novel, *Go Tell It on the Mountain* (1953). Two subsequent novels, *Giovanni's Room* (1956) and *Another Country* (1962), reflected Baldwin's preoccupation with his twin identity as homosexual and African-American. In his essays, short stories, and plays as well as novels, Baldwin's outlook was intensely social: he explored, in eloquent and impassioned prose, issues of race and racism, civil rights, sexuality, and religion. He also wrote about families, including sibling and parent-child relationships, as reflected in the short story "Sonny's Blues." Baldwin was probably most acclaimed for his essays, particularly those collected in *Notes of a Native Son* (1955) and *The Fire Next Time* (1963). He published one volume of short stories, *Going to Meet the Man* (1965).

Carol Bly (b. 1930)

A Minnesota native, Carol Bly is best known for her essays and short stories about rural and small-town Minnesotans. Born in Duluth, Bly earned her B.A. degree from Wellesley College and did graduate study at the University of Minnesota. She married the poet Robert Bly and, before they were divorced, helped him produce an influential literary magazine, raised a family, and performed numerous tasks, paid and volunteer, in her community. In her forties she began writing essays ("letters," she called them) for Minnesota Public Radio that were collected and published as *Letters from the Country* in 1981. Bly has also written two volumes of short stories, *Backbone* (1985) and *The Tomcat's Wife and Other Stories* (1992). Bly's work both celebrates and critiques small-town life. As one reviewer explains, she distills "the essences of small-town life—its . . . satisfactions and impoverishments, the contradictory pleasures of community and isolation, and . . . the difficulty of coming to a full exercise of individual capacity without seeming an alien, even a threat, to one's neighbors."

Robert Bly (b. 1926)

As a writer, editor, and translator, Robert Bly has had a powerful influence on contemporary American poetry. Born in Madison, Minnesota, Bly got his bachelor's degree from Harvard and his master's degree from the University of Iowa. In the 1950s, feeling that the American poetry then being written was too academic and remote from life, Bly founded his own small press and literary magazine (originally called *The Fifties*) to publish alternative work. Through his press he also translated and published the poetry of many important European and South American writers. Bly's own poems, collected in such volumes as *The Light Around the Body*, for which he won the National Book Award in 1968, and *What Have I Ever Lost by Dying?* (1992), are characteristically visionary, full of associative leaps, and sometimes surreal; he once described poetry as a "leaping around the unconscious." More recently, Bly has won fame for his *Iron John: A Book about Men* (1990) and as a much-sought-after leader of men's workshops and retreats.

Ray Bradbury (b. 1920)

Ray Bradbury was born in Waukegan, Illinois, and received no formal education beyond high school. From youth on, however, he aspired to write. In 1941 he published his first short story in the genre (science fiction) with which he was to become most intimately connected. Since then Bradbury has written prolifically for magazines, television, radio, theatre, and film. His works include *The Martian Chronicles, Fahrenheit 451, Dandelion Wine, Something Wicked This Way Comes*, and *The Stories of Ray Bradbury*.

Bertolt Brecht (1898–1956)

Bertolt Brecht was a German playwright and poet of intense political conscience whose work reflects some of the major cataclysmic events of the first half of the twentieth century. Born in Augsburg to a well-to-do family, Brecht studied medicine at the University of Munich before being drafted to serve as an orderly in a German military hospital during World War I. After the war he returned to Munich, began writing plays, and in 1924, settled in Berlin. A Marxist and an avant-garde playwright, Brecht developed the concept of "epic theater," a theater intended to stir audience members to heightened social and political consciousness. During his Berlin period he wrote (in collaboration with composer Kurt Weill) *The Threepenny Opera* (1928) and *Rise and Fall of the City of Mahagonny* (1929). He also wrote other plays attacking capitalism, war, and bureaucracy and calling for a new and more just political and social order. Brecht fled Hitler's Germany in 1933 and spent nearly fifteen years in exile in Denmark, Sweden, Finland, and the United States. After being investigated by the House Committee on Un-American Activities in 1947, he returned to Germany, settled in East Berlin, and founded the Berliner Ensemble, an influential theater company. Among Brecht's major later plays are *Mother Courage and Her Children, Galileo, The Good Woman of Setzuan*, and *The Caucasian Chalk Circle*. "Anecdotes of Mr. Keuner" is excerpted from *Tales from the Calendar* (1948), a collection of fables and prose poems. "Anecdotes" shows Brecht's characteristically political and social focus as well as his skill at aphoristic pronouncement.

Gwendolyn Brooks (b. 1917)

Born in Topeka, Kansas, Gwendolyn Brooks grew up in inner-city Chicago and graduated from high school and junior college there. She began writing poetry as a child, received encouragement from mentors, and published her first book of poetry, *A Street in Bronzeville,* in 1945. Her second book, *Annie Allen* (1949) was the first volume of poetry by an African-American to win a Pulitzer Prize. Though always focused on the experience of African-Americans, Brooks's work underwent an important evolution in the late 1960s, when she attended a conference with many new and younger black poets and began to write more exclusively to black audiences. In the late sixties and early seventies, her poetry became more self-consciously political as she championed the cause of black militants and feminists. Some of her books from this period are *Riot, Family Pictures,* and *Beckonings.* Brooks's poetry is a distinctive, energy-charged blend of many influences, including traditional Anglo-American rhymed verse, street talk, African chant, the biblical cadences of black Protestant preaching, and the improvisatory rhythms of jazz.

Raymond Carver (1938–1988)

In a career cut short by lung cancer, Raymond Carver established himself as a contemporary master of the short story. Born in Clatskanie, Oregon, the son of a sawmill worker and a waitress, Carver produced fiction that relentlessly chronicled the lives of working-class Americans. Collections of his short stories include *Will You Please Be Quiet, Please?, What We Talk About When We Talk About Love,* and *Cathedral.* Carver also wrote essays and poems, which are collected in *Fires: Essays, Poems, Stories, In a Marine Light,* and in the posthumously published *A New Path to the Waterfall.* The lean, spare, and often bleak character of his stories earned him the label "minimalist."

Anton Chekhov (1860–1904)

Anton Chekhov, a major short story writer and playwright, was born in rural Russia and earned a medical degree at Moscow University School of Medicine. Though he was educated as a physician, literature was his passion. At nineteen he began submitting humorous sketches to newspapers and magazines, and his first published collection of stories appeared in 1884. By the end of his life he had written some six hundred stories. During the last decade of his life Chekhov also produced several dramatic works that revolutionized the modern theater: *The Sea Gull, Uncle Vanya, The Three Sisters,* and *The Cherry Orchard.* Long plagued by tuberculosis, Chekhov died at a resort in Germany in 1904. Chekhov's work is characterized by a strict economy and objectivity. As he wrote, "The artist should be, not the judge of his characters and their conversations, but only an unbiased witness." This stance is evident in "Gooseberries," in which the writer presents us with "the characters and their conversations" while leaving judgment and interpretation to his readers.

Kate Chopin (1850–1904)

Born Katherine ("Kate") O'Flaherty in St. Louis, Missouri, Kate Chopin was educated at Sacred Heart Academy, a St. Louis boarding school. Her father died in a railroad accident when Kate was a child, and she was subsequently raised by her mother, grandmother, and great-grandmother, all widowed and independent women. In 1870 she married Oscar Chopin, a well-to-do Louisiana man, and lived with him and their growing family in New Orleans until 1879, when they moved to the Chopin plantation in central Louisiana. After Oscar's sudden death in 1882 Kate returned with her six children to St. Louis. There, in 1889, she began writing for publication, producing her first novel, *At Fault,* in 1890, and two collections of short stories—*Bayou Folk* (1894) and *A Night in Acadie* (1897). In 1899 she published the novel for which she is best known today, *The Awakening,* about a heroine whose voyage of self-discovery causes her to defy conventional notions of wifehood, motherhood, and womanhood. This book drew largely negative reviews from across the country, especially from male critics, who were angered by its controversial subject matter. Chopin's stories are mainly set against the culturally diverse background of rural Louisiana. They explore themes of female sexuality, the often imprisoning effects of social institutions and conventions on individual development, and the roles and status of women in nineteenth-century American society, a time when most married women were considered the legal property of their husbands.

Sandra Cisneros (b. 1954)

Sandra Cisneros's roots are strongly bicultural. She was born in Chicago to a Mexican father and a Chicana mother, and as she was growing up the family moved back and forth between urban homes in Chicago and Mexico City. Cisneros earned her B.A. degree from Loyola University in Chicago and an M.F.A. degree in creative writing from the University of Iowa Writers Workshop and has taught at various schools and universities in the United States. Her short stories are collected in *The House on Mango Street* (1984) and *Woman Hollering Creek and Other Stories* (1991). Also a poet acclaimed for her depictions of female experience, Cisneros has emerged as an important contemporary writer and a resonant voice in Chicana feminism.

Lucille Clifton (b. 1936)

A prominent contemporary African-American poet, Lucille Clifton was born in Depew, New York, and educated at Howard University and Fredonia State Teachers College. She published her first book of poems, *Good Times,* in 1969. Since then she has written several more volumes of poetry, among them *Two-Headed Woman, Good Woman: Poems and a Memoir 1969–1980,* and *Quilting: Poems 1987–1990,* as well as nonfiction and children's books.

Judith Ortiz Cofer (b. 1952)

Born in Hormigueros, Puerto Rico, Judith Ortiz Cofer grew up on a "border" between cultures. Her father was a career navy man, and during Cofer's childhood the family shuttled between Puerto Rico and the mainland United States, between Spanish language and English, and between Puerto Rican culture and American. Cofer describes the impact of this experience in "Primary Lessons" and other autobiographical writings. Some of Cofer's collections of poetry and prose are *Latin Women Pray, Among the Ancestors, Silent Dancing: A Partial Remembrance of a Puerto Rican Childhood,* and *The Latin Deli: Prose and Poetry.* She has also written a novel, *The Line of the Sun* (1989).

Emily Dickinson (1830–1886)

Emily Dickinson was born in Amherst, Massachusetts, where her father, Edward, was a prominent lawyer and citizen. She attended Amherst Academy and, briefly, the nearby Mount Holyoke Female Seminary. After leaving the seminary without graduating in 1848, Dickinson seldom went beyond the grounds of the family home in Amherst until the day of her death. There, in an upstairs room of the house, she wrote over 1,700 poems, which she stitched into "packets" of sixteen to twenty-four pages each. She was wary of publication, terming it "the Auction of the Mind," and only a dozen poems appeared in print during her lifetime. Others were published posthumously by family members and friends, and her complete poems did not appear until the 1950s. Dickinson's reclusive circumstances gave her the privacy and freedom she wanted for reading, thinking, and writing. Moreover, she was not completely isolated from the world. She lived among family and servants, maintained passionate friendships, and read voraciously—newspapers, contemporary poetry and fiction, and classics (especially Shakespeare). Many of Dickinson's poems are written in the simple iambic meters (see Appendix C) of hymns, but her verbal compression, suggestiveness, and astonishing metaphors make it impossible to label her poetry as "traditional." Tough-minded, irreverent, and stubbornly faithful to her own intuitions, Dickinson constantly pushed the limits of language—reinventing it, when necessary, to suit her ends. In her brother's words, "She saw things directly and just as they were. She abhorred sham."

Isak Dinesen (1885–1962)

Born in Rungstedlund, Denmark, Isak Dinesen (real name Karen Dinesen) was educated first in her hometown and later abroad, in Switzerland and France, and at the Royal Academy of Fine Arts in Copenhagen. In 1914 she married a distant cousin, Baron Bror Blixen, and purchased with him a coffee plantation in British East Africa, where she lived for the next seventeen years. Independent and impatient with social conventions, Dinesen enjoyed the life of an aristocrat-adventurer but also experienced suffering: she and Bror divorced, she lost her lover of several years in a plane crash, and, after a series of poor harvests, she was forced (in 1931) to sell the coffee farm. Returning to Denmark she began writing and publishing, in English, under the pen name of Isak ("one who laughs") Dinesen. Her collections of stories include *Seven Gothic Tales* (1934), *Winter's Tales* (1942), *Last Tales* (1957), and *Anecdotes of Destiny* (1958). *Out of Africa* (1937) and *Shadows on the Grass* (1960) are nonfiction memoirs of her experiences in Africa.

Michael Dorris (b. 1945)

Part white and part Modoc Indian, writer/teacher Michael Dorris has been a prominent contemporary advocate of Native American studies. Educated at Georgetown University (B.A., 1967) and Yale University (M.Phil., 1970), Dorris founded the Native American Studies department at Dartmouth College in the 1970s. In 1981 he married Louise Erdrich (see below), one of his former students and a writer with whom he has since collaborated. Dorris's books include the novel *A Yellow Raft on Blue Water, The Broken Chord: A Family's Ongoing Struggle with Fetal Alcohol Syndrome* (winner of the 1989 National Book Critics Circle Award), *The Crown of Columbus,* a novel he coauthored with Erdrich, and several works for young adults. His essays are gathered in *Paper Trail: Collected Essays, 1967–1992.*

Louise Erdrich (b. 1954)

Louise Erdrich was born in Minnesota and grew up in Wahpeton, North Dakota. Her mother was French-Chippewa, and both of her parents worked in the Bureau of Indian Affairs boarding school in Wahpeton. As a girl she wrote stories but displayed little interest in her Native American roots; this changed, however, in 1972 when she entered the Native American Studies program at Dartmouth College and studied under Michael Dorris (also a writer and part Native American), whom she eventually married. Erdrich went on to earn an M.A. degree in writing at Johns Hopkins University and published her first novel, *Love Medicine,* in 1984. Winner of the National Book Critics Circle Award, *Love Medicine* traces the stories of two Chippewa families through several decades of the twentieth century. In the novel's distinctive format, each chapter is told from a particular character's point of view, and individual chapters, such as "Saint Marie," reprinted in *Reading and Writing from Literature,* can be read in sequence or as largely independent units. Erdrich's other books include *Jacklight* and *Baptism of Desire* (poems), *The Beet Queen, Tracks, The Crown of Columbus* (a novel coauthored with Michael Dorris), *The Bingo Palace,* and *Tales of Burning Love.*

William Faulkner (1897–1962)

A "self-made" writer in the fullest sense, William Faulkner grew from humble beginnings to become a major American novelist and the 1950 winner of the Nobel Prize for literature. Faulkner was born in New Albany, Mississippi, and moved as a child to Oxford, Mississippi, where he spent most of his life. In 1918, without finishing high school, he enlisted in the Royal Canadian Air Force. Upon his return to the United States he attended school briefly and did odd jobs while dreaming of a life as a writer. His first published book, *The Marble Faun* (1924), was a collection of poems, but during a stay in New Orleans he met story writer Sherwood Anderson, who encouraged him to write fiction. A first novel, *Soldier's Pay,* came out in 1926, followed soon after by the novels that began to earn Faulkner a wider reputation: *Sartoris* (1929), *The Sound and the Fury* (1929), and *As I Lay Dying* (1930). In these and subsequent works Faulkner found his subject matter—his own South, the corrupt and violent South of myth and history, which he evoked obsessively in the people and landscapes of a fictional county named "Yoknapatawpha." Faulkner also developed a poetic, metaphoric, and syntactically complex prose style that is unique in American literature. "Barn Burning" is reprinted from *Collected Stories* (1950).

Robert Frost (1874–1963)

Though Robert Frost was born in San Francisco, California, his poetry is closely associated with rural New England, where he lived most of his life. While still a boy he moved there with his mother and sister following his father's death. He graduated from high school in Lawrence, Massachusetts (and eventually married a high school classmate), did some college work at Dartmouth and Harvard, and dedicated himself to becoming a poet. Success, however, came late; well into his thirties, Frost did odd jobs to keep his growing family out of poverty, and in 1912 he had to move to England to find a positive reception for his writing. Recognition came, first in England and then in America, with his first two books, *A Boy's Will* (1913) and *North of Boston* (1914). After moving back to New England in 1915 Frost saw critical acclaim for his work grow, and he soon became one of the most famous and widely honored poets in the United States, winning four Pulitzer prizes and reading a poem at the inauguration of President John F. Kennedy. In Frost's work, the ordinary rhythms of New England speech play with and against the poetic strictures of blank verse (see Appendix C) and rhyme. Much of the pleasure experienced in reading a Frost poem comes from the contrast between the spontaneous-sounding speech, on the one hand, and the attention to form, on the other. Frost's life was plagued by personal suffering and tragedy, and the tragic occasionally surfaces in his poetry, as in "Out, Out—." Poems like "Birches" and "Stopping by Woods on a Snowy Evening" evoke the scenes and images of rustic tranquility that are another familiar strain in Frost's work.

Athol Fugard (b. 1932)

A white native of South Africa, Athol Fugard is best known for his plays about apartheid and the deep political and racial divisions that have torn his country. Originally planning to enter a technical trade, Fugard excelled in academics and won a scholarship to the University of Cape Town; restless, however, he left school in 1953 and signed on as a crew member aboard a tramp steamer on which he was the only white seaman. Upon returning to South Africa he became a news writer, got married in 1956, and began both acting in and writing plays. He also helped organize an interracial theater in Cape Town at a time when such racial mixing was illegal in South Africa. Fugard's first major success,

Blood Knot (1961), the first play performed in South Africa with a mixed cast, was followed by *Boesman and Lena, A Lesson from Aloes, "Master Harold"* . . . *and the Boys,* and *The Road to Mecca,* among many others. Though Fugard's work focuses on issues of racial tension and injustice, his more general themes are intolerance and prejudice of all kinds, as evidenced in *The Road to Mecca,* in which an eccentrically creative heroine incurs the wrath of her conformity-minded neighbors.

Charlotte Perkins Gilman (1860–1935)

Charlotte Perkins Gilman was born in Hartford, Connecticut, to a distinguished family of independent thinkers but suffered an unstable and impoverished childhood. Her father abandoned the family when Charlotte was a small child, and she and her brother were raised by their mother and moved nineteen times in eighteen years. In 1884 Charlotte married Charles W. Stetson, a painter. After the birth of their child, a daughter, Charlotte fell into a deep depression and received treatments from Philadelphia physician S. Weir Mitchell, a specialist in nerve disorders. Mitchell's prescription of complete rest nearly drove Charlotte mad, and in 1888 she left her husband, fled to California, and obtained a divorce. Subsequently she devoted herself to lecturing and writing and emerged as a leading feminist theorist. Her major works include *Women and Economics* (1898) *The Man-Made World: Our Androcentric Culture* (1911), and the utopian novel *Herland* (1915). Gilman committed suicide in 1935 while dying of breast cancer. Her autobiography, *The Living of Charlotte Perkins Gilman,* was published posthumously.

Susan Glaspell (1882–1948)

Susan Glaspell was a native Midwesterner who spent much of her creative life in New England. In 1915 she and her husband, George Cram Cook, were instrumental in creating the Provincetown Players in Massachusetts, a group of amateur writers and actors who inaugurated "modern" American theater and drama. Also a short story writer and novelist, Glaspell is best remembered today for her plays, in which she explored such issues as women's experience and relations between the sexes. Major works include *Suppressed Desires* (1915), *The Verge* (1921), and *Alison's House,* which won a Pulitzer Prize in 1930.

Louise Glück (b. 1943)

Born in New York City, Louise Glück obtained her formal education at Sarah Lawrence College and Columbia University. Her first book of poems, *Firstborn,* was published in 1968, and since then she has taught and lectured at various colleges and universities in the United States while continuing to write. Some of her other poetry collections are *The Triumph of Achilles, Ararat,* and *The Wild Iris.*

Ellen Goodman (b. 1941)

A Pulitzer Prize–winning journalist, Ellen Goodman was born in Newton, Massachusetts, and earned her B.A. degree from Radcliffe College. After a job doing research for *Newsweek* magazine, she shifted to newspaper work in the mid-1960s and became a columnist for *The Boston Globe.* As a syndicated columnist, Goodman has been largely concerned with issues of family relationships and values, divorce, feminism, and changing lifestyles—what she once called the "life-and-death issues" of contemporary American society. Among her books and collections of columns are *Close to Home, Turning Points, At Large, Keeping in Touch, Making Sense,* and *Value Judgments.*

Thomas Hardy (1840–1928)

Thomas Hardy was born near Dorchester in rural Dorset, England. Though he trained as an architect, the young Hardy's passions for philosophy and poetry soon drove him to forsake architecture and become a writer. Beginning in the 1870s, he achieved widespread fame as a novelist, centering his fictional world in the countryside of his native Dorset (called "Wessex" in his novels). Among his best-known novels, published between 1874 and 1895, are *Far from the Madding Crowd, The Return of the Native, The Mayor of Casterbridge, Tess of the D'Urbervilles,* and *Jude the Obscure.* After 1896 he focused on writing poems, which were collected in *Wessex Poems* (1898) and two volumes, *Winter Words* and *Collected Poems,* published after his death. Like his novels, Hardy's poems reflect the traditions and rusticisms of the Dorset he knew in his youth.

Joy Harjo (b. 1951)

The work of Joy Harjo—poet, essayist, editor, and children's book writer—has been closely tied to her identity as a Creek Indian. Harjo was born in Tulsa, Oklahoma, in the heart of the Creek Nation. She attended school at the Institute of American Indian Arts in Santa Fe, New Mexico, and graduated with a B.A. degree from the University of New Mexico, Albuquerque, in 1976. In 1978 she earned an M.F.A. in creative writing from the University of Iowa Writers Workshop, and since then she has continued both to write and to teach. Among her books are *She Had Some Horses* (1983), *Secrets from the Center of the World* (1989), *In Mad Love and War* (1990), and *The Woman Who Fell from the Sky: Poems* (1994).

Linda Hogan (b. 1947)

Born in Denver, Colorado, Linda Hogan is a member of the Chickasaw tribe, and her Native American heritage figures prominently in her poetry, essays, fiction, and plays. Hogan earned an M.A. degree from the University of Colorado at Boulder in 1978, and since then has taught at numerous schools and universities, such as the TRIBES program in Colorado Springs, the University of Minnesota, and the University of Colorado, Boulder. She has also held such jobs as dental assistant, homemaker, secretary, waitress, and volunteer worker at the Minnesota Wildlife Rehabilitation Clinic. Hogan says she has a focal interest in "studying the relationship between humans and other species, and trying to create world survival skills out of what I learn from this." Her writings include *Calling Myself Home* (poems), *Mean Spirit: A Novel, The Book of Medicines: Poems, Dwellings: Reflections on the Natural World,* and *Solar Storms: A Novel.*

bell hooks (b. 1955?)

Writer and social critic bell hooks (real name Gloria Watkins) is a prominent figure in contemporary African-American feminism. Hooks grew up in Kentucky, reading voraciously and gaining confidence in the importance of her own voice through writing and public speaking. With her first book, *Ain't I a Woman: Black Women and Feminism* (1981), hooks began articulating a vision for radical social change that she has since developed in *Talking Back: Thinking Feminist, Thinking Black, Teaching to Transgress: Education as the Practice of Freedom, Art on My Mind: Visual Politics,* and other works. Though an "academic" (she has a Ph.D. and has taught at Yale and other prestigious institutions), hooks is known for her trenchant and accessible writing style. With her pen name, bell hooks honors her great-grandmother (Bell Hooks), "that figure in my childhood who . . . paved the way for me to speak."

Langston Hughes (1902–1967)

Regarded by some as the single most influential African-American poet of the twentieth century, Langston Hughes was born in Joplin, Missouri, and started writing poetry as a boy. He graduated from high school in Cleveland and attended college for a year at Columbia University. Tiring of formal education, Hughes traveled to Africa and Europe in the early 1920s before returning to the United States and eventually settling in Harlem, New York. Harlem was then the scene of the "Harlem Renaissance" in black literature, theater, music, and other arts. Hughes became a literary leader of the Renaissance and a tireless champion of African-American culture and writers. He went on to write over a dozen volumes of poetry, including *The Weary Blues* (1926) and *Montage of a Dream Deferred* (1951), as well as novels, stories, screenplays, plays, and histories. Strongly influenced by jazz, the blues, and spirituals, Hughes wrote, as he put it, "to explain and illuminate the Negro condition in America."

Fenton Johnson (b. 1953)

Fenton Johnson's most recent book is *Geography of the Heart: A Memoir* (1996), about his lover, Larry Rose, who died of AIDS in 1990.

James Joyce (1882–1941)

James Joyce is a central figure in modern literature. Born and classically educated in Dublin, Joyce spent most of his working life on the European Continent—in Paris, Zurich, and other cities. Dublin, however, furnished the themes, characters, and cultural backdrop for all of his writing. Joyce's first published book, *Chamber Music* (poems, 1907), was followed in 1914 by *Dubliners,* a collection of short stories. In 1914 the autobiographical novel *A Portrait of the Artist as a Young Man* also began to appear serially in the London journal *The Egoist.* Other works include the landmark and controversial *Ulysses* (1922), a densely woven modern epic of alienated urban humanity, and *Finnegans Wake* (1939).

Franz Kafka (1883–1924)

Franz Kafka was born in Prague, Czechoslovakia, the son of a well-to-do and domineering father. After earning a law degree in 1906, he went to work in Prague in an insurance office. In 1917 he contracted tuberculosis, and he spent his last days in a sanatorium in Austria. Kafka published little during his lifetime and requested that, upon his death, his friend Max Brod destroy his unpublished works. Brod, however, ignored this request and compiled the manuscripts of three novels that brought Kafka an international, posthumous fame: *The Trial, The Castle,* and *Amerika.* Other works, also published posthumously, include diaries, parables, and letters. The irony-ridden and often nightmarish landscapes of Kafka's fiction have seemed quintessentially "modern" to many readers, among them W. H. Auden, who wrote: "Had one to name the author who comes nearest to bearing the same kind of relation to our age as Dante, Shakespeare and Goethe bore to theirs, Kafka is the first one would think of."

Claire Kemp (b. 1936)

Born in Worcester, Massachusetts, Claire Kemp is a short story writer who lives in Florida.

D. H. Lawrence (1885–1930)

David Herbert Lawrence was born in Nottinghamshire, England, the son of a coal miner and a genteel and refined mother. He graduated from Nottingham University in 1908 and began writing poetry and fiction, including the major autobiographical novel, *Sons and Lovers* (1913). In 1912 he eloped with Frieda von Richthofen, the wife of a Nottingham professor, whom he later married and with whom he shared his intense and emotionally tempestuous life. In the 1910s Lawrence grew increasingly disaffected with the mechanized, routinized life of industrial society and began to wander widely in search of alternative modes of life. His journeys took him and Frieda to southern Europe, Ceylon, Australia, the southwestern United States, Mexico, and eventually back to Europe. Throughout this period he continued to write novels (*The Rainbow* and *Women in Love* are among the best) as well as the travel essays and poems that established him as one of the finest descriptive writers in English. He died, of tuberculosis, in France. Lawrence's writings exhibit deep and lifelong obsessions: an emphasis on the elemental force of human sexuality, a faith in the life-forming power of the unconscious as opposed to the sterility and deadness of life lived from the merely conscious mind, and a passion to restore connections among human beings and between human beings and the earth—connections that modern society, in Lawrence's view, has largely lost or destroyed.

Doris Lessing (b. 1919)

Doris Lessing was born in Persia, the daughter of English parents. When she was five the family moved to a farm in southern Rhodesia (now Zimbabwe).

Lessing remained in Africa until 1949, when she and her second husband and their child moved to England. Her first novel, *The Grass Is Singing* (1950), portrays the horrors of black-white relations in Africa, and injustices—racial, political, gender-based—have remained focal concerns of her work. Major writings include *The Golden Notebook* (1962), which narrates the growth of one woman's feminist consciousness; the five-novel *Children of Violence* series (1952–1969); *Canopus in Argos: Archives* (1979–1983), a multivolume sequence of nonrealistic novels; *The Good Terrorist* (1986); and *African Lands* (1992). Among Lessing's short story collections are *The Habit of Loving* (1957), *African Stories* (1964), and *Stories* (1978).

Naguib Mahfouz (b. 1911?)

Winner of the 1988 Nobel Prize for Literature, Naguib Mahfouz is generally regarded as Egypt's finest writer. He was born in Cairo (some sources say in 1911; others suggest 1912 or 1914), graduated from the University of Cairo, and did postgraduate study in philosophy. Many of Mahfouz's novels and stories depict the turbulence of Egypt's social and political past and the harsh lives of the Arab poor. Since the 1980s, Mahfouz's books (*Midaq Alley, The Thief and the Dogs, Miramar,* and many others) have been widely translated and become bestsellers in English-speaking countries.

Nancy Mairs (b. 1943)

Born in Long Beach, California, Nancy Mairs did her undergraduate work at Wheaton College and earned her M.F.A. and Ph.D. degrees from the University of Arizona. She has published books of poems but is best known as a writer of autobiographical essays, which are collected in *Plaintext, Carnal Acts, Ordinary Time: Cycles in Marriage, Fiction, and Renewal, Voice Lessons: On Becoming a (Woman) Writer,* and other volumes. Describing herself as a "radical feminist, pacifist, and cripple," Mairs writes frankly about her multiple sclerosis and other subjects usually ignored or shunned by what she terms "polite discourse." Mairs's persona is characteristically tough-minded, witty, and passionate; she writes, says one critic, "with all intellectual-emotional flags flying."

Katherine Mansfield (1888–1923)

Born in New Zealand, Katherine Mansfield (born Kathleen Beauchamp) was educated in England and spent most of her working life there. Following a disastrous marriage in her twenties, to a young musician, she obtained a divorce and in 1918 married the critic John Middleton Murry. Amid her family and personal problems and chronic ill health (she eventually died of tuberculosis), Mansfield devoted herself to writing. With such collections as *Bliss and Other Stories* (1920) and *The Garden Party and Other Stories* (1922), she established herself as a fiction writer of rare subtlety and as a daring experimenter with narrative technique. Today she is considered one of the major creators of the modern short story.

Terrence McNally (b. 1939)

Best known for his comedies and farces, playwright Terrence McNally was born in St. Petersburg, Florida, and graduated with a bachelor's degree from Columbia University. Subsequently he worked as a critic, editor, and stage manager as he was writing his first plays. His plays include *And Things That Go Bump in the Night, Bad Habits, The Ritz, Frankie and Johnny in the Claire de Lune* (which he rewrote for the Garry Marshall film *Frankie and Johnny*), *The Lisbon Traviata, Love! Valour! Compassion!,* and *Master Class.*

James Alan McPherson (b. 1943)

Born in Savannah, Georgia, James Alan McPherson earned his B.A. degree from Morris Brown College, a bachelor of laws degree from Harvard University, and an M.F.A. in creative writing from the University of Iowa (1969). In his early twenties he won first prize in a short story contest sponsored by the *Atlantic* magazine, and later he became a contributing editor to the *Atlantic.* Since 1981 McPherson has taught in the English Department at the University of Iowa. An African-American, McPherson has published two widely praised books of short stories, *Hue and Cry* (1969) and the Pulitzer Prize–winning *Elbow Room* (1977). While many of McPherson's characters are African-American, he has tried to transcend racial barriers in his work, regarding his characters less as "blacks" or "whites" than as individual people.

Thomas Moore (b. 1940)

Born in Detroit, Thomas Moore has been a professor of psychology and religious studies and a practicing psychotherapist. His books include *The Planets Within, Rituals of the Imagination, Dark Eros, Care of the Soul,* and *Soulmates.* Moore has also written numerous articles on Jungian and archetypal psychology for books and periodicals and has edited *A Blue Fire: Selected Writings* by archetypal psychologist James Hillman.

Gloria Naylor (b. 1950)

Born in New York City, Gloria Naylor earned her B.A. degree from Brooklyn College of the City University of New York in 1981 and an M.A. in African-American Studies from Yale University in 1983. Her first novel, *The Women of Brewster Place* (1982), which won the American Book Award for best first novel, is about seven African-American women living in an urban ghetto in the northern United States. Her other books include *Linden Hills,* about residents of an upper-middle-class black neighborhood, *Mama Day,* and *Bailey's Cafe* (1992). "Kiswana Browne" is reprinted from *The Women of Brewster Place.*

Joyce Carol Oates (b. 1938)

Born in Lockport, New York, Joyce Carol Oates was educated at Syracuse University and the University of Wisconsin. She taught at the Universities of Detroit and Windsor (Ontario) and since 1978 has been on the faculty at

Princeton University. An extraordinarily prolific writer, Oates has published dozens of books, including novels (e.g., *Black Water, Bellefleur, A Garden of Earthly Delights*), short stories, literary and social criticism, and plays. *Tone Clusters,* reprinted from her 1991 collection *Twelve Plays,* admits us to familiar Oates terrain: a place of instability and fear, the brutal side of American experience, a world in which people are repeatedly threatened—often violently—by dark forces from without and within. The play also exhibits the interest in formal experimentation that is characteristic of Oates's fiction and dramas.

Flannery O'Connor (1925–1964)

Flannery O'Connor was born in Savannah, Georgia, and attended school at Georgia State College for Women and the University of Iowa, from which she received an M.F.A. degree. As an undergraduate O'Connor was already writing and publishing stories. In 1952 she published her first novel, *Wise Blood.* Diagnosed in 1950 with lupus, an autoimmune disease that eventually claimed her life, O'Connor returned to live with her mother on the family farm in Milledgeville. There she devoted mornings to writing and afternoons to reading, letter writing, and the raising of peacocks. Though she published a second novel, *The Violent Bear It Away,* in 1960, O'Connor's greatest success was as a writer of short stories, which are collected in *A Good Man Is Hard to Find* (1955) and two volumes published after her death, *Everything That Rises Must Converge* (1965) and *The Complete Stories* (1971). O'Connor was devoutly Catholic and emphasized the pervasive influence of her Catholicism on her work. She was never, however, sentimentally religious, but more (in the words of a fellow novelist) like "an Old Testament prophet, crying out in our modern wilderness," exposing faithlessness, secularization, and human hypocrisy. "Her instruments," wrote a reviewer for *Time* magazine, "are a brutal irony, a slam-bang humor and a style of writing as balefully direct as a death sentence."

Sharon Olds (b. 1942)

Born in San Francisco, Sharon Olds graduated with a B.A. degree from Stanford University and a Ph.D. from Columbia University in 1972. Her collections of poems include *Satan Says, The Dead and the Living, The Gold Cell, The Matter of This World, The Sign of Saturn,* and *The Father.*

Mary Oliver (b. 1935)

Born in Cleveland, Ohio, Mary Oliver attended Ohio State University and Vassar College. *No Voyage and Other Poems* (1963) was her first book. It was followed by *The Night Traveler, Twelve Moons, Sleeping in the Forest,* and *American Primitive,* which won the Pulitzer Prize in 1984. *New and Selected Poems* won the National Book Award in 1992. Fellow poet Maxine Kumin has called Oliver an "indefatigable guide to the natural world" who is comfortable with being "on the margins of things, on the line between earth and sky, the thin membrane that separates human from what we loosely call animal."

Tillie Olsen (b. 1913)

Tillie Olsen was born in Omaha, Nebraska. She married in her early twenties, had four children, and struggled for many years to write amid the competing demands of homemaking and earning a humble living at secretarial and other jobs. Not until the 1950s, with the help of a fellowship and a grant, was she able to concentrate on writing and finish her first short story collection, *Tell Me a Riddle* (1961). The title story of that volume won the O. Henry award for best American short story, and the book established Olsen's fame as a writer about the poor, the socially disenfranchised, and women. In a later nonfiction work, *Silences* (1978), Olsen examined how class, gender, race, and other circumstances compel people into unnatural "silences." Olsen has also published *Yonnondio: From the Thirties* (1974), a novel set during the Great Depression, and has edited two books about mothers and daughters.

Eugene O'Neill (1888–1953)

The son of a famous actor, Eugene O'Neill grew up around theater but only began writing plays in his mid-twenties. His formal schooling was minimal (he spent a year at Princeton in 1906–1907 and took a playwriting class at Harvard in 1914). Most of his early education came through voracious and idiosyncratic reading of poets, romantic philosophers, and other iconoclasts and a series of experiences as gold prospector, seaman, and beachcomber that took him to Central and South America, Africa, and other parts of the globe. Abroad and in his native New York, O'Neill befriended down-and-outers, prostitutes, vagabonds, alcoholics, and other socially marginal persons who were to pose the themes and provide many of the characters for his dramas. O'Neill's first plays (mostly one-acts) were written in the 1910s and performed by experimental theater groups, notably the Provincetown Players in Provincetown, Cape Cod, Massachusetts, and in New York. *Beyond the Horizon* (1920) earned him his first of four Pulitzer Prizes, and with *The Emperor Jones* (1920), *The Hairy Ape* (1922), and *Desire Under the Elms* (1924), O'Neill emerged as the first American playwright of international stature. In 1936 he won the Nobel Prize for Literature. His powerful autobiographical play *Long Day's Journey into Night* was published posthumously in 1956. A fearless experimenter, O'Neill wrote plays of all lengths and in many forms and styles, including the expressionism (see Appendix C) of *The Hairy Ape*.

Dorothy Parker (1893–1967)

Dorothy Parker began her literary career as a fashion writer and drama critic but is best known for her poems, short stories, and sketches, which exhibit her trademark humor and often malicious wit. Many of her writings originally appeared in *The New Yorker*, with which she was intimately associated. Collections of short stories and sketches include *Laments for the Living* (1930), *After Such Pleasures* (1933), and *Here Lies* (1939).

Edgar Allan Poe (1809-1849)

The son of actor parents, Edgar Allan Poe was orphaned as a child and suffered a turbulent and lonely personal life. After a brief formal education and an abortive stint at West Point, Poe turned to writing and became one of the foremost literary editors and critics of his day. He also wrote poetry and tales of horror and the macabre, which were published in magazines and collected in *Tales of the Grotesque and Arabesque* (1840) and other volumes. Poe's influence cuts across literary genres and types. He did more than any other individual writer to establish the genre of the horror story; he wrote highly rhythmic, musical, and symbolic poetry that was internationally influential, especially in France; and his intricate stories of mystery and intrigue, such as "The Murders in the Rue Morgue" and "The Purloined Letter," make him the creator of the modern detective story.

Adrienne Rich (b. 1929)

An influential feminist poet and thinker, Adrienne Rich was born in Baltimore and grew up in an intellectual household. She graduated from Radcliffe College in 1951; in the same year her first book of poems, *A Change of World,* was published in the prestigious Yale Series of Younger Poets. In the decades since, Rich has published numerous volumes of poetry, as well as collections of essays and speeches. Her poems are collected in *The Fact of a Doorframe: Poems Selected and New 1950–1984, Time's Power: Poems 1985–1988, An Atlas of the Difficult World: Poems 1988–1991,* and *Dark Fields of the Republic: Poems 1991–1995.* For Rich, poetry never stands apart from life; it is always "political" in the broadest sense—about one's position in the world and how one is situated in relationship to history and to institutions (for instance, the institutions of patriarchy). Her major autobiographical essay, "When We Dead Awaken: Writing as Re-Vision" (reprinted in her 1979 prose collection, *On Lies, Secrets, and Silence*), tells the story of her evolution into feminist consciousness.

Rainer Maria Rilke (1875–1926)

Born in Prague, Rainer Maria Rilke began publishing poems in his teens and twenties. His growth as a poet, however, occurred slowly, and Rilke always insisted that the vocation of poet demands supreme patience, solitude, and perseverance. His work during the early 1900s was influenced by travels to Russia, where he encountered Russian religious art and novelist Leo Tolstoy; by contacts with the French sculptor Auguste Rodin, whom he served briefly as a secretary; and by studies of the French painter, Paul Cézanne. (Rilke's writings on Rodin and Cézanne offer brilliant meditations on the creative process.) Major works of Rilke's maturity include *The Book of Images, Stories of God, The Book of Hours, New Poems,* the autobiographical novel *The Notebooks of Malte Laurids Brigge,* and *Duino Elegies* and *Sonnets to Orpheus.* The French poet Paul Valéry called Rilke "a man who more than anyone else possessed all the wonderful anguish and secrets of the spirit." Matters of spiritual struggle and soulfulness figure prominently in Rilke's poetry, including "The Man Watching," reprinted in *Reading and Writing from Literature*.

Mary Robison (b. 1949)

Mary Robison was born in Washington, D. C., and graduated with an M.A. degree from Johns Hopkins University in 1977. She has been a writer in residence and a teacher at several colleges and universities. Her novels and short story collections include *Days*, *Oh!*, *An Amateur's Guide to the Night*, and *Believe Them*.

Richard Rodriguez (b. 1944)

The son of Mexican-American immigrants, Richard Rodriguez was born in San Francisco and attended Catholic schools in Sacramento. He earned a B.A. from Stanford University (1967), a master's degree from Columbia (1969), and did graduate work at the University of California, Berkeley, and in London. Rodriguez's first book, *Hunger of Memory: The Education of Richard Rodriguez* (1982), recounts his experiences growing up as a Chicano within a predominantly Anglo culture and educational system. Since 1981 Rodriguez has been a full-time writer and a columnist. Praised for his frank and sensitive autobiographical writing, he has also been controversial because of his opposition to bilingual education and affirmative action. Two of Rodriguez's recent books are *Days of Obligation: An Argument with My Mexican Father* and *Movements*.

Milcha Sanchez-Scott (b. 1954)

Milcha Sanchez-Scott was born on the island of Bali, the daughter of a Colombian father and an Indonesian mother. She went to school in England and later at the University of California, San Diego, from which she graduated. Her published plays include *Latina*, *Dog Lady* and *The Cuban Swimmer* (both written in 1982 and produced for the first time in 1984), *Roosters*, and *Evening Star*.

Scott Russell Sanders (b. 1945)

Born in Memphis, Tennessee, Scott Russell Sanders earned his undergraduate degree at Brown University and his Ph.D. at Cambridge University. He has published work on subjects ranging from science fiction and literary criticism to biography and folklore. "In all of my work," he remarks, "regardless of period or style, I am concerned with the ways in which human beings come to terms with the practical problems of living on a small planet, in nature and in communities." Among his books, written in the 1980s and the 1990s, are *Fetching the Dead: Stories*, *Hear the Wind Blow: American Folksongs Retold*, *The Paradise of Bombs*, *Staying Put: Making a Home in a Restless World*, and *Writing from the Center*.

Arthur Schopenhauer (1788–1860)

A major nineteenth-century German philosopher, Arthur Schopenhauer was born into a wealthy family and earned his doctorate in 1813. The following year he moved to Dresden, where he wrote the book for which he is best known, *The World as Will and Idea* (1818). In this work and others, Schopenhauer articulated a pessimistic philosophy that placed him at odds with the then dominant and more optimistic philosophy of G. W. F. Hegel. Largely ignored for many years, he became embittered and resigned a lectureship at a prestigious university to pursue, after 1831, a reclusive life as a writer. Only in the last decade of his life did he begin to receive widespread recognition. Schopenhauer's work, blending philosophies of West and East and stressing the centrality of the irrational in human behavior, influenced Freud, among others.

Leslie Marmon Silko (b. 1948)

Leslie Marmon Silko was born in Albuquerque, New Mexico, and grew up in the nearby village of Old Laguna. She is of mixed blood, including white, Laguna, and Plains Indian, and her cultural origins and traditions are at the heart of her writing. After attending Catholic schools in Albuquerque, Silko graduated with a B.A. from the University of New Mexico and briefly attended law school before deciding to be a writer and teacher. She published her first story in 1969 and since then has produced a volume of poems and several books of fiction, including *Ceremony* (1977, a novel), *Storyteller* (1981, a collection of stories and short prose interwoven with poetry and photographs), and *Almanac of the Dead* (1991, a novel). She has also published two more books of nonfiction, *Sacred Water: Narratives and Pictures* (1993) and *Yellow Woman and a Beauty of the Spirit: Essays on Native American Life Today* (1996). Not just about characters, Silko's fiction is about the healing and protective powers inherent in storytelling itself. This emphasis on the functionality of storytelling is the focus of "Language and Literature from a Pueblo Indian Perspective," the Silko piece reprinted in *Reading and Writing from Literature*.

Gary Soto (b. 1952)

A noted Chicano poet, essayist, and fiction writer, Gary Soto grew up in a working-class family in Fresno, California. He was employed as a laborer during his childhood, and a strong identification with the working poor stamps much of his work. Soto graduated from California State University, Fresno, in 1974 and earned an M.F.A. in creative writing from the University of California, Irvine, in 1976. In 1977 he published his first book, *The Elements of San Joaquín*, a collection of poems depicting the Fresno of his childhood. Since then he has written several books of prose memoirs, including *Living Up the Street: Narrative Recollections* and *Lesser Evils: Ten Quartets*, and numerous volumes of poetry, including *Black Hair*, *Home Course in Religion*, and *New and Selected Poems*.

Wole Soyinka (b. 1934)

Educated in England, Wole Soyinka is a Nigerian political activist who has had to flee his native land several times for criticizing the government. He is the author of *Swamp Dwellers*, *Death and the King's Horseman*, and over a dozen other plays that have made him Nigeria's leading playwright. In 1986 he was awarded the Nobel Prize for Literature. Though best known for his plays, Soyinka has also written novels, an autobiography, and several collections of poetry.

Jean Stafford (1915–1979)

Born in Covina, California, Jean Stafford graduated from the University of Colorado and studied abroad before turning to writing fiction. She wrote one work of nonfiction, *A Mother in History* (1966), about Lee Harvey Oswald's mother, and short stories that are gathered in *Children Are Bored on Sunday* (1953), *Bad Characters* (1964), and *The Collected Stories of Jean Stafford* (1969), which won a Pulitzer Prize.

Henry David Thoreau (1817–1862)

Essayist, poet, and naturalist, Henry David Thoreau was born in Concord, Massachusetts. Though he graduated from Harvard in 1837, he was mainly self-taught, studying surveying and other practical arts and steeping himself in the literary classics of East and West. Above all Thoreau studied nature, both from a naturalist's perspective and from that of a poet who detected symbols of human experience in even the minutest natural phenomena. Thoreau matured into one of the era's great iconoclasts, a supreme example of a countercultural thinker. Disgruntled by the materialism of midcentury America, he built a small cabin at Walden Pond (near Concord) in 1845 and lived there, in simple relationship with nature, for two years. As he put it, he "chose to be rich by making his wants few." This experience furnished the material for *Walden* (1854), his most famous book. Other major writings include *A Week on the Concord and Merrimack Rivers* (1849) and the essay "Resistance to Civil Government" (1849), an argument for the sanctity of individual conscience in relation to political majorities that was to influence Mahatma Gandhi and Martin Luther King, Jr., among others. Thoreau's *Journal,* which he kept for some twenty-three years, supplied the material for his published writings.

James Thurber (1894–1961)

American humorist James Thurber was born and grew up in Columbus, Ohio, and attended (but never graduated from) Ohio State University. In the 1920s he became a newspaper writer, worked briefly in France, and eventually settled in New York City, where he joined the staff of the recently founded *New Yorker* magazine, with which he was to maintain a lifelong association. Beginning in the late 1920s, Thurber's humorous sketches, stories, and line cartoons—distinguished by their simple style and often wildly imaginative subject matter— became a *New Yorker* fixture. His work is collected in such volumes as *My Life and Hard Times, Fables for Our Time, The Thurber Carnival,* and *My World— and Welcome to It,* which includes "The Secret Life of Walter Mitty."

Anne Tyler (b. 1941)

Born in Minneapolis, Minnesota, and educated at Duke University and Columbia, Anne Tyler published her first novel, *If Morning Ever Comes* (1964), when she was in her mid-twenties. Since then twelve more novels have followed, including *Dinner at the Homesick Restaurant, The Accidental Tourist, Breathing Lessons,* and *Ladder of Years.* Much of Tyler's fiction is concerned with the American family—as one critic has said, "ordinary families with extraordinary troubles."

Alice Walker (b. 1944)

Alice Walker was born in Eatonton, Georgia, the youngest of eight children of black sharecropper parents. She attended Spelman College, a black women's school in Atlanta, and graduated in 1965 from Sarah Lawrence College in New York, where she began writing what would become some of her first published works. She participated in the civil rights movement in Mississippi in 1966 and taught college before obtaining a fellowship at the Radcliffe Institute in Cambridge, Massachusetts, in 1971. Walker's books include novels (*The Third Life of Grange Copeland, Meridian,* and *Possessing the Secret of Joy,* among others), collections of short stories (*In Love & Trouble* and *You Can't Keep a Good Woman Down*), poems (such as *Revolutionary Petunias*), and essay collections (*In Search of Our Mothers' Gardens: Womanist Prose* and *Living by the Word: Selected Writings, 1973–1987*). *The Color Purple,* an epistolary novel (a novel in the form of a series of letters) that won a Pulitzer Prize in 1983, shows Walker's characteristic interest in formal experimentation. Much of Walker's work is about strong and independent-minded African-American women, such as Gracie Mae Still in the short story "Nineteen Fifty-five."

Walt Whitman (1819–1892)

Born near Huntington, Long Island, Walt Whitman received virtually no formal education and worked at a variety of jobs during his youth and early manhood—as a printer, schoolteacher, journalist, and carpenter. As a poet he developed relatively late, not publishing his first book until 1855, when he was thirty-six years old. Over time, however, this book, *Leaves of Grass,* revolutionized the writing of poetry in English and exerted significant impact on poets worldwide. In an impassioned "Preface" to the book Whitman rejected the constraints of traditional verse, with its meter and rhyme, and advocated a poetry that shapes itself freely out of the poet's own "beautiful blood and . . . brain." An obsessive and fastidious rewriter, Whitman revised and expanded *Leaves of Grass* for the rest of his life, taking the book through six different editions. During the Civil War he volunteered as a nurse, assisting and comforting the dying and wounded in army hospitals in and around Washington, D.C. Out of this experience he published *Drum-Taps,* a collection of vividly realistic war poems that was later absorbed into *Leaves of Grass.* In addition to being a radical innovator of poetic style, Whitman is famous for celebrating sex and the human body as focal subjects for great poetry.

William Carlos Williams (1883–1963)

Like many distinguished American poets, William Carlos Williams was a self-taught poet. His professional training was as a medical doctor, and he learned and practiced the art of poetry as an avocation. Born in Rutherford, New Jersey, Williams earned his M.D. degree from the University of Pennsylvania, where he became friends with Ezra Pound, who influenced his early poetry. Following postgraduate study in Germany, Williams returned to New Jersey, opened a medical practice, married, and devoted himself to medicine and writing. He published his first book of poems in 1909, and over the next five decades he turned out a prodigious amount of poetry, fiction, and essays. His books of poems are gathered in *Collected Poems of William Carlos Williams, 1909–1962* (two volumes, 1988–1989). Williams's spare yet sensuous free verse style, evident in "The Last Words of My English Grandmother," influenced a generation of American poets.

August Wilson (b. 1945)

August Wilson was born in Pittsburgh, Pennsylvania, the son of a black mother and a white father. Abandoned by their father, August and his siblings were raised by their mother in the Pittsburgh slums and, later, in a largely white community where August suffered racial harassment at school. Wilson dropped out of school at age fifteen and went on to work various jobs such as short-order cook and stock clerk. He also frequented the public library, where he steeped himself in the works of Ralph Ellison, Langston Hughes, Richard Wright, and other African-American writers. While books helped give Wilson confidence to write himself, he was also inspired by many other influences in his African-American culture and heritage: street talk, the rhythms of ordinary speech and conversation, political movements, and especially the music and language of the blues. Wilson was already writing fiction and poetry in the 1960s when he got caught up in the Black Power movement and helped found a black activist theater in Pittsburgh. He also began writing plays. Later, moving to Minnesota, he worked with the Playwrights Center of Minneapolis and founded the Black Horizons Theatre Company. Wilson's first commercial success, *Ma Rainey's Black Bottom* (1984)—about the legendary black blues singer—was voted Best Play of the Year 1984–85 by the New York Drama Critics Circle. Wilson's aim is to write a cycle of ten plays about the experience of African-Americans, one for each decade of the twentieth century. Thus far he has completed several plays in the cycle, in addition to *Ma Rainey: Fences* and *The Piano Lesson* (both Pulitzer Prize winners), *Joe Turner's Come and Gone, Two Trains Running,* and *Seven Guitars.*

William Butler Yeats (1865–1939)

Irish poet, playwright, and critic, William Butler Yeats was born near Dublin, the son of the lawyer and distinguished painter John Butler Yeats. William himself studied painting as a young man but soon abandoned art for writing, producing his first books of poems in the late 1880s. Yeats's poetry interweaves personal vision with history, mythology, psychology, mysticism, and other cultural influences. While many of his contemporaries wrote in free verse, Yeats breathed new life into old poetic forms, articulating his personal and symbolic vision in rhymed lines and tightly constructed stanzas. He was a leading advocate of Irish national art and served as president of the Irish National Theatre Society and codirector of Dublin's Abbey Theatre. In 1923 Yeats was awarded the Nobel Prize for Literature. Among his major collections of poetry are *In the Seven Woods* (1903), *The Wild Swans at Coole* (1917), *The Tower* (1928), and *Collected Poems* (definitive edition, 1956).

Author/Title Index

Subject Index

Text Credits